NINTH EDITION

 # Patterns for College Writing

A Rhetorical Reader and Guide

LAURIE G. KIRSZNER

UNIVERSITY OF THE SCIENCES IN PHILADELPHIA

STEPHEN R. MANDELL

DREXEL UNIVERSITY

BEDFORD / ST. MARTIN'S

Boston ◆ New York

For Bedford/St. Martin's

Senior Developmental Editor: Mikola De Roo
Production Editor: Bernard Onken
Production Supervisor: Jennifer Wetzel
Marketing Manager: Richard Cadman
Art Director: Lucy Krikorian
Text Design: Anna George
Copy Editor: Rosemary Winfield
Indexer: Riofrancos & Co. Indexes
Photo Research: Alice Lundoff
Cover Design: Lucy Krikorian
Cover Art: Henri Matisse, *Ivy in Flower,* 1953; colored paper, watercolor, pencil and brown paper tape on paper mounted on canvas, 112 × 112 in. (284.48 × 284.48 cm.); Dallas Museum of Art, Foundation for the Arts Collection, gift of the Albert and Mary Lasker Foundation.
Composition: Stratford Publishing Services, Inc.
Printing and Binding: R.R. Donnelley & Sons Company

President: Joan E. Feinberg
Editorial Director: Denise B. Wydra
Editor in Chief: Nancy Perry
Director of Marketing: Karen R. Melton
Director of Editing, Design, and Production: Marcia Cohen
Managing Editor: Erica T. Appel

Library of Congress Control Number: 2003100778

Manufactured in the United States of America.

9 8 7 6 5 4
f e d c b a

For information, write: Bedford/St. Martin's, 75 Arlington Street, Boston, MA 02116   (617-399-4000)

ISBN: 0-312-40431-X (paperback)
       0-312-40856-0 (hardcover)

Acknowledgments

For Peter Phelps (1936–1990), with thanks

Preface

Since it was first published, *Patterns for College Writing* has been adopted at over a thousand colleges and universities across the country. We have been delighted by the overwhelmingly positive response to the first eight editions of *Patterns,* and we continue to be gratified and awed by the many instructors who find *Patterns* to be the most accessible and most pedagogically sound rhetoric-reader they have ever used. In preparing this ninth edition, we have worked hard to fine-tune the features that have made *Patterns* the most popular composition reader available today and to develop new features that add to the book's usefulness for both instructors and students.

WHAT INSTRUCTORS AND STUDENTS LIKE ABOUT *PATTERNS FOR COLLEGE WRITING*

An Emphasis on Critical Reading

The opening chapter, "Introduction: Reading to Write," prepares students to become analytical readers and writers by showing them how to apply critical reading strategies to a typical selection and by providing sample responses to various kinds of writing prompts. Not only does this chapter orient students to the book's features, but it also prepares them to tackle reading and writing assignments in other courses.

Extensive Coverage of the Writing Process

Part One, "The Writing Process" (Chapters 1 through 3), functions as a "mini-rhetoric," offering advice on planning, writing, and revising as it introduces students to activities like brainstorming, clustering, journal writing, and editing. These chapters also include some twenty writing exercises to give students opportunities for immediate practice.

Detailed Coverage of the Patterns of Development

In Part Two, "Readings for Writers," Chapters 4 through 12 explain and illustrate the patterns of development that students typically use in their college writing assignments: narration, description, exemplification, process, cause and effect, comparison and contrast, classification and division, definition, and argumentation. Each chapter begins with a comprehensive introduction that presents a definition and a paragraph-length example of the pattern to be discussed and then explains the particular writing strategies and applications associated with it. Next, each chapter analyzes one or two annotated student papers to show how the pattern can be used in particular college writing situations. Chapter 13, "Combining the Patterns," illustrates how the various patterns of development discussed in Chapters 4 through 12 can work together in an essay.

A Diverse and Popular Selection of Readings

Varied in subject, style, and cultural perspective, the seventy professional selections engage students while providing them with outstanding models for writing. We have sought a balance between classic authors (George Orwell, Jessica Mitford, E. B. White, Martin Luther King Jr.) and newer voices (Deborah Tannen, Scott Russell Sanders, Amy Tan, Alice Walker) so that instructors have a broad range to choose from.

More Student Essays Than Any Competing Text

To provide students with realistic models for improving their own writing, we include sixteen sample essays (four new to this edition) by actual students. These essays are also available as transparency masters so that instructors can use them more effectively in the classroom. (The transparency masters are obtainable as a printed package and as files downloadable from the *Patterns for College Writing* Web site.)

Apparatus Designed to Help Students Learn

To help students as they read, write, and revise, each professional essay is preceded by an informative headnote and followed by four types of questions. These questions are designed to help students assess their understanding of the essay's content and of the writer's purpose and audience; to recognize the stylistic and structural techniques used to shape the essay; and to become sensitive to the nuances of language. Each essay is also accompanied by a Journal Entry prompt, Writing Workshop topics (suggestions for full-length writing assignments), and Thematic Connections identifying related readings in the text. Also following each essay is a Combining the Patterns feature that focuses student attention on different patterns used in the essay and possible alternatives to these patterns. Each chapter ends with a list of Writing Assignments, a Collaborative Activity, and an Internet Assignment. Many of these assignments and activities have been revised and updated to reflect the most current topics as well as the most up-to-date trends and sites available on the Web.

WHAT'S NEW IN THIS EDITION

Engaging New Readings

Twenty-four new essays treat topics of current interest, from dating to the environment to the workplace. Some are by well-known writers such as Barbara Ehrenreich, Annie Dillard, Richard Rodriguez, and Juan Williams, while others introduce newer yet equally compelling voices, including those of Suzanne Berne, Sherman Alexie, David Sedaris, and Gayle Rosenwald Smith. Five of the eight literature selections are also new.

Headnotes Situating the Readings in Time and Place

Revised and expanded for this edition, the headnotes provide students with a fuller cultural and historical context for each reading, helping them make connections between the readings and the historical, social, and economic forces that shaped them.

A Unique Grammar-in-Context Feature

A new Grammar in Context section now appears in the introduction to each rhetorical chapter. These ten sections offer specific advice on how to avoid common grammar, mechanical, and punctuation problems that are likely to arise in the context of a particular rhetorical pattern. Examples based on or drawn directly from the essays in the book show students how to eliminate these common problems in their own writing.

An Updated Book Companion Site, Including Online Grammar Practice

For students who need more practice in mastering specific grammatical skills, the Book Companion site at **bedfordstmartins.com/patterns** now includes Exercise Central for *Patterns for College Writing*—a unique online collection of over 7,000 exercise items conveniently arranged by topic. These exercises (also accessible at **bedfordstmartins.com/exercise-central**) enable students to practice essential grammar skills—those discussed in the Grammar in Context sections as well as other important grammar, mechanical, and punctuation issues—and to get immediate feedback on their progress.

A Focus on Visual Texts

In addition to the reading selections, every rhetorical chapter in the ninth edition includes a visual text — for example, a piece of fine art, a photograph, or an advertisement. Each visual text provides an accessible introduction to the pattern of development discussed in the chapter and visually reinforces the chapter's basic rhetorical concepts. Every visual is followed by questions that help students see how a particular pattern operates in visual form.

Two New Debates and a New Casebook in the Argumentation Chapter

In response to students' changing concerns, the chapter on argumentation now includes two new debates — one on the advantages and disadvantages of national ID cards and the other on the pros and cons of gay adoption — and a new casebook of four readings on the highly controversial topic of whether or not African Americans should be entitled to reparations for the enslavement of their ancestors.

Expanded Coverage of Writing Research Papers

The appendix "Writing a Research Paper" has been considerably expanded. This appendix takes students though the complete process of writing a research paper — from choosing a topic and doing research to avoiding plagiarism and documenting both print and online sources. The appendix also includes a wider selection of examples of MLA documentation style — especially for Internet sources and sources from the library's electronic databases. These examples have been updated in accordance with the 6th edition of the *MLA Handbook for Writers of Research Papers* (2003). The appendix closes with a new, fully documented student paper drawing on readings from the debate on national ID cards.

MORE SUPPORT FOR INSTRUCTORS THAN ANY OTHER READER

The extensive ancillary package available to instructors who adopt *Patterns* includes the following items:

- *An Instructor's Edition* incorporating *Resources for Instructors,* which gives instructors guidance in teaching from the text and provides sample answers to the questions following each reading. (*Resources for Instructors* is also available as a separate booklet.)
- *Transparency Masters* featuring ten peer-editing worksheets and sixteen sample student essays (available as a printed package and as files downloadable from the *Patterns for College Writing* Book Companion Site).

- *A Book Companion Site* <bedfordstmartins.com/patterns> offering additional argumentation support materials; a downloadable version of *Resources for Instructors to Accompany* PATTERNS FOR COLLEGE WRITING; downloadable files of the transparency masters and peer-editing worksheets; access to TopLinks, a database that guides students to the best links available on the most commonly chosen writing topics; and access to online grammar practice through Exercise Central, the largest collection of grammar exercises available.

Acknowledgments

As always, friends, colleagues, students, and family all helped this project along. Of particular value were the responses to questionnaires sent to users of the eighth edition, and we thank each of the instructors who responded so frankly and helpfully: Cathy Akers-Jordan, University of Michigan–Flint; Dan Baldwin, Muscatine Community College; Sandra Barnhill, South Plains College; Janice Bellinghiere, Grossmont College; Sharon Blackstock, Stark State College of Technology; Nan Bulish, Gonzaga University; Carlos Campo, Community College of Southern Nevada; Jennifer Clay, Okaloosa-Walton Community College; Richard Dery, Brookdale Community College; Brian Donahue, Gonzaga University; Lynn Hudson Ezzell, Cape Fear Community College; Rhonda Jones Franklin, Cape Fear Community College; Winborne H. Gautreaux, Southeastern Louisiana University; Lois Rauch Gibson, Coker College; Ken Haley, Paris Junior College; Beverly Holmes, Okaloosa-Walton Community College; Jeff Hoogeveen, Lincoln University; Linda Janakos, Santa Monica College; Clifford S. Johnson, St. Clair County Community College; Breneida Gale Lankford, University of Arkansas; Brigette LaPresto, Pikeville College; Eleanor Latham, Central Oregon Community College; Diann Mason, Paris Junior College; David McCracken, Coker College; Brandy McKenzie, Mount Hood Community College; Tracy Miller, Towson University; Julie Nichols, Okaloosa-Walton Community College; A. Myrna Nurse, Lincoln University; Diana Nystedt, Palo Alto College; Michael Pringle, Gonzaga University; Walter Radike, St. Clair County Community College; Angela Rasmussen, Spokane Community College; Douglas Robillard, University of Arkansas–Little Rock; Lynn Rotanz, Cape Fear Community College; Claudia Salewske, San Jose State University; Jenny Scheidt, Palo Alto College; Ursula Scott, Daytona Beach Community College: Advanced Technology Center; Vivian Thomlinson, Cameron University; Rebecca Wickham, University of Michigan–Flint; and Vivian Yenika-Agbaw, Bloomsburg University.

Special thanks go to Mark Gallaher, a true professional and a valued friend, for revising the headnotes and the *Resources for Instructors* for this edition. We are also grateful to Carolyn Lengel for her help in revising the MLA documentation guidelines in the appendix.

Through nine editions of *Patterns for College Writing,* we have enjoyed a wonderful working relationship with Bedford/St. Martin's. We have always found the editorial and production staff to be efficient, cooperative, and generous with their time and advice. As always, we appreciate the encouragement and advice of our longtime friend, editor in chief Nancy Perry. In addition, we thank Joan Feinberg, president of Bedford/St. Martin's, for her support for this project and for her trust in us. During our work on this edition, we have benefited from the insights, humor, and support of Mika De Roo, senior development editor. We are grateful to Bernie Onken, project editor, and to Jennifer Wetzel, production supervisor, for their work overseeing the production of this edition; to Lucy Krikorian, art director, for the attractive new design; to New Media editors Harriet Wald, Coleen O'Hanley, and David Mogolov for their work on the *Patterns for College Writing* Web site; and to associate editors Greg Johnson and Joanna Imm and editorial assistant Kristy Bredin for help with tasks large and small.

We are fortunate to have enjoyed our own twenty-five-year collaboration; we know how rare a successful partnership like ours is. We also know how lucky we are to have our families—Mark, Adam, and Rebecca Kirszner and Demi, David, and Sarah Mandell—to help keep us in touch with the things that really matter.

Laurie G. Kirszner
Stephen R. Mandell

Contents

3 Drafting and Revising   51

❖ PART TWO: READINGS FOR WRITERS   69

4 Narration   71

   "My earliest memories of Sam Cohen are of his chin, which I remember as fiercely hard and pointy."

   "Like me, perhaps, the people around me had in mind images from television and newspaper pictures: the collapsing buildings, the running office workers, the black plume of smoke against a bright blue sky. Like me, they were probably trying to superimpose those terrible images onto the industrious emptiness right in front of them."

"My Principle is the key to an understanding of all hierarchical systems, and therefore to an understanding of the whole structure of civilization."

"Cutting the lines at the Department of Motor Vehicles to renew my driver's license, getting out of speeding tickets and arriving late to work without a reprimand are my 'even uppers' for my physical limitations and for the difficulties caused by establishments not complying with the Americans with Disabilities Act."

"My confidence hit a new low when my friend Adeline told me that French children often make mistakes, but never with the sex of their nouns. 'It's just something we grow up with,' she said. 'We hear the gender once, and then think of it as part of the word. There's nothing to it.'"

"It was in the echo of that terrified woman's footfalls that I first began to know the unwieldy inheritance I'd come into — the ability to alter public space in ugly ways."

"Do we possess the character and courage to address a problem which so many nations, poorer than our own, have found it natural to correct?"

"Some boys are very tough. They're afraid of nothing. They are the ones who climb a wall and take a bow at the top. . . . They also jiggle and hop on the platform between the locked doors of the subway cars."

"My first view in the mirror blotted out the hurting. I'd seen some pretty conks, but when it's the first time, on your *own* head, the transformation, after the lifetime of kinks, is staggering."

"The process of creating my sleuth, Sharon McCone, and plotting her first case — *Edwin of the Iron Shoes* — presented a number of technical problems. Because female sleuths are in themselves a rarity, my imaginary friend could not be too unusual or too much of a super-woman if modern readers — both male and female — were to identify with her."

"If you do not think you will be able to change your appearance enough to slip past your date, you may have to find another way to depart. Back doors are the simplest; they are often located near the restrooms or are marked as fire exits. Do not open an emergency exit door if it is alarmed unless absolutely necessary; an alarm will only draw attention."

"You learn that you are only human flesh, not Superman, and that you can burn like a candle."

"For those who have the stomach for it, let us part the formaldehyde curtain."

"When Ulysses S. Grant and Robert E. Lee met in the parlor of a modest house at Appomattox Court House, Virginia, on April 9, 1865, to work out the terms for the surrender of Lee's Army of Northern Virginia, a great chapter in American life came to a close, and a great new chapter began."

"I'm interested in pay phones in general these days, especially when I get the feeling that they are about to go away. Technology, in the form of sleek little phones in our pockets, has swept on by them and made them begin to seem antique."

"This is a tale of two sisters from Calcutta, Mira and Bharati, who have lived in the United States for some 35 years, but who find themselves on different sides in the current debate over the status of immigrants."

"In fact, by focusing on liability and not teaching our kids to take risks, we are making their world more dangerous. When we were children, we had to learn to evaluate risks and handle them on our own."

11 Definition *491*

"My God, who *wouldn't* want a wife?"

"Whether a public function or service or regulation is or is not a burden depends on the income of the individual so helped or favored."

"My earliest memory of *tortillas* is my *Mamá* telling me not to play with them. I had bitten eyeholes in one and was wearing it as a mask at the dinner table."

"He worked six days a week, five of them until eight or nine at night, during a time when his own company had begun the four-day week for everyone but the executives. He worked like the Important People."

"The *Oxford Dictionary* defines the term *wife-beater* as:
  '1. A man who physically abuses his wife and
    2. Tank-style underwear shirts. Origin: based on the stereotype that physically abusive husbands wear that particular type of shirt.'"

13 Combining the Patterns   *651*

"I have learned much as a scavenger. I mean to put some of what I have learned down here, beginning with the practical art of Dumpster diving and proceeding to the abstract."

"I have been assured by a very knowing American of my acquaintance in London, that a young healthy child well nursed is at a year old a most delicious, nourishing, and wholesome food, whether stewed, roasted, baked, or boiled; and I make no doubt that it will equally serve in fricasee or a ragout."

"Who were these Saints? These crazy, loony, pitiful women?
Some of them, without a doubt, were our mothers and grandmothers."

"What *did* I see in my books? I had the idea that they were crucial for my academic success, though I couldn't have said exactly how or why. In the sixth grade I simply concluded that what gave a book its value was some major idea or theme it contained. If that core essence could be mined and memorized, I would become learned like my teachers."

❖ APPENDIX: WRITING A RESEARCH PAPER 707

Thematic Guide
to the Contents

READING AND WRITING

EDUCATION

BUSINESS AND WORK

SPORTS

RACE AND CULTURE

GENDER

NATURE AND THE ENVIRONMENT

MEDIA AND SOCIETY

HISTORY AND POLITICS

ETHICS

❖ Introduction: Reading to Write

On a purely practical level, you will read the selections in this text to answer study questions and prepare for class discussions. More significantly, however, you will also read to evaluate the ideas of others, to form judgments, and to develop original points of view. By introducing you to new ideas and new ways of thinking about familiar concepts, reading prepares you to respond critically to the ideas of others and to develop ideas of your own. When you understand what you read, you are able to form opinions, exchange ideas with others in conversation, ask and answer questions, and develop ideas that can be further explored in writing. For all of these reasons, reading is a vital part of your education.

READING CRITICALLY

Reading is a two-way street. Readers are presented with a writer's ideas, but they also bring their own responses and interpretations to what they read. After all, readers have different national, ethnic, cultural, and geographic backgrounds and different kinds of knowledge and experiences, and so they may react differently to a particular essay or story. For example, readers from an economically and ethnically homogeneous suburban neighborhood may have difficulty understanding a story about class conflict, but these readers may also be more objective than readers who are struggling with such conflict in their own lives.

These differences in reactions do not mean that every interpretation is acceptable, that an essay or story or poem may mean whatever a reader wants it to mean. Readers must make sure they are not distorting the writer's words, overlooking (or ignoring) significant details, or seeing things in an essay or story that do not exist. It is not important for all readers to agree on a particular interpretation of a work. It *is* important, however, for each reader to develop an interpretation that can be supported by the work itself.

The study questions that accompany the essays in this text encourage you to question writers' ideas. Although some of the questions (particularly those listed in the Comprehension assignments) call for fairly straightforward factual responses, other questions (particularly those in the Journal Entry assignments) invite more complex responses, reflecting your individual reaction to the selections.

READING ACTIVELY

When you read an essay in this text, or any work that you expect to discuss in class (and perhaps to write about), you should read it carefully — and you should read it more than once.

Before You Read

Before you read, look over the essay to get an overview of its content. If the selection has a **headnote** — a paragraph or two about the author and the work — begin by reading it. Next, skim the work to get a general sense of the writer's ideas. As you read, note the title and any internal headings as well as the use of boldface type, italics, and other design elements. Also pay special attention to the introductory and concluding paragraphs, where a writer is likely to make (or reiterate) key points.

As You Read

As you read, try to answer the following questions.

☑ **CHECKLIST: READING ACTIVELY**

- What is the writer's general subject?
- What is the writer's main point?
- Does the writer seem to have a particular purpose in mind?
- What kind of audience is the writer addressing?
- Are the writer's ideas consistent with your own?
- Do you have any knowledge that could challenge the writer's ideas?
- Is any information missing?
- Are any sequential or logical links missing?
- Can you identify themes or ideas that also appear in other works you have read?
- Can you identify parallels with your own experience?

HIGHLIGHTING AND ANNOTATING

As you read and reread, be sure to record your reactions in writing. These notations will help you understand the writer's ideas and your own thoughts about these ideas. Every reader develops a different system of recording such responses, but many readers use a combination of highlighting and annotating.

When you **highlight,** you mark the text with symbols. You might, for example, underline important ideas, box key terms, number a series of related points, circle an unfamiliar word (or place a question mark beside it), draw vertical lines in the margin beside a particularly interesting passage, draw arrows to connect related points, or star discussions of the work's central issues or themes.

When you **annotate,** you carry on a conversation with the text in marginal notes. You might, among other things, ask questions, suggest possible parallels with other reading selections or with your own experiences, argue with the writer's points, comment on the writer's style, or define unfamiliar terms and concepts.

The following paragraph, excerpted from Maya Angelou's "Finishing School" (page 89), illustrates the method of highlighting and annotating described above.

Date written?

Why does she mention this?

(Recently) a white woman from Texas, who would quickly describe herself as a (liberal,) asked me about my hometown. When I told her that in Stamps my grandmother had owned the only Negro general merchandise store since the turn of the century, she exclaimed, "Why, you were a (debutante)." Ridiculous and even ludicrous. But Negro girls in small Southern towns, whether poverty-stricken or just munching along on a few of life's necessities, were given as extensive and irrelevant preparations for adulthood as rich white girls shown in magazines. Admittedly the training was not the same. While white girls learned to waltz and sit gracefully with a tea cup balanced on their knees, we were lagging behind, learning the (mid-Victorian values) with very little money to indulge them. . . .

Serious or sarcastic?

Also true of boys? In North as well as South? True today?

*

What are these values?

Remember that this process of highlighting and annotating is not an end in itself but rather a step toward understanding what you have read. Annotations suggest questions; in your search for answers, you may ask your instructor for clarification, or you may raise particularly puzzling or provocative points during class discussion or in small study groups. After your questions have been answered, you will be able to discuss and write about what you have read with greater confidence, accuracy, and authority.

READING THE ESSAYS IN THIS BOOK

The selection that follows, "'What's in a Name?'" by Henry Louis Gates Jr., is typical of the essays in this text. It is preceded by a headnote that provides information about the author's life and career and provides a social, historical, and cultural context for the essay. As you read the headnote and the essay, highlight and annotate them carefully.

HENRY LOUIS GATES JR.

"What's in a Name?"

Henry Louis Gates Jr. was born in 1950 in Keyser, West Virginia, and grew up in the small town of Piedmont. Currently W. E. B. Du Bois Professor of Humanities and chair of the Afro-American Studies Department at Harvard, he has edited many collections of works by African-American writers and published several volumes of literary criticism. However, he is probably best known as a social critic whose books and articles for a general audience explore a wide variety of issues and themes, often focusing on issues of race and culture. In the following essay, which originally appeared in the journal *Dissent* in 1989, Gates recalls a childhood experience that occurred during the mid-1950s.

At that time, the first stirrings of the civil rights movement were under way, and in 1954 and 1955 the U.S. Supreme Court handed down decisions declaring racial segregation unconstitutional in public schools and other publicly financed venues. Still, much of the country—particularly the South—remained largely segregated until Congress passed the Civil Rights Act of 1964, which prohibited discrimination based on race, color, religion, or national origin in businesses (such as restaurants and theaters) covered by interstate commerce laws, as well as in employment. This was followed by the Voting Rights Act of 1965, which guaranteed equal access to the polls, and the Civil Rights Act of 1968, which prohibited discrimination in housing and real estate. At the time of the experience Gates recalls here, prejudice and discrimination against African Americans were the norm in many communities, including those outside the South.

> The question of color takes up much space in these pages, but the question of color, especially in this country, operates to hide the graver questions of the self.
>
> —JAMES BALDWIN, *1961*

> . . . blood, darky, Tar Baby, Kaffir, shine . . . moor, blackamoor, Jim Crow, spook . . . quadroon, meriney, red bone, high yellow . . . Mammy, porch monkey, home, homeboy, George . . . spearchucker, schwarze, Leroy, Smokey . . . mouli, buck. Ethiopian, brother, sistah. . . .
>
> —TREY ELLIS, *1989*

I had forgotten the incident completely, until I read Trey Ellis's essay "Remember My Name" in a recent issue of the *Village Voice* (June 13, 1989). But there, in the middle of an extended italicized list of the bynames of "the race" ("the race" or "our people" being the terms my parents used in polite or reverential discourse, "jigaboo" or "nigger" more commonly used in anger, jest, or pure disgust), it was: "George." Now the events of that very brief exchange return to mind so vividly that I wonder why I had forgotten it.

My father and I were walking home at dusk from his second job. He [2] "moonlighted" as a janitor in the evenings for the telephone company. Every day but Saturday, he would come home at 3:30 from his regular job at the paper mill, wash up, eat supper, then at 4:30 head downtown to his second job. He used to make jokes frequently about a union official who moonlighted. I never got the joke, but he and his friends thought it was hilarious. All I knew was that my family always ate well, that my brother and I had new clothes to wear, and that all of the white people in Piedmont, West Virginia, treated my parents with an odd mixture of resentment and respect that even we understood at the time had something directly to do with a small but certain measure of financial security.

He had left a little early that evening because I was with him and I had [3] to be in bed early. I could not have been more than five or six, and we had stopped off at the Cut-Rate Drug Store (where no black person in town but my father could sit down to eat, and eat off real plates with real silverware) so that I could buy some caramel ice cream, two scoops in a wafer cone, please, which I was busy licking when Mr. Wilson walked by.

Mr. Wilson was a very quiet man, whose stony, brooding, silent manner seemed designed to scare off any overtures of friendship, even from [4] white people. He was Irish, as was one-third of our village (another third being Italian), the more affluent among whom sent their children to "Catholic School" across the bridge in Maryland. He had white straight hair, like my Uncle Joe, whom he uncannily resembled, and he carried a black worn metal lunch pail, the kind that Riley* carried on the television show. My father always spoke to him, and for reasons that we never did understand, he always spoke to my father.

"Hello, Mr. Wilson," I heard my father say. [5]

"Hello, George." [6]

I stopped licking my ice cream cone, and asked my Dad in a loud voice [7] why Mr. Wilson had called him "George."

"Doesn't he know your name, Daddy? Why don't you tell him your [8] name? Your name isn't George."

For a moment I tried to think of who Mr. Wilson was mixing Pop up [9] with. But we didn't have any Georges among the colored people in Piedmont; nor were there colored Georges living in the neighboring towns and working at the mill.

"Tell him your name, Daddy." [10]

"He knows my name, boy," my father said after a long pause. "He calls [11] all colored people George."

A long silence ensued. It was "one of those things," as my Mom would [12] put it. Even then, that early, I knew when I was in the presence of "one of those things," one of those things that provided a glimpse, through a rent curtain, at another world that we could not affect but that affected us.

---

*EDS. NOTE—The lead character in a 1950s television program titled *The Life of Riley.*

There would be a painful moment of silence, and you would wait for it to give way to a discussion of a black superstar such as Sugar Ray or Jackie Robinson.

"Nobody hits better in a clutch than Jackie Robinson."   13

"That's right. Nobody."   14

I never again looked Mr. Wilson in the eye.   15

•   •   •

RESPONDING TO AN ESSAY

Once you have or read an essay carefully and recorded your initial reactions to it, you should be able to respond to specific questions about it.

The study questions that follow each essay in those chapters will guide you through the rest of the reading process and help you think critically about what you are reading. Five types of questions follow each essay:

Comprehension questions help you to measure your understanding of what the writer is saying.

Purpose and Audience questions ask you to consider why, and for whom, each selection was written and to examine the implications of the writer's choices in view of a particular purpose or intended audience.

Style and Structure questions encourage you to examine the decisions the writer has made about elements like arrangement of ideas, paragraphing, sentence structure, word choice, and imagery.

Vocabulary Projects ask you to define certain words, to consider the connotations of others, and to examine the writer's reasons for selecting particular words or patterns of language.

Journal Entry questions ask you to respond informally to what you read and to speculate freely about related ideas — perhaps exploring ethical issues raised by the selection or offering your opinions about the writer's statements. Briefer, less polished, and less structured than full-length essays, journal entries not only allow you to respond critically to a reading selection but may also suggest ideas for more formal kinds of writing.

Following these sets of questions are three additional features:

Writing Workshop assignments ask you to write essays structured according to the pattern of development explained and illustrated in the chapter.

Combining the Patterns questions focus on the various patterns of development — other than the essay's dominant pattern — that the writer uses. These questions ask why a writer uses particular patterns (narration, description, exemplification, process, cause and effect, comparison and contrast, classification and division, definition), what each pattern contributes to the essay, and what other choices the writer had.

Thematic Connections identify other readings in this book that deal with similar themes. Reading these related works will enhance your understanding and appreciation of the original work and perhaps give you material to write about.

Following are some examples of study questions and possible responses as well as a Writing Workshop assignment and Thematic Connections for "'What's in a Name?'" (pages 5–7). The numbers in parentheses after quotations refer to the paragraphs in which the quotations appear.

COMPREHENSION

1. *In paragraph 1, Gates wonders why he forgot about the exchange between his father and Mr. Wilson. Why do you think he forgot about it?* Gates may have forgotten about the incident simply because it was something that happened a long time ago, or because such incidents were commonplace when he was a child. Alternatively, he may *not* have forgotten the exchange between his father and Mr. Wilson but rather pushed it out of his mind because he found it so painful. (After all, he says he was never again able to look Mr. Wilson in the eye.)

2. *How is the social status of Gates's family different from that of other black families in Piedmont, West Virginia? How does Gates account for this difference?* Gates's family is different from other African-American families in town in that they are treated with "an odd mixture of resentment and respect" (2) by whites. Although other blacks are not permitted to eat at the drugstore, Mr. Gates is. Gates attributes this social status to his family's "small but certain measure of financial security" (2). Even so, when Mr. Wilson insults Mr. Gates, the privileged status of the Gates family is revealed to be false.

3. *What does Gates mean when he says, "It was 'one of those things,' as my Mom would put it" (12)?* Gates's comment indicates that the family learned to see such mistreatment as routine. In context, the word *things* in paragraph 12 refers to the kind of incident that gives Gates and his family a glimpse of the way the white world operates.

4. *Why does Gates's family turn to discussions of "black superstars" after a "painful moment of silence" (12) such as the one he describes?* Although Gates does not explain the family's behavior, we can infer that they speak of African-American heroes like prizefighter Sugar Ray Robinson and baseball player Jackie Robinson to make themselves feel better. Such discussions are a way of balancing the negative images of African Americans created by incidents such as the one Gates describes and of bolstering the low self-esteem the family felt as a result. These heroes seem to have won the respect denied to the Gates family; to mention them is to participate vicariously in their glory.

5. *Why do you think Gates "never again looked Mr. Wilson in the eye" (15)?* Gates may have felt that Mr. Wilson was somehow the enemy, not to be trusted, because he had insulted Gates's father. Or he may have been ashamed to look him in the eye because he believed his father should have insisted on being addressed properly.

PURPOSE AND AUDIENCE

1. *Why do you think Gates introduces his narrative with the two quotations he selects? How do you suppose he expects his audience to react to them? How do you react?* Gates begins with two quotations, both by African-American writers, written nearly thirty years apart. Baldwin's words seem to suggest that, in the United States, "the question of color" is a barrier to understanding "the graver questions of the self." That is, the labels *black* and *white* may mask more fundamental characteristics or issues. Ellis's list of names (many pejorative) for African Americans illustrates the fact that epithets can dehumanize people — they can, in effect, rob a person of his or her "self." This issue of the discrepancy between a name and what lies behind it is central to Gates's essay. In one sense, then, Gates begins with these two quotations because they are relevant to the issues he will discuss. More specifically, he is using the two quotations — particularly Ellis's string of unpleasant names — to arouse interest in his topic and provide an intellectual and emotional context for his story. He may also be intending to make his white readers uncomfortable and his black readers angry. How you react depends on your attitudes about race (and perhaps about language).

2. *What is the point of Gates's narrative? That is, why does he recount the incident?* Certainly Gates wishes to make readers aware of the awkward, and potentially dangerous, position of his father (and, by extension, of other African Americans) in a small southern town in the 1950s. He also shows us how names help to shape people's perceptions and actions: as long as Mr. Wilson can call all black men "George," he can continue to see them as insignificant and treat them as inferiors. The title of the piece suggests that the way names shape perceptions is the writer's main point.

3. *The title of this selection, which Gates places in quotation marks, is an allusion to act 2, scene 2 of Shakespeare's* Romeo and Juliet, *in which Juliet says, "What's in a name? That which we call a rose / By any other name would smell as sweet." Why do you think Gates chose this title? Does he expect his audience to recognize the quotation?* Because his work was originally published in a journal read by a well-educated audience, Gates probably expected readers to recognize the allusion (and also to be knowledgeable about 1950s race relations). Although Gates could not have been certain that all members of this audience would recognize the reference to *Romeo and Juliet,* he could have been reasonably sure that if they did, it would enhance their understanding of the selection. In Shakespeare's play, the two lovers are kept apart essentially because of their names: she is a Capulet and he is a Montague, and the two families are involved in a bitter feud. In the speech from which Gates takes the title quotation, Juliet questions the logic of such a situation. In her view, what a person is called should not determine how he or she is regarded — and this, of course, is Gates's point as well. Even if readers are not able to recognize the allusion, however, the title still foreshadows the selection's focus on names.

STYLE AND STRUCTURE

1. *Does paragraph 1 add something vital to the narrative, or would Gates's story make sense without the introduction? Could another kind of introduction work as well?* Gates's first paragraph supplies the context in which the incident is to be read — that is, it makes clear that Mr. Wilson's calling Mr. Gates "George" was not an isolated incident but rather part of a pattern of behavior that allowed those in positions of power to mistreat those they considered inferior. For this reason, it is an effective introduction. Although the narrative would make sense without paragraph 1, the story's full impact would probably not be as great. Still, Gates could have begun differently. For example, he could have started with the incident itself (paragraph 2) and interjected his comments about the significance of names later in the piece. He could also have begun with the exchange of dialogue in paragraphs 5 through 11 and then introduced the current paragraph 1 to supply the incident's context.

2. *What does the use of dialogue contribute to the narrative? Would the selection have a different impact without dialogue? Explain.* Gates was five or six years old when the incident occurred, and the dialogue helps to establish the child's innocence as well as his father's quiet acceptance of the situation. In short, the dialogue is a valuable addition to the piece because it creates two characters, one innocent and one resigned to injustice, both of whom stand in contrast to the voice of the adult narrator: wise, worldly, but also angry and perhaps ashamed, the voice of a man who has benefited from the sacrifices of men like Gates's father.

3. *Why do you think Gates supplies the specific details he chooses in paragraphs 2 and 3? In paragraph 4? Is all this information necessary?* The details Gates provides in paragraphs 2 and 3 help to establish the status of his family in Piedmont; because readers have this information, the fact that the family was ultimately disregarded and discounted by some whites emerges as deeply ironic. The information in paragraph 4 also contributes to this **irony**. Here we learn that Mr. Wilson was not liked by many whites, that he looked like Gates's Uncle Joe, and that he carried a lunch box — in other words, that he had no special status in the town apart from that conferred by race.

VOCABULARY PROJECTS

1. *Define each of the following words as it is used in this selection.*
   bynames (1) — nicknames
   measure (2) — extent or degree
   uncannily (4) — strangely
   rent (12) — torn
   ensued (12) — followed

2. *Consider the connotations of the words* colored *and* black, *both of which are used by Gates to refer to African Americans. What different associations does each word have? Why does Gates use both — for example,* colored *in paragraph 9 and* black *in paragraph 12? What is your response to the father's use of the term* boy *in paragraph 11?* In the 1950s, when the incident Gates describes took

place, the term *colored* was still widely used, along with *Negro,* to designate Americans of African descent. In the 1960s, the terms *Afro-American* and *black* replaced the earlier names, with *black* emerging as the preferred term and remaining dominant through the 1980s. Today, although *black* is still preferred by many, *African American* is used more and more often. Because the term *colored* is the oldest designation, it may seem old-fashioned and even racist today; *black,* which connoted a certain degree of militancy in the 1960s, is probably now considered a neutral term by most people. Gates uses both words because he is speaking from two time periods. In paragraph 9, re-creating the thoughts and words of a child in a 1950s southern town, he uses the term *colored;* in paragraph 12, the adult Gates, commenting in 1989 on the incident, uses *black.* The substitution of *African American* for the older terms might give the narrative a more contemporary flavor, but it might also seem awkward or forced—and, in paragraph 9, inappropriately formal. As far as the term *boy* is concerned, different readers are apt to have different responses. Although the father's use of the term can be seen as affectionate, it can also be seen as derisive in this context since it echoes the bigot's use of *boy* for all black males, regardless of age or accomplishments.

JOURNAL ENTRY

Do you think Gates's parents should have used experiences like the one in "'What's in a Name?'" to educate him about the family's social status in the community? Why do you think they chose instead to dismiss such incidents as "one of those things" (12)? Your responses to these questions should reflect your own opinions and judgments, based on your background and experiences as well as on your interpretation of the reading selection.

WRITING WORKSHOP

Write about a time when you, like Gates's father, could have spoken out in protest but chose not to. Would you make the same decision today? By the time you approach the Writing Workshop questions, you will have read an essay, highlighted and annotated it, responded to study questions about it, discussed it in class, and perhaps considered its relationship to other essays in the text. Often, your next step will be to write an essay in response to one of the Writing Workshop questions. (Chapters 1–3 follow Laura Bobnak, a first-year composition student, through the process of writing an essay on the topic described above.)

COMBINING THE PATTERNS

Although **narration** *is the pattern of development that dominates "'What's in a Name?'" and gives it its structure, Gates also uses* **exemplification,** *presenting an extended example to support his thesis. What is this example? What does it illustrate? Would several brief examples have been more convincing?* The extended example is the story of the encounter between Gates's father and Mr. Wilson, which compellingly illustrates the kind of behavior African Americans were often forced to adopt in the 1950s. Because Gates's introduction focuses on "the incident"

(1), one extended example is enough (although he alludes to other incidents in paragraph 12).

THEMATIC CONNECTIONS

- "Finishing School" (page 89)
- "An Idea Whose Time Has Come" (page 637)

As you read and think about the selections in this text, you should begin to see thematic links among them. Such parallels can add to your interest and understanding as well as give you ideas for group discussion and writing. For example, Maya Angelou's "Finishing School," another autobiographical essay by an African-American writer, has many similarities with Gates's. Both essays describe the uneasy position of a black child expected to conform to the white world's unfair code of behavior, and both deal squarely with the importance of being called by one's name. In fact, paragraph 26 of "Finishing School" offers some helpful insights into the problem Gates examines. Another related work is Manning Marable's "An Idea Whose Time Has Come," which supports the idea of having the U.S. government pay reparations to African Americans to compensate them for the evils of slavery. Marable's essay provides a wider historical context for the incident Gates describes, which took place nearly 100 years after slavery was abolished.

In the process of thinking about Gates's narrative, discussing it in class, or preparing to write an essay on a related topic (such as those listed under Writing Workshop), you might find it useful to consider (or reconsider) Angelou's and Marable's essays.

RESPONDING TO OTHER TEXTS

The first selection in Chapters 4 through 13 of this book is a visual text. It is followed by *Reading Images* questions, a *Journal Entry,* and *Thematic Connections* that will help you understand the image and shape your response to it.

The final selection in each chapter, a story or poem, is followed by *Reading Literature* questions, a *Journal Entry,* and *Thematic Connections.*

Note: At the end of each chapter, *Writing Assignments* offer additional practice in writing essays structured according to a particular pattern of development, a *Collaborative Activity* suggests an idea for a group project, and an *Internet Assignment* suggests an additional possibility for writing about the pattern.

PART ONE

THE WRITING PROCESS

Every reading selection in this book is the result of a struggle between a writer and his or her material. If a writer's struggle is successful, the finished work is welded together without a visible seam, and readers have no sense of the frustration the writer experienced while rearranging ideas or hunting for the right word. Writing is no easy business, even for a professional writer. Still, although no simple formula for good writing exists, some approaches are easier and more productive than others.

At this point you may be asking yourself, "So what? What has this got to do with me? I'm not a professional writer." True enough, but during the next few years you will be doing a good deal of writing. Throughout your college career, you will need to write midterms, final exams, lab reports, essays, and research papers. In your professional life, you may have to write progress reports, proposals, business correspondence, and memos. As diverse as these tasks may seem, they have something in common: they can be made easier if you are familiar with the **writing process** — the procedure experienced writers follow to produce a finished piece of writing.

THE STAGES OF THE WRITING PROCESS

- **Invention** (also called **prewriting**)   During invention, you decide what to write about and gather information to support or explain what you want to say.
- **Arrangement**   During arrangement, you decide how you are going to organize your ideas.
- **Drafting, revision, and editing**   During drafting and revision, you create several drafts as you reconsider ideas and refine your style and structure. During editing, you correct grammar, punctuation, spelling, and mechanics.

Although the writing process is usually presented as a series of neatly defined steps, this model does not reflect the way people actually write. For one thing, ideas do not always flow easily, and the central point you set out to develop does not always wind up in the essay you ultimately write. Writing often progresses in fits and starts, with ideas occurring sporadically or not at all. In fact, much good writing occurs when a writer gets stuck or confused but continues to work until ideas take shape on the page or on the screen.

Furthermore, because the writing process is so erratic, its three stages overlap. Most writers engage in invention, arrangement, and drafting and revision simultaneously — finding ideas, considering possible methods of organization, and looking for the right words all at the same time. In fact, writing is an idiosyncratic process: no two writers approach the writing process in exactly the same way. Some people outline; others do not. Some take elaborate notes during the prewriting stage; others keep track of everything in their heads.

The writing process discussed throughout this book illustrates the many choices writers may make at various stages of composition. But regardless of writers' different approaches, one thing is certain: the more you write, the better acquainted you will become with your personal writing process and with ways to modify it to suit various writing tasks. The three chapters that follow will help you define your needs as a writer and understand your options as you approach writing assignments both in college and beyond.

❖ 1
Invention

Invention, or **prewriting,** is an important part of the writing process. At this stage, you discover what interests you about your subject and what ideas you will develop in your essay. When you are given a writing assignment, you may be tempted to plunge into a first draft immediately. Before writing, however, you should consider the assignment, explore your subject, and decide what you want to say about it. Time spent on these concerns now will pay off later when you draft your essay.

UNDERSTANDING THE ASSIGNMENT

Almost everything you write in college will begin as an *assignment.* Some assignments will be direct and easy to understand:

Write about an experience that changed your life.

Discuss the procedure you used to synthesize ammonia.

Others will be more difficult and complex:

According to Wayne Booth, point of view is central to understanding modern fiction. In a short essay, discuss how Henry James uses point of view in *The Turn of the Screw.*

Before beginning to write, you need to understand what you are being asked to do. If the assignment is a written question, read it carefully several times, and underline its key words. If the assignment is read aloud by your instructor, be sure to copy it accurately. (A missed word—*compare* or *analyze,* for example—can make quite a difference.) If you are confused about anything, ask your instructor for clarification. Remember that no matter how well written an essay is, it will miss the mark if it does not address the assignment.

SETTING LIMITS

Once you understand the assignment, you should consider its *length, purpose, audience,* and *occasion* and your own *knowledge* of the subject. Each of these factors helps you determine what you will say about your subject and thus simplifies your writing task.

Length

Often, your instructor will specify an approximate length for a paper, and this word or page limit has a direct bearing on your paper's focus. For example, you would need a narrower topic for a two-page essay than for a ten-page one. Similarly, you could not discuss a question as thoroughly during an hour-long exam as you might in a paper prepared over several days.

If your instructor sets no page limit, consider how the nature of the assignment suggests its length. A *summary* of a chapter or an article, for instance, should be much shorter than the original, whereas an *analysis* of a poem will usually be longer than the poem itself. If you are uncertain about the appropriate length for your paper, consult your instructor.

Purpose

Your **purpose** also limits what you say and how you say it. For example, if you were writing a job application letter, you would not emphasize the same aspects of college life as you would in a letter to a friend. In the first case, you would want to persuade the reader to hire you, so you might include your grade-point average or a list of the relevant courses you took. In the second case, you would want to inform and perhaps entertain. To accomplish these aims, you might share anecdotes about dorm life or describe one of your favorite instructors. In each case, your purpose would help you determine what information to include to evoke a particular response in a specific audience.

In general, you can classify your purposes for writing according to your relationship to the audience. Thus, one purpose might be to express personal feelings or impressions to your readers. *Expressive* writing includes diaries, personal letters, journals, and often narrative and descriptive essays as well. Another purpose might be to inform readers about something. *Informative* writing includes essay exams, lab reports, book reports, expository essays, and some research papers. Your purpose might also be to persuade readers to think or act in a certain way. *Persuasive* writing includes editorials, argumentative essays, and many other essays and research papers.

In addition to these general purposes, you might have a more specific purpose — to analyze, entertain, hypothesize, assess, summarize, question, report, recommend, suggest, evaluate, describe, recount, request, instruct, and so on. For example, suppose you wrote a report on the incidence of homelessness in your community. Your general purpose might be to *inform* readers of the situation, but you might also want to *assess* the problem and *instruct* readers how to help those in need.

Audience

To be effective, your essay should be written with a particular **audience** in mind. An audience can be an *individual* (your instructor, for example), or it can be a *group* (like your classmates or coworkers). Your essay can address a *specialized* audience (such as a group of medical doctors or economists) or a *general* or *universal* audience whose members have little in common (such as the readers of a newspaper or newsmagazine).

In college, your audience is usually your instructor, and your purpose in most cases is to demonstrate your mastery of the subject matter, your reasoning ability, and your competence as a writer. Other audiences may include classmates, professional colleagues, or members of your community. Considering the age and gender of your audience, its political and religious values, its social and educational level, and its interest in your subject may help you define it. Certainly the approach you took in your report about homelessness in your community would depend on your intended audience. For example, a report written for students at a local middle school would be very different from one addressing a civic group or the city council — or the parents of those students.

Often, you will find that your audience is just too diverse to be categorized. In such cases, many writers imagine a universal audience and make points that they think will appeal to a variety of readers. Sometimes writers try to imagine one typical individual in the audience — perhaps a person they know — so that they can write to someone specific. At other times, writers identify a common denominator, a role that characterizes the entire audience. For instance, when a report on the dangers of smoking asserts, "Now is the time for health-conscious individuals to demand that cigarettes be removed from the market," it automatically casts its audience in the role of health-conscious individuals.

After you define your audience, you have to determine how much or how little its members know about your subject. This consideration helps you decide how much information your readers will need to understand the discussion. Are they highly informed? If so, you can make your points directly. Are they relatively uninformed? If this is the case, you will have to include definitions of key terms, background information, and summaries of basic research. Keep in mind that experts in one field will need background information in other fields. If, for example, you were writing an essay analyzing the characters in Joseph Conrad's *Heart of Darkness,* you could assume that the literature instructor who assigned the novel would not need a plot summary. However, if you wrote an essay for your history instructor that used *Heart of Darkness* to illustrate the evils of European colonialism in nineteenth-century Africa, you would probably include a short plot summary. (Even though your history instructor would know a lot about colonialism in Africa, she might not be familiar with the details of Conrad's work.)

Occasion

In general, the occasion for academic writing will be either an in-class writing exercise or an at-home assignment. In addition, different subject areas create different occasions for writing. A response suitable for a psychology or history class might not be acceptable for an English class.

Although college writing situations may seem artificial, they provide valuable practice for writing you do outside of college. Like these assignments, each writing task you do outside of college requires a special approach that suits the occasion. A memo to your coworkers, for instance, will be less formal and more limited in scope than a report to your company's president. An e-mail to members of an online discussion group might be strictly informational, whereas a letter to your state senator about preserving a local historic landmark would be persuasive as well as informational.

Knowledge

What you know (and do not know) about a subject limits what you can say about it. Before writing about any subject, ask yourself the following questions:

- What do I know about the subject?
- What do I need to find out?
- What do I think about the subject?

Different writing situations require different kinds of knowledge. A personal essay may draw on your own experiences and observations; a term paper will require you to gain new knowledge through research. Sometimes you will be able to increase your knowledge about a topic easily because you already know a lot about the general subject. At other times, you may need to select a topic particularly carefully so that you do not get out of your depth. In many cases, your page limit and the amount of time you are given to do the assignment will help you decide how much information you need to gather before you can begin.

☑ **CHECKLIST: SETTING LIMITS**

LENGTH

- Has your instructor specified a length?
- Does the nature of your assignment suggest a length?

PURPOSE

- Is your general purpose to express personal feelings? To inform? To persuade?
- In addition to your general purpose, do you have any more specific purposes?
- Does your assignment provide any guidelines about purpose?

AUDIENCE

- Is your audience a group or an individual?
- Are you going to address a specialized or a general audience?
- Should you take into consideration the audience's age, gender, education, biases, or political or social values?
- Should you cast your audience in a particular role?
- How much can you assume your audience knows about your subject?
- How much interest does your audience have in the subject?

OCCASION

- Are you writing an in-class exercise or an at-home assignment?
- Are you addressing a situation outside the academic setting?
- What special approaches does your occasion require?

KNOWLEDGE

- What do you know about your subject?
- What do you need to find out?
- What are your opinions about your subject?

EXERCISE 1

Decide whether or not each of the following topics is appropriate for the stated limits, and then write a few sentences to explain why each topic is or is not acceptable.

1. *A two-to-three-page paper*   A history of animal testing in medical research labs

2. *A two-hour final exam*   The effectiveness of bilingual education programs

3. *A one-hour in-class essay*   An interpretation of Andy Warhol's painting of Campbell's soup cans

4. *A letter to your college newspaper*   A discussion of your school's policy on alcoholic beverages

EXERCISE 2

Make a list of the different audiences to whom you speak or write in your daily life. (Consider all the different people you see regularly, such as family members, your roommate, instructors, your boss, your friends, and so on.) Then, record your answers to the following questions.

1. Do you speak or write to each person in the same way and about the same things? If not, how do your approaches to these people differ?

2. List some subjects that would interest some of these people but not others. How do you account for these differences?

3. Choose one of the following subjects, and describe how you would speak or write to each audience about it.
   • A local political issue
   • Your favorite television show
   • Mandatory drug testing
   • Plagiarism

MOVING FROM SUBJECT TO TOPIC

Although many essays begin as specific assignments or topics (see "A Student Writer," p. 24), some begin as broad areas of interest or concern. These general **subjects** always need to be narrowed to specific **topics** that can be reasonably discussed within the limits of the assignment. For example, a subject like stem-cell research could be interesting, but it is too complicated to write about for any college assignment except in a general way. You need to limit such a subject to a topic that can be covered within the time and space available.

Subject	Topic
Stem-cell research	Using stem-cell research to cure multiple sclerosis
Herman Melville's *Billy Budd*	Billy Budd as a Christ figure
Constitutional law	One result of the *Miranda* ruling
The Internet	The uses of the Internet in elementary school classrooms

Two strategies can help you narrow a subject to a workable topic: *questions for probing* and *freewriting*.

Questions for Probing

One way to move from a general subject to a specific topic is to examine your subject by asking a series of probing questions about it. These questions are useful because they reflect ways in which your mind operates — finding similarities and differences, for instance, or dividing a whole into its parts. By going through the questions on the following checklist, you can explore your subject systematically. Not all questions will work for every subject, but any question may elicit many different answers, and each answer is a possible topic for your essay.

✅ **CHECKLIST: QUESTIONS FOR PROBING**

What happened?
When did it happen?
Where did it happen?
Who did it?
What does it look like?
What are its characteristics?
What impressions does it make?
What are some typical cases or examples of it?
How did it happen?
What makes it work?
How is it made?
Why did it happen?
What caused it?
What does it cause?
What are its effects?
How is it like other things?
How is it different from other things?
What are its parts or types?
How can its parts or types be separated or grouped?
Do its parts or types fit into a logical order?
Into what categories can its parts or types be arranged?
On what basis can it be categorized?
How can it be defined?
How does it resemble other members of its class?
How does it differ from other members of its class?
What are its limits?

When applied to a subject, some of these questions can yield many workable topics, including some you might never have considered had you not asked the questions. For example, by applying this approach to the general subject "the Brooklyn Bridge," you can generate more ideas and topics than you need:

What happened? A short history of the Brooklyn Bridge

What does it look like? A description of the Brooklyn Bridge

How is it made? The construction of the Brooklyn Bridge

What are its effects? The impact of the Brooklyn Bridge on American writers

How does it differ from other members of its class? Innovations in the design of the Brooklyn Bridge

At this point in the writing process, you mainly want to discover possible topics, and the more ideas you have, the wider your choice. So write

down all the topics you think of. You can even repeat the process of probing several times to limit topics further. Once you have a list of topics,
eliminate those that are not suitable—those that do not interest you or
that are too complex or too simple to fit your assignment. When you have
discarded these less promising ideas, you should still have several left. You
can then select the topic that best suits your paper's length, purpose, audience, and occasion as well as your interests and your knowledge of the
subject.

🖳 COMPUTER STRATEGY

You can store the questions for probing listed on page 21 in a file that you
can open every time you have a new subject to probe. Make sure you also keep
a record of your answers. If the topic you have chosen is too difficult or too
narrow, you can return to the questions-for-probing file and select another
topic.

EXERCISE 3

Indicate whether the following are general subjects or specific topics that are
narrow enough for a short essay.

1. An argument against fast-food ads aimed at young children
2. A comparison of the salaries of professional basketball and football players
3. Two creation stories in the Book of Genesis
4. Canadian and U.S. immigration laws
5. The Haber process for the fixation of atmospheric nitrogen
6. The advantages of affirmative action programs
7. The advantages of term over whole life insurance
8. Managed health care
9. An analysis of a political cartoon in your local newspaper
10. Gender roles

EXERCISE 4

In preparation for writing a 750-word essay, choose two of the following subjects, and generate three or four topics from each by using as many of the questions for probing as you can.

1. Credit-card fraud
2. Censorship and the Internet
3. Identity theft
4. Gasoline prices
5. Substance abuse

6. Smoking

7. The minimum wage

8. Age discrimination

9. Women in combat

10. National ID cards

11. The drinking age

12. Rising college tuition

13. Grading

14. Television reality shows

15. The death penalty

Freewriting

Another strategy for moving from subject to topic is **freewriting.** You can use freewriting at any stage of the writing process—for example, to generate supporting information or to find a thesis. However, freewriting is a particularly useful way to narrow a general subject or assignment. When you freewrite, you write for a fixed period, perhaps five or ten minutes, without stopping and without paying attention to spelling, grammar, or punctuation. Your goal is to get your ideas down on paper so you can react to them and shape them. If you find you have nothing to say, write down anything until ideas begin to emerge—and in time they will. The secret is to *keep writing.* Try to focus on your subject, but don't worry if your ideas seem to wander off in other directions. The object of freewriting is to let your ideas flow. Often your best ideas will come to you from the unexpected connections you make as you write.

After completing your freewriting, read what you have written and look for ideas that you can write about. Some writers underline ideas they think they might explore in their essays. Any of these ideas could become essay topics, or they could become subjects for other freewriting exercises. You might want to freewrite again, using a new idea as your focus. This process of writing more and more narrowly focused freewriting exercises—called **looping**—can often yield a great deal of useful information and help you decide on a workable topic.

💻 COMPUTER STRATEGY

If you do your freewriting on a computer, you may find that staring at your own words causes you to go blank or lose your spontaneity. One possible solution is to turn down the brightness until the screen becomes dark and then to freewrite. This technique allows you to block out distracting elements and concentrate on your ideas. Once you finish freewriting, turn up the brightness, and see what you have. If you have come up with an interesting idea, you can move it onto a new page and use it as the subject of a new freewriting exercise.

▶ **A STUDENT WRITER: FREEWRITING**

After reading Henry Louis Gates Jr.'s "'What's in a Name?'" (page 5), Laura Bobnak, a student in a composition class, chose to write an essay in response to this Writing Workshop question:

> Write about a time when you, like Gates's father, could have spoken out in protest but chose not to. Would you make the same decision today?

In an attempt to narrow this assignment to a workable topic, Laura completed the following freewriting exercise:

> Write for ten minutes . . . ten minutes . . . at 9 o'clock in the morning— Just what I want to do in the morning—If you can't think of something to say, just write about anything. Right! Time to get this over with—An experience—should have talked—I can think of plenty of times I should have kept quiet! I should have brought coffee to class. I wonder what the people next to me are writing about. That reminds me. Next to me. Jeff Servin in chemistry. The time I saw him cheating. I was mad but I didn't do anything. I studied so hard and all he did was cheat. I was so mad. Nobody else seemed to care either. What's the difference between now and then? It's only a year and a half. . . . Honor code? Maturity? A lot of people cheated in high school. I bet I could write about this—Before and after, etc. My attitude then and now.

After some initial floundering, Laura discovered an idea that could be the basis for her essay. Although her discussion of the incident still had to be developed, Laura's freewriting had helped her discover a possible topic for her essay.

EXERCISE 5

Do a ten-minute freewriting exercise on one of the topics you generated in Exercise 4 (pages 22–23).

EXERCISE 6

Read what you have just written, underline the most interesting ideas, and choose one idea as a topic you might be able to write about in a short essay. Freewrite about this topic for another ten minutes to narrow it further and to generate ideas for your essay. Underline the ideas that seem most useful.

FINDING SOMETHING TO SAY

Once you have narrowed your subject to a workable topic, you need to find something to say about it. *Brainstorming* and *journal writing* are useful tools for generating ideas, and both strategies can be helpful at this stage of the writing process (and whenever you need to find additional material).

Brainstorming

Brainstorming is a very productive way of discovering ideas about your topic. You can brainstorm in a group, exchanging ideas with several students in your composition class and writing down the useful ideas that come up. You can also brainstorm on your own, quickly writing down every fact, idea, or association you can think of that relates to your topic. Your notes might include words, phrases, statements, questions, or even drawings or diagrams. Jot them down in the order in which you think of them. Some of the items may be inspired by your class notes; others may be ideas you got from reading or from talking with friends; still other items may be ideas you have begun to wonder about, points you thought of while moving from subject to topic, or thoughts that occurred to you as you brainstormed.

▶ **A STUDENT WRITER: BRAINSTORMING**

After she narrowed her subject by freewriting, Laura Bobnak decided to write about a time when she saw someone cheating and did not speak out. To limit her topic further and find something to say about it, she made the brainstorming notes shown on page 26. After reading these notes several times, Laura decided to concentrate on the differences between her attitude in high school and her current attitude. She knew that she could write a lot about this idea and relate it to the assignment, and she felt confident that her topic would be interesting both to her instructor and to the other students in the class.

Journal Writing

Journal writing can be a useful source of ideas at any stage of the writing process. Many writers routinely keep a journal, jotting down experiences or exploring ideas they may want to use when they write. They write journal entries even when they have no particular writing project in mind. Often these journal entries are the kernels from which longer pieces of writing develop. Your instructor may ask you to keep a writing journal, or you may decide to do so on your own. In either case, you will find that your journal entries are likely to be more narrowly focused than freewriting or brainstorming, perhaps examining a small part of a reading selection or even one particular statement. Sometimes you will write in your journal in

---

💻 **COMPUTER STRATEGY**

If you are a good typist, brainstorming on your computer can save you time and effort. Most word-processing programs make it easy to create bulleted or numbered lists. A computer also enables you to experiment with different ways of arranging and grouping items from your brainstorming notes.

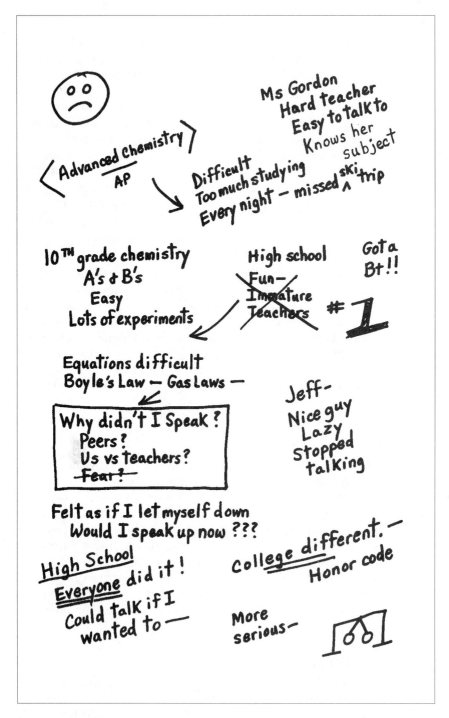

Brainstorming Notes

response to specific questions, like the Journal Entry assignments that appear throughout this book. Assignments such as these can help you start thinking about a reading selection you may later discuss in class or write about.

▶ **A STUDENT WRITER: JOURNAL WRITING**

In the journal entry Laura Bobnak wrote on the topic for her paper, she explores one idea from her brainstorming notes — her thoughts about her college's honor code.

> At orientation the dean of students talked about the college's honor code. She talked about how we were a community of scholars who were here for a common purpose — to take part in an intellectual conversation. According to her, the purpose of the honor code is to make sure this conversation continues uninterrupted. This idea sounded dumb at first, but now it makes more sense. If I saw someone cheating, I'd tell the instructor. First, though, I'd ask the *student* to go to the instructor. I don't see this as "telling" or "squealing." We're all here to get an education, and we should be able to assume everyone is being honest and fair. Besides, why should I go to all the trouble of studying while someone else does nothing and gets the same grade?

Even though Laura eventually included only a small part of this entry in her paper, writing in her journal helped her clarify her ideas about her topic.

🖥 **COMPUTER STRATEGY**

Keeping your writing journal in a computer file has some obvious advantages. Not only can you maintain a neat record of your ideas, but you can also easily move entries from your journal into an essay without retyping them.

GROUPING IDEAS

Once you have generated material for your essay, you will want to group ideas that belong together. *Clustering* and *outlining* can help you do this.

Clustering

Clustering is a way of visually arranging your ideas so that you can tell at a glance where ideas belong and whether or not you need to generate more information. Although you can use clustering at an earlier stage of the writing process, it is especially useful now for seeing how your ideas fit together. (Clustering can also help you narrow your paper's topic even further. If you find that your cluster diagram is too detailed, you can write about just one branch of the cluster.)

Begin clustering by writing your topic in the center of a sheet of paper. After circling the topic, surround it with the words and phrases that identify the major points you intend to discuss. (You can get ideas from your brainstorming notes, from your journal, and from your freewriting.) Circle these words and phrases and connect them to the topic in the center. Next, construct other clusters of ideas relating to each major point and draw lines connecting them to the appropriate point. By dividing and subdividing your points, you get more specific as you move outward from the center of the page. In the process, you identify the facts, details, examples, and opinions that illustrate and expand your main points.

▶ A STUDENT WRITER: CLUSTERING

Because Laura Bobnak was not particularly visually oriented, she chose not to use this method of grouping her ideas. If she had, however, her cluster diagram might have looked like this:

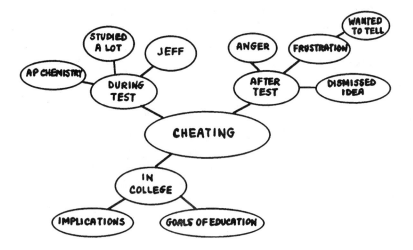

Making an Informal Outline

As an alternative or follow-up to clustering, you can organize your notes from brainstorming or other invention techniques into an **informal outline.** Quite often an informal outline is just a list of your major points presented in a tentative order. Sometimes, however, an informal outline will include supporting details or suggest a pattern of development. Informal outlines do not include all the major divisions and subdivisions of your paper or indicate the relative importance of your ideas the way formal outlines do; they simply suggest the shape of your emerging essay.

🖳 COMPUTER STRATEGY

If you use a computer, you can easily arrange the notes generated from your prewriting activities into an informal outline. You can make an informal outline by typing words or phrases from your prewriting notes and rearranging them until the order makes sense. Later, you can use the categories from this informal outline to construct a more formal outline.

▶ A STUDENT WRITER: MAKING AN INFORMAL OUTLINE

The following outline shows how Laura Bobnak grouped her ideas.

During test
  Found test hard
  Saw Jeff cheating

After test
  Got angry
  Wanted to tell
  Dismissed idea

In college
  Implications of cheating
  Goals of education

EXERCISE 7

Employing the invention strategies discussed in this chapter, prepare to write an essay about one topic you selected in Exercise 5 on page 24. First, use the questions for probing. Next, do five minutes of freewriting, and then brainstorm about your topic. Finally, select the ideas you plan to write about in your essay, and use either clustering or an informal outline to help you group these ideas.

UNDERSTANDING THESIS AND SUPPORT

Once you have grouped your ideas, you need to consider your essay's thesis.

A **thesis** is the main idea of your essay, its central point. The concept of *thesis and support*—stating your thesis and developing ideas that explain and expand it—is central to college writing. The essays you write will consist of several paragraphs: an *introduction* that presents your thesis statement, several *body paragraphs* that develop and support your thesis, and a *conclusion* that reinforces your thesis and provides closure. Your thesis holds this structure together; it is the center around which the rest of your essay develops.

Introductory paragraph
Thesis statement

Body paragraph (support for thesis)

Body paragraph (support for thesis)

Body paragraph (support for thesis)

Body paragraph (support for thesis)

Concluding paragraph
Restatement of thesis or review of key points

FORMULATING A THESIS

Defining the Thesis Statement

A **thesis statement** is more than a title, an announcement of your intent, or a statement of fact. Although a descriptive title orients your readers, it is seldom detailed enough to reveal your essay's purpose or direction. An announcement of your intent can reveal more, but it is stylistically distracting. Finally, a statement of fact — such as a historical fact or a statistic — is typically a dead end and therefore cannot be developed into an essay. A statement like "Alaska became a state in 1959" or "Tuberculosis is highly contagious" or "The population of Greece is about ten million" provides your essay with no direction. However, a judgment or opinion in response to a fact *can* be an effective thesis — for instance, "The continuing threat of tuberculosis, particularly in the inner cities, suggests it is necessary to administer more frequent diagnostic tests among high-risk populations."

Title:	Hybrid Cars: Pro and Con
Announcement:	I will examine the pros and cons of hybrid cars that use both gasoline and electricity.
Statement of fact:	Hybrid cars are more energy efficient than cars with standard gasoline engines.

Thesis statement:	Hybrid cars that use both gasoline and electricity would greatly decrease our country's dependence on foreign oil.
Title:	Orwell's "A Hanging"
Announcement:	This paper will discuss George Orwell's attitude toward the death penalty in his essay "A Hanging."
Statement of fact:	In his essay, Orwell describes a hanging that he witnessed in Burma.
Thesis statement:	In "A Hanging," George Orwell shows that capital punishment is not only unpleasant but immoral.
Title:	Speaking Out
Announcement:	This essay will discuss a time when I could have spoken out but did not.
Statement of fact:	Once I saw someone cheating and did not speak out.
Thesis statement:	As I look back on the situation, I wonder why I kept silent and what would have happened had I acted.

Deciding on a Thesis

No fixed rules determine when you formulate your thesis; the decision depends on the scope and difficulty of your assignment, your knowledge of the subject, and your method of writing. When you know a lot about a subject, you may be able to come up with a thesis before doing any invention activities (freewriting or brainstorming, for example). At other times, you may have to review all your material and then think of a single statement that communicates your position on the topic. Occasionally, your assignment may specify a thesis by telling you to take a particular position on a topic. Whatever the case, you should have a thesis statement in mind before you begin to write your first draft.

As you write, you will continue to discover new ideas, and you will probably move in directions that you did not anticipate. For this reason, the thesis statement that you develop at this stage of the writing process is only *tentative*. Still, because a tentative thesis gives you guidance and purpose, it is essential at the initial stages of writing. As you draft your essay, review your thesis statement in light of the points you make, and revise it accordingly.

Stating Your Thesis

It is a good idea to include a one-sentence statement of your thesis in your essay. An effective thesis statement has three characteristics.

1. *An effective thesis statement clearly expresses your essay's main idea.* It does more than state your topic; it indicates what you will say about your

topic, and it signals how you will approach your material. The following thesis statement, from the essay "Grant and Lee: A Study in Contrasts" by Bruce Catton (page 386), clearly communicates the writer's main idea:

> They [Grant and Lee] were two strong men, these oddly different generals, and they represented the strengths of two conflicting currents that, through them, had come into final collision.

This statement indicates that the essay will compare and contrast Grant and Lee. More specifically, it reveals that Catton will present the two Civil War generals as symbols of two historical currents that were also in opposition. If the statement had been less fully developed—for example, had Catton written, "Grant and Lee were quite different from each other"—it would have just echoed the essay's title.

2. *An effective thesis statement communicates your essay's purpose.* Whether your **purpose** is to evaluate or analyze or simply to describe or recount, your thesis statement should communicate that purpose to your readers. In general terms, your purpose may be to express personal feelings, to present information in a straightforward manner, or to persuade. Accordingly, your thesis can be *expressive,* conveying a mood or impression; it can be *informative,* perhaps listing the major points you will discuss or presenting an objective overview of the essay; or it can be *persuasive,* taking a strong stand or outlining the position you will argue.

Each of the following thesis statements communicates a different purpose:

To express feelings:	The city's homeless families live in heartbreaking surroundings.
To inform:	The plight of the homeless has become so serious that it is a major priority for many city governments.
To persuade:	The only responsible reaction to the crisis at hand is to renovate abandoned city buildings to create suitable housing for homeless families.

3. *An effective thesis statement is clearly worded.* To communicate your essay's main idea, an effective thesis statement—usually a single sentence—should be clearly and specifically worded. (It should also speak for itself. It is not necessary to write, "My thesis is that . . ." or "The thesis of this paper is. . . .") The thesis statement should give an accurate indication of what follows and not mislead readers about the essay's direction, emphasis, content, or point of view. Vague language, confusing abstractions, irrelevant details, and complex terminology have no place in a thesis statement. Keep in mind, too, that your thesis statement should not make promises that your essay is not going to keep. For example, if you are going to discuss just the *effects* of new immigration laws, your thesis statement should not emphasize the sequence of events that led to their passage.

Your thesis statement cannot, of course, include every point you will discuss in your paper. Still, it should be specific enough to indicate the direction and scope of your essay. The statement "New immigration laws have failed to stem the tide of illegal immigrants" does not give your essay much focus. Which immigration law will you be examining? Which illegal immigrants? The following sentence, however, *is* an effective thesis statement. It clearly indicates what the writer is going to discuss, and it establishes a specific direction and purpose for the essay.

> Because they do not take into account the economic causes of immigration, the 2002 immigration laws do little to decrease the number of illegal immigrants coming from Mexico into the United States.

Implying a Thesis

Like an explicitly stated thesis, an *implied* thesis conveys an essay's purpose, but it does not do so explicitly. Instead, the purpose is suggested by the selection and arrangement of the essay's points. Many professional writers prefer this option because an implied thesis is subtler than a stated thesis. (An implied thesis is especially useful in narratives, descriptions, and some arguments, where an explicit thesis would seem heavy-handed or arbitrary.) In most college writing, however, you should state your thesis to avoid any risk of being misunderstood or of wandering away from your topic.

▶ **A STUDENT WRITER: FORMULATING A THESIS**

After experimenting with different ways of arranging her ideas for her essay, Laura Bobnak eventually summed them up in a tentative thesis statement: "As I look back on the situation, I wonder why I kept silent and what would have happened had I acted."

EXERCISE 8

Assess the strengths and weaknesses of the following as thesis statements by asking yourself which statements would most effectively establish the direction of an essay, and why.

1. Myths are more than fairy tales.
2. Myths serve an important function in society.
3. Contrary to popular assumptions, myths are more than fairy tales; they express the underlying attitudes a society has toward important issues.
4. Today, almost two marriages in four will end in divorce.
5. Skiing, a popular sport for millions, is a major cause of winter injuries.
6. If certain reforms are not instituted immediately, our company will be bankrupt within two years.
7. Early childhood is an important period.

8. By using the proper techniques, parents can significantly improve the learning capabilities of their preschool children.

9. Fiction can be used to criticize society.

10. Fiction, in the hands of an able writer, can be a powerful tool for social change.

EXERCISE 9

Rewrite the following factual statements to make them effective thesis statements. Make sure each thesis statement is a clearly and specifically worded sentence.

1. A number of hospitals have refused to admit patients without health insurance because they fear that such patients do not have the resources to pay their bills.

2. Several recent Supreme Court decisions say that art containing a sexual theme is not necessarily pornographic.

3. Many women earn less money than men do, in part because they drop out of the workforce during their child-rearing years.

4. People who watch more than five hours of television a day tend to think the world is more violent than do people who watch less than two hours of television daily.

5. In recent years, the rate of suicide among teenagers — especially middle- and upper-middle-class teenagers — has risen dramatically.

EXERCISE 10

Read the following sentences from *Broca's Brain* by Carl Sagan. Then, formulate a one-sentence thesis statement that draws together the points Sagan makes about robots.

- "Robots, especially robots in space, have received derogatory notices in the press."

- "Each human being is a superbly constructed, astonishingly compact, self-ambulatory computer — capable on occasion of independent decision making and real control of his or her environment."

- "If we do send human beings to exotic environments, we must also send along food, air, water, waste recycling, amenities for entertainment, and companions."

- "By comparison, machines require no elaborate life-support systems, no entertainment, and no companionship, and we do not feel any strong ethical prohibitions against sending machines on one-way, or suicide, missions."

- "Even exceptionally simple computers — those that can be wired by a bright ten-year-old — can be wired to play perfect tic-tac-toe."

- "With this . . . set of examples of the state of development of machine intelligence, I think it is clear that a major effort over the next decade could produce much more sophisticated examples."
- "We appear to be on the verge of developing a wide variety of intelligent machines capable of performing tasks too dangerous, too expensive, too onerous, or too boring for human beings."
- "The main obstacle seems to be a very human problem, the quiet feeling that there is something threatening or 'inhuman' about machines."
- "But in many respects our survival as a species depends on our transcending such primitive chauvinisms."
- "There is nothing inhuman about an intelligent machine; it is indeed an expression of all those superb intellectual capabilities that only human beings . . . now possess."

EXERCISE 11

Go through as many steps as you need to formulate an effective thesis statement for an essay on the topic you developed in Exercise 7 (page 29).

❖ 2
Arrangement

Each of the tasks discussed in Chapter 1 represents choices you have to make about your topic and your material. Now, before you actually begin to write, you have another choice to make—how to arrange your material into an essay.

RECOGNIZING A PATTERN

Sometimes arranging your ideas will be easy because your assignment specifies a particular pattern of development. This may be the case in a composition class, where the instructor may assign, for example, a descriptive or a narrative essay. Also, certain assignments or exam questions suggest how your material should be structured. Probably no one will say to you "Write a narrative," but you will have assignments that begin "Give an account" or "Tell about." Likewise, teachers may not explicitly assign a process essay, but they may ask you to explain how something works. Similarly, an examination question might ask you to trace the circumstances leading up to an event. If you are perceptive, you will realize that this question calls for either a narrative or a cause-and-effect answer. The important thing is to recognize the clues such assignments give (or those you find in your topic or thesis statement) and to structure your essay accordingly.

One clue to structuring your essay may be found in the questions that proved most helpful when you probed your subject (see page 21). For example, if questions like "What happened?" and "When did it happen?" yielded the most useful information about your topic, you might consider structuring your paper as a narrative. The chart on page 38 links various questions to the patterns of development they suggest. Notice that the terms in the right-hand column—narration, description, and so on—identify patterns of development that can help order your ideas. Chapters 4 through 11 explain and illustrate each of these patterns.

☑ CHECKLIST: RECOGNIZING A PATTERN	
What happened? When did it happen? Where did it happen? Who did it?	Narration
What does it look like? What are its characteristics? What impression does it make?	Description
What are some typical cases or examples of it?	Exemplification
How did it happen? What makes it work? How is it made?	Process
Why did it happen? What caused it? What does it cause? What are its effects?	Cause and effect
How is it like other things? How is it different from other things?	Comparison and contrast

What are its parts or types?
How can its parts or types be
    separated or grouped?
Do its parts or types fit into a
    logical order?
Into what categories can its
    parts or types be arranged?
On what basis can it be
    categorized?
	Classification and division

What is it?
How does it resemble other
    members of its class?
How does it differ from other
    members of its class?
What are its limits?
	Definition

UNDERSTANDING THE PARTS OF THE ESSAY

No matter what pattern of development you use, your essay should have a beginning, a middle, and an end — that is, an *introduction,* a *body,* and a *conclusion.*

The Introduction

The **introduction** of your essay, usually one paragraph and rarely more than two, introduces your subject, engages your readers' interest, and often states your thesis.

You can introduce an essay and engage your readers' interest in a number of ways. (In each of the sample introductions that follow, the thesis statement is underlined.)

1. You can give some *background information* and then move directly to your thesis statement. This approach works well when you know that the audience is already interested in your topic and that you can therefore come directly to the point. This strategy is especially useful for exams, where there is no need (or time) for subtlety.

> With inflation slowing down, many companies have understandably lowered prices, and the oil industry should be no exception. Consequently, homeowners have begun wondering whether the relatively high price of home heating oil is justified given the economic climate. It makes sense, therefore, for us to start examining the pricing policies of the major American oil companies. (economics essay)

2. You can introduce an essay with a *definition* of a relevant term or concept. (Keep in mind, however, that the "According to *Webster's Dictionary*..." formula is overused and trite.) This technique is especially useful for research papers or exams, where the meaning of a specific term is crucial.

> Democracy is a form of government in which the ultimate authority is given to and exercised by the people. This may be so in theory, but some recent elections—especially the 2000 presidential election—have raised concerns about the future of democracy. Extensive voting-machine irregularities and ghost voting have seriously jeopardized people's faith in the democratic process. (political science exam)

3. You can begin your essay with an *anecdote* or *story* that leads readers to your thesis.

> Upon meeting the famous author James Joyce, a young student stammered, "May I kiss the hand that wrote *Ulysses?*" "No!" said Joyce. "It did a lot of other things, too." As this exchange shows, Joyce was a person who valued humor. His sense of humor is also present in his final work, *Finnegans Wake*, in which he uses humor to comment on the human condition. (English literature paper)

4. You can begin with a *question*.

> What was it like to live through the Holocaust? Elie Wiesel, in *One Generation After*, answers this question by presenting a series of accounts about ordinary people who found themselves imprisoned in Nazi death camps. As he does so, he challenges some of the assumptions we hold in our smug, materialistic society. (sociology book report)

5. You can begin with a *quotation*. If it arouses interest, it can encourage your audience to read further.

> "The rich are different," said F. Scott Fitzgerald more than seventy years ago. Apparently, they still are. <u>As any examination of the tax laws shows, the wealthy receive many more benefits than the middle class or the poor do.</u>   (business law paper)

6. You can begin with a *surprising statement*. An unexpected statement catches readers' attention and makes them want to read more.

> Believe it or not, most people who live in the suburbs are not white and rich. My family, for example, fits into neither of these categories. Ten years ago, my family and I came to the United States from Pakistan. My parents were poor then, and by some standards, they are still poor even though they both work two jobs. Still, they eventually saved enough to buy a small house in the suburbs of Chicago. <u>Throughout the country, there are many suburban families like mine who are working hard to make ends meet so that their children can get a good education and go to college.</u>   (composition essay)

7. You can begin with a *contradiction*. You can begin with an idea that most people believe is true and then get readers' attention by showing that it is inaccurate or ill advised.

> Many people think that after the Declaration of Independence was signed in 1776, the colonists defeated the British army in battle after battle. This commonly held belief is incorrect. The truth is that the colonial army lost most of its battles. <u>The British were defeated not because the colonial army was stronger, but because George Washington refused to be lured into a costly winner-take-all battle and because the British government lost interest in pursuing a costly war three thousand miles from home.</u>   (history paper)

8. You can begin with a *fact or statistic*.

> According to a recent government study, recipients of Medicare will spend $1.8 billion on drugs over the next ten years. This is an extraordinarily large amount of money, and it illustrates why lawmakers must decide on a plan to help older Americans with the cost of medications. <u>Without financial assistance, many elderly citizens will not be able to afford the drugs they need.</u>   (public policy essay)

No matter which strategy you select, your introduction should be consistent in tone with the rest of your essay. If it is not, it can misrepresent your intentions and even damage your credibility. (For this reason, it is a good idea not to write your introduction until after you have finished the rest of your rough draft.) A technical report, for instance, should have an introduction that reflects the formality and objectivity required by the occasion. The introduction to an autobiographical essay or a personal letter, however, may have a more informal, subjective tone.

EXERCISE 1

Look through magazine articles or the essays in this book, and find one example of each kind of introduction. Why do you think each introductory strategy was chosen? What other strategies might have worked?

The Body Paragraphs

The middle section, or **body,** of your essay develops your thesis. The body paragraphs present the support that convinces your audience that your thesis is reasonable. To do so, each body paragraph should be *unified, coherent,* and *well developed.* It should also follow a particular pattern of development and should clearly support your thesis.

• *Each body paragraph should be unified.* A paragraph has **unity** when every sentence relates directly to the main idea of the paragraph. Sometimes the main idea of a paragraph is stated in a **topic sentence.** Like a thesis statement, a topic sentence acts as a guidepost, making it easy for readers to follow the paragraph's discussion. Although the placement of a topic sentence depends on a writer's purpose and subject, beginning writers often make it the first sentence of a paragraph.

Sometimes the main idea of a paragraph is *implied* by the sentences in the paragraph. Professional writers frequently use this technique because they believe that in some situations — especially narratives and descriptions — a topic sentence can seem forced or awkward. As a beginning writer, however, you will find it helpful to use topic sentences to keep your paragraphs focused.

Whether or not you include an explicitly stated topic sentence, remember that each sentence in a paragraph should develop the paragraph's main idea. If the sentences in a paragraph do not support the main idea, the paragraph will lack unity.

In the following excerpt from a student essay, notice how the topic sentence (underlined) unifies the paragraph by summarizing its main idea:

> Built on the Acropolis overlooking the city of Athens in the fifth century B.C., the Parthenon illustrates the limitations of Greek architecture. As a temple of the gods, it was supposed to represent heavenly or divine perfection. However, although at first glance its structure seems to be perfect, on closer examination it becomes clear that it is a static, two-dimensional object. As long as you stand in the center of any of its four sides to look at it, its form appears to be perfect. The strong Doric columns seem to be equally spaced, one next to another, along all four of its sides. But if you take a step to the right or left, the Parthenon's symmetry is destroyed.

The explicit topic sentence, located at the beginning of the paragraph, enables readers to grasp the writer's point immediately. The examples that follow all relate to that point, making the paragraph focused and unified.

• *Each body paragraph should be coherent.*   A paragraph is coherent if its sentences are smoothly and logically connected to one another. **Coherence** can be achieved through three techniques. First, you can repeat **key words** to carry concepts from one sentence to another and to echo important terms. Second, you can use **pronouns** to refer to key nouns in previous sentences. Finally, you can use **transitions,** words or expressions that show chronological sequence, cause and effect, and so on (see the list of transitions on page 43). These three strategies for connecting sentences — which you can also use to connect paragraphs within an essay — indicate for your readers the exact relationships among your ideas.

The following paragraph, from George Orwell's "Shooting an Elephant" (page 117), uses repeated key words, pronouns, and transitions to achieve coherence:

> I got up. The Burmans were already racing past me across the mud. It was obvious that the elephant would never rise again, but he was not dead. He was breathing very rhythmically with long rattling gasps, his great mound of a side painfully rising and falling. His mouth was wide open — I could see far down into the caverns of pale pink throat. I waited a long time for him to die, but his breathing did not weaken. Finally I fired my two remaining shots into the spot where I thought his heart must be. The thick blood welled out of him like red velvet, but still he did not die. His body did not even jerk when the shots hit him, the tortured breathing continued without a pause. He was dying, very slowly and in great agony, but in some world remote from me where not even a bullet could damage him further. I felt that I had got to put an end to that dreadful noise. It seemed dreadful to see the great beast lying there, powerless to move and yet powerless to die, and not even be able to finish him. I sent back for my small rifle and poured shot after shot into his heart and down his throat. They seemed to make no impression. The tortured gasps continued as steadily as the ticking of a clock.

In the paragraph above, Orwell keeps his narrative coherent by using transitional expressions *(already, finally, when the shots hit him)* to signal the passing of time. He uses pronouns *(he, his)* in nearly every sentence to refer back to the elephant, the topic of his paragraph. Finally, he repeats key words like *shot* and *die* (and its variants *dead* and *dying*) to link the whole paragraph's sentences together. The result is a coherent, cohesive whole.

• *Each body paragraph should be well developed.*   A paragraph is well developed if it contains the **support** — examples, reasons, and so on — that readers need to understand its main idea. If a paragraph is not adequately developed, readers will feel they have been given only a partial picture of the subject.

If you decide you need more information in a paragraph, you can look back at your brainstorming notes. If this doesn't help, you can freewrite or brainstorm again, talk with friends and instructors, read more about your topic, or (with your instructor's permission) even do some research. Your assignment and your topic will determine the kind and amount of information you need.

TRANSITIONS

SEQUENCE OR ADDITION

again	first, . . . second, . . . third	next
also	furthermore	one . . . another
and	in addition	still
besides	last	too
finally	moreover	

TIME

afterward	finally	simultaneously
as soon as	immediately	since
at first	in the meantime	soon
at the same time	later	subsequently
before	meanwhile	then
earlier	next	until
eventually	now	

COMPARISON

also	in the same way
likewise	similarly
in comparison	

CONTRAST

although	in contrast	on the one hand . . .
but	instead	on the other hand . . .
conversely	nevertheless	still
despite	nonetheless	whereas
even though	on the contrary	yet
however		

EXAMPLES

for example	specifically
for instance	that is
in fact	thus
namely	

CONCLUSIONS OR SUMMARIES

as a result	in summary
in conclusion	therefore
in short	thus

CAUSES OR EFFECTS

as a result	so
because	then
consequently	therefore
since	

USING SUPPORT

TYPES OF SUPPORT

- **Examples**   Specific illustrations of a general idea or concept
- **Reasons**   Underlying causes or explanations
- **Facts**   Pieces of information that can be verified or proved
- **Statistics**   Numerical data (results of studies by reputable authorities or organizations, for example)
- **Details**   Parts or portions of a whole (steps in a process, for example)
- **Expert Opinions**   Statements by authorities in a particular field
- **Personal Experiences**   Events that you lived through

EFFECTIVE SUPPORT

- **Support should be relevant.**   Body paragraphs should clearly relate to your essay's thesis. Irrelevant material — material that does not pertain to the thesis — should be deleted.

- **Support should be specific.**   Body paragraphs should contain support that is specific, not general or vague. Specific examples, clear reasons, and precise explanations engage readers and communicate your ideas to them.

- **Support should be adequate.**   Body paragraphs should contain enough facts, reasons, and examples to support your thesis. How much support you need depends on your audience, your purpose, and your thesis.

- **Support should be representative.**   Body paragraphs should present support that is typical, not atypical. For example, suppose you write a paper in which you claim that flu shots do not work. Your support for this claim is the fact that your grandmother got the flu after she was vaccinated. This example is not representative because studies show that most people who get vaccinated do not get the flu. For this reason, your grandmother's illness was most likely a coincidence and unrelated to her vaccination.

- **Support should be documented.**   Support that comes from research (print sources and the Internet, for example) should be documented. (For more information on proper documentation, see Appendix A.) **Plagiarism** — failure to document the ideas and words of others — is not only unfair but also dishonest. For this reason, be sure to use proper documentation to acknowledge your debt to your sources. (Keep in mind that words and ideas that you borrow from the essays in this book must also be documented.)

The following student paragraph uses two examples to support its topic sentence:

> Just look at how males have been taught that extravagance is a positive characteristic. Scrooge, the main character of Dickens's *A Christmas Carol*, is portrayed as an evil man until he is rehabilitated — meaning that

he gives up his miserly ways and freely distributes gifts and money on Christmas day. This behavior, of course, is rewarded when people change their opinions about him and decide that perhaps he isn't such a bad person after all. Diamond Jim Brady is another interesting example. This individual was a financier who was known for his extravagant taste in women and food. On any given night, he would consume enough food to feed at least ten of the numerous poor who roamed the streets of late-nineteenth-century New York. Yet, despite his selfishness and infantile self-gratification, Diamond Jim Brady's name has become associated with the good life.

• *Each body paragraph should follow a particular pattern of development.* In addition to making sure that your body paragraphs are unified, coherent, and well developed, you need to organize each paragraph according to a specific pattern of development. (Chapters 4 through 11 each begin with a paragraph-length example of the pattern discussed in the chapter.)

• *Each body paragraph should clearly support the thesis statement.* No matter how many body paragraphs your essay has — three, four, five, or even more — each paragraph should introduce and develop an idea that supports the essay's thesis. Each paragraph's topic sentence should express one of these supporting points. The following diagram illustrates this thesis-and-support structure.

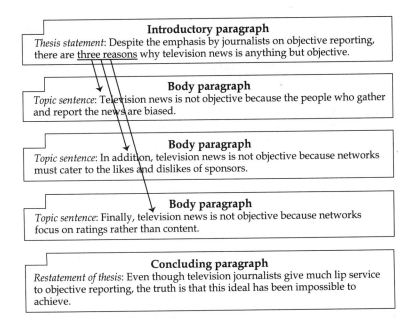

Introductory paragraph
Thesis statement: Despite the emphasis by journalists on objective reporting, there are <u>three reasons</u> why television news is anything but objective.

Body paragraph
Topic sentence: Television news is not objective because the people who gather and report the news are biased.

Body paragraph
Topic sentence: In addition, television news is not objective because networks must cater to the likes and dislikes of sponsors.

Body paragraph
Topic sentence: Finally, television news is not objective because networks focus on ratings rather than content.

Concluding paragraph
Restatement of thesis: Even though television journalists give much lip service to objective reporting, the truth is that this ideal has been impossible to achieve.

EXERCISE 2

Choose one body paragraph from an essay in this text. Using the criteria discussed on pages 41–45, decide whether the paragraph is unified, coherent, and well developed.

EXERCISE 3

Choose one essay in this text, and underline its thesis statement. Then, determine how each of its body paragraphs supports the thesis statement. (Note that in a long essay, several body paragraphs may develop a single point, and some paragraphs may serve as transitions from one point to another.)

The Conclusion

Since readers remember best what they read last, your **conclusion** is extremely important. Always end your essay in a way that reinforces your thesis and your purpose.

Like your introduction, your conclusion should be brief. In a short essay, it is rarely longer than a paragraph. Regardless of its length, however, your conclusion should be consistent with the rest of your essay. It should not introduce supporting material that you have not discussed earlier. Frequently, a conclusion will restate the thesis, summarizing your essay's main idea in different words, or review your key points. Like thesis statements, effective conclusions need no announcement, and you should avoid beginning your conclusion with the artificial phrase *In conclusion.*

Conclusions can be as challenging to construct as introductions. Here are several ways to conclude an essay:

1. You can conclude your essay by *reviewing your key points* or *restating your thesis.*

> Rotation of crops provided several benefits. It enriched soil by giving it a rest; it enabled farmers to vary their production; and it ended the cycle of "boom or bust" that had characterized the prewar South's economy when cotton was the primary crop. Of course, this innovation did not solve all the economic problems of the postwar South, but it did lay the groundwork for the healthy economy this region enjoys today.   (history exam)

2. You can end a discussion of a problem with a *recommendation of a course of action.*

> While there is still time, American engineering has to reassess its priorities. We no longer have the luxury of exotic and wasteful experiments. Instead, we need technology grounded in common sense and economic feasibility. That the international space station that is presently under construction seems to have few practical applications illustrates how far we have strayed from old-fashioned common sense and ingenuity.
> (engineering ethics report)

3. You can conclude with a *prediction*. Be sure, however, that your prediction follows logically from the points you have made in the essay. Your conclusion is no place to make new points or change direction.

> It is too late to save parts of the great swamps in northern Florida, but it is not too late to preserve the Everglades in the southern part of the state. With intelligent planning and an end to the dam building program

by the Army Corps of Engineers, we will be able to halt the destruction of what Native Americans called the "Timeless Swamp."

(environmental science essay)

4. You can end with a relevant *quotation*.

In *Walden*, Henry David Thoreau says, "The mass of men lead lives of quiet desperation." This sentiment is reinforced by a drive through the Hill District of our city. Perhaps the work of the men and women who run the clinic on Jefferson Street cannot totally change this situation, but it can give us hope to know that some people, at least, are working for the betterment of us all. (public health essay)

EXERCISE 4

Look through magazine articles or the essays in this book, and find one example of each kind of conclusion. Why do you think each concluding strategy was chosen? What other strategies might have worked?

CONSTRUCTING A FORMAL OUTLINE

At this point, you may decide to construct a **formal outline** to guide you as you write your essay. Whereas informal outlines are preliminary lists that simply remind you which points to make, formal outlines are detailed, multilevel constructions that indicate the exact order in which you will present your points. The complexity of your assignment determines which type of outline you need. For a short paper, an informal outline like the one on page 29 is usually sufficient. For a longer, more complex essay, however, you may need a formal outline.

Begin constructing a formal outline by reviewing your thesis statement and all the ideas you compiled during prewriting. As you examine this material, you will see that some ideas seem more important than others. One way to construct a formal outline is to copy down the main headings from your informal outline. Then, arrange ideas from your brainstorming notes or cluster diagram as subheadings under the appropriate headings. As you work on your outline, make sure that each idea you include supports your thesis. Ideas that don't fit should be reworded or discarded. As you revise your essay, continue to refer to your outline to make sure thesis and support are logically related. The guidelines on page 48 will help you prepare a formal outline.

▶ A STUDENT WRITER: CONSTRUCTING A FORMAL OUTLINE

The topic outline Laura Bobnak constructed follows the guidelines discussed on page 48. Notice that her outline focuses on the body of her paper and does not include the introduction or conclusion: these are usually developed after the body has been drafted. (Compare this formal

---

☑ **CHECKLIST: CONSTRUCTING A FORMAL OUTLINE**

- Write your thesis statement at the top of the page.
- Group main headings under roman numerals (I, II, III, IV, and so forth), and place them flush with the left-hand margin.
- Indent each subheading under the first word of the heading above it. Use capital letters before major points and numbers before subtopics.
- Capitalize the first letter of the first word of each heading.
- Make your outline as simple as possible, avoiding overly complex divisions of ideas. (Try not to go beyond third-level headings—1, 2, 3, and so on.)
- Your outline should be either a *topic outline,* with headings expressed as short phrases or single words ("Advantages and disadvantages") or a *sentence outline,* with headings expressed as complete sentences ("The advantages of advanced placement chemistry outweigh the disadvantages"). *Never use both phrases and complete sentences in the same outline.*
- Express all headings at the same level in parallel terms. (If roman numeral I is a noun, II, III, and IV should also be nouns.)
- Make sure each heading contains at least two subdivisions. You cannot have a *1* without a *2,* or an *a* without a *b.*
- Make sure your headings don't overlap.

---

outline with the informal outline on page 29 in which Laura simply grouped her brainstorming notes under three general headings.)

SPEAKING OUT

Thesis statement: As I look back on the situation, I wonder why I kept silent and what would have happened had I acted.

  I. The incident
     A. Taking test
     B. Witnessing cheating
     C. Reacting
        1. Anger
        2. Dismissal
 II. Reasons for keeping silent
     A. Other students' attitudes
     B. My fears
III. Current opinion of cheating
     A. Effects of cheating on education
        1. Undercuts the process
        2. Is unfair to teachers
     B. Effects of cheating on students

This outline enabled Laura to arrange her points so that they supported her thesis. As she went on to draft her essay, the outline reminded her to emphasize the contrast between her present and former attitudes toward cheating.

💻 COMPUTER STRATEGY

If you use a computer to construct a formal outline, you can easily arrange and rearrange your headings until your outline is logical and complete. (Many word-processing programs have an outline function that automatically indents and numbers items.) If you saved your prewriting notes in computer files, you can refer to them while working on your outline and perhaps add or modify headings to reflect what you find.

EXERCISE 5

Read the thesis you developed in Chapter 1, Exercise 11 (on page 35), as well as all the notes you made for the paper you are planning. Then, make a topic outline that lists the points you will discuss in your essay. When you are finished, check to make sure that your outline conforms to the guidelines in the checklist on page 48.

3
Drafting and Revising

After you decide on a tentative thesis and an arrangement for your ideas, you can begin to draft and revise your essay. Keep in mind that even as you carry out these activities, you may have to generate more material or revise your thesis statement or outline.

WRITING YOUR FIRST DRAFT

The purpose of your **first draft** is to get your ideas down on paper so you can react to them. Experienced writers know that the first draft is nothing more than a work in progress; it exists to be revised. With this in mind, you should be prepared to cross out and extensively rearrange material. In addition, don't be surprised if you think of new ideas as you write. If a new idea comes to you, follow it to its conclusion. Some of the best writing comes from unexpected turns or accidents. The following guidelines will help you prepare your first draft.

☑ **CHECKLIST: DRAFTING**

- *Begin with the body paragraphs.*   Because your essay will probably be revised extensively, don't take the time at this stage to write an introduction or conclusion. Let your thesis statement guide you as you draft the body paragraphs of your essay. When you have finished, you can write an appropriate introduction and conclusion.

- *Get your ideas down quickly.*   Don't worry about grammar or word choice, and try not to interrupt the flow of your writing with concerns about style.

- *Take regular breaks as you write.*   Don't continue writing until you are so exhausted you can't think straight. Many writers divide their writing into stages, perhaps completing one or two body paragraphs and then

(continued on next page)

(continued from previous page)

taking a short break. This strategy reduces fatigue and is more efficient than trying to write without stopping.

- *Write with revision in mind.* Triple-space so you will have room to make changes by hand on hard copy.
- *Leave yourself time to revise.* Remember, your first draft is called a *rough draft* for a good reason. All writing profits from revision, so allow enough time to write two or more drafts.

▶ A STUDENT WRITER: WRITING A FIRST DRAFT

Here is the first draft of Laura Bobnak's essay on the topic "Write about a time when you, like Henry Louis Gates's father, could have spoken out but chose not to. Would you make the same decision today?"

When I was in high school, I had an experience like the one Henry Louis Gates talks about in his essay. It was then that I saw a close friend cheat in chemistry class. As I look back on the situation, I wonder why I kept silent and what would have happened had I acted. 1

The incident I am going to describe took place during the final examination for my advanced placement chemistry class. I had studied hard for it, but even so, I found the test difficult. As I struggled to balance a particularly difficult equation, I noticed that my friend Jeff Servin, who was sitting across from me, was acting strangely. I noticed that he was copying material from a paper. After watching him for a while, I dismissed the incident and got back to my test. 2

After the test was over, I began to think about what I had seen. The more I thought about it the angrier I got. It seemed unfair that I had studied for weeks to memorize formulas and equations while all Jeff had done was to copy them onto a cheat sheet. For a moment I considered going to the teacher, but I quickly rejected this idea. After all, cheating was something everybody did. Besides, I was afraid if I told on Jeff, my friends would stop talking to me. 3

Now that I am in college I see the situation differently. I find it hard to believe that I could ever have been so calm about cheating. Cheating is certainly something that students should not take for granted. It undercuts the edu- 4 cation process and is unfair to teachers and to the majority of students who spend their time studying.

If I could go back to high school and relive the experi- 5 ence, I now know that I would have gone to the teacher. Naturally Jeff would have been angry at me, but at least I would have known I had the courage to do the right thing.

EXERCISE 1

Write a draft of the essay you have been working on in Chapters 1 and 2. Be sure to look back at the notes you made during prewriting as well as at your outline.

REVISING YOUR ESSAY

Revision is not something you do after your paper is finished. It is a continuing process during which you consider the logic and clarity of your ideas as well as how effectively they are presented. Revision is not simply a matter of proofreading or editing, of crossing out one word and substituting another or correcting errors in spelling and punctuation; revision involves reexamining and rethinking what you have written. In fact, you may even find yourself adding and deleting extensively, reordering whole sentences or paragraphs as you reconsider what you want to communicate to your audience. Revision can take a lot of time, so don't be discouraged if you have to go through three or four drafts of your essay before you think it is ready to hand in. The following pointers can help you when you revise your essay.

- *Give yourself a cooling-off period.* After you have written your first draft, put it aside for several hours or even a day or two if you can. This cooling-off period lets you distance yourself from your essay so that you can read it more objectively when you return to it. When you read it again, you will see things you missed the first time.

- *Work from a typed draft.* Because a typed or printed draft is neat and easy to read, you will be able to see connections and gaps more easily than you will if you work with a handwritten draft. In addition, type enables you to distance yourself from your work and evaluate it objectively.

- *Read your draft aloud.* Before you revise, read your draft aloud to help you spot choppy sentences, missing words, or phrases that do not sound right.

- *Take advantage of opportunities to get feedback.* Your instructor may organize peer critique sessions, hand out a revision checklist, refer students to a writing center, or schedule one-on-one conferences. Make use of as many of these opportunities for feedback as you can; each offers you a different way of gaining information about what you have written.

- *Try not to get overwhelmed.*   It is easy to become overwhelmed by all the feedback you get about your draft. To avoid this, approach revision as a systematic process. Don't just automatically make all the changes that people suggest; consider the impact and the validity of each change. Also ask yourself whether comments suggest larger issues that are not being addressed. For example, does a comment about choppy sentences in a paragraph simply suggest a need for you to add transitions, or does it require you to rethink your ideas?

- *Don't let your ego get in the way.*   Everyone likes praise, and receiving negative criticism is never pleasant. Experienced writers know, however, that they must get feedback if they are going to improve their work. Learn to see criticism — whether by an instructor or by your peers — as a necessary (if painful) part of the revision process.

- *Revise in stages.*   Deal with the large elements (essay and paragraph structure) before moving on to the smaller elements (sentence structure and word choice).

How you revise — what specific strategies you decide to use — depends on your own preference, your instructor's directions, and the time available. Like the rest of the writing process, revision varies from student to student and from assignment to assignment. Four of the most useful revision strategies are *revising with a checklist, revising with an outline, revising with a peer critique,* and *revising with an instructor's comments.*

Revising with a Checklist

If you have time, you can use the following checklist, adapting it to your own writing process.

☑ **CHECKLIST: REVISION**

- **Thesis statement**   Is it clear and specific? Does it indicate the direction your essay is taking? Is it consistent with the body of your essay? If you departed from your essay's original direction while you were writing, you may need to revise your thesis statement so that it accurately sums up the ideas and information now contained in the body. Or you may need to delete from the body any material that is unrelated to the thesis statement — or revise it so it *is* relevant.

- **Body**   Are the body paragraphs unified? Coherent? Well developed? If not, you might have to add more facts or examples or smoother transitions. Does each body paragraph follow a particular pattern of development? Do the points you make in these paragraphs support your thesis?

- **Introduction and conclusion**   Are they appropriate for your material, your audience, and your purpose? Are they interesting? Do they reinforce your thesis?

(continued on next page)

(continued from previous page)

- **Sentences**   Are they effective? Interesting? Varied in length and structure? Should any sentences be deleted, combined, or moved?
- **Words**   Should you make any substitutions?
- **Title**   Because it creates readers' first impression of your essay, your title should spark their interest. Usually, single-word titles ("Love") and cute ones ("The Cheery Cheerleader") do little to draw readers into your essay. To be effective, a title should reflect your purpose and your tone.

The essays in this book illustrate the various kinds of titles you can use.

Statement of essay's focus: "Grant and Lee: A Study in Contrasts"
Question: "Who Killed Benny Paret?"
Unusual angle: "How the Lawyers Stole Winter"
Controversy: "A Peaceful Woman Explains Why She Carries a Gun"
Provocative wording: "Sex, Lies, and Conversation"
Quotation: "The 'Black Table' Is Still There"

Revising with an Outline

If you do not have time to consult a detailed checklist, you can check your essay's structure by making a *review outline*. Either an informal outline or a formal one can show you whether you have omitted any important points. An outline can also show you whether your essay follows a particular pattern of development. Finally, an outline can clarify the relationship between your thesis statement and your body paragraphs.

Revising with a Peer Critique

Another revision strategy you may find helpful is seeking a *peer critique* — asking a friend to read your essay and comment on it. Sometimes a peer critique can be quite formal. An instructor may require students to exchange papers and evaluate their classmates' work according to certain standards, perhaps by completing a *peer editing worksheet*. (See pages 57–58 for an example.) Often, however, a peer critique is informal. Even if a friend is unfamiliar with your topic, he or she can still tell you honestly whether you are getting your point across — and maybe even advise you about how to communicate more effectively. (Remember, though, that your critic should be only your reader, not your ghostwriter.)

🖵 COMPUTER STRATEGY

When you revise on a computer, make sure that you do not delete text that you may need later. Move such information to the end of the draft or to a separate file. That way, if you change your mind about a deletion or if you find that you need information that you took out of a draft, you will be able to recover it easily.

The use of peer critiques mirrors the way people in the real world actually write. Businesspeople circulate reports to get feedback from coworkers; scientists and academics routinely collaborate when they write. (And, as you may have realized, even this book is the result of a collaboration.)

Your classmates can be quite helpful as you write the early drafts of your essay, providing suggestions that can guide you through the revision process. In addition, they can respond to questions you may have about your essay — for example, whether your introduction works or whether one of your supporting points needs more explanation or additional support. When friends ask *you* to critique their work, the guidelines below should help you.

✔ CHECKLIST: GUIDELINES FOR PEER CRITIQUES

- *Be positive.*   Remember that your purpose is to help other students improve their essays.
- *Be tactful.*   Be sure to emphasize the good points about the essay; mention one or two things the writer has done particularly well.
- *Be specific.*   Offer concrete suggestions about what the writer could do better. Vague words like *good* or *bad* provide little guidance.
- *Look at the big picture.*   If you are doing a critique orally, make sure you interact with the writer as you read. Ask questions, listen to responses, and explain your comments.
- *Be thorough.*   Don't focus on the mechanics of the paper. Although spelling and punctuation matter, you shouldn't expect these elements to be perfect in a first draft. At this stage, the clarity of the thesis statement, the effectiveness of the support, and the organization of the writer's ideas are much more important.
- *Be thorough.*   When possible, write down and explain your comments — either on a form your instructor provides or in the margins of the paper.

Revising with Your Instructor's Comments

Your instructor's marginal comments on a draft of your essay can also help you revise by suggesting changes in content, arrangement, or style. For example, these comments may question your logic, suggest a clearer thesis statement, ask for more explicit transitions, recommend that a paragraph be relocated, or even propose a new direction for your essay. They may also recommend stylistic changes or ask you to provide more support in one or more of your body paragraphs. You may decide to incorporate these suggestions into the next draft of your essay, or you may decide not to. Whatever the case, you should take your instructor's comments seriously and make reading and responding to them a part of your revision process.

💻 COMPUTER STRATEGY

A computer enables you to add, delete, and move information quickly and effortlessly. Still, it is usually not a good idea to begin revising directly on the computer screen. Since most screens show only a portion of a page, the connections between ideas are hard to see and to keep track of. Even with the split-screen option that some word-processing programs offer, you cannot view more than two sections of a draft at once or compare one draft to another. For these reasons, it is a good idea to revise on a hard copy of your essay. Once you have made your handwritten corrections, you can type them into your paper.

Your instructor may also encourage (or require) you to schedule a one-on-one conference. You should come to the conference prepared to discuss your paper. Read all your drafts carefully before you come to the conference, and bring a copy of your most recent draft as well as a list of any questions that you may have. During the conference, you can ask your instructor to clarify marginal comments or to help you revise a particular section of your essay that is giving you trouble. Make sure that you take notes during the conference so that you will have a record of what you and your instructor discussed. Remember that the more prepared for the conference you are, the more you will get out of it. (Some instructors use e-mail to answer questions and to give students feedback.)

▶ A STUDENT WRITER: REVISING A FIRST DRAFT

When she revised the first draft of her essay (pages 52–53), Laura followed the revision process discussed above. After writing her rough draft, she put it aside for a few hours and then reread it. Later, her instructor divided the class into small groups and had them read and write critiques of each other's papers. As a result of her own reading and three written critiques (one Peer Editing Worksheet is reproduced below), Laura was able to focus on a number of areas that needed revision.

PEER EDITING WORKSHEET

What is the essay's thesis? Is it clearly worded? Does it provide a focus for the rest of the essay? Is it appropriate for the assignment?

Thesis statement: "As I look back on the situation, I wonder why I kept silent and what would have happened had I acted." I don't really think the thesis talks about the second part of the assignment—would you have done the same thing today?

How clearly are the body paragraphs related to the essay's thesis? Which topic sentences could be more focused?

The topic sentences seem OK—each one seems to tell what the paragraph is about.

(continued on next page)

(continued from previous page)

How do the body paragraphs develop the essay's main idea? Where could the writer have used more detail?

Each of the body paragraphs tells a part of the narrative, but as I said before, the paragraph that deals with the second part of the assignment is missing. You could add more detail—really can't picture everything you're talking about.

Can you follow the writer's ideas? Does the essay need transitions?

I have no problem following your ideas. Maybe you could have added some more transitions, but I think the essay moves nicely.

Which points are especially clear? What questions do you have that are not answered in the essay?

I think the things you didn't like about Jeff's cheating were good. I'm not sure what AP chemistry is like, though. Do people cheat because it's hard?

If this were your essay, what would you change before you handed it in?

I'd change the thesis so it reflects the assignment. I'd add more detail and explain more about AP chemistry. Also, what were the other students doing while the cheating was going on?

Overall, do you think the paper is effective? Explain.

Good paper; cheating is an important issue, and I think your story really puts it in focus.

A peer editing worksheet for each pattern of development can be found on the *Patterns for College Writing* Web site at <bedfordstmartins.com/patterns>.

POINTS FOR SPECIAL ATTENTION: FIRST DRAFT

The Introduction

When she wrote her first draft, Laura knew that she would eventually have to present more detail in her introduction. (Because she was writing a first draft, she had spent little time on this section.) At this stage, though, she was more concerned with her thesis statement, and the students in her peer editing group said that they didn't think it addressed the second half of the assignment—to explain whether or not she would act differently today.

Keeping their comments in mind, Laura rewrote her introduction. First, she created a context for her discussion by more specifically linking her story to Gates's essay. Next, she decided to postpone mentioning her subject—cheating—until later in the paper, hoping that this strategy would stimulate the curiosity of her readers and make them want to read further. Finally, she revised her thesis statement to reflect the specific wording of the assignment.

The Body Paragraphs

The students in her peer editing group also said that Laura needed to expand her body paragraphs. Although she had expected that most of her readers would be familiar with courses like advanced placement chemistry, she discovered this was not the case. One student suggested she explain how challenging it was. In addition, some students in her group thought she should expand the paragraph in which she described her reaction to the cheating. They wondered what the other students had thought about the incident. Did they know? Did they care? Laura's classmates were curious, and they thought other readers would be, too.

Before revising the body paragraphs, Laura did some brainstorming to come up with additional ideas. She decided to describe the difficulty of advanced placement chemistry and the pressure that the students in the class had felt. She also decided to summarize discussions she had had with several of her classmates after the test. In addition, she wanted to explain in more detail her present views on cheating; she felt that the paragraph in which she presented these ideas did not contrast clearly enough with the paragraphs that dealt with her high school experiences.

To make sure that her sentences led smoothly into one another, Laura added transitions and rewrote entire sentences when necessary, signaling the progression of her thoughts by adding words and phrases like *therefore, for this reason, for example,* and *as a result.* In addition, she tried to repeat key words so that important concepts would be reinforced.

The Conclusion

Laura's biggest concern as she revised was to make sure her readers would see the connection between her essay and the assignment. To make this connection clear, she decided to mention in her conclusion a specific effect the incident had on her: its impact on her friendship with Jeff. She also decided to link her reactions to those of Henry Louis Gates Jr.: like him, she had been upset by the actions of someone she knew. By employing this strategy, she was able to bring her essay full circle and develop an idea she had alluded to in her introduction. Thus, rewriting her conclusion helped Laura to reinforce her thesis statement and provide closure to her essay.

▶ A STUDENT WRITER: REVISING A SECOND DRAFT

The following draft incorporates Laura's revisions as well as some preliminary editing of punctuation and grammar.

Speaking Out

In his essay "'What's in a Name?'" Henry Louis Gates Jr.   1
recalls an incident from his past in which his father did
not speak up. Perhaps he kept silent because he was afraid
or because he knew that nothing he said or did would change
the situation in Piedmont, West Virginia. Although I have
never encountered the kind of prejudice Gates describes, I
did have an experience in high school where, like Gates's
father, I could have spoken up but did not. As I now look
back on the situation, I know I would not make the same
decision today.

The incident I am going to describe took place during   2
the final examination in my advanced placement chemistry
class. The course was very demanding and required hours of
studying every night. Every day after school, I would meet
with other students to outline chapters and answer homework
questions. Sometimes we would even work on weekends. We
would often ask ourselves whether we had gotten in over our
heads. As the semester dragged on, it became clear to me,
as well as to the other students in the class, that passing
the course was not something we could take for granted. Test
after test came back with grades that were well below the
"As" and "Bs" I was used to getting in the regular chemistry
course I took in tenth grade. By the time we were ready to
take the final exam, most of us were worried that we would
fail the course—despite the teacher's assurances that she
would mark on a curve.

The final examination for advanced placement chemistry   3
was given on a Friday morning from nine to twelve o'clock.
As I struggled to balance a particularly complex equation,
I noticed that the person sitting across from me was acting
strangely. At first I thought I was imagining things, but
as I stared I saw Jeff Servin, my friend and study partner,
fumbling with his test booklet. About a minute passed before
I realized that he was copying material from a paper he had
taped inside the cuff of his shirt. After a short time, I
dismissed the incident and finished my test.

Surprisingly, when I mentioned the incident to others   4
in the class, they all knew what Jeff had done. The more I
thought about Jeff's actions, the angrier I got. It seemed

unfair that I had studied for weeks to memorize formulas and
equations while all Jeff had done was to copy them onto a
cheat sheet. For a moment I considered going to the teacher,
but I quickly rejected this idea. Cheating was nothing new to
me or to others in my school. Many of my classmates cheated
at one time or another. Most of us saw school as a war
between us and the teachers, and cheating was just another
weapon in our arsenal. The worst crime I could commit would
be to turn Jeff in. As far as I was concerned, I had no
choice. I fell in line with the values of my high school
classmates and dismissed the incident as "no big deal."

I find it hard to believe that I could ever have been   5
so complacent about cheating. The issues that were simple
in high school now seem complex. I now ask questions that
never would have occurred to me in high school. Interestingly, Jeff and I are no longer very close. Whenever I see
him, I have the same reaction Henry Louis Gates Jr. had when
he met Mr. Wilson after he had insulted his father — I have a
hard time looking him in the eye.

POINTS FOR SPECIAL ATTENTION: SECOND DRAFT

Laura could see that her second draft was stronger than her first, but
she decided she needed to arrange a conference with her instructor before
she could improve her draft further.

The Introduction

Although Laura was basically satisfied with her introduction, her
instructor identified one problem. Laura had assumed that everyone reading her essay would be familiar with Gates's essay. However, her instructor
pointed out that this might not be the case. So, he suggested that she add a
brief explanation of the problems Gates's father had faced, in order to
accommodate readers who didn't know about or remember Gates's comments.

The Body Paragraphs

After rereading her first body paragraph, Laura thought she could
sharpen its focus. Her instructor agreed, suggesting that she delete the first
sentence of the paragraph, which seemed too conversational. She also
decided that she could delete the sentences that explained how difficult
advanced placement chemistry was — even though she had added this

material at the suggestion of a classmate. After all, cheating, not advanced placement chemistry, was the subject of her paper. Her instructor told her that if she included this kind of detail, she ran the risk of distracting readers with an irrelevant discussion.

Her instructor also pointed out that in the second body paragraph, the first and second sentences did not seem to be connected, and so Laura decided to add a short discussion of her own reaction to the test to connect these two ideas. Her instructor also suggested that Laura add transitional words and phrases to the last part of the paragraph to clarify the sequence of events she described. Phrases like *at first, about a minute passed,* and *after a short time* would help readers follow her discussion.

Laura thought that the third body paragraph was her best, but even so, she felt that she needed to add some material. She and her instructor decided that she should expand the discussion of the students' reactions to cheating. More information — perhaps some dialogue — would help Laura make the point that cheating was condoned by the students in her class.

The Conclusion

Laura realized her conclusion began by mentioning her present attitude toward cheating and then suddenly shifted to the effect cheating had on her relationship with Jeff. Her instructor suggested that she remedy this situation by taking her discussion about her current view of cheating out of her conclusion and putting it in a separate paragraph. By doing this, she would be able to focus her conclusion on the effect cheating had on both Jeff and her. This strategy would enable Laura to present her views about cheating in more detail and also help her to end her essay forcefully.

The Title

Laura's original title was only a working title, and now she wanted one that would create interest and draw readers into her essay. She knew, however, that a humorous, cute, or catchy title would undermine the seriousness of her essay. After she and her instructor rejected a number of possibilities, they decided on "The Price of Silence." This title was thought provoking and also descriptive, and it prepared readers for what was to follow in the essay.

▶ **A STUDENT WRITER: PREPARING A FINAL DRAFT**

Based on the decisions she made during and after her conference, Laura revised and edited her draft and handed in this final version of her essay.

The Price of Silence

Introduction (provides background)
In his essay "'What's in a Name?'" Henry Louis Gates Jr. recalls an incident from his past in which his father encountered prejudice

1

and did not speak up. Perhaps he kept silent because he was afraid or because he knew that nothing he said or did would change the racial situation in Piedmont, West Virginia. Although I have never encountered the kind of prejudice Gates describes, I did have an experience in high school where, like Gates's father, I could have spoken out but did not. As I think back on the situation, I realize that I have outgrown the immaturity and lack of confidence that made me keep silent.

Thesis statement

Narrative begins

In my senior year in high school I, along with fifteen other students, took advanced placement chemistry. The course was very demanding and required hours of studying every night. As the semester dragged on, it became clear to me, as well as to the other students in the class, that passing the course was not something we could take for granted. Test after test came back with grades that were well below the "As" and "Bs" I was used to getting in the regular chemistry course I had taken in tenth grade. By the time we were ready to take the final exam, most of us were worried that we would fail the course—despite the teacher's assurances that she would mark on a curve.

2

Key incident occurs

The final examination for advanced placement chemistry was given on a Friday morning between nine o'clock and noon. I had studied all that week, but even so, I found the test difficult. I knew the material, but I had a hard time answering the long questions that were asked. As I struggled to balance a particularly complex equation, I noticed that the person sitting across from me was acting strangely. At first I thought I was imagining things, but as I stared I saw Jeff Servin, my friend and study partner, fumbling with his test booklet. About a minute passed before I realized that he was copying material from a

3

paper he had taped to the inside of his shirt cuff. After a short time, I stopped watching him and finished my test.

Narrative continues: reactions to the incident

It was not until after the test that I began thinking about what I had seen. Surprisingly, when I mentioned the incident to others in the class, they all knew what Jeff had done. Some even thought that Jeff's actions were justified. "After all," one student said, "the test was hard." But the more I thought about Jeff's actions, the angrier I got. It seemed unfair that I had studied for weeks to memorize formulas and equations while all Jeff had done was copy them onto a cheat sheet. For a moment I considered going to the teacher, but I quickly rejected this idea. Cheating was nothing new to me or to others in my school. Many of my classmates cheated at one time or another. Most of us saw school as a war between us and the teachers, and cheating was just another weapon in our arsenal. The worst crime I could commit

Narrative ends

would be to turn Jeff in. As far as I was concerned, I had no choice. I fell in line with the values of my high school classmates and dismissed the incident as "no big deal."

Analysis of key incident

Now that I am in college, however, I see the situation differently. I find it hard to believe that I could ever have been so complacent about cheating. The issues that were simple in high school now seem complex — especially in light of the honor code that I follow in college. I now ask questions that never would have occurred to me in high school. What, for example, are the implications of cheating? What would happen to the educational system if cheating became the norm? What are my obligations to all those who are involved in education? Aren't teachers and students interested in achieving a common goal? The answers to these questions give me a sense

4

5

of the far-reaching effects of my failure to act. If confronted with the same situation today, I know I would speak out regardless of the consequences.

Reinforcement of thesis

Jeff Servin is now a first-year student at the state university and, like me, was given credit for chemistry. I feel certain that by not turning him in, I failed not only myself but also Jeff. I gave in to peer pressure instead of doing what I knew to be right. The worst that would have happened to Jeff had I spoken up is that he would have had to repeat chemistry in summer school. By doing so, he would have proven to himself that he could, like the rest of us in the class, pass on his own. In the long run, this knowledge would have served him better than the knowledge that he could cheat whenever he faced a difficult situation.

6

Conclusion (aftermath of incident)

Interestingly, Jeff and I are no longer very close. Whenever I see him I have the same reaction Henry Louis Gates Jr. had when he met Mr. Wilson after he had insulted his father — I have a hard time looking him in the eye.

7

With each draft of her essay, Laura sharpened the focus of her discussion. In the process, she clarified her thoughts about her subject and reached some new and interesting conclusions. Although much of Laura's paper is a narrative, it also contains a contrast between her current ideas about cheating and the ideas she had in high school. Perhaps Laura could have explained the reasons behind her current ideas about cheating more fully. Even so, her paper gives a straightforward account of the incident and analyzes its significance without lapsing into clichés or simplistic moralizing. Especially effective is Laura's conclusion, in which she discusses the long-term effects of her experience. By placing this discussion at the end of her essay, she makes sure that her readers will not lose sight of the implications of her experience.

EXERCISE 2

Use the checklist on page 54 to help you revise your draft. If you prefer, outline your draft and use that outline to help you revise.

EXERCISE 3

Have another student read your second draft. Then, using the student's peer critique as your guide, revise your draft.

A NOTE ON EDITING

When you finish revising your essay, it is tempting to hand it in and breathe a sigh of relief. This is one temptation you should resist. You still have to edit your paper to correct many of the small problems that remain even after you revise.

When you edit, you put the finishing touches on your essay. You correct misspellings, check punctuation, search for grammatical errors, look at your paper's format, and consider any other surface features that might weaken its message or undermine your credibility. Editing is your last chance to make sure your paper says what you want it to say.

Of course, you could spend literally hours checking your essay for every possible error, but this approach would be time-consuming and impractical. As you edit, keep in mind that certain errors occur more frequently than others. By concentrating on these errors, and by keeping a record of the specific errors that you make most often, you will be able to edit your essays quickly and efficiently.

The following checklist includes many of the most common errors. Consult a handbook of grammar and usage for detailed discussions of ways to correct these errors.

☑ **CHECKLIST: EDITING**

- **Subject-verb agreement** Do all your verbs agree in number with their subjects? Remember that singular subjects take singular verbs, and plural subjects take plural verbs.
- **Verb tenses** Are all your verb tenses accurate and consistent? Do you avoid unnecessary shifts in tense?
- **Parallelism** Have you avoided faulty parallelism? Do you use matching words, phrases, or clauses to express equivalent ideas?
- **Clear pronoun reference** Do pronouns that refer back to specific nouns do so clearly? Be especially careful of unclear references involving *this*. To avoid this problem, always follow *this* with a word that clarifies the reference—*this problem, this event,* and so on.
- **Punctuation** Are any commas misplaced, missing, or unnecessary? Remember to use commas before coordinating conjunctions (such as *and* or *but*) that join independent clauses in compound sentences.

(continued on next page)

(continued from previous page)

- **Misspelled words and typos** Have you proofread for spelling as well as run a computer spell check? Be on the lookout for mistakes in capitalization as well as for improper spacing and omitted letters.

- **Commonly confused words** Have you proofread for words that are often confused with each other? Remember, for example, that *it's* is a contraction meaning "it is," and *its* is the possessive form of *it*.

- **Sentence fragments** Does each group of words punctuated as a sentence have both a subject and a verb? Does it make sense on its own, without being attached to another sentence?

- **Run-on sentences** Have you been careful not to connect two independent clauses without the necessary punctuation?

  Have you avoided comma splices? (A comma splice is an error in which two independent clauses are connected by a comma alone.) Correct a comma splice by adding an appropriate coordinating conjunction (*and* or *but,* for example), by changing the comma to a semicolon, or by making the clauses separate sentences.

  Have you avoided fused sentences? (A fused sentence is an error in which two independent clauses are connected without any punctuation.) Correct a fused sentence by adding an appropriate coordinating conjunction (*and* or *but,* for example) preceded by a comma, by adding a semicolon, or by making the clauses separate sentences.

- **Manuscript format** Have you followed your instructor's guidelines? Is your essay neat and clearly printed?

EXERCISE 4

Edit your essay, and then print out a final draft.

💻 COMPUTER STRATEGY

Just as you do when you revise, you should edit on a hard copy of your essay. Seeing your work on the printed page makes it easy for you to spot surface-level errors in spelling, grammar, and punctuation. Before you print, however, you can run a grammar check to find problems such as sentence fragments and sexist usage. Remember, though, that grammar checkers are far from perfect. They often miss problems (such as faulty modification), and they frequently highlight areas of text (such as long sentences) that may not contain an error. You can also run a spell check to find words that are misspelled, but keep in mind that a spell checker will not help you with many proper nouns, nor will it highlight words that are spelled correctly but used incorrectly — *there* for *their* or *form* for *from,* for example. For this reason, even if you run a spell check, you must still proofread carefully.

PART TWO

READINGS FOR WRITERS

The relationship between reading and writing is a complex one. Sometimes you will write an essay based on your own experience; more often than not, however, you will respond in writing to something that you have read. The essays in this book give you a chance to do both.

As you are probably aware, the fact that information appears in print or on the Internet does not mean you should take it at face value. Of course, most of the books and articles you read will be reliable, but some — especially material found on Web sites and in online discussion groups — will contain contradictions, biased ideas, or even inaccurate or misleading information. For this reason, your goal should not be simply to understand what you are reading but to assess the credibility of the writer and, eventually, to judge the soundness of his or her ideas.

When you read the essays that follow, you should approach them critically. In other words, you should question (and sometimes challenge) the writer's ideas — and, in the process, try to create new interpretations that you can explore in your writing. Approaching a text in this way is not easy, for it requires you to develop your own analytical and critical skills and your own set of standards to help you judge and interpret what you read. Only after you have read and critically evaluated a text can you begin to draw your ideas together and write about them.

Every reading selection in Chapters 4 through 13 is accompanied by a series of questions intended to guide you through the reading process. In many ways, these questions are a warm-up for the intellectual workout of writing a paper. The more time you devote to them, the more you will develop your analytical skills. In a real sense, then, these questions will help you develop the critical thinking skills that you will need as you write. In becoming a proficient reader, you will also gain confidence in yourself as a writer.

Each of the reading selections in Chapters 4 through 12 is organized around one dominant pattern of development. In your outside reading, however, you will often find more than one pattern used in a single piece of writing (as in Chapter 13, Combining the Patterns, page 651). When you write, then, do not feel you must follow these patterns blindly; instead, think of them as tools for making your writing more effective, and adapt them to your subject, your audience, and your writing purpose.

In addition to the reading selections, each chapter also includes a visual text—for example, a piece of fine art, an advertisement, or a photograph. By visually reinforcing the chapter's basic rhetorical concept, each visual text serves as a bridge to the chapter's essays. Following each visual is a set of questions designed to help you understand not just the image but also the pattern that is the chapter's focus.

4
Narration

WHAT IS NARRATION?

Narration tells a story by presenting events in an orderly, logical sequence. In the following paragraph from "The Stone Horse," essayist Barry Lopez recounts the history of the exploration of the California desert:

Topic sentence	Western man did not enter the California desert until the end of the eighteenth century, 250 years after Coronado brought his soldiers into the Zuni pueblos in a bewildered search for the cities of Cibola. The earliest appraisals of the land were cursory, hurried. People traveled *through* it, en route to Santa Fe or the California coastal settlements. Only
Narrative traces developments through the nineteenth century	miners tarried. In 1823 what had been Spain's became Mexico's, and in 1848 what had been Mexico's became America's; but the bare, jagged mountains and dry lake beds, the vast and uniform plains of creosote bush and yucca plants, remained as obscure as the northern Sudan until the end of the nineteenth century.

Narration can be the dominant pattern in many kinds of writing as well as in speech. Histories, biographies, and autobiographies follow a narrative form, as do personal letters, diaries, and journals. Narration is the dominant pattern in many works of fiction and poetry, and it is an essential part of casual conversation. Narration also underlies folk and fairy tales and radio and television news reports. In short, any time you tell what happened, you are using narration.

USING NARRATION

Although the purpose of a narrative may be simply to recount events or create a particular mood or impression, in college writing a narrative essay is more likely to present a sequence of events for the purpose of supporting a thesis. For instance, in a narrative about your first date, your purpose may be to show your readers that dating is a bizarre and often unpleasant ritual. Accordingly, you do not simply tell the story of your date. Rather, you select and arrange details to show your readers *why* dating is bizarre and unpleasant. As in any other kind of essay, you may state your thesis explicitly ("My experiences with dating have convinced me that this ritual should be abandoned entirely"), or you may imply your thesis through your selection and arrangement of events.

Narration can provide the structure for an entire essay, but narrative passages may also appear in essays that are not primarily narrative. In an *argumentative essay* supporting stricter gun-safety legislation, for example, you might devote one or two paragraphs to the story of a child accidentally killed by a handgun. In this chapter, however, we focus on narration as the dominant pattern of a piece of writing. During your college career, many of your assignments will call for such writing. In an English composition class, for instance, you may be asked to write about an experience that was important to your development as an adult; on a European history exam, you may need to relate the events that led up to Napoleon's defeat at the Battle of Waterloo; in a technical writing class, you may be asked to write a letter of complaint summarizing in detail a company's negligent actions. In each of these situations (as well as in many additional assignments), the piece of writing has a structure that is primarily narrative, and the narrative supports a particular thesis.

The skills you develop in narrative writing will also help you in other kinds of writing. A *process essay,* such as an explanation of a laboratory experiment, is like a narrative because it outlines a series of steps in chronological order; a *cause-and-effect essay,* such as your answer to an exam question that asks you to analyze the events that caused the Great Depression, also resembles a narrative in that it traces a sequence of events. A process essay, however, explains how to do something, and a cause-and-effect essay explains why events occur. Still, writing process and cause-and-effect essays will be easier after you master narration. (Process essays and cause-and-effect essays are dealt with in Chapters 7 and 8, respectively.)

PLANNING A NARRATIVE ESSAY

Including Enough Detail

Narratives, like other types of writing, need rich, specific details if they are to be convincing. Each detail should help to create a picture for the reader; even exact times, dates, and geographical locations can be helpful.

Look, for example, at the following paragraph from the essay "My Mother Never Worked," which appears later in this chapter:

> In the winter she sewed night after night, endlessly, begging cast-off clothing from relatives, ripping apart coats, dresses, blouses, and trousers to remake them to fit her four daughters and son. Every morning and every evening she milked cows, fed pigs and calves, cared for chickens, picked eggs, cooked meals, washed dishes, scrubbed floors, and tended and loved her children. In the spring she planted a garden once more, dragging pails of water to nourish and sustain the vegetables for the family. In 1936 she lost a baby in her sixth month.

In the paragraph above, the list of details gives the narrative authenticity and generates interest. The central figure in the narrative is a busy, productive woman, and readers know this because they are presented with an exhaustive catalog of her activities.

Varying Sentence Structure

When narratives present a long series of events, all the sentences can begin to sound alike: "She sewed dresses. She milked cows. She fed pigs. She fed calves. She cared for chickens." Such a predictable string of sentences may become monotonous for your readers. You can eliminate this monotony by varying your sentence structure — for instance, by using a variety of sentence openings or by combining simple sentences: "In the winter she sewed night after night, endlessly.[. . .] Every morning and every evening she milked cows, fed pigs and calves, cared for chickens."

Maintaining Clear Narrative Order

Many narratives present events in the exact order in which they occurred, moving from first event to last. Whether or not you follow a strict **chronological order** depends on the purpose of your narrative. If you are writing a straightforward account of a historical event or summarizing a record of poor management practices, you will probably want to move from beginning to end. In a personal experience essay or a fictional narrative, however, you may want to engage your readers' interest by beginning with an event from the middle of your story, or even from the end, and then presenting the events that led up to it. You may also decide to begin in the present and then use one or more **flashbacks** (shifts into the past) to tell your story.

Using Accurate Verb Tenses   **Verb tense** is extremely important in writing that recounts events in a fixed order because tenses indicate temporal (time) relationships — *earlier, simultaneous, later.* When you write a narrative, you must be careful to keep verb tenses consistent and accurate so your readers can follow the sequence of events. Naturally, you must shift tenses to reflect an actual time shift in your narrative. For instance, convention requires that you use present tense when discussing works of literature ("When Hamlet's mother *marries* his uncle . . . "), but a flashback to an earlier point in the story calls for a shift from present to past tense ("Before their marriage, Hamlet *was . . .*"). Nevertheless, you should avoid unwarranted shifts in verb tense; they will make your narrative confusing.

Using Transitions   Transitions — connecting words or phrases — help link events in time, enabling narratives to flow smoothly. Without them, narratives would lack coherence, and readers would be unsure of the correct sequence of events. Transitions can indicate the order in which events occur, and they also signal shifts in time. In narrative writing, the transitions commonly used for these purposes include *first, second, next, then, later, at the same time, meanwhile, immediately, soon, before, earlier, after, afterward, now,* and *finally.* In addition to these transitions, specific time markers — such as *three years later, in 1927, after two hours,* and *on January 3* — indicate how much time has passed between events. (A more complete list of transitions appears on page 43.)

STRUCTURING A NARRATIVE ESSAY

Like other essays, a narrative essay has an introduction, a body, and a conclusion. If your essay's thesis is explicitly stated, it will, in most cases, appear in the *introduction*. The *body* of your essay will recount the events that make up your narrative, following a clear and orderly plan. Finally, the *conclusion* will give your readers the sense that your story is complete, perhaps by restating your thesis or summarizing key points or events.

Suppose you are assigned a short history paper about the Battle of Waterloo. You plan to support the thesis that if Napoleon had kept more troops in reserve, he might have defeated the British troops serving under Wellington. Based on this thesis, you decide that the best way to organize your paper is to present the five major phases of the battle in chronological order. An informal outline of your essay might look like this:

Introduction:	Thesis statement — Had Napoleon kept more troops in reserve, he might have broken Wellington's line with another infantry attack and thus won the Battle of Waterloo.
Phase 1 of the battle:	Napoleon attacked the Château of Hougoumont.
Phase 2 of the battle:	The French infantry attacked the British lines.
Phase 3 of the battle:	The French cavalry staged a series of charges against the British lines that had not been attacked before; Napoleon committed his reserves.

Phase 4 of the battle:	The French captured La Haye Sainte, their first success of the day but an advantage that Napoleon, having committed troops elsewhere, could not maintain without reserves.
Phase 5 of the battle:	The French infantry was decisively defeated by the combined thrust of the British infantry and the remaining British cavalry.
Conclusion:	Restatement of thesis or review of key points or events.

By discussing the five phases of the battle in chronological order, you clearly support your thesis. As you expand your informal outline into a historical narrative, exact details, dates, times, and geographical locations are extremely important. Without them, your statements are open to question. In addition, to keep your readers aware of the order in which the events of the battle took place, you must select appropriate transitional words and phrases and pay careful attention to verb tenses.

REVISING A NARRATIVE ESSAY

When you revise a narrative essay, consider the items on the Revision Checklist on page 54. In addition, pay special attention to the items on the checklist below, which apply specifically to revising narrative essays.

☑ REVISION CHECKLIST: NARRATION

- Does your assignment call for narration?
- Does your essay's thesis communicate the significance of the events you discuss?
- Have you included enough specific detail?
- Have you varied your sentence structure?
- Is the order of events clear to readers?
- Have you varied sentence openings to avoid monotony?
- Do your transitions link events in time?

EDITING A NARRATIVE ESSAY

When you edit your narrative essay, follow the guidelines on the Editing Checklist on pages 66–67. In addition, focus on the grammar, mechanics, and punctuation issues that are most relevant to narrative essays. One of these issues — avoiding run-on sentences — is discussed on page 76.

For more practice in avoiding run-ons, visit **Exercise Central** at <bedfordstmartins.com/patterns/runons>.

GRAMMAR IN CONTEXT : Avoiding Run-on Sentences*

When writing narrative essays, particularly personal narratives and essays that include dialogue, writers can easily lose sight of sentence boundaries and create **run-on sentences.** There are two kinds of run-on sentences: fused sentences and comma splices.

A **fused sentence** occurs when two sentences are incorrectly joined without punctuation.

Two correct sentences: "The sun came out hot and bright, endlessly, day after day. The crops shriveled and died." (Smith-Yackel 97)

Fused sentence: The sun came out hot and bright, endlessly, day after day the crops shriveled and died.

A **comma splice** occurs when two sentences are incorrectly joined with just a comma.

Comma splice: The sun came out hot and bright, endlessly, day after day, the crops shriveled and died.

There are five ways to correct these errors.

1. **Use a period to create two separate sentences.**

   The sun came out hot and bright, endlessly, day after day. The crops shriveled and died.

2. **Join the sentences with a comma and a coordinating conjunction** (*and, or, nor, for, so, but, yet*).

   The sun came out hot and bright, endlessly, day after day, and the crops shriveled and died.

3. **Join the sentences with a semicolon.**

   The sun came out hot and bright, endlessly, day after day; the crops shriveled and died.

4. **Join the sentences with a semicolon and a transitional word or phrase (followed by a comma), such as** *however, therefore,* **or** *for example.* **(See page 43 for a list of transitional words and phrases.)**

   The sun came out hot and bright, endlessly, day after day; eventually, the crops shriveled and died.

5. **Create a complex sentence by adding a subordinating conjunction** (*although, because, if,* and so on) **or a relative pronoun** (*who, which, that,* and so on) **to one of the sentences.**

   As the sun came out hot and bright, endlessly, day after day, the crops shriveled and died.

---

*Eds. note — All the examples used below refer to an essay that appears later in this chapter.

☑ **EDITING CHECKLIST: NARRATION**

- Have you avoided run-on sentences?
- Have you avoided sentence fragments?
- Do your verb tenses enable readers to follow the sequence of events?
- Have you avoided unnecessary tense shifts?
- Have you punctuated dialogue correctly and capitalized where necessary?

▶ **A STUDENT WRITER: NARRATION**

The following essay is typical of the informal narrative writing many students are asked to do in English composition classes. It was written by Tiffany Forte in response to the assignment "Write an essay about a goal or dream you had when you were a child."

My Field of Dreams

Introduction   When I was young, I was told that when I   1
grew up I could be anything I wanted to be, and
I always took for granted that this was true.
I knew exactly what I was going to be, and I
would spend hours dreaming about how wonderful
my life would be when I grew up. One day, though,
Thesis statement   when I did grow up, I realized that things had
not turned out the way I had always expected
they would.

Narrative begins   When I was little, I never played with   2
baby dolls or Barbies. I wasn't like other
little girls; I was a tomboy. I was the only
girl in the neighborhood where I lived, so I
always played with boys. We would play army or
football or (my favorite) baseball.

Almost every summer afternoon, all the   3
boys in my neighborhood and I would meet by the
big oak tree to get a baseball game going. Surprisingly, I was always one of the first to be
picked for a team. I was very fast, and (for my
size) I could hit the ball far. I loved baseball more than anything, and I wouldn't miss a
game for the world.

My dad played baseball too, and every Fri-   4
day night I would go to the field with my mother

to watch him play. It was just like the big
leagues, with lots of people, a snack bar, and
lights that shone so high and bright you could
see them a mile away. I loved to go to my dad's
games. When all the other kids would wander off
and play, I would sit and cheer on my dad and
his team. My attention was focused on the field,
and my heart would jump with every pitch.

Even more exciting than my dad's games   5
were the major league games. The Phillies were
my favorite team, and I always looked forward
to watching them on television. My dad would
make popcorn, and we would sit and watch in
anticipation of a Phillies victory. We would
go wild, yelling and screaming at all the big
plays. When the Phillies would win, I would be
so excited I couldn't sleep; when they would
lose, I would go to bed angry just like my dad.

*Key experience
introduced
(par. 6–7)*

It was when my dad took me to my first   6
major league baseball game that I decided I
wanted to be a major league baseball player.
The excitement began when we pulled into the
parking lot of Veterans Stadium. There were
thousands of cars. As we walked from the car
to the stadium, my dad told me to hold on to
his hand and not to let go no matter what. When
we gave the man our tickets and entered the
stadium, I understood why. There were mobs of
people everywhere. They were walking around
the stadium and standing in long lines for hot
dogs, beer, and souvenirs. It was the most wonderful thing I had ever seen. When we got to
our seats, I looked down at the tiny baseball
diamond below and felt as if I were on top of
the world.

The cheering of the crowd, the singing,   7
and the chants were almost more than I could
stand. I was bursting with enthusiasm. Then,
in the bottom of the eighth inning, with the

score tied and two outs, Mike Schmidt came up
to bat and hit the game-winning home run. The
crowd went crazy. Everyone in the whole stadium
was standing, and I found myself yelling and
screaming along with everyone else. When Mike
Schmidt came out of the dugout to receive his
standing ovation, I felt a lump in my throat
and butterflies in my stomach. He was everyone's hero that night, and I could only imagine
the pride he must have felt. I slept the whole
way home and dreamed of what it would be like
to be the hero of the game.

*Narrative
continues*

The next day, when I met with the boys   8
at the oak tree, I told them that when I grew
up, I was going to be a major league baseball
player. They all laughed at me and said I could
never be a baseball player because I was a girl.
I told them that they were all wrong, and that
I would show them.

*Analysis of childhood
experiences*

In the years to follow I played girls'   9
softball in a competitive fast-pitch league,
and I was very good. I always wanted to play
baseball with the boys, but there were no mixed
leagues. After a few years, I realized that
the boys from the oak tree were right: I was
never going to be a major league baseball
player. I realized that what I had been told
when I was younger wasn't the whole truth.
What no one had bothered to tell me was that
I could be anything I wanted to be—as long as
it was something that was appropriate for a
girl to do.

Conclusion

In time, I would get over the loss of my   10
dream. I found new dreams, acceptable for a
young woman, and I moved on to other things.
Still, every time I watch a baseball game and
someone hits a home run, I get those same butterflies in my stomach and think, for just a
minute, about what might have been.

Points for Special Attention

Introduction   Tiffany's introduction is straightforward, yet it arouses reader interest by setting up a contrast between what she expected and what actually happened. Her optimistic expectation—that she could be anything she wanted to be—is contradicted by her thesis statement, encouraging readers to read on to discover how things turned out, and why.

Thesis Statement   Tiffany's assignment was to write about a goal or dream she had when she was a child, but her instructor made it clear that the essay should have an explicitly stated thesis that made a point about the goal or dream. Tiffany knew she wanted to write about her passion for baseball, but she also knew that just listing a series of events would not fulfill the assignment. Her thesis statement—"One day, though, when I did grow up, I realized that things had not turned out the way I had always expected they would"—puts her memories in context, suggesting that she will use them to support a general conclusion about the gap between dreams and reality.

Structure   The body of Tiffany's essay traces the chronology of her involvement with baseball—playing with the neighborhood boys, watching her father's games, watching baseball on television, and, finally, seeing her first major league game. Each body paragraph introduces a different aspect of her experience with baseball, culminating in the vividly described Phillies game. The balance of the essay (paragraphs 8–10) summarizes the aftermath of that game, gives a brief overview of Tiffany's later years in baseball, and presents her conclusion.

Detail   Personal narratives like Tiffany's need a lot of detail because the writers want readers to see and hear and feel what they did. To present an accurate picture, Tiffany includes all the significant sights and sounds she can remember: the big oak tree, the lights on the field, the popcorn, the excited cheers, the food and souvenir stands, the crowds, and so on. She also names Mike Schmidt ("everyone's hero"), his team, and the stadium in which she saw him play. Despite all these details, though, she omits some important information—for example, how old she was at each stage of her essay.

Verb Tense   Maintaining clear chronological order is very important in narrative writing, where unwarranted shifts in verb tenses can confuse readers. Knowing this, Tiffany avoids unnecessary tense shifts. In her conclusion, she shifts from past to present tense, but this shift is both necessary and clear. Elsewhere she uses *would* to identify events that recurred regularly. For example, in paragraph 5 she says, "My dad *would* make popcorn" rather than "My dad *made* popcorn," which would suggest that he did so only once.

Transitions   Tiffany's skillful use of transitional words and expressions links her sentences and moves her readers smoothly through her essay. In addition to transitional words like *when* and *then,* she uses specific time markers—"When I was little," "Almost every summer afternoon," "every Friday night," "As we walked," "The next day," "In the years to follow," and "After a few years"—to advance the narrative and carry her readers along.

Focus on Revision

In their responses to an earlier draft of Tiffany's essay, several students in her peer editing group recommended that she revise one particularly monotonous paragraph. (As one student pointed out, all its sentences began with the subject, making the paragraph seem choppy and its ideas disconnected.) Here is the paragraph from her draft:

> My dad played baseball too. I went to the field with my mother every Friday night to watch him play. It was just like the big leagues. There were lots of people and a snack bar. The lights shone so high and bright you could see them a mile away. I loved to go to my dad's games. All the other kids would wander off and play. I would sit and cheer on my dad and his team. My attention was focused on the field. My heart would jump with every pitch.

In the revised version of the paragraph (now paragraph 4 of her essay), Tiffany varies sentence length and opening strategies:

> My dad played baseball too, and every Friday night I would go to the field with my mother to watch him play. It was just like the big leagues, with lots of people, a snack bar, and lights that shone so high and bright you could see them a mile away. I loved to go to my dad's games. When all the other kids would wander off and play, I would sit and cheer on my dad and his team. My attention was focused on the field, and my heart would jump with every pitch.

After reading Tiffany's revised draft, another student suggested that she might still polish her essay a bit. For instance, she could add some dialogue, quoting the boys' taunts and her own reply in paragraph 8. She could also edit to eliminate **clichés** (overused expressions), substituting fresher, more original language for phrases like "I felt a lump in my throat and butterflies in my stomach" and "I felt as if I were on top of the world." In the draft of her essay, Tiffany followed up on these suggestions. (A sample peer editing worksheet for narration can be found on the *Patterns for College Writing* Web site at <bedfordstmartins.com/patterns>.)

The selections that follow illustrate some of the many possibilities open to writers of narratives. The first selection, a visual text, is followed by questions designed to illustrate how narration can operate in visual form.

From *Spider-Man* (Comic Book)

TM & © 2003, Marvel Characters Inc. Used with permission.

• • •

READING IMAGES

1. The five panels above tell part of a story of a conflict between Spider-Man and his enemy The Vulture. Make a list of the events depicted in the panels in the order in which they occur.

2. What visual elements link each panel to the one that follows? Can you identify any verbal transitions? What additional transitional words and phrases might help to move readers more smoothly through the story?

3. What do you think happened before the events depicted here? What do you suppose will happen next?

JOURNAL ENTRY

Write a narrative paragraph summarizing the story told in these panels. Begin with a sentence that identifies the characters and the setting. Next, write a sentence that summarizes the events that might have preceded the first panel. Then, tell the story the pictures tell. In your last sentence, bring the sequence of events to a logical close. Be sure to use present tense and to include all necessary transitions.

THEMATIC CONNECTIONS

- "Creating a Female Sleuth" (page 265)
- "On Fire" (page 280)
- "Whodunit — The Media?" (page 618)
- "The Park" (page 655)

SANDRA CISNEROS

Only Daughter

Born into a working-class family in 1954, Sandra Cisneros, the daughter of a Mexican-American mother and a Mexican father, spent much of her childhood shuttling between Chicago and Mexico City. A lonely, bookish child, Cisneros began writing privately at a young age but only began to find her voice when she was a creative writing student at Loyola University and later at the University of Iowa Writers' Workshop. Her best-known works are the novel *The House on Mango Street* (1983) and the short-story collection *Woman Hollering Creek* (1991); she has also published several collections of poetry. Cisneros's latest novel, *Caramelo,* appeared in 2002.

Background: In the following essay, which originally appeared in *Glamour* in 1990, Cisneros describes the difficulties of growing up as the only daughter in a Mexican-American family of six sons. Historically, sons have been valued over daughters in most cultures, as reflected in the following proverbs: "A house full of daughters is like a cellar full of sour beer" (Dutch); "Daughters pay nae [no] debts" (Scottish); "A stupid son is better than a crafty daughter" (Chinese); "A virtuous son is the sun of his family" (Sanskrit). This was largely the case because limited employment opportunities for women meant that sons were more likely to be able to provide financial support for aging parents. Contemporary research suggests that while a preference for sons has diminished considerably in industrialized nations, there continues to be a distinct preference for sons among many cultures in Asia and the Middle East, a fact that has raised concerns among medical ethicists worldwide. And even within the more traditional cultures of the industrialized world, old habits of mind regarding the role of women in society can die hard, as the attitudes of Cisneros's father suggest.

Once, several years ago, when I was just starting out my writing career, I was asked to write my own contributor's note for an anthology I was part of. I wrote: "I am the only daughter in a family of six sons. *That* explains everything."

Well, I've thought about that ever since, and yes, it explains a lot to me, but for the reader's sake I should have written: "I am the only daughter in a *Mexican* family of six sons." Or even: "I am the only daughter of a Mexican father and a Mexican-American mother." Or: "I am the only daughter of a working-class family of nine." All of these had everything to do with who I am today.

I was/am the only daughter and *only* a daughter. Being an only daughter in a family of six sons forced me by circumstance to spend a lot of time by myself because my brothers felt it beneath them to play with a *girl* in public. But that aloneness, that loneliness, was good for a would-be

writer—it allowed me time to think and think, to imagine, to read and prepare myself.

Being only a daughter for my father meant my destiny would lead me   4
to become someone's wife. That's what he believed. But when I was in the
fifth grade and shared my plans for college with him, I was sure he understood. I remember my father saying, "*Que bueno, ni'ja,* that's good." That
meant a lot to me, especially since my brothers thought the idea hilarious.
What I didn't realize was that my father thought college was good for
girls—good for finding a husband. After four years in college and two more
in graduate school, and still no husband, my father shakes his head even
now and says I wasted all that education.

In retrospect, I'm lucky my father believed daughters were meant for   5
husbands. It meant it didn't matter if I majored in something silly like
English. After all, I'd find a nice professional eventually, right? This allowed
me the liberty to putter about embroidering my little poems and stories
without my father interrupting with so much as a "What's that you're
writing?"

But the truth is, I wanted him to interrupt. I wanted my father to   6
understand what it was I was scribbling, to introduce me as "My only
daughter, the writer." Not as "This is only my daughter. She teaches." *Es
maestra*—teacher. Not even *profesora.*

In a sense, everything I have ever written has been for him, to win his   7
approval even though I know my father can't read English words, even
though my father's only reading includes the brown-ink *Esto* sports magazines from Mexico City and the bloody *¡Alarma!* magazines that feature yet
another sighting of *La Virgen de Guadalupe* on a tortilla or a wife's revenge
on her philandering husband by bashing his skull in with a *molcajete* (a
kitchen mortar made of volcanic rock). Or the *fotonovelas,* the little picture
paperbacks with tragedy and trauma erupting from the characters' mouths
in bubbles.

My father represents, then, the public majority. A public who is un-   8
interested in reading, and yet one whom I am writing about and for, and
privately trying to woo.

When we were growing up in Chicago, we moved a lot because of my   9
father. He suffered bouts of nostalgia. Then we'd have to let go of our flat,
store the furniture with mother's relatives, load the station wagon with
baggage and bologna sandwiches, and head south. To Mexico City.

We came back, of course. To yet another Chicago flat, another Chicago   10
neighborhood, another Catholic school. Each time, my father would seek
out the parish priest in order to get a tuition break, and complain or boast:
"I have seven sons."

He meant *siete hijos,* seven children, but he translated it as "sons." "I   11
have seven sons." To anyone who would listen. The Sears Roebuck
employee who sold us the washing machine. The short-order cook where
my father ate his ham-and-eggs breakfasts. "I have seven sons." As if he
deserved a medal from the state.

My papa. He didn't mean anything by that mistranslation, I'm sure. 12
But somehow I could feel myself being erased. I'd tug my father's sleeve
and whisper: "Not seven sons. Six! and *one daughter.*"

When my oldest brother graduated from medical school, he fulfilled 13
my father's dream that we study hard and use this—our heads, instead
of this—our hands. Even now my father's hands are thick and yellow,
stubbed by a history of hammer and nails and twine and coils and springs.
"Use this," my father said, tapping his head, "and not this," showing us
those hands. He always looked tired when he said it.

Wasn't college an investment? And hadn't I spent all those years in 14
college? And if I didn't marry, what was it all for? Why would anyone go to
college and then choose to be poor? Especially someone who had always
been poor.

Last year, after ten years of writing professionally, the financial rewards 15
started to trickle in. My second National Endowment for the Arts Fellowship. A guest professorship at the University of California, Berkeley. My
book, which sold to a major New York publishing house.

At Christmas, I flew home to Chicago. The house was throbbing, same 16
as always; hot *tamales* and sweet *tamales* hissing in my mother's pressure
cooker, and everybody—my mother, six brothers, wives, babies, aunts,
cousins—talking too loud and at the same time, like in a Fellini film,
because that's just how we are.

I went upstairs to my father's room. One of my stories had just been 17
translated into Spanish and published in an anthology of Chicano writing,
and I wanted to show it to him. Ever since he recovered from a stroke two
years ago, my father likes to spend his leisure hours horizontally. And
that's how I found him, watching a Pedro Infante* movie on Galavisión**
and eating rice pudding.

There was a glass filmed with milk on the bedside table. There were 18
several vials of pills and balled Kleenex. And on the floor, one black sock
and a plastic urinal that I didn't want to look at but looked at anyway.
Pedro Infante was about to burst into song, and my father was laughing.

I'm not sure if it was because my story was translated into Spanish, or 19
because it was published in Mexico, or perhaps because the story dealt
with Tepeyac, the *colonia* my father was raised in and the house he grew up
in, but at any rate, my father punched the mute button on his remote control and read my story.

I sat on the bed next to my father and waited. He read it very slowly. As 20
if he were reading each line over and over. He laughed at all the right places
and read lines he liked out loud. He pointed and asked questions: "Is this
So-and-so?" "Yes," I said. He kept reading.

When he was finally finished, after what seemed like hours, my father 21
looked up and asked: "Where can we get more copies of this for the relatives?"

---

*EDS. NOTE—Mexican actor.
**EDS. NOTE—A Spanish-language cable channel.

Of all the wonderful things that happened to me last year, that was the   22
most wonderful.

• • •

COMPREHENSION

1. What does Cisneros mean when she writes that being an only daughter in a family of six sons "explains everything" (1)?
2. What distinction does Cisneros make in paragraphs 2 and 3 between being "the only daughter" and being "only a daughter"?
3. What advantages does Cisneros see in being "the only daughter"? In being "only a daughter"?
4. Why does her father think she has wasted her education? What is her reaction to his opinion?
5. Why is her father's reaction to her story the "most wonderful" (22) thing that happened to Cisneros that year?

PURPOSE AND AUDIENCE

1. Although Cisneros uses many Spanish words in her essay, in most cases she defines or explains these words. What does this decision tell you about her purpose and audience?
2. What is Cisneros's thesis? What incidents and details support her point?
3. Do you think Cisneros intends to convey a sympathetic or an unsympathetic impression of her father? Explain.

STYLE AND STRUCTURE

1. Where does Cisneros interrupt a narrative passage to comment on or analyze events? What does this strategy accomplish?
2. Are the episodes presented in chronological order? Explain.
3. What transitional expressions does Cisneros use to introduce new episodes?
4. Cisneros quotes her father several times. What do we learn about him from his words?
5. Why does Cisneros devote so much space to describing her father in paragraphs 17-21? How does this portrait compare to the one she presents in paragraphs 9-11?

VOCABULARY PROJECTS

1. Define each of the following words as it is used in this selection.

   embroidering (5)   stubbed (13)

2. What is the difference in connotation between *sons* and *children*? Between *teacher* and *professor*? Do you think these distinctions are as significant as Cisneros seems to think they are? Explain.

JOURNAL ENTRY

In what sense do the number and gender(s) of your siblings "explain everything" about who you are today?

WRITING WORKSHOP

1. Write a narrative essay consisting of a series of related episodes that show how you gradually gained the approval and respect of one of your parents, another relative, or a friend.

2. In "Only Daughter," Cisneros traces the development of her identity as an adult, a female, and a writer. Write a narrative essay in which you trace the development of your own personal or professional identity.

3. Are male and female children treated differently in your family? Have your parents had different expectations for their sons and daughters? Write a narrative essay recounting one or more incidents that illustrate these differences (or the lack of differences). If you and your siblings are all of the same gender, or if you are an only child, write about another family you know well.

COMBINING THE PATTERNS

Cisneros structures her essay as a narrative in which she is the main character and her brothers barely appear. To give her readers a clearer understanding of how her father's attitude toward her differs from his attitude toward her brothers, Cisneros could have added one or more paragraphs of **comparison and contrast,** focusing on the different ways she and her brothers are treated. What specific points of contrast would readers find most useful? Where might such paragraphs be added?

THEMATIC CONNECTIONS

- "My Field of Dreams" (page 77)
- "Words Left Unspoken" (page 153)
- "Suicide Note" (page 357)
- "The Men We Carry in Our Minds" (page 456)

❖

Finishing School

Maya Angelou was born Marguerita Johnson in 1928 in St. Louis and spent much of her childhood in Stamps, Arkansas, living with her grandmother. She began her varied career as an actress and singer, appearing in several television dramas and films; in 1998, she made her debut as a director with the film *Down in the Delta.* In the 1960s, she served as northern coordinator for the Southern Christian Leadership Conference, the civil rights group organized by Martin Luther King Jr. A well-known poet, Angelou composed and read "On the Pulse of Morning" for Bill Clinton's 1993 presidential inauguration. The published version of the poem was a best-seller, and her recording of it won a Grammy award. She is currently on the faculty at Wake Forest University. It is likely, however, that Angelou will be best remembered for her series of autobiographical works, beginning with the critically acclaimed *I Know Why the Caged Bird Sings* (1969), which appeared at a time when African-American literature was just beginning to flower.

Background: In the following excerpt from *I Know Why the Caged Bird Sings,* Angelou recalls a difficult incident that occurred when she was growing up in racially segregated Stamps in the late 1930s. At this time, wealthy young white women, rather than complete a rigorous education, often attended "finishing schools," where they refined the social skills and artistic accomplishments deemed necessary for their future roles in polite society. While versions of such schools existed on a limited basis for the daughters of black professionals in urban areas, children of the poor and the working class—both black and white—were expected to learn practical skills that would provide them a means of employment. Such employment opportunities for rural black people were limited by and large to farm work; black women in particular were limited to domestic service in white households, the role for which Angelou describes her training in this essay.

Recently a white woman from Texas, who would quickly describe herself as a liberal, asked me about my hometown. When I told her that in Stamps my grandmother had owned the only Negro general merchandise store since the turn of the century, she exclaimed, "Why, you were a debutante." Ridiculous and even ludicrous. But Negro girls in small Southern towns, whether poverty-stricken or just munching along on a few of life's necessities, were given as extensive and irrelevant preparations for adulthood as rich white girls shown in magazines. Admittedly the training was not the same. While white girls learned to waltz and sit gracefully with a tea cup balanced on their knees, we were lagging behind, learning the mid-Victorian values with very little money to indulge them. . . .

We were required to embroider and I had trunkfuls of colorful dish- 2
towels, pillowcases, runners, and handkerchiefs to my credit. I mastered
the art of crocheting and tatting, and there was a lifetime's supply of
dainty doilies that would never be used in sacheted dresser drawers. It went
without saying that all girls could iron and wash, but the finer touches
around the home, like setting a table with real silver, baking roasts, and
cooking vegetables without meat, had to be learned elsewhere. Usually at
the source of those habits. During my tenth year, a white woman's kitchen
became my finishing school.

Mrs. Viola Cullinan was a plump woman who lived in a three-bedroom 3
house somewhere behind the post office. She was singularly unattractive
until she smiled, and then the lines around her eyes and mouth which
made her look perpetually dirty disappeared, and her face looked like the
mask of an impish elf. She usually rested her smile until late afternoon
when her woman friends dropped in and Miss Glory, the cook, served
them cold drinks on the closed-in porch.

The exactness of her house was inhuman. This glass went here and 4
only here. That cup had its place and it was an act of impudent rebellion to
place it anywhere else. At twelve o'clock the table was set. At 12:15 Mrs.
Cullinan sat down to dinner (whether her husband had arrived or not). At
12:16 Miss Glory brought out the food.

It took me a week to learn the difference between a salad plate, a bread 5
plate, and a dessert plate.

Mrs. Cullinan kept up the tradition of her wealthy parents. She was 6
from Virginia. Miss Glory, who was a descendant of slaves that had worked
for the Cullinans, told me her history. She had married beneath her (according to Miss Glory). Her husband's family hadn't had their money very
long and what they had "didn't 'mount to much."

As ugly as she was, I thought privately, she was lucky to get a husband 7
above or beneath her station. But Miss Glory wouldn't let me say a thing
against her mistress. She was very patient with me, however, over the
housework. She explained the dishware, silverware, and servants' bells. The
large round bowl in which soup was served wasn't a soup bowl, it was a
tureen. There were goblets, sherbet glasses, ice-cream glasses, wine glasses,
green glass coffee cups with matching saucers, and water glasses. I had a
glass to drink from, and it sat with Miss Glory's on a separate shelf from
the others. Soup spoons, gravy boat, butter knives, salad forks, and carving
platter were additions to my vocabulary and in fact almost represented a
new language. I was fascinated with the novelty, with the fluttering Mrs.
Cullinan and her Alice-in-Wonderland house.

Her husband remains, in my memory, undefined. I lumped him with 8
all the other white men that I had ever seen and tried not to see.

On our way home one evening, Miss Glory told me that Mrs. Cullinan 9
couldn't have children. She said that she was too delicate-boned. It was
hard to imagine bones at all under those layers of fat. Miss Glory went on
to say that the doctor had taken out all her lady organs. I reasoned that a

pig's organs included the lungs, heart, and liver, so if Mrs. Cullinan was walking around without those essentials, it explained why she drank alcohol out of unmarked bottles. She was keeping herself embalmed.

When I spoke to Bailey* about it, he agreed that I was right, but he also 10
informed me that Mr. Cullinan had two daughters by a colored lady and that I knew them very well. He added that the girls were the spitting image of their father. I was unable to remember what he looked like, although I had just left him a few hours before, but I thought of the Coleman girls. They were very light-skinned and certainly didn't look very much like their mother (no one ever mentioned Mr. Coleman).

My pity for Mrs. Cullinan preceded me the next morning like the 11
Cheshire cat's smile. Those girls, who could have been her daughters, were beautiful. They didn't have to straighten their hair. Even when they were caught in the rain, their braids still hung down straight like tamed snakes. Their mouths were pouty little cupid's bows. Mrs. Cullinan didn't know what she missed. Or maybe she did. Poor Mrs. Cullinan.

For weeks after, I arrived early, left late and tried very hard to make up 12
for her barrenness. If she had her own children, she wouldn't have had to ask me to run a thousand errands from her back door to the back doors of her friends. Poor old Mrs. Cullinan.

Then one evening Miss Glory told me to serve the ladies on the porch. 13
After I set the tray down and turned toward the kitchen, one of the women asked, "What's your name, girl?" It was the speckled-faced one. Mrs. Cullinan said, "She doesn't talk much. Her name's Margaret."

"Is she dumb?" 14

"No. As I understand it, she can talk when she wants to but she's usu- 15
ally quiet as a little mouse. Aren't you, Margaret?"

I smile at her. Poor thing. No organs and couldn't even pronounce my 16
name correctly.

"She's a sweet little thing, though." 17

"Well, that may be, but the name's too long. I'd never bother myself. I'd 18
call her Mary if I was you."

I fumed into the kitchen. That horrible woman would never have the 19
chance to call me Mary because if I was starving I'd never work for her. . . .

That evening I decided to write a poem on being white, fat, old, and 20
without children. It was going to be a tragic ballad. I would have to watch her carefully to capture the essence of her loneliness and pain.

The very next day, she called me by the wrong name. Miss Glory and I 21
were washing up the lunch dishes when Mrs. Cullinan came to the doorway. "Mary?"

Miss Glory asked, "Who?" 22

Mrs. Cullinan, sagging a little, knew and I knew. "I want Mary to go 23
down to Mrs. Randall's and take her some soup. She's not been feeling well for a few days."

---

* EDS. NOTE — Angelou's brother.

Miss Glory's face was a wonder to see. "You mean Margaret, ma'am. 24
Her name's Margaret."

"That's too long. She's Mary from now on. Heat that soup from last 25
night and put it in the china tureen and, Mary, I want you to carry it carefully."

Every person I knew had a hellish horror of being "called out of his 26
name." It was a dangerous practice to call a Negro anything that could be
loosely construed as insulting because of the centuries of their having been
called niggers, jigs, dinges, blackbirds, crows, boots, and spooks.

Miss Glory had a fleeting second of feeling sorry for me. Then as she 27
handed me the hot tureen she said, "Don't mind, don't pay that no mind.
Sticks and stones may break your bones, but words . . . You know, I been
working for her for twenty years."

She held the back door open for me. "Twenty years. I wasn't much 28
older than you. My name used to be Hallelujah. That's what Ma named
me, but my mistress give me 'Glory,' and it stuck. I likes it better too."

I was in the little path that ran behind the houses when Miss Glory 29
shouted, "It's shorter too."

For a few seconds it was a tossup over whether I would laugh (imagine 30
being named Hallelujah) or cry (imagine letting some white woman rename you for her convenience). My anger saved me from either outburst. I
had to quit the job, but the problem was going to be how to do it. Momma
wouldn't allow me to quit for just any reason.

"She's a peach. That woman is a real peach." Mrs. Randall's maid was 31
talking as she took the soup from me, and I wondered what her name used
to be and what she answered to now.

For a week I looked into Mrs. Cullinan's face as she called me Mary. 32
She ignored my coming late and leaving early. Miss Glory was a little
annoyed because I had begun to leave egg yolk on the dishes and wasn't
putting much heart in polishing the silver. I hoped that she would complain to our boss, but she didn't.

Then Bailey solved my dilemma. He had me describe the contents 33
of the cupboard and the particular plates she liked best. Her favorite
piece was a casserole shaped like fish and the green glass coffee cups. I
kept his instructions in mind, so on the next day when Miss Glory was
hanging out clothes and I had again been told to serve the old biddies on
the porch, I dropped the empty serving tray. When I heard Mrs. Cullinan
scream "Mary!" I picked up the casserole and two of the green glass cups
in readiness. As she rounded the kitchen door I let them fall on the tiled
floor.

I could never absolutely describe to Bailey what happened next, 34
because each time I got to the part where she fell on the floor and screwed
up her ugly face to cry, we burst out laughing. She actually wobbled around
on the floor and picked up shards of the cups and cried, "Oh, Momma.
Oh, dear Gawd. It's Mamma's china from Virginia. Oh Momma, I'm
sorry."

Miss Glory came running in from the yard and the women from the   35
porch crowded around. Miss Glory was almost as broken up as her mistress. "You mean to say she broke our Virginia dishes? What we gone do?"

Mrs. Cullinan cried louder. "That clumsy nigger. Clumsy little black   36
nigger."

Old speckled-face leaned down and asked, "Who did it, Viola? Was it   37
Mary? Who did it?"

Everything was happening so fast I can't remember whether her action   38
preceded her words, but I know that Mrs. Cullinan said, "Her name's Margaret, goddamn it, her name's Margaret." And she threw a wedge of broken
plate at me. It could have been the hysteria which put her aim off, but the
flying crockery caught Miss Glory right over her ear and she started
screaming.

I left the front door wide open so all the neighbors could hear.   39

Mrs. Cullinan was right about one thing. My name wasn't Mary.   40

• • •

COMPREHENSION

1. What is Angelou required to do in the white woman's kitchen? Why are these tasks so important to Mrs. Cullinan?

2. Why does Angelou feel sorry for Mrs. Cullinan at first? When does her attitude change? Why?

3. Why does Mrs. Cullinan's friend recommend that Angelou be called "Mary" (18)? Why does this upset Angelou so deeply?

4. When Angelou decides she wants to quit, she realizes she cannot quit "for just any reason" (30). How does Bailey help her resolve her dilemma?

5. What does Angelou actually learn through her experience?

PURPOSE AND AUDIENCE

1. Is Angelou writing for southerners, blacks, whites, or a general audience? Identify specific details that support your answer.

2. Angelou begins her narrative by summarizing a discussion between herself and a white woman. What is her purpose in doing this?

3. What is Angelou's thesis?

STYLE AND STRUCTURE

1. What exactly is a *finishing school*? What image does it usually call to mind? How is the use of this phrase **ironic** in view of its meaning in this selection?

2. How does Angelou signal the passage of time in this narrative? Identify some transitional phrases that move readers from one time period to another.

3. How does the use of dialogue highlight the contrast between the black and the white characters? In what way does this contrast strengthen the narrative?

4. What details does Angelou use to describe Mrs. Cullinan and her home to the reader? How does this detailed description help advance the narrative?

VOCABULARY PROJECTS

1. Define each of the following words as it is used in this selection.

tatting (2)	pouty (11)	dilemma (33)
sacheted (2)	barrenness (12)	shards (34)
impudent (4)	ballad (20)	
embalmed (9)	construed (26)	

2. According to your dictionary, what is the difference between *ridiculous* and *ludicrous* (1)? Between *soup bowl* and *tureen* (7)? Why do you think Angelou draws a distinction between the two words in each pair?

3. Try substituting an equivalent word for each of the following, paying careful attention to the context of each in the narrative.

perpetually (3)	station (7)	biddies (33)
exactness (4)	peach (31)	

Does Angelou's original choice seem more effective in all cases? Explain.

JOURNAL ENTRY

Have you ever received any training or education that you considered at the time to be "extensive and irrelevant preparations for adulthood" (1)? Do you now see any value in the experience?

WRITING WORKSHOP

1. Think about a time in your life when someone in a position of authority treated you unjustly. How did you react? Write a narrative essay in which you recount the situation and your responses to it.

2. Have you ever had an experience in which you were the victim of name calling — or in which you found yourself doing the name calling? Summarize the incident, including dialogue and description that will help your readers understand your motivations and reactions. Include a thesis statement that conveys your present attitude toward the incident.

3. Write a narrative essay that includes a brief summary of an incident from a work of fiction — specifically, an incident that serves as a character's initiation into adulthood. In your essay, focus on how the experience helps the character grow up.

COMBINING THE PATTERNS

Angelou's essay is a narrative, but it is rich with descriptive detail. Identify specific passages of the essay that are structured as **descriptions** of people and places. Is the description primarily visual, or does it incorporate other senses (sound, smell, taste, and touch) as well? Do you think any person, setting, or object should be described in greater detail? Explain.

THEMATIC CONNECTIONS

- "Midnight" (page 201)
- "The 'Black Table' Is Still There" (page 340)
- "Litigating the Legacy of Slavery" (page 627)

BONNIE SMITH-YACKEL*

❖
My Mother Never Worked

Although this narrative essay, which was first published in *Women: A Journal of Liberation* in 1975, is based on personal experience, it also makes a broader statement about how society values "women's work."

Background: Social Security is a federal insurance program that requires workers to contribute a percentage of their wages to a fund from which they may draw benefits if they become unemployed due to disability. After retirement, workers can receive a monthly income from this fund, which also provides a modest death benefit to survivors. The contribution is generally deducted directly from a worker's paycheck, and employers must contribute a matching amount. According to federal law, a woman who is a homemaker, who has never been a wage earner, is eligible for Social Security benefits only through the earnings of her deceased husband. (The same would be true for a man if the roles were reversed.) Therefore, a homemaker's survivors would not be eligible for the death benefit. Although the law has been challenged in the courts, the survivors of a homemaker who has never been a wage earner are still not entitled to a Social Security death benefit.

"Social Security Office." (The voice answering the telephone sounds very self-assured.)   1

"I'm calling about . . . my mother just died . . . I was told to call you and see about a . . . death-benefit check, I think they call it. . . ."   2

"I see. Was your mother on Social Security? How old was she?"   3

"Yes . . . she was seventy-eight. . . ."   4

"Do you know her number?"   5

"No . . . I, ah . . . don't you have a record?"   6

"Certainly. I'll look it up. Her name?"   7

"Smith. Martha Smith. Or maybe she used Martha Ruth Smith? . . . Sometimes she used her maiden name . . . Martha Jerabek Smith?"   8

"If you'd care to hold on, I'll check our records — it'll be a few minutes."   9

"Yes. . . ."   10

Her love letters — to and from Daddy — were in an old box, tied with ribbons and stiff, rigid-with-age leather thongs: 1918 through 1920; hers written on stationery from the general store she had worked in full-time and managed, single-handed, after her graduation from high school in 1913; and his, at first, on YMCA or Soldiers and Sailors Club stationery dispensed to the fighting men of World War I. He wooed her thoroughly   11

*In some previous editions of *Patterns for College Writing,* the author's name was mistakenly printed as Donna, not Bonnie. Bedford/St. Martin's regrets the error.

and persistently by mail, and though she reciprocated all his feelings for her, she dreaded marriage. . . .

"It's so hard for me to decide when to have my wedding day—that's all. 12 I've thought about these last two days. I have told you dozens of times that I won't be afraid of married life, but when it comes down to setting the date and then picturing myself a married woman with half a dozen or more kids to look after, it just makes me sick. . . . I am weeping right now— I hope that some day I can look back and say how foolish I was to dread it all."

They married in February, 1921, and began farming. Their first baby, a 13 daughter, was born in January, 1922, when my mother was 26 years old. The second baby, a son, was born in March, 1923. They were renting farms; my father, besides working his own fields, also was a hired man for two other farmers. They had no capital initially, and had to gain it slowly, work-ing from dawn until midnight every day. My town-bred mother learned to set hens and raise chickens, feed pigs, milk cows, plant and harvest a gar-den, and can every fruit and vegetable she could scrounge. She carried water nearly a quarter of a mile from the well to fill her wash boilers in order to do her laundry on a scrub board. She learned to shock grain, feed threshers, shock and husk corn, feed corn pickers. In September, 1925, the third baby came, and in June, 1927, the fourth child—both daughters. In 1930, my parents had enough money to buy their own farm, and that March they moved all their livestock and belongings themselves, 55 miles over rutted, muddy roads.

In the summer of 1930 my mother and her two eldest children re- 14 claimed a 40-acre field from Canadian thistles, by chopping them all out with a hoe. In the other fields, when the oats and flax began to head out, the green and blue of the crops were hidden by the bright yellow of wild mustard. My mother walked the fields day after day, pulling each mustard plant. She raised a new flock of baby chicks—500—and she spaded up, planted, hoed, and harvested a half-acre garden.

During the next spring their hogs caught cholera and died. No cash 15 that fall.

And in the next year the drought hit. My mother and father trudged 16 from the well to the chickens, the well to the calf pasture, the well to the barn, and from the well to the garden. The sun came out hot and bright, endlessly, day after day. The crops shriveled and died. They harvested half the corn, and ground the other half, stalks and all, and fed it to the cattle as fodder. With the price at four cents a bushel for the harvested crop, they couldn't afford to haul it into town. They burned it in the furnace for fuel that winter.

In 1934, in February, when the dust was still so thick in the Minnesota 17 air that my parents couldn't always see from the house to the barn, their fifth child—a fourth daughter—was born. My father hunted rabbits daily, and my mother stewed them, fried them, canned them, and wished out loud that she could taste hamburger once more. In the fall the shotgun brought prairie chickens, ducks, pheasant, and grouse. My mother plucked each bird, carefully reserving the breast feathers for pillows.

In the winter she sewed night after night, endlessly, begging cast-off clothing from relatives, ripping apart coats, dresses, blouses, and trousers to remake them to fit her four daughters and son. Every morning and every evening she milked cows, fed pigs and calves, cared for chickens, picked eggs, cooked meals, washed dishes, scrubbed floors, and tended and loved her children. In the spring she planted a garden once more, dragging pails of water to nourish and sustain the vegetables for the family. In 1936 she lost a baby in her sixth month. 18

In 1937 her fifth daughter was born. She was 42 years old. In 1939 a second son, and in 1941 her eighth child — and third son. 19

But the war had come, and prosperity of a sort. The herd of cattle had grown to 30 head; she still milked morning and evening. Her garden was more than a half acre — the rains had come, and by now the Rural Electricity Administration and indoor plumbing. Still she sewed — dresses and jackets for the children, housedresses and aprons for herself, weekly patching of jeans, overalls, and denim shirts. She still made pillows, using feathers she had plucked, and quilts every year — intricate patterns as well as patchwork, stitched as well as tied — all necessary bedding for her family. Every scrap of cloth too small to be used in quilts was carefully saved and painstakingly sewed together in strips to make rugs. She still went out in the fields to help with the haying whenever there was a threat of rain. 20

In 1959 my mother's last child graduated from high school. A year later the cows were sold. She still raised chickens and ducks, plucked feathers, made pillows, baked her own bread, and every year made a new quilt — now for a married child or for a grandchild. And her garden, that huge, undying symbol of sustenance, was as large and cared for as in all the years before. The canning, and now freezing, continued. 21

In 1969, on a June afternoon, mother and father started out for town so that she could buy sugar to make rhubarb jam for a daughter who lived in Texas. The car crashed into a ditch. She was paralyzed from the waist down. 22

In 1970 her husband, my father, died. My mother struggled to regain some competence and dignity and order in her life. At the rehabilitation institute, where they gave her physical therapy and trained her to live usefully in a wheelchair, the therapist told me: "She did fifteen pushups today — fifteen! She's almost seventy-five years old! I've never known a woman so strong!" 23

From her wheelchair she canned pickles, baked bread, ironed clothes, wrote dozens of letters weekly to her friends and her "half dozen or more kids," and made three patchwork housecoats and one quilt. She made balls and balls of carpet rags — enough for five rugs. And kept all her love letters. 24

"I think I've found your mother's records — Martha Ruth Smith; married to Ben F. Smith?" 25

"Yes, that's right." 26

"Well, I see that she was getting a widow's pension. . . ." 27

"Yes, that's right."   28
"Well, your mother isn't entitled to our $255 death benefit."   29
"Not entitled! But why?"   30
The voice on the telephone explains patiently: 31
"Well, you see — your mother never worked."   32

• • •

COMPREHENSION

1. What kind of work did Martha Smith do while her children were growing up? List some of the chores she performed.

2. Why aren't Martha Smith's survivors entitled to a death benefit when their mother dies?

3. How does the government define *work*?

PURPOSE AND AUDIENCE

1. What point is the writer trying to make? Why do you suppose her thesis is never explicitly stated?

2. This essay appeared in *Ms.* magazine and other publications whose audiences are sympathetic to feminist goals. Could it just as easily have appeared in a magazine whose audience was not? Explain.

3. Smith-Yackel mentions relatively little about her father in this essay. How can you account for this?

4. This essay was first published in 1975. Is it dated?

STYLE AND STRUCTURE

1. Is the title effective? If so, why? If not, what alternate title can you suggest?

2. Smith-Yackel could have outlined her mother's life without framing it with the telephone conversation. Why do you think she includes this frame?

3. What strategies does Smith-Yackel use to indicate the passing of time in her narrative?

4. This narrative piles details one on top of another almost like a list. Why does the writer list so many details?

5. In paragraphs 20 and 21, what is accomplished by the repetition of the word *still*?

VOCABULARY PROJECTS

1. Define each of the following words as it is used in this selection.

scrounge (13)	rutted (13)	intricate (20)
shuck (13)	reclaimed (14)	sustenance (21)
shock (13)	flax (14)	
husk (13)	fodder (16)	

2. Try substituting equivalent words for those italicized in this sentence:

   He *wooed* her *thoroughly* and *persistently* by mail, and though she *reciprocated* all his feeling for her, she *dreaded* marriage . . . (11).

   How do your substitutions change the sentence's meaning?

3. Throughout her narrative, Smith-Yackel uses concrete, specific verbs. Review her choice of verbs, particularly in paragraphs 13–24, and comment on how such verbs serve the essay's purpose.

JOURNAL ENTRY

Do you believe that a homemaker who has never been a wage earner should be entitled to a Social Security death benefit for her survivors? Explain your reasoning.

WRITING WORKSHOP

1. If you can, interview one of your parents or grandparents (or another person you know who might remind you of Smith-Yackel's mother) about his or her work, and write a chronological narrative based on what you learn. Include a thesis statement that your narrative can support.

2. Write Martha Smith's obituary as it might have appeared in her hometown newspaper. If you are not familiar with the form of an obituary, read a few in your local paper.

3. Write a narrative account of a typical day at the worst job you ever had. Include a thesis statement that expresses your negative feelings.

COMBINING THE PATTERNS

Because of the repetitive nature of the farm chores Smith-Yackel describes in her narrative, some passages come very close to explaining a **process,** a series of repeated steps that always occur in a predictable order. Identify several such passages. If Smith-Yackel's essay were written entirely as a process explanation, what material would have to be left out? How would these omissions change the essay?

THEMATIC CONNECTIONS

- "Midnight" (page 201)
- "On Fire" (page 280)
- "I Want a Wife" (page 505)
- "The Company Man" (page 517)

MARTIN GANSBERG

Thirty-Eight Who Saw Murder Didn't Call the Police

Martin Gansberg (1920–1995), a native of Brooklyn, New York, was a reporter and editor for the *New York Times* for forty-three years. The following article, written for the *Times* two weeks after the 1964 murder it recounts, earned Gansberg an award for excellence from the Newspaper Reporters Association of New York. Gansberg's thesis, though not explicitly stated, still retains its power.

Background: The events reported here took place on March 14, 1964, as contemporary American culture was undergoing a complex transition. The relatively placid years of the 1950s were giving way to more troubling times: the Civil Rights movement had led to social unrest in the South and in northern inner cities; the escalating war in Vietnam had created angry political divisions; President John F. Kennedy had been assassinated the previous fall; violent imagery was on the rise in television and film; a growing drug culture was becoming apparent. The brutal, senseless murder of Kitty Genovese — and, more important, her neighbors' failure to respond immediately to her cries for help — became a nationwide symbol for what was perceived as an evolving culture of violence and indifference. Even today, social scientists around the world debate the causes of "the Genovese syndrome."

For more than half an hour 38 respectable, law-abiding citizens in Queens watched a killer stalk and stab a woman in three separate attacks in Kew Gardens. 1

Twice their chatter and the sudden glow of their bedroom lights interrupted him and frightened him off. Each time he returned, sought her out, and stabbed her again. Not one person telephoned the police during the assault; one witness called after the woman was dead. 2

That was two weeks ago today. 3

Still shocked is Assistant Chief Inspector Frederick M. Lussen, in charge of the borough's detectives and a veteran of 25 years of homicide investigations. He can give a matter-of-fact recitation on many murders. But the Kew Gardens slaying baffles him — not because it is a murder, but because the "good people" failed to call the police. 4

"As we have reconstructed the crime," he said, "the assailant had three chances to kill this woman during a 35-minute period. He returned twice to complete the job. If we had been called when he first attacked, the woman might not be dead now." 5

This is what the police say happened beginning at 3:20 A.M. in the   6
staid, middle-class, tree-lined Austin Street area:

Twenty-eight-year-old Catherine Genovese, who was called Kitty by   7
almost everyone in the neighborhood, was returning home from her job as
manager of a bar in Hollis. She parked her red Fiat in a lot adjacent to the
Kew Gardens Long Island Rail Road Station, facing Mowbray Place. Like
many residents of the neighborhood, she had parked there day after day
since her arrival from Connecticut a year ago, although the railroad frowns
on the practice.

She turned off the lights of her car, locked the door, and started to   8
walk the 100 feet to the entrance of her apartment at 82-70 Austin Street,
which is in a Tudor building, with stores in the first floor and apartments
on the second.

The entrance to the apartment is in the rear of the building because   9
the front is rented to retail stores. At night the quiet neighborhood is
shrouded in the slumbering darkness that marks most residential areas.

Miss Genovese noticed a man at the far end of the lot, near a seven-   10
story apartment house at 82-40 Austin Street. She halted. Then, nervously,
she headed up Austin Street toward Lefferts Boulevard, where there is a call
box to the 102nd Police Precinct in nearby Richmond Hill.

She got as far as a street light in front of a bookstore before the man   11
grabbed her. She screamed. Lights went on in the 10-story apartment
house at 82-67 Austin Street, which faces the bookstore. Windows slid
open and voices punctuated the early-morning stillness.

Miss Genovese screamed: "Oh, my God, he stabbed me! Please help   12
me! Please help me!"

From one of the upper windows in the apartment house, a man called   13
down: "Let that girl alone!"

The assailant looked up at him, shrugged, and walked down Austin   14
Street toward a white sedan parked a short distance away. Miss Genovese
struggled to her feet.

Lights went out. The killer returned to Miss Genovese, now trying to   15
make her way around the side of the building by the parking lot to get to
her apartment. The assailant stabbed her again.

"I'm dying!" she shrieked. "I'm dying!"   16

Windows were opened again, and lights went on in many apartments.   17
The assailant got into his car and drove away. Miss Genovese staggered to
her feet. A city bus, 0-10, the Lefferts Boulevard line to Kennedy International Airport, passed. It was 3:35 A.M.

The assailant returned. By then, Miss Genovese had crawled to the   18
back of the building, where the freshly painted brown doors to the apartment house held out hope for safety. The killer tried the first door; she
wasn't there. At the second door, 82-62 Austin Street, he saw her slumped
on the floor at the foot of the stairs. He stabbed her a third time—fatally.

It was 3:50 by the time the police received their first call, from a man   19
who was a neighbor of Miss Genovese. In two minutes they were at the

scene. The neighbor, a 70-year-old woman, and another woman were the only persons on the street. Nobody else came forward.

The man explained that he had called the police after much delibera- 20 tion. He had phoned a friend in Nassau County for advice and then he had crossed the roof of the building to the apartment of the elderly woman to get her to make the call.

"I didn't want to get involved," he sheepishly told police. 21

Six days later, the police arrested Winston Moseley, a 29-year-old busi- 22 ness machine operator, and charged him with homicide. Moseley had no previous record. He is married, has two children and owns a home at 133–19 Sutter Avenue, South Ozone Park, Queens. On Wednesday, a court committed him to Kings County Hospital for psychiatric observation.

When questioned by the police, Moseley also said that he had slain 23 Mrs. Annie May Johnson, 24, of 146–12 133d Avenue, Jamaica, on Feb. 29 and Barbara Kralik, 15, of 174–17 140th Avenue, Springfield Gardens, last July. In the Kralik case, the police are holding Alvin L. Mitchell, who is said to have confessed to that slaying.

The police stressed how simple it would have been to have gotten 24 in touch with them. "A phone call," said one of the detectives, "would have done it." The police may be reached by dialing "0" for operator or SPring 7-3100.

Today witnesses from the neighborhood, which is made up of one- 25 family homes in the $35,000 to $60,000 range with the exception of the two apartment houses near the railroad station, find it difficult to explain why they didn't call the police.

A housewife, knowingly if quite casually, said, "We thought it was a 26 lovers' quarrel." A husband and wife both said, "Frankly, we were afraid." They seemed aware of the fact that events might have been different. A distraught woman, wiping her hands in her apron, said, "I didn't want my husband to get involved."

One couple, now willing to talk about that night, said they heard the 27 first screams. The husband looked thoughtfully at the bookstore where the killer first grabbed Miss Genovese.

"We went to the window to see what was happening," he said, "but the 28 light from our bedroom made it difficult to see the street." The wife, still apprehensive, added: "I put out the light and we were able to see better."

Asked why they hadn't called the police, she shrugged and replied: "I 29 don't know."

A man peeked out from a slight opening in the doorway to his apart- 30 ment and rattled off an account of the killer's second attack. Why hadn't he called the police at the time? "I was tired," he said without emotion. "I went back to bed."

It was 4:25 A.M. when the ambulance arrived to take the body of Miss 31 Genovese. It drove off. "Then," a solemn police detective said, "the people came out."

• • •

COMPREHENSION

1. How much time elapses between the first stabbing of Kitty Genovese and the time when the people finally come out?

2. What excuses do the neighbors make for not coming to Kitty Genovese's aid?

PURPOSE AND AUDIENCE

1. This article appeared in 1964. What effect was it intended to have on its audience? Do you think it has the same impact today, or has its impact changed or diminished?

2. What is the article's main point? Why does Gansberg imply his thesis rather than stating it explicitly?

3. What is Gansberg's purpose in describing the Austin Street area as "staid, middle-class, tree-lined" (6)?

4. Why do you suppose Gansberg provides the police department's phone number in his article? (Note that New York City did not have 911 emergency service in 1964.)

STYLE AND STRUCTURE

1. Gansberg is very precise in this article, especially in his references to time, addresses, and ages. Why?

2. The objective newspaper style is dominant in this article, but the writer's anger shows through. Point to words and phrases that reveal his attitude toward his material.

3. Because this article was originally set in the narrow columns of a newspaper, it has many short paragraphs. Would the narrative be more effective if some of these brief paragraphs were combined? If so, why? If not, why not? Give examples to support your answer.

4. Review the dialogue. Does it strengthen Gansberg's presentation? Would the article be more compelling without dialogue? Explain.

5. This article does not have a formal conclusion; nevertheless, the last paragraph sums up the writer's attitude. How?

VOCABULARY PROJECTS

1. Define each of the following words as it is used in this section.

stalk (1)	adjacent (7)	distraught (26)
baffles (4)	punctuated (11)	apprehensive (28)
staid (6)	sheepishly (21)	

2. The word *assailant* appears frequently in this article. Why is it used so often? What impact is this repetition likely to have on readers? What other words could have been used?

JOURNAL ENTRY

In a similar situation, would you have called the police? Would you have gone outside to help? What factors do you think might have influenced your decision?

WRITING WORKSHOP

1. In your own words, write a ten-sentence summary of the article. Try to reflect Gansberg's order and emphasis as well as his ideas, and be sure to include all necessary transitions.

2. Rewrite the article as if it were a diary entry of one of the thirty-eight people who watched the murder. Summarize what you saw, and explain why you decided not to call for help. (You may invent details that Gansberg does not include.)

3. If you have ever been involved in or witnessed a situation in which someone was in trouble, write a narrative essay about the incident. If people failed to help the person in trouble, explain why you think no one acted. If people did act, tell how. Be sure to account for your own actions.

COMBINING THE PATTERNS

Because the purpose of this newspaper article is to give basic factual information, it has no extended descriptions of the victim, the witnesses, or the crime scene. It also does not explain why those who watched did not act. Where might passages of **description** or **cause and effect** be added? How might such additions change the essay's impact on readers? Do you think they would strengthen the essay?

THEMATIC CONNECTIONS

- "Ground Zero" (page 158)
- "Samuel" (page 239)
- "Who Killed Benny Paret?" (page 321)
- "A Peaceful Woman Explains Why She Carries a Gun" (page 345)

BARBARA EHRENREICH

❖

Scrubbing in Maine

Born in 1941 to working-class parents in Butte, Montana, Barbara Ehrenreich went on to earn a Ph.D. in biology from New York's Rockefeller University. After deciding against a career as a research scientist, she devoted her attention to liberal political causes, which led to her becoming a professional writer and social critic. She has published articles and essays in many periodicals, including *Time*, *The Progressive*, and *The New Republic*. Her thirteen books include *The Worst Years of Our Lives: Irreverent Notes on a Decade of Greed* (1990) and *Blood Rites: The Origins and History of the Passions of War* (1997). For her most recent book, *Nickel and Dimed: On (Not) Getting By in America* (2001), Ehrenreich found employment at a variety of entry-level, minimum-wage jobs — such as waitressing in Florida restaurants and stocking shelves at a Minnesota Wal-Mart — to research the plight of the working poor.

Background: In this excerpt from *Nickel and Dimed*, Ehrenreich relates some of her experiences working for a large household cleaning service. In footnoted material not included here, she writes that such franchised services as Merry Maids and The Maids International have grown dramatically over the past twenty years as housework has become increasingly "outsourced." In the early twentieth century, most domestic workers were Irish and German immigrants, and by midcentury, African-American women and Japanese Americans on the West Coast replaced them until greater opportunities began to open up for these groups. Today, most household workers in the West are Hispanic (36.8 percent Hispanic overall), and most in New York are Caribbean (15.8 percent black overall). However, in the Midwest and other parts of the country (such as Maine, where Ehrenreich worked), most are white and Anglo, and many have lost public assistance benefits because of welfare reform.

I am rested and ready for anything when I arrive at The Maids' office 1
suite Monday at 7:30 A.M. I know nothing about cleaning services like this one, which, according to the brochure I am given, has over three hundred franchises nationwide, and most of what I know about domestics in general comes from nineteenth-century British novels and *Upstairs, Downstairs*. Prophetically enough, I caught a rerun of that very show on PBS over the weekend and was struck by how terribly correct the servants looked in their black-and-white uniforms and how much wiser they were than their callow, egotistical masters. We too have uniforms, though they are more oafish than dignified — ill-fitting and in an overloud combination of kelly-green pants and a blinding sunflower-yellow polo shirt. And, as is explained in writing and over the next day and a half of training, we too have a special code of decorum. No smoking anywhere, or at least not within

fifteen minutes of arrival at a house. No drinking, eating, or gum chewing in a house. No cursing in a house, even if the owner is not present, and — perhaps to keep us in practice — no obscenities even in the office. So this is Downstairs, is my chirpy first thought. But I have no idea, of course, just how far down these stairs will take me.

Forty minutes go by before anyone acknowledges my presence with more than a harried nod. During this time the other employees arrive, about twenty of them, already glowing in their uniforms, and breakfast on the free coffee, bagels, and doughnuts The Maids kindly provides for us. All but one of the others are female, with an average age I would guess in the late twenties, though the range seems to go from prom-fresh to well into the Medicare years. There is a pleasant sort of bustle as people get their breakfasts and fill plastic buckets with rags and bottles of cleaning fluids, but surprisingly little conversation outside of a few references to what people ate (pizza) and drank (Jell-O shots are mentioned) over the weekend. Since the room in which we gather contains only two folding chairs, both of them occupied, the other new girl and I sit cross-legged on the floor, silent and alert, while the regulars get sorted into teams of three or four and dispatched to the day's list of houses. One of the women explains to me that teams do not necessarily return to the same houses week after week, nor do you have any guarantee of being on the same team from one day to the next. This, I suppose, is one of the advantages of a corporate cleaning service to its customers: there are no sticky and possibly guilt-ridden relationships involved, because the customers communicate almost entirely with Tammy, the office manager, or with Ted, the franchise owner and our boss. The advantage to the cleaning person is harder to determine, since the pay compares so poorly to what an independent cleaner is likely to earn — up to $15 an hour, I've heard. While I wait in the inner room, where the phone is and Tammy has her desk, to be issued a uniform, I hear her tell a potential customer on the phone that The Maids charges $25 per person-hour. The company gets $25 and we get $6.65 for each hour we work? I think I must have misheard, but a few minutes later I hear her say the same thing to another inquirer. So the only advantage of working here as opposed to freelancing is that you don't need a clientele or even a car. You can arrive straight from welfare or, in my case, the bus station — fresh off the boat.

At last, after all the other employees have sped off in the company's eye-catching green-and-yellow cars, I am led into a tiny closet-sized room off the inner office to learn my trade via videotape. The manager at another maid service where I'd applied had told me she didn't like to hire people who had done cleaning before because they were resistant to learning the company's system, so I prepare to empty my mind of all prior house-cleaning experience. There are four tapes — dusting, bathrooms, kitchen, and vacuuming — each starring an attractive, possibly Hispanic young woman who moves about serenely in obedience to the male voiceover: For vacuuming, begin in the master bedroom; when dusting, begin with the room directly off the kitchen. When you enter a room, mentally divide it into sections no wider than your reach. Begin in the section to your left and, within each section, move from left to right and top to bottom. This way nothing is ever overlooked.

I like *Dusting* best, for its undeniable logic and a certain kind of austere beauty. When you enter a house, you spray a white rag with Windex and place it in the left pocket of your green apron. Another rag, sprayed with disinfectant, goes into the middle pocket, and a yellow rag bearing wood polish in the right-hand pocket. A dry rag, for buffing surfaces, occupies the right-hand pocket of your slacks. Shiny surfaces get Windexed, wood gets wood polish, and everything else is wiped dust-free with disinfectant. Every now and then Ted pops in to watch with me, pausing the video to underscore a particularly dramatic moment: "She how's she's working around the vase? That's an accident waiting to happen." If Ted himself were in a video, it would have to be a cartoon, because the only features sketched onto his pudgy face are brown buttonlike eyes and a tiny pug nose; his belly, encased in a polo shirt, overhangs the waistline of his shorts. "You know, all this was figured out with a stopwatch," he tells me with something like pride. When the video warns against oversoaking our rags with cleaning fluids, he pauses it to tell me there's a danger in under-soaking too, especially if it's going to slow me down. "Cleaning fluids are less expensive than your time." It's good to know that *something* is cheaper than my time, or that in the hierarchy of the company's values I rank above Windex.

Vacuuming is the most disturbing video, actually a double feature beginning with an introduction to the special backpack vacuum we are to use. Yes, the vacuum cleaner actually straps onto your back, a chubby fellow who introduces himself as its inventor explains. He suits up, pulling the straps tight across and under his chest and then says proudly into the camera: "See, I *am* the vacuum cleaner." It weighs only ten pounds, he claims, although, as I soon find out, with the attachments dangling from the strap around your waist, the total is probably more like fourteen. What about my petulant and much-pampered lower back? The inventor returns to the theme of human/machine merger: when properly strapped in, we too will be vacuum cleaners, constrained only by the cord that attaches us to an electrical outlet, and vacuum cleaners don't have backaches. Somehow all this information exhausts me, and I watch the second video, which explains the actual procedures for vacuuming, with the detached interest of a cineast. Could the model maid be an actual maid and the model home someone's actual dwelling? And who are these people whose idea of decorating is matched pictures of mallard ducks in flight and whose house is perfectly characterless and pristine even before the model maid sets to work?

At first I find the videos on kitchens and bathrooms baffling, and it takes me several minutes to realize why: there is no *water*, or almost no water, involved. I was taught to clean by my mother, a compulsive housekeeper who employed water so hot you needed rubber gloves to get into it and in such Niagara-like quantities that most microbes were probably crushed by the force of it before the soap suds had a chance to rupture their cell walls. But germs are never mentioned in the videos provided by The Maids. Our antagonists exist entirely in the visible world—soap scum, dust, counter crud, dog hair, stains, and smears—and are to be attacked by damp rag or, in hard-core cases, by Dobie (the brand of plastic scouring pad we use). We scrub only to remove impurities that might be detectable to a customer by hand or by eye; otherwise our only job is to wipe. Nothing is said about the possibility of transporting bacteria, by rag or by hand, from bathroom to kitchen or even from one house to the next. It is the "cosmetic touches" that the videos emphasize and that Ted, when he wanders back into the room, continually directs my eye to. Fluff up all throw pillows and arrange them symmetrically. Brighten up stainless steel sinks with baby oil. Leave all spice jars, shampoos, etc., with their labels facing outward. Comb out the fringes of Persian carpets with a pick. Use the vacuum cleaner to create a special, fernlike pattern in the carpets. The loose ends of toilet paper and paper towel rolls have to be given a special fold (the same one you'll find in hotel bathrooms). "Messes" of loose paper, clothing, or toys are to be stacked into "neat messes." Finally, the house is to be sprayed with the cleaning service's signature floral-scented air freshener, which will signal to the owners, the moment they return home, that, yes, their house has been "cleaned."

After a day's training I am judged fit to go out with a team, where I soon discover that life is nothing like the movies, at least not if the movie is *Dusting*. For one thing, compared with our actual pace, the training videos were all in slow motion. We do not walk to the cars with our buckets full of cleaning fluids and utensils in the morning, we run, and when we pull up to a house, we run with our buckets to the door. Liza, a good-natured woman in her thirties who is my first team leader, explains that we are given only so many minutes per house, ranging from under sixty for a 1½-bathroom apartment to two hundred or more for a multibathroom "first timer." I'd like to know why anybody worries about Ted's time limits if we're being paid by the hour but hesitate to display anything that might be interpreted as attitude. As we get to each house, Liza assigns our tasks, and I cross my fingers to ward off bathrooms and vacuuming. Even dusting, though, gets aerobic under pressure, and after about an hour of it—reaching to get door tops, crawling along floors to wipe baseboards, standing on my bucket to attack the higher shelves—I wouldn't mind sitting down with a tall glass of water. But as soon as you complete your assigned task, you report to the team leader to be assigned to help someone else. Once or twice, when the normal process of evaporation is deemed too slow, I am assigned to dry a scrubbed floor by putting rags under my feet and skating around on it. Usually, by the time I get out to the car and am dumping the dirty water used on floors and wringing out rags, the rest of the team is already in the car with the motor running. Liza assures me that they've never left anyone

7

behind at a house, not even, presumably, a very new person whom nobody knows.

In my interview, I had been promised a thirty-minute lunch break, but this turns out to be a five-minute pit stop at a convenience store, if that. I bring my own sandwich—the same turkey breast and cheese every day—as do a couple of the others; the rest eat convenience store fare, a bagel or doughnut salvaged from our free breakfast, or nothing at all. The two older married women I'm teamed up with eat best—sandwiches and fruit. Among the younger women, lunch consists of a slice of pizza, a "pizza pocket" (a roll of dough surrounding some pizza sauce), or a small bag of chips. Bear in mind we are not office workers, sitting around idling at the basal metabolic rate. A poster on the wall in the office cheerily displays the number of calories burned per minute at our various tasks, ranging from about 3.5 for dusting to 7 for vacuuming. If you assume an average of 5 calories per minute in a seven-hour day (eight hours minus time for travel between houses), you need to be taking in 2,100 calories in addition to the resting minimum of, say, 900 or so. I get pushy with Rosalie, who is new like me and fresh from high school in a rural northern part of the state, about the meagerness of her lunches, which consist solely of Doritos—a half bag from the day before or a freshly purchased small-sized bag. She just didn't have anything in the house, she says (though she lives with her boyfriend and his mother), and she certainly doesn't have any money to buy lunch, as I find out when I offer to fetch her a soda from a Quik Mart and she has to admit she doesn't have eighty-nine cents. I treat her to the soda, wishing I could force her, mommylike, to take milk instead. So how does she hold up for an eight- or even nine-hour day? "Well," she concedes, "I get dizzy sometimes." 8

How poor are they, my coworkers? The fact that anyone is working this job at all can be taken as prima facie evidence of some kind of desperation or at least a history of mistakes and disappointments, but it's not for me to ask. In the prison movies that provide me with a mental guide to comportment, the new guy doesn't go around shaking hands and asking, "Hi there, what are you in for?" So I listen, in the cars and when we're assembled in the office, and learn, first, that no one seems to be homeless. Almost everyone is embedded in extended families or families artificially extended with housemates. People talk about visiting grandparents in the hospital or sending birthday cards to a niece's husband; single mothers live with their own mothers or share apartments with a coworker or boyfriend. Pauline, the oldest of us, owns her own home, but she sleeps on the living room sofa, while her four grown children and three grandchildren fill up the bedrooms. 9

But although no one, apparently, is sleeping in a car, there are signs, even at the beginning, of real difficulty if not actual misery. Half-smoked cigarettes are returned to the pack. There are discussions about who will come up with fifty cents for a toll and whether Ted can be counted on for prompt reimbursement. One of my teammates gets frantic about a 10 painfully impacted wisdom tooth and keeps making calls from our houses to try to locate a source of free dental care. When my — or, I should say, Liza's — team discovers there is not a single Dobie in our buckets, I suggest that we stop at a convenience store and buy one rather than drive all the way back to the office. But it turns out I haven't brought any money with me and we cannot put together $2 between the four of us.

The Friday of my first week at The Maids is unnaturally hot for Maine in early September — 95 degrees, according to the digital time-and-temperature displays offered by banks that we pass. I'm teamed up with the sad-faced Rosalie and our leader, Maddy, whose sullenness, under the circumstances, is almost a relief after Liza's relentless good cheer. Liza, I've learned, is the highest-ranking cleaner, a sort of supervisor really, and said to be something of a snitch, but Maddy, a single mom of maybe twenty-seven or so, has worked for only three months and broods about her child care problems. Her boyfriend's sister, she tells me on the drive to our first house, watches her eighteen-month-old for $50 a week, which is a stretch on The Maids' pay, plus she doesn't entirely trust the sister, but a real day care center could be as much as $90 a week. After polishing off the first house, no problem, we grab "lunch" — Doritos for Rosalie and a bag of Pepperidge Farm Goldfish for Maddy — and head out into the exurbs for what our instruction sheet warns is a five-bathroom spread and a first-timer to boot. Still, the size of the place makes us pause for a moment, buckets in hand, before searching out an appropriately humble entrance. It sits there like a beached ocean liner, the prow cutting through swells of green turf, windows without number. "Well, well," Maddy says, reading the owner's name from our instruction sheet. "Mrs. W. and her big-ass house. I hope she's going to give us lunch."

Mrs. W. is not in fact happy to see us, grimacing with exasperation when the black nanny ushers us into the family room or sunroom or den or whatever kind of specialized space she is sitting in. After all, she already has the nanny, a cooklike person, and a crew of men doing some sort of finishing touches on the construction to supervise. No, she doesn't want to take us around the house, because she already explained everything to the office on the phone, but Maddy stands there, with Rosalie and me behind her, until she relents. We are to move everything on all surfaces, she instructs during the tour, and get underneath and be sure to do every bit of the several miles, I calculate, of baseboards. And be mindful of the baby, who's napping and can't have cleaning fluids of any kind near her.

Then I am let loose to dust. In a situation like this, where I don't even know how to name the various kinds of rooms, The Maids' special system turns out to be a lifesaver. All I have to do is keep moving from left to right, within rooms and between rooms, trying to identify landmarks so I don't accidentally do a room or a hallway twice. Dusters get the most complete biographical overview, due to the necessity of lifting each object and tchotchke individually, and I learn that Mrs. W. is an alumna of an important women's college, now occupying herself by monitoring her investments and the baby's bowel movements. I find special charts for this latter purpose, with spaces for time of day, most recent fluid intake, consistency, and color. In the master bedroom, I dust a whole shelf of books on pregnancy, breastfeeding, the first six months, the first year, the first two years — and I wonder what the child care–deprived Maddy makes of all this. Maybe there's been some secret division of the world's women into breeders and drones, and those at the maid level are no longer supposed to be reproducing at all. Maybe this is why our office manager, Tammy, who was once a maid herself, wears inch-long fake nails and tarty little outfits — to show she's advanced to the breeder caste and can't be sent out to clean anymore.

It is hotter inside than out, un-air-conditioned for the benefit of the baby, I suppose, but I do all right until I encounter the banks of glass doors that line the side and back of the ground floor. Each one has to be Windexed, wiped, and buffed — inside and out, top to bottom, left to right, until it's as streakless and invisible as a material substance can be. Outside, I can see the construction guys knocking back Gatorade, but the rule is that no fluid or food item can touch a maid's lips when she's inside a house. Now, sweat, even in unseemly quantities, is nothing new to me. I live in a subtropical area where even the inactive can expect to be moist nine months out of the year. I work out, too, in my normal life and take a certain macho pride in the *V*s of sweat that form on my T-shirt after ten minutes or more on the StairMaster. But in normal life fluids lost are immediately replaced. Everyone in yuppie-land — airports, for example — looks like a nursing baby these days, inseparable from their plastic bottles of water. Here, however, I sweat without replacement or pause, not in individual drops but in continuous sheets of fluid soaking through my polo shirt, pouring down the backs of my legs. The eyeliner I put on in the morning — vain twit that I am — has long since streaked down onto my cheeks, and I could wring my braid out if I wanted to. Working my way through the living room(s), I wonder if Mrs. W. will ever have occasion to realize that every single doodad and *objet* through which she expresses her unique, individual self is, from another vantage point, only an obstacle between some thirsty person and a glass of water.

When I can find no more surfaces to wipe and have finally exhausted the supply of rooms, Maddy assigns me to do the kitchen floor. OK, except that Mrs. W. is *in* the kitchen, so I have to go down on my hands and knees practically at her feet. No, we don't have sponge mops like the one I use in my own house; the hands-and-knees approach is a definite selling point for corporate cleaning services like The Maids. "We clean floors the old-fashioned way — *on our hands and knees*" (emphasis added), the brochure for a competing firm boasts. In fact, whatever advantages there may be to the hands-and-knees approach — you're closer to your work, of course, and less likely to miss a grimy patch — are undermined by the artificial drought imposed by The Maids' cleaning system. We are instructed to use less than half a small bucket of lukewarm water for a kitchen and all adjacent scrubbable floors (breakfast nooks and other dining areas), meaning that within

14

15

a few minutes we are doing nothing more than redistributing the dirt evenly around the floor. There are occasional customer complaints about the cleanliness of our floors—for example, from a man who wiped up a spill on his freshly "cleaned" floor only to find the paper towel he employed for this purpose had turned gray. A mop and a full bucket of hot soapy water would not only get a floor cleaner but would be a lot more dignified for the person who does the cleaning. But it is this primal posture of submission—and of what is ultimately anal accessibility—that seems to gratify the consumers of maid services.

I don't know, but Mrs. W.'s floor is hard—stone, I think, or at least a   16 stonelike substance—and we have no knee pads with us today. I had thought in my middle-class innocence that knee pads were one of Monica Lewinsky's prurient fantasies, but no, they actually exist, and they're usually a standard part of our equipment. So here I am on my knees, working my way around the room like some fanatical penitent crawling through the stations of the cross, when I realize that Mrs. W. is staring at me fixedly—so fixedly that I am gripped for a moment by the wild possibility that I may have once given a lecture at her alma mater and she's trying to figure out where she's seen me before. If I were recognized, would I be fired? Would she at least be inspired to offer me a drink of water? Because I have decided that if water is actually offered, I'm taking it, rules or no rules, and if word of this infraction gets back to Ted, I'll just say I thought it would be rude to refuse. Not to worry, though. She's just watching that I don't leave out some stray square inch, and when I rise painfully to my feet again, blinking through the sweat, she says, "Could you just scrub the floor in the entryway while you're at it?"

I rush home to the Blue Haven at the end of the day, pull down the   17 blinds for privacy, strip off my uniform in the kitchen—the bathroom being too small for both a person and her discarded clothes—and stand in the shower for a good ten minutes, thinking all this water is *mine*. I have paid for it, in fact, I have earned it. I have gotten through a week at The Maids without mishap, injury, or insurrection. My back feels fine, meaning I'm not feeling it at all; even my wrists, damaged by carpal tunnel syndrome years ago, are issuing no complaints. Coworkers warned me that the first time they donned the backpack vacuum they felt faint, but not me. I am strong and I am, more than that, good. Did I toss my bucket of filthy water onto Mrs. W.'s casual white summer outfit? No. Did I take the wand of my vacuum cleaner and smash someone's Chinese porcelain statues or Hummel figurines? Not once. I was at all times cheerful, energetic, helpful, and as competent as a new hire can be expected to be. If I can do one week, I can do another, and might as well, since there's never been a moment for job-hunting. The 3:30 quitting time turns out to be a myth; often we don't return to the office until 4:30 or 5:00. And what did I think? That I was going to go out to interviews in my soaked and stinky postwork condition? I decide to reward myself with a sunset walk on Old Orchard Beach.

On account of the heat, there are still a few actual bathers on the   18 beach, but I am content to sit in shorts and T-shirt and watch the ocean pummel the sand. When the sun goes down I walk back into the town to find my car and am amazed to hear a sound I associate with cities like New York and Berlin. There's a couple of Peruvian musicians playing in the little grassy island in the street near the pier, and maybe fifty people — locals and vacationers — have gathered around, offering their bland end-of-summer faces to the sound. I edge my way through the crowd and find a seat where I can see the musicians up close — the beautiful young guitarist and the taller man playing the flute. What are they doing in this rinky-dink blue-collar resort, and what does the audience make of this surprise visit from the dark-skinned South? The melody the flute lays out over the percussion is both utterly strange and completely familiar, as if it had been imprinted in the minds of my own peasant ancestors centuries ago and forgotten until this very moment. Everyone else seems to be as transfixed as I am. The musicians wink and smile at each other as they play, and I see then that they are the secret emissaries of a worldwide lower-class conspiracy to snatch joy out of degradation and filth. When the song ends, I give them a dollar, the equivalent of about ten minutes of sweat.

• • •

COMPREHENSION

1. How is Ehrenreich different from the other maids?

2. Why do women choose to work for The Maids when they could make a good deal more money as independent cleaners?

3. In paragraph 6, Ehrenreich notes that she is surprised to find that the system of cleaning kitchens and bathrooms employed by The Maids is very different from her own cleaning practices. In what ways is it different?

4. What "cosmetic touches" (6) do The Maids emphasize? Why?

5. How is Ehrenreich's actual job different from the job depicted on the training videos?

6. What "signs [. . .] of real difficulty if not actual misery" (10) does Ehrenreich detect in her coworkers? What, if anything, does she do to help them?

7. Why, according to Ehrenreich, do The Maids scrub floors on their hands and knees?

8. Do you think Ehrenreich has more in common with her coworkers or with Mrs. W.? How do you think Mrs. W. would react if she knew more about Ehrenreich's background?

PURPOSE AND AUDIENCE

1. At the end of paragraph 1, Ehrenreich states her thesis. Restate this thesis in your own words. Is Ehrenreich exaggerating her situation, or does her essay actually support this thesis? (In other words, exactly "how far down these stairs" did Ehrenreich go?)

2. What do you think Ehrenreich actually hopes to accomplish here? Does she want readers to feel admiration for her? Sympathy for her coworkers? Anger at their employers? Or does she have a more ambitious purpose? Does she achieve her purpose?

3. The last paragraph describes a scene in which Peruvian musicians play for the public. What is the purpose of this paragraph? In what way does this interlude enlighten Ehrenreich about the people with whom she has been working?

4. In paragraphs 9 and 10, Ehrenreich pauses in her narrative to focus on the economic plight of her coworkers. Are these paragraphs necessary? Are they consistent with her purpose? Do they support her thesis?

STYLE AND STRUCTURE

1. List some of the transitional expressions (for example, "Forty minutes go by" [2]) that move readers from one time period to another.

2. Ehrenreich's portrayal of Mrs. W. is negative, even contemptuous. What specific words and phrases does the author use to convey this negative attitude? Is this characterization fair? Do you think her coworkers share her feelings?

3. Do Ehrenreich's descriptions of her coworkers make them come alive as individuals? Give examples of some effective description. Would dialogue have strengthened these characterizations? If so, where could it have been added?

4. In paragraph 2, Ehrenreich sarcastically notes that The Maids "kindly" provided a free breakfast. Where else does she use sarcasm? Is it effective?

VOCABULARY PROJECTS

1. Define each of the following words as it is used in this selection.

callow (1)	meagerness (8)	primal (15)
oafish (1)	prima facie (9)	prurient (16)
decorum (1)	comportment (9)	penitent (16)
harried (2)	exurbs (11)	infraction (16)
petulant (5)	relents (12)	insurrection (17)
cineast (5)	drones (13)	pummel (18)
pristine (5)		

2. Note the use of brand names (for cleaning products and snack foods) in this selection. Would the substitution of generic names have made any difference? Should more brand names have been used? Where? Explain.

JOURNAL ENTRY

Do you think Ehrenreich got any personal satisfaction out of her experience as a maid that her coworkers did not get? Do you think she feels in any way superior to them? Explain.

WRITING WORKSHOP

1. Write a letter of resignation from one of the maids to the owner of The Maids. Structure your letter as a narrative that traces your complaints from your first day on the job to your last. State your thesis—your reasons for quitting—in your first paragraph.

2. Write a sales brochure in the form of a narrative, reviewing a typical visit by The Maids to a house or apartment. Emphasize the highly trained employees, efficient service, and positive results. Your purpose is to attract new business.

3. Write a narrative essay that traces your ideal career path for the next ten years. Begin with the job you hope to have when you graduate from college, and move on to the positions you hope to have you become more skilled in your field. Be sure to use clear transitions to show how you hope to move from one job to the next.

COMBINING THE PATTERNS

Although this is a narrative, Ehrenreich implicitly compares herself to the other maids. Should she have developed the similarities and differences between them more fully? What new material could she have added to turn this into a **comparison-and-contrast** essay?

THEMATIC CONNECTIONS

- "Finishing School" (page 89)
- "The Peter Principle" (page 207)
- "The Men We Carry in Our Minds" (page 456)
- Declaration of Sentiments and Resolutions (page 563)

GEORGE ORWELL

❖

Shooting an Elephant

George Orwell (1903–1950) was born Eric Blair in Bengal, India, where his father was a British civil servant. Rather than attend university, Orwell joined the Imperial Police in neighboring Burma (now renamed Myanmar), where he served from 1922 to 1927. Finding himself increasingly opposed to British colonial rule, Orwell left Burma to live and write in Paris and London. A political liberal and fierce moralist, Orwell is best known today for his novels *Animal Farm* (1945) and *1984* (1949), which portray the dangers of totalitarianism. In "Shooting an Elephant," written in 1936, he recalls an incident from his days in Burma that clarified his thinking about British colonial rule.

Background: The British had gradually taken over Burma through a succession of wars beginning in 1824; by 1885, the domination was complete. Like a number of other European countries, Britain had forcibly established colonial rule in countries throughout the world during the eighteenth and nineteenth centuries, primarily to exploit local resources. This empire building, known as *imperialism*, was justified by the belief that European culture was superior to the cultures of the indigenous peoples, particularly in Asia and Africa. Therefore, imperialist nations claimed, it was "the white man's burden" to bring civilization to these "heathen" lands. In most cases, such control could be achieved only through forcible oppression. Anti-imperialist sentiment began to grow in the early twentieth century, but colonial rule continued until midcentury in much of the less developed world. Not until the late 1940s did many European colonies begin to achieve independence. The British ceded home rule to Burma in 1947.

In Moulmein, in Lower Burma, I was hated by large numbers of people—the only time in my life that I have been important enough for this to happen to me. I was sub-divisional police officer of the town, and in an aimless, petty kind of way anti-European feeling was very bitter. No one had the guts to raise a riot, but if a European woman went through the bazaars alone somebody would probably spit betel juice over her dress. As a police officer I was an obvious target and was baited whenever it seemed safe to do so. When a nimble Burman tripped me up on the football field and the referee (another Burman) looked the other way, the crowd yelled with hideous laughter. This happened more than once. In the end the sneering yellow faces of young men that met me everywhere, the insults hooted after me when I was at a safe distance, got badly on my nerves. The young Buddhist priests were the worst of all. There were several thousands of them in the town and none of them seemed to have anything to do except stand on street corners and jeer at Europeans.

All this was perplexing and upsetting. For at that time I had already   2
made up my mind that imperialism was an evil thing and the sooner I
chucked up my job and got out of it the better. Theoretically — and secretly,
of course — I was all for the Burmese and all against their oppressors,
the British. As for the job I was doing, I hated it more bitterly than I can
perhaps make clear. In a job like that you see the dirty work of Empire at
close quarters. The wretched prisoners huddling in the stinking cages of
the lockups, the grey, cowed faces of the long-term convicts, the scarred
buttocks of the men who had been flogged with bamboos — all these
oppressed me with an intolerable sense of guilt. But I could get nothing
into perspective. I was young and ill-educated and I had had to think
out my problems in the utter silence that is imposed on every Englishman
in the East. I did not even know that the British Empire is dying, still less
did I know that it is a great deal better than the younger empires that are
going to supplant it.* All I knew was that I was stuck between my hatred of
the empire I served and my rage against the evil-spirited little beasts who
tried to make my job impossible. With one part of my mind I thought of
the British Raj** as an unbreakable tyranny, as something clamped down,
in *saecula saeculorum*,*** upon the will of prostrate peoples; with another
part I thought that the greatest joy in the world would be to drive a bayo-
net into a Buddhist priest's guts. Feelings like these are the normal by-
products of imperialism; ask any Anglo-Indian official, if you can catch
him off duty.

One day something happened which in a roundabout way was enlight-   3
ening. It was a tiny incident in itself, but it gave me a better glimpse than I
had had before of the real nature of imperialism — the real motives for
which despotic governments act. Early one morning the sub-inspector at a
police station the other end of the town rang me up on the phone and said
that an elephant was ravaging the bazaar. Would I please come and do
something about it? I did not know what I could do, but I wanted to see
what was happening and I got on to a pony and started out. I took my rifle,
an old .44 Winchester and much too small to kill an elephant, but I
thought the noise might be useful *in terrorem*.† Various Burmans stopped
me on the way and told me about the elephant's doings. It was not, of
course, a wild elephant, but a tame one which had gone "must."‡ It had
been chained up, as tame elephants always are when their attack of "must"
is due, but on the previous night it had broken its chain and escaped. Its
mahout,¶ the only person who could manage it when it was in that state,
had set out in pursuit, but had taken the wrong direction and was now
twelve hours' journey away, and in the morning the elephant had suddenly

---

*EDS. NOTE — Orwell was writing in 1936, when Hitler and Stalin were in power
and World War II was only three years away.
**EDS. NOTE — Sovereignty.
***EDS. NOTE — From time immemorial.
†EDS. NOTE — For the purpose of frightening.
‡EDS. NOTE — Was in heat, a condition likely to wear off.
¶EDS. NOTE — A keeper and driver of an elephant.

reappeared in the town. The Burmese population had no weapons and were quite helpless against it. It had already destroyed somebody's bamboo hut, killed a cow, and raided some fruit-stalls and devoured the stock; also it had met the municipal rubbish van and, when the driver jumped out and took to his heels, had turned the van over and inflicted violences upon it.

The Burmese sub-inspector and some Indian constables were waiting   4 for me in the quarter where the elephant had been seen. It was a very poor quarter, a labyrinth of squalid bamboo huts, thatched with palm-leaf, winding all over a steep hillside. I remember that it was a cloudy, stuffy morning at the beginning of the rains. We began questioning people as to where the elephant had gone, and, as usual, failed to get any definite information. That is invariably the case in the East; a story always sounds clear enough at a distance, but the nearer you get to the scene of events the vaguer it becomes. Some of the people said that the elephant had gone in one direction, some said that he had gone in another, some professed not even to have heard of an elephant. I had almost made up my mind that the whole story was a pack of lies, when we heard yells a little distance away. There was a loud, scandalized cry of "Go away, child! Go away this instant!" and an old woman with a switch in her hand came round the corner of a hut, violently shooing away a crowd of naked children. Some more women followed, clicking their tongues and exclaiming; evidently there was something that the children ought not to have seen. I rounded the hut and saw a man's dead body sprawling in the mud. He was an Indian, a black Dravidian coolie,* almost naked, and he could not have been dead many minutes. The people said that the elephant had come suddenly upon him round the corner of the hut, caught him with its trunk, put its foot on his back, and ground him into the earth. This was the rainy season and the ground was soft, and his face had scored a trench a foot deep and a couple of yards long. He was lying on his belly with arms crucified and head sharply twisted to one side. His face was coated with mud, the eyes wide open, the teeth bared and grinning with an expression of unendurable agony. (Never tell me, by the way, that the dead look peaceful. Most of the corpses I have seen looked devilish.) The friction of the great beast's foot had stripped the skin from his back as neatly as one skins a rabbit. As soon as I saw the dead man I sent an orderly to a friend's house nearby to borrow an elephant rifle. I had already sent back the pony, not wanting it to go mad with fright and throw me if it smelled the elephant.

The orderly came back in a few minutes with a rifle and five cartridges,   5 and meanwhile some Burmans had arrived and told us that the elephant was in the paddy** fields below, only a few hundred yards away. As I started forward practically the whole population of the quarter flocked out of the houses and followed me. They had seen the rifle and were all shouting excitedly that I was going to shoot the elephant. They had not shown much interest in the elephant when he was merely ravaging their homes, but it

---

* Eds. note — An unskilled laborer.
** Eds. note — Wet land in which rice grows.

was different now that he was going to be shot. It was a bit of fun to them, as it would be to an English crowd; besides they wanted the meat. It made me vaguely uneasy. I had no intention of shooting the elephant—I had merely sent for the rifle to defend myself if necessary—and it is always unnerving to have a crowd following you. I marched down the hill, looking and feeling a fool, with the rifle over my shoulder and an ever-growing army of people jostling at my heels. At the bottom, when you got away from the huts, there was a metalled road and beyond that a miry waste of paddy fields a thousand yards across, not yet ploughed but soggy from the first rains and dotted with coarse grass. The elephant was standing eight yards from the road, his left side towards us. He took not the slightest notice of the crowd's approach. He was tearing up bunches of grass, beating them against his knees to clean them and stuffing them into his mouth.

I had halted on the road. As soon as I saw the elephant I knew with perfect certainty that I ought not to shoot him. It is a serious matter to shoot a working elephant—it is comparable to destroying a huge and costly piece of machinery—and obviously one ought not to do it if it can possibly be avoided. And at that distance, peacefully eating, the elephant looked no more dangerous than a cow. I thought then and I think now that his attack of "must" was already passing off; in which case he would merely wander harmlessly about until the mahout came back and caught him. Moreover, I did not in the least want to shoot him. I decided that I would watch him for a little while to make sure that he did not turn savage again, and then go home. 6

But at that moment I glanced round at the crowd that had followed me. It was an immense crowd, two thousand at the least and growing every minute. It blocked the road for a long distance on either side. I looked at the sea of yellow faces above the garish clothes—faces all happy and excited over this bit of fun, all certain that the elephant was going to be shot. They were watching me as they would watch a conjurer about to perform a trick. They did not like me, but with the magical rifle in my hands I was momentarily worth watching. And suddenly I realized that I should have to shoot the elephant after all. The people expected it of me and I had got to do it; I could feel their two thousand wills pressing me forward, irresistibly. And it was at this moment, as I stood there with the rifle in my hands, that I first grasped the hollowness, the futility of the white man's dominion in the East. Here was I, the white man with his gun, standing in front of the unarmed native crowd—seemingly the leading actor of the piece; but in reality I was only an absurd puppet pushed to and fro by the will of those yellow faces behind. I perceived in this moment that when the white man turns tyrant it is his own freedom that he destroys. He becomes a sort of hollow, posing dummy, the conventionalized figure of a sahib.* For it is 7

*Eds. note—An official. The term was used among Hindus and Muslims in colonial India.

the condition of his rule that he shall spend his life in trying to impress the "natives," and so in every crisis he has got to do what the "natives" expect of him. He wears a mask, and his face grows to fit it. I had got to shoot the elephant. I had committed myself to doing it when I sent for the rifle. A sahib has got to act like a sahib; he has got to appear resolute, to know his own mind and do definite things. To come all that way, rifle in hand, with two thousand people marching at my heels, and then to trail feebly away, having done nothing—no, that was impossible. The crowd would laugh at me. And my whole life, every white man's life in the East, was one long struggle not to be laughed at.

But I did not want to shoot the elephant. I watched him beating his 8 bunch of grass against his knees, with the preoccupied grandmotherly air that elephants have. It seemed to me that it would be murder to shoot him. At that age I was not squeamish about killing animals, but I had never shot an elephant and never wanted to. (Somehow it always seems worse to kill a *large* animal.) Besides, there was the beast's owner to be considered. Alive, the elephant was worth at least a hundred pounds; dead, he would only be worth the value of his tusks, five pounds, possibly. But I had got to act quickly. I turned to some experienced-looking Burmans who had been there when we arrived, and asked them how the elephant had been behaving. They all said the same thing: he took no notice of you if you left him alone, but he might charge if you went too close to him.

It was perfectly clear to me what I ought to do. I ought to walk up to 9 within, say, twenty-five yards of the elephant and test his behavior. If he charged I could shoot, if he took no notice of me it would be safe to leave him until the mahout came back. But also I knew that I was going to do no such thing. I was a poor shot with a rifle and the ground was soft mud into which one would sink at every step. If the elephant charged and I missed him, I should have about as much chance as a toad under a steamroller. But even then I was not thinking particularly of my own skin, only of the watchful yellow faces behind. For at that moment, with the crowd watching me, I was not afraid in the ordinary sense, as I would have been if I had been alone. A white man mustn't be frightened in front of "natives"; and so, in general, he isn't frightened. The sole thought in my mind was that if anything went wrong those two thousand Burmans would see me pursued, caught, trampled on, and reduced to a grinning corpse like that Indian up the hill. And if that happened it was quite probable that some of them would laugh. That would never do. There was only one alternative. I shoved the cartridges into the magazine and lay down on the road to get a better aim.

The crowd grew very still, and a deep, low, happy sigh, as of people who 10 see the theatre curtain go up at last, breathed from innumerable throats. They were going to have their bit of fun after all. The rifle was a beautiful German thing with cross-hair sights. I did not then know that in shooting an elephant one would shoot to cut an imaginary bar running from ear-hole to ear-hole. I ought, therefore, as the elephant was sideways on, to have aimed straight at his ear-hole; actually I aimed several inches in front of this, thinking the brain would be further forward.

When I pulled the trigger I did not hear the bang or feel the kick — one never does when a shot goes home — but I heard the devilish roar of glee that went up from the crowd. In that instant, in too short a time, one would have thought, even for the bullet to get there, a mysterious, terrible change had come over the elephant. He neither stirred nor fell, but every line on his body had altered. He looked suddenly stricken, shrunken, immensely old, as though the frightful impact of the bullet had paralyzed him without knocking him down. At last, after what seemed a long time — it might have been five seconds, I dare say — he sagged flabbily to his knees. His mouth slobbered. An enormous senility seemed to have settled upon him. One could have imagined him thousands of years old. I fired again into the same spot. At the second shot he did not collapse but climbed with desperate slowness to his feet and stood weakly upright, with legs sagging and head drooping. I fired a third time. That was the shot that did for him. You could see the agony of it jolt his whole body and knock the last remnant of strength from his legs. But in falling he seemed for a moment to rise, for as his hind legs collapsed beneath him he seemed to tower upwards like a huge rock toppling, his trunk reaching skywards like a tree. He trumpeted, for the first and only time. And then down he came, his belly towards me, with a crash that seemed to shake the ground even where I lay.

I got up. The Burmans were already racing past me across the mud. It was obvious that the elephant would never rise again, but he was not dead. He was breathing very rhythmically with long rattling gasps, his great mound of a side painfully rising and falling. His mouth was wide open — I could see far down into the caverns of pale pink throat. I waited a long time for him to die, but his breathing did not weaken. Finally, I fired my two remaining shots into the spot where I thought his heart must be. The thick blood welled out of him like red velvet, but still he did not die. His body did not even jerk when the shots hit him, the tortured breathing continued without a pause. He was dying, very slowly and in great agony, but in some world remote from me where not even a bullet could damage him further. I felt that I had got to put an end to that dreadful noise. It seemed dreadful to see the great beast lying there, powerless to move and yet powerless to die, and not even to be able to finish him. I sent back for my small rifle and poured shot after shot into his heart and down his throat. They seemed to make no impression. The tortured gasps continued as steadily as the ticking of a clock.

In the end I could not stand it any longer and went away. I heard later that it took him half an hour to die. Burmans were bringing dahs* and baskets even before I left, and I was told they had stripped his body almost to the bones by the afternoon.

---

*Eds. note — Heavy knives.

Afterwards, of course, there were endless discussions about the shoot-   14
ing of the elephant. The owner was furious, but he was only an Indian and
could do nothing. Besides, legally I had done the right thing, for a mad
elephant has to be killed, like a mad dog, if its owner fails to control
it. Among the Europeans opinion was divided. The older men said I was
right, the younger men said it was a damn shame to shoot an elephant for
killing a coolie, because an elephant was worth more than any damn Cor-
inghee coolie. And afterwards I was very glad that the coolie had been
killed; it put me legally in the right and it gave me a sufficient pretext for
shooting the elephant. I often wondered whether any of the others grasped
that I had done it solely to avoid looking a fool.

● ● ●

COMPREHENSION

1. Why is Orwell "hated by large numbers of people" (1) in Burma? Why does
   he have mixed feelings toward the Burmese people?

2. Why do the local officials want something done about the elephant? Why
   does the crowd want Orwell to shoot the elephant?

3. Why does Orwell finally decide to kill the elephant? What makes him hesitate at first?

4. Why does Orwell say at the end that he was glad the coolie had been
   killed?

PURPOSE AND AUDIENCE

1. One of Orwell's purposes in telling his story is to show how it gave him a
   glimpse of "the real nature of imperialism" (3). What does he mean? How
   does his essay illustrate this purpose?

2. Do you think Orwell wrote this essay to inform or to persuade his audience? How did Orwell expect his audience to react to his ideas? How can
   you tell?

3. What is the essay's thesis?

STYLE AND STRUCTURE

1. What does Orwell's first paragraph accomplish? Where does the introduction end and the narrative itself begin?

2. The essay includes almost no dialogue. Why do you think Orwell's voice as
   narrator is the only one readers hear? Is the absence of dialogue a strength
   or a weakness? Explain.

3. Why do you think Orwell devotes so much attention to the elephant's
   misery (11–12)?

4. Orwell's essay includes a number of editorial comments, which appear
   within parentheses or dashes. How would you characterize these comments? Why are they set off from the text?

5. Consider the following statements: "Some of the people said that the elephant had gone in one direction, some said that he had gone in another" (4); "Among the Europeans opinion was divided. The older men said I was right, the younger men said it was a damn shame to shoot an elephant" (14). How do these comments reinforce the theme expressed in paragraph 2 ("All I knew was that I was stuck between my hatred of the empire I served and my rage against the evil-spirited little beasts")? What other comments reinforce this theme?

VOCABULARY PROJECTS

1. Define each of the following words as it is used in this selection.

baited (1)	despotic (3)	conjurer (7)
perplexing (2)	labyrinth (4)	dominion (7)
oppressors (2)	squalid (4)	magazine (9)
lockups (2)	professed (4)	cross-hair (10)
flogged (2)	ravaging (5)	remnant (11)
supplant (2)	miry (5)	trumpeted (11)
prostrate (2)	garish (7)	pretext (14)

2. Because Orwell is British, he frequently uses words or expressions that an American writer would not be likely to use. Substitute a contemporary American word or phrase for each of the following, making sure it is appropriate in Orwell's context.

raise a riot (1)	rubbish van (3)	a bit of fun (5)
rang me up (3)	inflicted violences (3)	I dare say (11)

What other expressions might need to be "translated" for a contemporary American audience?

JOURNAL ENTRY

Do you think Orwell is a coward? Do you think he is a racist? Explain your feelings.

WRITING WORKSHOP

1. Orwell says that even though he hated British imperialism and sympathized with the Burmese people, he found himself a puppet of the system. Write a narrative essay about a time when you had to do something that went against your beliefs or convictions.

2. Orwell's experience taught him something not only about himself but also about something beyond himself—the way British imperialism worked. Write a narrative essay that reveals how an incident in your life taught you something about some larger social or political force as well as about yourself.

3. Write an objective, factual newspaper article recounting the events Orwell describes.

COMBINING THE PATTERNS

Implicit in this narrative essay is an extended **comparison and contrast** that highlights the differences between Orwell and the Burmese people. Review the essay, and list the most obvious differences Orwell perceives between himself and them. Do you think his perceptions are accurate? If all of the differences were set forth in a single paragraph, how might such a paragraph change your perception of Orwell's dilemma? Of his character?

THEMATIC CONNECTIONS

- "Thirty-Eight Who Saw Murder Didn't Call the Police" (page 101)
- "Just Walk On By" (page 223)
- "The Untouchable" (page 498)

❖

Indian Education (Fiction)

Sherman Alexie, the son of a Coeur d'Alene Indian father and a Spokane Indian mother, was born in 1966 and grew up on the Spokane Reservation in Wellpinit, Washington, home to some 1,100 Spokane tribal members. A precocious child who endured much teasing from his fellow classmates on the reservation and who realized as a teenager that his educational opportunities there were extremely limited, Alexie made the unusual decision to attend high school off the reservation in nearby Reardon. Later a scholarship student at Gonzaga University, he received a bachelor's degree in American studies from Washington State University at Pullman. While in college, he began publishing poetry; within a year of graduation, his first collection, *The Business of Fancydancing* (1992), appeared. This was followed by *The Lone Ranger and Tonto Fistfight in Heaven* (1993), a short-story collection, and the novels *Reservation Blues* (1995) and *Indian Killer* (1996), all of which have garnered numerous awards and honors. Alexie also wrote the screenplay for the highly acclaimed film *Smoke Signals* (1998) and most recently wrote and directed *The Business of Fancydancing* (2002), a hit at film festivals across the country.

Background: By the mid-1800s, most Native American tribes had been overwhelmed by the superior weapons of the U.S. military and confined to reservations. Beginning in the late 1800s and continuing into the 1950s, government policymakers established boarding schools for Native American youth to help them assimilate into the dominant culture and thus become "civilized." To this end, children were forcibly removed from their homes for long periods of time to separate them from native traditions. At the boarding schools, they were given a cursory academic education and spent most of their time studying Christian teachings and laboring to contribute to the cost of their schooling. Students were punished for speaking their own languages or practicing their own religions. Responding to protests from the American Indian Movement in the 1970s, the government began to send fewer Native Americans to boarding schools and retreated from its goal of assimilation at boarding schools and at newly established reservation schools. Still, government funding for Native American schools remains considerably lower than for other public schools, and students often make do with inadequate and antiquated facilities, equipment, and textbooks. In part because of such educational failures, few Native American students go on to college, and the incidence of alcohol and drug abuse among Native Americans is higher than in any other U.S. population.

First Grade

My hair was too short and my U.S. Government glasses were horn-rimmed, ugly, and all that first winter in school, the other Indian boys chased me from one corner of the playground to the other. They pushed

1

me down, buried me in the snow until I couldn't breathe, thought I'd never breathe again.

They stole my glasses and threw them over my head, around my out- 2
stretched hands, just beyond my reach, until someone tripped me and sent me falling again, facedown in the snow.

I was always falling down; my Indian name was Junior Falls Down. 3
Sometimes it was Bloody Nose or Steal-His-Lunch. Once, it was Cries-Like-a-White-Boy, even though none of us had seen a white boy cry.

Then it was a Friday morning recess and Frenchy SiJohn threw snow- 4
balls at me while the rest of the Indian boys tortured some other *top-yogh-yaught* kid, another weakling. But Frenchy was confident enough to torment me all by himself, and most days I would have let him.

But the little warrior in me roared to life that day and knocked Frenchy 5
to the ground, held his head against the snow, and punched him so hard that my knuckles and the snow made symmetrical bruises on his face. He almost looked like he was wearing war paint.

But he wasn't the warrior. I was. And I chanted *It's a good day to die, it's a* 6
good day to die, all the way down to the principal's office.

Second Grade

Betty Towle, missionary teacher, redheaded and so ugly that no one ever 7
had a puppy crush on her, made me stay in for recess fourteen days straight.

"Tell me you're sorry," she said. 8

"Sorry for what?" I asked. 9

"Everything," she said and made me stand straight for fifteen minutes, 10
eagle-armed with books in each hand. One was a math book; the other was English. But all I learned was that gravity can be painful.

For Halloween I drew a picture of her riding a broom with a scrawny 11
cat on the back. She said that her God would never forgive me for that.

Once, she gave the class a spelling test but set me aside and gave me a 12
test designed for junior high students. When I spelled all the words right, she crumpled up the paper and made me eat it.

"You'll learn respect," she said. 13

She sent a letter home with me that told my parents to either cut my 14
braids or keep me home from class. My parents came in the next day and dragged their braids across Betty Towle's desk.

"Indians, indians, indians." She said it without capitalization. She 15
called me "indian, indian, indian."

And I said, *Yes, I am. I am Indian. Indian, I am.* 16

Third Grade

My traditional Native American art career began and ended with my 17
very first portrait: *Stick Indian Taking a Piss in My Backyard.*

As I circulated the original print around the classroom, Mrs. Schluter 18
intercepted and confiscated my art.

Censorship, I might cry now. *Freedom of expression,* I would write in edito- 19
rials to the tribal newspaper.

In third grade, though, I stood alone in the corner, faced the wall, and 20
waited for the punishment to end.

I'm still waiting. 21

Fourth Grade

"You should be a doctor when you grow up," Mr. Schluter told me, 22
even though his wife, the third grade teacher, thought I was crazy beyond
my years. My eyes always looked like I had just hit-and-run someone.

"Guilty," she said. "You always look guilty." 23

"Why should I be a doctor?" I asked Mr. Schluter. 24

"So you can come back and help the tribe. So you can heal people." 25

That was the year my father drank a gallon of vodka a day and the 26
same year that my mother started two hundred different quilts but never
finished any. They sat in separate, dark places in our HUD house and wept
savagely.

I ran home after school, heard their Indian tears, and looked in the 27
mirror. *Doctor Victor,* I called myself, invented an education, talked to my
reflection. *Doctor Victor to the emergency room.*

Fifth Grade

I picked up a basketball for the first time and made my first shot. No. I 28
missed my first shot, missed the basket completely, and the ball landed in
the dirt and sawdust, sat there just like I had sat there only minutes before.

But it felt good, that ball in my hands, all those possibilities and 29
angles. It was mathematics, geometry. It was beautiful.

At that same moment, my cousin Steven Ford sniffed rubber cement 30
from a paper bag and leaned back on the merry-go-round. His ears rang,
his mouth was dry, and everyone seemed so far away.

But it felt good, that buzz in his head, all those colors and noises. It 31
was chemistry, biology. It was beautiful.

Oh, do you remember those sweet, almost innocent choices that the Indian 32
boys were forced to make?

Sixth Grade

Randy, the new Indian kid from the white town of Springdale, got into 33
a fight an hour after he first walked into the reservation school.

Stevie Flett called him out, called him a squawman, called him a pussy, 34
and called him a punk.

Randy and Stevie, and the rest of the Indian boys, walked out into the 35
playground.

"Throw the first punch," Stevie said as they squared off. 36

"No," Randy said. 37

"Throw the first punch," Stevie said again. 38

"No," Randy said again. 39

"Throw the first punch!" Stevie said for the third time, and Randy 40
reared back and pitched a knuckle fastball that broke Stevie's nose.

We all stood there in silence, in awe. 41

That was Randy, my soon-to-be first and best friend, who taught me 42
the most valuable lesson about living in the white world: *Always throw the
first punch.*

Seventh Grade

I leaned through the basement window of the HUD house and kissed 43
the white girl who would later be raped by her foster-parent father, who
was also white. They both lived on the reservation, though, and when the
headlines and stories filled the papers later, not one word was made of
their color.

Just Indians being Indians, someone must have said somewhere and they 44
were wrong.

But on the day I leaned through the basement window of the HUD 45
house and kissed the white girl, I felt the good-byes I was saying to my
entire tribe. I held my lips tight against her lips, a dry, clumsy, and ultimately stupid kiss.

But I was saying good-bye to my tribe, to all the Indian girls and 46
women I might have loved, to all the Indian men who might have called me
cousin, even brother.

I kissed that white girl and when I opened my eyes, she was gone from 47
the reservation, and when I opened my eyes, I was gone from the reservation, living in a farm town where a beautiful white girl asked my name.

"Junior Polatkin," I said, and she laughed. 48

After that, no one spoke to me for another five hundred years. 49

Eighth Grade

At the farm town junior high, in the boys' bathroom, I could hear 50
voices from the girls' bathroom, nervous whispers of anorexia and bulimia.
I could hear the white girls' forced vomiting, a sound so familiar and natural to me after years of listening to my father's hangovers.

"Give me your lunch if you're just going to throw it up," I said to one of 51
those girls once.

I sat back and watched them grow skinny from self-pity. 52

Back on the reservation, my mother stood in line to get us commodities. 53
We carried them home, happy to have food, and opened the canned beef
that even the dogs wouldn't eat.

But we ate it day after day and grew skinny from self-pity. 54

There is more than one way to starve. 55

Ninth Grade

At the farm town high school dance, after a basketball game in an over- 56
heated gym where I had scored twenty-seven points and pulled down
thirteen rebounds, I passed out during a slow song.

As my white friends revived me and prepared to take me to the emer- 57
gency room where doctors would later diagnose my diabetes, the Chicano
teacher ran up to us.

"Hey," he said. "What's that boy been drinking? I know all about these 58
Indian kids. They start drinking real young."

Sharing dark skin doesn't necessarily make two men brothers. 59

Tenth Grade

I passed the written test easily and nearly flunked the driving, but still 60
received my Washington State driver's license on the same day that Wally
Jim killed himself by driving his car into a pine tree.

No traces of alcohol in his blood, good job, wife and two kids. 61

"Why'd he do it?" asked a white Washington State trooper. 62

All the Indians shrugged their shoulders, looked down at the ground. 63

"Don't know," we all said, but when we look in the mirror, see the his- 64
tory of our tribe in our eyes, taste failure in the tap water, and shake with
old tears, we understand completely.

Believe me, everything looks like a noose if you stare at it long enough. 65

Eleventh Grade

Last night I missed two free throws which would have won the game 66
against the best team in the state. The farm town high school I play for is
nicknamed the "Indians," and I'm probably the only actual Indian ever to
play for a team with such a mascot.

This morning I pick up the sports page and read the headline: INDIANS 67
LOSE AGAIN.

Go ahead and tell me none of this is supposed to hurt me very much. 68

Twelfth Grade

I walk down the aisle, valedictorian of this farm town high school, and 69
my cap doesn't fit because I've grown my hair longer than it's ever been.
Later, I stand as the school-board chairman recites my awards, accomplishments, and scholarships.

I try to remain stoic for the photographers as I look toward the future. 70

Back home on the reservation, my former classmates graduate: a few can't 71
read, one or two are just given attendance diplomas, most look forward to
the parties. The bright students are shaken, frightened, because they don't
know what comes next.

They smile for the photographer as they look back toward tradition. 72

* * *

The tribal newspaper runs my photograph and the photograph of my for-   73
mer classmates side by side.

Postscript: Class Reunion

Victor said, "Why should we organize a reservation high school re-   74
union? My graduating class has a reunion every weekend at the Powwow
Tavern."

• • •

READING LITERATURE

1. Instead of linking events with transitional phrases that establish chronology, Alexie uses internal headings to move readers through the story. How
   do these headings indicate the passage of time? Are these headings
   enough, or do you think Alexie should have opened each section of the
   story with a transitional phrase? (Try to suggest some possibilities.)

2. The narrator's experiences in each grade in school are illustrated by one or
   more specific incidents. What do these incidents have in common? What
   do they reveal about the narrator? About his schools?

3. Explain the meaning of each of these statements in the context of the
   story:
   • "There is more than one way to starve" (55).
   • "Sharing dark skin doesn't necessarily make two men brothers" (59).
   • "Believe me, everything looks like a noose if you stare at it long
     enough" (65).

JOURNAL ENTRY

What does the "Postscript: Class Reunion" section (74) tell readers about
Indian education? Is this information consistent with what we have learned in
the rest of the story, or does it come as a surprise? Explain.

THEMATIC CONNECTIONS

WRITING ASSIGNMENTS FOR NARRATION

1. Trace the path you expect to follow to establish yourself in your chosen profession, considering possible obstacles you may face and how you expect to deal with them. Include a thesis statement that conveys the importance of your goals. If you like, you may refer to some essays elsewhere in this book that focus on work — for example, "The Peter Principle" (page 207), "On Fire" (page 280), or "The Men We Carry in Our Minds" (page 456).

2. Write a personal narrative in which you look back from some point in the far future on your own life as you hope it will be seen by others. Use third person if you like, and write your own obituary; or use first person, assessing your life in the form of a letter to your great-grandchildren.

3. Write a news article recounting in objective terms the events described in an essay that appears elsewhere in this text — for example, "Who Killed Benny Paret?" (page 321) or "Grant and Lee: A Study in Contrasts" (page 386). Include a descriptive headline.

4. Write a historical narrative tracing the roots of your family or your hometown or community. Be sure to include specific detail, dialogue, and descriptions of people and places.

5. Write an account of one of these "firsts": your first date; your first serious argument with your parents; your first experience with physical violence or danger; your first extended stay away from home; your first encounter with someone whose culture was very different from your own; your first experience with the serious illness or death of a close friend or relative. Make sure your essay includes a thesis statement that your narrative can support.

6. Both George Orwell and Martin Gansberg deal with the consequences of failing to act. Write an essay or story in which you recount what would have happened if Orwell had *not* shot the elephant or if one of the eyewitnesses *had* called the police right away.

7. Maya Angelou's "finishing school" was Mrs. Cullinan's kitchen. Write about a similar person or place that helped you develop into the person you are today. What did you learn from this person or place, and how did this knowledge serve you later?

8. Write a short narrative telling what happened in a class, a short story, a television show, a conversation, a fable or fairy tale, or a narrative poem. Include as many details as you can.

9. Write a narrative about a time when you were an outsider, isolated because of social, intellectual, or ethnic differences between you and others. Did you resolve the problems your isolation created? Explain. If you like, you may refer to the Angelou or Orwell essays in this chapter or to "Just Walk On By" (page 223).

10. Imagine a meeting between any two people who appear in this chapter's reading selections. Using dialogue as well as narrative, write an account of this meeting.

11. Narrate the history of an object that is of great value to you. If you do not know the object's history, you can research the history of that object or create one based on what you do know. Throughout the essay, use the

story of the object's history to reveal something about yourself. For example, a ring that you inherited from your grandmother might illustrate your closeness to her; similarly, an autographed baseball might be the impetus for your interest in coaching a professional baseball team.

12. Using Alexie's story as a model, write the story of your own education.

COLLABORATIVE ACTIVITY FOR NARRATION

Working with a group of students of about your own age, write a history of your television-viewing habits. Start by working individually to list all your most-watched television shows in chronological order, beginning as far back as you can remember. Then compile a single list that reflects a consensus of the group's preferences, perhaps choosing one or two representative programs for each stage of your life (preschool, elementary school, and so on). Have a different student write a paragraph on each stage, describing the chosen programs in as much detail as possible. Finally, combine the individual paragraphs to create a narrative essay that traces the group's changing tastes in television shows. The essay's thesis statement should express what your group's television preferences reveal about your generation's development.

INTERNET ASSIGNMENT FOR NARRATION

Choose an important local or national event that you remember hearing about, and use the following Web sites to help you locate newspaper or magazine articles about the event to find out more. Then, imagining that you have witnessed the event firsthand, write a narrative of what you experienced. Refer to Martin Gansberg's "Thirty-Eight Who Saw Murder Didn't Call the Police" to see how to use dialogue in your narrative.

Poynter Institute
<poynter.org/links/>
A list of links to journalistic sources including journalism organizations and libraries, research, newspapers, and radio and television channels.

The Len-Net Entertainment Web
<lni.net/cowabunga/>
This site offers links to media-related sites, including links to local newspapers across the United States.

Media Link
<kidon.com/media-link/index.shtml/>
This site offers links and in-depth information about news sources in virtually every nation in the world.

❖ 5
Description

WHAT IS DESCRIPTION?

You use **description** to tell readers about the physical characteristics of a person, place, or thing. Description relies on the five senses — sight, hearing, taste, touch, and smell. In the following paragraph from "Knoxville: Summer 1915," James Agee uses sight, sound, and touch to re-create a scene for his audience:

Topic sentence	It is not of games children play in the evening that I want to speak now, it is of a contemporaneous atmosphere that has little to do with them; that of fathers and families, each in his space of
Description using sight	lawn, his shirt fishlike pale in the unnatural light and his face nearly anonymous, hosing their lawns. The hoses were attached to spigots that stood out of the brick foundations of the houses. The nozzles were variously set but usually so there was a long
Description using touch	sweet stream of spray, the nozzle wet in the hand, the water trickling the right forearm and the peeled-back cuff, and the water whishing out a long loose and low-curved cone, and so gentle a sound.
Description using sound	First an insane noise of violence in the nozzle, then the still irregular sound of adjustment, then the smoothing into steadiness and a pitch as accurately tuned to the size and style of stream as any violin. So many qualities of sound out of one hose: so many choral differences out of those several hoses that were in earshot. Out of any one hose, the almost dead silence of the release, and the short still arch of the separate big drops, silent as a held breath, and the only noise the flattering noise on leaves and the slapped grass at the fall of each big drop. That, and the intense hiss with the intense stream; that, and the same intensity not growing

less but growing more quiet and delicate with the turn of the nozzle, up to that extreme tender whisper when the water was just a wide bell of film.

A descriptive essay tells what something looks like or what it feels like, sounds like, smells like, or tastes like. However, description often goes beyond personal sense impressions: novelists can create imaginary landscapes, historians can paint word pictures of historical figures, and scientists can describe physical phenomena they have never actually seen. When you write description, you use language to create a vivid impression for your readers.

Writers of descriptive essays often use an implied thesis when they describe a person, place, or thing. This technique allows them to convey an essay's **dominant impression**—the mood or quality that is emphasized in the piece of writing—subtly through the selection and arrangement of details. When they use description to support a particular point, however, many writers prefer to use an explicitly stated thesis. This strategy lets readers see immediately what point the writer is making—for example, "The sculptures that adorn Philadelphia's City Hall are a catalog of nineteenth-century artistic styles." Whether you state or imply your thesis, the details of your descriptive essay must work together to create a single dominant impression. In many cases your thesis may be just a statement of the dominant impression; sometimes, however, your thesis may go further and make a point about that dominant impression.

USING DESCRIPTION

Before we make judgments about the world, before we compare or contrast or classify our experiences, we describe. In your college writing, you use description in many different kinds of assignments. In a comparison-and-contrast essay, for example, you may describe the appearance of two cars to show that one is more desirable than the other. In an argumentative essay, you may describe a fish kill in a local river to show that industrial waste dumping is a problem. Through description, you communicate your view of the world to your readers. If your readers come to understand or share your view, they are more likely to accept your observations, your judgments, and your conclusions. Therefore, in almost every essay you write, knowing how to write effective description is important.

Understanding Objective and Subjective Description

Description can be objective or subjective. In an **objective description,** you focus on the object itself rather than on your personal reactions to it. Your purpose is to present a precise, literal picture of your subject. Many writing situations require exact descriptions of apparatus or conditions, and in these cases your goal is to construct an accurate picture for your audience. A biologist describing what he sees through a microscope and a historian describing a Civil War battlefield would both write objectively. The biologist would not, for instance, say how exciting his observations were, nor would the historian say how disappointed she was at the outcome of the battle. Many newspaper reporters also try to achieve this objectivity, as do writers of technical reports, scientific papers, and certain types of business correspondence. Still, objectivity is an ideal that writers strive for but never fully achieve. In fact, in selecting some details and leaving out others, writers are making subjective decisions.

In the following descriptive passage, Thomas Marc Parrott aims for objectivity by giving his readers all the factual information they need to visualize Shakespeare's theater:

> When James Burbage built the Theatre in 1576 he naturally designed it along the lines of inn-yards in which he had been accustomed to play. The building had two entrances — one in front for the audience; one in the rear for actors, musicians, and the personnel of the theatre. Inside the building a rectangular platform projected far out into what was called "the yard" — we know the stage of the Fortune ran halfway across the "yard," some twenty-seven and a half feet.

Note that Parrott is not interested in responding to or evaluating the theater he describes. Instead, he chooses words that convey sizes, shapes, and distances, such as *two* and *rectangular*. Only one word in the paragraph — *naturally* — suggests an opinion.

In contrast to objective description, **subjective description** conveys your personal response to your subject. Your perspective is not necessarily expressed explicitly, in a direct statement. Often it is revealed indirectly, through your choice of words and phrasing. If an English composition assignment asks you to describe a place that has special meaning to you, you could give a subjective reaction to your topic by selecting and emphasizing details that show your feelings about the place. For example, you could write a subjective description of your room by focusing on particular objects — your desk, your window, and your bookshelves — and explaining the meanings these things have for you. Thus, your desk could be a "warm brown rectangle of wood whose surface contains the scratched impressions of a thousand school assignments."

A subjective description should convey not just a literal record of sights and sounds but also their significance. For example, if you objectively described a fire, you might include its temperature, duration, and scope. In addition, you might describe, as accurately as possible, the fire's color, movement, and intensity. If you subjectively described the fire, however, you would try to re-create for your audience a sense of how the fire made you feel — your reactions to the crackling noise, to the dense smoke, to the sudden destruction.

In the following passage, notice how Mark Twain subjectively describes a sunset on the Mississippi River:

> I still kept in mind a certain wonderful sunset which I witnessed when steamboating was new to me. A broad expanse of the river was turned to blood; in the middle distance the red hue brightened into gold, through which a solitary log came floating, black and conspicuous; in one place a long, slanting mark lay sparkling upon the water; in another the surface was broken by boiling, tumbling rings, that were as many-tinted as an opal.

In this passage, Twain conveys his strong emotional reaction to the sunset by using vivid, powerful images such as the river "turned to blood," the "solitary log [. . .] black and conspicuous," and the "boiling, tumbling rings." He also chooses words that suggest great value, such as *gold* and *opal*.

Neither objective nor subjective description exists independently. Objective descriptions usually contain some subjective elements, and subjective descriptions need some objective elements to convey a sense of reality. The skillful writer adjusts the balance between objectivity and subjectivity to suit the topic, thesis, audience, purpose, and occasion of an essay.

Using Objective and Subjective Language

As the passages by Parrott and Twain illustrate, both objective and subjective descriptions depend on specific and concrete words to appeal to readers' senses. But these two types of description use different kinds of language. Objective descriptions rely on precise, factual language that presents a writer's observations without conveying his or her attitude toward the subject. Subjective descriptions, however, often use richer or more suggestive language. They are more likely to rely on the **connotations** of words, their emotional associations, than on their **denotations,** or more direct meanings. In addition, they may deliberately provoke the reader's imagination with striking phrases or vivid language, including **figures of speech** like simile, metaphor, and personification.

A **simile** uses *like* or *as* to compare two dissimilar things. These comparisons occur frequently in everyday speech — for example, when someone claims to be "happy as a clam," "free as a bird," or "hungry as a bear." As a rule, however, you should avoid overused expressions like these in your writing. Effective writers constantly strive to create original similes. In his essay "The Way to Rainy Mountain," for instance, N. Scott Momaday uses a striking simile to describe the ruggedness of the Black Hills when he says, "the land was *like iron.*" In the same essay, he describes shadows from clouds "that move upon the grain *like water.*"

A **metaphor** compares two dissimilar things without using *like* or *as.* Instead of saying that something is *like* something else, a metaphor says it *is* something else. Twain uses a metaphor when he says "A broad expanse of river was turned to blood."

Personification speaks of concepts or objects as if they were endowed with life or human characteristics. If you say that the wind whispered or that an engine died, you are using personification.

In addition to these figures of speech, writers of subjective descriptions also use allusions to enrich their writing. An **allusion** is a reference to a person, place, event, or quotation that the writer assumes readers will recognize. In "Letter from Birmingham Jail" (page 570), for example, Martin Luther King Jr. enriches his argument by alluding to biblical passages and proverbs with which he expects his audience of clergy to be familiar.

Your purpose and audience determine whether you should use objective or subjective description. An assignment that specifically asks for reactions calls for a subjective description. Legal, medical, technical, business, and scientific writing assignments, however, frequently require objective descriptions because their primary purpose is to give the audience factual information. (Even in these areas, of course, figures of speech may be used. Scientists often use such language to describe an unfamiliar object or concept to an audience. In their pioneering article on the structure of DNA, for example, James Watson and Francis Crick use a simile when they describe a molecule of DNA as looking like two spiral staircases winding around each other.)

Selecting Details

Sometimes inexperienced writers pack their descriptions with empty abstract words like *nice, great, terrific,* or *awful,* substituting their own reactions to an object for the qualities of the object itself. To produce an effective description, however, you must do more than just *say* something is wonderful—you must use details that evoke this response in your readers, as Twain does with the sunset. (Twain does in fact use the word *wonderful* at the beginning of his description, but he then goes on to supply many concrete details that make the scene he describes vivid and specific.)

All good descriptive writing, whether objective or subjective, relies on specific detail. Your aim is not simply to *tell* readers what something looks like but to *show* them. Every person, place, or thing has its special characteristics, and you should use your powers of observation to detect them. Then, you need to select the concrete words that will enable your readers to imagine what you describe. Don't be satisfied with "He looked angry" when you can say "His face flushed, and one corner of his mouth twitched as he tried to control his anger." What's the difference? In the first case, you simply identify the man's emotional state. In the second, you provide enough detail so that readers can tell not only that he was angry but also how he revealed the intensity of his anger.

Of course, you could have provided even more detail by describing the man's beard, his wrinkles, or any number of other features. Keep in mind, however, that not all details are equally useful or desirable. You should take care to include only those that contribute to the dominant impression you wish to create. Thus, in describing a man's face to show how angry he was, you would probably not include the shape of his nose or the color of his hair. (After all, a person's hair color does not change when he or she gets angry.) In fact, the number of particulars you use is less important than their quality and appropriateness. You should select and use only those details relevant to your purpose.

Factors like the level, background, and knowledge of your audience also influence the kinds of details you include. For example, a description of a DNA molecule written for first-year college students would contain more basic details than a description written for junior biology majors. In addition, the more advanced description would contain details—the sequence of amino acid groups, for instance—that might be inappropriate for first-year students.

PLANNING A DESCRIPTIVE ESSAY

Organizing Details

When you plan a descriptive essay, you usually begin by writing down descriptive details in no particular order. You then arrange these details in a way that supports your thesis and communicates your dominant impression. As you consider how to arrange your details, you have a number of options. For example, you can move from a specific description of an object to a general description of other things around it. Or you can reverse this order, beginning with the general and proceeding to the specific. You can also progress from the least important feature to the most important one, from the smallest to the largest item, from the least unusual to the most unusual detail, or from left to right, right to left, top to bottom, or bottom to top. Another option you have is to combine approaches, using different organizing schemes in different parts of the essay. The strategy you choose depends on the dominant impression you want to convey, your thesis, and your purpose and audience.

Using Transitions

Be sure to include all the transitional words and phrases readers will need to follow your description. Without them, readers will have difficulty understanding the relationship between one detail and another. Throughout your description, and especially in the topic sentences of your body paragraphs, use words or phrases that indicate the spatial arrangement of details. In descriptive essays, the transitions commonly used include *above, adjacent to, at the bottom, at the top, behind, below, beyond, in front of, in the middle, next to, over, under, through,* and *within.* A more complete list of transitions appears on page 43.

STRUCTURING A DESCRIPTIVE ESSAY

Descriptive essays begin with an *introduction* that presents the thesis or establishes the dominant impression that the rest of the essay will develop. Each *body paragraph* includes details that support the thesis or convey the dominant impression. The *conclusion* reinforces the thesis or dominant impression, perhaps echoing an idea stated in the introduction or using a particularly effective simile or metaphor.

Suppose your English composition instructor has asked you to write a short essay describing a person, place, or thing. After thinking about the assignment for a day or two, you decide to write an objective description of the National Air and Space Museum in Washington, D.C., because you have visited it recently and many details are fresh in your mind. The museum is large and has many different exhibits, so you know you will not be able to describe them all. Therefore, you decide to concentrate on one, the heavier-than-air flight exhibit, and you choose as your topic the display that you remember most vividly—Charles Lindbergh's airplane, *The Spirit of St. Louis.* You begin by brainstorming to recall all the details you can. When you read over your notes, you realize that the organizing scheme of your essay could reflect your actual experience in the museum. You decide to present the details of the airplane in the order in which your eye took them in, from front to rear. The dominant impression you wish to create is how small and fragile *The Spirit of St. Louis* appears, and your thesis statement communicates this impression. An informal outline for your essay might look like this:

Introduction:	Thesis statement—It is startling that a plane as small as *The Spirit of St. Louis* could fly across the Atlantic.
Front of plane:	Single engine, tiny cockpit
Middle of plane:	Short wing span, extra gas tanks
Rear of plane:	Limited cargo space filled with more gas tanks
Conclusion:	Restatement of thesis or review of key points or details

REVISING A DESCRIPTIVE ESSAY

When you revise a descriptive essay, consider the items on the Revision Checklist on pages 54–55. In addition, pay special attention to the items on the checklist below, which apply specifically to descriptive essays.

☑ **REVISION CHECKLIST: DESCRIPTION**

- Does your assignment call for description?
- Does your descriptive essay clearly communicate its thesis or dominant impression?

(continued on next page)

(continued from previous page)

- Is your description primarily objective or subjective?
- If your description is primarily objective, have you used precise, factual language?
- If your description is primarily subjective, have you used figures of speech?
- Have you included enough specific details?
- Have you arranged your details in a way that supports your thesis and communicates your dominant impression?
- Have you used the transitional words and phrases that readers need to follow your description?

EDITING A DESCRIPTIVE ESSAY

When you edit your descriptive essay, follow the guidelines in the Editing Checklist on pages 66–67. In addition, focus on the grammar, mechanics, and punctuation issues that are most relevant to descriptive essays. One of these issues—avoiding misplaced and dangling modifiers—is discussed below.

For more practice in avoiding misplaced and dangling modifiers, visit **Exercise Central** at **<bedfordstmartins.com/patterns/modifiers>**.

GRAMMAR IN CONTEXT : Avoiding Misplaced and Dangling Modifiers*

When writing descriptive essays, you use modifying words and phrases to describe people, places, and objects. Because these modifiers are important in descriptive essays, you need to place them correctly to ensure that they point clearly to the words they describe.

Avoiding Misplaced Modifiers   A **misplaced modifier** appears to modify the wrong word because it is placed incorrectly in the sentence. Sentences that contain these errors are always illogical and frequently humorous.

> **Misplaced:**   E. B. White's son swam in the lake wearing an old bathing suit. (Was the lake wearing a bathing suit?)

> **Misplaced:**   In alliance with the Comanches, the southern Plains were ruled by the Kiowa. (Did the southern Plains have an alliance with the Comanches?)

In the sentences above, the phrases *wearing an old bathing suit* and *in alliance with the Comanches* appear to modify words that they cannot logically mod-

---
*EDS. NOTE—All the examples below refer to essays that appear later in this chapter.

ify. You can correct these errors and avoid confusion by moving each modifier so that it is as close as possible to the word it is supposed to modify.

Correct: Wearing an old bathing suit, E. B. White's son swam in the lake.

Correct: In alliance with the Comanches, the Kiowa ruled the southern Plains.

Avoiding Dangling Modifiers A dangling modifier "dangles" because it modifies a word (or group of words) that does not appear in the sentence. Often these modifiers come at the beginning of sentences (as present or past participle phrases) and unintentionally modify the words that come immediately after them.

Dangling: Startled by a sound, their eyes locked. (Were their eyes startled?)

Dangling: Standing on the corner, the cranes, jackhammers, and bulldozers work feverishly at ground zero. (Are the cranes, jackhammers, and bulldozers standing on the corner?)

In the preceding sentences, the phrases *startled by a sound* and *standing on the corner* modify *eyes* and *cranes, jackhammers, and bulldozers,* respectively. However, these sentences make no sense. How can eyes be startled? How can cranes, jackhammers, and bulldozers stand on a corner? The sentences do not contain the word that each phrase is supposed to modify. In each case, you can correct the problem by supplying the missing word and rewriting the sentence accordingly.

Correct: Startled by a sound, Annie Dillard locked eyes with the weasel.

Correct: Standing on the corner, people watch the cranes, jackhammers, and bulldozers work feverishly at ground zero.

☑ EDITING CHECKLIST: DESCRIPTION

- Have you avoided misplaced modifiers?
- Have you avoided dangling modifiers?
- Have you used figures of speech effectively?
- Have you avoided empty abstract words like *nice, great,* and *terrific*?

▶ **STUDENT WRITERS: DESCRIPTION**

Each of the following student essays illustrates the principles of effective description. The first one, an objective description of a trailer, was written by James Greggs for a sociology class. The assignment was to write a description of the service learning project in which he and some classmates participated. The second essay, a subjective description of an area in

Burma (renamed Myanmar after a military coup in 1989), was written by Mary Lim for her composition class. Her assignment was to write an essay about a place that had a profound effect on her.

Building and Learning

Introduction

Throughout the United States, houses not only reflect the lives of the people who live in them, but they also reflect the diversity of the American population. Some are large and ostentatious, others are modest but well maintained, while still others are badly in need of repair. Unfortunately, most college students know little about homes other than those in their own neighborhood. I too was fairly sheltered until I participated in a service learning project for my sociology class. For this project, I, along with some classmates, added a deck to a trailer in which three elderly people lived. We gained a great deal of satisfaction from this project, and we *Thesis statement* also got to see a way of life that we never knew existed.

1

Description of area around the trailer

The trailer on which we worked was located at the end of a small rural road about thirty minutes from campus. Patches of green and brown grass dotted the land around the trailer, and in the far right-hand corner of the property stood three tall poplar trees. Although the bushes in the front of the trailer were trimmed, the woods behind the trailer were overgrown, threatening to overrun the property. (We were told that members of a local church were supposed to come once a month to trim the hedges and cut back the woods.) Dominating the right front corner of the lawn was a circular concrete basin that looked like a large birdbath and housed a white well pipe with a rusted blue cap. About thirty feet to the left of the concrete basin stood a telephone pole and a bright red metal mailbox.

2

General description of the trailer

Like the property on which it stood, the trailer was well maintained. It was approximately thirty-five feet long and six and a half feet high; it rested on cinderblocks, which raised it about three feet off the ground. Under the trailer was an overturned white plastic chair. The trailer itself was nearly covered with sheets of white vinyl siding that ran horizontally, except for the bottom panels on the right side, which ran vertically. The vinyl panels closest to the roof were slightly discolored with dirt and green moss. 3

Specific description of the trailer

At the far left of the trailer was a small window—about two feet wide and one foot high. Next to the window was an aluminum door that was painted a dark brick red and outlined in green trim. It had one window at eye level that was divided by metal strips into four small sections. The number "24" in white plastic letters was glued to the door below this window. To the right of the door was a one-hundred-watt light bulb in a black ceramic socket. Next to the light was a large window that was actually two vertical rows of three windows—each the same size as the small window on the left. Farther to the right were two of the smaller windows arranged vertically. Each of the small windows tilted upward at almost a ninety-degree angle and was framed with silver metal strips. Outlining each of these windows was a pair of green metal shutters. 4

Description of steps and walkway

The deck we built replaced three white plastic steps that had led up to the trailer. A white metal handrail stood to the right side of these steps. It had been newly painted and was connected to the body of the trailer by a heart-shaped piece of metal. In front of the steps, two worn gray wooden boards, each about two feet wide and ten feet long, served as a walkway to the road. 5

Description of new deck

6

The finished deck provided a much better entranceway than the steps did and also gave the trailer a brighter appearance. It was not very large — ten feet by eight feet — but it extended from the doorway to the area underneath the windows immediately to the right of the door. We built the deck out of pressure-treated lumber so it wouldn't rot or need painting. We also built four steps that led from the deck to the lawn and a wooden railing that surrounded the deck and ran down the right side of the steps. After we finished, we bought two white plastic chairs at a local thrift store and placed them, along with the chair that was under the trailer, on the deck.

Conclusion

7

Both the residents of the trailer and our class benefited from the service learning project. The residents of the trailer were happy with the deck because it gave them a place to sit when the weather was good. They also were proud of their trailer's new look. Those of us who worked on the project expanded our view of the world and learned how other kinds of people live. Above all, we learned that we could make a difference in other people's lives.

Points for Special Attention

Objective Description   James Greggs, a student in a sociology course that had a service learning component, wrote this paper describing the project in which he participated. James knew that his instructor wanted an objective description because she told the class not to include any subjective comments in the body of the paper. She told them that they could, if they wished, discuss their feelings about the project in their introductions and conclusions.

Objective Language   Because his essay is an objective description, James keeps his description straightforward. His factual, concrete language concentrates on the size, shape, and construction of the trailer as well as on its surroundings. He uses specific measurements to convey the dimensions of the trailer and to show the relationship of each part of the trailer to the other parts, and he uses figures of speech to help his readers visualize what he is describing—the "circular concrete basin that looked like a large birdbath," for example (2).

Structure   James structures his description by moving from far to near. He begins by describing the land on which the trailer stands. He then directs his readers' attention to specific areas—for example, the woods behind the trailer and the telephone pole and red mailbox in front of it. James gives a general description of the trailer and then, as he moves from left to right, considers its specific features. Finally, he focuses on the deck, following a general description of the deck with specific details about its construction. In his introduction, James provides the context for this description and states his thesis; in his conclusion, he restates his thesis and then evaluates his service learning experience.

Selection of Detail   James's instructor defined his audience as people who would know what service learning is but who would not know about the specific project in which he participated. For this reason, James does not include a definition of service learning or explain how it fits into the sociology curriculum. He does, however, provide a detailed description of the trailer and the work that he and his classmates did.

Focus on Revision

The peer critics of James's paper identified three areas that they thought needed work. One student said that James should have included descriptions of the people who lived in the trailer. This student thought that without these descriptions, readers could not appreciate the impact the deck had on the residents. Another student suggested that James add more detail about the deck itself. She thought the deck should be the main focus of the paper, and for this reason, she thought James should spend more time describing it. As a result of these criticisms, James decided to write a short paragraph (and insert it between paragraphs 2 and 3) describing the residents of the trailer. He also decided to add more detail about the deck itself—for example, the wishbone pattern formed by the floorboards and the decorative elements on the railing. Finally, a third student thought the description of the trailer's windows in paragraph 4 went on too long, so in his final draft, James condensed paragraph 4. (A sample peer editing worksheet for description can be found on the *Patterns for College Writing* Web site at <bedfordstmartins.com/patterns>.)

Unlike "Building and Learning," Mary Lim's essay uses subjective description so that readers can share, as well as understand, her experience.

The Valley of Windmills

Introduction   In my native country of Burma, strange happenings and exotic scenery are not unusual, for Burma is a mysterious land that in some areas   1 seems to have been ignored by time. Mountains stand jutting their rocky peaks into the clouds as they have for thousands of years. Jungles are so dense with exotic vegetation that human beings or large animals cannot even enter. But one of the most fascinating areas in Burma is

Description (identifying the scene)

the Valley of Windmills, nestled between the tall mountains near the fertile and beautiful city of Taungaleik. In this valley there is beautiful and breathtaking scenery, but there are also old, massive, and gloomy structures that can disturb a person deeply.

Description (moving toward the valley)

The road to Taungaleik twists out of the coastal flatlands into those heaps of slag, shale, and limestone that are the Tennesserim Mountains in the southern part of Burma. The air grows rarer and cooler, and stones become grayer, the highway a little more precarious at its edges, until, ahead, standing in ghostly sentinel across the lip of a pass, is a line of

2

Description (immediate view)

squat forms. They straddle the road and stand at intervals up hillsides on either side. Are they boulders? Are they fortifications? Are they broken wooden crosses on graves in an abandoned cemetery?

These dark figures are windmills standing in the misty atmosphere. They are immensely old and distinctly evil, some merely turrets, some with remnants of arms hanging derelict from their snouts, and most of them covered with dark green moss. Their decayed but still mas-sive forms seem to turn and sneer at visitors.

3

Description (more distant view)

Down the pass on the other side is a circular green plateau that lies like an arena below, where there are still more windmills. Massed in the plain behind them, as far as the eye can see, in every field, above every hut, stand ten thousand iron windmills, silent and sailless. They seem to await only a call from a watchman to clank, whirr, flap, and groan into action.

Visitors suddenly feel cold. Perhaps it is a
sense of loneliness, the cool air, the desolation, or the weirdness of the arcane windmills —
but something chills them.

Conclusion

Description (windmills contrasted with city)

Thesis statement

As you stand at the lip of the valley,   4
contrasts rush as if to overwhelm you. Beyond,
glittering on the mountainside like a solitary
jewel, is Taungaleik in the territory once
occupied by the Portuguese. Below, on rolling
hillsides, are the dark windmills, still enveloped in morning mist. These ancient windmills
can remind you of the impermanence of life and
the mystery that still surrounds these hills.
In a strange way, the scene in the valley can
disturb you, but it also can give you an insight
into the contrasts that seem to define our
lives here in my country.

Points for Special Attention

Subjective Description   One of the first things her classmates noticed when they read Mary's essay was her use of vivid details. The road to Taungaleik is described in specific terms: it twists "out of the coastal flatlands" into the mountains, which are "heaps of slag, shale, and lime-stone." The iron windmills are decayed and stand "silent and sailless" on a green plateau that "lies like an arena." Through her use of detail, Mary creates her dominant impression of the Valley of Windmills as dark, mysteri-ous, and disquieting. The point of her essay — the thesis — is stated in the last paragraph: the Valley of Windmills embodies the contrasts that char-acterize life in Burma.

Subjective Language   By describing the windmills, Mary conveys the sense of foreboding she felt. When she first introduces them, she ques-tions whether these "squat forms" are "boulders," "fortifications," or "bro-ken wooden crosses," each of which has a menacing connotation. After telling readers what they are, she uses personification, describing the wind-mills as dark, evil, sneering figures with "arms hanging derelict." She sees them as ghostly sentinels awaiting "a call from a watchman" to spring into action. With this figure of speech, Mary skillfully re-creates the unearthly quality of the scene.

Structure   Mary's purpose in writing this paper was to give her read-ers the experience of actually being in the Valley of Windmills. She uses an organizing scheme that takes readers along the road to Taungaleik, up into the Tennesserim Mountains, and finally to the pass where the windmills wait. From her perspective on the lip of the valley, she describes the details closest to her and then those farther away, as if following the movement of her eyes. She ends by bringing her readers back to the lip of the valley, contrasting Taungaleik "glittering on the mountainside" with the windmills "enveloped in morning mist." With her description, Mary builds up to her thesis about the nature of life in her country. She withholds the explicit statement of her main point until her last paragraph, when readers are fully prepared for it.

Focus on Revision

One of Mary's peer critics thought that the essay's thesis about life in Burma needed additional support. The student pointed out that although Mary's description is quite powerful, it does not really convey the contrasts she alludes to in her conclusion. Mary decided that adding another paragraph in which she discusses something about her life (perhaps her reasons for visiting the windmills) could help supply this missing information. She could, for example, tell her reader that right after her return from the valley, she found out that a friend had been accidentally shot by border guards and that it was this event that caused her to characterize the windmills as she did. Such information would help to explain the somber mood of the passage and underscore the ideas presented in the conclusion. (A sample peer editing worksheet for description can be found on the *Patterns for College Writing* Web site at <bedfordstmartins.com/patterns>.)

The following selections illustrate various ways in which description can shape an essay. As you read them, pay particular attention to the differences between objective and subjective description. The first selection, a visual text, is followed by questions designed to illustrate how description can operate in visual form.

❖

Girls in Front of 9/11 Mural (Photo)

• • •

READING IMAGES

1. The wall painting in the photograph above commemorates the first anniversary of the destruction of the towers at the World Trade Center by terrorists. What details does the wall painting include? What determines how these details are arranged?

2. What dominant impression do you think the photographer is trying to create? In what way do the details in the photograph communicate this dominant impression?

3. Is the photographer who took the picture of the wall painting presenting a subjective or objective view of the subject? On what do you base your conclusion?

JOURNAL ENTRY

What is the difference between the impact of the original wall painting and the impact of the photo? Which do you find more moving? Why?

THEMATIC CONNECTIONS

LEAH HAGER COHEN

❖

Words Left Unspoken

Although she herself is not deaf, Leah Hager Cohen (b. 1967) lived for much of her childhood at the Lexington School for the Deaf in Queens, New York, where her mother was a teacher and her father was an administrator. (Both her paternal grandparents were deaf.) A graduate of the Columbia University School of Journalism, Cohen has been a writing instructor at Emerson College in Boston and an interpreter for deaf students in mainstream classes. Her books include *Glass, Paper, Beans: Revelations on the Nature and Value of Ordinary Things* (1997) and a novel, *Heat Lightning* (1998).

Background: There are some one million deaf people in the United States and more than twenty million who are hearing impaired. Hearing loss is often a result of the aging process, but children may also be born deaf or lose their hearing at an early age, usually because of inner ear or other infections. While improvements in hearing aids and cochlear implants have helped to mitigate some types of hearing loss, they are of only marginal help to those who are profoundly deaf. A growing segment of the deaf population has begun to urge that deafness be viewed not as an infirmity but rather as a cultural marker. Much debate has surrounded the question of whether deaf children should be educated to participate in the mainstream oral culture or whether they should be taught to communicate through sign language and thus become part of a deaf culture. One of Cohen's goals in *Train Go Sorry* (1994), from which the following essay is taken, was to convince readers that deafness is "not a pathology but a cultural identity."

My earliest memories of Sam Cohen are of his chin, which I remember as fiercely hard and pointy. Not pointy, my mother says, jutting; Grandpa had a strong, jutting chin. But against my very young face it felt like a chunk of honed granite swathed in stiff white bristles. Whenever we visited, he would lift us grandchildren up, most frequently by the elbows, and nuzzle our cheeks vigorously. This abrasive ritual greeting was our primary means of communication. In all my life, I never heard him speak a word I could understand.

Sometimes he used his voice to get our attention. It made a shapeless, gusty sound, like a pair of bellows sending up sparks and soot in a blacksmith shop. And he made sounds when he was eating, sounds that, originating from other quarters, would have drawn chiding or expulsion from the table. He smacked his lips and sucked his teeth; his chewing was moist and percussive; he released deep, hushed moans from the back of his throat, like a dreaming dog. And he burped out loud. Sometimes it was all Reba, Andy, and I could do not to catch one another's eyes and fall into giggles.

Our grandfather played games with us, the more physical the better. He loved that hand game: he would extend his, palms up, and we would hover ours, palms down, above his, and lower them, lower, lower, until they were just nesting, and *slap!* he'd have sandwiched one of our hands, trapping it between his. When we reversed, I could never even graze his, so fast would he snatch them away, like a big white fish.

He played three-card monte* with us, arranging the cards neatly between his long fingers, showing us once the jack of diamonds smirking, red and gold, underneath. And then, with motions as swift and implausible as a Saturday morning cartoon chase, his hands darted and faked and blurred and the cards lay still, face down and impassive. When we guessed the jack's position correctly, it was only luck. When we guessed wrong, he would laugh — a fond, gravelly sound — and pick up the cards and begin again.

He mimicked the way I ate. He compressed his mouth into dainty proportions as he nibbled air and carefully licked his lips and chewed tiny, precise bites, his teeth clicking, his eyelashes batting as he gazed shyly from under them. He could walk exactly like Charlie Chaplin and make nickels disappear, just vanish, from both his fists and up his sleeves; we never found them, no matter how we crawled over him, searching. All of this without any words.

He and my grandmother lived in the Bronx, in the same apartment my father and Uncle Max had grown up in. It was on Knox Place, near Mosholu Parkway, a three-room apartment below street level. The kitchen was a tight squeeze of a place, especially with my grandmother bending over the oven, blocking the passage as she checked baked apples or stuffed cabbage, my grandfather sitting with splayed knees at the dinette. It was easy to get each other's attention in there; a stamped foot sent vibrations clearly over the short distance, and an outstretched arm had a good chance of connecting with the other party.

The living room was ampler and dimmer, with abundant floor and table lamps to accommodate signed conversation. Little windows set up high revealed the legs of passersby. And down below, burrowed in black leather chairs in front of the television, we children learned to love physical comedy. Long before the days of closed captioning, we listened to our grandfather laugh out loud at the snowy black-and-white antics of Abbott and Costello, Laurel and Hardy, the Three Stooges.

During the time that I knew him, I saw his hairline shrink back and his eyes grow remote behind pairs of progressively thicker glasses. His athlete's bones shed some of their grace and nimbleness; they began curving in on themselves as he stood, arms folded across his sunken chest. Even his long, thin smile seemed to recede deeper between his nose and his prominent chin. But his hands remained lithe, vital. As he teased and argued and chatted and joked, they were the instruments of his mind, the conduits of his thoughts.

3

4

5

6

7

8

---

*Eds. note — A sleight-of-hand card game often played on urban streets, in which the dealer gets onlookers to place bets that they can pick the jack of diamonds.

As far as anyone knows, Samuel Kolominsky was born deaf (according to Lexington* records, his parents "failed to take note until child was about one and a half years old"). His birthplace was Russia, somewhere near Kiev. Lexington records say he was born in 1908; my grandmother says it was 1907. He was a child when his family fled the czarist pogroms. Lexington records have him immigrating in 1913, at age five; my grandmother says he came to this country when he was three. Officials at Ellis Island altered the family name, writing down Cohen, but they did not detect his deafness, so Sam sailed on across the last ribbon of water to America.   9

His name-sign at home: *Daddy*. His name-sign with friends: the thumb and index finger, perched just above the temple, rub against each other like grasshopper legs. One old friend attributes this to Sam's hair, which was blond and thick and wavy. Another says it derived from his habit of twisting a lock between his fingers.   10

Lexington records have him living variously at Clara, Moore, Siegel, Tehema, and Thirty-eighth streets in Brooklyn and on Avenue C in Manhattan. I knew him on Knox Place, and much later on Thieriot Avenue, in the Bronx. Wherever he lived, he loved to walk, the neighborhoods revolving silently like pictures in a Kinetoscope,** unfurling themselves in full color around him.   11

Shortly before he died, when I was thirteen, we found ourselves walking home from a coffee shop together on a warm night. My family had spent the day visiting my grandparents at their apartment. My grandmother and the rest of the family were walking half a block ahead; I hung back and made myself take my grandfather's hand. We didn't look at each other. His hand was warm and dry. His gait was uneven then, a long slow beat on the right, catch-up on the left. I measured my steps to his. It was dark except for the hazy pink cones of light cast by streetlamps. I found his rhythm, and breathed in it. That was the longest conversation we ever had.   12

He died before I was really able to converse in sign. I have never seen his handwriting. I once saw his teeth, in a glass, on the bathroom windowsill. Now everything seems like a clue.   13

•   •   •

COMPREHENSION

1. Why was Cohen's grandfather unable to speak? How did Cohen communicate with him?

2. What kind of relationship did Cohen have with her grandfather? Warm? Distant?

3. What is the significance of the essay's title? What does Cohen mean when she says, "That was the longest conversation we ever had" (12)?

---

*EDS. NOTE — The Lexington School for the Deaf, where Cohen's grandfather was once a student.

**EDS. NOTE — A device for viewing a sequence of moving pictures as it rotates over a light source, creating the illusion of motion.

4. In paragraph 13, Cohen says that now, after her grandfather's death, "everything seems like a clue." What does she mean?

5. What do you think the "words left unspoken" are? Is the speaker of these words Cohen, her grandfather, or both? Explain.

PURPOSE AND AUDIENCE

1. Does "Words Left Unspoken" have an explicitly stated thesis? Why or why not?

2. What dominant impression is Cohen trying to create in this essay? How successful is she?

3. How much do you think Cohen expects her readers to know about deaf culture? How can you tell?

STYLE AND STRUCTURE

1. Why do you think Cohen begins her essay with a description of her grandfather's chin?

2. What is the organizing principle of this essay? Would another organizing principle be more effective? Explain.

3. Are you able to picture Cohen's grandfather after reading her description? Do you think she expects you to?

4. Does Cohen develop her description fully enough? At what points could she have provided more detail?

5. What figures of speech does Cohen use in this essay? Where might additional figures of speech be helpful?

VOCABULARY PROJECTS

1. Define each of the following words as they are used in this selection.

honed (1)   abundant (7)
expulsion (2)   prominent (8)
percussive (2)   lithe (8)
smirking (4)   conduits (8)
splayed (6)   gait (12)

2. Supply a synonym for each of the words listed above. In what way is each synonym different from the original word?

JOURNAL ENTRY

In what ways does Cohen's grandfather fit the traditional stereotype of a grandfather? In what ways does he not fit this stereotype?

WRITING WORKSHOP

1. Write a description of a person. Concentrate on one specific feature or quality that you associate with this person (as Cohen does in her essay).

2. Choose three or four members of your family, and write a one-paragraph description of each. Combine these descriptions into a "family album" essay that has an introduction, a thesis statement, and a conclusion.

3. Write an essay in which you describe your earliest memories of a family member or close family friend. Before you write, decide on the dominant impression you want to convey.

COMBINING THE PATTERNS

Cohen uses **narration** to develop paragraph 9. Why does she include this narrative paragraph? Does it add to or detract from the dominant impression she is trying to convey? Explain.

THEMATIC CONNECTIONS

- "Only Daughter" (page 84)
- "The Way to Rainy Mountain" (page 169)
- "Mother Tongue" (page 462)

SUZANNE BERNE

❖

Ground Zero

Suzanne Berne grew up in Warrenton, Virginia, and Washington, D.C., and holds degrees from Wesleyan University and the Iowa Writers' Workshop at the University of Iowa. She has worked as a journalist and has also published book reviews and personal essays as well as two well-received novels, *A Crime in the Neighborhood* (1997) and *A Perfect Arrangement* (2001). She has taught writing at Harvard University and currently lives near Boston. In the following essay, which appeared on the *New York Times* op-ed page in April 2002, Berne describes a personal pilgrimage to the site of the former World Trade Center in New York City.

Background: The September 11, 2001, terrorist attacks that destroyed the twin towers of New York's World Trade Center and severely damaged the Pentagon stunned the nation and the world. People watched in horror as camera crews recorded the collapse of the towers while victims jumped to their deaths. The three hijacked aircraft that crashed into these targets, and a fourth that crashed into a field in rural Pennsylvania, caused the deaths of some three thousand people. An outpouring of grief, outrage, fear, and patriotism consumed the nation in the ensuing months as the possibility of war loomed large. While many, like Berne, have felt drawn to visit "ground zero" (as it has come to be called), some family members of the victims—particularly of those whose unidentified remains are still at the site—have expressed concern that it not become a tourist attraction. As of early 2003, plans for rebuilding at the site and creating a memorial to those who died in the attacks have still not been finalized.

On a cold, damp March morning, I visited Manhattan's financial district, a place I'd never been, to pay my respects at what used to be the World Trade Center. Many other people had chosen to do the same that day, despite the raw wind and spits of rain, and so the first thing I noticed when I arrived on the corner of Vesey and Church Streets was a crowd. 1

Standing on the sidewalk, pressed against aluminum police barricades, wearing scarves that flapped into their faces and woolen hats pulled over their ears, were people apparently from everywhere. Germans, Italians, Japanese. An elegant-looking Norwegian family in matching shearling coats. People from Ohio and California and Maine. Children, middle-aged couples, older people. Many of them were clutching cameras and video recorders, and they were all craning to see across the street, where there was nothing to see. 2

At least, nothing is what it first looked like, the space that is now ground zero. But once your eyes adjust to what you are looking at, "nothing" becomes something much more potent, which is absence. 3

But to the out-of-towner, ground zero looks at first simply like a con-   4
struction site. All the familiar details are there: the wooden scaffolding; the
cranes, the bulldozers and forklifts; the trailers and construction workers
in hard hats; even the dust. There is the pound of jackhammers, the steady
beep-beep-beep of trucks backing up, the roar of heavy machinery.

So much busyness is reassuring, and it is possible to stand looking at   5
the cranes and trucks and feel that mild curiosity and hopefulness so often
inspired by construction sites.

Then gradually your eyes do adjust, exactly as if you have stepped from   6
a dark theater into a bright afternoon, because what becomes most striking about this scene is the light itself.

Ground zero is a great bowl of light, an emptiness that seems weirdly   7
spacious and grand, like a vast plaza amid the dense tangle of streets in
lower Manhattan. Light reflecting off the Hudson River vaults into the site,
soaking everything—especially on an overcast morning—with a watery
glow. This is the moment when absence begins to assume a material form,
when what is not there becomes visible.

Suddenly you notice the periphery, the skyscraper shrouded in black   8
plastic, the boarded windows, the steel skeleton of the shattered Winter
Garden. Suddenly there are the broken steps and cracked masonry in front
of Brooks Brothers. Suddenly there are the firefighters, the waiting ambulance on the other side of the pit, the police on every corner. Suddenly
there is the enormous cross made of two rusted girders.

And suddenly, very suddenly, there is the little cemetery attached to   9
St. Paul's Chapel, with tulips coming up, the chapel and grounds miraculously undamaged except for a few plastic-sheathed gravestones. The iron
fence is almost invisible beneath a welter of dried pine wreaths, banners,
ribbons, laminated poems and prayers and photographs, swags of paper
cranes, withered flowers, baseball hats, rosary beads, teddy bears. And flags,
flags everywhere, little American flags fluttering in the breeze, flags on
posters drawn by Brownie troops, flags on T-shirts, flags on hats, flags
streaming by, tied to the handles of baby strollers.

It takes quite a while to see all of this; it takes even longer to come up   10
with something to say about it.

An elderly man standing next to me had been staring fixedly across   11
the street for some time. Finally he touched his son's elbow and said:
"I watched those towers being built. I saw this place when they weren't
there." Then he stopped, clearly struggling with, what for him, was a
double negative, recalling an absence before there was an absence. His son,
waiting patiently, took a few photographs. "Let's get out of here," the man
said at last.

Again and again I heard people say, "It's unbelievable." And then they   12
would turn to each other, dissatisfied. They wanted to say something more
expressive, more meaningful. But it *is* unbelievable, to stare at so much devastation, and know it for devastation, and yet recognize that it does not
look like the devastation one has imagined.

Like me, perhaps, the people around me had in mind images from tele- 13
vision and newspaper pictures: the collapsing buildings, the running office
workers, the black plume of smoke against a bright blue sky. Like me, they
were probably trying to superimpose those terrible images onto the industrious emptiness right in front of them. The difficulty of this kind of mental revision is measured, I believe, by the brisk trade in World Trade Center
photograph booklets at tables set up on street corners.

Determined to understand better what I was looking at, I decided to 14
get a ticket for the viewing platform beside St. Paul's. This proved no easy
task, as no one seemed to be able to direct me to South Street Seaport,
where the tickets are distributed. Various police officers whom I asked for
directions, waved me vaguely toward the East River, differing degrees of
boredom and resignation on their faces. Or perhaps it was a kind of incredulousness. Somewhere around the American Stock Exchange, I asked a
security guard for help and he frowned at me, saying, "You want tickets to
the disaster?"

Finally I found myself in line at a cheerfully painted kiosk, watching a 15
young juggler try to entertain the crowd. He kept dropping the four red
balls he was attempting to juggle, and having to chase after them. It was
noon; the next available viewing was at 4 P.M.

Back I walked, up Fulton Street, the smell of fish in the air, to wander 16
again around St. Paul's. A deli on Vesey Street advertised a view of the
World Trade Center from its second-floor dining area. I went in and
ordered a pastrami sandwich, uncomfortably aware that many people
before me had come to that same deli for pastrami sandwiches who would
never come there again. But I was here to see what I could, so I carried my
sandwich upstairs and sat down beside one of the big plate-glass windows.

And there, at last, I got my ticket to the disaster. 17

I could see not just into the pit now, but also its access ramp, which 18
trucks had been traveling up and down since I had arrived that morning.
Gathered along the ramp were firefighters in their black helmets and black
coats. Slowly they lined up, and it became clear that this was an honor
guard, and that someone's remains were being carried up the ramp toward
the open door of an ambulance.

Everyone in the dining room stopped eating. Several people stood up, 19
whether out of respect or to see better, I don't know. For a moment, everything paused.

Then the day flowed back into itself. Soon I was outside once more, 20
joining the tide of people washing around the site. Later, as I huddled with
a little crowd on the viewing platform, watching people scrawl their names
or write "God Bless America" on the plywood walls, it occurred to me that
a form of repopulation was taking effect, with so many visitors to this
place, thousands of visitors, all of us coming to see the wide emptiness
where so many were lost. And by the act of our visiting—whether we are

motivated by curiosity or horror or reverence or grief, or by something confusing that combines them all — that space fills up again.

•   •   •

COMPREHENSION

1. What does Berne mean when she says that as her eyes adjust to what she is seeing, "'nothing' becomes something much more potent, which is absence" (3)?

2. Why does it take "quite a while" (10) to see all the details at ground zero? Why does it take "even longer" (10) to think of something to say about it?

3. According to Berne, how were the television pictures of ground zero different from the actual experience of seeing it?

4. In what way does the area around ground zero contrast with the site itself? How does Berne react to this contrast?

5. What does Berne mean in her conclusion when she says that with so many visitors coming to see ground zero, a form of "repopulation" is taking place? Do you think she is being ironic?

PURPOSE AND AUDIENCE

1. Does Berne state or imply her thesis? Why do you think she makes the decision she does? State Berne's thesis in your own words.

2. What is Berne's purpose in writing this essay?

3. What assumptions does Berne make about her readers' ideas about ground zero? How can you tell?

STYLE AND STRUCTURE

1. Why does Berne begin her essay by saying that she had never before visited Manhattan's financial district?

2. What organizational scheme does Berne use? What are the advantages and disadvantages of this scheme?

3. In paragraph 3, Berne says that ground zero at first looks like "nothing"; in paragraph 4, she says that it looks like a construction site. Then, in paragraph 7, she describes ground zero as "a great bowl of light." And finally, in her conclusion, she refers to it as a pit. Why do you think Berne describes ground zero in so many different ways?

4. Berne leaves a space between paragraphs 17 and 18. In what way does the space (as well as paragraph 17) reinforce a shift in the focus of her essay?

5. Why does Berne end her essay with a description of the crowd standing on the viewing platform? Why do you suppose she feels the need to include these observations?

6. In paragraphs 8 and 9, Berne repeats the word *suddenly*. What is the effect of this repetition? Could she have achieved this effect some other way?

VOCABULARY PROJECTS

1. Define each of the following words as it is used in this selection.

   shearling (2)
   potent (3)
   periphery (8)
   laminated (9)
   devastation (12)
   incredulousness (14)
   repopulation (20)

2. A **paradox** is a seemingly contradictory statement that may nonetheless be true. Find examples of paradoxes in "Ground Zero." Why do you think Berne uses these paradoxes in this essay?

3. List ten striking visual details that Berne uses to describe people and objects. Can you think of other details that she could have used?

4. What does the term *ground zero* mean? What connotations does this term have?

JOURNAL ENTRY

What did you feel when you first saw newspaper or magazine images of ground zero? In what ways were your reactions similar to or different from Berne's?

WRITING WORKSHOP

1. Write an essay in which you describe what you saw on the morning of September 11, 2001, when terrorists destroyed the World Trade Center. Make sure that you include a thesis and that you use your description to convey your reactions to the event.

2. Like Berne, write a description of a place from several different vantage points. Make sure each of your perspectives provides different information about the place you are describing.

3. Write a subjective description of a scene that you remember from your childhood. In your thesis statement and in your conclusion, explain how your adult impressions of the scene differ from those of your childhood.

COMBINING THE PATTERNS

In addition to containing a great deal of description, this essay also uses **comparison and contrasts.** In paragraphs 1 through 10, what two ways of seeing ground zero are being compared? What points about each view of ground zero does Berne compare?

THEMATIC CONNECTIONS

ANNIE DILLARD

❖
Living Like Weasels

Annie Dillard was born in 1945 and grew up in Pittsburgh, Pennsylvania, developing an intense interest in the natural world at an early age. After receiving degrees from Hollins College in Virginia, she began working on a series of meditative essays examining the ecology of rural Virginia that provided the basis for her first book, *A Pilgrim at Tinker Creek* (1974), which won the Pulitzer Prize for nonfiction. Since then, she has published subsequent essay collections — most recently *For the Time Being* (1999) — as well as two volumes of memoirs, *An American Childhood* (1987) and *A Writing Life* (1989); the novel *The Living* (1992); and several poetry collections, including *Mornings Like This: Found Poems* (1995). She is currently Writer in Residence at Wesleyan College.

Background: Dillard's work continues a long tradition of nature writing in the United States, extending back at least to Henry David Thoreau's 1854 classic *Walden,* which was in turn influenced by Ralph Waldo Emerson's 1836 essay *Nature.* Both Emerson and Thoreau saw in nature a kind of mystical unity and spiritual dynamism that civilized humanity needed to learn to appreciate. In the following generation, naturalist John Muir spurred a newborn preservation movement that led to the establishment of the National Park Service and the founding of ecological groups such as the Sierra Club, of which he was the first president from 1892 until his death in 1914. In Muir's footsteps came Aldo Leopold, whose 1949 *A Sand County Almanac* promoted a "land ethic" that established the basis for environmental awareness; Marjorie Stoneman Douglas, whose 1947 *The Everglades: River of Grass* helped spark interest in saving this natural wonder; and Rachel Carson, whose books from *Under the Sea* (1941) to *Silent Spring* (1962) found a wide readership and largely created the current ecology movement. Among Dillard's contemporaries carrying on this tradition are Wendell Barry, Gretel Ehrlich, Barry Lopez, Gary Snyder, and many others.

A weasel is wild. Who knows what he thinks? He sleeps in his underground den, his tail draped over his nose. Sometimes he lives in his den for two days without leaving. Outside, he stalks rabbits, mice, muskrats, and birds, killing more bodies than he can eat warm, and often dragging the carcasses home. Obedient to instinct, he bites his prey at the neck, either splitting the jugular vein at the throat or crunching the brain at the base of the skull, and he does not let go. One naturalist refused to kill a weasel who was socketed into his hand deeply as a rattlesnake. The man could in no way pry the tiny weasel off, and he had to walk half a mile to water, the weasel dangling from his palm, and soak him off like a stubborn label.

And once, says Ernest Thompson Seton — once, a man shot an eagle out of the sky. He examined the eagle and found the dry skull of a weasel

1

2

fixed by the jaws to his throat. The supposition is that the eagle had pounced on the weasel and the weasel swiveled and bit as instinct taught him, tooth to neck, and nearly won. I would like to have seen that eagle from the air a few weeks or months before he was shot: was the whole weasel still attached to his feathered throat, a fur pendant? Or did the eagle eat what he could reach, gutting the living weasel with his talons before his breast, bending his beak, cleaning the beautiful airborne bones?

I have been thinking about weasels because I saw one last week. I startled a weasel who startled me, and we exchanged a long glance. 3

Near my house in Virginia is a pond — Hollins Pond. It covers two acres of bottomland near Tinker Creek with six inches of water and six thousand lily pads. There is a fifty-five mph highway at one end of the pond, and a nesting pair of wood ducks at the other. Under every bush is a muskrat hole or a beer can. The far end is an alternating series of fields and woods, fields and woods, threaded everywhere with motorcycle tracks — in whose bare clay wild turtles lay eggs. 4

One evening last week at sunset, I walked to the pond and sat on a downed log near the shore. I was watching the lily pads at my feet tremble and part over the thrusting path of a carp. A yellow warbler appeared to my right and flew behind me. It caught my eye; I swiveled around — and the next instant, inexplicably, I was looking down at a weasel, who was looking up at me. 5

Weasel! I had never seen one wild before. He was ten inches long, thin as a curve, a muscled ribbon, brown as fruitwood, soft-furred, alert. His face was fierce, small and pointed as a lizard's; he would have made a good arrowhead. There was just a dot of chin, maybe two brown hairs' worth, and then the pure white fur began that spread down his underside. He had two black eyes I did not see, any more than you see a window. 6

The weasel was stunned into stillness as he was emerging from beneath an enormous shaggy wild-rose bush four feet away. I was stunned into stillness, twisted backward on the tree trunk. Our eyes locked, and someone threw away the key. 7

Our look was as if two lovers, or deadly enemies, met unexpectedly on an overgrown path when each had been thinking of something else: a clearing blow to the gut. It was also a bright blow to the brain, or a sudden beating of brains, with all the charge and intimate grate of rubbed balloons. It emptied our lungs. It felled the forest, moved the fields, and drained the pond; the world dismantled and tumbled into that black hole of eyes. If you and I looked at each other that way, our skulls would split and drop to our shoulders. But we don't. We keep our skulls. 8

He disappeared. This was only last week, and already I don't remember what shattered the enchantment. I think I blinked, I think I retrieved my brain from the weasel's brain, and tried to memorize what I was seeing, and the weasel felt the yank of separation, the careening splashdown into 9 real life and the urgent current of instinct. He vanished under the wild rose. I waited motionless, my mind suddenly full of data and my spirit with pleadings, but he didn't return.

Please do not tell me about "approach-avoidance conflicts." I tell you   10
I've been in that weasel's brain for sixty seconds, and he was in mine. Brains are private places, muttering through unique and secret tapes — but the weasel and I both plugged into another tape simultaneously, for a sweet and shocking time. Can I help it if it was a blank?

What goes on in his brain the rest of the time? What does a weasel   11
think about? He won't say. His journal is tracks in clay, a spray of feathers, mouse blood and bone: uncollected, unconnected, loose-leaf, and blown.

I would like to learn, or remember, how to live. I come to Hollins Pond   12
not so much to learn how to live as, frankly, to forget about it. That is, I don't think I can learn from a wild animal how to live in particular — shall I suck warm blood, hold my tail high, walk with my footprints precisely over the prints of my hands? — but I might learn something of mindlessness, something of the purity of living in the physical senses and the dignity of living without bias or motive. The weasel lives in necessity and we live in choice, hating necessity and dying at the last ignobly in its talons. I would like to live as I should, as the weasel lives as he should. And I suspect that for me the way is like the weasel's: open to time and death painlessly, notic-ing everything, remembering nothing, choosing the given with a fierce and pointed will.

I missed my chance. I should have gone for the throat. I should have   13
lunged for that streak of white under the weasel's chin and held on, held on through mud and into the wild rose, held on for a dearer life. We could live under the wild rose wild as weasels, mute and uncomprehending. I could very calmly go wild. I could live two days in the den, curled, leaning on mouse fur, sniffing bird bones, blinking, licking, breathing musk, my hair tangled in the roots of grasses. Down is a good place to go, where the mind is single. Down is out, out of your ever-loving mind and back to your careless senses. I remember muteness as a prolonged and giddy fast, where every moment is a feast of utterance received. Time and events are merely poured, unremarked, and ingested directly, like blood pulsed into my gut through a jugular vein. Could two live that way? Could two live under the wild rose, and explore by the pond, so that the smooth mind of each is as everywhere present to the other, and as received and as unchallenged, as falling snow?

We could, you know. We can live any way we want. People take vows of   14
poverty, chastity, and obedience — even of silence — by choice. The thing is to stalk your calling in a certain skilled and supple way, to locate the most tender and live spot and plug into that pulse. This is yielding, not fighting. A weasel doesn't "attack" anything; a weasel lives as he's meant to, yielding at every moment to the perfect freedom of single necessity.

*　*　*

I think it would be well, and proper, and obedient, and pure, to grasp your one necessity and not let it go, to dangle from it limp wherever it takes you. Then even death, where you're going no matter how you live, cannot you part. Seize it and let it seize you up aloft even, till your eyes burn out and drop; let your musky flesh fall off in shreds, and let your very bones unhinge and scatter, loosened over fields, over fields and woods, lightly, thoughtless, from any height at all, from as high as eagles.

15

• • •

COMPREHENSION

1. Why has Dillard been thinking of weasels?
2. What qualities does Dillard admire in weasels?
3. In what ways would Dillard like to be like a weasel? What does she mean in paragraph 12 when she says, "I would like to learn, or remember, how to live"?
4. Why, in paragraph 13, does Dillard say, "I missed my chance"?

PURPOSE AND AUDIENCE

1. Does Dillard state or imply her thesis? Why do you think she makes the choice she does? Explain.
2. Do you think Dillard is writing to an audience of animal lovers? Nature enthusiasts? A general audience? Explain.
3. Dillard's essay reads much like a journal. Usually, journal entries have no purpose other than to record a writer's ideas and observations. Does Dillard do more than simply record her ideas and observations? Do you think she has a definite purpose in mind? If so, what is this purpose?

STYLE AND STRUCTURE

1. What dominant impression does Dillard try to create? Is she successful? Explain.
2. In what order does Dillard arrange the details in her description? What does she achieve with this arrangement? Would another arrangement have been more effective?
3. Why does Dillard begin her essay with an objective description of the weasel? At what point does she begin her subjective description?
4. In paragraph 2, Dillard tells the story of an eagle with "the dry skull of a weasel fixed by the jaws to his throat." Why does she repeat this image in paragraph 13 and again in her conclusion? What ideas does this image convey for Dillard?
5. In paragraph 13, Dillard imagines what it would be like to live like a weasel. Does she actually think it would be possible for her to live like a weasel? Explain.

VOCABULARY PROJECTS

1. Define each of the following words as it is used in this selection.

   swiveled (2)
   inexplicably (5)
   grate (8)
   simultaneously (10)
   ignobly (12)
   talons (12)
   musk (13)
   ingested (13)
   supple (14)

2. Make a list of the adjectives that Dillard uses to describe the weasel. What conclusion can you draw from these adjectives about her attitude toward this animal?

3. Find examples of similes, metaphors, and personification. In what way do these figures of speech help Dillard make her point?

JOURNAL ENTRY

Write about an animal that you would like to live like. What appeals to you about this animal? What qualities does it have that you admire?

WRITING WORKSHOP

1. Describe an animal that you have either encountered in the wild or had as a pet. Write an essay in which you describe the animal and discuss the qualities that you admire in this animal.

2. Find a picture of an animal in a magazine or on the Internet. Then, write both a subjective and an objective description of the same animal.

3. Write an essay in which you describe Annie Dillard from the point of view of the weasel that she encounters. In your description, make sure that you make apparent what the weasel thinks of Dillard. (You can view a picture of Dillard on the Internet at <wardy.org/dillard.html>.) Your essay can be either serious or humorous.

COMBINING THE PATTERNS

What purpose does **comparison and contrast** serve in paragraph 12? In what way does this comparison prepare readers for the discussion to follow?

THEMATIC CONNECTIONS

- "Scrubbing in Maine" (page 106)
- "Shades of Green" (page 480)
- "Burdens" (page 509)

N. SCOTT MOMADAY

❖

The Way to Rainy Mountain

N. Scott Momaday was born in 1934 in Lawton, Oklahoma, of Kiowa ancestry. He holds degrees from the University of New Mexico and Stanford University and has taught English at a number of colleges; he is currently on the faculty at the University of Arizona. In 1969, Momaday won a Pulitzer Prize for his first novel, *House Made of Dawn* (1968). He followed this book with *The Way to Rainy Mountain* (1968), in which he retells Kiowa legends and folktales. Momaday has also published collections of poetry and stories, as well as a memoir, *The Names* (1976).

Background: The following essay, excerpted from the introduction to *The Way to Rainy Mountain*, focuses both on the landscape of Momaday's childhood and on his Kiowa grandmother. The Kiowa tribe, originally from western Canada, migrated in the early 1700s to what is now western Montana. From there, they traveled to the Black Hills of South Dakota and later to the central plains of Oklahoma. Through their contact with the Crow Indians, they came to worship the sun, and an annual Sun Dance brought various autonomous groups of Kiowa together for a week of ritual. By the 1800s, the Kiowa were considered fierce warriors both by neighboring tribes and by settlers arriving from the East. They were famous buffalo hunters, using the animal for food as well as for the raw materials used in their daily lives. They were also skilled artists known for their intricate beadwork and paintings on buffalo hides depicting their culture, religion, and history. After tribal leaders signed treaties with the United States government in the late 1800s, many Kiowa were quick to assimilate, often doing so in a single generation. Like Momaday, those growing up in the twentieth century and later have often sought to embrace the heritage and traditions of their ancestors.

A single knoll rises out of the plain in Oklahoma, north and west of   1
the Wichita Range. For my people, the Kiowas, it is an old landmark, and
they gave it the name Rainy Mountain. The hardest weather in the world is
there. Winter brings blizzards, hot tornadic winds arise in the spring, and
in summer the prairie is an anvil's edge. The grass turns brittle and brown,
and it cracks beneath your feet. There are green belts along the rivers
and creeks, linear groves of hickory and pecan, willow and witch hazel. At a
distance in July or August the steaming foliage seems almost to writhe in
fire. Great green-and-yellow grasshoppers are everywhere in the tall grass,
popping up like corn to sting the flesh, and tortoises crawl about on the
red earth, going nowhere in the plenty of time. Loneliness is an aspect of
the land. All things in the plain are isolate; there is no confusion of objects
in the eye, but *one* hill or *one* tree or *one* man. To look upon that landscape
in the early morning, with the sun at your back, is to lose the sense of

proportion. Your imagination comes to life, and this, you think, is where Creation was begun.

I returned to Rainy Mountain in July. My grandmother had died in the spring, and I wanted to be at her grave. She had lived to be very old and at last infirm. Her only living daughter was with her when she died, and I was told that in death her face was that of a child. 2

I like to think of her as a child. When she was born, the Kiowas were living that last great moment of their history. For more than a hundred years they had controlled the open range from the Smoky Hill River to the Red, from the headwaters of the Canadian to the fork of the Arkansas and Cimarron. In alliance with the Comanches, they had ruled the whole of the southern Plains. War was their sacred business, and they were among the finest horsemen the world has ever known. But warfare for the Kiowas was preeminently a matter of disposition rather than of survival, and they never understood the grim, unrelenting advance of the U.S. Cavalry. When at last, divided and ill-provisioned, they were driven onto the Staked Plains in the cold rains of autumn, they fell into panic. In Palo Duro Canyon they abandoned their crucial stores to pillage and had nothing then but their lives. In order to save themselves, they surrendered to the soldiers at Fort Sill and were imprisoned in the old stone corral that now stands as a military museum. My grandmother was spared the humiliation of those high gray walls by eight or ten years, but she must have known from birth the affliction of defeat, the dark brooding of old warriors. 3

Her name was Aho, and she belonged to the last culture to evolve in North America. Her forebears came down from the high country in western Montana nearly three centuries ago. They were a mountain people, a mysterious tribe of hunters whose language has never been positively classified in any major group. In the late seventeenth century they began a long migration to the south and east. It was a long journey toward the dawn, and it led to a golden age. Along the way the Kiowas were befriended by the Crows, who gave them the culture and religion of the Plains. They acquired horses, and their ancient nomadic spirit was suddenly free of the ground. They acquired Tai-me, the sacred Sun Dance doll, from that moment the object and symbol of their worship, and so shared in the divinity of the sun. Not least, they acquired the sense of destiny, therefore courage and pride. When they entered upon the southern Plains, they had been transformed. No longer were they slaves to the simple necessity of survival; they were a lordly and dangerous society of fighters and thieves, hunters and priests of the sun. According to their origin myth, they entered the world through a hollow log. From one point of view, their migration was the fruit of an old prophecy, for indeed they emerged from a sunless world. 4

Although my grandmother lived out her long life in the shadow of Rainy Mountain, the immense landscape of the continental interior lay like memory in her blood. She could tell of the Crows, whom she had never seen, and of the Black Hills, where she had never been. I wanted to see in 5 reality what she had seen more perfectly in the mind's eye, and traveled fifteen hundred miles to begin my pilgrimage.

Yellowstone, it seemed to me, was the top of the world, a region of 6 deep lakes and dark timber, canyons and waterfalls. But, beautiful as it is, one might have the sense of confinement there. The skyline in all directions is close at hand, the high wall of the woods and deep cleavages of shade. There is a perfect freedom in the mountains, but it belongs to the eagle and the elk, the badger and the bear. The Kiowas reckoned their stature by the distance they could see, and they were bent and blind in the wilderness.

Descending eastward, the highland meadows are a stairway to the 7 plain. In July the inland slope of the Rockies is luxuriant with flax and buckwheat, stonecrop and larkspur. The earth unfolds and the limit of the land recedes. Clusters of trees and animals grazing far in the distance cause the vision to reach away and wonder to build upon the mind. The sun follows a longer course in the day, and the sky is immense beyond all comparison. The great billowing clouds that sail upon it are shadows that move upon the grain like water, dividing light. Farther down, in the land of the Crows and Blackfeet, the plain is yellow. Sweet clover takes hold of the hills and bends upon itself to cover and seal the soil. There the Kiowas paused on their way; they had come to the place where they must change their lives. The sun is at home in the plains. Precisely there does it have the certain character of a god. When the Kiowas came to the land of the Crows, they could see the dark lees of the hills at dawn across the Bighorn River, the profusion of light on the grain shelves, the oldest deity ranging after the solstices. Not yet would they veer southward to the caldron of the land that lay below; they must wean their blood from the northern winter and hold the mountains a while longer in their view. They bore Tai-me in procession to the east.

A dark mist lay over the Black Hills, and the land was like iron. At the 8 top of a ridge I caught sight of Devil's Tower upthrust against the gray sky as if in the birth of time the core of the earth had broken through its crust and the motion of the world was begun. There are things in nature that engender an awful quiet in the heart of man; Devil's Tower is one of them. Two centuries ago, because they could not do otherwise, the Kiowas made a legend at the base of the rock. My grandmother said:

> "Eight children were there at play, seven sisters and their brother. Suddenly the boy was struck dumb; he trembled and began to run upon his hands and feet. His fingers became claws, and his body was covered with fur. Directly there was a bear where the boy had been. The sisters were terrified; they ran, and the bear after them. They came to the stump of a great tree, and the tree spoke to them. It bade them climb upon it, and as they did so, it began to rise into the air. The bear came to kill them, but they were just beyond its reach. It reared against the tree and scored the bark all around with its claws. The seven sisters were borne into the sky, and they became the stars of the Big Dipper."

From that moment, and so long as the legend lives, the Kiowas have kinsmen in the night sky. Whatever they were in the mountains, they could be no more. However tenuous their well-being, however much they had suffered and would suffer again, they had found a way out of the wilderness.

My grandmother had a reverence for the sun, a holy regard that now is all but gone out of mankind. There was a wariness in her, and an ancient awe. She was a Christian in her later years, but she had come a long way about, and she never forgot her birthright. As a child she had been to the Sun Dances; she had taken part in those annual rites, and by them she had learned the restoration of her people in the presence of Tai-me. She was about seven when the last Kiowa Sun Dance was held in 1887 on the Washita River above Rainy Mountain Creek. The buffalo were gone. In order to consummate the ancient sacrifice—to impale the head of a buffalo bull upon the medicine tree—a delegation of old men journeyed into Texas, there to beg and barter for an animal from the Goodnight herd. She was ten when the Kiowas came together for the last time as a living Sun Dance culture. They could find no buffalo; they had to hang an old hide from the sacred tree. Before the dance could begin, a company of soldiers rode out from Fort Sill under orders to disperse the tribe. Forbidden without cause the essential act of their faith, having seen the wild herds slaughtered and left to rot upon the ground, the Kiowas backed away forever from the medicine tree. That was July 20, 1890, at the great bend of the Washita. My grandmother was there. Without bitterness, and for as long as she lived, she bore a vision of deicide.

Now that I can have her only in memory, I see my grandmother in the several postures that were peculiar to her: standing at the wood stove on a winter morning and turning meat in a great iron skillet; sitting at the south window, bent above her beadwork, and afterwards, when her vision had failed, looking down for a long time into the fold of her hands; going out upon a cane, very slowly as she did when the weight of age came upon her; praying. I remember her most often at prayer. She made long, rambling prayers out of suffering and hope, having seen many things. I was never sure that I had the right to hear, so exclusive were they of all mere custom and company. The last time I saw her she prayed standing by the side of her bed at night, naked to the waist, the light of a kerosene lamp moving upon her dark skin. Her long, black hair, always drawn and braided in the day, lay upon her shoulders and against her breasts like a shawl. I do not speak Kiowa, and I never understood her prayers, but there was something inherently sad in the sound, some merest hesitation upon the syllables of sorrow. She began in a high and descending pitch, exhausting her breath to silence; then again and again—and always the same intensity of effort, of something that is, and is not, like urgency in the human voice. Transported so in the dancing light among the shadows of her room, she seemed beyond the reach of time. But that was illusion; I think I knew that I should not see her again.

•   •   •

COMPREHENSION

1. What is the significance of the essay's title?
2. What does Momaday mean when he says that his grandmother was born when the Kiowas were living the "last great moment of their history" (3)?
3. How did meeting the Crows change the Kiowa (4)?
4. What effect did the soldiers have on the religion of the Kiowa?
5. What significance does Momaday's grandmother have for him? What does she represent?

PURPOSE AND AUDIENCE

1. Is Momaday writing only to express emotions, or does he have other purposes as well? Explain.
2. What assumptions does Momaday make about his audience? How do you know?
3. Why do you think Momaday includes the legend of Devil's Tower in his essay?

STYLE AND STRUCTURE

1. Why do you think Momaday begins his essay with a description of Rainy Mountain?
2. What determines the order in which Momaday arranges details in his description of his grandmother?
3. Why do you think Momaday ends his essay with a description of his grandmother praying?
4. Momaday includes many passages that describe landscapes. What do these descriptions add to readers' understanding of Momaday's grandmother?

VOCABULARY PROJECTS

1. Define each of the following words as it is used in this selection.

infirm (2)	billowing (7)	consummate (9)
preeminently (3)	profusion (7)	impale (9)
nomadic (4)	engender (8)	deicide (9)
luxuriant (7)	tenuous (8)	inherently (10)

2. Find three examples of figurative language in the essay. How do these examples help Momaday convey his impressions to his readers?

JOURNAL ENTRY

Which people in your family connect you to your ethnic or cultural heritage? How do they do so?

WRITING WORKSHOP

1. Write an essay describing a grandparent or any other older person who has had a great influence on you. Make sure that you include background information as well as a detailed physical description.

2. Describe a place that has played an important part in your life. Include a narrative passage that conveys the significance of the place to your readers.

3. Describe a ritual—such as a wedding or a confirmation—that you have witnessed or participated in.

COMBINING THE PATTERNS

Momaday weaves passages of **narration** throughout this descriptive essay. Bracket the narrative passages that Momaday uses in this essay, and explain how each one helps him describe his grandmother.

THEMATIC CONNECTIONS

- "Indian Education" (page 126)
- "Only Daughter" (page 84)
- "My Mother Never Worked" (page 96)
- "Words Left Unspoken" (page 153)

E. B. WHITE

❖
Once More to the Lake

Elwyn Brooks White was born in 1899 in Mount Vernon, New York, and graduated from Cornell University in 1921. He joined the newly founded *New Yorker* in 1925 and was associated with the magazine until his death in 1985. In 1937, White moved his family to a farm in Maine and began a monthly column for *Harper's* magazine entitled "One Man's Meat." A collection of some of these essays appeared under the same title in 1942. In addition to this and other essay collections, White published two popular children's books, *Stuart Little* (1945) and *Charlotte's Web* (1952). He also wrote a classic writer's handbook, *The Elements of Style* (1959), a revision of a text by one of his Cornell professors, William Strunk.

Background: In this 1941 *Harper's* essay, White writes of returning to a Maine lake where he and his parents began summering when he was a child thirty-six years earlier. He takes along his son. In a sense, his essay is a reflection on continuity and change. While much had remained the same at this rural retreat over the intervening years, the world outside had undergone a significant transformation. Auto and air travel had become commonplace; the invention of innumerable electrical appliances and machines had revolutionized the home and the workplace; movies had gone from primitive silent, black-and-white shorts to sophisticated productions with opulent soundtracks and sometimes color; a new and greatly expanded generation of consumer products had been spurred by the rise of national advertising. Moreover, the country had suffered through World War I, enjoyed a great economic expansion, experienced a period of social revolution, and been devastated by a great economic depression with high rates of unemployment. It is within this context that White relives his childhood through the eyes of his son.

One summer, along about 1904, my father rented a camp on a lake in 1
Maine and took us all there for the month of August. We all got ringworm from some kittens and had to rub Pond's Extract on our arms and legs night and morning, and my father rolled over in a canoe with all his clothes on; but outside of that the vacation was a success and from then on none of us ever thought there was any place in the world like that lake in Maine. We returned summer after summer—always on August 1st for one month. I have since become a salt-water man, but sometimes in summer there are days when the restlessness of the tides and the fearful cold of the sea water and the incessant wind which blows across the afternoon and into the evening make me wish for the placidity of a lake in the woods. A few weeks ago this feeling got so strong I bought myself a couple of bass hooks and a spinner and returned to the lake where we used to go, for a week's fishing and to revisit old haunts.

I took along my son, who had never had any fresh water up his nose 2
and who had seen lily pads only from train windows. On the journey over
to the lake I began to wonder what it would be like. I wondered how time
would have marred this unique, this holy spot — the coves and streams, the
hills that the sun set behind, the camps and the paths behind the camps. I
was sure that the tarred road would have found it out and I wondered in
what other ways it would be desolated. It is strange how much you can
remember about places like that once you allow your mind to return into
the grooves which lead back. You remember one thing, and that suddenly
reminds you of another thing. I guess I remembered clearest of all the early
mornings, when the lake was cool and motionless, remembered how the
bedroom smelled of the lumber it was made of and the wet woods whose
scent entered through the screen. The partitions in the camp were thin and
did not extend clear to the top of the rooms, and as I was always the first up
I would dress softly so as not to wake the others, and sneak out into the
sweet outdoors and start out in the canoe, keeping close along the shore in
the long shadows of the pines. I remembered being very careful never to
rub my paddle against the gunwale for fear of disturbing the stillness of
the cathedral.

The lake had never been what you would call a wild lake. There were 3
cottages sprinkled around the shores, and it was in farming country
although the shores of the lake were quite heavily wooded. Some of the
cottages were owned by nearby farmers, and you would live at the shore
and eat your meals at the farmhouse. That's what our family did. But
although it wasn't wild, it was a fairly large and undisturbed lake and there
were places in it which, to a child at least, seemed infinitely remote and
primeval.

I was right about the tar: it led to within half a mile of the shore. But 4
when I got back there, with my boy, and we settled into a camp near a farmhouse and into the kind of summertime I had known, I could tell that it
was going to be pretty much the same as it had been before — I knew it,
lying in bed the first morning, smelling the bedroom, and hearing the boy
sneak quietly out and go off along the shore in a boat. I began to sustain
the illusion that he was I, and therefore, by simple transposition, that I was
my father. This sensation persisted, kept cropping up all the time we were
there. It was not an entirely new feeling, but in this setting it grew much
stronger. I seemed to be living a dual existence. I would be in the middle of
some simple act, I would be picking up a bait box or laying down a table
fork, or I would be saying something, and suddenly it would be not I but
my father who was saying the words or making the gesture. It gave me a
creepy sensation.

We went fishing the first morning. I felt the same damp moss covering 5
the worms in the bait can, and saw the dragonfly alight on the tip of my
rod as it hovered a few inches from the surface of the water. It was the
arrival of this fly that convinced me beyond any doubt that everything was
as it always had been, that the years were a mirage and there had been no

years. The small waves were the same, chucking the rowboat under the chin as we fished at anchor, and the boat was the same boat, the same color green and the ribs broken in the same places, and under the floor-boards the same freshwater leavings and débris — the dead helgramite,* the wisps of moss, the rusty discarded fishhook, the dried blood from yesterday's catch. We stared silently at the tips of our rods, at the dragonflies that came and went. I lowered the tip of mine into the water, tentatively, pensively dislodging the fly, which darted two feet away, poised, darted two feet back, and came to rest again a little farther up the rod. There had been no years between the ducking of this dragonfly and the other one — the one that was part of memory. I looked at the boy, who was silently watching his fly, and it was my hands that held his rod, my eyes watching. I felt dizzy and didn't know which rod I was at the end of.

We caught two bass, hauling them in briskly as though they were 6 mackerel, pulling them over the side of the boat in a businesslike manner without any landing net, and stunning them with a blow on the back of the head. When we got back for a swim before lunch, the lake was exactly where we had left it, the same number of inches from the dock, and there was only the merest suggestion of a breeze. This seemed an utterly enchanted sea, this lake you could leave to its own devices for a few hours and come back to, and find that it had not stirred, this constant and trustworthy body of water. In the shallows, the dark, water-soaked sticks and twigs, smooth and old, were undulating in clusters on the bottom against the clean ribbed sand, and the track of the mussel was plain. A school of minnows swam by, each minnow with its small individual shadow, doubling the attendance, so clear and sharp in the sunlight. Some of the other campers were in swimming, along the shore, one of them with a cake of soap, and the water felt thin and clear and unsubstantial. Over the years there had been this person with the cake of soap, this cultist, and here he was. There had been no years.

Up to the farmhouse to dinner through the teeming, dusty field, the 7 road under our sneakers was only a two-track road. The middle track was missing, the one with the marks of the hooves and the splotches of dried, flaky manure. There had always been three tracks to choose from in choosing which track to walk in; now the choice was narrowed down to two. For a moment I missed terribly the middle alternative. But the way led past the tennis court, and something about the way it lay there in the sun reassured me; the tape had loosened along the backline, the alleys were green with plantains and other weeds, and the net (installed in June and removed in September) sagged in the dry noon, and the whole place steamed with midday heat and hunger and emptiness. There was a choice of pie for dessert, and one was blueberry and one was apple, and the waitresses were the same country girls, there having been no passage of time, only the

---

*EDS. NOTE — An insect larva often used as bait.

illusion of it as in a dropped curtain — the waitresses were still fifteen; their hair had been washed, that was the only difference — they had been to the movies and seen the pretty girls with the clean hair.

Summertime, oh summertime, pattern of life indelible, the fade-proof lake, the woods unshatterable, the pasture with the sweetfern and the juniper forever and ever, summer without end; this was the background, and the life along the shore was the design, the cottages with their innocent and tranquil design, their tiny docks with the flagpole and the American flag floating against the white clouds in the blue sky, the little paths over the roots of the trees leading from camp to camp and the paths leading back to the outhouses and the can of lime for sprinkling, and at the souvenir counters at the store the miniature birch-bark canoes and the post cards that showed things looking a little better than they looked. This was the American family at play, escaping the city heat, wondering whether the newcomers in the camp at the head of the cove were "common" or "nice," wondering whether it was true that the people who drove up for Sunday dinner at the farmhouse were turned away because there wasn't enough chicken.   8

It seemed to me, as I kept remembering all this, that those times and those summers had been infinitely precious and worth saving. There had been jollity and peace and goodness. The arriving (at the beginning of August) had been so big a business in itself, at the railway station the farm wagon drawn up, the first smell of the pineladen air, the first glimpse of the smiling farmer, and the great importance of the trunks and your father's enormous authority in such matters, and the feel of the wagon under you for the long ten-mile haul, and at the top of the last long hill catching the first view of the lake after eleven months of not seeing this cherished body of water. The shouts and cries of the other campers when they saw you, and the trunks to be unpacked, to give up their rich burden. (Arriving was less exciting nowadays, when you sneaked up in your car and parked it under a tree near the camp and took out the bags and in five minutes it was all over, no fuss, no loud wonderful fuss about trunks.)   9

Peace and goodness and jollity. The only thing that was wrong now, really, was the sound of the place, an unfamiliar nervous sound of the outboard motors. This was the note that jarred, the one thing that would sometimes break the illusion and set the years moving. In those other summertimes all motors were inboard; and when they were at a little distance, the noise they made was a sedative, an ingredient of summer sleep. They were one-cylinder and two-cylinder engines, and some were make-and-break and some were jump-spark, but they all made a sleepy sound across the lake. The one-lungers throbbed and fluttered, and the twin-cylinder ones purred and purred, and that was a quiet sound too. But now the campers all had outboards. In the daytime, in the hot mornings, these motors made a petulant, irritable sound; at night, in the still evening when the afterglow lit the water, they whined about one's ears like mosquitoes.   10

My boy loved our rented outboard, and his great desire was to achieve singlehanded mastery over it, and authority, and he soon learned the trick of choking it a little (but not too much), and the adjustment of the needle valve. Watching him I would remember the things you could do with the old one-cylinder engine with the heavy flywheel, how you could have it eating out of your hand if you got really close to it spiritually. Motor boats in those days didn't have clutches, and you would make a landing by shutting off the motor at the proper time and coasting in with a dead rudder. But there was a way of reversing them, if you learned the trick, by cutting the switch and putting it on again exactly on the final dying revolution of the flywheel, so that it would kick back against compression and begin reversing. Approaching a dock in a strong following breeze, it was difficult to slow up sufficiently by the ordinary coasting method, and if a boy felt he had complete mastery over his motor, he was tempted to keep it running beyond its time and then reverse it a few feet from the dock. It took a cool nerve, because if you threw the switch a twentieth of a second too soon you could catch the flywheel when it still had speed enough to go up past center, and the boat would leap ahead, charging bull-fashion at the dock.

We had a good week at the camp. The bass were biting well and the sun shone endlessly, day after day. We would be tired at night and lie down in the accumulated heat of the little bedrooms after the long hot day and the breeze would stir almost imperceptibly outside and the smell of the swamp drift in through the rusty screens. Sleep would come easily and in the morning the red squirrel would be on the roof, tapping out his gay routine. I kept remembering everything, lying in bed in the mornings—the small steamboat that had a long rounded stern like the lip of a Ubangi,* how quietly she ran on the moonlight sails, when the older boys played their mandolins and the girls sang and we ate doughnuts dipped in sugar, and how sweet the music was on the water in the shining night, and what it had felt like to think about girls then. After breakfast we would go up to the store and the things were in the same place—the minnows in a bottle, the plugs and spinners disarranged and pawed over by the youngsters from the boys' camp, the fig newtons and the Beeman's gum. Outside, the road was tarred and cars stood in front of the store. Inside, all was just as it had always been, except there was more Coca-Cola and not so much Moxie** and root beer and birch beer and sarsaparilla.*** We would walk out with a bottle of pop apiece and sometimes the pop would backfire up our noses and hurt. We explored the streams, quietly, where the turtles slid off the

11

---

*Eds. note—A member of an African tribe known for wearing mouth ornaments that stretch the lips into a saucerlike shape.

**Eds. note—A soft drink that was popular in the early twentieth century.

***Eds. note—A sweetened carbonated beverage flavored with birch oil and sassafras.

sunny logs and dug their way into the soft bottom; and we lay on the town wharf and fed worms to the tame bass. Everywhere we went I had trouble making out which was I, the one walking at my side, the one walking in my pants.

One afternoon while we were there at that lake a thunderstorm came up. It was like the revival of an old melodrama that I had seen long ago with childish awe. The second-act climax of the drama of the electrical disturbance over a lake in America had not changed in any important respect. This was the big scene, still the big scene. The whole thing was so familiar, the first feeling of oppression and heat and a general air around camp of not wanting to go very far away. In midafternoon (it was all the same) a curious darkening of the sky, and a lull in everything that had made life tick; and then the way the boats suddenly swung the other way at their moorings with the coming of a breeze out of the new quarter, and the premonitory rumble. Then the kettle drum, then the snare, then the bass drum and cymbals, then crackling light against the dark, and the gods grinning and licking their chops in the hills. Afterward the calm, the rain steadily rustling in the calm lake, the return of light and hope and spirits, and the campers running out in joy and relief to go swimming in the rain, their bright cries perpetuating the deathless joke about how they were getting simply drenched, and the children screaming with delight at the new sensation of bathing in the rain, and the joke about getting drenched linking the generations in a strong indestructible chain. And the comedian who waded in carrying an umbrella. 12

When the others went swimming my son said he was going in too. He pulled his dripping trunks from the line where they had hung all through the shower, and wrung them out. Languidly, and with no thought of going in, I watched him, his hard little body, skinny and bare, saw him wince slightly as he pulled up around his vitals the small, soggy, icy garment. As he buckled the swollen belt suddenly my groin felt the chill of death. 13

• • •

COMPREHENSION

1. In what ways are the writer and his son alike? In what ways are they different? What does White mean when he says, "I seemed to be living a dual existence" (4)?

2. In paragraph 5, White says there seem to be "no years" between past and present; elsewhere, he senses that things are different. How do you account for these conflicting feelings?

3. Why does White feel disconcerted when he discovers that the road to the farmhouse has two tracks, not three? What do you make of his comment that "now the choice was narrowed down to two" (7)?

4. In what way does sound "break the illusion and set the years moving" (10)?

5. To what is White referring in the last sentence?

PURPOSE AND AUDIENCE

1. What is the thesis of this essay? Is it stated or implied?

2. Do you think White expects the ending of his essay to be a surprise to his audience? Explain.

3. To what age group do you think this essay would appeal most? Why?

STYLE AND STRUCTURE

1. List the specific changes that have taken place on the lake. Does White emphasize these changes or play them down? Explain.

2. What ideas and images does White repeat throughout his essay? What is the purpose of this repetition?

3. White goes to great lengths to describe how things look, feel, smell, taste, and sound. How does this help him achieve his purpose in this essay?

4. In what way does White's conclusion refer to the first paragraph of the essay?

VOCABULARY PROJECTS

1. Define each of the following words as it is used in this selection.

placidity (1)	pensively (5)	melodrama (12)
gunwale (2)	jollity (9)	premonitory (12)
primeval (3)	petulant (10)	perpetuating (12)
transposition (4)	imperceptibly (11)	languidly (13)

2. Underline ten words in the essay that refer to one of the five senses. Make a list of synonyms you could use for these words. How close do your substitutions come to capturing White's meaning?

JOURNAL ENTRY

Do you identify more with the father or the son in this essay? Why?

WRITING WORKSHOP

1. Write a description of a scene you remember from your childhood. In your essay, discuss how your current view of the scene differs from the view you had when you were a child.

2. Assume you are a travel agent. Write a descriptive brochure designed to bring tourists to the lake. Be specific, and stress the benefits White mentions in his essay.

3. Write an essay in which you describe yourself from the perspective of one of your parents. Make sure your description conveys both the qualities your parent likes and the qualities he or she would want to change.

COMBINING THE PATTERNS

White opens his essay with a short narrative about his first trip to the lake in 1904. How does this use of **narration** provide a context for the entire essay?

THEMATIC CONNECTIONS

- "Only Daughter" (page 84)
- "How the Lawyers Stole Winter" (page 402)
- "The Men We Carry in Our Minds" (page 456)
- "Tortillas" (page 513)

KATE CHOPIN

❖
The Storm (Fiction)

Kate Chopin (1851–1904) was born Catherine O'Flaherty, the daughter of a St. Louis businessman father of Irish descent and a French-American mother. In 1870, she married Oscar Chopin and moved with him to New Orleans, where he was a cotton merchant. After suffering business reversals, the Chopins relocated to Cloutierville, Louisiana, to be closer to Oscar's extended Creole family. Oscar Chopin died suddenly in 1882, and Kate Chopin, left with six children to raise, returned to St. Louis. There she began writing short stories, many set in the colorful Creole country of central Louisiana, that appeared in a variety of popular publications. Her first collection, *Bayou Folk,* was published in 1894, followed by *A Night in Arcadie* in 1897. Her literary success was cut short, however, with the publication of her first novel, *The Awakening* (1899), a story of adultery that outraged many of her critics and readers because it was told sympathetically from a woman's perspective. Her work languished until the middle of the twentieth century, when it was rediscovered, largely by the feminist literary movement.

Background: The following story was apparently written about the same time as *The Awakening,* but Chopin never attempted to publish it. Its frank sexuality—franker than that depicted in her controversial novel—and its focus on a liaison between two lovers (Calixta and Alcée) who are married to others would have been deemed too scandalous for middle-class readers of the day. Even within the more liberal Creole culture where the story is set, Calixta's actions would have been outrageous. While Creole men were expected and even encouraged to have mistresses (usually black or mixed-race women), Creole wives were expected to remain true to their wedding vows. The Creoles themselves were descendants of the early Spanish and French settlers in Louisiana, and they lived lives quite separate from—and, they believed, superior to—those whose ancestors were British. Their language came to be a mix of French and English, as did their mode of dress and cuisine. A strong Creole influence can still be found in New Orleans and the surrounding Louisiana countryside; Mardi Gras, for example, is a Creole tradition.

I

The leaves were so still that even Bibi thought it was going to rain. 1
Bobinôt, who was accustomed to converse on terms of perfect equality with his little son, called the child's attention to certain sombre clouds that were rolling with sinister intention from the west, accompanied by a sullen, threatening roar. They were at Friedheimer's store and decided to remain there till the storm had passed. They sat within the door on two empty kegs. Bibi was four years old and looked very wise.

183

"Mama'll be 'fraid, yes," he suggested with blinking eyes. 2

"She'll shut the house. Maybe she got Sylvie helpin' her this evenin'," 3
Bobinôt responded reassuringly.

"No; she ent got Sylvie. Sylvie was helpin' her yistiday," piped Bibi. 4

Bobinôt arose and going across to the counter purchased a can of 5
shrimps, of which Calixta was very fond. Then he returned to his perch
on the keg and sat stolidly holding the can of shrimps while the storm
burst. It shook the wooden store and seemed to be ripping great furrows
in the distant field. Bibi laid his little hand on his father's knee and was not
afraid.

II

Calixta, at home, felt no uneasiness for their safety. She sat at a side 6
window sewing furiously on a sewing machine. She was greatly occupied
and did not notice the approaching storm. But she felt very warm and
often stopped to mop her face on which the perspiration gathered in
beads. She unfastened her white sacque at the throat. It began to grow
dark, and suddenly realizing the situation she got up hurriedly and went
about closing windows and doors.

Out on the small front gallery she had hung Bobinôt's Sunday clothes 7
to air and she hastened out to gather them before the rain fell. As she
stepped outside, Alcée Laballière rode in at the gate. She had not seen him
very often since her marriage, and never alone. She stood there with
Bobinôt's coat in her hands, and the big rain drops began to fall. Alcée rode
his horse under the shelter of a side projection where the chickens had
huddled and there were plows and a harrow piled up in the corner.

"May I come and wait on your gallery till the storm is over, Calixta?" 8
he asked.

"Come 'long in, M'sieur Alcée." 9

His voice and her own startled her as if from a trance, and she seized 10
Bobinôt's vest. Alcée, mounting to the porch, grabbed the trousers and
snatched Bibi's braided jacket that was about to be carried away by a sudden gust of wind. He expressed an intention to remain outside, but it was
soon apparent that he might as well have been out in the open: the water
beat in upon the boards in driving sheets, and he went inside, closing the
door after him. It was even necessary to put something beneath the door to
keep the water out.

"My! what a rain! It's good two years since it rain' like that," exclaimed 11
Calixta as she rolled up a piece of bagging and Alcée helped her to thrust it
beneath the crack.

She was a little fuller of figure than five years before when she married; 12
but she had lost nothing of her vivacity. Her blue eyes still retained their
melting quality; and her yellow hair, dishevelled by the wind and rain,
kinked more stubbornly than ever about her ears and temples.

The rain beat upon the low, shingled roof with a force and clatter that   13
threatened to break an entrance and deluge them there. They were in the
dining room — the sitting room — the general utility room. Adjoining was
her bed room, with Bibi's couch along side her own. The door stood open,
and the room with its white, monumental bed, its closed shutters, looked
dim and mysterious.

Alcée flung himself into a rocker and Calixta nervously began to   14
gather up from the floor the lengths of a cotton sheet which she had been
sewing.

"If this keeps up, *Dieu sait** if the levees goin' to stan' it!" she exclaimed.   15
"What have you got to do with the levees?"   16
"I got enough to do! An' there's Bobinôt with Bibi out in that storm —   17
if he only didn't left Friedheimer's!"
"Let us hope, Calixta, that Bobinôt's got sense enough to come in out   18
of a cyclone."

She went and stood at the window with a greatly disturbed look on her   19
face. She wiped the frame that was clouded with moisture. It was stiflingly
hot. Alcée got up and joined her at the window, looking over her shoulder.
The rain was coming down in sheets obscuring the view of far-off cabins
and enveloping the distant wood in a gray mist. The playing of the lightning was incessant. A bolt struck a tall chinaberry tree at the edge of the
field. It filled all visible space with a blinding glare and the crash seemed to
invade the very boards they stood upon.

Calixta put her hands to her eyes, and with a cry, staggered backward.   20
Alcée's arm encircled her, and for an instant he drew her close and spas-
modically to him.

"*Bonté!*"** she cried, releasing herself from his encircling arm and   21
retreating from the window, "the house'll go next! If I only knew w'ere Bibi
was!" She would not compose herself; she would not be seated. Alcée
clasped her shoulders and looked into her face. The contact of her warm,
palpitating body when he had unthinkingly drawn her into his arms, had
aroused all the old-time infatuation and desire for her flesh.

"Calixta," he said, "don't be frightened. Nothing can happen. The   22
house is too low to be struck, with so many tall trees standing about.
There! aren't you going to be quiet? say, aren't you?" He pushed her hair
back from her face that was warm and steaming. Her lips were as red and
moist as pomegranate seed. Her white neck and a glimpse of her full, firm
bosom disturbed him powerfully. As she glanced up at him the fear in her
liquid blue eyes had given place to a drowsy gleam that unconsciously
betrayed a sensuous desire. He looked down into her eyes and there was
nothing for him to do but to gather her lips in a kiss. It reminded him of
Assumption.

---

*EDS. NOTE — God knows.
**EDS. NOTE — Goodness!

"Do you remember—in Assumption, Calixta?" he asked in a low voice 23
broken by passion. Oh! she remembered; for in Assumption he had kissed
her and kissed and kissed her; until his senses would well nigh fail, and to
save her he would resort to a desperate flight. If she was not an immaculate
dove in those days, she was still inviolate; a passionate creature whose very
defenselessness had made her defense, against which his honor forbade
him to prevail. Now—well, now—her lips seemed in a manner free to be
tasted, as well as her round, white throat and her whiter breasts.

They did not heed the crashing torrents, and the roar of the elements 24
made her laugh as she lay in his arms. She was a revelation in that dim,
mysterious chamber; as white as the couch she lay upon. Her firm, elastic
flesh that was knowing for the first time its birthright, was like a creamy
lily that the sun invites to contribute its breath and perfume to the undying life of the world.

The generous abundance of her passion, without guile or trickery, was 25
like a white flame which penetrated and found response in depths of his
own sensuous nature that had never yet been reached.

When he touched her breasts they gave themselves up in quivering 26
ecstasy, inviting his lips. Her mouth was a fountain of delight. And when
he possessed her, they seemed to swoon together at the very borderland of
life's mystery.

He stayed cushioned upon her, breathless, dazed, enervated, with his 27
heart beating like a hammer upon her. With one hand she clasped his
head, her lips lightly touching his forehead. The other hand stroked with a
soothing rhythm his muscular shoulders.

The growl of the thunder was distant and passing away. The rain beat 28
softly upon the shingles, inviting them to drowsiness and sleep. But they
dared not yield.

The rain was over; and the sun was turning the glistening green world 29
into a palace of gems. Calixta, on the gallery, watched Alcée ride away. He
turned and smiled at her with a beaming face; and she lifted her pretty chin
in the air and laughed aloud.

III

Bobinôt and Bibi, trudging home, stopped without at the cistern to 30
make themselves presentable.

"My! Bibi, w'at will yo' mama say! You ought to be asham'. You oughtn' 31
put on those good pants. Look at 'em! An' that mud on yo' collar! How you
got that mud on yo' collar, Bibi? I never saw such a boy!" Bibi was the picture of pathetic resignation. Bobinôt was the embodiment of serious solicitude as he strove to remove from his own person and his son's the signs of
their tramp over heavy roads and through wet fields. He scraped the mud
off Bibi's bare legs and feet with a stick and carefully removed all traces
from his heavy brogans. Then, prepared for the worst—the meeting with
an over-scrupulous housewife, they entered cautiously at the back door.

Calixta was preparing supper. She had set the table and was dripping   32
coffee at the hearth. She sprang up as they came in.

"Oh, Bobinôt! You back! My! but I was uneasy. W'ere you been during   33
the rain? An' Bibi? he ain't wet? he ain't hurt?" She had clasped Bibi and
was kissing him effusively. Bobinôt's explanations and apologies which he
had been composing all along the way, died on his lips as Calixta felt him
to see if he were dry, and seemed to express nothing but satisfaction at
their safe return.

"I brought you some shrimps, Calixta," offered Bobinôt, hauling the   34
can from his ample side pocket and laying it on the table.

"Shrimps! Oh, Bobinôt! you too good fo' anything!" and she gave him   35
a smacking kiss on the cheek that resounded. "*J'vous réponds,** we'll have a
feas' tonight! umph-umph!"

Bobinôt and Bibi began to relax and enjoy themselves, and when the   36
three sated themselves at table they laughed much and so loud that anyone
might have heard them as far away as Laballière's.

IV

Alcée Laballière wrote to his wife, Clarisse, that night. It was a loving   37
letter, full of tender solicitude. He told her not to hurry back, but if she and
the babies liked it at Biloxi, to stay a month longer. He was getting on
nicely; and though he missed them, he was willing to bear the separation a
while longer — realizing that their health and pleasure were the first things
to be considered.

V

As for Clarisse, she was charmed upon receiving her husband's letter.   38
She and the babies were doing well. The society was agreeable; many of her
old friends and acquaintances were at the bay. And the first free breath
since her marriage seemed to restore the pleasant liberty of her maiden
days. Devoted as she was to her husband, their intimate conjugal life was
something which she was more than willing to forego for a while.

So the storm passed and everyone was happy.   39

• • •

READING LITERATURE

1. How does the storm help set in motion the action of the story? List the
   events caused by the storm.

2. Is the last line of the story to be taken literally, or is it meant to be **ironic**
   (that is, does it actually suggest the opposite meaning)? Explain.

3. What do specific, concrete details tell us about Calixta?

---

*EDS. NOTE — I tell you.

JOURNAL ENTRY

On one level, the story's title refers to the storm that takes place through much of the story. To what else could the story's title refer?

THEMATIC CONNECTIONS

- "The Men We Carry in our Minds" (page 456)
- "Sex, Lies, and Conversation" (page 407)
- "The Ways We Lie" (page 470)

WRITING ASSIGNMENTS FOR DESCRIPTION

1. Choose a character from a work of fiction or a film who you think is truly interesting. Write a descriptive essay that conveys what makes this character so special.

2. Describe a particularly memorable sporting event you have attended. Include both your own reactions and the reactions of other spectators.

3. Locate some photographs of your relatives. Describe three of these pictures, including details that provide insight into the lives of the people you discuss. Use your descriptive paragraphs to support a thesis about your family.

4. Visit an art museum, and select a painting that interests you. Study it carefully, and then write an essay-length description of it. Before you write, decide how you will organize your details and whether you will write a subjective or an objective description.

5. Select an object that you are familiar with, and write an objective description of it. Include a diagram.

6. Assume you are writing a letter to someone in another country who knows little about life in the United States. Describe to this person something that you consider to be typically American — a baseball stadium or a shopping mall, for example.

7. Visit your college library, and write an objective description of the reference area. Be specific, and select an organizing scheme before you begin your essay. Your purpose is to acquaint students with some of the reference materials they will use.

8. Describe your neighborhood to a visitor who knows nothing about it. Include as much specific detail as you can.

9. After reading "Ground Zero," write a description of a sight or scene that fascinated, surprised, or shocked you. Your description should explain why you were so deeply affected by what you saw.

10. Write an essay in which you describe an especially frightening horror film. What specific sights and sounds make this film so horrifying? Include a thesis statement that assesses the film's success as a horror film. (Be careful not to merely recount the plot of the film.)

COLLABORATIVE ACTIVITY FOR DESCRIPTION

Working in groups of three or four students, select a famous person — one you can reasonably expect your classmates to recognize. Then, work as a group to write a physical description of that individual, including as much physical detail as possible. (Avoid any details that will be an instant giveaway.) Give your description a general title — *politician, television star,* or *person in the news,* for example. Finally, have one person read the description aloud to the class, and see whether your classmates can guess the person's identity.

INTERNET ASSIGNMENT FOR DESCRIPTION

Visiting the following Web sites, find a painting or photograph that captures your interest. Imagine that you are inside the scene depicted in the artwork, and write a description of what you see and experience. If there is a person in the painting, evoke that person's experience. This exercise calls for imagination — going beyond what you see in the painting or photograph to think about the effects of what you see on your other senses. Think about the details of the image — the mood, lighting, texture, color, brushstrokes, or shadows — to help you capture the overall impression of the artwork.

The Whitney Museum of American Art
<whitney.org>

The Museum of Modern Art
<moma.org>

International Center for Photography
<icp.org>

❖ 6
Exemplification

WHAT IS EXEMPLIFICATION?

Exemplification uses one or more particular cases, or **examples,** to illustrate or explain a general point or an abstract concept. In the following paragraph from *Sexism and Language,* Alleen Pace Nilsen uses a number of well-chosen examples to illustrate her statement that the armed forces use words that have positive masculine connotations to encourage recruitment:

Topic sentence

The armed forces, particularly the Marines, use the positive masculine connotation as part of their recruitment psychology. They promote the idea that to join the Marines (or the Army, Navy, or Air Force) guarantees that you will become a man. But this brings up a problem, because much of the work that is necessary to keep a large organization running is what is traditionally thought of as *woman's work.* Now, how can the Marines ask someone who has signed up for a *man-sized job* to do *woman's work?* Since they can't, they euphemize and give the jobs titles that are more prestigious or, at least, don't make people think of females.

Series of related examples

Waitresses are called *orderlies,* secretaries are called *clerk-typists,* nurses are called *medics,* assistants are called *adjutants,* and cleaning up an area is called *policing* the area. The same kind of word glorification is used in civilian life to bolster a man's ego when he is doing such tasks as cooking and sewing. For example, a *chef* has higher prestige than a *cook* and a *tailor* has higher prestige than a *seamstress.*

USING EXEMPLIFICATION

You have probably noticed, when watching television talk shows or listening to classroom discussions, that the most interesting and persuasive exchanges take place when the participants support their points with specific examples. Sweeping generalizations and vague statements are not nearly as effective as specific observations, anecdotes, details, and opinions. It is one thing to say, "The mayor is corrupt and should not be reelected" and another to illustrate your point by saying, "The mayor should not be reelected because he has fired two city workers who refused to contribute to his campaign fund, has put his family and friends on the city payroll, and has used public employees to make improvements to his home." The same principle applies to writing: many of the most effective essays use examples extensively. Exemplification is used in every kind of writing situation to explain and clarify, to add interest, and to persuade.

Using Examples to Explain and Clarify

On a midterm exam in a film course, you might write, "Even though horror movies seem modern, they really aren't." You may think your statement is perfectly clear, but if this is all you say about horror movies, you should not be surprised if your exam comes back with a question mark in the margin next to this sentence. After all, you have only made a general statement or claim about your subject. It is not specific, nor does it anticipate readers' questions about the ways in which horror movies are not modern. To be certain your audience knows exactly what you mean, state your point precisely: "Despite the fact that horror movies seem modern, two of the most memorable ones are adaptations of nineteenth-century Gothic novels." Then, use examples to ensure clarity and avoid ambiguity. For example, you could illustrate your point by discussing two films — *Frankenstein,* directed by James Whale, and *Dracula,* directed by Todd Browning — and linking them to the nineteenth-century novels on which they are based. With the benefit of these specific examples, readers would know what you mean — that the literary roots of such movies are in the past, not that their cinematic techniques or production methods are dated. Moreover, readers would know which particular horror movies you are discussing.

Using Examples to Add Interest

Writers use well-chosen examples to add interest as well as clarify their points. Laurence J. Peter and Raymond Hull do this in their essay "The Peter Principle," which appears later in this chapter. Their claim that each employee in a system rises to a level of authority at which he or she is incompetent is not particularly engaging. This statement becomes interesting, however, when it is supported by specific examples — the affable foreman who becomes the indecisive supervisor, the exacting mechanic who becomes the disorganized foreman, and the effective battlefield general who becomes the ineffective and self-destructive field marshal.

When you use exemplification, look for examples that are interesting as well as pertinent. Test the effectiveness of your examples by putting yourself in your readers' place. If you don't find your essay lively and absorbing, chances are your readers won't either. If this is the case, try to add more engaging, more spirited examples. After all, your goal is to communicate ideas to your readers, and imaginative examples can make the difference between an engrossing essay and one that is a chore to read.

Using Examples to Persuade

Although you may use examples to explain your ideas or to add interest to your essay, examples are also an effective way of persuading people that what you are saying is reasonable and worth considering. A few well-chosen examples can provide effective support for otherwise unconvincing general statements. For instance, a statement that school districts across the country cannot cope with the large number of students with limited English skills needs support. If you make such a statement on an exam, you need to back it up with appropriate examples — such as the fact that in one state, North Carolina, the number of students with limited English skills increased from 8,900 in 1993 to 52,500 in 2002. Similarly, a statement in a biology paper that DDT should continue to be banned is unconvincing without persuasive examples such as these to support it:

- Although DDT has been banned since December 31, 1972, traces are still being found in the eggs of various fish and waterfowl.

- Certain lakes and streams still cannot be used for sport and recreation because DDT levels are dangerously high, presumably because of farmland runoff.

- Because of its stability as a compound, DDT does not degrade quickly; therefore, existing residues will threaten the environment well into the twenty-first century.

Using Examples to Test Your Thesis

Examples can help you test your own ideas as well as the ideas of others. For instance, suppose you plan to write a paper for a composition class about students' writing skills. Your tentative thesis is that writing well is an inborn talent and that teachers can do little to help people write better. But is this really true? Has it been true in your own life? To test your point, you brainstorm about the various teachers you have had who tried to help you improve your writing.

As you assemble your list, you remember Mrs. Colson, a teacher you had when you were a junior in high school. She was strict, required lots of writing, and seemed to accept nothing less than perfection. At the time neither you nor your classmates liked her; in fact, her nickname was Warden Colson. But looking back, you recall her one-on-one conferences, her organized lessons, and her pointed comments. You also remember her careful review of essay tests, and you realize that after being in her class, you felt much more comfortable taking such tests. After examining some papers that you saved, you are surprised to see how much your writing actually improved that year. These examples lead you to reevaluate your ideas and to revise your tentative thesis. You conclude that even though some people seem to have a natural flair for writing, a good teacher can make a difference.

PLANNING AN EXEMPLIFICATION ESSAY

Providing Enough Examples

Unfortunately, no general rule exists to tell you how many examples you need to support your ideas. The number you use depends on your thesis statement. If, for instance, your thesis is that an educational institution, like a business, needs careful financial management, a detailed examination of one college or university could work well. In this case, a single example might provide all the information you need to make your point.

If, however, your thesis is that conflict between sons and fathers is a major theme in the writing of Franz Kafka, more than one example would be necessary. A single example would show only that the theme is present in *one* of Kafka's works. In this case, the more examples you include, the more effectively you prove your point. Of course, for some thesis statements, even several examples would not be enough. Examples alone, for instance, could not demonstrate convincingly that children from small families have more successful careers than children from large families. This thesis would have to be supported with a statistical study—that is, by collecting and interpreting numerical data representing a great many examples.

Selecting a sufficient *range* of examples is just as important as choosing an appropriate number. If you want to persuade readers that Colin Powell was an able general, you should choose examples from several stages of his military career. Likewise, if you want to convince readers that outdoor advertising is ruining the scenic views from major highways, you should discuss an area larger than your immediate neighborhood. Your objective in each case is to select a cross section of examples appropriate for the boundaries of your topic.

Choosing Representative Examples

Just as professional pollsters take great pains to ensure that their samples reflect the makeup of the group they are polling, you should make sure that your examples fairly represent the group you are discussing. If you want to support a ban on smoking in all public buildings, you should not limit your examples to restaurants. To be convincing, you should include examples involving many public places, such as office buildings, hotel lobbies, and sports stadiums. For the same reason, one person's experience is not enough to support a conclusion about many others unless you can establish that the experience is typical.

If you decide that you cannot cite enough representative examples to support your thesis, reexamine it. Rather than switching to a new topic, try to narrow your thesis. After all, the only way your paper will be convincing is if your readers believe that your thesis is supported by your examples and that your examples fairly represent the scope of your topic.

Of course, to be convincing you must not only choose examples effectively but also *use* them effectively. You should keep your thesis statement in mind as you write, taking care not to get so involved with one example that you digress from your main point. No matter how carefully developed, no matter how specific, lively, and appropriate, your examples accomplish nothing if they do not support your essay's main idea.

Using Transitions

Be sure to use transitional words and phrases to introduce your examples. Without them, readers will have difficulty seeing the connection between an example and the general statement that it is illustrating. In some cases, transitions will help you connect your examples to your thesis statement ("*Another* successful program for the homeless provides telephone answering services for job seekers"). At other times, transitions will link examples to topic sentences ("*For instance,* I have written articles for my college newspaper"). In exemplification essays, the most frequently used transitions include *for example, for instance, in fact, namely, specifically, that is,* and *thus.* A more complete list of transitions appears on page 43.

STRUCTURING AN EXEMPLIFICATION ESSAY

Exemplification essays usually begin with an *introduction* that includes the thesis statement, which is supported by examples in the body of the essay. Each *body paragraph* may develop a separate example, present a point illustrated by several brief examples, or explore one aspect of a single extended example that is developed throughout the essay. The *conclusion* reinforces the main idea of the essay, perhaps restating the thesis. At times, however, variations of this basic pattern are advisable and even necessary. For instance, beginning your paper with a striking example might stimulate your reader's interest and curiosity; ending with one might vividly reinforce your thesis.

Exemplification presents one special organizational problem. If you do not select your examples carefully and arrange them effectively, your paper can become a thesis statement followed by a list or by ten or fifteen brief, choppy paragraphs. One way to avoid this problem is to develop your best examples fully in separate paragraphs and to discard the others. Another effective strategy is to group related examples in individual paragraphs.

Within each paragraph, you can arrange examples *chronologically,* beginning with those that occurred first and moving to those that occurred later. You can also arrange examples in order of *increasing complexity,* beginning with the simplest and moving to the most difficult or complex. Finally, you can arrange examples in order of *importance,* beginning with those that are less significant and moving to those that are most significant or persuasive.

The following informal outline for a paper evaluating the nursing care at a hospital illustrates one way to arrange examples. Notice how the writer presents his examples in order of increasing importance under three general headings — *patient rooms, emergency room,* and *clinics.*

Introduction:	Thesis statement — Because of its focus on the patient, the nursing care at Montgomery Hospital can serve as a model for other medical facilities.

In Patient Rooms

Example 1:	Being responsive
Example 2:	Establishing rapport
Example 3:	Delivering bedside care

In Emergency Room

Example 4:	Staffing treatment rooms
Example 5:	Circulating among patients in the waiting room
Example 6:	Maintaining good working relationships with physicians

In Clinics

Example 7:	Preparing patients
Example 8:	Assisting during treatment
Example 9:	Instructing patients after treatment
Conclusion:	Restatement of thesis or review of key points or examples

REVISING AN EXEMPLIFICATION ESSAY

When you revise an exemplification essay, consider the items on the Revision Checklist on page 54. In addition, pay special attention to the items on the checklist below, which apply specifically to exemplification essays.

☑ REVISION CHECKLIST: EXEMPLIFICATION

- Does your assignment call for exemplification?
- Does your essay have a clear thesis statement that identifies the point or concept that you will illustrate?

(continued on next page)

(continued from previous page)

- Do your examples explain and clarify your thesis statement?
- Have you provided enough examples?
- Have you chosen clear and representative examples?
- Are your examples persuasive?
- Do your examples add interest?
- Have you used transitional words and phrases that reinforce the connection between your examples and your thesis statement?

EDITING AN EXEMPLIFICATION ESSAY

When you edit your exemplification essay, follow the guidelines on the Editing Checklist on page 66. In addition, focus on the grammar, mechanics, and punctuation issues that are most relevant to exemplification essays. One of these issues — using commas in a series — is discussed below. For more practice in using commas in a series, visit **Exercise Central** at **<bedfordstmartins.com/patterns/commas>**.

GRAMMAR IN CONTEXT : Using Commas in a Series*

When you write an exemplification essay, you often use a series of examples to support a statement or to illustrate a point. When you give a series of examples, you must remember to separate them with commas.

- Always use commas to separate three or more items — words, phrases, or clauses — in a series.

In "Just Walk On By," Brent Staples says, "I was <u>surprised,</u> <u>embarrassed,</u> and <u>dismayed</u> all at once" (224).

In "Just Walk On By," Staples observes that the woman thought she was being stalked <u>by a mugger,</u> <u>by a rapist,</u> or <u>by something worse</u> (224).

In "The Peter Principle," Lawrence Peter says, "For example my principal's main concerns were <u>that all window shades be at the same level,</u> <u>that class-rooms should be quiet,</u> and <u>that no one step on or near the rose beds</u>" (Peter and Hull 207).

According to Jonathan Kozol in "The Human Cost of an Illiterate Society," <u>illiterates cannot help with homework,</u> <u>they cannot write notes to teachers,</u> and <u>they cannot read school notices</u> (231).

NOTE: Although newspaper and magazine writers routinely leave out the comma before the coordinating conjunction that comes before the last item in a series of three or more items, you should always include this comma in your college writing.

---

*All the examples below refer to essays that appear later in this chapter.

- Do not use a comma after the final element in a series of three or more items.

Incorrect: Staples was <u>shocked</u>, <u>horrified</u>, and <u>disillusioned</u>, to be taken for a mugger.

Correct: Staples was <u>shocked</u>, <u>horrified</u>, and <u>disillusioned</u> to be taken for a mugger.

- Do not use commas if all the elements in a series of three or more items are separated by coordinating conjunctions (*and, or, but,* and so on).

Peter and Hull believe that the Peter Principle controls everyone <u>in business</u> and <u>in government</u> and <u>in education</u>. (no commas)

☑ **EDITING CHECKLIST: EXEMPLIFICATION**

- Have you used commas to separate three or more items in a series?
- Have you made sure not to use a comma after the last element in a series?
- Have you made sure not to use a comma in a series with items that are separated by coordinating conjunctions?
- Are all the elements in a series stated in **parallel** terms (see page 370)?

▶ STUDENT WRITERS: EXEMPLIFICATION

Exemplification is frequently used in nonacademic writing situations, such as business reports, memos, and proposals. One of the most important situations in which you will use exemplification is in a letter in which you apply for a job. Kristy Bredin's letter of application to a prospective employer appears below. (Grace Ku's essay on page 201 illustrates a more conventional academic use of exemplification.)

> 1028 Geissinger Street
> Bethlehem, PA 18018
> September 7, 2003

> Kim Goldstein
> <u>Rolling Stone</u>
> 1290 Avenue of the Americas
> New York, NY 10104

> Dear Ms. Goldstein:

Introduction   I am writing to apply for the editorial intern-   1
ship with <u>Rolling Stone</u> magazine that you posted

on Moravian College's employment Web site. I
have been subscribing to your magazine for
several years, and I admire the quality and
thoroughness of the articles. I believe that my

Thesis statement

studies in English and music and my work with
undergraduate publications qualify me for the
internship you advertised.

I am currently a senior at Moravian College,   2
where I am pursuing degrees in English (B.A.
with a concentration in creative writing) and

Series of brief
examples

music (B.A.). Throughout my college career, I
have maintained a 3.3 average and have served
as both secretary and president of the Literary
Society. After I graduate in May, I would like
to find a full-time position in publishing. For
this reason, I am looking for an internship
such as yours that would give me administrative
and editorial experience as well as insight into
a large-scale production process. An internship
with Rolling Stone would also enable me to read,
edit, and perhaps write articles about a subject that I have studied extensively—music.

Series of brief
examples

For an undergraduate, I have considerable ex-   3
perience in editing. I have worked as a tutor
in Moravian's Writing Center; as a literature
editor for Manuscript, Moravian's literary
magazine; and as a features editor for the
Comenian, the student newspaper. In addition,
my work as a music major has made me meticulous
and accurate—both vital traits in editing
manuscripts. Finally, I have already had some
professional editing experience through my
internship this semester with Taylor and Francis (Routledge) Publishing in New York.

Conclusion

I believe that my education and experience make   4
me a good candidate for your position. I have

enclosed my résumé, reference letters, information on Moravian's internship program, and
several writing samples for your consideration. You can contact me at work by phone at
(610) 625-6731 or by e-mail at <stkab02@moravian
.edu>. I will be available for an interview
anytime after September 23. I look forward to
meeting with you to discuss my qualifications.

Sincerely,

Kristy Bredin

Kristy Bredin

Points for Special Attention

Organization   Exemplification is ideally suited for letters of application. The only way that Kristy can support her claims about her qualifications for the internship at *Rolling Stone* is to illustrate her educational and
professional qualifications. For this reason, the body of her letter is divided
into two categories—her educational record and her editorial experience.
Each of the body paragraphs has a clear purpose and function. The second
paragraph contains a series of brief examples pertaining to Kristy's educational record. The third paragraph contains examples of her editorial experience. These examples tell the prospective employer what qualifies Kristy
for the internship. Within these two body paragraphs, she arranges her
examples in order of increasing importance. Because her practical experience as an editor relates directly to the position for which she is applying,
Kristy considers this her strongest point and presents it last.

Kristy ends her letter on a strong note, expressing her willingness to be
interviewed and giving the date after which she will be available for an
interview. Because people remember best what they read last, a strong conclusion is essential here, just as it is in other writing situations.

Persuasive Examples   To support a thesis convincingly, examples
should convey specific information, not generalizations. Saying "I am a
good student who is not afraid of responsibility" means very little. It is far
better to say, as Kristy does, "I have maintained a 3.3 average and have
served as both secretary and president of the Literary Society." A letter of
application should specifically show a prospective employer how your
strengths and background correspond to the employer's needs; well-
chosen examples can help you accomplish this.

Focus on Revision

After reading her letter, the students in Kristy's peer editing group identified several areas that they thought needed work. One student thought that Kristy should have mentioned her computer experience. She had taken a desktop publishing course as an elective and worked with publishing and graphics software when she was the features editor of the student newspaper. Kristy agreed that this expertise would make her a more attractive candidate for the job and thought that she could work these examples into her third paragraph. Another student asked Kristy to explain how her experience as secretary and president of the Literary Society relates to the job for which she is applying. If her purpose is to show that she is able to assume responsibility, she should say so; if it is to illustrate that she can supervise others, she should make this clear. Finally, a student suggested that she expand the discussion of her internship with Taylor and Francis Publishing in New York. Examples of her duties there would be persuasive because they would give her prospective employer a clear idea of her extensive experience as an editor. (A peer editing worksheet for exemplification can be found on the *Patterns for College Writing* Web site at <bedfordstmartins.com/patterns>.)

The following essay by Grace Ku was written for a composition class in response to the assignment "Write an essay about the worst job you (or someone you know) ever had."

Midnight

Introduction

It was eight o'clock, and like millions of other Americans, I was staring at the television set wondering what kind of lesson Mr. Huxtable was going to teach his children next on The Cosby Show. I was glued to the set like an average eleven-year-old couch potato while leisurely eating a can of cold Chef Boyardee spaghetti in my empty living room. As I watched the show, I gradually fell asleep on the floor fully clothed in a pair of blue jeans and a T-shirt, wondering when my parents would come home. Around midnight I woke up to a rustling noise: my parents had finally arrived from a

Thesis statement

long day at work. I could see in their tired faces the grief and hardship of working at a dry-cleaning plant.

Transitional paragraph provides background

Although my parents lived in the most technologically advanced country in the world,

1

2

their working conditions were like those of nineteenth-century factory workers. Because they were immigrants with little formal education and spoke broken English, they could get only physically demanding jobs. Therefore, they worked at a dry-cleaning plant that was as big as a factory, a place where smaller cleaners sent their clothes to be processed.

Series of brief examples: physical demands

My parents had to meet certain quotas.   3
Each day they had to clean and press several hundred garments — shirts, pants, and other clothing. By themselves, every day, they did the work of four laborers. The muscles of my mother's shoulders and arms became as hard as iron from working with the press, a difficult job even for a man. In addition to pressing, my father operated the washing machines. As a result, a strong odor of oil was permanently embedded in his work clothes.

Example: long hours

Not only were my parents' jobs physically   4
demanding, but they also required long hours. My parents went to work at five o'clock in the morning and came home anytime between nine o'clock at night and midnight. They worked over twelve hours daily at the dry-cleaning plant, where an eight-hour work day and labor unions did not exist. During that time, they were allowed to take only two ten- to twenty-minute breaks — one for lunch and one for dinner. They did not stop even when they were burned by the hot press or by the steam rising from it. The

Example: frequent burns

scars on their arms made it obvious that they worked at a dry-cleaning plant. Their burned skin would blister and later peel off, exposing their raw flesh. In time, these injuries would heal, but other burns would soon follow.

Example: low pay

Along with having to work overtime without   5
compensation and suffering injuries without treatment, my parents were paid below minimum wage. These two people (who did the work of

four) together received a paycheck equivalent to that of a single worker. They used this money to feed and care for a household of five people.

Conclusion   As my parents silently entered our home   6 around midnight, they did not have to complain about their jobs. I could see their anguish in their faces and their fatigue in the languid movements of their bodies. Their eyes looked

Restatement of thesis   toward me, saying, "We hate our jobs, but we work so our children will have better lives than we do."

Points for Special Attention

Organization   Grace Ku begins her introduction by describing herself as an eleven-year-old sitting on the floor watching television. At first, her behavior seems typical of many American children, but two things suggest problems: first, she is eating her cold dinner out of a can, and second, even though it is late in the evening, she is still waiting for her parents to return from work. This opening prepares readers for her thesis that her parents' jobs produce only grief and hardship.

In the body of her essay, Grace presents the examples that support her thesis statement. In paragraph 2, she sets the stage for the discussion to follow, explaining that her parents' working conditions were similar to those of nineteenth-century factory workers, and in paragraph 3 she presents a series of examples that illustrate how physically demanding her parents' jobs were. In the remaining body paragraphs, she gives three other examples to show how unpleasant the jobs were — how long her parents worked, how often they were injured, and how little they were paid. Grace concludes her essay by returning to the scene in her introduction, using a quotation that is intended to stay with her readers after they have finished the essay.

Enough Examples   Certainly no single example, no matter how graphic, could adequately support the thesis of this essay. To establish the pain and difficulty of her parents' jobs, Grace uses several examples. Although more examples could add depth to the essay, the ones she uses are vivid and compelling enough to reinforce her thesis that her parents had to endure great hardship to make a living.

Representative Examples   Grace selects examples that illustrate the full range of her subject. She draws from the daily experience of her parents and does not include examples that are atypical. She also includes enough detail so that her readers, who she assumes do not know much about working in a dry-cleaning plant, will understand her points. She does not, however, use so much detail that her readers get bogged down and lose interest.

Effective Examples   All of Grace's examples support her thesis statement. While developing these examples, she never loses sight of her main idea; consequently, she does not get sidetracked in irrelevant discussions. She also avoids the temptation to preach to her readers about the injustice of her parents' situation. By allowing her examples to speak for themselves, Grace presents a powerful portrait of her parents and their hardships.

Focus on Revision

After reading this draft, a peer critic thought Grace could go into more detail about her parents' situation and could explain her examples in more depth — perhaps writing about the quotas her parents had to meet or the other physical dangers of their jobs. Grace herself thought she should expand the discussion in paragraph 5 about her parents' low wages, perhaps anticipating questions some of her readers might have about working conditions. For example, was it legal for her parents' employer to require them to work overtime without compensation or to pay them less than the minimum wage? If not, how was the employer able to get away with such practices? Grace also thought she should move the information about her parents' work-related injuries from paragraph 4 to paragraph 3, where she discusses the physical demands of their jobs. Finally, she decided to follow the advice of another student and include comments by her parents to make their experiences more immediate to readers. (A peer editing worksheet for exemplification can be found on the *Patterns for College Writing* Web site at <bedfordstmartins.com/patterns>.)

The reading selections that appear in this chapter all depend on exemplification to explain and clarify, to add interest, or to persuade. The first selection, a visual text, is followed by questions designed to illustrate how exemplification can operate in visual form.

ALEX WILLIAMS, JOEL GORDON, CHARLES GATEWOOD, AND BOB DAEMMRICH*

❖ ## Four Tattoos (Photos)

Alex Williams, "~~Lisa~~, Karen"

Joel Gordon, "Rose"

Bob Daemmrich, "Jiminy Cricket"

Charles Gatewood, "Body Art"

---

*Photos shown clockwise from top left.

• • •

READING IMAGES

1. How would you describe each of the four tattoos pictured on the previous page? List the prominent features of each, and then write a sentence or two that describes each of them.

2. After studying the four pictures on the previous page (and reviewing your answer to question 1), write a one-sentence general statement that sums up your ideas about tattoos. For example, why do you think people get tattoos? Do you see them as a way for people to express themselves? As a way of demonstrating individuality? As a form of rebellion?

3. Do you think you have enough examples to support the general statement you made in paragraph 2? Explain.

JOURNAL ENTRY

Would you ever get a tattoo? Write a paragraph in which you answer this question. Use your answers to the questions above to support the main idea in your topic sentence. (If you have a tattoo, explain why you decided to get it.)

THEMATIC CONNECTIONS

- "Medium Ash Brown" (page 254)
- "My First Conk" (page 260)
- "The Embalming of Mr. Jones" (page 285)
- "The Wife-Beater" (page 521)

LAURENCE J. PETER AND RAYMOND HULL

❖ The Peter Principle

Laurence J. Peter (1919–1990), an academic and education specialist, and Raymond Hull (1919–1985), a humorist and playwright, collaborated on the 1969 best-seller *The Peter Principle: Why Things Always Go Wrong*. In the preface to the book, Hull explained that he had become increasingly appalled at the number of problems people experienced with businesses and organizations, from those of trifling significance (bills going to an old address despite numerous attempts to give the business a new one) to ones of catastrophic importance (bridges collapsing only a few years after construction). Dr. Peter, Hull discovered during an impromptu conversation, had the explanation for such widespread ineptitude: within any hierarchy, employees tend to be promoted to a level at which they are incompetent to perform the duties of the position. Within a short time of the publication of their book, the term *Peter Principle* had entered the language.

Background: During the 1950s, large corporations—touted as examples of an evolutionary leap forward in business organization structure—were widely perceived as models of efficiency. By the late 1960s, however, large bureaucracies seemed to be increasingly unresponsive, riddled with red tape, and demoralizing for workers. Peter and Hull's idea that most corporations were run by executives and managers who were simply out of their depth flew in the face of conventional 1950s wisdom and provided an explanation for 1960s corporate failings. More than forty years later, the meteoric rise and subsequent crash of many Web-based business ventures and the stunning demise of supposedly model corporations such as Enron and WorldCom suggests that little has changed.

When I was a boy I was taught that the men upstairs knew what they were doing. I was told, "Peter, the more you know, the further you go." So I stayed in school until I graduated from college and then went forth into the world clutching firmly these ideas and my new teaching certificate. During the first year of teaching I was upset to find that a number of teachers, school principals, supervisors, and superintendents appeared to be unaware of their professional responsibilities and incompetent in executing their duties. For example my principal's main concerns were that all window shades be at the same level, that classrooms should be quiet, and that no one step on or near the rose beds. The superintendent's main concerns were that no minority group, no matter how fanatical, should ever be offended and that all official forms be submitted on time. The children's education appeared farthest from the administrator's mind.

At first I thought this was a special weakness of the school system in which I taught so I applied for certification in another province. I filled out the special forms, enclosed the required documents, and complied will-ingly with all the red tape. Several weeks later, back came my application and all the documents!

No, there was nothing wrong with my credentials; the forms were cor-rectly filled out; an official departmental stamp showed that they had been received in good order. But an accompanying letter said, "The new regula-tions require that such forms cannot be accepted by the Department of Education unless they have been registered at the Post Office to ensure safe delivery. Will you please remail the forms to the Department, making sure to register them this time?"   3

I began to suspect that the local school system did not have a monop-oly on incompetence.   4

As I looked further afield, I saw that every organization contained a number of persons who could not do their jobs.   5

A Universal Phenomenon

Occupational incompetence is everywhere. Have you noticed it? Proba-bly we have all noticed it.   6

We see indecisive politicians posing as resolute statesmen and the "authoritative source" who blames his misinformation on "situational imponderables." Limitless are the public servants who are indolent and insolent, military commanders whose behavioral timidity belies their dreadnought rhetoric, and governors whose innate servility prevents their actually governing. In our sophistication, we virtually shrug aside the immoral cleric, corrupt judge, incoherent attorney, author who cannot write, and English teacher who cannot spell. At universities we see procla-mations authored by administrators whose own office communications are hopelessly muddled, and droning lectures from inaudible or incompre-hensible instructors.   7

Seeing incompetence at all levels of every hierarchy—political, legal, educational, and industrial—I hypothesized that the cause was some inherent feature of the rules governing the placement of employees. Thus began my serious study of the ways in which employees move upward through a hierarchy, and of what happens to them after promotion.   8

For my scientific data hundreds of case histories were collected. Here are three typical examples.   9

Municipal Government File, Case No. 17

J. S. Minion* was a maintenance foreman in the public works depart-ment of Excelsior City. He was a favorite of the senior officials at City Hall. They all praised his unfailing affability.   10

"I like Minion," said the superintendent of works. "He has good judg-ment and is always pleasant and agreeable."   11

---

*Some names have been changed, in order to protect the guilty.

This behavior was appropriate for Minion's position: he was not sup- 12
posed to make policy, so he had no need to disagree with his superiors.

The superintendent of works retired and Minion succeeded him. Min- 13
ion continued to agree with everyone. He passed to his foreman every suggestion that came from above. The resulting conflicts in policy, and the
continual changing of plans, soon demoralized the department. Complaints poured in from the Mayor and other officials, from taxpayers and
from the maintenance-workers' union.

Minion still says "Yes" to everyone, and carries messages briskly back 14
and forth between his superiors and his subordinates. Nominally a superintendent, he actually does the work of a messenger. The maintenance
department regularly exceeds its budget, yet fails to fulfill its program of
work. In short, Minion, a competent foreman, became an incompetent
superintendent.

Service Industries File, Case No. 3

E. Tinker was exceptionally zealous and intelligent as an apprentice at 15
G. Reece Auto Repair Inc., and soon rose to journeyman mechanic. In this
job he showed outstanding ability in diagnosing obscure faults, and endless patience in correcting them. He was promoted to foreman of the repair
shop.

But here his love of things mechanical and his perfectionism became 16
liabilities. He will undertake any job that he thinks looks interesting, no
matter how busy the shop may be. "We'll work it in somehow," he says.

He will not let a job go until he is fully satisfied with it. 17

He meddles constantly. He is seldom to be found at his desk. He is usu- 18
ally up to his elbows in a dismantled motor and while the man who should
be doing the work stands watching, other workmen sit around waiting to
be assigned new tasks. As a result the shop is always overcrowded with
work, always in a muddle, and delivery times are often missed.

Tinker cannot understand that the average customer cares little about 19
perfection—he wants his car back on time! He cannot understand that
most of his men are less interested in motors than in their pay checks. So
Tinker cannot get on with his customers or with his subordinates. He was
a competent mechanic, but is now an incompetent foreman.

Military File, Case No. 8

Consider the case of the late renowned General A. Goodwin. His 20
hearty, informal manner, his racy style of speech, his scorn for petty regula-
tions, and his undoubted personal bravery made him the idol of his men.
He led them to many well-deserved victories.

When Goodwin was promoted to field marshal he had to deal, not 21
with ordinary soldiers, but with politicians and allied generalissimos.

He would not conform to the necessary protocol. He could not turn 22
his tongue to the conventional courtesies and flatteries. He quarreled with
all the dignitaries and took to lying for days at a time, drunk and sulking,

in his trailer. The conduct of the war slipped out of his hands into those of his subordinates. He had been promoted to a position that he was incompetent to fill.

An Important Clue

In time I saw that all such cases had a common feature. The employee   23
had been promoted from a position of competence to a position of incompetence. I saw that, sooner or later, this could happen to every employee in every hierarchy.

Hypothetical Case File, Case No. 1

Suppose you own a pill-rolling factory, Perfect Pill Incorporated. Your   24
foreman pill roller dies of a perforated ulcer. You need a replacement. You naturally look among your rank-and-file pill rollers.

Miss Oval, Mrs. Cylinder, Mr. Ellipse, and Mr. Cube all show various   25
degrees of incompetence. They will naturally be ineligible for promotion. You will choose — other things being equal — your most competent pill roller, Mr. Sphere, and promote him to foreman.

Now suppose Mr. Sphere proves competent as foreman. Later, when   26
your general foreman, Legree, moves up to Works Manager, Sphere will be eligible to take his place.

If, on the other hand, Sphere is an incompetent foreman, he will get no   27
more promotion. He has reached what I call his "level of incompetence." He will stay there till the end of his career.

Some employees, like Ellipse and Cube, reach a level of incompetence   28
in the lowest grade and are never promoted. Some, like Sphere (assuming he is not a satisfactory foreman), reach it after one promotion.

E. Tinker, the automobile repair-shop foreman, reached his level of   29
incompetence on the third stage of the hierarchy. General Goodwin reached his level of incompetence at the very top of the hierarchy.

So my analysis of hundreds of cases of occupational incompetence led   30
me on to formulate *The Peter Principle:*

In a Hierarchy Every Employee Tends to Rise to His Level of Incompetence.

A New Science!

Having formulated the Principle, I discovered that I had inadvertently   31
founded a new science, hierarchiology, the study of hierarchies.

The term "hierarchy" was originally used to describe the system of   32
church government by priests graded into ranks. The contemporary meaning includes any organization whose members or employees are arranged in order of rank, grade, or class.

Hierarchiology, although a relatively recent discipline, appears to have   33
great applicability to the fields of public and private administration.

This Means You!

My Principle is the key to an understanding of all hierarchical systems, 34 and therefore to an understanding of the whole structure of civilization. A few eccentrics try to avoid getting involved with hierarchies, but everyone in business, industry, trade-unionism, politics, government, the armed forces, religion, and education is so involved. All of them are controlled by the Peter Principle.

Many of them, to be sure, may win a promotion or two, moving from 35 one level of competence to a higher level of competence. But competence in that new position qualifies them for still another promotion. For each individual, for *you*, for *me*, the final promotion is from a level of competence to a level of incompetence.*

So, given enough time—and assuming the existence of enough ranks 36 in the hierarchy—each employee rises to, and remains at, his level of incompetence. Peter's Corollary states:

In time, every post tends to be occupied by an employee who is incompetent to carry out its duties.

Who Turns the Wheels?

You will rarely find, of course, a system in which *every* employee has 37 reached his level of incompetence. In most instances, something is being done to further the ostensible purposes for which the hierarchy exists.

Work is accomplished by those employees who have not yet reached their level of incompetence.

• • •

COMPREHENSION

1. What things disillusioned Peter during his first year of teaching? What did he find out about organizations?

2. What is the Peter Principle? According to Peter and Hull, what happens when employees reach their "level of incompetence"?

3. What do Peter and Hull mean by *hierarchiology* (31)? How did hierarchiology lead Peter to the Peter Principle?

4. If the Peter Principle operates in hierarchies such as corporations, who does the work?

---

*The phenomena of "percussive sublimation" (commonly referred to as "being kicked upstairs") and of "the lateral arabesque" are not, as the casual observer might think, exceptions to the Principle. They are only pseudo-promotions.[. . .]

PURPOSE AND AUDIENCE

1. Is this essay aimed at a general or an expert audience? What led you to your conclusion?

2. What is the essay's thesis? At what point in the essay does it appear? Why do you think Peter and Hull wait so long to state it?

3. How serious are Peter and Hull? What words or phrases indicate whether their purpose is to instruct or to entertain — or both?

STYLE AND STRUCTURE

1. Why do you think Peter and Hull begin the essay with an example? Why do they present a series of brief examples before introducing the typical case histories?

2. Why do Peter and Hull say they collected hundreds of case histories for data? How are the three case histories analyzed here typical?

3. Does the reliance on hypothetical examples strengthen or weaken the writers' case? Explain.

4. Do Peter and Hull use a sufficient range of examples? Explain.

VOCABULARY PROJECTS

1. Define each of the following words as it is used in this selection.

imponderables (7)	incomprehensible (7)	protocol (22)
indolent (7)	hypothesized (8)	subordinates (22)
insolent (7)	hierarchy (8)	eccentrics (34)
dreadnought (7)	minion (10)	ostensible (37)
inaudible (7)	dismantled (18)	

2. Do Peter and Hull use **figures of speech** in their discussion? Why do you think they do or do not?

JOURNAL ENTRY

What examples of the Peter Principle have you encountered in your life?

WRITING WORKSHOP

1. Do Peter and Hull overstate their case? Write a letter to them in the form of an exemplification essay pointing out the weaknesses of their position.

2. Study a school, business, or organization with which you are familiar. Write an exemplification essay showing how the Peter Principle applies (or does not apply).

3. Do you know someone who has progressed to the highest level of his or her incompetence? Supporting your thesis with a single extended example, write an exemplification essay showing how the Peter Principle applies.

COMBINING THE PATTERNS

Peter and Hull use a series of narrative examples. What are the advantages and disadvantages of using **narration** here? Would other kinds of examples—such as statistics—have been more effective? Explain.

THEMATIC CONNECTIONS

- "Shooting an Elephant" (page 117)
- "Walt and Ray: Your Trusted Friends" (page 414)
- "The Company Man" (page 517)

DAVID J. BIRNBAUM

The Catbird Seat

David J. Birnbaum was born in 1963 in Brooklyn, New York, and is a graduate of New York University. A manager with AT&T, he also contributes essays to a number of publications. As he describes in the following essay, he lost the use of his legs in an auto accident and now uses a wheelchair to move about.

Background: Approximately 19 percent of Americans, representing about 49 million people, have some form of disability, and almost half of these are considered severely disabled. An estimated 15 percent (about 38 million people) have disabilities that limit their physical activity. The 1990 Americans with Disabilities Act, to which Birnbaum refers in paragraph 11, requires that reasonable accommodation be made for people with disabilities in areas of educational opportunity, employment, government services, and access to businesses open to the general public, and it further prohibits discrimination against people with disabilities. Noncompliance with the act can result in fines, and perceived noncompliance has resulted in a number of lawsuits, which have raised questions about who can legitimately be considered disabled and what, in fact, constitutes "reasonable" accommodation. As Birnbaum suggests, due to various ambiguities in the wording of the act and to some of the loopholes contained in it, many establishments are still not in full compliance; this remains a sore point for advocates of the disabled.

1   I wasn't in a hurry to get back to my hospital room, but I had a lot on my mind. I was adjusting to my new fate, quadriplegia. Besides, I had been waiting at least three minutes for the elevator, which in teen-age time is three years. When I heard the ding, I dashed into the car, unintentionally cutting off the handful of other riders.

2   "What's the big hurry?" a pregnant woman asked. An elderly Asian man chimed in: "Leave the young man alone. He's in a wheelchair!"

3   That was the first time I felt my new place in society. A few months later, my friend Roy and I were in the back of a ticketholders' line that was clogging 34th Street waiting to see *The Empire Strikes Back* at the Murray Hill cinema. Suddenly an usher appeared and asked us to follow him into the theater. Despite the drizzle, the other patrons didn't seem to mind that we were cutting ahead. I was the only one in line that had a chair to sit in. Yet I didn't have to wait. Thereafter, I began to cut ahead often. Cashing a check at Chase, I'd ignore the velvet ropes and go straight to a teller. Registering for classes at N.Y.U., I cut three lines in one day: department approval, course selection, and, finally, registrar payment. Older people who only a few months earlier would have ignored a teen-ager with long

hair began acting very friendly. Senior citizens still smile at me 17 years after I crashed my car in Park Slope, breaking my neck, just days before my 18th birthday. Are they trying to cheer me up? Maybe they just see me as nonthreatening. They're probably thinking, "This guy is less than half my age, but I can still beat him up."

Soon after leaving the hospital, I realized I could now break rules. I would sneak cans of beer into concerts at Madison Square Garden. At the queue where teen-agers are routinely patted down, the guards held up the process for me: "Please step back, we gotta wheelchair coming through!"   4

When I leave Staples, I tell the security guard that I need the plastic shopping basket to carry my goods to my van. He nods his head trustingly, on the assumption that I'll unload and return it. I have five of these red baskets in my hallway closet. I don't know what I'm going to do with them. I just get a kick driving them home.   5

Before I left Jamaica last January, I hid a box of Cuban cigars in my canvas case. As I passed through customs at Newark International Airport, a woman in a brown uniform looked at my two large bags suspiciously. Perusing the card I filled out on the plane, she asked, "Nothing to declare?"   6

"Nothing."   7

"What's the canvas bag for?"   8

"It's a portable handicap shower seat," I replied truthfully.   9

"Oh . . . I'm so sorry. Go ahead."   10

Cutting the lines at the Department of Motor Vehicles to renew my driver's license, getting out of speeding tickets and arriving late to work without a reprimand are my "even uppers" for my physical limitations and for the difficulties caused by establishments not complying with the Americans with Disabilities Act. I had to sit behind the last row in a theater, separated from my college friends, only once before I stopped being too proud to accept the senior citizens' discount offered by sympathetic employees. When the purser offered to bump me up into first class on that flight from Jamaica, I didn't say: "No, thank you. I've accepted my disability, I have a successful career and live independently. Please treat me like everyone else." I didn't care whether she was condescending, sympathizing or patronizing. I was just glad to be in "2B" sipping Chardonnay while I eyed the coach passengers frantically seeking space for their carry-on luggage and duty-free rum.   11

After sneaking my cigars through customs, I headed upstairs to get a taxi. Three carloads of tired travelers, dragging luggage with and without wheels, were waiting for a single elevator to arrive. I waited like an Olympic sprinter anticipating the starting gun. I began inching my wheelchair forward, but accidentally wheeled over some guy's foot.   12

"Oww!" he turned around, saw my wheelchair and then followed nervously with, "Oh, I'm ss . . . sss . . . sorry." He stepped to the side, leaving me perfectly positioned in front of the sliding aluminum doors. The "L" on   13 the display lighted, the ding went off, the doors opened, and I swiftly pushed my chair forward into the car.

"What's wrong with you?" A well-tanned girl asked me angrily. I looked her in the eye with cockiness, expecting my usual support from others. But it didn't come. 14

"Have some respect, for God's sake!" she continued, holding the door open for a middle-aged man with dark glasses and a white cane. 15

There in the elevator, as everyone looked at me in disgust, I learned the pecking order: blind trumps wheelchair; wheelchair trumps pregnant; pregnant trumps old; old trumps whatever is left. 16

• • •

COMPREHENSION

1. What "new place in society" does Birnbaum occupy after his accident (3)?

2. In what ways does Birnbaum take advantage of his new status?

3. According to Birnbaum, how are cutting in line, avoiding speeding tickets, and getting to work late his "even uppers" (11)?

4. What incident causes Birnbaum to realize that there are limitations to the advantages he gets from his disability?

PURPOSE AND AUDIENCE

1. What preconceptions about the disabled does Birnbaum assume his readers have? How can you tell?

2. Why does Birnbaum wait until paragraph 16 to state his thesis? Should he have stated it sooner? Explain.

3. Birnbaum is aiming his essay at a general audience. How would his essay be different if he were addressing health-care professionals? Other people with disabilities?

4. What is Birnbaum's purpose in writing this essay? For example, does he want to educate his readers? To persuade them? Or does he have some other purpose?

STYLE AND STRUCTURE

1. Birnbaum's essay begins with an example. Is this a good choice? Should he have included a more formal introduction?

2. All of Birnbaum's examples are drawn from his own experience. Does this reliance on personal experience make his essay less convincing than it would otherwise be? Explain.

3. How does Birnbaum arrange his examples? Is this arrangement effective? Explain.

4. In what ways are the ideas in Birnbaum's first example (1–3) echoed in his conclusion?

VOCABULARY PROJECTS

1. Define each of the following words as it is used in this selection.

   quadriplegia (1) patronizing (11)
   reprimand (11) Chardonnay (11)
   purser (11) trumps (16)
   condescending (11)

2. What terms does Birnbaum use to define his condition? What other terms could he use? What different connotations do these terms have?

3. To be in the *catbird seat* is to have a position of power or prominence. Why does Birnbaum use this term as his title? Is he being serious or ironic?

JOURNAL ENTRY

Do you think the disabled have advantages that others do not have? Do you think Birnbaum should have special privileges because of his disability?

WRITING WORKSHOP

1. Write a letter to Birnbaum in which you agree or disagree with his actions. Do you, for example, think that he should reject the benefits that are conferred on him because he is disabled? Or do you think that these benefits are legitimate compensation for his physical limitations?

2. A **stereotype** is an oversimplified concept or image. Write an essay in which you discuss three stereotypes of disabled people that many people share. How accurate are these stereotypes? What could (or should) be done to eliminate them?

3. Write an editorial for your school newspaper in which you discuss how your school could do more to help students with physical disabilities. To support your thesis, include specific examples of changes that could be made.

COMBINING THE PATTERNS

Choose four or five examples that Birnbaum uses in his essay. What other patterns of development does he use in presenting these examples? Does any single pattern predominate? If so, why?

THEMATIC CONNECTIONS

- "Words Left Unspoken" (page 153)
- "The Men We Carry in Our Minds" (page 456)
- "On Dumpster Diving" (page 660)

DAVID SEDARIS

❖

Make That a Double

Born in 1956 in Johnson City, New York, humorist David Sedaris grew up in North Carolina and attended Kent State University and several other schools before graduating from the Art Institute of Chicago. A diarist from an early age, he began performing from his diaries while in Chicago, where his work was discovered by a National Public Radio (NPR) producer. Sedaris's first nationwide performance was on NPR's *Morning Edition* in 1992, and his quirky story of working as a Christmas elf at Macy's department store was an immediate hit. He became an NPR regular, as well as a contributor to *Harper's* and *Details.* His first collection of essays, *Barrel Fever,* appeared in 1994 and was followed by three subsequent collections, most recently the best-selling *Me Talk Pretty One Day* (2000). Sedaris, who currently lives in Paris with his companion (the Hugh mentioned in this essay) won the Thurber Prize for American Humor in 2001.

Background: In the following selection from *Me Talk Pretty One Day,* Sedaris takes a comic look at the difficulties he encountered while trying to master the gender of French nouns. Although many French people speak English, they have a long tradition — extending back to the establishment of the French Academy in 1635 — of keeping the French language pure. Over the last fifty years, numerous attempts have been made to limit the number of Anglicisms that have crept into the language. In 1994, for example, a law was passed that required all products advertised in France to be translated into French terms. (The Ministry of Culture, for example, has mandated that *e-mail* be officially referred to as *message electronique.*) Groups such as the Association for the Defense of the French Language have even demanded that all information on Web sites that originate in France must be written in French. In light of this national preoccupation with language, Sedaris's concern for not mangling French grammar seems justified.

There are, I have noticed, two basic types of French spoken by Americans vacationing in Paris: the Hard Kind and the Easy Kind. The Hard Kind involves the conjugation of wily verbs and the science of placing them alongside various other words in order to form such sentences as "I go him say good afternoon" and "No, not to him I no go it him say now." 1

The second, less complicated form of French amounts to screaming English at the top of your lungs, much the same way you'd shout at a deaf person or the dog you thought you could train to stay off the sofa. Doubt and hesitation are completely unnecessary, as Easy French is rooted in the premise that, if properly packed, the rest of the world could fit within the confines of Reno, Nevada. The speaker carries no pocket dictionary and 2 never suffers the humiliation that inevitably comes with pointing to the menu and ordering the day of the week. With Easy French, eating out involves a simple "BRING ME A STEAK."

Having undertaken the study of Hard French, I'll overhear such requests and glare across the room, thinking, "That's *Mister* Steak to you, buddy." Of all the stumbling blocks inherent in learning this language, the greatest for me is the principle that each noun has a corresponding sex that affects both its articles and its adjectives. Because it is a female and lays eggs, a chicken is masculine. *Vagina* is masculine as well, while the word *masculinity* is feminine. Forced by the grammar to take a stand one way or the other, *hermaphrodite* is male and *indecisiveness* female.

I spent months searching for some secret code before I realized that common sense has nothing to do with it. *Hysteria, psychosis, torture, depression:* I was told that if something is unpleasant, it's probably feminine. This encouraged me, but the theory was blown by such masculine nouns as *murder, toothache,* and *Rollerblade.* I have no problem learning the words themselves, it's the sexes that trip me up and refuse to stick.

What's the trick to remembering that a sandwich is masculine? What qualities does it share with anyone in possession of a penis? I'll tell myself that a sandwich is masculine because if left alone for a week or two, it will eventually grow a beard. This works until it's time to order and I decide that because it sometimes loses its makeup, a sandwich is undoubtedly feminine.

I just can't manage to keep my stories straight. Hoping I might learn through repetition, I tried using gender in my everyday English. "Hi, guys," I'd say, opening a new box of paper clips, or "Hey, Hugh, have you seen my belt? I can't find her anywhere." I invented personalities for the objects on my dresser and set them up on blind dates. When things didn't work out with my wallet, my watch drove a wedge between my hairbrush and my lighter. The scenarios reminded me of my youth, when my sisters and I would enact epic dramas with our food. Ketchup-wigged french fries would march across our plates, engaging in brief affairs or heated disputes over carrot coins while burly chicken legs guarded the perimeter, ready to jump in should things get out of hand. Sexes were assigned at our discretion and were subject to change from one night to the next — unlike here, where the corncob and the string bean remain locked in their rigid masculine roles. Say what you like about southern social structure, but at least in North Carolina a hot dog is free to swing both ways.

Nothing in France is free from sexual assignment. I was leafing through the dictionary, trying to complete a homework assignment, when I noticed the French had prescribed genders for the various land masses and natural wonders we Americans had always thought of as sexless. Niagara Falls is feminine and, against all reason, the Grand Canyon is masculine. Georgia and Florida are female, but Montana and Utah are male. New England is a she, while the vast area we call the Midwest is just one big guy.

I wonder whose job it was to assign these sexes in the first place. Did he do his work right there in the sanitarium, or did they rent him a little office where he could get away from all the noise?

There are times when you can swallow the article and others when it   8
must be clearly pronounced, as the word has two different meanings, one masculine and the other feminine. It should be fairly obvious that I cooked an omelette in a frying pan rather than in a wood stove, but it bothers me to make the same mistakes over and over again. I wind up exhausting the listener before I even get to the verb.

My confidence hit a new low when my friend Adeline told me that   9
French children often make mistakes, but never with the sex of their nouns. "It's just something we grow up with," she said. "We hear the gender once, and then think of it as part of the word. There's nothing to it."

It's a pretty grim world when I can't even feel superior to a toddler.   10
Tired of embarrassing myself in front of two-year-olds, I've started referring to everything in the plural, which can get expensive but has solved a lot of my problems. In saying *a melon,* you need to use the masculine article. In saying *the melons,* you use the plural article, which does not reflect gender and is the same for both the masculine and the feminine. Ask for two or ten or three hundred melons, and the number lets you off the hook by replacing the article altogether. A masculine kilo of feminine tomatoes presents a sexual problem easily solved by asking for two kilos of tomatoes. I've started using the plural while shopping, and Hugh has started using it in our cramped kitchen, where he stands huddled in the corner, shouting, "What do we need with four pounds of tomatoes?"

I answer that I'm sure we can use them for something. The only hard   11
part is finding someplace to put them. They won't fit in the refrigerator, as I filled the last remaining shelf with the two chickens I bought from the butcher the night before, forgetting that we were still working our way through a pair of pork roasts the size of Duraflame logs. "We could put them next to the radios," I say, "or grind them for sauce in one of the blenders. Don't get so mad. Having four pounds of tomatoes is better than having no tomatoes at all, isn't it?"

Hugh tells me that the market is off-limits until my French improves.   12
He's pretty steamed, but I think he'll get over it when he sees the CD players I got him for his birthday.

•   •   •

COMPREHENSION

1. According to Sedaris, what are the two kinds of French spoken by Americans in Paris? What is the difference between the two?

2. Why does Sedaris find the fact that every noun in French is either masculine or feminine a major "stumbling block" (3)?

3. What strategies does Sedaris use to try to remember the gender of nouns? Are they successful?

4. Why does Sedaris find the pronunciation of French nouns difficult?

5. Why does Sedaris begin referring to everything in the plural? How does this strategy lessen his embarrassment?

PURPOSE AND AUDIENCE

1. At whom are Sedaris's comments aimed? Those who know French? Those who speak only English? Both? How can you tell?

2. What is the thesis of this essay? At what point in the essay is it stated?

3. Do you think Sedaris has a serious message to communicate, or do you think his essay's purpose is simply to entertain his readers? Explain.

STYLE AND STRUCTURE

1. What information does Sedaris provide in his introduction? Why do you think he provides this information?

2. Does Sedaris ever establish a connection between "Hard French" and the gender of French nouns? Should he have made this relationship clearer?

3. What points does Sedaris make in each of his body paragraphs? How do the examples in these paragraphs help him to support these points?

4. Do you think Sedaris uses enough examples? Would additional examples have been more persuasive?

5. Sedaris uses a two-sentence paragraph to end his essay. How effective is this conclusion? What alternatives can you suggest?

VOCABULARY PROJECTS

1. Define each of the following words as it is used in this selection.

   humiliation (2)   indecisiveness (3)
   inevitably (2)   hysteria (4)
   inherent (3)   discretion (6)
   hermaphrodite (3)   sanitarium (7)

2. Although nouns in English do not have gender the way French nouns do, certain English nouns do have male or female connotations. Make a list of twenty occupational nouns — ten that you consider male and ten that you consider female. Then, for each noun, decide if there is a gender-neutral equivalent (for example, *letter carrier* for *mailman* or *server* for *waiter* or *waitress*). What might be gained or lost by substituting the gender-neutral term for the original term?

JOURNAL ENTRY

Assume that you are learning to speak English as a second language. What aspect of the language do you think would give you the most trouble? Why?

WRITING WORKSHOP

1. Review the list of occupational terms that you generated for Vocabulary Project 2 above. Then, write an essay in which you discuss whether gender-neutral terms should be substituted for terms that have gender associations. Would our society be different if everyone used only gender-neutral nouns? How?

2. Write about your effort to learn a foreign language. Give examples of the things you found especially difficult. Explain why and how you did (or did not) overcome your difficulties. (If English is not your first language, write about the difficulties English presented when you first started speaking it.)

3. List the words and expressions that you use only at work, only at home, and only with your friends. (These may be **slang, jargon,** or technical terms.) Then, write an essay that examines how your different uses of English reflect the roles you play in different situations.

COMBINING THE PATTERNS

The essay's primary pattern of development is **exemplification.** Does Sedaris use any other patterns? How would a paragraph of **comparison and contrast**—comparing French to English—help support his thesis? Do you think that Sedaris should have included such a paragraph? Why or why not?

THEMATIC CONNECTIONS

- "Sex, Lies, and Conversation" (page 407)
- "Mother Tongue" (page 462)
- "The Wife-Beater" (page 521)
- "Strange Tools" (page 697)

BRENT STAPLES

❖

Just Walk On By: A Black Man Ponders His Power to Alter Public Space

Born in Chester, Pennsylvania, in 1951, Brent Staples received his bachelor's degree from Widener University in 1973 and his doctorate in psychology from the University of Chicago in 1982. Staples joined the staff of the *New York Times* in 1985, writing on culture and politics, and he became a member of its editorial board in 1990. His columns appear regularly on the paper's op-ed pages. Staples has also written a memoir, *Parallel Time: Growing Up in Black and White* (1994), about his escape from the poverty and violence of his childhood.

Background: "Just Walk On By" originally appeared in *Ms.* magazine in 1986. In it, Staples reflects on the many times people have reacted to him as a potential threat solely because of his gender and the color of his skin. His essay can be read in light of current controversies surrounding racial profiling of criminal suspects, which occurs, according to the American Civil Liberties Union, "when the police target someone for investigation on the basis of that person's race, national origin, or ethnicity. Examples of profiling are the use of race to determine which drivers to stop for minor traffic violations ('driving while black') and the use of race to determine which motorists or pedestrians to search for contraband." Although law enforcement officials have often denied that they profile criminals solely on the basis of race, a number of studies have shown a high prevalence of police profiling directed primarily at African and Hispanic Americans. A number of states have enacted laws barring racial profiling, and some people have won court settlements when they objected to being interrogated by police solely because of their race. Following the terrorist attacks of September 11, 2001, people of Arab descent have been targets of heightened interest at airports and elsewhere, which has added to the continuing controversy surrounding the association of criminal behavior with particular ethnic groups.

My first victim was a woman—white, well dressed, probably in her early twenties. I came upon her late one evening on a deserted street in Hyde Park, a relatively affluent neighborhood in an otherwise mean, impoverished section of Chicago. As I swung onto the avenue behind her, there seemed to be a discreet, uninflammatory distance between us. Not so. She cast back a worried glance. To her, the youngish black man—a broad six feet two inches with a beard and billowing hair, both hands shoved into the pockets of a bulky military jacket—seemed menacingly close. After a few more quick glimpses, she picked up her pace and was soon running in earnest. Within seconds she disappeared into a cross street.

That was more than a decade ago. I was 22 years old, a graduate stu-   2
dent newly arrived at the University of Chicago. It was in the echo of that
terrified woman's footfalls that I first began to know the unwieldy inheritance I'd come into—the ability to alter public space in ugly ways. It was
clear that she thought herself the quarry of a mugger, rapist, or worse. Suffering a bout of insomnia, however, I was stalking sleep, not defenseless
wayfarers. As a softy who is scarcely able to take a knife to a raw chicken—
let alone hold it to a person's throat—I was surprised, embarrassed, and
dismayed all at once. Her flight made me feel like an accomplice in tyranny.
It also made it clear that I was indistinguishable from the muggers who
occasionally seeped into the area from the surrounding ghetto. That first
encounter, and those that followed, signified that a vast, unnerving gulf lay
between nighttime pedestrians—particularly women—and me. And I soon
gathered that being perceived as dangerous is a hazard in itself. I only
needed to turn a corner into a dicey situation, or crowd some frightened,
armed person in a foyer somewhere, or make an errant move after being
pulled over by a policeman. Where fear and weapons meet—and they often
do in urban America—there is always the possibility of death.

In that first year, my first away from my hometown, I was to become   3
thoroughly familiar with the language of fear. At dark, shadowy intersections in Chicago, I could cross in front of a car stopped at a traffic light and
elicit the *thunk, thunk, thunk, thunk* of the driver—black, white, male, or
female—hammering down the door locks. On less traveled streets after
dark, I grew accustomed to but never comfortable with people who crossed
to the other side of the street rather than pass me. Then there were the
standard unpleasantries with police, doormen, bouncers, cab drivers, and
others whose business it is to screen out troublesome individuals *before*
there is any nastiness.

I moved to New York nearly two years ago and I have remained an avid   4
night walker. In central Manhattan, the near-constant crowd cover mini-
mizes tense one-on-one street encounters. Elsewhere—visiting friends in
SoHo, where sidewalks are narrow and tightly spaced buildings shut out
the sky—things can get very taut indeed.

Black men have a firm place in New York mugging literature. Norman   5
Podhoretz in his famed (or infamous) 1963 essay, "My Negro Problem—
and Ours," recalls growing up in terror of black males; they "were tougher
than we were, more ruthless," he writes—and as an adult on the Upper
West Side of Manhattan, he continues, he cannot constrain his nervous-
ness when he meets black men on certain streets. Similarly, a decade later,
the essayist and novelist Edward Hoagland extols a New York where once
"Negro bitterness bore down mainly on other Negroes." Where some see
mere panhandlers, Hoagland sees "a mugger who is clearly screwing up his
nerve to do more than just *ask* for money." But Hoagland has "the New
Yorker's quick-hunch posture for broken-field maneuvering," and the bad
guy swerves away.

I often witness that "hunch posture," from women after dark on the warrenlike streets of Brooklyn where I live. They seem to set their faces on neutral and, with their purse straps strung across their chests bandolier style, they forge ahead as though bracing themselves against being tackled. I understand, of course, that the danger they perceive is not a hallucination. Women are particularly vulnerable to street violence, and young black males are drastically overrepresented among the perpetrators of that violence. Yet these truths are no solace against the kind of alienation that comes of being ever the suspect, against being set apart, a fearsome entity with whom pedestrians avoid making eye contact. 6

It is not altogether clear to me how I reached the ripe old age of 22 without being conscious of the lethality nighttime pedestrians attributed to me. Perhaps it was because in Chester, Pennsylvania, the small, angry industrial town where I came of age in the 1960s, I was scarcely noticeable against a backdrop of gang warfare, street knifings, and murders. I grew up one of the good boys, had perhaps a half-dozen fist fights. In retrospect, my shyness of combat has clear sources. 7

Many things go into the making of a young thug. One of those things is the consummation of the male romance with the power to intimidate. An infant discovers that random flailings send the baby bottle flying out of the crib and crashing to the floor. Delighted, the joyful babe repeats those motions again and again, seeking to duplicate the feat. Just so, I recall the points at which some of my boyhood friends were finally seduced by the perception of themselves as tough guys. When a mark cowered and surrendered his money without resistance, myth and reality merged—and paid off. It is, after all, only manly to embrace the power to frighten and intimidate. We, as men, are not supposed to give an inch of our lane on the highway; we are to seize the fighter's edge in work and in play and even in love; we are to be valiant in the face of hostile forces. 8

Unfortunately, poor and powerless young men seem to take all this nonsense literally. As a boy, I saw countless tough guys locked away; I have since buried several, too. They were babies, really—a teenage cousin, a brother of 22, a childhood friend in his mid-twenties—all gone down in episodes of bravado played out in the streets. I came to doubt the virtues of intimidation early on. I chose, perhaps even unconsciously, to remain a shadow—timid, but a survivor. 9

The fearsomeness mistakenly attributed to me in public places often has a perilous flavor. The most frightening of these confusions occurred in the late 1970s and early 1980s when I worked as a journalist in Chicago. One day, rushing into the office of a magazine I was writing for with a deadline story in hand, I was mistaken for a burglar. The office manager called security and, with an ad hoc posse, pursued me through the labyrinthine halls, nearly to my editor's door. I had no way of proving who I was. I could only move briskly toward the company of someone who knew me. 10

Another time I was on assignment for a local paper and killing time 11
before an interview. I entered a jewelry store on the city's affluent Near
North Side. The proprietor excused herself and returned with an enormous red Doberman pinscher straining at the end of a leash. She stood,
the dog extended toward me, silent to my questions, her eyes bulging
nearly out of her head. I took a cursory look around, nodded, and bade her
good night. Relatively speaking, however, I never fared as badly as another
black male journalist. He went to nearby Waukegan, Illinois, a couple of
summers ago to work on a story about a murderer who was born there.
Mistaking the reporter for the killer, police hauled him from his car at
gunpoint and but for his press credentials would probably have tried to
book him. Such episodes are not uncommon. Black men trade tales like
this all the time.

In "My Negro Problem—and Ours," Podhoretz writes that the hatred 12
he feels for blacks makes itself known to him through a variety of
avenues—one being his discomfort with that "special brand of paranoid
touchiness" to which he says blacks are prone. No doubt he is speaking
here of black men. In time, I learned to smother the rage I felt at so often
being taken for a criminal. Not to do so would surely have led to madness—via that special "paranoid touchiness" that so annoyed Podhoretz at
the time he wrote the essay.

I began to take precautions to make myself less threatening. I move 13
about with care, particularly late in the evening. I give a wide berth to nervous people on subway platforms during the wee hours, particularly when
I have exchanged business clothes for jeans. If I happen to be entering a
building behind some people who appear skittish, I may walk by, letting
them clear the lobby before I return, so as not to seem to be following
them. I have been calm and extremely congenial on those rare occasions
when I've been pulled over by the police.

And on late-evening constitutionals along streets less traveled by, I 14
employ what has proved to be an excellent tension-reducing measure: I
whistle melodies from Beethoven and Vivaldi and the more popular classical composers. Even steely New Yorkers hunching toward nighttime desti-
nations seem to relax, and occasionally they even join in the tune. Virtually
everybody seems to sense that a mugger wouldn't be warbling bright,
sunny selections from Vivaldi's *Four Seasons*. It is my equivalent of the cow-
bell that hikers wear when they know they are in bear country.

• • •

COMPREHENSION

1. Why does Staples characterize the woman he encounters in paragraph 1
   as a "victim"?

2. What does Staples mean when he says he has the power to "alter public
   space" (2)?

3. Why does Staples walk the streets at night?

4. What things does Staples say go "into the making of a young thug" (8)? According to Staples, why are young, poor, and powerless men especially likely to become thugs?

5. In what ways does Staples attempt to make himself less threatening?

PURPOSE AND AUDIENCE

1. What is Staples's thesis? Does he state it or imply it?

2. Does Staples use logic, emotion, or a combination of the two to appeal to his readers? How appropriate is his strategy?

3. What preconceptions does Staples assume his audience has? In what ways does he challenge these preconceptions?

4. What is Staples trying to accomplish with his first sentence? Do you think he succeeds? Why or why not?

STYLE AND STRUCTURE

1. Why does Staples mention Norman Podhoretz? Could he make the same points without referring to Podhoretz's essay?

2. Staples begins his essay with an anecdote. How effective is this strategy? Do you think another opening strategy would be more effective? Explain.

3. Does Staples present enough examples to support his thesis? Are they representative? Would other types of examples be more convincing? Explain.

4. In what order does Staples present his examples? Would another order be more effective? Explain.

VOCABULARY PROJECTS

1. Define each of the following words as it is used in this selection.

discreet (1)	quarry (2)	constrain (5)
uninflammatory (1)	insomnia (2)	bravado (9)
billowing (1)	wayfarers (2)	constitutionals (14)

2. In his essay, Staples uses the word *thug*. List as many synonyms as you can for this word. Do these words convey the same idea, or are there differences in connotation? Explain.

JOURNAL ENTRY

Have you ever been in a situation such as the ones Staples describes, where you perceived someone (or someone perceived you) as threatening? How did you react? After reading Staples's essay, do you think you would react the same way now?

WRITING WORKSHOP

1. Use your journal entry to help you write an essay in which you use an extended example to support this statement: "When walking alone at night, you can (or cannot) be too careful."

2. Relying on examples from your own experience, write an essay in which you discuss what part you think race plays in people's reactions to Staples. Do you think his perceptions are accurate?

3. How accurate is Staples's observation concerning the "male romance with the power to intimidate" (8)? What does he mean by this statement? What examples from your own experience support (or do not support) the idea that this "romance" is an element of male upbringing in our society?

COMBINING THE PATTERNS

In paragraph 8, Staples uses **cause and effect** to demonstrate what goes "into the making of a young thug." Would several **examples** have better illustrated how a youth becomes a thug?

THEMATIC CONNECTIONS

- "The 'Black Table' Is Still There" (page 340)
- "Brains versus Brawn" (page 371)
- "The Men We Carry in Our Minds" (page 456)
- "The Threat of National ID" (page 586)

JONATHAN KOZOL

❖
The Human Cost of an Illiterate Society

Jonathan Kozol was born in Boston in 1936 and graduated from Harvard University in 1958. After studying in England, he began teaching in public schools in Boston's inner city. His experiences there provided the source material for his first book, *Death at an Early Age* (1967), a startling indictment of the system's failure to provide an adequate education to poor, mostly minority children. In the years since, Kozol—himself a child of privilege—has continued to use firsthand experience to write about the poorest in our society, sometimes angrily, sometimes movingly, but always with respect and sympathy. His books have focused on homelessness, on the inequities between schools in poor neighborhoods and those in affluent ones, and, most recently, on the lives of children in a South Bronx housing project.

Background: Kozol's *Illiterate America* (1985) examines the human and financial costs of illiteracy in the United States. The book estimates that more than 35 million Americans read below the level needed to function in society. A comprehensive survey published in 1993 seemed to support Kozol's estimates, reporting that more than 40 million adults—as much as 23 percent of the population—scored at the lowest of five levels on a series of standardized reading tests. Some critics have claimed that these results are misleading because the lowest level included some people who could not read at all and others who were functional readers who could perform some reading tasks required at higher levels. Still, literacy in the United States remains a matter of concern. In a recent report by the Educational Testing Service, analysis of the results of the 1993 U.S. study and a later international literacy study found that the United States ranked only twelfth in terms of literacy among twenty comparably wealthy nations and ranked first or second in terms of inequality in the distribution of literacy skills.

PRECAUTIONS. READ BEFORE USING.
Poison: Contains sodium hydroxide (caustic soda-lye).
Corrosive: Causes severe eye and skin damage, may cause blindness.
Harmful or fatal if swallowed.
If swallowed, give large quantities of milk or water.
Do not induce vomiting.
Important: Keep water out of can at all times to prevent contents from violently erupting. . . .
                              – Warning on a can of Drano

Questions of literacy, in Socrates' belief, must at length be judged   1
as matters of morality. Socrates could not have had in mind the moral

compromise peculiar to a nation like our own. Some of our Founding Fathers did, however, have this question in their minds. One of the wisest of those Founding Fathers (one who may not have been most compassionate but surely was more prescient than some of his peers) recognized the special dangers that illiteracy would pose to basic equity in the political construction that he helped to shape.

"A people who mean to be their own governors," James Madison wrote, "must arm themselves with the power knowledge gives. A popular government without popular information or the means of acquiring it, is but a prologue to a farce or a tragedy, or perhaps both."   2

Tragedy looms larger than farce in the United States today. Illiterate citizens seldom vote. Those who do are forced to cast a vote of questionable worth. They cannot make informed decisions based on serious print information. Sometimes they can be alerted to their interests by aggressive voter education. More frequently, they vote for a face, a smile, or a style, not for a mind or character or body of beliefs.   3

The number of illiterate adults exceeds by 16 million the entire vote cast for the winner in the 1980 presidential contest. If even one third of all illiterates could vote, and read enough and do sufficient math to vote in their self-interest, Ronald Reagan would not likely have been chosen president. There is, of course, no way to know for sure. We do know this: Democracy is a mendacious term when used by those who are prepared to countenance the forced exclusion of one third of our electorate. So long as 60 million people are denied significant participation, the government is neither of, nor for, nor by, the people. It is a government, at best, of those two-thirds whose wealth, skin color, or parental privilege allows them opportunity to profit from the provocation and instruction of the written word.   4

The undermining of democracy in the United States is one "expense" that sensitive Americans can easily deplore because it represents a contradiction that endangers citizens of all political positions. The human price is not so obvious at first.   5

Since I first immersed myself within this work I have often had the following dream: I find that I am in a railroad station or a large department store within a city that is utterly unknown to me and where I cannot understand the printed words. None of the signs or symbols is familiar. Everything looks strange: like mirror writing of some kind. Gradually I understand that I am in the Soviet Union. All the letters on the walls around me are Cyrillic. I look for my pocket dictionary but I find that it has been mislaid. Where have I left it? Then I recall that I forgot to bring it with me when I packed my bags in Boston. I struggle to remember the name of my hotel. I try to ask somebody for directions. One person stops and looks at me in a peculiar way. I lose the nerve to ask. At last I reach into my wallet for an ID card. The card is missing. Have I lost it? Then I remember that my card was confiscated for some reason, many years before. Around this point, I wake up in a panic.   6

This panic is not so different from the misery that millions of adult   7
illiterates experience each day within the course of their routine existence
in the U.S.A.

Illiterates cannot read the menu in a restaurant.   8

They cannot read the cost of items on the menu in the *window* of the   9
restaurant before they enter.

Illiterates cannot read the letters that their children bring home from   10
their teachers. They cannot study school department circulars that tell them
of the courses that their children must be taking if they hope to pass the
SAT exams. They cannot help with homework. They cannot write a letter
to the teacher. They are afraid to visit in the classroom. They do not want
to humiliate their child or themselves.

Illiterates cannot read instructions on a bottle of prescription medi-   11
cine. They cannot find out when a medicine is past the year of safe consumption; nor can they read of allergenic risks, warnings to diabetics, or
the potential sedative effect of certain kinds of nonprescription pills. They
cannot observe preventive health care admonitions. They cannot read
about "the seven warning signs of cancer" or the indications of blood-
sugar fluctuations or the risks of eating certain foods that aggravate the
likelihood of cardiac arrest.

Illiterates live, in more than literal ways, an uninsured existence. They   12
cannot understand the written details on a health insurance form. They
cannot read the waivers that they sign preceding surgical procedures. Several women I have known in Boston have entered a slum hospital with the
intention of obtaining a tubal ligation and have emerged a few days later
after having been subjected to a hysterectomy. Unaware of their rights, in-
cognizant of jargon, intimidated by the unfamiliar air of fear and atmosphere of ether that so many of us find oppressive in the confines even of
the most attractive and expensive medical facilities, they have signed their
names to documents they could not read and which nobody, in the hectic
situation that prevails so often in those overcrowded hospitals that serve
the urban poor, had even bothered to explain.

Childbirth might seem to be the last inalienable right of any female   13
citizen within a civilized society. Illiterate mothers, as we shall see, already
have been cheated of the power to protect their progeny against the likelihood of demolition in deficient public schools and, as a result, against
the verbal servitude within which they themselves exist. Surgical denial of
the right to bear that child in the first place represents an ultimate denial,
an unspeakable metaphor, a final darkness that denies even the twilight
gleamings of our own humanity. What greater violation of our biological,
our biblical, our spiritual humanity could possibly exist than that which
takes place nightly, perhaps hourly these days, within such overburdened
and benighted institutions as the Boston City Hospital? Illiteracy has many
costs; few are so irreversible as this.

Even the roof above one's head, the gas or other fuel for heating that   14
protects the residents of northern city slums against the threat of illness in

the winter months become uncertain guarantees. Illiterates cannot read the lease that they must sign to live in an apartment which, too often, they cannot afford. They cannot manage check accounts and therefore seldom pay for anything by mail. Hours and entire days of difficult travel (and the cost of bus or other public transit) must be added to the real cost of whatever they consume. Loss of interest on the check accounts they do not have, and could not manage if they did, must be regarded as another of the excess costs paid by the citizen who is excluded from the common instruments of commerce in a numerate society.

"I couldn't understand the bills," a woman in Washington, D.C., 15 reports, "and then I couldn't write the checks to pay them. We signed things we didn't know what they were."

Illiterates cannot read the notices that they receive from welfare offices 16 or from the IRS. They must depend on word-of-mouth instruction from the welfare worker—or from other persons whom they have good reason to mistrust. They do not know what rights they have, what deadlines and requirements they face, what options they might choose to exercise. They are half-citizens. Their rights exist in print but not in fact.

Illiterates cannot look up numbers in a telephone directory. Even if 17 they can find the names of friends, few possess the sorting skills to make use of the yellow pages; categories are bewildering and trade names are beyond decoding capabilities for millions of nonreaders. Even the emergency numbers listed on the first page of the phone book—"Ambulance," "Police," and "Fire"—are too frequently beyond the recognition of nonreaders.

Many illiterates cannot read the admonition on a pack of cigarettes. 18 Neither the Surgeon General's warning nor its reproduction on the package can alert them to the risks. Although most people learn by word of mouth that smoking is related to a number of grave physical disorders, they do not get the chance to read the detailed stories which can document this danger with the vividness that turns concern into determination to resist. They can see the handsome cowboy or the slim Virginia lady lighting up a filter cigarette; they cannot heed the words that tell them that this product is (not "may be") dangerous to their health. Sixty million men and women are condemned to be the unalerted, high-risk candidates for cancer.

Illiterates do not buy "no-name" products in the supermarkets. They 19 must depend on photographs or the familiar logos that are printed on the packages of brand-name groceries. The poorest people, therefore, are denied the benefits of the least costly products.

Illiterates depend almost entirely upon label recognition. Many labels, 20 however, are not easy to distinguish. Dozens of different kinds of Campbell's soup appear identical to the nonreader. The purchaser who cannot read and does not dare to ask for help, out of the fear of being stigmatized (a fear which is unfortunately realistic), frequently comes home with something which she never wanted and her family never tasted.

Illiterates cannot read instructions on a pack of frozen food. Packages   21
sometimes provide an illustration to explain the cooking preparations; but
illustrations are of little help to someone who must "boil water, drop the
food — *within* its plastic wrapper — in the boiling water, wait for it to sim-
mer, instantly remove."

Even when labels are seemingly clear, they may be easily mistaken. A   22
woman in Detroit brought home a gallon of Crisco for her children's dinner. She thought that she had bought the chicken that was pictured on the
label. She had enough Crisco now to last a year — but no more money to go
back and buy the food for dinner.

Recipes provided on the packages of certain staples sometimes tempt   23
a semiliterate person to prepare a meal her children have not tasted. The
longing to vary the uniform and often starchy content of low-budget meals
provided to the family that relies on food stamps commonly leads to ruin-
ous results. Scarce funds have been wasted and the food must be thrown
out. The same applies to distribution of food-surplus produce in emergency conditions. Government inducements to poor people to "explore the
ways" by which to make a tasty meal from tasteless noodles, surplus
cheese, and powdered milk are useless to nonreaders. Intended as benevo-
lent advice, such recommendations mock reality and foster deeper feelings
of resentment and of inability to cope. (Those, on the other hand, who cautiously refrain from "innovative" recipes in preparation of their children's
meals must suffer the opprobrium of "laziness," "lack of imagination. . . .")

Illiterates cannot travel freely. When they attempt to do so, they en-   24
counter risks that few of us can dream of. They cannot read traffic signs
and, while they often learn to recognize and to decipher symbols, they cannot manage street names which they haven't seen before. The same is true
for bus and subway stops. While ingenuity can sometimes help a man or
woman to discern directions from familiar landmarks, buildings, cemeter-
ies, churches, and the like, most illiterates are virtually immobilized. They
seldom wander past the streets and neighborhoods they know. Geographical paralysis becomes a bitter metaphor for their entire existence. They are
immobilized in almost every sense we can imagine. They can't move up.
They can't move out. They cannot see beyond. Illiterates may take an oral
test for drivers' permits in most sections of America. It is a questionable
concession. Where will they go? How will they get there? How will they get
home? Could it be that some of us might like it better if they stayed where
they belong?

Travel is only one of many instances of circumscribed existence.   25
Choice, in almost all of its facets, is diminished in the life of an illiterate
adult. Even the printed TV schedule, which provides most people with the
luxury of preselection, does not belong within the arsenal of options in
illiterate existence. One consequence is that the viewer watches only what
appears at moments when he happens to have time to turn the switch.
Another consequence, a lot more common, is that the TV set remains in
operation night and day. Whatever the program offered at the hour when

he walks into the room will be the nutriment that he accepts and swallows. Thus, to passivity, is added frequency — indeed, almost uninterrupted continuity. Freedom to select is no more possible here than in the choice of home or surgery or food.

"You don't choose," said one illiterate woman. "You take your wishes 26 from somebody else." Whether in perusal of a menu, selection of highways, purchase of groceries, or determination of affordable enjoyment, illiterate Americans must trust somebody else: a friend, a relative, a stranger on the street, a grocery clerk, a TV copywriter.

"All of our mail we get, it's hard for her to read. Settin' down and writ- 27 ing a letter, she can't do it. Like if we get a bill . . . we take it over to my sister-in-law. . . . My sister-in-law reads it."

Billing agencies harass poor people for the payment of the bills for 28 purchases that might have taken place six months before. Utility companies offer an agreement for a staggered payment schedule on a bill past due. "You have to trust them," one man said. Precisely for this reason, you end up by trusting no one and suspecting everyone of possible deceit. A submerged sense of distrust becomes the corollary to a constant need to trust. "They are cheating me. . . . I have been tricked. . . . I do not know. . . ."

Not knowing: This is a familiar theme. Not knowing the right word for 29 the right thing at the right time is one form of subjugation. Not knowing the world that lies concealed behind those words is a more terrifying feeling. The longitude and latitude of one's existence are beyond all easy apprehension. Even the hard, cold stars within the firmament above one's head begin to mock the possibilities for self-location. Where am I? Where did I come from? Where will I go?

"I've lost a lot of jobs," one man explains. "Today, even if you're a jani- 30 tor, there's still reading and writing. . . . They leave a note saying 'Go to room so-and-so. . . .' You can't do it. You can't read it. You don't know."

"The hardest thing about it is that I've been places where I didn't know 31 where I was. You don't know where you are. . . . You're lost."

"Like I said: I have two kids. What do I do if one of my kids starts chok- 32 ing? I go running to the phone. . . . I can't look up the hospital phone number. That's if we're at home. Out on the street, I can't read the sign. I get to a pay phone. 'Okay, tell us where you are. We'll send an ambulance.' I look at the street sign. Right there, I can't tell you what it says. I'd have to spell it out, letter for letter. By that time, one of my kids would be dead. . . . These are the kinds of fears you go with, every single day. . . ."

"Reading directions, I suffer with. I work with chemicals. . . . That's 33 scary to begin with. . . ."

"You sit down. They throw the menu in front of you. Where do you go 34 from there? Nine times out of ten you say, 'Go ahead. Pick out something for the both of us.' I've eaten some weird things, let me tell you!"

Menus. Chemicals. A child choking while his mother searches for a 35 word she does not know to find assistance that will come too late. Another mother speaks about the inability to help her kids to read: "I can't read to them. Of course that's leaving them out of something they should have. Oh, it matters. You *believe* it matters! I ordered all these books. The kids belong to a book club. Donny wanted me to read a book to him. I told Donny: 'I can't read.' He said: 'Mommy, you sit down. I'll read it to you.' I tried it one day, reading from the pictures. Donny looked at me. He said, 'Mommy, that's not right.' He's only five. He knew I couldn't read. . . ."

A landlord tells a woman that her lease allows him to evict her if her 36 baby cries and causes inconvenience to her neighbors. The consequence of challenging his words conveys a danger which appears, unlikely as it seems, even more alarming than the danger of eviction. Once she admits that she can't read, in the desire to maneuver for the time in which to call a friend, she will have defined herself in terms of an explicit impotence that she cannot endure. Capitulation in this case is preferable to self-humiliation. Resisting the definition of oneself in terms of what one cannot do, what others take for granted, represents a need so great that other imperatives (even one so urgent as the need to keep one's home in winter's cold) evaporate and fall away in face of fear. Even the loss of home and shelter, in this case, is not so terrifying as the loss of self.

"I come out of school. I was sixteen. They had their meetings. The 37 directors meet. They said that I was wasting their school paper. I was wasting pencils. . . ."

Another illiterate, looking back, believes she was not worthy of her 38 teacher's time. She believes that it was wrong of her to take up space within her school. She believes that it was right to leave in order that somebody more deserving could receive her place.

Children choke. Their mother chokes another way: on more than 39 chicken bones.

People eat what others order, know what others tell them, struggle not 40 to see themselves as they believe the world perceives them. A man in California speaks about his own loss of identity, of self-location, definition:

"I stood at the bottom of the ramp. My car had broke down on the 41 freeway. There was a phone. I asked for the police. They was nice. They said to tell them where I was. I looked up at the signs. There was one that I had seen before. I read it to them: ONE WAY STREET. They thought it was a joke. I told them I couldn't read. There was other signs above the ramp. They told me to try. I looked around for somebody to help. All the cars was going by real fast. I couldn't make them understand that I was lost. The cop was nice. He told me: 'Try once more.' I did my best. I couldn't read. I only knew the sign above my head. The cop was trying to be nice. He knew that I was trapped. 'I can't send out a car to you if you can't tell me where you are.' I felt afraid. I nearly cried. I'm forty-eight years old. I only said: 'I'm on a one-way street. . . .' "

The legal problems and the courtroom complications that confront 42 illiterate adults have been discussed above. The anguish that may underlie such matters was brought home to me this year while I was working on this book. I have spoken [in an earlier part of the book] of a sudden phone call from one of my former students, now in prison for a criminal offense. Stephen is not a boy today. He is twenty-eight years old. He called to ask me to assist him in his trial, which comes up next fall. He will be on trial for murder. He has just knifed and killed a man who first enticed him to his home, then cheated him, and then insulted him—as "an illiterate subhuman."

Stephen now faces twenty years to life. Stephen's mother was illiterate. 43 His grandparents were illiterate as well. What parental curse did not destroy was killed off finally by the schools. Silent violence is repaid with interest. It will cost us $25,000 yearly to maintain this broken soul in prison. But what is the price that has been paid by Stephen's victim? What is the price that will be paid by Stephen?

Perhaps we might slow down a moment here and look at the realities 44 described above. This is the nation that we live in. This is a society that most of us did not create but which our President and other leaders have been willing to sustain by virtue of malign neglect. Do we possess the character and courage to address a problem which so many nations, poorer than our own, have found it natural to correct?

The answers to these questions represent a reasonable test of our belief 45 in the democracy to which we have been asked in public school to swear allegiance.

• • •

COMPREHENSION

1. Why is illiteracy a danger to a democratic society?
2. According to Kozol, why do our reactions to the problem of illiteracy in America test our belief in democracy?
3. What does Kozol mean when he says that an illiterate person leads a "circumscribed existence" (25)? How does being illiterate limit a person's choices?
4. What legal problems and courtroom complications confront illiterate adults?
5. According to Kozol, what is being done to solve the problem of illiteracy in the United States?

PURPOSE AND AUDIENCE

1. What is Kozol's thesis? Where does he state it?
2. Kozol aims his essay at a general audience. How does he address the needs of this audience? In what ways would his discussion differ if it were intended for an audience of reading specialists? Of politicians?
3. Is Kozol's purpose to inform, to persuade, to express emotions, or some combination of these three? Does he have additional, more specific purposes as well? Explain.

STYLE AND STRUCTURE

1. Why does Kozol introduce his essay with references to Socrates and James Madison? How does this strategy help him support his thesis?

2. In paragraph 6, Kozol recounts a dream that he often has. Why does he include this anecdote? How does it help him move from his introduction to the body of his essay?

3. Kozol uses many short examples to make his point. Do you think fewer examples developed in more depth would be more effective? Why or why not?

4. How effective is Kozol's use of statistics? Do the statistics complement or undercut his illustrations of the personal cost of illiteracy?

VOCABULARY PROJECTS

1. Define each of the following words as it is used in this selection.

prescient (1)	sedative (11)	opprobrium (23)
farce (2)	admonitions (11)	concession (24)
mendacious (4)	incognizant (12)	firmament (29)
countenance (4)	jargon (12)	capitulation (36)
Cyrillic (6)	numerate (14)	

2. Reread paragraphs 24 and 25, and determine which words or phrases convey Kozol's feelings toward his subject. Rewrite these two paragraphs, eliminating as much subjective language as you can. Do you think your changes make the paragraphs more appealing or less so to a general audience? To a group of sociologists? To a group of reading teachers?

JOURNAL ENTRY

Keep a detailed record of your activities for a day. Then, discuss the difficulty you would have carrying out each activity in your daily routine if you were illiterate.

WRITING WORKSHOP

1. Using your journal entry as a starting point, write an essay in which you describe the tasks you would have difficulty accomplishing if you could not read. Include an explicit thesis statement, and use examples to illustrate your points.

2. People have not always had to read to function in society. Six hundred years ago, in fact, most people could not read. Similarly, many people today are not computer literate. Write an essay giving examples of the kinds of jobs a person cannot hold today if he or she cannot use a computer.

3. Using Kozol's essay as source material, write an essay in which your thesis is Madison's statement, "A people who mean to be their own governors must arm themselves with the power knowledge gives" (2). Be sure to document any information you borrow from Kozol.

COMBINING THE PATTERNS

Why does Kozol choose to end his essay with a **narrative** about Stephen, one of his former students, who is in jail awaiting trial for murder? How does this anecdote help Kozol set up his concluding remarks in paragraphs 44 and 45?

THEMATIC CONNECTIONS

- "Words Left Unspoken" (page 153)
- "Mother Tongue" (page 462)
- "The Untouchable" (page 498)
- "Strange Tools" (page 697)

❖

Samuel (Fiction)

Grace Paley (b. 1922) grew up in New York City and attended Hunter College there. Initially interested in poetry, she began writing short fiction in the 1950s, at the same time raising a family and participating in a number of political causes. Her stories have been published in the collections *Little Disturbances of Man* (1959), *Enormous Changes at the Last Minute* (1974), and *Later the Same Day* (1985). Her *Collected Stories* appeared in 1994 and was nominated for a National Book Award.

Background: "Samuel" was originally published in *The Atlantic Monthly* and was reprinted in Paley's 1974 collection of stories. The story is set at a time when the social and political upheavals of the 1960s had led to complex rifts within society. Much of the younger generation was rebelling against government policies and cultural conformity, while many older people felt fearful of or antagonistic toward the young people and minorities who were challenging the status quo. "Samuel" touches on these complexities and raises difficult questions about responsibility and loss.

Some boys are very tough. They're afraid of nothing. They are the ones who climb a wall and take a bow at the top. Not only are they brave on the roof, but they make a lot of noise in the darkest part of the cellar where even the super hates to go. They also jiggle and hop on the platform between the locked doors of the subway cars.   1

Four boys are jiggling on the swaying platform. Their names are Alfred, Calvin, Samuel, and Tom. The men and women in the cars on either side watch them. They don't like them to jiggle or jump but don't want to interfere. Of course some of the men in the cars were once brave boys like these. One of them had ridden the tail of a speeding truck from New York to Rockaway Beach without getting off, without his sore fingers losing hold. Nothing happened to him then or later. He had made a compact with other boys who preferred to watch: starting at Eighth Avenue and Fifteenth Street, he would get to some specified place, maybe Twenty-third and the river, by hopping the tops of the moving trucks. This was hard to do when one truck turned a corner in the wrong direction and the nearest truck was a couple of feet too high. He made three or four starts before succeeding. He had gotten this idea from a film at school called *The Romance of Logging*. He had finished high school, married a good friend, was in a responsible job, and going to night school.   2

These two men and others looked at the four boys jumping and jiggling on the platform and thought, It must be fun to ride that way, especially now the weather is nice and we're out of the tunnel and way high over the Bronx. Then they thought, These kids do seem to be acting sort of   3 stupid. They *are* little. Then they thought of some of the brave things they had done when they were boys and jiggling didn't seem so risky.

The ladies in the car became very angry when they looked at the four boys. Most of them brought their brows together and hoped the boys could see their extreme disapproval. One of the ladies wanted to get up and say, be careful you dumb kids, get off that platform or I'll call a cop. But three of the boys were Negroes and the fourth was something else she couldn't tell for sure. She was afraid they'd be fresh and laugh at her and embarrass her. She wasn't afraid they'd hit her, but she was afraid of embarrassment. Another lady thought, their mothers never know where they are. It wasn't true in this particular case. Their mothers all knew that they had gone to see the missile exhibit on Fourteenth Street.   4

Out on the platform, whenever the train accelerated, the boys would raise their hands and point them up to the sky to act like rockets going off, then they rat-tat-tatted the shatterproof glass pane like machine guns, although no machine guns had been exhibited.   5

For some reason known only to the motorman, the train began a sudden slowdown. The lady who was afraid of embarrassment saw the boys jerk forward and backward and grab the swinging guard chains. She had her own boy at home. She stood up with determination and went to the door. She slid it open and said, "You boys will be hurt. You'll be killed. I'm going to call the conductor if you don't just go into the next car and sit down and be quiet."   6

Two of the boys said, "Yes'm," and acted as though they were about to go. Two of them blinked their eyes a couple of times and pressed their lips together. The train resumed its speed. The door slid shut, parting the lady and the boys. She leaned against the side door because she had to get off at the next stop.   7

The boys opened their eyes wide at each other and laughed. The lady blushed. The boys looked at her and laughed harder. They began to pound each other's back. Samuel laughed the hardest and pounded Alfred's back until Alfred coughed and the tears came. Alfred held tight to the chain hook. Samuel pounded him even harder when he saw the tears. He said, "Why you bawling? You a baby, huh?" and laughed. One of the men whose boyhood had been more watchful than brave became angry. He stood up straight and looked at the boys for a couple of seconds. Then he walked in a citizenly way to the end of the car, where he pulled the emergency cord. Almost at once, with a terrible hiss, the pressure of air abandoned the brakes and the wheels were caught and held.   8

People standing in the most secure places fell forward, then backward. Samuel had let go of his hold on the chain so he could pound Tom as well as Alfred. All the passengers in the cars whipped back and forth, but he pitched only forward and fell head first to be crushed and killed between the cars.   9

The train had stopped hard, halfway into the station, and the conductor called at once for the trainmen who knew about this kind of death   10 and how to take the body from the wheels and brakes. There was silence except for passengers from the other cars who asked, What happened! What happened! The ladies waited around wondering if he might be an only child. The men recalled other afternoons with very bad endings. The little boys stayed close to each other, leaning and touching shoulders and arms and legs.

When the policeman knocked at the door and told her about it, 11 Samuel's mother began to scream. She screamed all day and moaned all night, though the doctors tried to quiet her with pills.

Oh, oh, she hopelessly cried. She did not know how she could ever find 12 another boy like that one. However, she was a young woman and she became pregnant. Then for a few months she was hopeful. The child born to her was a boy. They brought him to be seen and nursed. She smiled. But immediately she saw that this baby wasn't Samuel. She and her husband together have had other children, but never again will a boy exactly like Samuel be known.

●   ●   ●

READING LITERATURE

1. The story begins with the observation, "Some boys are very tough." Is Samuel really tough? What do you think Paley wants her readers to realize about Samuel?

2. What point do you think the story makes about bravery? Which of the characters do you consider brave? Why?

3. What effect does the incident have on the other characters? What do their reactions reveal about them?

JOURNAL ENTRY

Do you consider Samuel a hero? Is it true, as the narrator asserts, that "never again will a boy exactly like Samuel be known" (12)?

THEMATIC CONNECTIONS

- "Thirty-Eight Who Saw Murder Didn't Call the Police" (page 101)
- "Who Killed Benny Paret?" (page 321)
- "Why Boys Don't Play with Dolls" (page 335)
- "The Men We Carry in Our Minds" (page 456)

WRITING ASSIGNMENTS FOR EXEMPLIFICATION

1. Interview several businesspeople in your community. Begin by explaining the Peter Principle to them if they are unfamiliar with it. Then, ask them to express their feelings about this concept, and take notes on their responses. Finally, write an essay about your findings that includes quotations from your notes.

2. Write a humorous essay about a ritual, ceremony, or celebration you experienced and the types of people who participated in it. Make a point about the event, and use the participants as examples to support your point.

3. Write an essay in which you establish that you are an optimistic or a pessimistic person. Use examples to support your case.

4. If you could change three or four things at your school, what would they be? Use examples from your own experience to support your recommendations, and tie your recommendations together with a single thesis statement.

5. Write an essay in which you discuss two or three of the greatest challenges facing the United States today. If you like, you may refer to essays in this chapter, such as "Just Walk On By" (page 223) or "The Human Cost of an Illiterate Society" (page 229), or to essays elsewhere in this book, such as "Two Ways to Belong in America" (page 397) or "On Dumpster Diving" (page 670).

6. Using your family and friends as examples, write an essay in which you suggest some of the positive or negative characteristics of Americans.

7. Write an essay in which you present your formula for achieving success in college. You may, if you wish, talk about things like scheduling time, maintaining a high energy level, and learning how to relax. Use examples from your own experience to make your point. You may wish to refer to "College Pressures" (page 447).

8. Write an exemplification essay in which you discuss how cooperation has helped you achieve some important goal. Support your thesis with a single well-developed example.

9. Choose an event that you believe illustrates a less-than-admirable moment in your life. Write an essay explaining your feelings.

10. The popularity of the TV talent show *American Idol* revealed once again Americans' long-standing infatuation with music icons. Choose several pop groups or stars, old and new—such as Elvis Presley, the Beatles, Michael Jackson, Madonna, Jay-Z, Jennifer Lopez, Nirvana, Destiny's Child, and Eminem, to name only a handful of examples—and use them to illustrate the characteristics that you think make pop music so enduring.

COLLABORATIVE ACTIVITY FOR EXEMPLIFICATION

The following passage appeared in a handbook given to parents of entering students at a midwestern university:

> The freshman experience is like no other—at once challenging, exhilarating, and fun. Students face academic challenges as they are exposed to

many new ideas. They also face personal challenges as they meet many new people from diverse backgrounds. It is a time to mature and grow. It is an opportunity to explore new subjects and familiar ones. There may be no more challenging and exciting time of personal growth than the first year of university study.

Working in groups of four, brainstorm to identify examples that support or refute the idea that there "may be no more challenging and exciting time of personal growth" than the first year of college. Then, choose one person from each group to tell the class the position the group took and explain the examples you collected. Finally, work together to write an essay that presents your group's position. Have one student write the first draft, two others revise this draft, and the last student edit and proofread the revised draft.

INTERNET ASSIGNMENT FOR EXEMPLIFICATION

Using examples from your own experience and from the Internet, write an exemplification essay in which you explain the importance of protecting the privacy rights of individuals. Use the following Web sites to gain an understanding of current privacy issues and policies.

Federal Trade Commission
<ftc.gov/privacy/index.html>
The FTC's site is designed to educate consumers and businesses about the importance of protecting the privacy of personal information.

Electronic Privacy Information Center
<epic.org>
This site has news articles and other information about privacy and civil liberties issues in the information age.

Privacy Times
<privacytimes.com>
Privacy Times is a newsletter that covers information law and policy.

❖ 7
Process

WHAT IS PROCESS?

A **process** essay explains how to do something or how something occurs. It presents a sequence of steps and shows how those steps lead to a particular result. In the following paragraph from *Language in Thought and Action,* the semanticist S. I. Hayakawa uses process to explain how an editor of a dictionary decides on a word's definition:

> **Process presents series of steps in chronological order**
>
> To define a word, then, the dictionary-editor places before him the stack of cards illustrating that word; each of the cards represents an actual use of the word by a writer of some literary or historical importance. He reads the cards carefully, discards some, rereads the rest, and divides up the stack according to what he thinks are the several senses of the word. Finally, he writes his definitions, following the hard-and-fast rule that each definition *must* be based on what the quotations in front of him reveal about the meaning of the word. The editor cannot be influenced by what *he* thinks a given word *ought* to mean. He must work according to the cards or not at all.
>
> **Topic sentence**

Process, like narration, presents events in chronological order. Unlike a narrative, however, a process essay explains a particular series of events that produces the same outcome whenever it is duplicated. Because these events form a sequence with a fixed order, clarity is extremely important. Whether your readers are actually going to perform the process or are simply trying to understand how it occurs, your essay must make clear the exact order of the individual steps as well as their relationships to one another and to the process as a whole. This means that you need to provide clear, logical transitions between the steps in a process, and you also need to present the steps in *strict* chronological order — that is, in the exact order in which they occur or are to be performed.

Depending on its purpose, a process essay can be either a set of *instructions* or a *process explanation.*

Understanding Instructions

Instructions enable readers to perform a process. A recipe, a handout about using your library's online databases, and the operating manual for your DVD player are all written as instructions. So are directions for locating an office building in Washington, D.C., or driving from Houston to Pensacola. Instructions use the present tense and, like commands, the imperative mood, speaking directly to readers: "*Disconnect* the system, and *check* the electrical source."

Understanding Process Explanations

The purpose of a **process explanation** is not to enable readers to perform a process but rather to help them understand how it is carried out. Such essays may examine anything from how silkworms spin their cocoons to how Michelangelo and Leonardo da Vinci painted their masterpieces on plaster walls and ceilings. A process explanation may use the first person *(I, we)* or the third *(he, she, it, they),* the past tense or the present. Because its readers need to understand the process, not perform it, a process explanation does not use the second person *(you)* or the imperative mood (commands). The style of a process explanation varies, depending on whether a writer is explaining a process that takes place regularly or one that occurred in the past and on whether the writer or someone else carries out the steps. The chart below suggests some of the options available to writers of process explanations.

	First person	*Third person*
Present tense	"After I place the chemicals in the tray, I turn out the lights in the darkroom." *(habitual process performed by the writer)*	"After photographers place the chemicals in the tray, they turn out the lights in the darkroom." *(habitual process performed by someone other than the writer)*
Past tense	"After I placed the chemicals in the tray, I turned out the lights in the darkroom." *(process performed in the past by the writer)*	"After the photographer placed the chemicals in the tray, she turned out the lights in the darkroom." *(process performed in the past by someone other than the writer)*

USING PROCESS

College writing frequently calls for instructions or process explanations. In a biology paper on genetic testing, you might devote a paragraph to an explanation of the process of amniocentesis; in an editorial about the negative side of fraternity life, you might include a brief outline of the process of pledging. You can also organize an entire paper around a process pattern: in a literature essay, you might trace the steps through which a fictional character reaches some new insight; on a finance midterm, you might explain the procedure for approving a commercial loan.

You can use either kind of process writing to persuade or simply to present information. If its purpose is persuasive, a process paper may take a strong stand like "Applying for food stamps is a needlessly complex process that discourages many qualified recipients" or "The process of slaughtering baby seals is inhumane and sadistic." Many process essays, however, communicate nothing more debatable than the procedure for blood typing. Even in such a case, though, a process should have a clear thesis statement that identifies the process and perhaps tells why it is performed: "Typing their own blood can familiarize students with some fundamental laboratory procedures."

PLANNING A PROCESS ESSAY

As you plan a process essay, remember that your primary goal is to depict the process accurately. This means that you need to distinguish between what usually or always happens and what occasionally or rarely happens, between necessary steps and optional ones. You should also mentally test all the steps in sequence to be sure that the process really works as you say it does, checking carefully for omitted steps or incorrect information. If you are writing about a process you witnessed, try to test your explanation by observing the process again.

Accommodating Your Audience

As you write, remember to keep your readers' needs in mind. When necessary, explain the reasons for performing the steps, describe unfamiliar materials or equipment, define terms, and warn readers about possible problems that may occur during the process. (Sometimes you may even need to include illustrations.) Besides complete information, your readers need a clear and consistent discussion without ambiguities or surprises. For this reason, you should avoid unnecessary shifts in tense, person, voice, and mood. You should also include appropriate articles (*a, an,* and *the*) so that your discussion moves smoothly, like an essay—not abruptly, like a cookbook.

Using Transitions

Throughout your essay, be sure to use transitional words and phrases to ensure that each step, each stage, and each paragraph leads logically to the next. Transitions like *first, second, meanwhile, after this, next, then, at the same time, when you have finished,* and *finally* help to establish sequential and chronological relationships so that readers can follow the process. A more complete list of transitions appears on page 43.

STRUCTURING A PROCESS ESSAY

Like other essays, a process essay generally consists of three sections. The *introduction* identifies the process and indicates why and under what circumstances it is performed. This section may include information about materials or preliminary preparations, or it may present an overview of the process, perhaps even listing its major stages. The paper's thesis is also usually stated in the introduction.

Each paragraph in the *body* of the essay typically treats one major stage of the process. Each stage may group several steps, depending on the nature and complexity of the process. These steps are presented in chronological order, interrupted only for essential definitions, explanations, or cautions. Every step must be included and must appear in its proper place.

A short process essay may not need a formal *conclusion*. If an essay does have a conclusion, however, it will often briefly review the procedure's major stages. Such an ending is especially useful if the paper has outlined a technical procedure that may seem complicated to general readers. The conclusion may also reinforce the thesis by summarizing the results of the process or explaining its significance.

Suppose you are taking a midterm examination in a course in childhood and adolescent behavior. One essay question calls for a process explanation: "Trace the stages that children go through in acquiring language." After thinking about the question, you formulate the following thesis statement: "Although individual cases may differ, most children acquire language in a predictable series of stages." You then plan your essay and develop an informal outline, which might look like this:

Introduction:	Thesis statement—Although individual cases may differ, most children acquire language in a predictable series of stages.
First stage (two to twelve months):	Prelinguistic behavior, including "babbling" and appropriate responses to nonverbal cues.
Second stage (end of first year):	Single words as commands or requests; infant catalogs his or her environment.
Third stage (beginning of second year):	Expressive jargon (flow of sounds that imitates adult speech); real words along with jargon.
Fourth and final stage (middle of second year to beginning of third year):	Two-word phrases; longer strings; missing parts of speech.
Conclusion:	Restatement of thesis or review of major stages of process.

This essay, when completed, will show not only what the stages of the process are but also how they relate to one another. In addition, it will support the thesis that children learn language through a well-defined process.

REVISING A PROCESS ESSAY

When you revise a set of instructions or a process explanation, consider the items on the Revision Checklist on page 54. In addition, pay special attention to the items on the checklist below, which apply specifically to revising process essays.

☑ REVISION CHECKLIST: PROCESS

- Does your assignment call for a set of instructions or a process explanation?
- Does your writing style clearly and consistently indicate whether you are writing a set of instructions or a process explanation?
- Does your essay have a clearly stated thesis that identifies the process and perhaps tells why it is (or was) performed?
- Have you included all necessary reminders and cautions?
- Have you included all necessary steps?
- Are the steps presented in strict chronological order?
- Do transitions clearly indicate where one step ends and the next begins?

EDITING A PROCESS ESSAY

When you edit your process essay, follow the guidelines on the Editing Checklist on page 66. In addition, focus on the grammar, mechanics, and punctuation issues that are most relevant to process essays. One of these issues—avoiding unnecessary shifts in tense, person, voice, and mood—is discussed below.

For more practice in avoiding unnecessary shifts, visit **Exercise Central** at **<bedfordstmartins.com/patterns/shifts>**.

GRAMMAR IN CONTEXT : Avoiding Unnecessary Shifts*

To explain a process to readers, you need to use consistent verb tense (past or present), person (second or third), voice (active or passive), and mood (statements or commands). Unnecessary shifts in tense, person, voice, or mood can confuse readers and make it difficult for them to follow your process.

Avoiding Shifts in Tense   Use present tense for a process that is performed regularly.

"The next step is to have at Mr. Jones with a thing called a trocar" (Mitford 287).

---

*Most of the examples below refer to essays that appear later in this chapter.

Use past tense for a process that was performed in the past.

"He peeled the potatoes and thin-sliced them into a quart-sized Mason fruit jar, . . ." (Malcolm X 260).

Shift from present to past tense only when you need to indicate a change in time: Usually, I study several days before a test, but this time I studied the night before.

Avoiding Shifts in Person Use first or third person for process explanations.

First person (*I*): "Now that I had my sleuth, the next question was what kind of case she should solve" (Muller 267).

First person (*we*): "We decided to use my bathroom to dye our hair" (Hunt 254)

Third person (*he*): "The embalmer, having allowed an appropriate interval to elapse, returns to the attack, but now he brings into play the skill and equipment of sculptor and cosmetician" (Mitford 288).

Use second person for instructions.

Second person (*you*): "If you want to avoid injury, you should begin gradually" (Miksitz 252).

When you give instructions, be careful not to shift from third to second person.

Incorrect: If a person wants to avoid injury, you should begin gradually.

Correct (second person): If you want to avoid injury, you should begin gradually.

NOTE: For an unusual use of second person in a process explanation, see Larry Brown's essay "On Fire" on page 280.

Avoiding Shifts in Voice Use active voice when you want to emphasize the person performing the action.

"During the final typing of the manuscript, I checked and rechecked my clues" (Muller 269).

Use passive voice to emphasize the action itself, not the person performing it.

"The patching and filling completed, Mr. Jones is now shaved, washed, and dressed" (Mitford 289).

Do not shift between the active and the passive voice, especially within a sentence, unless your intent is to change your emphasis.

Incorrect: The first draft was completed, and then I started the second draft.

Correct (active voice): I completed the first draft, and then I started the second draft.

Avoiding Shifts in Mood   Use the indicative mood (statements) for process explanations.

"He draped the towel around my shoulders, over my rubber apron, and began again vaselining my hair" (Malcolm X 261).

Use the imperative mood (commands) only in instructions.

"Call a friend or relative for help" (Piven et al. 272).

Be careful not to shift from the imperative mood to the indicative mood.

Incorrect: First, assemble your materials, and then you should check to make sure you have everything you need.

Correct (imperative):   First, assemble your materials, and then check to make sure you have everything you need.

Correct (indicative):   First, you should assemble your materials, and then you should check to make sure you have everything you need.

✓ EDITING CHECKLIST: PROCESS

- Have you used commas correctly in a series of three or more steps, including a comma before the *and*?
- Have you used parallel structure for items in a series?
- Have you avoided unnecessary shifts in tense?
- Have you avoided unnecessary shifts in person?
- Have you avoided unnecessary shifts in voice?
- Have you avoided unnecessary shifts in mood?

▶ **STUDENT WRITERS: PROCESS**

The following student essays, Joseph Miksitz's set of instructions and Melany Hunt's explanation of how a process was conducted, were both written in response to the same assignment: "Write an essay in which you give instructions for a process that can change a person's appearance — or explain a process that changed your own appearance in some way."

Pumping Iron

Introduction   Students of high school and college age are   1
often dissatisfied with their appearance. They
see actors and models on television and in magazines, and they want to be thinner, stronger,

or better looking. Sometimes this quest for
perfection gets young adults into trouble,
leading them to eating disorders or drug use.

Thesis statement A healthier way for young adults to improve
their appearance is through a weight-training
program, which can increase not only their
strength but also their self-esteem.

Overview of the process; getting started   If you want to avoid injury, you should 2
begin gradually. In the first week, you might
lift weights only two days, concentrating on
thigh and calf muscles in the lower body and
on triceps, biceps, chest, back, and shoulders
in the upper body. For the next three or four
weeks, lift three days a week, adding more exercises each week. By the fourth week, you will
probably start to feel stronger. At this point,
you can begin a four-day lifting program, which
many experts believe is the most productive and
shows the best results.

Steps in process of upper-body workout   On Monday and Thursday, concentrate on 3
your upper body. Begin with the bench press
(to work chest muscles) and then move on to the
military press (for the shoulders). After that,
work your back muscles with the lat pull-down
exercise on the Universal machine or with some
heavy and light dead lifts. Finally, concentrate
on your arms, doing bicep curls, tricep extensions, and wrist curls (for the forearms). To
cool down, do a few sets of sit-ups.

Steps in process of lower-body workout   On Tuesday and Friday, focus on your lower 4
body with a leg workout. Start with the leg
press. (Always begin your workout with your most
strenuous exercise, which is usually the exercise that works the largest muscles.) Next, do
some leg extensions to build the thigh muscles in
the front of your leg, and then move on to leg
curls to strengthen your hamstring muscle. After
that, do calf raises to work your calf muscles.
When you are finished, be sure to stretch all the
major muscles to prevent tightness and injuries.

Warnings and reminders

Of course, a balanced weight-training pro- 5
gram involves more than just lifting weights.
During your weight training, you should eat
four high-protein/high-carbohydrate meals a
day, limiting fat and eating four or five serv-
ings of fruit and vegetables daily. You should
also monitor your progress carefully, paying
attention to your body's aches and pains and
consulting a professional trainer when necessary—especially if you think you may have
injured yourself.

Conclusion

Above all, don't let your weight-training 6
regimen take over your life. If you integrate
it into the rest of your life, balancing exercise with school, work, and social activities,
a weight-training program can make you look and
feel terrific.

Points for Special Attention

Introduction   The first paragraph of Joseph Miksitz's essay includes a thesis statement that presents the advantages of embarking on a weight-training program. Joseph begins with an overview of the image problems faced by young adults and then narrows his focus to present weight training as a possible solution to those problems.

Structure   After his introduction, Joseph includes a paragraph that presents guidelines for getting started. The third and fourth paragraphs enumerate the steps in each of the two processes he describes—upper- and lower-body workouts. In his fifth paragraph, Joseph includes reminders and cautions so that his readers will get the most out of their exercise program while avoiding overexertion or injury. (The parenthetical sentence in paragraph 4 offers another helpful tip.) In his conclusion, Joseph advises readers to keep their exercise program in perspective and (echoing his thesis statement) reminds them of its benefits.

Purpose and Style   Because Joseph's readers should be able to perform the process themselves, he wrote it as a set of instructions. Therefore, he uses the second person (*"you* will probably start to feel stronger"), and the present tense, with many of his verbs in the form of commands (*"Begin* with the bench press").

Transitions   To make his essay clear and easy to follow, Joseph includes transitions that indicate the order in which each step is to be performed ("After that," "Next," "Finally") as well as specific time markers ("On Monday and Thursday," "On Tuesday and Friday") to distinguish the two related processes his essay discusses.

Focus on Revision

Joseph is careful to name various parts of the body and to identify different exercises as well as the general objective of each. He has, however, omitted many other key details, as several students noted in their peer critiques of his essay. For example, how much time should be spent on each exercise? What exactly is a bench press? A bicep curl? How are "light" and "heavy" defined? How many is "some" leg extensions or "a few sets" of sit-ups? How many repetitions of each exercise are necessary? What specific danger signs should alert readers to possible overexertion or injury? Is the routine Joseph describes appropriate for females as well as males? When revising his essay, Joseph kept in mind that most members of his audience would not be familiar with the processes he describes. He therefore added much more detailed explanations. (A sample peer editing worksheet for process can be found on the *Patterns for College Writing* Web site at <bedfordstmartins.com/patterns>.)

In contrast to "Pumping Iron," Melany Hunt's essay is a process explanation.

Medium Ash Brown

Introduction   The beautiful chestnut-haired woman pic-   1
tured on the box seemed to beckon to me. I
reached for the box of Medium Ash Brown hair
dye just as my friend Veronica grabbed the box
labeled Sparkling Sherry. I can't remember our
reasons for wanting to change our hair color,
but they seemed to make sense at the time. Maybe
we were just bored. I do remember that the
idea of transforming our appearance came up unexpectedly. Impulsively, we decided to change
our hair color — and, we hoped, ourselves — that
Thesis statement   very evening. Now I know that some impulses
should definitely be resisted.

Materials assembled   We decided to use my bathroom to dye our   2
hair. Inside each box of hair color, we found
two little bottles and a small tube wrapped in
a page of instructions. Attached to the instruction page itself were two very large, one-size-
fits-all plastic gloves, which looked and felt

like plastic sandwich bags. The directions recommended having some old towels around to soak up any spills or drips that might occur. Under the sink we found some old, frayed towels that I figured my mom had forgotten about, and we spread them around the bathtub. After we

First stage of process: preparing the dye

put our gloves on, we began the actual dyeing process. First we poured the first bottle into the second, which was half-full of some odd-smelling liquid. The smell was not much better after we combined the two bottles. The directions advised us to cut off a small section of hair to use as a sample. For some reason, we decided to skip this step.

Second stage of process: applying the dye

At this point, Veronica and I took turns leaning over the tub to wet our hair for the dye. The directions said to leave the dye on the hair for fifteen to twenty minutes, so we found a little timer and set it for fifteen minutes. Next, we applied the dye to our hair. Again, we took turns squeezing the bottle in order to cover all our hair. We then wrapped the old towels around our sour-smelling hair and went outside to get some fresh air.

Third stage of process: rinsing

After the fifteen minutes were up, we rinsed our hair. According to the directions, we were to add a little water and scrub as if we were shampooing our hair. The dye lathered up, and we rinsed our hair until the water ran clear. So far, so good.

Last stage of process: applying conditioner

The last part of the process involved applying the small tube of conditioner to our hair (because dyed hair becomes brittle and easily damaged). We used the conditioner as directed, and then we dried our hair so that we could see the actual color. Even before I looked in the mirror, I heard Veronica's gasp.

Outcome of process

"Nice try," I said, assuming she was just trying to make me nervous, "but you're not funny."

"Mel," she said, "look in the mirror."   7
Slowly, I turned around. My stomach turned into
a lead ball when I saw my reflection. My hair
was the putrid greenish-brown color of a winter
lawn, dying in patches yet still a nice green
in the shade.

The next day in school, I wore my hair tied   8
back under a baseball cap. I told only my close
friends what I had done. After they were finished laughing, they offered their deepest,
most heartfelt condolences. They also offered
many suggestions — none very helpful — on what to
do to get my old hair color back.

Conclusion   It is now three months later, and I still   9
have no idea what prompted me to dye my hair.
My only consolation is that I resisted my first
impulse — to dye my hair a wild color, like blue
or fuchsia. Still, as I wait for my hair to
grow out, and as I assemble a larger and larger
collection of baseball caps, it is small consolation indeed.

Points for Special Attention

Structure In her opening paragraph, Melany's thesis statement makes it very clear that the experience she describes is not one she would recommend to others. The temptation she describes in her introduction's first few sentences lures readers into her essay just as the picture on the box lured her. Her second paragraph lists the contents of the box of hair dye and explains how she and her friend assembled the other necessary materials. Then, she explains the first stage in the process, preparing the dye. Paragraphs 3–5 describe the other stages in the process in chronological order, and paragraphs 6–8 record Melany's and Veronica's reactions to their experiment. In paragraph 9, Melany sums up the impact of her experience and once again expresses her annoyance with herself for her impulsive act.

Purpose and Format Melany's purpose is *not* to enable others to duplicate the process she explains; on the contrary, she is trying to discourage readers from doing what she did. Consequently, she presents her process not as a set of instructions but as a process explanation, using first person and past tense to explain the actions of herself and her friend. She also largely eliminates cautions and reminders that her readers, who are not likely to undertake the process, will not need to know.

Detail   Melany's essay includes vivid descriptive detail that gives readers a clear sense of the process and its outcome. Throughout, her emphasis is on the negative aspects of the process — the "odd-smelling liquid" and the "putrid greenish-brown color" of her hair, for instance — and this emphasis is consistent with her essay's purpose.

Transitions   To move readers smoothly through the process, Melany includes clear transitions ("First," "At this point," "Next," "then") and clearly identifies the beginning of the process ("After we put our gloves on, we began the actual dyeing process") and the end ("The last part of the process").

Focus on Revision

Students who read Melany's essay thought that it was clearly written and structured and that its ironic, self-mocking tone was well suited to her audience and purpose. They felt, however, that some minor revisions would make her essay even more effective. Paragraph 2, for example, still needed a bit of work. For one thing, this paragraph began quite abruptly: paragraph 1 recorded the purchase of the hair dye, and paragraph 2 opened with the sentence "We decided to use my bathroom to dye our hair," leaving readers wondering how much time had passed between purchase and application. Because the thesis rests on the idea of the foolishness of an impulsive gesture, it is important for readers to understand that the girls presumably went immediately from the store to Melany's house. After thinking about this criticism, Melany decided to write a clearer opening for paragraph 2: "As soon as we paid for the dye, we returned to my house, where, eager to begin our transformation, we locked ourselves in my bathroom. Inside each box . . . ." She also decided to divide paragraph 2 into two paragraphs, one describing the materials and another beginning with "After we put our gloves on," which introduces the first step in the process.

Another possible revision Melany considered was to develop Veronica's character further. Although both girls purchase and apply hair color, readers never learn what happens to Veronica. Melany knew she could easily add a brief paragraph after paragraph 7, describing Veronica's "Sparkling Sherry" hair in humorous terms, and she planned to do so in her paper's final draft. (A sample peer editing worksheet for process can be found on the *Patterns for College Writing* Web site at <www.bedfordstmartins.com/patterns>.)

The reading selections that follow illustrate how varied the purposes of process writing can be. The first selection, a visual text, is followed by questions designed to illustrate how process can operate in visual form.

❖ MICHAEL P. GADOMSKI

Jack-o'-Lantern (Photo)

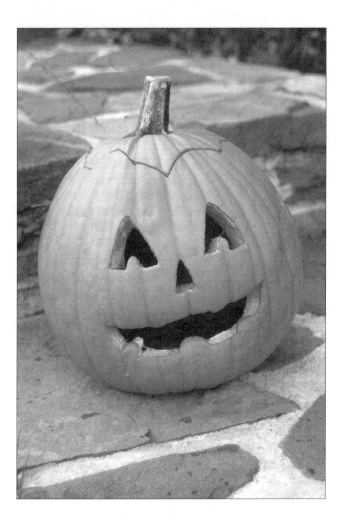

• • •

READING IMAGES

1. Look closely at the photograph above. How is this jack-o'-lantern different from the pumpkin from which it was carved?

2. List the steps involved in the process of carving a pumpkin into a jack-o'-lantern. Where does the process begin? Where does it end?

3. What cautions and reminders might be helpful to someone who has never made a jack-o'-lantern?

JOURNAL ENTRY

Write a set of instructions for someone who has never made a jack-o'-lantern. Using commands and present tense, explain each step in the order in which it occurs, including all necessary cautions and reminders.

THEMATIC CONNECTIONS

- "Why Boys Don't Play with Dolls" (page 335)
- "How the Lawyers Stole Winter" (page 402)
- "Tortillas" (page 513)

❖

My First Conk

Malcolm X was born Malcolm Little in Omaha, Nebraska, in 1925. As a young man, he had a number of run-ins with the law, and he wound up in prison on burglary charges before he was twenty-one. There he pursued his education and was influenced by the writings of Elijah Muhammed, the founder of the Black Muslims (now known as the Nation of Islam), a black separatist organization. On his release from prison, Malcolm X became a highly visible member of this group and a disciple of its leader. He left the movement in 1963, later converting to orthodox Islam and founding a rival African-American political organization. He was assassinated in 1965.

Background: In 1964, *The Autobiography of Malcolm X* (written with Alex Haley) was published. In the following excerpt from that book, he describes the painful and painstaking process many African-American men once endured to achieve a style of straight hair called a "conk." (The term probably comes from Congolene, the brand name of one commercial hair straightener.) First popularized in the 1920s by black entertainers such as Cab Calloway, the style continued to be fashionable until the 1960s, when more natural styles, including the Afro, became a symbol of black pride, and conked hair was seen as a self-loathing attempt to imitate whites. Ironically, perhaps, some contemporary African Americans still distinguish between "good" (that is, naturally straight) and "bad" (that is, naturally curly) hair. Today, cosmetically straightened hair (a process that is no longer so arduous) is considered one fashion option among many, including closely cropped hair, braids, cornrows, and dreadlocks.

Shorty soon decided that my hair was finally long enough to be conked. 1
He had promised to school me in how to beat the barber shops' three- and four-dollar price by making up congolene, and then conking ourselves.

I took the little list of ingredients he had printed out for me, and went 2
to a grocery store, where I got a can of Red Devil lye, two eggs, and two medium-sized white potatoes. Then at a drugstore near the poolroom, I asked for a large jar of vaseline, a large bar of soap, a large-toothed comb and a fine-toothed comb, one of those rubber hoses with a metal spray-head, a rubber apron, and a pair of gloves.

"Going to lay on that first conk?" the drugstore man asked me. I 3
proudly told him, grinning, "Right!"

Shorty paid six dollars a week for a room in his cousin's shabby apart- 4
ment. His cousin wasn't at home. "It's like the pad's mine, he spends so much time with his woman," Shorty said. "Now, you watch me—"

He peeled the potatoes and thin-sliced them into a quart-sized Mason 5
fruit jar, then started stirring them with a wooden spoon as he gradually

poured in a little over half the can of lye. "Never use a metal spoon; the lye will turn it black," he told me.

A jelly-like, starchy-looking glop resulted from the lye and potatoes, 6
and Shorty broke in the two eggs, stirring real fast—his own conk and dark face bent down close. The congolene turned pale-yellowish. "Feel the jar," Shorty said. I cupped my hand against the outside, and snatched it away. "Damn right, it's hot, that's the lye," he said. "So you know it's going to burn when I comb it in—it burns bad. But the longer you can stand it, the straighter the hair."

He made me sit down, and he tied the string of the new rubber apron 7
tightly around my neck, and combed up my bush of hair. Then, from the big vaseline jar, he took a handful and massaged it hard all through my hair and into the scalp. He also thickly vaselined my neck, ears and forehead. "When I get to washing out your head, be sure to tell me anywhere you feel any little stinging," Shorty warned me, washing his hands, then pulling on the rubber gloves, and tying on his own rubber apron. "You always got to remember that any congolene left in burns a sore into your head."

The congolene just felt warm when Shorty started combing it in. But 8
then my head caught fire.

I gritted my teeth and tried to pull the sides of the kitchen table 9
together. The comb felt as if it was raking my skin off.

My eyes watered, my nose was running. I couldn't stand it any longer; 10
I bolted to the washbasin. I was cursing Shorty with every name I could think of when he got the spray going and started soap lathering my head.

He lathered and spray-rinsed, lathered and spray-rinsed, maybe ten or 11
twelve times, each time gradually closing the hot-water faucet, until the rinse was cold, and that helped some.

"You feel any stinging spots?" 12

"No," I managed to say. My knees were trembling. 13

"Sit back down, then. I think we got it all out okay." 14

The flame came back as Shorty, with a thick towel, started drying my 15
head, rubbing hard. *"Easy, man, easy!"* I kept shouting.

"The first time's always worst. You get used to it better before long. You 16
took it real good, homeboy. You got a good conk."

When Shorty let me stand up and see in the mirror, my hair hung 17
down in limp, damp strings. My scalp still flamed, but not as badly; I could bear it. He draped the towel around my shoulders, over my rubber apron, and began again vaselining my hair.

I could feel him combing, straight back, first the big comb, then the 18
fine-tooth one.

Then, he was using a razor, very delicately, on the back of my neck. 19
Then, finally, shaping the sideburns.

My first view in the mirror blotted out the hurting. I'd seen some 20
pretty conks, but when it's the first time, on your *own* head, the transformation, after the lifetime of kinks, is staggering.

The mirror reflected Shorty behind me. We both were grinning and   21
sweating. And on top of my head was this thick, smooth sheen of shining
red hair—real red—as straight as any white man's.

How ridiculous I was! Stupid enough to stand there simply lost in   22
admiration of my hair now looking "white," reflected in the mirror in
Shorty's room. I vowed that I'd never again be without a conk, and I never
was for many years.

This was my first really big step toward self-degradation: when I   23
endured all of that pain, literally burning my flesh to have it look like a
white man's hair. I had joined that multitude of Negro men and women in
America who are brainwashed into believing that the black people are "inferior"—and white people "superior"—that they will even violate and muti-
late their God-created bodies to try to look "pretty" by white standards.

Look around today, in every small town and big city, from two-bit   24
catfish and soda-pop joints into the "integrated" lobby of the Waldorf-
Astoria, and you'll see conks on black men. And you'll see black women
wearing these green and pink and purple and red and platinum-blonde wigs.
They're all more ridiculous than a slapstick comedy. It makes you wonder if
the Negro has completely lost his sense of identity, lost touch with himself.

You'll see the conk worn by many, many so-called "upper class"   25
Negroes, and, as much as I hate to say it about them, on all too many
Negro entertainers. One of the reasons that I've especially admired some of
them, like Lionel Hampton and Sidney Poitier, among others, is that they
have kept their natural hair and fought to the top. I admire any Negro man
who has never had himself conked, or who has had the sense to get rid of
it—as I finally did.

I don't know which kind of self-defacing conk is the greater shame—   26
the one you'll see on the heads of the black so-called "middle class" and
"upper class," who ought to know better, or the one you'll see on the heads
of the poorest, most downtrodden, ignorant black men. I mean the legal-
minimum-wage ghetto-dwelling kind of Negro, as I was when I got my first
one. It's generally among these poor fools that you'll see a black kerchief
over the man's head, like Aunt Jemima; he's trying to make his conk last
longer, between trips to the barbershop. Only for special occasions is this
kerchief-protected conk exposed—to show off how "sharp" and "hip" its
owner is. The ironic thing is that I have never heard any woman, white or
black, express any admiration for a conk. Of course, any white woman with
a black man isn't thinking about his hair. But I don't see how on earth a
black woman with any race pride could walk down the street with any
black man wearing a conk—the emblem of his shame that he is black.

To my own shame, when I say all of this, I'm talking first of all about 27
myself—because you can't show me any Negro who ever conked more
faithfully than I did. I'm speaking from personal experience when I say of
any black man who conks today, or any white-wigged black woman, that if
they gave the brains in their heads just half as much attention as they do
their hair, they would be a thousand times better off.

• • •

COMPREHENSION

1. What exactly is a conk? Why does Malcolm X want to get his hair conked? What does the conk symbolize to him at the time he gets it? What does it symbolize at the time he writes about it?

2. List the materials Shorty asks Malcolm X to buy. Is the purpose of each explained? If so, where?

3. Outline the major stages in the procedure Malcolm X describes. Are they presented in chronological order? Which, if any, of the major stages are out of place?

PURPOSE AND AUDIENCE

1. Why was this selection written as a process explanation instead of as a set of instructions?

2. This selection has an explicitly stated thesis that makes its purpose clear. What is this thesis?

3. *The Autobiography of Malcolm X* was published in 1964, when many African Americans regularly straightened their hair. Is the thesis of this excerpt from the book still relevant today?

4. Why do you think Malcolm X includes so many references to the pain and discomfort he endured as part of the process?

5. What is the relationship between Malcolm X's personal experience and the universal statement he is making about conking?

STYLE AND STRUCTURE

1. Identify some of the transitional words Malcolm X uses to move from step to step.

2. Only about half of this selection is devoted to the process explanation. Where does the process begin? Where does it end?

3. In paragraphs 22–26, Malcolm X encloses several words in quotation marks, occasionally prefacing them with the phrase *so-called*. What is the effect of these quotation marks?

VOCABULARY PROJECTS

1. Define each of the following words as it is used in this selection.

vowed (22)	mutilate (23)	downtrodden (26)
self-degradation (23)	slapstick (24)	emblem (26)
multitude (23)	self-defacing (26)	

2. Because this is an informal piece of writing, Malcolm X uses many **colloquialisms** and **slang** terms. Substitute a more formal word for each of the following.

beat (1)	glop (6)	"sharp" (26)
pad (4)	real (6)	"hip" (26)

Evaluate the possible impact of your substitutions. Do they improve the essay or weaken it?

JOURNAL ENTRY

Did you ever engage in behavior that you later came to view as unacceptable as your beliefs changed or as your social consciousness developed? What made you change your attitude toward this behavior?

WRITING WORKSHOP

1. Write a process explanation of an unpleasant experience you or someone you know has often gone through in order to conform to others' standards of physical beauty (for instance, dieting or undertaking strenuous exercise). Include a thesis statement that conveys your disapproval of the process.

2. Rewrite Malcolm X's process explanation as he might have written it when he still considered conking a desirable process, worth all the trouble. Include all his steps, but change his thesis and choose words that make conking sound painless and worthwhile.

3. Rewrite this essay as a set of instructions that Shorty might have written for a friend who is about to help someone conk his hair. Begin by telling the friend what materials to purchase.

COMBINING THE PATTERNS

Although "My First Conk" is very detailed, it does not include an extended **definition** of a conk. Do you think a definition paragraph should be added? If so, where could it be inserted? What patterns could be used to develop such a definition?

THEMATIC CONNECTIONS

- "Finishing School" (page 89)
- "Medium Ash Brown" (page 254)
- "Slavery Isn't the Issue" (page 632)

MARCIA MULLER

Creating a Female Sleuth

Marcia Muller (b. 1944) grew up in Detroit and received her B.A. in English and her M.A. in journalism from the University of Michigan. She wrote for magazines and worked for an editorial service before publishing her first novel, *Edwin of the Iron Shoes* (1977), a detective story featuring private investigator Sharon McCone as its central character. Since then, Muller has written more than twenty books in the McCone series, most recently *Dead Midnight* (2002), as well as mysteries solved by other female sleuths. The winner of many awards, she has also edited a number of fiction collections, often with her husband, the mystery writer Bill Pronzini. In this essay, first published in *The Writer* in 1978, Muller explains how she created Sharon McCone.

Background: Most critics trace the fictional detective back to Edgar Allan Poe's 1841 short story "The Murders in the Rue Morgue" and later Poe tales centering on the brilliant and eccentric amateur C. Auguste Dupin. The English writer Wilkie Collins published what is considered the first detective novel, *The Moonstone,* in 1868. Some twenty years later, Arthur Conan Doyle introduced Sherlock Holmes, probably literature's most famous detective. The genre blossomed in the early twentieth century when scores of new detective series appeared, with central characters such as G. K. Chesterton's cerebral priest, Father Brown; Dorothy L. Sayers's genteel Lord Peter Wimsey; S. S. Van Dine's wealthy connoisseur Philo Vance; and the hardboiled private investigators Sam Spade and Philip Marlowe (both precursors of a long line of fictional PIs), created by Dashiell Hammett and Raymond Chandler, respectively. While there had been series devoted to amateur female sleuths — such as Agatha Christie's elderly Jane Marple and plucky teenager Nancy Drew (ghostwritten by various writers, all using the pseudonym Carolyn Keene) — other than P. D. James's Cordelia Gray, who appeared in 1972, Muller's Sharon McCone was the first fictional female private investigator. She was soon joined by Sue Grafton's Kinsey Millhone, Liza Cody's Anna Lee, and Sara Paretsky's V. I. Warshawsky, among many others.

Several years ago, a friend handed me my first whodunit as I was about 1
to embark on a long bus ride. I finished the book before I reached my destination and, upon arrival, went straight to the paperback racks for another. I was hooked.

In the years that followed, my puzzle-prone friends and I noticed that 2
one figure was missing from the mystery scene. There were scores of male sleuths, both hard- and soft-boiled. There were old ladies with knitting needles and noses for secrets. There were even a few dedicated and hardworking policewomen. But nowhere, at that time, could we find a female private eye.

Obviously, I decided, if I wanted to read about such a character, I 3
would first have to write about her.

The process of creating my sleuth, Sharon McCone, and plotting her 4
first case—*Edwin of the Iron Shoes*—presented a number of technical problems. Because female sleuths are in themselves a rarity, my imaginary
friend could not be too unusual or too much of a super-woman if modern readers—both male and female—were to identify with her. She also
needed to have a background that would make her choice of profession
believable.

On the other hand, like all detectives, she had to be somewhat larger 5
than life. She had to be the sort of person who would do things you and I
might never dream of: stalk her quarry through the highways and byways
of the city; stand her ground with hostile cops; grapple hand-to-hand with
dangerous criminals.

In order to reconcile these seeming opposites, I chose to give Sharon 6
a normal, perhaps pedestrian, family background and upbringing that
produced a well-adjusted, uncomplicated adult. Sharon's problems are
those we've all experienced at one time: an affectionate but nosy mother
who, fortunately, lives 500 miles away; the frustration of not finding a
decent job after graduating from college with a sociology major; the lack of
an interesting man in one's life; too high a rent for too small a studio
apartment.

Marital status, which affects a female investigator's freedom of move- 7
ment far more than a male's, was easy to decide, particularly when the
police lieutenant in charge of Sharon's first murder case turned out to be
attractive, if a bit of a smart-aleck. Sharon is single.

For the background that would qualify her for a career as a private 8
investigator, I chose department-store security, a relatively easy field to
break into. Where else could a nice girl learn to fire a .38 Special or flip a
grown man over with a judo hold? I decided that Sharon was bored with
guarding dresses on the sales floor, had gone off to college, and then
returned to investigative work when she realized the demand for sociologists was nil. Further training with a big security agency equipped her for a
position as staff investigator at a San Francisco legal cooperative in time
for her first big case.

With this plausible basis for my sleuth's choice of occupation and a 9
number of down-to-earth character traits, I gave my imagination free rein.
I wanted to make Sharon's physical attributes stand out in the reader's
mind, and at the same time to avoid the old, overused mirror-on-the-wall
device ("As I stood before the mirror and brushed my hair, I thought about
the case and noticed gray strands among the black.") Therefore, I decided
to make Sharon a person with Scotch-Irish ancestry, whose one-eighth
Shoshone Indian blood dominates her appearance. Her unusual looks,
coupled with her name, cause people to comment, "McCone? But you look
like an Indian!"—and this enabled me to dispense with a great deal of
description.

Larger Than Life

Now I was really getting into the larger-than-life qualities, or, more accurately, the larger-than-author traits. Sharon is much taller than I, so she can more easily wrestle with criminals. She never has to worry about her weight, presumably because she does not sit at a typewriter all day. She is more independent than the average soul, delights in asserting herself, and, of course, is much braver.

These admirable qualities were all very well to list, but the next problem was how to express them in action. When I began writing up her first case, I found my heroine in a given situation and asked myself: "All right, what would *I* do?" The answer, inevitably, was something like "Run." Since this was not working out, I conditioned myself to think of what I would do if I were brave, tall, an expert at judo, and so on, each time taking it a step farther. I discovered it was better to have Sharon act ridiculously brave, even foolhardy, and moderate her actions later, than to start off timidly, because a timid response to a situation was more difficult to correct in a rewrite.

Touchier yet was the problem of emotional balance: how was Sharon to deal with the rough situations that came up in the course of her work without sacrificing her femininity? The qualities of empathy and intuition would be great assets to her, because as a woman she might realize or even be told things that ordinary investigative methods would not turn up. Still, she couldn't cry at every bump and bruise, or lose her gun in her purse at the crucial moment. Again, I constantly had to consider what I would do if I were a trained professional, how I would condition and curb my natural responses. I constantly made adjustments for this balance in every draft of the novel, and am still making adjustments now, as I guide my sleuth through her second case.

A mechanical aid in getting acquainted with my character was writing the biographical sketch, a detailed run-down on Sharon's history, preferences and opinions from her own point of view. I wrote this in the first person, as if she were standing up to introduce herself to a group. Throughout the writing process, this "biography" was there to help refresh my memory as to details. It was no substitute, however, for getting to know my character through writing about her.

Two Rules for Plotting

Now that I had my sleuth, the next question was what kind of case she should solve. In short, what was my plot to be?

I had a setting I wanted to explore: an enclave of antique and junk shops, loosely based on several such areas in San Francisco, and I wanted to center on one particular shop containing an assortment of strange objects, including a department store mannequin named Edwin, who wore a pair of ornate iron shoes. I also had a problem for Sharon to solve: the dead body of the proprietor on the floor of the shop, with Edwin as the only witness to the murder.

With this in mind, I began to play the game of "what if." I started with 16
the very obvious questions: What if the proprietor had a fortune in antiques hidden in the shop? What if she had a jealous lover? What if several powerful real-estate syndicates were after the land the shop was on? What if, beneath her ordinary exterior, the victim hid some criminal secret? The answers to these and other often laughable questions gave the basis for my solution.

Knowing my solution was the real key to a plot that held together. I 17
needed to have some ending, however tentative, in mind at all times, or I couldn't plant clues or make my suspects act properly suspicious. Without a solution, I didn't know what the clues pointed to or why my characters needed to behave strangely. This has become my first unbreakable rule of plotting.

My second unbreakable rule, to keep the plot as flexible as possible, 18
may sound like a direct contradiction to the first. I found, however, that I had to be willing to modify my original solution or even throw it out and replace it with another when characters and events indicated this was necessary.

For example, I reached a point in my whodunit where all the loose ends 19
were tying up nicely. Everything pointed to my chosen killer, his motives were coming clear, and my sleuth had won over the nasty police lieutenant by her clever use of logic. Elated, I took a breath to count pages and realized that I was only halfway through the book!

This is the kind of situation in which you need all the flexibility you 20
can muster. I looked over what I had written and concluded that this would be not only a very short book, but also a very boring one. Everything pointed clearly to the killer. His motives were too pat and ordinary. I began once more to play "what if."

What if, at the height of his bedazzlement with Sharon's logic, the 21
police lieutenant receives a phone call, and then smugly announces to her that the supposed murderer himself was dead? That he was knifed in his own apartment, in fact, and that the apartment had been searched?

Of course, the answer was that I had to get myself a new killer. What if 22
the sleazy bail bondsman that the victim had been consorting with . . . ? The new solution was more interesting all around, and it gave me the extra pages I needed.

Plot Control

This experience taught me the difficulty of keeping the plot of a who- 23
dunit in hand even after you think you know what it is. I had to keep track of events that happened weeks, even years, before my opening action, all of which led up to the initial crime. There were also facts that had to be withheld from the reader as long as possible, and clues the reader had to be given. A number of characters were engaged in suspicious activities that may or may not have had something to do with the murder. How was I to keep track of all this?

Several mechanical devices helped. The first, a sketch of what really   24
happened, was like a well-detailed short story. I started at the beginning of
my mystery, two years before the murder, when the antique shop proprietor needed a great deal more money than her shop could bring in. I followed the course of events from there to the day she ended up dead on the
shop floor, and finally ended the sketch with the arrest of her killer. The
sketch was available for reference as my plot unfolded and the past was
explained. And, in accordance with the flexibility rule, it was discarded and
rewritten when the solution changed.

A second device was the sketch of each main character. While not as   25
detailed as the biography of the heroine, it contained much the same types
of information: background, important life events, outstanding physical
and personality traits. These sketches helped me keep the characters' motivations in mind and to keep details about their lives consistent.

The most useful device for plot control was my time chart. It took the   26
form of a grid, with major characters plotted across the top and chapters
or time frames plotted down the side; it covered the same period as the
sketch of what really happened.

In the squares under each character on the chart, I noted what he or   27
she was doing during every time period. In this way, I avoided such embarrassing situations as finding that the murderer was really with my detective
when he was supposed to have been doing in his second victim. I usually
plotted only three to five chapters ahead at a time, finding that the things
characters said and did often suggested new complications or scenes. However, I imagine this type of chart could be adapted nicely to complete pre-
planning as well.

The rewrite was my final check of how well my plot hung together.   28
This was when I went back and inserted clues I had forgotten, brought out
necessary facets of a suspect's character, and smoothed over inconsistencies and cut and cleaned up style. My experience with rewrites has been
rewarding: the wicked-looking bone-handled knife which, as the murder
weapon, plays a large part in my whodunit, didn't even exist until the
rewrite, when a critic friend pointed out that a small paring knife made a
pretty silly instrument of violent death.

During the final typing of the manuscript, I checked and rechecked my   29
clues. I believe in playing fair with the reader, and I wanted to make sure I'd
given him every clue Sharon came across in solving the case. Rather than
have Sharon say: "I realized something that told me who the killer was," I
had her carry on a mental conversation with Edwin, the heavy-footed mannequin. At its end, she says: "Edwin, why didn't you tell me?" The conversation provides the reader with all the clues he needs to solve the murders
along with Sharon. And I will be delighted to hear of readers who solve my
whodunit ahead of my sleuth!

•   •   •

COMPREHENSION

1. According to Muller, what motivated her to create her "female sleuth"?

2. Muller believed that her detective had to be someone with whom readers could identify and yet also someone "larger than life" (5). Why? List some of the characteristics that help Sharon McCone satisfy both these requirements.

3. What advantages does Muller's fictional detective have because she is female? What disadvantages does she have?

4. What are Muller's "unbreakable rule[s] of plotting" (17–18)? Why are they "unbreakable"?

5. What problems did Muller encounter in plotting her novel? How did she solve them? What "mechanical devices" (24) did she devise to help her control her plot?

PURPOSE AND AUDIENCE

1. This essay was first published in 1978, a year after the first Sharon McCone detective novel appeared in print. Are today's readers more or less likely than those of twenty-five years ago to be interested in the development of the female detective? Explain.

2. Do you think Muller expects her audience to be familiar with the conventions of a typical detective story? How can you tell?

3. Muller states her thesis in paragraph 3. Paraphrase this one-sentence paragraph. Should she have stated her thesis earlier? Explain.

STYLE AND STRUCTURE

1. Where does the actual discussion of the process of creating a female sleuth begin? How does Muller signal the start of this process to her readers?

2. List the major stages in the process Muller followed to create Sharon McCone.

3. What transitional expressions does Muller use to guide readers through the process and connect one stage to the next?

4. Are any of the elements that are typically included in a process explanation missing from this essay? For example, does Muller include warnings and reminders? If so, where? If not, why not?

5. Although Muller is a professional writer discussing her craft, her style is, for the most part, quite informal. Give examples of her informal language. What does Muller gain by using this kind of language instead of more formal language?

VOCABULARY PROJECTS

1. Define each of the following words as it is used in this selection.

quarry (5)   nil (8)
pedestrian (6)   plausible (9)

foolhardy (11)   pat (20)
elated (19)   facets (28)

2. Muller's essay includes a number of words traditionally associated with detective stories — for example, *sleuth* (title) and *whodunit* (1). What other such words can you identify? What do they add to the essay?

3. What adjectives does Muller use to describe Sharon McCone? Which of these adjectives, if any, could not be used to describe a male detective?

JOURNAL ENTRY

Review the steps in Muller's writing process, and compare them with the steps in the writing process outlined in Chapters 1 through 3 of this text. How are the two processes alike? How are they different? How do you account for the differences?

WRITING WORKSHOP

1. Rewrite Muller's process explanation as a brief "how-to" essay aimed at writers who want to write a detective story.

2. Write a process explanation telling how you would write a story that features another kind of nontraditional detective — for example, a member of an ethnic or racial minority or a person with a disability. What "technical problems" would you have, and how would you solve them?

3. Write a process essay in which you explain how you would create a different kind of character altogether — for example, a villain in a romance novel or a comic book or movie superhero with unusual powers.

COMBINING THE PATTERNS

Although this essay explains a process, Muller uses a good deal of **description** as well. Is this description primarily *subjective* or *objective*? Should she have included additional passages of description?

THEMATIC CONNECTIONS

- "Why Boys Don't Play with Dolls" (page 335)
- "Sex, Lies, and Conversation" (page 407)
- Declaration of Sentiments and Resolutions (page 563)

JOSHUA PIVEN, DAVID BORGENICHT, AND JENNIFER WORICK

❖

How to Escape from a Bad Date

Joshua Piven and David Borgenicht are the authors of the runaway best-seller *The Worst-Case Scenario Survival Handbook* (1999), for which they consulted numerous experts to enable them to provide advice for such dilemmas as "How to Break into a Parked Car" and "How to Escape from a Mountain Lion." The success of the book sparked a series that now includes *The Worst-Case Scenario Travel Handbook* (2001), *The Worst-Case Scenario Handbook: Golf* (2002), *The Worst-Case Scenario Handbook: Holidays* (2002), and the upcoming *The Worst-Case Scenario Handbook: College,* as well as the reality-television show *Worst-Case Scenario.* In 2002, they collaborated on *The Worst-Case Scenario Handbook: Sex and Dating* with Jennifer Worick, who is also the author of *My Fabulous Life: Musings on a Marvelous Me* (2001), *Nancy Drew's Guide to Life* (2001), and *The Art of Belly Dancing* (2002).

Background: The United States has a long history of "how-to," advice, and self-improvement books dating back to Benjamin Franklin's *Poor Richard's Almanack* (1732–1757), but beginning in the 1930s, the genre proliferated when publications such as Dale Carnegie's *How to Win Friends and Influence People* topped the best-seller lists. The "Self-Help" and "How-To" sections are now among the largest in many bookstores, and the success of the *for Dummies* series suggests the wide range of topics covered by such advice books. The books in the *Worst-Case Scenario* series, however, are generally shelved in bookstore "Humor" sections because they offer tongue-in-cheek advice that is not really intended to be followed. Such parodies have been popular at least since Shepherd Mead's 1952 *How to Succeed in Business without Really Trying;* other examples include *The Official Preppy Handbook* (1980) and *Life for Real Dummies* (1998). More specifically, the *Sex and Dating* entry parodies such relationship-oriented how-to books as 1999's *The Rules: Time-Tested Secrets for Capturing the Heart of Mr. Right,* aimed at the kind of young urban singles depicted in the television series *Sex and the City.*

Fake an Emergency

1. Excuse Yourself from the Table.

Tell your date that you are going to the restroom to "wash up." Take your cell phone with you. If you do not have one, locate a restaurant phone that's out of your date's line of vision. Bring a restaurant matchbook or a business card that includes the restaurant's phone number.

2. Call a Friend or Relative for Help.

Tell them to call you (either on your cell phone or on the restaurant's phone) and pretend there has been an emergency. Believable emergencies are:

- Personal Crisis: "My friend just broke up with her husband—she's having a breakdown. I have to go."
- Business Crisis: "My boss just called—she's in Seattle for a major presentation, and has lost all her files. I have to e-mail them to her immediately."
- Health Crisis: "My sister just called—our grandmother is alone and ill."

3. Leave Quickly before Your Date Can Protest.

Apologize, but refuse any attempt your date makes to accompany you. 3 If you leave swiftly and without hesitation, your date won't have time to understand what's happening or to object.

Slip Away Unnoticed

1. Identify Your Escape Route.

Observe your surroundings. Take note of the exits, especially the back 4 doors. Look for the best way out and an alternative.

2. Plan to Alter Your Appearance.

Think about your most distinctive features and figure out how to hide 5 or disguise them. The person you are trying to leave is going to see a figure moving past and away at a distance and will be focusing on the first impression. If you are not familiar to him and are uninteresting, you will not get a second look.

3. Excuse Yourself from the Table.

Move to the restroom or any private area with a mirror to begin your 6 transformation. Your date will probably wait only two or three minutes before expecting you to return, so act quickly, before he begins looking for you.

4. Add or Remove Clothing.

Layering garments will change your body shape and even suggest a dif- 7 ferent gender. A long coat will obscure your body type. Hats are especially useful because they conceal your hair and facial features. Eyeglasses, whether added or removed, work wonders. A shopping bag is a handy prop and can be used to hold your belongings.

5. Change Your Walk and Posture.

If you usually walk quickly, move slowly. If you stand up straight, 8 hunch over. To alter your gait, slip a pebble in one shoe or bind one of your knees with a piece of string or cloth.

6. Use or Remove Cosmetics.

Lipstick can change the shape of your mouth, heighten the color in 9 your cheeks and nose, and even give you tired eyes if dabbed and blended

Add—or remove—eyeglasses. Roll or unroll your sleeves; tuck in or untuck your blouse. Modify your hairstyle.

on your eyelids. An eyebrow pencil can be used to add age lines, change the shape of your eyes and brows, or create facial hair.

7. Change Your Hairstyle or Color.

A rubberband, hairspray, water, or any gooey substance can be useful for changing a hairstyle, darkening your hair, or altering a hairline. Borrow flour from the kitchen to lighten or gray your hair color.

10

8. Adopt a Cover Role.

A waiter in the restaurant may have an apron and be carrying a tray. If [11] you can manage to procure these items, add or subtract a pair of eyeglasses and alter your hairline or hairstyle, you can become invisible as you are moving out of the restaurant, into the kitchen, and out the rear door. Or you can take on the role of a maintenance worker; carry a convenient potted plant out the front door and no one will think twice.

9. Make Your Move.

Do not look at your date. [12]

Slip Out the Window

If you do not think you will be able to change your appearance enough [13] to slip past your date, you may have to find another way to depart. Back doors are the simplest; they are often located near the restrooms or are marked as fire exits. Do not open an emergency exit door if it is alarmed unless absolutely necessary; an alarm will only draw attention. If there are no accessible alternate doors, you will need to find a window.

1. Locate a Usable Window.

Avoid windows with chicken wire or large plate glass. Bathroom win- [14] dows often work best. If you are not on the ground floor, be sure there is a fire escape.

2. Attempt to Open the Window.

Do not immediately break the window, no matter how dire your need [15] to get out.

3. Prepare to Break the Window If You Cannot Open It.

Make sure no one is around. If you can, lock the bathroom door. [16]

4. Find an Implement to Break the Window.

Try to avoid using your elbow, fist, or foot. Suitable implements are: [17]

- Wastebasket
- Toilet plunger
- Handbag or briefcase
- Paper towel dispenser

5. Strike the Center of the Glass with the Implement

If the hand holding the implement will come within a foot of the win- [18] dow as you break it, wrap it with a jacket or sweater before attempting to break the glass. If no implement is available, use your heavily wrapped hand; be sure you wrap your arm as well, beyond the elbow.

Strike the center of the glass with the implement.

6. Punch Out Any Remaining Shards of Glass.

Cover your fist with a jacket or sweater before removing the glass.   19

7. Make Your Escape.

Do not worry about any minor nicks and cuts. Run.   20

Get Your Date to Leave

1. Say Something Offensive.

If you know your date is of a particular religion or ethnicity, make   21
inappropriate comments.

2. Behave Inappropriately.

Do things that you think he will find unattractive or distasteful: chew   22
with your mouth open, eat with your fingers, argue with the waiter, close
your eyes and pretend to sleep, light matches and drop them on your plate,
ignore everything he says, and/or call someone else on your cell phone.

3. Send Your Date on a "Fool's Errand."

- Tell him you want to go to a specific nightclub, but explain that it gets 23
very crowded and that if you are not in line by a certain time (say, fifteen minutes from then), you won't get in. Tell your date that you have
arranged to have your friend stop by the restaurant with guest passes,
but that if your date does not go ahead to the nightclub to get in line,
you'll never make it inside. If your date wants your cell phone number,
give the number willingly but make sure you change one digit. Promise
you will see your date within half an hour. Never show.

- Fake an allergy attack, and insist that he leave in search of the appropriate over-the-counter allergy medicine. Explain that you must have
been allergic to something in the drink/appetizer/food/taxicab, and
that if you do not obtain your medicine you will break out in hives.
When your date dutifully leaves, slip away.

Be Aware

Blind dates are the riskiest form of dating—it is best to check out a 24
potential suitor extensively before the date.

- Have a friend agree to check out your potential suitor and call you
before you enter the bar/restaurant. Send your friend in with a cell
phone. Situate yourself at a bar nearby, and await her call. Have her
contact you when she has identified the mark.

- If you discover unsavory facts about someone you're supposed to meet,
call immediately to cancel the date. Blame work and say that you have
to stay late at the office, or say that you're experiencing car trouble. A
more permanent solution is to say that an old flame has reentered your
life; this will prevent your blind date from calling you again and asking
for a rain check.

• • •

COMPREHENSION

1. According to the authors, what four basic strategies can be used by someone who wants to escape from a bad date?

2. Which of the four strategies seems most realistic? Why?

3. What kind of date do the authors seem to be imagining? Where does the
date take place? How can you tell? Can the "escape" strategies the authors
describe be used for other kinds of dates as well?

PURPOSE AND AUDIENCE

1. Do the authors expect their advice to be taken seriously? How do you
know?

2. What purpose do visuals usually serve in instructions? What purpose do the visuals serve in this selection?

3. What thesis is implied in this set of instructions? Write a sentence that could serve as the thesis statement. Should such a sentence be added?

4. Is the intended audience of this selection men, women, or both? How can you tell?

5. The writers never define what they mean by a "bad date." Why not?

STYLE AND STRUCTURE

1. This selection is neither structured nor formatted like the other essays in this text. What does it include that other essays do not? What elements are missing that other essays include?

2. What features tell you that this is a set of instructions rather than a process explanation?

3. Instructions are directed at people who will actually perform the process described. Is that the case here? Explain.

4. Where do the authors include the cautions and reminders that characterize instructions? Are these warnings and reminders actually necessary here?

5. Look carefully at the steps listed under each of the essay's four headings. How do the authors move readers from one step to the next? Would transitional words and expressions be helpful additions? If so, which ones? Explain.

VOCABULARY PROJECTS

1. Define each of the following words as it is used in this selection.

obscure (7)   dire (15)
gait (8)   implement (17)
procure (11)   unsavory (24)

2. Despite its informal style and tone, "How to Escape from a Bad Date" uses some terms—for example, "escape route" (4) and "prop" (7)—designed to make it sound like an authentic set of instructions. Identify other examples of such language. Do these expressions make the selection seem more serious? More credible?

JOURNAL ENTRY

Think about a date you wanted to "escape" from but couldn't. Which of the strategies presented here might have been useful to you?

WRITING WORKSHOP

1. Although this is a humorous essay, the writers nevertheless do give some useful advice. Write a new version of these instructions, including only

those steps that you see as realistic and sensible. In your introduction, give some reasons that someone might need to escape from a date; in your conclusion, make recommendations for avoiding such problems in the future.

2. Rewrite one of the selection's four sections, replacing the authors' specific advice with advice of your own — for example, your own steps for faking an emergency or getting your date to leave. Add an introduction and a conclusion to make your instructions into a complete essay.

3. Write a set of instructions for how to escape from a bad party.

COMBINING THE PATTERNS

"How to Escape from a Bad Date" presents the steps in a process but considers neither the causes nor the effects of the "escape." What might cause someone to need to escape from a date? What might the effects of such an escape be? Should the authors have included sections of **cause and effect** to answer these questions?

THEMATIC CONNECTIONS

- "Sex, Lies, and Conversation" (page 407)
- "The Ways We Lie" (page 470)

❖
On Fire

Larry Brown was born in 1951 into a farming family in Oxford, Mississippi. After serving as a marine during the Vietnam War, he attended the University of Mississippi and held a variety of odd jobs until he joined the Oxford Fire Department in 1973. Promoted to captain in 1986, Brown retired from firefighting in 1990 in order to pursue full time a writing career that had begun in 1986 with the publication of a collection of short stories, *Facing the Music*. This book was followed by the novel *Dirty Work* (1989), as well as *Joe* (1991) and *Father and Son* (1996), both of which won the Southern Book Critics' Award for fiction. Brown's most recent book is the autobiography *Billy Ray's Farm* (2001). The following selection is from Brown's *On Fire: A Personal Account of Life and Death and Choices* (1994), a series of diary-like entries about his life as a firefighter in a small town.

Background: Firefighting goes back to ancient times: it is known, for example, that the Roman government employed about 7,000 firefighters by the first century A.D. The first fire department in the United States was established in 1653 in New Amsterdam (now New York City), and other cities soon followed suit. Currently, there are some thirty thousand fire departments in the United States and approximately one million firefighters, 74 percent of whom are volunteers. On average each year, firefighters are called to two million fires, and one hundred firefighters die in the line of duty (that number was catastrophically higher in 2001 because of the 343 New York City firefighters killed in the aftermath of the terrorist attacks on the World Trade Center).

You learn early to go in low, that heat and smoke rise into the ceiling, that cooler air is near the floor. You learn to button your collar tightly around your neck, to pull the gauntlets of your gloves up over the cuffs of your coat, that embers can go anywhere skin is exposed. You learn that you are only human flesh, not Superman, and that you can burn like a candle.

You try to go easy on the air that's inside the tank on your back, try to be calm and not overly exert yourself, try and save some of your strength. You learn about exhaustion and giving it all you've got, then having to reach back and pull up some more. Suck it up and go.

You learn eventually not to let your legs tremble when you're pressing hard on the gas or the diesel pedal, when you're driving into something that is unknown.

One day if you make rank you will be promoted to driver or pump operator or lieutenant and you will discover what it feels like to roll up to a burning structure, a house that somebody lives in, or a university dormitory where hundreds of people live, or a business upon whose commerce somebody's livelihood depends. You will change in that moment, stop being a nozzleman and become instead the operator of the apparatus the nozzlemen are pulling lines from, and you will know then that the knowledge pushed into your head at dry training sessions in the fire station must now be applied to practical use, quickly, with no mistakes, because there are men you know whose lives are going to depend on a steady supply of water, at the right pressure, for as long as it takes to put the fire out.

And on that first time you'll probably be like I was, scared shitless. But you can't let that stop you from doing your job. 5

You learn the difficulty of raising a ladder and pulling the rope and raising the extensions up to a second-floor window, and the difficulty of climbing that ladder with a charged inch-and-a-half line and then opening it and staying on the ladder without falling. 6

You learn of ropes and safety belts, insulated gloves to move downed high-voltage lines, nozzle pressure and friction loss and the rule of thumb for a two-and-a-half-inch nozzle. You learn to check the flow pressure on a fire hydrant and what burning plastic tastes like, the way it will make you gag and cough and puke when those fumes get into your lungs and you know that something very bad has come inside your body. You see death and hear the sounds of the injured. Some days you look at the fire phone and have a bad feeling, smoke more cigarettes, glance at the phone, and sometimes it rings. Sometimes you're wrong and the night passes without trouble. 7

You learn to love a job that is not like sacking groceries or working in a factory or painting houses, because everybody watches you when you come down the street. You wear a blue uniform with silver or brass or gold, and you get free day-old doughnuts from the bakery shop down the street. At Christmas people bring in pies, cakes, cookies, ham, smoked sausage, cheese, half-pints of whiskey. They thank you for your work in a season of good cheer. One freezing December night the whole department gathers with eighty steaks and Wally parks his wheeled cooker and dumps in sixty or seventy pounds of charcoal to cook them and you have drinks and play Bingo for prizes that businesses in your town have donated, a rechargeable flashlight from the auto supply, a hot-air popcorn popper from a department store, a case of beer from the grocery down the street. 8

You lay out hose in the deadly summer heat on a street with no shade, hook it all up, hundreds and hundreds of feet of it, put closed nozzles on the end of the hose, and run the pressure up to three hundred psi* and hold it for five minutes. If a piece bursts and creates a waterstorm on the street, you remove that section from the line and throw it away. Then you shut it down and drain it and write down the identification number of every piece of hose that survived the test and put it all back on the truck, thirteen hundred feet of it, and you make new bends and turns so the rubber coating inside it won't kink and start to dry-rot. 9

---

*EDS. NOTE — Pounds per square inch.

You learn the major arteries of the body and the names of the bones 10
and how to splint a leg or an arm, how to tie off and cut an umbilical cord.
You learn to read blood pressure, administer oxygen. You see amounts of
blood that are unbelievable, not realizing until it's actually spilled how
much the human body holds. You crawl up under taxpayers' houses for
their dogs, go inside culverts where snakes may be hiding for their cats.
You learn to do whatever is called for.

No two days are ever the same and you're thankful for that. You dread 11
the winter and the advent of ice. On an August day you pray that the city
will behave and let you lie under the air conditioner and read a good book,
draw easy money.

You learn that your muscles and bones and tendons get older and that 12
you cannot remain young forever. You test the pump on the truck every
day when you come on duty, make sure it's full of fuel, clean, full of water,
that the extinguishers are up. You check that your turnouts* are all
together, hanging on the hook that has your name written above it, and
that both your gloves are in your coat pocket. You make sure your flashlight works. You test the siren and the lights because everything has to be
in readiness. You shut it all down and stand back and look at the deep red
Imron paint, the gold leafing and lettering, the chrome valves and caps, the
shiny chains and levers, the fluid-filled pressure gauges, the beds filled with
woven nylon, the nozzles folded back into layers of hose, the hydrant
wrenches snug in their holders, everything on this magnificent machine.
You learn every inch of your truck and you know which compartments
hold the forcible entry tools, the exhaust fans for removing smoke from a
house, the power saws, the portable generator, the pike poles, the scoops,
the salvage covers, the boltcutters, the axes, the ropes, the rappelling gear.
You look at all of it over and over again and then you go inside the fire station and get a cup of coffee, sit down with a magazine or a newspaper, and
once more, you wait for whatever comes your way.

• • •

COMPREHENSION

1. What process does Brown describe?
2. Into what general stages can you group the individual steps in the process?
3. Does Brown seem to consider some steps more important than others? If
   so, how does he indicate this?
4. What does Brown see as the good and bad points of his job?

PURPOSE AND AUDIENCE

1. For whom is this essay intended? Firefighters? A general audience? How
   can you tell?

---

*EDS. NOTE — Firefighter's apparel.

2. What impressions of firefighting does Brown wish to convey? Do you think he achieves his purpose?

3. Does this essay have an explicitly stated thesis? If so, where is it? Do you think an explicit thesis statement is necessary here?

STYLE AND STRUCTURE

1. What words and phrases are repeated in this essay? Do these repetitions strengthen or weaken the essay? Explain your reasoning.

2. In paragraph 1, Brown uses a **simile** when he says that one of the things firefighters learn is that they "can burn like a candle." Where else does he use similes or other **figures of speech**? How does such language enhance the essay?

3. Brown uses a variety of stylistic devices in his essay. Comment on the effectiveness of each of these devices: sentence fragments; contractions; long, rhythmic sentences; juxtaposition of long and short paragraphs.

4. How do you interpret the essay's title? Do you think Brown intends it to have more than one meaning?

5. Throughout his essay, Brown repeatedly uses the pronoun *you.* Some readers might find this usage too general or too informal for a discussion of such a serious subject. Why do you suppose Brown chooses this pronoun instead of the more usual *I* or *he?* Does *you* refer to his readers? Explain.

6. How is this essay like and unlike the typical process explanation? For example, does it include steps presented in chronological order? A list of materials and equipment? Warnings and cautions? How do you account for any departures from the pattern of the typical process explanation?

7. Is paragraph 8 a digression, or is it part of the process? Explain.

VOCABULARY PROJECTS

1. Define each of the following words as it is used in this selection.

gauntlets (1)   advent (11)
culverts (10)   rappelling (12)

2. Brown uses **slang,** professional **jargon,** and impolite language in this essay. Identify one or two examples of each, and explain why it is used instead of a more formal, neutral, or polite term.

JOURNAL ENTRY

Brown clearly has mixed feelings about his job. What conflicting emotions do you see in his essay?

WRITING WORKSHOP

1. Recast "On Fire" as a letter of application for a position with a different fire department or as an application for promotion. Use process to

structure the body of the essay, and write in the first person and the present tense. Try to be somewhat less emotional and subjective than Brown, but be sure to stress what a valuable employee you have been.

2. Write a process essay about a difficult job you have (or have had). As you explain your day-to-day routine, try to convey the challenges of your job to readers.

3. Use the material in Brown's essay to help you write a set of instructions directed at firefighter trainees. Be honest about the tasks required, and try to balance the positive and negative aspects of the job.

COMBINING THE PATTERNS

In paragraph 8, Brown comments that firefighting is "a job that is not like sacking groceries or working in a factory or painting houses, because everybody watches you when you come down the street," but he does not go beyond this comment to compare firefighting to other occupations. Do you think this essay would be strengthened if it began or ended with a **comparison-and-contrast** paragraph that explained exactly how different firefighting is from other jobs? How would the addition of such an opening or closing paragraph change the essay?

THEMATIC CONNECTIONS

- "Scrubbing in Maine" (page 106)
- "Ground Zero" (page 158)
- "Midnight" (page 201)
- "The Men We Carry in Our Minds" (page 456)

❖

The Embalming of Mr. Jones

Jessica Mitford (1917–1996) was born in Batsford Mansion, England, to a wealthy, aristocratic family. She rebelled against her sheltered upbringing, became involved in left-wing politics, and eventually immigrated to the United States. Mitford wrote two volumes of autobiography — *Daughters and Rebels* (1960), about her eccentric family, and *A Fine Old Conflict* (1976). In the 1950s, she began a career in investigative journalism, which produced the books *The American Way of Death* (1963), about abuses in the funeral business; *Kind and Usual Punishment* (1973), about the U.S. prison system; and *The American Way of Birth* (1992), about the crisis in American obstetrical care.

Background: "The Embalming of Mr. Jones" is excerpted from *The American Way of Death,* a scathing critique of the funeral industry in the United States. The book prompted angry responses from morticians but also led to increased governmental regulation, culminating in a 1984 Federal Trade Commission ruling requiring funeral homes to disclose in writing the prices for all goods and services as well as certain consumer rights; barring funeral homes from forcing consumers to purchase more than they really want; and forbidding funeral directors from misleading consumers regarding state laws governing the disposal of bodies. Still, critics of the industry charge that many abuses continue. While funeral services can be purchased for less than a thousand dollars, the standard rate is between two and four thousand dollars — and can go much higher. The difference in cost is based largely on the price of a casket, and grieving family members are often strongly pressured into buying the most expensive caskets, which may be marked up as much as 500 percent. Advocates for reform suggest that consumers choose cremation over burial (of the approximately 2.5 million people who died in the United States in 2000, only some 600,000 were cremated) and that they hold memorial services in churches or other settings, where costs are much lower than in funeral homes.

Embalming is indeed a most extraordinary procedure, and one must wonder at the docility of Americans who each year pay hundreds of millions of dollars for its perpetuation, blissfully ignorant of what it is all about, what is done, how it is done. Not one in ten thousand has any idea of what actually takes place. Books on the subject are extremely hard to come by. They are not to be found in most libraries or bookshops.

In an era when huge television audiences watch surgical operations in the comfort of their living rooms, when, thanks to the animated cartoon, the geography of the digestive system has become familiar territory even to the nursery school set, in a land where the satisfaction of curiosity about almost all matters is a national pastime, the secrecy surrounding embalming can, surely, hardly be attributed to the inherent gruesomeness of the

1

2

subject. Custom in this regard has within this century suffered a complete reversal. In the early days of American embalming, when it was performed in the home of the deceased, it was almost mandatory for some relative to stay by the embalmer's side and witness the procedure. Today, family members who might wish to be in attendance would certainly be dissuaded by the funeral director. All others, except apprentices, are excluded by law from the preparation room.

A close look at what does actually take place may explain in large measure the undertaker's intractable reticence concerning a procedure that has become his major *raison d'être.** Is it possible he fears that public information about embalming might lead patrons to wonder if they really want this service? If the funeral men are loath to discuss the subject outside the trade, the reader may, understandably, be equally loath to go on reading at this point. For those who have the stomach for it, let us part the formaldehyde curtain. [. . .]

The body is first laid out in the undertaker's morgue — or rather, Mr. Jones is reposing in the preparation room — to be readied to bid the world farewell.

The preparation room in any of the better funeral establishments has the tiled and sterile look of a surgery, and indeed the embalmer-restorative artist who does his chores there is beginning to adopt the term "derma-surgeon" (appropriately corrupted by some mortician-writers as "demi-surgeon") to describe his calling. His equipment, consisting of scalpels, scissors, augers, forceps, clamps, needles, pumps, tubes, bowls, and basin, is crudely imitative of the surgeon's as is his technique, acquired in a nine- or twelve-month post-high-school course in an embalming school. He is supplied by an advanced chemical industry with a bewildering array of fluids, sprays, pastes, oils, powders, creams, to fix or soften tissue, shrink or distend it as needed, dry it here, restore the moisture there. There are cosmetics, waxes, and paints to fill and cover features, even plaster of Paris to replace entire limbs. There are ingenious aids to prop and stabilize the cadaver: a Vari-Pose Head Rest, the Edwards Arm and Hand Positioner, the Repose Block (to support the shoulders during the embalming), and the Throop Foot Positioner, which resembles an old-fashioned stocks.

Mr. John H. Eckels, president of the Eckels College of Mortuary Science, thus describes the first part of the embalming procedure: "In the hands of a skilled practitioner, this work may be done in a comparatively short time and without mutilating the body other than by slight incision — so slight that it scarcely would cause serious inconvenience if made upon a living person. It is necessary to remove all the blood, and doing this not only helps in the disinfecting, but removes the principal cause of disfigurements due to discoloration."

Another textbook discusses the all-important time element: "The earlier this is done, the better, for every hour that elapses between death and

---

*Eds. note — Reason for being (French).

embalming will add to the problems and complications encountered. . . ." Just how soon should one get going on the embalming? The author tells us, "On the basis of such scanty information made available to this profession through its rudimentary and haphazard system of technical research, we must conclude that the best results are to be obtained if the subject is embalmed before life is completely extinct—that is, before cellular death has occurred. In the average case, this would mean within an hour after somatic death." For those who feel that there is something a little rudimentary, not to say haphazard, about this advice, a comforting thought is offered by another writer. Speaking of fears entertained in early days of premature burial, he points out, "One of the effects of embalming by chemical injection, however, has been to dispel fears of live burial." How true; once the blood is removed, chances of live burial are indeed remote.

To return to Mr. Jones, the blood is drained out through the veins and replaced by embalming fluid pumped in through the arteries. As noted in *The Principles and Practices of Embalming,* "every operator has a favorite injection and drainage point—a fact which becomes a handicap only if he fails or refuses to forsake his favorites when conditions demand it." Typical favorites are the carotid artery, femoral artery, jugular vein, subclavian vein. There are various choices of embalming fluid. If Flextone is used, it will produce a "mild, flexible rigidity. The skin retains a velvety softness, the tissues are rubbery and pliable. Ideal for women and children." It may be blended with B. and G. Products Company's Lyf-Lyk tint, which is guaranteed to reproduce "nature's own skin texture . . . the velvety appearance of living tissue." Suntone comes in three separate tints: Suntan; Special Cosmetic Tint, a pink shade "especially indicated for young female subjects"; and Regular Cosmetic Tint, moderately pink. 8

About three to six gallons of a dyed and perfumed solution of formaldehyde, glycerin, borax, phenol, alcohol, and water is soon circulating through Mr. Jones, whose mouth has been sewn together with a "needle directed upward between the upper lip and gum and brought out through the left nostril," with the corners raised slightly "for a more pleasant expression." If he should be buck-toothed, his teeth are cleaned with Bon Ami and coated with colorless nail polish. His eyes, meanwhile, are closed with flesh-tinted eye caps and eye cement. 9

The next step is to have at Mr. Jones with a thing called a trocar. This is a long, hollow needle attached to a tube. It is jabbed into the abdomen, poked around the entrails and chest cavity, the contents of which are pumped out and replaced with "cavity fluid." This done, and the hole in the abdomen sewed up, Mr. Jones's face is heavily creamed (to protect the skin from burns which may be caused by leakage of the chemicals), and he is covered with a sheet and left unmolested for a while. But not for long— there is more, much more, in store for him. He has been embalmed, but not yet restored, and the best time to start restorative work is eight to ten hours after embalming, when the tissues have become firm and dry. 10

The object of all this attention to the corpse, it must be remembered, is   11
to make it presentable for viewing in an attitude of healthy repose. "Our
customs require the presentation of our dead in the semblance of normal-
ity . . . unmarred by the ravages of illness, disease or mutilation," says Mr. J.
Sheridan Mayer in his *Restorative Art.* This is rather a large order since few
people die in the full bloom of health, unravaged by illness and unmarked
by some disfigurement. The funeral industry is equal to the challenge: "In
some cases the gruesome appearance of a mutilated or disease-ridden subject may be quite discouraging. The task of restoration may seem impossible and shake the confidence of the embalmer. This is the time for
intestinal fortitude and determination. Once the formative work is begun
and affected tissues are cleaned or removed, all doubts of success vanish. It
is surprising and gratifying to discover the results which may be obtained."

The embalmer, having allowed an appropriate interval to elapse, re-   12
turns to the attack, but now he brings into play the skill and equipment
of sculptor and cosmetician. Is a hand missing? Casting one in plaster of
Paris is a simple matter. "For replacement purposes, only a cast of the back
of the hand is necessary; this is within the ability of the average operator
and is quite adequate." If a lip or two, a nose or an ear should be missing,
the embalmer has at hand a variety of restorative waxes with which to
model replacements. Pores and skin texture are simulated by stippling
with a little brush, and over this cosmetics are laid on. Head off? Decapitation cases are rather routinely handled. Ragged edges are trimmed, and
head joined to torso with a series of splints, wires, and sutures. It is a good
idea to have a little something at the neck — a scarf or high collar — when
time for viewing comes. Swollen mouth? Cut out tissue as needed from
inside the lips. If too much is removed, the surface contour can easily be
restored by padding with cotton. Swollen necks and cheeks are reduced by
removing tissue through vertical incisions made down each side of the
neck. "When the deceased is casketed, the pillow will hide the suture incisions. . . . as an extra precaution against leakage, the suture may be painted
with liquid sealer."

The opposite condition is more likely to be present itself — that of ema-   13
ciation. His hypodermic syringe now loaded with massage cream, the
embalmer seeks out and fills the hollowed and sunken areas by injection.
In this procedure the backs of the hands and fingers and the underchin
area should not be neglected.

Positioning the lips is a problem that recurrently challenges the inge-   14
nuity of the embalmer. Closed too tightly, they tend to give a stern, even
disapproving expression. Ideally, embalmers feel, the lips should give the
impression of being ever so slightly parted, the upper lip protruding
slightly for a more youthful appearance. This takes some engineering,
however, as the lips tend to drift apart. Lip drift can sometimes be reme-
died by pushing one or two straight pins through the inner margin of the
lower lip and then inserting them between the two front upper teeth. If Mr.
Jones happens to have no teeth, the pins can just as easily be anchored in

his Armstrong Face Former and Denture Replacer. Another method to maintain lip closure is to dislocate the lower jaw, which is then held in its new position by a wire run through holes which have been drilled through the upper jaws at the midline. As the French are fond of saying, *il faut souffrir pour être belle.**

If Mr. Jones has died of jaundice, the embalming fluid will very likely turn him green. Does this deter the embalmer? Not if he has intestinal fortitude. Masking pastes and cosmetics are heavily laid on, burial garments and casket interiors are color-correlated with particular care, and Jones is displayed beneath rose-colored lights. Friends will say, "How *well* he looks." Death by carbon monoxide, on the other hand, can be rather a good thing from an embalmer's viewpoint: "One advantage is the fact that this type of discoloration is an exaggerated form of a natural pink coloration." This is nice because the healthy glow is already present and needs but little attention.

The patching and filling completed, Mr. Jones is now shaved, washed, and dressed. Cream-based cosmetic, available in pink, flesh, suntan, brunette, and blonde, is applied to his hands and face, his hair is shampooed and combed (and, in the case of Mrs. Jones, set), his hands manicured. For the horny-handed son of toil special care must be taken; cream should be applied to remove ingrained grime, and the nails cleaned. "If he were not in the habit of having them manicured in life, trimming and shaping is advised for better appearance — never questioned by kin."

Jones is now ready for casketing (this is the present participle of the verb "to casket"). In this operation his right shoulder should be depressed slightly "to turn the body a bit to the right and soften the appearance of lying flat on the back." Positioning the hands is a matter of importance, and special rubber positioning blocks may be used. The hands should be cupped slightly for a more lifelike, relaxed appearance. Proper placement of the body requires a delicate sense of balance. It should lie as high as possible in the casket, yet not so high that the lid, when lowered, will hit the nose. On the other hand, we are cautioned, placing the body too low "creates the impression that the body is in a box."

Jones is next wheeled into the appointed slumber room where a few last touches may be added — his favorite pipe placed in his hand or, if he was a great reader, a book propped into position. (In the case of little Master Jones a Teddy bear may be clutched.) Here he will hold open house for a few days, visiting hours 10 A.M. to 9 P.M.

• • •

COMPREHENSION

1. How, according to Mitford, has the public's knowledge of embalming changed? How does she explain this change?

---

*EDS. NOTE — It is necessary to suffer in order to be beautiful.

2. To what other professionals does Mitford liken the embalmer? Are these analogies flattering or critical? Explain.

3. What are the major stages in the process of embalming and restoration?

PURPOSE AND AUDIENCE

1. Mitford's purpose in this essay is to convince her audience of something. What is her thesis?

2. Do you think Mitford expects her audience to agree with her thesis? How can you tell?

3. In one of her books, Mitford refers to herself as a *muckraker*, one who informs the public of misconduct. Does she achieve this status here? Cite specific examples.

4. Mitford's tone in this essay is subjective, even judgmental. What effect does her tone have on you? Does it encourage you to trust her? Should she present her facts in a more objective way? Explain.

STYLE AND STRUCTURE

1. Identify the stylistic features that distinguish this process explanation from a set of instructions.

2. In this selection, as in many process essays, a list of necessary materials comes before the procedure. What additional details does Mitford include in her list in paragraph 5? How do these additions affect you?

3. Locate Mitford's remarks about the language of embalming. How do her comments about euphemisms, newly coined words, and other aspects of language help to support her thesis?

4. Throughout the essay, Mitford quotes various experts. How does she use their remarks to support her thesis?

5. What phrases serve as transitions between the various stages of Mitford's process?

6. Mitford uses a good deal of sarcasm and loaded language in this essay. Identify some examples. Does this kind of language strengthen or weaken her essay?

VOCABULARY PROJECTS

1. Define each of the following words as it is used in this selection.

perpetuation (1)	rudimentary (7)	stippling (12)
inherent (2)	haphazard (7)	emaciation (13)
mandatory (2)	entertained (7)	recurrently (14)
dissuaded (2)	pliable (8)	jaundice (15)
intractable (3)	repose (11)	toil (16)
reticence (3)	unravaged (11)	
loath (3)	fortitude (11)	

2. Substitute another word for each of the following.

territory (2)   ingenious (5)   presentable (11)
gruesomeness (2)   jabbed (10)

What effect does each of your changes have on Mitford's meaning?

3. Reread paragraphs 5–9 carefully. Then, list all the words in this section of the essay that suggest surgical technique and all the words that suggest cosmetic artistry. What do your lists tell you about Mitford's intent in these paragraphs?

JOURNAL ENTRY

What are your thoughts about the way your religion or culture deals with death and dying? What practices, if any, make you uncomfortable? Why?

WRITING WORKSHOP

1. Rewrite this process explanation as a set of instructions for undertakers, condensing it so that your essay is about five hundred words long. Unlike Mitford, keep your essay objective.

2. In the role of a funeral director, write a letter to Mitford in which you take issue with her essay. Explain the practice of embalming as necessary and practical. Unlike Mitford, design your process explanation to defend the practice.

3. Write an explanation of a process that you personally find disgusting — or delightful. Make your attitude clear in your thesis statement and in your choice of words.

COMBINING THE PATTERNS

Although Mitford structures this essay as a process, many passages rely heavily on subjective **description**. Where is her focus on descriptive details most obvious? What is her purpose in describing particular individuals and objects as she does? How do these descriptive passages help to support her essay's thesis?

THEMATIC CONNECTIONS

- "My First Conk" (page 260)
- "The Ways We Lie" (page 470)
- "A Modest Proposal" (page 676)

SHIRLEY JACKSON

❖
The Lottery (Fiction)

Shirley Jackson (1919–1965) was born in California and graduated from Syracuse University in 1940. She is best known for her subtly macabre stories of horror and suspense, most notably her best-selling novel *The Haunting of Hill House* (1959), which Stephen King has called "one of the greatest horror stories of all time." She also published wryly humorous reflections on her experiences as a wife and mother of four children. Many of her finest stories and novels were anthologized after her death.

Background: "The Lottery" first appeared in *The New Yorker* in 1948, three years after the end of World War II. Jackson was living somewhat uneasily in the New England college town of Bennington, Vermont, a village very similar to the setting of "The Lottery." She felt herself an outsider there in many ways: a sophisticated intellectual in an isolated, closely knit community suspicious of strangers. Here, Jackson (whose husband was Jewish) experienced frequent encounters with anti-Semitism. Moreover, the full atrocity of Germany's wartime program to exterminate Jews, now called the Holocaust, had led many social critics to contemplate humanity's terrible capacity for evil. Most Americans of the time, however, wished to put the horrors of the war behind them, and many readers reacted with outrage to Jackson's tale of an annual small-town ritual, calling it "nasty," "nauseating," even "perverted." Others immediately recognized its genius, its power, and its many layers of meaning. This classic is now one of the most widely anthologized of twentieth-century short stories.

The morning of June 27th was clear and sunny, with the fresh warmth   1
of a full-summer day; the flowers were blossoming profusely and the grass was richly green. The people of the village began to gather in the square, between the post office and the bank, around ten o'clock; in some towns there were so many people that the lottery took two days and had to be started on June 26th, but in this village, where there were only about three hundred people, the whole lottery took less than two hours, so it could begin at ten o'clock in the morning and still be through in time to allow the villagers to get home for noon dinner.

The children assembled first, of course. School was recently over for   2
the summer, and the feeling of liberty sat uneasily on most of them; they tended to gather together quietly for a while before they broke into boisterous play, and their talk was still of the classroom and the teacher, of books and reprimands. Bobby Martin had already stuffed his pockets full of stones, and the other boys soon followed his example, selecting the smoothest and roundest stones; Bobby and Harry Jones and Dickie Delacroix—the villagers pronounced his name "Dellacroy"—eventually made a great pile of stones in one corner of the square and guarded it

against the raids of the other boys. The girls stood aside, talking among themselves, looking over their shoulders at the boys, and the very small children rolled in the dust or clung to the hands of their older brothers or sisters.

Soon the men began to gather, surveying their own children, speaking of planting and rain, tractors and taxes. They stood together, away from the pile of stones in the corner, and their jokes were quiet and they smiled rather than laughed. The women, wearing faded house dresses and sweaters, came shortly after their menfolk. They greeted one another and exchanged bits of gossip as they went to join their husbands. Soon the women, standing by their husbands, began to call to their children, and the children came reluctantly, having to be called four or five times. Bobby Martin ducked under his mother's grasping hand and ran, laughing, back to the pile of stones. His father spoke up sharply, and Bobby came quickly and took his place between his father and his oldest brother.

The lottery was conducted — as were the square dances, the teenage club, the Halloween program — by Mr. Summers, who had time and energy to devote to civic activities. He was a round-faced, jovial man and he ran the coal business, and people were sorry for him, because he had no children and his wife was a scold. When he arrived in the square, carrying the black wooden box, there was a murmur of conversation among the villagers, and he waved and called "Little late today, folks." The postmaster, Mr. Graves, followed him, carrying a three-legged stool, and the stool was put in the center of the square and Mr. Summers set the black box down on it. The villagers kept their distance, leaving a space between themselves and the stool, and when Mr. Summers said, "Some of you fellows want to give me a hand?" there was a hesitation before two men, Mr. Martin and his oldest son, Baxter, came forward to hold the box steady on the stool while Mr. Summers stirred up the papers inside it.

The original paraphernalia for the lottery had been lost long ago, and the black box now resting on the stool had been put into use even before Old Man Warner, the oldest man in town, was born. Mr. Summers spoke frequently to the villagers about making a new box, but no one liked to upset even as much tradition as was represented by the black box. There was a story that the present box had been made with some pieces of the box that had preceded it, the one that had been constructed when the first people settled down to make a village here. Every year, after the lottery, Mr. Summers began talking about a new box, but every year the subject was allowed to fade off without anything's being done. The black box grew shabbier each year; by now it was no longer completely black but splintered badly along one side to show the original wood color, and in some places faded and stained.

Mr. Martin and his oldest son, Baxter, held the black box securely on the stool until Mr. Summers had stirred the papers thoroughly with his hand. Because so much of the ritual had been forgotten or discarded, Mr. Summers had been successful in having slips of paper substituted for the chips of wood that had been used for generations. Chips of wood, Mr. Summers had argued, had been all very well when the village was tiny, but now that the population was more than three hundred and likely to keep on growing, it was necessary to use something that would fit more easily into the black box. The night before the lottery, Mr. Summers and Mr. Graves made up the slips of paper and put them in the box, and it was then taken to the safe of Mr. Summers' coal company and locked up until Mr. Summers was ready to take it to the square the next morning. The rest of the year, the box was put away, sometimes one place, sometimes another; it had spent one year in Mr. Graves' barn and another year underfoot in the post office, and sometimes it was set on a shelf in the Martin grocery and left there.

There was a great deal of fussing to be done before Mr. Summers 7 declared the lottery open. There were the lists to make up—of heads of families, heads of households in each family, members of each household in each family. There was the proper swearing-in of Mr. Summers by the postmaster, as the official of the lottery; at one time, some people remembered, there had been a recital of some sort, performed by the official of the lottery, a perfunctory, tuneless chant that had been rattled off duly each year; some people believed that the official of the lottery used to stand just so when he said or sang it, others believed that he was supposed to walk among the people, but years and years ago this part of the ritual had been allowed to lapse. There had been, also, a ritual salute, which the official of the lottery had had to use in addressing each person who came up to draw from the box, but this also had changed with time, until now it was felt necessary only for the official to speak to each person approaching. Mr. Summers was very good at all this; in his clean white shirt and blue jeans, with one hand resting carelessly on the black box, he seemed very proper and important as he talked interminably to Mr. Graves and the Martins.

Just as Mr. Summers finally left off talking and turned to the as- 8 sembled villagers, Mrs. Hutchinson came hurriedly along the path to the square, her sweater thrown over her shoulders, and slid into place in the back of the crowd. "Clean forgot what day it was," she said to Mrs. Delacroix, who stood next to her, and they both laughed softly. "Thought my old man was out back stacking wood," Mrs. Hutchinson went on, "and then I looked out the window and the kids were gone, and then I remembered it was the twenty-seventh and came a-running." She dried her hands on her apron, and Mrs. Delacroix said, "You're in time, though. They're still talking away up there."

Mrs. Hutchinson craned her neck to see through the crowd and found 9 her husband and children standing near the front. She tapped Mrs. Delacroix on the arm as a farewell and began to make her way through the crowd. The people separated good-humoredly to let her through; two or three people said, in voices just loud enough to be heard across the crowd, "Here comes your Missus, Hutchinson," and "Bill, she made it after all." Mrs. Hutchinson reached her husband, and Mr. Summers, who had been waiting, said cheerfully, "Thought we were going to have to get on without you, Tessie." Mrs. Hutchinson said, grinning, "Wouldn't have me leave m'dishes in the sink, now, would you, Joe?" and soft laughter ran through the crowd as the people stirred back into position after Mrs. Hutchinson's arrival.

"Well, now," Mr. Summers said soberly, "guess we better get started, get   10
this over with, so's we can go back to work. Anybody ain't here?"

"Dunbar," several people said. "Dunbar, Dunbar."   11

Mr. Summers consulted his list. "Clyde Dunbar," he said. "That's   12
right. He's broke his leg, hasn't he? Who's drawing for him?"

"Me, I guess," a woman said, and Mr. Summers turned to look at her.   13
"Wife draws for her husband," Mr. Summers said. "Don't you have a grown boy to do it for you, Janey?" Although Mr. Summers and everyone else in the village knew the answer perfectly well, it was the business of the official of the lottery to ask such questions formally. Mr. Summers waited with an expression of polite interest while Mrs. Dunbar answered.

"Horace's not but sixteen yet," Mrs. Dunbar said regretfully. "Guess I   14
gotta fill in for the old man this year."

"Right," Mr. Summers said. He made a note on the list he was holding.   15
Then he asked, "Watson boy drawing this year?"

A tall boy in the crowd raised his hand. "Here," he said. "I'm drawing   16
for m'mother and me." He blinked his eyes nervously and ducked his head as several voices in the crowd said things like "Good fellow, Jack," and "Glad to see your mother's got a man to do it."

"Well," Mr. Summers said, "guess that's everyone. Old Man Warner   17
make it?"

"Here," a voice said, and Mr. Summers nodded.   18

A sudden hush fell on the crowd as Mr. Summers cleared his throat   19
and looked at the list. "All ready?" he called. "Now, I'll read the names — heads of families first — and the men come up and take a paper out of the box. Keep the paper folded in your hand without looking at it until everyone has had a turn. Everything clear?"

The people had done it so many times that they only half listened to   20
the directions; most of them were quiet, wetting their lips, not looking around. Then Mr. Summers raised one hand high and said, "Adams." A man disengaged himself from the crowd and came forward. "Hi, Steve," Mr. Summers said, and Mr. Adams said, "Hi, Joe." They grinned at one another humorlessly and nervously. Then Mr. Adams reached into the black box and took out a folded paper. He held it firmly by one corner as he turned and went hastily back to his place in the crowd, where he stood a little apart from his family, not looking down at his hand.

"Allen." Mr. Summers said. "Anderson. . . . Betham."   21

"Seems like there's no time at all between lotteries any more," Mrs.   22
Delacroix said to Mrs. Graves in the back row. "Seems like we got through the last one only last week."

"Time sure goes fast," Mrs. Graves said.   23

"Clark. . . . Delacroix."   24

"There goes my old man," Mrs. Delacroix said. She held her breath   25
while her husband went forward.

"Dunbar," Mr. Summers said, and Mrs. Dunbar went steadily to the   26
box while one of the women said, "Go on, Janey," and another said, "There
she goes."

"We're next," Mrs. Graves said. She watched while Mr. Graves came   27
around from the side of the box, greeted Mr. Summers gravely, and
selected a slip of paper from the box. By now, all through the crowd there
were men holding the small folded papers in their large hands, turning
them over and over nervously. Mrs. Dunbar and her two sons stood
together, Mrs. Dunbar holding the slip of paper.

"Harburt. . . . Hutchinson."   28

"Get up there, Bill," Mrs. Hutchinson said, and the people near her   29
laughed.

"Jones."   30

"They do say," Mr. Adams said to Old Man Warner, who stood next to   31
him, "that over in the north village they're talking of giving up the lottery."

Old Man Warner snorted. "Pack of crazy fools," he said. "Listening to   32
the young folks, nothing's good enough for *them*. Next thing you know,
they'll be wanting to go back to living in caves, nobody work any more, live
that way for a while. Used to be a saying about 'Lottery in June, corn be
heavy soon.' First thing you know, we'd all be eating stewed chickweed and
acorns. There's *always* been a lottery," he added petulantly. "Bad enough to
see young Joe Summers up there joking with everybody."

"Some places have already quit lotteries," Mrs. Adams said.   33

"Nothing but trouble in *that*," Old Man Warner said stoutly. "Pack of   34
young fools."

"Martin." And Bobby Martin watched his father go forward. "Over-   35
dyke. . . . Percy."

"I wish they'd hurry," Mrs. Dunbar said to her older son. "I wish they'd   36
hurry."

"They're almost through," her son said.   37

"You get ready to run tell Dad," Mrs. Dunbar said.   38

Mr. Summers called his own name and then stepped forward precisely   39
and selected a slip from the box. Then he called, "Warner."

"Seventy-seventh year I been in the lottery," Old Man Warner said as he   40
went through the crowd. "Seventy-seventh time."

"Watson." The tall boy came awkwardly through the crowd. Someone   41
said, "Don't be nervous, Jack," and Mr. Summers said, "Take your time, son."

"Zanini."   42

After that, there was a long pause, a breathless pause, until Mr. Sum-   43
mers, holding his slip of paper in the air, said, "All right fellows." For a
minute, no one moved, and then all the slips of paper were opened. Sud-

denly, all the women began to speak at once, saying, "Who is it," "Who's got it?," "Is it the Dunbars?," "Is it the Watsons?" Then the voices began to say, "It's Hutchinson. It's Bill," "Bill Hutchinson's got it."

"Go tell your father," Mrs. Dunbar said to her older son. 44

People began to look around to see the Hutchinsons. Bill Hutchinson 45
was standing quiet, staring down at the paper in his hand. Suddenly, Tessie Hutchinson shouted to Mr. Summers, "You didn't give him time enough to take any paper he wanted. I saw you. It wasn't fair!"

"Be a good sport, Tessie," Mrs. Delacroix called, and Mrs. Graves said, 46
"All of us took the same chance."

"Shut up, Tessie," Bill Hutchinson said. 47

"Well, everyone," Mr. Summers said, "That was done pretty fast, and 48
now we've got to be hurrying a little more to get it done in time." He consulted his next list. "Bill," he said, "you draw for the Hutchinson family. You got any other households in the Hutchinsons?"

"There's Don and Eva," Mrs. Hutchinson yelled. "Make *them* take their 49
chance!"

"Daughters draw with their husbands' families, Tessie," Mr. Summers 50
said gently. "You know that as well as anyone else."

"It wasn't *fair*," Tessie said. 51

"I guess not, Joe," Bill Hutchinson said regretfully. "My daughter 52
draws with her husband's family, that's only fair. And I've got no other family except the kids."

"Then, as far as drawing for families is concerned, it's you," Mr. Sum- 53
mers said in explanation, "and as far as drawing for households is concerned, that's you, too. Right?"

"Right," Bill Hutchinson said. 54

"How many kids, Bill?" Mr. Summers asked formally. 55

"Three," Bill Hutchinson said. "There's Bill, Jr., and Nancy, and little 56
Dave. And Tessie and me."

"All right, then," Mr. Summers said. "Harry, you got their tickets back?" 57

Mr. Graves nodded and held up the slips of paper. "Put them in the 58
box, then," Mr. Summers directed. "Take Bill's and put it in."

"I think we ought to start over," Mrs. Hutchinson said, as quietly as she 59
could. "I tell you it wasn't *fair*. You didn't give him time enough to choose. *Every*body saw that."

Mr. Graves had selected the five slips and put them in the box, and he 60
dropped all the papers but those onto the ground, where the breeze caught them and lifted them off.

"Listen, everybody," Mrs. Hutchinson was saying to the people around 61
her.

"Ready, Bill?" Mr. Summers asked, and Bill Hutchinson, with one 62
quick glance around at his wife and children, nodded.

"Remember," Mr. Summers said, "take the slips and keep them folded 63
until each person has taken one. Harry, you help little Dave." Mr. Graves took the hand of the little boy, who came willingly with him up to the box.

"Take a paper out of the box, Davy," Mr. Summers said. Davy put his hand into the box and laughed. "Take just *one* paper," Mr. Summers said. "Harry, you hold it for him." Mr. Graves took the child's hand and removed the folded paper from the tight fist and held it while little Dave stood next to him and looked up at him wonderingly.

"Nancy next," Mr. Summers said. Nancy was twelve, and her school 64 friends breathed heavily as she went forward, switching her skirt, and took a slip daintily from the box. "Bill, Jr.," Mr. Summers said, and Billy, his face red and his feet over-large, nearly knocked the box over as he got a paper out. "Tessie," Mr. Summers said. She hesitated for a minute, looking around defiantly, and then set her lips and went up to the box. She snatched a paper out and held it behind her.

"Bill," Mr. Summers said, and Bill Hutchinson reached into the box 65 and felt around, bringing his hand out at last with the slip of paper in it.

The crowd was quiet. A girl whispered, "I hope it's not Nancy," and the 66 sound of the whisper reached the edges of the crowd.

"It's not the way it used to be," Old Man Warner said clearly. "People 67 ain't the way they used to be."

"All right," Mr. Summers said. "Open the papers. Harry, you open little 68 Dave's."

Mr. Graves opened the slip of paper and there was a general sigh 69 through the crowd as he held it up and everyone could see that it was blank. Nancy and Bill, Jr., opened theirs at the same time, and both beamed and laughed, turning around to the crowd and holding their slips of paper above their heads.

"Tessie," Mr. Summers said. There was a pause, and then Mr. Summers 70 looked at Bill Hutchinson, and Bill unfolded his paper and showed it. It was blank.

"It's Tessie," Mr. Summers said, and his voice was hushed. "Show us 71 her paper, Bill."

Bill Hutchinson went over to his wife and forced the slip of paper out 72 of her hand. It had a black spot on it, the black spot Mr. Summers had made the night before with the heavy pencil in the coal-company office. Bill Hutchinson held it up, and there was a stir in the crowd.

"All right, folks," Mr. Summers said. "Let's finish quickly." 73

Although the villagers had forgotten the ritual and lost the original 74 black box, they still remembered to use stones. The pile of stones the boys had made earlier was ready; there were stones on the ground with the blowing scraps of paper that had come out of the box. Mrs. Delacroix selected a stone so large she had to pick it up with both hands and turned to Mrs. Dunbar. "Come on," she said. "Hurry up."

Mrs. Dunbar had small stones in both hands, and she said, gasping 75 for breath, "I can't run at all. You'll have to go ahead and I'll catch up with you."

The children had stones already, and someone gave little Davy 76 Hutchinson a few pebbles.

Tessie Hutchinson was in the center of a cleared space by now, and she 77 held her hands out desperately as the villagers moved in on her. "It isn't fair," she said. A stone hit her on the side of the head.

Old Man Warner was saying, "Come on, come on, everyone." Steve 78 Adams was in the front of the crowd of villagers, with Mrs. Graves beside him.

"It isn't fair, it isn't right," Mrs. Hutchinson screamed, and then they 79 were upon her.

● ● ●

READING LITERATURE

1. List the stages in the process of the lottery. Then, identify passages that explain the reasons behind each step. How logical are these explanations?

2. What is the significance of the fact that the process has continued essentially unchanged for so many years? What does this fact suggest about the people in the town?

3. Do you see this story as an explanation of a brutal process carried out in one particular town, or do you see it as a universal statement about dangerous tendencies in modern society—or in human nature? Explain your reasoning.

JOURNAL ENTRY

What do you think it would take to stop a process like the lottery? What could be done—and who would have to do it?

THEMATIC CONNECTIONS

- "Thirty-Eight Who Saw Murder Didn't Call the Police" (page 101)
- "Shooting an Elephant" (page 117)
- "Samuel" (page 239)

WRITING ASSIGNMENTS FOR PROCESS

1. Both Larry Brown and Jessica Mitford describe the process of doing a job. Write an essay in which you summarize the steps you took in applying for, performing, or quitting a job.

2. Write a set of instructions explaining in objective terms how the lottery Shirley Jackson describes should be conducted. Imagine you are setting these steps down in writing for generations of your fellow townspeople to follow.

3. Write a consumer-oriented article for your school newspaper in which you explain how to apply for financial aid, a work-study job, a student internship, or permanent employment in your field.

4. List the steps in the process you follow when you study for an important exam. Then, interview two friends about how they study, and take notes about their usual routine. Finally, combine the most helpful strategies into a set of instructions aimed at students entering your school.

5. Write a set of instructions explaining how to use a print reference work or an online database with which you are familiar. Assume your audience is not familiar with the research tool you are using.

6. Think of a series of steps in a bureaucratic process, a process you had to go through to accomplish something—getting a driver's license or becoming a U.S. citizen, for instance. Write an essay in which you explain that process, and include a thesis statement that evaluates the efficiency of that process.

7. Imagine you have encountered a visitor from another country (or another planet) who is not familiar with a social ritual you take for granted. Try to outline the steps involved in one such ritual—for instance, choosing sides for a game or pledging a fraternity or sorority.

8. Write a process essay explaining how you went about putting together a collection, a scrapbook, a portfolio, or an album of some kind. Be sure your essay makes clear why you collected or compiled your materials.

9. Explain how a certain ritual or ceremony is conducted in your religion. Make sure someone of another faith will be able to understand the process, and include a thesis statement that explains why the ritual is important to you.

10. Think of a process you believe should be modified or discontinued. (Examples might include getting a passport or applying to college.) Formulate a persuasive thesis that presents your negative feelings, and then explain the process so that you make your objections to it clear to your readers.

COLLABORATIVE ACTIVITY FOR PROCESS

Working with three other students, create an illustrated instructional pamphlet to help new students survive four of your college's first "ordeals"—for example, registering for classes, purchasing textbooks, eating in the cafeteria, and moving into a dorm. Before beginning, decide as a group which processes to write about, whether you want your pamphlet to be practical and serious or humorous and irreverent, and what kind of illustrations it should include. Then, decide which of you will write about which process—each student should do one—and who will be responsible for the illustrations. When all of you are ready, assemble your individual efforts into a single piece of writing.

INTERNET ASSIGNMENT FOR PROCESS

Write a letter to a friend giving him or her instructions for doing Internet research for a school project. Before you start to write, visit the following Web sites about the Internet so you can better understand the process your friend will need to go through when doing research on the Internet, and think carefully about what resources and steps will be most useful to him or her.

NetLearn: Internet Learning Resources Directory
<rgu.ac.uk/~sim/research/netlearn/callist.htm>
This site provides links to resources for learning and teaching Internet skills, including use of the Web, e-mail, and other Internet tools.

Conducting Research on the Internet
<library.albany.edu/internet/research.html>
This site, sponsored by the University at Albany libraries, offers a list of ways to search the Internet and includes links to other Internet tutorials.

Using the Internet
<sofweb.vic.edu.au/internet/research.htm>
This site offers information on planning how you will use the Internet for research projects, strategies for searching and evaluating resources, and a helpful worksheet of questions to think about when evaluating sources.

Bedford/St. Martin's Interactive Research Tutorials
<bedfordstmartins.com/english_research/demos.htm>
This site offers tutorials on such skills as conducting Web searches and using online library catalogues.

❖ 8
Cause and Effect

WHAT IS CAUSE AND EFFECT?

Process describes *how* something happens; **cause and effect** analyzes *why* something happens. Cause-and-effect essays examine causes, describe effects, or do both. In the following paragraph, journalist Tom Wicker considers the effects of a technological advance on a village in India:

Cause

Effects

Topic sentence

When a solar-powered water pump was provided for a well in India, the village headman took it over and sold the water, until stopped. The new liquid abundance attracted hordes of unwanted nomads. Village boys who had drawn water in buckets had nothing to do, and some became criminals. The gap between rich and poor widened, since the poor had no land to benefit from irrigation. Finally, village women broke the pump, so they could gather again around the well that had been the center of their social lives. Moral: technological advances have social, cultural, and economic consequences, often unanticipated.

Cause and effect, like narration, links situations and events together in time, with causes preceding effects. But causality involves more than sequence: cause-and-effect analysis explains why something happened — or is happening — and predicts what probably will happen.

Sometimes many different causes can be responsible for one effect. For example, as the following diagram illustrates, many elements may contribute to an individual's decision to leave his or her country of origin and come to the United States.

Causes   *Effect*

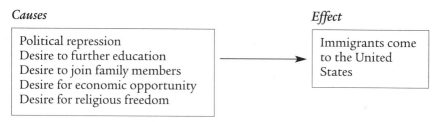

Similarly, many different effects can be produced by a single cause. Immigration, for instance, has had a variety of effects on the United States:

Cause   *Effects*

USING CAUSE AND EFFECT

Of course, causal relationships are rarely as neat as these boxes suggest; in fact, such relationships are often subtle and complex. As you examine situations that seem suited to cause-and-effect analysis, you will discover that most complex situations involve numerous causes and many different effects.

Consider this example. For more than twenty years, from the 1960s to the 1980s, the college-board scores of high school seniors steadily declined. The decline began soon after television became popular, and therefore many people concluded that the two events were connected. This idea is plausible because children did seem to be reading less in order to watch television more, and reading comprehension is one of the chief skills the tests evaluate.

But many other elements might have contributed to the decline of test scores. During the same period, for example, many schools reduced the number of required courses and deemphasized traditional subjects and skills, such as reading. Adults were reading less than they used to, and perhaps they were not encouraging their children to read. Furthermore, during the 1960s and 1970s, many colleges changed their policies and admitted students who previously would not have qualified. These new admission standards encouraged students who would not have taken college boards in earlier years to take the tests. Therefore, the scores may have been lower because they measured the top third of high school seniors rather than the top fifth. In any case, the reason for the lower scores is not clear. Perhaps television was the main cause after all, but nobody knows for sure. In such a case, it is easy — too easy — to claim a cause-and-effect relationship without the evidence to support it.

Just as the drop in scores may have had many causes, television watching may have had many effects. For instance, it may have made those same students better observers and listeners even if they did less well on standardized written tests. It may have encouraged them to have a national or even international outlook instead of a narrower local perspective. In other words, even if watching television did limit young people in some ways, it may also have expanded their horizons in other ways.

To give a balanced analysis, try to consider all causes and effects, not just the most obvious ones or the first ones you think of. For example, suppose a professional basketball team, recently stocked with the best players money can buy, has had a mediocre season. Because the individual players are talented and were successful under other coaches, fans blame the current coach for the team's losing streak and want him fired. But is the coach alone responsible? Maybe the inability of the players to function well as a team is responsible for their poor performance. Perhaps some of the players are suffering from injuries, personal problems, or drug dependency. Or maybe the drop in attendance at games has affected the team's morale. Clearly, other elements besides the new coach could have caused the losing streak. (And, of course, the team's losing streak might have any number of consequences, from declining attendance at games to the city's refusal to build a new arena.) When you write about such a situation, you need to be very careful to identify these complex causes and effects.

Understanding Main and Contributory Causes

Even when you have identified several causes of an effect, one — the main cause — is always more important than the others — the contributory causes. Understanding the distinction between the **main** (most important) **cause** and the **contributory** (less important) **causes** is vital for planning a cause-and-effect paper because once you identify the main cause, you can emphasize it in your paper and downplay the other causes. How, then, can you tell which cause is most important? Sometimes the main cause is obvious, but often it is not, as the following example shows.

During one winter a number of years ago, an unusually large amount of snow accumulated on the roof of the Civic Center Auditorium in Hartford, Connecticut, and the roof fell in. Newspapers reported that the weight of the snow had caused the collapse, and they were partly right. Other buildings, however, had not been flattened by the snow, so the main cause seemed to lie elsewhere. Insurance investigators eventually decided that the design of the roof, not the weight of the snow (which was a contributory cause), was the main cause of the collapse.

The cause-and-effect relationships summarized above are shown in this diagram:

Main cause | *Contributory cause*
Roof design | Weight of snow
Effect
Roof collapse

Because the main cause is not always the most obvious one, you should be sure to consider the significance of each cause very carefully as you plan your essay—and to continue to evaluate the importance of each cause as you write and revise.

Understanding Immediate and Remote Causes

Another important distinction is the difference between an immediate cause and a remote cause. An **immediate cause** closely precedes an effect and is therefore relatively easy to recognize. A **remote cause** is less obvious, perhaps because it involves something in the past or far away. Assuming that the most obvious cause is always the most important can be dangerous as well as shortsighted.

For example, consider again the Hartford roof collapse. Most people agreed that the snow was the immediate, or most obvious, cause of the roof collapse. But further study by insurance investigators suggested remote causes that were not so apparent. The design of the roof was the most important remote cause of the collapse, but other remote causes were also examined. Perhaps the materials used in the roof's construction were partly to blame. Maybe maintenance crews had not done their jobs properly, or necessary repairs had not been made. If you were the insurance investigator analyzing the causes of this event, you would want to assess all possible contributing factors rather than just the most obvious. If you did not consider the remote as well as the immediate causes, you would reach an oversimplified and perhaps incorrect conclusion.

This diagram shows the cause-and-effect relationships summarized above:

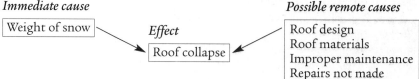

Immediate cause
Possible remote causes
Weight of snow
Effect
Roof collapse
Roof design
Roof materials
Improper maintenance
Repairs not made

Remote causes can be extremely important. In the roof-collapse situation, as we have seen, a remote cause—the roof design—was actually the main cause of the accident.

Understanding Causal Chains

Sometimes an effect can also be a cause. This is true in a **causal chain,** where A causes B, B causes C, C causes D, and so on, as shown here:

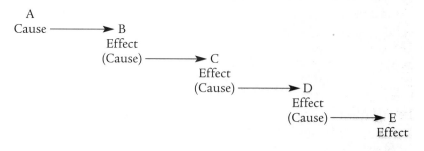

A
Cause ⟶ B
Effect
(Cause) ⟶ C
Effect
(Cause) ⟶ D
Effect
(Cause) ⟶ E
Effect

In causal chains, the result of one action is the cause of another. Leaving out any link in the chain, or putting any link in improper order, destroys the logic and continuity of the chain.

A simple example of a causal chain starts with the conclusion of World War II in 1945. Beginning in 1946, as thousands of American soldiers returned home, the U.S. birth rate began to rise dramatically. As the numbers of births increased, the creation of goods and services to meet the needs of this growing population also increased. As advertisers competed to attract this group's attention to various products, the so-called baby-boom generation became more and more visible. Consequently, baby boomers were perceived as more and more powerful — as voters as well as consumers. As a result, this group's emergence became a major factor in shaping American political, social, cultural, and economic life.

Here is another example of a causal chain. In the last thirty years, the bicycle as a form of transportation for children has become increasingly rare, with fewer than 1 percent of children now riding bicycles to school. In addition, fewer and fewer children ride bicycles for recreation. Causes cited for this decline include the absence of sidewalks in many newer suburban communities, parents' rising fears about crime and traffic accidents, the rise in the number of students who schedule back-to-back after-school activities (perhaps due in part to the increased number of households in which both parents work), the growing popularity of computer games, and the increased availability of after-school jobs for teenagers (who often need cars, not bikes, to get to work). The decreasing number of children who ride bikes has contributed to a corresponding steady decline, since the 1970s, in the sale of bicycles.

As a result of the decline in bicycle sales, bicycle thefts have decreased sharply, and bicycle deaths involving children under sixteen have also dropped dramatically (although this is due in part to increased use of helmets). At the same time, however, the number of American children who are obese has doubled since the mid-1980s — in part because they got less exercise. So, factors like fewer sidewalks and more working teenagers led to a decline in bicycle sales, which in turn has had a far-reaching impact.

If your analysis of a situation reveals a causal chain, this discovery can be useful in your writing. The very operation of a causal chain suggests an organizational pattern for a paper, and following the chain helps you to discuss items in their logical order. Be careful, however, to keep your emphasis on the causal connections and not to lapse into narration.

Avoiding *Post Hoc* Reasoning

When developing a cause-and-effect paper, you should not assume that just because event A *precedes* event B, event A has *caused* event B. This illogical assumption, called **post hoc reasoning,** equates a chronological sequence with causality. When you fall into this trap — assuming, for instance, that you failed an exam because a black cat crossed your path the day before — you are mistaking coincidence for causality.

Consider a classic example of *post hoc* reasoning. Until the late nineteenth century, many scientists accepted the notion of spontaneous generation—that is, they believed living things could arise directly from nonliving matter. To support their beliefs, they pointed to specific situations. For instance, they observed that maggots, the larvae of the housefly, seemed to arise directly from the decaying flesh of dead animals.

These scientists were confusing sequence with causality, assuming that just because the presence of decaying meat preceded the appearance of maggots, the two were connected in a causal relationship. In fact, because the dead animals were exposed to the air, flies were free to lay eggs in the animals' bodies, and these eggs hatched into maggots. Therefore, the living maggots were not a direct result of the presence of nonliving matter. Although these scientists were applying the best technology and scientific theory of their time, hindsight reveals that their conclusions were not valid.

A more recent example of *post hoc* reasoning occurred after medical researchers published findings reporting that female centenarians—women who reached the age of one hundred—were four times as likely to have given birth when they were past forty as were women in a control group who died at the age of seventy-three. Researchers saw no causal connection between childbirth after forty and long life, suggesting only that the centenarians might have been predisposed to live longer because they reached menopause later than the other women. Local television newscasts and tabloid newspapers, however, misinterpreted the implications of the study, presenting the relationship between late childbearing and long life as a causal one. In a vivid example of *post hoc* reasoning, one promotional spot for a local television newscast proclaimed, "Having kids late in life can help you live longer."

In your writing as well as in your observations, it is neither logical nor fair to assume that a causal relationship exists unless clear, strong evidence supports the connection. When you revise a cause-and-effect paper, make sure you have not confused words like *because, therefore,* and *consequently* (words that indicate a causal relationship) with words like *subsequently, later,* and *afterward* (words that indicate a chronological relationship). When you use a word like *because,* you are signaling to readers that you are telling *why* something happened; when you use a word like *later,* you are only showing *when* it happened.

Being able to identify and analyze cause-and-effect relationships; to distinguish causes from effects and recognize causal chains; and to distinguish immediate from remote, main from contributory, and logical from illogical causes are all skills that will improve your writing. Understanding the nature of the cause-and-effect relationship will help you decide when and how to use this pattern in a paper.

PLANNING A CAUSE-AND-EFFECT ESSAY

After you have sorted out the cause-and-effect relationships you will write about, you are ready to plan your paper. You have three basic options—to discuss causes, to discuss effects, or to discuss both causes and effects. Often your assignment will suggest which of these options to use. Here are a few likely topics for cause-and-effect treatment:

Focus on finding causes	Identify some possible causes of collective obsessional behavior. (psychology exam)
	Discuss the factors that have contributed to the declining population of state mental hospitals. (social work paper)
Focus on describing or predicting effects	Evaluate the probable effects of moving elementary school children from a highly structured classroom to a relatively open classroom. (education paper)
	Discuss the impact of World War I on two of Ernest Hemingway's characters. (literature exam)
Focus on both causes and effects	The 1840s were volatile years in Europe. Choose one social, political, or economic event that occurred during those years, analyze its causes, and briefly note how the event influenced later developments in European history. (history exam)

Purpose and Thesis

Of course, a cause-and-effect essay usually does more than just enumerate causes or effects. For example, an economics paper treating the major effects of the Vietnam War on the U.S. economy could be a straightforward presentation of factual information—an attempt to inform readers of the war's economic impact. It is more likely, however, that the paper would indicate the significance of the war's effects, not just list them. In fact, cause-and-effect analysis often requires you to judge various factors so that you can assess their relative significance.

When you formulate a thesis statement, be sure that it identifies the relationships among the specific causes or effects you will discuss. This thesis statement should tell your readers three things: the points you plan to consider, the position you will take, and whether your emphasis is on causes, effects, or both. Your thesis statement may also indicate explicitly or implicitly the cause or effect you consider most important and the order in which you will treat your points.

Order and Sequence

When deciding on the sequence in which you will present causes or effects, you have several options. One option, of course, is chronological order: you can present causes or effects in the order in which they occurred. Another option is to introduce the main cause first and then the contributory causes — or to do just the opposite. If you want to stress positive consequences, begin by briefly discussing the negative ones; if you plan to emphasize negative results, summarize the less important positive effects first. Still another possibility is to begin by dismissing any events that were *not* causes and then explain what the real causes were. This method is especially effective if you think your readers are likely to jump to *post hoc* conclusions. Finally, you can begin with the most obvious causes or effects and move on to more subtle factors — and then to your analysis and conclusion.

Using Transitions

Cause-and-effect essays rely on clear transitions — *the first cause, the second cause; one result, another result* — to distinguish causes from effects and to help move readers through the discussion. In essays that analyze complex causal relationships, transitions are even more important because they can help readers distinguish main from contributory causes (*the most important cause, another cause*) and immediate from remote causes (*the most obvious cause, a less apparent cause*). Transitions are also essential in a causal chain, where they can help readers sort out the sequence (*then, next*) as well as the causal relationships (*because, as a result, for this reason*). A more complete list of transitions appears on page 43.

STRUCTURING A CAUSE-AND-EFFECT ESSAY

Finding Causes

Suppose you are planning the social work paper mentioned earlier: "Discuss the factors that have contributed to the declining population of state mental hospitals." Your assignment specifies an effect — the declining population of state mental hospitals — and asks you to discuss possible causes, which might include the following:

- An increasing acceptance of mental illness in our society
- Prohibitive costs of in-patient care
- Increasing numbers of mental-health professionals, facilitating treatment outside of hospitals

Many health professionals, however, believe that the most important cause is the development and use of psychotropic drugs, such as chlorpromazine (Thorazine), which can alter behavior. To emphasize this cause in your paper, you could formulate the following thesis statement:

Less important causes	Although society's increasing acceptance of the mentally ill, the high cost of in-patient care, and the rise in the number of health professionals have
Effect	all been influential in reducing the population of state mental hospitals, the most important cause
Most important cause	of this reduction is the development and use of psychotropic drugs.

This thesis statement fully prepares your readers for your essay. It identifies the points you will consider, and it reveals your position — your assessment of the relative significance of the causes you identify. It states the less important causes first and indicates their secondary importance with *although*. In the body of your essay, the less important causes would come first so that the essay could gradually build up to the most convincing material. An informal outline for your paper might look like this:

Introduction:	Thesis statement — Although society's increasing acceptance of the mentally ill, the high cost of in-patient care, and the rise in the number of health professionals have all been influential in reducing the population of state mental hospitals, the most important cause of this reduction is the development and use of psychotropic drugs.
First cause:	Increasing acceptance of the mentally ill
Second cause:	High cost of in-patient care
Third cause:	Rise in the number of health professionals
Fourth (and most important) cause:	Development and use of psychotropic drugs
Conclusion:	Restatement of thesis or summary of key points

Describing or Predicting Effects

Suppose you were planning the education paper mentioned earlier: "Evaluate the probable effects of moving elementary school children from a highly structured classroom to a relatively open classroom." Here you would focus on effects rather than on causes. After brainstorming and deciding which specific points to discuss, you might formulate this thesis statement:

Cause	Moving children from a highly structured classroom to a relatively open one is desirable because it is
Effects	likely to encourage more independent play, more flexibility in forming friendship groups, and, ultimately, more creativity.

This thesis statement clearly tells readers the stand you will take and the main points you will consider in your essay. The thesis also clearly specifies that these points are *effects* of the open classroom. After introducing the cause, your essay would treat these three effects in the order in which they are presented in the thesis statement, building up to the most important point. An informal outline of your paper might look like this:

Introduction:	Thesis statement—Moving children from a highly structured classroom to a relatively open one is desirable because it is likely to encourage more independent play, more flexibility in forming friendship groups, and, ultimately, more creativity.
First effect:	More independent play
Second effect:	More flexible friendship groups
Third (and most important) effect:	More creativity
Conclusion:	Restatement of thesis or summary of key points

REVISING A CAUSE-AND-EFFECT ESSAY

When you revise a cause-and-effect essay, consider the items on the Revision Checklist on page 54. In addition, pay special attention to the items on the checklist below, which apply specifically to cause-and-effect essays.

☑ REVISION CHECKLIST: CAUSE AND EFFECT

- Does your assignment call for a discussion of causes, of effects, or of both causes and effects?
- Does your essay have a clearly stated thesis that indicates your focus and the significance of the causes and/or effects you discuss?
- Have you considered all possible causes and all possible effects?
- Have you distinguished between the main (most important) cause and the contributory (less important) causes?
- Have you distinguished between immediate and remote causes?
- Have you identified a causal chain in your reasoning?
- Have you avoided *post hoc* reasoning?
- Have you used transitional words and phrases to show how the causes and/or effects you discuss are related?

EDITING A CAUSE-AND-EFFECT ESSAY

When you edit your cause-and-effect essay, follow the guidelines on the Editing Checklist on page 66. In addition, focus on the grammar, mechanics, and punctuation issues that are most relevant to cause-and-effect essays. Two of these issues—avoiding faulty "the reason is because" constructions and using *affect* and *effect* correctly—are discussed below.

For more practice in avoiding faulty constructions and commonly confused words, visit **Exercise Central** at **<bedfordstmartins.com/ patterns/faultyconstructions>** or **<bedfordstmartins.com/patterns/ confusedwords>**.

GRAMMAR IN CONTEXT : **Avoiding Faulty Constructions; *Affect* and *Effect****

Avoiding "the reason is because"   When you discuss causes and effects, you may find yourself writing the phrase "the reason is." If you follow this phrase with *because* ("the reason is *because*"), you will create an error.

The word *because* means "for the reason that." Therefore, it is redundant to say "the reason is because" (which literally means "the reason is for the reason that"). You can correct this error by substituting *that* for *because* ("the reason is *that*").

> **Incorrect:**   As Malcolm Gladwell notes, one reason for the decline in violent crime is because quality-of-life crimes have declined.

> **Correct:**   As Malcolm Gladwell notes, one reason for the decline in violent crime is that quality-of-life crimes have declined.

Using *Affect* and *Effect* Correctly   When you write a cause-and-effect essay, you will most likely use the words *affect* and *effect* quite often. For this reason, it is important that you know the difference between *affect* and *effect*.

Affect, usually a verb, means "to influence."

> "The relationships of family members to each other are affected by television's powerful competition in both obvious and subtle ways" (Winn 329).

Effect, usually a noun, means "a result."

> "For surely the hours that children spend in a one-way relationship with television people, an involvement that allows for no communication or interaction, must have some effect on their relationships with real-life people" (Winn 329).

NOTE: *Effect* can also be a verb meaning "to bring about" ("She worked hard to effect change in the community").

---

*The examples below refer to essays that appear later in this chapter.

☑ **EDITING CHECKLIST: CAUSE AND EFFECT**

- Have you used verb tenses correctly to distinguish among events that happened earlier, at the same time, and later?
- Have you placed a comma **after** every dependent clause introduced by *because* ("Because the rally was so crowded, we left early") but *not* used a comma **before** a dependent clause introduced by *because* ("We left early because the rally was so crowded")?
- Have you used "the reason is that" (not "the reason is because")?
- Have you used *affect* and *effect* correctly?

▶ **A STUDENT WRITER: CAUSE AND EFFECT**

The following midterm exam, written for a history class, analyzes both the causes and effects of the Irish potato famine that occurred during the 1840s. Notice how the writer, Evelyn Pellicane, concentrates on causes but also discusses briefly the effects of this tragedy, just as the exam question directs.

> *Question:* The 1840s were volatile years in Europe. Choose one social, political, or economic event that occurred during those years, analyze its causes, and briefly note how the event influenced later developments in European history.

The Irish Famine, 1845-1849

Thesis statement   The Irish famine, which brought hardship 1
and tragedy to Ireland during the 1840s, was
caused and prolonged by four basic factors: the
failure of the potato crop, the landlord-tenant
system, errors in government policy, and the
long-standing prejudice of the British toward
Ireland.

First cause   The immediate cause of the famine was the 2
failure of the potato crop. In 1845, potato
disease struck the crop, and potatoes rotted
in the ground. The 1846 crop also failed, and
before long people were eating weeds. The 1847
crop was healthy, but there were not enough
potatoes to go around, and in 1848 the blight
struck again, leading to more and more evictions
of tenants by landlords.

Second cause   The tenants' position on the land had never 3
been very secure. Most had no leases and could

be turned out by their landlords at any time.
If a tenant owed rent, he was evicted — or,
worse, put in prison, leaving his family to
starve. The threat of prison caused many tenants to leave their land; those who could leave
Ireland did so, sometimes with money provided
by their landlords. Some landlords did try to
take care of their tenants, but most did not.
Many were absentee landlords who spent their
rent money abroad.

Third cause

Government policy errors, although not an   4
immediate cause of the famine, played an important role in creating an unstable economy
and perpetuating starvation. In 1846, the government decided not to continue selling corn,
as it had during the first year of the famine,
claiming that low-cost purchases of corn by
Ireland had paralyzed British trade by inter-
fering with free enterprise. Therefore, 1846
saw a starving population, angry demonstrations,
and panic; even those with money were unable to
buy food. Still, the government insisted that
if it sent food to Ireland, prices would rise
in the rest of the United Kingdom and that this
would be unfair to hardworking English and
Scots. As a result, no food was sent. Throughout the years of the famine, the British government aggravated an already grave situation:
they did nothing to improve agricultural operations, to help people adjust to another crop,
to distribute seeds, or to reorder the landlord-
tenant system that made the tenants' position
so insecure.

Fourth cause

At the root of this poor government policy   5
was the long-standing British prejudice against
the Irish. Hostility between the two countries
went back some six hundred years, and the British were simply not about to inconvenience
themselves to save the Irish. When the Irish so
desperately needed grain to replace the damaged

potatoes, it was clear that grain had to be imported from England. This meant, however, that the Corn Laws, which had been enacted to keep the price of British corn high by taxing imported grain, had to be repealed. The British were unwilling to repeal the Corn Laws. Even when they did supply cornmeal, they made no attempt to explain to the Irish how to cook this unfamiliar food. Moreover, the British government was determined to make Ireland pay for its own poor, and so it forced the collection of taxes. Since many landlords just did not have the tax money, they were forced to evict their tenants. The British government's callous and indifferent treatment of the Irish has been called genocide.

Effects

As a result of this devastating famine, 6 the population of Ireland was reduced from about nine million to about six and one-half million. During the famine years, men roamed the streets looking for work, begging when they found none. Epidemics of "famine fever" and dysentery reduced the population drastically. The most important historical result of the famine, however, was the massive immigration to the United States, Canada, and Great Britain of poor, unskilled people who had to struggle to fit into a skilled economy and who brought with them a deep-seated hatred of the British. (This same hatred remained strong in Ireland itself—so strong that at the time of World War II, Ireland, then independent, remained neutral rather than coming to England's aid.) Irish immigrants faced slums, fever epidemics, joblessness, and hostility—even anti-Catholic and anti-Irish riots—in Boston, New York, London, Glasgow, and Quebec. In Ireland itself, poverty and discontent continued, and by 1848 those emigrating from Ireland included a more highly skilled class of farmer, the ones Ireland needed to recover and to survive.

*Conclusion (includes
restatement of thesis)*

The Irish famine, one of the great trage-   7
dies of the nineteenth century, was a natural
disaster compounded by the insensitivity of
the British government and the archaic agricultural system of Ireland. Although the deaths
that resulted depleted Ireland's resources
even more, the men and women who immigrated
to other countries permanently enriched those
nations.

Points for Special Attention

Structure   This is a relatively long essay; if it were not so clearly organized, it would be difficult to follow. Because the essay was to focus primarily on causes, Evelyn first introduces the effect — the famine itself — and then considers its causes. After she examines the causes, she moves on to the results of the famine, treating the most important result last. In this essay, then, the famine is first treated as an effect and then, toward the end, as a cause. In fact, it is the central link in a causal chain.

Evelyn devotes one paragraph to her introduction and one to each cause; she sums up the famine's results in a separate paragraph and devotes the final paragraph to her conclusion. (Depending on a particular paper's length and complexity, more — or less — than one paragraph may be devoted to each cause or effect.) An informal outline for her paper might look like this:

Introduction (including thesis statement)
First cause: Failure of the potato crop
Second cause: The landlord-tenant system
Third cause: Errors in government policy
Fourth cause: British prejudice
Results of the famine
Conclusion

Because Evelyn sees all the causes as important and interrelated, she does not present them in order of increasing importance. Instead, she begins with the immediate cause of the famine — the failure of the potato crop — and then digs more deeply until she arrives at the most remote cause, British prejudice. The immediate cause is also the main (most important) cause, for the other situations had existed before the famine began.

Transitions   The cause-and-effect relationships in this essay are both subtle and complex because Evelyn considers a series of relationships as well as an intricate causal chain. Throughout the essay, many words suggest cause-and-effect connections: *so, therefore, because, as a result, since, led to, brought about, caused,* and the like. These words help readers sort out the causal connections.

Answering an Exam Question   Before planning and writing her answer, Evelyn read the exam question carefully. She noted that it asked for both causes and effects but that its wording directed her to spend more time on causes ("analyze") than on effects ("briefly note"), so she organized her discussion to conform to these directions. In addition, she indicated *explicitly* which are the causes ("government policy [. . .] played an important role") and which are the effects ("The most important historical result").

Evelyn's purpose is to convey factual information and, in doing so, to demonstrate her understanding of the course material. Rather than waste her limited time choosing a clever opening strategy or making elaborate attempts to engage her audience, Evelyn begins her essay with a direct statement of her thesis.

Evelyn has obviously been influenced by outside sources; the ideas in the essay are not completely her own. Because this is an exam, however, and because the instructor expected that students would base their essays on class notes and assigned readings, Evelyn does not have to document her sources.

Focus on Revision

Because this essay was written as an exam answer, Evelyn had no time — and no need — to revise it further. If she had been preparing this assignment outside of class, however, she might have done more. For example, she could have added a more arresting opening, such as a brief eyewitness account of the famine's effects. Her conclusion — appropriately brief and straightforward for an exam answer — could also have been strengthened, perhaps with the addition of information about the nation's eventual recovery. Finally, the addition of statistics, quotations by historians, or a brief summary of Irish history before the famine could have further enriched the essay. (A sample peer editing worksheet for cause and effect can be found on the *Patterns for College Writing* Web site at <bedfordstmartins.com/patterns>.)

All the selections that follow focus on cause-and-effect relationships. Some readings focus on causes, others on effects. The first selection, a visual text, is followed by questions designed to illustrate how cause and effect can operate in visual form.

LOUIS REQUENA

❖

Major League Baseball Brawl (Photo)

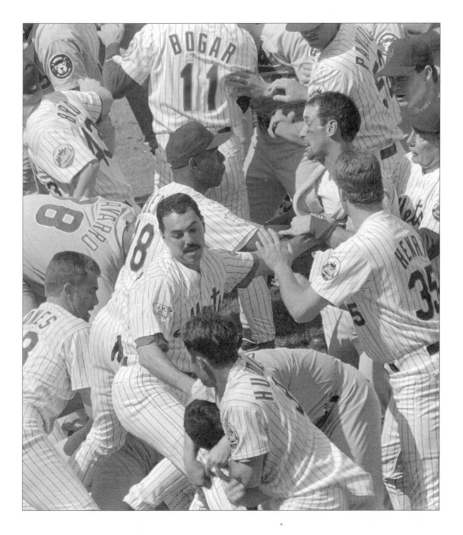

• • •

READING IMAGES

1. Study the photo above. What might have caused the situation on the field? Consider remote as well as immediate causes.

2. What outcomes might you expect as a result of this fight? Consider the effects on the players on the field, on the players waiting in the dugout, and on the fans in the stands.

3. Consider the fight on the field as part of a causal chain. Diagram that chain of events, using arrows to point from one event to the next.

JOURNAL ENTRY

Write a paragraph in which you suggest ways to prevent situations such as the one shown in the picture. For example, might high fines deter players from losing their tempers?

THEMATIC CONNECTIONS

- "My Field of Dreams" (page 77)
- "Who Killed Benny Paret?" (page 321)
- "Whodunit—The Media?" (page 618)

❖
Who Killed Benny Paret?

Norman Cousins (1915–1990) was born in Union City, New Jersey, and graduated from Columbia University's Teachers College in 1933. He began his career in journalism writing for the *New York Evening Post* and *Current History* magazine. In 1940, Cousins joined the *Saturday Review*, where he served as editor from 1942 to 1978. A noted social critic, Cousins lectured widely on world affairs. An adjunct professor in the department of psychiatry at the UCLA School of Medicine from 1978 until his death, he is particularly remembered for his many books urging a positive outlook to combat illness, including *Anatomy of an Illness* (1979).

Background: Cousins's 1962 essay "Who Killed Benny Paret?" focuses on a brutal boxing match at Madison Square Garden that resulted in the death of one of the boxers. The event, witnessed by millions of shocked television viewers, led to demands from many quarters that professional boxing be banned altogether. As a result, a number of rules for professional boxing were changed, but boxing remains an inherently dangerous sport. There have been an estimated five hundred ring deaths in the last century; as recently as 2002, a professional boxer died following a knockout in the ring. In addition, many boxers suffer from chronic latent brain damage, known medically as *pugilistica dementia*. In answering the question posed by his essay's title, Cousins takes a strong stand against violence in boxing.

Sometime about 1935 or 1936 I had an interview with Mike Jacobs, the prize-fight promoter. I was a fledgling reporter at that time; my beat was education but during the vacation season I found myself on varied assignments, all the way from ship news to sports reporting. In this way I found myself sitting opposite the most powerful figure in the boxing world. [1]

There was nothing spectacular in Mr. Jacobs' manner or appearance; but when he spoke about prize fights, he was no longer a bland little man but a colossus who sounded the way Napoleon must have sounded when he reviewed a battle. You knew you were listening to Number One. His saying something made it true. [2]

We discussed what to him was the only important element in successful promoting—how to please the crowd. So far as he was concerned, there was no mystery to it. You put killers in the ring and the people filled your arena. You hire boxing artists—men who are adroit at feinting, parrying, weaving, jabbing, and dancing, but who don't pack dynamite in their fists—and you wind up counting your empty seats. So you searched for the killers and sluggers and maulers—fellows who could hit with the force of a baseball bat. [3]

I asked Mr. Jacobs if he was speaking literally when he said people came out to see the killer. [4]

"They don't come out to see a tea party," he said evenly. "They come out to see the knockout. They come out to see a man hurt. If they think anything else, they're kidding themselves."

Recently, a young man by the name of Benny Paret was killed in the ring. The killing was seen by millions; it was on television. In the twelfth round, he was hit hard in the head several times, went down, was counted out, and never came out of the coma.

The Paret fight produced a flurry of investigations. Governor Rockefeller was shocked by what happened and appointed a committee to assess the responsibility. The New York State Boxing Commission decided to find out what was wrong. The District Attorney's office expressed its concern. One question that was solemnly studied in all three probes concerned the action of the referee. Did he act in time to stop the fight? Another question had to do with the role of the examining doctors who certified the physical fitness of the fighters before the bout. Still another question involved Mr. Paret's manager; did he rush his boy into the fight without adequate time to recuperate from the previous one?

In short, the investigators looked into every possible cause except the real one. Benny Paret was killed because the human fist delivers enough impact, when directed against the head, to produce a massive hemorrhage in the brain. The human brain is the most delicate and complex mechanism in all creation. It has a lacework of millions of highly fragile nerve connections. Nature attempts to protect this exquisitely intricate machinery by encasing it in a hard shell. Fortunately, the shell is thick enough to withstand a great deal of pounding. Nature, however, can protect a man against everything except man himself. Not every blow to the head will kill a man — but there is always the risk of concussion and damage to the brain. A prize fighter may be able to survive even repeated brain concussions and go on fighting, but the damage to his brain may be permanent.

In any event, it is futile to investigate the referee's role and seek to determine whether he should have intervened to stop the fight earlier. That is not where the primary responsibility lies. The primary responsibility lies with the people who pay to see a man hurt. The referee who stops a fight too soon from the crowd's viewpoint can expect to be booed. The crowd wants the knockout; it wants to see a man stretched out on the canvas. This is the supreme moment in boxing. It is nonsense to talk about prize fighting as a test of boxing skills. No crowd was ever brought to its feet screaming and cheering at the sight of two men beautifully dodging and weaving out of each other's jabs. The time the crowd comes alive is when a man is hit hard over the heart or the head, when his mouthpiece flies out, when the blood squirts out of his nose or eyes, when he wobbles under the attack and his pursuer continues to smash at him with pole-axe impact.

Don't blame it on the referee. Don't even blame it on the fight managers. Put the blame where it belongs — on the prevailing mores that regard prize fighting as a perfectly proper enterprise and vehicle of entertainment.

No one doubts that many people enjoy prize fighting and will miss it if it should be thrown out. And that is precisely the point.

• • •

COMPREHENSION

1. Why, according to Mike Jacobs, do people come to see a prizefight? Does Cousins agree with him?

2. What was the immediate cause of Paret's death? What remote causes did the investigators consider? What, according to Cousins, was the main cause? That is, where does the "primary responsibility" (9) lie?

3. Why does Cousins believe that "it is futile to investigate the referee's role" (9)?

4. Cousins ends his essay with "And that is precisely the point." What is the "point" to which he refers?

PURPOSE AND AUDIENCE

1. This persuasive essay has a strong thesis. What is it?

2. This essay appeared on May 5, 1962, a month after Paret died. What do you suppose its impact was on its audience? Is the impact the same today, or has it changed?

3. At whom is this essay aimed — boxing enthusiasts, sportswriters, or a general audience? On what do you base your conclusion?

4. Does Cousins expect his audience to agree with his thesis? How does he try to win sympathy for his position?

STYLE AND STRUCTURE

1. Does Cousins include enough detail to convince readers? Explain. Where, if anywhere, might more detail be helpful?

2. Sort out the complex cause-and-effect relationships discussed in paragraph 9.

3. What strategy does Cousins use in his conclusion? Is it effective? Explain your reasoning.

VOCABULARY PROJECTS

1. Define each of the following words as it is used in this selection.

promoter (1)	feinting (3)	lacework (8)
fledgling (1)	parrying (3)	encasing (8)
colossus (2)	maulers (3)	intervened (9)

2. The specialized vocabulary of boxing is prominent in this essay, but the facts Cousins presents would apply equally well to any sport in which violence is a potential problem.

a. Imagine that you are writing a similar essay about football, hockey, rugby, or another sport. Think about your audience and substitute an appropriate equivalent word or phrase for each of the following:

promoter (1)	feinting, parrying, weaving,	knockout (5)
prize fights (2)	jabbing, and dancing (3)	referee (7)
in the ring (3)	killers and sluggers	fighters/fight (7)
boxing artists (3)	and maulers (3)	

b. Rewrite this sentence so that it suits the sport you have chosen: "The crowd wants the knockout; it wants to see a man stretched out on the canvas. [. . .] It is nonsense to talk about prize fighting as a test of boxing skills. No crowd was ever brought to its feet screaming and cheering at the sight of two men beautifully dodging and weaving out of each other's jabs" (9).

JOURNAL ENTRY

Do Cousins's graphic descriptions convince you that boxing should be outlawed? Explain.

WRITING WORKSHOP

1. Write a cause-and-effect essay examining how the demands of the public affect a professional sport. (You might examine violence in hockey or football, for example, or the ways in which an individual player cultivates an image for the fans.)

2. Write a cause-and-effect essay about a time when, in response to peer pressure, you encouraged someone to do something you felt was dishonest or unwise. Be sure to identify the causes for your actions.

3. Why do you think a young person might turn to a career in boxing? Write a cause-and-effect essay in which you examine the possible motives.

COMBINING THE PATTERNS

This essay begins with five paragraphs of **narration** that summarize a meeting between Cousins and Mike Jacobs. What function does this narrative introduction serve in this essay? Once Paret's death is mentioned and the persuasive portion of the essay begins, Cousins never resumes the narrative. Do you think he should have returned to this narrative? If so, where might he have continued the story?

THEMATIC CONNECTIONS

- "Thirty-Eight Who Saw Murder Didn't Call the Police" (page 101)
- "Shooting an Elephant" (page 117)
- "The Lottery" (page 292)

MARIE WINN

❖

Television: The Plug-In Drug

Marie Winn was born in 1936 in Prague, in what is now the Czech Republic, and came to the United States in 1939. She was educated at Radcliffe College and Columbia University. As a freelance writer, Winn has contributed articles to the *New York Times Magazine, Parade,* and *Smithsonian* magazine. She has written books for children and also for parents and teachers, including *The Plug-In Drug: Television, Computers, and Family Life* (1977, revised 2002), *Children without Childhood* (1983), and *Unplugging the Plug-In Drug* (1987). Her recent work has focused on urban wildlife; in 1998 she published *Red-Tails in Love: A Wildlife Drama in Central Park.*

Background: Referred to as early as 1961 as a "vast wasteland" (by the then chairman of the Federal Communications Commission, no less), television has had its critics all along, particularly in relation to the effect of television watching on children. Some three thousand books and articles have been published on the subject, and current research suggests that the average young person watches twenty-eight hours of television a week (which, with the proliferation of cable channels devoted to children and the spread of videos and DVDs, may be a low estimate). Studies show that children who spend four or more hours a day in front of the set do less schoolwork, have poorer reading and social skills, and are more likely to be overweight. In addition, much controversy surrounds the effects of television violence and advertising on young viewers. In this excerpt from *The Plug-In Drug* (which was republished in a new revised and updated edition in 2002), Winn considers the effects of television not only on children but on how family members relate to one another. (Winn's observations are even more relevant now than when she originally wrote her essay: today 66 percent of children live in a household with three or more television sets, and 54 percent have one in their own rooms.)

Not much more than fifty years after the introduction of television into American society, the medium has become so deeply ingrained in daily life that in many states the TV set has attained the rank of a legal necessity, safe from repossession in case of debt along with clothes and cooking utensils. Only in the early years after television's introduction did writers and commentators have sufficient perspective to separate the activity of watching television from the actual content it offers the viewer. In those days writers frequently discussed the effects of television on family life. However, a curious myopia afflicted those first observers: almost without exception they regarded television as a favorable, beneficial, indeed, wondrous influence upon the family. 1

"Television is going to be a real asset in every home where there are children," predicted a writer in 1949. 2

"Television will take over your way of living and change your children's 3
habits, but this change can be a wonderful improvement," claimed another
commentator.

"No survey's needed, of course, to establish that television has brought 4
the family together in one room," wrote the *New York Times*'s television
critic in 1949.

The early articles about television were almost invariably accompanied 5
by a photograph or illustration showing a family cozily sitting together
before the television set, Sis on Mom's lap, Buddy perched on the arm of
Dad's chair, Dad with his arm around Mom's shoulder. Who could have
guessed that twenty or so years later Mom would be watching a drama in
the kitchen, the kids would be looking at cartoons in their room, while
Dad would be taking in the ball game in the living room?

Of course television sets were enormously expensive when they first 6
came on the market. The idea that by the year 2000 more than three quarters of all American families would own two or more sets would have
seemed preposterous. The splintering of the multiple-set family was something the early writers did not foresee. Nor did anyone imagine the number
of hours children would eventually devote to television, the changes television would effect upon child-rearing methods, the increasing domination
of family schedules by children's viewing requirements — in short, the power
of television to dominate family life.

As children's consumption of the new medium increased together 7
with parental concern about the possible effects of so much television
viewing, a steady refrain helped soothe and reassure anxious parents. "Television always enters a pattern of influences that already exist: the home,
the peer group, the school, the church and culture generally," wrote the
authors of an early and influential study of television's effects on children.
In other words, if the child's home life is all right, parents need not worry
about the effects of too much television watching.

But television did not merely influence the child; it deeply influenced 8
that "pattern of influences" everyone hoped would ameliorate the new
medium's effects. Home and family life have changed in important ways
since the advent of television. The peer group has become television-
oriented, and much of the time children spend together is occupied by
television viewing. Culture generally has been transformed by television.
Participation in church and community activities has diminished, with
television a primary cause of this change. Therefore it is improper to assign
to television the subsidiary role its many apologists insist it plays. Television is not merely one of a number of important influences upon today's
child. Through the changes it has made in family life, television emerges as
the important influence in children's lives today.

The Quality of Life

Television's contribution to family life has been an equivocal one. For 9
while it has, indeed, kept the members of the family from dispersing, it has

not served to bring them together. By its domination of the time families spend together, it destroys the special quality that distinguishes one family from another, a quality that depends to a great extent on what a family does, what special rituals, games, recurrent jokes, familiar songs, and shared activities it accumulates.

Yet parents have accepted a television-dominated family life so com-   10
pletely that they cannot see how the medium is involved in whatever problems they might be having. A first-grade teacher reports:

> I have one child in the group who's an only child. I wanted to find out more about her family life because this little girl was quite isolated from the group, didn't make friends, so I talked to her mother. Well, they don't have time to do anything in the evening, the mother said. The parents come home after picking up the child at the baby-sitter's. Then the mother fixes dinner while the child watches TV. Then they have dinner and the child goes to bed. I said to this mother. "Well, couldn't she help you fix dinner? That would be a nice time for the two of you to talk," and the mother said, "Oh, but I'd hate to have her miss *Zoom*. It's such a good program!"

Several decades ago a writer and mother of two boys aged three and   11
seven described her family's television schedule in a newspaper article. Though some of the programs her kids watched then have changed, the situation she describes remains the same for great numbers of families today:

> We were in the midst of a full-scale War. Every day was a new battle and every program was a major skirmish. We agreed it was a bad scene all around and were ready to enter diplomatic negotiations. . . . In principle we have agreed on 2½ hours of TV a day, *Sesame Street, Electric Company* (with dinner gobbled up in between) and two half-hour shows between 7 and 8:30, which enables the grown-ups to eat in peace and prevents the two boys from destroying one another. Their pre-bedtime choice is dreadful, because, as Josh recently admitted, "There's nothing much on I really like." So . . . it's *What's My Line* or *To Tell the Truth*. . . . Clearly there is a need for first-rate children's shows at this time. . . .

Consider the "family life" described here: Presumably the father comes   12
home from work during the *Sesame Street–Electric Company* stint. The children are either watching television, gobbling their dinner, or both. While the parents eat their dinner in peaceful privacy, the children watch another hour of television. Then there is only a half-hour left before bedtime, just enough time for baths, getting pajamas on, brushing teeth, and so on. The children's evening is regimented with an almost military precision. They watch their favorite programs, and when there is "nothing much on I really like," they watch whatever else is on — because *watching* is the important thing. Their mother does not see anything amiss with watching programs just for the sake of watching; she only wishes there were some first-rate children's shows on at those times.

Without conjuring up fantasies of bygone eras with family games and   13
long, leisurely meals, the question arises: isn't there a better family life

available than this dismal, mechanized arrangement of children watching television for however long is allowed them, evening after evening?

Of course, families today still do things together at times: go camp- 14 ing in the summer, go to the zoo on a nice Sunday, take various trips and expeditions. But their ordinary daily life together is diminished—those hours of sitting around at the dinner table, the spontaneous taking up of an activity, the little games invented by children on the spur of the moment when there is nothing else to do, the scribbling, the chatting, and even the quarreling, all the things that form the fabric of a family, that define a childhood. Instead, the children have their regular schedule of television programs and bedtime, and the parents have their peaceful dinner together.

The author of the quoted newspaper article notes that "keeping a fam- 15 ily sane means mediating between the needs of both children and adults." But surely the needs of the adults in that family were being better met than the needs of the children. The kids were effectively shunted away and rendered untroublesome, while their parents enjoyed a life as undemanding as that of any childless couple. In reality, it is those very demands that young children make upon a family that lead to growth, and it is the way parents respond to those demands that builds the relationships upon which the future of the family depends. If the family does not accumulate its backlog of shared experiences, shared everyday experiences that occur and recur and change and develop, then it is not likely to survive as anything other than a caretaking institution.

Family Rituals

Ritual is defined by sociologists as "that part of family life that the 16 family likes about itself, is proud of and wants formally to continue." Another text notes that "the development of a ritual by a family is an index of the common interest of its members in the family as a group."

What has happened to family rituals, those regular, dependable, recur- 17 rent happenings that gave members of a family a feeling of belonging to a home rather than living in it merely for the sake of convenience, those experiences that act as the adhesive of family unity far more than any material advantages?

Mealtime rituals, going-to-bed rituals, illness rituals, holiday rituals— 18 how many of these have survived the inroads of the television set?

A young woman who grew up near Chicago reminisces about her 19 childhood and gives an idea of the effects of television upon family rituals:

As a child I had millions of relatives around—my parents both come from relatively large families. My father had nine brothers and sisters. And so every holiday there was this great swoop-down of aunts, uncles, and millions of cousins. I just remember how wonderful it used to be. These thousands of cousins would come and everyone would play and ultimately, after dinner, all the women would be in the front of the house, drinking coffee and talking, all the men would be in the back of the house, drinking and smoking, and all the kids would be all over the place, playing hide and seek. Christmas time was particularly nice because everyone always brought all their toys and games. Our house had a couple of rooms with go-through closets, so there were always kids running in a great circle route. I remember it was just wonderful.

And then all of a sudden one year I remember becoming suddenly aware of how different everything had become. The kids were no longer playing Monopoly or Clue or the other games we used to play together. It was because we had a television set which had been turned on for a football game. All of that socializing that had gone on previously had ended. Now everyone was sitting in front of the television set, on a holiday, at a family party! I remember being stunned by how awful that was. Somehow the television had become more attractive.

As families have come to spend more and more of their time together 20 engaged in the single activity of television watching, those rituals and pastimes that once gave family life its special quality have become more and more uncommon. Not since prehistoric times, when cave families hunted, gathered, ate, and slept, with little time remaining to accumulate a culture of any significance, have families been reduced to such a sameness.

Real People

The relationships of family members to each other are affected by television's powerful competition in both obvious and subtle ways. For surely the hours that children spend in a one-way relationship with television people, an involvement that allows for no communication or interaction, must have some effect on their relationships with real-life people.

Studies show the importance of eye-to-eye contact, for instance, in 22 real-life relationships, and indicate that the nature of one's eye-contact patterns, whether one looks another squarely in the eye or looks to the side or shifts one's gaze from side to side, may play a significant role in one's success or failure in human relationships. But no eye contact is possible in the child-television relationship, although in certain children's programs people purport to speak directly to the child and the camera fosters this illusion by focusing directly upon the person being filmed. How might such a distortion affect a child's development of trust, of openness, of an ability to relate well to *real* people?

Bruno Bettelheim suggested an answer: 23

Children who have been taught, or conditioned, to listen passively most of the day to the warm verbal communications coming from the TV screen, to the deep emotional appeal of the so-called TV personality, are often unable to respond to real persons because they arouse so much less feeling than the skilled actor. Worse, they lose the ability to learn from reality because life experiences are much more complicated than the ones they see on the screen. . . .

A teacher makes a similar observation about her personal viewing 24
experiences:

> I have trouble mobilizing myself and dealing with real people after watching a few hours of television. It's just hard to make that transition from watching television to a real relationship. I suppose it's because there was no effort necessary while I was watching, and dealing with real people always requires a bit of effort. Imagine, then, how much harder it might be to do the same thing for a small child, particularly one who watches a lot of television every day.

But more obviously damaging to family relationships is the elimination of opportunities to talk and converse, or to argue, to air grievances between parents and children and brothers and sisters. Families frequently use television to avoid confronting their problems, problems that will not go away if they are ignored but will only fester and become less easily resolvable as time goes on. 25

A mother reports: 26

> I find myself, with three children, wanting to turn on the TV set when they're fighting. I really have to struggle not to do it because I feel that's telling them this is the solution to the quarrel—but it's so tempting that I often do it.

A family therapist discusses the use of television as an avoidance mechanism: 27

> In a family I know the father comes home from work and turns on the television set. The children come and watch with him and the wife serves them their meal in front of the set. He then goes and takes a shower, or works on the car or something. She then goes and has her own dinner in front of the television set. It's a symptom of a deeper-rooted problem, sure. But it would help them all to get rid of the set. It would be far easier to work on what the symptom really means without the television. The television simply encourages a double avoidance of each other. They'd find out more quickly what was going on if they weren't able to hide behind the TV. Things wouldn't necessarily be better, of course, but they wouldn't be anesthetized.

A number of research studies done when television was a relatively new 28
medium demonstrated that television interfered with family activities and the formation of family relationships. One survey showed that 78 percent of the respondents indicated no conversation taking place during viewing except at specified times such as commercials. The study noted: "The television atmosphere in most households is one of quiet absorption on the part of family members who are present. The nature of the family social life during a program could be described as 'parallel' rather than interactive, and the set does seem to dominate family life when it is on." Thirty-six percent of the respondents in another study indicated that television viewing was the only family activity participated in during the week.

The situation has only worsened during the intervening decades. 29 When the studies were made, the great majority of American families had only one television set. Though the family may have spent more time watching TV in those early days, at least they were all together while they watched. Today the vast majority of all families have two or more sets, and nearly a third of all children live in homes with four or more TVs. The most telling statistic: almost 60 percent of all families watch television during meals, and not necessarily at the same TV set. When do they talk about what they did that day? When do they make plans, exchange views, share jokes, tell about their triumphs or little disasters? When do they get to be a real family?

Undermining the Family

Of course television has not been the only factor in the decline of fam- 30 ily life in America. The steadily rising divorce rate, the increase in the number of working mothers, the trends towards people moving far away from home, the breakdown of neighborhoods and communities — all these have seriously affected the family.

Obviously the sources of family breakdown do not necessarily come 31 from the family itself, but from the circumstances in which the family finds itself and the way of life imposed upon it by those circumstances. As Urie Bronfenbrenner has suggested:

> When those circumstances and the way of life they generate undermine relationships of trust and emotional security between family members, when they make it difficult for parents to care for, educate, and enjoy their children, when there is no support or recognition from the outside world for one's role as a parent, and when time spent with one's family means frustration of career, personal fulfillment, and peace of mind, then the development of the child is adversely affected.

Certainly television is not the single destroyer of American family life. 32 But the medium's dominant role in the family serves to anesthetize parents into accepting their family's diminished state and prevents them from struggling to regain some of the richness the family once possessed.

One research study alone seems to contradict the idea that television 33 has a negative impact on family life. In their important book *Television and the Quality of Life*, sociologists Robert Kubey and Mihaly Csikszentmihalyi observe that the heaviest viewers of TV among their subjects were "no less likely to spend time with their families" than the lightest viewers. Moreover, those heavy viewers reported feeling happier, more relaxed, and satisfied when watching TV with their families than light viewers did. Based on these reports, the researchers reached the conclusion that "television viewing harmonizes with family life."

Using the same data, however, the researchers made another observa- 34 tion about the heavy and light viewers: ". . . families that spend substantial portions of their time together watching television are likely to experience greater percentages of their family time feeling relatively passive and un-challenged compared with families who spend small proportions of their time watching TV."

At first glance the two observations seem at odds: the heavier viewers feel happy and satisfied, yet their family time is more passive and unchal-lenging—less satisfying in reality. But when one considers the nature of the television experience, the contradiction vanishes. Surely it stands to reason that the television experience is instrumental in preventing view-ers from recognizing its dulling effects, much as a mind-altering drug might do. 35

In spite of everything, the American family muddles on, dimly aware that something is amiss but distracted from an understanding of its plight by an endless stream of television images. As family ties grow weaker and vaguer, as children's lives become more separate from their parents', as par-ents' educational role in their children's lives is taken over by the media, the school, and the peer group, family life becomes increasingly more un-satisfying for both parents and children. All that seems to be left is love, an abstraction that family members know is necessary but find great diffi-culty giving to each other since the traditional opportunities for express-ing it within the family have been reduced or eliminated. 36

• • •

COMPREHENSION

1. How did early observers view television? How, in general, does Winn's view differ from theirs?

2. How has the nature of family television viewing changed since its incep-tion? How does Winn account for this change?

3. How does television keep families apart? In what sense does Winn see tele-vision as a threat to the very nature of the family?

4. What definition of *ritual* does Winn quote (16)? According to Winn, how has television affected these rituals?

5. What other factors besides television does Winn see as having a negative effect on the family?

PURPOSE AND AUDIENCE

1. Winn states her thesis in paragraph 8. What is it?

2. In paragraphs 23 and 31, Winn quotes two noted psychologists. What effect do you think she expects their words to have on her audience?

3. What effect do you believe the young woman's testimony in paragraph 19 is calculated to have on Winn's readers?

4. Do you think Winn presents enough evidence to support her thesis? Ex-plain your position.

5. In paragraph 20, Winn makes an **analogy** between modern families and cave families. What is her purpose in doing this? Is this a valid analogy?

STYLE AND STRUCTURE

1. Winn does not state her thesis until paragraph 8. What does she do in the paragraphs that precede this?

2. The length of Winn's paragraphs varies considerably. What effect do you think short paragraphs such as paragraphs 2, 3, 4, and 18 are likely to have on readers?

3. From what sources does Winn draw the many quotations she uses in this essay? How does the varied nature of these quotations help support her thesis?

4. This essay includes four headings: "The Quality of Life," "Family Rituals," "Real People," and "Undermining the Family." What functions do these headings serve? Could they be omitted? Should they be? Why or why not?

5. At the end of the essay, Winn addresses the findings of a study that contradicts her thesis. Should she also have addressed other issues that might have challenged her thesis? If so, which ones? Do you think she adequately refutes the conclusions of the study? Does placing the opposing study at the end of the essay strengthen or weaken her essay? Explain.

6. This is a fairly long essay. Is it *too* long? What, if anything, could Winn have cut?

VOCABULARY PROJECTS

1. Define each of the following words as it is used in this selection.

myopia (1)	recurrent (9)	inroads (18)
preposterous (6)	regimented (12)	purport (22)
splintering (6)	leisurely (13)	fosters (22)
ameliorate (8)	mechanized (13)	fester (25)
advent (8)	mediating (15)	diminished (32)
subsidiary (8)	shunted (15)	amiss (36)
apologists (8)	rendered (15)	abstraction (36)
equivocal (9)	adhesive (17)	

2. One effect of television has been on our vocabulary: television has spawned new words (for example, *sitcom*) and suggested new uses for old words (for instance, *tube*). List as many television-inspired words as you can, and define each.

JOURNAL ENTRY

What effects — positive or negative — do you think television has had on your life? What would your life be like without it?

WRITING WORKSHOP

1. Write an essay in which you consider the effects (including any possible future effects) of one of these inventions on the American family: the cell phone, e-mail, the microwave, the VCR, the Walkman, Nintendo, the telephone answering machine, the pager, the MP3 player.

2. Write a cause-and-effect essay in which you discuss the *positive* effects of television on American society.

3. Winn's essay, although recently updated for this book, is over thirty-five years old, and both television and viewers have changed considerably since she wrote "Television: The Plug-In Drug." Write a cause-and-effect essay about television in which you consider developments that Winn does not take into account—for example, the popularity of reality-based programs and the availability of satellite dishes.

COMBINING THE PATTERNS

Winn's essay relies on several patterns of development besides cause and effect. Where does she use **narration? Definition? Exemplification?** Why does she use each of these patterns?

THEMATIC CONNECTIONS

- "Once More to the Lake" (page 175)
- "The Human Cost of an Illiterate Society" (page 229)
- "Whodunit—The Media?" (page 618)

KATHA POLLITT

❖
Why Boys Don't Play with Dolls

Katha Pollitt (b. 1949) grew up in Brooklyn, New York, and now lives on Manhattan's Upper West Side. A graduate of Radcliffe College, she won the *Mademoiselle* undergraduate poetry contest in 1971. Pollitt has taught in the graduate writing program at New York University and the graduate program in liberal studies at the New School for Social Research, and she has published hundreds of book reviews and essays, as well as poetry, in a variety of periodicals, including *The Atlantic Monthly, The New Yorker, Harper's, Mother Jones,* and *Dissent.* A popular lecturer on feminist issues, she has also written the books *Reasonable Creatures: Essays on Women and Feminism* (1994) and *Subject to Debate: Sense and Dissents on Women, Politics, and Culture* (2001).

Background: In the following essay, which originally appeared in the *New York Times Magazine,* Pollitt considers the effects of gender stereotyping as it is reflected in the different toys given to little girls and to little boys. While the twentieth century saw the introduction of many toys that appealed to both girls and boys — wagons, pogo sticks, board games, hula hoops, and video games such as Pokémon — the majority of toys were marketed either for boys or for girls: at the turn of the century, train sets and cap guns for boys, baby dolls and crayons for girls; ten years later, Erector sets and toy cars for boys, Raggedy Ann dolls for girls. The introduction of the Barbie doll in the 1950s was matched by a proliferation of cowboy gear for boys. In the 1960s, the must-have toys were G.I. Joe and Hot Wheels versus the Easy Bake oven; in the 1970s, action figures versus Holly Hobbie dolls; in the 1980s, He-Man and the Masters of the Universe versus She-Ra and My Little Pony. Among the more recent popular toys introduced for boys was the Bionicle series of biomechanical action heroes; girls got the Bratz dolls ("with a passion for fashion") and the Diva Starz fashion dolls.

It's 28 years since the founding of NOW,* and boys still like trucks and girls still like dolls. Increasingly, we are told that the source of these robust preferences must lie outside society — in prenatal hormonal influences, brain chemistry, genes — and that feminism has reached its natural limits. What else could possibly explain the love of preschool girls for party dresses or the desire of toddler boys to own more guns than Mark from Michigan.

True, recent studies claim to show small cognitive differences between the sexes: he gets around by orienting himself in space, she does it by

---

*EDS. NOTE — The National Organization for Women (NOW) was founded in 1966.

2

remembering landmarks. Time will tell if any deserve the hoopla with which each is invariably greeted, over the protests of the researchers themselves. But even if the results hold up (and the history of such research is not encouraging), we don't need studies of sex-differentiated brain activity in reading, say, to understand why boys and girls still seem so unalike.

The feminist movement has done much for some women, and something for every woman, but it has hardly turned America into a playground free of sex roles. It hasn't even got women to stop dieting or men to stop interrupting them.

Instead of looking at kids to "prove" that differences in behavior by sex are innate, we can look at the ways we raise kids as an index to how unfinished the feminist revolution really is, and how tentatively it is embraced even by adults who fully expect their daughters to enter previously male-dominated professions and their sons to change diapers.

I'm at a children's birthday party. "I'm sorry," one mom silently mouths to the mother of the birthday girl, who has just torn open her present—Tropical Splash Barbie. Now, you can love Barbie or you can hate Barbie, and there are feminists in both camps. But *apologize* for Barbie? Inflict Barbie, against your own convictions, on the child of a friend you know will be none too pleased?

Every mother in that room had spent years becoming a person who had to be taken seriously, not least by herself. Even the most attractive, I'm willing to bet, had suffered over her body's failure to fit the impossible American ideal. Given all that, it seems crazy to transmit Barbie to the next generation. Yet to reject her is to say that what Barbie represents—being sexy, thin, stylish—is unimportant, which is obviously not true, and children know it's not true.

Women's looks matter terribly in this society, and so Barbie, however ambivalently, must be passed along. After all, there are worse toys. The Cut and Style Barbie styling head, for example, a grotesque object intended to encourage "hair play." The grown-ups who give that probably apologize, too.

How happy would most parents be to have a child who flouted sex conventions? I know a lot of women, feminists, who complain in a comical, eyeball-rolling way about their sons' passion for sports: the ruined weekends, obnoxious coaches, macho values. But they would not think of discouraging their sons from participating in this activity they find so foolish. Or do they? Their husbands are sports fans, too, and they like their husbands a lot.

Could it be that even sports-resistant moms see athletics as part of manliness? That if their sons wanted to spend the weekend writing up their diaries, or reading, or baking, they'd find it disturbing? Too antisocial? Too lonely? Too gay?

Theories of innate differences in behavior are appealing. They let parents off the hook—no small recommendation in a culture that holds moms, and sometimes even dads, responsible for their children's every misstep on the road to bliss and success.

They allow grown-ups to take the path of least resistance to the domi-   11
nant culture, which always requires less psychic effort, even if it means
more actual work: just ask the working mother who comes home exhausted
and nonetheless finds it easier to pick up her son's socks than make him
do it himself. They let families buy for their children, without too much
guilt, the unbelievably sexist junk that the kids, who have been watching
commercials since birth, understandably crave.

But the thing the theories do most of all is tell adults that the *adult*   12
world—in which moms and dads still play by many of the old rules even as
they question and fidget and chafe against them—is the way it's supposed
to be. A girl with a doll and a boy with a truck "explain" why men are from
Mars and women are from Venus, why wives do housework and husbands
just don't understand.

The paradox is that the world of rigid and hierarchical sex roles evoked   13
by determinist theories is already passing away. Three-year-olds may indeed
insist that doctors are male and nurses female, even if their own mother is
a physician. Six-year-olds know better. These days, something like half of
all medical students are female, and male applications to nursing school
are inching upward. When tomorrow's three-year-olds play doctor, who's
to say how they'll assign the roles?

With sex roles, as in every area of life, people aspire to what is possible   14
and conform to what is necessary. But these are not fixed, especially today.
Biological determinism may reassure some adults about their present, but
it is feminism, the ideology of flexible and converging sex roles, that fits
our children's future. And the kids, somehow, know this.

That's why, if you look carefully, you'll find that for every kid who fits a   15
stereotype, there's another who's breaking one down. Sometimes it's the
same kid—the boy who skateboards *and* takes cooking in his after-school
program; the girl who collects stuffed animals *and* A-pluses in science.

Feminists are often accused of imposing their "agenda" on children.   16
Isn't that what adults always do, consciously or unconsciously? Kids aren't
born religious, or polite, or kind, or able to remember where they put their
sneakers. Inculcating these behaviors, and the values behind them, is a
tremendous amount of work, involving many adults. We don't have a
choice, really, about *whether* we should give our children messages about
what it means to be male and female—they're bombarded with them from
morning till night.

The question, as always, is what do we want those messages to be?   17

• • •

COMPREHENSION

1. How does Pollitt assess the accomplishments of the feminist movement?

2. Who (or what) does Pollitt blame for the fact that the "feminist revolution" is "unfinished" (4)?

3. Why, according to Pollitt, do mothers continue to "transmit Barbie to the
   next generation" (6)? Does she think they are wrong to do so? Explain.

4. How does Pollitt account for the fact that women do not discourage their sons from playing sports? Does she think they should?

5. What is Pollitt's asessment of "theories of innate differences in behavior" (10) between girls and boys?

6. What dangers does Pollitt see in encouraging girls to play with dolls and boys to play with trucks? Do you see any dangers in this behavior?

7. What **paradox** does Pollitt identify beginning in paragraph 13? Why is this a paradox?

8. In paragraph 14, Pollitt says, "With sex roles, as in every area of life, people aspire to what is possible and conform to what is necessary." What does she mean?

PURPOSE AND AUDIENCE

1. What is Pollitt's thesis? Does she state it explicitly? Do you agree with her?

2. In paragraphs 5–7, Pollitt relates an anecdote about a birthday party. What purpose does this anecdote serve in the essay?

3. How does Pollitt expect her audience to react to her essay? Do you think she wants them to change their behavior or simply to reexamine their priorities? Explain.

STYLE AND STRUCTURE

1. According to Pollitt, what is the main cause of the gender differences in toy preferences? What other causes does she suggest? Can you think of others?

2. Use a causal chain to explain why a female child might choose to play with dolls instead of with trucks.

3. When Pollitt says, "A girl with a doll and a boy with a truck 'explain' why [. . .] wives do housework and husbands just don't understand" (12), is she guilty of *post hoc* reasoning? Explain.

4. Pollitt ends her essay with a one-sentence conclusion. Is this an effective strategy, or should she have developed the paragraph further—for example, by suggesting answers to the question she poses?

VOCABULARY PROJECTS

1. Define each of the following words as it is used in this selection.

robust (1)	flouted (8)	hierarchical (13)
cognitive (2)	innate (10)	determinist (13)
hoopla (2)	chafe (12)	inculcating (16)

2. Throughout this essay, Pollitt uses the word *kids* rather than *children*. What different connotations do these two words have? Do you think she made the right choice?

JOURNAL ENTRY

In the essay's first sentence, Pollitt says that "boys still like trucks and girls still like dolls." Does your experience support this conclusion?

WRITING WORKSHOP

1. Write a cause-and-effect essay titled "Why Girls Don't Play with Trucks." Support your thesis with information from your personal experience and observations.

2. How do you think playing with Barbie dolls might actually change the way a young girl thinks or behaves? Write a cause-and-effect essay that explains the specific effects of various aspects of playing with this particular doll.

3. What kinds of toys or games do you see as having a negative effect on young children? Write a cause-and-effect essay that identifies and accounts for these negative consequences. In your conclusion, make some recommendations on how to solve the problems these toys or games create.

COMBINING THE PATTERNS

Although this is a cause-and-effect essay, it also compares boys and girls (and, by extension, men and women). What specific differences does Pollitt see between the two genders? Do you think she should have spent more time on developing a **comparison and contrast** between males and females? What additional information would she have to provide?

THEMATIC CONNECTIONS

- "My Field of Dreams" (page 77)
- "Sex, Lies, and Conversation" (page 407)
- "I Want a Wife" (page 505)

LAWRENCE OTIS GRAHAM

❖

The "Black Table" Is Still There

Lawrence Otis Graham was born in 1962 into one of the few African-American families then living in an upper-middle-class community in Westchester County, near New York City. A graduate of Princeton University and Harvard Law School, Graham works as a corporate attorney in Manhattan and teaches at Fordham University. He is the author of some dozen books, most recently *Our Kind of People: Inside the Black Middle Class* (1999) and *Proversity: Getting Past Face Value* (2001). The following essay, originally published in the *New York Times* in 1991, is included in Graham's 1995 essay collection, *Member of the Club: Reflections on Life in a Racially Polarized Society.*

Background: In "The 'Black Table' Is Still There," Graham returns to his largely white junior high school and discovers to his dismay how little has changed since the 1970s. Since the 1950s, the United States government has strongly supported integration of public schools. For example, the Supreme Court in 1955 found segregation of public schools unconstitutional; the Civil Rights Act of 1964 required public school systems to implement integration programs; and in 1971, the Supreme Court upheld court-ordered busing as a means of achieving integration. The results of these policies were dramatic. From the mid-1960s to 1972, the number of African-American students attending desegregated schools jumped from 12 percent to 44 percent. By the 1990s, however, this had begun to change as the Supreme Court began to lift desegregation orders in response to local school boards' promises to desegregate voluntarily through magnet schools and the like. According to one study, since 1989 the percentage of African-American students attending segregated schools has increased in twenty states and declined in only thirteen. Ironically, as Graham observes, when students are given the choice, self-segregation seems to become the norm.

During a recent visit to my old junior high school in Westchester County, I came upon something that I never expected to see again, something that was a source of fear and dread for three hours each school morning of my early adolescence: the all-black lunch table in the cafeteria of my predominantly white suburban junior high school.

As I look back on 27 years of often being the first and only black person integrating such activities and institutions as the college newspaper, the high school tennis team, summer music camps, our all-white suburban neighborhood, my eating club at Princeton, or my private social club at Harvard Law School, the one scenario that puzzled me the most then and now is the all-black lunch table.

Why was it there? Why did the black kids separate themselves? What did the table say about the integration that was supposedly going on in home rooms and gym classes? What did it say about the black kids? The white kids? What did it say about me when I refused to sit there, day after day, for three years?

Each afternoon, at 12:03 P.M., after the fourth period ended, I found myself among 600 12-, 13-, and 14-year-olds who marched into the brightly-lit cafeteria and dashed for a seat at one of the 27 blue formica lunch tables.   4

No matter who I walked in with — usually a white friend — no matter what mood I was in, there was one thing that was certain: I would not sit at the black table.   5

I would never consider sitting at the black table.   6

What was wrong with me? What was I afraid of?   7

I would like to think that my decision was a heroic one, made in order to express my solidarity with the theories of integration that my community was espousing. But I was just 12 at the time, and there was nothing heroic in my actions.   8

I avoided the black table for a very simple reason: I was afraid that by sitting at the black table I'd lose all my white friends. I thought that by sitting there I'd be making a racist, anti-white statement.   9

Is that what the all-black table means? Is it a rejection of white people? I no longer think so.   10

At the time, I was angry that there was a black lunch table. I believed that the black kids were the reason why other kids didn't mix more. I was ready to believe that their self-segregation was the cause of white bigotry.   11

Ironically, I even believed this after my best friend (who was white) told me I probably shouldn't come to his bar mitzvah because I'd be the only black and people would feel uncomfortable. I even believed this after my Saturday afternoon visit, at age 10, to a private country club pool prompted incensed white parents to pull their kids from the pool in terror.   12

In the face of this blatantly racist (anti-black) behavior I still somehow managed to blame only the black kids for being the barrier to integration in my school and my little world. What was I thinking?   13

I realize now how wrong I was. During that same time, there were at least two tables of athletes, an Italian table, a Jewish girls' table, a Jewish boys' table (where I usually sat), a table of kids who were into heavy metal music and smoking pot, a table of middle-class Irish kids. Weren't these tables just as segregationist as the black table? At the time, no one thought so. At the time, no one even acknowledged the segregated nature of these other tables.   14

Maybe it's the color difference that makes all-black tables or all-black groups attract the scrutiny and wrath of so many people. It scares and angers people; it exasperates. It did those things to me, and I'm black.   15

As an integrating black person, I know that my decision *not* to join the black lunch table attracted its own kinds of scrutiny and wrath from my classmates. At the same time that I heard angry words like "Oreo" and "white boy" being hurled at me from the black table, I was also dodging   16 impatient questions from white classmates: "Why do all those black kids sit together?" or "Why don't you ever sit with the other blacks?"

The black lunch table, like those other segregated tables, is a comment   17
on the superficial inroads that integration has made in society. Perhaps I should be happy that even this is a long way from where we started. Yet, I can't get over the fact that the 27th table in my junior high school cafeteria is still known as the "black table" — 14 years after my adolescence.

• • •

COMPREHENSION

1. What exactly is the "black table"?

2. In paragraph 1, Graham says that on a recent visit to his old junior high school he "came upon something that [he] never expected to see again." Why do you think the sight of the all-black lunch table was such a surprise to him?

3. In Graham's junior high school, what factors determined where students sat?

4. Why didn't Graham sit at the black table when he was in junior high?

5. When he was a junior high school student, whom did Graham blame for the existence of the exclusively black lunch table? Whom or what does he now see as the cause of the table's existence?

PURPOSE AND AUDIENCE

1. What is Graham's thesis?

2. Rather than introducing outside supporting information — such as statistics, interviews with educators, or sociological studies — Graham relies on his own opinions and on anecdotal evidence to support his thesis. Do you think this is enough? Explain.

3. What is Graham's purpose in giving background information about himself in this essay — for example, in paragraphs 2 and 12? How does this information affect your reaction to him as a person? Your reaction to his essay? Do you think he needs to supply additional information about himself or his school? If so, what kind of information would be helpful?

4. Do you think Graham's primary purpose is to criticize a system he despises, to change his audience's views about segregated lunch tables, or to justify his own behavior? Explain your conclusion.

5. In paragraph 5, Graham tells readers that he usually entered the cafeteria with a white friend; in paragraph 12, he reveals that his best friend was white. Why do you suppose he wants his audience to know these facts?

STYLE AND STRUCTURE

1. Throughout his essay Graham asks **rhetorical questions.** Identify as many of these questions as you can. Are they necessary? Provocative? Distracting? Explain.

2. In paragraph 16, Graham quotes his long-ago classmates. What do these quotations reveal? Should he have included more of them?

3. Is Graham's focus on finding causes, describing effects, or both? Explain.

4. This essay uses first-person pronouns and contractions. Do you think Graham would have more credibility if he used a style that was less personal and more formal? Why or why not?

VOCABULARY PROJECTS

1. Define each of the following words as it is used in this selection.

scenario (2)	incensed (12)	scrutiny (15)
espousing (8)	blatantly (13)	inroads (17)

2. Does the phrase *black table* have a negative connotation for you? Do you think this is Graham's intention? What other names could he give to the table that might present it in a more neutral, even positive, light? What names could he give to the other tables he lists in paragraph 14?

JOURNAL ENTRY

Graham sees the continued presence of the black table as a serious problem. Do you agree?

WRITING WORKSHOP

1. In paragraph 14, Graham mentions other lunch tables that were limited to certain groups and asks, "Weren't these tables just as segregationist as the black table?" Answer his question in a cause-and-effect essay that explains why you believe "black tables" still exist.

2. In addition to self-segregated lunch tables, many colleges also have single-race social clubs, dormitories, fraternities, and even graduation ceremonies. Do you see such self-segregation as something that divides our society (that is, as a cause) or as something that reflects divisions that already exist (that is, as an effect)? Write an essay in which you discuss this issue, supporting your thesis with examples from your own experience.

3. Do the people in your school or workplace tend to segregate themselves according to race, gender, or some other principle? Do you see a problem in such behavior? Write a memo to your school's dean of students or to your employer explaining what you believe causes this pattern and what effects, positive or negative, you have observed.

COMBINING THE PATTERNS

In paragraph 14, Graham uses **classification and division.** What is he categorizing? What categories does he identify? What other categories might he include? Why is this pattern of development particularly appropriate for this essay?

THEMATIC CONNECTIONS

- "Just Walk On By" (page 223)
- "College Pressures" (page 447)
- "Slavery Isn't the Issue" (page 632)
- "An Idea Whose Time Has Come" (page 637)

LINDA M. HASSELSTROM

A Peaceful Woman Explains Why She Carries a Gun

Linda M. Hasselstrom (b. 1943) grew up in rural South Dakota, the daughter of a cattle ranching family. After receiving a master's degree in journalism from the University of Missouri, she returned to South Dakota to run her own ranch and now lives in Cheyenne, Wyoming. A highly respected poet, essayist, and writing teacher, she often focuses in her work on everyday life in the American West. Her publications include the poetry collections *Caught by One Wing* (1984), *Roadkill* (1987), and *Dakota Bones* (1991); the essay collection *Land Circle* (1991); and two books about ranching, *Feels Like Far: A Rancher's Life on the Great Plains* (1999) and *Between Grass and Sky: Where I Live and Work* (2002). In this essay from *Land Circle,* Hasselstrom explains her reluctant decision to become licensed to carry a concealed handgun.

Background: Hasselstrom's gun ownership can certainly be considered in the context of the ongoing debate over how (and even whether) stricter gun safety measures should be enacted in the United States. But equally important is the fact that her reason for carrying a gun is to protect herself from sexual assault. A study by the Bureau of Justice Statistics found that in 1997, some 115,000 women reported being raped in this country, with another 79,000 victims of rape attempts. A Department of Justice survey of women the following year found 333,000 incidents of rape and sexual assault, three times the number actually reported to the police. This discrepancy suggests that rape continues to be significantly underreported.

I am a peace-loving woman. But several events in the past 10 years have 1
convinced me I'm safer when I carry a pistol. This was a personal decision, but because handgun possession is a controversial subject, perhaps my reasoning will interest others.

I live in western South Dakota on a ranch 25 miles from the nearest 2
town: for several years I spent winters alone here. As a free-lance writer, I travel alone a lot — more than 100,000 miles by car in the last four years. With women freer than ever before to travel alone, the odds of our encountering trouble seem to have risen. Distances are great, roads are deserted, and the terrain is often too exposed to offer hiding places.

A woman who travels alone is advised, usually by men, to protect her- 3
self by avoiding bars and other "dangerous situations," by approaching her car like an Indian scout, by locking doors and windows. But these precautions aren't always enough. I spent years following them and still found myself in dangerous situations. I began to resent the idea that just because I am female, I have to be extra careful.

A few years ago, with another woman, I camped for several weeks in the   4
West. We discussed self-defense, but neither of us had taken a course in it.
She was against firearms, and local police told us Mace was illegal. So we
armed ourselves with spray cans of deodorant tucked into our sleeping
bags. We never used our improvised Mace because we were lucky enough to
camp beside people who came to our aid when men harassed us. But on
one occasion we visited a national park where our assigned space was less
than 15 feet from other campers. When we returned from a walk, we found
our closest neighbors were two young men. As we gathered our cooking
gear, they drank beer and loudly discussed what they would do to us after
dark. Nearby campers, even families, ignored them: rangers strolled past,
unconcerned. When we asked the rangers point-blank if they would protect us, one of them patted my shoulder and said, "Don't worry, girls.
They're just kidding." At dusk we drove out of the park and hid our camp
in the woods a few miles away. The illegal spot was lovely, but our enjoyment of that park was ruined. I returned from the trip determined to
reconsider the options available for protecting myself.

At that time, I lived alone on the ranch and taught night classes in   5
town. Along a city street I often traveled, a woman had a flat tire, called for
help on her CB radio, and got a rapist who left her beaten. She was afraid
to call for help again and stayed in her car until morning. For that reason,
as well as because CBs work best along line-of-sight, which wouldn't help
much in the rolling hills where I live, I ruled out a CB.

As I drove home one night, a car followed me. It passed me on a narrow   6
bridge while a passenger flashed a blinding spotlight in my face. I braked
sharply. The car stopped, angled across the bridge, and four men jumped
out. I realized the locked doors were useless if they broke the windows of
my pickup. I started forward, hoping to knock their car aside so I could
pass. Just then another car appeared, and the men hastily got back in their
car. They continued to follow me, passing and repassing. I dared not go
home because no one else was there. I passed no lighted houses. Finally
they pulled over to the roadside, and I decided to use their tactic: fear.
Speeding, the pickup horn blaring, I swerved as close to them as I dared as
I roared past. It worked: they turned off the highway. But I was frightened
and angry. Even in my vehicle I was too vulnerable.

Other incidents occurred over the years. One day I glanced out at a   7
field below my house and saw a man with a shotgun walking toward a
pond full of ducks. I drove down and explained that the land was posted. I
politely asked him to leave. He stared at me, and the muzzle of the shotgun
began to rise. In a moment of utter clarity I realized that I was alone on the
ranch, and that he could shoot me and simply drive away. The moment
passed: the man left.

One night, I returned home from teaching a class to find deep tire ruts   8
in the wet ground of my yard, garbage in the driveway, and a large gas tank
empty. A light shone in the house: I couldn't remember leaving it on. I was
too embarrassed to drive to a neighboring ranch and wake someone up. An

hour of cautious exploration convinced me the house was safe, but once inside, with the doors locked, I was still afraid. I kept thinking of how vulnerable I felt, prowling around my own house in the dark.

My first positive step was to take a kung fu class, which teaches evasive or protective action when someone enters your space without permission. I learned to move confidently, scanning for possible attackers. I learned how to assess danger and techniques for avoiding it without combat. 9

I also learned that one must practice several hours every day to be good at kung fu. By that time I had married George: when I practiced with him, I learned how *close* you must be to your attacker to use martial arts, and decided a 120-pound woman dare not let a six-foot, 220-pound attacker get that close unless she is very, very good at self-defense. I have since read articles by several women who were extremely well trained in the martial arts, but were raped and beaten anyway. 10

I thought back over the times in my life when I had been attacked or threatened and tried to be realistic about my own behavior, searching for anything that had allowed me to become a victim. Overall, I was convinced that I had not been at fault. I don't believe myself to be either paranoid or a risk-taker, but I wanted more protection. 11

With some reluctance I decided to try carrying a pistol. George had always carried one, despite his size and his training in martial arts. I practiced shooting until I was sure I could hit an attacker who moved close enough to endanger me. Then I bought a license from the county sheriff, making it legal for me to carry the gun concealed. 12

But I was not yet ready to defend myself. George taught me that the most important preparation was mental: convincing myself I could actually *shoot a person*. Few of us wish to hurt or kill another human being. But there is no point in having a gun; in fact, gun possession might increase your danger unless you know you can use it. I got in the habit of rehearsing, as I drove or walked, the precise conditions that would be required before I would shoot someone. 13

People who have not grown up with the idea that they are capable of protecting themselves — in other words, most women — might have to work hard to convince themselves of their ability, and of the necessity. Handgun ownership need not turn us into gunslingers, but it can be part of believing in, and relying on, *ourselves* for protection. 14

To be useful, a pistol has to be available. In my car, it's within instant reach. When I enter a deserted rest stop at night, it's in my purse, with my hand on the grip. When I walk from a dark parking lot into a motel, it's in my hand, under a coat. At home, it's on the headboard. In short, I take it with me almost everywhere I go alone. 15

Just carrying a pistol is not protection; avoidance is still the best approach to trouble. Subconsciously watching for signs of danger, I believe I've become more alert. Handgun use, not unlike driving, becomes instinctive. Each time I've drawn my gun — I have never fired it at another human being — I've simply found it in my hand. 16

I was driving the half-mile to the highway mailbox one day when I saw 17
a vehicle parked about midway down the road. Several men were standing
in the ditch, relieving themselves. I have no objection to emergency urination, but I noticed they'd dumped several dozen beer cans in the road.
Besides being ugly, cans can slash a cow's feet or stomach.

The men noticed me before they finished and made quite a perfor- 18
mance out of zipping their trousers while walking toward me. All four of
them gathered around my small foreign car, and one of them demanded
what the hell I wanted.

"This is private land. I'd appreciate it if you'd pick up the beer cans." 19

"What beer cans?" said the belligerent one, putting both hands on the 20
car door and leaning in my window. His face was inches from mine, and
the beer fumes were strong. The others laughed. One tried the passenger
door, locked; another put his foot on the hood and rocked the car. They
circled, lightly thumping the roof, discussing my good fortune in meeting
them and the benefits they were likely to bestow upon me. I felt very small
and very trapped and they knew it.

"The ones you just threw out," I said politely. 21

"I don't see no beer cans. Why don't you get out here and show them to 22
me, honey?" said the belligerent one, reaching for the handle inside my door.

"Right over there," I said, still being polite. " — there, and over there." I 23
pointed with the pistol, which I'd slipped under my thigh. Within one
minute the cans and the men were back in the car and headed down the
road.

I believe this incident illustrates several important principles. The men 24
were trespassing and knew it: their judgment may have been impaired by
alcohol. Their response to the polite request of a woman alone was to use
their size, numbers, and sex to inspire fear. The pistol was a response in the
same language. Politeness didn't work: I couldn't match them in size or
number. Out of the car, I'd have been more vulnerable. The pistol just
changed the balance of power. It worked again recently when I was driving
in a desolate part of Wyoming. A man played cat-and-mouse with me for 30
miles, ultimately trying to run me off the road. When his car passed mine
with only two inches to spare, I showed him my pistol, and he disappeared.

When I got my pistol, I told my husband, revising the old Colt slogan, 25
"God made men *and women,* but Sam Colt made them equal." Recently I
have seen a gunmaker's ad with a similar sentiment. Perhaps this is an idea
whose time has come, though the pacifist inside me will be saddened if the
only way women can achieve equality is by carrying weapons.

We must treat a firearm's power with caution. "Power tends to corrupt, 26
and absolute power corrupts absolutely," as a man (Lord Acton) once said.
A pistol is not the only way to avoid being raped or murdered in today's
world, but, intelligently wielded, it can shift the balance of power and provide a measure of safety.

• • •

COMPREHENSION

1. According to Hasselstrom, why does she carry a gun? In one sentence, summarize her rationale.

2. List the specific events that led Hasselstrom to her decision to carry a gun.

3. Other than carrying a gun, what means of protecting herself did Hasselstrom try? Why did she find them unsatisfactory? Can you think of other strategies she could have adopted instead of carrying a gun?

4. Where in the essay does Hasselstrom express her reluctance to carry a gun?

5. In paragraph 13, Hasselstrom says, "Gun possession might increase your danger unless you know you can use it." Where else does she touch on the possible pitfalls of carrying a gun?

6. What does Hasselstrom mean when she says, "The pistol just changed the balance of power" (paragraph 24)?

PURPOSE AND AUDIENCE

1. How does paragraph 1 establish Hasselstrom's purpose for writing this essay? What other purpose might she have?

2. What purpose does paragraph 5 serve? Is it necessary?

3. Do you think this essay is aimed at men, at women, or at both? Why?

4. Do you think Hasselstrom expects her readers to agree with her position? Where does she indicate that she expects them to challenge her? How does she address this challenge?

STYLE AND STRUCTURE

1. This essay is written in the first person, and it relies heavily on personal experience. Do you see this as a strength or a weakness? Explain.

2. What is the main cause in this cause-and-effect essay — that is, what is the most important reason Hasselstrom gives for carrying a gun? Can you identify any contributory causes?

3. Could you argue that simply being a woman is justification enough for carrying a gun? Do you think this is Hasselstrom's position? Explain.

4. Think of Hasselstrom's essay as the first step in a possible causal chain. What situations might result from her decision to carry a gun?

5. In paragraph 25, Hasselstrom says, "The pacifist inside me will be saddened if the only way women can achieve equality is by carrying weapons." In her title and elsewhere in the essay, Hasselstrom characterizes herself as a "peaceful woman." Do you think she is successful in using language like this to portray herself as a peace-loving woman who only reluctantly carries a gun? Why or why not?

VOCABULARY PROJECTS

1. Define each of the following words as it is used in this selection.

   posted (7)   belligerent (20)   wielded (26)
   muzzle (7)   bestow (20)

2. Some of the words and phrases Hasselstrom uses in this essay suggest that she sees her pistol as an equalizer, something that helps to compensate for her vulnerability. Identify the words and phrases she uses to characterize her gun in this way.

JOURNAL ENTRY

Do you agree that carrying a gun is Hasselstrom's only choice, or do you think there are other steps she could take to ensure her safety? Explain.

WRITING WORKSHOP

1. Hasselstrom lives in a rural area, and the scenarios she describes apply to rural life. Rewrite this essay as "A Peaceful Urban (or Suburban) Woman Explains Why She Carries a Gun."

2. What reasons might a "peace-loving" man have for carrying a gun? Write a cause-and-effect essay outlining such a man's motives, using any of Hasselstrom's reasons that might apply to him as well.

3. Write a cause-and-effect essay presenting reasons to support a position that opposes Hasselstrom's: "A Peaceful Woman (or Man) Explains Why She (or He) Will Not Carry a Gun."

COMBINING THE PATTERNS

Several times in her essay, Hasselstrom uses **narrative** to support her position. Identify these narrative passages. Are they absolutely essential to the essay? Could they be briefer? Could some be deleted? Explain.

THEMATIC CONNECTIONS

- "Shooting an Elephant" (page 117)
- "How the Lawyers Stole Winter" (page 402)
- "The Wife-Beater" (page 521)

MALCOLM GLADWELL

❖

The Tipping Point

Born in England in 1963, Malcolm Gladwell grew up in Canada and received his bachelor's degree in history from the University of Toronto in 1984. From 1987 to 1996, he reported for the *Washington Post,* first as a science writer and then as the paper's New York City bureau chief. Since 1996, he has been a staff writer for *The New Yorker.* He published his first book, *The Tipping Point: How Little Things Can Make a Big Difference,* in 2000.

Background: In a recent interview, Gladwell noted that "the word 'tipping point' [. . .] comes from the world of epidemiology. It's the name given to that moment in an epidemic when a virus reaches critical mass. It's the boiling point. It's the moment on the graph when the line starts to shoot straight upwards.[. . .] When I heard that phrase for the first time I remember thinking — wow. What if everything has a tipping point? Wouldn't it be cool to try and look for tipping points in business, or in social policy, or in advertising or in any number of other nonmedical areas?" In the following excerpt from his book, Gladwell considers the factors that precipitated the dramatic decrease in violent crime in the United States, and particularly in New York City, over the course of the 1990s. Between 1973 and 1993, incidents of violent crime nationwide ranged from 3.5 million to over 4 million annually. From 1993 to 1998, that rate dropped precipitously to slightly more than 2 million and has since then remained steady or declined slightly. Declines in New York City crime rates accounted for 25 percent of this drop. Prior to 1993, the number of murders in New York City was routinely over 2,000 yearly, a figure that had fallen 70 percent by 1999 (the lowest homicide rate in the city since 1964), while overall crime rates had fallen 50 percent. The FBI has recognized New York City as the "Safest Large City in America."

During the 1990s violent crime declined across the United States for a number of fairly straightforward reasons. The illegal trade in crack cocaine, which had spawned a great deal of violence among gangs and drug dealers, began to decline. The economy's dramatic recovery meant that many people who might have been lured into crime got legitimate jobs instead, and the general aging of the population meant that there were fewer people in the age range — males between eighteen and twenty-four — that is responsible for the majority of all violence. The question of why crime declined in New York City, however, is a little more complicated. In the period when the New York epidemic tipped down, the city's economy hadn't improved. It was still stagnant. In fact, the city's poorest neighborhoods had just been hit hard by the welfare cuts of the early 1990s. The waning of the crack cocaine epidemic in New York was clearly a factor, but then again, it had been in steady decline well before crime dipped. As for the aging of the population, because of heavy immigration to New York in the 1980s, the city was getting younger in the 1990s, not older. In any case, all of these trends are long-term changes that one would expect to have gradual effects. In New York the decline was anything but gradual. Something else clearly played a role in reversing New York's crime epidemic.

The most intriguing candidate for that "something else" is called the   2
Broken Windows theory. Broken Windows was the brainchild of the criminologists James Q. Wilson and George Kelling. Wilson and Kelling argued that crime is the inevitable result of disorder. If a window is broken and left unrepaired, people walking by will conclude that no one cares and no one is in charge. Soon, more windows will be broken, and the sense of anarchy will spread from the building to the street on which it faces, sending a signal that anything goes. In a city, relatively minor problems like graffiti, public disorder, and aggressive panhandling, they write, are all the equivalent of broken windows, invitations to more serious crimes:

> Muggers and robbers, whether opportunistic or professional, believe they reduce their chances of being caught or even identified if they operate on streets where potential victims are already intimidated by prevailing conditions. If the neighborhood cannot keep a bothersome panhandler from annoying passersby, the thief may reason, it is even less likely to call the police to identify a potential mugger or to interfere if the mugging actually takes place.

This is an epidemic theory of crime. It says that crime is contagious — just as a fashion trend is contagious — that it can start with a broken window and spread to an entire community. The Tipping Point in this epidemic, though, isn't a particular kind of person [. . .]. It's something physical like graffiti. The impetus to engage in a certain kind of behavior is not coming · from a certain kind of person but from a feature of the environment.

In the mid-1980s Kelling was hired by the New York Transit Authority   3
as a consultant, and he urged them to put the Broken Windows theory into practice. They obliged, bringing in a new subway director by the name of David Gunn to oversee a multibillion-dollar rebuilding of the subway system. Many subway advocates, at the time, told Gunn not to worry about graffiti, to focus on the larger questions of crime and subway reliability, and it seemed like reasonable advice. Worrying about graffiti at a time when the entire system was close to collapse seems as pointless as scrubbing the decks of the *Titanic* as it headed toward the icebergs. But Gunn insisted. "The graffiti was symbolic of the collapse of the system," he says. "When you looked at the process of rebuilding the organization and morale, you had to win the battle against graffiti. Without winning that battle, all the management reforms and physical changes just weren't going to happen. We were about to put out new trains that were worth about ten million bucks apiece, and unless we did something to protect them, we knew just what would happen. They would last one day and then they would be vandalized."

Gunn drew up a new management structure and a precise set of goals   4
and timetables aimed at cleaning the system line by line, train by train. He
started with the number seven train that connects Queens to midtown
Manhattan, and began experimenting with new techniques to clean off
the paint. On stainless-steel cars, solvents were used. On the painted cars,
the graffiti were simply painted over. Gunn made it a rule that there
should be no retreat, that once a car was "reclaimed" it should never be
allowed to be vandalized again. "We were religious about it," Gunn said.
At the end of the number one line in the Bronx, where the trains stop
before turning around and going back to Manhattan, Gunn set up a cleaning station. If a car came in with graffiti, the graffiti had to be removed
during the changeover, or the car was removed from service. "Dirty" cars,
which hadn't yet been cleansed of graffiti, were never to be mixed with
"clean" cars. The idea was to send an unambiguous message to the vandals
themselves.

"We had a yard up in Harlem on One hundred thirty-fifth Street where   5
the trains would lay up over night," Gunn said. "The kids would come the
first night and paint the side of the train white. Then they would come the
next night, after it was dry, and draw the outline. Then they would come
the third night and color it in. It was a three-day job. We knew the kids
would be working on one of the dirty trains, and what we would do is wait
for them to finish their mural. Then we'd walk over with rollers and paint
it over. The kids would be in tears, but we'd just be going up and down,
up and down. It was a message to them. If you want to spend three nights
of your time vandalizing a train, fine. But it's never going to see the light
of day."

Gunn's graffiti cleanup took from 1984 to 1990. At that point, the   6
Transit Authority hired William Bratton to head the transit police, and the
second stage of the reclamation of the subway system began. Bratton was,
like Gunn, a disciple of Broken Windows. He describes Kelling, in fact, as
his intellectual mentor, and so his first step as police chief was as seemingly
quixotic as Gunn's. With felonies — serious crimes — on the subway system
at an all-time high, Bratton decided to crack down on fare-beating. Why?
Because he believed that, like graffiti, fare-beating could be a signal, a small
expression of disorder that invited much more serious crimes. An estimated 170,000 people a day were entering the system, by one route or
another, without paying a token. Some were kids, who simply jumped over
the turnstiles. Others would lean backward on the turnstiles and force
their way through. And once one or two or three people began cheating the
system, other people — who might never otherwise have considered evading the law — would join in, reasoning that if some people weren't going to
pay, they shouldn't either, and the problem would snowball. The problem
was exacerbated by the fact fare-beating was not easy to fight. Because
there was only $1.25 at stake, the transit police didn't feel it was worth
their time to pursue it, particularly when there were plenty of more serious
crimes happening down on the platform and in the trains.

Bratton is a colorful, charismatic man, a born leader, and he quickly   7
made his presence felt. His wife stayed behind in Boston, so he was free to
work long hours, and he would roam the city on the subway at night, getting a sense of what the problems were and how best to fight them. First,
he picked stations where fare-beating was the biggest problem, and put as
many as ten policemen in plainclothes at the turnstiles. The team would
nab fare-beaters one by one, handcuff them, and leave them standing, in a
daisy chain, on the platform until they had a "full catch." The idea was to
signal, as publicly as possible, that the transit police were now serious
about cracking down on fare-beaters. Previously, police officers had been
wary of pursuing fare-beaters because the arrest, the trip to the station
house, the filling out of necessary forms, and the waiting for those forms
to be processed took an entire day — all for a crime that usually merited no
more than a slap on the wrist. Bratton retrofitted a city bus and turned it
into a rolling station house, with its own fax machines, phones, holding
pen, and fingerprinting facilities. Soon the turnaround time on an arrest
was down to an hour. Bratton also insisted that a check be run on all those
arrested. Sure enough, one out of seven arrestees had an outstanding warrant for a previous crime, and one out of twenty was carrying a weapon of
some sort. Suddenly it wasn't hard to convince police officers that tackling
fare-beating made sense. "For the cops it was a bonanza," Bratton writes.
"Every arrest was like opening a box of Cracker Jack. What kind of toy am I
going to get? Got a gun? Got a knife? Got a warrant? Do we have a murderer here? . . . After a while the bad guys wised up and began to leave their
weapons home and pay their fares." Under Bratton, the number of ejec-
tions from subway stations — for drunkenness, or improper behavior —
tripled within his first few months in office. Arrests for misdemeanors, for
the kind of minor offenses that had gone unnoticed in the past, went up
fivefold between 1990 and 1994. Bratton turned the transit police into an
organization focused on the smallest infractions, on the details of life
underground.

After the election of Rudolph Giuliani as mayor of New York in 1994,   8
Bratton was appointed head of the New York City Police Department, and
he applied the same strategies to the city at large. He instructed his officers
to crack down on quality-of-life crimes: on the "squeegee men" who came
up to drivers at New York City intersections and demanded money for
washing car windows, for example, and on all the other above-ground
equivalents of turnstile-jumping and graffiti. "Previous police administration had been handcuffed by restrictions," Bratton says. "We took the
handcuffs off. We stepped up enforcement of the laws against public
drunkenness and public urination and arrested repeat violators, including
those who threw empty bottles on the street or were involved in even relatively minor damage to property. . . . If you peed in the street, you were
going to jail." When crime began to fall in the city — as quickly and dramatically as it had in the subways — Bratton and Giuliani pointed to the same

cause. Minor, seemingly insignificant quality-of-life crimes, they said, were Tipping Points for violent crime.

• • •

COMPREHENSION

1. Why, according to Gladwell, did violent crime decline in the United States during the 1990s? Why does he see New York City's situation as "more complicated" (1)?

2. What is the "Broken Windows" theory (2)? In what sense are broken windows "invitations to more serious crimes"? How might the Broken Windows theory be used to explain the decline in crime in New York City?

3. What does Gladwell mean by "an epidemic theory of crime" (2)? What does he see as the "Tipping Point" of the epidemic?

4. What steps did New York City take to "put the Broken Windows theory into practice" (3)? Why did subway director David Gunn begin by eliminating graffiti on the trains?

5. Why did William Bratton, head of the transit police, begin his job with a crackdown on fare-beating?

6. What unexpected "bonanza" (7) did the crackdown on fare-beaters produce?

7. How did Mayor Giuliani continue to apply the strategies used by Gunn and Bratton? On what specific quality-of-life crimes did he focus?

PURPOSE AND AUDIENCE

1. Gladwell states his thesis at the end of paragraph 1: "Something else clearly played a role in reversing New York's crime epidemic." What is that "something else"? Do you think he should have identified it in his thesis statement instead of waiting? Explain.

2. Gladwell quotes quite extensively from Wilson and Kelling's research and from comments by both David Gunn and William Bratton. Why? Is this a successful strategy?

STYLE AND STRUCTURE

1. Where does this essay focus on finding causes? Where does it focus on describing effects?

2. In paragraph 2, Gladwell explains the Broken Windows theory. Is his explanation an example of a causal chain? In what sense is fare-beating (described in paragraph 6) an example of a causal chain?

3. Paragraphs 3–5 describe the steps taken by David Gunn to clean graffiti off subway cars; paragraph 7 presents a detailed explanation of how William Bratton attacked the problem of fare-beating. Why does Gladwell devote so much time to explaining these processes?

4. Could Gladwell be accused of *post hoc* reasoning? That is, could you argue that quality-of-life crimes did not cause violent crimes but simply preceded them in time? Explain.

VOCABULARY PROJECTS

1. Define each of the following words as it is used in this selection.

   lured (1)   exacerbated (6)
   impetus (2)   charismatic (7)
   reclamation (6)   retrofitted (7)
   mentor (6)   bonanza (7)

2. Consider the various quality-of-life crimes Gladwell identifies — for example, vandalism, aggressive panhandling, fare-beating, "squeegee men," public drunkenness, and public urination. Write a one-sentence definition of each crime.

JOURNAL ENTRY

How has the number (or the kind) of crimes in your neighborhood changed in the years in which you have lived there? How do you account for these changes?

WRITING WORKSHOP

1. What changes have you observed in your community (or in your school) that you believe have led to a decline in your quality of life? How have these changes had a negative impact on your life?

2. What small changes in your school could have a positive effect on students' quality of life? Write a cause-and-effect essay in which you discuss how some specific changes could have a positive effect on the student body.

3. Using a **causal chain** to structure your essay, trace the gradual decline — or improvement — of a service or institution with which you are familiar.

COMBINING THE PATTERNS

This cause-and-effect essay explains two **processes,** one in paragraphs 3–5 and another in paragraph 7. What changes would Gladwell have to make to these two passages if he wanted to expand each of them into a self-contained **process explanation**?

THEMATIC CONNECTIONS

- "Thirty-Eight Who Saw Murder Didn't Call the Police" (page 101)
- "Just Walk On By" (page 223)
- "On Dumpster Diving" (page 660)

JANICE MIRIKITANI

Suicide Note (Poetry)

Janice Mirikitani, a third-generation Japanese American, was born in San Francisco in 1942 and graduated from the University of California at Los Angeles in 1962. In her poetry, Mirikitani often considers how racism in the United States affects Asian Americans, particularly the thousands of Japanese Americans held in internment camps during World War II. Her collections include *Awake in the River* (1978), *Shedding Silence* (1987), and *We Are the Dangerous: Selected Poems* (1995). She has also edited anthologies of Japanese-American and third world literature, as well as several volumes giving voice to children living in poverty. For many years, she has been president of the Glide Foundation, which sponsors numerous outreach programs for the poor and homeless of San Francisco. Mirikitani is also a noted choreographer.

Background: The following poem, which appears in *Shedding Silence*, takes the form of a suicide note written by a young Asian-American college student to her family and reveals the extreme pressure to excel placed on her by her parents and her culture. The theme, however, is one that has considerable relevance beyond the Asian-American community. Tragically, some five thousand teenagers and young adults commit suicide annually in the United States (there are thirty to fifty times as many attempts), and suicide is the third leading cause of death among fifteen- to twenty-four-year-olds. Among college students, suicide is the second leading cause of death; as of this writing, it is estimated that some one thousand college students will take their lives in 2002. Although this number is somewhat lower than for young people who are not enrolled in college, many experts believe that it is on the rise.

How many notes written . . .
ink smeared like birdprints in snow.

not good enough   not pretty enough   not smart enough

dear mother and father.
I apologize   5
for disappointing you.
I've worked very hard,

       not good enough

harder, perhaps to please you.
If only I were a son, shoulders broad   10
as the sunset threading through pine,
I would see the light in my mother's
eyes, or the golden pride reflected

in my father's dream
of my wide, male hands worthy of work   15
and comfort.
I would swagger through life
muscled and bold and assured,
drawing praises to me
like currents in the bed of wind, virile   20
with confidence.

   not good enough   not strong enough   not good enough
I apologize.
Tasks do not come easily.
Each failure, a glacier.   25
Each disapproval, a bootprint.
Each disappointment,
ice above my river.
So I have worked hard.
                    not good enough   30
My sacrifice I will drop
bone by bone, perched
on the ledge of my womanhood,
fragile as wings.

                    not strong enough   35

It is snowing steadily
surely not good weather
for flying — this sparrow
sillied and dizzied by the wind
on the edge.   40

                    not smart enough
I make this ledge my altar
to offer penance.
This air will not hold me,
the snow burdens my crippled wings,   45
my tears drop like bitter cloth
softly into the gutter below.
   not good enough   not strong enough   not smart enough

                  Choices thin as shaved
                  ice. Notes shredded   50
                  drift like snow

on my broken body,
cover me like whispers
of sorries
sorries.   55
Perhaps when they find me

they will bury
my bird bones beneath
a sturdy pine
and scatter my feathers like   60
unspoken song
over this white and cold and silent
breast of earth.

•   •   •

READING LITERATURE

1. An author's note that originally introduced this poem explained the main cause of the student's death:

   An Asian-American college student was reported to have jumped to her death from her dormitory window. Her body was found two days later under a deep cover of snow. Her suicide note contained an apology to her parents for having received less than a perfect four-point grade average.

   What other causes might have contributed to her suicide?

2. Why does the speaker believe her life would be happier if she were male? Do you think she is correct?

3. What words, phrases, and images are repeated in this poem? What effect do these repetitions have on you?

JOURNAL ENTRY

Whom (or what) do you blame for teenage suicides such as the one the poem describes? How might the causes of such deaths be eliminated?

THEMATIC CONNECTIONS

- "Only Daughter" (page 84)
- "College Pressures" (page 447)
- "The Company Man" (page 517)

WRITING ASSIGNMENTS FOR CAUSE AND EFFECT

1. "Who Killed Benny Paret?" (page 323), "On Dumpster Diving" (page 670), and "Thirty-Eight Who Saw Murder Didn't Call the Police" (page 103) all encourage readers, either directly or indirectly, to take action rather than remaining uninvolved. Using information gleaned from these essays (or from others in the text) as support for your thesis, write an essay in which you explore either the possible consequences of apathy, the possible causes of apathy, or both.

2. Write an updated version of one of this chapter's essays. For example, you might reconsider Winn's points in light of the increasing influence of cable television in the thirty-five years since "Television: The Plug-In Drug" was written or explore the kinds of pressure that Lawrence Otis Graham ("The 'Black Table' Is Still There") might face as a middle-school student today.

3. Various technological and social developments have contributed to the decline of formal letter writing. One of these is the telephone; another is e-mail. Consider some other possible causes, and write an essay explaining why letter writing has become less popular. You may also consider the *effects* of this decline. (Alternatively, you might approach the same topic from a different viewpoint: you might write an essay discussing the effects of increased letter writing in the form of e-mail.)

4. How do you account for the popularity of one of the following phenomena: reality TV, fast food, rap music, Internet chat rooms, sensationalist tabloids like the *Star*? Write an essay in which you consider remote as well as immediate causes for the success of the phenomenon you choose.

5. Between 1946 and 1964, the U.S. birth rate increased considerably. Some of the effects attributed to this baby boom include the 1960s anti-war movement, an increase in the crime rate, and the development of the women's movement. Write an essay in which you explore some possible effects on the nation's economy and politics of the baby-boom generation's growing older. What trends would you expect to find now that baby boomers have reached middle age? When they reach retirement age?

6. Write an essay in which you trace a series of events in your life that constitutes a causal chain. Indicate clearly both the sequence of events and the causal connections among them, and be careful not to confuse coincidence with causality.

7. Consider the effects, or possible effects, of one of these scientific developments on your life and/or on the lives of your contemporaries: genetic engineering, space exploration, the Internet, human cloning. Consider negative as well as positive effects.

8. Almost half of American marriages now end in divorce. To what do you attribute this high divorce rate? Be as specific as possible, citing "case studies" of families with which you are familiar.

9. What do you see as the major cause of any *one* of these problems: acquaintance rape, binge drinking among college students, voter apathy, school

shootings, academic cheating? Based on your identification of its causes, formulate some specific solutions for the problem you select.

10. Write an essay in which you consider the likely effects of a severe, protracted shortage of one of the following commodities: food, rental housing, medical care, computer hardware, reading matter. You may consider a community-, city-, or statewide shortage or a nation- or worldwide crisis.

11. Write an essay in which you explore the causes and/or effects of increased violence among children in the United States. If you choose to cite the media as a main cause, you might refer to the essays on media violence in Chapter 12, "Argumentation."

12. Write an essay exploring the causes and effects of the trend toward longer lifespans among adults in contemporary times. (An example of a cause might be advances in medicine; an effect could be a larger population of senior citizens.) In your thesis statement, be sure to focus on what this trend might mean for future generations — politically, socially, and economically.

COLLABORATIVE ACTIVITY FOR CAUSE AND EFFECT

Working in groups of four, discuss your thoughts about the increasing homeless population, and then list four *effects* the presence of homeless people is having on you, your community, and our nation. Assign each member of your group to write a paragraph explaining one of the effects the group identifies. Then arrange the paragraphs in order of increasing importance, moving from the least to the most significant consequence. Finally, work together to turn your individual paragraphs into an essay: write an introduction, a conclusion, and transitions between paragraphs, and include a thesis statement in paragraph 1.

INTERNET ASSIGNMENT FOR CAUSE AND EFFECT

Write an essay in which you describe the effects of food irradiation, genetically modified food, or the use of pesticides on consumers' health. Visit the following Web sites to learn about the possible advantages and disadvantages of these food industry practices.

Center for Food Safety & Applied Nutrition
<vm.cfsan.fda.gov>
The site contains an overview and history of the Food and Drug Administration, as well as articles and information on specific programs and special topics such as biotechnology, food labeling, and nutrition.

Consumers International
<consumersinternational.org/campaigns/irradiation/irrad.html>
This report from Consumers International discusses the advantages and disadvantages of food irradiation.

Foundation for Food Irradiation Education
<food-irradiation.com>
This site, which contains articles, links to other Web sites, and a students' corner, supports the adoption of food irradiation.

Organic Consumers Association (OCA)
<organicconsumers.org/organlink.htm>
The OCA is a grassroots nonprofit organization that deals with issues of food safety, industrial agriculture, genetic engineering, corporate account-ability, and environmental sustainability. Its Web site offers an overview of the pro-organic, anti-irradiation, and anti–genetically engineered food positions but also includes general information and a vast archive of articles from newspapers, magazines, and other publications on these subjects.

❖ 9
Comparison and Contrast

WHAT IS COMPARISON AND CONTRAST?

In the narrowest sense, *comparison* shows how two or more things are similar, and *contrast* shows how they are different. In most writing situations, however, the two related processes of **comparison and contrast** are used together. In the following paragraph from *Disturbing the Universe,* scientist Freeman Dyson compares and contrasts two different styles of human endeavor, which he calls "the gray and the green":

Topic sentence (outlines elements of comparison)

 In everything we undertake, either on earth or in the sky, we have a choice of two styles, which I call the gray and the green. The distinction between the gray and green is not sharp. Only at the extremes of the spectrum can we say without qualification, this is green and that is gray. The difference between green and gray is better explained by examples than by definitions. Factories are gray, gardens are green. Physics is gray, biology is green. Plutonium is gray, horse manure is green. Bureaucracy is gray, pioneer communities are green. Self-reproducing machines are gray, trees and children are green. Human technology is gray, God's technology is green. Clones are gray, clades* are green. Army field manuals are gray, poems are green.

Point-by-point comparison

A special form of comparison, called **analogy,** explains one thing by comparing it to a second thing that is more familiar than the first. In the following paragraph from *The Shopping Mall High School,* Arthur G. Powell, Eleanor Farrar, and David K. Cohen use analogy to shed light on the nature of contemporary American high schools:

 If Americans want to understand their high schools at work, they should imagine them as shopping malls. Secondary education is another

---

*EDS. NOTE—A group of organisms that evolved from a common ancestor.

consumption experience in an abundant society. Shopping malls attract a broad range of customers with different tastes and purposes. Some shop at Sears, others at Woolworth's or Bloomingdale's. In high schools a broad range of students also shop. They too can select from an astonishing variety of products and services conveniently assembled in one place with ample parking. Furthermore, in malls and schools many different kinds of transactions are possible. Both institutions bring hopeful purveyors and potential purchasers together. The former hope to maximize sales but can take nothing for granted. Shoppers have a wide discretion not only about what to buy but also about whether to buy.

USING COMPARISON AND CONTRAST

Throughout our lives, we are bombarded with information from newspapers, television, radio, the Internet, and personal experience: the police strike in Memphis; city workers walk out in Philadelphia; the Senate debates government spending; taxes are raised in New Jersey. Somehow we must make sense of the jumbled facts and figures that surround us. One way we have of understanding information like this is to put it side by side with other data and then to compare and contrast. Do the police in Memphis have the same complaints as the city workers in Philadelphia? What are the differences between the two situations? Is the national debate on spending analogous to the New Jersey debate on taxes? How do they differ? We make similar distinctions every day about matters that directly affect us. When we make personal decisions, we consider alternatives, asking ourselves whether one option seems better than another. Should I major in history or business? What job opportunities will each major offer me? Should I register as a Democrat or a Republican, or should I join a third party? What are the positions of each political party on government spending, health care, and taxes? To answer questions like these, we use comparison and contrast.

PLANNING A COMPARISON-AND-CONTRAST ESSAY

Because comparison and contrast is central to our understanding of the world, this way of thinking is often called for in papers and on essay examinations:

Compare and contrast the attitudes toward science and technology expressed in Fritz Lang's *Metropolis* and George Lucas's *Star Wars*. (film)

What are the similarities and differences between mitosis and meiosis? (biology)

Discuss the relative merits of establishing a partnership or setting up a corporation. (business law)

Discuss the advantages and disadvantages of bilingual education. (education)

Recognizing Comparison-and-Contrast Assignments

You are not likely to sit down and say to yourself, "I think I'll write a comparison-and-contrast essay today. Now what can I write about?" Instead, your assignment will suggest comparison and contrast, or you will decide comparison and contrast suits your purpose. In the preceding examples, for instance, the instructors have phrased their questions to tell students how to treat the material. When you read these questions, certain key words and phrases — *compare and contrast, similarities and differences, relative merits, advantages and disadvantages* — indicate that you should use a comparison-and-contrast pattern to organize your essay. Sometimes you may not even need a key phrase. Consider the question, "Which of the two Adamses, John or Samuel, had the greater influence on the timing and course of the American Revolution?" Here the word *greater* is enough to suggest a contrast.

Even when your assignment is not worded to suggest comparison and contrast, your purpose may point to this pattern of development. For instance, when you evaluate, you frequently use comparison and contrast. If, as a student in a management course, you are asked to evaluate two health-care systems, you can begin by researching the standards experts use in their evaluations. You can then compare each system's performance with those standards and contrast the systems with each other, concluding perhaps that both systems meet minimum standards but that one is more cost-efficient than the other. Or, if you are evaluating two of this year's new cars for a consumer newsletter, you might establish some criteria — fuel economy, safety features, handling, comfort, style — and compare and contrast the cars with respect to each criterion. If each of the cars is better in different categories, your readers will have to decide which features matter most to them.

Establishing a Basis for Comparison

Before you can compare and contrast two things, you must be sure a **basis of comparison** exists — that is, that the two things have enough in common to justify the comparison. For example, although cats and dogs are very different, they share several common elements: they are mammals, they make good pets, and so forth. Without these common elements, there would be no basis for analysis, and no comparison would be possible.

A comparison should lead you beyond the obvious. For instance, at first the idea of a comparison-and-contrast essay based on an analogy between bees and people might seem absurd: after all, these two creatures differ in species, physical structure, and intelligence. In fact, their differences are so obvious that an essay based on them might seem pointless. But after further analysis, you might decide that bees and people have quite a few similarities. Both are social animals that live in complex social structures, and both have tasks to perform and roles to fulfill in their respective societies. Therefore, you *could* write about them, but you would focus on the common elements that seem most provocative — social structures and roles — rather than on dissimilar elements. If you tried to draw an analogy between bees and SUVs or humans and golf tees, however, you would run into trouble. Although some points of comparison could be found, they would be trivial. Why bother to point out that both bees and SUVs can travel great distances or that both people and tees are needed to play golf? Neither statement establishes a significant basis for comparison.

When two subjects are very similar, it is the contrast that may be worth writing about. And when two subjects are not very much alike, you may find that the similarities are enlightening.

Selecting Points for Discussion

After you decide which subjects to compare and contrast, you need to select the points you want to discuss. You do this by determining your emphasis — on similarities, differences, or both — and the major focus of your paper. If your purpose in comparing two types of house plants is to explain that one is easier to grow than the other, you would select points having to do with plant care, not those having to do with plant biology.

When you compare and contrast, make sure you treat the same (or at least similar) elements for each subject you discuss. For instance, if you were going to compare and contrast two novels, you might consider the following elements in both works:

Novel A	*Novel B*
Major characters	Major characters
Minor characters	Minor characters
Themes	Themes

Try to avoid the common error of discussing entirely different elements for each subject. Such an approach obscures any basis of comparison that might exist. The two novels, for example, could not be meaningfully compared or contrasted if you discussed dissimilar elements:

Novel A	*Novel B*
Major characters	Plot
Minor characters	Author's life
Themes	Symbolism

Formulating a Thesis Statement

After selecting the points you want to discuss, you are ready to formulate your thesis statement. This thesis statement should tell readers what to expect in your essay, identifying not only the subjects to be compared and contrasted but also the point you will make about them. Your thesis statement should also indicate whether you will concentrate on similarities or differences or balance the two. In addition, it may list the points of comparison and contrast in the order in which they will be discussed in the essay.

The structure of your thesis statement can indicate the emphasis of your essay. As the following sentences illustrate, a thesis statement should highlight the central concern of the essay by presenting it in the independent, rather than the dependent, clause of the sentence. The structure of the first thesis statement emphasizes similarities, and the structure of the second highlights differences:

> Despite the fact that television and radio are distinctly different media, they use similar strategies to appeal to their audiences.
>
> Although Melville's *Moby-Dick* and London's *The Sea Wolf* are both about the sea, the minor characters, major characters, and themes of *Moby-Dick* establish its greater complexity.

STRUCTURING A COMPARISON-AND-CONTRAST ESSAY

Like every other type of essay in this book, a comparison-and-contrast essay has an introduction, several body paragraphs, and a conclusion. Within the body of your paper, you can use either of two basic comparison-and-contrast patterns—*subject by subject* or *point by point*. As you might expect, each organizational pattern has advantages and disadvantages. In general, you should use subject-by-subject comparison when your purpose is to emphasize overall similarities or differences, and you should use point-by-point comparison when your purpose is to emphasize individual points of similarity or difference.

Using Subject-by-Subject Comparison

In a **subject-by-subject comparison,** you essentially write a separate essay about each subject, but you discuss the same points for both subjects. In discussing each subject, you use your basis for comparison to guide your selection of points, and you arrange these points in some logical order, usually in order of their increasing significance. The following informal outline illustrates a subject-by-subject comparison:

Introduction:	Thesis statement—Despite the fact that television and radio are distinctly different media, they use similar strategies to appeal to their audiences.

Television audiences
Point 1:	Men
Point 2:	Women
Point 3:	Children

Radio audiences
Point 1:	Men
Point 2:	Women
Point 3:	Children
Conclusion:	Restatement of thesis or review of key points

Subject-by-subject comparisons are most appropriate for short, un-complicated papers. In longer papers, where many points are made about each subject, this organizational pattern demands too much of your read-ers, requiring them to keep track of all your points throughout your paper. In addition, because of the length of each section, your paper may seem like two completely separate essays. For longer or more complex papers, then, it is usually best to use point-by-point comparison.

Using Point-by-Point Comparison

In a **point-by-point comparison,** you first make a point about one subject and then follow it with a comparable point about the other. This alternating pattern continues throughout the body of your essay until all your points have been made. The following informal outline illustrates a point-by-point comparison:

Introduction:	Thesis statement—Although Melville's *Moby-Dick* and London's *The Sea Wolf* are both about the sea, the minor characters, major characters, and themes of *Moby-Dick* establish its greater complexity.

Minor characters
Book 1:	*The Sea Wolf*
Book 2:	*Moby-Dick*

Major characters
Book 1:	*The Sea Wolf*
Book 2:	*Moby-Dick*

Themes
Book 1:	*The Sea Wolf*
Book 2:	*Moby-Dick*
Conclusion:	Restatement of thesis or review of key points

Point-by-point comparisons are especially useful for longer, more complicated essays in which you discuss many different points. (If you treat only one or two points of comparison, you should consider a subject-by-subject organization.) In a point-by-point essay, readers can follow comparisons or contrasts more easily and do not have to wait several para-graphs to find out, for example, the differences between minor characters in *Moby-Dick* and *The Sea Wolf* or to remember on page five what was said on page three. Nevertheless, it is easy to fall into a monotonous, back-and-forth movement between points when you write a point-by-point compari-son. To avoid this problem, vary sentence structure as you move from point to point.

Using Transitions

Transitions are especially important in comparison-and-contrast essays because you must supply readers with clear signals that indicate whether you are discussing similarities or differences. Without these cues, readers will have trouble following your train of thought and may lose track of the significance of the points you are making. Some transitions indicating comparison and contrast are listed in the box below. A more complete list of transitions appears on page 43.

USEFUL TRANSITIONS FOR COMPARISON AND CONTRAST

COMPARISON

just as . . . so	in comparison
like	similarly
likewise	in the same way

CONTRAST

although	nevertheless
but	nonetheless
conversely	on the contrary
despite	on the one hand . . . on the other hand . . .
even though	still
however	unlike
in contrast	whereas
instead	yet

Longer essays frequently contain *transitional paragraphs* that connect one part of an essay to another. A transitional paragraph can be a single sentence that signals a shift in focus or a longer paragraph that provides a concise summary of what was said before. In either case, transitional paragraphs enable readers to pause and consider what has already been said before moving on to a new point.

REVISING A COMPARISON-AND-CONTRAST ESSAY

When you revise your comparison-and-contrast essay, consider the items on the Revision Checklist on page 54. In addition, pay special attention to the items on the checklist below, which apply specifically to comparison-and-contrast essays.

☑ **REVISION CHECKLIST: COMPARISON AND CONTRAST**

- Does your assignment call for comparison and contrast?
- What basis for comparison exists between the two subjects you are comparing?

(continued on next page)

(continued from previous page)

- Does your essay have a clear thesis statement that identifies both the subjects you are comparing and the points you are making about them?
- Do you discuss the same or similar points for both subjects?
- If you have written a subject-by-subject comparison, have you included a transition paragraph that connects the two sections of the essay?
- If you have written a point-by-point comparison, have you included appropriate transitions and varied your sentence structure to indicate your shift from one point to another?
- Is the organizational pattern of your essay suited to your purpose?
- Have you included transitional words and phrases that indicate whether you are discussing similarities or differences?

EDITING A COMPARISON-AND-CONTRAST ESSAY

When you edit your comparison-and-contrast essay, follow the guidelines on the Editing Checklist on page 66. In addition, focus on the grammar, mechanics, and punctuation issues that are most relevant to comparison-and-contrast essays. One of these issues — using parallel structure — is discussed below.

For more practice in using parallelism, visit **Exercise Central** at **<bedfordstmartins.com/patterns/parallelism>**.

GRAMMAR IN CONTEXT : Using Parallelism

Parallelism — the use of matching nouns, verbs, phrases, or clauses to express the same or similar ideas — is frequently used in comparison-and-contrast essays to highlight the similarities or differences between one point and another.*

- Always use parallel structure with paired items or with items in a series.

"I am an American citizen and she is not" (Mukherjee 397).

"For women, as for girls, intimacy is the fabric of relationships, and talk is the thread from which it is woven" (Tannen 408).

"Lee was tidewater Virginia, and in his background were family, culture, and tradition . . . the age of chivalry transplanted to a New World which was making its own legends and its own myths" (Catton 386).

---

*The quotations used as examples below come from essays that appear later in this chapter, except for the Dyson quotation, which is from the paragraph that appears on p. 363.

"When I was a boy, my friends and I would come home from school each day, change our clothes . . . , and go outside until dinnertime" (Daly 402).

According to Eric Schlosser, Walt Disney was a role model for Ray Kroc because he was intelligent, focused, and successful (418).

- Be sure to use parallel structure with paired items linked by correlative conjunctions (*not only/but also, both/and, neither/nor, either/or,* and so on).

"In everything we undertake, **either** on earth **or** in the sky, we have a choice of two styles, which I call the gray and the green" (Dyson 363).

Not only does Kroc admire Disney, **but** he **also** respects him (Schlosser 418).

- Finally, use parallel structure to emphasize the contrast between paired items linked by *as* or *than*.

"Women's conversational habits are **as** frustrating to men **as** men's are to women" (Tannen 410).

As Deborah Tannen observes, most men are socialized to communicate through actions **rather than** to communicate through conversation (408).

☑ **EDITING CHECKLIST: COMPARISON AND CONTRAST**

- Have you used parallel structure with parallel elements in a series?
- Have you used commas to separate three or more parallel elements in a series?
- Have you used parallel structure with paired items linked by correlative conjunctions?
- Have you used parallel structure with paired items linked by *as* or *than*?

▶ **STUDENT WRITERS: COMPARISON AND CONTRAST**

Both of the following essays illustrate comparison and contrast. The first, by Mark Cotharn, is a subject-by-subject comparison. The second, by Margaret Depner, is a point-by-point comparison. Both were written for a composition class in which the instructor asked students to write an essay comparing two educational experiences.

Brains versus Brawn

Introduction   When people think about discrimination, 1

they usually associate it with race or gender.

But discrimination can take another form. For

example, a person can gain an unfair advantage

at a job interview by being attractive or know-

ing someone who works at the company or by being

able to talk about something (like sports) that has nothing to do with the job. Certainly, the people who do not get the job would claim that they were discriminated against, and to some extent they would be right. As a high school athlete, I experienced both sides of discrimination. When I was a sophomore in high school, I benefited from discrimination. When I was a junior, however, I was penalized by it, treated as if there were no place for me in a classroom. As a result, I learned that discrimination, whether it helps you or hinders you, is wrong.

Thesis statement (emphasizing differences)

First subject: Mark helped by discrimination

At my high school, football was everything, and the entire town supported the local team. In the summer, merchants would run special football promotions. Adults would wear shirts with the team's logo, students would collect money to buy equipment, and everyone would go to the games and cheer the team on. Coming out of junior high school, I was considered an exceptional athlete who was eventually going to start as the varsity quarterback. Because of my status, I was enthusiastically welcomed by the high school. Before I entered the school, the varsity coach even visited my home, and the principal called my parents and told them how well I was going to do.

Status of football

I knew that high school would be different from junior high, but I wasn't prepared for the treatment I received from my teachers. Many of them talked to me as if I were their friend, not their student. My math teacher used to keep me after class just to talk football; he would even give me a note so I could be late for my next class. My biology teacher told me I could skip the afternoon labs so I would have some time for myself before practice. Several of my teachers told me that during football season I didn't have to hand in homework because it might distract me during practice. My Spanish teacher

Treatment by teachers

2

3

even told me that if I didn't do well on a test,
I could take it over after the season. Everything I did seemed to be perfect.

Mark's reaction to
treatment

In spite of this favorable treatment, I   4
continued to study hard. I knew that if I wanted
to go to a good college, I would have to get
good grades, and I resented the implication
that the only way I could get good grades was
by getting special treatment. I had always been
a good student, and I had no intention of
changing my study habits now that I was in high
school. Each night after practice, I stayed up
late outlining my notes and completing my class
assignments. Any studying I couldn't do during
the week, I would complete on the weekends. Of
course my social life suffered, but I didn't
care. I took pride in the fact that I never had
to take advantage of the special treatment my
teachers were offering me.

Transitional
paragraph: signals
shift from one
subject to another

Then one day the unthinkable happened. The   5
township redrew the school-district lines, and
I suddenly found myself assigned to a new high
school — one that was academically more demanding than the one I attended and, what was worse,
one that had a weak football team. When my parents appealed to the school board to let me
stay at my current school, they were told that
no exceptions could be made. If the board made
a change for me, it would have to make changes
for others, and that would lead to chaos. My
principal and my coach also tried to get the
board to change its decision, but they got
the same response. So in my junior year, at
the height of my career, I changed schools.

Second subject: Mark
hurt by discrimination

Unlike the people at my old school, no one   6
at my new school seemed to care much about high
school football. Many of the students attended
the games, but their primary focus was on getting into college. If they talked about football
at all, they usually discussed the regional

Status of football

college teams. As a result, I didn't have the status I had when I attended my former school. When I met with the coach before school started, he told me the football team was weak. He also told me that his main goal was to make sure everyone on the team had a chance to play. So, even though I would start, I would have to share the quarterback position with two seniors. Later that day I saw the principal, who told me that although sports were an important part of school, academic achievement was more important. He made it clear that I would play football only as long as my grades did not suffer.

Treatment by teachers

Unlike the teachers at my old school, the   7
teachers at my new school did not give any special treatment to athletes. When I entered my new school, I was ready for the challenge. What I was not ready for was the hostility of most of my new teachers. From the first day, in just about every class, my teachers made it obvious they had already made up their minds about what kind of student I was going to be. Some teachers told me I shouldn't expect any special consideration just because I was the team's quarterback. One even said in front of the class that I would have to study as hard as the other students if I expected to pass. I was hurt and embarrassed by these comments. I didn't expect anyone to give me anything, and I was ready to get the grades I deserved. After all, I had gotten good grades up to this point, and I had no reason to think that the situation would

Mark's reaction to treatment

change. Even so, my teachers' preconceived ideas upset me.

Just as I had in my old school, I studied   8
hard, but I didn't know how to deal with the prejudice I faced. At first, it really bothered me and even affected my performance on the football field. However, after awhile, I decided

that the best way to show my teachers that I was
not the stereotypical jock was to prove to them
what kind of student I really was. In the long
run, far from discouraging me, their treatment
motivated me, and I decided to work even harder
in the classroom than I did on the football
field. I didn't care if the football team lost
every game as long as I did my best in every
class I had. By the end of high school, not only
had the team won half of its games (a record
season), but I had also proved to my teachers
that I was a good student. (I still remember
the surprised look on the face of my chemistry
teacher when she handed my first exam back to
me and told me that I had received the second
highest grade in the class.)

Conclusion   Before I graduated, I talked to the teach-   9
ers about how they had treated me during my
junior year. Some admitted they had been harder
on me than on the rest of the students, but
others denied they had ever discriminated
against me. Eventually, I realized that they
would never understand what they had done. Even
so, my experience did have some positive effects. I learned that you should judge people
on their merits, not by some preconceived
Restatement of thesis   standard. In addition, I learned that although
some people are talented intellectually, others
possess special skills that should also be
valued. And, as I found out, discriminatory
treatment, whether it helps you or hinders you,
is no substitute for fairness.

Points for Special Attention

Basis for Comparison   Mark knew he could easily compare his two
experiences. Both involved high school, and both focused on the treatment he had received as an athlete. In one case, Mark was treated better
than other students because he was the team's quarterback; in the other,
he was stereotyped as a "dumb jock" because he was a football player. Mark
also knew that his comparison would make an interesting (and perhaps

unexpected) point—that discrimination is unfair, even when it gives a person an advantage.

Selecting Points for Comparison   Mark wanted to make certain that he would discuss the same (or at least similar) points for the two experiences he was going to compare. As he planned his essay, Mark consulted his brainstorming notes and made the following informal outline:

Experience 1 *(gained an advantage)*	**Experience 2** *(was put at a disadvantage)*
Status of football	Status of football
Treatment by teachers	Treatment by teachers
My reaction	My reaction

Structure   Mark's essay makes three points about each of the two experiences he compares. Because his purpose was to convey the overall differences between the two experiences, he decided to use a subject-by-subject strategy. In addition, Mark thought he could make his case more convincingly if he discussed the first experience fully before moving on to the next one, and he believed readers would have no trouble keeping his individual points in mind as they read. Of course, Mark could have decided to do a point-by-point comparison. He rejected this strategy, though, because he thought that shifting back and forth between subjects would distract readers from his main point.

In Mark's case, a subject-by-subject comparison made more sense than a point-by-point comparison. Occasionally, however, the choice is a matter of preference—a writer might simply like one strategy better than the other.

Transitions   Without adequate transitions, a subject-by-subject comparison can read like two separate essays. Notice that in Mark's essay, paragraph 5 functions as a transitional paragraph that connects the two sections of the essay. In it, Mark sets up the comparison by telling how he suddenly found himself assigned to another high school.

In addition to connecting the sections of an essay, transitional words and phrases can identify similarities and differences for readers. Notice, for example, how the transitional word *however* emphasizes the contrast between the following sentences from paragraph 1:

Without transition
When I was a sophomore in high school, I benefited from discrimination. When I was a junior, I was penalized by it.

With transition
When I was a sophomore in high school, I benefited from discrimination. When I was a junior, *however,* I was penalized by it.

Topic Sentences   Like transitional phrases, topic sentences help to guide readers through an essay. When reading a comparison-and-contrast essay, readers can easily forget the points that are being compared, especially if the paper is long or complex. Direct, clearly stated topic sentences act as guideposts, alerting readers to the comparisons and contrasts you are making. For example, Mark's straightforward topic sentence at the beginning of paragraph 5 dramatically signals the movement from one experience to the other ("Then one day the unthinkable happened"). In addition, as in any effective comparison-and-contrast essay, each point discussed in connection with one subject is also discussed in connection with the other. Mark's topic sentences reinforce this balance:

First subject
At my high school, football was everything.

Second subject
Unlike the people at my old school, no one at my new school seemed to care much about high school football.

Focus on Revision

Mark's peer critics thought he could have spent more time talking about what he did to counter the preconceptions about athletes that teachers in *both* his schools had. One student pointed out that the teachers at both schools seemed to think athletes were weak students. The only difference was that the teachers at Mark's first school were willing to make allowances for athletes, while the teachers at his second school were not. The student thought that although Mark alluded to this fact, he should have made his point more explicitly. After rereading his essay along with his classmates' comments, Mark decided to add information about how demanding football practice was. Without this information, readers would have a hard time understanding how difficult it was for him to keep up with his studies. Another peer critic thought Mark should concede that some student athletes do fit the teachers' stereotypes, although many do not. This information would reinforce his thesis and help him demonstrate how unfair his treatment was. (A peer editing worksheet for comparison and contrast can be found on the *Patterns for College Writing* Web site at <bedfordstmartins.com/patterns>.)

Unlike the preceding essay, Margaret Depner's paper is a point-by-point comparison.

The Big Move

Introduction   The adjustment began when I was a sophomore   1
in high school. I was fifteen — a typical Ameri-
can teenager. I lived to talk on the telephone,
hang out at the mall, watch lots of television,
and go to the movies. Everything about my life
seemed satisfying. I loved my neighborhood, my

school, and my friends. But suddenly everything changed. One night my parents told me that my father had been transferred and that we were going to move to England. I felt as if everything I had grown to love was being torn away from me. I was going to have to start over, and I did not want to go. My parents dismissed my pleas and told me in no uncertain terms that I had no choice in the matter. My fate was sealed. When we finally arrived in England, I was so frightened that I felt sick. Not only would I have to get used to a new neighborhood and a new school, but I would also have to get used to a new way of life.

Thesis statement (emphasizing differences)

First point: adjusting to a new neighborhood

The first thing I had to adjust to was living in a new neighborhood. The Boston suburb we had left was a known quantity, and perhaps for this reason, I liked it. At home we lived in a new development that was just starting to get built up. There were houses everywhere, with a few small trees scattered in between. Our house had a large lawn that my brother and I tried to avoid cutting whenever we could. Moms carting children around in minivans was a common sight. My dad belonged to a neighborhood watch program and coached a girls' soccer team. My mom had a part-time job and rushed around on weekends catching up on all the things she could not do during the week. Every fall, kids came to the door selling Girl Scout cookies or raising money to fight heart disease. Every spring and summer, lawnmowers hummed away on Saturday mornings, and everyone went to church on Sunday. Everything was familiar...almost predictable. 2

Neighborhood in U.S.

Neighborhood in England

Our neighborhood outside of London, however, was far different from what I was used to. The house we lived in was cozy but much smaller than the house we had left in the United States. It had a cute little lawn in front — 3 which my brother and I still argued about cutting — and was exactly like the house next door. Near our house was a forest in which out-laws were said to have lived several hundred years ago. Most of the women in the neighborhood worked full time to supplement their husbands' income, and my mother was no exception. She got a job with my father's company and was very busy most of the time. There was no need for a neighborhood watch program because there was almost no crime. (The only crimes I ever heard about were a parked car that was sideswiped and a cat that had allegedly been stolen.) Although there was a soccer team, girls weren't allowed to play on it. (In England soccer is considered a boy's game, like tackle football.) Some things were the same, however. Just as they did at home, people cut their lawns on Saturday — with a push mower, not a power mower — and went to church every Sunday.

Second point: adjusting to a new school

School in U.S.

The next thing I had to adjust to was attending a new school. In the United States, I had attended a large suburban public high school. It had been built in the 1970s and held over two thousand students. Sweatshirts and jeans were the most common articles of clothing for the students, and informality was a way of life. Several of my teachers even encouraged students to call them by their first names and to talk in class whenever they had something to say. I was able to choose from a long list of classes and take almost any course I wanted to. The atmosphere in class was relaxed, to say the least. Some students had private conversations during class and paid little attention to the teacher. The only time they focused on the class was when the teacher called on them or when they made a funny comment or a sarcastic remark. We frequently had no homework, and we didn't study much, except for a test. Although most of us

4

wanted to go on to college, none of us seemed to take learning seriously. Those who did were usually teased by the rest of us.

School in England

5 The school I attended in England was quite different from the one I attended in the United States. It was small even by English standards — only four hundred students — and the building was over three hundred years old. All the students wore uniforms — a black blazer, a freshly ironed white shirt, and a pleated skirt if you were female or black pants if you were male. The teachers were the epitome of formality: you called them "Sir" or "Ma'am" and always showed respect; I never dreamed of using their first names. The atmosphere in the classroom was also quite formal. Students worked quietly and spoke to the teachers only when they were called on. When we were called on, our teachers expected us to respond intelligently. No one joked or made sarcastic remarks. All of us were serious about our work. I spent hours studying each night and wrote a thousand-word essay each week. I always had papers to hand in or a tutorial to prepare for. Eventually, I got used to the workload and was able to budget my time so I could go out on the weekends.

Third point: adjusting to a new way of life

Life in U.S.

6 My greatest challenge, however, was adjusting to a new way of life. In the United States, my social life was predictable, if not very interesting. Most of my friends lived in my neighborhood within walking distance of my house. I spent hours talking on the phone each night. Every Friday, my friends and I would hang out at the local mall or go to the movies. On Saturday we would get together at someone's house and watch TV or rent a movie. Sometimes we would go to a party or take a train into the city and go to Quincy Market. During the summer, my friends and I would go to the beach or just lie around the house complaining that we had

nothing to do. Although occasionally I would volunteer to help a teacher, my friends and I did not consider it acceptable to be too involved with school. Once, when I tried out for a school play, my friends teased me for weeks.

Life in England   In England my social life was quite dif- 7 ferent. Most of my friends lived almost an hour away. There were no malls to hang out in, we never went to the movies, and I spent little time on the phone. At first, my whole life seemed upside down, but gradually I grew to like it. I found new things to do. I got interested in sports and other school activities. I became involved in community service, joined the debating team, and was elected to student council. Instead of hanging out at the mall, my friends and I went to plays and concerts in London. During the summer, I went on trips to Spain and to the Isle of Wight. Perhaps the most interesting thing I did was meet people from all over the world and find out about their customs. And I don't ever remember sitting around the house wondering what to do.

Conclusion   In my one year in England, I accomplished 8 more than I had dreamed I would before I left the United States. It was hard to give up everything that was familiar to me, but for the first time I understood what my mother had meant when she said, "Sometimes, you need to lose something to gain something." By the end of the year, when we returned home, I knew that the year had changed me and that I would never be the same person I had been before.

Points for Special Attention

Structure   Margaret's purpose in writing this essay was to highlight several specific differences between her two educational experiences. As a result, she chose to write a point-by-point comparison. She introduces three points of contrast between her two subjects, and she is careful to present the same kind of information about each point for each subject. With this method of organization, she can be sure her readers will easily understand the specific differences between her life in the United States and her life in England. Had Margaret used a subject-by-subject comparison, her readers would have had to keep turning back to match points she made about the second subject to those she made about the first.

Topic Sentences   Without clear topic sentences, Margaret's readers would have a difficult time determining where each discussion of life in the United States ended and each one about life in England began. Margaret makes sure that her readers can follow her discussion by distinguishing the two subjects of her comparison with topic sentences that make the contrast between them clear:

> The Boston suburb we had left was a known quantity, and perhaps for this reason, I liked it.
> Our neighborhood outside of London, however, was far different from what I was used to.

> In the United States I had attended a large suburban public high school. The school I attended in England was quite different from the one I attended in the United States.

> In the United States, my social life was predictable, if not very interesting. In England my social life was quite different.

Transitions   In addition to the clear and straightforward topic sentences, Margaret also includes transitional sentences that help readers move through the essay. Notice that by establishing a parallel structure, these sentences form a pattern that reinforces the essay's thesis:

> The first thing I had to adjust to was living in a new neighborhood.
> The next thing I had to adjust to was attending a new school.
> My greatest challenge, however, was adjusting to a new way of life.

Focus on Revision

Margaret's peer critics thought the biggest strength of her essay was its use of detail, which made the contrast between the United States and England clear. One student, however, thought that even more detail would improve her essay. For example, in paragraph 3, Margaret could describe her London suburb more precisely than she does. In paragraph 7, she could provide insight into how her English friends were different from her friends in the United States. Margaret agreed with these suggestions and also thought she could improve her conclusion. After rereading it, she decided it was not much more than a loose collection of ideas that added little to the discussion. An anecdote that summed up her feelings about leaving England would be an improvement. So would a summary of how her experience changed her life once she returned to the United States. (A peer editing worksheet for comparison and contrast can be found on the *Patterns for College Writing* Web site at <bedfordstmartins.com/patterns>.)

The selections that follow illustrate both point-by-point and subject-by-subject comparison. The first selection, a pair of visual texts, is followed by questions designed to illustrate how comparison and contrast can operate in visual form.

The Kiss (Sculpture)

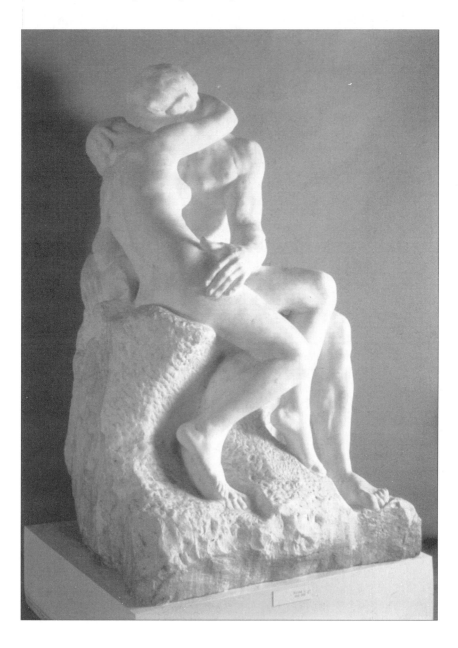

ROBERT INDIANA

❖
LOVE (Sculpture)

• • •

READING IMAGES

1. What significant characteristics do the two sculptures pictured on these facing pages share? Do they share enough characteristics to establish a basis for comparison? Explain.

2. Make a list of points you could discuss if you were comparing the two sculptures.

3. What general statement could you make about these two sculptures? Do the points you listed in question 2 provide enough support for this general statement?

JOURNAL ENTRY

How does each sculpture convey the idea of love? Which one do you believe conveys this idea more effectively? Why?

THEMATIC CONNECTIONS

- "The Storm" (page 183)
- "How to Escape from a Bad Date" (page 272)
- "Sex, Lies, and Conversation" (page 407)

BRUCE CATTON

Grant and Lee: A Study in Contrasts

Bruce Catton (1899–1978) was born in Petoskey, Michigan, and attended
Oberlin College. His studies were interrupted by his service during World
War I, after which he worked as a journalist and then for various govern-
ment agencies. Catton edited *American Heritage* magazine from 1954 until
his death. He was a notable authority on the American Civil War; among
his many books on the subject are *Mr. Lincoln's Army* (1951); *A Stillness at
Appomattox* (1953), which won both a Pulitzer Prize and a National Book
Award; and *Gettysburg: The Final Fury* (1974). Catton also wrote a memoir,
Waiting for the Morning Train (1972), in which he recalls listening as a young
boy to the reminiscences of Union Army veterans.

Background: "Grant and Lee: A Study in Contrasts," which first
appeared in a collection of historical essays entitled *The American Story,*
focuses on the two generals who headed the opposing armies during the
Civil War. Robert E. Lee led the Army of Northern Virginia, the backbone
of the Confederate forces, throughout much of the war. Ulysses S. Grant
was commander in chief of the Union troops. By the spring of 1865,
although it seemed almost inevitable that the Southern forces would be
defeated, Lee made an attempt to lead his troops to join another Confederate army in North Carolina. Finding himself virtually surrounded by
Grant's forces near the small town of Appomattox Court House, Lee chose
to surrender to Grant. The following essay considers these two great generals in terms of both their differences and their important similarities.

1   When Ulysses S. Grant and Robert E. Lee met in the parlor of a modest
house at Appomattox Court House, Virginia, on April 9, 1865, to work out
the terms for the surrender of Lee's Army of Northern Virginia, a great
chapter in American life came to a close, and a great new chapter began.

2   These men were bringing the Civil War to its virtual finish. To be sure,
other armies had yet to surrender, and for a few days the fugitive Confederate government would struggle desperately and vainly, trying to find some
way to go on living now that its chief support was gone. But in effect it was
all over when Grant and Lee signed the papers. And the little room where
they wrote out the terms was the scene of one of the poignant, dramatic
contrasts in American history.

3   They were two strong men, these oddly different generals, and they
represented the strengths of two conflicting currents that, through them,
had come into final collision.

4   Back of Robert E. Lee was the notion that the old aristocratic concept
might somehow survive and be dominant in American life.

5   Lee was tidewater Virginia, and in his background were family, culture,
and tradition . . . the age of chivalry transplanted to a New World which

was making its own legends and its own myths. He embodied a way of life that had come down through the age of knighthood and the English country squire. America was a land that was beginning all over again, dedicated to nothing much more complicated than the rather hazy belief that all men had equal rights and should have an equal chance in the world. In such a land Lee stood for the feeling that it was somehow of advantage to human society to have pronounced inequality in the social structure. There should be a leisure class, backed by ownership of land; in turn, society itself should be keyed to the land as the chief source of wealth and influence. It would bring forth (according to this deal) a class of men with a strong sense of obligation to the community; men who lived not to gain advantage for themselves, but to meet the solemn obligations which had been laid on them by the very fact that they were privileged. From them the country would get its leadership; to them it could look for the higher values — of thought, of conduct, of personal deportment — to give it strength and virtue.

Lee embodied the noblest elements of this aristocratic ideal. Through 6
him, the landed nobility justified itself. For four years, the Southern states had fought a desperate war to uphold the ideals for which Lee stood. In the end, it almost seemed as if the Confederacy fought for Lee; as if he himself was the Confederacy . . . the best thing that the way of life for which the Confederacy stood could ever have to offer. He had passed into legend before Appomattox. Thousands of tired, underfed, poorly clothed Confederate soldiers, long since past the simple enthusiasm of the early days of the struggle, somehow considered Lee the symbol of everything for which they had been willing to die. But they could not quite put this feeling into words. If the Lost Cause, sanctified by so much heroism and so many deaths, had a living justification, its justification was General Lee.

Grant, the son of a tanner on the Western frontier, was everything Lee 7
was not. He had come up the hard way and embodied nothing in particular except the eternal toughness and sinewy fiber of the men who grew up beyond the mountains. He was one of a body of men who owed reverence and obeisance to no one, who were self-reliant to a fault, who cared hardly anything for the past but who had a sharp eye for the future.

These frontier men were the precise opposites of the tidewater aristo- 8
crats. Back of them, in the great surge that had taken people over the Alleghenies and into the opening Western country, there was a deep, implicit dissatisfaction with a past that had settled into grooves. They stood for democracy, not from any reasoned conclusion about the proper ordering of human society, but simply because they had grown up in the middle of democracy and knew how it worked. Their society might have privileges, but they would be privileges each man had won for himself. Forms and patterns meant nothing. No man was born to anything, except perhaps to a chance to show how far he could rise. Life was competition.

Yet along with this feeling had come a deep sense of belonging to a 9
national community. The Westerner who developed a farm, opened a shop,

or set up in business as a trader, could hope to prosper only as his own community prospered — and his community ran from the Atlantic to the Pacific and from Canada down to Mexico. If the land was settled, with towns and highways and accessible markets, he could better himself. He saw his fate in terms of the nation's own destiny. As its horizons expanded, so did his. He had, in other words, an acute dollars-and-cents stake in the continued growth and development of his country.

And that, perhaps, is where the contrast between Grant and Lee becomes most striking. The Virginia aristocrat, inevitably, saw himself in relation to his own region. He lived in a static society which could endure almost anything except change. Instinctively, his first loyalty would go to the locality in which that society existed. He would fight to the limit of endurance to defend it, because in defending it he was defending everything that gave his own life its deepest meaning. 10

The Westerner, on the other hand, would fight with an equal tenacity for the broader concept of society. He fought so because everything he lived by was tied to growth, expansion, and a constantly widening horizon. What he lived by would survive or fall with the nation itself. He could not possibly stand by unmoved in the face of an attempt to destroy the Union. He would combat it with everything he had, because he could only see it as an effort to cut the ground out from under his feet. 11

So Grant and Lee were in complete contrast, representing two diametrically opposed elements in American life. Grant was the modern man emerging; beyond him, ready to come on the stage, was the great age of steel and machinery, of crowded cities and a restless burgeoning vitality. Lee might have ridden down from the old age of chivalry, lance in hand, silken banner fluttering over his head. Each man was the perfect champion of his cause, drawing both his strengths and his weaknesses from the people he led. 12

Yet it was not all contrast, after all. Different as they were — in background, in personality, in underlying aspiration — these two great soldiers had much in common. Under everything else, they were marvelous fighters. Furthermore, their fighting qualities were really very much alike. 13

Each man had, to begin with, the great virtue of utter tenacity and fidelity. Grant fought his way down the Mississippi Valley in spite of acute personal discouragement and profound military handicaps. Lee hung on in the trenches at Petersburg after hope itself had died. In each man there was an indomitable quality . . . the born fighter's refusal to give up as long as he can still remain on his feet and lift his two fists. 14

Daring and resourcefulness they had, too; the ability to think faster and move faster than the enemy. These were the qualities which gave Lee the dazzling campaigns of Second Manassas and Chancellorsville and won Vicksburg for Grant. 15

Lastly, and perhaps greatest of all, there was the ability, at the end, to turn quickly from war to peace once the fighting was over. Out of the way these two men behaved at Appomattox came the possibility of a peace of reconciliation. It was a possibility not wholly realized, in the years to come, but which did, in the end, help the two sections to become one nation 16 again . . . after a war whose bitterness might have seemed to make such a reunion wholly impossible. No part of either man's life became him more than the part he played in this brief meeting in the McLean house at Appomattox. Their behavior there put all succeeding generations of Americans in their debt. Two great Americans, Grant and Lee—very different, yet under everything very much alike. Their encounter at Appomattox was one of the great moments of American history.

• • •

COMPREHENSION

1. What took place at Appomattox Court House on April 9, 1865? Why did the meeting at Appomattox signal the closing of "a great chapter in American life" (1)?

2. How does Robert E. Lee represent aristocracy? How does Ulysses S. Grant represent Lee's opposite?

3. According to Catton, where is it that "the contrast between Grant and Lee becomes most striking" (10)?

4. What similarities does Catton see between the two men?

5. Why, according to Catton, are "succeeding generations of Americans" (16) in debt to Grant and Lee?

PURPOSE AND AUDIENCE

1. Catton's purpose in contrasting Grant and Lee is to make a general statement about the differences between two currents in American history. Summarize these differences. Do you think the differences still exist today? Explain.

2. Is Catton's purpose in comparing Grant and Lee the same as his purpose in contrasting them? That is, do their similarities also make a statement about U.S. history? Explain.

3. State the essay's thesis in your own words.

STYLE AND STRUCTURE

1. Does Catton use subject-by-subject or point-by-point comparison? Why do you think he chooses the structure he does?

2. In this essay, topic sentences are extremely helpful to the reader. Explain the functions of the following sentences: "Grant . . . was everything Lee was not" (7); "So Grant and Lee were in complete contrast" (12); "Yet it was not all contrast, after all" (13); "Lastly, and perhaps greatest of all" (16).

3. Catton uses transitions skillfully in his essay. Identify the transitional words or expressions that link each paragraph to the preceding one.

4. Why do you suppose Catton provides the background for the meeting at Appomattox but presents no information about the dramatic meeting itself?

VOCABULARY PROJECTS

1. Define each of the following words as it is used in this selection.

poignant (2)   obeisance (7)   tenacity (14)
chivalry (5)   implicit (8)   fidelity (14)
deportment (5)   inevitably (10)   indomitable (14)
sanctified (6)   diametrically (12)   reconciliation (16)
embodied (7)   burgeoning (12)
sinewy (7)   aspiration (13)

2. Look up **synonyms** for each of the following words, and determine which synonyms would and would not be as effective as the word used in this essay. Explain your choices.

deportment (5)   obeisance (7)   indomitable (14)
sanctified (6)   diametrically (12)

JOURNAL ENTRY

Compare your attitudes about the United States to those held by Grant and by Lee. With which man do you agree?

WRITING WORKSHOP

1. Write a "study in contrasts" about two people you know well — two teachers, your parents, two relatives, two friends — or about two fictional characters with whom you are very familiar. Be sure to include a thesis statement.

2. Write a dialogue between two people you know that reveals their contrasting attitudes toward school, work, or any other subject.

3. Write an essay about two individuals from a period of American history other than the Civil War to make the same points Catton makes. Do some research if necessary.

COMBINING THE PATTERNS

In several places, Catton uses **exemplification** to structure a paragraph. For instance, in paragraph 7, he uses examples to support the topic sentence "Grant, the son of a tanner on the Western frontier, was everything Lee was not." Identify three paragraphs that use examples to support the topic sentence, and bracket the examples. In what ways do these examples in these paragraphs reinforce the similarities and differences between Grant and Lee?

THEMATIC CONNECTIONS

- The Declaration of Independence (page 557)
- "Letter from Birmingham Jail" (page 570)
- "An Idea Whose Time Has Come" (page 637)

IAN FRAZIER

❖

Dearly Disconnected

Born in 1951 in Cleveland, Ohio, Ian Frazier graduated from Harvard University, where he was on the staff of the *Harvard Lampoon*. He went on to become a *New Yorker* staff writer for many years, and his first books were the humor collections *Dating Your Mom* (1986) and *Nobody Better, Better Than Nobody* (1987). His later works, beginning with *Great Plains* (1989) and including most recently *The Fish's Eye: Essays about Angling and the Out of Doors* (2002), have often focused on his love of rural Montana, where he spends part of each year. Frazier also writes about American culture and society in essays such as the following ode to the pay telephone.

Background: Telephone technology was perfected in 1876, and the first United States telephone company was organized in 1878. The popularity of this new invention spread quickly, and by 1880 close to 200,000 telephones were in use nationwide. The earliest pay telephones were often installed in hotels and other businesses open to the public and supervised by attendants who collected money directly from users. The first coin-operated telephone was installed in a Hartford, Connecticut, bank in 1889, and by 1902 there were 81,000 pay phones in the United States. The first outdoor pay telephone appeared on a Cincinnati corner in 1905, but such phones were not immediately popular, perhaps because people did not wish to have private conversations on a public street. Early telephone booths — especially those in hotel lobbies — were often elaborate, carpeted closets constructed of expensive woods, but later in the century metal and glass booths became more common. As of 1960, the Bell Company had installed one million pay telephones in the United States. These phones were, of course, a boon to people who could not afford home service. Moreover, in the days before cell phones, pay phones were virtually the only means that people away from their homes and offices had for calling others.

Before I got married I was living by myself in an A-frame cabin in   1
northwestern Montana. The cabin's interior was a single high-ceilinged room, and at the center of the room, mounted on the rough-hewn log that held up the ceiling beam, was a telephone. I knew no one in the area or indeed the whole state, so my entire social life came to me through that phone. The woman I would marry was living in Sarasota, Florida, and the distance between us suggests how well we were getting along at the time. We had not been in touch for several months; she had no phone. One day she decided to call me from a pay phone. We talked for a while, and after her coins ran out I jotted the number on the wood beside my phone and called her back. A day or two later, thinking about the call, I wanted to talk to her again. The only number I had for her was the pay phone number I'd written down.

The pay phone was on the street some blocks from the apartment 2
where she stayed. As it happened, though, she had just stepped out to do
some errands a few minutes before I called, and she was passing by on the
sidewalk when the phone rang. She had no reason to think that a public
phone ringing on a busy street would be for her. She stopped, listened to it
ring again, and picked up the receiver. Love is pure luck; somehow I had
known she would answer, and she had known it would be me.

Long afterwards, on a trip to Disney World in Orlando with our two 3
kids, then aged six and two, we made a special detour to Sarasota to show
them the pay phone. It didn't impress them much. It's just a nondescript
Bell Atlantic pay phone on the cement wall of a building, by the vestibule.
But its ordinariness and even boringness only make me like it more; ordinary places where extraordinary events have occurred are my favorite kind.
On my mental map of Florida that pay phone is a landmark looming above
the city it occupies, and a notable, if private, historic site.

I'm interested in pay phones in general these days, especially when I get 4
the feeling that they are about to go away. Technology, in the form of sleek
little phones in our pockets, has swept on by them and made them begin to
seem antique. My lifelong entanglement with pay phones dates me; when I
was young they were just there, a given, often as stubborn and uncongenial
as the curbstone underfoot. They were instruments of torture sometimes.
You had to feed them fistfuls of change in those pre-phone-card days, and
the operator was a real person who stood maddeningly between you and
whomever you were trying to call. And when the call went wrong, as communication often does, the pay phone gave you a focus for your rage. Pay
phones were always getting smashed up, the receivers shattered to bits
against the booth, the coin slots jammed with chewing gum, the cords
yanked out and unraveled to the floor.

You used to hear people standing at pay phones and cursing them. I 5
remember the sound of my own frustrated shouting confined by the glass
walls of a phone booth—the kind you don't see much anymore, with a
little ventilating fan in the ceiling that turned on when you shut the
double-hinged glass door. The noise that fan made in the silence of a
phone booth was for a while the essence of romantic, lonely-guy melancholy for me. Certain specific pay phones I still resent for the unhappiness
they caused me, and others I will never forgive, though not for any fault of
their own. In the C concourse of the Salt Lake City airport there's a row of
pay phones set on the wall by the men's room just past the concourse
entry. While on a business trip a few years ago, I called home from a phone
in that row and learned that a friend had collapsed in her apartment and
was in the hospital with brain cancer. I had liked those pay phones before,
and had used them often; now I can't even look at them when I go by.

There was always a touch of seediness and sadness to pay phones, and 6
a sense of transience. Drug dealers made calls from them, and shady types
who did not want their whereabouts known, and otherwise respectable
people planning assignations, and people too poor to have phones of their

own. In the movies, any character who used a pay phone was either in trouble or contemplating a crime. Pay phones came with their own special atmospherics and even accessories sometimes — the predictable bad smells and graffiti, of course, as well as cigarette butts, soda cans, scattered pamphlets from the Jehovah's Witnesses, and single bottles of beer (empty) still in their individual, street-legal paper bags. Mostly, pay phones evoked the mundane: "Honey, I'm just leaving. I'll be there soon." But you could tell that a lot of undifferentiated humanity had flowed through these places, and that in the muteness of each pay phone's little space, wild emotion had howled.

Once, when I was living in Brooklyn, I read in the newspaper that a South American man suspected of dozens of drug-related contract murders had been arrested at a pay phone in Queens. Police said that the man had been on the phone setting up a murder at the time of his arrest. The newspaper story gave the address of the pay phone, and out of curiosity one afternoon I took a long walk to Queens to take a look at it. It was on an undistinguished street in a middle-class neighborhood, by a florist's shop. By the time I saw it, however, the pay phone had been blown up and/or firebombed. I had never before seen a pay phone so damaged; explosives had blasted pieces of the phone itself wide open in metal shreds like frozen banana peels, and flames had blackened everything and melted the plastic parts and burned the insulation off the wires. Soon after, I read that police could not find enough evidence against the suspected murderer and so had let him go.

The cold phone outside a shopping center in Bigfork, Montana, from which I called a friend in the West Indies one winter when her brother was sick; the phone on the wall of the concession stand at Redwood Pool, where I used to stand dripping and call my mom to come and pick me up; the sweaty phones used almost only by men in the hallway outside the maternity ward at Lenox Hill Hospital in New York; the phone by the driveway of the Red Cloud Indian School in South Dakota where I used to talk with my wife while priests in black slacks and white socks chatted on a bench nearby; the phone in the old wood-paneled phone booth with leaded glass windows in the drugstore in my Ohio hometown — each one is as specific as a birthmark, a point on earth unlike any other. Recently I went back to New York City after a long absence and tried to find a working pay phone. I picked up one receiver after the next without success. Meanwhile, as I scanned down the long block, I counted half a dozen or more pedestrians talking on their cell phones.

It's the cell phone, of course, that's putting the pay phone out of business. The pay phone is to the cell phone as the troubled and difficult older sibling is to the cherished newborn. People even treat their cell phones like babies, cradling them in their palms and beaming down upon them lovingly as they dial. You sometimes hear people yelling on their cell phones, but almost never yelling at them. Cell phones are toylike, nearly magic, and we get a huge kick out of them, as often happens with technological advances until the new wears off. Somehow I don't believe people had a similar honeymoon period with pay phones back in their early days, and they certainly have no such enthusiasm for them now. When I see a cell-phone user gently push the little antenna and fit the phone back into its brushed-vinyl carrying case and tuck the case inside his jacket beside his heart, I feel sorry for the beat-up pay phone standing in the rain.

People almost always talk on cell phones while in motion — driving, walking down the street, riding on a commuter train. The cell phone took the transience the pay phone implied and turned it into VIP-style mobility and speed. Even sitting in a restaurant, the person on a cell phone seems importantly busy and on the move. Cell-phone conversations seem to be unlimited by ordinary constraints of place and time, as if they represent an almost-perfect form of communication whose perfect state would be telepathy. 10

And yet no matter how we factor the world away, it remains. I think this is what drives me so nuts when a person sitting next to me on a bus makes a call from her cell phone. Yes, this busy and important caller is at no fixed point in space, but nevertheless I happen to be beside her. The job of providing physical context falls on me; I become her call's surroundings, as if I'm the phone booth wall. For me to lean over and comment on her cell-phone conversation would be as unseemly and unexpected as if I were in fact a wall; and yet I have no choice, as a sentient person, but to hear what my chatty fellow traveler has to say. 11

Some middle-aged guys like me go around complaining about this kind of thing. The more sensible approach is just to accept it and forget about it, because there's not much we can do. I don't think that pay phones will completely disappear. Probably they will survive for a long while as clumsy old technology still of some use to those lagging behind, and as a backup if ever the superior systems should temporarily fail. Before pay phones became endangered I never thought of them as public spaces, which of course they are. They suggested a human average; they belonged to anybody who had a couple of coins. Now I see that, like public schools and public transportation, pay phones belong to a former commonality our culture is no longer quite so sure it needs. 12

I have a weakness for places — for old battlefields, car-crash sites, houses where famous authors lived. Bygone passions should always have an address, it seems to me. Ideally, the world would be covered with plaques and markers listing the notable events that occurred at each particular spot. A sign on every pay phone would describe how a woman broke up with her fiancé here, how a young ballplayer learned that he had made the team. Unfortunately, the world itself is fluid, and changes out from under us; the rocky islands that the pilot Mark Twain was careful to avoid in the Mississippi are now stone outcroppings in a soybean field. Meanwhile, our passions proliferate into illegibility, and the places they occur can't hold them. Eventually pay phones will become relics of an almost-vanished landscape, and of a time when there were fewer of us and our sto- 13 ries were on an earlier page. Romantics like me will have to reimagine our passions as they are — unmoored to earth, like an infinitude of cell-phone messages flying through the atmosphere.

•   •   •

COMPREHENSION

1. Why does Frazier see the pay phone in Florida as a "landmark" and a "historic site" (3)?
2. Why are pay phones in danger of disappearing?
3. Why does Frazier feel nostalgic about pay phones?
4. In what ways are cell phones different from pay phones?
5. What bothers Frazier most about cell phones?

PURPOSE AND AUDIENCE

1. At what point in the essay does Frazier state his thesis? Why do you think he states it where he does?
2. What preconceptions about pay phones does Frazier seem to think his readers have? How can you tell?
3. What is Frazier's purpose in this essay? To instruct? To convince? To entertain? Does he have some other purpose? Explain.
4. Does the title of this essay accurately reflect its thesis? Suggest some other titles that Frazier could have used.

STYLE AND STRUCTURE

1. Why does Frazier open his essay with a story about how he phoned his wife? What does this story add to his essay?
2. Is this essay organized as a subject-by-subject comparison or a point-by-point comparison? Why do you think Frazier chose this arrangement?
3. What transition does Frazier use to signal his movement from one subject to another?
4. Does Frazier make the same (or similar) points about both pay phones and cell phones? Are there any points he should have made but didn't?
5. What strategy does Frazier use in his conclusion? Is this strategy effective? Why or why not?

VOCABULARY PROJECTS

1. Define each of the following words as it is used in this selection.

A-frame (1)	curbstone (4)	concourse (5)
nondescript (3)	unraveled (4)	assignations (6)
uncongenial (4)	ventilating (5)	atmospherics (6)

evoked (6)	muteness (6)	proliferate (13)
mundane (6)	concession stand (8)	infinitude (13)
undifferentiated (6)	commonality (12)	

2. This essay contains a number of rather difficult words. Choose a paragraph that contains several of these words (paragraph 6, for example), and rewrite it in more accessible language. Then, evaluate what has been gained and lost as a result of your substitutions.

JOURNAL ENTRY

Identify an object about which you feel as intensely as Frazier feels about pay phones, and explain the role this object has played in your life.

WRITING WORKSHOP

1. Write an essay in which you, like Frazier, tell how a technological device — a cell phone or a digital camera, for example — changed your life. Make sure you compare your life before you began using the object with your life after you started to use it. Your essay can be either serious or humorous.

2. Write an essay in which you compare an example of new technology with an example of old technology — e-mail and regular mail, for example. Make sure you discuss the positive and negative aspects of each.

3. Interview your parents or grandparents, and ask them about their attitudes toward cell phones. Then, write an essay in which you compare their attitudes to your own.

COMBINING THE PATTERNS

This essay contains a number of **exemplification** paragraphs — for example, paragraphs 6 and 8. What do these paragraphs add to the essay?

THEMATIC CONNECTIONS

- "Once More to the Lake" (page 175)
- "Television: The Plug-In Drug" (page 325)
- "How the Lawyers Stole Winter" (page 402)

BHARATI MUKHERJEE

❖
Two Ways to Belong in America

Born in 1940 in Calcutta, India, novelist Bharati Mukherjee attended the University of Calcutta before immigrating to the United States in 1961. After receiving an M.F.A. from the University of Iowa, she moved with her husband to Canada, where she taught at McGill University. Now a naturalized U.S. citizen, she teaches at the University of California at Berkeley. Mukherjee's novels include *Tiger's Daughter* (1972), *Jasmine* (1989), *Leave It to Me* (1997), and *Desirable Daughters* (2002); her story collections are *Darkness* (1975) and the prize-winning *The Middleman and Other Stories* (1988). Her fiction often explores the tensions between the traditional role of women in Indian society and their very different role in the United States.

Background: The following essay, originally published in 1996, was written in response to proposals in Congress (eventually defeated) to enact legislation denying government benefits, such as Social Security, to resident aliens. (Not to be confused with illegal immigrants, resident aliens — also called legal permanent residents — are immigrants who live in the United States legally, sometimes for their whole lives, but choose not to apply for citizenship. Most work and pay taxes like any citizen.) According to the 2000 census, the United States population includes more than 30 million foreign-born residents, accounting for about 11 percent of the population. Of these, 9.3 million are legal permanent residents, 9.2 million are naturalized citizens, and an estimated 8.5 million are in the country illegally; most of the rest are refugees seeking political asylum and students and temporary workers with visas. Although various issues related to immigration policy have been hotly debated for many years, particularly as large numbers of immigrants entered the country in the 1990s, the terrorist attacks of September 2001 have led to widespread calls for greater restrictions and closer screenings of foreigners who want to enter the United States, especially those applying for student visas.

This is a tale of two sisters from Calcutta, Mira and Bharati, who have   1
lived in the United States for some 35 years, but who find themselves on different sides in the current debate over the status of immigrants. I am an American citizen and she is not. I am moved that thousands of long-term residents are finally taking the oath of citizenship. She is not.

Mira arrived in Detroit in 1960 to study child psychology and pre-   2
school education. I followed her a year later to study creative writing at the University of Iowa. When we left India, we were almost identical in appearance and attitude. We dressed alike, in saris; we expressed identical views on politics, social issues, love, and marriage in the same Calcutta convent-school accent. We would endure our two years in America, secure our degrees, then return to India to marry the grooms of our father's choosing.

Instead, Mira married an Indian student in 1962 who was getting his business administration degree at Wayne State University. They soon acquired the labor certifications necessary for the green card of hassle-free residence and employment.

Mira still lives in Detroit, works in the Southfield, Mich., school system, and has become nationally recognized for her contributions in the fields of pre-school education and parent-teacher relationships. After 36 years as a legal immigrant in this country, she clings passionately to her Indian citizenship and hopes to go home to India when she retires.

In Iowa City in 1963, I married a fellow student, an American of Canadian parentage. Because of the accident of his North Dakota birth, I bypassed labor-certification requirements and the race-related "quota" system that favored the applicant's country of origin over his or her merit. I was prepared for (and even welcomed) the emotional strain that came with marrying outside my ethnic community. In 33 years of marriage, we have lived in every part of North America. By choosing a husband who was not my father's selection, I was opting for fluidity, self-invention, blue jeans and T-shirts, and renouncing 3,000 years (at least) of case-observant, "pure culture" marriage in the Mukherjee family. My books have often been read as unapologetic (and in some quarters overenthusiastic) texts for cultural and psychological "mongrelization." It's a word I celebrate.

Mira and I have stayed sisterly close by phone. In our regular Sunday morning conversations, we are unguardedly affectionate. I am her only blood relative on this continent. We expect to see each other through the looming crises of aging and ill health without being asked. Long before Vice President Gore's "Citizenship U.S.A." drive, we'd had our polite arguments over the ethics of retaining an overseas citizenship while expecting the permanent protection and economic benefits that come with living and working in America.

Like well-raised sisters, we never said what was really on our minds, but we probably pitied one another. She, for the lack of structure in my life, the erasure of Indianness, the absence of an unvarying daily core. I, for the narrowness of her perspective, her uninvolvement with the mythic depths or the superficial pop culture of this society. But, now, with the scapegoatings of "aliens" (documented or illegal) on the increase, and the targeting of long-term legal immigrants like Mira for new scrutiny and new self-consciousness, she and I find ourselves unable to maintain the same polite discretion. We were always unacknowledged adversaries, and we are now, more than ever, sisters.

"I feel used," Mira raged on the phone the other night. "I feel manipulated and discarded. This is such an unfair way to treat a person who was invited to stay and work here because of her talent. My employer went to the I.N.S. and petitioned for the labor certification. For over 30 years, I've invested my creativity and professional skills into the improvement of *this* country's pre-school system. I've obeyed all the rules, I've paid my taxes, I love my work, I love my students, I love the friends I've made. How dare America now change its rules in midstream? If America wants to make new rules curtailing benefits of legal immigrants, they should apply only to immigrants who arrive after those rules are already in place."

To my ears, it sounded like the description of a long-enduring, comfortable yet loveless marriage, without risk or recklessness. Have we the right to demand, and to expect, that we be loved? (That, to me, is the subtext of the arguments by immigration advocates.) My sister is an expatriate, professionally generous and creative, socially courteous and gracious, and that's as far as her Americanization can go. She is here to maintain an identity, not to transform it.

I asked her if she would follow the example of others who have decided to become citizens because of the anti-immigration bills in Congress. And here, she surprised me. "If America wants to play the manipulative game, I'll play it, too," she snapped. "I'll become a U.S. citizen for now, then change back to India when I'm ready to go home. I feel some kind of irrational attachment to India that I don't to America. Until all this hysteria against legal immigrants, I was totally happy. Having my green card meant I could visit any place in the world I wanted to and then come back to a job that's satisfying and that I do very well."

In one family, from two sisters alike as peas in a pod, there could not be a wider divergence of immigrant experience. America spoke to me — I married it — I embraced the demotion from expatriate aristocrat to immigrant nobody, surrendering those thousands of years of "pure culture," the saris, the delightfully accented English. She retained them all. Which of us is the freak?

Mira's voice, I realize, is the voice not just of the immigrant South Asian community but of an immigrant community of the millions who have stayed rooted in one job, one city, one house, one ancestral culture, one cuisine, for the entirety of their productive years. She speaks for greater numbers than I possibly can. Only the fluency of her English and the anger, rather than fear, born of confidence from her education, differentiate her from the seamstresses, the domestics, the technicians, the shop owners, the millions of hard-working but effectively silenced documented immigrants as well as their less fortunate "illegal" brothers and sisters.

Nearly 20 years ago, when I was living in my husband's ancestral homeland of Canada, I was always well-employed but never allowed to feel part of the local Quebec or larger Canadian society. Then, through a Green Paper that invited a national referendum on the unwanted side effects of "nontraditional" immigration, the Government officially turned against its immigrant communities, particularly those from South Asia.

I felt then the same sense of betrayal that Mira feels now. I will never forget the pain of that sudden turning, and the casual racist outbursts the Green Paper elicited. That sense of betrayal had its desired effect and drove me, and thousands like me, from the country.

Mira and I differ, however, in the ways in which we hope to interact with the country that we have chosen to live in. She is happier to live in America as expatriate Indian than as an immigrant American. I need to feel like a part of the community I have adopted (as I tried to feel in Canada as well). I need to put roots down, to vote and make the difference that I can. The price that the immigrant willingly pays, and that the exile avoids, is the trauma of self-transformation.

• • •

COMPREHENSION

1. At first, how long did Mukherjee and her sister intend to stay in America? Why did they change their plans?

2. What does Mukherjee mean when she says she welcomed the "emotional strain" of "marrying outside [her] ethnic community" (5)?

3. In what ways is Mukherjee different from her sister? What kind of relationship do they have?

4. Why does Mukherjee's sister feel used? Why does she think America has changed "its rules in midstream" (8)?

5. According to Mukherjee, how is her sister like all immigrants who "have stayed rooted in one job, one city, one house, one ancestral culture, one cuisine, for the entirety of their productive years" (12)?

PURPOSE AND AUDIENCE

1. What is Mukherjee's thesis? At what point does she state it?

2. At whom is Mukherjee aiming her remarks? Immigrants like herself? Immigrants like her sister? General readers? Explain.

3. What is Mukherjee's purpose? Is she trying to inform? To move readers to action? To accomplish something else? Explain.

STYLE AND STRUCTURE

1. What basis for comparison exists between Mukherjee and her sister? Where in the essay does Mukherjee establish this basis of comparison?

2. Is this essay a point-by-point or a subject-by-subject comparison? Why do you think Mukherjee chose the option she did?

3. What points does Mukherjee discuss for each subject? Should she have discussed any other points?

4. What transitional words and phrases does Mukherjee use to signal shifts from one point to another?

5. How effective is Mukherjee's conclusion? Does it summarize the major points of the essay? Would another strategy be more effective? Explain.

VOCABULARY PROJECTS

1. Define each of the following words as it is used in this selection.

certifications (3)	perspective (7)	superficial (7)
mongrelization (5)	mythic (7)	scrutiny (7)

| discretion (7) | divergence (11) | saris (11) |
| curtailing (8) | expatriate (11) | trauma (15) |

2. What, according to Mukherjee, is the difference between an *immigrant* and an *exile* (15)? What are the connotations of these two words? Do you think the distinction Mukherjee makes is valid?

JOURNAL ENTRY

Do you think Mukherjee respects her sister's decision? From your perspective, which sister has made the right decision?

WRITING WORKSHOP

1. Assume that the sister, Mira, has just read Mukherjee's essay and wants to respond to it. Write a letter from Mira in which you compare her position about assimilation to that of Mukherjee. Make sure you explain Mira's position and address Mukherjee's points about assimilation.

2. Have you ever moved from one town or city to another? Write an essay in which you compare the two places. Your thesis statement should indicate whether you are emphasizing similarities or differences and convey your opinion of the new area to which you moved. (If you have never moved, write an essay comparing two places you are familiar with — your college and your high school, for example.)

3. Assume you had to move to another country. Where would you move? Would you, like Mukherjee, assimilate into your new culture or, like her sister, retain your own cultural values? Write an essay in which you compare life in your new country to life in the United States. Make sure your thesis reflects your attitude toward assimilation. If you have already moved from another country, compare your life in the United States with your life in your country of origin.

COMBINING THE PATTERNS

Do you think Mukherjee should have used **cause and effect** to structure a section explaining why she and her sister are so different? Explain what such a section would add to or take away from the essay.

THEMATIC CONNECTIONS

- "Only Daughter" (page 84)
- "The Way to Rainy Mountain" (page 169)
- "The Untouchable" (page 498)
- "Strange Tools" (page 697)

CHRISTOPHER B. DALY

❖

How the Lawyers Stole Winter

Born in Boston in 1954, Christopher B. Daly received a B.A. from Harvard and an M.A. in history from the University of North Carolina at Chapel Hill. A veteran journalist, Daly spent ten years working at the Associated Press and another seven years covering New England for the *Washington Post.* He has taught journalism and writing at Harvard and Brandeis; currently he is a visiting professor at Boston University as well as a freelance writer. His work has appeared in a variety of magazines and journals, and he is coauthor of *Like a Family* (1987), a prize-winning social history of the industrialization of the South.

Background: In the following essay, which originally appeared in *The Atlantic Monthly,* Daly recalls the fun he and his boyhood friends had during the winter when they skated unsupervised on a local pond. Today, however, this activity would not be permitted in many communities because of the threat of lawsuits should someone drown. Lawsuits have been on the rise in the United States since the mid-1970s, sparked primarily by two events: the 1976 decision by the American Bar Association to allow its attorney members to advertise and a 1977 Supreme Court decision that made it easier for people to file lawsuits. For example, New York City's payout for lawsuits jumped from $24 million in 1977 to $114 million in 1985. One tort-reform advocacy group claims that a lawsuit is filed every ten seconds of every working hour in the United States and that the $163 billion that is paid out every year in damages and lawyers' fees increases taxes and the prices of consumer products.

When I was a boy, my friends and I would come home from school each day, change our clothes (because we were not allowed to wear "play clothes" to school), and go outside until dinnertime. In the early 1960s in Medford, a city on the outskirts of Boston, that was pretty much what everybody did. Sometimes there might be flute lessons, or an organized Little League game, but usually not. Usually we kids went out and played.

In winter, on our way home from the Gleason School, we would go past Brooks Pond to check the ice. By throwing heavy stones on it, hammering it with downed branches, and, finally, jumping on it, we could figure out if the ice was ready for skating. If it was, we would hurry home to grab our skates, our sticks, and whatever other gear we had, and then return to play hockey for the rest of the day. When the streetlights came on, we knew it was time to jam our cold, stiff feet back into our green rubber snow boots and get home for dinner.

I had these memories in mind recently when I moved, with my wife and two young boys, into a house near a lake even closer to Boston, in the city of Newton. As soon as Crystal Lake froze over, I grabbed my skates and headed out. I was not the first one there, though: the lawyers had beaten me to the lake. They had warned the town recreation department to put it off limits. So I found a sign that said DANGER, THIN ICE. NO SKATING.

Knowing a thing or two about words myself, I put my own gloss on the sign. I took it to mean *When the ice is thin, there is danger and there should be no skating.* Fair enough, I thought, but I knew that the obverse was also true: *When the ice is thick, it is safe and there should be skating.* Finding the ice plenty thick, I laced up my skates and glided out onto the miraculous glassy surface of the frozen lake. My wife, a native of Manhattan, would not let me take our two boys with me. But for as long as I could, I enjoyed the free, open-air delight of skating as it should be. After a few days others joined me, and we became an outlaw band of skaters.

What we were doing was once the heart of winter in New England — and a lot of other places, too. It was clean, free exercise that needed no StairMasters, no health clubs, no appointments, and hardly any gear. Sadly, it is in danger of passing away. Nowadays it seems that every city and town and almost all property holders are so worried about liability and lawsuits that they simply throw up a sign or a fence and declare that henceforth there shall be no skating, and that's the end of it.

As a result, kids today live in a world of leagues, rinks, rules, uniforms, adults, and rides — rides here, rides there, rides everywhere. It is not clear that they are better off; in some ways they are clearly *not* better off.

When I was a boy skating on Brooks Pond, there were no grown-ups around. Once or twice a year, on a weekend day or a holiday, some parents might come by with a thermos of hot cocoa. Maybe they would build a fire (which we were forbidden to do), and we would gather round.

But for the most part the pond was the domain of children. In the absence of adults, we made and enforced our own rules. We had hardly any gear — just some borrowed hockey gloves, some hand-me-down skates, maybe an elbow pad or two — so we played a clean form of hockey, with no high-sticking, no punching, and almost no checking. A single fight could ruin the whole afternoon. Indeed, as I remember it, thirty years later, it was the purest form of hockey I ever saw — until I got to see the Russian national team play the game.

But before we could play, we had to check the ice. We became serious junior meteorologists, true connoisseurs of cold. We learned that the best weather for pond skating is plain, clear cold, with starry nights and no snow. (Snow not only mucks up the skating surface but also insulates the ice from the colder air above.) And we learned that moving water, even the gently flowing Mystic River, is a lot less likely to freeze than standing water. So we skated only on the pond. We learned all the weird whooping and cracking sounds that ice makes as it expands and contracts, and thus when to leave the ice.

Do kids learn these things today? I don't know. How would they? We don't let them. Instead we post signs. Ruled by lawyers, cities and towns everywhere try to eliminate their legal liability. But try as they might, they cannot eliminate the underlying risk. Liability is a social construct; risk is a natural fact. When it is cold enough, ponds freeze. No sign or fence or ordinance can change that.

In fact, by focusing on liability and not teaching our kids how to take   11
risks, we are making their world more dangerous. When we were children, we had to learn to evaluate risks and handle them on our own. We had to learn, quite literally, to test the waters. As a result, we grew up to be savvier about ice and ponds than any kid could be who has skated only under adult supervision on a rink.

When I was a boy, despite the risks we took on the ice no one I knew   12
ever drowned. The only people I heard about who drowned were graduate students at Harvard or MIT who came from the tropics and were living through their first winters. Not knowing (after all, how could they?) about ice on moving water, they would innocently venture out onto the half-frozen Charles River, fall through, and die. They were literally out of their element.

Are we raising a generation of children who will be out of their ele-   13
ment? And if so, what can we do about it? We cannot just roll back the calendar. I cannot tell my six-year-old to head down to the lake by himself to play all afternoon—if for no other reason than that he would not find twenty or thirty other kids there, full of the collective wisdom about cold and ice that they had inherited, along with hockey equipment, from their older brothers and sisters. Somewhere along the line that link got broken.

The whole setting of childhood has changed. We cannot change it   14
again overnight. I cannot send my children out by themselves yet, but at least some of the time I can go out there with them. Maybe that is a start.

As for us, last winter was a very unusual one. We had ferocious cold   15
(near-zero temperatures on many nights) and tremendous snows (about a hundred inches in all). Eventually a strange thing happened. The town gave in—sort of. Sometime in January the recreation department "opened" a section of the lake, and even dispatched a snowplow truck to clear a good-sized patch of ice. The boys and I skated during the rest of winter. Ever vigilant, the town officials kept the THIN ICE signs up, even though their own truck could safely drive on the frozen surface. And they brought in "lifeguards" and all sorts of rules about the hours during which we could skate and where we had to stay.

But at least we were able to skate in the open air, on real ice.   16

And it was still free.   17

•   •   •

COMPREHENSION

1. What did Daly and his friends do when they came home from school in the 1960s?

2. According to Daly, why is winter "in danger of passing away" (5)?

3. During the 1960s, how did children make sure the ice was safe to skate on? Why don't children learn these things today?

4. According to Daly, in what ways has "the whole setting of childhood" (14) changed? What does he propose to do about this situation?

5. What does Daly mean when he says that "by focusing on liability and not teaching our kids how to take risks, we are making their world more dangerous" (11)?

PURPOSE AND AUDIENCE

1. At what point does Daly state his thesis? Why does he wait so long to state it? Should he have stated it sooner?

2. What is Daly's purpose in writing his essay? What does he hope to accomplish?

3. Does Daly think his readers will be sympathetic, neutral, or hostile to his ideas? How can you tell?

4. How would you expect an audience of Daly's contemporaries to react to his essay? Would Daly's children and their friends have a different reaction?

5. What is Daly's purpose in mentioning StairMasters and health clubs in paragraph 5? How might he expect his audience of fairly affluent, well-educated adults to react?

STYLE AND STRUCTURE

1. How does the introduction of this essay prepare readers for the discussion that follows?

2. Does Daly use a subject-by-subject or a point-by-point method of comparison (or a combination of the two)? What is the advantage of the strategy he uses?

3. Daly refers to THIN ICE signs at the beginning and end of his essay. Why does he refer to the signs at these key points in his essay? Do the words *thin ice* suggest any meaning beyond the literal one? Explain.

4. What transitional words and phrases indicate that Daly is shifting from one subject to another? From one point to another? Does the essay need more transitions? If so, where?

5. Daly's essay has a one-sentence conclusion. Should it be expanded? If so, how? If not, why not?

VOCABULARY PROJECTS

1. Define each of the following words as it is used in this selection.

   gloss (4)   domain (8)
   liability (5)   connoisseurs (9)

2. Underline all the uses of the words *risk* and *liability* in Daly's essay. Do these words have the same meaning each time he uses them?

JOURNAL ENTRY

Do you agree with Daly's assertion that because of the threat of lawsuits and liability, children are being raised not to take risks? Are there other explanations for the rules and uniformity Daly observes?

WRITING WORKSHOP

1. Write an essay comparing how you performed a particular activity when you were a child with how you perform the same activity now. Make sure you focus on the differences and, like Daly, draw some conclusion about the present.

2. Write a letter to Daly in which you compare his memories of winter with your own. In your essay, address Daly's contention that children today are brought up not to take risks.

3. Write an essay in which you compare your own willingness to take risks with that of one of your friends or family members.

COMBINING THE PATTERNS

Daly ends his essay with a **narrative** about a particularly cold winter. Does the narrative contain enough detail? Would more detail make this paragraph more effective? Explain.

THEMATIC CONNECTIONS

- "Ground Zero" (page 158)
- "The Way to Rainy Mountain" (page 169)
- "Once More to the Lake" (page 175)
- "Television: The Plug-In Drug" (page 325)

DEBORAH TANNEN

❖

Sex, Lies, and Conversation

Deborah Tannen was born in Brooklyn, New York, in 1945. She graduated from the State University of New York at Binghamton, was awarded a doctorate from the University of California at Berkeley, and currently teaches at Georgetown University. Tannen has written and edited several scholarly books on the problems of communicating across cultural, class, ethnic, and sexual divides. She has also presented her research to the general public in newspapers and magazines and in her best-selling books *That's Not What I Meant!* (1986), *You Just Don't Understand: Women and Men in Conversation* (1990), and *Talking from 9 to 5* (1994). Her latest book is *I Only Say This Because I Love You* (2001).

Background: "Sex, Lies, and Conversation" was written in conjunction with the publication of *You Just Don't Understand,* which Tannen wrote because the single chapter in *That's Not What I Meant!* on the difficulties men and women have communicating with one another had gotten such an overwhelming response. She realized the chapter might raise some controversy — that discussing their different communication styles might be used to malign men or to put women at a disadvantage — and indeed some critics have seen her work as reinforcing stereotypes. Still, her work on the subject, along with that of other writers (most notably John Gray in his *Men Are from Mars, Women Are from Venus* series), has proved enormously popular, and much research (and debate) is being carried on about male and female differences in terms of brain function, relational styles and expectations, and evolutionary roles.

1   I was addressing a small gathering in a suburban Virginia living room — a women's group that had invited men to join them. Throughout the evening, one man had been particularly talkative, frequently offering ideas and anecdotes, while his wife sat silently beside him on the couch. Toward the end of the evening, I commented that women frequently complain that their husbands don't talk to them. This man quickly concurred. He gestured toward his wife and said, "She's the talker in our family." The room burst into laughter; the man looked puzzled and hurt. "It's true," he explained. "When I come home from work I have nothing to say. If she didn't keep the conversation going, we'd spend the whole evening in silence."

2   This episode crystallizes the irony that although American men tend to talk more than women in public situations, they often talk less at home. And this pattern is wreaking havoc with marriage.

3   The pattern was observed by political scientist Andrew Hacker in the late '70s. Sociologist Catherine Kohler Riessman reports in her new book *Divorce Talk* that most of the women she interviewed — but only a few of

the men—gave lack of communication as the reason for their divorces. Given the current divorce rate of nearly 50 percent, that amounts to millions of cases in the United States every year—a virtual epidemic of failed conversation.

In my own research, complaints from women about their husbands most often focused not on tangible inequities such as having given up the chance for a career to accompany a husband to his, or doing far more than their share of daily life-support work like cleaning, cooking, social arrangements, and errands. Instead, they focused on communication: "He doesn't listen to me," "He doesn't talk to me." I found, as Hacker observed years before, that most wives want their husbands to be, first and foremost, conversational partners, but few husbands share this expectation of their wives.   4

In short, the image that best represents the current crisis is the stereotypical cartoon scene of a man sitting at the breakfast table with a newspaper held up in front of his face, while a woman glares at the back of it, wanting to talk.   5

Linguistic Battle of the Sexes

How can women and men have such different impressions of communication in marriage? Why the widespread imbalance in their interests and expectations?   6

In the April issue of *American Psychologist,* Stanford University's Eleanor Maccoby reports the results of her own and others' research showing that children's development is most influenced by the social structure of peer interactions. Boys and girls tend to play with children of their own gender, and their sex-separate groups have different organizational structures and interactive norms.   7

I believe these systematic differences in childhood socialization make talk between women and men like cross-cultural communication, heir to all the attraction and pitfalls of that enticing but difficult enterprise. My research on men's and women's conversations uncovered patterns similar to those described for children's groups.   8

For women, as for girls, intimacy is the fabric of relationships, and talk is the thread from which it is woven. Little girls create and maintain friendships by exchanging secrets; similarly, women regard conversation as the cornerstone of friendship. So a woman expects her husband to be a new and improved version of a best friend. What is important is not the individual subjects that are discussed but the sense of closeness, of a life shared, that emerges when people tell their thoughts, feelings, and impressions.   9

Bonds between boys can be as intense as girls', but they are based less on talking, more on doing things together. Since they don't assume talk is the cement that binds a relationship, men don't know what kind of talk women want, and they don't miss it when it isn't there.   10

Boys' groups are larger, more inclusive, and more hierarchical, so boys must struggle to avoid the subordinate position in the group. This may   11 play a role in women's complaints that men don't listen to them. Some men really don't like to listen, because being the listener makes them feel one-down, like a child listening to adults or an employee to a boss.

But often when women tell men, "You aren't listening," and the men 12 protest, "I am," the men are right. The impression of not listening results from misalignments in the mechanics of conversation. The misalignment begins as soon as a man and a woman take physical positions. This became clear when I studied videotapes made by psychologist Bruce Dorval of children and adults talking to their same-sex best friends. I found that at every age, the girls and women faced each other directly, their eyes anchored on each other's faces. At every age, the boys and men sat at angles to each other and looked elsewhere in the room, periodically glancing at each other. They were obviously attuned to each other, often mirroring each other's movements. But the tendency of men to face away can give women the impression they aren't listening even when they are. A young woman in college was frustrated: Whenever she told her boyfriend she wanted to talk to him, he would lie down on the floor, close his eyes, and put his arm over his face. This signaled to her, "He's taking a nap." But he insisted he was listening extra hard. Normally, he looks around the room, so he is easily distracted. Lying down and covering his eyes helped him concentrate on what she was saying.

Analogous to the physical alignment that women and men take in 13 conversation is their topical alignment. The girls in my study tended to talk at length about one topic, but the boys tended to jump from topic to topic. The second-grade girls exchanged stories about people they knew. The second-grade boys teased, told jokes, noticed things in the room, and talked about finding games to play. The sixth-grade girls talked about problems with a mutual friend. The sixth-grade boys talked about 55 different topics, none of which extended over more than a few turns.

Listening to Body Language

Switching topics is another habit that gives women the impression 14 men aren't listening, especially if they switch to a topic about themselves. But the evidence of the 10th-grade boys in my study indicates otherwise. The 10th-grade boys sprawled across their chairs with bodies parallel and eyes straight ahead, rarely looking at each other. They looked as if they were riding in a car, staring out the windshield. But they were talking about their feelings. One boy was upset because a girl had told him he had a drinking problem, and the other was feeling alienated from all his friends.

Now, when a girl told a friend about a problem, the friend responded 15 by asking probing questions and expressing agreement and understanding. But the boys dismissed each other's problems. Todd assured Richard that his drinking was "no big problem" because "sometimes you're funny when you're off your butt." And when Todd said he felt left out, Richard responded, "Why should you? You know more people than me."

Women perceive such responses as belittling and unsupportive. But   16
the boys seemed satisfied with them. Whereas women reassure each other
by implying, "You shouldn't feel bad because I've had similar experiences,"
men do so by implying, "You shouldn't feel bad because your problems
aren't so bad."

There are even simpler reasons for women's impression that men don't   17
listen. Linguist Lynette Hirschman found that women make more listener-
noise, such as "mhm," "uhuh," and "yeah," to show "I'm with you." Men,
she found, more often give silent attention. Women who expect a stream of
listener-noise interpret silent attention as no attention at all.

Women's conversational habits are as frustrating to men as men's are   18
to women. Men who expect silent attention interpret a stream of listener-
noise as overreaction or impatience. Also, when women talk to each other
in a close, comfortable setting, they often overlap, finish each other's sentences, and anticipate what the other is about to say. This practice, which I
call "participatory listenership," is often perceived by men as interruption,
intrusion, and lack of attention.

A parallel difference caused a man to complain about his wife, "She   19
just wants to talk about her own point of view. If I show her another view,
she gets mad at me." When most women talk to each other, they assume a
conversationalist's job is to express agreement and support. But many men
see their conversational duty as pointing out the other side of an argument. This is heard as disloyalty by women, and refusal to offer the requi-
site support. It is not that women don't want to see other points of view,
but that they prefer them phrased as suggestions and inquiries rather than
as direct challenges.

In his book *Fighting for Life*, Walter Ong points out that men use "ago-   20
nistic," or warlike, oppositional formats to do almost anything; thus discussion becomes debate, and conversation a competitive sport. In contrast,
women see conversation as a ritual means of establishing rapport. If Jane
tells a problem and June says she has a similar one, they walk away feeling
closer to each other. But this attempt at establishing rapport can backfire
when used with men. Men take too literally women's ritual "troubles talk,"
just as women mistake men's ritual challenges for real attack.

The Sounds of Silence

These differences begin to clarify why women and men have such dif-   21
ferent expectations about communication in marriage. For women, talk
creates intimacy. Marriage is an orgy of closeness: you can tell your feelings
and thoughts, and still be loved. Their greatest fear is being pushed away.
But men live in a hierarchical world, where talk maintains independence
and status. They are on guard to protect themselves from being put down
and pushed around.

This explains the paradox of the talkative man who said of his silent   22
wife, "She's the talker." In the public setting of a guest lecture, he felt challenged to show his intelligence and display his understanding of the

lecture. But at home, where he has nothing to prove and no one to defend against, he is free to remain silent. For his wife, being home means she is free from the worry that something she says might offend someone, or spark disagreement, or appear to be showing off; at home she is free to talk.

The communication problems that endanger marriage can't be fixed by mechanical engineering. They require a new conceptual framework about the role of talk in human relationships. Many of the psychological explanations that have become second nature may not be helpful, because they tend to blame either women (for not being assertive enough) or men (for not being in touch with their feelings). A sociolinguistic approach by which male-female conversation is seen as cross-cultural communication allows us to understand the problem and forge solutions without blaming either party.

Once the problem is understood, improvement comes naturally, as it did to the young woman and her boyfriend who seemed to go to sleep when she wanted to talk. Previously, she had accused him of not listening, and he had refused to change his behavior, since that would be admitting fault. But then she learned about and explained to him the differences in women's and men's habitual ways of aligning themselves in conversation. The next time she told him she wanted to talk, he began, as usual, by lying down and covering his eyes. When the familiar negative reaction bubbled up, she reassured herself that he really was listening. But then he sat up and looked at her. Thrilled, she asked why. He said, "You like me to look at you when we talk, so I'll try to do it." Once he saw their differences as cross-cultural rather than right and wrong, he independently altered his behavior.

Women who feel abandoned and deprived when their husbands won't listen to or report daily news may be happy to discover their husbands trying to adapt once they understand the place of small talk in women's relationships. But if their husbands don't adapt, the women may still be comforted that for men, this is not a failure of intimacy. Accepting the difference, the wives may look to their friends or family for that kind of talk. And husbands who can't provide it shouldn't feel their wives have made unreasonable demands. Some couples will still decide to divorce, but at least their decisions will be based on realistic expectations.

In these times of resurgent ethnic conflicts, the world desperately needs cross-cultural understanding. Like charity, successful cross-cultural communication should begin at home.

•   •   •

COMPREHENSION

1. What pattern of communication does Tannen identify at the beginning of her essay?

2. According to Tannen, what do women complain about most in their marriages?

3. What gives women the impression that men do not listen?

4. What characteristics of women's speech do men find frustrating?

5. According to Tannen, what can men and women do to remedy the communication problems that exist in most marriages?

PURPOSE AND AUDIENCE

1. What is Tannen's thesis?

2. What is Tannen's purpose in writing this essay? Do you think she wants to inform or to persuade? On what do you base your conclusion?

3. Is Tannen writing to an expert audience or an audience of general readers? To men, women, or both? How can you tell?

STYLE AND STRUCTURE

1. What does Tannen gain by stating her thesis in paragraph 2 of the essay? Would there be any advantage in postponing the thesis statement until the end? Explain.

2. Is this essay a subject-by-subject or a point-by-point comparison? What does Tannen gain by organizing her essay the way she does?

3. Throughout her essay, Tannen cites scholarly studies and quotes statistics. How effectively does this information support her points? Could she have made a strong case without this material? Why or why not?

4. Would you say Tannen's tone is hopeful, despairing, sarcastic, angry, or something else? Explain.

5. Tannen concludes her essay with a far-reaching statement. What do you think she hopes to accomplish with this conclusion? Is she successful? Explain your reasoning.

VOCABULARY PROJECTS

1. Define each of the following words as it is used in this selection.

concurred (1)	pitfalls (8)	rapport (20)
crystallizes (2)	subordinate (11)	ritual (20)
inequities (4)	misalignment (12)	orgy (21)
imbalance (6)	analogous (13)	sociolinguistic (23)
peer (7)	alienated (14)	forge (23)
organizational (7)	intrusion (18)	

2. Where does Tannen use professional **jargon** in this essay? Would the essay be more or less effective without these words? Explain.

JOURNAL ENTRY

Based on your own observations of male-female communication, how accurate is Tannen's analysis? Can you relate an anecdote from your own life that illustrates (or contradicts) her thesis?

WRITING WORKSHOP

1. In another essay, Tannen contrasts the communication patterns of male and female students in classroom settings. After observing a few of your own classes, write an essay in which you, too, draw a comparison between the communication patterns of your male and female classmates.

2. Write an essay in which you compare the way male and female characters speak in films or on television. Use examples to support your points.

3. Write an essay in which you compare the vocabulary used in two different sports. Does one sport use more violent language than the other? For example, baseball uses the terms *bunt* and *sacrifice,* and football uses the terms *blitz* and *bomb*. Use as many examples as you can to support your points.

COMBINING THE PATTERNS

Tannen begins her essay with an anecdote. Why does she begin with a paragraph of **narration?** How does this story set the tone for the rest of the essay?

THEMATIC CONNECTIONS

- "Why Boys Don't Play with Dolls" (page 335)
- "The Men We Carry in Our Minds" (page 456)
- "I Want a Wife" (page 505)
- "The Wife-Beater" (page 521)

ERIC SCHLOSSER

Walt and Ray: Your Trusted Friends

Born in 1959 in New York City, Eric Schlosser received a bachelor's degree in American history from Princeton University and went on to Oxford University, where he studied the history of the British monarchy. An award-winning investigative journalist, he has contributed to *Rolling Stone* and *The New Yorker,* and—as a correspondent for *The Atlantic Monthly* since 1996—he has written about marijuana laws, families of homicide victims, prisons, and the pornography business. In 2001, Schlosser published *Fast Food Nation: The Dark Side of the All-American Meal,* a witty and unsettling account of how the fast-food industry, led by McDonald's, has changed the way much of the world produces, as well as thinks about, food. The following selection from that book focuses on Ray Kroc, McDonald's legendary founder, and the similarities between his empire and that of Walt Disney.

Background: The rise of the McDonald's Corporation and the growth of the Walt Disney Company, including the opening of the original Disneyland theme park, were the result of significant changes that occurred in consumer culture during the 1950s. Following the economic depression of the 1930s and the war years of the 1940s, when many products were in relatively short supply, the 1950s saw an economic boom and a consequent rise in consumer spending. For example, automobile sales, which had slumped to 70,000 in 1945, leaped to more than 6.5 million by 1950 and would continue to increase throughout the decade. The mobility afforded by the automobile allowed Americans to travel widely and thus gain access to many different businesses. Moreover, the growth of television ownership—from virtually none in the late 1940s to sales of fifteen million in 1951 and total ownership of more than fifty million by 1960—created a new outlet for advertising that sparked increased consumer desire and led to a growth in nationwide business chains. The 1950s also continued the twentieth century's promise that convenience was an inevitable outgrowth of technological advancement. As more and more labor-saving appliances became part of every suburban home, both McDonald's and Disney's Tomorrowland offered glimpses of a future when people would be free from household drudgery.

Before entering the Ray A. Kroc Museum, you have to walk through McStore. Both sit on the ground floor of McDonald's corporate headquarters, located at One McDonald's Plaza in Oak Brook, Illinois. The headquarters building has oval windows and a gray concrete façade—a look that must have seemed space-age when the building opened three decades ago. Now it seems stolid and drab, an architectural relic of the Nixon era. It resembles the American embassy compounds that always used to attract antiwar protesters, student demonstrators, flag burners. The eighty-acre campus of Hamburger University, McDonald's managerial training center, is a short drive from headquarters. Shuttle buses constantly go back and forth between the campus and McDonald's Plaza, ferrying clean-cut young men and women in khakis who've come to study for their "Degree in Hamburgerology." The course lasts two weeks and trains a few thousand managers, executives, and franchisees each year. Students from out of town stay at the Hyatt on the McDonald's campus. Most of the classes are devoted to personnel issues, teaching lessons in teamwork and employee motivation, promoting "a common McDonald's language" and "a common McDonald's culture." Three flagpoles stand in front of McDonald's Plaza, the heart of the hamburger empire. One flies the Stars and Stripes, another flies the Illinois state flag, and the third flies a bright red flag with golden arches.

You can buy bean-bag McBurglar dolls at McStore, telephones shaped   2
like french fries, ties, clocks, key chains, golf bags and duffel bags, jewelry, baby clothes, lunch boxes, mouse pads, leather jackets, postcards, toy trucks, and much more, all of it bearing the stamp of McDonald's. You can buy T-shirts decorated with a new version of the American flag. The fifty white stars have been replaced by a pair of golden arches.

At the back of McStore, past the footsteps of Ronald McDonald sten-   3
ciled on the floor, past the shelves of dishes and glassware, a bronze bust of Ray Kroc marks the entrance to his museum. Kroc was the founder of the McDonald's Corporation, and his philosophy of QSC and V—Quality, Service, Cleanliness, and Value—still guide it. The man immortalized in bronze is balding and middle-aged, with smooth cheeks and an intense look in his eyes. A glass display case nearby holds plaques, awards, and letters of praise. "One of the highlights of my sixty-first birthday celebration," President Richard Nixon wrote in 1974, "was when Tricia suggested we needed a 'break' on our drive to Palm Springs, and we turned in at McDonald's. I had heard for years from our girls that the 'Big Mac' was really something special, and while I've often credited Mrs. Nixon with making the best hamburgers in the world, we are both convinced that McDonald's runs a close second. . . . The next time the cook has a night off we will know where to go for fast service, cheerful hospitality—and probably one of the best food buys in America." Other glass cases contain artifacts of Kroc's life, mementos of his long years of struggle and his twilight as a billionaire. The museum is small and dimly lit, displaying each object with reverence. The day I visited, the place was empty and still. It didn't feel like a traditional museum, where objects are coolly numbered, catalogued, and described. It felt more like a shrine.

Many of the exhibits at the Ray A. Kroc Museum incorporate neat   4
technological tricks. Dioramas appear and then disappear when certain buttons are pushed. The voices of Kroc's friends and coworkers—one of them identified as a McDonald's "vice president of individuality"—boom from speakers at the appropriate cue. Darkened glass cases are suddenly illuminated from within, revealing their contents. An artwork on the wall,

when viewed from the left, displays an image of Ray Kroc. Viewed from the right, it shows the letters QSC and V. The museum does not have a life-size, Audio-Animatronic version of McDonald's founder telling jokes and anecdotes. But one wouldn't be out of place. An interactive exhibit called "Talk to Ray" shows video clips of Kroc appearing on the *Phil Donahue Show,* being interviewed by Tom Snyder, and chatting with Reverend Robert Schuller at the altar of Orange County's Crystal Cathedral. "Talk to Ray" permits the viewer to ask Kroc as many as thirty-six predetermined questions about various subjects; old videos of Kroc supply the answers. The exhibit wasn't working properly the day of my visit. Ray wouldn't take my questions, and so I just listened to him repeating the same speeches.

The Disneyesque tone of the museum reflects, among other things,   5
many of the similarities between the McDonald's Corporation and the Walt Disney Company. It also reflects the similar paths of the two men who founded these corporate giants. Ray Kroc and Walt Disney were both from Illinois; they were born a year apart, Disney in 1901, Kroc in 1902; they knew each other as young men, serving together in the same World War I ambulance corps; and they both fled the Midwest and settled in southern California, where they played central roles in the creation of new American industries. The film critic Richard Schickel has described Disney's powerful inner need "to order, control, and keep clean any environment he inhabited." The same could easily be said about Ray Kroc, whose obsession with cleanliness and control became one of the hallmarks of his restaurant chain. Kroc cleaned the holes in his mop wringer with a toothbrush.

Kroc and Disney both dropped out of high school and later added the   6
trappings of formal education to their companies. The training school for Disney's theme-park employees was named Disneyland University. More importantly, the two men shared the same vision of America, the same optimistic faith in technology, the same conservative political views. They were charismatic figures who provided an overall corporate vision and grasped the public mood, relying on others to handle the creative and financial details. Walt Disney neither wrote, nor drew the animated classics that bore his name. Ray Kroc's attempts to add new dishes to McDonald's menu — such as Kolacky, a Bohemian pastry, and the Hulaburger, a sandwich featuring grilled pineapple and cheese — were unsuccessful. Both men, however, knew how to find and motivate the right talent. While Disney was much more famous and achieved success sooner, Kroc may have been more influential. His company inspired more imitators, wielded more power over the American economy — and spawned a mascot even more famous than Mickey Mouse.

Despite all their success as businessmen and entrepreneurs, as cultural   7
figures and advocates for a particular brand of Americanism, perhaps the most significant achievement of these two men lay elsewhere. Walt Disney and Ray Kroc were masterful salesmen. They perfected the art of selling things to children. And their success led many others to aim marketing

efforts at kids, turning America's youngest consumers into a demographic group that is now avidly studied, analyzed, and targeted by the world's largest corporations.

Walt and Ray

Ray Kroc took the McDonald brothers' Speedee Service System and spread it nationwide, creating a fast food empire. Although he founded a company that came to symbolize corporate America, Kroc was never a buttoned-down corporate type. He was a former jazz musician who'd played at speakeasies — and at a bordello, on at least one occasion — during Prohibition. He was a charming, funny, and indefatigable traveling salesman who endured many years of disappointment, a Willy Loman who finally managed to hit it big in his early sixties. Kroc grew up in Oak Park, Illinois, not far from Chicago. His father worked for Western Union. As a high school freshman, Ray Kroc discovered the joys of selling while employed at his uncle's soda fountain. "That was where I learned you could influence people with a smile and enthusiasm," Kroc recalled in his autobiography, *Grinding It Out,* "and sell them a sundae when what they'd come for was a cup of coffee."

Over the years, Kroc sold coffee beans, sheet music, paper cups, Florida real estate, powdered instant beverages called "Malt-a-Plenty" and "Shake-a-Plenty," a gadget that could dispense whipped cream or shaving lather, square ice cream scoops, and a collapsible table-and-bench combination called "Fold-a-Nook" that retreated into the wall like a Murphy bed. The main problem with square scoops of ice cream, he found, was that they slid off the plate when you tried to eat them. Kroc used the same basic technique to sell all these things: he tailored his pitch to fit the buyer's tastes. Despite one setback after another, he kept at it, always convinced that success was just around the corner. "If you believe in it, and you believe in it hard," Kroc later told audiences, "it's impossible to fail. I don't care what it is — you can get it!"

Ray Kroc was selling milk-shake mixers in 1954 when he first visited the new McDonald's Self-Service Restaurant in San Bernardino. The McDonald brothers were two of his best customers. The Multimixer unit that Kroc sold could make five milk shakes at once. He wondered why the McDonald brothers needed eight of the machines. Kroc had visited a lot of restaurant kitchens, out on the road, demonstrating the Multimixer — and had never seen anything like the McDonald's Speedee Service System. "When I saw it," he later wrote, "I felt like some latter-day Newton who'd just had an Idaho potato caromed off his skull." He looked at the restaurant "through the eyes of a salesman" and envisioned putting a McDonald's at busy intersections all across the land.

Richard and "Mac" McDonald were less ambitious. They were clearing $100,000 a year in profits from the restaurant, a huge sum in those days. They already owned a big house and three Cadillacs. They didn't like to travel. They'd recently refused an offer from the Carnation Milk Company, which thought that opening more McDonald's would increase the sales of milk shakes. Nevertheless, Kroc convinced the brothers to sell him the right to franchise McDonald's nationwide. The two could stay at home, while Kroc traveled the country, making them even richer. A deal was signed. Years later Richard McDonald described his first memory of Kroc, a moment that would soon lead to the birth of the world's biggest restaurant chain: "This little fellow comes in, with a high voice, and says, 'hi.'"

After finalizing the agreement with the McDonald brothers, Kroc sent   12
a letter to Walt Disney. In 1917 the two men had both lied about their ages to join the Red Cross and see battle in Europe. A long time had clearly passed since their last conversation. "Dear Walt," the letter said. "I feel somewhat presumptuous addressing you in this way yet I feel sure you would not want me to address you any other way. My name is Ray A. Kroc . . . I look over the Company A picture we had taken at Sound Beach, Conn., many times and recall a lot of pleasant memories." After the warm-up came the pitch: "I have very recently taken over the national franchise of the McDonald's system. I would like to inquire if there may be an opportunity for a McDonald's in your Disneyland Development."

Walt Disney sent Kroc a cordial reply and forwarded his proposal to   13
an executive in charge of the theme park's concessions. Disneyland was still under construction, its opening was eagerly awaited by millions of American children, and Kroc may have had high hopes. According to one account, Disney's company asked Kroc to raise the price of McDonald's french fries from ten cents to fifteen cents; Disney would keep the extra nickel as payment for granting the concession; and the story ends with Ray Kroc refusing to gouge his loyal customers. The account seems highly unlikely, a belated effort by someone at McDonald's to put the best spin on a sales pitch that went nowhere. When Disneyland opened in July of 1955—an event that Ronald Reagan cohosted for ABC—it had food stands run by Welch's, Stouffer's, and Aunt Jemima's, but no McDonald's. Kroc was not yet in their league. His recollection of Walt Disney as a young man, briefly mentioned in *Grinding It Out,* is not entirely flattering. "He was regarded as a strange duck," Kroc wrote of Disney, "because whenever we had time off and went out on the town to chase girls, he stayed in camp drawing pictures."

Whatever feelings existed between the two men, Walt Disney proved in   14
many respects to be a role model for Ray Kroc. Disney's success had come much more quickly. At the age of twenty-one he'd left the Midwest and opened his own movie studio in Los Angeles. He was famous before turning thirty. In *The Magic Kingdom* (1997) Steven Watts describes Walt Disney's efforts to apply the techniques of mass production to Hollywood moviemaking. He greatly admired Henry Ford and introduced an assembly line and a rigorous division of labor at the Disney Studio, which was soon depicted as a "fun factory." Instead of drawing entire scenes, artists were given narrowly defined tasks, meticulously sketching and inking Disney

characters while supervisors watched them and timed how long it took them to complete each cel. During the 1930s the production system at the studio was organized to function like that of an automobile plant. "Hundreds of young people were being trained and fitted," Disney explained, "into a machine for the manufacture of entertainment."

The working conditions at Disney's factory, however, were not always fun. In 1941 hundreds of Disney animators went on strike, expressing support for the Screen Cartoonists Guild. The other major cartoon studios in Hollywood had already signed agreements with the union. Disney's father was an ardent socialist, and Disney's films had long expressed a populist celebration of the common man. But Walt's response to the strike betrayed a different political sensibility. He fired employees who were sympathetic to the union, allowed private guards to rough up workers on the picket line, tried to impose a phony company union, brought in an organized crime figure from Chicago to rig a settlement, and placed a full-page ad in *Variety* that accused leaders of the Screen Cartoonists Guild of being Communists. The strike finally ended when Disney acceded to the union's demands. The experience left him feeling embittered. Convinced that Communist agents had been responsible for his troubles, Disney subsequently appeared as a friendly witness before the House Un-American Activities Committee, served as a secret informer for the FBI, and strongly supported the Hollywood blacklist. During the height of labor tension at his studio, Disney had made a speech to a group of employees, arguing that the solution to their problems rested not with a labor union, but with *a good day's work*. "Don't forget this," Disney told them, "it's the law of the universe that the strong shall survive and the weak must fall by the way, and I don't give a damn what idealistic plan is cooked up, nothing can change that." 15

Decades later, Ray Kroc used similar language to outline his own political philosophy. Kroc's years on the road as a traveling salesman—carrying his own order forms and sample books, knocking on doors, facing each new customer alone, and having countless doors slammed in his face—no doubt influenced his view of humanity. "Look, it is ridiculous to call this an industry," Kroc told a reporter in 1972, dismissing any high-minded analysis of the fast food business. "This is not. This is rat eat rat, dog eat dog. I'll kill 'em, and I'm going to kill 'em before they kill me. You're talking about the American way of survival of the fittest." 16

While Disney backed right-wing groups and produced campaign ads for the Republican Party, Kroc remained aloof from electoral politics—with one notable exception. In 1972, Kroc gave $250,000 to President Nixon's reelection campaign, breaking the gift into smaller donations, funneling the money through various state and local Republican committees. Nixon had every reason to like McDonald's, long before tasting one of its hamburgers. Kroc had never met the president; the gift did not stem from any personal friendship or fondness. That year the fast food industry was lobbying Congress and the White House to pass new legislation— 17 known as the "McDonald's bill"—that would allow employers to pay six-teen- and seventeen-year-old kids wages 20 percent lower than the mini-mum wage. Around the time of Kroc's $250,000 donation, McDonald's crew members earned about $1.60 an hour. The subminimum wage pro-posal would reduce some wages to $1.28 an hour.

The Nixon administration supported the McDonald's bill and permit-   18
ted McDonald's to raise the price of its Quarter Pounders, despite the mandatory wage and price controls restricting other fast food chains. The size and the timing of Kroc's political contribution sparked Democratic accusations of influence peddling. Outraged by the charges, Kroc later called his critics "sons of bitches." The uproar left him wary of backing political candidates. Nevertheless, Kroc retained a soft spot for Calvin Coolidge, whose thoughts on hard work and self-reliance were promi-nently displayed at McDonald's corporate headquarters.

Better Living

Despite a passionate opposition to socialism and to any government   19
meddling with free enterprise, Walt Disney relied on federal funds in the 1940s to keep his business afloat. The animators' strike had left the Disney Studio in a precarious financial condition. Disney began to seek govern-ment contracts—and those contracts were soon responsible for 90 percent of his studio's output. During World War II, Walt Disney produced scores of military training and propaganda films, including *Food Will Win the War, High-Level Precision Bombing,* and *A Few Quick Facts about Venereal Disease.* After the war, Disney continued to work closely with top military officials and military contractors, becoming America's most popular exponent of Cold War science. For audiences living in fear of nuclear annihilation, Walt Disney became a source of reassurance, making the latest technical ad-vances seem marvelous and exciting. His faith in the goodness of American technology was succinctly expressed by the title of a film that the Disney Studio produced for Westinghouse Electric: *The Dawn of Better Living.*

Disney's passion for science found expression in "Tomorrowland," the   20
name given to a section of his theme park and to segments of his weekly television show. Tomorrowland encompassed everything from space travel to the household appliances of the future, depicting progress as a relent-less march toward greater convenience for consumers. And yet, from the very beginning, there was a dark side to this Tomorrowland. It celebrated technology without moral qualms. Some of the science it espoused later proved to be not so benign—and some of the scientists it promoted were unusual role models for the nation's children.

In the mid-1950s Wernher von Braun cohosted and helped produce a   21
series of Disney television shows on space exploration. "Man in Space" and the other Tomorrowland episodes on the topic were enormously popular and fueled public support for an American space program. At the time, von Braun was the U.S. Army's leading rocket scientist. He had served in

the same capacity for the German army during World War II. He had been an early and enthusiastic member of the Nazi party, as well as a major in the SS. At least 20,000 slave laborers, many of them Allied prisoners of war, died at Dora-Nordhausen, the factory where von Braun's rockets were built. Less than ten years after the liberation of Dora-Nordhausen, von Braun was giving orders to Disney animators and designing a ride at Disneyland called Rocket to the Moon. Heinz Haber, another key Tomorrowland adviser — and eventually the chief scientific consultant to Walt Disney Productions — spent much of World War II conducting research on high-speed, high-altitude flight for the Luftwaffe Institute for Aviation Medicine. In order to assess the risks faced by German air force pilots, the institute performed experiments on hundreds of inmates at the Dachau concentration camp near Munich. The inmates who survived these experiments were usually killed and then dissected. Haber left Germany after the war and shared his knowledge of aviation medicine with the U.S. Army Air Force. He later cohosted Disney's "Man in Space" with von Braun. When the Eisenhower administration asked Walt Disney to produce a show championing the civilian use of nuclear power, Heinz Haber was given the assignment. He hosted the Disney broadcast called "Our Friend the Atom" and wrote a popular children's book with the same title, both of which made nuclear fission seem fun, instead of terrifying. "Our Friend the Atom" was sponsored by General Dynamics, a manufacturer of nuclear reactors. The company also financed the atomic submarine ride at Disneyland's Tomorrowland.

The future heralded at Disneyland was one in which every aspect of American life had a corporate sponsor. Walt Disney was the most beloved children's entertainer in the country. He had unrivaled access to impressionable young minds — and other corporations, with other agendas to sell, were eager to come along for the ride. Monsanto built Disneyland's House of the Future, which was made of plastic. General Electric backed the Carousel of Progress, which featured an Audio-Animatronic housewife, standing in her futuristic kitchen, singing about "a great big beautiful tomorrow." Richfield Oil offered utopian fantasies about cars and a ride aptly named Autopia. "Here you leave Today," said the plaque at the entrance to Disneyland, "and enter the world of Yesterday, Tomorrow, and Fantasy." 22

At first, Disneyland offered visitors an extraordinary feeling of escape; 23 people had never seen anything like it. The great irony, of course, is that Disney's suburban, corporate world of Tomorrow would soon become the Anaheim of Today. Within a decade of its opening, Disneyland was no longer set amid a rural idyll of orange groves, it was stuck in the middle of cheap motels, traffic jams on the Santa Ana freeway, fast food joints, and industrial parks. Walt Disney frequently slept at his small apartment above the firehouse in Disneyland's Main Street, USA. By the early 1960s, the hard realities of Today were more and more difficult to ignore, and Disney began dreaming of bigger things, of Disney World, a place even farther removed from the forces he'd helped to unleash, a fantasy that could be even more thoroughly controlled.

Among other cultural innovations, Walt Disney pioneered the market- 24 ing strategy now known as "synergy." During the 1930s, he signed licensing agreements with dozens of firms, granting them the right to use Mickey Mouse on their products and in their ads. In 1938 *Snow White* proved a turning point in film marketing: Disney had signed seventy licensing deals prior to the film's release. Snow White toys, books, clothes, snacks, and records were already for sale when the film opened. Disney later used television to achieve a degree of synergy beyond anything that anyone had previously dared. His first television broadcast, *One Hour in Wonderland* (1950), culminated in a promotion for the upcoming Disney film *Alice in Wonderland*. His first television series, *Disneyland* (1954), provided weekly updates on the construction work at his theme park. ABC, which broadcast the show, owned a large financial stake in the Anaheim venture. Disneyland's other major investor, Western Printing and Lithography, printed Disney books such as *The Walt Disney Story of Our Friend the Atom*. In the guise of televised entertainment, episodes of *Disneyland* were often thinly disguised infomercials, promoting films, books, toys, an amusement park — and, most of all, Disney himself, the living, breathing incarnation of a brand, the man who neatly tied all the other commodities together into one cheerful, friendly, patriotic idea.

Ray Kroc could only dream, during McDonald's tough early years, of 25 having such marketing tools at his disposal. He was forced to rely instead on his wits, his charisma, and his instinct for promotion. Kroc believed completely in whatever he sold and pitched McDonald's franchises with an almost religious fervor. He also knew a few things about publicity, having auditioned talent for a Chicago radio station in the 1920s and performed in nightclubs for years. Kroc hired a publicity firm led by a gag writer and a former MGM road manager to get McDonald's into the news. Children would be the new restaurant chain's target customers. The McDonald brothers had aimed for a family crowd, and now Kroc improved and refined their marketing strategy. He'd picked the right moment. America was in the middle of a baby boom; the number of children had soared in the decade after World War II. Kroc wanted to create a safe, clean, all-American place for kids. The McDonald's franchise agreement required every new restaurant to fly the Stars and Stripes. Kroc understood that how he sold food was just as important as how the food tasted. He liked to tell people that he was really in show business, not the restaurant business. Promoting McDonald's to children was a clever, pragmatic decision. "A child who loves our TV commercials," Kroc explained, "and brings her grandparents to a McDonald's gives us two more customers."

The McDonald's Corporation's first mascot was Speedee, a winking 26 little chef with a hamburger for a head. The character was later renamed Archie McDonald. Speedy was the name of Alka-Seltzer's mascot, and it seemed unwise to imply any connection between the two brands. In 1960, Oscar Goldstein, a McDonald's franchisee in Washington, D.C., decided to sponsor *Bozo's Circus,* a local children's television show. Bozo's appearance at a McDonald's restaurant drew large crowds. When the local NBC station canceled *Bozo's Circus* in 1963, Goldstein hired its star — Willard Scott, later the weatherman on NBC's *Today* show — to invent a new clown who could make restaurant appearances. An ad agency designed the outfit, Scott came up with the name Ronald McDonald, and a star was born. Two years later the McDonald's Corporation introduced Ronald McDonald to the rest of the United States through a major ad campaign. But Willard Scott no longer played the part. He was deemed too overweight; McDonald's wanted someone thinner to sell its burgers, shakes, and fries.

The late-1960s expansion of the McDonald's restaurant chain coin- 27 cided with declining fortunes at the Walt Disney Company. Disney was no longer alive, and his vision of America embodied just about everything that kids of the sixties were rebelling against. Although McDonald's was hardly a promoter of whole foods and psychedelia, it had the great advantage of seeming new — and there was something trippy about Ronald McDonald, his clothes, and his friends. As McDonald's mascot began to rival Mickey Mouse in name recognition, Kroc made plans to create his own Disneyland. He was a highly competitive man who liked, whenever possible, to settle the score. "If they were drowning to death," Kroc once said about his business rivals, "I would put a hose in their mouth." He planned to buy 1,500 acres of land northeast of Los Angeles and build a new amusement park there. The park, tentatively called Western World, would have a cowboy theme. Other McDonald's executives opposed the idea, worried that Western World would divert funds from the restaurant business and lose millions. Kroc offered to option the land with his own money, but finally listened to his close advisers and scrapped the plan. The McDonald's Corporation later considered buying Astro World in Houston. Instead of investing in a large theme park, the company pursued a more decentralized approach. It built small Playlands and McDonaldlands all over the United States.

The fantasy world of McDonaldland borrowed a good deal from Walt 28 Disney's Magic Kingdom. Don Ament, who gave McDonaldland its distinctive look, was a former Disney set designer. Richard and Robert Sherman — who had written and composed, among other things, all the songs in Disney's *Mary Poppins,* Disneyland's "It's a Great, Big, Beautiful Tomorrow" and "It's a Small World, After All" — were enlisted for the first McDonaldland commercials. Ronald McDonald, Mayor McCheese, and the other characters in the ads made McDonald's seem like more than just another place to eat. McDonaldland — with its hamburger patch, apple pie trees, and Fillet-O-Fish fountain — had one crucial thing in common with Disneyland. Almost everything in it was for sale. McDonald's soon loomed large in the imagination of toddlers, the intended audience for the ads.

The restaurant chain evoked a series of pleasing images in a youngster's mind: bright colors, a playground, a toy, a clown, a drink with a straw, little pieces of food wrapped up like a present. Kroc had succeeded, like his old Red Cross comrade, at selling something intangible to children, along with their fries.

• • •

COMPREHENSION

1. In what ways are Walt Disney and Ray Kroc alike? What does Schlosser see as their most significant achievement?

2. What did Kroc obtain from the McDonald brothers? What did he do that they were unable or unwilling to do?

3. In what respects was Disney a role model for Kroc? How were the two men's political and social views alike?

4. According to Schlosser, what is "the great irony" of Disneyland (23)?

5. In what ways were Disney's Magic Kingdom and McDonaldland alike? What did both these fantasy worlds "sell" to children?

PURPOSE AND AUDIENCE

1. What is the thesis of this essay? Where does it appear?

2. What do you think Schlosser hoped to suggest in his title by using the phrase "your trusted friends"? What other titles might have worked?

3. This essay is a chapter from Schlosser's book *Fast Food Nation,* a pointed exposé of the fast-food industry in the United States. In what way do you think this essay contributes to the book's purpose? What do you think Schlosser hopes to accomplish by comparing Kroc to Disney?

STYLE AND STRUCTURE

1. Schlosser begins his essay with a four-paragraph description of the Ray A. Kroc Museum. What does this description add to the essay? Would a different introduction have been more effective?

2. What specific points does Schlosser make about both Kroc and Disney? Does he stress their similarities or their differences?

3. Is the essay organized primarily as a point-by-point or a subject-by-subject comparison? Why do you think Schlosser organized it the way he did?

4. What basis for comparison exists between Kroc and Disney? Do you think the two men share enough characteristics to justify a comparison?

5. Schlosser ends his essay by saying, "Kroc had succeeded, like his old Red Cross comrade [Disney], at selling something intangible to children, along with their fries" (28). What does he mean?

VOCABULARY PROJECTS

1. Define each of the following words as it is used in this selection.

façade (1)
franchisees (1)
dioramas (4)
Animatronic (4)
interactive (4)
optimistic (6)
charismatic (6)

entrepreneurs (7)
gouge (13)
populist (15)
embittered (15)
subsequently (15)
precarious (19)
encompassed (20)

qualms (20)
synergy (24)
culminated (24)
pragmatic (25)
psychedelia (27)

2. Make a list of five adjectives Schlosser uses to describe Kroc and five adjectives he uses to describe Disney. What qualities do these adjectives emphasize?

JOURNAL ENTRY

Do you think Kroc and Disney should be admired for their achievements? What facts about the two men lead you to your conclusion?

WRITING WORKSHOP

1. Write an essay in which you compare and contrast two people you know in terms of their attitudes toward their jobs.

2. Compare the way you study with the way someone you know studies. How are your study habits different from theirs?

3. Compare two businesses with which you are familiar — for example, home-improvement stores, clothing stores, or fast-food restaurants. In what way are these two businesses similar? In what way are they different? Do these businesses sell something "intangible" along with their merchandise?

COMBINING THE PATTERNS

Schlosser uses several **cause-and effect** paragraphs in his essay — paragraph 19, for example. Identify some of these cause-and-effect paragraphs. Why does he include these paragraphs? What do they contribute to the essay?

THEMATIC CONNECTIONS

- "The Peter Principle" (page 207)
- "The Ways We Lie" (page 470)
- "Tortillas" (page 513)
- "On Dumpster Diving" (page 660)

Sadie and Maud (Poetry)

Poet Gwendolyn Brooks (1917–2000) was born in Topeka, Kansas, and graduated from Wilson Junior College in Chicago, where she lived most of her life. She was on the faculty of Columbia College and Northeastern Illinois State College, and she was named the poet laureate of Illinois. Her first volume of poetry was *A Street in Bronzeville* (1945), named for the African-American neighborhood on the South Side of Chicago where she grew up. Among her many later collections are *Annie Allen* (1949), for which she was the first African American to win a Pulitzer Prize; *Riot* (1969), based on the violent unrest that gripped many inner-city neighborhoods following the assassination of Martin Luther King Jr.; and *Blacks* (1987). She also published books for children, a novel, and two volumes of memoir. The following poem is from *A Street in Bronzeville*.

Background: Because restrictive laws in Chicago in the 1940s prevented blacks from buying property outside of Bronzeville, the area was home to African Americans from all income levels as well as to many thriving black-owned businesses. Still, the opportunities available to women like Sadie and Maud in the 1940s were limited. Only about 12 percent of African Americans completed four years of high school (although numbers were higher in the North than in the South), and many fewer went on to college. Six out of ten African-American women were employed in low-paying domestic service positions, while fewer than 1 percent held professional positions, primarily as teachers in segregated schools.

Maud went to college.
Sadie stayed at home.
Sadie scraped life
With a fine-tooth comb.

She didn't leave a tangle in.   5
Her comb found every strand.
Sadie was one of the livingest chits
In all the land.

Sadie bore two babies
Under her maiden name.   10
Maud and Ma and Papa
Nearly died of shame.

When Sadie said her last so-long
Her girls struck out from home.
(Sadie had left as heritage   15
Her fine-tooth comb.)

Maud, who went to college,
Is a thin brown mouse.
She is living all alone
In this old house.   20

• • •

READING LITERATURE

1. What two ideas are being compared in the poem? In what way does the speaker let readers know when she is shifting her focus from one subject to another?

2. How accurate do you think the speaker's portrayals are? Is the speaker stereotyping the characters?

3. What comment do you think the poem is making about education? About society? About women? About African-American women?

JOURNAL ENTRY

Brooks wrote "Sadie and Maud" in 1945. What changes do you think she would have to make if she wrote her poem today?

THEMATIC CONNECTIONS

- "Finishing School" (page 89)
- Declaration of Sentiments and Resolutions (page 563)
- "Strange Tools" (page 697)

❖

WRITING ASSIGNMENTS FOR COMPARISON AND CONTRAST

1. Find a description of the same news event in two different magazines or newspapers. Write a comparison-and-contrast essay in which you discuss the similarities and differences between these two stories.

2. In the library, locate two children's books on the same subject — one written in the 1950s and one written within the last ten years. Write an essay discussing which elements are the same and which are different. Include a thesis statement that makes a point about the significance of the differences between the two books.

3. Write a comparison-and-contrast essay in which you show how your participation in an activity has either increased or decreased your enthusiasm for it. For example, has participating in a sport made you more enthusiastic about it than you were when you were just a fan? Or has knowing what actually goes on in the sport made you less enthusiastic?

4. Write an essay about a relative or friend you knew when you were a child. Consider in what respects your opinion of this person has changed.

5. Write an essay in which you compare and contrast the expectations that college professors and high school teachers have for their students, citing your own experiences as examples.

6. Since you started college, how have you changed? Write an essay that answers this question.

7. Taking careful notes, watch a local television news program and then a national news broadcast. Write an essay in which you compare the two programs, paying particular attention to the news content and to the broadcasting styles of the journalists.

8. Write an essay in which you compare your own early memories of school with those of a parent or an older relative.

9. How are the attitudes toward education different among students who work to finance their own education and students who do not? Your thesis statement should explain what differences exist and why.

10. Compare and contrast the college experiences of commuters and students who live in dorms on campus. Interview people in your classes to use as examples.

11. Write an essay in which you compare any two groups that have divergent values — vegetarians and meat eaters or smokers and nonsmokers, for example.

COLLABORATIVE ACTIVITY FOR COMPARISON AND CONTRAST

Form groups of four students. Assume that your college has hired the groups as consultants to suggest solutions for several problems students have been complaining about. Select the four areas — food, campus safety, parking, and class scheduling, for example — that you think are most in need of improvement. Then, as a group, write a short report to your college in which you describe the present conditions in these areas and compare them to the improvements you envision. (Be sure to organize your report as a comparison-

and-contrast essay.) Finally, have one person from each group read the group's report to the class. Decide as a class which group has the best suggestion.

INTERNET ASSIGNMENT FOR COMPARISON AND CONTRAST

Write an essay in which you compare and contrast the media coverage of men's and women's professional athletics. Use the following Web sites to familiarize yourself with how men's and women's sports are covered by the media.

CNN Sports Illustrated
<cnnsi.com>
This site offers up-to-the-minute sports coverage.

ESPN.com
<espn.go.com/main.html>
This site covers both men's and women's sports teams on both collegiate and professional levels.

Feminist Majority Foundation
<feminist.org/gateway/sp_exec2.html>
This site includes a spotlight on women's sports, links to sports magazines, information on grants and scholarships for athletes, and links to publications covering such topics as inequity and sex discrimination in sports.

10
Classification and Division

WHAT IS CLASSIFICATION AND DIVISION?

Division is the process of breaking a whole into parts; **classification** is the process of sorting individual items into categories. In the following paragraph from "Pregnant with Possibility," Gregory J. E. Rawlins divides Americans into categories based on their access to computer technology:

<table>
<tr>
<td>Topic sentence
identifies
categories</td>
<td>Today's computer technology is rapidly turning us into three completely new races: the superpoor, the rich, and the superrich. The superpoor are perhaps eight thousand in every ten thousand of us. The rich—me and you—make up most of the remaining two thousand, while the superrich are perhaps the last two of every ten thousand. Roughly speaking, the decisions of two superrich people control what almost two thousand of us do, and our decisions, in turn, control what the remaining eight thousand do. These groups are really like races since the group you're born into often determines which group your children will be born into.</td>
</tr>
</table>

Through **classification and division,** we can make sense of seemingly random ideas by putting scattered bits of information into useful, coherent order. By breaking a large group into smaller categories and assigning individual items to larger categories, we are able to identify relationships between a whole and its parts and among the parts themselves. (Remember, though, that classification involves more than simply comparing two items or enumerating examples; when you classify, you sort examples into a variety of different categories.)

In countless practical situations, classification and division brings order to chaos. Items in a Sunday newspaper are *classified* in clearly defined sections—international news, sports, travel, entertainment, and so on—so that hockey scores, for example, are not mixed up with real estate listings. Similarly, department stores are *divided* into different departments so that

431

managers can assign merchandise to particular areas and shoppers can know where to look for a particular item. Thus, order is brought to newspapers and department stores — and to supermarkets, biological hierarchies, and libraries — when a whole is divided into categories or sections and individual items are assigned to one or another of these subgroups.

Understanding Classification

Even though the interrelated processes of classification and division invariably occur together, they are two separate operations. When you *classify,* you begin with individual items and sort them into categories. Since most things have several different attributes, they can be classified in several different ways. For example, the most obvious way to classify the students who attend your school might be according to their year in college. But you could also classify students according to their major, racial or ethnic background, home state, grade-point average, or any number of other principles. The **principle of classification** you choose — the quality your items have in common — would depend on how you wished to approach the members of this large and diverse group.

Understanding Division

Division is the opposite of classification. When you *divide,* you start with a whole (an entire class) and break it into its individual parts. For example, you might start with the large general class *television shows* and divide it into categories: *comedy, drama, action/adventure,* and so forth. You could then divide each of these still further. *Action/adventure programs,* for example, might include *Westerns, police shows, spy dramas,* and so on — and each of these categories could be divided as well. Eventually, you would need to identify a particular principle of classification to help you assign specific programs to one category or another — that is, to classify them.

USING CLASSIFICATION AND DIVISION

Whenever you write an essay, you use classification and division to bring order to the invention stage of the writing process. For example, when you brainstorm, as Chapter 1 explains, you begin with your paper's topic and list all the related points you can think of. Next, you *divide* your topic into logical categories and *classify* the items in your brainstorming notes into one category or another, perhaps narrowing, expanding, or eliminating some categories — or some points — as you go along. This picking and choosing, sorting and grouping, enables you to condense and shape your material until it eventually suggests a thesis and the main points of your essay.

More specifically, certain topics and questions, because of the way they are worded, immediately suggest a classification-and-division pattern. Suppose, for example, you are asked, "What kinds of policies can be used to direct and control the national economy?" Here, the word *kinds* suggests classification and division. Other words — such as *types, varieties, aspects,* and *categories* — can also serve as clues.

PLANNING A CLASSIFICATION-AND-DIVISION ESSAY

Once you decide to use a classification-and-division pattern, you need to identify a principle of classification. Every group of people, things, or ideas can be categorized in many ways. When you are at your college bookstore with limited funds, the cost of different books may be the only principle of classification you use when deciding which ones to buy. As you consider which books to carry across campus, however, weight may matter more. Finally, as you study and read, the usefulness of the books will determine which ones you concentrate on. Similarly, when you organize an essay, the principle of classification you choose is determined by your writing situation — your assignment, your purpose, your audience, and your special knowledge and interests.

Selecting and Arranging Categories

After you define your principle of classification and apply it to your topic, you should select your categories by dividing a whole class into parts and grouping a number of different items together within each part. Next, you should decide how you will treat the categories in your essay. Just as a comparison-and-contrast essay makes comparable points about its subjects, so your classification-and-division essay should treat all categories similarly. When you discuss comparable points for each category, your readers are able to understand your distinctions among categories as well as your definition of each category.

Finally, you should arrange your categories in some logical order, so that readers can see how the categories are related and what their relative importance is. Whatever order you choose, it should be consistent with your purpose and with your essay's thesis.

☑ CHECKLIST: ESTABLISHING CATEGORIES

- *All the categories should result from the same principle.* If you decide to divide *television shows* into *soap operas, police shows,* and the like, it is not logical to include *children's programs,* for this category results from one principle (target audience) while the others result from another principle (genre). Similarly, if you were classifying undergraduates at your school according to their year, you would not include *students receiving financial aid.*

- *All the categories should be at the same level.* In the series *comedy, drama, action/adventure,* and *Westerns,* the last item, *Westerns,* does not belong because it is at a lower level — that is, it is a subcategory of *action/adventure.* Likewise, *sophomores* (a subcategory of *undergraduates*) does not belong in the series *undergraduates, graduate students, continuing education students.*

(continued on next page)

(continued from previous page)

- *You should treat all categories that are significant and relevant to your discussion.* Include enough categories to make your point, with no important omissions and no overlapping categories. In a review of a network's fall television lineup, the series *sitcoms, soap operas, police shows,* and *detective shows* is incomplete because it omits important categories like *news programs, game shows, reality shows,* and *documentaries;* moreover, *detective shows* may overlap with *police shows.* In the same way, the series *freshmen, sophomores, juniors,* and *transfers* is illogical: the important group *seniors* has been omitted, and *transfers* may include *freshmen, sophomores,* and *juniors.*

Formulating a Thesis Statement

Like other kinds of essays, a classification-and-division essay should have a thesis. Your thesis statement should identify your subject, present the categories you will discuss, and perhaps show readers the relationships of your categories to one another and to the subject as a whole. In addition, your thesis statement should tell your readers why your categories are significant or establish their relative value. For example, simply listing different kinds of investments would be pointless. Instead, your thesis statement might note their relative strengths and weaknesses and pehaps make recommendations based on your assessment. Similarly, a term paper about a writer's major works would accomplish little if it merely categorized his or her writings. Instead, your thesis statement should communicate your evaluation of these works, perhaps demonstrating that some deserve higher public regard than others.

Using Transitions

When you write a classification-and-division essay, you use transitional words and phrases both to introduce your categories (*the first category, one category,* and so on) and to move readers from one category to the next (*the second category, the next category, another category,* and so on). In addition, transitional words and expressions can show readers the relationships between categories — for example, whether one category is more important than another (*a more important category, the most important category,* and so on). A more complete list of transitions appears on page 43.

STRUCTURING A CLASSIFICATION-AND-DIVISION ESSAY

Once you have formulated your essay's thesis and established your categories, you should plan your classification-and-division essay around the same three major sections that other essays have: introduction, body, and conclusion. Your *introduction* should orient your readers by mentioning your topic, the principle by which your material is classified, and the individual categories you plan to discuss; your thesis is also usually stated in the introduction. In the subsequent *body paragraphs,* you should treat the categories one by one in the same order as in your introduction. Finally, your *conclusion* should restate your thesis, summing up the points you have made and perhaps considering their implications.

Suppose you are preparing a term paper on Mark Twain's nonfiction works for an American literature course. You have read selections from *Roughing It, Life on the Mississippi,* and *The Innocents Abroad.* Besides these travel narratives, you have read parts of Twain's autobiography as well as some of his correspondence and essays. When you realize that the works you have studied can easily be classified as four different types of Twain's nonfiction — travel narratives, essays, letters, and autobiography — you decide to use classification and division to structure your essay. Therefore, you first divide the large class *Twain's nonfiction prose* into major categories — his travel narratives, essays, autobiography, and letters. Then you classify the individual works, assigning each work to one of these categories, which you will discuss one at a time. Your purpose is to persuade readers to reconsider the reputations of some of these works, and you formulate your thesis accordingly. You might then prepare a formal outline like this one for the body of your paper:

> *Thesis statement:* Most readers know Mark Twain as a novelist, but his nonfiction works — his travel narratives, essays, letters, and especially his autobiography — deserve more attention.

I. Travel narratives
   A. *Roughing It*
   B. *The Innocents Abroad*
   C. *Life on the Mississippi*

II. Essays
   A. "Fenimore Cooper's Literary Offenses"
   B. "How to Tell a Story"
   C. "The Awful German Language"

III. Letters
   A. To W. D. Howells
   B. To his family

IV. Autobiography

Because this will be a long paper, each of the outline's divisions will have several subdivisions, and each subdivision might require several paragraphs.

This outline illustrates all the characteristics of an effective classification-and-division essay. To begin with, Twain's nonfiction works are classified according to a single principle of classification — literary genre. (Depending on your purpose, of course, another principle — such as theme or subject matter — could work just as well.) In addition to illustrating a single principle of classification, the outline reveals that the paper's categories are on the same level (each is a different literary genre) and that all relevant categories are included. Had you left out *essays,* for example, you would have been unable to classify several significant works of nonfiction.

This outline also arranges the four categories so they will support your thesis most effectively. Because you believe Twain's travel narratives are somewhat overrated, you plan to discuss them early in your paper. Similarly, because you think the autobiography would make your best case for the merit of the nonfiction works as a whole, you decide it should be placed last. (Of course, you could arrange your categories in several other orders, such as shorter to longer works or least to most popular, depending on the thesis your paper will support.)

Finally, this outline helps you to treat all categories comparably in your paper. Now, you should identify each main point in your rough draft and compare the order of points from category to category. Your case would be weakened if, for example, you inadvertently skipped style in your discussion of Twain's letters while discussing style for every other category. This omission might lead your readers to suspect that you had not done enough research on the letters or that the style of Twain's letters did not measure up to the style of his other works.

REVISING A CLASSIFICATION-AND-DIVISION ESSSAY

When you revise a classsification-and-division essay, consider the items on the Revision Checklist on page 54. In addition, pay special attention to the items on the checklist below, which apply specifically to revising classification-and-division essays.

✅ REVISION CHECKLIST: CLASSIFICATION AND DIVISION

- Does your assignment call for classification and division?
- Have you identified a principle of classification for your material?
- Have you identified the categories you plan to discuss and decided how you will treat them?
- Have you arranged your categories in a logical order?
- Have you treated all categories similarly?
- Does your essay have a clearly stated thesis that identifies your subject and the categories you will discuss and indicates the significance of your classification?
- Have you used transitional words and phrases to show the relationships among categories?

EDITING A CLASSIFICATION-AND-DIVISION ESSAY

When you edit your classification-and-division essay, you should follow the guidelines on the Editing Checklist on page 66. In addition, you should focus on the grammar, mechanics, and punctuation issues that are most relevant to classification-and-division essays. One of these issues — using a colon to introduce your categories — is discussed below.

For more practice in using colons correctly, visit **Exercise Central** at **<bedfordstmartins.com/patterns/colons>**.

GRAMMAR IN CONTEXT : Using a Colon to Introduce Your Categories

When you state the thesis of a classification-and-division essay, you often give readers an overview of your essay by listing the categories you will discuss. Frequently, you introduce this list of categories with a **colon,** a punctuation mark whose purpose is to direct readers to look ahead for a series, list, clarification, or explanation.

When you use a colon to introduce your categories, the colon must be preceded by a complete sentence.*

Correct: "I see four kinds of pressure working on college students today: economic pressure, parental pressure, peer pressure, and self-induced pressure" (Zinsser 448).

Incorrect: Four kinds of pressure working on college students today are: economic pressure, parental pressure, peer pressure, and self-induced pressure.

In any list or series of three or more categories, the categories should be separated by commas, with a comma preceding the *and* that separates the last two items. This last comma prevents confusion by ensuring that readers will be able to see at a glance exactly how many categories you are discussing.

Correct: economic pressure, parental pressure, peer pressure, and self-induced pressure (four categories)

Incorrect: economic pressure, parental pressure, peer pressure and self-induced pressure (without the final comma, it might appear that only three categores are being discussed)

NOTE: Items in a list or series are always stated in **parallel** terms.

☑ EDITING CHECKLIST: CLASSIFICATION AND DIVISION

- Do you introduce your list of categories with a colon preceded by a complete sentence?
- Are the items on your list of categories separated by commas?
- Do you include a comma before the *and* that connects the last two items in your list?
- Do you state the items on your list in parallel terms?

---

*The quotation used as an example below comes from the essay "College Pressures," which appears later in this chapter.

► A STUDENT WRITER: CLASSIFICATION AND DIVISION

The following classification-and-division essay was written by Josie Martinez for an education course. Her assignment was to look back at her own education and to consider what she had learned so far. The essay divides a whole — college classes — into four categories.

What I Learned (and Didn't Learn) in College

Introduction

College classes are as varied as the students who take them. As a result, a class that is perfect for one student — in size, format, subject matter, and teaching style — may be the same class that another student hates and learns little or nothing from. Nevertheless, despite the variety of experiences that different students have with different courses, most college classes can be classified into one of four categories.

Categories identified

First, there are courses that students love — ideal learning environments in which they enjoy both the subject matter and the professor-student interaction. Far from these ideal courses are those that students find completely worthless in terms of subject matter, atmosphere, and teaching style. Somewhere between these two extremes are two kinds of courses that can be classified into another pair of opposites: those courses that students expect to enjoy and learn much from but are disappointing and those courses that students are initially not interested in but that exceed their expectations. Knowing that these four categories exist can help students accept the fact that one disappointing class is not a disaster.

Thesis statement

First category: ideal class

One of the best college courses that I have taken so far as a college student was my Shakespeare class. The professor who taught it had a great sense of humor and was liberal in terms of what she allowed in her classroom — for example, controversial Shakespeare adaptations and virtually any discussion, relevant or irrelevant. The students in the class — English majors and non-English majors, those who were interested in the plays as theater and those who preferred to study them as literature — shared an enthusiasm for Shakespeare, and they were eager to engage in lively discussions of the material. This class gave us a thorough knowledge of Shakespeare's plays (tragedies, histories, comedies) as well as an understanding of his life. We also developed our analytical skills through our discussions of the plays and films as well as through special projects, which included a character profile presentation and an abstract art presentation in which we related a work of art to one of the plays. This class was an ideal learning environment not only because of the wealth of material that we were exposed to but also because of the respect with which our professor treated us: we were her colleagues, and she was as willing to learn from us as we were to learn from her.

Second category: worthless class

In contrast to this ideal class, one of the most worthless courses I have taken in college was Movement Education. As an education major, I expected to like this class, and several other students who had taken it told me that it was both easy and enjoyable. The class consisted of playing children's games and learning the theory behind what made certain activities appropriate and inappropriate for children of various ages. The only requirement for this class was that we had to write note cards explaining how to play each game so that we could use them for reference in our future teaching experiences. Unfortunately, I never really enjoyed the games we played, and I have long since discarded my note cards and forgotten how to play the games — or even what they were.

4

Third category: disappointing class

Although I looked forward to taking Intro- 5
duction to Astronomy, I was very disappointed
in this class. I had hoped to satisfy my curiosity about the universe outside our solar system, but the instructor devoted most of the
semester to a detailed study of the earth and
the other bodies in our own solar system. In
addition, a large part of our work included
charting orbits and processing distance equations—work that I found both difficult and
boring. Furthermore, we spent little class time
learning how to use a telescope and locate
objects in the sky. In short, I gained little
information from the class, learning only how
to solve equations that I would never confront
again and how to chart orbits that had already
been charted.

Fourth category: unexpectedly valuable class

In direct contrast to my astronomy class, 6
a religion class called Paul and the Early
Church was much more rewarding than I had
anticipated. Having attended Catholic school
for thirteen years, I assumed that this course
would offer me little that was new to me. However, because the class took a historical
approach to studying Paul's biblical texts, I
found that I learned more about Christianity
than I had in all my previous religion classes.
We learned about the historical validity of
Paul and other texts in the Bible and how they
were derived from various sources and passed
orally through several generations before being
written down and translated into different
languages. In this way, we studied the texts
primarily for their linguistic value, determining the significance of certain words and how
various meanings can be derived from different
translations of the same passage. This class
was unlike any of my other religion classes
in that it encouraged me to study the texts
objectively, leaving me with a new and valuable

understanding of material I had been exposed to for most of my life.

Conclusion   Although each student's learning experi-   7
ence in college will be different—because
every student has a different learning style,
is interested in different subjects, and takes
courses at different schools taught by different professors—all college students' experiences are similar in one respect. All students
Summary of four   will encounter the same kinds of courses: those
categories   that are ideal, those that are worthless, those
that they learn little from despite their inter-
est in the subject, and those that they learn
from and become engaged in despite their low
Restatement of thesis   expectations. Understanding that these categories exist is important because it can teach
students that even if one course is a disappointment, another will be more interesting—
or even exciting. For this reason, they should
not be discouraged by a course they do not
like; the best classes are almost certainly
still in their future.

Points for Special Attention

Thesis and Support   Josie's purpose in writing this essay was to communicate to her professor and the other students in her education class what she had learned from the classes she had taken so far in college. Knowing that other students in her class would not have taken most of the same courses, Josie knew she had to provide a lot of detail. She was also careful to include a thesis that made her purpose clear to her readers.

Organization   As she reviewed the various courses she had taken and took stock of their strengths and weaknesses, Josie saw a classification scheme emerging. As soon as she noticed this, she organized her material into four categories. Rather than discuss the four kinds of classes from best to worst or from worst to best, Josie decided to present them as two opposing pairs: ideal class and worthless class, surprisingly disappointing class and unexpectedly worthwhile class.

Overview of Categories   In paragraph 2, Josie gives readers an overview of the four categories she discusses in her essay. She could have listed these categories at the end of paragraph 1, but she thought she needed to give more explanation to readers before she went on to state her thesis and discuss the categories that would support it.

Transitions between Categories   Josie uses clear topic sentences to move readers from one category to the next and indicate the relationship of each category to another.

"One of the best college courses that I have taken so far as a college student was my Shakespeare class." (par. 3)

"In contrast to this ideal class, one of the most worthless courses I have taken in college was Movement Education." (par. 4)

"Although I looked forward to taking Introduction to Astronomy, I was very disappointed in this class." (par. 5)

"In direct contrast to my astronomy class, a religion class called Paul and the Early Church was much more rewarding than I had anticipated." (par. 6)

These four sentences distinguish the four categories from one another and also help to communicate Josie's direction and emphasis.

Focus on Revision

An earlier draft of Josie's essay, which she discussed with her classmates in a peer editing session, did not include very helpful topic sentences. Instead, the sentences were vague and unfocused.

"One class I took in college was a Shakespeare course."

"Another class I took was Movement Education."

"I looked forward to taking Introduction to Astronomy."

"My experience with a religion class was very different."

Although her first-draft thesis statement listed the categories and explained how they differed, Josie's classmates advised her to revise her topic sentences so it would be clear which category she was discussing in each body paragraph. Josie took the advice of her peer editing group and revised these topic sentences. After reading her next draft, she felt confident that her categories — listed in paragraph 2, in her topic sentences, and again in her conclusion — were clear and distinct.

Even after making these revisions, however, Josie felt her paper needed some additional fine-tuning. In her final draft, she planned to add some material to paragraphs 4 and 5. At first, because she had dismissed Movement Education as completely worthless and Introduction to Astronomy as disappointing, Josie felt she did not have to say much about them. When she reread her paper, however, she realized she needed to explain the shortcomings of the two classes more fully so others would understand why they had little value for her. (A sample peer editing worksheet for classification and division can be found on the *Patterns for College Writing* Web site at <bedfordstmartins.com/patterns>.)

Each of the following selections is developed by means of classification and division. In some cases, the pattern is used to explain ideas; in others, it is used to persuade the reader. The first selection, a pair of visual texts, is followed by questions designed to illustrate how classification and division can operate in visual form.

Medical Exam of Male Immigrants, 1907 (Photo)

❖

Aliens Debarred from the United States by Causes: 1892–1931 (Chart)

TABLE 104.—*Aliens debarred, by causes, 1892–1931*

Period or year (ended June 30)—	Idiots	Imbeciles	Feeble-minded	Insane persons	Epileptics	Constitutional psychopathic inferiority	Surgeon's certificate of mental defect which may affect alien's ability to earn a living, other than idiots, imbeciles, feeble-minded, epileptics, insanity, constitutional psychopathic inferiority	Tuberculosis (noncontagious)	Loathsome or dangerous contagious diseases	Surgeon's certificate of physical defect which may affect alien's ability to earn a living, other than loathsome or dangerous contagious diseases or noncontagious tuberculosis[1]	Chronic alcoholism	Paupers or likely to become public charges
1892–1907	211			628				6	13,822			54,255
1908	20	45	121	159	25			6	2,900	870		3,710
1909	18	42	121	141	26			8	2,382	370		4,402
1910	16	40	125	169	29			5	3,123	312		15,918
1911	12	26	126	111	33			15	2,831	3,055		12,039
1912	10	44	110	105	28			15	1,733	2,288		8,160
1913	18	54	483	175	23			2	2,562	4,208		7,946
1914	14	68	995	172	25			4	3,253	6,537		15,756
1915	6	27	302	98	30		29	1	1,701	925		15,557
1916	5	17	224	123	28		46	3	1,153	1,657		10,392
1917	9	19	224	112	34	3	55	7	1,495	1,679	10	7,881
1918	4	5	19	64	31	20	10	17	469	305	24	2,825
1919	1	7	29	48	19	37	9	3	385	334	10	4,002
1920	9	20	49	56	27	38	9	11	541	353	8	5,308
1921	10	31	63	93	11	39	15	4	856	620	5	5,875
1922	7	35	70	82	12	31	22	14	672	573	2	5,531
1923	10	17	74	72	15	55	22	5	955	646	3	8,242
1924	4	21	80	65	20	69	41	9	1,486	706	5	8,134
1925	3	10	39	47	13	25	14	1	562	345	8	3,031
1926	6	9	64	48	13	67	30	8	507	199	8	3,595
1927	1	4	31	26	8	28	26	3	308	113	4	1,848
1928			10	13	3	7	1	1	196	103		344
1929		1	2	18	1	1		2	171	98		269
1930	1		3	11	3	7	4	1	102	59		252
1931			2	4	1	12	1		68	35		112

[1] Prior to 1915 includes both mental and physical defects.

• • •

READING IMAGES

1. Look closely at the chart pictured above, paying special attention to the categories listed across the top. (These twelve categories indicate the various causes for which potential immigrants could be prevented from entering the United States.) What different principles of classification might be used to assign these categories into groups? Which principle of classification seems to make the most sense? Why?

2. Guided by the principle of classification you selected in question 1 above, arrange the various categories into three or four logical groups.

3. Study the photograph at left. What is happening? What relationship do you see between this photo and the chart? Be as specific as you can.

JOURNAL ENTRY

Write a paragraph that summarizes the information in the chart on page 445, focusing on dates and categories, not on statistics. Explain your emotional response to the chart and to the photograph on page 444. When you have finished, give your paragraph a title that sums up your reaction.

THEMATIC CONNECTIONS

- "Words Left Unspoken" (page 153)
- "The Catbird Seat" (page 214)
- "Burdens" (page 509)
- "Why Fear National ID Cards?" (page 590)

WILLIAM ZINSSER

❖ _____

College Pressures

Born in 1922 in New York City, William Zinsser graduated from Princeton University in 1944. He worked at the *New York Herald Tribune* as a feature and editorial writer, and he was a columnist for *Life* magazine and the *New York Times.* Zinsser has also taught English at Yale University and is the author of several books on writing, including *On Writing Well: The Classic Guide to Writing Nonfiction* (25th anniversary edition, 2001). He has also written works on American culture, including *Spring Training* (1989), about the culture of baseball, and *Easy to Remember: Great American Songwriters and Their Songs* (2001).

Background: While the following essay focuses on the kinds of pressures facing Yale students in 1979, many of these remain relevant for college students today: the need to develop time management and study skills appropriate for college work, the desire for good grades, familial expectations, the need to find employment in a potentially competitive job market after graduation. In addition, many college students today face pressures unknown to most students twenty-five years ago. According to the U.S. Department of Education's National Center for Education Statistics, only about 25 percent of current undergraduates fit the "traditional" model of eighteen- to twenty-two-year-old full-time students still supported primarily by their parents. Increasingly, college undergraduates are adults, supporting themselves—and sometimes families—and funding their own education through full- or part-time employment. Moreover, the average student faces some $17,000 of college-related debt by the time he or she graduates.

Dear Carlos: I desperately need a dean's excuse for my chem   1
midterm which will begin in about 1 hour. All I can say is that
I totally blew it this week. I've fallen incredibly, inconceivably
behind.

Carlos: Help! I'm anxious to hear from you. I'll be in my room   2
and won't leave it until I hear from you. Tomorrow is the last
day for. . . .

Carlos: I left town because I started bugging out again. I stayed   3
up all night to finish a take home make-up exam and am typing
it to hand in on the 10th. It was due on the 5th. P.S. I'm going
to the dentist. Pain is pretty bad.

Carlos: Probably by Friday I'll be able to get back to my studies.   4
Right now I'm going to take a long walk. This whole thing has
taken a lot out of me.

Carlos: I'm really up the proverbial creek. The problem is I   5
really *bombed* the history final. Since I need that course for my
major. . . .

Carlos: Here follows a tale of woe. I went home this weekend, 6
had to help my Mom, & caught a fever so didn't have much time
to study. My professor. . . .

Carlos: Aargh! Nothing original but everything's piling up at 7
once. To be brief, my job interview. . . .

Hey Carlos, good news! I've got mononucleosis. 8

Who are these wretched supplicants, scribbling notes so laden with 9
anxiety, seeking such miracles of postponement and balm? They are men
and women who belong to Bradford College, one of the twelve residential
colleges at Yale University, and the messages are just a few of the hundreds
that they left for their dean, Carlos Hortas — often slipped under his door
at 4 A.M. — last year.

But students like the ones who wrote those notes can also be found on 10
campuses from coast to coast — especially in New England and at many
other private colleges across the country that have high academic standards and highly motivated students. Nobody could doubt that the notes
are real. In their urgency and their gallows humor they are authentic voices
of a generation that is panicky to succeed.

My own connection with the message writers is that I am master of 11
Bradford College. I live in its Gothic quadrangle and know the students
well. (We have 485 of them.) I am privy to their hopes and fears — and also
to their stereo music and their piercing cries in the dead of night ("Does
anybody ca-a-are?"). If they went to Carlos to ask how to get through tomorrow, they come to me to ask how to get through the rest of their lives.

Mainly I try to remind them that the road ahead is a long one and that 12
it will have more unexpected turns than they think. There will be plenty of
time to change jobs, change careers, change whole attitudes and approaches.
They don't want to hear such liberating news. They want a map — right
now — that they can follow unswervingly to career security, financial security, Social Security, and, presumably, a prepaid grave.

What I wish for all students is some release from the clammy grip of 13
the future. I wish them a chance to savor each segment of their education
as an experience in itself and not as a grim preparation for the next step. I
wish them the right to experiment, to trip and fall, to learn that defeat is as
instructive as victory and is not the end of the world.

My wish, of course, is naive. One of the few rights that America does 14
not proclaim is the right to fail. Achievement is the national god, venerated
in our media — the million-dollar athlete, the wealthy executive — and glorified in our praise of possessions. In the presence of such a potent state
religion, the young are growing up old.

I see four kinds of pressure working on college students today: eco- 15
nomic pressure, parental pressure, peer pressure, and self-induced pressure.
It is easy to look around for villains — to blame the colleges for charging
too much money, the professors for assigning too much work, the parents
for pushing their children too far, the students for driving themselves too
hard. But there are no villains, only victims.

"In the late 1960s," one dean told me, "the typical question that I got from students was 'Why is there so much suffering in the world?' or 'How can I make a contribution?' Today it's 'Do you think it would look better for getting into law school if I did a double major in history and political science, or just majored in one of them?'" Many other deans confirmed this pattern. One said: "They're trying to find an edge—the intangible something that will look better on paper if two students are about equal."

Note the emphasis on looking better. The transcript has become a sacred document, the passport to security. How one appears on paper is more important than how one appears in person. *A* is for Admirable and *B* is for Borderline, even though, in Yale's official system of grading, *A* means "excellent" and *B* means "very good." Today, looking very good is no longer good enough, especially for students who hope to go on to law school or medical school. They know that entrance into the better schools will be an entrance into the better law firms and better medical practices where they will make a lot of money. They also know that the odds are harsh. Yale Law School, for instance, matriculates 170 students from an applicant pool of 3,700; Harvard enrolls 550 from a pool of 7,000.

It's all very well for those of us who write letters of recommendation for our students to stress the qualities of humanity that will make them good lawyers or doctors. And it's nice to think that admission officers are really reading our letters and looking for the extra dimension of commitment or concern. Still, it would be hard for a student not to visualize these officers shuffling so many transcripts studded with *A*s that they regard a *B* as positively shameful.

The pressure is almost as heavy on students who just want to graduate and get a job. Long gone are the days of the "gentleman's *C*," when students journeyed through college with a certain relaxation, sampling a wide variety of courses—music, art, philosophy, classics, anthropology, poetry, religion—that would send them out as liberally educated men and women. If I were an employer I would rather employ graduates who have this range and curiosity than those who narrowly pursued safe subjects and high grades. I know countless students whose inquiring minds exhilarate me. I like to hear the play of their ideas. I don't know if they're getting *A*s or *C*s, and I don't care. I also like them as people. The country needs them, and they will find satisfying jobs. I tell them to relax. They can't.

Nor can I blame them. They live in a brutal economy. Tuition, room, and board at most private colleges now comes to at least $7,000, not counting books and fees.* This might seem to suggest that the colleges are getting rich. But they are equally battered by inflation. Tuition covers only 60 percent of what it costs to educate a student, and ordinarily the remainder comes from what colleges receive in endowments, grants, and gifts. Now the remainder keeps being swallowed by cruel costs—higher every year—of just opening the doors. Heating oil is up. Insurance is up. Postage

---

*EDS. NOTE—Zinsser's essay was published in 1979; the figures quoted for tuition and other expenses would be much higher today.

is up. Health-premium costs are up. Everything is up. Deficits are up. We are witnessing in America the creation of a brotherhood of paupers—colleges, parents, and students, joined by the common bond of debt.

Today it is not unusual for a student, even if he works part time at col- 21 lege and full time during the summer, to accrue $5,000 in loans after four years—loans that he must start to repay within one year after graduation. Exhorted at commencement to go forth into the world, he is already behind as he goes forth. How could he not feel under pressure throughout college to prepare for this day of reckoning? I have used "he" incidentally, only for brevity. Women at Yale are under no less pressure to justify their expensive education to themselves, their parents, and society. In fact, they are probably under more pressure. For although they leave college superbly equipped to bring fresh leadership to traditionally male jobs, society hasn't yet caught up with this fact.

Along with economic pressure goes parental pressure. Inevitably, the 22 two are deeply intertwined.

I see many students taking pre-medical courses with joyless tenacity. 23 They go off to their labs as if they were going to the dentist. It saddens me because I know them in other corners of their life as cheerful people.

"Do you want to go to medical school?" I ask them. 24

"I guess so," they say, without conviction, or "Not really." 25

"Then why are you going?" 26

"Well, my parents want me to be a doctor. They're paying all this 27 money and . . ."

Poor students, poor parents. They are caught in one of the oldest webs 28 of love and duty and guilt. The parents mean well; they are trying to steer their sons and daughters toward a secure future. But the sons and daughters want to major in history or classics or philosophy—subjects with no "practical" value. Where's the payoff on the humanities? It's not easy to persuade such loving parents that the humanities do indeed pay off. The intellectual faculties developed by studying subjects like history and classics—an ability to synthesize and relate, to weigh cause and effect, to see events in perspective—are just the faculties that make creative leaders in business or almost any general field. Still, many fathers would rather put their money on courses that point toward a specific profession—courses that are pre-law, pre-medical, pre-business, or, as I sometimes heard it put, "pre-rich."

But the pressure on students is severe. They are truly torn. One part of 29 them feels obliged to fulfill their parents' expectations; after all, their parents are older and presumably wiser. Another part tells them that the expectations that are right for their parents are not right for them.

I know a student who wants to be an artist. She is very obviously an 30 artist and will be a good one—she has already had several modest exhibits. Meanwhile she is growing as a well-rounded person and taking humanistic subjects that will enrich the inner resources out of which her art will grow. But her father is strongly opposed. He thinks that an artist is a "dumb" thing to be. The student vacillates and tries to please everybody. She keeps up with her art somewhat furtively and takes some of the "dumb" courses her father wants her to take—at least they are dumb courses for her. She is a free spirit on a campus of tense students—no small achievement in itself—and she deserves to follow her muse.

Peer pressure and self-induced pressure are also intertwined, and they begin almost at the beginning of freshman year. 31

"I had a freshman student I'll call Linda," one dean told me, "who came in and said she was under terrible pressure because her roommate, Barbara, was much brighter and studied all the time. I couldn't tell her that Barbara had come in two hours earlier to say the same thing about Linda." 32

The story is almost funny—except that it's not. It's symptomatic of all the pressures put together. When every student thinks every other student is working harder and doing better, the only solution is to study harder still. I see students going off to the library every night after dinner and coming back when it closes at midnight. I wish they could sometimes forget about their peers and go to a movie. I hear the clacking of typewriters in the hours before dawn. I see the tension in their eyes when exams are approaching and papers are due: *"Will I get everything done?"* 33

Probably they won't. They will get sick. They will get "blocked." They will sleep. They will oversleep. They will bug out. *Hey Carlos, help!* 34

Part of the problem is that they do more than they are expected to do. A professor will assign five-page papers. Several students will start writing ten-page papers to impress him. Then more students will write ten-page papers, and a few will raise the ante to fifteen. Pity the poor student who is still just doing the assignment. 35

"Once you have twenty or thirty percent of the student population deliberating overexerting," one dean points out, "it's bad for everybody. When a teacher gets more and more effort from his class, the student who is doing normal work can be perceived as not doing well. The tactic works, psychologically." 36

Why can't the professor just cut back and not accept longer papers? He can, and he probably will. But by then the term will be half over and the damage done. Grade fever is highly contagious and not easily reversed. Besides, the professor's main concern is with his course. He knows his students only in relation to the course and doesn't know that they are also overexerting in their other courses. Nor is it really his business. He didn't sign up for dealing with the student as a whole person and with all the emotional baggage the student brought along from home. That's what deans, masters, chaplains, and psychiatrists are for. 37

To some extent this is nothing new: a certain number of professors have always been self-contained islands of scholarship and shyness, more comfortable with books than with people. But the new pauperism has widened the gap still further, for professors who actually like to spend time with students don't have as much time to spend. They also are overexerting. If they are young, they are busy trying to publish in order not to perish, hanging by their fingernails onto a shrinking profession. If they are old 38 and tenured, they are buried under the duties of administering departments — as departmental chairmen or members of committees — that have been thinned out by the budgetary axe.

Ultimately it will be the students' own business to break the circles in 39 which they are trapped. They are too young to be prisoners of their parents' dreams and their classmates' fears. They must be jolted into believing in themselves as unique men and women who have the power to shape their own future.

"Violence is being done to the undergraduate experience," says Carlos 40 Hortas. "College should be open-ended: at the end it should open many, many roads. Instead, students are choosing their goal in advance, and their choices narrow as they go along. It's almost as if they think that the country has been codified in the type of jobs that exist — that they've got to fit into certain slots. Therefore, fit into the best-paying slot.

"They ought to take chances. Not taking chances will lead to a life of 41 colorless mediocrity. They'll be comfortable. But something in the spirit will be missing."

I have painted too drab a portrait of today's students, making them 42 seem a solemn lot. That is only half of their story; if they were so dreary I wouldn't so thoroughly enjoy their company. The other half is that they are easy to like. They are quick to laugh and to offer friendship. They are not introverts. They are usually kind and are more considerate of one another than any student generation I have known.

Nor are they so obsessed with their studies that they avoid sports and 43 extracurricular activities. On the contrary, they juggle their crowded hours to play on a variety of teams, perform with musical and dramatic groups, and write for campus publications. But this in turn is one more cause of anxiety. There are too many choices. Academically, they have 1,300 courses to select from; outside class they have to decide how much spare time they can spare and how to spend it.

This means that they engage in fewer extracurricular pursuits than 44 their predecessors did. If they want to row on the crew and play in the symphony they will eliminate one; in the '60s they would have done both. They also tend to choose activities that are self-limiting. Drama, for instance, is flourishing in all twelve of Yale's residential colleges as it never has before. Students hurl themselves into these productions — as actors, directors, carpenters, and technicians — with a dedication to create the best possible play, knowing that the day will come when the run will end and they can get back to their studies.

They also can't afford to be the willing slave of organizations like the 45 *Yale Daily News.* Last spring at the one-hundredth anniversary banquet of that paper — whose past chairmen include such once and future kings as Potter Stewart, Kingman Brewster, and William F. Buckley, Jr.* — much was

---

*EDS. NOTE — Stewart is a former U.S. Supreme Court Justice; Brewster is a former president of Yale; and Buckley is a conservative editor and columnist.

made of the fact that the editorial staff used to be small and totally committed and that "newsies" routinely worked fifty hours a week. In effect they belonged to a club; Newsies is how they defined themselves at Yale. Today's student will write one or two articles a week, when he can, and he defines himself as a student. I've never heard the word Newsie except at the banquet.

If I have described the modern undergraduate primarily as a driven creature who is largely ignoring the blithe spirit inside who keeps trying to come out and play, it's because that's where the crunch is, not only at Yale but throughout American education. It's why I think we should all be worried about the values that are nurturing a generation so fearful of risk and so goal-obsessed at such an early age. 46

I tell students that there is no one "right" way to get ahead — that each of them is a different person, starting from a different point and bound for a different destination. I tell them that change is a tonic and that all the slots are not codified nor the frontiers closed. One of my ways of telling them is to invite men and women who have achieved success outside the academic world to come and talk informally with my students during the year. They are heads of companies or ad agencies, editors of magazines, politicians, public officials, television magnates, labor leaders, business executives, Broadway producers, artists, writers, economists, photographers, scientists, historians — a mixed bag of achievers. 47

I ask them to say a few words about how they got started. The students assume that they started in their present profession and knew all along that it was what they wanted to do. Luckily for me, most of them got into their field by a circuitous route, to their surprise, after many detours. The students are startled. They can hardly conceive of a career that was not pre-planned. They can hardly imagine allowing the hand of God or chance to nudge them down some unforeseen trail. 48

•   •   •

COMPREHENSION

1. What advice does Zinsser give students when they bring their problems to him?

2. What does Zinsser wish for his students? Why does he believe his wish is naive?

3. What four kinds of pressure does Zinsser identify?

4. Whom does Zinsser blame for the existence of the pressures? Explain.

5. How, according to Zinsser, is his evaluation of students different from their own and from their potential employers' assessments?

6. Why does Zinsser believe that women are probably under even more pressure than men?

7. How does what Zinsser calls the "new pauperism" (38) affect professors?

8. Who, according to Zinsser, is ultimately responsible for eliminating college pressures? Explain.

9. In what sense are sports and other extracurricular activities another source of anxiety for students? How do students adapt to this pressure?

PURPOSE AND AUDIENCE

1. In your own words, state Zinsser's thesis. Is his intent in this essay simply to expose a difficult situation or to effect change? Explain.

2. On what kind of audience do you think this essay would have the most significant impact: students, teachers, parents, potential employers, graduate school admissions committees, or college administrators? Why?

3. What do you think Zinsser hopes to accomplish in paragraphs 42–46? How might the essay be different without this section?

4. What assumptions does Zinsser make about his audience? Do you think these assumptions are valid? Explain.

STYLE AND STRUCTURE

1. Evaluate the essay's introductory strategy. What impact do you think the notes to Carlos are likely to have on readers?

2. Identify the boundaries of Zinsser's actual classification. How does he introduce the first category? How does he indicate that his treatment of the final category is complete?

3. What function do paragraphs 22 and 31 serve in the essay?

4. Zinsser is careful to explain that when he refers to students as *he,* he includes female students as well. However, he also refers to professors as *he* (for example, in paragraphs 35–37). Assuming that not all professors at Yale are male, what other stylistic options does Zinsser have in this situation?

5. At various points in the essay, Zinsser quotes deans and students at Yale. What is the effect of these quotations?

6. Zinsser notes that his categories are "intertwined" (22, 31). In what ways do the categories overlap? Does this overlap weaken the essay? Explain.

7. What, if anything, seems to determine the order in which Zinsser introduces his categories? Is this order effective? Why or why not?

VOCABULARY PROJECTS

1. Define each of the following words as it is used in this selection.

proverbial (5)	intangible (16)	blithe (46)
supplicants (9)	accrue (21)	tonic (47)
balm (9)	exhorted (21)	codified (47)
privy (11)	tenacity (23)	
venerated (14)	faculties (28)	

2. At times Zinsser uses religious language — *national god, sacred document* — to describe the students' quest for success. Identify other examples of such language, and explain why it is used.

JOURNAL ENTRY

Which of the pressures Zinsser identifies has the strongest impact on you? Why? Do you have any other pressures that Zinsser does not mention?

WRITING WORKSHOP

1. Zinsser describes problems faced by students at an elite private college in the late 1970s. Are the pressures you experience as a college student similar to or different from the ones Zinsser identifies? Classify your own college pressures, and write an essay with a thesis statement that takes a strong stand against the forces responsible for these pressures.

2. Write a classification essay in which you support a thesis about college students' drive for success. Categorize students you know either by the degree of their need to succeed or by the different ways in which they wish to succeed.

3. Zinsser takes a negative view of the college pressures he identifies. Using his four categories, write an essay that argues that in the long run, these pressures are not only necessary but valuable.

COMBINING THE PATTERNS

Exemplification is an important secondary pattern in this classification-and-division essay. Identify as many passages of exemplification as you can. What do these examples add to Zinsser's essay? What other kinds of examples might be helpful to readers?

THEMATIC CONNECTIONS

- "The 'Black Table' Is Still There" (page 340)
- "Suicide Note" (page 357)
- "The Company Man" (page 517)

SCOTT RUSSELL SANDERS

❖

The Men We Carry in Our Minds

Scott Russell Sanders was born in 1945 in Memphis, Tennessee, and grew up in a poor rural family. A scholarship student, he graduated first in his class from Brown University. Now a professor of English at Indiana University, he has written science fiction, folk tales, children's stories, essays, and novels. Among his many books are *Stone Country* (1985), about Indiana's limestone region; the novel *The Invisible Company* (1989); the picture books *Aurora Means Dawn* (1998) and *The Floating House* (1999); and a recent essay collection, *The Force of Spirit* (2000). "The Men We Carry in Our Minds" appeared in his 1987 collection *The Paradise of Bombs*. Sanders writes here of his college years in the mid-1960s when, having grown up among poor working-class men, he was baffled by the vehemence of female classmates who argued that society favored all males over females and that men had "cornered the world's pleasures."

Background: In terms of men's higher educational and professional attainment, these women were correct. In 1970, female college undergraduates in the United States numbered some three million, while the figure for male undergraduates was some four million. More strikingly, women accounted for only 2.5 percent of law degrees, 8.4 percent of medical degrees, 3.6 percent of M.B.A.s, and 13 percent of Ph.D.s. By 2000, however, female undergraduates surpassed male undergraduates by 1 million and are projected to increase that lead by almost 2.5 million by 2011. According to the most recent statistics, women now account for some 44 percent of law degrees, 41 percent of M.D.s, 38 percent of M.B.A.s, and 41 percent of Ph.D.s. Half of all managerial and professional positions are held by women, and 40 percent of U.S. businesses are female-owned. Nevertheless, women have yet to hold executive positions in numbers similar to men, and they are still, on average, paid less than men who do comparable work.

The first men, besides my father, I remember seeing were black convicts and white guards, in the cottonfield across the road from our farm on the outskirts of Memphis. I must have been three or four. The prisoners wore dingy gray-and-black zebra suits, heavy as canvas, sodden with sweat. Hatless, stooped, they chopped weeds in the fierce heat, row after row, breathing the acrid dust of boll-weevil poison. The overseers wore dazzling white shirts and broad shadowy hats. The oiled barrels of their shotguns flashed in the sunlight. Their faces in memory are utterly blank. Of course those men, white and black, have become for me an emblem of racial hatred. But they have also come to stand for the twin poles of my early vision of manhood—the brute toiling animal and the boss.

When I was a boy, the men I knew labored with their bodies. They were marginal farmers, just scraping by, or welders, steel workers, carpenters;

1

2

they swept floors, dug ditches, mined coal, or drove trucks, their forearms ropy with muscle; they trained horses, stoked furnaces, built tires, stood on assembly lines wrestling parts onto cars and refrigerators. They got up before light, worked all day long whatever the weather, and when they came home at night they looked as though somebody had been whipping them. In the evenings and on weekends they worked on their own places, tilling gardens that were lumpy with clay, fixing broken-down cars, hammering on houses that were always too drafty, too leaky, too small.

The bodies of the men I knew were twisted and maimed in ways visible and invisible. The nails of their hands were black and split, the hands tattooed with scars. Some had lost fingers. Heavy lifting had given many of them finicky backs and guts weak from hernias. Racing against conveyor belts had given them ulcers. Their ankles and knees ached from years of standing on concrete. Anyone who had worked for long around machines was hard of hearing. They squinted, and the skin of their faces was creased like the leather of old work gloves. There were times, studying them, when I dreaded growing up. Most of them coughed, from dust or cigarettes, and most of them drank cheap wine or whiskey, so their eyes looked bloodshot and bruised. The fathers of my friends always seemed older than the mothers. Men wore out sooner. Only women lived into old age. 3

As a boy I also knew another sort of men, who did not sweat and break down like mules. They were soldiers, and so far as I could tell they scarcely worked at all. During my early school years we lived on a military base, an arsenal in Ohio, and every day I saw GIs in the guardshacks, on the stoops of barracks, at the wheels of olive drab Chevrolets. The chief fact of their lives was boredom. Long after I left the Arsenal I came to recognize the sour smell the soldiers gave off as that of souls in limbo. They were all waiting—for wars, for transfers, for leaves, for promotions, for the end of their hitch—like so many braves waiting for the hunt to begin. Unlike the warriors of older tribes, however, they would have no say about when the battle would start or how it would be waged. Their waiting was broken only when they practiced for war. They fired guns at targets, drove tanks across the churned-up fields of the military reservation, set off bombs in the wrecks of old fighter planes. I knew this was all play. But I also felt certain that when the hour for killing arrived, they would kill. When the real shooting started, many of them would die. This was what soldiers were *for,* just as a hammer was for driving nails. 4

Warriors and toilers: those seemed, in my boyhood vision, to be the chief destinies for men. They weren't the only destinies, as I learned from having a few male teachers, from reading books, and from watching television. But the men on television—the politicians, the astronauts, the generals, the savvy lawyers, the philosophical doctors, the bosses who gave orders to both soldiers and laborers—seemed as remote and unreal to me as the figures in tapestries. I could no more imagine growing up to become one of these cool, potent creatures than I could imagine becoming a prince. 5

A nearer and more hopeful example was that of my father, who had escaped from a red-dirt farm to a tire factory, and from the assembly line to the front office. Eventually he dressed in a white shirt and tie. He carried himself as if he had been born to work with his mind. But his body, remembering the earlier years of slogging work, began to give out on him in his fifties, and it quit on him entirely before he turned sixty-five. Even such a partial escape from man's fate as he had accomplished did not seem possible for most of the boys I knew. They joined the Army, stood in line for jobs in the smoky plants, helped build highways. They were bound to work as their fathers had worked, killing themselves or preparing to kill others.

A scholarship enabled me not only to attend college, a rare enough feat in my circle, but even to study in a university meant for the children of the rich. Here I met for the first time young men who had assumed from birth that they would lead lives of comfort and power. And for the first time I met women who told me that men were guilty of having kept all the joys and privileges of the earth for themselves. I was baffled. What privileges? What joys? I thought about the maimed, dismal lives of most of the men back home. What had they stolen from their wives and daughters? The right to go five days a week, twelve months a year, for thirty or forty years to a steel mill or a coal mine? The right to drop bombs and die in war? The right to feel every leak in the roof, every gap in the fence, every cough in the engine, as a wound they must mend? The right to feel, when the layoff comes or the plant shuts down, not only afraid but ashamed?

I was slow to understand the deep grievances of women. This was because, as a boy, I had envied them. Before college, the only people I had ever known who were interested in art or music or literature, the only ones who read books, the only ones who ever seemed to enjoy a sense of ease and grace were the mothers and daughters. Like the menfolk, they fretted about money, they scrimped and made-do. But, when the pay stopped coming in, they were not the ones who had failed. Nor did they have to go to war, and that seemed to me a blessed fact. By comparison with the narrow, ironclad days of fathers, there was an expansiveness, I thought, in the days of mothers. They went to see neighbors, to shop in town, to run errands at school, at the library, at church. No doubt, had I looked harder at their lives, I would have envied them less. It was not my fate to become a woman, so it was easier for me to see the graces. Few of them held jobs outside the home, and those who did filled thankless roles as clerks and waitresses. I didn't see, then, what a prison a house could be, since houses seemed to me brighter, handsomer places than any factory. I didn't realize — because such things were never spoken of — how often women suffered from men's bullying. I did learn about the wretchedness of abandoned wives, single mothers, widows; but I also learned about the wretchedness of lone men. Even then I could see how exhausting it was for a mother to cater all day to the needs of young children. But if I had been asked, as a boy, to choose between tending a baby and tending a machine, I think I would have chosen the baby. (Having now tended both, I know I would choose the baby.)

So I was baffled when the women at college accused me and my sex of having cornered the world's pleasures. I think something like my bafflement has been felt by other boys (and by girls as well) who grew up in dirt-poor farm country, in mining country, in black ghettos, in Hispanic barrios, in the shadows of factories, in Third World nations—any place where the fate of men is as grim and bleak as the fate of women. Toilers and warriors. I realize now how ancient these identities are, how deep the tug they exert on men, the undertow of a thousand generations. The miseries I saw, as a boy, in the lives of nearly all men I continue to see in the lives of many—the body-breaking toil, the tedium, the call to be tough, the humiliating powerlessness, the battle for a living and for territory.

When the women I met at college thought about the joys and privileges of men, they did not carry in their minds the sort of men I had known in my childhood. They thought of their fathers, who were bankers, physicians, architects, stockbrokers, the big wheels of the big cities. These fathers rode the train to work or drove cars that cost more than any of my childhood houses. They were attended from morning to night by female helpers, wives and nurses and secretaries. They were never laid off, never short of cash at month's end, never lined up for welfare. These fathers made decisions that mattered. They ran the world.

The daughters of such men wanted to share in this power, this glory. So did I. They yearned for a say over their future, for jobs worthy of their abilities, for the right to live at peace, unmolested, whole. Yes, I thought, yes yes. The difference between me and these daughters was that they saw me, because of my sex, as destined from birth to become like their fathers, and therefore as an enemy to their desires. But I knew better. I wasn't an enemy, in fact or in feeling. I was an ally. If I had known, then, how to tell them so, would they have believed me? Would they now?

• • •

COMPREHENSION

1. What does Sanders mean in paragraph 1 when he characterizes the black convicts and white guards as "an emblem of racial hatred"? In what sense do they represent "the twin poles of [his] early vision of manhood"?

2. When he was a child, what did Sanders expect to become when he grew up? Why? How did he escape this destiny?

3. What advantages did Sanders initially attribute to women? Why? What challenged his assumptions?

4. What kind of men did the women Sanders met in college carry in their minds? Why did the women see Sanders as "an enemy to their desires" (11)? How did he defend himself against their charges?

PURPOSE AND AUDIENCE

1. What purpose do you think Sanders had in mind when he wrote this essay? Is his essay intended as a personal memoir, or does he have another agenda? Explain.

2. What is the essay's thesis?

3. Is this essay directed primarily at workers like the ones Sanders observed when he was growing up or at the "children of the rich" (7)? At men or at women? On whom would you expect it to have the greatest impact? Explain.

STYLE AND STRUCTURE

1. What is Sanders categorizing in this essay? What categories does he name? What other, unnamed categories does he identify?

2. What principle of classification determines the categories Sanders discusses?

3. What, if anything, determines the order in which Sanders discusses his categories?

4. Is the treatment of the various categories in this essay balanced, or does Sanders give more attention to some than to others? If some categories are given more attention, does this weaken the essay? Explain.

VOCABULARY PROJECTS

1. Define each of the following words as it is used in this selection.

acrid (1)	finicky (3)	expansiveness (8)
boll weevil (1)	slogging (6)	undertow (9)
overseers (1)	fretted (8)	unmolested (11)
maimed (3)	ironclad (8)	

2. Invent descriptive titles for the categories Sanders does not name. Be sure to include categories that cover women's roles as well as men's, and be sure your categories do not overlap.

JOURNAL ENTRY

Do you agree with Sanders when he suggests that men have harder lives than women do? What is your reaction to his parenthetical comment at the end of paragraph 8?

WRITING WORKSHOP

1. Imagine the possible kinds of work available to you in the field you expect to study. Write a classification-and-division essay in which you discuss several categories of possible future employment, arranging them from least to most desirable.

2. Consider the adult workers you know best—your relatives, friends' parents, employers, teachers—and other workers with whom you come in contact on a regular basis (store clerks or waiters, for example). Write a classification-and-division essay in which you devise categories that distinguish different types of workers. Then discuss these categories of workers in terms of how fortunate (or unfortunate) they are. Consider income level, job security, working conditions, prestige, and job satisfaction in your discussion of each category. In your essay's introduction and conclusion, consider how the employment categories you have devised are like or unlike Sanders's.

3. What kinds of jobs do you see as "dream jobs"? Why? List as many of these ideal jobs as you can, and group them into logical categories. Then write an essay with a thesis statement that explains the value you see in these jobs.

COMBINING THE PATTERNS

After he establishes his categories, Sanders uses **description** to characterize workers and distinguish them from one another. Identify and evaluate the descriptive passages that serve these two purposes. Is any category of worker identified but not described? Explain.

THEMATIC CONNECTIONS

- "Scrubbing in Maine" (page 106)
- "On Fire" (page 282)
- "I Want a Wife" (page 505)

AMY TAN

❖

Mother Tongue

Amy Tan was born in 1952 in Oakland, California, the daughter of recent Chinese immigrants. She studied linguistics at San Francisco State University and began a career as a corporate communications specialist. In 1984, Tan began to write stories as a sort of do-it-yourself therapy. At the same time, she began thinking about the contradictions she faced as a highly Americanized Chinese American who was also the daughter of immigrant parents. Three years later, she published *The Joy Luck Club* (1987), a best-selling novel (made into a movie in 1993) about four immigrant Chinese women and their American-born daughters. Later works include *The Hundred Secret Senses* (1995) and *The Bonesetter's Daughter* (2001), as well as two children's books. In this 1990 essay, Tan considers her mother's heavily Chinese-influenced English, as well as the different "Englishes" she herself uses, especially in communicating with her mother. She then goes on to ponder the potential limitations of growing up with immigrant parents who do not speak fluent English.

Background: The children of Asian immigrants tend to be highly assimilated and are often outstanding students, in part because their parents expect them to work hard and do well. Most who were born in the United States speak and read English fluently. Yet on standardized tests, while they generally score much higher than average in math, their verbal scores are a bit lower than average. For example, average SAT scores for all student test-takers beginning college in 2002 were 504 on the verbal section and 516 on the math section; the average scores for Asian-American students were 501 on the verbal section and 569 on the math section. In some cases, this lower verbal score means that an Asian-American student's combined score limits his or her college choices. Moreover, as Tan suggests, Asian-American students' performance on such standardized tests may lead teachers to discourage them from pursuing degrees in fields outside of math and science.

I am not a scholar of English or literature. I cannot give you much 1 more than personal opinions on the English language and its variations in this country or others.

I am a writer. And by that definition, I am someone who has always 2 loved language. I am fascinated by language in daily life. I spend a great deal of my time thinking about the power of language — the way it can evoke an emotion, a visual image, a complex idea, or a simple truth. Language is the tool of my trade. And I use them all — all the Englishes I grew up with.

Recently, I was made keenly aware of the different Englishes I do use. I 3 was giving a talk to a large group of people, the same talk I had already given to half a dozen other groups. The nature of the talk was about my writing, my life, and my book, *The Joy Luck Club*. The talk was going along well enough, until I remembered one major difference that made the whole talk sound wrong. My mother was in the room. And it was perhaps the first time she had heard me give a lengthy speech, using the kind of English I have never used with her. I was saying things like, "The intersection of memory upon imagination" and "There is an aspect of my fiction that relates to thus-and-thus"—a speech filled with carefully wrought grammatical phrases, burdened, it suddenly seemed to me, with nominalized forms, past perfect tenses, conditional phrases, all the forms of standard English that I had learned in school and through books, the forms of English I did not use at home with my mother.

Just last week, I was walking down the street with my mother, and I 4 again found myself conscious of the English I was using, and the English I do use with her. We were talking about the price of new and used furniture and I heard myself saying this: "Not waste money that way." My husband was with us as well, and he didn't notice any switch in my English. And then I realized why. It's because over the twenty years we've been together I've often used that same kind of English with him, and sometimes he even uses it with me. It has become our language of intimacy, a different sort of English that relates to family talk, the language I grew up with.

So you'll have some idea of what this family talk I heard sounds like, 5 I'll quote what my mother said during a recent conversation which I videotaped and then transcribed. During this conversation my mother was talking about a political gangster in Shanghai who had the same last name as her family's, Du, and how the gangster in his early years wanted to be adopted by her family, which was rich by comparison. Later, the gangster became more powerful, far richer than my mother's family, and one day showed up at my mother's wedding to pay his respects. Here's what she said in part:

"Du Yusong having business like fruit stand. Like off the street kind. 6 He is Du like Du Zong—but not Tsung-ming Island people. The local people call putong, the river east side, he belong to that side local people. The man want to ask Du Zong father take him in like become own family. Du Zong father wasn't looking down on him, but didn't take seriously, until that man big like become a mafia. Now important person very hard to inviting him. Chinese way, come only to show respect, don't stay for dinner. Respect for making big celebration, he shows up. Mean gives lots of respect. Chinese custom. Chinese social life that way. If too important won't have to stay too long. He come to my wedding. I didn't see. I heard it. I gone to boy's side, they have YMCA dinner. Chinese age I was nineteen."

You should know that my mother's expressive command of English 7 belies how much she actually understands. She reads the *Forbes* report, listens to *Wall Street Week*, converses daily with her stockbroker, reads all of Shirley MacLaine's books with ease—all kinds of things I can't begin to understand. Yet some of my friends tell me they understand 50 percent of what my mother says. Some say they understand 80 to 90 percent. Some say they understand none of it, as if she were speaking pure Chinese. But to me, my mother's English is perfectly clear, perfectly natural. It's my mother's tongue. Her language, as I hear it, is vivid, direct, full of observation and imagery. This was the language that helped shape the way I saw things, expressed things, made sense of the world.

Lately, I've been giving more thought to the kind of English my mother speaks. Like others, I have described it to people as "broken" or "fractured" English. But I wince when I say that. It has always bothered me that I can think of no way to describe it other than "broken," as if it were damaged and needed to be fixed, as if it lacked a certain wholeness and soundness. I've heard other terms used, "limited English," for example. But they seem just as bad, as if everything is limited, including people's perceptions of the limited English speaker. 8

I know this for a fact, because when I was growing up, my mother's "limited" English limited *my* perception of her. I was ashamed of her English. I believed that her English reflected the quality of what she had to say. That is, because she expressed them imperfectly her thoughts were imperfect. And I had plenty of empirical evidence to support me: the fact that people in department stores, at banks, and at restaurants did not take her seriously, did not give her good service, pretended not to understand her, or even acted as if they did not hear her. 9

My mother has long realized the limitations of her English as well. When I was fifteen, she used to have me call people on the phone to pretend I was she. In this guise, I was forced to ask for information or even complain and yell at people who had been rude to her. One time it was a call to her stockbroker in New York. She had cashed out her small portfolio and it just so happened we were going to go to New York the next week, our very first trip outside California. I had to get on the phone and say in an adolescent voice that was not very convincing, "This is Mrs. Tan." 10

And my mother was standing in the back whispering loudly, "Why he don't send me check, already two weeks late. So mad he lie to me, losing me money." 11

And then I said in perfect English, "Yes, I'm getting rather concerned. You had agreed to send the check two weeks ago, but it hasn't arrived." 12

Then she began to talk more loudly. "What he want, I come to New York tell him front of his boss, you cheating me?" And I was trying to calm her down, make her be quiet, while telling the stockbroker, "I can't tolerate any more excuses. If I don't receive the check immediately I am going to have to speak to your manager when I'm in New York next week." And sure enough, the following week there we were in front of this astonished stockbroker, and I was sitting there red-faced and quiet, and my mother, the real Mrs. Tan, was shouting at his boss in her impeccable broken English. 13

We used a similar routine just five days ago, for a situation that was far less humorous. My mother had gone to the hospital for an appointment, to find out about a benign brain tumor a CAT scan had revealed a month 14 ago. She said she had spoken very good English, her best English, no mistakes. Still, she said, the hospital did not apologize when they said they had lost the CAT scan and she had come for nothing. She said they did not seem to have any sympathy when she told them she was anxious to know the exact diagnosis, since her husband and son had both died of brain tumors. She said they would not give her any more information until the next time and she would have to make another appointment for that. So she said she would not leave until the doctor called her daughter. She wouldn't budge. And when the doctor finally called her daughter, me, who spoke in perfect English — lo and behold — we had assurances the CAT scan would be found, promises that a conference call on Monday would be held, and apologies for any suffering my mother had gone through for a most regrettable mistake.

I think my mother's English almost had an effect on limiting my possibilities in life as well. Sociologists and linguists probably will tell you that a person's developing language skills are more influenced by peers. But I do think that the language spoken in the family, especially in immigrant families which are more insular, plays a large role in shaping the language of the child. And I believe that it affected my results on achievement tests, IQ tests, and the SAT. While my English skills were never judged as poor, compared to math, English could not be considered my strong suit. In grade school I did moderately well, getting perhaps B's, sometimes B-pluses, in English and scoring perhaps in the sixtieth or seventieth percentile on achievement tests. But those scores were not good enough to override the opinion that my true abilities lay in math and science, because in those areas I achieved A's and scored in the ninetieth percentile or higher.

This was understandable. Math is precise; there is only one correct answer. Whereas, for me at least, the answers on English tests were always a judgment call, a matter of opinion and personal experience. Those tests were constructed around items like fill-in-the-blank sentence completion, such as "Even though Tom was _____, Mary thought he was _____." And the correct answer always seemed to be the most bland combinations of thoughts, for example, "Even though Tom was shy, Mary thought he was charming," with the grammatical structure "even though" limiting the correct answer to some sort of semantic opposites, so you wouldn't get answers like, "Even though Tom was foolish, Mary thought he was ridiculous." Well, according to my mother, there were very few limitations as to what Tom could have been and what Mary might have thought of him. So I never did well on tests like that.

The same was true with word analogies, pairs of words in which you were supposed to find some sort of logical, semantic relationship — for example, "*Sunset* is to *nightfall* as _____ is to _____." And here you would be presented with a list of four possible pairs, one of which showed the same kind of relationship: *red* is to *stoplight*, *bus* is to *arrival*, *chills* is to *fever*, *yawn* is to *boring*. Well, I could never think that way. I knew what the tests were asking, but I could not block out of my mind the images already created by the first pair, "*sunset* is to *nightfall*"—and I would see a burst of colors against a darkening sky, the moon rising, the lowering of a curtain of stars. And all the other pairs of words—red, bus, stoplight, boring—just threw up a mass of confusing images, making it impossible for me to sort out something as logical as saying: "A sunset precedes nightfall" is the same as "a chill precedes a fever." The only way I would have gotten that answer right would have been to imagine an associative situation, for example, my being disobedient and staying out past sunset, catching a chill at night, which turns into feverish pneumonia as punishment, which indeed did happen to me.

I have been thinking about all this lately, about my mother's English, about achievement tests. Because lately I've been asked, as a writer, why there are not more Asian Americans represented in American literature. Why are there few Asian Americans enrolled in creative writing programs? Why do so many Chinese students go into engineering? Well, these are broad sociological questions I can't begin to answer. But I have noticed in surveys—in fact, just last week—that Asian students, as a whole, always do significantly better on math achievement tests than in English. And this makes me think that there are other Asian-American students whose English spoken in the home might also be described as "broken" or "limited." And perhaps they also have teachers who are steering them away from writing and into math and science, which is what happened to me. 18

Fortunately, I happen to be rebellious in nature and enjoy the challenge of disproving assumptions made about me. I became an English major my first year in college, after being enrolled as pre-med. I started writing nonfiction as a freelancer the week after I was told by my former boss that writing was my worst skill and I should hone my talents toward account management. 19

But it wasn't until 1985 that I finally began to write fiction. And at first I wrote using what I thought to be wittily crafted sentences, sentences that would finally prove I had mastery over the English language. Here's an example from the first draft of a story that later made its way into *The Joy Luck Club*, but without this line: "That was my mental quandary in its nascent state." A terrible line, which I can barely pronounce. 20

Fortunately, for reasons I won't get into today, I later decided I should envision a reader for the stories I would write. And the reader I decided upon was my mother because these were stories about mothers. So with this reader in mind—and in fact she did read my early drafts—I began to write stories using all the Englishes I grew up with: the English I spoke to my mother, which for lack of a better term might be described as "simple"; the English she used with me, which for lack of a better term might be described as "broken"; my translation of her Chinese, which could certainly be described as "watered down"; and what I imagined to be her translation of her Chinese if she could speak in perfect English, her internal language, and for that I sought to preserve the essence, but neither an 21

English nor a Chinese structure. I wanted to capture what language ability tests can never reveal: her intent, her passion, her imagery, the rhythms of her speech and the nature of her thoughts.

Apart from what any critic had to say about my writing, I knew I had succeeded where it counted when my mother finished reading my book and gave me her verdict: "So easy to read." 22

• • •

COMPREHENSION

1. What is Tan classifying in this essay? What individual categories does she identify?

2. Where does Tan identify the different categories she discusses in "Mother Tongue"? Should she have identified these categories earlier? Why or why not?

3. Does Tan illustrate each category she identifies? Does she treat all categories equally? If she does not, do you see this as a problem? Explain.

4. In what specific situations does Tan say her mother's "limited English" was a handicap? In what other situations might Mrs. Tan face difficulties?

5. What effects have her mother's English had on Tan's life?

6. How does Tan account for the difficulty she had in answering questions on achievement tests, particularly word analogies? Do you think her problems in this area can be explained by the level of her family's language skills, or might other factors have contributed to the problem? Explain.

7. In paragraph 18, Tan considers the possible reasons for the lack of Asian Americans in the fields of language and literature. What explanations does she offer? What other explanations can you think of?

PURPOSE AND AUDIENCE

1. Why do you suppose Tan opens her essay by explaining her qualifications? Why, for example, does she tell her readers that she is "not a scholar of English or literature" (1) but rather a writer who is "fascinated by language in daily life" (2)?

2. Do you think Tan expects most of her readers to be Asian American? To be familiar with Asian-American languages and culture? How can you tell?

3. Is Tan's primary focus in this essay on language or on her mother? Explain your conclusion.

STYLE AND STRUCTURE

1. This essay's style is relatively informal. For example, Tan uses I to refer to herself and addresses her readers as you. Identify other features that characterize her style as informal. Do you think Tan would strengthen her credibility if she were to use a more formal style? Explain your reasoning.

2. In paragraph 6, Tan quotes a passage of her mother's speech. What purpose does Tan say is served by this quotation? What impression does it give of her mother? Do you think this effect is what Tan intended? Explain.

3. In paragraphs 10 through 13, Tan juxtaposes her mother's English with her own. What point do these quoted passages make?

4. The expression used in Tan's title, "Mother Tongue," is also used in paragraph 7. What does this expression generally mean? What does it seem to mean in this essay?

5. In paragraph 20, Tan quotes a "terrible line" from an early draft of part of her novel *The Joy Luck Club*. Why do you suppose she quotes this line? How is it different from the style she uses in "Mother Tongue"?

VOCABULARY PROJECTS

1. Define each of the following words as it is used in this selection.

nominalized (3)	guise (10)	semantic (16)
belies (7)	impeccable (13)	quandary (20)
empirical (9)	insular (15)	nascent (20)

2. In paragraph 8, Tan discusses the different words that might be used to describe her mother's spoken English. Which term seems most accurate? Do you agree with Tan that these words are unsatisfactory? What other term for her mother's English would be both neutral and accurate?

JOURNAL ENTRY

In paragraph 9, Tan says that when she was growing up she was sometimes ashamed of her mother because of her limited English proficiency. Have you ever felt ashamed of a parent (or a friend) because of his or her inability to "fit in" in some way? How do you feel now about your earlier reaction?

WRITING WORKSHOP

1. What different "Englishes" (or other languages) do you use in your day-to-day life as a student, employee, friend, and family member? Write a classification-and-division essay in which you identify, describe, and illustrate each kind of language and explain the purpose it serves.

2. What kinds of problems are faced today by a person whose English is as limited as that of Mrs. Tan? Write a classification-and-division essay that identifies and explains the kinds of problems you might encounter if the level of your spoken English were comparable to hers.

3. Tan's essay focuses on spoken language, but people also use different kinds of *written* language in different situations. Write a classification-and-division essay that identifies and analyzes three different kinds of written English: one appropriate for your parents, one for a teacher or employer, and one for a friend. Illustrate each kind of language with an extended example in which you write about your plans for your future. In your thesis statement, explain why you need all three kinds of language.

COMBINING THE PATTERNS

Tan develops her essay with a series of anecdotes about her mother and about herself. How does this use of **narration** strengthen her essay? Could she have made her point about the use of different "Englishes" without these anecdotes? What other strategy could she have used?

THEMATIC CONNECTIONS

- "Only Daughter" (page 84)
- "Words Left Unspoken" (page 153)
- "The Human Cost of an Illiterate Society" (page 229)

STEPHANIE ERICSSON

❖

The Ways We Lie

Stephanie Ericsson (b. 1953) grew up in San Francisco and began writing as a teenager. She has been a screenwriter and an advertising copywriter and has published several books based on her own life. *Shamefaced: The Road to Recovery* and *Women of AA: Recovering Together* (both 1985) focus on her experiences with addiction; *Companion through the Darkness: Inner Dialogues on Grief* (1993) deals with the sudden death of her husband; and *Companion into the Dawn: Inner Dialogues on Loving* (1994) is a collection of essays.

Background: The following piece originally appeared as the cover article in the January 1993 issue of the *Utne Reader,* which was devoted to the theme of lies and lying. The subject had particular relevance after a year in which the honesty of Bill Clinton—the newly elected U.S. president—had been questioned. It also followed the furor surrounding the confirmation hearings of U.S. Supreme Court nominee Clarence Thomas, who denied allegations by attorney Anita Hill of workplace sexual harassment; the question was who was telling the truth and who was not. Six years later, President Clinton would be accused of perjury and would face a Senate impeachment trial. More recently, lying has featured prominently in the news again as executives at Enron, Arthur Andersen, Adelphia Communications, Tyco, WorldCom, and other major corporations have been charged with committing fraud, falsifying records, and illegally manipulating company information at the expense of employees and shareholders.

1 The bank called today and I told them my deposit was in the mail, even though I hadn't written a check yet. It'd been a rough day. The baby I'm pregnant with decided to do aerobics on my lungs for two hours, our three-year-old daughter painted the living-room couch with lipstick, the IRS put me on hold for an hour, and I was late to a business meeting because I was tired.

2 I told my client the traffic had been bad. When my partner came home, his haggard face told me his day hadn't gone any better than mine, so when he asked, "How was your day?" I said, "Oh, fine," knowing that one more straw might break his back. A friend called and wanted to take me to lunch. I said I was busy. Four lies in the course of a day, none of which I felt the least bit guilty about.

3 We lie. We all do. We exaggerate, we minimize, we avoid confrontation, we spare people's feelings, we conveniently forget, we keep secrets, we justify lying to the big-guy institutions. Like most people, I indulge in small falsehoods and still think of myself as an honest person. Sure I lie, but it doesn't hurt anything. Or does it?

4 I once tried going a whole week without telling a lie, and it was paralyzing. I discovered that telling the truth all the time is nearly impossible. It means living with some serious consequences: The bank charges me $60

in overdraft fees, my partner keels over when I tell him about my travails, my client fires me for telling her I didn't feel like being on time, and my friend takes it personally when I say I'm not hungry. There must be some merit to lying.

But if I justify lying, what makes me any different from slick politicians or the corporate robbers who raided the S&L industry? Saying it's okay to lie one way and not another is hedging. I cannot seem to escape the voice deep inside me that tells me: When someone lies, someone loses.

What far-reaching consequences will I, or others, pay as a result of my lie? Will someone's trust be destroyed? Will someone else pay *my* penance because I ducked out? We must consider the *meaning of our actions*. Deception, lies, capital crimes, and misdemeanors all carry meanings. *Webster's* definition of *lie* is specific:

1: a false statement or action especially made with the intent to deceive;
2: anything that gives or is meant to give a false impression.

A definition like this implies that there are many, many ways to tell a lie. Here are just a few.

The White Lie

A man who won't lie to a woman has very little consideration
for her feelings.
— BERGEN EVANS

The white lie assumes that the truth will cause more damage than a simple, harmless untruth. Telling a friend he looks great when he looks like hell can be based on a decision that the friend needs a compliment more than a frank opinion. But, in effect, it is the liar deciding what is best for the lied to. Ultimately, it is a vote of no confidence. It is an act of subtle arrogance for anyone to decide what is best for someone else.

Yet not all circumstances are quite so cut-and-dried. Take, for instance, the sergeant in Vietnam who knew one of his men was killed in action but listed him as missing so that the man's family would receive indefinite compensation instead of the lump-sum pittance the military gives widows and children. His intent was honorable. Yet for twenty years this family kept their hopes alive, unable to move on to a new life.

Facades

Et tu, Brute?
— CAESAR*

We all put up facades to one degree or another. When I put on a suit to go to see a client, I feel as though I am putting on another face, obeying the

---

*EDS. NOTE — "And you, Brutus?" (Latin). In Shakespeare's play *Julius Caesar,* Caesar asks this question when he sees Brutus, whom he has believed to be his friend, among the conspirators who are stabbing him.

expectation that serious businesspeople wear suits rather than sweatpants. But I'm a writer. Normally, I get up, get the kid off to school, and sit at my computer in my pajamas until four in the afternoon. When I answer the phone, the caller thinks I'm wearing a suit (though the UPS man knows better).

But facades can be destructive because they are used to seduce others into an illusion. For instance, I recently realized that a former friend was a liar. He presented himself with all the right looks and the right words and offered lots of new consciousness theories, fabulous books to read, and fascinating insights. Then I did some business with him, and the time came for him to pay me. He turned out to be all talk and no walk. I heard a plethora of reasonable excuses, including in-depth descriptions of the big break around the corner. In six months of work, I saw less than a hundred bucks. When I confronted him, he raised both eyebrows and tried to convince me that I'd heard him wrong, that he'd made no commitment to me. A simple investigation into his past revealed a crowded graveyard of disenchanted former friends.

Ignoring the Plain Facts

> Well, you must understand that Father Porter is only human. . . .
> – A MASSACHUSETTS PRIEST

In the '60s, the Catholic Church in Massachusetts began hearing complaints that Father James Porter was sexually molesting children. Rather than relieving him of his duties, the ecclesiastical authorities simply moved him from one parish to another between 1960 and 1967, actually providing him with a fresh supply of unsuspecting families and innocent children to abuse. After treatment in 1967 for pedophilia, he went back to work, this time in Minnesota. The new diocese was aware of Father Porter's obsession with children, but they needed priests and recklessly believed treatment had cured him. More children were abused until he was relieved of his duties a year later. By his own admission, Porter may have abused as many as a hundred children.

Ignoring the facts may not in and of itself be a form of lying, but consider the context of this situation. If a lie is *a false action done with the intent to deceive,* then the Catholic Church's conscious covering for Porter created irreparable consequences. The church became a co-perpetrator with Porter.

Deflecting

> When you have no basis for an argument, abuse the plaintiff.
> – CICERO

I've discovered that I can keep anyone from seeing the true me by being selectively blatant. I set a precedent of being up-front about intimate issues, but I never bring up the things I truly want to hide; I just let people assume I'm revealing everything. It's an effective way of hiding.

Any good liar knows that the way to perpetuate an untruth is to deflect 15
attention from it. When Clarence Thomas exploded with accusations that
the Senate hearings were a "high-tech lynching," he simply switched the
focus from a highly charged subject to a radioactive subject. Rather than
defending himself, he took the offensive and accused the country of
racism. It was a brilliant maneuver. Racism is now politically incorrect in
official circles—unlike sexual harassment, which still rewards those who
can get away with it.

Some of the most skillful deflectors are passive-aggressive people who, 16
when accused of inappropriate behavior, refuse to respond to the accusations. This you-don't-exist stance infuriates the accuser, who, understandably, screams something obscene out of frustration. The trap is sprung and
the act of deflection successful, because now the passive-aggressive person
can indignantly say, "Who can talk to someone as unreasonable as you?"
The real issue is forgotten and the sins of the original victim become the
focus. Feeling guilty of name-calling, the victim is fully tamed and crawls
into a hole, ashamed. I have watched this fighting technique work thousands of times in disputes between men and women, and what I've learned
is that the real culprit is not necessarily the one who swears the loudest.

Omission

The cruelest lies are often told in silence.
— R. L. STEVENSON

Omission involves telling most of the truth minus one or two key facts 17
whose absence changes the story completely. You break a pair of glasses
that are guaranteed under normal use and get a new pair, without mentioning that the first pair broke during a rowdy game of basketball. Who
hasn't tried something like that? But what about omission of information
that could make a difference in how a person lives his or her life?

For instance, one day I found out that rabbinical legends tell of 18
another woman in the Garden of Eden before Eve. I was stunned. The
omission of the Sumerian goddess Lilith from Genesis—as well as her
demonization by ancient misogynists as an embodiment of female evil—
felt like spiritual robbery. I felt like I'd just found out my mother was really
my stepmother. To take seriously the tradition that Adam was created out
of the same mud as his equal counterpart, Lilith, redefines all of Judeo-
Christian history.

Some renegade Catholic feminists introduced me to a view of Lilith 19
that had been suppressed during the many centuries when this strong goddess was seen only as a spirit of evil. Lilith was a proud goddess who defied
Adam's need to control her, attempted negotiations, and when this failed,
said adios and left the Garden of Eden.

This omission of Lilith from the Bible was a patriarchal strategy to 20
keep women weak. Omitting the strong-woman archetype of Lilith from
Western religions and starting the story with Eve the Rib has helped keep

Christian and Jewish women believing they were the lesser sex for thousands of years.

Stereotypes and Clichés

> Where opinion does not exist, the status quo becomes stereotyped and all originality is discouraged.
> – BERTRAND RUSSELL

Stereotype and cliché serve a purpose as a form of shorthand. Our   21
need for vast amounts of information in nanoseconds has made the stereotype vital to modern communication. Unfortunately, it often shuts down original thinking, giving those hungry for the truth a candy bar of misinformation instead of a balanced meal. The stereotype explains a situation with just enough truth to seem unquestionable.

All the "isms"—racism, sexism, ageism, et al.—are founded on and   22
fueled by the stereotype and the cliché, which are lies of exaggeration, omission, and ignorance. They are always dangerous. They take a single tree and make it a landscape. They destroy curiosity. They close minds and separate people. The single mother on welfare is assumed to be cheating. Any black male could tell you how much of his identity is obliterated daily by stereotypes. Fat people, ugly people, beautiful people, old people, large-breasted women, short men, the mentally ill, and the homeless all could tell you how much more they are like us than we want to think. I once admitted to a group of people that I had a mouth like a truck driver. Much to my surprise, a man stood up and said, "I'm a truck driver, and I never cuss." Needless to say, I was humbled.

Groupthink

> Who is more foolish, the child afraid of the dark, or the man afraid of the light?
> – MAURICE FREEHILL

Irving Janis, in *Victims of GroupThink,* defines this sort of lie as a psycho-   23
logical phenomenon within decision-making groups in which loyalty to the group has become more important than any other value, with the result that dissent and the appraisal of alternatives are suppressed. If you've ever worked on a committee or in a corporation, you've encountered groupthink. It requires a combination of other forms of lying—ignoring facts, selective memory, omission, and denial, to name a few.

The textbook example of groupthink came on December 7, 1941. From   24
as early as the fall of 1941, the warnings came in, one after another, that Japan was preparing for a massive military operation. The Navy command in Hawaii assumed Pearl Harbor was invulnerable—the Japanese weren't stupid enough to attack the United States' most important base. On the other hand, racist stereotypes said the Japanese weren't smart enough to

invent a torpedo effective in less than 60 feet of water (the fleet was docked in 30 feet); after all, U.S. technology hadn't been able to do it.

On Friday, December 5, normal weekend leave was granted to all the   25
commanders at Pearl Harbor, even though the Japanese consulate in Hawaii was busy burning papers. Within the tight, good-ole-boy cohesiveness of the U.S. command in Hawaii, the myth of invulnerability stayed well entrenched. No one in the group considered the alternatives. The rest is history.

Out-and-Out Lies

> The only form of lying that is beyond reproach is lying for its
> own sake.
>   – OSCAR WILDE

Of all the ways to lie, I like this one the best, probably because I get   26
tired of trying to figure out the real meanings behind things. At least I can trust the bald-faced lie. I once asked my five-year-old nephew, "Who broke the fence?" (I had seen him do it.) He answered, "The murderers." Who could argue?

At least when this sort of lie is told it can be easily confronted. As the   27
person who is lied to, I know where I stand. The bald-faced lie doesn't toy with my perceptions — it argues with them. It doesn't try to refashion reality, it tries to refute it. *Read my lips.* . . . No sleight of hand. No guessing. If this were the only form of lying, there would be no such thing as floating anxiety or the adult-children of alcoholics movement.

Dismissal

> Pay no attention to that man behind the curtain! I am the
> Great Oz!
>   – THE WIZARD OF OZ

Dismissal is perhaps the slipperiest of all lies. Dismissing feelings, per-   28
ceptions, or even the raw facts of a situation ranks as a kind of lie that can do as much damage to a person as any other kind of lie.

The roots of many mental disorders can be traced back to the dis-   29
missal of reality. Imagine that a person is told from the time she is a tot that her perceptions are inaccurate. *"Mommy, I'm scared."* "No, you're not, darling." *"I don't like that man next door, he makes me feel icky."* "Johnny, that's a terrible thing to say, of course you like him. You go over there right now and be nice to him."

I've often mused over the idea that madness is actually a sane reaction   30
to an insane world. Psychologist R. D. Laing supports this hypothesis in *Sanity, Madness & the Family,* an account of his investigations into families of schizophrenics. The common thread that ran through all of the families he studied was a deliberate, staunch dismissal of the patient's perceptions from a very early age. Each of the patients started out with an accurate grasp of reality, which, through meticulous and methodical

dismissal, was demolished until the only reality the patient could trust was catatonia.

Dismissal runs the gamut. Mild dismissal can be quite handy for forgiving the foibles of others in our day-to-day lives. Toddlers who have just learned to manipulate their parents' attention sometimes are dismissed out of necessity. Absolute attention from the parents would require so much energy that no one would get to eat dinner. But we must be careful and attentive about how far we take our "necessary" dismissals. Dismissal is a dangerous tool, because it's nothing less than a lie. 31

Delusion

> We lie loudest when we lie to ourselves.
> – ERIC HOFFER

I could write the book on this one. Delusion, a cousin of dismissal, is the tendency to see excuses as facts. It's a powerful lying tool because it filters out information that contradicts what we want to believe. Alcoholics who believe that the problems in their lives are legitimate reasons for drinking rather than results of the drinking offer the classic example of deluded thinking. Delusion uses the mind's ability to see things in myriad ways to support what it wants to be the truth. 32

But delusion is also a survival mechanism we all use. If we were to fully contemplate the consequences of our stockpiles of nuclear weapons or global warming, we could hardly function on a day-to-day level. We don't want to incorporate that much reality into our lives because to do so would be paralyzing. 33

Delusion acts as an adhesive to keep the status quo intact. It shamelessly employs dismissal, omission, and amnesia, among other sorts of lies. Its most cunning defense is that it cannot see itself. 34

> The liar's punishment . . . is that he cannot believe anyone else.
> – GEORGE BERNARD SHAW

These are only a few of the ways we lie. Or are lied to. As I said earlier, it's not easy to entirely eliminate lies from our lives. No matter how pious we may try to be, we will still embellish, hedge, and omit to lubricate the daily machinery of living. But there is a world of difference between telling functional lies and living a lie. Martin Buber* once said, "The lie is the spirit committing treason against itself." Our acceptance of lies becomes a cultural cancer that eventually shrouds and reorders reality until moral garbage becomes as invisible to us as water is to a fish. 35

How much do we tolerate before we become sick and tired of being sick and tired? When will we stand up and declare our *right* to trust? When do we stop accepting that the real truth is in the fine print? Whose lips do 36

---

*EDS. NOTE — Austrian-born Judaic philosopher (1878–1965).

we read this year when we vote for president? When will we stop being so reticent about making judgments? When do we stop turning over our personal power and responsibility to liars?

Maybe if I don't tell the bank the check's in the mail I'll be less tolerant of the lies told me every day. A country song I once heard said it all for me: "You've got to stand for something or you'll fall for anything."

• • •

COMPREHENSION

1. List and define each of the ten kinds of lies Ericsson identifies.

2. Why, in Ericsson's view, is each kind of lie necessary?

3. According to Ericsson, what is the danger of each kind of lie?

4. Why does Ericsson like "out-and-out lies" (26–27) best?

5. Why is dismissal the "slipperiest of all lies" (28)?

PURPOSE AND AUDIENCE

1. Is Ericsson's thesis simply that "there are many, many ways to tell a lie" (7)? Or is she defending—or attacking—the process of lying? Try to state her thesis in a single sentence.

2. Do you think Ericsson's choice of examples reveals a political bias? If so, do you think she expects her intended audience to share her views? Explain.

STYLE AND STRUCTURE

1. Despite the seriousness of her subject matter, Ericsson's essay is informal; her opening paragraphs are especially personal and breezy. Why do you think she uses this kind of opening? Do you think her decision makes sense? Why or why not?

2. Ericsson introduces each category of lie with a quotation. What function do these quotations serve? Would the essay be more or less effective without them? Explain your conclusion.

3. In addition to a heading and a quotation, what other elements does Ericsson include in her discussion of each kind of lie? Are all the discussions parallel—that is, does each include *all* the standard elements, and *only* those elements? If not, do you think this lack of balance is a problem? Explain.

4. What, if anything, determines the order in which Ericsson arranges her categories? Should any category be relocated? Explain.

5. Throughout her essay, Ericsson uses **rhetorical questions.** Why do you suppose she uses this stylistic device?

6. Ericsson occasionally cites the views of experts. Why does she do so? If she wished to cite additional experts, what professional backgrounds or fields of study do you think they should represent? Why?

7. In paragraph 29, Ericsson says, "Imagine that a person is told from the time she is a tot. . . ." Does she use *she* in similar contexts elsewhere in the essay? Do you find the feminine form of the personal pronoun appropriate or distracting? Explain.

8. Paragraphs 35–37 constitute Ericsson's conclusion. How does this conclusion parallel the essay's introduction in terms of style, structure, and content?

VOCABULARY PROJECTS

1. Define each of the following words as it is used in this selection.

travails (4)	deflectors (16)	staunch (30)
hedging (5)	passive-aggressive (16)	catatonia (30)
pittance (9)	misogynists (18)	gamut (31)
facades (10)	counterpart (18)	foibles (31)
plethora (11)	archetype (20)	reticent (36)
pedophilia (12)	nanoseconds (21)	
blatant (14)	obliterated (22)	

2. Ericsson uses many **colloquialisms** in this essay—for example, "I could write the book on this one" (32). Identify as many of these expressions as you can. Why do you think she uses colloquialisms instead of more formal expressions? Do they have a positive or negative effect on your reaction to her ideas? Explain.

JOURNAL ENTRY

In paragraph 3, Ericsson says, "We lie. We all do." Later in the paragraph she comments, "Sure I lie, but it doesn't hurt anything. Or does it?" Answer her question.

WRITING WORKSHOP

1. Choose three or four of Ericsson's categories, and write a classification-and-division essay called "The Ways I Lie." Base your essay on personal experience, and include an explicit thesis statement that defends these lies—or is sharply critical of their use.

2. In paragraph 22, Ericsson condemns stereotypes. Write a classification-and-division essay with the following thesis statement: "Stereotypes are sometimes inaccurate, often negative, and always dangerous." In your essay, consider the stereotypes applied to four of the following groups: the disabled, the overweight, the elderly, teenagers, welfare recipients, housewives, immigrants.

3. Using the thesis provided in question 2, write a classification-and-division essay that considers the stereotypes applied to four of the following occupations: police officers, librarians, used-car dealers, flight attendants, lawyers, construction workers, rock musicians, accountants.

COMBINING THE PATTERNS

A dictionary **definition** is a familiar — even tired — strategy for an essay's intro-duction. Would you advise Ericsson to delete the definition in paragraph 6 for this reason, or do you believe it is necessary? Explain.

THEMATIC CONNECTIONS

- "'What's in a Name?'" (page 5)
- "Thirty-Eight Who Saw Murder Didn't Call the Police" (page 101)
- "The Lottery" (page 292)

JEDEDIAH PURDY

❖ Shades of Green

Jedediah Purdy (b. 1975) grew up on a farm in rural West Virginia where he was home-schooled until he was fourteen by parents who were part of the "back-to-the-land" movement. He later attended Phillips Exeter Academy and then returned to West Virginia for a year to work in environmental politics. Purdy graduated from Harvard University in 1997 and went on to write for *The American Prospect,* focusing on culture, technology, politics, and the environment. His book *For Common Things: Irony, Trust, and Commitment in America* was published in 1999. A second book, *Being America: Liberty, Commerce, and Violence in an American World,* appeared in 2003. Purdy recently earned a degree from the Yale School of Law. The following essay on the environmental movement originally appeared in *The American Prospect.*

Background: The environmental movement in the United States traces its roots to the founding of the Audubon Society in 1886 and the Sierra Club in 1892. Theodore Roosevelt, president of the United States from 1901 to 1909 and an early environmental champion, was instrumental in the acquisition of public lands that would form the basis of the National Park System. By the middle of the century, wilderness preservationists had succeeded in blocking numerous development projects they saw as environmentally threatening. Eventually, concerns about air and water pollution and other environmental problems led to a greater politicization of the movement and resulted in the first Earth Day demonstrations in 1970 and the establishment of the U.S. Environmental Protection Agency that same year. Since then, the movement has been further radicalized by organizations such as Greenpeace that have engaged in acts of civil disobedience in an effort to preserve endangered species and habitats, as well as by those whose goal is environmental justice for marginalized human populations. At the same time, backlash from pro-business factions has resulted in the weakening of some environmental restrictions.

More than two-thirds of Americans call themselves environmentalists. 1 Their rank includes every serious presidential candidate, a growing list of corporate executives, some of the country's most extreme radicals, and ordinary people from just about every region, class, and ethnic group. Even allowing for some hypocrisy, finding consensus so tightly overlaid on division is reason for a closer look.

In fact, there are several environmentalisms in this country, and there 2 have been for a long time. They are extensions of some of the most persistent strands of American thought and political culture. They stand for different and sometimes conflicting policy agendas, and their guiding concerns are often quite widely divergent. Recently, though, they have begun to contemplate a set of issues that promises to transform each of them — and to expand environmental politics from its traditional concern with a limited number of wild places and species to a broader commitment to the environment as the place where we all live, all the time.

The oldest and most familiar version of environmental concern might be called romantic environmentalism. Still a guiding spirit of the Sierra Club and the soul of the Wilderness Society and many regional groups, this environmentalism arises from love of beautiful landscapes: the highest mountains, deepest canyons, and most ancient forests. As a movement, it began in the late nineteenth century when America's wealthy discovered outdoor recreation and, inspired by writers like Sierra Club founder John Muir, developed a reverence for untamed places. For these American romantics, encounters with the wild promised to restore bodies and spirits worn down by civilized life. Today's romantic environmentalists blend this ambition with a delight in whales, wolves, and distant rain forests. More than any other environmentalists, they—still disproportionately white and prosperous—feel a spiritual attachment to natural places.

Muir's environmentalism contains the idea that our true selves await us in the wild. Another type, managerial environmentalism, puts the wild at our service. This approach is a direct descendant of the Progressive era's hopeful reformism, specifically of Teddy Roosevelt's forestry policies; it makes its basic task the fitting together of ecology and economy to advance human ends. Pragmatic, market oriented, but respectful of public institutions, managerial environmentalists design trading schemes for pollution permits at the Natural Resources Defense Council, head up programs at the Environmental Protection Agency (EPA) to collaborate with businesses in developing clean technologies, and envision global environmental standards advancing alongside free trade accords. In their wild-eyed moments, they imagine a high-tech economy that follows nature in producing no waste or, like *The New Republic*'s senior editor Gregg Easterbrook, genetic engineering that will turn carnivores into grass eaters and bring lion and lamb together at last. Although it began among policy makers, this managerial attitude is gaining ground in the optimistic culture of Silicon Valley and has many adherents younger than 35.

The environmental justice movement is another thing entirely. Only an idea a decade ago, this effort to address the relationships among race, poverty, and environmental harm has come to rapid prominence. Grassroots projects in inner cities and industrial areas around the country have drawn attention to urban air pollution, lead paint, transfer stations for municipal garbage and hazardous waste, and other environmental dangers that cluster in poor and minority neighborhoods. Eight years ago, romantic environmentalism was virtually the only movement that engaged students on college campuses; now young activists are equally likely to talk about connections between the environment and social justice or, on an international scale, the environment and human rights.

Environmental justice follows the tradition of social inclusion and concern for equity that had its last great triumphs during the civil rights movement and the War on Poverty. Some of its landmark moments are court cases ruling that federal projects can be challenged when they concentrate environmental harm in minority areas, which have begun to extend the principles of civil rights to environmental policy.

The environmental justice movement also reflects the populist streak   7
that emerges in American politics wherever an isolated community finds itself up against big and anonymous institutions. Activists and community members tend to mistrust big business and government alike. The constituency of the environmental justice movement often perceives the gap between the prosperous and the poor, between whites and minorities, between mainstream culture and their own communities, as much more basic than the difference between the EPA and Monsanto. All outsiders are on the other side of that gap—an impression that has been reinforced where some local Sierra Club chapters have ignored community health issues and have endorsed proposals to put waste dumps in poor neighborhoods rather than in pristine valleys.

Environmental justice advocates have little patience for romantic envi-   8
ronmentalism, and their culture of perpetual embattlement is worlds away from managerial optimism. When "environmentalists" of such different experiences and sensibilities address the same issue, it is no surprise that misunderstanding and acrimony sometimes result. This tension was evident two years ago when the Sierra Club came close to endorsing strict controls on immigration to slow development and resource use in this country. The organization's justice-oriented members were outraged, as they had been over the waste-siting disputes a few years earlier. For the pure romantics, the concerns about poor communities and international equity didn't seem "environmental" at all. Meanwhile, the impassioned dispute was all rather alien to the measured rationality of the managerial environmentalists' plans for efficient resource use.

But our several environmentalisms are learning from their interactions,   9
and it is possible that the lessons will be good for them all. Romantic environmentalism has long withheld itself from cities, suburbs, and factories, sometimes following Muir in treating these as fallen places where nothing beautiful will grow. The other environmentalisms have challenged this idea by insisting that "the environment" means the space where we live and work, that the built environment of Manhattan and the industrial environment of the lower Mississippi matter as much as the ecosystem of Yellowstone.

The change brings environmental concern home to cities and neigh-   10
borhoods, where people live. This domesticated environmentalism is crystallized in the debates about sprawl, "smart growth," and the design of communities. It is powered by the recognition that the way we now pursue the things we seem to want—space, light, some trees, a little peace and quiet—can leave us feeling overcrowded and isolated, spending too much time in our cars, living and working in spaces that do not inspire our affection. Communities that decide to make walking or bicycling easy, develop dense housing in return for set-asides of open space, and foster neigh-

borhoods where living, working, and shopping all happen on the same block, are addressing an environmental problem with an environmental solution. This is an environmentalism that urges not just setting aside a piece of wilderness for occasional visits but changing the way we live every day — the way we spend our money, build our homes, and move from place to place.

Attention to these domesticated environmental concerns thus corrects a huge blind spot in romantic environmentalism's sometimes exclusive commitment to wilderness. It can also help to bridge a basic gap in the policy proposals of managerial environmentalism. Those proposals concentrate on technological innovation: taxing greenhouse gases, devising permit systems for pollution, and otherwise inventing better devices for living as we already do. The paradox that dogs the managers is that because their policy proposals generally cost money to ordinary people, big industry, or both, they stand little chance without a ground swell of popular support; yet they are just the thing to induce a fit of napping in the average citizen, whose visceral concern for the environment does not carry over into an interest in the tax code. Policies that foster, say, responsible logging, farming for stewardship, or sustainable grazing on public lands have more appeal when they come not as insights of microeconomic analysis and resource management but as part of a proposal that the work we do in nature is more appealing and honorable when it respects nature's requirements. Most of us care little about supply and demand curves, but a fair amount about where we live and how we work. Because it is close to the grain of everyday experience, the language of livable communities and environmentally responsible work can make environmental policy-designers more politically effective.

As for the environmental justice movement, it fits here as the Alabama bus boycotts fit into the 1964 Civil Rights Act. It fights against particular, sometimes quite outrageous, injustices. Its work is right and necessary but not usually connected with a broader agenda for sustaining dignified communities. Yet such an agenda needs not just constituents who are suburbanites upset by sprawl, but the people who suffer most from poor policies on toxics, land use, and transportation: the urban and rural poor. Moreover, a systematic response to the systematic problems those communities face is the only just way to end their thousands of brushfire struggles.

So one possible result of the present trends in environmental politics is a broader, more effective environmental movement. Such a movement might propose that we should need neither to withdraw our innermost selves to the woods nor to experience our neighborhoods as a species of oppression. It would make the human environment a complete and honored portion of environmental politics. Pursuing such goals would require romantics to bring some of their aspirations home from the wilderness, policy specialists to get their hands dirty in a political culture that does not yield to economists' graphs, and environmental justice activists to find reason to turn their populist anger to projects on common ground. None of our several environmentalisms will go away, and none should, but they are all better off with the recognition that the environment is very much a political, cultural, and human affair.

•   •   •

COMPREHENSION

1. Why, according to Purdy, does the environmental movement deserve "a closer look" (1)?

2. How does Purdy believe the focus of environmentalism has changed in recent years?

3. What is "romantic environmentalism" (3)? Where did it originate?

4. What is "managerial environmentalism" (4)? How is it different from "romantic environmentalism"?

5. What is the "environmental justice" movement (5)? Why, according to Purdy, do its supporters "have little patience for romantic environmentalism" (8)? How are they different from managerial environmentalists?

6. What is "domesticated environmentalism" (10)?

7. What advantage does Purdy see in the existence of the "several environmentalisms" (9) he discusses? How does their existence strengthen the environmental movement?

8. What possible outcome does Purdy think may result from today's trends in environmental politics?

PURPOSE AND AUDIENCE

1. In paragraph 2, Purdy says, "In fact, there are several environmentalisms in this country, and there have been for a long time." Is this his thesis statement, or does his thesis appear somewhere else? Explain.

2. Does Purdy seem to favor one category of environmentalism over the others? What makes you think so?

3. Does Purdy seeem optimistic or pessimistic about the future of our nation's environmental politics?

STYLE AND STRUCTURE

1. List the topics Purdy covers for his first category, "romantic environmentalism" (3). Does he cover the same topics for his other categories? If not, should he have added information to any category?

2. How does Purdy introduce each category? Does he need more specific signals to alert readers to the introduction of a new category? If so, where?

3. Do you think Purdy should have listed the categories he planned to discuss? If so, where might he have inserted such a list?

4. Is "domesticated environmentalism" (10) a separate category in Purdy's classification, or does it overlap with any of the others? Is it on the same level of importance as the other categories? Explain.

VOCABULARY PROJECTS

1. Define each of the following words as it is used in this selection.

divergent (2)   populist (7)   ecosystem (9)
pragmatic (4)   constituency (7)   visceral (11)
accords (4)   perpetual (8)   stewardship (11)
inclusion (6)   acrimony (8)

2. Explain the meaning of each of these expressions in the context in which it appears.

"encounters with the wild" (3)
"culture of perpetual embattlement" (8)
"'smart growth'" (10)
"brushfire struggles" (12)

JOURNAL ENTRY

Which kind of environmentalism do you see as most important? Why?

WRITING WORKSHOP

1. Apply each of Purdy's categories of environmentalism to one specific change that could be made in your own community. Begin by considering the kind of project that might be inspired by the values and priorities of "romantic environmentalism." How could such a project improve your community's environment and make life better for its residents? Then, consider each of Purdy's other categories in turn. In your thesis statement, set priorities, indicating which kind of change is most important.

2. Write a classification-and-division essay in which you classify three kinds of people in terms of their attitudes toward the environment. You can use Purdy's categories, or you can devise (and define) three or four categories of your own. In developing your essay, be sure to give examples of each kind of person's characteristic attitudes and behavior.

3. Classify your friends in terms of their interest and involvement in politics. Your principle of classification might be their relative degree of involvement (from total apathy to active participation), the nature of their politics (from conservative to liberal), or the kind of political issues they believe are most important (the environment, gun safety, or free trade, for example). Be sure to include a thesis statement in which you list your categories.

COMBINING THE PATTERNS

If he were to expand this essay, Purdy might add more **description** to his discussion of romantic environmentalism. What might he describe? Do you think he should add such description?

THEMATIC CONNECTIONS

- "Living Like Weasels" (page 164)
- "Burdens" (page 509)
- "On Dumpster Diving" (page 660)

EDWIN BROCK

Five Ways to Kill a Man (Poetry)

Edwin Brock (1927–1997) was born in London, England. As a young man, he served in the Royal Navy for two years, and he later worked as a police officer. His first poetry collection, *An Attempt at Exorcism,* was published in 1959. He went on to work as an advertising copywriter, while publishing over a dozen further poetry collections. He is also the author of the novel *The Little White God* (1962) and the memoir *Here, Now, Always* (1977).

Background: In the following 1963 poem, the first stanza refers to the crucifixion of Jesus, as described in the New Testament. Nailing a victim to a pole or cross was a form of capital punishment practiced in ancient times, especially by the Romans. The second stanza of the poem refers to the battling of knights suited in armor during the European Middle Ages. The third stanza refers to the trench warfare and mustard gas bombs used by German and British forces during World War I. These bombs caused severe blistering, blindness, and respiratory failure, resulting in many casualties. The fourth stanza refers to the aerial bombing conducted during World War II—the German attacks on London, the Japanese attack on Pearl Harbor, and the U.S. atomic bombs dropped on Hiroshima and Nagasaki in Japan.

There are many cumbersome ways to kill a man:
you can make him carry a plank of wood
to the top of a hill and nail him to it. To do this
properly you require a crowd of people
wearing sandals, a cock that crows, a cloak   5
to dissect, a sponge, some vinegar and one
man to hammer the nails home.

Or you can take a length of steel,
shaped and chased in a traditional way,
and attempt to pierce the metal cage he wears.   10
But for this you need white horses,
English trees, men with bows and arrows,
at least two flags, a prince and a
castle to hold your banquet in.

Dispensing with nobility, you may, if the wind   15
allows, blow gas at him. But then you need
a mile of mud sliced through with ditches,
not to mention black boots, bomb craters,
more mud, a plague of rats, a dozen songs
and some round hats made of steel.   20

In an age of aeroplanes, you may fly
miles above your victim and dispose of him by
pressing one small switch. All you then
require is an ocean to separate you, two
systems of government, a nation's scientists,   25
several factories, a psychopath and
land that no one needs for several years.

These are, as I began, cumbersome ways
to kill a man. Simpler, direct, and much more neat
is to see that he is living somewhere in the middle   30
of the twentieth century, and leave him there.

•   •   •

READING LITERATURE

1. What five ways to kill a man does the speaker identify?
2. What other examples can you give for each category?
3. When the speaker uses the word *you,* to whom is he referring?

JOURNAL ENTRY

Why does the speaker see the first four methods of killing as "cumbersome" (1)? Why is the final method "Simpler, direct, and much more neat" (29)?

THEMATIC CONNECTIONS

- "Thirty-Eight Who Saw Murder Didn't Call the Police" (page 101)
- "Ground Zero" (page 158)
- "The Lottery" (page 292)

WRITING ASSIGNMENTS FOR CLASSIFICATION AND DIVISION

1. Choose a film you have seen recently, and list all the elements that you consider significant—plot, direction, acting, special effects, and so on. Then further subdivide each category (for instance, listing each of the special effects). Using this list as an organizational guide, write a review of the film.

2. Write an essay in which you classify the teachers or bosses you have had into several distinct categories and make a judgment about the relative effectiveness of the individuals in each group. Give each category a name, and be sure your essay has a thesis statement.

3. What fashion styles do you observe on your college campus? Establish four or five distinct categories, and write an essay in which you classify students on the basis of how they dress. Give each group a descriptive title.

4. Do some research to help you identify the subclasses of a large class of animals or plants. Write an essay in which you enumerate and describe the subclasses in each class for an audience of elementary school students.

5. Violence in sports is considered by many to be a serious problem. Write an essay in which you express your views on this problem. Use a classification-and-division structure, categorizing information according to sources of violence (such as the players, the nature of the game, and the fans).

6. Classify television shows according to type (action, drama, and so forth), audience (preschoolers, school-age children, adults, and so forth), or any other logical principle. Write an essay based on your system of classification, making sure to include a thesis statement. For instance, you might assert that the relative popularity of one kind of program over others reveals something about television watchers, or that one kind of program shows signs of becoming obsolete.

7. Write a lighthearted essay discussing kinds of snack foods, cartoons, pets, status symbols, toys, shoppers, vacations, weight-loss diets, hairstyles, or drivers.

8. Write an essay in which you assess the relative merits of several different politicians, news broadcasts, or academic majors.

9. What kinds of survival skills does a student need to get through college successfully? Write a classification-and-division essay in which you identify and discuss several kinds of skills, indicating why each category is important. If you like, you may write your essay in the form of a letter to a beginning college student.

10. After attending a party, lecture, or concert, write an essay in which you divide the people you observe there into categories according to some logical principle. Include a thesis statement that indicates how different the various groups are.

11. Based on your own experiences as a student, as well as on your observations of your peers, classify types of students based on their study habits. Is one way of studying more effective than the others? Explain why the study habits of each type of student do or do not work well.

COLLABORATIVE ACTIVITY FOR CLASSIFICATION AND DIVISION

Working in groups, devise a classification system that encompasses all the different kinds of popular music favored by the members of your group. You may begin with general categories like country, pop, and rhythm and blues, but you should also include more specific categories, such as rap and heavy metal, in your classification system. After you decide on categories and subcategories that represent the tastes of all members of your group, fill in examples for each category. Then devise several different options for arranging your categories into an essay.

INTERNET ASSIGNMENT FOR CLASSIFICATION AND DIVISION

Imagine that you are a writer for *Beat* magazine and have been asked to write a feature article titled "American Music of the New Millennium." Referring to the following Web sites, use a classification-and-division structure to discuss the types of music you think represent the future of the music industry. Be sure to give each type of music a name and describe its characteristics so as to give your audience a sense of the differences between the categories.

Spin Magazine
<spin.com>
Along with articles on bands and "pop life," this site contains audio and video clips of new music.

New Music Box
<newmusicbox.org>
This magazine from the American Music Center includes articles, interviews, a calendar, news sections, and sound and audio files.

NewMusicNow.org
<newmusicnow.org>
This site features contemporary works for orchestra by American composers. Visitors can listen to pieces of music, explore their background, and learn about composers.

Rolling Stone Magazine
<rollingstone.com>
This site offers up-to-date music news, reviews, and interviews with various popular music groups and artists of various genres.

Definition

WHAT IS DEFINITION?

A **definition** tells what a term means and how it is different from other terms in its class. In the following paragraph from "Altruistic Behavior," anthropologist Desmond Morris defines *altruism,* the key term of his essay:

Topic sentence	Altruism is the performance of an unselfish act. As a pattern of behavior, this act must have two
Extended definition defines term by enumeration and negation	properties: it must benefit someone else, and it must do so to the disadvantage of the benefactor. It is not merely a matter of being helpful; it is helpfulness at a cost to yourself.

Most people think of definition in terms of dictionaries, which give brief, succinct explanations—called **formal definitions**—of what words mean. But definition also includes explaining what something, or even someone, *is*—that is, its essential nature. Sometimes a definition requires a paragraph, an essay, or even a whole book. These longer, more complex definitions are called **extended definitions.**

Understanding Formal Definitions

Look at any dictionary, and you will notice that all definitions have a standard three-part structure. First, they present the *term* to be defined, then the general *class* it is a part of, and finally the *qualities that differentiate it* from the other terms in the same class.

Term	Class	Differentiation
behaviorism	a theory	that regards the objective facts of a subject's actions as the only valid basis for psychological study
cell	a unit of protoplasm	with a nucleus, cytoplasm, and an enclosing membrane

naturalism	a literary movement	whose original adherents believed that writers should treat life with scientific objectivity
mitosis	a process	of nuclear division of cells, consisting of prophase, metaphase, anaphase, and telophase
authority	a power	to command and require obedience

Understanding Extended Definitions

An extended definition includes the three basic parts of a formal definition—the term, its class, and its distinguishing characteristics. Beyond these essentials, an extended definition does not follow a set pattern of development. Instead, it uses whatever strategies best suit the term being defined and the writing situation. In fact, any one (or more than one) of the essay patterns illustrated in this book can be used to structure a definition essay.

USING DEFINITION

Supplying a formal definition of each term you use is seldom necessary or desirable. Readers will either know what a word means or be able to look it up. Sometimes, however, defining your terms is essential—for example, when a word has several meanings, each of which might fit your context, or when you want to use a word in a special way.

When taking an exam, of course, you are likely to encounter questions that require extended definitions. You might, for example, be asked to define *behaviorism;* tell what a *cell* is; explain the meaning of the literary term *naturalism;* include a comprehensive definition of *mitosis* in your answer; or define *authority.* Such exam questions cannot always be answered in one or two sentences. In fact, the definitions they call for often require several paragraphs.

Extended definitions are useful in many academic assignments besides exams. For example, definitions can explain abstractions like *freedom,* controversial terms like *right to life,* or **slang** terms (informal expressions whose meanings may vary from locale to locale or change as time passes). In a particular writing situation, a definition may be essential because a term has more than one meaning, because you are using it in an unusual way, or because you are fairly certain that the term will be unfamiliar to your readers.

Many extended-definition essays include short formal definitions like those in dictionaries. In such an essay, a brief formal definition can introduce readers to the extended definition, or it can help to support the essay's thesis. In addition, essays in which other patterns of development are dominant often incorporate brief definitions to clarify points or explain basic information for the reader.

PLANNING A DEFINITION ESSAY

You can organize a definition essay according to one or more of the patterns of development described in this book, or you can use other strategies. This section explains both approaches.

Using Patterns of Development

As you plan your essay and jot down your ideas about the term or subject you will define, you will see which other patterns are most useful. For example, the formal definitions of the five terms discussed on pages 491–92 could be expanded with five different patterns of development.

• *Exemplification* To explain *behaviorism,* you could give examples. Carefully chosen cases could show how this theory of psychology applies to different situations. These examples could help readers see exactly how behaviorism works and what it can and cannot account for. Often, examples are the clearest way to explain something unusual, especially when it is unfamiliar to your readers. Defining dreams as "the symbolic representation of mental states" might convey little to readers who do not know much about psychology, but a few examples would help you make your point. Many students have dreams about taking exams—perhaps dreaming that they are late for the test, that they remember nothing about the course, or that they are writing their answers in disappearing ink. You might explain the nature of dreams by interpreting these particular dreams, which may reflect anxiety about a course or about school in general.

• *Description* You can explain the nature of something by describing it. For example, the concept of a *cell* is difficult to grasp from just a formal definition, but your readers would understand the concept more clearly if you were to describe what a cell looks like, possibly with the aid of a diagram or two. Concentrating on the cell membrane, cytoplasm, and nucleus, you could detail each structure's appearance and function. These descriptions would enable readers to visualize the whole cell and understand its workings. Of course, description involves more than the visual: a definition of a tsunami might describe the sounds and the appearance of this enormous ocean wave, and a definition of Parkinson's disease might include a description of how its symptoms feel to a patient.

• *Comparison and contrast* An extended definition of *naturalism* could use a comparison-and-contrast structure. Naturalism is one of several major movements in American literature, so its literary aims could be contrasted with those of other literary movements, such as romanticism or realism. Or you might compare and contrast the plots and characters of several naturalistic works with those of romantic or realistic works. Any time you need to define something unfamiliar, you can compare it to something familiar to your readers. For example, your readers may never have heard of the Chinese dish called sweet-and-sour cabbage, but you can help them imagine it by saying it tastes something like cole slaw. You can also define a thing by contrasting it with something unlike it, especially if the two have some qualities in common. One way to explain the British sport of rugby is by contrasting it with American football, which is not as violent.

• *Process* Because mitosis is a process, an extended definition of *mitosis* should be organized as a process explanation. By tracing the process from stage to stage, you would be able to clearly define this type of cell division for your readers. Process is also a suitable pattern for objects that must be defined in terms of what they do. For example, because a computer carries out certain processes, an extended definition of a computer would probably include a process explanation.

• *Classification and division* You could define *authority* by using classification and division. Basing your extended definition on the model developed by the German sociologist Max Weber, you could divide the class *authority* into the subclasses *traditional authority, charismatic authority,* and *legal-bureaucratic authority.* By explaining each type of authority, you could clarify this very broad term for your readers. In both extended and formal definitions, classification and division can be very useful. By identifying the class that something belongs to, you are explaining what kind of thing it is. For instance, *monetarism* is an economic theory; *The Adventures of Huckleberry Finn* is a novel; *emphysema* is a disease. Likewise, by dividing a class into subclasses, you are defining something more specifically. Emphysema, for instance, is a disease of the lungs and can therefore be classified with tuberculosis but not with appendicitis.

Using Other Strategies

In addition to using various patterns of development, you can expand a definition by using other strategies:

- You can define a term by using **synonyms** (words with similar meanings).
- You can define a term by using *negation* (telling what it is *not*).
- You can define a term by using *enumeration* (listing its characteristics).
- You can define a term by using **analogies** (comparisons that identify similarities between the term and something dissimilar).
- You can define a term by discussing its *origin and development* (the word's derivation, original meaning, and usages).

Phrasing Your Definition

Whatever form your definitions take, make certain that they are clear and that they actually define your terms. Be sure to provide a true definition, not just a descriptive statement such as "Happiness is a four-day weekend." Also, remember that repetition is not definition, so don't include the term you are defining in your definition. For instance, the statement "abstract art is a school of artists whose works are abstract" clarifies nothing for your readers. Finally, define as precisely as possible. Name the class of the term you are defining—"mitosis is *a process in which* a cell divides"—and define this class as narrowly and as accurately as you can. Be specific when you differentiate your term from other members of its class. Careful attention to the language and structure of your definition will help readers understand your meaning.

STRUCTURING A DEFINITION ESSAY

A definition essay should have an *introduction,* a *body,* and a *conclusion.* Although a formal definition strives for objectivity, an extended definition may not. Instead, it may define a term in a way that reflects your attitude toward the subject or your reason for defining it. For example, your extended-definition paper about literary *naturalism* might argue that the significance of this movement's major works has been underestimated by literary scholars. Similarly, your definition of *authority* might criticize its abuses. In such cases, the thesis statement provides a focus for a definition essay, telling readers *your* approach to the definition.

Suppose your assignment is to write a short paper for your introductory psychology course. You decide to examine *behaviorism.* First, you have to determine whether your topic is appropriate for a definition essay. If the topic suggests a response such as "The true nature of A is B" or "A means B," then it is a definition. Of course, you can define the word in one sentence, or possibly two. But to explain the *concept* of behaviorism and its position in the field of psychology, you must go beyond the dictionary.

Second, you have to decide what kinds of explanations are most suitable for your topic and for your intended audience. If you are trying to define *behaviorism* for readers who know very little about psychology, you might use comparisons that relate behaviorism to your readers' experiences, such as how they were raised or how they train their pets. You might also use examples, but the examples would relate not to psychological experiments or clinical treatment but to experiences in everyday life. If, however, you are directing your paper to your psychology instructor, who obviously already knows what behaviorism is, your purpose is to show that you know, too. One way to do this is to compare behaviorism to other psychological theories; another way is to give examples of how behaviorism works in practice. You could also briefly summarize the background and history of the theory. (In a long paper, you might use all of these strategies.)

After considering your paper's scope and audience, you might decide that because behaviorism is somewhat controversial, your best strategy is to supplement a formal definition with examples showing how behaviorist assumptions and methods are applied in specific situations. These examples, drawn from your class notes and textbook, will support your thesis that behaviorism is a valid approach for treating certain psychological dysfunctions. Together, your examples will define *behaviorism* as it is understood today.

An informal outline for your essay might look like this:

Introduction:	Thesis statement—Contrary to its critics' objections, behaviorism is a valid approach for treating a wide variety of psychological dysfunctions.
Background:	Definition of behaviorism, including its origins and evolution
First example:	The use of behaviorism to help psychotics function in an institutional setting
Second example:	The use of behaviorism to treat neurotic behavior, such as chronic anxiety, a phobia, or a pattern of destructive acts
Third example:	The use of behaviorism to treat normal but antisocial or undesirable behavior, such as heavy smoking or overeating
Conclusion:	Restatement of thesis or review of key points

Notice how the three examples in this paper define behaviorism with the complexity, detail, and breadth that a formal definition could not duplicate. This definition is more like a textbook explanation, and, in fact, textbook explanations are often written as extended definitions.

REVISING A DEFINITION ESSAY

When you revise a definition essay, consider the items on the Revision Checklist on page 54. In addition, pay special attention to the items on the checklist below, which apply specifically to revising definition essays.

☑ REVISION CHECKLIST: DEFINITION

- Does your assignment call for definition?
- Does your essay include a clearly stated thesis that identifies the term you will define and communicates your approach to the definition?
- Have you included a formal definition of your subject? Of any additional key terms?
- Have you identified a pattern or patterns of development that you can use to expand your definition?
- Have you used other strategies—such as synonyms, negation, enumeration, or analogies—to expand your definition?
- Have you discussed the origin and development of the term you are defining?

EDITING A DEFINITION ESSAY

When you edit your definition essay, follow the guidelines on the Editing Checklist on page 66. In addition, focus on the grammar, mechanics, and punctuation issues that are most relevant to definition essays. One of these issues—avoiding the phrases *is when* and *is where* in formal definitions—is discussed below.

For more practice in avoiding faulty constructions, visit **Exercise Central** at **<bedfordstmartins.com/patterns/faultyconstructions>**.

GRAMMAR IN CONTEXT : Avoiding *is when* and *is where*

Many extended definitions include one or more one-sentence formal definitions. As you have learned, each of these definitions must include the term you are defining, the class to which the term belongs, and the characteristics that distinguish the term from other terms in the same class.

Sometimes, however, when you are defining a term or concept, you may find yourself using the phrase *is when* or *is where*. If this is the case, your definition is not complete because it omits the class to which the term belongs. In fact, the use of *is when* or *is where* indicates that you are actually presenting an example of the term and not a definition. You can avoid this error by making certain that the form of the verb *be* in your definition is always followed by a noun.*

Incorrect: As described in the essay "The Untouchable," *prejudice* is when someone forms an irrational bias or negative opinion of a person or group (Mahtab 498).

Correct: As described in the essay "The Untouchable," *prejudice* is an irrational bias or negative opinion of a person or group (Mahtab 498).

Incorrect: According to John Kenneth Galbraith, a *burden* is where certain people object to supporting a government social program (509–10).

Correct: According to John Kenneth Galbraith, a *burden* is a government social program that certain people do not support (509–10).

☑ **EDITING CHECKLIST: DEFINITION**

- Have you avoided using *is when* and *is where* in your formal definitions?
- Have you used the present tense for your definition—even if you have used the past tense elsewhere in your essay?
- If you have used a definition from a dictionary, have you italicized the term you are defining (or underlined to indicate italics) and placed the definition itself in quotation marks?

---

*The examples below refer to essays that appear later in this chapter.

▶ **A STUDENT WRITER: DEFINITION**

The following student essay, written by Ajoy Mahtab for a composition course, defines the untouchables, members of a caste that is shunned in India. In his essay, Ajoy, who grew up in Calcutta, presents a thesis that is sharply critical of the practice of ostracizing untouchables.

The Untouchable

Introduction:
background

A word that is extremely common in India   1
yet uncommon to the point of incomprehension in
the West is the word <u>untouchable</u>. It is a word
that has had extremely sinister connotations
throughout India's history. A rigorously
worked-out caste system existed in traditional
Indian society. At the top of the social ladder sat the Brahmins, the clan of the priest-
hood. These people had renounced the material
world for a spiritual one. Below them came the
Kshatriyas, or the warrior caste. This caste
included the kings and all their nobles along
with their armies. Third on the social ladder
were the Vaishyas, who were the merchants of
the land. Trade was their only form of livelihood. Last came the Shudras — the menials.
Shudras were employed by the prosperous as
sweepers and laborers. Originally a person's
caste was determined only by his profession.
Thus, if the son of a merchant joined the army,
he automatically converted from a Vaishya to
a Kshatriya. However, the system soon became
hereditary and rigid. Whatever one's occupation, one's caste was determined from birth
according to the caste of one's father.

Outside of this structure were a group of   2
people, human beings treated worse than dogs
and shunned far more than lepers, people who
were not considered even human, people who
defiled with their very touch. These were the

Formal definition

Achhoots: the untouchables. The word <u>untouch-</u>
<u>able</u> is commonly defined as "that which cannot
or should not be touched." In India, however,

Historical background   it was taken to a far greater extreme. The untouchables of a village lived in a separate community downwind of the borders of the village. They had a separate water supply, for they would make the village water impure if they were to drink from it. When they walked, they were made to bang two sticks together continuously so that passersby could avoid an untouchable's shadow. Tied to their waists, trailing behind them, was a broom that would clean the ground they had walked on. The penalty for not following these or any other rules was death for the untouchable and, in many instances, for the entire untouchable community.

Present situation   One of the pioneers of the fight against   3
untouchability was Mahatma Gandhi. Thanks to his efforts and those of many others, untouchability no longer presents anything like the horrific picture painted earlier. In India today, in fact, recognition of untouchability is punishable by law. Theoretically, there is no such thing as untouchability anymore. But old traditions linger on, and such a deep-rooted fear passed down from generation to generation cannot disappear overnight. Even today, caste is an important factor in most marriages. Most Indian surnames reveal a person's caste immediately, and so it is a difficult thing to hide. The shunning of the untouchable is more prevalent in South India, where the general public is much more devout, than in the North. Some people would rather starve than share food and water with an untouchable. This concept is very difficult to accept in the West, but it is true all the same.

Example   I remember an incident from my childhood.   4
I could not have been more than eight or nine at the time. I was on a holiday staying at my family's house on the river Ganges. There was

a festival going on and, as is customary, we were giving the servants small presents. I was handing them out when an old lady, bent with age, slowly hobbled into the room. She stood in the far corner of the room all alone, and no one so much as looked at her. When the entire line ended, she stepped hesitantly forward and stood in front of me, looking down at the ground. She then held a cloth stretched out in front of her. I was a little confused about how I was supposed to hand her her present, since both her hands were holding the cloth. Then, with the help of prompting from someone behind me, I learned that I was supposed to drop the gift into the cloth without touching the cloth it- self. It was only later that I found out that she was an untouchable. This was the first time I had actually come face to face with prejudice, and it felt like a slap in the face. That inci- dent was burned into my memory, and I do not think I will ever forget it.

Conclusion begins   The word <u>untouchable</u> is not often used in   5 the West, and when it is, it is generally used as a complimentary term. For example, an avid fan might say of an athlete, "He was absolutely untouchable. Nobody could even begin to compare with him." It seems rather ironic that a word could be so favorable in one culture and so derogatory in another. Why does a word that gives happiness in one part of the world cause pain in another? Why does the same word have different meanings to different people around the globe? Why do certain words cause rifts and others forge bonds? I do not think anyone can tell me the answer.

Conclusion continues   No actual parallel can be found today that   6 compares to the horrors of untouchability. For an untouchable, life itself was a crime. The day was spent just trying to stay alive. From

Thesis statement

```
the misery of the untouchables, the world should
learn a lesson: isolating and punishing any
group of people is dehumanizing and immoral.
```

Points for Special Attention

Thesis Statement   Ajoy Mahtab's assignment was to write an extended definition of a term he assumed would be unfamiliar to his audience. Because he had definite ideas about the unjust treatment of the untouchables, Ajoy wanted his essay to have a strong thesis that communicated his disapproval. Still, because he knew his American classmates would need a good deal of background information before they would accept such a thesis, he decided not to present it in his introduction. Instead, he decided to lead up to his thesis gradually and state it at the end of his essay. When other students in the class reviewed his draft, this subtlety was one of the points they reacted to most favorably.

Structure   Ajoy's introduction establishes the direction of his essay by introducing the word he will define; he then places this word in context by explaining India's rigid caste system. In paragraph 2, he gives the formal definition of the word *untouchable* and goes on to sketch the term's historical background. Paragraph 3 explains the status of the untouchables in present-day India, and paragraph 4 gives a vivid example of Ajoy's first encounter with an untouchable. As he begins his conclusion in paragraph 5, Ajoy brings his readers back to the word his essay defines. Here he uses two strategies to add interest: he contrasts a contemporary American usage of *untouchable* with its derogatory meaning in India, and he asks a series of **rhetorical questions** (questions asked for effect and not meant to be answered). In paragraph 6, Ajoy presents a summary of his position to lead into his thesis statement.

Patterns of Development   This essay uses a number of strategies commonly encountered in extended definitions: it includes a formal definition, explains the term's origin, and explores some of the term's connotations. In addition, the essay incorporates several familiar patterns of development. For instance, paragraph 1 uses classification and division to explain India's caste system; paragraphs 2 and 3 use brief examples to illustrate the plight of the untouchable; and paragraph 4 presents a narrative. Each of these patterns enriches the definition.

Focus on Revision

Because the term Ajoy defined was so unfamiliar to his classmates, many of the peer editing worksheets his classmates filled in asked for more information. One suggestion in particular—that he draw an **analogy** between the unfamiliar term *untouchable* and a more familiar concept—appealed to Ajoy as he planned his revision. Another student suggested that Ajoy could compare untouchables to other groups who are shunned—for example, people with AIDS. Although Ajoy states in his conclusion that no parallel exists, an attempt to find common ground between untouchables and other groups could make his essay more meaningful to his readers—and bring home to them an idea that is distinctly foreign. Such a connection could also make his conclusion especially powerful. (A sample peer editing worksheet for definition can be found on the *Patterns for College Writing* Web site at <bedfordstmartins.com/patterns>.)

The selections that follow use exemplification, description, narration, and other methods of developing extended definitions. The first selection, a visual text, is followed by questions designed to illustrate how definition can operate in visual form.

❖

U.S. Census 2000 Form (Questionnaire)

→ **NOTE: Please answer BOTH Questions 7 and 8.**

7. **Is Person 1 Spanish/Hispanic/Latino?** *Mark* ☒ *the* ***"No"*** *box if* ***not*** *Spanish/Hispanic/Latino.*

- ☐ **No,** not Spanish/Hispanic/Latino
- ☐ Yes, Mexican, Mexican Am., Chicano
- ☐ Yes, other Spanish/Hispanic/Latino — *Print group.* ↙
- ☐ Yes, Puerto Rican
- ☐ Yes, Cuban

| | | | | | | | | | | | | | | | | | | | | | | |

8. **What is Person 1's race?** *Mark* ☒ ***one or more races*** *to indicate what this person considers himself/herself to be.*

- ☐ White
- ☐ Black, African Am., or Negro
- ☐ American Indian or Alaska Native — *Print name of enrolled or principal tribe.* ↙

| | | | | | | | | | | | | | | | | | | | | | | |

- ☐ Asian Indian
- ☐ Chinese
- ☐ Filipino
- ☐ Other Asian — *Print race.* ↙
- ☐ Japanese
- ☐ Korean
- ☐ Vietnamese
- ☐ Native Hawaiian
- ☐ Guamanian or Chamorro
- ☐ Samoan
- ☐ Other Pacific Islander — *Print race.* ↙

| | | | | | | | | | | | | | | | | | | | | | | |

- ☐ Some other race — *Print race.* ↙

| | | | | | | | | | | | | | | | | | | | | | | |

• • •

READING IMAGES

1. In a single complete sentence, define yourself in terms of your race, religion, or ethnicity (whatever is most important to you).

2. Look at the U.S. Census questions above. Which boxes would you mark? Do you see this choice as an accurate expression of what you consider yourself to be? Explain.

3. Only recently has the Bureau of the Census permitted respondents to mark "one or more races" to indicate their ethnic identity. Do you think this option is a good idea? Why or why not?

JOURNAL ENTRY

Why do you think the government needs to know "what [a] person considers himself/herself to be"? Do you think it is important for the government to know how people define themselves, or do you consider this information to be an unwarranted violation of a person's privacy? Explain.

THEMATIC CONNECTIONS

- "Only Daughter" (page 84)
- "Indian Education" (page 126)
- "The 'Black Table' Is Still There" (page 340)
- "Two Ways to Belong in America" (page 397)
- "Mother Tongue" (page 462)

JUDY BRADY

I Want a Wife

Judy Brady was born in San Francisco in 1937 and earned a B.F.A. in painting from the University of Iowa in 1962. She has raised two daughters,
worked as a secretary, and published articles on many social issues. Diag-
nosed with breast cancer in 1980, she became active in the politics of cancer and has edited *Women and Cancer* (1990) and *One in Three: Women with
Cancer Confront an Epidemic* (1991). She also helped found the Toxic Links
Coalition, an organization devoted to lobbying for cancer and environmental issues.

Background: Brady has been active in the women's movement since
1969, and "I Want a Wife" first appeared in the premiere issue of the feminist *Ms.* magazine in 1972. That year represented perhaps the height of
the feminist movement in the United States. The National Organization
for Women, established in 1966, had hundreds of chapters around the
country. The Equal Rights Amendment, barring discrimination against
women, passed in Congress (although it has been ratified by only thirty-
five of the necessary thirty-eight states), and Congress also passed Title IX
of the Education Amendments Act, which required equal opportunity (in
sports as well as academics) for all students in any school that receives
federal funding. At that time, women accounted for just under 40 percent
of the labor force (up from 23 percent in 1950), a number that has grown
to almost 50 percent today. Of mothers with children under the age of
eighteen, fewer than 40 percent were employed in 1970; today, three-
quarters work, 38 percent of them full-time and year-round. As for stay-at-
home fathers, their numbers have increased from virtually zero to close to
three million.

I belong to that classification of people known as wives. I am A Wife. 1
And, not altogether incidentally, I am a mother.

Not too long ago a male friend of mine appeared on the scene fresh 2
from a recent divorce. He had one child, who is, of course, with his ex-wife.
He is looking for another wife. As I thought about him while I was ironing
one evening, it suddenly occurred to me that I, too, would like to have a
wife. Why do I want a wife?

I would like to go back to school so that I can become economically 3
independent, support myself, and, if need be, support those dependent
upon me. I want a wife who will work and send me to school. And while I
am going to school I want a wife to take care of my children. I want a wife
to keep track of the children's doctor and dentist appointments. And to
keep track of mine, too. I want a wife to make sure my children eat properly
and are kept clean. I want a wife who will wash the children's clothes and
keep them mended. I want a wife who is a good nurturant attendant to my

children, who arranges for their schooling, makes sure that they have an adequate social life with their peers, takes them to the park, the zoo, etc. I want a wife who takes care of the children when they are sick, a wife who arranges to be around when the children need special care, because, of course, I cannot miss classes at school. My wife must arrange to lose time at work and not lose the job. It may mean a small cut in my wife's income from time to time, but I guess I can tolerate that. Needless to say, my wife will arrange and pay for the care of the children while my wife is working.

I want a wife who will take care of *my* physical needs. I want a wife who   4
will keep my house clean. A wife who will pick up after my children, a wife who will pick up after me. I want a wife who will keep my clothes clean, ironed, mended, replaced when need be, and who will see to it that my personal things are kept in their proper place so that I can find what I need the minute I need it. I want a wife who cooks the meals, a wife who is a *good* cook. I want a wife who will plan the menus, do the necessary grocery shopping, prepare the meals, serve them pleasantly, and then do the cleaning up while I do my studying. I want a wife who will care for me when I am sick and sympathize with my pain and loss of time from school. I want a wife to go along when our family takes a vacation so that someone can continue to care for me and my children when I need a rest and change of scene.

I want a wife who will not bother me with rambling complaints about   5
a wife's duties. But I want a wife who will listen to me when I feel the need to explain a rather difficult point I have come across in my course of studies. And I want a wife who will type my papers for me when I have written them.

I want a wife who will take care of the details of my social life. When   6
my wife and I are invited out by my friends, I want a wife who will take care of the babysitting arrangements. When I meet people at school that I like and want to entertain, I want a wife who will have the house clean, will prepare a special meal, serve it to me and my friends, and not interrupt when I talk about things that interest me and my friends. I want a wife who will have arranged that the children are fed and ready for bed before my guests arrive so that the children do not bother us. I want a wife who takes care of the needs of my guests so that they feel comfortable, who makes sure that they have an ashtray, that they are passed the hors d'oeuvres, that they are offered a second helping of the food, that their wine glasses are replenished when necessary, that their coffee is served to them as they like it. And I want a wife who knows that sometimes I need a night out by myself.

I want a wife who is sensitive to my sexual needs, a wife who makes love   7
passionately and eagerly when I feel like it, a wife who makes sure that I am satisfied. And, of course, I want a wife who will not demand sexual attention when I am not in the mood for it. I want a wife who assumes the complete responsibility for birth control, because I do not want more children. I want a wife who will remain sexually faithful to me so that I do not have to clutter up my intellectual life with jealousies. And I want a wife who

understands that *my* sexual needs may entail more than strict adherence to monogamy. I must, after all, be able to relate to people as fully as possible.

If, by chance, I find another person more suitable as a wife than the wife I already have, I want the liberty to replace my present wife with another one. Naturally, I will expect a fresh new life; my wife will take the children and be solely responsible for them so that I am left free.   8

When I am through with school and have a job, I want my wife to quit working and remain at home so that my wife can more fully and completely take care of a wife's duties.   9

My God, who *wouldn't* want a wife?   10

• • •

COMPREHENSION

1. In one sentence, define what Brady means by *wife*. Does this ideal wife actually exist? Explain.

2. List some of the specific duties of the wife Brady describes. Into what five general categories does Brady arrange these duties?

3. What complaints does Brady apparently have about the life she actually leads? To what does she seem to attribute her problems?

4. Under what circumstances does Brady say she would consider leaving her wife? What would happen to the children if she left?

PURPOSE AND AUDIENCE

1. This essay was first published in *Ms.* magazine. In what sense is it appropriate for the audience of this feminist publication? Where else can you imagine it appearing?

2. Does this essay have an explicitly stated thesis? If so, where is it? If the thesis is implied, paraphrase it.

3. Do you think Brady *really* wants the kind of wife she describes? Explain.

STYLE AND STRUCTURE

1. Throughout the essay, Brady repeats the words "I want a wife." What is the effect of this repetition?

2. The first and last paragraphs of this essay are quite brief. Does this weaken the essay? Why or why not?

3. In enumerating a wife's duties, Brady frequently uses the verb *arrange*. What other verbs does she use repeatedly? How do these verbs help her make her point?

4. Brady never uses the personal pronouns *he* or *she* to refer to the wife she defines. Why not?

5. Comment on Brady's use of phrases like *of course* (2, 3, and 7), *needless to say* (3), *after all* (7), *by chance* (8), and *naturally* (8). What do these expressions contribute to the sentences in which they appear? To the essay as a whole?

VOCABULARY PROJECTS

1. Define each of the following words as it is used in this selection.

   nurturant (3)   adherence (7)
   replenished (6)   monogamy (7)

2. Going beyond the dictionary definitions, decide what Brady means to suggest by the following words. Is she using any of these words sarcastically? Explain.

   proper (4)   necessary (6)   suitable (8)
   pleasantly (4)   demand (7)   free (8)
   bother (6)   clutter up (7)

JOURNAL ENTRY

Is Brady's 1972 characterization of a wife still accurate today? Which of the characteristics she describes have remained the same? Which have changed? Why?

WRITING WORKSHOP

1. Write an essay in which you define your ideal spouse.

2. Write an essay entitled "I Want a Husband." Taking an **ironic** stance, use society's notions of the ideal husband to help you shape your definition.

3. Read "The Company Man" (page 517). Using ideas gleaned from that essay and "I Want a Wife," as well as your own ideas, write a definition essay called "The Ideal Couple." Your essay can be serious or humorous. Develop your definition with examples.

COMBINING THE PATTERNS

Like most definition essays, "I Want a Wife" uses several patterns of development. Which ones does it use? Which of these do you consider most important for supporting Brady's thesis? Why?

THEMATIC CONNECTIONS

- "My Mother Never Worked" (page 96)
- "Sex, Lies, and Conversation" (page 407)
- "The Men We Carry in Our Minds" (page 456)

Burdens

One of the twentieth century's most influential economists, John Kenneth Galbraith was born in 1908 in Ontario, Canada, the son of a farmer. He studied agriculture at the University of Toronto and received advanced degrees in economics at the University of California at Berkeley. He became a U.S. citizen in 1937. Galbraith has taught economics at Harvard and Princeton and has held a number of important government positions, most notably as economic advisor to Democratic presidents John F. Kennedy and Lyndon B. Johnson in the 1960s. He is the author of more than thirty books for general readers, including *The Affluent Society* (1958), *The Age of Uncertainty* (1977), and *The Good Society* (1996).

Background: The following essay first appeared on the op-ed page of the *New York Times* in 1995, at the peak of the debate in Congress over reducing welfare and other benefits to the poor and the unemployed. The taxpayer-supported antipoverty programs that were passed by Congress in the 1960s have long been controversial. On the one side are those (such as Galbraith) who advocate a more equal distribution of wealth in the United States. These people maintain that wealthy citizens and large corporations should be taxed at high rates so that the government can provide housing, food subsidies, and educational opportunities for those who are less well off. On the other side are those who advocate essentially equal tax rates for all, tax reductions for corporations that create jobs, and fewer government regulations and services. For these critics, aid to the economically disadvantaged has become a "burden" to taxpayers; Galbraith here finds it ironic that other types of government expenditures are not so defined. (Note that much of this "burden" was eliminated by the Welfare Reform Act of 1998.)

In these last years, and notably in these past months, we have heard much of the burden imposed by government on the citizen. Nothing has been more emphasized in speech and possibly also in thought. This comment is not meant to regret this concern, as some might suppose: rather, it is to clarify the way the word *burden* is now employed. It has a very special connotation, of which all who cherish good or anyhow accepted English usage should be aware.

As now used, *burden* applies only to a very specific range of government activities. Many are not a burden and are not to be so described. Defense expenditure is definitely not a burden; indeed, increases therein are now being proposed. That there is now no wholly plausible enemy does not affect the situation. Similarly, in recent years large sums, in a range upward from $50 billion, have been appropriated to bail out failed financial institutions, specifically the savings and loan associations. This was not a burden. A clear distinction must be made between a burden and an admittedly unfortunate and costly financial misadventure.

Social Security is not a burden; in no politically acceptable discourse is it so described. Nor are farm price and income supports, although recipients regularly command incomes of a hundred grand or more. Medicare is basically not a burden and is not to be so described. There are many lesser items of expenditure that are not a burden, including health care for members of the Congress.

On the other hand, some functions of government are a heavy burden. Notable are welfare payments, especially those to unmarried mothers and their children. Likewise expenditures for food stamps and child nutrition. While Medicare is not a burden, Medicaid is a real burden.*

Education is a somewhat special case. While private education is not a burden, public education, especially in our cities, can be a very heavy load. Here, as elsewhere, burden bears no necessary relation to cost.

And here one sees the rule by which students of contemporary English usage should be guided. Whether a public function or service or regulation is or is not a burden depends on the income of the individual so helped or favored.

As with all linguistic rules there can be exceptions. The National Endowment for the Arts, support to public broadcasting, a few other items not specifically designed for the poor, are a burden. The exceptions, as ever, make the rule.

It is the generally accepted purpose of language to convey meaning. All who use or hear the word *burden* should know the precise and subtle meaning that it conveys. Basically something is a burden when it is not for the rich, not for the merely affluent, but for the poor.

● ● ●

COMPREHENSION

1. How does Galbraith define *burden*? Where does he give his formal definition of the word? Why do you think he presents this definition where he does?

2. In paragraph 1, when Galbraith speaks of "all who cherish good or anyhow accepted English usage," what distinction do you think he means to make between *good* and *accepted* English? Why is this distinction important?

3. What distinction does Galbraith draw between a burden and "an admittedly unfortunate and costly financial misadventure" (2)?

4. What examples does Galbraith give of programs that are burdens? Of those that are not burdens? What do the programs in each group have in common?

---

*EDS. NOTE—Medicare is health insurance for retired people that is supported by government funds and by individual contributions. Medicaid is health insurance for the poor and disabled that is supported only by government funds.

5. Why, according to Galbraith, is education a "special case" (5)?

6. Why do the National Endowment for the Arts and public broadcasting qualify as burdens even though they are not designed for the poor? Does Galbraith state the reason or merely imply it? Why?

PURPOSE AND AUDIENCE

1. The original title of this essay was "Our Forked Tongue." A person who speaks with a forked tongue is someone who is taking two different positions at the same time — in other words, a liar. What effect do you think Galbraith might have expected the title "Our Forked Tongue" to have on his readers? Do you think this title was a good choice? Why or why not?

2. Is Galbraith's purpose in this essay to criticize social priorities or to criticize the use of language to justify those priorities? Do you think his primary target is government or individuals? Explain your reasoning.

STYLE AND STRUCTURE

1. Where does Galbraith define by enumeration? By negation? Why is negation a particularly effective strategy for this essay?

2. How could Galbraith use additional strategies to strengthen his definition? For example, could he discuss the origin and development of the word *burden*? Could he use **synonyms** or **analogies?** If so, where?

3. How would you characterize Galbraith's tone in this essay? Does he seem to be angry or bitter, or does he seem disheartened by what he observes?

4. Where does Galbraith use **sarcasm?** Do you think the sarcasm is appropriate? Necessary? Do you think Galbraith could reach more readers by adopting a more neutral tone? Explain your reasoning.

5. Do you think the essay would be more convincing if Galbraith had provided historical background for the social and political situation he describes — for example, discussions of other programs that were (or were not) perceived as burdens? Why or why not?

6. In paragraph 3, Galbraith sets down a rule: "Medicare is basically not a burden and is not to be so described." Where else does he use this kind of language? Who does he imply has established these rules? What is his attitude toward these rule makers?

VOCABULARY PROJECTS

1. Define each of the following words as it is used in this selection.

therein (2)   plausible (2)   discourse (3)

2. Look up the word *burden* in a dictionary. How does the dictionary's primary definition differ from Galbraith's? How do you account for this difference?

JOURNAL ENTRY

Contrary to what Galbraith says in paragraph 3, some people today *do* see Social Security and Medicare as burdens. Do you? Why or why not?

WRITING WORKSHOP

1. Write an essay in which you define *burden* on a personal level by giving examples of the kinds of things you consider burdens. You might also want to develop your definition essay with comparison and contrast, exploring the differences between a *burden* and a *responsibility*.

2. What state, local, or national government program do you consider to be the biggest burden on citizens? Why? Write a definition essay in which you support your thesis with a single extended example.

3. Sometimes a person can be a burden. Define *burden* by explaining in what sense you find a particular friend or family member to be a burden to you—or in what respects you believe you are or have been a burden to someone else.

COMBINING THE PATTERNS

What pattern does Galbraith use most often to develop his definition? Where does he use this pattern? Could he have used **narration** to support his thesis? Where? Do you think he *should* have expanded his essay with a paragraph or two of narrative? Why or why not?

THEMATIC CONNECTIONS

- "The Human Cost of an Illiterate Society" (page 229)
- "The Ways We Lie" (page 470)
- "On Dumpster Diving" (page 660)
- "A Modest Proposal" (page 676)

JOSÉ ANTONIO BURCIAGA

❖

Tortillas

José Antonio Burciaga (1940–1996) was born in El Chuco, Texas, and served in the U.S. Air Force from 1960 to 1964. He graduated from the University of Texas at El Paso in 1968 and attended the Corcoran School of Art and the San Francisco Art Institute. Burciaga was the founder of *Disseños Literarios,* a publishing company in California, as well as the comedy troupe Culture Clash. He contributed fiction, poetry, and articles to many anthologies as well as to journals and newspapers. He also published several books of poems, drawings, and essays, including the poetry collection *Undocumented Love* (1992) and the essay collection *Drink Cultura* (1993). "Tortillas," originally titled "I Remember Masa," was first published in *Weedee Peepo* (1988), a collection of essays in Spanish and English.

Background: Tortillas have been a staple of Mexican cooking for thousands of years. These thin, round griddlecakes made of cornmeal *(masa)* are often eaten with every meal, and the art of making them is still passed from generation to generation (although they now are widely available commercially as well). The earliest Mexican immigrants introduced them to the United States, and in the last twenty-five years tortillas, along with many other popular items of Mexican cuisine, have entered the country's culinary landscape (as, over the decades, has a wide variety of other "ethnic" foods like pizza, egg rolls, bagels, and gyros). Still, tortillas have special meaning for Mexican Americans, and in this essay Burciaga discusses the role of the tortilla within his family's culture.

My earliest memory of *tortillas* is my *Mamá* telling me not to play with them. I had bitten eyeholes in one and was wearing it as a mask at the dinner table. 1

As a child, I also used *tortillas* as hand warmers on cold days, and my family claims that I owe my career as an artist to my early experiments with *tortillas.* According to them, my clowning around helped me develop a strong artistic foundation. I'm not so sure, though. Sometimes I wore a *tortilla* on my head, like a *yarmulke,* and yet I never had any great urge to convert from Catholicism to Judaism. But who knows? They may be right. 2

For Mexicans over the centuries, the *tortilla* has served as the spoon and the fork, the plate and the napkin. *Tortillas* originated before the Mayan civilizations, perhaps predating Europe's wheat bread. According to Mayan mythology, the great god Quetzalcoatl, realizing that the red ants knew the secret of using maize as food, transformed himself into a black ant, infiltrated the colony of red ants, and absconded with a grain of corn. (Is it any wonder that to this day, black ants and red ants do not get along?) Quetzalcoatl then put maize on the lips of the first man and woman, 3

Oxomoco and Cipactonal, so that they would become strong. Maize festivals are still celebrated by many Indian cultures of the Americas.

When I was growing up in El Paso, *tortillas* were part of my daily life. I 4 used to visit a *tortilla* factory in an ancient adobe building near the open *mercado* in Ciudad Juárez. As I approached, I could hear the rhythmic slapping of the *masa* as the skilled vendors outside the factory formed it into balls and patted them into perfectly round corn cakes between the palms of their hands. The wonderful aroma and the speed with which the women counted so many dozens of *tortillas* out of warm wicker baskets still linger in my mind. Watching them at work convinced me that the most handsome and *deliciosas tortillas* are handmade. Although machines are faster, they can never adequately replace generation-to-generation experience. There's no place in the factory assembly line for the tender slaps that give each *tortilla* character. The best thing that can be said about mass-producing *tortillas* is that it makes it possible for many people to enjoy them.

In the *mercado* where my mother shopped, we frequently bought 5 *taquitos de nopalitos,* small tacos filled with diced cactus, onions, tomatoes, and *jalapeños.* Our friend Don Toribio showed us how to make delicious, crunchy *taquitos* with dried, salted pumpkin seeds. When you had no money for the filling, a poor man's *taco* could be made by placing a warm *tortilla* on the left palm, applying a sprinkle of salt, then rolling the *tortilla* up quickly with the fingertips of the right hand. My own kids put peanut butter and jelly on *tortillas,* which I think is truly bicultural. And speaking of fast foods for kids, nothing beats a *quesadilla,* a *tortilla* grilled-cheese sandwich.

Depending on what you intend to use them for, *tortillas* may be made 6 in various ways. Even a run-of-the-mill *tortilla* is more than a flat corn cake. A skillfully cooked homemade *tortilla* has a bottom and a top; the top skin forms a pocket in which you put the filling that folds your *tortilla* into a taco. Paper-thin *tortillas* are used specifically for *flautas,* a type of taco that is filled, rolled, and then fried until crisp. The name *flauta* means *flute,* which probably refers to the Mayan bamboo flute; however, the only sound that comes from an edible *flauta* is a delicious crunch that is music to the palate. In México *flautas* are sometimes made as long as two feet and then cut into manageable segments. The opposite of *flautas* is *gorditas,* meaning *little fat ones.* These are very thick small *tortillas.*

The versatility of *tortillas* and corn does not end here. Besides being 7 tasty and nourishing, they have spiritual and artistic qualities as well. The Tarahumara Indians of Chihuahua, for example, concocted a corn-based beer called *tesgüino,* which their descendants still make today. And everyone has read about the woman in New Mexico who was cooking her husband a *tortilla* one morning when the image of Jesus Christ miraculously appeared on it. Before they knew what was happening, the man's breakfast had become a local shrine.

Then there is *tortilla* art. Various Chicano artists throughout the 8 Southwest have, when short of materials or just in a whimsical mood, used a dry *tortilla* as a small, round canvas. And a few years back, at the height of the Chicano movement, a priest in Arizona got into trouble with the Church after he was discovered celebrating mass using a *tortilla* as the host. All of which only goes to show that while the *tortilla* may be a lowly corn cake, when the necessity arises, it can reach unexpected distinction.

• • •

COMPREHENSION

1. What exactly is a tortilla?
2. List the functions — both practical and whimsical — tortillas serve.
3. In paragraph 7, Burciaga cites the "spiritual and artistic qualities" of tortillas. Do you think he is being serious? Explain your reasoning.

PURPOSE AND AUDIENCE

1. Burciaga states his thesis explicitly in his essay's final sentence. Paraphrase this thesis. Why do you think he does not state it sooner?
2. Do you think Burciaga expects most of his readers to be of Hispanic descent? To be familiar with tortillas? How can you tell?
3. Why do you think Burciaga uses humor in this essay? Is it consistent with his essay's purpose? Could the humor have a negative effect on his audience? Explain.
4. Why are tortillas so important to Burciaga? Is it just their versatility he admires, or do they represent something more to him?

STYLE AND STRUCTURE

1. Where does Burciaga provide a formal definition of *tortilla*? Why does he locate this formal definition at this point in his essay?
2. Burciaga uses many Spanish words, but he defines only some of them — for example, *taquitos de nopalitos* and *quesadilla* in paragraph 5 and *flautas* and *gorditas* in paragraph 6. Why do you think he defines some Spanish terms but not others? Should he have defined them all?
3. Does Burciaga use **synonyms** or negation to define *tortilla*? Does he discuss the word's origin? If so, where? If not, do you think any of these strategies would improve his essay? Explain.

VOCABULARY PROJECTS

1. Define each of the following words as it is used in this selection.

   yarmulke (2)   absconded (3)   concocted (7)
   maize (3)   adobe (4)

2. Look up each of the following words in a Spanish-English dictionary and (if possible) supply its English equivalent.

mercado (4)   *deliciosas* (4)
masa (4)   *jalapeños* (5)

JOURNAL ENTRY

Explore some additional uses — practical or frivolous — for tortillas that Burciaga does not discuss.

WRITING WORKSHOP

1. Write an essay in which you define a food that is important to your family, ethnic group, or circle of friends. Use several patterns of development, as Burciaga does. Assume that your audience is not very familiar with the food you define.

2. Relying primarily on description and exemplification, define a food that is sure to be familiar to all your readers. Do not name the food until your essay's last sentence.

3. Write an essay defining a food — but include a thesis statement that paints a very favorable portrait of a much-maligned food (for example, Spam or brussels sprouts) or a very negative picture of a popular food (for example, chocolate or ice cream).

COMBINING THE PATTERNS

Burciaga uses several patterns of development in his extended definition. Where, for example, does he use **description, narration, process,** and **exemplification**? Does he use any other patterns? Explain.

THEMATIC CONNECTIONS

- "Once More to the Lake" (page 175)
- "Walt and Ray: Your Trusted Friends" (page 414)
- "The Park" (page 655)

ELLEN GOODMAN

❖

The Company Man

Ellen Goodman was born in 1941 in Newton, Massachusetts, and graduated from Radcliffe College in 1963. She joined the *Boston Globe* in 1967
and is now a columnist and associate editor at the newspaper. Her regular
column, "At Large," has been syndicated since 1976 and now appears in
more than four hundred newspapers nationwide. She has published several volumes of her columns, including *Close to Home* (1975) and *Value Judgments* (1993). She cowrote her most recent book, *I Know Just What You Mean*
(2001), with novelist Patricia O'Brien. Goodman received a Pulitzer Prize
for commentary in 1980.

Background: The concept of the "company man" dates from the
1950s, when employees — almost exclusively male and particularly in large
corporations — were expected to virtually give over their lives to their jobs
if they expected to climb the corporate ladder. Any questioning of company policy or procedures, any sort of nonconformity, was implicitly discouraged. By the early 1970s, when Goodman's column appeared, however,
the countercultural movements of the 1960s had led some, particularly
younger people, to challenge such values and to view large corporations
with distrust. It is within this context that Goodman defines a particularly
grim vision of the "company man." More recently, some companies have
modified their corporate culture to allow for more original thinking and
more flexible work schedules. Nevertheless, the company man — now, of
course, just as likely to be a woman — still exists.

1   He worked himself to death, finally and precisely, at 3:00 A.M. Sunday
morning.

2   The obituary didn't say that, of course. It said that he died of a coronary thrombosis — I think that was it — but everyone among his friends
and acquaintances knew it instantly. He was a perfect Type A, a workaholic,
a classic, they said to each other and shook their heads — and thought for
five or ten minutes about the way they lived.

3   This man who worked himself to death finally and precisely at 3:00 A.M.
Sunday morning — on his day off — was fifty-one years old and a vice-
president. He was, however, one of six vice-presidents, and one of three
who might conceivably — if the president died or retired soon enough —
have moved to the top spot. Phil knew that.

4   He worked six days a week, five of them until eight or nine at night,
during a time when his own company had begun the four-day week for
everyone but the executives. He worked like the Important People. He had
no outside "extracurricular interests," unless, of course, you think about a
monthly golf game that way. To Phil, it was work. He always ate egg salad

sandwiches at his desk. He was, of course, overweight, by 20 or 25 pounds. He thought it was okay, though, because he didn't smoke.

On Saturdays, Phil wore a sports jacket to the office instead of a suit, because it was the weekend. 5

He had a lot of people working for him, maybe sixty, and most of them liked him most of the time. Three of them will be seriously considered for his job. The obituary didn't mention that. 6

But it did list his "survivors" quite accurately. He is survived by his wife, Helen, forty-eight years old, a good woman of no particular marketable skills, who worked in an office before marrying and mothering. She had, according to her daughter, given up trying to compete with his work years ago, when the children were small. A company friend said, "I know how much you will miss him." And she answered, "I already have." 7

"Missing him all these years," she must have given up part of herself which had cared too much for the man. She would be "well taken care of." 8

His "dearly beloved" eldest of the "dearly beloved" children is a hardworking executive in a manufacturing firm down South. In the day and a half before the funeral, he went around the neighborhood researching his father, asking the neighbors what he was like. They were embarrassed. 9

His second child is a girl, who is twenty-four and newly married. She lives near her mother and they are close, but whenever she was alone with her father, in a car driving somewhere, they had nothing to say to each other. 10

The youngest is twenty, a boy, a high-school graduate who has spent the last couple of years, like a lot of his friends, doing enough odd jobs to stay in grass and food. He was the one who tried to grab at his father, and tried to mean enough to him to keep the man at home. He was his father's favorite. Over the last two years, Phil stayed up nights worrying about the boy. 11

The boy once said, "My father and I only board here." 12

At the funeral, the sixty-year-old company president told the forty-eight-year-old widow that the fifty-one-year-old deceased had meant much to the company and would be missed and would be hard to replace. The widow didn't look him in the eye. She was afraid he would read her bitterness and, after all, she would need him to straighten out the finances — the stock options and all that. 13

Phil was overweight and nervous and worked too hard. If he wasn't at the office, he was worried about it. Phil was a Type A, a heart-attack natural. You could have picked him out in a minute from a lineup. 14

So when he finally worked himself to death, at precisely 3:00 A.M. Sunday morning, no one was really surprised. 15

By 5:00 P.M. the afternoon of the funeral, the company president had begun, discreetly of course, with care and taste, to make inquiries about his replacement. One of three men. He asked around: "Who's been working the hardest?" 16

• • •

COMPREHENSION

1. In one sentence, define *the company man*. What does Goodman's extended definition convey that your one-sentence definition lacks?

2. When Phil's widow is told by a friend, "I know how much you will miss him," she answers, "I already have" (7). What does she mean?

3. Why does Phil's oldest son go around the neighborhood researching his father?

4. Why doesn't Phil's widow look the company president in the eye?

5. What kind of man will the company president seek for Phil's replacement?

PURPOSE AND AUDIENCE

1. What point is Goodman trying to make in this essay? Does she succeed? Explain.

2. What assumptions does Goodman make about her readers? What effect do you think she hopes the essay will have on her audience?

3. Why does Goodman imply her thesis and not state it?

STYLE AND STRUCTURE

1. Why does Goodman state the time of Phil's death at both the beginning and the end of her essay?

2. Is there a reason why Goodman waits until the end of paragraph 3 before she refers to the company man by name? Explain.

3. What is the effect of the bits of dialogue Goodman includes?

4. Goodman tells Phil's story in a flat, impersonal way. How does this tone help her achieve her purpose?

5. Why does Goodman put quotation marks around the phrases *extracurricular interests* (4), *survivors* (7), *missing him all these years, well taken care of* (8), and *dearly beloved* (9)?

VOCABULARY PROJECTS

1. Define each of the following words as it is used in this selection.

   coronary thrombosis (2)   classic (2)   stock options (13)
   workaholic (2)   conceivably (3)

2. This essay's style and vocabulary are quite informal. Substitute a more formal word or phrase for each of these expressions:

   top spot (3)   odd jobs (11)   all that (13)
   okay (4)   grab at (11)   a heart-attack natural (14)

   How does each substitution change the sentence in which it appears?

JOURNAL ENTRY

Do you know anyone like Phil? What do you think really motivates people like him? Do you believe such forces drive women as well as men?

WRITING WORKSHOP

1. Write an essay defining the workaholic student (or the procrastinating student). As Goodman does, use a narrative to support your thesis.

2. Write a definition essay in which you define the company man (or the company woman), but use comparison and contrast to organize your definition.

3. Write a brief obituary for Phil, one that might appear in his company's newsletter. Using the title "A Valued Employee," develop the obituary as a definition essay. Your aim is to show readers what traits such an employee must have — and to present those traits as desirable ones.

COMBINING THE PATTERNS

Goodman relies on **narration** to develop her definition. Is this a good choice? Why? What other patterns of development would be helpful?

THEMATIC CONNECTIONS

- "Midnight" (page 201)
- "The Peter Principle" (page 207)
- "Suicide Note" (page 357)

GAYLE ROSENWALD SMITH

❖ The Wife-Beater

Gayle Rosenwald Smith was born in 1951 in Philadelphia and received her bachelor's degree from the University of Pennsylvania. A graduate of the University of Miami School of Law, she currently practices family law. She has published articles in a variety of journals and periodicals and is co-author of *What Every Woman Should Know about Divorce and Custody* (1998). The following essay appeared in the *Philadelphia Inquirer* in 2001.

Background: As Smith notes here, *wife-beater* is a slang term for a type of sleeveless undershirt that has in recent years achieved an air of "fashion" status. An Internet search of the term found a number of businesses that, in fact, market such shirts as "wife-beaters." A Texas-based firm offers adult-sized shirts emblazoned with the slogan, as well as "Lil' Wife Beater" shirts for babies. The firm's Web site—which is accompanied by the beat of a rap recording about "smashing" women—includes a background screen showing a woman being spanked, and provides a link to a "Wife Beater Hall of Fame." It also offers to send a second shirt at half price to any customer convicted of domestic violence (proof of conviction required, photos not acceptable). Many Web sites have sprung up condemning this business, but one of the site's customers is a victim of domestic violence who hands out shirts to police officers, judges, and others whose professional conduct she believes condones domestic violence. In another twist, a feminist retail site offers a "Wife Beater Beater" shirt with a cartoon image of a woman kicking a man in the groin.

Everybody wears them. The Gap sells them. Fashion designers Dolce and Gabbana have lavished them with jewels. Their previous greatest resurgence occurred in the 1950s, when Marlon Brando's Stanley Kowalski wore one in Tennessee Williams' *A Streetcar Named Desire*. They are all the rage. 1

What are they called? 2

The name is the issue. For they are known as "wife-beaters." 3

A Web search shows that kids nationwide are wearing the skinny-ribbed white T-shirts that can be worn alone or under another shirt. Women have adopted them with the same gusto as men. A search of boutiques shows that these wearers include professionals who wear them, adorned with designer accessories, under their pricey suits. They are available in all colors, sizes and price ranges. 4

Wearers under 25 do not seem to be disturbed by the name. But I sure am. 5

It's an odd name for an undershirt. And even though the ugly stereotypes behind the name are both obvious and toxic, it appears to be cool to say the name without fear of (or without caring about) hurting anyone. 6

That the name is fueled by stereotype is now an academically estab- 7
lished fact, although various sources disagree on exactly when shirt and
name came together. The *Oxford Dictionary* defines the term *wife-beater* as:

1. A man who physically abuses his wife and
2. Tank-style underwear shirts. Origin: based on the stereotype that physically abusive husbands wear that particular type of shirt.

The *World Book Dictionary* locates the origin of the term *wife-beater* in 8
the 1970s, from the stereotype of the Midwestern male wearing an undershirt while beating his wife. The shirts are said to have been popular in
the 1980s at all types of sporting events, especially ones at which one sits in
the sun and develops "wife-beater marks." The undershirts also attained
popularity at wet T-shirt contests, in which the wet, ribbed tees accentuated contestants' breasts.

In an article in the style section of the *New York Times,* Jesse Scheid- 9
lower, principal editor of the *Oxford English Dictionary*'s American office,
says the association of the undershirt and the term *wife-beater* arose in 1997
from varied sources, including gay and gang subcultures and rap music.

In the article, some sources argued that the reference in the term was 10
not to spousal abuse per se but to popular-culture figures such as Ralph
Cramden and Tony Soprano. And what about Archie Bunker?

It's not just the name that worries me. Fashion headlines reveal 11
that we want to overthrow '90s grunge and return to shoulder pads and
hardware-studded suits. Am I reading too much into a fashion statement
that the return is also to male dominance where physical abuse is acceptable as a means of control?

There has to be a better term. After all, it's a pretty rare piece of cloth- 12
ing that can make both men and women look sexier. You'd expect a term
connoting flattery — not violence.

Wearers under 25 may not want to hear this, but here it is. More than 13
4 million women are victims of severe assaults by boyfriends and husbands each year. By conservative estimate, family violence occurs in 2 million families each year in the United States. Average age of the batterer: 31.

Possibly the last statistic is telling. Maybe youth today would rather 14
ignore the overtones of the term *wife-beater.* It is also true, however, that the
children of abusers often learn the behavior from their elders.

Therein lies perhaps the worst difficulty: that this name for this shirt 15
teaches the wrong thing about men. Some articles quote women who felt
the shirts looked great, especially on guys with great bodies. One woman
stated that it even made guys look "manly."

So *manly* equals *violent*? Not by me, and I hope not by anyone on any 16
side of age 25.

• • •

COMPREHENSION

1. Why is Smith "disturbed" (5) by the name "wife-beater"?

2. In paragraph 3, Smith says, "The name is the issue"; in paragraph 11, she says "It's not just the name that worries me." What does she mean by each statement? Does she contradict herself?

3. What relationship does Smith see between the name of a sleeveless under-shirt and the prevalence of family violence? Does she believe there is—or could be—a causal connection? If so, which is the cause, and which is the effect?

4. In paragraph 12, Smith acknowledges that the shirt "can make both men and women look sexier." Does this remark in any way undercut her credibility? Explain.

5. How, according to Smith, does calling a shirt a wife-beater teach women "the wrong thing about men" (15)?

PURPOSE AND AUDIENCE

1. How do you think Smith expects her audience to react to her opening statement ("Everybody wears them")?

2. Why do you think Smith wrote this essay? Is her purpose to change the name of the T-shirt, or does she seem to have a more ambitious purpose? Explain.

3. Twice in her essay, Smith mentions a group she calls "wearers under 25" (5, 13). Does she seem to be directing her remarks at these young adults or at older readers? At wearers of the shirts or at a more general audience?

4. Restate Smith's thesis in your words.

STYLE AND STRUCTURE

1. Why do you think Smith begins her essay by explaining the popularity of sleeveless undershirts? Is this an effective strategy?

2. In paragraph 7, Smith reproduces a formal definition from the *Oxford Dictionary*. Why does she include this definition when she has already defined her term? What, if anything, does the formal definition add?

3. Where does Smith present information on the history of the wife-beater? Why does she include this kind of information?

4. Where does Smith quote statistics? Do you see this information as relevant or incidental to her argument?

VOCABULARY PROJECTS

1. Define each of the following words as it is used in this selection.

resurgence (1)   accentuated (8)
gusto (4)   per se (10)
toxic (6)   connoting (12)

2. In paragraph 12, Smith says, "There has to be a better term." Can you think of a "better term"—one that does not suggest violence—for the shirt Smith describes?

JOURNAL ENTRY

Do you agree with Smith that there is a danger in the casual use of terms like *wife-beater,* or do you think she is exaggerating the problem?

WRITING WORKSHOP

1. Relying primarily on description and exemplification, define an article of clothing that is essential to your wardrobe. Begin by checking an unabridged dictionary to learn the item's history and the origin of its name.

2. Using comparison and contrast to structure your essay, define what a particular item of clothing means to you and to one of your parents.

3. Do members of your religious or ethnic group wear an item of clothing that is not well known to others? Define the article of clothing, and explain its significance and its history in terms that outsiders can understand.

COMBINING THE PATTERNS

Do you think that Smith should have spent more time in this essay on developing the **cause-and-effect** relationship, if any, between the "wife-beater" shirt and family violence? What additional information would she have to provide?

THEMATIC CONNECTIONS

- "My First Conk" (page 260)
- "A Peaceful Woman Explains Why She Carries a Gun" (page 345)
- "Violent Films Cry 'Fire' in Crowded Theaters" (page 612)

❖
"Hope" Is the Thing with Feathers (Poetry)

Emily Dickinson (1830–1886) was born into a prominent Amherst, Massachusetts, family, attended a local grammar school, and spent one year at Mount Holyoke Female Seminary. While in her twenties, Dickinson began to have doubts about organized religion, and at the age of thirty, she stopped attending church and withdrew almost entirely from society as well, spending the rest of her life in the family home. Dickinson began writing poetry at an early age, but she had little success in publishing her work because editors deemed her poems too quirky and unconventional in theme and style. She eventually gave up any hope of reaching a wide audience although she continued to write, composing over seventeen hundred poems by the time of her death. Some of these were collected posthumously in heavily edited versions, and these initial volumes of her work achieved surprising success. It was not until the twentieth century, however, that Dickinson was recognized as a major American poet with a wholly distinctive voice.

Background: To understand Dickinson's lack of success during her lifetime, it is necessary to recognize that poets of the mid-nineteenth century—especially female poets—were expected to express conventionally uplifting sentiments in traditional forms. Here, for example, are some lines from a poem by Phoebe Cary (1824–1871), a poet who was popular in her day but is now forgotten:

> Sometimes, I think, the things we see
> Are shadows of the things to be;
> That what we plan we build;
> That every hope that hath been crossed,
> And every dream we thought was lost,
> In heaven shall be fulfilled.

Compared to this, Dickinson's meditation on hope is nothing short of revolutionary.

"Hope" is the thing with feathers —
That perches in the soul —
And sings the tune without the words —
And never stops — at all —

And sweetest — in the Gale — is heard —   5
And sore must be the storm —
That could abash the little Bird —
That kept so many warm —

I've heard it in the chillest land —
And on the strangest Sea —   10
Yet, never, in Extremity,
It asked a crumb — of Me.

• • •

READING LITERATURE

1. This poem defines *hope* by comparing it to a bird. According to the speaker, in what respects is hope like a bird? Can you think of other similarities?

2. What do you think the speaker means when she says that hope "sings the tune without the words" (3)?

3. What words could be substituted for each of the following?

   "thing" (1)   "chillest" (9)
   "perches" (2)   "crumb" (12)

   How might your substitutions change the poem?

JOURNAL ENTRY

Write a paragraph in which you use a different pattern — **exemplification** or **narration,** for instance — to define *hope*.

THEMATIC CONNECTIONS

- "Ground Zero" (page 158)
- "Suicide Note" (page 357)
- The Declaration of Independence (page 557)

WRITING ASSIGNMENTS FOR DEFINITION

1. Choose a document or ritual that is a significant part of your religious or cultural heritage. Define it, using any pattern or combination of patterns you choose, but make sure to include a formal definition somewhere in your essay. Assume your readers are not familiar with the term you are defining.

2. Define an abstract term — for example, *stubbornness, security, courage,* or *fear* — by making it concrete. You can develop your definition with a series of brief examples or with an extended narrative that illustrates the characteristic you are defining.

3. The readings in this chapter define (among other things) a food, a family role, an occupational role, and an item of clothing. Write an essay in which you use examples and description to define one of these topics — for instance, sushi (food), a stepmother (family role), the modern baseball player (occupational role), or chador (item of clothing).

4. Do some research to learn the meaning of one of these medical conditions: angina, migraine, Down syndrome, attention deficit disorder, schizophrenia, autism, osteoporosis, Alzheimer's disease. Then, write an extended definition essay explaining the condition to an audience of high school students.

5. Use an extended example to support a thesis in an essay that defines *racism, sexism,* or another type of bigoted behavior.

6. Choose a term that is central to one of your courses — for instance, *naturalism, behaviorism,* or *authority* — and write an essay in which you define the term. Assume that your audience is made up of students who have not yet taken the course. You may begin with an overview of the term's origin if you believe this is appropriate. Then, develop your essay with examples and **analogies** that will facilitate your audience's understanding of the term.

7. Assume your audience is from a culture that is not familiar with modern American pastimes. Write a definition essay for this audience in which you describe the form and function of a Frisbee, a Barbie doll, an action figure, a skateboard, or a video game.

8. Review any one of the following narrative essays from Chapter 4, and use it to help you develop an extended definition of one of the following terms.

   "Finishing School" or "Only Daughter" — prejudice

   "My Mother Never Worked" or "Scrubbing in Maine" — work

   "Thirty-Eight Who Saw Murder Didn't Call the Police" — apathy

   "Shooting an Elephant" — power

9. What constitutes an education? Define the term *education* by identifying several different sources of knowledge, formal or informal, and explaining what each contributes. You might read — or reread — "Finishing School" (page 89), "Indian Education" (page 126), "The Human Cost of an Illiterate Society" (page 229), or "Strange Tools" (page 697).

10. What qualifies someone as a hero? Developing your essay with a single extended example or a series of examples, define the word *hero*. Include a formal definition, and try to incorporate at least one paragraph in which you define the term by explaining and illustrating what a hero is *not*.

COLLABORATIVE ACTIVITY FOR DEFINITION

Working as a group, choose one of the following words to define: *pride, hope, sacrifice, courage, justice*. Then, define the term with a series of extended examples drawn from films that members of your group have seen, with each of you developing an illustrative paragraph based on a different film. (Before beginning, your group may decide to focus on one particular genre of film.) When each paragraph has been read by everyone in the group, work together to formulate a thesis that asserts the vital importance of the quality your examples have defined. Finally, write suitable opening and closing paragraphs for the essay, and arrange the body paragraphs in a logical order, adding transitions where necessary.

INTERNET ASSIGNMENT FOR DEFINITION

After visiting the following Web sites, write an essay in which you define the term *Industrial Revolution*. To give your readers a better understanding of the effects of industrialization, develop your definition by considering changes that it led to in the areas of art, science, technology, medicine, working conditions, and/or transportation.

IRWeb: The Industrial Revolution
<tqjunior.advanced.org/4132/index.htm>
This educational site about the Industrial Revolution contains information, links to other sites, and games, including an Industrial Revolution quiz.

Internet Modern History Sourcebook: The Industrial Revolution
<fordham.edu/halsall/mod/modsbook14.html>
This site offers original texts written during the Industrial Revolution, including lectures and discussions about the process of industrialization and the social and political effects of the revolution. It also features literary responses to the revolution.

The Industrial Revolution: A Trip to the Past
<members.aol.com/mhirotsu/kevin/trip2.html>
This site discusses advances in art, science, medicine, and transportation.

❖ 12
Argumentation

WHAT IS ARGUMENTATION?

Argumentation is a reasoned, logical way of asserting the soundness of a position, belief, or conclusion. Argumentation takes a stand—supported by evidence—and urges people to share the writer's perspective and insights. In the following paragraph from his essay "Holding Cell," Jerome Groopman argues that with its decision to limit therapeutic cloning, the President's Council on Bioethics has prevented scientists from carrying out important medical research that could possibly save lives:

Issue identified	The President's Council on Bioethics, chaired by Dr. Leon R. Kass, presented its long-awaited report on human cloning to the White House on July 10, 2002. The council unanimously advised against "cloning to produce children," commonly called "reproductive cloning." But on "cloning for biomedical research"—therapeutic cloning to produce stem cells to try to ameliorate disease—it split. Of the seventeen members, ten (including Kass)
Background presents both sides of issue	voted against it. They couched their rejection as a compromise since they called not for a permanent ban but for a four-year moratorium. This moratorium, according to the letter accompanying the report, would allow "a thorough federal review . . . to clarify the issues and foster a public consensus about how to proceed." It would also give researchers time to seek alternative ways to generate stem cells. But for scientists and, more importantly, for the millions of patients with incurable maladies, the compromise is a painful disappointment.
Topic sentence (takes a stand)	It shackles potentially lifesaving research and provides no clear framework to advance the ethical debate. What's more, the arguments deployed on its behalf don't withstand scrutiny.

Argumentation can be used to convince other people to accept (or at least acknowledge the validity of) your position; to defend your position, even if others cannot be convinced to agree; or to question or refute a position you believe to be misguided, untrue, dangerous, or evil (without necessarily offering an alternative).

UNDERSTANDING ARGUMENTATION AND PERSUASION

Although the terms *persuasion* and *argumentation* are frequently used interchangeably, they do not mean the same thing. **Persuasion** is a general term that refers to the method by which a writer moves an audience to adopt a belief or follow a course of action. To persuade an audience, a writer relies on various appeals — to the emotions, to reason, or to ethics.

Argumentation is the appeal to reason. In an argument, a writer connects a series of statements so that they lead logically to a conclusion. Argumentation is different from persuasion in that it does not try to move an audience to action; its primary purpose is to demonstrate that certain ideas are valid and others are not. And, unlike persuasion, argumentation has a formal structure: an argument makes points, supplies evidence, establishes a logical chain of reasoning, refutes opposing arguments, and accommodates the views of an audience.

As the selections in this chapter demonstrate, however, most effective arguments combine several appeals: even though their primary appeal is to reason, they may also appeal to emotions. For example, you could use a combination of logical and emotional appeals to argue against lowering the drinking age in your state from twenty-one to eighteen. You could appeal to *reason* by constructing an argument leading to the conclusion that the state should not condone policies that have a high probability of injuring or killing citizens. You could support your conclusion by presenting statistics showing that alcohol-related traffic accidents kill more teenagers than disease does. You could also cite a study showing that when the drinking age was raised from eighteen to twenty-one, fatal accidents declined. In addition, you could include an appeal to the *emotions* by telling a particularly sad story about an eighteen-year-old alcoholic or by pointing out how an increased number of accidents involving drunk drivers would cost taxpayers more money and could even cost some of them their lives. These appeals to your audience's emotions could strengthen your argument by widening its appeal. Keep in mind, however, that in an effective argument emotion does not take the place of logic; it supports and reinforces it.

The appeals you choose and how you balance them depend in part on your purpose and your sense of your audience. As you consider what strategies to use, remember that some extremely effective appeals are unfair. Although most people would agree that lies, threats, misleading statements, and appeals to greed and prejudice are unacceptable ways of reaching an audience, such appeals are used frequently in daily conversation, political campaigns, and even international diplomacy. Nevertheless, in your college writing you should use only those appeals that most people would consider fair.

PLANNING AN ARGUMENTATIVE ESSAY

Choosing a Topic

In an argumentative essay, as in all writing, choosing the right topic is important. Ideally, your topic should be one in which you have an intellectual or emotional stake. Still, you should be open-minded and willing to consider all sides of a question. If the evidence goes against your position, you should be willing to change your thesis. And you should be able, from the outset, to consider your topic from other people's viewpoints; this will help you determine how much they know about your topic, what their beliefs are, and how they are likely to react. You can then use this knowledge to build your case. If you cannot be open-minded, you should choose another topic that you can deal with more objectively.

Other factors should also influence your selection of a topic. First, you should be well informed about your topic. In addition, you should choose an issue narrow enough to be treated effectively in the space available to you, or be willing to confine your discussion to one aspect of a broad issue. It is also important to consider your purpose—what you expect your argument to accomplish and how you wish your audience to respond. If your topic is so far-reaching that you cannot identify what you want to convince readers to think, or if your purpose is so idealistic that your expectations of their response are impossible or unreasonable, your essay will suffer.

Taking a Stand

After you have chosen your topic, you are ready to take your stand—to state the position you will argue in the form of a thesis. Consider the following thesis statement:

> Education is the best way to address the problem of increased drug use among teenagers.

This thesis statement says that increased drug use is a problem among teenagers, that there is more than one possible solution to this problem, and that education is a better solution than any other. In your argument, you will have to support each of these three points logically and persuasively.

After stating your thesis, you should examine it to make sure it is *debatable*. There is no point in arguing a statement of fact or a point that most people accept as self-evident. A good argumentative thesis contains a proposition that at least some people would object to. A good way to test the suitability of your thesis for an argumentative essay is to formulate an

antithesis, a statement that asserts the opposite position. If you know that some people would support the antithesis, you can be certain that your thesis is indeed debatable.

Thesis: Because immigrants have contributed much to the development of the United States, immigration quotas should be relaxed.

Antithesis: Even though immigrants have contributed much to the development of the United States, immigration quotas should not be relaxed.

Analyzing Your Audience

Before writing any essay, you should analyze the characteristics, values, and interests of your audience. In argumentation, it is especially important to consider what beliefs or opinions your readers are likely to have and whether your audience is likely to be friendly, neutral, or hostile to your thesis. It is probably best to assume that some, if not most, of your readers are at least skeptically neutral—that they are open to your ideas but need to be convinced. This assumption will keep you from making claims you cannot support. If your position is controversial, you should assume that an informed and determined opposition is looking for holes in your argument.

In an argumentative essay, you face a dual challenge. You must appeal to readers who are neutral or even hostile to your position, and you must influence those readers so that they are more receptive to your viewpoint. For example, it would be relatively easy to convince college students that tuition should be lowered or instructors that faculty salaries should be raised. You could be reasonably sure, in advance, that each group would agree with your position. But argument requires more than just telling people what they already believe. It would be much harder to convince college students that tuition should be raised to pay for an increase in instructors' salaries or to persuade instructors to forgo raises so that tuition can remain the same. Remember, your audience will not just take your word for the claims you make. You must provide evidence that will support your thesis and reasoning that will lead logically to your conclusion.

Gathering and Documenting Evidence

All the points you make in your paper must be supported. If they are not, your audience will dismiss them as unfounded, irrelevant, or unclear. Sometimes you can support a statement with appeals to emotion, but most of the time you support the points of your argument by appealing to reason—by providing **evidence,** facts and opinions in support of your position.

As you gather evidence and assess its effectiveness, keep in mind that evidence in an argumentative essay never proves anything conclusively. If it did, there would be no debate and hence no point in arguing. The best that evidence can do is convince your audience that an assertion is reasonable and worth considering.

Kinds of Evidence   Evidence can be *fact* or *opinion*. Facts are statements that most people agree are true and that can be verified independently. Facts — including statistics — are the most commonly used type of evidence. It is a fact, for example, that fewer people per year were killed in automobile accidents in the 1990s than in the 1970s. Facts may be drawn from your own experience as well as from reading and observation. It may, for instance, be a fact that you yourself may have had a serious automobile accident. Quite often, facts are more convincing when they are supplemented by **opinions,** or interpretations of facts. To connect your facts about automobile accidents to the assertion that the installation of side-impact airbags in all SUVs as well as cars could reduce deaths still further, you could cite the opinions of an expert — consumer advocate Ralph Nader, for example. His statements, along with the facts and statistics you have assembled and your own interpretations of those facts and statistics, could convince readers that your solution to the problem of highway deaths is reasonable.

Keep in mind that not all opinions are equally convincing. The opinions of experts are more convincing than are those of individuals who have less knowledge of an issue. Your personal opinions can be excellent evidence (provided you are knowledgeable about your subject), but they are usually less convincing to your audience than expert opinions. In the final analysis, what is important is not just the quality of the evidence but also the credibility of the person offering it.

What kind of evidence might change readers' minds? That depends on the readers, the issue, and the facts at hand. Put yourself in the place of your readers, and ask what would make them receptive to your thesis. Why, for example, should a student agree to pay higher tuition? You might concede that tuition is high but point out that it has not been raised for three years, while the college's costs have kept going up. The cost of heating and maintaining the buildings has increased, and professors' salaries have not, with the result that several excellent teachers have recently left the college for higher-paying jobs. Furthermore, cuts in federal and state funding have already caused a reduction in the number of courses offered. Similarly, how could you convince a professor to agree to accept no raise at all, especially in light of the fact that faculty salaries have not kept up with inflation? You could say that because cuts in government funding have already reduced course offerings and because the government has also reduced funds for student loans, any further rise in tuition to pay faculty salaries will cause some students to drop out — and that in turn would cost some instructors their jobs. As you can see, the evidence and reasoning you use in an argument depend to a great extent on whom you want to persuade and what you know about them.

Criteria for Evidence   As you select and review material, choose your evidence with the following three criteria in mind:

1. Your evidence should be *relevant.* It should support your thesis and be pertinent to your argument. As you present evidence, be careful not to concentrate so much on a specific example that you lose sight of the point you are supporting. Such digressions may confuse your readers. For example, in arguing for mandatory HIV testing for all health-care workers, one student made the point that AIDS is at epidemic proportions. To illustrate this point, he offered a discussion of the bubonic plague in fourteenth-century Europe. Although interesting, this example was not relevant. To show its relevance, the student would have to link his discussion to his assertions about AIDS, possibly by comparing the spread of the bubonic plague in the fourteenth century to the spread of AIDS in Africa today.

2. Your evidence should be *representative.* It should represent the full range of opinions about your subject, not just one side. For example, in an essay in which you argued against the use of animals in medical experimentation, you would not just use information provided by animal rights activists. You would also use information supplied by medical researchers, pharmaceutical companies, and possibly medical ethicists. In addition, the examples and expert opinions you include should be typical, not aberrant. Suppose you are writing an essay in support of building a trash-to-steam plant in your city. To support your thesis, you present the example of Baltimore, which has a successful trash-to-steam program. As you consider your evidence, ask yourself if Baltimore's experience with trash-to-steam is typical. Did other cities have less success? Take a close look at the opinions that disagree with the position you plan to take. If you understand your opposition, you will be able to refute it effectively when you write your paper.

3. Your evidence should be *sufficient.* Include enough evidence to support your claims. The amount of evidence you need depends on the length of your paper, your audience, and your thesis. It stands to reason that you would use fewer examples in a two-page paper than in a ten-page research assignment. Similarly, an audience that is favorably disposed to your thesis might need only one or two examples to be convinced, whereas a skeptical audience would need many more. As you develop your thesis, think about the amount of support you will need to write your paper. You may decide that a narrower, more limited thesis will be easier to support than one that is more inclusive.

Documentation of Evidence   As soon as you decide on a topic, you should begin to gather your evidence. Sometimes you will be able to use your own ideas and observations to support your claims. Most of the time, however, you will have to use the print and electronic resources of the library or search the Internet to locate the information you need. Whenever you use such evidence in your paper, you have to **document** it by providing the source of the information. (When documenting sources, follow the documentation format recommended by the Modern Language Association, which is explained in the Appendix of this book. If you don't document your sources, your readers are likely to dismiss your evidence, thinking that it may be inaccurate, unreliable, or simply false. **Documentation** gives readers the ability to evaluate the sources you cite and to consult them if they wish. When you document sources, you are telling your readers that you are honest and have nothing to hide. Documentation also helps you avoid **plagiarism** — presenting the ideas or words of others as if they were your own. Certainly you don't have to document every idea you use in your paper. (**Common knowledge** — information you could easily find in several reference sources, for example — can be presented without documentation.) You must, however, document any use of a direct quotation as well as any ideas that are the original conclusions of your source.

Dealing with the Opposition

When gathering evidence, keep in mind that you cannot ignore arguments against your position. In fact, you should specifically address the most obvious — and sometimes the not-so-obvious — objections to your case. Try to anticipate the objections that a reasonable person would have to your thesis. By directly addressing these objections in your essay, you will help convince readers that your arguments are sound. This part of an argument, called **refutation,** is essential to making the strongest case possible.

You can *refute* opposing arguments by showing that they are unsound, unfair, or weak. Frequently, you will present contrasting evidence to show the weakness of your opponent's points and to reinforce your own case. Careful use of definition and cause-and-effect analysis may also prove effective. In the following passage from the classic essay "Politics and the English Language," George Orwell refutes an opponent's argument:

> I said earlier that the decadence of our language is probably curable. Those who deny this would argue, if they produced an argument at all, that language merely reflects existing social conditions, and that we cannot influence its development by any direct tinkering with words and constructions. So far as the general tone or spirit of a language goes, this may be true, but it is not true in detail. Silly words and expressions have often disappeared, though not through any evolutionary process but owing to the conscious actions of a minority.

Orwell begins by stating the point he wants to make, goes on to define the argument against his position, and then identifies its weakness. Later in the essay, Orwell bolsters his argument by presenting two examples that support his point.

When an opponent's argument is so compelling that it cannot be easily dismissed, you should concede its strength. By acknowledging that a point is well taken, you reinforce the impression that you are a fair-minded person. If possible, identify the limitations of the opposing position and then move your argument to more solid ground. Often an opponent's strong point addresses only *one* facet of a multifaceted problem.

When planning an argumentative essay, write down all possible arguments against your thesis that you can identify. Then, as you marshal your evidence, decide which points you will refute, keeping in mind that careful readers will expect you to refute the most compelling of your opponent's arguments. Take care, though, not to distort an opponent's argument by making it seem weaker than it actually is. This technique, called creating a *straw man,* can backfire and actually turn fair-minded readers against you.

Understanding Rogerian Argument

Psychologist Carl Rogers has written about how to argue without assuming an adversarial relationship. According to Rogers, traditional strategies of argument rely on confrontation — proving that an opponent's position is wrong. With this method of arguing, one person is "wrong" and one is "right." By attacking an opponent and repeatedly hammering home the message that his or her arguments are incorrect or misguided, a writer forces the opponent into a defensive position. The result is conflict, disagreement, and frequently ill will and hostility.

Rogers recommends that you think of the members of your audience as colleagues, not adversaries. With this approach, now known as **Rogerian argument,** you enter into a cooperative relationship with readers. Instead of refuting opposing arguments, you negotiate to determine points of agreement. The result is that you collaborate to find solutions that are mutually satisfying. By adopting a conciliatory attitude, you demonstrate your respect for opposing points of view and your willingness to compromise and work toward a position that both you and those who disagree with you will find acceptable. To use a Rogerian strategy in your writing, follow the guidelines below.

☑ GUIDELINES FOR USING ROGERIAN ARGUMENT

- Begin by summarizing opposing viewpoints.
- Carefully consider the position of those who disagree with you. What are their legitimate concerns? If you were in their place, how would you react?
- Present opposing points of view accurately and fairly. Demonstrate your respect for the ideas of those who disagree with you.
- Concede the strength of a compelling opposing argument.
- Acknowledge the concerns that you and your opposition share.
- Point out to readers how they will benefit from the position you are defining.
- Present the evidence that supports your point of view.

USING DEDUCTIVE AND INDUCTIVE ARGUMENTS

In an argument, you move from evidence to conclusion in two ways. One method, called **deductive reasoning,** proceeds from a general premise or assumption to a specific conclusion. Deduction is what most people mean when they speak of logic. Using strict logical form, deduction holds that if all the statements in the argument are true, the conclusion must also be true. The other method of moving from evidence to conclusion is called **inductive reasoning.** Induction proceeds from individual observations to a more general conclusion and uses no strict form. It requires only that all the relevant evidence be stated and that the conclusion fit the evidence better than any other conclusion would. Most written arguments use a combination of deductive and inductive reasoning, but it is simpler to discuss and illustrate them separately.

Using Deductive Arguments

The basic form of a deductive argument is a **syllogism.** A syllogism consists of a *major premise,* which is a general statement; a *minor premise,* which is a related but more specific statement; and a *conclusion,* which has to be drawn from those premises. Consider the following example:

Major premise:	All Olympic runners are fast.
Minor premise:	Jesse Owens was an Olympic runner.
Conclusion:	Therefore, Jesse Owens was fast.

As you can see, if you grant each of the premises, then you must also grant the conclusion—and it is the only conclusion you can properly draw. You cannot conclude that Jesse Owens was slow, because that conclusion contradicts the premises. Nor can you conclude (even if it is true) that Jesse Owens was tall, because that conclusion goes beyond the premises.

Of course this argument seems obvious, and it is much simpler than an argumentative essay would be. But a deductive argument's premises can be fairly elaborate. The Declaration of Independence, which appears later in this chapter, has at its core a deductive argument that might be summarized in this way:

Major premise:	Tyrannical rulers deserve no loyalty.
Minor premise:	King George III is a tyrannical ruler.
Conclusion:	Therefore, King George III deserves no loyalty.

The major premise is a truth that the Declaration claims is self-evident. Much of the Declaration consists of evidence to support the minor premise that King George is a tyrannical ruler. And the conclusion, because it is drawn from those premises, has the force of irrefutable logic: the king deserves no loyalty from his American subjects, who are therefore entitled to revolt against him.

When a conclusion follows logically from the major and minor premises, then the argument is said to be *valid*. But if the syllogism is not logical, the argument is not valid and the conclusion is not sound. For example, the following syllogism is not logical:

Major premise:	All dogs are animals.
Minor premise:	All cats are animals.
Conclusion:	Therefore, all dogs are cats.

Of course the conclusion is absurd. But how did we wind up with such a ridiculous conclusion when both premises are obviously true? The answer is that although both cats and dogs are animals, cats are not included in the major premise of the syllogism, which deals only with dogs. Therefore, the form of the syllogism is defective, and the argument is invalid. Here is another example of an invalid argument:

Major premise:	All dogs are animals.
Minor premise:	Ralph is an animal.
Conclusion:	Therefore, Ralph is a dog.

Here an error in logic occurs because the minor premise refers to a term in the major premise that is *undistributed*—that is, it covers only some of the items in the class it denotes. (To be valid, the minor premise must refer to the term in the major premise that is *distributed*—that is, it covers *all* the items in the class it denotes.) In the major premise, *dogs* is the distributed term; it designates *all dogs*. The minor premise, however, refers to *animals*, which is undistributed because it refers only to animals that are dogs. As the minor premise establishes, Ralph is an animal, but it does not follow that he is a dog. He could be a cat, a horse, or even a human being.

Even if a syllogism is valid—that is, correct in its form—its conclusion will not necessarily be *true*. The following syllogism draws a false conclusion:

Major premise:	All dogs are brown.
Minor premise:	My poodle Toby is a dog.
Conclusion:	Therefore, Toby is brown.

As it happens, Toby is black. The conclusion is false because the major premise is false: many dogs are *not* brown. If Toby were actually brown, the conclusion would be correct, but only by chance, not by logic. To be *sound*, a syllogism must be both logical and true.

The advantage of a deductive argument is that if you convince your audience to accept your major and minor premises, the force of logic should bring them to accept your conclusion. Therefore, you should try to select premises that you know your audience accepts or that are *self-evident*—that is, premises that most people believe to be true. Do not assume, however, that "most people" refers only to your friends and acquaintances. Consider, too, those who may hold different views. If you think that your premises are too controversial or difficult to establish firmly, you should use inductive reasoning.

Using Inductive Arguments

Inductive arguments move from specific examples or facts to a general conclusion. Unlike deduction, induction has no distinctive form, and its conclusions are less definitive than those of syllogisms whose forms are valid and whose premises are clearly true. Still, much inductive thinking (and writing based on that thinking) tends to follow a certain process. First, you usually decide on a question to be answered — or, especially in scientific work, you identify a tentative answer to such a question, called a *hypothesis*. Then, you gather all the evidence you can find that is relevant to the question and that may be important to finding the answer. Finally, you move from your evidence to your conclusion by making an *inference* that answers the question and takes the evidence into account. Here is a very simple example of the inductive process:

Question:	How did that living-room window get broken?
Evidence:	There is a baseball on the living-room floor.
	The baseball was not there this morning.
	Some children were playing baseball this afternoon.
	They were playing in the vacant lot across from the window.
	They stopped playing a little while ago.
	They aren't in the vacant lot now.
Conclusion:	One of the children hit or threw the ball through the window. Then they all ran away.

The conclusion, because it takes all of the evidence into account, seems obvious. But if it turned out that the children had been playing volleyball, not baseball, that one additional piece of evidence would make the conclusion doubtful — and the true answer could not be inferred. Even if the conclusion is believable, you cannot necessarily assume it is true: after all, the window could have been broken in some other way. For example, perhaps a bird flew against it, and perhaps the baseball in the living room had gone unnoticed all day, making the second piece of "evidence" on the list above not true.

Because inductive arguments tend to be more complicated than the preceding example, it is not always easy to move from the evidence you have collected to a sound conclusion. Of course, the more information you gather, the smaller the gap between your evidence and your conclusion. Still, whether large or small, the crucial step from evidence to conclusion always involves what is called an **inductive leap.** For this reason, inductive conclusions are never certain, only highly probable. Although induction does not point to any particular type of conclusion the way deduction does, making sure that your evidence is *relevant, representative,* and *sufficient* (see page 534) can increase the probability that your conclusion will be sound.

Considering possible conclusions is a good way to avoid reaching an unjustified or false conclusion. In the preceding example, a hypothesis like this one might follow the question:

| Hypothesis: | One of those children playing baseball broke the living-room window. |

Many people stop reasoning at this point, without considering the evidence. But when the gap between your evidence and your conclusion is too great, you may reach a hasty conclusion or one that is not borne out by the facts. This well-named error is called **jumping to a conclusion** because it amounts to a premature inductive leap. In induction, the hypothesis is merely the starting point. The rest of the inductive process continues as if the question were still to be answered—as in fact it is until all the evidence has been taken into account.

Using Toulmin Logic

Another approach for structuring arguments has been advanced by philosopher Stephen Toulmin. Known as **Toulmin logic,** this method is an effort to describe argumentation as it actually occurs in everyday life. Toulmin puts forth a model that divides arguments into three parts: the *claim,* the *grounds,* and the *warrant.* The **claim** is the main point of the essay. Usually the claim is stated directly as the thesis, but in some arguments it may be implied. The **grounds**—the material a writer uses to support the claim—can be evidence (facts or expert opinion) or appeals to the emotions or values of the audience. The **warrant** is the inference that connects the claim to the grounds. It can be a belief that is taken for granted or an assumption that underlies the argument.

In its simplest form, an argument following Toulmin logic would look like this:

Claim:	Carol should be elected class president.
Grounds:	Carol is an honor student.
Warrant:	A person who is an honor student would make a good class president.

When you formulate an argument using Toulmin logic, you can still use inductive and deductive reasoning. You derive your claim inductively from facts and examples, and you connect the grounds and warrant to your claim deductively. For example, the deductive argument in the Declaration of Independence that was summarized on page 537 can be represented this way:

Claim:	King George III deserves no loyalty.
Grounds:	King George III is a tyrannical ruler. (supported by facts and examples)
Warrant:	Tyrannical rulers deserve no loyalty.

As Toulmin points out, the clearer your warrant, the more likely readers will be to agree with it. Notice that in the two preceding examples, the warrants are very explicit.

Recognizing Fallacies

Fallacies are statements that may sound reasonable or true but are deceptive and dishonest. When your readers detect them, such statements can turn even a sympathetic audience against your position. Here are some of the more common fallacies that you should avoid:

Begging the Question Begging the question is a logical fallacy that assumes in the premise what the arguer should be trying to prove in the conclusion. This tactic asks readers to agree that certain points are self-evident when they are not.

> The unfair and shortsighted legislation that limits free trade is clearly a threat to the American economy.

Restrictions against free trade may or may not be unfair and shortsighted, but emotionally loaded language does not constitute proof. The statement begs the question because it assumes what it should be proving—that restrictive legislation is dangerous.

Argument from Analogy An **analogy** is a form of comparison that explains something unfamiliar by comparing it to something more familiar. Although analogies can explain abstract or unclear ideas, they do not constitute proof. An argument based on an analogy frequently ignores important dissimilarities between the two things being compared. When this occurs, the argument is fallacious.

> The overcrowded conditions in some parts of our city have forced people together like rats in a cage. Like rats, they will eventually turn on one another, fighting and killing until a balance is restored. It is therefore necessary that we vote to appropriate funds to build low-cost housing.

No evidence is offered that people behave like rats under these or any other conditions. Just because two things have some characteristics in common, you should not assume they are alike in other respects.

Personal Attack (Argument *Ad Hominem*) This fallacy tries to divert attention from the facts of an argument by attacking the motives or character of the person making the argument.

> The public should not take seriously Dr. Mason's plan for upgrading county health services. He is a recovering alcoholic whose second wife recently divorced him.

This attack on Dr. Mason's character says nothing about the quality of his plan. Sometimes a connection exists between a person's private and public lives—for example, in a case of conflict of interest. However, no evidence of such a connection is presented here.

Hasty or Sweeping Generalization Sometimes called *jumping to a conclusion,* this fallacy occurs when a conclusion is reached on the basis of too little evidence.

Because our son Marc really benefited socially from going to nursery school, I am convinced that every child should go.

Perhaps other children would benefit from nursery school, and perhaps not, but no conclusion about children in general can be reached on the basis of one child's experience.

False Dilemma (*Either/Or Fallacy*) This fallacy occurs when you suggest that only two alternatives exist even though there may be others.

We must choose between life and death, between intervention and genocide. There can be no neutral position on this issue.

An argument like this oversimplifies issues and forces people to choose between extremes instead of exploring more moderate positions.

Equivocation This fallacy occurs when the meaning of a key term changes at some point in an argument. Equivocation makes it seem as if a conclusion follows from premises when it actually does not.

As a human endeavor, computers are a praiseworthy and even remarkable accomplishment. But how human can we hope to be if we rely on computers to make our decisions?

The use of *human* in the first sentence refers to the entire human race. In the second sentence *human* means "merciful" or "civilized." By subtly shifting this term to refer to qualities characteristic of people as opposed to machines, the writer makes the argument seem more sound than it is.

Red Herring This fallacy occurs when the focus of an argument is changed to divert the audience from the actual issue.

The mayor has proposed building a new baseball-only sports stadium. How can he even consider allocating millions of dollars to this scheme when so many professional baseball players are being paid high salaries?

The focus of this argument should be the merits of the sports stadium. Instead, the writer shifts to the irrelevant issue of athletes' high salaries.

You Also (*Tu Quoque*) This fallacy asserts that an opponent's argument has no value because the opponent does not follow his or her own advice.

How can that judge favor stronger penalties for convicted drug dealers? During his confirmation hearings, he admitted he had smoked marijuana as a student.

Appeal to Doubtful Authority Often people will attempt to bolster an argument with references to experts or famous people. These appeals are valid when the person quoted or referred to is an expert in the area being discussed. They are not valid, however, when the individuals cited have no expertise on the issue.

> According to Ted Koppel, interest rates will remain low during the next fiscal year.

Although Ted Koppel is a respected journalist, he is not an expert in business or finance. Therefore, his pronouncements about interest rates are no more than a personal opinion or, at best, an educated guess.

Misleading Statistics   Although statistics are a powerful form of factual evidence, they can be misrepresented or distorted in an attempt to influence an audience.

> Women will never be competent firefighters; after all, 50 percent of the women in the city's training program failed the exam.

Here the writer has neglected to mention that there were only two women in the program. Because this statistic is not based on a large enough sample, it cannot be used as evidence to support the argument.

Post Hoc, Ergo Propter Hoc* (After This, Therefore Because of This)**   This fallacy, known as ***post hoc reasoning, assumes that because two events occur close together in time, the first must be the cause of the second.

> Every time a Republican is elected president a recession follows. If we want to avoid another recession, we should elect a Democrat as our next president.

Even if it were true that recessions always occur during the tenure of Republican presidents, no causal connection has been established. (See pages 307–308.)

***Non Sequitur* (It Does Not Follow)**   This fallacy occurs when a statement does not logically follow from a previous statement.

> Disarmament weakened the United States after World War I. Disarmament also weakened the United States after the Vietnam War. For this reason, efforts to control guns will weaken the United States.

The historical effects of disarmament have nothing to do with current efforts to control the sale of guns. Therefore, the conclusion is a *non sequitur.*

Using Transitions

Transitional words and phrases are extremely important in argumentative essays. Without these words and phrases, readers will find it difficult to follow your logic and could lose track of your argument.

Argumentative essays frequently use transitions to signal a shift in focus. For example, paragraphs that present the specific points of your argument can signal their purpose with transitions such as *first, second, third, in addition,* and *finally.* In the same way, paragraphs that refute opposing arguments can signal their purpose with transitions such as *still, nevertheless, however,* and *yet.* Transitional words and phrases — such as *therefore* and *for these reasons* — are also useful when you are presenting your argument's conclusions.

USEFUL TRANSITIONS FOR ARGUMENTATION

all in all	in summary
finally	in conclusion
first, second, third	in other words
for example	nevertheless
for instance	on the one hand . . . on the other hand
for these reasons	still
however	thus
in addition	therefore
in brief	as a result
in short	yet

A more complete list of transitions appears on page 43.

STRUCTURING AN ARGUMENTATIVE ESSAY

An argumentative essay, like other kinds of essays, has an *introduction,* a *body,* and a *conclusion.* But an argumentative essay has its own special structure, one that ensures that ideas are presented logically and convincingly. The Declaration of Independence follows the classic design typical of many arguments:

Introduction:	Introduces the issue
	States the thesis
Body:	Induction — offers evidence to support the thesis
	Deduction — uses syllogisms to support the thesis
	States the arguments against the thesis and refutes them
Conclusion:	Restates the thesis in different words
	Makes a forceful closing statement

Jefferson begins the Declaration by presenting the issue that the document addresses: the obligation of the people of the American colonies to tell the world why they must separate from Great Britain. Next, Jefferson states his thesis that because of the tyranny of the British king, the colonies must replace his rule with another form of government. In the body of the Declaration, he offers as evidence twenty-eight examples of injustice endured by the colonies. Following the evidence, Jefferson refutes counterarguments by explaining how time and time again the colonists have appealed to the British for redress, but without result. In his concluding paragraph, he restates the thesis and reinforces it one final time. He ends with a flourish: speaking for the representatives of the United States, he explicitly dissolves all political connections between England and America.

Not all arguments, however, follow this pattern. Your material, your thesis, your purpose, your audience, the type of argument you are writing, and the limitations of your assignment all help you determine the strategies you use. If your thesis is especially novel or controversial, for example, the refutation of opposing arguments may come first. In this instance, opposing positions might even be mentioned in the introduction — provided they are discussed more fully later in the argument.

Suppose your journalism instructor gives you the following assignment:

> Select a controversial topic that interests you, and write a brief editorial about it. Direct your editorial to readers who do not share your views, and try to convince them that your position is reasonable. Be sure to acknowledge the view your audience holds and to refute possible criticisms of your argument.

You are well informed about one local issue because you have just read a series of articles on it. A citizens' group is lobbying for a local ordinance that would authorize government funding for parochial schools in your community. Since you have also recently studied the constitutional doctrine of separation of church and state in your American government class, you know you could argue fairly and strongly against the position taken by this group.

An informal outline of your essay might look like this:

Issue introduced:	Should public tax revenues be spent on aid to parochial schools?
Thesis statement:	Despite the pleas of citizen groups like Parochial School Parents United, using tax dollars to support church-affiliated schools directly violates the U.S. Constitution.
Evidence (deduction):	Explain general principle of separation of church and state in the Constitution.
Evidence (induction):	Present recent examples of court cases interpreting and applying this principle.
Evidence (deduction):	Explain how the Constitution and the court cases apply to your community's situation.

Opposition refuted:	Identify and respond to arguments used by Parochial School Parents United. Concede the point that parochial schools educate many children who would otherwise have to be educated in public schools at taxpayers' expense.
Conclusion:	Restate the thesis; end with a strong closing statement.

REVISING AN ARGUMENTATIVE ESSAY

When you revise an argumentative essay, consider the items on the Revision Checklist on page 55. In addition, pay special attention to the items on the checklist below, which apply specifically to argumentative essays.

☑ REVISION CHECKLIST: ARGUMENTATION

- Does your assignment call for argumentation?
- Have you chosen a topic about which you can argue effectively?
- Do you have a debatable thesis?
- Have you considered the beliefs and opinions of your audience?
- Is your evidence relevant, representative, and sufficient?
- Have you documented evidence that you have gathered from sources?
- Have you made an effort to address your audience's possible objections to your position?
- Have you refuted opposing arguments?
- Have you used inductive or deductive reasoning (or a combination of the two) to move from your evidence to your conclusion?
- Have you avoided logical fallacies?
- Have you used appropriate transitional words and phrases?

EDITING AN ARGUMENTATIVE ESSAY

When you edit your argumentative essay, follow the guidelines on the Editing Checklist on page 67. In addition, focus on the grammar, mechanics, and punctuation issues that are most relevant to argumentative essays. One of these issues — using coordinating and subordinating conjunctions to link ideas — is discussed below.

For more practice in using coordinating and subordinating conjunctions, visit **Exercise Central** at **<bedfordstmartins.com/patterns/ conjunctions>**.

GRAMMAR IN CONTEXT : Using Coordinating and Subordinating Conjunctions*

When you write an argumentative essay, you often have to use conjunctions to express the logical and sequential relationships between ideas. Conjunctions are especially important because they help readers follow your reasoning so that they will be persuaded by your argument. For this reason, you should be certain that the conjunctions you select clearly and accurately communicate the connections between the ideas you are discussing.

Using Coordinating Conjunctions   A **compound sentence** is made up of two or more independent clauses (simple sentences) connected by a coordinating conjunction. **Coordinating conjunctions** join two independent clauses that contain ideas of equal importance and indicate how those ideas are related.

> *independent clause*   *independent clause*
> [People can disobey unjust laws], or [they can be oppressed by them].

COORDINATING CONJUNCTIONS

and (indicates addition)
but, yet (indicate contrast or contradiction)
nor (indicates an elimination of alternatives)
or (indicates alternatives)
so, for (indicate a cause-and-effect connection)

> According to William Safire, a national ID card would give the police almost unlimited surveillance power, and it would give businesses unprecedented access to personal information (587).

> "A national ID card would not prevent all threats of terrorism, but it would make it more difficult for potential terrorists to hide in open view" (Dershowitz 591).

> Oliver Stone does not believe that his movie drove people to commit murder, nor does he believe that it should be banned (608–609).

When you use a coordinating conjunction to join two independent clauses, always place a comma before the coordinating conjunction.

---

*Eds. NOTE — All the examples below either quote from or comment on essays that appear later in this chapter.

Using Subordinating Conjunctions   A **complex sentence** is made up of one independent clause (simple sentence) and one or more dependent clauses. (A dependent clause cannot stand alone as a sentence.) Subordinating conjunctions link dependent and independent clauses that contain ideas of unequal importance and indicate how those ideas are related.

independent clause   *dependent clause*

[According to Michael Zimecki, film executives should be sued] [so that they will stop making violent movies] (614–15).

SUBORDINATING CONJUNCTIONS

SUBORDINATING CONJUNCTION	RELATIONSHIP BETWEEN CLAUSES
after, before, since, until, when, whenever, while	Time
as, because, since	Reason or cause
in order that, so that	Result or effect
even if, if, unless	Condition
although, even though, though	Contrast

"Reparations are a dangerous, even evil, idea because they contradict the moral authority of black America's claim to equal rights" (Williams 634).

"Though claims for slavery reparations have moved near the front of national and international policy discussions in the past few years, the movement has deep historical roots" (Ogletree 629).

"Until there is more of a consensus on the best choice, we cannot take chances on a doubtful alternative when children's lives are concerned" (Adkins 598).

"If the AAP recommendations become law, they would likely apply not only to second-parent adoptions, but to other adoptions by gay couples or singles" (Birtha 602).

When you use a subordinating conjunction to join two clauses, place a comma after the dependent clause when it comes *before* the independent clause. Do not use a comma when the dependent clause comes *after* the independent clause.

When they signed the Declaration of Independence, Thomas Jefferson and the others knew that they were committing treason. (comma)

Thomas Jefferson and the others knew that they were committing treason when they signed the Declaration of Independence. (no comma)

☑ **EDITING CHECKLIST: ARGUMENTATION**

- Have you used coordinating conjunctions correctly to connect two or more independent clauses?
- Do the coordinating conjunctions accurately express the relationship between the ideas in the independent clauses?
- Have you placed a comma before the coordinating conjunction?
- Have you used subordinating conjunctions correctly to connect an independent clause and one or more dependent clauses?
- Do the subordinating conjunctions accurately express the relationship between the ideas in the dependent and independent clauses?
- Have you placed a comma after the dependent clause when it comes before the independent clause?
- Have you remembered not to use a comma when the dependent clause comes after the independent clause?

▶ **A STUDENT WRITER: ARGUMENTATION**

The following editorial, written by Matt Daniels for his college newspaper, illustrates a number of the techniques discussed earlier in the chapter.

An Argument against the Anna Todd Jennings
Scholarship

Introduction

Summary of controversy

Recently, a dispute has arisen over the "Caucasian-restricted" Anna Todd Jennings scholarship.* Anna Jennings died in 1955, and her will established a trust that granted a scholarship of up to $15,000 for a deserving student. Unfortunately, Jennings, who had certain racist views, limited her scholarship to "Caucasian students." After much debate with family and friends, I, a white, well-qualified, and definitely deserving student, have decided

Thesis statement

not to apply for the scholarship. It is my view that despite arguments to the contrary, applying for the Anna Todd Jennings scholarship furthers the racist ideas that were held by its founder.

1

---

*Eds. note — This essay discusses an actual situation, but the name of the scholarship has been changed here.

Argument (deductive)

Most people would agree that racism in any   2
form is an evil that should be opposed. The
Anna Todd Jennings scholarship is a subtle but
nonetheless dangerous expression of racism. It
explicitly discriminates against African Americans, Asians, Latinos, Native Americans, and
others. By providing a scholarship for whites
only, Anna Jennings frustrates the aspirations
of groups who until recently had been virtually
kept out of the educational mainstream. On this
basis alone, students should refuse to apply
and should actively work to encourage the school
to challenge the racist provisions of Anna Todd
Jennings's will. Such challenges have been
upheld by the courts: the striking down of a
similar clause in the will of the eighteenth-
century financier Stephen Girard is just one
example.

Argument (inductive)

The school itself must share some blame   3
in this case. Students who applied for the Anna
Todd Jennings scholarship were unaware of its
restrictions. The director of the financial
aid office has acknowledged that he knew about
the racial restrictions of the scholarship but

Evidence

thought that students should have the right to
apply anyway. In addition, the materials distributed by the financial aid office gave no
indication that the award was limited to Cau-
casians. Students were required to fill out
forms, submit financial statements, and forward transcripts. In addition to this material,
all students were told to attach a recent photograph to their application. Little did the
applicants know that the sole purpose of this
innocuous little picture was to distinguish
whites from nonwhites. By keeping secret the
restrictions of the scholarship, the school has
put students in the position of unwittingly

Conclusion
(based on evidence)

endorsing Anna Jennings's racism. Thus, both
the school and the unsuspecting students have

been in collusion with the administrators of
the Anna Todd Jennings trust.

*Refutation of opposing
argument*

The problem facing students is how best to   4
deal with the generosity of a racist. A recent
edition of the school paper contained several
letters saying that students should accept Anna
Jennings's scholarship money. One student said,
"If we do not take that money and use our education to topple the barriers of prejudice, we
are giving the money to those who will use the
money in the opposite fashion." This argument,
although attractive, is flawed. If an individual accepts a scholarship with racial restrictions, then he or she is actually endorsing the
principles behind it. If a student does not
want to appear to endorse racism, then he or
she should reject the scholarship, even if this
action causes hardship or gives adversaries a
momentary advantage. To do otherwise is to further the cause of the individual who set up the
scholarship. The best way to register a protest
is to work to change the requirement for the
scholarship and to encourage others not to
apply as long as the racial restrictions exist.

*Refutation of opposing
argument*

A recent letter to this newspaper made the   5
point that a number of other restricted scholarships are available at the school and no one
seems to question them. For example, one is
for the children of veterans, another is for
women, and yet another is earmarked for African
Americans. Even though these scholarships have
restrictions, to assume that all restrictions
are the same is to make a hasty generalization.
Women, African Americans, and the children of
veterans are groups that deserve special treatment. Both women and African Americans have
been discriminated against for years, and many
educational opportunities have been denied
them. Earmarking scholarships for them is
simply a means of restoring some measure of

equality. The children of veterans have been
singled out because their parents have rendered
an extraordinary service to their country.
Whites, however, do not fall into either of
these categories. Special treatment for them
is based solely on race and has nothing to do
with any objective standard of need or merit.

Conclusion   I hope that by refusing to apply for the   6
Anna Todd Jennings scholarship, I have encour-
aged other students to think about the issues

Restatement of thesis involved in their own decisions. All of us have
a responsibility to ourselves and to society.
If we truly believe that racism in all its forms
is evil, then we have to make a choice between

Concluding statement   sacrifice and hypocrisy. Faced with these
options, our decision should be clear: accept
the loss of funds as an opportunity to explore
your values and fight for principles in which
you believe; if you do, this opportunity is
worth far more than any scholarship.

Points for Special Attention

Gathering Evidence   Because of his involvement with his subject,
Matt Daniels was able to support his points with examples from his own
experience and did not have to do much research. Still, Matt did have to
spend a lot of time thinking about ideas and selecting evidence. He had to
review the requirements for the scholarship and decide on the arguments
he would make. In addition, he reviewed an article that appeared in the
school newspaper and the letters students wrote in response to the article.
He then chose material that would add authority to his arguments.

Certainly statistics, studies, and expert testimony, if they exist, would
strengthen Matt's argument. But even without such evidence, an argument
such as this one, based on strong logic and personal experience, can be
quite compelling.

Refuting Opposing Arguments   Matt devotes two paragraphs to
presenting and refuting arguments made by those who believe qualified
students should apply for the scholarship despite its racial restrictions. He
begins this section by asking a **rhetorical question** — a question asked not
to elicit an answer but to further the argument. He goes on to refute what
he considers the two best arguments against his thesis — that students

should take the money and work to fight racism and that other scholarships at the school have restrictions. Matt refutes these arguments by identifying a flaw in the logic of the first argument and by pointing to a fallacy, a hasty generalization, in the second.

Audience   Because his essay was written as an editorial for his college newspaper, Matt assumed his audience would be familiar with the issue he was discussing. Letters to the editor of the paper convinced him that his position was controversial, so he decided that his readers, mostly students and instructors, would have to be persuaded that his points were valid. To achieve this purpose, he is careful to present himself as a reasonable person, to explain issues that he believes are central to his case, and to avoid *ad hominem* attacks. In addition, he avoids sweeping generalizations and name-calling and includes many details to support his assertions and convince readers that his points are worth considering.

Organization   Matt uses several strategies discussed earlier in this chapter. He begins his essay by introducing the issue he is going to discuss and then states his thesis: "Applying for the Anna Todd Jennings scholarship furthers the racist ideas that were held by its founder."

Because Matt had given a good deal of thought to his subject, he was able to construct two fairly strong arguments to support his position. His first argument is deductive. He begins by stating a premise that he believes is self-evident—that racism should be opposed. The rest of this argument follows a straightforward deductive pattern:

Major premise:	Racism should be opposed.
Minor premise:	The Anna Todd Jennings scholarship is racist.
Conclusion:	Therefore, the Anna Todd Jennings scholarship should be opposed.

Matt ends his first argument with factual evidence that reinforces his conclusion: the successful challenge to the will of financier Stephen Girard, which limited admittance to Girard College in Philadelphia to white male orphans.

Matt's second argument is inductive, asserting that the school has put students in the position of unknowingly supporting racism. The argument begins with Matt's hypothesis and presents the fact that even though the school is aware of the racist restrictions of the scholarship, it has done nothing to make students aware of them. According to Matt, the school's knowledge (and tacit approval) of the situation leads to the conclusion that the school is in collusion with those who manage the scholarship.

In his fourth and fifth paragraphs, Matt refutes two criticisms of his argument. Although his conclusion is rather brief, it does effectively reinforce and support his main idea. Matt ends his essay by recommending a course of action to his fellow students.

Focus on Revision

Matt constructed a solid argument that addresses his central issue very effectively. However, some students on the newspaper's editorial board thought he should add a section giving more information about Anna Todd Jennings and her bequest. These students believed that such information would help them understand the implications of accepting her money. As it now stands, the essay dismisses Anna Todd Jennings as a racist, but biographical material and excerpts from her will — both of which appeared in the school paper — would enable readers to grasp the extent of her prejudice. Matt decided to follow up on this advice and to strengthen his conclusion as well. He thought that including the exact words of Anna Todd Jennings's will would help him to reinforce his points forcefully and memorably. (A peer editing worksheet for argumentation can be found on the *Patterns for College Writing* Web site at <bedfordstmartins .com/patterns>.)

The essays that follow represent a wide variety of topics, and the purpose of each essay is to support a controversial thesis. In the two debates, two essays that take opposing stands on the same issue are paired. In the debate casebooks, several essays on a single topic are presented to offer a greater variety of viewpoints. The first selection, a visual text, is followed by questions designed to illustrate how argumentation can operate in visual form.

❖ Thanks to Modern Science . . . (Ad)

• • •

READING IMAGES

1. What points does the ad's headline make? Does the rest of the ad support the headline?

2. How would you describe the picture that accompanies the ad? In what way does the picture reinforce the message of the text?

3. Does this ad appeal primarily to logic, to emotions, or to both? Explain.

4. List the specific points the ad makes. Which points are supported by evidence? Which points should be supported by evidence but are not? In what way does this lack of support affect your response to the ad?

JOURNAL ENTRY

Overall, do you find this ad convincing? Write a short letter to the ACLU in which you present your position. Be sure to refer to specific parts of the ad to support your argument.

THEMATIC CONNECTIONS

- "Thirty-Eight Who Saw Murder Didn't Call the Police" (page 101)
- "A Peaceful Woman Explains Why She Carries a Gun" (page 345)
- "Five Ways to Kill a Man" (page 487)
- "Whodunit — The Media?" (page 618)

THOMAS JEFFERSON

The Declaration of Independence

Thomas Jefferson was born in 1743 in what is now Albemarle County, Virginia, and attended the College of William and Mary. A lawyer, he was elected to Virginia's colonial legislature in 1769 and began a distinguished political career that strongly influenced the early development of the United States. In addition to his participation in the Second Continental Congress of 1775–1776, which ratified the Declaration of Independence, he served as governor of Virginia; as minister to France; as secretary of state under President George Washington; as vice president under John Adams; and finally as president from 1801 to 1809. After his retirement, he founded the University of Virginia. He died on July 4, 1826.

Background: By the early 1770s, many residents of the original thirteen American colonies had come to believe that King George III and his ministers, both in England and in the New World, wielded too much power over the colonists. In particular, they objected to a series of taxes imposed on them by the British Parliament, and, being without political representation, they asserted that "taxation without representation" amounted to tyranny. In response to a series of laws passed by Parliament in 1774 to limit the political and geographic freedom of the colonists, representatives of each colony met at the Continental Congress of 1774 to draft a plan of reconciliation, but it was rejected. As cries for independence increased, British soldiers and state militias began to engage in armed conflict, which by 1776 had become a full-fledged civil war. On June 11, 1776, the Second Continental Congress chose Jefferson, Benjamin Franklin, and several other delegates to draft a declaration of independence. The draft was written entirely by Jefferson, with suggestions and revisions contributed by other commission members. Jefferson's Declaration of Independence challenges a basic assumption of its time — that the royal monarch rules by divine right — and in so doing became one of the most important political documents in world history.

When in the course of human events, it becomes necessary for one people to dissolve the political bonds which have connected them with another, and to assume among the powers of the earth, the separate and equal station to which the Laws of Nature and of Nature's God entitle them, a decent respect to the opinions of mankind requires that they should declare the causes which impel them to the separation.

We hold these truths to be self-evident, that all men are created equal, that they are endowed by their Creator with certain unalienable rights, that among these are life, liberty and the pursuit of happiness. That to secure these rights, governments are instituted among men, deriving their just powers from the consent of the governed. That whenever any form of government becomes destructive to these ends, it is the right of the people to alter or to abolish it, and to institute new government, laying its foundation on such principles and organizing its powers in such form, as to them shall seem most likely to effect their safety and happiness. Prudence, indeed, will dictate that governments long established should not be changed for light and transient causes; and accordingly all experience hath shown, that mankind are more disposed to suffer, while evils are sufferable, than to right themselves by abolishing the forms to which they are accustomed. But when a long rain of abuses and usurpations, pursuing invariably the same object, evinces a design to reduce them under absolute despotism, it is their right, it is their duty, to throw off such government, and to provide new guards for their future security. Such has been the patient sufferance of these Colonies; and such is now the necessity which constrains them to alter their former systems of government. This history of the present king of Great Britain is a history of repeated injuries and usurpations, all having in direct object the establishment of an absolute tyranny over these States. To prove this, let facts be submitted to a candid world.

He has refused his assent to laws, the most wholesome and necessary for the public good.   3

He has forbidden his Governors to pass laws of immediate and pressing importance, unless suspended in their operation till his assent should be obtained; and when so suspended, he has utterly neglected to attend to them.   4

He has refused to pass other laws for the accommodation of large districts of people, unless those people would relinquish the right of representation in the legislature, a right inestimable to them and formidable to tyrants only.   5

He has called together legislative bodies at places unusual, uncomfortable, and distant from the depository of their public records, for the sole purpose of fatiguing them into compliance with his measure.   6

He has dissolved representative houses repeatedly, for opposing with manly firmness his invasions on the rights of people.   7

He has refused for a long time, after such dissolutions, to cause others to be elected; whereby the legislative powers, incapable of annihilation, have returned to the people at large for their exercise; the State remaining in the meantime exposed to all the dangers of invasion from without and convulsions within.   8

He has endeavoured to prevent the population of these states; for that purpose obstructing the laws for naturalization of foreigners; refusing to pass others to encourage their migration hither, and raising the conditions of new appropriations of lands.   9

He has obstructed the administration of justice, by refusing his assent to laws for establishing judiciary powers.   10

He has made judges dependent on his will alone, for the tenure of their offices, and the amount and payment of their salaries.   11

He has erected a multitude of new offices, and sent hither swarms of 12 officers to harass our people, and eat out their substance.

He has kept among us, in times of peace, standing armies without the 13 consent of our legislatures.

He has affected to render the military independent of and superior to 14 the civil power.

He has combined with others to subject us to a jurisdiction foreign 15 to our constitution, and unacknowledged by our laws; giving his assent to their acts of pretended legislation:

For quartering large bodies of troops among us: 16

For protecting them, by a mock trial, from punishment for any mur- 17 ders which they should commit on the inhabitants of these States:

For cutting off our trade with all parts of the world: 18

For imposing taxes on us without our consent: 19

For depriving us in many cases of the benefits of trial by jury: 20

For transporting us beyond seas to be tried for pretended offences: 21

For abolishing the free system of English laws in a neighbouring 22 Province, establishing therein an arbitrary government, and enlarging its boundaries so as to render it at once an example and fit instrument for introducing the same absolute rule into these Colonies:

For taking away our Charters, abolishing our most valuable laws, and 23 altering fundamentally the forms of our governments:

For suspending our own legislatures, and declaring themselves 24 invested with power to legislate for us in all cases whatsoever.

He has abdicated government here, by declaring us out of his protec- 25 tion and waging war against us.

He has plundered our seas, ravaged our coasts, burnt our towns, and 26 destroyed the lives of our people.

He is at this time transporting large armies of foreign mercenaries to 27 complete the works of death, desolation and tyranny, already begun with circumstances of cruelty and perfidy scarcely paralleled in the most bar-barous ages, and totally unworthy the head of a civilized nation.

He has constrained our fellow citizens taken captive on the high seas 28 to bear arms against their country, to become the executioners of their friends and brethren, or to fall themselves by their hands.

He has excited domestic insurrections amongst us, and has endeav- 29 oured to bring on the inhabitants of our frontiers, the merciless Indian savages, whose known rule of warfare, is an undistinguished destruction of all ages, sexes, and conditions.

In every stage of these oppressions we have petitioned for redress in the 30 most humble terms: our repeated petitions have been answered only by repeated injury. A prince whose character is thus marked by every act which may define a tyrant is unfit to be the ruler of a free people.

Nor have we been wanting in attention to our British brethren. We 31 have warned them from time to time of attempts by their legislature to extend an unwarrantable jurisdiction over us. We have reminded them of the circumstances of our emigration and settlement here. We have appealed to their native justice and magnanimity, and we have conjured them by the ties of our common kindred to disavow these usurpations, which would inevitably interrupt our connections and correspondence. They too have been deaf to the voice of justice and of consanguinity. We must, therefore, acquiesce in the necessity, which denounces our separation, and hold them, as we hold the rest of mankind, enemies in war, in peace friends.

We, therefore, the Representatives of the United States of America, in   32
General Congress assembled, appealing to the Supreme Judge of the world for the rectitude of our intentions, do, in the name, and by authority of the good people of these Colonies, solemnly publish and declare, That these United Colonies are, and of right ought to be, Free and Independent States; that they are absolved from all allegiance to the British Crown, and that all political connection between them and the state of Great Britain, is and ought to be totally dissolved; and that as Free and Independent States, they have full power to levy war, conclude peace, contract alliances, establish commerce, and to do all other acts and things which Independent States may of right do. And for the support of this declaration, with a firm reliance on the protection of Divine Providence, we mutually pledge to each other our lives, our fortunes, and our sacred honor.

•   •   •

COMPREHENSION

1. What "truths" does Jefferson assert are "self-evident"?

2. What does Jefferson say is the source from which governments derive their powers?

3. What reasons does Jefferson give to support his premise that the United States should break away from Great Britain?

4. What conclusions about the British crown does Jefferson draw from the evidence he presents?

PURPOSE AND AUDIENCE

1. What is the major premise of Jefferson's argument? Should Jefferson have done more to establish the truth of this premise?

2. The Declaration of Independence was written during a period now referred to as the Age of Reason. In what ways has Jefferson tried to make his document appear reasonable?

3. For what audience (or audiences) was the document intended? Which groups of readers would have been most likely to accept it? Explain.

4. How effectively does Jefferson anticipate and refute the opposition?

5. In paragraph 31, following the list of grievances, why does Jefferson address his "British brethren"?

6. At what point does Jefferson state his thesis? Why does he state it where he does?

STYLE AND STRUCTURE

1. Does the Declaration of Independence rely primarily on inductive or deductive reasoning? Identify examples of each.

2. What techniques does Jefferson use to create smooth and logical transitions from one paragraph to another?

3. Why does Jefferson list all of his twenty-eight grievances? Why doesn't he just summarize them or mention a few representative grievances?

4. Jefferson begins the last paragraph of the Declaration of Independence with "We, therefore." How effective is this conclusion? Explain.

VOCABULARY PROJECTS

1. Define each of the following words as it is used in this selection.

station (1)	evinces (2)	tenure (11)
impel (1)	despotism (2)	jurisdiction (15)
self-evident (2)	sufferance (2)	arbitrary (22)
endowed (2)	candid (2)	insurrections (29)
deriving (2)	depository (6)	disavow (31)
prudence (2)	dissolutions (8)	consanguinity (31)
transient (2)	annihilation (8)	rectitude (32)
usurpations (2)	appropriations (9)	levy (32)

2. Underline ten words that have negative connotations. How does Jefferson use these words to help him make his point? Do you think words with more neutral connotations would strengthen or weaken his case? Why?

3. What words does Jefferson use that are rarely used today? Would the Declaration of Independence be more meaningful to today's readers if it were updated, with more familiar words substituted? To help you formulate your response, try rewriting a paragraph or two, and assess your updated version.

JOURNAL ENTRY

Do you think Jefferson is being fair to the king? Do you think he should be?

WRITING WORKSHOP

1. Following Jefferson's example, write a declaration of independence from your school, job, family, or any other institution with which you are associated.

2. Write an essay in which you state a grievance you share with other members of some group, and then argue for the best way to eliminate the grievance.

3. In an argumentative essay written from the point of view of King George III, try to convince the colonists that they should not break away from Great Britain. If you can, refute some of the points Jefferson lists in the Declaration.

COMBINING THE PATTERNS

The middle section of the Declaration of Independence is developed by means of **exemplification;** it presents a series of examples to support Jefferson's assertion that the colonists have experienced "repeated injuries and usurpations" (2). Are these examples relevant? Representative? Sufficient? What other pattern of development could Jefferson have used to support his assertion?

THEMATIC CONNECTIONS

- "The 'Black Table' Is Still There" (page 340)
- "Grant and Lee: A Study in Contrasts" (page 386)
- "Letter from Birmingham Jail" (page 570)
- "Litigating the Legacy of Slavery" (page 627)

ELIZABETH CADY STANTON

❖
Declaration of Sentiments and Resolutions, Seneca Falls Convention, 1848

Elizabeth Cady was born in Johnstown, New York, in 1815 and attended the Troy Female Seminary. At the age of twenty-five, she married the writer and abolitionist Henry Brewster Stanton, joining him in the struggle to end slavery. She also became active in the woman suffrage movement, lobbying for the right of women to vote. This movement had its genesis in the United States at the first Woman's Rights Convention, which was organized by Stanton and other early petitioners for women's rights and held in Seneca Falls, New York, in July 1848. There, the following declaration was first presented, amended, and then unanimously adopted by the three hundred delegates. (All the resolutions were passed unanimously except for the one calling for women's right to vote, which was thought by some to be extreme enough to discredit the larger feminist movement.) Stanton went on to lead the National Woman Suffrage Movement from 1869 to 1890 and to coedit *Revolution,* a feminist periodical. A popular lecturer and skilled writer, she continued to work toward the goal of equality for women until her death in 1902.

Background: Conventional wisdom of the day held that women were, in general, far inferior to men in terms of intelligence and rationality, so the Founding Fathers' "all men are created equal" did not seem to apply to them. In fact, the idea for the Seneca Falls Convention was spurred by Stanton's experiences at the 1840 World Anti-Slavery Convention in London, which she attended with her husband and which refused to admit women delegates to the floor. When made public, the Declaration of Sentiments was universally derided by the press and by contemporary religious leaders — even Henry Stanton thought his wife had gone too far — and it had little practical effect. The Civil War interrupted the budding women's rights movement, but at its close, when emancipated African-American men were granted the right to vote, the movement picked up steam again. Its leaders lobbied for an amendment to the U.S. Constitution allowing women to vote and pressed state legislatures for voting rights as well. It was a long road, however. By 1913, only twelve states had extended voting rights to women, and not until the Nineteenth Amendment to the Constitution was ratified in 1920 did women achieve this right nationally.

Declaration of Sentiments

When, in the course of human events, it becomes necessary for one 1 portion of the family of man to assume among the people of the earth a position different from that which they have hitherto occupied, but one to which the laws of nature and of nature's God entitle them, a decent respect to the opinions of mankind requires that they should declare the causes that impel them to such a course.

We hold these truths to be self-evident: that all men and women are created equal; that they are endowed by their Creator with certain inalienable rights; that among these are life, liberty, and the pursuit of happiness; that to secure these rights governments are instituted, deriving their just powers from the consent of the governed. Whenever any form of government becomes destructive of these ends, it is the right of those who suffer from it to refuse allegiance to it, and to insist upon the institution of a new government, laying its foundation on such principles, and organizing its powers in such form, as to them shall seem most likely to effect their safety and happiness. Prudence, indeed, will dictate that governments long established should not be changed for light and transient causes; and accordingly all experience hath shown that mankind are more disposed to suffer, while evils are sufferable, than to right themselves by abolishing the forms to which they were accustomed. But when a long train of abuses and usurpations, pursuing invariably the same object, evinces a design to reduce them under absolute despotism, it is their duty to throw off such government, and to provide new guards for their future security. Such has been the patient sufferance of the women under this government, and such is now the necessity which constrains them to demand the equal station to which they are entitled. 2

The history of mankind is a history of repeated injuries and usurpations on the part of man toward woman, having in direct object the establishment of an absolute tyranny over her. To prove this, let facts be submitted to a candid world. 3

He has never permitted her to exercise her inalienable right to the elective franchise. 4

He has compelled her to submit to laws, in the formation of which she had no voice. 5

He has withheld from her rights which are given to the most ignorant and degraded men — both natives and foreigners. 6

Having deprived her of this first right of a citizen, the elective franchise, thereby leaving her without representation in the halls of legislation, he has oppressed her on all sides. 7

He has made her, if married, in the eye of the law, civilly dead. 8

He has taken from her all right in property, even to the wages she earns. 9

He has made her, morally, an irresponsible being, as she can commit many crimes with impunity, provided they be done in the presence of her husband. In the covenant of marriage, she is compelled to promise obedience to her husband, he becoming, to all intents and purposes, her master — the law giving him power to deprive her of her liberty, and to administer chastisement. 10

He has so framed the laws of divorce, as to what shall be the proper causes, and in case of separation, to whom the guardianship of the chil- 11 dren shall be given, as to be wholly regardless of the happiness of women — the law, in all cases, going upon the false supposition of the supremacy of man, and giving all power into his hands.

After depriving her of all rights as a married woman, if single, and the owner of property, he has taxed her to support a government which recognizes her only when her property can be made profitable to it. 12

He has monopolized nearly all the profitable employments, and from those she is permitted to follow, she receives but a scanty remuneration. He closes against her all the avenues to wealth and distinction which he considers most honorable to himself. As a teacher of theology, medicine, or law, she is not known. 13

He has denied her the facilities for obtaining a thorough education, all colleges being closed against her. 14

He allows her in Church, as well as State, but a subordinate position, claiming Apostolic authority for her exclusion from the ministry, and, with some exceptions, from any public participation in the affairs of the Church. 15

He has created a false public sentiment by giving to the world a different code of morals for men and women, by which moral delinquencies which exclude women from society, are not only tolerated, but deemed of little account in man. 16

He has usurped the prerogative of Jehovah himself, claiming it as his right to assign for her a sphere of action, when that belongs to her conscience and to her God. 17

He has endeavored, in every way that he could, to destroy her confidence in her own powers, to lessen her self-respect, and to make her willing to lead a dependent and abject life. 18

Now, in view of this entire disenfranchisement of one-half the people of this country, their social and religious degradation — in view of the unjust laws above mentioned, and because women do feel themselves aggrieved, oppressed, and fraudulently deprived of their most sacred rights, we insist that they have immediate admission to all the rights and privileges which belong to them as citizens of the United States. 19

In entering upon the great work before us, we anticipate no small amount of misconception, misrepresentation, and ridicule; but we shall use every instrumentality within our power to effect our object. We shall employ agents, circulate tracts, petition the State and National legislatures, and endeavor to enlist the pulpit and the press in our behalf. We hope this Convention will be followed by a series of Conventions embracing every part of the country. 20

Resolutions

Whereas, The great precept of nature is conceded to be, that "man shall pursue his own true and substantial happiness." Blackstone in his Commentaries remarks, that this law of Nature being coeval with mankind, and dictated by God himself, is of course superior in obligation to 21 any other. It is binding over all the globe, in all countries and at all times; no human laws are of any validity if contrary to this, and such of them as are valid, derive all their force, and all their validity, and all their authority, mediately and immediately, from this original; therefore,

Resolved, That such laws as conflict, in any way, with the true and sub- 22 stantial happiness of woman, are contrary to the great precept of nature and of no validity, for this is "superior in obligation to any other."

Resolved, That all laws which prevent woman from occupying such a 23 station in society as her conscience shall dictate, or which place her in a position inferior to that of man, are contrary to the great precept of nature, and therefore of no force or authority.

Resolved, That woman is man's equal—was intended to be so by the 24 Creator, and the highest good of the race demands that she should be recognized as such.

Resolved, That the women of this country ought to be enlightened 25 in regard to the laws under which they live, that they may no longer publish their degradation by declaring themselves satisfied with their present position, nor their ignorance, by asserting that they have all the rights they want.

Resolved, That inasmuch as man, while claiming for himself intel- 26 lectual superiority, does accord to woman moral superiority, it is preeminently his duty to encourage her to speak and teach, as she has an opportunity, in all religious assemblies.

Resolved, That the same amount of virtue, delicacy, and refinement of 27 behavior that is required of woman in the social state, should also be required of man, and the same transgressions should be visited with equal severity on both man and woman.

Resolved, That the objection of indelicacy and impropriety, which is 28 so often brought against woman when she addresses a public audience, comes with a very ill-grace from those who encourage, by their attendance, her appearance on the stage, in the concert, or in feats of the circus.

Resolved, That woman has too long rested satisfied in the circum- 29 scribed limits which corrupt customs and a perverted application of the Scriptures have marked out for her, and that it is time she should move in the enlarged sphere which her great Creator has assigned her.

Resolved, That it is the duty of the women of this country to secure to 30 themselves their sacred right to the elective franchise.

Resolved, That the equality of human rights results necessarily from the 31 fact of the identity of the race in capabilities and responsibilities.

Resolved, therefore, That, being invested by the Creator with the same 32 capabilities, and the same consciousness of responsibility for their exercise, it is demonstrably the right and duty of woman, equally with man, to promote every righteous cause by every righteous means; and especially in regard to the great subjects of morals and religion, it is self-evidently her right to participate with her brother in teaching them, both in private and in public, by writing and by speaking, by any instrumentalities proper to be used, and in any assemblies proper to be held; and this being a self-evident truth growing out of the divinely implanted principles of human nature, any custom or authority adverse to it, whether modern or wearing the hoary sanction of antiquity, is to be regarded as a self-evident falsehood, and at war with mankind.

Resolved, That the speedy success of our cause depends upon the zeal- 33 ous and untiring efforts of both men and women, for the overthrow of the monopoly of the pulpit, and for the securing to woman an equal participation with men in the various trades, professions, and commerce.*

•   •   •

COMPREHENSION

1. According to Stanton, why is it necessary for women to declare their sentiments?

2. What truths does Stanton say are "self-evident" (2)?

3. What injuries does Stanton list? Which injuries seem most important?

4. What type of reception does Stanton expect the Declaration of Sentiments and Resolutions to receive? What does she propose to do about this reception?

5. What conclusion does Stanton draw? According to her, what self-evident right do women have? What does she believe should be regarded as "a self-evident falsehood" (32)?

PURPOSE AND AUDIENCE

1. Is Stanton addressing men, women, or both? How can you tell? Does she consider one segment of her audience to be more receptive to her argument than another? Explain.

2. What strategies does Stanton use to present herself as a reasonable person? Do you think she is successful? Explain.

3. What is Stanton's thesis? At what point does she state it? Why do you think she states it when she does?

4. What is Stanton's purpose? Do you think she actually expects to change people's ideas and behavior, or does she have some other purpose in mind?

STYLE AND STRUCTURE

1. Does Stanton present her argument inductively or deductively? Why do you think she chose this arrangement?

2. The Declaration of Sentiments and Resolutions imitates the tone, style, and, in some places, the wording of the Declaration of Independence. What are the advantages of this strategy? What are the disadvantages?

———

*EDS. NOTE — This last resolution was given by Lucretia Mott at the actual convention. All the previous resolutions were previously drafted by Elizabeth Cady Stanton.

3. In paragraphs 2 and 32, Stanton mentions "self-evident" truths. Are these truths really self-evident? Should Stanton have done more to establish the validity of these statements?

4. What are the major and minor premises of Stanton's argument? Do these premises lead logically to her conclusion?

5. In what way do transitional words and phrases help Stanton move readers from one section of her argument to another? Are the transitions effective?

6. Should Stanton have specifically refuted arguments against her position? Could she be accused of ignoring her opposition?

VOCABULARY PROJECTS

1. Define each of the following words as it is used in this selection.

hitherto (1)	station (2)	validity (21)
impel (1)	franchise (4)	transgressions (27)
inalienable (2)	degraded (6)	indelicacy (28)
allegiance (2)	impunity (10)	impropriety (28)
dictate (2)	chastisement (10)	circumscribed (29)
sufferable (2)	subordinate (15)	sphere (29)
invariably (2)	delinquencies (16)	antiquity (32)
sufferance (2)	abject (18)	zealous (33)
constrains (2)	disenfranchisement (19)	

2. Today, many people would consider the style of some of the passages in the Declaration of Sentiments and Resolutions stiff and overly formal. Find a paragraph that fits this description, and rewrite it using less formal diction. What is lost in your revision, and what is gained?

JOURNAL ENTRY

Review the injuries to women that Stanton lists. How many of these wrongs have been corrected? How many have yet to be addressed?

WRITING WORKSHOP

1. Choose an issue that you care about, and write your own Declaration of Sentiments and Resolutions. Like Stanton, echo the phrasing of the Declaration of Independence in your essay.

2. Reread your journal entry, and select one of the injuries to women that has not yet been corrected. Write a letter to the editor of your school newspaper in which you argue that this issue needs to be resolved. In your essay, refer specifically to the Declaration of Sentiments and Resolutions.

3. When the Declaration of Sentiments and Resolutions was voted on at the Seneca Falls Convention in 1848, the only resolution not passed unanimously was the one that called for women to win the right to vote (30). Write a letter to the convention in which you call on the delegates to vote for this resolution. Make sure you refute the main argument against this

resolution — that it would alienate so many people that it would discredit the entire feminist movement.

COMBINING THE PATTERNS

Like the Declaration of Independence, the Declaration of Sentiments and Resolutions is partly developed by **exemplification.** A series of examples support Stanton's assertion that women now "demand the equal station to which they are entitled" (2). How effective are these examples? Are they relevant? Representative? Sufficient?

THEMATIC CONNECTIONS

- "My Mother Never Worked" (page 96)
- "I Want a Wife" (page 505)
- The Declaration of Independence (page 557)
- "In Search of Our Mothers' Gardens" (page 686)

MARTIN LUTHER KING JR.

Letter from Birmingham Jail

Martin Luther King Jr. was born in Atlanta, Georgia, in 1929. He attended Morehouse College and Crozer Theological Seminary, and after receiving his doctorate in theology from Boston University in 1955, he became pastor of the Dexter Avenue Baptist Church in Montgomery, Alabama. There, he organized a 382-day bus boycott that led to the 1956 Supreme Court decision outlawing segregation on Alabama's buses. As leader of the Southern Christian Leadership Conference, he was instrumental in securing the civil rights of black Americans, using methods based on a philosophy of nonviolent protest. His books include *Stride towards Freedom* (1958) and *Why We Can't Wait* (1964). In 1964, he was awarded the Nobel Peace Prize. He was assassinated in 1968 in Memphis, Tennessee.

Background: In the mid-1950s, long-standing state support for segregation of the races and discrimination against blacks had begun to be challenged from a variety of quarters. Supreme Court decisions in 1954 and 1955 declared segregation in public schools and other publicly financed venues unconstitutional, while calls for an end to discrimination were being made by blacks and whites alike. Their actions took the form of marches, boycotts, and sit-ins (organized protests in which participants refuse to move from a public area). Many whites, however, particularly in the South, vehemently resisted any change in race relations. By 1963, when King organized a campaign against segregation in Birmingham, Alabama, tensions ran deep. He and his followers met fierce opposition from the police as well as from white moderates, who considered him an "outside agitator." During the demonstrations, King was arrested and jailed for eight days. He wrote his "Letter from Birmingham Jail" to white clergymen to explain his actions and answer those who urged him to call off the demonstrations.

April 16, 1963

My Dear Fellow Clergymen:

While confined here in the Birmingham city jail, I came across your recent statement calling my present activities "unwise and untimely." Seldom do I pause to answer criticism of my work and ideas. If I sought to answer all the criticisms that cross my desk, my secretaries would have little time for anything other than such correspondence in the course of the day, and I would have no time for constructive work. But since I feel that you are men of genuine good will and that your criticisms are sincerely set forth, I want to try to answer your statement in what I hope will be patient and reasonable terms.

I think I should indicate why I am here in Birmingham, since you have been influenced by the view which argues against "outsiders coming in." I have the honor of serving as president of the Southern Christian Leadership Conference, an organization operating in every southern state, with headquarters in Atlanta, Georgia. We have some eighty-five affiliated organizations across the South, and one of them is the Alabama Christian Movement for Human Rights. Frequently we share staff, educational, and financial resources with our affiliates. Several months ago the affiliate here in Birmingham asked us to be on call to engage in a nonviolent direct-action program if such were deemed necessary. We readily consented, and when the hour came we lived up to our promise. So I, along with several members of my staff, am here because I was invited here. I am here because I have organizational ties here.

But more basically, I am in Birmingham because injustice is here. Just   3
as the prophets of the eighth century B.C. left their villages and carried their "thus saith the Lord" far beyond the boundaries of their home towns, and just as the Apostle Paul left his village of Tarsus and carried the gospel of Jesus Christ to the far corners of the Greco-Roman world, so am I compelled to carry the gospel of freedom beyond my own home town. Like Paul, I must constantly respond to the Macedonian call for aid.

Moreover, I am cognizant of the interrelatedness of all communities   4
and states. I cannot sit idly by in Atlanta and not be concerned about what happens in Birmingham. Injustice anywhere is a threat to justice everywhere. We are caught in an inescapable network of mutuality, tied in a single garment of destiny. Whatever affects one directly, affects all indirectly. Never again can we afford to live with the narrow, provincial, "outside agitator" idea. Anyone who lives inside the United States can never be considered an outsider anywhere within its bounds.

You deplore the demonstrations taking place in Birmingham. But   5
your statement, I am sorry to say, fails to express a similar concern for the conditions that brought about the demonstrations. I am sure that none of you would want to rest content with the superficial kind of social analysis that deals merely with effects and does not grapple with underlying causes. It is unfortunate that demonstrations are taking place in Birmingham, but it is even more unfortunate that the city's white power structure left the Negro community with no alternative.

In any nonviolent campaign there are four basic steps: collection of the   6
facts to determine whether injustices exist; negotiation; self-purification; and direct action. We have gone through all these steps in Birmingham. There can be no gainsaying the fact that racial injustice engulfs this community. Birmingham is probably the most thoroughly segregated city in the United States. Its ugly record of brutality is widely known. Negroes have experienced grossly unjust treatment in courts. There have been more unsolved bombings of Negro homes and churches in Birmingham than in any other city in the nation. These are the hard, brutal facts of the case. On the basis of these conditions, Negro leaders sought to negotiate with the city fathers. But the latter consistently refused to engage in good-faith negotiation.

Then, last September, came the opportunity to talk with leaders of 7 Birmingham's economic community. In the course of the negotiations, certain promises were made by the merchants — for example, to remove the stores' humiliating racial signs. On the basis of these promises, the Reverend Fred Shuttlesworth and the leaders of the Alabama Christian Movement for Human Rights agreed to a moratorium on all demonstrations. As the weeks and months went by, we realized that we were the victims of a broken promise. A few signs, briefly removed, returned; the others remained.

As in so many past experiences, our hopes had been blasted, and the 8 shadow of deep disappointment settled upon us. We had no alternative except to prepare for direct action, whereby we would present our very bodies as means of laying our case before the conscience of the local and the national community. Mindful of the difficulties involved, we decided to undertake a process of self-purification. We began a series of workshops on nonviolence, and we repeatedly asked ourselves: "Are you able to accept blows without retaliating?" "Are you able to endure the ordeal of jail?" We decided to schedule our direct-action program for the Easter season, realizing that except for Christmas, this is the main shopping period of the year. Knowing that a strong economic-withdrawal program would be the by-product of direct action, we felt that this would be the best time to bring pressure to bear on the merchants for the needed change.

Then it occurred to us that Birmingham's mayoral election was coming up in March, and we speedily decided to postpone action until after election day. When we discovered that the Commissioner of Public Safety, Eugene "Bull" Connor, had piled up enough votes to be in the run-off, we decided again to postpone action until the day after the run-off so that the demonstrations could not be used to cloud the issues. Like many others, we waited to see Mr. Connor defeated, and to this end we endured postponement after postponement. Having aided in this community need, we felt that our direct-action program could be delayed no longer.

You may well ask, "Why direct action? Why sit-ins, marches, and so 10 forth? Isn't negotiation a better path?" You are quite right in calling for negotiation. Indeed, this is the very purpose of direct action. Nonviolent direct action seeks to create such a crisis and foster such a tension that a community which has constantly refused to negotiate is forced to confront the issue. It seeks so to dramatize the issue that it can no longer be ignored. My citing the creation of tension as part of the work of the nonviolent-resistor may sound rather shocking. But I must confess that I am not afraid of the word "tension." I have earnestly opposed violent tension, but there is a type of constructive, nonviolent tension which is necessary for growth. Just as Socrates felt that it was necessary to create a tension in the mind so that individuals could rise from the bondage of myths and half-truths to the unfettered realm of creative analysis and objective appraisal, so must we see the need for nonviolent gadflies to create the kind of tension in society that will help men rise from the dark depths of prejudice and racism to the majestic heights of understanding and brotherhood.

The purpose of our direct-action program is to create a situation so   11
crisis-packed that it will inevitably open the door to negotiation. I therefore concur with you in your call for negotiation. Too long has our beloved
Southland been bogged down in a tragic effort to live in monologue rather
than dialogue.

One of the basic points in your statement is that the action that I and   12
my associates have taken in Birmingham is untimely. Some have asked:
"Why didn't you give the new city administration time to act?" The only
answer that I can give to this query is that the new Birmingham administration must be prodded about as much as the outgoing one, before it will
act. We are sadly mistaken if we feel that the election of Albert Boutwell
as mayor will bring the millennium to Birmingham. While Mr. Boutwell
is a much more gentle person than Mr. Connor, they are both segrega-
tionists, dedicated to maintenance of the status quo. I have hoped that Mr.
Boutwell will be reasonable enough to see the futility of massive resistance
to desegregation. But he will not see this without pressure from devotees
of civil rights. My friends, I must say to you that we have not made a single
gain in civil rights without determined legal and nonviolent pressure.
Lamentably, it is an historical fact that privileged groups seldom give up
their privileges voluntarily. Individuals may see the moral light and voluntarily give up their unjust posture; but, as Reinhold Niebuhr* has reminded us, groups tend to be more immoral than individuals.

We know through painful experience that freedom is never voluntarily   13
given by the oppressor; it must be demanded by the oppressed. Frankly, I
have yet to engage in a direct-action campaign that was "well timed" in the
view of those who have not suffered unduly from the disease of segregation. For years now I have heard the word "Wait!" It rings in the ear of every
Negro with piercing familiarity. This "Wait" has almost always meant
"Never." We must come to see, with one of our distinguished jurists, that
"justice too long delayed is justice denied."

We have waited for more than 340 years for our constitutional and   14
God-given rights. The nations of Asia and Africa are moving with jetlike
speed toward gaining political independence, but we still creep at horse-
and-buggy pace toward gaining a cup of coffee at a lunch counter. Perhaps
it is easy for those who have never felt the stinging darts of segregation to
say, "Wait." But when you have seen vicious mobs lynch your mothers and
fathers at will and drown your sisters and brothers at whim; when you have
seen hate-filled policemen curse, kick, and even kill your black brothers
and sisters; when you see the vast majority of your twenty million Negro
brothers smothering in an airtight cage of poverty in the midst of an affluent society; when you suddenly find your tongue twisted and your
speech stammering as you seek to explain to your six-year-old daughter
why she can't go to the public amusement park that has just been advertised on television, and see tears welling up in her eyes when she is told that

---

*EDS. NOTE — American religious and social thinker (1892–1971).

Funtown is closed to colored children, and see ominous clouds of inferiority beginning to form in her little mental sky, and see her beginning to distort her personality by developing an unconscious bitterness toward white people; when you have to concoct an answer for a five-year-old son who is asking, "Daddy, why do white people treat colored people so mean?"; when you take a cross-country drive and find it necessary to sleep night after night in the uncomfortable corners of your automobile because no motel will accept you; when you are humiliated day in and day out by nagging signs reading "white" and "colored"; when your first name becomes "nigger," your middle name becomes "boy" (however old you are) and your last name becomes "John," and your wife and mother are never given the respected title "Mrs."; when you are harried by day and haunted at night by the fact that you are a Negro, living constantly at tiptoe stance, never quite knowing what to expect next, and are plagued with inner fears and outer resentments; when you are forever fighting a degenerating sense of "nobodiness" — then you will understand why we find it difficult to wait. There comes a time when the cup of endurance runs over, and men are no longer willing to be plunged into the abyss of despair. I hope, sirs, you can understand our legitimate and unavoidable impatience.

You express a great deal of anxiety over our willingness to break laws. 15 This is certainly a legitimate concern. Since we so diligently urge people to obey the Supreme Court's decision of 1954 outlawing segregation in the public schools, at first glance it may seem rather paradoxical for us consciously to break laws. One may well ask: "How can you advocate breaking some laws and obeying others?" The answer lies in the fact that there are two types of laws: just and unjust. I would be the first to advocate obeying just laws. One has not only a legal but a moral responsibility to obey just laws. Conversely, one has a moral responsibility to disobey unjust laws. I would agree with St. Augustine* that "an unjust law is no law at all."

Now, what is the difference between the two? How does one determine 16 whether a law is just or unjust? A just law is a man-made code that squares with the moral law or the law of God. An unjust law is a code that is out of harmony with the moral law. To put it in the terms of St. Thomas Aquinas:** An unjust law is a human law that is not rooted in eternal law and natural law. Any law that uplifts human personality is just. Any law that degrades human personality is unjust. All segregation statutes are unjust because segregation distorts the soul and damages the personality. It gives the segregator a false sense of superiority and the segregated a false sense of inferiority. Segregation, to use the terminology of the Jewish philosopher Martin Buber, substitutes an "I-it" relationship for an "I-thou" relationship and ends up relegating persons to the status of things. Hence segregation is not only politically, economically, and sociologically unsound, it is morally wrong and sinful. Paul Tillich*** has said

---

*EDS. NOTE — Early church father and philosopher (354–430).
**EDS. NOTE — Italian philosopher and theologian (1225–1274).
***EDS. NOTE — American philosopher and theologian (1886–1965).

that sin is separation. Is not segregation an existential expression of man's tragic separation, his awful estrangement, his terrible sinfulness? Thus it is that I can urge men to obey the 1954 decision of the Supreme Court, for it is morally right; and I can urge them to disobey segregation ordinances, for they are morally wrong.

Let us consider a more concrete example of just and unjust laws. An 17 unjust law is a code that a numerical or power majority group compels a minority group to obey but does not make binding on itself. This is *difference* made legal. By the same token, a just law is a code that a majority compels a minority to follow and that it is willing to follow itself. This is *sameness* made legal.

Let me give another explanation. A law is unjust if it is inflicted on a 18 minority that, as a result of being denied the right to vote, had no part in enacting or devising the law. Who can say that the legislature of Alabama which set up that state's segregation laws was democratically elected? Throughout Alabama all sorts of devious methods are used to prevent Negroes from becoming registered voters, and there are some counties in which, even though Negroes constitute a majority of the population, not a single Negro is registered. Can any law enacted under such circumstances be considered democratically structured?

Sometimes a law is just on its face and unjust in its application. For 19 instance, I have been arrested on a charge of parading without a permit. Now, there is nothing wrong in having an ordinance which requires a permit for a parade. But such an ordinance becomes unjust when it is used to maintain segregation and to deny citizens the First-Amendment privilege of peaceful assembly and protest.

I hope you are able to see the distinction I am trying to point out. In no 20 sense do I advocate evading or defying the law, as would the rabid segregationist. That would lead to anarchy. One who breaks an unjust law must do so openly, lovingly, and with a willingness to accept the penalty. I submit that an individual who breaks a law that conscience tells him is unjust, and who willingly accepts the penalty of imprisonment in order to arouse the conscience of the community over its injustice, is in reality expressing the highest respect for law.

Of course, there is nothing new about this kind of civil disobedience. It 21 was evidenced sublimely in the refusal of Shadrach, Meshach, and Abednego* to obey the laws of Nebuchadnezzar, on the ground that a higher moral law was at stake. It was practiced superbly by the early Christians, who were willing to face hungry lions and the excruciating pain of chopping blocks rather than submit to certain unjust laws of the Roman Empire. To a degree, academic freedom is a reality today because Socrates practiced civil disobedience. In our own nation, the Boston Tea Party represented a massive act of civil disobedience.

---

*EDS. NOTE — In the Book of Daniel, three men who were thrown into a blazing fire for refusing to worship a golden statue.

We should never forget that everything Adolph Hitler did in Germany   22
was "legal" and everything the Hungarian freedom fighters did in Hungary
was "illegal." It was "illegal" to aid and comfort a Jew in Hitler's Germany.
Even so, I am sure that, had I lived in Germany at the time, I would have
aided and comforted my Jewish brothers. If today I lived in a Communist country where certain principles dear to the Christian faith are suppressed, I would openly advocate disobeying that country's anti-religious
laws.

I must make two honest confessions to you, my Christian and Jewish   23
brothers. First, I must confess that over the past few years I have been
gravely disappointed with the white moderate. I have almost reached the
regrettable conclusion that the Negro's great stumbling block in his stride
toward freedom is not the White Citizens Counciler or the Ku Klux Klan-
ner, but the white moderate, who is more devoted to "order" than to justice; who prefers a negative peace which is the absence of tension to a
positive peace which is the presence of justice; who constantly says, "I agree
with you in the goal you seek, but I cannot agree with your methods of
direct action"; who paternalistically believes he can set the timetable for
another man's freedom; who lives by a mythical concept of time and who
constantly advised the Negro to wait for a "more convenient season." Shal-
low understanding from people of good will is more frustrating than
absolute misunderstanding from people of ill will. Lukewarm acceptance
is much more bewildering than outright rejection.

I had hoped that the white moderate would understand that law and   24
order exist for the purpose of establishing justice and that when they fail
in this purpose they become the dangerously structured dams that block
the flow of social progress. I had hoped that the white moderate would
understand that the present tension in the South is a necessary phase of
the transition from an obnoxious negative peace, in which the Negro passively accepted his unjust plight, to a substantive and positive peace, in
which all men will respect the dignity and worth of human personality.
Actually, we who engage in nonviolent direct action are not the creators of
tension. We merely bring to the surface the hidden tension that is already
alive. We bring it out in the open, where it can be seen and dealt with. Like
a boil that can never be cured so long as it is covered up but must be
opened with all its ugliness to the natural medicines of air and light, injustice must be exposed, with all the tension its exposure creates, to the light
of human conscience and the air of national opinion, before it can be cured.

In your statement you assert that our actions, even though peaceful,   25
must be condemned because they precipitate violence. But is this a logical
assertion? Isn't this like condemning a robbed man because his possession
of money precipitated the evil act of robbery? Isn't this like condemning
Socrates because his unswerving commitment to truth and his philosophical inquiries precipitated the act by the misguided populace in which they
made him drink hemlock? Isn't this like condemning Jesus because his
unique God-consciousness and never-ceasing devotion to God's will pre-

cipitated the evil act of crucifixion? We must come to see that, as the federal courts have consistently affirmed, it is wrong to urge an individual to cease his efforts to gain his basic constitutional rights because the quest may precipitate violence. Society must protect the robbed and punish the robber.

I had also hoped that the white moderate would reject the myth concerning time in relation to the struggle for freedom. I have just received a letter from a white brother in Texas. He writes: "All Christians know that the colored people will receive equal rights eventually, but it is possible that you are in too great a religious hurry. It has taken Christianity almost two thousand years to accomplish what it has. The teachings of Christ take time to come to earth." Such an attitude stems from a tragic misconception of time, from the strangely irrational notion that there is something in the very flow of time that will inevitably cure all ills. Actually, time itself is neutral; it can be used either destructively or constructively. More and more I feel that the people of ill will have used time much more effectively than have the people of good will. We will have to repent in this generation not merely for the hateful words and actions of the bad people, but for the appalling silence of the good people. Human progress never rolls in on wheels of inevitability; it comes through the tireless efforts of men willing to be co-workers with God, and without this hard work, time itself becomes an ally of the forces of social stagnation. We must use time creatively, in the knowledge that the time is always ripe to do right. Now is the time to make real the promise of democracy and transform our pending national elegy into a creative psalm of brotherhood. Now is the time to lift our national policy from the quicksand of racial injustice to the solid rock of human dignity.

You speak of our activity in Birmingham as extreme. At first I was rather disappointed that fellow clergymen would see my nonviolent efforts as those of an extremist. I began thinking about the fact that I stand in the middle of two opposing forces in the Negro community. One is a force of complacency, made up in part of Negroes who, as a result of long years of oppression, are so drained of self-respect and a sense of "somebodiness" that they have adjusted to segregation; and in part of a few middle-class Negroes who, because of a degree of academic and economic security and because in some ways they profit by segregation, have become insensitive to the problems of the masses. The other force is one of bitterness and hatred, and it comes perilously close to advocating violence. It is expressed in the various black nationalist groups that are springing up across the nation, the largest and best-known being Elijah Muhammad's Muslim movement. Nourished by the Negro's frustration over the continued existence of racial discrimination, this movement is made up of people who have lost faith in America, who have absolutely repudiated Christianity, and who have concluded that the white man is an incorrigible "devil."

I have tried to stand between these two forces, saying that we need emulate neither the "do-nothingism" of the complacent nor the hatred and despair of the black nationalist. For there is the more excellent way of love and nonviolent protest. I am grateful to God that, through the influence of the Negro church, the way of nonviolence became an integral part of our struggle.

If this philosophy had not emerged, by now many streets of the South would, I am convinced, be flowing with blood. And I am further convinced that if our white brothers dismiss as "rabble-rousers" and "outside agitators" those of us who employ nonviolent direct action, and if they refuse to support our nonviolent efforts, millions of Negroes will, out of frustration and despair, seek solace and security in black-nationalist ideologies—a development that would inevitably lead to a frightening racial nightmare. 29

Oppressed people cannot remain oppressed forever. The yearning for freedom eventually manifests itself, and that is what has happened to the American Negro. Something within has reminded him of his birthright of freedom, and something without has reminded him that it can be gained. Consciously or unconsciously, he has been caught up by the *Zeitgeist,* and with his black brothers of Africa and his brown and yellow brothers of Asia, South America, and the Caribbean, the United States Negro is moving with a sense of great urgency toward the promised land of racial justice. If one recognizes this vital urge that has engulfed the Negro community, one should readily understand why public demonstrations are taking place. The Negro has many pent-up resentments and latent frustrations, and he must release them. So let him march; let him make prayer pilgrimages to the city hall; let him go on freedom rides—and try to understand why he must do so. If his repressed emotions are not released in nonviolent ways, they will seek expression through violence; this is not a threat but a fact of history. So I have not said to my people, "Get rid of your discontent." Rather, I have tried to say that this normal and healthy discontent can be channeled into the creative outlet of nonviolent direct action. And now this approach is being termed extremist. 30

But though I was initially disappointed at being categorized as an extremist, as I continued to think about the matter I gradually gained a measure of satisfaction from the label. Was not Jesus an extremist for love: "Love your enemies, bless them that curse you, do good to them that hate you, and pray for them which despitefully use you, and persecute you." Was not Amos an extremist for justice: "let justice roll down like waters and righteousness like an everflowing stream." Was not Paul an extremist for the Christian gospel: "I bear in my body the marks of the Lord Jesus." Was not Martin Luther an extremist: "Here I stand; I cannot do otherwise, so help me God." And John Bunyan: "I will stay in jail to the end of my days before I make a butchery of my conscience." And Abraham Lincoln: "This nation cannot survive half slave and half free." And Thomas Jefferson: "We hold these truths to be self-evident, that all men are created equal. . . ." So the question is not whether we will be extremists, but what kind of extremists we will be. Will we be extremists for hate or for love? Will we be extremists for the preservation of injustice or for the extension of justice? In that dramatic scene of Calvary's hill three men were crucified. We must never 31 forget that all three were crucified for the same crime — the crime of extremism. Two were extremists for immorality, and thus fell below their environment. The other, Jesus Christ, was an extremist for love, truth, and goodness, and thereby rose above his environment. Perhaps the South, the nation, and the world are in dire need of creative extremists.

I hoped that the white moderate would see this need. Perhaps I was too 32 optimistic; perhaps I expected too much. I suppose I should have realized that few members of the oppressor race can understand the deep groans and passionate yearnings of the oppressed race, and still fewer have the vision to see that injustice must be rooted out by strong, persistent, and determined action. I am thankful, however, that some of our white brothers in the South have grasped the meaning of this social revolution and committed themselves to it. They are still all too few in quantity, but they are big in quality. Some — such as Ralph McGill, Lillian Smith, Harry Golden, James McBride Dabbs, Ann Braden, and Sarah Patton Boyle — have written about our struggle in eloquent and prophetic terms. Others have marched with us down nameless streets of the South. They have languished in filthy, roach-infested jails, suffering the abuse and brutality of policemen who view them as "dirty nigger-lovers." Unlike so many of their moderate brothers and sisters, they have recognized the urgency of the movement and sensed the need for powerful "action" antidotes to combat the disease of segregation.

Let me take note of my other major disappointment. I have been so 33 greatly disappointed with the white church and its leadership. Of course, there are some notable exceptions. I am not unmindful of the fact that each of you has taken some significant stands on this issue. I commend you, Reverend Stallings, for your Christian stand on this past Sunday, in welcoming Negroes to your worship service on a nonsegregated basis. I commend the Catholic leaders of this state for integrating Spring Hill College several years ago.

But despite these notable exceptions, I must honestly reiterate that I 34 have been disappointed with the church. I do not say this as one of those negative critics who can always find something wrong with the church. I say this as a minister of the gospel, who loves the church; who was nurtured in its bosom; who has been sustained by its spiritual blessings and who will remain true to it as long as the cord of life shall lengthen.

When I was suddenly catapulted into the leadership of the bus protest 35 in Montgomery, Alabama, a few years ago, I felt we would be supported by the white church. I felt that the white ministers, priests, and rabbis of the South would be among our strongest allies. Instead, some have been outright opponents, refusing to understand the freedom movement and misrepresenting its leaders; all too many others have been more cautious than courageous and have remained silent behind the anesthetizing security of stained-glass windows.

In spite of my shattered dreams, I came to Birmingham with the hope 36 that the white religious leadership of this community would see the justice of our cause and, with deep moral concern, would serve as the channel through which our just grievances could reach the power structure. I had hoped that each of you would understand. But again I have been disappointed.

There was a time when the church was very powerful—in the time when the early Christians rejoiced at being deemed worthy to suffer for what they believed. In those days the church was not merely a thermometer that recorded the ideas and principles of popular opinion; it was a thermostat that transformed the mores of society. Whenever the early Christians entered a town, the people in power became disturbed and immediately sought to convict the Christians for being "disturbers of the peace" and "outside agitators." But the Christians pressed on, in the conviction that they were "a colony of heaven," called to obey God rather than man. Small in number, they were big in commitment. They were too God-intoxicated to be "astronomically intimidated." By their effort and example they brought an end to such ancient evils as infanticide and gladiatorial contests. 37

Things are different now. So often the contemporary church is a weak, ineffectual voice with an uncertain sound. So often it is an archdefender of the status quo. Far from being disturbed by the presence of the church, the power structure of the average community is consoled by the church's silent—and often even vocal—sanction of things as they are. 38

But the judgment of God is upon the church as never before. If today's church does not recapture the sacrificial spirit of the early church, it will lose its authenticity, forfeit the loyalty of millions, and be dismissed as an irrelevant social club with no meaning for the twentieth century. Every day I meet young people whose disappointment with the church has turned into outright disgust. 39

Perhaps I have once again been too optimistic. Is organized religion too inextricably bound to the status quo to save our nation and the world? Perhaps I must turn my faith to the inner spiritual church, the church within the church, as the true *ekklesia** and the hope of the world. But again I am thankful to God that some noble souls from the ranks of organized religion have broken loose from the paralyzing chains of conformity and joined us as active partners in the struggle for freedom. They have left their secure congregations and walked the streets of Albany, Georgia, with us. They have gone down the highways of the South on torturous rides for freedom. Yes, they have gone to jail with us. Some have been dismissed from their churches, have lost the support of their bishops and fellow ministers. But they have acted in the faith that right defeated is stronger than evil triumphant. Their witness has been the spiritual salt that has preserved the true meaning of the gospel in these troubled times. They have carved a tunnel of hope through the dark mountain of disappointment. 40

I hope the church as a whole will meet the challenge of this decisive hour. But even if the church does not come to the aid of justice, I have no despair about the future. I have no fear about the outcome of our struggle 41

---

*EDS. NOTE—Greek word for the early Christian church.

in Birmingham, even if our motives are at present misunderstood. We will reach the goal of freedom in Birmingham and all over the nation, because the goal of America is freedom. Abused and scorned though we may be, our destiny is tied up with America's destiny. Before the pilgrims landed at Plymouth, we were here. Before the pen of Jefferson etched the majestic words of the Declaration of Independence across the pages of history, we were here. For more than two centuries our forebears labored in this country without wages; they made cotton king; they built the homes of their masters while suffering gross injustice and shameful humiliation—and yet out of a bottomless vitality they continued to thrive and develop. If the inexpressible cruelties of slavery could not stop us, the opposition we now face will surely fail. We will win our freedom because the sacred heritage of our nation and the eternal will of God are embodied in our echoing demands.

Before closing I feel impelled to mention one other point in your state- 42
ment that has troubled me profoundly. You warmly commended the Birmingham police for keeping "order" and "preventing violence." I doubt that you would have so warmly commended the police force if you had seen its dogs sinking their teeth into unarmed, nonviolent Negroes. I doubt that you would so quickly commend the policemen if you were to observe their ugly and inhumane treatment of Negroes here in the city jail; if you were to watch them push and curse old Negro women and young Negro girls; if you were to see them slap and kick old Negro men and young boys; if you were to observe them, as they did on two occasions, refuse to give us food because we wanted to sing our grace together. I cannot join you in your praise of the Birmingham police department.

It is true that the police have exercised a degree of discipline in han- 43
dling the demonstrators. In this sense they have conducted themselves rather "nonviolently" in public. But for what purpose? To preserve the vile system of segregation. Over the past few years I have consistently preached that nonviolence demands that the means we use must be as pure as the ends we seek. I have tried to make clear that it is wrong to use immoral means to attain moral ends. But now I must affirm that it is just as wrong, or perhaps even more so, to use moral means to preserve immoral ends. Perhaps Mr. Connor and his policemen have been rather nonviolent in public, as was Chief Pritchett in Albany, Georgia, but they have used the moral means of nonviolence to maintain the immoral end of racial injustice. As T. S. Eliot has said, "The last temptation is the greatest treason: To do the right deed for the wrong reason."

I wish you had commended the Negro sit-inners and demonstrators of 44
Birmingham for their sublime courage, their willingness to suffer, and their amazing discipline in the midst of great provocation. One day the South will recognize its real heroes. They will be the James Merediths,* with the noble sense of purpose that enables them to face jeering and

---

*Eds. note—James Meredith was the first African American to enroll at the University of Mississippi.

hostile mobs, and with the agonizing loneliness that characterizes the life of the pioneer. They will be old, oppressed, battered Negro women, symbolized in a seventy-two-year old woman in Montgomery, Alabama, who rose up with a sense of dignity and with her people decided not to ride segregated buses, and who responded with ungrammatical profundity to one who inquired about her weariness: "My feets is tired, but my soul is at rest." They will be the young high school and college students, the young ministers of the gospel and a host of their elders, courageously and nonviolently sitting in at lunch counters and willingly going to jail for conscience's sake. One day the South will know that when these disinherited children of God sat down at lunch counters, they were in reality standing up for what is best in the American dream and for the most sacred values in our Judaeo-Christian heritage, thereby bringing our nation back to those great wells of democracy which were dug deeply by the founding fathers in their formulation of the Constitution and the Declaration of Independence.

Never before have I written so long a letter. I'm afraid it is much too long to take your precious time. I can assure that it would have been much shorter if I had been writing from a comfortable desk, but what else can one do when he is alone in a narrow jail cell, other than write long letters, think long thoughts, and pray long prayers? 45

If I have said anything in this letter that overstates the truth and indicates an unreasonable impatience, I beg you to forgive me. If I have said anything that understates the truth and indicates my having a patience that allows me to settle for anything less than brotherhood, I beg God to forgive me. 46

I hope this letter finds you strong in the faith. I also hope that circumstances will soon make it possible for me to meet each of you, not as an integrationist or a civil-rights leader but as a fellow clergyman and a Christian brother. Let us all hope that the dark clouds of racial prejudice will soon pass away and the deep fog of misunderstanding will be lifted from our fear-drenched communities, and in some not too distant tomorrow the radiant stars of love and brotherhood will shine over our great nation with all their scintillating beauty. 47

> Yours for the cause of Peace and Brotherhood,
> Martin Luther King Jr.

• • •

COMPREHENSION

1. King says he seldom answers criticism. Why not? Why, then, does he decide to do so in this instance?

2. Why do the other clergymen consider King's activities to be "unwise and untimely" (1)?

3. What reasons does King give for the demonstrations? Why does he think it is too late for negotiations?

4. What does King say *wait* means to black people?

5. What are the two types of laws King defines? What is the difference between the two?

6. What does King find illogical about the claim that the actions of his followers precipitate violence?

7. Why is King disappointed in the white church?

PURPOSE AND AUDIENCE

1. Why, in the first paragraph, does King establish his setting (the Birmingham city jail) and define his intended audience?

2. Why does King begin his letter with a reference to his audience as "men of genuine good will" (1)? Is this phrase ironic in light of his later criticism of them? Explain.

3. What indication is there that King is writing his letter to an audience other than his fellow clergymen?

4. What is the thesis of this letter? Is it stated or implied?

STYLE AND STRUCTURE

1. Where does King seek to establish that he is a reasonable person?

2. Where does King address the objections of his audience?

3. As in the Declaration of Independence, transitions are important in King's letter. Identify the transitional words and phrases that connect the different parts of his argument.

4. Why does King cite Jewish, Catholic, and Protestant philosophers to support his position?

5. King relies heavily on appeals to authority (Augustine, Aquinas, Buber, Tillich, and so forth). Why do you think he uses this strategy?

6. King uses both induction and deduction in his letter. Find an example of each, and explain how they function in the argument.

7. Throughout the body of his letter, King criticizes his audience of white moderates. In his conclusion, however, he seeks to reestablish a harmonious relationship with them. How does he do this? Is he successful?

VOCABULARY PROJECTS

1. Define each of the following words as it is used in this selection.

affiliate (2)	devotee (12)	reiterate (34)
cognizant (4)	estrangement (16)	intimidate (37)
mutuality (4)	ordinances (16)	infanticide (37)
provincial (4)	anarchy (20)	inextricably (40)
gainsay (6)	elegy (26)	scintillating (47)
unfettered (10)	incorrigible (27)	
millennium (12)	emulate (28)	

2. Locate five **allusions** to the Bible in this essay. How do these allusions help King express his ideas?

3. In paragraph 14, King refers to his "cup of endurance." To what is this a reference? How is the original phrase worded?

JOURNAL ENTRY

Do you believe King's remarks go too far? Do you believe they do not go far enough? Explain.

WRITING WORKSHOP

1. Write an argumentative essay in which you support a deeply held belief of your own. Assume that your audience, like King's, is not openly hostile to your position.

2. Assume that you are a militant political leader writing a letter to Martin Luther King Jr. Argue that King's methods do not go far enough. Be sure to address potential objections to your position. You might want to search the Internet or read some newspapers and magazines from the 1960s to help you prepare your argument. (Be sure to document all material you borrow from your sources. See the Appendix for information on documentation formats.)

3. Read your local newspaper for several days, collecting articles about a controversial subject that interests you. Using information from the articles, take a position on the issue, and write an essay supporting it. (Be sure to document all material you borrow from your sources. See the Appendix for information on documentation formats.)

COMBINING THE PATTERNS

In "Letter from Birmingham Jail," King includes several passages of **narration.** Find two of these passages, and discuss what use King makes of narration. Why do you think narration plays such an important part in King's argument?

THEMATIC CONNECTIONS

- "Finishing School" (page 89)
- "The 'Black Table' Is Still There" (page 340)
- "Two Ways to Belong in America" (page 397)

❖ DEBATE:
Should U.S. Citizens Be Required to Carry National Identity Cards?

On the morning of September 11, 2001, two commercial passenger planes, hijacked by Al-Qaeda terrorists, slammed into the two towers of New York's World Trade Center. By 10:30 that morning, the two buildings lay in ruins, and over 2,800 people were dead. As the towers burned, another hijacked passenger plane hit the Pentagon in Washington, D.C., killing almost two hundred people, and a fourth plane, which was thought to be headed for either the Capitol building or the White House, was forced by passengers to crash in a field in Shanksville, Pennsylvania. Not since the Japanese attack on Pearl Harbor in 1941 had the United States been attacked on its own soil; never before had so many American civilians lost their lives in a single incident. The effects of these acts of terrorism were immediate: fighter jets patrolled the skies over many major cities in the United States, President George W. Bush declared a national state of emergency, and the armed forces were put on high alert.

In response to the events of September 11, the federal government instituted a number of programs designed to combat terrorism and increase national security. Although many of these policies met little or no resistance, some — such as instituting military tribunals and setting up a network of civilian informants — caused so much controversy that they were either scaled back or eliminated entirely. One proposed program — a system of national identity cards — has attracted a great deal of attention. Asserting that it goes too far, detractors claim that the plan is an unnecessary extension of governmental power that would deprive people of fundamental civil liberties. They point out that every time the country has curtailed civil liberties — for example, by confining Japanese Americans in internment camps during World War II — Americans later regretted it. Supporters of national ID cards say that they too are reluctant to undermine the principals on which the country was founded. They argue, however, that the need to protect civil liberties must be tempered by the need to defend the country against the real security threats that it faces. For them, national ID cards represent a middle ground between instituting extreme measures to ensure security and preserving individual liberties at all costs.

The two writers in this debate hold opposite opinions concerning national identity cards. In "The Threat of National ID," William Safire asserts that both the government and commercial marketers are exploiting the public's fears to "sell" them on the idea of national identity cards. In "Why Fear National ID Cards?" Alan M. Dershowitz argues that even though national identity cards do take away some measure of personal freedom, their advantages far outweigh their disadvantages.

WILLIAM SAFIRE

❖

The Threat of National ID

Born in New York City in 1929, William Safire attended Syracuse University for two years before becoming a reporter for the *New York Herald Tribune*. He later became a television producer for WNBC in New York, worked in public relations, and in 1961 opened his own public relations firm. From 1968 to 1973, he served as speechwriter to President Richard Nixon, after which he joined the *New York Times* as a political columnist, a position he still holds today. His columns are widely syndicated, and he won a Pulitzer Prize for commentary in 1978. He is the author of over twenty books on politics and language as well as several novels.

Background: Safire bases his argument against a national identity card in part on the fact that "U.S. citizens [are] protected by the Fourth Amendment." The Fourth Amendment to the U.S. Constitution reads, "The right of the people to be secure in their persons, houses, papers, and effects, against unreasonable searches and seizures, shall not be violated, and no warrants shall issue but upon probable cause, supported by oath or affirmation, and particularly describing the place to be searched, and the persons or things to be seized." This amendment has been broadly interpreted as guaranteeing to U.S. citizens a right to privacy from government intrusion. It provides the basis, for example, for the U.S. Supreme Court's 1973 *Roe v. Wade* ruling that struck down antiabortion statutes. An increasingly conservative Supreme Court, however, has tended to interpret the amendment more narrowly. Most recently, for example, the Court ruled that the Fourth Amendment does not prevent school districts from conducting drug testing of any student engaged in extracurricular activities, whether or not there is a reasonable suspicion of drug use.

1   A device is now available to help pet owners find lost animals. It's a little chip implanted under the skin in the back of the neck; any animal shelter can quickly scan lost dogs or cats and pick up the address of the worried owner.

2   That's a good side of identification technology. There's a bad side: fear of terrorism has placed Americans in danger of trading our "right to be let alone" for the false sense of security of a national identification card.

3   All of us are willing to give up some of our personal privacy in return for greater safety. That's why we gladly suffer the pat-downs and "wanding" at airports, and show a local photo ID before boarding. Such precautions contribute to our peace of mind.

4   However, the fear of terror attack is being exploited by law enforcement sweeping for suspects as well as by commercial marketers seeking prospects. It has emboldened the zealots of intrusion to press for the holy grail of snoopery—a mandatory national ID.

Police unconcerned with the sanctity of an individual's home have 5
already developed heat sensors to let them look inside people's houses. The
federal "Carnivore" surveillance system feeds on your meatiest e-mail.
Think you can encrypt your way to privacy? The Justice Department is
proud of its new "Magic Lantern": all attempts by computer owners to
encode their messages can now be overwhelmed by an electronic bug the
F.B.I. can plant on your keyboard to read every stroke.

But in the dreams of Big Brother and his cousin, Big Marketing, noth- 6
ing can compare to forcing every person in the United States—under
penalty of law—to carry what the totalitarians used to call "papers."

The plastic card would not merely show a photograph, signature and 7
address, as driver's licenses do. That's only the beginning. In time, and
with exquisite refinements, the card would contain not only a fingerprint,
description of DNA and the details of your eye's iris, but a host of other
information about you.

Hospitals would say: How about a chip providing a complete medical 8
history in case of emergencies? Merchants would add a chip for credit
rating, bank accounts, and product preferences, while divorced spouses
would lobby for a rundown of net assets and yearly expenditures. Politicians would like to know voting records and political affiliation. Cops, of
course, would insist on a record of arrests, speeding tickets, E-Z pass auto
movements, and links to suspicious Web sites and associates.

All this information and more is being collected already. With a 9
national ID system, however, it can all be centered in a single dossier, even
pressed on a single card—with a copy of that card in a national databank,
supposedly confidential but available to any imaginative hacker.

What about us libertarian misfits who take the trouble to try to "opt 10
out"? We will not be able to travel, or buy on credit, or participate in
tomorrow's normal life. Soon enough, police as well as employers will consider those who resist full disclosure of their financial, academic, medical,
religious, social, and political affiliations to be suspect.

The universal use and likely abuse of the national ID—a discredit 11
card—will trigger questions like: When did you begin subscribing to these
publications, and why were you visiting that spicy or seditious Web site?
Why are you afraid to show us your papers on demand? Why are you paying cash? What do you have to hide?

Today's diatribe will be scorned as alarmist by the same security- 12
mongers who shrugged off our attorney general's attempt to abolish
habeas corpus (which libertarian protests and the Bush administration's
sober second thoughts seem to be aborting). But the lust to take advantage
of the public's fear of terrorist penetration by penetrating everyone's private lives—this time including the lives of U.S. citizens protected by the
Fourth Amendment—is gaining popularity.

Beware: It is not just an efficient little card to speed you through lines 13
faster or to buy you sure-fire protection from suicide bombers. A national
ID card would be a ticket to the loss of much of your personal freedom. Its

size could then be reduced for implantation under the skin in the back of your neck.

• • •

COMPREHENSION

1. According to Safire, why are most people willing to give up their privacy? In what ways does he believe that law enforcement officials are already taking advantage of this situation?

2. What does Safire mean when he says that national ID cards give Americans a "false sense of security" (2)? Do you agree with him?

3. Why won't people be able to choose not to carry national ID cards?

4. What does Safire mean in paragraph 6 when he says, "But in the dreams of Big Brother and his cousin, Big Marketing, nothing can compare to forcing every person in the United States — under penalty of law — to carry what the totalitarians used to call 'papers'"?

5. What are the advantages of national ID cards? What are the dangers of such cards?

PURPOSE AND AUDIENCE

1. Does Safire see his readers as friendly, hostile, or neutral? How can you tell?

2. Is Safire's purpose primarily to change people's ideas or to change their behavior?

3. What preconceptions does Safire seem to think his readers have about his subject?

STYLE AND STRUCTURE

1. Safire begins his essay with a discussion of lost animals. How effective is this strategy? Would another opening strategy have been more effective?

2. Is Safire's argument primarily inductive or deductive? Explain.

3. What evidence does Safire use to support his points? Do you think he includes enough support? Explain.

4. What opposing arguments does Safire refute? How effective are these refutations?

5. Throughout his essay, Safire uses **rhetorical questions** as a stylistic device to move his argument along. Find some examples of his use of rhetorical questions. How effective is this technique? Would another strategy — such as the use of direct statements or transitional words and phrases — be more effective?

6. What strategy does Safire use to conclude his essay? Is this a wise choice? Could he be accused of overstating his case?

VOCABULARY PROJECTS

1. Define each of the following words as it is used in this selection.

   implanted (1)   sanctity (5)   dossier (9)
   exploited (4)   encrypt (5)   seditious (11)
   emboldened (4)   totalitarians (6)   diatribe (12)
   mandatory (4)   exquisite (7)   habeas corpus (12)

2. In his conclusion, Safire uses **colloquialisms.** Do such informal expressions help him make his point more clearly, or do they undercut his credibility?

JOURNAL ENTRY

Would you be willing to give up your personal privacy for more personal security? Or do you believe that the benefits of increased surveillance are not worth the cost?

WRITING WORKSHOP

1. Do you agree or disagree with Safire? Do you think national ID cards are necessary for national security, or do you think they are an unjustified invasion of privacy? Be specific, and use information from your own experience or from "The Threat of National ID" to support your points.

2. Write an essay in which you take two of Safire's points and refute them, either by questioning their accuracy or by demonstrating flaws in their logic.

3. What specific steps—other than national ID cards—do you think the national government should take to protect Americans from terrorism?

COMBINING THE PATTERNS

In his essay, Safire includes several **exemplification** paragraphs. How do examples help him make his point? Should he have included more examples? Different kinds of examples? Why or why not?

THEMATIC CONNECTIONS

- "Ground Zero" (page 158)
- "A Peaceful Woman Explains Why She Carries a Gun" (page 345)
- "The Tipping Point" (page 351)

ALAN M. DERSHOWITZ

❖

Why Fear National ID Cards?

Alan Dershowitz was born in Brooklyn, New York, in 1938. A graduate of Brooklyn College and the Yale School of Law, he was the youngest tenured professor in the history of Harvard Law School. He has long been an avid proponent of civil liberties, taking on many controversial cases—including the defenses of O. J. Simpson and Mike Tyson. In a recent article, he argued that suspected terrorists should be offered the best legal defense possible. Dershowitz's many books include *The Abuse Excuse* (1994), *Supreme Injustice: How the High Court Hijacked Election 2000* (2001), *Shouting Fire: Civil Liberties in a Turbulent Age* (2002), and *Why Terrorism Works* (2002). He has also published more than three hundred op-ed columns syndicated throughout the country and appeared on numerous television talk shows.

Background: National identity cards have long been associated with highly repressive governments. They were required under the Nazi regime in Germany, which used them to deny basic civil liberties to "undesirables." Communist dictators used national identity cards to control dissenters, and in South Africa the system of apartheid was enforced through national identity cards. In the United States today, some people—both liberal and conservative—oppose them because of their potential for governmental abuse. For example, they could be used to monitor almost every aspect of a person's life, required for check cashing, travel, and admission to public facilities such as airports and hospitals. Critics contend that with national identity cards, the government could easily compile a national database that would track the behavior of every man, woman, and child in the United States.

1   At many bridges and tunnels across the country, drivers avoid long delays at the toll booths with an unobtrusive device that fits on a car's dashboard. Instead of fumbling for change, they drive right through; the device sends a radio signal that records their passage. They are billed later. It's a tradeoff between privacy and convenience: the toll-takers know more about you—when you entered and left Manhattan, for instance—but you save time and money.

2   An optional national identity card could be used in a similar way, offering a similar kind of tradeoff: a little less anonymity for a lot more security. Anyone who had the card could be allowed to pass through airports or building security more expeditiously, and anyone who opted out could be examined much more closely.

3   As a civil libertarian, I am instinctively skeptical of such tradeoffs. But I support a national identity card with a chip that can match the holder's fingerprint. It could be an effective tool for preventing terrorism, reducing

the need for other law-enforcement mechanisms—especially racial and ethnic profiling—that pose even greater dangers to civil liberties.

I can hear the objections: What about the specter of Big Brother? What 4 about fears of identity cards leading to more intrusive measures? (The National Rifle Association, for example, worries that a government that registered people might also decide to register guns.) What about fears that such cards would lead to increased deportation of illegal immigrants?

First, we already require photo ID's for many activities, including fly- 5 ing, driving, drinking, and check-cashing. And fingerprints differ from photographs only in that they are harder to fake. The vast majority of Americans routinely carry photo ID's in their wallets and pocketbooks. These ID's are issued by state motor vehicle bureaus and other public and private entities. A national card would be uniform and difficult to forge or alter. It would reduce the likelihood that someone could, intentionally or not, get lost in the cracks of multiple bureaucracies.

The fear of an intrusive government can be addressed by setting crite- 6 ria for any official who demands to see the card. Even without a national card, people are always being asked to show identification. The existence of a national card need not change the rules about when ID can properly be demanded. It is true that the card would facilitate the deportation of illegal immigrants. But President Bush has proposed giving legal status to many of the illegal immigrants now in this country. And legal immigrants would actually benefit from a national ID card that could demonstrate their status to government officials.

Finally, there is the question of the right to anonymity. I don't believe 7 we can afford to recognize such a right in this age of terrorism. No such right is hinted at in the Constitution. And though the Supreme Court has identified a right to privacy, privacy and anonymity are not the same. American taxpayers, voters, and drivers long ago gave up any right of anonymity without loss of our right to engage in lawful conduct within zones of privacy. Rights are a function of experience, and our recent experiences teach that it is far too easy to be anonymous—even to create a false identity—in this large and decentralized country. A national ID card would not prevent all threats of terrorism, but it would make it more difficult for potential terrorists to hide in open view, as many of the September 11 hijackers apparently managed to do.

A national ID card could actually enhance civil liberties by reducing 8 the need for racial and ethnic stereotyping. There would be no excuse for hassling someone merely because he belongs to a particular racial or ethnic group if he presented a card that matched his print and that permitted his name to be checked instantly against the kind of computerized criminal-history retrieval systems that are already in use. (If there is too much personal information in the system, or if the information is being used improperly, that is a separate issue. The only information the card need contain is name, address, photo, and print.)

From a civil liberties perspective, I prefer a system that takes a little bit 9 of freedom from all to one that takes a great deal of freedom and dignity from the few — especially since those few are usually from a racially or ethnically disfavored group. A national ID card would be much more effective in preventing terrorism than profiling millions of men simply because of their appearance.

• • •

COMPREHENSION

1. In paragraph 1, Dershowitz makes an analogy between a national ID card and an EZ Pass transmitter on a car. How are they alike?

2. According to Dershowitz, why is the tradeoff between privacy and convenience acceptable?

3. What are some fears that people have concerning national ID cards? Does Dershowitz believe these fears are justified?

4. According to Dershowitz, what could the government do to make sure national ID cards do not excessively curtail people's civil liberties?

5. What does Dershowitz mean in paragraph 7 when he says, "No such right [to anonymity] is hinted at in the Constitution"?

PURPOSE AND AUDIENCE

1. What audience does Dershowitz seem to be addressing — those who support national ID cards or those who oppose them? Explain.

2. In paragraph 3, Dershowitz attempts to establish his credentials as a civil libertarian. Why does he do this? How successful is he?

3. At what points in the essay does Dershowitz concede the legitimacy of opposing arguments? How effective is this strategy?

STYLE AND STRUCTURE

1. In paragraphs 1 and 2, Dershowitz draws an analogy between national ID cards and EZ Pass transmitters. Why does he use this analogy? What point is he trying to make?

2. What arguments against national ID cards does Dershowitz refute? Why does he devote so much of his essay — paragraphs 4 to 7 — to refutation?

3. Dershowitz does not present his arguments in favor of national ID cards until paragraph 8. Why does he wait so long to make his case?

4. What evidence does Dershowitz use to support his point? Would other kinds of evidence strengthen his case? Explain.

5. How well does Dershowitz summarize his argument in his final paragraph? What new point does he introduce? Is this a wise strategy?

VOCABULARY PROJECTS

1. Define each of the following words as it is used in this selection.

   intrusive (4)   facilitate (6)
   bureaucracies (5)   perspective (9)

2. What does Dershowitz mean by the phrase *civil libertarian*? What connotations does it have?

JOURNAL ENTRY

Do you agree with Dershowitz when he says that a national ID card could actually "enhance civil liberties by reducing the need for racial and ethnic stereotyping" (8)?

WRITING WORKSHOP

1. Who makes a better argument, Safire or Dershowitz? Write an essay in which you summarize the positions of both writers and then take a stand in support of one or the other. Include your reasons for preferring one over the other, and use material from both essays to support your thesis.

2. How do you think Dershowitz would respond to Safire's argument? Assuming that you are Dershowitz, write a letter to Safire that responds to the specific points that Safire makes in his essay.

3. Write an essay in which you respond to Dershowitz's statement, "From a civil liberties perspective, I prefer a system that takes a little bit of freedom from all to one that takes a great deal of freedom and dignity from a few—especially since those few are usually from a racially or ethnically disfavored group" (9). Use examples from personal experience (your own or someone else's) to support your thesis.

COMBINING THE PATTERNS

In paragraph 7, Dershowitz uses **comparison and contrast** to discuss the terms *privacy* and *anonymity*. How clear is the distinction he makes between these two terms? Should he have provided **formal definitions** of both terms in his discussion? What would be the advantages and disadvantages of such a strategy?

THEMATIC CONNECTIONS

- "Just Walk On By" (page 223)
- "Two Ways to Belong in America" (page 397)
- "Five Ways to Kill a Man" (page 487)
- The Declaration of Independence (page 557)

Should Gay and Lesbian Couples Be Allowed to Adopt?

Some studies have shown that over 500,000 children are in foster care and that over 100,000 of these children are waiting to be adopted. Unfortunately, each year only 20,000 qualified parents adopt such children. Many children in foster care are considered "unadoptable" because they are too old, have significant health problems, or are members of minority groups. Frequently, child welfare agencies place these "unwanted" children into foster-care homes, some of which are substandard. The lack of qualified adoptive parents has trapped thousands of children in a foster-care system that is stretched to its limits, and the results have been disastrous. For example, a child in foster care may have lived in as many as twenty homes by the time he or she is eighteen. In Florida, a child in the foster-care system was "lost" and never located. In Arkansas, the foster-care system was deemed so inefficient that it was placed under court supervision. Not surprisingly, children in foster care suffer from substance abuse, delinquency, and academic problems to a much greater degree than children raised with their birth parents in two-parent households.

In response to this situation, many states have liberalized their foster-care and adoption policies. To find suitable couples, welfare agencies have made the options of adoption and foster care available to a wider range of adults — many of whom would have been ineligible in the past — including single people, people with physical disabilities, and low-income families. Many gay and lesbian couples are attempting to join this group, but they are facing resistance. Supporters of gay and lesbian rights say that gay parents should be judged by the same standards that heterosexual parents are: if they are stable, loving, and caring, they should be allowed to adopt or serve as foster parents. In other words, a parent's sexual orientation should not be a criterion in determining adoption or foster-care eligibility. Many people — some of them well intentioned — strongly oppose this position. They claim that a family should consist of a mother and father who are married to each other. In addition, they say that children need both male and female role models. Finally, they say that gays and lesbians do not have stable relationships and for this reason would not be good parents. So far, most states do not allow gays and lesbians to adopt or to serve as foster parents, but the situation — at least in some states — is changing. The supreme courts of Delaware, Illinois, Massachusetts, New Jersey, New York, Pennsylvania, and Vermont, as well as the lower courts in many other states, have ruled in favor of gay adoption.

The two writers in this debate hold opposite opinions concerning adoption by gay and lesbian couples. In "Traditional Mother and Father: Still the Best Choice for Children," Tom Adkins asserts that until there is compelling evidence to suggest that children adopted by gay couples will not face irreparable harm, children should continue to be placed solely with heterosexual couples. In "Laws Should Support Loving Households, Straight or Not," Becky Birtha states that the well-being of the children, not the prospective parents' sexual orientation, should be the only issue considered in adoption and foster-care cases.

TOM ADKINS

❖

Traditional Mother and Father: Still the Best Choice for Children

Tom Adkins (b. 1958) grew up in Plymouth Meeting, Pennsylvania. He attended West Chester University and then toured the country as a rock artist until 1984, when he settled into a career in real estate. Disillusioned with the Clinton presidency, Adkins began to express his concerns in letters to the *Philadelphia Inquirer,* which published sixty of them over the course of two years and eventually invited him to write an op-ed article. This led to more op-ed articles (in the *Washington Times* and elsewhere) and eventually to national notoriety. Today, Adkins publishes a Web magazine, CommonConservative.com, and has appeared as a commentator on such television programs as *Hannity & Colmes, Beyond the News, Politically Incorrect,* and *It's Your Call with Lynn Doyle.* His first book is to be published in 2003.

Background: Adkins suggests in the following essay that gay and lesbian couples may be unsuitable as parents in part because they are relatively unstable, implying that their relationships tend to be shorter than those of heterosexual couples. Although many advocates for gay and lesbian rights question this assertion, particularly when compared to the relationships of unmarried heterosexual couples, they also argue that extending marriage rights to same-sex couples would lead to greater long-term stability. At this point, close to five thousand corporations, educational institutions, and municipalities in the United States extend "marriage" benefits to cohabitating same-sex partners by allowing gay and lesbian employees to register their domestic partnerships. In a controversial 1999 decision, the Vermont Supreme Court ruled that same-sex couples could enter into civil unions that provide many of the legal benefits of marriage; in the two years after this ruling, over four thousand couples registered for civil unions, including a large number of non-Vermonters for whom the legal benefits would not apply. Increasing numbers of same-sex couples are exchanging vows in formal commitment ceremonies, and newspapers such as the *New York Times* have begun to report such ceremonies along with traditional marriage announcements. Still, same-sex couples in the United States are a long way from having their unions recognized by state and federal governments.

There are all sorts of prizes in politics. The White House. The governor's mansion. A congressional seat. Since gays have left the closet and entered the political arena, those prizes have rightfully become available to them. 1

But political prizes come by the will of voters. Social prizes are different. A few motivated people in the right places can often coerce public pol- 2

icy. Now gays have their eyes set on a critical prize: children — more specifically, who has rights to adopt children.

On February 4, 2002, the American Academy of Pediatrics released a   3
controversial policy statement on those rights, claiming that children
could be brought up with equally good results by gay or by heterosexual
parents. The AAP points to 31 published studies that "prove" its case. But
these studies are far from airtight. Each one had already been thoroughly
sliced and diced in the report *No Basis: What the Studies Don't Tell Us about
Same Sex Parenting,* written by quantitative analysts Robert Lerner and
Althea Nagai and published by the Ethics and Public Policy Center. Lerner
and Nagai had debunked these studies as unsound, often politically motivated fiction. Lerner told me that "the studies are fatally flawed in methodology, technique, and analysis. Some didn't even have control groups."

The AAP authors told me that they'd never heard of the Lerner/Nagai   4
study and that they had not been able to find much contrary evidence. Yet
University of Southern California sociologists Judith Stacey and Timothy
Biblarz reviewed studies showing that while "psychologically fine," daughters of lesbian couples are more likely to be sexually promiscuous and
engage in lesbian experimentation (though Stacey believes that gay parents may be better parents than heterosexuals). In her recent book *Children
as Trophies,* sociologist Patricia Morgan pored over 144 academic papers
and concluded that same-sex parenting fosters homosexual behavior and
confused gender roles, and that such children often suffer serious psychological problems later in life.

Stacey of USC points out that no one can get an accurate, broad-based   5
sample "as long as you have a closet." And lead AAP author Ellen Perrin
admits, "We need more longitudinal research to see effects of different
kinds of family structures."

In other words, there are huge holes in the data, conflicting reports,   6
and almost no review of contrary evidence. Yet everyone is taking sides. So
why would an institution like the AAP make a sweeping, one-sided policy
statement likely to be used in pediatric guidance and court cases? It
appears the AAP has slipped into the trap of politics.

People generally expect a nonpartisan stance when an organization   7
like AAP endorses a practice or social movement that affects children. Yet
recently, the AAP has taken decidedly liberal stances on numerous issues —
in favor of gun control, and against mandated parental disclosure for children seeking abortions. Once again, it appears the AAP has assumed a
political stance. If so, that calls into question the credibility of any AAP
policy statements. In this case, with incomplete and conflicting evidence,
children may be exposed to irreparable harm. Yet the AAP is willing to use
orphans as little trophies in the political wars.

To be fair, AAP chair Joseph Hagan points out that the AAP study   8
"concerns itself primarily with children who are already in the [gay] family.
There are already special needs such as health insurance, health decisions,

legal responsibilities, inheritance, and such." Quite true, and not necessarily a direct endorsement of gay adoption.

But the report's attitude is quite clear. Barbara Howard, a co-author of the AAP statement, said, "Lesbian-parented daughters may experiment with lesbian sex more than a control group, but is this necessarily a problem?" Apparently, not for the AAP. 9

In the middle of all this lies the Gay Paradox: On one hand, gay people demand we accept them as parental equals. On the other, popular gay culture seems preoccupied with emphasizing its unstable, dark side, frightening away those who seek a truly unvarnished inspection of this issue. Sorry, you can't have it both ways. 10

Most of us can't pick our parents. But those who take on this immense responsibility for the less fortunate have rightly created a long, expensive, and complicated adoption process. Now, they must weed through supposedly objective organizations who make sweeping and conflicting declarations with little or no real evidence and disregard warning flags. Without real data on alternatives, society is forced to favor the sure thing: a loving, responsible mother and father. That is still the best certain choice—not grandpa, not same-sex parents, and not single mothers, the single most highly correlated poverty factor for children. 11

The real question is, should parentless children be given to loving gay parents or loving heterosexual parents? Until there is more of a consensus on the best choice, we cannot take chances on a doubtful alternative when children's lives are concerned. 12

• • •

COMPREHENSION

1. What does Adkins mean in paragraph 2 when he says, "Now gays have their eyes set on a critical prize: children"? Why does he see the right to adopt children as a "prize"?

2. What does the policy statement of the American Academy of Pediatrics (AAP) say about children brought up by gay parents? Why is this policy statement controversial?

3. What potential negative effects of gay parenting does Adkins mention?

4. In paragraph 5, Adkins quotes one of the authors of the AAP policy statement who says, "We need more longitudinal research to see effects of different kinds of family structures." If this is the case, why, according to Adkins, does the AAP endorse gay parenting?

5. In paragraph 8, Adkins concedes that the AAP policy statement focuses primarily on the "special needs" of children who are already in gay families. What does he mean when he says that acknowledging this fact is "not necessarily a direct endorsement of gay adoption" (8)?

6. According to Adkins, what responsibility do those who control the adoption process have to children?

PURPOSE AND AUDIENCE

1. Does Adkins assume that his readers are familiar with the issues involved in gay adoption? How can you tell?

2. What efforts does Adkins make to convince his readers that he is being fair? Is he successful?

3. What is Adkins's thesis? Why does he state it where he does?

4. Does Adkins reveal any of his own biases in his essay? Explain.

STYLE AND STRUCTURE

1. Adkins begins his essay by discussing the difference between political prizes and social prizes. Is his distinction clear? Is this is an effective opening strategy? Why or why not?

2. Adkins spends most of his essay refuting the AAP policy statement. What faults does he find with the report's methodology and with its conclusion?

3. In paragraph 7, Adkins accuses the AAP of playing politics. How fair is this accusation? Why, according to Adkins, does this challenge "the credibility of any AAP policy statements" (7)?

4. Does Adkins present a fair cross-section of opinion about gay parenting? Should he have made more of an effort to include (and refute) studies that supported gay adoption?

5. In paragraph 11, Adkins says, "Without real data on alternatives, society is forced to favor the sure thing: a loving, responsible mother and father." In other words, the burden is on gay advocates to prove that gay adoption causes no harm. Is this conclusion fair? Is it logical?

6. In paragraph 12, Adkins sums up his position with the statement, "The real question is, should parentless children be given to loving gay parents or loving heterosexual parents?" Is this statement accurate, or is it an example of a **false dilemma?**

VOCABULARY PROJECTS

1. Define each of the following words as it is used in this selection.

pediatrics (3)	longitudinal (5)	control group (9)
methodology (3)	nonpartisan (7)	declarations (11)
promiscuous (4)	credibility (7)	correlated (11)
fosters (4)	irreparable (7)	consensus (12)

2. In paragraph 3, Adkins uses the term *sliced and diced*. Is this language appropriate for this essay's purpose and subject matter? What is the effect of its use here? What other term could Adkins have used?

JOURNAL ENTRY

Do you agree that gay adoption should wait until "there is more of a consensus on the best choice," or should parentless children be given to "loving gay parents" now (12)?

WRITING WORKSHOP

1. Assume that you are the director of an adoption agency and that you have received an adoption application from a gay couple. Write a letter to the couple in which you either grant or deny their request to adopt. Be specific. If you wish, you may refer to Adkins's essay or the essay by Becky Birtha on page 601.

2. Write an essay in which you expand your journal entry. Make sure that you include a thesis statement and that you specifically refute the arguments against your position.

3. Write an essay in which you set your own criteria for adoptive parents. Explain why these specific criteria should govern adoptions, and be sure to refute the major objections to any of your criteria.

COMBINING THE PATTERNS

Paragraphs 3 through 5 are developed primarily by means of **exemplification.** Does Adkins provide enough examples? In what way do these examples help him set up his argument in paragraphs 11 and 12?

THEMATIC CONNECTIONS

- "The Lottery" (page 292)
- "The Tipping Point" (page 351)
- "A Modest Proposal" (page 676)

BECKY BIRTHA

❖

Laws Should Support Loving Households, Straight or Not

Born in Hampton, Virginia, in 1948, Becky Birtha is of Irish, Cherokee, Catawba, and African ancestry and is named for a great-grandmother who began life as a slave. She grew up in Philadelphia and attended Case Western Reserve University and the State University of New York at Buffalo, where she earned a B.S. in children's studies. She also holds an M.F.A. in creative writing from Vermont College. Birtha has published several collections of poetry, including *The Forbidden Poems* (1991), as well as the short-story collections *For Nights Like This One* (1983) and *Lover's Choice* (1987). She is a lesbian adoptive parent, as well as an adoption consultant.

Background: The American Academy of Pediatrics report mentioned here and in the previous essay by Tom Adkins recommends that in a same-sex relationship, children born to or adopted by one partner should be allowed to be adopted by the other partner. A larger question is whether same-sex couples should have the same right as heterosexual couples to adopt children to whom neither has a biological tie. In many states where single-parent foster care and adoption are allowed, gay and lesbian individuals have been allowed to serve as foster parents or to adopt because social services agencies wanted to reduce the number of hard-to-place children. This situation began to change as gay men and lesbians became more visible politically, bringing on a kind of backlash. Currently, legislatures in Florida, Utah, Mississippi, and Arkansas have enacted laws prohibiting gay and lesbian foster care and/or adoption, and several other states have introduced legislation unfavorable to gay and lesbian families. These actions have led to cases such as the one brought to national attention in Florida, where five foster children with AIDS are threatened with losing the only parents they have known, a gay male couple, both nurses, who are not allowed to adopt them.

The American Academy of Pediatrics, 55,000 physicians strong, has taken a giant step forward on behalf of 1 million to 9 million children who are growing up with gay or lesbian parents. The organization's policy statement, issued February 4, 2002, states that children born to or adopted by a parent in a same-sex couple have the right to be adopted by their nonlegal parent, entitling them to custody, visitation, and child support, as well as health benefits and inheritance rights from both parents. 1

The pediatricians say parents' sexual orientation alone cannot predict their ability to provide a supportive home environment for children. I wholeheartedly agree. Like race, gender, or being able-bodied, sexual orientation isn't linked to good or bad parenting. 2

Opponents of the policy suggest the data the AAP used to reach its conclusion are limited and flawed. However, 31 different research studies are cited in its technical report, gleaned from numerous books and scholarly journals and spanning a 20-year period from 1981 to 2001.

Others argue that legalizing gay adoption is a political issue, not a medical one. But the AAP's concern isn't really whether gays have the right to parent children; it's whether children of gays have the right to have parents. These pediatricians have seen gay parents unable to sign a medical consent for treatment of a child they have raised from birth and now view this as an issue of the health, safety, and well-being of children who didn't choose — but happen to have — same-gender parents.

Some question whether gay people are capable of making lasting commitments. Gay men, lesbians, and other sexual minorities don't just happen to become parents. Children, whether newborn, adopted, or from a former marriage or relationship, enter a gay couple's lives only after the couple have gone through much soul-searching, planning, and effort, whether through attempts at donor insemination, stringently screened home studies, or negotiated custody agreements. These are serious commitments.

Those who say it is wrong to deny a child two heterosexual parents miss the point. The children in question already have parents. They are not about to gain a parent of the opposite sex, whether their second parent's rights are legally recognized or not. Certainly, children should grow up with adult role models of both genders. As every single mother of sons knows, grandfathers and uncles can contribute here. Undoubtedly, each of us knows someone who was raised by a single parent and is a productive, responsible, and heterosexual adult.

Still, probably the greatest fear is that children raised by gays or lesbians will be homosexual themselves. And if they are? As one lesbian friend of mine commented, "There will be gay adults in the next generation, just as there have been gay people in every generation in history." Most of them won't come from gay-parented families. They never have.

One study found young adults with lesbian mothers slightly more likely to consider same-sex partners but not to identify themselves as homosexual. In another study, children of heterosexual parents are presented as more aggressive, bossy, negative, and domineering than other children. Apparently, there are also advantages to being raised by gay parents.

If the AAP recommendations become law, they would likely apply not only to second-parent adoptions, but to other adoptions by gay couples or singles. I think of the 134,000* children in foster care in the United States who wait to be adopted. These kids are school-age or teenage. Some have learning and emotional problems, and many of them have been waiting for years. Maybe there would be a few more homes for them.

If anything, gay parenting and the AAP's encouragement of two-parent families can be seen as a move toward, not away from, traditional family values. Any gay parent hurrying to the day-care center at 6 P.M. can tell you

---

*EDS. NOTE — Estimates vary widely.

that he has more in common with straight parents than his child-free gay friends do.

New Jersey has taken the lead in recognizing second-parent and joint 11 adoptions, and other states would do well to follow. I applaud the AAP in its conviction that children should grow up in families in which parents are protective, caring, loving, and, regardless of sexual orientation, recognized as parents by the law.

• • •

COMPREHENSION

1. What is the adoption policy recommended by the American Academy of Pediatrics?

2. What criticisms do the opponents of this policy put forward?

3. According to Birtha, what is the greatest fear people have about having children raised by gay or lesbian parents? How does she address these concerns?

4. According to Birtha, what would happen if the AAP recommendations became law?

5. How, according to Birtha, is gay parenting "a move toward, not away from, traditional family values" (10)? Do you agree? Explain.

PURPOSE AND AUDIENCE

1. Birtha states her thesis in paragraph 2 of her essay, while Adkins (in the previous essay) waits until his conclusion to state his thesis. How do you account for this difference?

2. Does Birtha see her readers as hostile, receptive, or neutral toward her position? Explain.

3. What steps does Birtha take to calm the fears of readers who might oppose gay adoption? Are these strategies effective?

4. Birtha is an adoptive parent and an adoption professional. Should she have mentioned these facts in her essay? Why or why not?

STYLE AND STRUCTURE

1. What strategy does Birtha use in her introduction? How effective do you think it is? Explain.

2. Birtha begins refuting arguments against her thesis in paragraph 3. Why do you think she addresses these arguments so soon?

3. Birtha introduces her refutations with the phrases "Opponents . . . suggest" (3), "Others argue" (4), and "Some question" (5). She also introduces evidence with phrases such as "One study found" (8) and "In another study" (8). Should Birtha have been more specific? Do such general references undercut her credibility? Explain.

4. List the arguments that Birtha presents to support her thesis. How effective are these arguments?

5. In paragraph 4, Birtha says, "But the AAP's concern isn't really whether gays have the right to parent children; it's whether children of gays have the right to have parents." What distinction is Birtha making? Does this distinction make sense to you? Explain.

6. Birtha ends her essay by saying, "New Jersey has taken the lead in recognizing second-parent and joint adoptions" (11). Why does she introduce this piece of information in her conclusion? Do you believe this is an effective strategy?

7. What transitions does Birtha use to move her readers from one point to another? How successfully do these transitions guide readers through the argument?

VOCABULARY PROJECTS

1. Define each of the following words as it is used in this selection.

orientation (2) scholarly (3) stringently (5)
gleaned (3) insemination (5) domineering (8)

2. In paragraph 10, Birtha uses the term *family values.* What does this term mean? Should she have used a more precise term?

JOURNAL ENTRY

Which of the two essays in this debate do you find more convincing? Why?

WRITING WORKSHOP

1. Do you think it is in society's interest to allow the children of a gay or lesbian parent to be adopted by the parent's partner? Write an essay in which you present your view on this issue. Make sure that you include a thesis and that you refute the main arguments against your position.

2. Write an essay in which you take two of Birtha's points and refute them, either by questioning their accuracy or by identifying flaws in their logic.

3. Research your state's policy toward gay adoption rights. Then, write a letter to your state representative in which you argue that the current policy is sound — or that it should be modified.

COMBINING THE PATTERNS

Paragraph 8 is developed by means of **cause and effect.** What point is Birtha making in paragraph 8? Could she have made the same point by using another pattern of development — for example, comparison and contrast?

THEMATIC CONNECTIONS

- "Why Boys Don't Play with Dolls" (page 335)
- "The Men We Carry in Our Minds" (page 456)

❖ DEBATE CASEBOOK:
Does Media Violence Cause Societal Violence?

Violence is a disturbing and sometimes frightening undercurrent of life in the United States. In any given year, more murders occur in any one of our major cities than in all of the British Isles combined. This fact has not been lost on lawmakers, especially those running for reelection. Violent behavior (and how to curb it) has been a frequent issue in elections. Although the causes of violent crime are complex, some people look for a single cause that will point to a quick fix for the problem. In the 1950s, for example, parents and educators blamed graphically violent comic books for an increase in "juvenile delinquency." In the 1970s, pressure from Congress caused Hollywood to institute a rating system so that parents could judge the suitability of movies. More recently, lawmakers mandated that a V-chip, enabling parents to block violent or sexually explicit programs, be built into all new television sets.

The debate about the connection between media violence and violent behavior heats up whenever a particularly horrible crime is linked to a movie. In one case, for example, two teenagers, Sarah Edmondson and Ben Darras, went on a murder spree and at their murder trial tried unsuccessfully to blame their actions on Oliver Stone's movie *Natural Born Killers*. One of the murder victims, Bill Savage, was an acquaintance of the bestselling writer John Grisham. In response to the murder, Grisham wrote "Unnatural Killers," an essay in which he argues that Hollywood has the responsibility to stop glamorizing and glorifying murder and mayhem. (This essay was included in the Debate Casebook in the previous edition of *Patterns for College Writing*.) According to Grisham, there are two ways to curtail the gratuitous violence that has become a staple of many Hollywood movies. The first, says Grisham, is to send a message to producers like Oliver Stone, by boycotting movies that encourage violence. The second is to sue. To Grisham, it is inconceivable that the makers of movies do not to know the effects of the steady diet of violence they feed the American public, and for this reason, Grisham believes they should be held legally accountable for the damage their products cause:

> It will take only one large verdict against the likes of Oliver Stone, and his production company, and perhaps the screenwriter, and the studio itself, and the party will be over. The verdict will come from the heartland, far away from Southern California, in some small courtroom with no cameras. A jury will finally say enough is enough; that the demons placed in Sarah Edmondson's mind were not solely of her making.

In 1996, a civil lawsuit was filed by Patsy Byers, a paralyzed victim of Sarah and Ben's crime spree, against Oliver Stone and Warner Brothers, who produced the film, as well as against the two assailants and their families' insurance companies. After several appeals, the suit was dismissed in 2001. The judge in the case ruled that the plaintiffs had not presented any evidence that Stone or the students had intended to incite violence, and he rejected the argument that the movie was not protected by the First Amendment. (Perhaps as a result of this decision, Grisham decided not to grant permission to include "Unnatural Killers" in this Debate Casebook.)

The three essays in this casebook examine the issue of media violence. In "Memo to John Grisham" Stone responds to Grisham's criticism, accusing Grisham of leading a witch hunt. According to Stone, Grisham has singled out his film for blame, ignoring the more direct causes of the crimes committed by those who saw his movie. In "Violent Films Cry 'Fire' in Crowded Theaters," attorney Michael Zimecki argues that legal precedents exist for finding filmmakers negligent when they make movies that glorify violence. Finally, in "Whodunit—The Media?" Maggie Cutler argues that the link between violent media and violent behavior has never been conclusively established. It is, she says, the media's need for a scapegoat and for easy answers that makes video games, movies, and music easy targets.

❖ ──────────────────────────────────

Memo to John Grisham: What's Next — "A Movie Made Me Do It"?

Controversial filmmaker Oliver Stone was born in New York City in 1946 and educated at Yale. After serving in the Vietnam War, he studied film at New York University and in the following years wrote screenplays for violent but well-received films like *Midnight Express* (1978) and *Scarface* (1983). His directorial debut came with *Salvador* (1986), about the revolution then taking place in El Salvador; it was followed that same year by *Platoon*, a drama set during the Vietnam War, which won the Academy Award for best picture and earned Stone the award for best director. His films *JFK* (1991) and *Nixon* (1995) sparked considerable debate about the fictionalization of film biography.

Background: Stone's most controversial film, however, is *Natural Born Killers* (1994), about a young couple who go on a crime spree, killing fifty-two people and becoming media stars in the process. Condemned for its apparent glorification of casual murder, the movie, according to Stone, was intended as a satire of the media's obsession with violence. While not a box-office hit, the film found a cult audience after it was released on videotape. In 1995, however, two teenagers went on a crime spree that was allegedly influenced by Stone's film. One of the murder victims was a friend of best-selling author John Grisham; consequently, Grisham wrote an essay in response to the murders, "Unnatural Killers," in which he argues that film makers and film studios need to either stop glamorizing violence or be held legally responsible for crime sprees like the one he describes. In the following essay, commissioned by *LA Weekly* as a response to "Unnatural Killers," Stone argues that his film had no influence on the couple who killed Grisham's friend and that Grisham's advocacy of "silencing artists" is only a small step from taking away freedom of speech altogether. Other copycat crimes associated with *Natural Born Killers* include the 1994 decapitation of a thirteen-year-old Texas girl by a fourteen-year-old boy who told police he "wanted to be famous like the natural born killers" and the 1995 murder of a Georgia truck driver by four people in their twenties after they had watched the movie nineteen times.

The hunt for witches to explain society's ills is ancient in our blood, but unholy for that nonetheless. The difference is that now we do not blame the village hag and her black cat, but the writer and the photographer and the filmmaker. Increasingly indicted by art and fearful of technology, our society scours them for scapegoats, in the process ignoring Shakespeare, who reminds us that artists do not invent nature but merely hold up to it a mirror. That the mirror now is electronic or widescreen or cyberspace is all the more intimidating to the unschooled, and the more tempting to the lawyers.

John Grisham predictably draws upon the superstition about the magical power of pictures to conjure up the undead specter of censorship. Too sophisticated to clamor for government intervention, he calls instead for civil action. Victims of crimes should, he declares, rise up against the purveyors of culture high and low and demand retribution, thereby "sending a message" about the mood of the popular mind. And so we arrive at yet another, more modern, more typically American superstition: that the lawsuit is the answer to everything. Fall victim to a crime acted out in the movies and all you have to do is haul the director into court. Has your father been brutalized? Sue Oedipus and call Hamlet as a witness. Do you hate your mother? Blame Medea and Joan Crawford.* And has your lawyer-husband been unfaithful? Why, then slap a summons on John Grisham, since, after all, he wrote *The Firm*.

Grisham is at pains to insist that before seeing my film *Natural Born Killers*, accused murderers Ben Darras (18) and Sarah Edmondson (19) had "never hurt anyone." But, even by his own admission, Ben and Sarah are deeply disturbed youths with histories of drug and/or alcohol abuse and psychiatric treatment. Ben's alcoholic father divorced his mother twice, then committed suicide. Grisham mentions as if it is insignificant that Sarah carried a gun because she feared that Ben would attack her. Far from never having hurt anyone, it seems Ben and Sarah had for years been hurting themselves and their families, and it was only a matter of time until they externalized their anger.

It is likely that, whether they had seen *Natural Born Killers* or *The Green Berets* or a *Tom and Jerry* cartoon the night before their first crime, Ben and Sarah would have behaved in exactly the way they did. And it is equally clear that the specific identity of the victim was entirely irrelevant. "Ben was quite anxious to kill someone," Grisham states, and Sarah was ready to help. And at the crucial moment when the carefully twisted springs of their psyches finally uncoiled, as they were bound to do, not I nor Newt Gingrich nor Father Sullivan of Boys Town could or did influence them.**

Did *Natural Born Killers* have an impact on members of its audience? Undoubtedly. Did it move some to a heightened sensitivity toward violence? It did, some. Does it reveal a truth about the media's obsession with the senseless sensational? Ask O. J. Simpson. But did it drive Ben and Sarah to commit two murders? No. If they are guilty, perhaps a negligent or abusive upbringing, combined with defects in their psyches, *did*. Parents,

---

*EDS. NOTE — Oedipus, Hamlet, and Medea are tragic figures of classical drama. Former Hollywood star Joan Crawford was accused of child abuse by her adopted daughter in a best-selling memoir.

**EDS. NOTE — Gingrich, former speaker of the U.S. House of Representatives, recommended homes like Boys Town as refuges for youths from troubled families.

school, and peers shape children from their earliest days, not films. And, once grown and gone horribly wrong, those children must answer for their actions—not Hollywood directors. An elementary principle of our civilization is that people are responsible for their own actions. If Dan White, the killer of San Francisco Supervisor Harvey Milk and Mayor George Moscone, could claim that "Twinkies made me do it," what's next—"A movie made me do it"?

A recent study showed that the average teenager spends 1,500 hours a   6
year watching television, compared with 1,100 hours a year in school. According to the study, most programs contain violence, and fully half of these violent acts do not depict the victim's injuries or pain. Astonishingly, only 16 percent of all programs show the long-term effects of violence, while three-quarters of the time, perpetrators of violence on television go unpunished. Is it just possible that these 15,000 hours of mostly violent TV programming might have had slightly more effect on these two youngsters than two hours of *Natural Born Killers*?

Grisham points to "at least several" anonymous youths who claim to   7
have committed crimes under the influence "to some degree" of my film. Leaving aside the self-serving vagueness of this statement, we might ask: How many thousands of murders have been committed under the influence of alcohol? Yet Grisham does not call for the breweries and distilleries to be shut down by lawsuits. How many homicidal lunatics have purchased guns? Yet he mounts no campaign to close the weapons factories. Even if we admit, for the sake of argument, that Ben and Sarah were influenced by a film, only a lawyer in search of a client could see in this an indictment of the entertainment industry and not of the teenage killers and those who reared them.

Grisham disparages the First Amendment (which also protects the   8
films that have sprung from Grisham's own brainless works of fiction) and those who believe in it. He has nothing to say, however, about the Second Amendment, which permits gun-toting crazies to litter the American landscape with bodies. To my mind, his priorities are severely distorted. But then, the First Amendment protects even the views of those who don't believe in it. In America, we call that freedom of speech.

It gives me a shiver of fear when an influential lawyer and writer   9
argues, as Grisham does, that a particular work of art *should never have been allowed to be made*. Strangle art in its infancy, he suggests, and society will be a better place. One might more persuasively argue that cold-blooded murderers should be strangled in their infancy. Yet as with human infants, we can never know the outcome of nascent art, and so both must be protected and nurtured, precisely for society's sake. For it is only a small step from silencing art to silencing artists, and then to silencing those who support them, and so on, until, while we may one day live in a lawyer's paradise, we will surely find ourselves in a human hell.

● ● ●

COMPREHENSION

1. In paragraph 1, Stone says that the function of an artist is to hold a mirror up to nature. What does he mean? How does this statement help explain why he made a movie as violent as *Natural Born Killers*?

2. In paragraphs 1 and 2, Stone calls Grisham's attack against *Natural Born Killers* a witch hunt. What does he mean? Do you agree?

3. In criticizing Grisham's article, Stone implies that Grisham is engaging in *post hoc* reasoning. At what point in his essay does Stone suggest this? Do you agree that Grisham's article is flawed by *post hoc* reasoning? Why or why not?

4. According to Stone, what impact does *Natural Born Killers* have on audiences? What impact does he say television has on viewers?

5. In paragraphs 7 and 8, Stone says that Grisham targets his movie while ignoring other possible causes of violence. What other causes can you identify? How persuasive is Stone's line of reasoning?

PURPOSE AND AUDIENCE

1. What preconceptions does Stone have about movie violence? Does he expect his readers to share his ideas? How do you know?

2. Do you think Stone respects his readers' intelligence, or does he talk down to his audience? Explain.

3. Why do you think Stone wrote this essay? What is his purpose?

4. Is Stone's argument likely to appeal to those who already think television and movies are too violent? Does he make any attempt to appeal to readers who are hostile to his position? If so, where?

STYLE AND STRUCTURE

1. Stone begins his essay by comparing Grisham's attack against *Natural Born Killers* to a witch hunt. Is this a good strategy? Is it likely to alienate some of his readers? Why or why not?

2. Where does Stone attempt to refute Grisham's major points? How successful is he in doing so?

3. In paragraph 5, Stone concedes some points to his opposition. Is this a good strategy, or should he have denied any connection between movie violence and societal violence?

4. In paragraph 8, Stone asks why those who want to censor him don't consider the implications of the Second Amendment, "which permits gun-toting crazies to litter the American landscape with bodies." What effect does the phrase *gun-toting crazies* have on you? Is Stone overstating his case? Why or why not?

5. How effective is Stone's conclusion? Does it adequately restate his position? Is his point about lawyers valid or is it an *ad hominem* attack? Explain.

VOCABULARY PROJECTS

1. Define each of the following words as it is used in this selection.

   scapegoats (1)   retribution (2)
   cyberspace (1)   perpetrators (6)
   specter (2)   nascent (9)

2. At times, Stone's feelings come through. Underline words and phrases in the essay that show his attitude toward Grisham. How would you describe his tone?

JOURNAL ENTRY

Do you believe there is a link between movie violence and societal violence? Do you think that seeing a movie such as *Natural Born Killers* can cause someone to do something he or she would not normally do?

WRITING WORKSHOP

1. Do you believe, as Stone does, that filmmakers should not be legally responsible for the consequences of their films? Or do you agree with Grisham, who says that filmmakers, like car manufacturers, are involved in a commercial enterprise and should be held liable for damages caused by their products? Write an essay in which you argue for one side or the other.

2. Stone says that people like Grisham are creating a society in which people no longer have to take responsibility for their actions. Do you agree with Stone? Write an essay in which you argue for or against this position. Use your own experiences as well as examples from the news to support your points.

3. Assume you are either Ben Darras or Sarah Edmondson. Write a letter to Stone in which you argue that he is responsible for the crime you committed. Use the facts of the case as presented in Grisham's and Stone's essays to bolster your argument.

COMBINING THE PATTERNS

Stone includes several paragraphs organized according to a **cause-and-effect** pattern. Find two of these paragraphs, and determine how they help Stone support his thesis.

THEMATIC CONNECTIONS

- "Thirty-Eight Who Saw Murder Didn't Call the Police" (page 101)
- "Who Killed Benny Paret?" (page 321)
- "Burdens" (page 509)

MICHAEL ZIMECKI

❖

Violent Films Cry "Fire" in Crowded Theaters

Michael Zimecki was born in Detroit in 1950 and received degrees from the University of Pittsburgh and Carnegie Mellon. For many years, he was a medical writer affiliated with the University of Pittsburgh Medical School. After receiving a law degree from Duquesne University, he established a private practice in Pittsburgh.

Background: Zimecki contributed the following essay to the *National Law Journal* in 1996 in the aftermath of the torching of a New York City subway token booth attendant, a crime that was similar to a scene depicted in the movie *The Money Train*. (The following year, a Kentucky teenager killed three girls after firing on a prayer group; this crime was allegedly influenced by a dream sequence in *The Basketball Diaries* in which Leonardo DiCaprio played a student who gunned down his classmates.) Up through the 1960s, Hollywood adhered to a fairly strict production code that stringently limited onscreen violence. This code included the provision that "methods of crime shall not be explicitly presented." Its purpose was, in part, to ensure that movie violence would not lead viewers to copycat crimes. That code was extensively revised in 1966, however, opening the door to the graphic depictions of violence that prevail today. In this essay, Zimecki argues that such violent images in the media undoubtedly contribute to real-life violence.

The late Richard Weaver, professor of rhetoric at the University of Chicago, was fond of reminding his students that "ideas have consequences." 1

Bad ideas can have abominable consequences. Nevertheless, U.S. courts 2 have permitted moviemakers, magazine publishers, and other members of the mass media to represent some of the most odious and repulsive scenes imaginable, "on the confidence," as Circuit Judge Alvin B. Run once said, "that the benefits society reaps from the free flow and exchange of ideas outweigh the costs society endures by receiving reprehensible or dangerous ideas." *Herceg v. Hustler Magazine Inc.,* 814 F.2d 1017 (1987).

In 1995, a few days after Thanksgiving, a group of five young men 3 torched a subway token booth in Brooklyn, N.Y., trapping the toll clerk inside. He died of his burns within the week. The act that caused his death bore an eerie resemblance to two scenes from the recently released Columbia Pictures movie *Money Train*. In the movie, a pyromaniac sets token booths on fire by squirting a flammable liquid through the token slots and throwing in a lighted match.

Senate Majority Leader Bob Dole, the *Wall Street Journal,* the head of 4 the New York Transit Authority and New York's police commissioners were quick to blame the movie for sparking a copycat crime. As it turned out, the movie may not have been responsible. Shortly after his arrest, the youth accused of squirting the flammable liquid denied that the movie had any connection to the incident. In a letter to the *New York Times,* Jack Valenti, President and CEO of the Motion Picture Association of America, could scarcely contain his glee.

For its part, Columbia Pictures steadfastly maintained that it was   5
merely holding a mirror up to life, noting that its film was based on a series of attacks in New York subway stations in 1988.

It may be premature to conclude that *Money Train* did or did not play a   6
part in the 1995 Thanksgiving incident: As of this writing, police have declined to say whether any of the men in custody saw the movie. Moreover, two suspects remain at large, and the match-thrower, who could face a capital murder charge, has not been identified.

One thing is certain: Life and art exert a strong tug on each other.   7

Money Train was not the only such example. In 1993, a Pennsylvania   8
youth died after he attempted to duplicate a scene from *The Program.* In a peculiar display of male bravado, he lay down on the center line of a highway and was run over by a car.

In an earlier era, the perpetrators of the 1974 Hi-Fi Murders in Ogden,   9
Utah, forced their victims to drink liquid Drano after watching a similar scene in the Clint Eastwood picture *Magnum Force.*

That same year, a 9-year-old girl was raped with a bottle by a group of   10
juveniles at a San Francisco beach — just days after the nationwide telecast of the film *Born Innocent,* which showed a young girl being sexually assaulted with a plunger. The parents of the San Francisco girl subsequently sued NBC for her physical and emotional injuries, alleging that they were attributable to the broadcaster's negligence and recklessness in airing the film. *Olivia N. v. National Broadcasting Co. Inc.,* 178 Cal. Rptr. 888, 126 Cal. App. 3d 488 (1982). Although the suit proved to be unsuccessful, it was nonetheless a signal attempt to expand tort liability for speech outside the area of defamation.

Courts Support Filmmakers

U.S. courts have routinely rejected attempts to hold filmmakers liable   11
in tort for the harm they cause. Plaintiffs' attorneys seeking recovery on a theory of strict products liability have encountered some of the same difficulties that have impeded anti-gun and anti-tobacco litigation: Movies are meant to be seen, just as guns are meant to be fired and cigarettes to be smoked, and there is nothing defective about a product that accomplishes its purpose all too well. In fact, brutally violent films are especially popular box-office fare.

The biggest obstacle to plaintiffs' attorneys, however, isn't the courts'   12
rejection of claims based on negligence, nuisance, or products liability. It's the courts' narrow interpretation of "incitement."

Speech that advocates violence but that does not incite imminent   13
harm is protected by the First Amendment under the U.S. Supreme
Court's holding in *Brandenburg v. Ohio,* 396 U.S. 444, 23 L.Ed.2d 430, 89
S.Ct. 1827 (1969).

In *Brandenburg,* the high court overturned the conviction of a Klans-   14
man under Ohio's criminal syndicalism statute for saying that "there
might have to be some revengence [sic] taken," if "our President, our Congress, our Supreme Court continues to suppress the white, Caucasian
race." The finding of the court was that the mere advocacy of violence is
not enough.

As Justice William O. Douglas wrote in his concurring opinion, the   15
line between what is permissible and what is not is "the line between ideas
and overt acts." The Klansman was on the constitutionally protected side
of the line because he was not advocating violent deeds now, in the temporal present; his message had an abstract, rather than an urgent, quality. By
contrast, someone who falsely shouts "fire" in a crowded theater has im-
permissibly crossed the line because his speech is "brigaded with action."

But what about a film that shouts "fire" in that same, proverbially   16
crowded theater? Film industry executives maintain that movies portray
violence but do not advocate it; to the contrary, industry spokespeople
claim, the perpetrators of movie violence typically get their comeuppance
by film's end.

Unfortunately, filmmakers say one thing while showing another. As   17
social psychologist Albert Bandura observed more than 20 years ago, the
message of most violent films is not that "crime does not pay," but rather
that the wages of violent sin are pretty good except for an occasional
mishap.

Indifferent to the anti-social repercussions of their cinematic special   18
effects, violent movies such as *Money Train* advocate violence implicitly, if
not explicitly. Violence is as much a product of external reinforcement as
internal pathology. By modeling, legitimizing, and sanctioning violence,
movies do not just loosen restraints on those who are already predisposed
to violence. Violent movies actively promote aggressive behavior as a social
norm.

Legally Flawed Definition

By any definition other than the legal one, this would constitute   19
"incitement." The rub, of course, is that harm delayed is no harm at all
under the *Brandenburg* standard, which distinguishes violence that takes to
the streets from violence that erupts in the theater. While fine in theory,
the *Brandenburg* concept of "speech brigaded with action" gets reduced in
practice to "Take it outside, boys!" — which is poor advice to a schoolchild
and hardly more sagacious as a constitutional principle.

The difference between a risk of eventual harm and immediate bodily   20
injury has been minimized of late in the toxic torts arena, where medical

monitoring awards embrace the principle that a polluter should not be allowed to escape responsibility for his actions simply because environmentally induced cancers are late-developing. Violence, too, can fester for years.

Unfortunately, constitutional law has been slow to appreciate the toxic power of words, slow to recognize that exposure to cruel and degrading images is like exposure to a carcinogen, slower still to understand that speech and act occupy a continuum of cause and effect. 21

The premiere of *Money Train* may not have been a substantial factor in bringing about the death of subway token clerk Harry Kaufman. But movies are a significant cause of the violence that has become so prevalent in our society. Film-inspired violence may not be "imminent" in the constitutional sense, but the constitutional difference between "I will kill you now" and "I will kill you later" is cold comfort to the victims of movie-modeled murder. 22

The problem is that we, as a society, are becoming increasingly deadened and desensitized to violence through repeated exposure to its display. Under *Brandenburg,* the onslaught continues. But film industry executives should take heed: Violence is now so imminent in our society that a wrong look can get you shot on many street corners. The hour has come at last, and the rough beast that the poet William Butler Yeats warned about is already born.* As we continue to split hairs, failing to address the need for legislation, we can take comfort in the cliché, "Enjoy yourself. It's later than you think." 23

● ● ●

COMPREHENSION

1. According to Zimecki, why have courts in the United States allowed moviemakers and magazine publishers "to represent some of the most odious and repulsive scenes imaginable" (2)?

2. In paragraph 7, Zimecki says, "Life and art exert a strong tug on each other." What does he mean? What examples does he offer to support this statement?

3. Why have courts routinely rejected attempts to hold filmmakers liable on the theory of product liability? How has the narrow interpretation of *incitement* created an obstacle for plaintiffs?

4. According to Zimecki, in what way do certain types of film shout "fire" in a crowded theater?

5. What does Zimecki mean when he says, "Unfortunately, constitutional law has been slow to appreciate the toxic power of words" (21)?

---

*EDS. NOTE—"And what rough beast, its hour come round at last, / Slouches toward Bethlehem to be born?" (from "The Second Coming" by William Butler Yeats).

PURPOSE AND AUDIENCE

1. At what point does Zimecki state his thesis? Why does he wait as long as he does?

2. Is this essay aimed at an audience of lawyers or at a more general audience? How do you know?

3. What is Zimecki's purpose in writing this essay? Is it to change attitudes? To bring about legislation? To change policy? Explain.

STYLE AND STRUCTURE

1. Zimecki begins his essay with a quotation by Richard Weaver. Why do you think he chose this quotation? What other strategies could he have used to introduce his essay?

2. This essay appeared in the *National Law Journal*. If Zimecki were to rewrite the essay for *People* magazine, what kinds of changes would he need to make? What additional information would he need to provide? Explain.

3. Do you think Zimecki undercuts his case by conceding the point that "*Money Train* may not have been a substantial factor in bringing about the death of subway token clerk Harry Kaufman" (22)? Why or why not?

4. What evidence does Zimecki use to support his assertions? Why do you think he chose this type of support?

5. Zimecki concludes his essay with a quotation that he admits is a cliché. How effective is this strategy? Would another quotation be more effective? Explain your reasoning.

VOCABULARY PROJECTS

1. Define each of the following words as it is used in this selection.

repulsive (2)	negligence (10)	brigaded (15)
reaps (2)	defamation (10)	repercussions (18)
endures (2)	tort (11)	pathology (18)
reprehensible (2)	liability (11)	norm (18)
pyromaniac (3)	incitement (12)	sagacious (19)
capital (6)	advocacy (14)	toxic (21)
attributable (10)	impermissibly (15)	carcinogen (21)

2. What is the dictionary definition of *incitement*? What additional meanings does Zimecki say the word has acquired?

JOURNAL ENTRY

Do you believe the courts should hold filmmakers responsible for the effects of their movies? What might be the possible effects on movies of such a change in policy?

WRITING WORKSHOP

1. Write an essay in which you argue that moviemakers should not be held responsible for the consequences of their films. Consider the effect on free expression of holding moviemakers liable years after their movies are released. Make sure you refute Zimecki's arguments against your position.

2. Using as evidence several violent movies you have seen, write an essay in which you argue that by glorifying violence, certain films encourage violent behavior.

3. How do you think Zimecki would respond to Stone's essay? Choose a section of Stone's essay, and refute it using any of Zimecki's points that are relevant to the issue.

COMBINING THE PATTERNS

In paragraph 15, Zimecki uses **comparison and contrast** to make his point. What point is he making? Would a paragraph of cause and effect be just as effective here? Why or why not?

THEMATIC CONNECTIONS

- "Thirty-Eight Who Saw Murder Didn't Call the Police" (page 101)
- "How the Lawyers Stole Winter" (page 402)
- "The Wife-Beater" (page 521)

❖

Whodunit — The Media?

Maggie Cutler is the pen name of Lynn Phillips (b. 1944), a New York–based writer who graduated from Radcliffe College. Early in her career, Cutler worked as an assistant editor on the historic documentary films *Salesman* (1968) and *Monterey Pop* (1969). She was also a staff writer for the 1970s television series *Mary Hartman, Mary Hartman*, a cult-favorite spoof of soap operas. She has contributed to a variety of periodicals, ranging from *National Lampoon* to *Glamour* to *The Nation*, and she has also written for Web-based projects including Vaguepolitix.com and Nerve.com. In the following essay, she considers the effect of media violence on children and young adults.

Background: In 1999, the most recent year for which statistics have been compiled, juveniles accounted for 16 percent of violent crime arrests nationwide, and 1,763 of those arrested for homicide were under the age of eighteen (down from 1993's peak of 4,330). Another 1999 survey showed that a majority of teachers and students believed violence to be a problem in schools. A quarter of the students surveyed and 16 percent of teachers said that they themselves had been victims of student-perpetrated violence. Most experts agree that children who are at risk for violent behavior can be identified at a young age and that early intervention is the most effective deterrent.

Will girls imitate the new, kickass heroines in the Japanese animé *Card-* 1 *captors*? Will the impressionable 12-year-olds exposed to trailers for MGM's *Disturbing Behavior* forever after associate good teen behavior with lobotomies? Did Nine Inch Nails and the video game *DOOM* inspire the Trench-coat Mafia's bloodbath at Columbine? Thousands of studies have been done to try to answer variants of the question: Does media violence lead to real-life violence, making children more antisocial and aggressive?

Like most complex issues, discussions about the impact of media vio- 2 lence on children suffer from that commonest of media problems: fudge. Almost any simple statement on the subject obscures the complexity of the facts, half-facts, and "results suggest" findings of the past forty years. The right-wing Parents Television Council, for example, announces that the per-hour rate in the United States of sexual and violent material and coarse language combined almost tripled from 1989 to 1999. But while PTC president Brent Bozell castigates the media for lowering standards of acceptable speech and behavior, he doesn't mention that in the final years of this avalanche of dreck the juvenile crime rate *dropped* more than 30 percent. Or, again, in August 1999 the Senate Judiciary Committee, headed by Orrin Hatch, reported confidently that "Television alone is responsible for 10 percent of youth violence." Given the overall juvenile crime count in

1997, the report implied, some 250 murders and 12,100 other violent crimes would not have been committed if it weren't for the likes of *Batman Beyond.*

But this, of course, is deeply misleading. One of the reasons so many   3
media violence studies have been done is that the phenomenon may be too complex to study conclusively. There's no way, after all, to lock two clones in a black box, feed them different TV, movie, and video-game diets, and open the box years later to determine that, yes, it was definitely those Bruce Lee epics that turned clone A into Jesse Ventura, while clone B's exposure to the movie *Babe* produced a Pee Wee Herman.

It has been hard, in other words, for media violence studies to shake   4
the ambiguity of correlations. Several studies have shown that violent boys tend to watch more TV, choose more violent content and get more enjoyment out of it. But the studies admittedly can't show exactly how or why that happens. Do temperamentally violent kids seek out shows that express feelings they already have, or are they in it for the adrenaline boost? Do the sort of parents who let kids pig out on gore tend to do more than their share of other hurtful things that encourage violent behavior? To what extent is violent media producing little Johnny's aggression — or inspiring it, making it appear glamorous, righteous, acceptably gratuitous, fun, or "normal" — and to what extent is it merely satisfying little Johnny's greater-than-average longings for the mayhem, vengeance, superhuman power, and sweet revenge that most people, at times, secretly crave?

According to James Garbarino, author of *Lost Boys: Why Our Sons Turn*   5
Violent and How We Can Save Them, it makes no sense to talk about violent media as a direct cause of youth violence. Rather, he says, "it depends": Media violence is a risk factor that, working in concert with others, can exacerbate bad behavior.

Like Orrin Hatch's committee, Garbarino estimates the effect of vio-   6
lent media on juvenile violence at about 10 percent, but his ecology-of-violence formulation is far less tidy than the Hatch committee's pop-psych model. Garbarino himself reports in an e-mail that he would like to see media violence treated as a public health problem — dammed at its Hollywood source the way sewage treatment plants "reduce the problem of cholera." Nevertheless, his ecology model of how juvenile violence emerges from complex, interacting factors means that hyperaggressive, "asset poor" kids are likely to be harmed by graphic depictions of violence, while balanced, "asset rich" kids are likely to remain unscathed. A few studies have even found that a "cathartic effect" of media violence makes some kids *less* aggressive. This wide range of individual variance makes policy prescriptions a tricky matter.

The American Psychological Association's Commission on Violence   7
and Youth (1994) mentions violent media as only one among many factors in juvenile violence. It stresses that inborn temperament, early parental abuse or neglect, poverty, cognitive impairment, plus a deficiency of corrective influences or role models in various combinations will put a child at

greater risk for violence, both as perpetrator and as victim. The APA found that many damaged kids' lives can be salvaged with early intervention. By the age of 8, these at-risk kids can be identified. Once identified they can be taught skills that enable them to resolve conflicts peacefully. The APA adds that parental guidance along with reducing kids' exposure to graphic violence can help keep them out of the correctional system. But for the kids most at risk, reducing representational violence is obviously no cure. So this past fall, when Senators John McCain and Joseph Lieberman ordered the entertainment industry to stop advertising its nastier products to young children or else face (shudder) regulation, it was fair of media critics to castigate them for exploiting the media violence problem for its bipartisan glow rather than attempting to find the least coercive, most effective ways of keeping children safe and sane.

Perhaps the biggest problem in mitigating the effect of media violence on children is that it's hard to nail down just what "violent media" means to actual kids. As with adult pornography, we all think we know what it is until we have to define it. That's because kids not only process content differently depending on their temperament, background, and circumstances, they seem to process it differently at different ages, too. 8

A series of often-cited studies known as Winick and Winick (1979) charted distinct stages in media processing abilities. Fairly early, from about 6 until about 10, most — but not all — kids are learning to deal with media much as adults do: interactively rather than passively. In her 1985 book, *Watching* Dallas: *Soap Opera and the Melodramatic Imagination,* Ien Ang of the University of Western Sydney in Australia showed that different adult viewers rewrote the "messages" of shows to suit their own views. So a wise little girl whose parents discuss media with her might enjoy *Wrestlemania* as an amusing guide to crazy-guys-to-avoid, while an angry, abandoned, slow-witted child is more likely to enter its world of insult and injury with uncritical awe. 9

At first blush, measures like content labeling would seem to make more sense for the 2-to-6 set because young kids do get confused about reality, fantasy, information, and advertising. But again, what constitutes "violent" content isn't always obvious. The Winicks found that young children whose parents fought a lot responded with more distress to representations of people yelling and screaming — because it seemed real — than to blatant violence for which they had no frame of reference. Should there be a label for "loud and emotional"? And if so, should we slap it on *La Bohème*? 10

Because representational violence is so hard to define, the recently reported Stanford media effects studies, which focused on third and fourth graders, ducked the problem. The study team, headed by Thomas Robinson, simply worked with teachers, parents, and kids to help children lower their overall media use voluntarily. As a result of the six-month program, which involved classroom instruction, parental support, and peer pressure, kids used media about 30 percent less than usual. And, they found, verbal and physical aggression levels subsequently dropped 25 percent on aver- 11 age. These numbers are being taken especially seriously because they were established "in the field" rather than in the lab, so that the verbal and physical aggression measured was actual, not simulated by, say, asking a child to kick or insult a doll. As media violence studies predicted, the more aggressive kids were to begin with, the more their behavior improved when they consumed less of whatever it was they normally consumed.

Although the Stanford study—perhaps to stay popular with granters— 12 is being promoted as a study on media violence, it is really a study of media overuse, self-awareness, and the rewards of self-discipline. Its clearest finding wasn't that media violence is always harmful but that too much mediated experience seems to impair children's ability to interact well with other people. Follow-up studies at Stanford will show whether the remarkable benefits of its media reduction program last over a longer period. If they do, such classes may be a helpful addition to school curriculums in conjunction, perhaps, with courses in conflict resolution. But in any case, its results demonstrate less the effects of specific content than what could be called "the rule of the real."

The rule of the real says that however strong media influences may be, 13 real life is stronger. Real love, real money, real political events, and real-life, unmediated interpersonal experience all shape kids' lives, minds, and behavior more powerfully than any entertainment products. Even media seen or understood as real—news, documentaries, interviews—will have more impact than that which a kid knows is make-believe. As the Winicks found, kids understand early that cartoon violence is a joke, not a model. Even wrestling, once kids figure out that it's staged, gets processed differently from, say, a schoolyard beating.

Without belittling the importance of media research, it's time that the 14 rule of the real governed policy as well. After all, boys whose dads do hard time tend to end up in jail, while boys who see *Fight Club* tend to end up in film clubs; it's more likely that the Santana High killer decided to shoot up his school after seeing the anniversary coverage of Columbine than because he watched *The Mummy*. Abused young women don't kill their battering husbands because they grew up watching *Charlie's Angels*, and teens who hear no criticism of the Gulf War tend to want another. Given limited energies and resources, if our politicians really wanted to reduce youth violence, they would push to reform prison policies, provide supervised after-school activities for teens, and get early, comprehensive help to high-risk children. As a community, we would do better to challenge the corporate conglomeration of news outlets than to legislate the jugs 'n' jugular quotient in *Tomb Raider,* its labeling, or ad placements—and this is true even though the stuff kids like is often quite nasty, and even though the better part of the scientific establishment now agrees that such excitements are less than benign. But setting priorities like these is hard because, while the real may rule children's lives as it rules our own, it's much more fun to imagine controlling their dreams.

• • •

COMPREHENSION

1. According to Cutler, why is it difficult to discuss the problem of media violence?

2. In paragraph 4, Cutler says, "It has been hard, in other words, for media violence studies to shake the ambiguity of correlations." What does she mean by this statement?

3. Why does Cutler believe it so difficult to define the term *media violence*?

4. How did the Stanford media effects studies approach the problem of media violence? According to Cutler, how effective was the Stanford approach?

5. According to Cutler, how should the problem of media violence be approached?

PURPOSE AND AUDIENCE

1. How would you describe Cutler's tone in this essay? Is she friendly? Concerned? Sarcastic? Distant? Angry? Something else?

2. What transitions does Cutler use to move her argument from one point to another? How effectively do these transitions move readers through the essay? Are any transitions missing?

3. Cutler is the author of a biweekly satirical column that focuses on the confusion between politics, media, and sex in American culture. Should she have mentioned this fact in her essay? Explain.

4. At what points in the essay does Cutler reveal her own biases?

STYLE AND STRUCTURE

1. Are the tone and language of Cutler's introduction consistent with the tone and language of the rest of the essay? Would a different introduction have been more effective?

2. Throughout much of her essay, Cutler discusses the difficulty of studying the effects of media violence. In what way does this discussion help her construct her argument? Is this an effective strategy?

3. Do any of the statements in the following excerpt from paragraph 7 of this essay lack adequate support? Would more support have strengthened this excerpt? Explain.

> The APA [American Psychological Association] adds that parental guidance along with reducing kids' exposure to graphic violence can help keep them out of the correctional system. But for the kids most at risk, reducing representational violence is obviously no cure. So this past fall, when Senators John McCain and Joseph Lieberman ordered the entertainment industry to stop advertising its nastier products to young children or else face (shudder) regulation, it was fair of media critics to castigate them for exploiting the media violence problem for its bipartisan glow rather than attempting to find the least coercive, most effective ways of keeping children safe and sane.

4. At what point in the essay does Cutler refute arguments against her thesis? Does she address opposing arguments effectively?

5. Cutler waits until her last paragraph to present her argument. Why does she do this? Is this a good decision?

6. In her conclusion, Cutler offers a number of suggestions for reducing youth violence. Do these suggestions flow naturally out of her essay, or is Cutler introducing new issues that need further discussion? Explain.

VOCABULARY PROJECTS

1. Define each of the following words as it is used in this selection.

lobotomies (1)	asset (6)	bipartisan (7)
fudge (2)	unscathed (6)	uncritical (9)
ambiguity (4)	variance (6)	peer (11)
correlations (4)	cognitive (7)	processed (13)
mayhem (4)	deficiency (7)	conglomeration (14)
exacerbate (5)	perpetrator (7)	quotient (14)
hyperaggressive (6)	representational (7)	benign (14)

2. Throughout her essay, Cutler uses a number of colloquial expressions—for example, *kickass* (1)—as well as contractions. She also repeatedly uses the word *kids* (rather than *children*). Is this kind of language consistent with Cutler's purpose and audience, or is it inappropriate? Explain.

JOURNAL ENTRY

Go to the Internet, and research the Columbine shootings (1). Then write a journal entry in which you discuss what influences other than the media could have caused the shooters to behave as they did.

WRITING WORKSHOP

1. Do you agree or disagree with Cutler's position on the impact of media violence on children? Write a letter to Cutler in which you state your position. Be sure to address the specific points she makes in her essay.

2. Do your own survey of violent media. Go to a video arcade, or view several recent movies that have been rated R for violent content. Then write an essay in which you present your findings. On the basis of your observations, do you think some of these video games or films are so violent that they could trigger violent behavior in some individuals? Be specific.

3. As Cutler points out, some studies have shown a link between violent video games and movies and aggressive behavior in children, but no studies have shown conclusively that excessive viewing of these games and movies actually causes children to go out and commit crimes. Even so, some parents and educators have called for limitations on (or outright banning of) this material. Do you believe some kind of censorship should

be imposed? Write an essay in which you take a stand on this issue. If you like, consult other sources, but be sure to document all words and ideas that you borrow from your sources.

COMBINING THE PATTERNS

Paragraphs 8 through 10 are developed by means of **definition.** What is the function of these paragraphs? In what way do they help Cutler further her argument?

THEMATIC CONNECTIONS

❖ DEBATE CASEBOOK:
Should African Americans Receive Reparations for Slavery?

In every session of Congress since 1989, Democratic Representative John Conyers (Michigan), ranking member of the House Judiciary Committee, has introduced a bill to establish a committee to study the residual effects of slavery on African Americans and possibly to recommend payment of reparations. So far, of the 435 members of Congress, only 31 have agreed to cosponsor his bill. In addition, public opinion polls show that almost 70 percent of the general population does not support reparations. Recently, however, a number of high-profile lawsuits have renewed debate on this issue.

Supporters of reparations usually point to the history of broken promises that occurred both during and after the Civil War. Special Field Order Number 15, issued by General William T. Sherman on January 16, 1865, gave each family of freed African Americans "a plot of not more than forty acres of tillable ground" formerly owned by slaveholders along parts of the South Carolina, Georgia, and Florida coasts. Sherman also recommended lending each family an army mule. Several months later, the Freedmen's Bureau began distributing 850,000 acres of confiscated or abandoned land to freed slaves, but this plan was discontinued when Andrew Johnson assumed the presidency after Lincoln's assassination and allowed the former Confederate slaveholders to reclaim their land. In succeeding years, lawmakers such as Thaddeus Stevens periodically introduced reparations bills, only to see them defeated.

The movement for reparations picked up speed in 1988, when Congress issued an apology as well as payment to Japanese Americans who had been imprisoned in American internment camps during World War II. Reparations have also been paid to other groups: the German government paid reparations to victims of the Holocaust, and the American government paid reparations to some Native American tribes. As a result, organizations such as the National Coalition of Blacks for Reparations in America and the Reparations Coordinating Committee renewed demands for reparations, this time in the form of lawsuits against the federal government and private businesses. Randall Robinson, president of the TransAfrica Forum and author of *The Debt: What America Owes to Blacks* (2000), expresses the position of reparations advocates when he says, "When the black living suffer real and current consequences as a result of the wrong committed by a younger America, then contemporary America must be caused to shoulder responsibility for these wrongs until such wrongs have been adequately compensated and righted."

Those people, both blacks and whites, who do not support reparations say that by adopting the rhetoric of victimhood, the slave-reparations movement ignores the achievements of African Americans who faced slavery and triumphed. They point out that the main arguments in favor of reparations are fraught with inconsistencies and inaccuracies. For example, even if one assumes a debt exists, it is not clear to whom the debt is owed or who owes it. Would money be given to all African Americans, or just to those who could conclusively trace their lineage to a slave ancestor? And who would pay? All Americans, even those whose ancestors came to this country after the Civil War? Or only that tiny minority who owned slaves? Detractors also point out that historically, reparations have been paid only to individuals (or to their immediate family members) who suffered or were hurt. Never have reparations been paid to all members of a group — for example, all Japanese Americans or all Jews. In addition, detractors question the underlying assumption of the supporters of reparations — that all African Americans currently suffer from the effects of slavery. This contention, they say, has never been proven. Besides, it ignores the existence of a large and prosperous black middle class and the recent growth in the number of black-owned businesses. Finally, detractors worry about the resentment and antagonism that they say would occur among nonblacks if trillions of dollars in reparations were paid to African Americans.

The writers in this debate casebook hold a variety of opinions concerning reparations for slavery. In "Litigating the Legacy of Slavery," Charles J. Ogletree Jr. argues that reparations are necessary for "undoing the damage" of slavery for those who have not benefited from affirmative action programs or from integration. In "Slavery Isn't the Issue," Juan Williams asserts that reparations will do irreparable damage to African Americans. In "An Idea Whose Time Has Come," Manning Marable contends that whites have an obligation to recognize the legacy of slavery and to pay African Americans their back wages. Finally, Linda Chavez argues in "Demands for Reparations" that the time for reparations has long past and that the best we can do as a country is to make sure that everyone is given an equal chance to achieve.

CHARLES J. OGLETREE JR.

Litigating the Legacy of Slavery

Charles J. Ogletree Jr. was born in 1952, the son of farm workers in central California. He holds B.A. and M.A. degrees from Stanford University and earned his law degree from Harvard in 1978. He began his legal career as a public defender in Washington, D.C., and entered private practice in 1985, the year he was appointed visiting professor at Harvard Law School, where he is now Jesse Climenko Professor of Law. At Harvard, he directs the Criminal Justice Institute as well as the Saturday School, which provides academic support for disadvantaged students. A prominent legal theorist and ardent proponent of civil rights, he is the author of numerous articles and coauthor of the book *Beyond the Rodney King Story: An Investigation of Police Conduct in Minority Communities* (1994). Ogletree has also served as moderator for a variety of public television panels focusing on issues of justice and fairness and is cochair of the Reparations Coordinating Committee.

Background: To get a sense of the scope that slave reparations might take, consider the shipping company CSX, which Ogletree mentions as one of the firms named in the lawsuit discussed in the essay. According to a *USA Today* article, one railroad company operating prior to the Civil War and now a part of CSX paid slave owners up to $150 for each slave it rented yearly; in contemporary currency, that figure would be $3,737. Another railroad company, also now part of CSX, valued its slave holdings at the end of the Civil War at $128,773, which would equal $1.4 million today. And these figures represent only a fraction of the slave labor attributed to railroads alone. Energy and mining companies, along with the early tobacco industry, relied on slave labor, and insurance companies that are still in existence profited from the slave and cotton trades. Moreover, some of the country's wealthiest universities received significant donations from slave owners. According to Ogletree, all of these companies and institutions could and should be sued for reparations.

Last Tuesday, a group of lawyers filed a federal class-action lawsuit in New York on behalf of all African-American descendants of slaves. The lawsuit seeks compensation from a number of defendants for profits earned through slave labor and the slave trade.

This lawsuit is limited to Fleet-Boston, Aetna, CSX, and other to-be-named companies. The broader reparations movement seeks to explore the historical role that other private institutions and government played during slavery and the era of legal racial discrimination that followed. The goal of these historical investigations is to bring American society to a new reckoning with how our past affects the current conditions of African-Americans and to make America a better place by helping the truly disadvantaged.

The Reparations Coordinating Committee, of which I am a cochair- 3
man, will proceed with its own plans to file wide-ranging reparations lawsuits late this autumn. The committee is a group of lawyers, academics,
public officials, and activists that has conducted extensive research and
begun to identify parties to sue and claims to be raised.

The shape of a reparations strategy can already be seen. Among private 4
defendants, corporations will be prominent, as last week's lawsuit shows.
Other private institutions — Brown University, Yale University, and Harvard Law School — have made headlines recently as the beneficiaries of
grants and endowments traced back to slavery and are probable targets.
Naming the government as a defendant is also central to any reparations
strategy; public officials guaranteed the viability of slavery and the segregation that followed it.

A number of recent examples illustrate the possibilities for making 5
reparations claims nationally and internationally. In South Africa, reparations have been part of the work of the Truth and Reconciliation Commission, which seeks to compensate people with clear material needs who
suffered under apartheid because of their race. It was also in South Africa
that, in the final documents of a racism conference sponsored by the
United Nations, slavery was defined as a "crime against humanity," a legal
determination that may enable the reparations movement to extend its
reach to international forums.

In the United States, just three years ago the federal government 6
reached a consent decree with a class of over 20,000 black farmers to compensate for years of discrimination by the Department of Agriculture. The
case represents the largest civil-rights settlement by the government ever,
with a likely payout of about $2 billion. Previously, the government also
approved significant compensation for Japanese-Americans interned during World War II and paid reparations to black survivors of the Rosewood,
Florida, race riots.

Although these precedents differ from a slavery-based reparations claim 7
in that they involved classes of individuals who were both alive and easily
identified, they nonetheless indicate government willingness to acknowledge past wrongs and remedy them. It is important that in each case the
government waived its immunity from suit, thereby lifting the ordinary
bar that prevents lawsuits against a sovereign.

Bringing the government into litigation will also generate a public 8
debate on slavery and the role its legacy continues to play in our society.
The opportunity to use expert witnesses and conduct extensive discovery,
to get facts and documentation, makes the courtroom an ideal venue for
this debate.

A full and deep conversation on slavery and its legacy has never taken 9
place in America; reparations litigation will show what slavery meant, how
it was profitable, and how it has continued to affect the opportunities of
millions of black Americans.

Litigation is required to promote this discussion because political 10
accountability has not been forthcoming. In each Congressional session

since 1989, Representative John Conyers has introduced a bill to study slavery reparations and it has quickly died each time.

Though claims for slavery reparations have moved near the front of national and international policy discussions in the past few years, the movement has deep historical roots. Those roots go back at least as far as the unkept promise in 1864 of "40 acres and a mule" to freed slaves, which acknowledged our country's debt to the newly emancipated. 11

Indeed, the civil rights movement has long been organized, in part, around the notion that slavery and the century of legal discrimination that followed have had enduring and detrimental effects on American minorities. 12

The reparations movement should not, I believe, focus on payments to individuals. The damage has been done to a group — African-American slaves and their descendants — but it has not been done equally within the group. The reparations movement must aim at undoing the damage where that damage has been most severe and where the history of race in America has left its most telling evidence. The legacy of slavery and racial discrimination in America is seen in well-documented racial disparities in access to education, health care, housing, insurance, employment, and other social goods. The reparations movement must therefore focus on the poorest of the poor — it must finance social recovery for the bottom-stuck, providing an opportunity to address comprehensively the problems of those who have not substantially benefited from integration or affirmative action. 13

The root of "reparations" is "to repair." This litigation strategy could give us an opportunity to fully address the legacy of slavery in a spirit of repair. 14

• • •

COMPREHENSION

1. What is the goal of the class-action lawsuit Ogletree mentions in paragraph 1? According to Ogletree, what is the goal of the reparations movement?

2. Why does Ogletree believe that "naming the government as a defendant is . . . central to any reparations strategy" (4)?

3. According to Ogletree, what is the relationship between slavery and the present condition of African Americans?

4. How will litigation promote the discussion of slavery and its legacy?

5. Why does Ogletree believe that reparations should not be paid to individuals?

PURPOSE AND AUDIENCE

1. What was Ogletree's purpose in writing this essay? What do you think he hoped to accomplish?

2. How would you characterize the tone of this essay? Frustrated? Threatening? Confident? Angry? Something else? Explain.

3. Why does Ogletree tell his readers in paragraph 3 that he is cochair of the Reparations Coordinating Committee? What effect might this information have on readers?

4. Where does Ogletree state his thesis? Given his audience, is this a wise decision?

STYLE AND STRUCTURE

1. Ogletree introduces his essay by describing the class-action lawsuit brought on behalf of African Americans. Why does he begin this way? Is this a successful strategy?

2. In paragraph 5, Ogletree presents a series of examples intended to illustrate "the possibilities for making reparations claims nationally and internationally." How convincing are these examples?

3. In paragraph 7, Ogletree concedes that the situations he discusses are not exactly parallel to the situation of African Americans. Does this admission undermine his case?

4. In paragraph 9, Ogletree says, "A full and deep conversation on slavery and its legacy has never taken place in America." Is this statement self-evident, or should Ogletree have presented evidence to support it?

5. Ogletree does not refute arguments against his thesis. Should he have done so? Explain.

VOCABULARY PROJECTS

1. Define each of these words as it is used in this selection.

class action (1)	apartheid (5)	sovereign (7)
reckoning (2)	consent (6)	documentation (8)
extensive (3)	compensation (6)	legacy (9)
prominent (4)	interned (6)	accountability (10)
reconciliation (5)	precedents (7)	disparities (13)

2. Ogletree uses the word *litigation* throughout his essay. What is the **denotation** of this word? What are its **connotations**? In what way do these connotations affect your response to paragraphs 8 through 10?

JOURNAL ENTRY

Do you think that corporations and educational institutions that have benefitted financially from slavery should be required to pay reparations to African Americans?

WRITING WORKSHOP

1. According to Juan Williams (page 633), "any payment of reparations will spark waves of racial resentment" (3) that will ultimately hurt African Americans as a group. Write a letter in which Ogletree responds to Williams's statement. Use material from both essays to support your points.

2. In an editorial printed in the *New York Times,* columnist Brent Staples says that by portraying African Americans as victims, reparations supporters "subvert the true story of blacks in the United States." According to Staples, this story is one of "extraordinary achievement" in the face of great obstacles. Do you agree with this critique of the reparations movement, or do you, like Ogletree, believe that paying reparations is the best way to improve the lives "of those who have not substantially benefited from integration or affirmative action" (13)?

3. Expand your journal entry into an essay. If you wish, you can gather some specific information about this topic from the other essays in this debate casebook. Be sure that you document all ideas that you get from your sources. (See the Appendix for information on MLA documentation format.)

COMBINING THE PATTERNS

Ogletree develops his conclusion by presenting a **definition.** How effective is this strategy? What other strategy could he have used?

THEMATIC CONNECTIONS

- "Indian Education" (page 126)
- "My First Conk" (page 260)
- "How the Lawyers Stole Winter" (page 402)

JUAN WILLIAMS

Slavery Isn't the Issue

Born in 1954 in Colon, Puerto Rico, Juan Williams graduated from Haverford College in 1976 and that year began his career as a reporter and columnist for the *Washington Post*. He is the author of *Eyes on the Prize: America's Civil Rights Years 1954–1965* (1987) and *Thurgood Marshall: American Revolutionary* (1998), a biography of the first African-American Supreme Court justice. He has written television documentaries and also served as a panelist on *Capital Gang* and as cohost of *Crossfire*. He is currently a senior correspondent for National Public Radio. Williams has called himself "part of a generation of black writers who feel less compelled to be advocates and, instead, simply recount the truth of the black triumph."

Background: One impetus behind black reparations for slavery is the disparity in income between blacks and whites in the United States. According to recent statistics, the median household income for black families is $29,407, and the comparable figure for white families is $46,305. Yet this gap narrows significantly when the incomes of married couples are compared: the median income of black married couples is approximately $51,000 while that of white couples is around $60,000 (though this is due, in part, to the fact that more black couples include two wage earners). Over the last twenty years, the income of black families has increased steadily, and the current black poverty rate is at an all-time low (26 percent compared to 8 percent for whites). Still, only 46 percent of blacks are homeowners, compared to 74 percent of whites, and the net worth of the average black household is less than one-quarter the net wealth of the average U.S. household. How much of this disparity has to do with the residual effects of slavery, as supporters of reparations contend, and how much of it can be attributed to other factors, such as the reluctance of African Americans as a group to invest in the stock market, is still a source of much debate.

Once upon a time, the black reparations movement amounted to 40 acres and a mule for ex-slaves. Now that legendary but long discarded idea has been transformed into lawsuits against several American companies that allegedly profited more than a century ago from the always immoral but once legal trade in slaves. The legitimate offer to help emancipated slaves get a start in life as free men has now been twisted into a strange scheme to squeeze money out of any company with distant ties to the bitter business of slavery.

The real news here is that lawyers and academics behind this effort have apparently given up trying to get the U.S. government to pay reparations for slavery. The statute of limitations has long since expired on any direct claim of reparations for former slaves. And the slaves are long dead.

So are the slave owners. Even a federal court dominated by liberal judges has ruled that there is no jurisdiction to hear a reparations case against the federal government. So now the faltering legal spotlight has shifted to pressuring private companies.

The consequences of this misguided adventure in racial politics have 3 not changed. Whether government or industry foots the bill, any payment of reparations will spark waves of racial resentment. Charges of extortion will be made against black people as a whole, not only by whites but also by Hispanics and Asians, and especially by the large number of recent immigrants scrambling to make it on their own.

If reparations become a reality, black Americans already battling pre- 4 sumptions of inferiority (they are less hardworking, less intelligent, and less patriotic, according to whites questioned by pollsters) will also bear the weight of being demeaned as less able than any Mexican immigrant or Bosnian refugee. The newcomers, after all, are not asking for reparations — they only want a chance to make it in America. The result will be a further segregation of low-income black people from the mainstream.

On a political level, the cost of reparations may be even higher. Repara- 5 tions will mean an end to the moral responsibility that all Americans, especially white Americans, have for the history of slavery, legal segregation, and the continuing racism in our national life. That white guilt opens the door to the idea of national obligation to repair the damage of racism. Once the first reparations check is written, that moral responsibility will disappear, and the door will shut on all claims for affirmative action in private industry, government, and academia. It may also bring a collapse of the already tenuous support for social-welfare programs that are a key to repairing the horrors of public schools in big cities, high rates of poverty among children, and jails overflowing with young black men.

Democrats as well as Republicans have rejected efforts to raise the 6 reparations issue in Congress for a dozen years, and polls show that nearly 70 percent of whites stand in opposition to even an apology for slavery. The minute any company starts writing reparations checks, all the collective white guilt that fuels support for social policy to help poor black people will be exhausted. The debt will be paid and forgotten.

Given the devastating consequences contained in this Trojan Horse, 7 why does the reparations movement march on?

On a simple level, it is about the alluring possibility of a bonanza pay- 8 day for some of the lawyers involved. And there are still people who think they might get a check for thousands of dollars if some company somewhere issues a reparation check. The IRS is dealing with increasing numbers of people who have been duped into believing that they can claim a "Slavery Rebate" on their tax forms. (Last year 80,000 taxpayers made that claim.)

But greed aside, the reparations movement is also evidence of the grow- 9 ing strength of black America. Some of the best-educated, most affluent black people in world history are properly flexing their political muscles. Randall Robinson, author of a best-selling book calling for reparations, has told interviewers that the key issue is that black people have "decided for ourselves that they are our due."

In a diverse nation, the demands of a strong and vocal black commu- 10 nity cannot be ignored. No matter how farfetched the legal claim may be, there will be press conferences and college conferences to review the horrors of slavery. The devastation that slavery visited on black people is beyond debate, and so is the history of exploitation of former slaves once they were set free without compensation for their labor.

But that sound argument is now being contorted into claims that 11 black America is still feeling the impact of slavery. That stretch is necessary for the lawyers behind the reparations movement to support the idea that there are victims of slavery alive to serve as plaintiffs in a lawsuit. But while racist attitudes persist, it's hard to make the case that slavery is the issue when black Americans are enjoying record levels of educational attainment and income.

One intriguing way to look at reparations is as an effort by the rising 12 black middle class to take control of the massive budgets dedicated to social-welfare policy. In the current lawsuits the money from reparations is designated for a treasury that would be controlled by a black elite and used as they see fit to improve life in black America. What is now national policy for dealing with black poverty would become a matter of a black national-ist agenda.

That is as sure a road to racial separatism as you can get. Scandals are 13 sure to follow as money goes to black entrepreneurs who may be friends of the people handing out the money. And inevitably some black nationalists will complain that those controlling the money are addressing the wrong needs. Even without infighting and scandals it is obscene to think of this modern generation of black Americans profiting from the blood money drawn nearly 140 years ago from the exploitation of slaves.

There is nothing wrong with a fantasy about every black person get- 14 ting a check for all that black people have gone through. But too much time spent in fantasy land is wasted time. If this reparations movement goes on much longer, history will view it as self-indulgent hysteria by people intoxicated by their rising power. The passion that currently goes for reparations would better be spent in other areas, such as confronting teachers' unions, civil-rights leaders, and everyone else involved in our fail-ure to educate minority kids.

Reparations are a dangerous, even evil, idea because they contradict 15 the moral authority of black America's claim to equal rights. Pushing them through would only hurt race relations by encouraging negative stereotypes about blacks at a time when the nation is more diverse and the need for interracial understanding is at its greatest.

• • •

COMPREHENSION

1. According to Williams, why have lawyers for the reparations movement switched their attention from suing the federal government to pressuring private companies?

2. What does Williams think the results of the reparations movement will be?

3. According to Williams, what really motivates those who support the reparations movement?

4. Why does Williams see the claim that "black America is still feeling the impact of slavery" (11) as a "stretch"?

5. Why does Williams think that the payment of reparations would ultimately lead to "racial separatism" (13)?

6. According to Williams, how could time and money be better spent by the people in the reparations movement?

PURPOSE AND AUDIENCE

1. At what point does Williams state his thesis? What is this thesis?

2. What does Williams hope to achieve with this essay? Do you think he succeeds?

3. Williams has a reputation for being a political moderate. Does his tone in this essay seem "moderate"? Would a different tone have better suited his purpose? Explain.

4. How does Williams attempt to assure his readers that he is being fair? Is he successful?

STYLE AND STRUCTURE

1. Why do you think Williams begins his essay with the phrase, "Once upon a time" (1)?

2. What points does Williams present to support his thesis? Should he have made any other points? What evidence does Williams present to support each of his points? Should he have supplied more or different kinds of evidence? Explain.

3. In paragraph 7, Williams asks a question. In what way does asking this question help him advance his argument?

4. In paragraph 10, Williams concedes a point to his opposition. What is this point? How effectively does he counter this point in paragraph 11? In what way do his concession and refutation further his argument?

5. Are there any places in this essay where Williams overstates his case? If so, how do you react to these overstatements?

6. What strategy does Williams use in his conclusion? How effective is this strategy?

VOCABULARY PROJECTS

1. Define each of these words as it is used in this selection.

   reparations (1)   demeaned (4)   designated (12)
   discarded (1)   tenuous (5)   separatism (13)
   emancipated (1)   alluring (8)   entrepreneurs (13)
   extortion (3)   affluent (9)   intoxicated (14)
   presumptions (4)   exploitation (10)   stereotypes (15)
   inferiority (4)   plaintiffs (11)

2. List some of the adjectives Williams uses to characterize the reparations movement and those who support it. How do these adjectives convey his attitude?

3. In paragraph 7, Williams calls reparations a "Trojan Horse." What is the meaning of this term? How does it apply to reparations?

JOURNAL ENTRY

Do you, like Williams, believe that reparations would do irreparable damage to African Americans?

WRITING WORKSHOP

1. Write an essay in which you agree or disagree with Williams's statement, "Reparations are a dangerous, even evil, idea because they contradict the moral authority of black America's claim to equal rights" (15). Make sure that you present evidence to support your points.

2. Assume that you are an African American who believes that a "Slavery Rebate" (8) is justified. Write a letter to your congressional representative in which you state your position. Assure him or her that you know such a rebate does not presently exist but that you believe one is warranted. Be specific, using your own ideas, as well as ideas presented in any essay in this debate casebook, for support.

3. In his essay "An Idea Whose Time Has Come" (p. 637), Manning Marable says, "Reparations could begin America's Third Reconstruction, the final chapter in the 400-year struggle to abolish slavery and its destructive consequences" (12). Write a response from Williams to Marable's statement. Use material from both Marable's and Williams's essays to support your points.

COMBINING THE PATTERNS

Paragraphs 3 through 5 are developed by means of **cause and effect.** How does this strategy help Williams develop his argument?

THEMATIC CONNECTIONS

- "The 'Black Table' Is Still There" (page 340)
- "Two Ways to Belong in America" (page 397)
- "Burdens" (page 509)

❖

An Idea Whose Time Has Come

Manning Marable was born in Dayton, Ohio, in 1950 and graduated from Earlham College, a Quaker school in Richmond, Indiana. After receiving an M.A. from the University of Wisconsin and a Ph.D. from the University of Maryland, he became a professor of political economy first at Tuskegee Institute and later at Fisk University, both historically black colleges. He currently directs the African-American Studies program at Columbia University. He is the author of numerous articles, as well as several books, including *From the Grassroots: Black Political Essays* (1980) and *Beyond Black and White: Transforming African-American Politics* (1995).

Background: Jim Crow laws, named for a racially stereotyped character in an early nineteenth-century minstrel song, began to be passed in Southern states immediately following the Civil War. Aimed at limiting the political and economic power of former slaves, such laws were initially declared illegal by the United States government, leading to a period known as Reconstruction, a brief era of gains in civil rights for African Americans. By 1877, however, the federal government had essentially stopped enforcing restrictions against Jim Crow, and white Southerners launched an all-out attack on African-American empowerment that included mob violence, economic disenfranchisement, limited access to voting, and legalized segregation. These actions ensured second-class citizenship for African Americans, along with substandard educational, employment, and even medical care. An 1896 Supreme Court decision upheld the constitutionality of separate facilities for blacks and whites. And although Northern states did not impose as many Jim Crow restrictions as Southern states did, de facto segregation was still the norm. Not until the 1950s and 1960s did laws that prohibited such blatant discrimination go into effect.

In 1854 my great-grandfather, Morris Marable, was sold on an auction 1 block in Georgia for $500. For his white slave master, the sale was just "business as usual." But to Morris Marable and his heirs, slavery was a crime against our humanity. This pattern of human-rights violations against enslaved African-Americans continued under Jim Crow segregation for nearly another century.

The fundamental problem of American democracy in the twenty-first 2 century is the problem of "structural racism": the deep patterns of socioeconomic inequality and accumulated disadvantage that are coded by race, and constantly justified in public discourse by both racist stereotypes and white indifference. Do Americans have the capacity and vision to dismantle these structural barriers that deny democratic rights and opportunities to millions of their fellow citizens?

This country has previously witnessed two great struggles to achieve a 3 truly multicultural democracy.

The First Reconstruction (1865–1877) ended slavery and briefly gave   4
black men voting rights, but gave no meaningful compensation for two
centuries of unpaid labor. The promise of "40 acres and a mule" was for
most blacks a dream deferred.

The Second Reconstruction (1954–1968), or the modern civil-rights   5
movement, outlawed legal segregation in public accommodations and
gave blacks voting rights. But these successes paradoxically obscure the
tremendous human costs of historically accumulated disadvantage that
remain central to black Americans' lives.

The disproportionate wealth that most whites enjoy today was first   6
constructed from centuries of unpaid black labor. Many white institutions, including Ivy League universities, insurance companies, and banks,
profited from slavery. This pattern of white privilege and black inequality
continues today.

Demanding reparations is not just about compensation for slavery   7
and segregation. It is, more important, an educational campaign to highlight the contemporary reality of "racial deficits" of all kinds, the unequal
conditions that impact blacks regardless of class. Structural racism's barriers include "equity inequity," the absence of black capital formation that is
a direct consequence of America's history. One third of all black households actually have negative net wealth. In 1998 the typical black family's
net wealth was $16,400, less than one fifth that of white families. Black
families are denied home loans at twice the rate of whites.

Blacks remain the last hired and first fired during recessions. During   8
the 1990–91 recession, African-Americans suffered disproportionately. At
Coca-Cola, 42 percent of employees who lost their jobs were black. At
Sears, 54 percent were black. Blacks have significantly shorter life expec-
tancies, in part due to racism in the health establishment. Blacks are statistically less likely than whites to be referred for kidney transplants or
early-stage cancer surgery.

In criminal justice, African-Americans constitute only one seventh   9
of all drug users. Yet we account for 35 percent of all drug arrests, 55 percent of drug convictions, and 75 percent of prison admissions for drug
offenses.

White Americans today aren't guilty of carrying out slavery and segre-   10
gation. But whites have a moral and political responsibility to acknowledge the continuing burden of history's structural racism.

A reparations trust fund could be established, with the goal of closing   11
the socioeconomic gaps between blacks and whites. Funds would be targeted specifically toward poor, disadvantaged communities with the greatest need, not to individuals. Let's eliminate the racial unfairness in capital
markets that perpetuates black poverty. A national commitment to expand
black homeownership, full employment, and quality health care would
benefit all Americans, regardless of race.

Reparations could begin America's Third Reconstruction, the final   12
chapter in the 400-year struggle to abolish slavery and its destructive con-

sequences. As Malcolm X said in 1961, hundreds of years of racism and labor exploitation are "worth more than a cup of coffee at a white café. We are here to collect back wages."

• • •

COMPREHENSION

1. What is "structural racism"? Why does Marable believe it is "the fundamental problem of democracy in the twenty-first century" (2)?

2. According to Marable, what "two great struggles to achieve a truly multicultural democracy" (3) has America faced? Does he see these struggles as successful? Explain.

3. What does Marable believe the demand for reparations will achieve?

4. Why, according to Marable, do whites have a responsibility to "acknowledge the continuing burden of history's structural racism" (10)?

5. What form does Marable want reparations to take? Why does he believe that both blacks and whites would benefit from reparations?

6. What did Malcolm X mean when he said in 1961 that African Americans' long experience with racism "is worth more than a cup of coffee at a white café" (12)? How does this statement support Marable's argument?

PURPOSE AND AUDIENCE

1. Does Marable expect his readers to agree with him? How can you tell?

2. Where does Marable state his thesis? Where else in the essay might he have stated it?

3. How does Marable try to convince readers that he is being fair? How successful is he?

STYLE AND STRUCTURE

1. Why does Marable begin his essay by discussing his great-grandfather? Can you think of another way he could have opened his essay?

2. What evidence does Marable present to support his points? How compelling is this evidence? What other kinds of evidence could he have presented?

3. In paragraph 10, Marable concedes the point that white Americans today have no direct involvement with slavery. He then goes on to say that in spite of this fact, whites have an obligation to take responsibility for the negative effects of racism. Does his concession help or hurt his argument?

4. Is Marable's argument primarily inductive or deductive? Explain.

5. How does Marable's use of the terms *First Reconstruction, Second Reconstruction,* and *Third Reconstruction* help him to structure his essay? Is his use of these terms misleading in any way?

6. How effective is Marable's conclusion? Do you, like Marable, believe that reparations would be "the final chapter in the 400-year struggle to abolish slavery" (12), or do you think he overstates his case?

VOCABULARY PROJECTS

1. Define each of these words as it is used in this selection.

structural (2)	paradoxically (5)	contemporary (7)
stereotypes (2)	accumulated (5)	recession (8)
indifference (2)	disproportionate (6)	disproportionately (8)
dismantle (2)	reparations (7)	socioeconomic (11)
deferred (4)	segregation (7)	consequences (12)

2. What does Marable mean by the term *structural racism*? Does he define this term adequately? What, if anything, does he gain by using this term?

JOURNAL ENTRY

Do you, like Marable, believe that "reparations could begin America's Third Reconstruction" (12), or do you believe that reparations would have negative consequences for the country?

WRITING WORKSHOP

1. Write an essay in which you agree or disagree with Marable's contention that "whites have a moral and political responsibility to acknowledge the continuing burden of history's structural racism" (10)? You can use information from Marable's essay and from your own experience to support your argument.

2. In "Demands for Reparations" (page 642), Linda Chavez says, "The nation might well have been a better place if, immediately after the Civil War, every former slave had been given 40 acres and a mule, as the government promised. But the best we can hope for now is that we recommit ourselves to the simple goal of treating all men as equals and affording every American equal opportunity to achieving what he or she can" (9). Write a letter from Marable to Chavez in which he responds to her statement. Use material from both writers' essays to support your points.

3. Do you, like Marable, believe that the fundamental problem for America in this century is "structural racism" (2)? Write an essay in which you agree or disagree with Marable's contention. Be sure you begin your essay by defining *structural racism*. You can use your own experience as well as information from the other essays in this debate casebook to support your points.

COMBINING THE PATTERNS

Paragraph 6 is developed by means of **cause and effect.** What point does this paragraph make? In what way does this paragraph advance Marable's argument?

THEMATIC CONNECTIONS

- "Finishing School" (page 89)
- "Shooting an Elephant" (page 117)
- "Indian Education" (page 126)

❖
Demands for Reparations

Linda Chavez was born in 1947 in Albuquerque, New Mexico, to a father of Spanish descent and a mother whose roots were Anglo-Irish. She received a bachelor's degree in English literature from the University of Colorado, where she became active in affirmative action causes and remedial education programs for minorities. Disenchanted with the increasing radicalism of these movements in education, Chavez began to campaign against issues such as racial quotas and bilingual education, first as a lobbyist for the National Education Association and later as staff director of the U.S. Commission on Civil Rights under President Ronald Reagan. She is the author of *Out of the Barrio: Toward a New Politics of Hispanic Assimilation* (1991) and *An Unlikely Conservative: The Transformation of an Ex-Liberal (Or How I Became the Most Hated Hispanic in America)* (2002). She also served as president of U.S. English, an organization dedicated to making English the country's official language, and is a fellow at the Manhattan Institute as well as a syndicated columnist.

Background: In *The Debt: What America Owes to Blacks* (2000), the book Chavez is responding to in this essay, Randall Robinson makes the argument that many African Americans, especially those living in poverty, are still suffering the effects of slavery and Jim Crow segregation policies. Denied any compensation for their ancestors' labor over some 250 years, after the Civil War most former slaves had little capital with which to start new lives—to buy farmland, for example, or to open businesses. Enforced discrimination further denied opportunity to them and their descendants. Although significant gains have been made over the last thirty years, Robinson argues that too many blacks have been left behind, disadvantaged economically by historical forces over which they have no control. What he proposes is a government-funded trust that would provide first-rate educational opportunities to at least two generations of African-American children, including family support and residential programs where needed. The government's liability, according to Robinson, is derived from its use of slave labor to build much of the nation's capital and its use of income raised by taxes on slave-produced commodities, such as cotton and sugar. In this essay, Chavez attempts to refute Robinson's basic argument.

Should America pay reparations to the descendants of African slaves 1 forcibly brought here 300 or more years ago? It's a question that has been raised many times since the Thirteenth Amendment abolished slavery some 130 years ago and has most recently gained attention because of a book written by Randall Robinson, *The Debt: What America Owes to Blacks*.

Robinson, the president of TransAfrica, is not a man to be dismissed 2 lightly. Perhaps more than anyone outside South Africa, he is responsible for ending apartheid in that nation through his unrelenting effort to promote economic sanctions against the government there. But is he right now to argue that America should pay today for sins committed more than 100 years ago? And how do we decide when to compensate victims of a terrible wrong perpetrated by the government itself?

The idea of giving money to individuals who have suffered some grave wrong is well-rooted in the American legal system. It is, after all, the basis of our civil-tort law. Our system even provides for compensation to the direct descendants and heirs of actual victims, for example, the spouse or children of someone killed in an airplane crash involving some negligence on the part of the manufacturer or airline. Moreover, the United States government has paid reparations before, $20,000 each to some 82,000 Japanese Americans forcibly removed from their homes during World War II, and sent to internment camps in several states.

So, why not do the same thing now for blacks, as Robinson and others argue? There is no question that what was done to blacks was incomparably worse than anything suffered by Japanese Americans or anyone else in America for that matter. The problem is time. It is simply impossible to right an injustice committed in the distant past, and any attempt to do so can create as many difficulties as it alleviates. It was possible to repay Japanese Americans for the property they lost and the time they spent in the camps, because we knew who they were and could document their actual losses.

But it is nearly impossible to know generations later what a particular loss or gain to an individual might mean for his descendants. Of course, that does not stop someone whose ancestors were mistreated from feeling resentment — and wanting some satisfaction for the wrongs done. And this seems to be at the root of what Robinson hopes to achieve, a kind of national catharsis over slavery.

"If you're ever to get past this, it must be gotten out and dealt with. Whatever awful thing was done to you must be drawn out and exorcised," he writes. But his prescription for how blacks should deal with the pain of the enslavement of their forebears is a recipe for racial hatred, not healing.

"You are owed," he tells blacks. "You were caused to endure terrible things. The fault is not yours. There is nothing wrong with you. They did this to you."

Does Robinson really believe that any amount of money — or government social programs, which is what he hopes will emerge from this dialogue — can compensate for the resentments toward all whites that such talk engenders among blacks? Americans are often accused of having short memories, and indeed, we do, perhaps because we are such a young nation. But memory can be a bad thing as well as a good one, especially if the memories we choose to forget are a litany of injustices, slights, and wrongs done to our ancestors. Such memories are the cause of wars, feuds, and racial animosity. Just look at those places where such memories are constantly reinforced and renewed: Northern Ireland, the Balkans, Rwanda, the Middle East. No, the time for reparations for slavery has long since passed.

The nation might well have been a better place if, immediately after the   9
Civil War, every former slave had been given 40 acres and a mule, as the
government promised. But the best we can hope for now is that we recommit ourselves to the simple goal of treating all men as equals and affording
every American equal opportunity to achieve what he or she can.

• • •

COMPREHENSION

1. Why does Chavez think that Randall Robinson is "not a man to be dismissed lightly" (2)?

2. What is the legal history of "giving money to individuals who have suffered some grave wrong" (3)? Why, according to Chavez, is the situation
   different for African Americans?

3. What does Chavez think will be the result of Robinson's ideas for compensating African Americans for "the pain of the enslavement of their
   forebears" (6)?

4. Why does Chavez think that the time for compensation "has long since
   passed" (8)?

5. In paragraph 8, Chavez says, "memory can be a bad thing as well as a good
   one." What does she mean?

6. What, according to Chavez, is the appropriate way to address the grievances of African Americans?

PURPOSE AND AUDIENCE

1. Does Chavez assume that her readers are familiar with Robinson's book?
   How can you tell? Do you think she should have given readers more information about Robinson?

2. Paraphrase Chavez's thesis. Why does she state it where she does?

3. Does Chavez ever mount a personal (*ad hominem*) attack against Robinson,
   or does she restrict her criticism to his book?

STYLE AND STRUCTURE

1. Chavez begins her essay with a question. Does she ever answer this question? If so, where? If not, should she have done so?

2. Chavez's essay is essentially a refutation of Robinson's ideas. What specific
   ideas does she discuss? How effective are her refutations?

3. Should Chavez have provided more evidence to support her points? What
   kind of evidence might be helpful?

4. Where does Chavez concede points to Robinson? How effective are these
   concessions?

5. Chavez also begins paragraph 8 with a question. Does she answer this
   question? In what way does this paragraph further her argument?

6. How compelling is Chavez's conclusion? What other strategy could she have used? Would another strategy have been more efective?

VOCABULARY PROJECTS

1. Define each of these words as it is used in this section.

abolished (1)	negligence (3)	catharsis (5)
apartheid (2)	internment (3)	forebears (6)
unrelenting (2)	incomparably (4)	endure (7)
perpetrated (2)	alleviates (4)	recommit (9)

2. In paragraph 8, Chavez repeats the word *memories*. Is this an effective use of repetition, or should she have used synonyms? Can you suggest alternative words?

JOURNAL ENTRY

Is it time, as Chavez suggests, for African Americans to put the experiences of slavery behind them, or is it time, as Robinson suggests, for the nation to get the experiences of slavery out in the open so that they can be "dealt with" (6)?

WRITING WORKSHOP

1. In his book *The Debt: What America Owes to Blacks,* Robinson says, "The life and responsibilities of a society or nation are not circumscribed by the life spans of mortal constituents. Social rights, wrongs, obligations, and responsibilities flow eternal." Write a letter in which you respond to Robinson's statement.

2. Expand your journal entry into an essay. Use material from Chavez's essay as well as material from any of the other essays in this debate casebook to support your points.

3. Who do you think makes the stronger case — those who support reparations or those who oppose them? Take one position or the other, and argue in favor of it. Use material from at least two of the essays in this debate casebook to make your case.

COMBINING THE PATTERNS

Paragraphs 6 and 7 are developed by means of **comparison and contrast.** What two things are being compared? How does this comparison set the stage for the rest of Chavez's argument?

THEMATIC CONNECTIONS

- "The Human Cost of an Illiterate Society" (page 229)
- "Five Ways to Kill a Man" (page 487)
- "Letter from Birmingham Jail" (page 570)

❖

WRITING ASSIGNMENTS FOR ARGUMENTATION

1. Write an essay in which you discuss whether parents have a right to spank their children. If your position is that they do, under what circumstances? What limitations should there be? If your position is that they do not, how should parents discipline children? In what ways should they deal with inappropriate behavior?

2. Assume that a library in your town has decided that certain books are objectionable and has removed them from the shelves. Write a letter to the local paper in which you argue for or against the library's actions. Make a list of the major arguments that might be advanced against your position, and try to refute some of them in your essay. Remember to respect the views of your audience and to address them in a respectful manner.

3. In Great Britain, cities began installing video surveillance systems in public areas in the 1970s. Police departments claim that these cameras enable the police to do their jobs more efficiently. Opponents of the cameras say that the police are creating a society in which the right of personal privacy has been severely compromised. How do you feel about this issue? Assume that the police department in your city is proposing to install cameras in the downtown area as well as in other pedestrian areas. Write an editorial for your local paper in which you present your views on the topic.

4. Write an essay in which you discuss under what circumstances, if any, animals should be used for scientific experimentation.

5. Write an essay in which you argue for or against the proposition that women soldiers should be able to serve in combat situations.

6. Research some criminal cases that resulted in the death penalty. Write an essay in which you use these accounts to support your arguments either for or against the death penalty. Don't forget to give credit to your sources. See the Appendix for information about documentation.

7. Write an argumentative essay in which you discuss whether there are any situations in which a nation has an obligation to go (or not to go) to war.

8. Since the events of September 11, 2001, the idea of arming pilots of commercial passenger planes has been debated. Those opposed to arming pilots claim that the risks — that a gun will fall into the hands of hijackers or that a passenger will be accidentally shot — outweigh any benefits. Those who support the idea say that the pilot is the last line of defense and must be able to defend the cockpit from terrorists. As a result of public pressure in favor of arming pilots, a small trial program has been instituted. Do you think that all pilots of commercial airplanes should be armed? Write an essay in which you present your views on this subject.

9. In the Declaration of Independence, Jefferson says that all individuals are entitled to "life, liberty, and the pursuit of happiness." Write an essay in which you argue that these rights are not absolute.

10. Write an argumentative essay on one of these topics: Should high school students be required to recite the Pledge of Allegiance at the start of each school day? Should college students be required to do community service? Should public school teachers be required to pass periodic competency

tests? Should the legal drinking age be raised (or lowered)? Should states be required to educate the children of illegal immigrants?

COLLABORATIVE ACTIVITY FOR ARGUMENTATION

Working with three other students, select a controversial topic—one not covered in any of the debates in this chapter—that interests all of you. (You can review the Writing Assignments for Argumentation listed above to get ideas.) State your topic the way a topic is stated in a formal debate:

Resolved: The United States should ban all human cloning.

Then, divide into two two-member teams, and decide which team will take the pro position and which will take the con. Each team should list the arguments on its side of the issue and then write two or three paragraphs summarizing its position. Finally, each team should stage a ten-minute debate—five minutes for each side—in front of the class. (The pro side presents its argument first.) At the end of each debate, the class should discuss which team has presented the stronger arguments.

INTERNET ASSIGNMENT FOR ARGUMENTATION: SHOULD U.S. CITIZENS BE REQUIRED TO CARRY NATIONAL IDENTITY CARDS?

Write an essay in which you argue for or against the implementation of national identity cards in the United States. Use the following Web sites to explore the two viewpoints and their implications.

American Association of Motor Vehicles Administrators
<aamva.net/IDSecurity>
The American Association of Motor Vehicles Administrators (AAMVA) site offers additional resources on legislation, statistical information, and press releases regarding the national ID debate and the AAMVA's plan to convert the states' driver's license programs into an effective national ID system.

Electronic Privacy Information Center
<epic.org/privacy/id_cards>
This national ID cards Web page, sponsored by the Electronic Privacy Information Center, gives links to several articles and current news features regarding the use of national ID cards all over the world and several resources for additional information.

CATO Institute
<cato.org/tech/tk/010928-tk.html>
This site, sponsored by the CATO Institute's department of telecommunications and technology, features an article by Adam Thierer that discusses problems that might arise with implementing a national ID card.

Computer Professionals for Social Responsibility
<cpsr.org/program/natlID/natlIDfaq.html>
Sponsored by Computer Professionals for Social Responsibility, this site includes a helpful FAQ list about plans for national ID implementation

and its relation to terrorism. The site also specifically addresses how certain systems might and might not work.

Smart Cards
<opinionjournal.com/extra/?id=95001336>
In this article for *Opinion Journal,* Larry Ellison, CEO of Oracle Corp., writes in support of a unified national ID system and offers ways of forming one based on the security and ID systems already in place.

INTERNET ASSIGNMENT FOR ARGUMENTATION: SHOULD GAY AND LESBIAN COUPLES BE ALLOWED TO ADOPT?

Focusing on one of the following three issues — the prejudice experienced by children of gay and lesbian parents, the example that homosexual parents set for their children, and the influence that homosexual parents have on their child's sexual orientation — write an essay that argues for or against adoption rights for gays and lesbians. Use the following Web sites for additional background information to support your argument.

American Civil Liberties Union
<aclu.org/LesbianGayRights/LesbianGayRightsMain.cfm>
This American Civil Liberties Union page for lesbian and gay rights includes ACLU press releases, legal documents, and other resources regarding parenting and adoption issues.

Same-Sex Parenting: Are Lesbians and Gays Good Parents?
<religioustolerance.org/hom_pare.htm>
This site includes research on the effectiveness of parenting and child development in homosexual households, as well as an overview of the legal status of same-sex adoptions in various states and countries.

Technical Report: Coparent or Second-Parent Adoption by Same-Sex Parents
<aap.org/policy/020008t.html>
From the American Academy of Pediatrics, this report discusses the current legal situation of homosexual parents, options for homosexuals who want children, and the development of children who grow up in households headed by homosexuals.

Family Research Council
<frc.org/get/cu02c2.cfm>
This site includes several feature articles sponsored by the Family Research Council that provide arguments against allowing homosexual men and women to adopt.

INTERNET ASSIGNMENT FOR ARGUMENTATION: DOES MEDIA VIOLENCE CAUSE SOCIETAL VIOLENCE?

Write an essay in which you argue for or against holding the television and movie industries responsible for violence in our society. Use the following Web sites to explore the two viewpoints and their implications.

Media Violence
<media-awareness.ca/eng/issues/violence/default.htm>

This site, sponsored by the Media Awareness Network, includes feature articles, statistics, and legislation on media violence.

Culture Shock
<pbs.org/wgbh/cultureshock/index_1.html>
This companion site to the PBS series *Culture Shock* deals with art, cultural values, and freedom of expression in the arts.

Center for Educational Priorities
<cep.org/index.html>
This educational site "track[s] the powerful influences of television, media and telecommunications policy as they affect children and the learning process."

INTERNET ASSIGNMENT FOR ARGUMENTATION: SHOULD AFRICAN AMERICANS RECEIVE REPARATIONS FOR SLAVERY?

On May 1, 2002, Deadria Farmer-Paellmann, a New York legal researcher and activist, filed a lawsuit against several corporations that profited from slavery. According to a *USA Today* article by James Cox that appeared on February 21, 2002 (see the first Web site listed below for the full article), those companies include New York Life Insurance, J. P. Morgan, Chase Manhattan Bank, FleetBoston Financial Group, Aetna, AIG, Brown Bros., and Harriman Lehman Bros. Imagine you are either a representative of one of these companies who must defend your firm against a proposed lawsuit or Ms. Farmer-Paellmann. Argue either that reparations are unjust and that the company should not have to pay them, or that the company's actions require it to compensate the descendants of slaves in some fashion.

Corporations Challenged by Reparations Activists
<usatoday.com/money/general/2002/02/21/slave-reparations
.htm#more>
This *USA Today* article provides background information on proposed reparations lawsuits against major corporations and information about several companies' involvement in slavery in the United States.

Slavery Reparations
<racerelations.about.com/library/weekly/blreparations.htm>
This About.com site gives a brief overview of the reparations issue and highlights the key arguments for and against the payment of reparations to descendants of slaves.

The Case for Slavery Reparations
<news.mpr.org/features/200011/13_williamsb_reparations/>
The site for Minnesota Public Radio features a transcription of Bryant Williams's discussion (aired November 2000) in which he supports reparations.

Slavery Reparations Would Only Increase Racial Hostility, Libertarians Say
<lp.org/press/archive.php?function=view&record=600>
This site features a Libertarian Party press release that opposes reparations and argues that they would increase racial tensions rather than alleviate them.

❖ 13
Combining the Patterns

Most paragraphs combine several patterns of development. In the following paragraph, for example, Paul Hoffman uses narration, exemplification, and cause and effect to explain why we tend to see numbers as more than "instruments of enumeration."

Topic sentence The idea that numbers are not mere instruments of enumeration but are sacred, perfect, friendly, lucky, or evil goes back to antiquity. In the **Narration** sixth century B.C. Pythagoras, whom schoolchildren associate with the famous theorem that in a right triangle the square of the hypotenuse always equals the sum of the squares of its sides, not only performed brilliant mathematics but made a religion out of numbers. In numerology, the number 12 has **Exemplification** always represented completeness, as in the 12 months of the year, the 12 signs of the zodiac, the 12 hours of the day, the 12 gods of Olympus, the 12 labors of Hercules, the 12 tribes of Israel, the 12 apostles of Jesus, the 12 days of Christmas, and, more recently perhaps, the 12 eggs in an egg carton. Since 13 ex- **Cause and effect** ceeds 12 by only one, the number lies just beyond completeness and, hence, is restless to the point of being evil.

Like paragraphs, essays do not usually follow a single pattern of development; in fact, nearly every essay, including those in this text, combines a variety of patterns. Even though an essay may be organized primarily as, say, a comparison and contrast, it is still likely to include paragraphs, and even groups of paragraphs, shaped by other patterns of development. In fact, combining various patterns in a single essay gives writers the flexibility to express their ideas most effectively. (For this reason, each essay in Chapters 4 through 12 of this text is followed by Combining the Patterns questions that focus on how the essay uses other patterns of development along with its dominant pattern.)

STRUCTURING AN ESSAY BY COMBINING THE PATTERNS

Essays that combine various patterns of development, like essays structured primarily by a single pattern, include an introductory paragraph, several body paragraphs, and a concluding paragraph. The introduction typically ends with the thesis statement that gives the essay its focus, and the conclusion often restates that thesis or summarizes the essay's main points. Each body paragraph (or group of paragraphs) is structured according to the pattern of development that best suits the material it develops.

Suppose you are planning your answer to the following question on a take-home essay exam for a sociology of religion course:

What factors attract people to cults? For what reasons do they join? Support your answer with specific examples that illustrate how cults recruit and retain members.

The wording of this exam question clearly suggests both **cause and effect** ("for what reasons") and **exemplification** ("specific examples"); in addition, you may decide to develop your response with **definition** and **process.** An informal outline for your essay might look like this:

Introduction:	Definition of *cult* (defined by negation — telling what it is *not* — and by comparison and contrast with *religion*). Thesis statement: Using aggressive recruitment tactics and isolating potential members from their families and past lives, cults appeal to new recruits by offering them a highly structured environment.
Cause and effect:	Why people join cults
Process:	How cults recruit new members
Exemplification:	Tactics cults use to retain members (series of brief examples)
Conclusion:	Restatement of thesis or review of key points

This essay will supply all the information the exam question asks for, with material organized and developed clearly and logically.

COMBINING THE PATTERNS: REVISING AND EDITING

When you revise an essay that combines several patterns of development, consider the items on the Revision Checklist on page 54 as well as any of the more specific revision checklists in Chapters 4 through 12 that apply to the patterns in your essay. As you edit your essay, refer to the Editing Checklist on page 66 and to the individual editing checklists in Chapters 4 through 12. You may also wish to consult the Grammar in Context sections that appear throughout the book, as well as the one that follows.

GRAMMAR IN CONTEXT : **Agreement with Indefinite Pronouns***

A **pronoun** is a word that takes the place of a noun or another pronoun in a sentence. Unlike most pronouns, an **indefinite pronoun** (*anyone, either, each,* and so on) does not refer to a specific person or thing.

For more practice in avoiding agreement problems with indefinite pronouns, visit **Exercise Central** at **‹bedfordstmartins.com/patterns /indefinitepronouns›**.

Subject-Verb Agreement   Pronouns must agree in number with their verbs: singular pronouns (*I, he, she, it,* and so on) take singular verbs, and plural pronouns (*we, they,* and so on) take plural verbs.

"I have learned much as a scavenger" (Eighner 661).

"We were free like comets in the heavens" (Truong 656).

Indefinite pronouns also must agree in number with their verbs: singular indefinite pronouns take singular verbs, and plural indefinite pronouns take plural verbs. Most indefinite pronouns are singular.

SINGULAR INDEFINITE PRONOUNS				
another	anyone	everyone	one	each
either	neither	anything	everything	

"Everyone was darker or lighter than we were" (Truong 657).

"Everything seems to stink" (Eighner 666).

Some indefinite pronouns are plural.

PLURAL INDEFINITE PRONOUNS				
both	many	few	several	others

"Many are discarded for minor imperfections that can be pared away" (Eighner 663).

---

*EDS. NOTE — All the examples below either quote from or comment on essays that appear later in this chapter.

Note: A few indefinite pronouns—*some, all, any, more, most,* and *none*—may be either singular or plural, depending on their meaning in the sentence.

Singular: <u>Some</u> of the pain her female ancestors suffered <u>is</u> described in Alice Walker's essay "In Search of Our Mothers' Gardens." (*Some* refers to *pain,* so the verb is singular.)

Plural: "<u>Some</u> of them, without a doubt, <u>were</u> our mothers and grandmothers" (Walker 687). (*Some* refers to *them,* so the verb is plural.)

Pronoun-Antecedent Agreement   An **antecedent** is the noun or pronoun to which a pronoun refers. Pronouns must agree in number with their antecedents.

Use a singular pronoun to refer to a singular indefinite pronoun antecedent.

<u>Each</u> day has <u>its</u> surprises for Lars Eighner and his dog Lizbeth.

Use a plural pronoun to refer to a plural indefinite pronoun antecedent.

<u>Many</u> of the people who pass Eighner and Lizbeth avert <u>their</u> eyes.

Note: Although the indefinite pronoun *everyone* is singular, it is often used with a plural pronoun in everyday speech and informal writing.

Informal: <u>Everyone</u> turns <u>their</u> heads when Eighner and Lizbeth walk by.

This usage is generally acceptable in informal situations, but college writing requires correct pronoun-antecedent agreement.

Correct: <u>Everyone</u> turns <u>his or her</u> head when Eighner and Lizbeth walk by.

Correct: <u>People</u> turn <u>their</u> heads when Eighner and Lizbeth walk by.

The essays in this chapter illustrate how different patterns of development work together in a single piece of writing. The first two essays—"The Park" by Michael Huu Truong, a student, and "On Dumpster Diving" by Lars Eighner—include annotations that identify the various patterns these writers use. Truong's essay relies primarily on narration, description, and exemplification to express his memories of childhood. Eighner's combines sections of definition, exemplification, classification and division, cause and effect, comparison and contrast, and process; at the same time, he tells the story (narration) and provides vivid details (description) of his life as a homeless person. Following these annotated essays are three additional selections that combine patterns: Jonathan Swift's classic satire "A Modest Proposal," Alice Walker's essay "In Search of Our Mothers' Gardens," and Richard Rodriguez's autobiographical essay "Strange Tools." Each of the essays in this chapter is followed by the same types of questions that accompany the other reading selections in the text.

▶ **A STUDENT WRITER: COMBINING THE PATTERNS**

This essay was written by Michael Huu Truong for a first-year composition course in response to the assignment "Write an essay about the person and/or place that defined your childhood."

The Park

Background

My childhood did not really begin until thirteen years ago, when I first came to this country from the rural jungle of Vietnam. I can't really remember much from this period, and the things I do remember are vague images that I have no desire or intention to discuss. However, my childhood in the States was a lot different, especially after I met my friend

Thesis statement

James. While it lasted, it was paradise.

Narrative begins

It was a cold wintry day in February after a big snowstorm—the first I'd ever seen. My

Description: effects of cold

lips were chapped, my hands were frozen stiff, and my cheeks were burning from the biting wind, and yet I loved it. I especially loved

Comparison and contrast: U.S. vs. Vietnam

the snow. I had come from a country where the closest things to snow were white paint and cotton balls. But now I was in America. On that frosty afternoon, I was determined to build a snowman. I had seen them in books, and I had heard they could talk. I knew they could come alive, and I couldn't wait.

"Eyryui roeow ierog," said a voice that came out of nowhere. I turned around, and right

Description: James

in my face was a short, red-faced (probably from the cold wind) Korean kid with a dirty, runny nose. I responded, "Wtefkjkr ruyjft gsdfr" in my own tongue. We understood each other perfectly, and we expressed our under-

Narration: the first day

standing with a smile. Together, we built our first snowman. We were disappointed that evening when the snowman just stood there; however, I was happy because I had made my first friend.

1

2

3

Analogies

Ever since then we've been a team like Abbott and Costello (or when my cousin joined us, The Three Stooges). The two of us were inseparable. We could've made the greatest Krazy Glue commercial ever.   4

Narration: what they did that summer

The summer that followed the big snowstorm, from what I can recall, was awesome. We were free like comets in the heavens, and we did whatever our hearts wanted. For the most part, our desires were fulfilled in a little park across the street. This park was ours; it was like our own planet guarded by our own robot army (disguised as trees). Together we fought against the bigger people who always tried to invade and take over our world. The enemy could never conquer our fortress because they would have to destroy our robots, penetrate our force field, and then defeat us; this last feat would be impossible.   5

Narrative continues

This park was our fantasy land where everything we wished for came true and everything we hated was banished forever. We banished vegetables, cheese, bigger people, and — of course — girls. The land was enchanted, and we could be whatever we felt like. We were super ninjas one day and millionaires the next; we became the heroes we idolized and lived the lives we dreamed about. I had the strength of Bruce Lee and Superman; James possessed the power of Clint Eastwood and the Bionic Man. My weapons were the skills of Bruce and a cape. James, however, needed a real weapon for Clint, and the weapon he made was awesome. The Death Ray could destroy a building with one blast, and it even had a shield so James was always protected. Even with all his mighty weapons and gadgets, though, he was still no match for Superman and Bruce Lee. Every day, we fought until death (or until our parents called us for dinner).   6

Examples: what they banished

Examples: superhero fantasies

Narrative continues

When we became bored with our super pow- 7
ers, the park became a giant spaceship. We
traveled all over the Universe, conquering and
exploring strange new worlds and mysterious

Examples: new worlds and planets

planets. Our ship was a top-secret indestructible space warship called the X-007. We went
to Mars, Venus, Pluto, and other alien planets,
destroying all the monsters we could find. When
necessary, our spacecraft was transformed into
a submarine for deep-sea adventures. We found
lost cities, unearthed treasures, and saved
Earth by destroying all the sea monsters that
were plotting against us. We became heroes —
just like Superman, Bruce Lee, the Bionic Man,
and Clint Eastwood.

Cause and effect: prospect of school leads to problems

James and I had the time of our lives in 8
the park that summer. It was great — until we
heard about the horror of starting school.
Shocked and terrified, we ran to our fortress
to escape. For some reason, though, our magic
kingdom had lost its powers. We fought hard
that evening, trying to keep the bigger people
out of our planet, but the battle was soon
lost. Bruce Lee, Superman, the Bionic Man,
and Clint Eastwood had all lost their special
powers.

Narrative continues

School wasn't as bad as we'd thought it 9
would be. The first day, James and I sat there
with our hands folded. We didn't talk or move,
and we didn't dare look at each other (we
would've cracked up because we always made
these goofy faces). Even though we had pens
that could be transformed into weapons, we
were still scared.

Description: school

Everyone was darker or lighter than we 10
were, and the teacher was speaking a strange
language (English). James and I giggled as she
talked. We giggled softly when everyone else
talked, and they laughed out loud when it was
our turn to speak.

Narrative continues

The day dragged on, and all we wanted 11
to do was go home and rebuild our fortress.
Finally, after an eternity, it was almost three
o'clock. James and I sat at the edge of our
seats as we counted under our breath: "10, 9,
8, 7, 6, 5, 4, 3, 2, 1." At last the bell
sounded. We dashed for the door and raced home
and across the street — and then we stopped. We
stood still in the middle of the street with
our hearts pounding like the beats of a drum.
The cool September wind began to pick up, and

Description: the fence

everything became silent. We stood there and
watched the metal of the fence reflect the
beautiful colors of the sun. It was beautiful,
and yet we hated everything about it. The new
metal fence separated us from our fortress,
our planet, our spaceship, our submarine — and,
most important of all, our heroes and our
dreams.

We stood there for a long time. As the sun 12
slowly turned red and sank beneath the ground,
so did our dreams, heroes, and hearts. Darkness
soon devoured the park, and after a while we
walked home with only the memories of the summer that came after the big snowstorm.

Points for Special Attention

Writing a Personal Experience Essay   Michael's instructor specified that he was to write an essay about a person or place to help his readers — other students — understand what his childhood was like. Because it
was a personal experience essay, Michael was free to use the first-person
pronouns *I* and *we* as well as contractions, neither of which would be
acceptable in a more formal essay.

Thesis Statement   Because Michael's primary purpose in this essay
was to communicate personal feelings and impressions, an argumentative
thesis statement (such as "If every television in the United States disappeared, more people would have childhoods like mine") would have been
inappropriate. Still, Michael states his thesis explicitly in order to unify his
essay around the dominant impression he wants to convey: "While it
lasted, it was paradise."

Combining the Patterns   Michael also had more specific purposes, and these determined the patterns that shape his essay. His essay's dominant pattern is *narration,* but to help students visualize the person (James) and the place (the park) he discusses, he includes sections that *describe* and give concrete, specific *examples* as well as summarize his daily routine. These patterns work together to create an essay that *defines* the nature of his childhood.

Transitions   The transitions between the individual sentences and paragraphs of Michael's essay—"now," "Ever since," "The summer that followed the big snowstorm"—serve primarily to move readers through time. This is appropriate because narration is the dominant pattern governing his essay's overall structure.

Detail   Michael's essay is full of specific detail—for example, quoted bits of dialogue in paragraph 3 and names of his heroes and of particular games (and related equipment and weapons) elsewhere. The descriptive details that re-create the physical scenes—in particular, the snow, cold, frost, and wind of winter and the sun reflected in the fence—are vivid enough to help readers visualize the places Michael writes about.

Figures of Speech   Michael's essay describes a time when his imagination wandered without the restraints of adulthood. Appropriately, he uses **similes, metaphors,** and **personification**—"We were free like comets in the heavens"; "The park became a giant spaceship"; "We found lost cities, unearthed treasures, and saved Earth"; "darkness soon devoured the park"—to evoke the time and place he describes.

Focus on Revision

Michael's assignment asked him to write about his childhood, and he chose to focus on his early years in the United States. When his peer editing group discussed his essay, however, a number of students were curious about his life in Vietnam. Some of them thought he should add a paragraph summarizing the "vague images" he remembered of his earlier childhood, perhaps contrasting it with his life in the United States, as he does in passing in paragraph 2. An alternate suggestion, made by one classmate, was that Michael consider deleting the sentence that states he has "no desire or intention" to discuss this part of his life, since it raises issues his essay does not address. After thinking about these ideas, Michael decided to revise his essay by adding a brief paragraph about his life in Vietnam, contrasting the park and his friendship with James to some of his earlier memories. (A sample peer editing worksheet for combining the patterns can be found on the *Patterns for College Writing* Web site at <bedfordstmartins.com/patterns>.)

Each of the following essays combines several patterns, blending strategies to achieve the writer's purpose.

LARS EIGHNER

❖ ────────────────────────────────

On Dumpster Diving

Lars Eighner (b. 1948) dropped out of the University of Texas at Austin after his third year and took a job at a state mental hospital. After leaving his job over a policy dispute in 1988 and falling behind in his rent payments, Eighner became homeless. For three years, he traveled between Austin and Los Angeles with his dog, Lizbeth, earning what money he could from writing stories for magazines. Eighner's memories of his experiences living on the street, *Travels with Lizbeth* (1993), was written on a computer he found in a Dumpster. The following chapter from that book details the practical dangers as well as the many possibilities he discovered in his "Dumpster diving." (Eighner now lives in Austin and operates an online writing course at <io.com/~eighner/wrtmain.html#ga>.)

Background: Although the number of homeless people is difficult to measure accurately, homelessness has become a highly visible issue over the last two decades. It is estimated, for example, that as many as ten million people experienced homelessness in this country in the late 1980s alone. There were a number of causes for this surge in homelessness. Perhaps most important, a booming real estate market led to a significant drop in affordable housing in many areas of the country. In a number of cities, single-room-occupancy hotels, which had long provided cheap lodging, were being demolished or converted into luxury apartments. At the same time, new technologies left many unskilled workers jobless. Government policies against detaining the nondangerous mentally ill against their will also played a significant role. (About a quarter of all homeless people are thought to be mentally ill.) Currently, the U.S. Department of Health and Human Services estimates that some 600,000 men, women, and children are homeless every night in the United States.

This chapter was composed while the author was homeless. The present tense has been preserved.

Definition: Dumpster

Long before I began Dumpster diving I was impressed with Dumpsters, enough so that I wrote the Merriam-Webster research service to discover what I could about the word *Dumpster.* I learned from them that it is a proprietary word belonging to the Dempsey Dumpster company. Since then I have dutifully capitalized the word, although it was lowercased in almost all the citations Merriam-Webster photocopied for me. Dempsey's word is too apt. I have never heard these things called anything but Dumpsters. I do not know anyone who knows the generic name for these objects. From time to time I have heard a wino or hobo give

some corrupted credit to the original and call them
Dipsy Dumpsters.

*Narration: Eighner's
story begins*

I began Dumpster diving about a year before I be- 2
came homeless.

Definition: diving

I prefer the word *scavenging* and use the word 3
scrounging when I mean to be obscure. I have heard
people, evidently meaning to be polite, use the word *foraging,* but I prefer to reserve that word for gathering
nuts and berries and such, which I do also according to
the season and the opportunity. *Dumpster diving* seems
to me to be a little too cute and, in my case, inaccurate
because I lack the athletic ability to lower myself into
the Dumpsters as the true divers do, much to their increased profit.

I like the frankness of the word *scavenging,* which I 4
can hardly think of without picturing a big black snail
on an aquarium wall. I live from the refuse of others.
I am a scavenger. I think it a sound and honorable
niche, although if I could I would naturally prefer to
live the comfortable consumer life, perhaps — and only
perhaps — as a slightly less wasteful consumer, owing to
what I have learned as a scavenger.

*Narration:
story continues*

While Lizbeth and I were still living in the shack on 5
Avenue B as my savings ran out, I put almost all my
sporadic income into rent. The necessities of daily life I
began to extract from Dumpsters. Yes, we ate from them.
Except for jeans, all my clothes came from Dumpsters.

*Exemplification: things
found in Dumpsters*

Boom boxes, candles, bedding, toilet paper, a virgin male
love doll, medicine, books, a typewriter, dishes, furnish-
ings, and change, sometimes amounting to many dollars — I acquired many things from Dumpsters.

Thesis statement

I have learned much as a scavenger. I mean to put 6
some of what I have learned down here, beginning with
the practical art of Dumpster diving and proceeding to
the abstract.

What is safe to eat? 7

After all, the finding of objects is becoming some- 8
thing of an urban art. Even respectable employed people
will sometimes find something tempting sticking out
of a Dumpster or standing beside one. Quite a number
of people, not all of them of the bohemian type, are
willing to brag that they found this or that piece of
trash. But eating from Dumpsters is what separates the
dilettanti from the professionals. Eating safely from
the Dumpsters involves three principles: using the

senses and common sense to evaluate the condition of the found materials, knowing the Dumpsters of a given area and checking them regularly, and seeking always to answer the question "Why was this discarded?"

Comparison and contrast: Dumpster divers vs. others

Perhaps everyone who has a kitchen and a regular supply of groceries has, at one time or another, made a sandwich and eaten half of it before discovering mold on the bread or got a mouthful of milk before realizing the milk had turned. Nothing of the sort is likely to happen to a Dumpster diver because he is constantly reminded that most food is discarded for a reason. Yet a lot of perfectly good food can be found in Dumpsters. 9

Classification and division: different kinds of food found in Dumpsters and their relative safety

Canned goods, for example, turn up fairly often in the Dumpsters I frequent. All except the most phobic people will be willing to eat from a can, even if it came from a Dumpster. Canned goods are among the safest foods to be found in Dumpsters but are not utterly foolproof. 10

Although very rare with modern canning methods, botulism is a possibility. Most other forms of food poisoning seldom do lasting harm to a healthy person, but botulism is almost certainly fatal and often the first symptom is death. Except for carbonated beverages, all canned goods should contain a slight vacuum and suck air when first punctured. Bulging, rusty, and dented cans and cans that spew when punctured should be avoided, especially when the contents are not very acidic or syrupy. 11

Heat can break down the botulin, but this requires much more cooking than most people do to canned goods. To the extent that botulism occurs at all, of course, it can occur in cans on pantry shelves as well as in cans from Dumpsters. Need I say that home-canned goods are simply too risky to be recommended. 12

From time to time one of my companions, aware of the source of my provisions, will ask, "Do you think these crackers are really safe to eat?" For some reason it is most often the crackers they ask about. 13

This question has always made me angry. Of course I would not offer my companion anything I had doubts about. But more than that, I wonder why he cannot evaluate the condition of the crackers for himself. I have no special knowledge and I have been wrong before. Since he knows where the food comes from, it seems to me he ought to assume some of the responsibility for deciding what he will put in his mouth. For 14 myself I have few qualms about dry foods such as crackers, cookies, cereal, chips, and pasta if they are free of visible contaminates and still dry and crisp. Most often such things are found in the original packaging, which is not so much a positive sign as it is the absence of a negative one.

Raw fruits and vegetables with intact skins seem   15
perfectly safe to me, excluding of course the obviously rotten. Many are discarded for minor imperfections that can be pared away. Leafy vegetables, grapes, cauliflower, broccoli, and similar things may be contaminated by liquids and may be impractical to wash.

Candy, especially hard candy, is usually safe if it has   16
not drawn ants. Chocolate is often discarded only because it has become discolored as the cocoa butter deemulsified. Candying, after all, is one method of food preservation because pathogens do not like very sugary substances.

All of these foods might be found in any Dumpster   17
and can be evaluated with some confidence largely on the basis of appearance. Beyond these are foods that cannot be correctly evaluated without additional information.

I began scavenging by pulling pizzas out of the   18
Dumpster behind a pizza delivery shop. In general, prepared food requires caution, but in this case I knew when the shop closed and went to the Dumpster as soon as the last of the help left.

Such shops often get prank orders; both the orders   19
and the products made to fill them are called *bogus*. Because help seldom stays long at these places, pizzas are often made with the wrong topping, refused on delivery for being cold, or baked incorrectly. The products to be discarded are boxed up because inventory is kept by counting boxes: A boxed pizza can be written off; an unboxed pizza does not exist.

I never placed a bogus order to increase the supply   20
of pizzas and I believe no one else was scavenging in this Dumpster. But the people in the shop became suspicious and began to retain their garbage in the shop overnight. While it lasted I had a steady supply of fresh, sometimes warm pizza. Because I knew the Dumpster I knew the source of the pizza, and because I visited the Dumpster regularly I knew what was fresh and what was yesterday's.

The area I frequent is inhabited by many afflu-   21
ent college students. I am not here by chance; the

Cause and effect: why Eighner visits certain Dumpsters; why students throw out food

Dumpsters in this area are very rich. Students throw out many good things, including food. In particular they tend to throw everything out when they move at the end of a semester, before and after breaks, and around midterm, when many of them despair of college. So I find it advantageous to keep an eye on the academic calendar.

Students throw food away around breaks because they do not know whether it has spoiled or will spoil before they return. A typical discard is a half jar of peanut butter. In fact, nonorganic peanut butter does not require refrigeration and is unlikely to spoil in any reasonable time. The student does not know that, and since it is Daddy's money, the student decides not to take a chance. Opened containers require caution and some attention to the question "Why was this discarded?" But in the case of discards from student apartments, the answer may be that the item was thrown out through carelessness, ignorance, or wastefulness. This can sometimes be deduced when the item is found with many others, including some that are obviously perfectly good. 22

Some students, and others, approach defrosting a freezer by chucking out the whole lot. Not only do the circumstances of such a find tell the story, but also the mass of frozen goods stays cold for a long time and items may be found still frozen or freshly thawed. 23

Yogurt, cheese, and sour cream are items that are often thrown out while they are still good. Occasionally I find cheese with a spot of mold, which of course I just pare off, and because it is obvious why such a cheese was discarded, I treat it with less suspicion than an apparently perfect cheese found in similar circumstances. Yogurt is often discarded, still sealed, only because the expiration date on the carton had passed. This is one of my favorite finds because yogurt will keep for several days, even in warm weather. 24

Students throw out canned goods and staples at the end of semesters and when they give up college at midterm. Drugs, pornography, spirits, and the like are often discarded when parents are expected — Dad's Day, for example. And spirits also turn up after big party weekends, presumably discarded by the newly reformed. Wine and spirits, of course, keep perfectly well even once opened, but the same cannot be said of beer. 25

My test for carbonated soft drinks is whether they still fizz vigorously. Many juices or other beverages are 26 too acidic or too syrupy to cause much concern, provided they are not visibly contaminated. I have discovered nasty molds in the vegetable juices, even when the product was found under its original seal; I recommend that such products be decanted slowly into a clear glass. Liquids always require some care. One hot day I found a large jug of Pat O'Brien's Hurricane mix. The jug had been opened but was still ice cold. I drank three large glasses before it became apparent to me that someone had added rum to the mix, and not a little rum. I never tasted the rum, and by the time I began to feel the effects I had already ingested a very large quantity of the beverage. Some divers would have considered this a boon, but being suddenly intoxicated in a public place in the early afternoon is not my idea of a good time.

Example: a liquid that requires care

I have heard of people maliciously contaminating discarded food and even handouts, but mostly I have heard of this from people with vivid imaginations who have had no experience with Dumpsters themselves. Just before the pizza shop stopped discarding its garbage at night, jalapeños began showing up on most of the thrown-out pizzas. If indeed this was meant to discourage me, it was a wasted effort because I am a native Texan.   27

For myself, I avoid game, poultry, pork, and egg-based foods, whether I find them raw or cooked. I seldom have the means to cook what I find, but when I do I avail myself of plentiful supplies of beef, which is often in very good condition. I suppose fish becomes disagreeable before it becomes dangerous. Lizbeth is happy to have any such thing that is past its prime and, in fact, does not recognize fish as food until it is quite strong.   28

Home leftovers, as opposed to surpluses from restaurants, are very often bad. Evidently, especially among students, there is a common type of personality that carefully wraps up even the smallest leftover and shoves it into the back of the refrigerator for six months or so before discarding it. Characteristic of this type are the reused jars and margarine tubs to which the remains are committed. I avoid ethnic foods I am unfamiliar with. If I do not know what it is supposed to look like when it is good, I cannot be certain I will be able to tell if it is bad.   29

No matter how careful I am I still get dysentery at least once a month, oftener in warmer weather. I do not   30 want to paint too romantic a picture. Dumpster diving has serious drawbacks as a way of life.

Process: how to scavenge

I learned to scavenge gradually, on my own. Since then I have initiated several companions into the trade. I have learned that there is a predictable series of stages a person goes through in learning to scavenge. 31

At first the new scavenger is filled with disgust and self-loathing. He is ashamed of being seen and may lurk around, trying to duck behind things, or he may try to dive at night. (In fact, most people instinctively look away from a scavenger. By skulking around, the novice calls attention to himself and arouses suspicion. Diving at night is ineffective and needlessly messy.) 32

Every grain of rice seems to be a maggot. Everything seems to stink. He can wipe the egg yolk off the found can, but he cannot erase from his mind the stigma of eating garbage. 33

That stage passes with experience. The scavenger finds a pair of running shoes that fit and look and smell brand-new. He finds a pocket calculator in perfect working order. He finds pristine ice cream, still frozen, more than he can eat or keep. He begins to understand: People throw away perfectly good stuff, a lot of perfectly good stuff. 34

At this stage, Dumpster shyness begins to dissipate. The diver, after all, has the last laugh. He is finding all manner of good things that are his for the taking. Those who disparage his profession are the fools, not he. 35

He may begin to hang on to some perfectly good things for which he has neither a use nor a market. Then he begins to take note of the things that are not perfectly good but are nearly so. He mates a Walkman with broken earphones and one that is missing a battery cover. He picks up things that he can repair. 36

At this stage he may become lost and never recover. Dumpsters are full of things of some potential value to someone and also of things that never have much intrinsic value but are interesting. All the Dumpster divers I have known come to the point of trying to acquire everything they touch. Why not take it, they reason, since it is all free? This is, of course, hopeless. Most divers come to realize that they must restrict themselves to items of relatively immediate utility. But in some cases the diver simply cannot control himself. I 37 have met several of these pack-rat types. Their ideas of the values of various pieces of junk verge on the psychotic. Every bit of glass may be a diamond, they think, and all that glisters,* gold.

Cause and effect: why Eighner gains weight when he scavenges

I tend to gain weight when I am scavenging. Partly 38 this is because I always find far more pizza and doughnuts than water-packed tuna, nonfat yogurt, and fresh vegetables. Also I have not developed much faith in the reliability of Dumpsters as a food source, although it has been proven to me many times. I tend to eat as if I have no idea where my next meal is coming from. But mostly I just hate to see food go to waste and so I eat much more than I should. Something like this drives the obsession to collect junk.

Cause and effect: why Eighner collects junk

As for collecting objects, I usually restrict myself 39 to collecting one kind of small object at a time, such as pocket calculators, sunglasses, or campaign buttons. To live on the street I must anticipate my needs to a certain extent: I must pick up and save warm bedding I find in August because it will not be found in Dumpsters in November. As I have no access to health care, I often hoard essential drugs, such as antibiotics and antihistamines. (This course can be recommended only to those with some grounding in pharmacology. Antibiotics, for example, even when indicated are worse than useless if taken in insufficient amounts.) But even if I had a home with extensive storage space, I could not save everything that might be valuable in some contingency.

I have proprietary feelings about my Dumpsters. As 40 I have mentioned, it is no accident that I scavenge from ones where good finds are common. But my limited experience with Dumpsters in other areas suggests to me that even in poorer areas, Dumpsters, if attended with sufficient diligence, can be made to yield a livelihood. The rich students discard perfectly good kiwi fruit; poorer people discard perfectly good apples. Slacks and Polo shirts are found in one place; jeans and T-shirts in the other. The population of competitors rather than the affluence of the dumpers most affects the feasibility of survival by scavenging. The large number of competitors is what puts me off the idea of trying to scavenge in places like Los Angeles.

Comparison and contrast: Dumpsters in rich and poorer areas

Curiously, I do not mind my direct competition, 41 other scavengers, so much as I hate the can scroungers.

---

*EDS. NOTE — Glitters.

Cause and effect: why
people scrounge cans

People scrounge cans because they have to have a   42
little cash. I have tried scrounging cans with an able-
bodied companion. Afoot a can scrounger simply cannot
make more than a few dollars in a day. One can extract
the necessities of life from the Dumpsters directly with
far less effort than would be required to accumulate the
equivalent value in cans. (These observations may not
hold in places with container redemption laws.)

Can scroungers, then, are people who must have   43
small amounts of cash. These are drug addicts and
winos, mostly the latter because the amounts of cash
are so small. Spirits and drugs do, like all other commodities, turn up in Dumpsters and the scavenger will
from time to time have a half bottle of a rather good
wine with his dinner. But the wino cannot survive on
these occasional finds; he must have his daily dose to
stave off the DTs. All the cans he can carry will buy
about three bottles of Wild Irish Rose.

I do not begrudge them the cans, but can   44
scroungers tend to tear up the Dumpsters, mixing the
contents and littering the area. They become so specialized that they can see only cans. They earn my contempt by passing up change, canned goods, and readily
hockable items.

There are precious few courtesies among scavengers.   45
But it is common practice to set aside surplus items:
pairs of shoes, clothing, canned goods, and such. A true

Comparison and
contrast: can
scroungers vs.
true scavengers

scavenger hates to see good stuff go to waste, and what
he cannot use he leaves in good condition in plain sight.

Can scroungers lay waste to everything in their   46
path and will stir one of a pair of good shoes to the bottom of a Dumpster, to be lost or ruined in the muck.
Can scroungers will even go through individual garbage cans, something I have never seen a scavenger do.

Individual garbage cans are set out on the public   47
easement only on garbage days. On the other days going
through them requires trespassing close to a dwelling.

Cause and effect: why
scavengers do not go
through individual
garbage cans

Going through individual garbage cans without scat-
tering litter is almost impossible. Litter is likely to
reduce the public's tolerance of scavenging. Individual
cans are simply not as productive as Dumpsters; people
in houses and duplexes do not move so often and for
some reason do not tend to discard as much useful
material. Moreover, the time required to go through
one garbage can that serves one household is not much
less than the time required to go through a Dumpster
that contains the refuse of twenty apartments.

But my strongest reservation about going through   48
individual garbage cans is that this seems to me a very
personal kind of invasion to which I would object if I
were a householder. Although many things in Dumpsters are obviously meant never to come to light, a
Dumpster is somehow less personal.

I avoid trying to draw conclusions about the people   49
who dump in the Dumpsters I frequent. I think it would
be unethical to do so, although I know many people
will find the idea of scavenger ethics too funny for
words.

Examples: things
found in Dumpsters

Dumpsters contain bank statements, correspon-   50
dence, and other documents, just as anyone might
expect. But there are also less obvious sources of information. Pill bottles, for example. The labels bear the
name of the patient, the name of the doctor, and the
name of the drug. AIDS drugs and antipsychotic medicines, to name but two groups, are specific and are
seldom prescribed for any other disorders. The plastic
compacts for birth-control pills usually have complete
label information.

Despite all of this sensitive information, I have   51
had only one apartment resident object to my going
through the Dumpster. In that case it turned out the
resident was a university athlete who was taking bets
and who was afraid I would turn up his wager slips.

Occasionally a find tells a story. I once found a small   52
paper bag containing some unused condoms, several
partial tubes of flavored sexual lubricants, a partially
used compact of birth-control pills, and the torn pieces
of a picture of a young man. Clearly she was through
with him and planning to give up sex altogether.

Dumpster things are often sad — abandoned teddy   53
bears, shredded wedding books, despaired-of sales kits.
I find many pets lying in state in Dumpsters. Although
I hope to get off the streets so that Lizbeth can have a
long and comfortable old age, I know this hope is not
very realistic. So I suppose when her time comes she
too will go into a Dumpster. I will have no better place
for her. And after all, it is fitting, since for most of her
life her livelihood has come from the Dumpster. When
she finds something I think is safe that has been spilled
from a Dumpster, I let her have it. She already knows
the route around the best ones. I like to think that if
she survives me she will have a chance of evading the
dog catcher and of finding her sustenance on the route.

Silly vanities also come to rest in the Dumpsters. I 54
am a rather accomplished needleworker. I get a lot of
material from the Dumpsters. Evidently sorority girls,
hoping to impress someone, perhaps themselves, with
their mastery of a womanly art, buy a lot of embroider-
by-number kits, work a few stitches horribly, and eventually discard the whole mess. I pull out their stitches,
turn the canvas over, and work an original design. Do
not think I refrain from chuckling as I make gifts from
these kits.

I find diaries and journals. I have often thought of 55
compiling a book of literary found objects. And perhaps I will one day. But what I find is hopelessly commonplace and bad without being, even unconsciously,
camp. College students also discard their papers. I am
horrified to discover the kind of paper that now merits
an A in an undergraduate course. I am grateful, however, for the number of good books and magazines the
students throw out.

In the area I know best I have never discovered ver- 56
min in the Dumpster, but there are two kinds of kitty
surprise. One is alley cats whom I meet as they leap,
claws first, out of Dumpsters. This is especially thrilling
when I have Lizbeth in tow. The other kind of kitty surprise is a plastic garbage bag filled with some ponder-
ous, amorphous mass. This always proves to be used
cat litter.

City bees harvest doughnut glaze and this makes 57
the Dumpster at the doughnut shop more interesting.
My faith in the instinctive wisdom of animals is always
shaken whenever I see Lizbeth attempt to catch a bee in
her mouth, which she does whenever bees are present.
Evidently some birds find Dumpsters profitable, for
birdie surprise is almost as common as kitty surprise of
the first kind. In hunting season all kinds of small game
turn up in Dumpsters, some of it, sadly, not entirely
dead. Curiously, summer and winter, maggots are uncommon.

The worst of the living and near-living hazards of 58
the Dumpsters are the fire ants. The food they claim is
not much of a loss, but they are vicious and aggressive.
It is very easy to brush against some surface of the
Dumpster and pick up half a dozen or more fire ants,
usually in some sensitive area such as the underarm.
One advantage of bringing Lizbeth along as I make
Dumpster rounds is that, for obvious reasons, she is

very alert to ground-based fire ants. When Lizbeth recognizes a fire-ant infestation around our feet, she does the Dance of the Zillion Fire Ants. I have learned not to ignore this warning from Lizbeth, whether I perceive the tiny ants or not, but to remove ourselves at Lizbeth's first *pas de bourée*.* All the more so because the ants are the worst in the summer months when I wear flip-flops if I have them. (Perhaps someone will misunderstand this. Lizbeth does the Dance of the Zillion Fire Ants when she recognizes more fire ants than she cares to eat, not when she is being bitten. Since I have learned to react promptly, she does not get bitten at all. It is the isolated patrol of fire ants that falls in Lizbeth's range that deserves pity. She finds them quite tasty.)

Process: how to go through a Dumpster

By far the best way to go through a Dumpster is to 59 lower yourself into it. Most of the good stuff tends to settle at the bottom because it is usually weightier than the rubbish. My more athletic companions have often demonstrated to me that they can extract much good material from a Dumpster I have already been over.

To those psychologically or physically unprepared 60 to enter a Dumpster, I recommend a stout stick, preferably with some barb or hook at one end. The hook can be used to grab plastic garbage bags. When I find canned goods or other objects loose at the bottom of a Dumpster, I lower a bag into it, roll the desired object into the bag, and then hoist the bag out — a procedure more easily described than executed. Much Dumpster diving is a matter of experience for which nothing will do except practice.

Dumpster diving is outdoor work, often surprisingly pleasant. It is not entirely predictable; things of 61 interest turn up every day and some days there are finds of great value. I am always very pleased when I can turn up exactly the thing I most wanted to find. Yet in spite of the element of chance, scavenging more than most other pursuits tends to yield returns in some proportion to the effort and intelligence brought to bear. It is very sweet to turn up a few dollars in change from a Dumpster that has just been gone over by a wino.

The land is now covered with cities. The cities are 62 full of Dumpsters. If a member of the canine race is ever able to know what it is doing, then Lizbeth knows that when we go around to the Dumpsters, we are

---

*EDS. NOTE — A ballet step.

hunting. I think of scavenging as a modern form of self-reliance. In any event, after having survived nearly ten years of government service, where everything is geared to the lowest common denominator, I find it refreshing to have work that rewards initiative and effort. Certainly I would be happy to have a sinecure again, but I am no longer heartbroken that I left one.

Cause and effect: results of Eighner's experiences as a scavenger

I find from the experience of scavenging two rather deep lessons. The first is to take what you can use and let the rest go by. I have come to think that there is no value in the abstract. A thing I cannot use or make useful, perhaps by trading, has no value however rare or fine it may be. I mean useful in some broad sense — some art I would find useful and some otherwise. 63

I was shocked to realize that some things are not worth acquiring, but now I think it is so. Some material things are white elephants that eat up the possessor's substance. The second lesson is the transience of material being. This has not quite converted me to a dualist,* but it has made some headway in that direction. I do not suppose that ideas are immortal, but certainly mental things are longer lived than other material things. 64

Once I was the sort of person who invests objects with sentimental value. Now I no longer have those objects, but I have the sentiments yet. 65

Many times in our travels I have lost everything but the clothes I was wearing and Lizbeth. The things I find in Dumpsters, the love letters and rag dolls of so many lives, remind me of this lesson. Now I hardly pick up a thing without envisioning the time I will cast it aside. This I think is a healthy state of mind. Almost everything I have now has already been cast out at least once, proving that what I own is valueless to someone. 66

Anyway, I find my desire to grab for the gaudy bauble has been largely sated. I think this is an attitude I share with the very wealthy — we both know there is plenty more where what we have came from. Between us are the rat-race millions who nightly scavenge the cable channels looking for they know not what. 67

I am sorry for them. 68

•   •   •

*EDS. NOTE — Someone who believes that the world consists of two opposing forces, such as mind and matter.

COMPREHENSION

1. In your own words, give a one-sentence definition of *Dumpster diving*.

2. List some of Eighner's answers to the question "Why was this discarded?" (8). What additional reasons can you think of?

3. What foods does Eighner take particular care to avoid? Why?

4. In paragraph 30, Eighner comments, "Dumpster diving has serious drawbacks as a way of life." What drawbacks does he cite in his essay? What additional drawbacks are implied? Can you think of others?

5. Summarize the stages in the process of learning to scavenge.

6. In addition to food, what else does Eighner scavenge for? Into what general categories do these items fall?

7. Why does Eighner hate can scroungers?

8. What lessons has Eighner learned as a Dumpster diver?

PURPOSE AND AUDIENCE

1. In paragraph 6, Eighner states his purpose: to record what he has learned as a Dumpster diver. What additional purposes do you think he had in setting his ideas down on paper?

2. Do you think most readers are apt to respond to Eighner's essay with sympathy? Pity? Impatience? Contempt? Disgust? How do you react? Why?

3. Why do you think Eighner chose not to provide any background about his life—his upbringing, education, or work history—before he became homeless? Do you think this decision was a wise one? How might such information (for example, any of the details in the headnote that precedes the essay) have changed readers' reactions to his discussion?

4. In paragraph 8, Eighner presents three principles one must follow to eat safely from a Dumpster; in paragraphs 59–60 he explains how to go through a Dumpster; and throughout the essay he includes many cautions and warnings. Clearly, he does not expect his audience to take up Dumpster diving. What, then, is his purpose in including such detailed explanations?

5. When Eighner begins paragraph 9 with "Perhaps everyone who has a kitchen," he encourages readers to identify with him. In what other ways does he help readers imagine themselves in his place? Are these efforts successful? Explain.

6. What effect do you think the essay's last sentence is calculated to have on readers? What effect does it have on you?

STYLE AND STRUCTURE

1. Eighner opens his essay with a fairly conventional strategy: extended definitions of *Dumpster* and *Dumpster diving*. What techniques does he use in paragraphs 1 through 3 to develop these definitions? Is beginning with definitions the best strategy for this essay? Why or why not?

2. This long essay contains four one-sentence paragraphs. Why do you think Eighner isolates these sentences? Do you think any of them should be combined with an adjacent paragraph? Explain your reasoning.

3. As the introductory comment notes, Eighner chose to retain the present tense even though he was no longer homeless when the essay was published. Why do you think he decided to preserve the present tense? Was this a good decision?

4. Eighner's essay includes a number of lists that catalog items with which he came in contact (for example, in paragraphs 5 and 50). Identify as many of these lists as you can. Why do you think Eighner includes such extensive lists?

VOCABULARY PROJECTS

1. Define each of the following words as it is used in this selection.

proprietary (1)	decanted (26)	contingency (39)
niche (4)	ingested (26)	feasibility (40)
sporadic (5)	avail (28)	stave (43)
bohemian (8)	skulking (32)	commonplace (55)
dilettanti (8)	stigma (33)	vermin (56)
phobic (10)	pristine (34)	sinecure (62)
pared (15)	dissipate (35)	transience (64)
de-emulsified (16)	disparage (35)	gaudy (67)
pathogens (16)	intrinsic (37)	bauble (67)
staples (25)		

2. In paragraph 3, Eighner suggests several alternative words for *diving* as he uses it in his essay. Consult a dictionary to determine the connotations of each of his alternatives. What are the pros and cons of substituting one of these words for *diving* in Eighner's title and throughout the essay?

JOURNAL ENTRY

In paragraphs 21–25, Eighner discusses the discarding of food by college students. Does your own experience support his observations? Do you think he is being too hard on students, or does his characterization seem accurate?

WRITING WORKSHOP

1. Write an essay about a homeless person you have seen in your community. Use any patterns you like to structure your paper. When you have finished, annotate your essay to identify the patterns you have used.

2. Write a memo to your school's dean of students recommending steps that can be taken on your campus to redirect discarded (but edible) food to the homeless. Use process and exemplification to structure your memo.

3. Taking Eighner's point of view and using information from his essay, write an argumentative essay with a thesis statement that takes a strong

stand against homelessness and recommends government and/or private measures to end it. If you like, you may write your essay in the form of a statement by Eighner to a congressional committee.

COMBINING THE PATTERNS

Review the annotations that identify each pattern of development used in this essay. Which patterns seem to be most effective in helping you understand and empathize with the life of a homeless person? Why?

THEMATIC CONNECTIONS

- "The Human Cost of an Illiterate Society" (page 229)
- "The Untouchable" (page 498)
- "Burdens" (page 509)
- The Declaration of Independence (page 557)

JONATHAN SWIFT

❖ ───────────────────────────────

A Modest Proposal

Jonathan Swift (1667–1745) was born in Dublin, Ireland, and spent much of his life journeying between his homeland, where he had a modest income as an Anglican priest, and England, where he wished to be part of the literary establishment. The author of many satires and political pamphlets, he is best known today for *Gulliver's Travels* (1726), a sharp satire that, except among academics, is now read primarily as a fantasy for children.

Background: At the time that Swift wrote "A Modest Proposal," Ireland had been essentially under British rule since 1171, with the British often brutally suppressing rebellions by the Irish people. When Henry VIII of England declared a Protestant Church of Ireland, many of the Irish remained fiercely Roman Catholic, and this led to even greater contention. By the early 1700s, the English-controlled Irish Parliament had passed laws that severely limited the rights of Irish Catholics, and British trade policies had begun to seriously depress the Irish economy. A fierce advocate for the Irish people in their struggle under British rule, Swift published several works supporting the Irish cause. The following sharply ironic essay was written during the height of a terrible famine in Ireland, at a time when the British were proposing a devastating tax on the impoverished Irish citizenry. Note that Swift does not write in his own voice here but adopts the persona of one who does not recognize the barbarity of his "solution."

It is a melancholy object to those who walk through this great town* 1 or travel in the country, when they see the streets, the roads, and cabin doors, crowded with beggars of the female sex, followed by three, four, or six children, all in rags and importuning every passenger for an alms. These mothers, instead of being able to work for their honest livelihood, are forced to employ all their time in strolling to beg sustenance for their helpless infants, who, as they grow up, either turn thieves for want of work, or leave their dear native country to fight for the Pretender in Spain, or sell themselves to the Barbadoes.**

I think it is agreed by all parties that this prodigious number of chil- 2 dren in the arms, or on the backs, or at the heels of their mothers, and frequently of their fathers, is in the present deplorable state of the kingdom a very great additional grievance; and therefore whoever could find out a fair, cheap, and easy method of making these children sound, useful members of the commonwealth would deserve so well of the public as to have his statue set up for a preserver of the nation.

─────────────

*Eds. note — Dublin.

**Eds. note — Many young Irishmen left their country to fight as mercenaries in Spain's civil war or to work as indentured servants in the West Indies.

But my intention is very far from being confined to provide only for   3
the children of professed beggars; it is of a much greater extent, and shall
take in the whole number of infants at a certain age who are born of parents in effect as little able to support them as those who demand our charity in the streets.

As to my own part, having turned my thoughts for many years upon   4
this important subject, and maturely weighed the several schemes of the
other projectors, I have always found them grossly mistaken in their com-
putation. It is true, a child just dropped from its dam may be supported by
her milk for a solar year, with little other nourishment; at most not above
the value of two shillings, which the mother may certainly get, or the value
in scraps, by her lawful occupation of begging; and it is exactly at one year
old that I propose to provide for them in such a manner as instead of being
a charge upon their parents or the parish, or wanting food and raiment for
the rest of their lives, they shall on the contrary contribute to the feeding,
and partly to the clothing, of many thousands.

There is likewise another great advantage in my scheme, that it will   5
prevent those involuntary abortions, and that horrid practice of women
murdering their bastard children, alas, too frequent among us, sacrificing
the poor innocent babies, I doubt, more to avoid the expense than the
shame, which would move tears and pity in the most savage and inhuman
breast.

The number of souls in this kingdom being usually reckoned one mil-   6
lion and a half, of these I calculate there may be about two hundred thousand couples whose wives are breeders, from which number I subtract
thirty thousand couples who are able to maintain their own children,
although I apprehend there cannot be so many under the present distress
of the kingdom; but this being granted, there will remain an hundred and
seventy thousand breeders. I again subtract fifty thousand for those
women who miscarry, or whose children die by accident or disease within
the year. There only remain an hundred and twenty thousand children of
poor parents annually born. The question therefore is, how this number
shall be reared and provided for, which, as I have already said, under the
present situation of affairs, is utterly impossible by all the methods hitherto proposed. For we can neither employ them in handicraft nor agriculture; we neither build houses (I mean in the country) nor cultivate land.
They can very seldom pick up livelihood by stealing till they arrive at six
years old, except where they are of towardly parts,* although I confess they
learn the rudiments much earlier, during which time they can however be
looked upon only as probationers, as I have been informed by a principal
gentleman in the country of Cavan, who protested to me that he never
knew above one or two instances under the age of six, even in a part of the
kingdom so renowned for the quickest proficiency in that art.

---

*EDS. NOTE—Precocious.

I am assured by our merchants that a boy or a girl before twelve years   7
old is no salable commodity; and even when they come to this age, they
will not yield above three pounds, or three pounds and half a crown at
most on the Exchange; which cannot turn to account either to the parents
or the kingdom, the charge of nutriment and rags having been at least four
times that value.

I shall now therefore humbly propose my own thoughts, which I hope   8
will not be liable to the least objection.

I have been assured by a very knowing American of my acquaintance   9
in London, that a young healthy child well nursed is at a year old a most delicious, nourishing, and wholesome food, whether stewed, roasted, baked,
or boiled; and I make no doubt that it will equally serve in fricasee or a
ragout.

I do therefore humbly offer it to public consideration that of the hun-   10
dred and twenty thousand children, already computed, twenty thousand
may be reserved for breed, whereof only one fourth part to be males, which
is more than we allow to sheep, black cattle, or swine; and my reason is
that these children are seldom the fruits of marriage, a circumstance not
much regarded by our savages, therefore one male will be sufficient to serve
four females. That the remaining hundred thousand may at a year old be
offered in sale to the persons of quality and fortune through the kingdom,
always advising the mother to let them suck plentifully in the last month,
so as to render them plump and fat for a good table. A child will make two
dishes at an entertainment for friends; and when the family dines alone,
the fore or hind quarter will make a reasonable dish, and seasoned with a
little pepper or salt, will be very good boiled on the fourth day, especially in
winter.

I have reckoned upon a medium that a child just born will weigh   11
twelve pounds, and in a solar year if tolerably nursed increaseth to twenty-
eight pounds.

I grant this food will be somewhat dear, and therefore very proper for   12
landlords, who, as they have already devoured most of the parents, seem to
have the best title to the children.

Infant's flesh will be in season throughout the year, but more plentiful   13
in March, and a little before and after. For we are told by a grave author, an
eminent French physician,* that fish being a prolific diet, there are more
children born in Roman Catholic countries about nine months after Lent,
than at any other season; therefore, reckoning a year after Lent, the markets will be more glutted than usual, because the number of popish infants
is at least three to one in this kingdom; and therefore it will have one other
collateral advantage, by lessening the number of Papists** among us.

I have already computed the charge of nursing a beggar's child (in   14
which list I reckon all cottagers, laborers, and four fifths of the farmers) to

---

*Eds. note — François Rabelais, a sixteenth-century satirical writer.
**Eds. note — Roman Catholics.

be about two shillings per annum, rags included; and I believe no gentleman would repine to give ten shillings for the carcass of a good fat child, which, as I have said, will make four dishes of excellent nutritive meat, when he hath only some particular friend or his own family to dine with him. Thus the squire will learn to be a good landlord, and grow popular among the tenants; the mother will have eight shillings net profit, and be fit for work till she produces another child.

Those who are more thrifty (as I must confess the times require) may 15 flay the carcass; the skin of which artificially* dressed will make admirable gloves for ladies, and summer boots for fine gentlemen.

As to our city of Dublin, shambles** may be appointed for this pur- 16 pose in the most convenient parts of it, and butchers we may be assured will not be wanting; although I rather recommend buying the children alive, and dressing them hot from the knife as we do roasting pigs.

A very worthy person, a true lover of his country, and whose virtues I 17 highly esteem, was lately pleased in discoursing on this matter to offer a refinement upon my scheme. He said that many gentlemen of his kingdom, having of late destroyed their deer, he conceived that the want of venison might be well supplied by the bodies of young lads and maidens, not exceeding fourteen years of age nor under twelve, so great a number of both sexes in every county being now ready to starve for want of work and service; and these to be disposed of by their parents, if alive, or otherwise by their nearest relations. But with due deference to so excellent a friend and so deserving a patriot I cannot be altogether in his sentiments; for as to the males, my American acquaintance assured me from frequent experience that their flesh was generally tough and lean, like that of our schoolboys, by continual exercise, and their taste disagreeable; and to fatten them would not answer the charge. Then as to the females, it would, I think with humble submission, be a loss to the public, because they soon would become breeders themselves; and besides, it is not improbable that some scrupulous people might be apt to censure such a practice (although indeed very unjustly) as a little bordering upon cruelty; which, I confess, hath always been with me the strongest objection against any project, how well soever intended.

But in order to justify my friend, he confessed that this expedient was 18 put into his head by the famous Psalmanazar,*** a native of the island Formosa, who came from thence to London above twenty years ago, and in conversation told my friend that in his country when any young person happened to be put to death, the executioner sold the carcass to the persons of quality as a prime dainty; and that in his time the body of a plump girl of fifteen, who was crucified for an attempt to poison the emperor, was

---

　　*Eds. note — Skillfully.
　　**Eds. note — A slaughterhouse or meat market.
　　***Eds. note — Frenchman who passed himself off as a native of Formosa (present-day Taiwan).

sold to the Imperial Majesty's prime minister of state, and other great mandarins of the court, in joints from the gibbet, at four hundred crowns. Neither indeed can I deny that if the same use were made of several plump young girls in this town, who without one single groat to their fortunes cannot stir abroad without a chair,* and appear at the playhouse and assemblies in foreign fineries which they never will pay for, the kingdom would not be the worse.

Some persons of a desponding spirit are in great concern about the vast number of poor people who are aged, diseased, or maimed, and I have been desired to employ my thoughts what course may be taken to ease the nation of so grievous an encumbrance. But I am not in the least pain upon that matter, because it is very well known that they are every day dying and rotting by cold and famine, and filth and vermin, as fast as can be reasonably expected. And as to the younger laborers, they are now in almost as hopeful a condition. They cannot get work, and consequently pine away for want of nourishment to a degree that if any time they are accidentally hired to common labor, they have not strength to perform it; and thus the country and themselves are happily delivered from the evils to come. 19

I have too long digressed, and therefore shall return to my subject. I think the advantages by the proposal which I have made are obvious and many, as well as of the highest importance. 20

For first, as I have already observed, it would greatly lessen the number of Papists, with whom we are yearly overrun, being the principal breeders of the nation as well as our most dangerous enemies; and who stay at home on purpose to deliver the kingdom to the Pretender, hoping to take their advantage by the absence of so many good Protestants, who have chosen rather to leave their country than to stay at home and pay tithes against their conscience to an Episcopal curate. 21

Secondly, the poorer tenants will have something valuable of their own, which by law may be made liable to distress,** and help to pay their landlord's rent, their corn and cattle being already seized and money a thing unknown. 22

Thirdly, whereas the maintenance of an hundred thousand children, from two years old and upwards, cannot be computed at less than ten shillings a piece per annum, the nation's stock will be thereby increased fifty thousand pounds per annum, besides the profit of a new dish introduced to the tables of all gentlemen of fortune in the kingdom who have any refinement in taste. And the money will circulate among ourselves, the goods being entirely of our own growth and manufacture. 23

Fourthly, the constant breeders, besides the gain of eight shillings sterling per annum by the sale of their children, will be rid of the charge for maintaining them after the first year. 24

---

*EDS. NOTE — A sedan chair; that is, a portable, covered chair designed to seat one person and then to be carried by two men.

**EDS. NOTE — Property could be seized by creditors.

Fifthly, this food would likewise bring great custom to taverns, where the vintners will certainly be so prudent as to procure the best receipts* for dressing it to perfection, and consequently have their houses frequented by all the fine gentlemen, who justly value themselves upon their knowledge in good eating; and a skillful cook, who understands how to oblige his guests, will contrive to make it as expensive as they please.

Sixthly, this would be a great inducement to marriage, after which all wise nations have either encouraged by rewards or enforced by laws and penalties. It would increase the care and tenderness of mothers toward their children, when they were sure of a settlement for life to the poor babes, provided in some sort by the public, to their annual profit instead of expense. We should see an honest emulation among the married women, which of them could bring the fattest child to the market. Men would become as fond of their wives during the time of pregnancy as they are now of their mares in foal, their cows in calf, or sows when they are ready to farrow; nor offer to beat or kick them (as is too frequent a practice) for fear of miscarriage.

Many other advantages might be enumerated. For instance, the addition of some thousand carcasses in our exportation of barreled beef, the propagation of swine's flesh, and improvements in the art of making good bacon, so much wanted among us by the great destruction of pigs, too frequent at our tables, which are no way comparable in taste or magnificence to a well-grown, fat, yearling child, which roasted whole will make a considerable figure at a lord mayor's feast or other public entertainment. But this and many others I omit, being studious of brevity.

Supposing that one thousand families in this city would be constant customers for infants' flesh, besides others who might have it at merry meetings, particularly weddings and christenings, I compute that Dublin would take off annually about twenty thousand carcasses, and the rest of the kingdom (where probably they will be sold somewhat cheaper) the remaining eighty thousand.

I can think of no one objection that will possibly be raised against this proposal, unless it should be urged that the number of people will be thereby much lessened in the kingdom. This I freely own, and it was indeed one principal design in offering it to the world. I desire the reader will observe; that I calculate my remedy for this one individual kingdom of Ireland and for no other that ever was, is, or I think ever can be upon earth. Therefore, let no man talk to me of other expedients: of taxing our absentees at five shillings a pound: of using neither clothes nor household furniture except what is of our own growth and manufacture: of utterly rejecting the materials and instruments that promote foreign luxury: of curing the expensiveness of pride, vanity, idleness, and gaming in our women: of introducing a vein of parsimony, prudence, and temperance: of learning to love our country, in the want of which we differ even from

25

26

27

28

29

---

*Eds. note — Recipes.

Lowlanders and the inhabitants of Topinamboo:* of quitting our animosities and factions, nor acting any longer like the Jews,** who were murdering one another at the very moment their city was taken: of being a little cautious not to sell our country and conscience for nothing: of teaching landlords to have at least one degree of mercy toward their tenants: lastly, of putting a spirit of honesty, industry, and skill into our shopkeepers; who, if a resolution could now be taken to buy only our native goods, would immediately unite to cheat and exact upon us in the price, the measure, and the goodness, nor could ever yet be brought to make one fair proposal of just dealing, though often and earnestly invited to it.

Therefore, I repeat, let no man talk to me of these and the like expedients, till he hath at least some glimpse of hope that there will ever be some hearty and sincere attempt to put them in practice.***   30

But as to myself, having been wearied out for many years with offering vain, idle, visionary thoughts, and at length utterly despairing of success, I fortunately fell upon this proposal, which, as it is wholly new, so it hath something solid and real, of no expense and little trouble, full in our own power, and whereby we can incur no danger in disobliging England. For this kind of commodity will not bear exploration, the flesh being of too tender a consistence to admit a long continuance in salt, although perhaps I could name a country which would be glad to eat up our whole nation without it.   31

After all, I am not so violently bent upon my own opinion as to reject any offer proposed by wise men, which shall be found equally innocent, cheap, easy, and effectual. But before something of that kind shall be advanced in contradiction to my scheme, and offering a better, I desire the author or authors will be pleased maturely to consider two points. First, as things now stand, how they will be able to find food and raiment for an hundred thousand useless mouths and backs. And secondly, there being a round million of creatures in human figure throughout this kingdom, whose sole subsistence put into a common stock would leave them in debt two million of pounds sterling, adding those who are beggars by profession to the bulk of farmers, cottagers, and laborers, with their wives and children who are beggars in effect; I desire those politicians who dislike my overture, and may perhaps be so bold to attempt an answer, that they will first ask the parents of these mortals whether they would not at this day think it a great happiness to have been sold for food at a year old in this manner I prescribe, and thereby have avoided such a perpetual scene of misfortunes as they have since gone through by the oppression of landlords, the impossibility of paying rent without money or trade, the want of   32

---

*EDS. NOTE — A place in the Brazilian jungle.
**EDS. NOTE — In the first century B.C., the Roman general Pompey was able to conquer Jerusalem in part because the citizenry was divided among rival factions.
***EDS. NOTE — Note that these measures represent Swift's true proposal.

common sustenance, with neither house nor clothes to cover them from the inclemencies of the weather, and the most inevitable prospect of entailing the like or greater miseries upon their breed forever.

I profess, in the sincerity of my heart, that I have not the least personal interest in endeavoring to promote this necessary work, having no other motive than the public good of my country, by advancing our trade, providing for infants, relieving the poor, and giving some pleasure to the rich. I have no children by which I can propose to get a single penny; the youngest being nine years old, and my wife past childbearing. 33

• • •

COMPREHENSION

1. What problem does Swift identify? What general solution does he recommend?

2. What advantages does Swift see in his plan?

3. What does he see as the alternative to his plan?

4. What clues indicate that Swift is not serious about his proposal?

5. In paragraph 29, Swift lists and rejects a number of "other expedients." What are they? Why do you think he presents and rejects these ideas?

PURPOSE AND AUDIENCE

1. Swift's target here is the British government, in particular its poor treatment of the Irish. How would you expect British government officials to respond to his proposal? How would you expect Irish readers to react?

2. What do you think Swift hoped to accomplish in this essay? Do you think his purpose was simply to amuse and shock, or do you think he wanted to change people's minds—or even inspire them to take some kind of action? Explain.

3. In paragraphs 6, 14, 23, and elsewhere, Swift presents a series of mathematical calculations. What effect do you think he expected these computations to have on his readers?

4. Explain why each of the following groups might have been offended by this essay: women, Catholics, butchers, poor people.

5. How do you think Swift expected the appeal in his conclusion to affect his audience?

STYLE AND STRUCTURE

1. In paragraph 6, Swift uses the word *breeders* to refer to fertile women. What connotations does this word have? Why does he use it rather than a more neutral alternative?

2. What purpose does paragraph 8 serve in the essay? Do the other short paragraphs have the same function? Explain.

3. Swift's remarks are presented as an argument. Where, if anywhere, does he anticipate and refute his readers' objections?

4. Swift applies to infants many words usually applied to animals who are slaughtered to be eaten—for example, *fore or hind quarter* (10) and *carcass* (15). Identify as many examples of this kind of usage as you can. Why do you think Swift uses such words?

5. Throughout his essay, Swift cites the comments of others—"our merchants" (7), "a very knowing American of my acquaintance" (9), and "an eminent French physician" (13), for example. Cite additional examples. What, if anything, does he accomplish by referring to these people?

6. A **satire** is a piece of writing that uses wit, **irony,** and ridicule to attack foolishness, incompetence, or evil. How does "A Modest Proposal" fit this definition of satire?

7. Evaluate the strategy Swift uses to introduce each advantage he cites in paragraphs 21 through 26.

8. Swift uses a number of parenthetical comments in his essay—for example, in paragraphs 14, 17, and 26. Identify all of his parenthetical comments, and consider what they contribute to the essay.

9. Swift begins paragraph 20 with "I have too long digressed, and therefore shall return to my subject." Has he in fact been digressing? Explain.

VOCABULARY PROJECTS

1. Define each of the following words as it is used in this selection.

importuning (1)	rudiments (6)	encumbrance (19)
alms (1)	nutriment (7)	tithes (21)
prodigious (2)	repine (14)	vintners (25)
professed (3)	flay (15)	expedients (29)
dam (4)	scrupulous (17)	parsimony (29)
reckoned (6)	censure (17)	temperance (29)
apprehend (6)	desponding (19)	raiment (32)

2. The title states that Swift's proposal is a "modest" one; elsewhere he says that he proposes his ideas "humbly" (8). Why do you think he chooses these words? Does he really mean to present himself as modest and humble?

JOURNAL ENTRY

What is your emotional reaction to this essay? Do you find it amusing or offensive? Why?

WRITING WORKSHOP

1. Write a "modest proposal," either straightforward or satirical, for solving a problem in your school or community.

2. Write a "modest proposal" for achieving one of these national goals:
   - Making health care more affordable
   - Improving gun safety
   - Eliminating binge drinking on college campuses
   - Improving public education
   - Eliminating teenage pregnancy
   - Reducing the use of illegal drugs

3. Write a letter to an executive of the tobacco industry, a television network, or an industry that threatens the environment. In your letter, set forth a "modest proposal" for making the industry more responsible.

COMBINING THE PATTERNS

What patterns of development does Swift use in his argument? Annotate the essay to identify each pattern. Use the annotations accompanying "On Dumpster Diving" (page 660) as a guide.

THEMATIC CONNECTIONS

- "The Embalming of Mr. Jones" (page 285)
- "The Irish Famine, 1845–1849" (page 314)
- "I Want a Wife" (page 505)
- The Declaration of Independence (page 557)

ALICE WALKER

In Search of Our Mothers' Gardens

Born in 1944 in Eatontown, Georgia, one of eight children in a family of sharecroppers, Alice Walker began her writing career in the late 1960s. She had published four volumes of well-received fiction when her novel *The Color Purple* (1982) first brought her to wide public attention. This best-seller won the Pulitzer Prize for fiction and served as the basis for a popular film directed by Steven Spielberg. Since then, Walker has published a number of novels, poetry collections, and volumes of memoirs. A writer who often explores feminist and antiracist themes, she has also published several highly influential collections of essays, including *In Search of Our Mothers' Gardens* (1983).

Background: This title essay from Walker's 1983 collection was written in 1974, a time when the gains of the civil rights movement and the appearance of new African-American writers had resulted in a flowering of the black literary tradition in America. In particular, the writers of the Harlem Renaissance of some fifty years earlier—Langston Hughes, Jean Toomer, and Zora Neale Hurston, to name a few—were being reexamined after years of relative neglect. Their works were being introduced into college literature courses, and they themselves were becoming the subject of academic study. Even the work of less well-known figures—like the eighteenth-century poet Phillis Wheatley, who adopted a voice like that of her white owners—received increased interest. In this essay, Walker is particularly interested in examining the traditions of the black woman artist and considering how so many black women over the years had to suppress their creativity because of a racist and sexist culture that turned them into "mules."

I described her own nature and temperament. Told how they needed a larger life for their expression. . . . I pointed out that in lieu of proper channels, her emotions had overflowed into paths that dissipated them. I talked, beautifully I thought, about an art that would be born, an art that would open the way for women the likes of her. I asked her to hope, and build up an inner life against the coming of that day. . . . I sang, with a strange quiver in my voice, a promise song.

> —JEAN TOOMER,
> *"Avey,"* Cane

The poet speaking to a prostitute who falls asleep while he's talking— 1

When the poet Jean Toomer walked through the South in the early 2 twenties, he discovered a curious thing: black women whose spirituality was so intense, so deep, so *unconscious,* that they were themselves unaware of the richness they held. They stumbled blindly through their lives: creatures so abused and mutilated in body, so dimmed and confused by pain, that they considered themselves unworthy even of hope. In the selfless abstractions their bodies became to the men who used them, they became more than "sexual objects," even more than mere women: they became "Saints." Instead of being perceived as whole persons, their bodies became shrines, what was thought to be their minds became temples suitable for worship. These crazy Saints stared out at the world, wildly, like lunatics — or quietly, like suicides; and the "God" that was in their gaze was as mute as a great stone.

Who were these Saints? These crazy, loony, pitiful women? 3

Some of them, without a doubt, were our mothers and grandmothers. 4

In the still heat of the post-Reconstruction South, this is how they 5 seemed to Jean Toomer: exquisite butterflies trapped in an evil honey, toiling away their lives in an era, a century, that did not acknowledge them, except as "the *mule* of the world." They dreamed dreams that no one knew — not even themselves, in any coherent fashion — and saw visions no one could understand. They wandered or sat about the countryside crooning lullabies to ghosts, and drawing the mother of Christ in charcoal on courthouse walls.

They forced their minds to desert their bodies and their striving spir- 6 its sought to rise, like frail whirlwinds from the hard red clay. And when those frail whirlwinds fell, in scattered particles, upon the ground, no one mourned. Instead, men lit candles to celebrate the emptiness that remained, as people do who enter a beautiful but vacant space to resurrect a God.

Our mothers and grandmothers, some of them: moving to music not 7 yet written. And they waited.

They waited for a day when the unknown thing that was in them 8 would be made known; but guessed, somehow in their darkness, that on the day of their revelation they would be long dead. Therefore to Toomer they walked, and even ran, in slow motion. For they were going nowhere immediate, and the future was not yet within their grasp. And men took our mothers and grandmothers, "but got no pleasure from it." So complex was their passion and their calm.

To Toomer, they lay vacant and fallow as autumn fields, with harvest 9 time never in sight: and he saw them enter loveless marriages, without joy; and become prostitutes, without resistance, and become mothers of children, without fulfillment.

For these grandmothers and mothers of ours were not Saints, but 10 Artists; driven to a numb and bleeding madness by the springs of creativity in them for which there was no release. They were Creators, who lived lives of spiritual waste, because they were so rich in spirituality — which is the basis of Art — that the strain of enduring their unused and unwanted talent drove them insane. Throwing away this spirituality was their pathetic attempt to lighten the soul to a weight their work-worn, sexually abused bodies could bear.

What did it mean for a black woman to be an artist in our grandmothers' time? In our great-grandmothers' day? It is a question with an answer cruel enough to stop the blood.   11

Did you have a genius of a great-great-grandmother who died under some ignorant and depraved white overseer's lash? Or was she required to bake biscuits for a lazy backwater tramp, when she cried out in her soul to paint watercolors of sunsets, or the rain falling on the green and peaceful pasturelands? Or was her body broken and forced to bear children (who were more often than not sold away from her)—eight, ten, fifteen, twenty children—when her one joy was the thought of modeling heroic figures of rebellion, in stone or clay?   12

How was the creativity of the black woman kept alive, year after year and century after century, when for most of the years black people have been in America, it was a punishable crime for a black person to read or write? And the freedom to paint, to sculpt, to expand the mind with an action did not exist. Consider, if you can bear to imagine it, what might have been the result if singing, too, had been forbidden by law. Listen to the voices of Bessie Smith, Billie Holiday, Nina Simone, Roberta Flack, and Aretha Franklin, among others, and imagine those voices muzzled for life. Then you may begin to comprehend the lives of our "crazy," "Sainted" mothers and grandmothers. The agony of the lives of women who might have been Poets, Novelists, Essayists, and Short Story Writers (over a period of centuries), who died with their real gifts stifled within them.   13

And, if this were the end of the story, we would have cause to cry out in my paraphrase of Okot p'Bitek's* great poem: 14

O, my clanswomen
Let us all cry together!
Come, Let us mourn the death of our mother,
The death of a Queen
The ash that was produced
By a great fire!
O, this homestead is utterly dead
Close the gates
With *lacari* thorns,
For our mother
The creator of the Stool is lost!
And all the young women
Have perished in the wilderness!

But this is not the end of the story, for all the young women—our mothers and grandmothers, *ourselves*—have not perished in the wilderness. And if we ask ourselves why, and search for and find the answer, we will know beyond all efforts to erase it from our minds, just exactly who, and of what, we black American women are.   15

---

*EDS. NOTE—(1931–1982) Ugandan writer and anthropologist.

One example, perhaps the most pathetic, most misunderstood one, 16
can provide a backdrop for our mothers' work: Phillis Wheatley,* a slave in
the 1700s.

Virginia Woolf,** in her book *A Room of One's Own,* wrote that in order 17
for a woman to write fiction she must have two things, certainly: a room of
her own (the key and lock) and enough money to support herself.

What then are we to make of Phillis Wheatley, a slave, who owned not 18
even herself? This sickly, frail black girl who required a servant of her own
at times—her health was so precarious—and who, had she been white,
would have been easily considered the intellectual superior of all women
and most of the men in the society of her day.

Virginia Woolf wrote further, speaking of course not of our Phillis, 19
that "any woman born with a great gift in the sixteenth century [insert
"eighteenth century," insert "black woman," insert "born or made a slave"]
would certainly have gone crazed, shot herself, or ended her days in some
lonely cottage outside the village, half witch, half wizard [insert "Saint"],
feared and mocked at. For it needs little skill and psychology to be sure
that a highly gifted girl who had tried to use her gift for poetry would have
been so thwarted and hindered by contrary instincts [add "chains, guns,
the lash, the ownership of one's body by someone else, submission to an
alien religion"], that she must have lost her health and sanity to a certainty."

The key words, as they relate to Phillis, are "contrary instincts." For 20
when we read the poetry of Phillis Wheatley—and when we read the
novels of Nella Larsen or the oddly false-sounding autobiography of that
freest of all black women writers, Zora Hurston***—evidence of "contrary
instincts" is everywhere. Her loyalties were completely divided, as was,
without question, her mind.

But how could this be otherwise? Captured at seven, a slave of wealthy, 21
doting whites who instilled in her the "savagery" of the Africa they "res-
cued" her from . . . one wonders if she was even able to remember her
homeland as she had known it, or as it really was.

Yet, because she did try to use her gift for poetry in a world that made 22
her a slave, she was "so thwarted and hindered by . . . contrary instincts,
that she . . . lost her health. . . ." In the last years of brief life, burdened
not only with the need to express her gift but also with a penniless, friend-
less "freedom" and several small children for whom she was forced to do
strenuous work to feed, she lost her health, certainly. Suffering from mal-
nutrition and neglect and who knows what mental agonies, Phillis Wheatley died.

---

*EDS. NOTE—Eventually achieving her freedom, Wheatley (1753?–1784) pub-
lished several volumes of poetry and is considered the first important African-American
writer in the United States.
**EDS. NOTE—Early-twentieth-century English essayist and novelist.
***EDS. NOTE—Larsen (1891–1964) wrote realistic novels about black and white
relations; Hurston (1903–1960) is noted for his folklore research and novels and stories
that reproduce southern black dialect.

So torn by "contrary instincts" was black, kidnapped, enslaved Phillis 23
that her description of "the Goddess" — as she poetically called the Liberty
she did not have — is ironically, cruelly humorous. And, in fact, has held
Phillis up to ridicule for more than a century. It is usually read prior to
hanging Phillis's memory as that of a fool. She wrote:

> The Goddess comes, she moves divinely fair,
> Olive and laurel binds her *golden* hair.
> Wherever shines this native of the skies,
> Unnumber'd charms and recent graces rise. [My italics]

It is obvious that Phillis, the slave, combed the "Goddess's" hair every 24
morning; prior, perhaps, to bringing in the milk, or fixing her mistress's
lunch. She took her imagery from the one thing she saw elevated above all
others.

With the benefit of hindsight we ask, "How could she?" 25

But at last, Phillis, we understand. No more snickering when your stiff, 26
struggling, ambivalent lines are forced on us. We know now that you were
not an idiot or a traitor; only a sickly little black girl, snatched from your
home and country and made a slave; a woman who still struggled to sing
the song that was your gift, although in a land of barbarians who praised
you for your bewildered tongue. It is not so much what you sang, as that
you kept alive, in so many of our ancestors, *the notion of song.*

Black women are called, in the folklore that so aptly identifies one's 27
status in society, "the *mule* of the world," because we have been handed the
burdens that everyone else — *everyone* else — refused to carry. We have also
been called "Matriarchs," "Superwomen," and "Mean and Evil Bitches."
Not to mention "Castraters" and "Sapphire's Mama." When we have
pleaded for understanding, our character has been distorted; when we have
asked for simple caring, we have been handed empty inspirational appella-
tions, then stuck in the farthest corner. When we have asked for love, we
have been given children. In short, even our plainer gifts, our labors of
fidelity and love, have been knocked down our throats. To be an artist and a
black woman, even today, lowers our status in many respects, rather than
raises it: and yet, artists we will be.

Therefore we must fearlessly pull out of ourselves and look at and 28
identify with our lives the living creativity some of our great-grandmothers
were not allowed to know. I stress *some* of them because it is well known
that the majority of our great-grandmothers knew, even without "knowing" it, the reality of their spirituality, even if they didn't recognize it
beyond what happened in the singing at church — and they never had any
intention of giving it up.

How they did it — those millions of black women who were not Phillis 29
Wheatley, or Lucy Terry or Frances Harper or Zora Hurston or Nella

Larsen or Bessie Smith; or Elizabeth Catlett, or Katherine Dunham,* either—brings me to the title of this essay, "In Search of Our Mothers' Gardens," which is a personal account that is yet shared, in its theme and its meaning, by all of us. I found, while thinking about the far-reaching world of the creative black woman, that often the truest answer to a question that really matters can be found very close.

In the late 1920s my mother ran away from home to marry my father. Marriage, if not running away, was expected of seventeen-year-old girls. By the time she was twenty, she had two children and was pregnant with a third. Five children later, I was born. And this is how I came to know my mother: she seemed a large, soft, loving-eyed woman who was rarely impatient in our home. Her quick, violent temper was on view only a few times a year, when she battled with the white landlord who had the misfortune to suggest to her that her children did not need to go to school. 30

She made all the clothes we wore, even my brothers' overalls. She made all the towels and sheets we used. She spent the summers canning vegetables and fruits. She spent the winter evenings making quilts enough to cover all our beds. 31

During the "working" day, she labored beside—not behind—my father in the fields. Her day began before sunup, and did not end until late at night. There was never a moment for her to sit down, undisturbed, to unravel her own private thoughts; never a time free from interruption—by work or the noisy inquiries of her many children. And yet, it is to my mother—and all our mothers who were not famous—that I went in search of the secrets of what has fed that muzzled and often mutilated, but vibrant, creative spirit that the black woman has inherited, and that pops out in wild and unlikely places to this day. 32

But when, you will ask, did my overworked mother have time to know or care about feeding the creative spirit? 33

The answer is so simple that many of us have spent years discovering it. We have constantly looked high, when we should have looked high—and low. 34

For example: in the Smithsonian Institution in Washington, D.C., there hangs a quilt unlike any other in the world. In fanciful, inspired, and yet simple and identifiable figures, it portrays the story of the Crucifixion. It is considered rare, beyond price. Though it follows no known pattern of quilt-making, and though it is made of bits and pieces of worthless rags, it is obviously the work of a person of powerful imagination and deep spiritual feeling. Below this quilt I saw a note that says it was made by "an anonymous Black woman in Alabama, a hundred years ago." 35

---

*EDS. NOTE—Successful black female artists; the first five were writers, Smith was a singer and songwriter, Catlett a sculptor, and Dunham a dancer and choreographer.

If we could locate this "anonymous" black woman from Alabama, she 36
would turn out to be one of our grandmothers—an artist who left her
mark in the only materials she could afford, and in the only medium her
position in society allowed her to use.

As Virginia Woolf wrote further, in *A Room of One's Own:* 37

> Yet genius of a sort must have existed among women as it must have
> existed among the working class. [Change this to "slaves" and "the wives
> or the daughters of sharecroppers."] Now and again an Emily Brontë or a
> Robert Burns [change this to "a Zora Hurston or a Richard Wright"]
> blazes out and proves its presence. But certainly it never got itself on to
> paper. When, however, one reads of a witch being ducked, of a woman pos-
> sessed by devils [or "Sainthood"], of a wise woman selling herbs [our root
> workers], or even a very remarkable man who had a mother, then I think
> we are on the track of a lost novelist, a suppressed poet, of some mute and
> inglorious Jane Austen. . . . Indeed, I would venture to guess that Anon,
> who wrote so many poems without signing them, was often a woman. . . .

And so our mothers and grandmothers have, more often than not anon- 38
ymously, handed on the creative spark, the seed of the flower they themselves never hoped to see: or like a sealed letter they could not plainly read.

And so it is, certainly, with my own mother. Unlike "Ma" Rainey's* 39
songs, which retained their creator's name even while blasting forth from
Bessie Smith's mouth, no song or poem will bear my mother's name. Yet so
many of the stories that I write, that we all write, are my mother's stories.
Only recently did I fully realize this: that through years of listening to my
mother's stories of her life, I have absorbed not only the stories themselves,
but something of the manner in which she spoke, something of the
urgency that involves the knowledge that her stories—like her life—must
be recorded. It is probably for this reason that so much of what I have written is about characters whose counterparts in real life are so much older
than I am.

But the telling of these stories, which came from my mother's lips as 40
naturally as breathing, was not the only way my mother showed herself as
an artist. For stories, too, were subject to being distracted, to dying without
conclusion. Dinners must be started, and cotton must be gathered before
the big rains. The artist that was and is my mother showed itself to me only
after many years. This is what I finally noticed:

Like Mem, a character in *The Third Life of Grange Copeland,* my mother 41
adorned with flowers whatever shabby house we were forced to live in. And
not just your typical straggly country stand of zinnias, either. She planted
ambitious gardens—and still does—with over fifty different varieties of
plants that bloom profusely from early March until late November. Before she left home for the fields, she watered her flowers, chopped up the
grass, and laid out new beds. When she returned from the fields she might

---

*EDS. NOTE—Blues singer and songwriter of the early twentieth century.

divide clumps of bulbs, dig a cold pit, uproot and replant roses, or prune branches from her taller bushes or trees — until night came and it was too dark to see.

Whatever she planted grew as if by magic, and her fame as a grower of flowers spread over three counties. Because of her creativity with her flowers, even my memories of poverty are seen through a screen of blooms — sunflowers, petunias, roses, dahlias, forsythia, spirea, delphiniums, verbena . . . and on and on.

And I remember people coming to my mother's yard to be given cuttings from her flowers; I hear again the praise showered on her because whatever rocky soil she landed on, she turned into a garden. A garden so brilliant with colors, so original in its design, so magnificent with life and creativity, that to this day people drive by our house in Georgia — perfect strangers and imperfect strangers — and ask to stand or walk in my mother's art.

I notice that it is only when my mother is working in her flowers that she is radiant, almost to the point of being invisible — except as Creator: hand and eye. She is involved in work her soul must have. Ordering the universe in the image of her personal conception of Beauty.

Her face, as she prepares the Art that is her gift, is a legacy of respect she leaves to me, for all that illuminates and cherishes life. She has handed down respect for the possibilities — and the will to grasp them.

For her, so hindered and intruded upon in so many ways, being an artist has still been a daily part of her life. This ability to hold on, even in very simple ways, is work black women have done for a very long time.

This poem is not enough, but it is something, for the woman who literally covered the holes in our walls with sunflowers:

They were women then
My mama's generation
Husky of voice — Stout of
Step
With fists as well as
Hands
How they battered down
Doors
And ironed
Starched white
Shirts
How they led
Armies
Headragged Generals
Across mined
Fields
Booby-trapped
Kitchens
To discovery books
Desks

A place for us
How they knew what we
Must know
Without knowing a page
Of it
Themselves.

Guided by my heritage of a love of beauty and a respect for strength — 48
in search of my mother's garden, I found my own.

And perhaps in Africa over two hundred years ago, there was just such 49
a mother; perhaps she painted vivid and daring decorations in oranges and
yellows and greens on the walls of her hut; perhaps she sang — in a voice
like Roberta Flack's — *sweetly* over the compounds of her village; perhaps
she wove the most stunning mats or told the most ingenious stories of all
the village storytellers. Perhaps she was herself a poet — though only her
daughter's name is signed to the poems that we know.

Perhaps Phillis Wheatley's mother was also an artist. 50

Perhaps in more than Phillis Wheatley's biological life is her mother's 51
signature made clear.

•   •   •

COMPREHENSION

1. Why does Walker describe southern black women in the 1920s as "crazy, loony, pitiful women" (3)? What strengths did these women have?

2. In paragraph 5, Walker describes southern black women as "exquisite butterflies trapped in an evil honey." What is this "evil honey"? What does Walker believe poet Jean Toomer means when he characterizes these women as "the mule of the world"?

3. What is the "music not yet written" (7) to which Walker says these women moved? What, according to Walker, were they waiting for?

4. Walker sees the women not as saints but as something else. How does she characterize them? Why?

5. In paragraph 11, Walker asks, "What did it mean for a black woman to be an artist in our grandmothers' time?" In paragraph 13, she asks how their creativity was kept alive. Paraphrase her answers to these questions.

6. Why, according to Walker, is what she describes in paragraphs 1 through 14 "not the end of the story"? What is the rest of this story?

7. Paraphrase the story of Phillis Wheatley's life. What does her story contribute to Walker's essay?

8. What, specifically, does Walker believe black women should do? In what sense should they see their mothers and grandmothers as positive examples? As negative examples? Why does she call this essay "In Search of Our Mothers' Gardens"?

9. How does Walker link herself with her mother and grandmother? What legacy have they left her?

PURPOSE AND AUDIENCE

1. This essay was first published in *Ms.*, a feminist magazine. In what sense is it a feminist essay?

2. In this essay, Walker addresses African-American women. What does she advise her readers? Do you think her recommendations are relevant to women of other races? To men? Why or why not?

3. What is Walker's thesis? Do you think she expects her audience to be sympathetic to this position? Explain your reasoning.

STYLE AND STRUCTURE

1. The essay opens with a quotation from noted African-American novelist and poet Jean Toomer. Is this an effective opening strategy? Why do you think Walker begins her essay this way?

2. Throughout her essay Walker (sometimes quoting Toomer) uses elaborate **figures of speech** to describe the women she is writing about. Give examples of some of the metaphors she uses, and evaluate their effectiveness. Do you think she uses too many figures of speech?

3. In paragraphs 14, 23, and 37, Walker quotes three women writers; in paragraph 47, she presents a poem of her own. What do these excerpts have in common? Do you think they are distracting digressions or vital components of the essay? Explain.

4. Is Walker's tone sorrowful? Bitter? Regretful? Strident? On what do you base your conclusion?

5. Why does Walker summarize her own mother's life in paragraphs 30 through 32? What is the connection between the life of Walker's mother and the life of Phillis Wheatley? Do you think the biographical information Walker provides about these two women is necessary? Why or why not?

6. Walker introduces some of her key ideas with questions. For example, in paragraph 3 she asks, "Who were these Saints?" Where else does she ask questions? Does she answer them? Why do you suppose she uses this strategy instead of making direct statements?

VOCABULARY PROJECTS

1. Define each of the following words as it is used in this selection.

overseer (12)	barbarians (26)	counterparts (39)
lash (12)	matriarchs (27)	

2. What images are usually associated with the word *garden*? Is *garden* simply a metaphor for art in this essay, or does it have other meanings as well?

JOURNAL ENTRY

In paragraph 27, Walker says, "To be an artist and a black woman, even today, lowers our status in many respects, rather than raises it." Do you agree with Walker's statement? Do you think it is true for all women? For any artist?

WRITING WORKSHOP

1. In what sense might you see yourself as an artist? What kinds of creative expression do you believe constitute your own garden? Using a series of examples, develop an essay about these ideas.

2. Interview your mother or grandmother (or another female relative) on the subject of the creative outlets available to women of her generation—and the obstacles to those outlets. Use narration, exemplification, and cause and effect to shape an essay about your relative's experiences and those of her peers.

3. Think about the various kinds of art Walker discusses in this essay—everything from poetry to quilting to singing to gardening. Do you consider all her examples legitimate kinds of art, or do you have different standards? Write a definition of *art* using classification and division as well as exemplification to develop your definition.

COMBINING THE PATTERNS

What patterns of development does Walker use in her essay? Annotate the essay to identify each pattern. Use the annotations accompanying "On Dumpster Diving" (page 660) as a guide.

THEMATIC CONNECTIONS

- "My Mother Never Worked" (page 96)
- "The Way to Rainy Mountain" (page 169)
- "The Men We Carry in Our Minds" (page 456)
- "Mother Tongue" (page 462)

RICHARD RODRIGUEZ

Strange Tools

The son of working-class immigrants from Mexico, Richard Rodriguez (b. 1944) grew up in Sacramento, California, and received an undergraduate degree from Stanford University and a doctorate in English Renaissance literature from the University of California at Berkeley. He initially sought a career as a college educator but abandoned that pursuit to become a full-time writer. His first book, the highly praised *Hunger of Memory* (1981), was a series of essays tracing the story of his education and its influence on his relationship with his parents. His later books include *Days of Obligation: An Argument with My Mexican Father* (1992) and *Brown: The Last Discovery of America* (2002), a meditation on personal identity at cultural borderlines. A regular essayist on *NewsHour with Jim Lehrer* on public television, Rodriguez is also a frequent commentator on National Public Radio, a correspondent with the Pacific News Service, and contributing editor to a number of periodicals.

Background: Earlier in *Hunger of Memory,* from which the following selection is excerpted, Rodriguez describes discovering as a graduate student the book *The Uses of Literacy* by Richard Hoggart. In this book, Hoggart defines a certain kind of student as a "scholarship boy," a child of uneducated working-class parents who himself strives desperately for academic achievement, "who has to be more and more alone if he is going to 'get on.'" Such a child's gradual mental and emotional separation from his family, his growing allegiance to the classroom, his wrenching sense of personal loss, his anxiety even as he succeeds at school — all these qualities Rodriguez recognized immediately as markers of his own childhood, exacerbated by his parents' limited English skills. As Rodriguez concludes, "If, because of my schooling, I had grown culturally separated from my parents, my education finally had given me ways of speaking and caring about that fact."

From an early age I knew that my mother and father could read and   1
write both Spanish and English. I had observed my father making his way through what, I now suppose, must have been income tax forms. On other occasions I waited apprehensively while my mother read onion-paper letters airmailed from Mexico with news of a relative's illness or death. For both my parents, however, reading was something done out of necessity and as quickly as possible. Never did I see either of them read an entire book. Nor did I see them read for pleasure. Their reading consisted of work manuals, prayer books, newspapers, recipes.

Richard Hoggart imagines how, at home,   2

> ... [The scholarship boy] sees strewn around, and reads regularly himself, magazines which are never mentioned at school, which seem not to

belong to the world to which the school introduces him; at school he hears about and reads books never mentioned at home. When he brings those books into the house they do not take their place with other books which the family are reading, for often there are none or almost none; his books look, rather, like strange tools.

In our house each school year would begin with my mother's careful instruction: "Don't write in your books so we can sell them at the end of the year." The remark was echoed in public by my teachers, but only in part: "Boys and girls, don't write in your books. You must learn to treat them with great care and respect."

OPEN THE DOORS OF YOUR MIND WITH BOOKS, read the red and white   3
poster over the nun's desk in early September. It soon was apparent to me that reading was the classroom's central activity. Each course had its own book. And the information gathered from a book was unquestioned. READ TO LEARN, the sign on the wall advised in December. I privately wondered: What was the connection between reading and learning? Did one learn something only by reading it? Was an idea only an idea if it could be written down? In June, CONSIDER BOOKS YOUR BEST FRIENDS. Friends? Reading was, at best, only a chore. I needed to look up whole paragraphs of words in a dictionary. Lines of type were dizzying, the eye having to move slowly across the page, then down, and across. . . . The sentences of the first books I read were coolly impersonal. Toned hard. What most bothered me, however, was the isolation reading required. To console myself for the loneliness I'd feel when I read, I tried reading in a very soft voice. Until: "Who is doing all that talking to his neighbor?" Shortly after, remedial reading classes were arranged for me with a very old nun.

At the end of each school day, for nearly six months, I would meet with   4
her in the tiny room that served as the school's library but was actually only a storeroom for used textbooks and a vast collection of *National Geographics*. Everything about our sessions pleased me: the smallness of the room; the noise of the janitor's broom hitting the edge of the long hallway outside the door; the green of the sun, lighting the wall; and the old woman's face blurred white with a beard. Most of the time we took turns. I began with my elementary text. Sentences of astonishing simplicity seemed to me lifeless and drab: "The boys ran from the rain . . . She wanted to sing . . . The kite rose in the blue." Then the old nun would read from her favorite books, usually biographies of early American presidents. Playfully she ran through complex sentences, calling the words alive with her voice, making it seem that the author somehow was speaking directly to me. I smiled just to listen to her. I sat there and sensed for the very first time some possibility of fellowship between a reader and a writer, a communication, never *intimate* like that I heard spoken words at home convey, but one nonetheless *personal*.

One day the nun concluded a session by asking me why I was so reluc-   5
tant to read by myself. I tried to explain; said something about the way written words made me feel all alone — almost, I wanted to add but didn't,

as when I spoke to myself in a room just emptied of furniture. She studied my face as I spoke; she seemed to be watching more than listening. In an uneventful voice she replied that I had nothing to fear. Didn't I realize that reading would open up whole new worlds? A book could open doors for me. It could introduce me to people and show me places I never imagined existed. She gestured toward the bookshelves. (Bare-breasted African women danced, and the shiny hubcaps of automobiles on the back covers of the *Geographic* gleamed in my mind.) I listened with respect. But her words were not very influential. I was thinking then of another consequence of literacy, one I was too shy to admit but nonetheless trusted. Books were going to make me "educated." *That* confidence enabled me, several months later, to overcome my fear of the silence.

In fourth grade I embarked upon a grandiose reading program. "Give   6
me the names of important books," I would say to startled teachers. They soon found out that I had in mind "adult books." I ignored their suggestion of anything I suspected was written for children. (Not until I was in college, as a result, did I read *Huckleberry Finn* or *Alice's Adventures in Wonderland.*) Instead, I read *The Scarlet Letter* and Franklin's *Autobiography.* And whatever I read I read for extra credit. Each time I finished a book, I reported the achievement to a teacher and basked in the praise my effort earned. Despite my best efforts, however, there seemed to be more and more books I needed to read. At the library I would literally tremble as I came upon whole shelves of books I hadn't read. So I read and I read and I read: *Great Expectations;* all the short stories of Kipling; *The Babe Ruth Story;* the entire first volume of the *Encyclopaedia Britannica* (A–ANSTEY); the *Iliad; Moby Dick; Gone with the Wind; The Good Earth; Ramona; Forever Amber; The Lives of the Saints; Crime and Punishment; The Pearl.* . . . Librarians who initially frowned when I checked out the maximum ten books at a time started saving books they thought I might like. Teachers would say to the rest of the class, "I only wish the rest of you took reading as seriously as Richard obviously does."

But at home I would hear my mother wondering, "What do you see in   7
your books?" (Was reading a hobby like her knitting? Was so much reading even healthy for a boy? Was it the sign of "brains"? Or was it just a convenient excuse for not helping around the house on Saturday mornings?) Always, "What do you see . . . ?"

What *did* I see in my books? I had the idea that they were crucial for my   8
academic success, though I couldn't have said exactly how or why. In the sixth grade I simply concluded that what gave a book its value was some major idea or theme it contained. If that core essence could be mined and memorized, I would become learned like my teachers. I decided to record in a notebook the themes of the books that I read. After reading *Robinson Crusoe,* I wrote that its theme was "the value of learning to live by oneself." When I completed *Wuthering Heights,* I noted the danger of "letting emotions get out of control." Rereading these brief moralistic appraisals usually left me disheartened. I couldn't believe that they were really the source

of reading's value. But for many more years, they constituted the only means I had of describing to myself the educational value of books.

In spite of my earnestness, I found reading a pleasurable activity. I came to enjoy the lonely good company of books. Early on weekday mornings, I'd read in my bed. I'd feel a mysterious comfort then, reading in the dawn quiet — the bluegray silence interrupted by the occasional churning of the refrigerator motor a few rooms away or the more distant sounds of a city bus beginning its run. On weekends I'd go to the public library to read, surrounded by old men and women. Or, if the weather was fine, I would take my books to the park and read in the shade of a tree. A warm summer evening was my favorite reading time. Neighbors would leave for vacation and I would water their lawns. I would sit through the twilight on the front porches or in backyards, reading to the cool, whirling sounds of the sprinklers.

I also had favorite writers. But often those writers I enjoyed most I was least able to value. When I read William Saroyan's *The Human Comedy*, I was immediately pleased by the narrator's warmth and the charm of his story. But as quickly I became suspicious. A book so enjoyable to read couldn't be very "important." Another summer I determined to read all the novels of Dickens. Reading his fat novels, I loved the feeling I got — after the first hundred pages — of being at home in a fictional world where I knew the names of the characters and cared about what was going to happen to them. And it bothered me that I was forced away at the conclusion, when the fiction closed tight, like a fortune-teller's fist — the futures of all the major characters neatly resolved. I never knew how to take such feelings seriously, however. Nor did I suspect that these experiences could be part of a novel's meaning. Still, there were pleasures to sustain me after I'd finish my books. Carrying a volume back to the library, I would be pleased by its weight. I'd run my fingers along the edge of the pages and marvel at the breadth of my achievement. Around my room, growing stacks of paperback books reenforced my assurance.

I entered high school having read hundreds of books. My habit of reading made me a confident speaker and writer of English. Reading also enabled me to sense something of the shape, the major concerns, of Western thought. (I was able to say something about Dante and Descartes and Engels and James Baldwin in my high school term papers.) In these various ways, books brought me academic success as I hoped that they would. But I was not a good reader. Merely bookish, I lacked a point of view when I read. Rather, I read in order to acquire a point of view. I vacuumed books for epigrams, scraps of information, ideas, themes — anything to fill the hollow within me and make me feel educated. When one of my teachers suggested to his drowsy tenth-grade English class that a person could not have a "complicated idea" until he had read at least two thousand books, I heard the remark without detecting either its irony or its very complicated truth. I merely determined to compile a list of all the books I had ever read. Harsh with myself, I included only once a title I might have read several times. (How, after all, could one read a book more than once?) And I included only those books over a hundred pages in length. (Could anything shorter be a book?)

There was yet another high school list I compiled. One day I came 12 across a newspaper article about the retirement of an English professor at a nearby state college. The article was accompanied by a list of the "hundred most important books of Western Civilization." "More than anything else in my life," the professor told the reporter with finality, "these books have made me all that I am." That was the kind of remark I couldn't ignore. I clipped out the list and kept it for the several months it took me to read all of the titles. Most books, of course, I barely understood. While reading Plato's *Republic*, for instance, I needed to keep looking at the book jacket comments to remind myself what the text was about. Nevertheless, with the special patience and superstition of a scholarship boy, I looked at every word of the text. And by the time I reached the last word, relieved, I convinced myself that I had read *The Republic*. In a ceremony of great pride, I solemnly crossed Plato off my list.

* * *

COMPREHENSION

1. What do Rodriguez's parents read, and for what purpose? What is their attitude toward books?

2. How is Rodriguez's home like the home of the "scholarship boy" (2) described by Richard Hoggart?

3. What attitude toward books is communicated to Rodriguez at school?

4. Why does Rodriguez have to take remedial reading classes? What does he learn in his sessions with the elderly nun? How do her ideas about the purpose of reading differ from his?

5. How does Rodriguez finally "overcome [his] fear of the silence" (5)?

6. What motivates Rodriguez to begin his "grandiose reading program" (6)? How does his mother react to his reading?

7. Why does Rodriguez write down the theme of each book he reads?

8. What benefits does Rodriguez derive from his reading?

PURPOSE AND AUDIENCE

1. In paragraph 11, speaking of his high school years, Rodriguez says, "But I was not a good reader. Merely bookish, I lacked a point of view when I read. Rather, I read to acquire a point of view." What does he mean? Does Rodriguez's essay illustrate that he has now acquired a point of view? Explain.

2. Do you think Rodriguez's purpose here is to promote the importance of reading? To analyze his own misguided efforts to educate himself? To reveal something about his upbringing or about his education? Might he have several different purposes?

3. Rodriguez grew up in a bilingual household. Do you think his essay has relevance only for those from bilingual families, or do you think his comments apply just as well to a broader audience? Explain.

STYLE AND STRUCTURE

1. Throughout this essay, Rodriguez lists specific titles of books that he has read. Why? Are these lists essential, or could he have omitted them? Explain.

2. Paragraph 7 is much shorter than the other paragraphs in this essay. Why? What purpose does this paragraph serve?

3. In paragraph 9, Rodriguez paints a picture of the "dawn quiet" during which he reads each day. What does this passage reveal about him?

4. In paragraph 10, Rodriguez compares the conclusion of a book to a "fortune-teller's fist." What does he mean?

VOCABULARY PROJECTS

1. Define each of the following words as it is used in this selection.

fellowship (4)   earnestness (9)
grandiose (6)   sustain (10)
basked (6)

2. What does Rodriguez mean in paragraph 11 when he says he "vacuumed books"? What other expression could you substitute for this phrase?

JOURNAL ENTRY

In paragraph 3, Rodriguez gives three examples of slogans that appeared on posters in his classroom. Create several new slogans designed to promote reading in the elementary school classroom, and describe how each poster might be illustrated.

WRITING WORKSHOP

1. Write an essay in which you discuss the role that books played in the household in which you grew up. What did your parents read, and for what purpose? What did you learn from their reading habits and attitudes? How are your own reading habits and attitudes like and unlike theirs?

2. Clearly, books changed Rodriguez's life. What activity had a similar impact on you? Write an essay in which you explain how your character and personality were shaped by the activity you pursued.

3. Make a list of five or six childhood books you remember with affection, and then write a combined book review in which you try to explain why these books are memorable. Include brief plot summaries (in present tense) and evaluations as well as a thesis statement that ties the books together and communicates their importance.

COMBINING THE PATTERNS

What patterns of development does Rodriguez use? Annotate the essay to identify each pattern. Use the annotations accompanying "On Dumpster Diving" (page 660) as a guide.

THEMATIC CONNECTIONS

- "Only Daughter" (page 84)
- "The Human Cost of an Illiterate Society" (page 229)
- "Television: The Plug-In Drug" (page 325)
- "Mother Tongue" (page 462)

WRITING ASSIGNMENTS FOR COMBINING THE PATTERNS

1. Reread Michael Huu Truong's essay at the beginning of this chapter. Responding to the same assignment he was given ("Write an essay about the person and/or place that defined your childhood"), use several different patterns to communicate to readers what your childhood was like.

2. Write an essay about the political, social, or economic events that you believe have dominated and defined your life, or a stage in your life. Use **cause and effect** and any other patterns you think are appropriate to explain and illustrate why these events were important to you and how they affected you.

3. Develop a thesis statement that draws a general conclusion about the nature, quality, or effectiveness of advertising in print media (in newspapers or magazines or on billboards). Write an essay that supports this thesis statement with a series of very specific paragraphs. Use the patterns of development that best help you to characterize particular advertisements.

4. Exactly what do you think it means to be an American? Write a **definition** essay that answers this question, developing your definition with whatever patterns best serve your purpose.

5. Many of the essays in this text recount the writers' personal experiences. Identify one essay in which a writer describes experiences that are either similar to your own or in sharp contrast to your own. Then write a **comparison-and-contrast** essay in which you *either* compare *or* contrast your experiences with those of the writer. Use several different patterns to develop your essay.

COLLABORATIVE ACTIVITY FOR COMBINING THE PATTERNS

Working in pairs, choose an essay from Chapters 4 through 12 of this text. Then, working individually, identify the various patterns of development used in the essay. When you have finished, compare notes with the other student in your group. Have both of you identified the same patterns in the essay? If not, try to reach a consensus. Working together, write a paragraph summarizing why each pattern is used and explaining how the various patterns work together to support the essay's thesis.

INTERNET ASSIGNMENT FOR COMBINING THE PATTERNS

Write an essay in which you consider the moral and ethical implications of new breakthroughs in cloning. Use several different patterns to support your thesis and to illustrate the potential benefits and/or dangers of cloning. Visit the following Web sites to learn more about the process of cloning and the future possibilities it suggests.

Time Newsfile: Cloning
<time.com/time/newsfiles/cloning>
This site sponsored by *Time* magazine offers information about the cloning process, futurist scenarios, and a discussion of the ethics of cloning.

Actionbioscience.org
<actionbioscience.org/biotech>
This site, sponsored by BioScience Productions, Inc., an organization promoting bioscience literacy, includes links to articles on cloning and the ethical issues surrounding cloning technology, as well as links to other sites on the cloning debate.

Human Cloning Foundation
<humancloning.org>
This nonprofit group's site links to interviews, frequently asked questions, essays about the benefits of human cloning, and lists of books and movies that address human cloning issues.

APPENDIX

Writing a Research Paper

When you write a research paper, you supplement your own ideas with material from books, articles, television programs, the Internet, and electronic databases. As you research and write, remember what you have learned about the writing process, and keep in mind that your main task is to present ideas clearly and convincingly. You will have an easier time writing a research paper if you follow an orderly process:

1. Choose a topic.
2. Look for sources.
3. Narrow your topic.
4. Do research.
5. Take notes.
6. Watch out for plagiarism.
7. Draft a thesis statement.
8. Make an outline.
9. Write your paper.
10. Document your sources.

STEP 1: CHOOSING A TOPIC

The first step in writing a research paper is finding a topic to write about. Before you decide on a topic, ask yourself the following questions:

- What is my page limit?
- When is my paper due?
- How many sources am I expected to use?

The answers to these questions can help you make sure your topic is neither too broad nor too narrow.

When Caitlin Byrne, a student in a college composition course, was asked to write a three- to five-page research paper due in five weeks, she knew she wanted to write about what could have been done to prevent the kind of terrorist violence that occurred on September 11, 2001. Caitlin was interested in airport security—especially since an hour-long delay at a security checkpoint had recently caused her to miss a flight. She realized, however, that the general topic "airport security" would be too broad for a short paper and that a topic like "my long delay at the airport" would be much too narrow. "What can be done to improve airport security?", however, might work well: she could discuss the topic in the required number of pages and would be able to complete her paper within the time limit.

STEP 2: LOOKING FOR SOURCES

To get an overview of your topic and see if you can find enough to write about, you could begin by going to the Internet and doing a keyword search. You should also survey the resources of your library. (First, arrange a meeting with a college librarian, who can answer questions, give you suggestions, and point you toward helpful resources.)

In the library, begin by looking at the *subject catalog* or its *online central information system* to see what books and articles about your topic are listed there. (Frequently, the online central information system contains the library's catalog as well as a number of databases you can search.) For example, under the general topic "airport security," Caitlin found a variety of books, numerous articles, and four government studies on her topic.

STEP 3: NARROWING YOUR TOPIC

As you survey the library's resources, the material you find should help you narrow your topic further.

Caitlin discovered a number of books and articles that focused on airport security. Several of them dealt with racial profiling—searching people solely on the basis of their race. Two or three of these articles suggested that the government could eliminate racial profiling by creating a national identity card that each citizen could carry. Caitlin knew from her instructor's guidelines that the purpose of her paper should be either to *present information* (for example, to discuss what was being done around the country to increase airport security), or to *make a point* (for example, that some form of national ID card could speed up airport security checks as well as eliminate racial profiling). Caitlin decided on the second option.

STEP 4: DOING RESEARCH

Once you have narrowed your topic, you need to gather information. Begin by going back to the library and checking out any books you think will be useful. Next, photocopy any periodical articles you need, and make copies of material on microfilm or microfiche. If you use a computer database such as Expanded Academic ASAP or FirstSearch, print out the text of any articles you plan to use or download them onto a diskette. You can also browse the Web for possible sources. (Remember, though, that the quality and reliability of material found on the Web can vary, so use only information from reliable sources — a Web page sponsored by a well-known national publication or organization or by a university, for example.)

When Caitlin searched the Web using the keywords *airport security* and *racial profiling,* she found an article on racial profiling that was published in *The Atlantic Monthly.* Her instructor told her that this publication was well-respected and usually reliable so she could be sure that the writer was someone who knew a lot about his subject.

STEP 5: TAKING NOTES

Once you have gathered the material you will need, read it carefully, writing down any information you think you can use in your paper. As you take notes, record relevant information in a computer file you set up for your paper.

When you use information from a source in your paper, you do not always *quote* the exact words of your source. In fact, most often you *paraphrase* or *summarize* a source, putting its ideas into your own words. For this reason, most of your notes should be in the form of paraphrase or summary.

When you **paraphrase,** you put the ideas of a source into your own words, following the order and emphasis of the original. You paraphrase when you want to make a discussion easier to understand while still conveying a clear sense of the original. Here is a passage from "Why Fear National ID Cards?" by Alan M. Dershowitz (page 590), an article Caitlin uses in her paper, followed by her paraphrase.

Original: Finally, there is the question of the right to anonymity. I don't believe we can afford to recognize such a right in this age of terrorism. No such right is hinted at in the Constitution. And though the Supreme Court has identified a right to privacy, privacy and anonymity are not the same. American taxpayers, voters, and drivers long ago gave up any right of anonymity without loss of our right to engage in lawful conduct with zones of privacy. Rights are a function of experience, and our recent experiences teach that it is far too easy to be anonymous — even to create a false identity — in this large and decentralized country. A national ID card would not prevent all threats of terrorism, but it would make it more difficult for potential terrorists to hide in open view, as many of the September 11 hijackers apparently managed to do.

Paraphrase: According to Alan Dershowitz, a right to anonymity would undercut the country's ability to deal with terrorism. The right to anonymity is not recognized by the United States Constitution, and there is a clear difference between anonymity and privacy, a right that the

> Constitution does acknowledge. As anyone who files a tax
> return or obtains a social security card knows, many daily
> activities require people to give up a certain degree of
> anonymity. In many other areas of our lives, however, we
> have a great deal of personal privacy. A national ID card
> would make it harder for terrorists to use this privacy to
> live among us and to travel freely. At the same time, it
> would give people the security of knowing that hijackers
> could not carry out their plans as easily as they did on
> September 11 (591).

When you write a **summary,** you also put the ideas of a source into your own words. But unlike a paraphrase, a summary condenses a passage, giving only the general meaning of the original. Here is Caitlin's summary of the original passage quoted above.

> **Summary:** According to Alan Dershowitz, a national ID card
> would require every citizen to give up a certain degree of
> anonymity, but it would also make it difficult for people
> to move anonymously around the country and engage in
> terrorist activities.

When you **quote,** you restate the exact words of a source, enclosing them in quotation marks. Because too many quotations can distract readers, quote only when an author's words are memorable or when you want to give readers the flavor of the original.

To show readers that you are using a source and to integrate source material smoothly into your paper, introduce paraphrases, summaries, and quotations with a phrase that identifies the source or its author. You can position this identifying phrase at various places in a sentence. You can also use different words to introduce source material—for example, *points out, observes, comments, notes, remarks,* and *concludes.*

> **Identifying Phrase at the Beginning:** According to the article "Why
> Fear National ID Cards?," "A national ID card would not
> prevent all threats of terrorism, but it would make it
> more difficult for potential terrorists to hide in open
> view, as many of the September 11 hijackers apparently
> managed to do" (591).

> **Identifying Phrase at the End:** "A national ID card would not pre-
> vent all threats of terrorism, but it would make it more
> difficult for potential terrorists to hide in open view,
> as many of the September 11 hijackers apparently managed
> to do," claims Alan Dershowitz (591).

> **Identifying Phrase in the Middle:** "A national ID card would not
> prevent all threats of terrorism," observes constitutional
> law expert Alan Dershowitz, "but it would make it more
> difficult for potential terrorists to hide in open view,
> as many of the September 11 hijackers apparently managed
> to do" (591).

STEP 6: WATCHING OUT FOR PLAGIARISM

As a rule, document any words or ideas from an outside source that are not **common knowledge** — information most readers will probably know or factual information widely available in reference works. When you present information from another source as if it were your own (whether intentionally or unintentionally), you are committing **plagiarism** — and plagiarism is theft. You can avoid plagiarism by understanding what you must document and what you do not have to document.

☑ GUIDELINES FOR AVOIDING PLAGIARISM

YOU MUST DOCUMENT

- Word-for-word quotations from a print or online source
- Ideas from a print or online source that you put in your own words
- Tables, charts, graphs, or statistics from a print or online source

YOU DO NOT NEED TO DOCUMENT

- Your own ideas
- Common knowledge
- Familiar quotations

Avoiding Common Errors That Lead to Plagiarism

Whenever you consult a source to get ideas for your writing, be careful to avoid the errors that commonly lead to plagiarism. The following paragraph from William Safire's essay "The Threat of National ID" (page 586) and the four rules listed after it will help you understand and avoid these common errors.

Original: Today's diatribe will be scorned as alarmist by the same security-mongers who shrugged off our attorney general's attempt to abolish habeas corpus (which libertarian protests and the Bush administration's sober second thoughts seem to be aborting). But the lust to take advantage of the public's fear of terrorist penetration by penetrating everyone's private lives — this time including the lives of U.S. citizens protected by the Fourth Amendment — is gaining popularity. (Safire, William. "The Threat of National ID." *Patterns for College Writing.* 9th ed. Ed. Laurie G. Kirszner and Stephen R. Mandell. New York: Bedford, 2004. 586-88.)

1. Identify Your Source

Plagiarism: Even though the government has pulled back from its most extreme plans to defeat terrorists, there is still a danger that the government will undermine our Fourth Amendment rights.

Even though the writer does not quote Safire directly, she still must identify him as the source of her paraphrased material. She can do this by adding an identifying phrase as well as documentation.

> **Correct:** According to William Safire, even though the government has pulled back from its most extreme plans to defeat terrorists, there is still a danger that the government will undermine our Fourth Amendment rights (587).

2. Place Borrowed Words in Quotation Marks

> **Plagiarism:** According to William Safire, the government as well as big business is increasingly willing to take advantage of the public's fear of terrorist penetration by penetrating everyone's private lives (587).

Although the writer cites Safire as her source, the passage incorrectly uses Safire's exact words without quoting them. The writer must either place the borrowed words in quotation marks or paraphrase them.

> **Correct (Borrowed Words in Quotation Marks):** According to William Safire, the government as well as big business is increasingly willing to "take advantage of the public's fear of terrorist penetration by penetrating everyone's private lives" (587).

> **Correct (Borrowed Words Paraphrased):** According to William Safire, the government as well as big business is increasingly willing to use the excuse of terrorism to extend the scope of its surveillance power (587).

3. Use Your Own Wording

> **Plagiarism:** Those who criticize plans for a national ID card will be dismissed as excessive by the same people who had no problem when the attorney general attempted to do away with habeas corpus protection. (Thankfully, the administration seems to have decided to abandon these plans.) Even so, the drive to exploit people's fear of terrorism by intruding into their private affairs — thus violating the Fourth Amendment — is becoming increasingly popular (Safire 587).

Even though the writer acknowledges Safire as her primary source, and even though she does not use Safire's exact words, her passage closely follows the order, emphasis, syntax, and phrasing of the original. In the following passage, the writer uses her own wording, quoting one distinctive phrase from her source.

> **Correct:** Unfortunately, many people have no problem with the government's plan for a national ID card. According to William Safire, these people do not realize the danger

```
of the government's "lust to take advantage of the pub-
lic's fear of terrorist penetration" (587). As Safire
makes clear, this intrusion into people's private lives
clearly violates the Fourth Amendment (587).
```

4. Distinguish Your Ideas from the Source's Ideas

Plagiarism: Unfortunately, many people have no problem with the government's plan for a national ID card. These people are afraid and want to be protected, and they do not realize that government is more than willing to take advantage of their fears. Its attempt to institute a national ID card is simply another unwarranted (and dangerous) incursion into "the lives of U.S. citizens protected by the Fourth Amendment" (Safire 587).

In the preceding passage, it appears that only the quotation in the last sentence is borrowed from Safire's article. In fact, the ideas in the second sentence are also Safire's. The writer should use an identifying phrase (such as "According to Safire") to acknowledge the borrowed material in this sentence and to indicate where it begins.

Correct: Unfortunately, many people have no problem with the government's plan for a national ID card. According to William Safire, these people are afraid and want to be protected, and they do not realize that government is more than willing to take advantage of their fears (587). Its attempt to institute a national ID card is simply another unwarranted (and dangerous) incursion into "the lives of U.S. citizens protected by the Fourth Amendment" (587).

Avoid Plagiarism with Online Sources

Most students are aware that using long passages (or entire articles) from a print source without documenting the source constitutes plagiarism. Unfortunately, many of the same people assume that borrowing material found on a Web site or elsewhere online without documentation is acceptable. However, such borrowing is also plagiarism. Perhaps these students feel differently about online borrowing because it is so easy to cut and paste from an online source into a text document. They may also see copying online material as acceptable because—with authors often unidentified online—no one appears to be taking credit for the source. No matter what the explanation is for many students' casual treatment of online sources, instructors will consider the use of undocumented words or ideas from online sources to be just as serious as the same kind of plagiarism from a print source. Therefore, you must document words or ideas you get from online sources as well as from print sources.

It should go without saying that downloading entire papers from Web sites that sell essays to college students and turning them in as your own work is plagiarism. Such conduct is unethical. It is unfair to you, your instructor, and your fellow students, and it subverts the learning process, which is the main purpose of going to college.

STEP 7: DRAFTING A THESIS STATEMENT

After you have taken notes, review the information you have gathered and draft a **thesis statement** — a single sentence that states the main idea of your paper and tells readers what to expect.

After completing her research, Caitlin Byrne came up with the following thesis statement for her paper on airport security.

> **Thesis Statement:** If every U.S. citizen had a national ID card or a Safe Traveler Card, airports could screen for terrorists more effectively than they do now and avoid procedures that single out individuals solely on the basis of race.

STEP 8: MAKING AN OUTLINE

Once you have drafted a thesis statement, you are ready to make an outline from your notes. Your outline, which covers just the body paragraphs of your paper, can be either a *topic outline* (in which each idea is expressed in a word or short phrase) or a *sentence outline* (in which each idea is expressed in a complete sentence). When it is finished, your outline will be your guide as you write your paper.

After reviewing her notes, Caitlin Byrne constructed the following sentence outline for her paper. Notice that she uses roman numerals for first-level headings, capital letters for second-level headings, and arabic numerals for third-level headings.

> **Thesis Statement:** If every US citizen had a national ID card or a Safe Traveler Card, airports could screen for terrorists more effectively than they do now and avoid procedures that single out individuals solely on the basis of race.
>
> I. To avoid charges of harassing people of Middle Eastern descent, many airports have instituted a policy of searching passengers at random.
>   A. Random searches have advantages.
>   1. Random searches occasionally detect people who would not be detected by racial profiling.
>   2. Random searches encourage security personnel to scrutinize all passengers.
>   B. Random searches also have disadvantages.
>   1. Random searches waste time and resources on people who pose no threat.

2. Security personnel focus on passengers randomly selected by a computer and not on specific passengers.

II. Other strategies are more effective for screening airline passengers, but they also have disadvantages.
    A. Routine preflight security checks for all passengers are effective.
       1. They are time consuming.
       2. They are expensive.
    B. New developments in airport security could alleviate problems.
       1. They have not been perfected.
       2. They are expensive.

III. The cheapest and most efficient airport security method is some type of Safe Traveler Card or national ID card.
    A. These cards have many advantages.
       1. They would be small and cost little to produce.
       2. They would be like EZ Pass devices and simple to use.
       3. Airport officials would be able to scan the cards.
       4. Airport officials would be able to obtain background information from government databases.
    B. These cards have drawbacks.
       1. They work only for travelers who do not mind volunteering personal information to obtain a card.
       2. They would not prevent passengers with "clean" backgrounds from bringing weapons or explosives on board.
       3. Some people believe that these cards would deprive people of their privacy.

IV. Syndicated columnist William Safire and constitutional law expert Alan Dershowitz have different positions concerning national ID cards.
    A. According to Safire, both the government and law-enforcement agencies could exploit national ID cards.
       1. Businesses could discover people's credit rating, bank accounts, and product preference.
       2. The advantages of ID cards would undermine people's right to privacy.
    B. Dershowitz believes that the advantages of national ID cards outweigh their disadvantages.
       1. The national ID card would be only a little more intrusive than a photo ID or a social security card.
       2. It would reduce or eliminate the need for racial profiling.

      3. Airport security officials could do instant background checks on everyone.
      4. The personal information in the system would stay in the system and never be made public.
V. Even though Safe Traveler Cards and national ID cards have drawbacks, the alternatives are also problematic.
  A. Racial profiling could once more be used to screen passengers.
      1. Racial profiling would have identified the September 11 terrorists as they passed through airports.
      2. Racial profiling is discriminatory.
  B. Religion could be used as a criterion to screen passengers.
      1. Religious profiling would have identified the September 11 terrorists.
      2. Religious profiling presents the same problems as racial profiling.
  C. Age and gender could also be considered.
      1. Most September 11 terrorists were males between eighteen and forty.
      2. Profiling on the basis of age or gender can lead to discrimination.
  D. Behavioral characteristics could be used to screen passengers.
      1. Behavioral profiling would have identified the September 11 terrorists.
      2. Behavioral profiling would not work with passengers who knew what behavior security officials were looking for.

STEP 9: WRITING YOUR PAPER

Once you have decided on a thesis and written an outline, you are ready to write a draft of your paper. Start by arranging your notes in the order in which you will use them. Follow your outline as you write, but don't be afraid to depart from it if new ideas occur to you.

Begin your paper with an **introduction** that includes your thesis statement. Usually your introduction will be a single paragraph, but sometimes it will be longer.

In the **body** of your paper, you support your thesis statement, with each body paragraph developing a single idea. Support your points with summaries, paraphrases, and quotations from your sources, as well as with your own ideas and opinions. Your body paragraphs should have clear topic sentences so that your readers will know exactly what points you are making, and you should use transitional words and phrases to help readers follow the progression of your ideas.

Finally, your **conclusion** should give readers a sense of completion. Like your introduction, your conclusion is usually a single paragraph, but it can be longer. It should reinforce your thesis statement and your paper's main ideas and should end with a sentence that will stay with readers.

Remember that you will probably write several drafts of your paper before you submit it. You can use the Revision Checklist on page 54 to help you revise and edit your paper.

Caitlin Byrne's completed paper on airport security appears on page 727.

STEP 10: DOCUMENTING YOUR SOURCES

When you **document** a source, you tell readers where you have found the information that you have used in your paper. The Modern Language Association (MLA) recommends the following documentation style for research papers.* This format consists of *parenthetical references* within a paper that refer to a *Works Cited* list at the end of the paper.

Parenthetical References in the Text

A parenthetical reference should include just enough information to guide readers to a specific entry in your Works Cited list. A typical parenthetical reference consists of the author's last name and the page number: (Safire 2). If you use more than one work by the same author, include a shortened form of the title in the parenthetical reference: (Safire, "National ID" 4). Notice that there is no *p.* or comma before the page number.

Whenever possible, introduce information with a phrase that includes the author's name. (If you do this, include the page number in parentheses.)

▶ According to Alan Dershowitz, the national ID card would be only a little more intrusive than a photo ID card or a social security card (591).

Place documentation so that it does not interrupt the flow of your ideas, preferably at the end of a sentence.

The format for parenthetical references departs from these guidelines in four special situations:

WHEN YOU ARE CITING A WORK BY TWO AUTHORS

▶ Ever since the Bush administration suggested national ID cards, civil libertarians have attacked the idea (Kladstrup and Walker 27).

---

*For further information, see the sixth edition of the *MLA Handbook for Writers of Research Papers* (New York: Mod. Lang. Assn., 2003) or the MLA Web site at <mla.org>.

WHEN YOU ARE CITING A WORK WITHOUT A LISTED AUTHOR

▶ After screeners at airports were made federal employees, the
government upgraded their training ("Airport Screeners" 54).

WHEN YOU ARE CITING AN INDIRECT SOURCE

If you use a statement by one author that is quoted in the work of
another author, indicate this by including the abbreviation qtd. in
("quoted in").

▶ When speaking about racial profiling, William Bryson says,
"The effects of such actions on the rights that Americans
take for granted is devastating" (qtd. in Seidman 45).

WHEN YOU ARE CITING AN ELECTRONIC SOURCE

Sources from the Internet or from library databases frequently do not
contain page numbers. If the electronic source uses paragraph, section, or
screen numbers, use the abbreviation par., sec., or the full word screen,
followed by the corresponding number, in your documentation. If the citation includes an author name, place a comma after the name.

▶ Random searches are not only time consuming, but they are
also highly inefficient (Richmond, par. 16).

If the electronic source has no page numbers or markers of any kind,
include just the name(s) of the author(s). Readers will be able to tell that
the citation refers to an electronic source when they consult the Works
Cited list.

▶ The problem with random searching is that security personnel
focus on a list of passengers randomly selected by a computer
and not on specific passengers (Cambanis and Daniel).

GUIDELINES FOR FORMATTING QUOTATIONS

SHORT QUOTATIONS. Quotations of no more than four typed lines
are run in with the text of your paper. End punctuation comes after the parenthetical reference (which follows the quotation marks).

According to two constitutional law experts, when one
group is singled out for scrutiny, "agents are more likely
to miss dangerous persons who take care not to fit the
profile" (Cole and Dempsey 170).

LONG QUOTATIONS. Quotations of more than four lines are set off
from the text of your paper. Indent a long quotation ten spaces (or one inch)
from the left-hand margin, and do not enclose the passage in quotation
marks. The first line of a long quotation is not indented even if it is the beginning of a paragraph. If a quoted passage has more than one paragraph,
indent the first line of each paragraph after the first one three additional

spaces (or one-quarter inch). Introduce a long quotation with a colon, and place the parenthetical reference one space *after* the end punctuation.

> According to David Cole and James Dempsey, September 11
> caused the American public to become more concerned about
> national security and less concerned about the personal
> liberties of those they considered to be possible terror-
> ists:
>
> > Before September 11, about 80 percent of the
> > American public considered racial profiling
> > wrong. . . . After September 11, however, polls
> > reported the fact that 60 percent of the Ameri-
> > can public favored racial profiling, at least as
> > long as it was directed at Arabs and Muslims.
> > (168)

Note: Ellipsis points indicate that the student has deleted words from the quotation.

The Works Cited List

The Works Cited list includes all the works you cite (refer to) in your paper. Use the following guidelines to prepare your list.

The following sample Works Cited entries cover the situations you will encounter most often. Follow the formats exactly as they appear here.

Books

BOOK BY ONE AUTHOR

List the author, last name first. State the full title, including any subtitle, and underline it. Include the city of publication and a shortened form of the publisher's name—for example, *Prentice* for *Prentice Hall* or *Random* for *Random House, Inc.* Use the abbreviation *UP* for *University Press,* as in *Princeton UP* and *U of Chicago P.* End with the date of publication.

▶ Brown, Charles T. The Rock and Roll Story: From the Sounds
     of Rebellion to an American Art Form. Englewood Cliffs:
     Prentice, 1983.

BOOK BY TWO OR THREE AUTHORS

List second and subsequent authors, first name first, in the order in which they are listed on the book's title page.

▶ Coe, Sophie D., and Michael D. Coe. The True History of
     Chocolate. New York: Thames, 1996.

BOOK BY MORE THAN THREE AUTHORS

Either list all authors in the order in which they are listed on the book's title page, with second and subsequent authors cited first name

---

GUIDELINES FOR PREPARING THE WORKS CITED LIST

- Begin the Works Cited list on a new page after the last page of your paper.
- Number the Works Cited page as the next page of the paper.
- Center the heading `Works Cited` one inch from the top of the page; do not underline the heading or put it in quotation marks.
- Double-space the list.
- List entries alphabetically according to the author's last name.
- Alphabetize unsigned articles according to the first major word of the title.
- Begin each entry flush with the left-hand margin.
- Indent second and subsequent lines five spaces (or one-half inch).
- Separate each division of the entry — author, title, and publication information — by a period and one space.

---

first, or list only the first author, followed by *et al.* ("and others"). Whichever method you choose, the parenthetical citations used in the text must match: if you use all the authors' names on the Works Cited page, you must use them all in the parenthetical citations; if you use *et al.* on the Works Cited page, you must use it in the parenthetical citations.

▶   Roark, James L., Michael P. Johnson, Patricia Cline Cohen, Sarah Stage, Alan Lawson, and Susan M. Hartmann. The American Promise: A History of the United States. 2nd ed. New York: Bedford, 2002.

▶   Roark, James L., et al. The American Promise: A History of the United States. 2nd ed. New York: Bedford, 2002.

TWO OR MORE BOOKS BY THE SAME AUTHOR

List two or more books by the same author in alphabetical order according to title. In each entry after the first, type three unspaced hyphens (followed by a period) instead of the author's name.

▶   Angelou, Maya. Gather Together in My Name. New York: Bantam, 1980.

---. I Know Why the Caged Bird Sings. New York: Bantam, 1985.

EDITED BOOK

▶   Dickinson, Emily. The Complete Poems of Emily Dickinson. Ed. Thomas H. Johnson. New York: Little, 1990.

TRANSLATION

▶   García Márquez, Gabriel. Love in the Time of Cholera. Trans. Edith Grossman. New York: Knopf, 1988.

REVISED EDITION

▶ Gans, Herbert J. The Urban Villagers: Group and Class in the
      Life of Italian-Americans. 2nd ed. New York: Free, 1982.

ANTHOLOGY

▶ Kirszner, Laurie G., and Stephen R. Mandell, eds. Patterns
      for College Writing: A Rhetorical Reader and Guide. 9th
      ed. New York: Bedford, 2004.

ESSAY IN AN ANTHOLOGY

▶ Zimecki, Michael. "Violent Films Cry 'Fire' in Crowded
      Theaters." Patterns for College Writing: A Rhetorical
      Reader and Guide. 9th ed. Ed. Laurie G. Kirszner and
      Stephen R. Mandell. New York: Bedford, 2004. 612-15.

MORE THAN ONE ESSAY IN THE SAME ANTHOLOGY

List each essay separately with a cross-reference to the entire anthology.

▶ Zimecki, Michael. "Violent Films Cry 'Fire' in Crowded
      Theaters." Kirszner and Mandell 612-15.

▶ Kirszner, Laurie G., and Stephen R. Mandell, eds. Patterns
      for College Writing: A Rhetorical Reader and Guide. 9th
      ed. New York: Bedford, 2004.

▶ Stone, Oliver. "Memo to John Grisham: What's Next—'A Movie
      Made Me Do It'?" Kirszner and Mandell 607-609.

SECTION OR CHAPTER OF A BOOK

▶ Gordimer, Nadine. "Once upon a Time." Jump and Other
      Stories. New York: Farrar, 1991.

INTRODUCTION, PREFACE, FOREWORD, OR AFTERWORD

▶ Ingham, Patricia. Introduction. Martin Chuzzlewit. By
      Charles Dickens. London: Penguin, 1999. x-xxxii.

MULTIVOLUME WORK

▶ Malory, Thomas. Le Morte D'Arthur. Ed. Janet Cowen. 2 vols.
      London: Penguin, 1986.

ARTICLE IN A REFERENCE WORK

For familiar reference works that publish new editions regularly,
include only the edition (if given) and the year of publication.

▶ "Civil Rights." The World Book Encyclopedia. 2002 ed.

For less familiar reference works, provide a full citation.

▶ Wagle, Greta. "Geisel, Theodor [Seuss]." The Encyclopedia of
   American Literature. Ed. Steven R. Serafin. New York:
   Continuum, 1999.

Periodicals

ARTICLE IN A JOURNAL WITH CONTINUOUS PAGINATION THROUGHOUT AN ANNUAL VOLUME

Some scholarly journals have continuous pagination; that is, one issue might end on page 234, and the next would then begin with page 235. In this case, the volume number is followed by the date of publication in parentheses.

▶ Allen, Dennis W. "Horror and Perverse Delight: Faulkner's
   'A Rose for Emily.'" Modern Fiction Studies 30 (1984):
   685-96.

ARTICLE IN A JOURNAL WITH SEPARATE PAGINATION IN EACH ISSUE

For a journal in which each issue begins with page 1, the volume number is followed by a period and the issue number and then by the date. Leave no space after the period.

▶ Lindemann, Erika. "Teaching as a Rhetorical Art." CEA Forum
   15.2 (1985): 9-12.

ARTICLE IN A MONTHLY MAGAZINE

If an article does not appear on consecutive pages—for example, if it begins on page 66, skips to page 68, skips again from page 71 to page 74, and continues on page 76—include only the first page, followed by a plus sign.

▶ Bowden, Mark. "The Kabul-Ki Dance." Atlantic Monthly Nov.
   2002: 66+.

ARTICLE IN A WEEKLY MAGAZINE (UNSIGNED/SIGNED)

▶ "Face Value: The Acceptable Face of Capitalism?" Economist
   14 Dec. 2002: 51.

▶ Sebald, W. G. "A Natural History of Destruction." New Yorker
   4 Nov. 2002: 66-77.

ARTICLE IN A NEWSPAPER

Include the newspaper's name as it appears at the top of the first page, but do not include an introductory article (*New York Times* not *The New York Times*).

▶ Angier, Natalie. "Weighing the Grandma Factor." New York
   Times 5 Nov. 2002: F1+.

If an edition is specified, place a comma after the date, and list the edition before the colon, abbreviating *edition* as *ed.*

▶ Haberman, Clyde. "Is Graffiti 'Art'?" New York Times 22 Oct. 1996, late ed.: B1.

EDITORIAL OR LETTER TO THE EDITOR

▶ "High Taxes Kill Cities." Editorial. Philadelphia Inquirer 8 Aug. 1995, late ed., sec. 1: 17.

REVIEW IN A NEWSPAPER

▶ Scott, A. O. "Forever Obsessing about Obsession." Rev. of Adaptation, dir. Spike Jonze. New York Times 6 Dec. 2002: F1+.

REVIEW IN A WEEKLY OR BIWEEKLY MAGAZINE

▶ Urquhart, Brian. "The Prospect of War." Rev. of The Threatening Storm: The Case for Invading Iraq, by Kenneth M. Pollack. New York Review of Books 19 Dec. 2002: 16-22.

REVIEW IN A MONTHLY MAGAZINE

▶ Jones, Kent. "The Lay of the Land." Rev. of Sunshine State, dir. John Sayles. Film Commentary May/June 2002: 22-24.

Electronic Sources

When citing Internet sources appearing on the Web, include both the date of electronic publication (if available) and the date you accessed the source. In addition, include the URL (electronic address) in angle brackets. (*Note:* MLA style requires that you break URLs only after a slash.)

Warning: Using information from an Internet source—especially an anonymous one—is risky. Contributors are not necessarily experts on a topic, and they are frequently misinformed. Unless you can be certain that the information you are obtaining from these sources is reliable, do not use it. You can check the reliability of an Internet source by consulting the guidelines printed in many college handbooks or by asking your instructor or librarian for guidance.

ENTIRE INTERNET SITE (SCHOLARLY PROJECT, INFORMATION DATABASE, JOURNAL, OR PROFESSIONAL WEB SITE)

▶ International Dialects of English Archive. 1998. Dept. of Theatre and Film, U of Kansas. 4 Dec. 2002 <http://www.ku.edu/~idea/>

▶ The Dickens Project. Ed. Jon Michael Varese. 1998. U of California, Santa Cruz. 2 Dec. 2002 <http://humwww.ucsc.edu /dickens>.

PERSONAL WEB SITE

▶ Lynch, Jack. Home page. 2 Jan. 2003 <http://
    andromeda.rutgers.edu/~jlynch>.

ENTIRE ONLINE BOOK

▶ Fielding, Henry. The History of Tom Jones, a Foundling.
    Ed. William Allan Nielson. New York: Collier, 1917.
    Bartleby.com: Great Books Online. Ed. Steven van
    Leeuwen. Sept. 2000. 29 Nov. 2002 <http://
    www.bartleby.com/301>.

▶ Austen, Jane. Pride and Prejudice. 1813. 30 Nov. 2002
    <http://www.online-literature.com/austen/
    prideprejudice>.

PART OF AN ONLINE BOOK

▶ Radford, Dollie. "At Night." Poems. London, 1910. Victorian
    Women Writers Project. Ed. Perry Willett. Nov. 1995.
    Indiana U. 17 Mar. 2003 <http://www.indiana.edu/~letrs
    /vwwp/radford/radpoems.html#p29>.

ARTICLE IN A SCHOLARLY JOURNAL

▶ Condie, Kent C., and Jane Silverstone. "The Crust of the
    Colorado Plateau: New Views of an Old Arc." Journal
    of Geology 107.4 (1999). 9 Aug. 1999 <http://
    www.journals.uchicago.edu/JG/journal/issues/v107n4/
    990034/990034.html>.

ARTICLE IN AN ONLINE REFERENCE BOOK OR ENCYCLOPEDIA

▶ "Croatia." The 1997 World Factbook. 30 Mar. 1998. Central
    Intelligence Agency. 30 Dec. 1998 <http://www.odci.gov/
    cia/publications/factbook/country-frame.html>.

ARTICLE IN AN ONLINE NEWSPAPER

▶ Krim, Jonathan. "FCC Preparing to Overhaul Telecom, Media
    Rules." Washington Post 3 Jan. 2003. 6 Jan. 2003
    <http://www.washingtonpost.com/wp-dyn/articles/
    A3541-2003Jan2.html>.

ONLINE EDITORIAL

▶ "Ersatz Eve." Editorial. New York Times on the Web 28 Dec.
    2002. 5 Jan. 2003 <http://www.nytimes.com/2002/12/28/
    opinion/28SAT2.html>.

ARTICLE IN AN ONLINE MAGAZINE

▶ Press, Eyal, and Jennifer Washburn. "The At-Risk-Youth
      Industry." Atlantic Online Dec. 2002. 3 Jan. 2003
      <http://www.theatlantic.com/issues/2002/12/press.htm>

REVIEW IN AN ONLINE PERIODICAL

▶ Chocano, Carina. "Sympathy for the Misanthrope." Rev. of
      Curb Your Enthusiasm, dir. Robert Weide, prod. Larry
      David. Salon 17 Sept. 2002. 4 Dec. 2002 <http://
      www.salon.com/ent/tv/diary/2002/09/17/curb/index.html>.

WORK FROM A LIBRARY SUBSCRIPTION SERVICE

▶ Prince, Stephen. "Why Do Film Scholars Ignore Media Vio-
      lence?" Chronicle of Higher Education. 10 Aug. 2001:
      B18. EBSCO. City U of New York, City College Lib. 14
      Feb. 2003 <http://www.epnet.com/>.

POSTING TO A DISCUSSION LIST

Be sure to include the phrase "Online posting."

▶ Thune, W. Scott. "Emotion and Rationality in Argument."
      Online posting. 23 Mar. 1997. CCCC/97 Online. 11 Nov.
      1997 <http://www.missouri.edu/HyperNews/get/cccc98
      /proplink/12.html>.

MATERIAL ACCESSED ON A CD-ROM, DVD, DISKETTE, OR MAGNETIC TAPE

In addition to the publication information, include the medium (CD-ROM, for example) and the distribution vendor, if relevant (UMI-Proquest, for example).

▶ Aristotle. "Poetics." The Complete Works of Aristotle. Ed.
      Jonathan Barnes. 2 vols. Princeton: Princeton UP, 1984.
      CD-ROM. Clayton: InteLex, 1994.

▶ "Feminism." The Oxford English Dictionary. 2nd ed. DVD. New
      York: Oxford UP, 1992.

E-MAIL

▶ De Roo, Mikola. "Re: Headnotes." E-mail to Laurie G.
      Kirszner. 13 Dec. 2002.

SYNCHRONOUS COMMUNICATION

When citing from a synchronous communication, such as a MOO or MUD, you should include the name of the speaker, a description of the event, the date of the event, and the name of the forum.

▶ Harris, Lee. "Titles." Online lecture. 14 Nov. 2000. Diver-
        sity University MOO. 16 Nov. 2000 <telnet://moo.du.org>.

DOWNLOADED SOFTWARE

▶ CryptoHeaven. Vers. 2.1.3. 30 Nov. 2002 <http://
        linux-ny.tucows.webusenet.com/internet/adnload
        /231445_94803.html>.

MATERIAL ACCESSED THROUGH AN ONLINE SERVICE

Frequently, online services like America Online and Lexis-Nexis enable
you to access material without providing a URL. If you access such material by using a keyword, provide the keyword (following the date of access)
at the end of the entry.

▶ "Kafka, Franz." Compton's Encyclopedia Online. Vers. 2.0.
        1997. American Online. 8 June 1998. Keyword: Compton's.

If, instead of using a keyword, you follow a series of paths, list the paths
separated by semicolons.

▶ "Elizabeth Adams." History Resources. 11 Nov. 1997. America
        Online. 28 June 1999. Path: Research: Biography; Women
        in Science; Biographies.

Other Nonprint Sources

TELEVISION OR RADIO PROGRAM

▶ "Prime Suspect 3." Writ. Lynda La Plante. Mystery! PBS.
        WNET, New York. 28 Apr. 1994.

VIDEOTAPE, MOVIE, RECORD, OR SLIDE PROGRAM

▶ Murray, Donald, perf. Interview with John Updike. Dir. Bruce
        Schwartz. Videocassette. Harcourt, 1997.

PERSONAL INTERVIEW

▶ Garcetti, Gilbert. Personal interview. 7 May 1994.

SAMPLE STUDENT RESEARCH PAPER IN MLA STYLE

Here is Caitlin Byrne's final essay on the topic of airport security. The
essay follows the conventions of MLA documentation style. It has been
reproduced in a narrower format than you will have on a standard
(8½" × 11") sheet of paper.

Byrne 1

Caitlin Byrne

Professor Hernandez

HUM 101

9 Apr. 2003

Airport Insecurity

Introduction

After the September 11, 2001, terrorist attacks on New York's World Trade Towers and the Pentagon, the debate surrounding racial profiling in airports intensified. Many people believed that profiling was the best way to identify possible terrorists, but many others worried about violations of civil liberties. While some airports began to target passengers based solely on their Middle Eastern origins, others instituted random searches instead. Neither of these techniques seems likely to eliminate terrorism. Now, many experts in government and in airport security are recommending the use of a national ID

Thesis statement

card or a Safe Traveler Card. If every US citizen had such a card, airlines could screen for terrorists more effectively than they do now and avoid procedures that single out individuals solely on the basis of race.

Pargraph combines Caitlin's own ideas, a paraphrase and quotation from Cambanis and Daniel, and a paraphrase and quotation from Cole and Dempsey

The events of September 11 dramatically revealed the shortcomings of airport security. Clearly, what was needed was a way of identifying terrorists before they got on airplanes. In an attempt to avoid charges of harassing people of Middle Eastern descent, many airlines decided that in addition to searching carry-on baggage, they would also search passengers at random. Although random searches are highly inefficient, they do occasionally detect people who would not have been identified by racial profiling. In fact, benign-looking passengers have been caught smuggling drugs and even concealing explosives.

Byrne 2

In one case, for example, "agents caught a pregnant Irish woman who tried to board an El Al flight from London to Tel Aviv with a bomb hidden in her luggage by her boyfriend" (Cambanis and Daniel). Moreover, random searches encourage security personnel to scrutinize all passengers, not just some of them. According to two constitutional law experts, when one group is singled out for scrutiny, "agents are more likely to miss dangerous persons who take care not to fit the profile" (Cole and Dempsey 170).

Paragraph contains a paraphrase from the Cambanis and Daniel article

Although they may have some limited success, however, random searches are less likely to detect terrorists than are searches based on racial profiling. Many critics of random searches believe that airports are wasting their time and resources searching children or elderly people who pose no legitimate threat. The problem with random searching is that security personnel focus on a list of passengers randomly selected by a computer and not on specific passengers (Cambanis and Daniel). For this reason, passengers whose names are not on the list can usually board a plane without much difficulty.

Paragraph combines Caitlin's ideas with a paraphrase from the Easterbrook article

Routine preflight security checks for all passengers are another strategy for detecting potential terrorists. Although they are more effective than random searches, they can be expensive and extremely time-consuming, in some cases requiring passengers to come to the airport two to three hours early. According to Gregg Easterbrook, new developments in airport security—such as full-body X-ray systems and mechanized bomb detectors—that the Transportation Security Administration is currently

Byrne 3

testing may alleviate these problems, but they are still a long way from being perfected. And even if they were available, the cost of installing them would be beyond the reach of most airports (179).

Perhaps the cheapest and most efficient security method is a so-called Safe Traveler Card or a national ID card. A Safe Traveler Card or national ID card would be about the size of a credit card, contain a computer chip, and cost little to produce. In some ways, these cards are like the EZ Pass devices that enable people to drive on highways, bridges, and tunnels without having to stop and pay tolls (Dershowitz 590). By scanning the card, airport security officials would be able to obtain background information from government databases for every passenger: flying history, residence, credit-card spending, travel habits, phone records, criminal background, and fingerprint and iris patterns (Safire 587). It is easy to see how such a card could expedite security checks at airports. One swipe of the card, and security officials could tell at a glance whether a person should be searched or let through.

As attractive as Safe Traveler Cards or national ID cards are, they are not without drawbacks. For one thing, as Easterbrook notes, these cards would expedite security procedures only for travelers who do not mind volunteering such information to obtain a card. Moreover, they would not prevent passengers with "clean" backgrounds from bringing weapons or explosives on board, as was the case in the September 11 attacks. Perhaps the biggest drawback is that some people believe that these cards would deprive people of their

Paragraph uses material from the Dershowitz and Safire articles to support Caitlin's own conclusions

Paragraph contains a paraphrase from the Easterbrook article

Byrne 4

privacy and that for this reason, their disadvantages outweigh their advantages (168).

Paragraph contains quotation and summary of ideas in the Safire article

According to syndicated columnist William
Safire, both the government and law-enforcement
agencies could exploit national ID cards. By
tapping into the computer databases, these agencies could obtain a great deal of personal data
about an individual. For example, they could
tell what magazines people subscribed to, what
Web sites they visited, and their political
affiliation. In addition, businesses could discover people's "credit rating, bank accounts,
and product preferences" (Safire 587). Safire
acknowledges the advantages of such cards but
concludes that they would undermine the Fourth
Amendment and compromise people's right to privacy (Safire 587).

Paragraph contains quotations and a summary from the Dershowitz article

Constitutional law expert Alan Dershowitz
disagrees with Safire's contentions. He concedes
that national ID cards would lessen a person's
anonymity, but he believes that this small loss
would be offset by a great increase in personal
security. To Dershowitz—a self-proclaimed civil
libertarian—the tradeoff would be well worth it.
According to Dershowitz, the national ID card
would be only a little more intrusive than a
photo ID card or a social security card. Best of
all, it would reduce or eliminate the need for
racial profiling: "Anyone who had the [national
ID] card could be allowed to pass through airports or building security more expeditiously,
and anyone who opted out could be examined much
more closely" (590). Such cards would enable
airport security officials to do instant background checks on everyone. The personal information in the system would stay in the system and

never be made public. The only information on
the card would be a person's "name, address,
photo, and [finger]print" (Dershowitz 591).

*Paragraph contains
Caitlin's own ideas
as well as a long
quotation from the
Cole and Dempsey
article*

    As both Safire and Dershowitz point out,
Safe Traveler Cards or national ID cards have
drawbacks, but the alternatives are also problematic. One alternative — racial profiling —
has been harshly criticized as discriminatory.
Nevertheless, the Transportation Security Administration — which was established in February 2002
to federalize airport security — has recently
been rethinking its ban on racial profiling.
One reason for this policy reversal is that the
government now believes that it was the taboo
against racial profiling that kept authorities
from questioning the September 11 terrorists as
they passed through airports. Another reason is
that since the attacks, the American public has
changed its opinion regarding racial profiling —
at least in airports. According to David Cole
and James X. Dempsey, September 11 caused the
American public to become more concerned about
national security and less concerned about the
personal liberties of those they considered to
be possible terrorists:

> Before September 11, about 80 percent
> of the American public considered
> racial profiling wrong. . . . After
> September 11, however, polls reported
> the fact that 60 percent of the Amer-
> ican public favored racial profiling,
> at least as long as it was directed at
> Arabs and Muslims. (168)

Those who favor racial profiling believe that it
would be better for security personnel to focus
on people who would be more likely to be involved

Byrne 6

in terrorism than to waste time and money on random searches of innocent people.

Paragraph uses two examples from the CNN article to support Caitlin's own conclusion

Even though racial profiling may be effective (and might even have prevented the acts of September 11), it raises disturbing questions about personal liberties and civil rights. One example of the problems that occur with racial profiling is the case of the Arab software developer who was removed from his flight simply because the pilot felt uncomfortable flying with him. This action was taken despite the fact that the passenger was a United States citizen who purchased his ticket through a corporate travel agency ("Airlines"). Another case of racial profiling involved a passenger who refused to sit next to another passenger because she thought he looked suspicious. This "suspicious" passenger was also escorted off the plane and, after questioning, was asked to board a different flight. In both these situations, a national ID card or Safe Traveler Card could easily have spared the passengers embarrassment and enabled them to continue their flights ("Airlines").

Paragraph contains a quotation from Taylor and statistics from Mooney

One way to avoid racial profiling would be to use some criterion (or combination of criteria) other than race to screen passengers. One possible criterion could be religion. For example, the knowledge that all "of the people who have hijacked airliners for the purpose of murdering Americans have been Arab men" who practice a form of radical Islam that is "committed to mass-murdering Americans" (Taylor) might lead to the increased scrutiny of Islamic Arab men — but not of all Arab men. In this case, most Arab Americans would be eliminated from suspicion because only 23 percent of Arab Americans are

Muslim, while 77 percent are Christians (Mooney).

Age and gender could also be considered when constructing a profile of terrorists. Most of those who committed the acts of September 11 were men between the ages of eighteen and forty (Mooney 2). So, it would make sense for security personnel to concentrate on Arab men who are between these ages and who practice some form of radical Islam. However, both these criteria single out individuals on the basis of a single characteristic, and for many people, this is disturbing. Using religion, age, or gender as a basis for questioning leads to discrimination—much like the racial discrimination that results from racial profiling.

Paragraph contains a paraphrase from the Easterbrook article followed by Caitlin's own conclusions

Another way to avoid racial profiling would be to use behavior as a screening criterion. For example, terrorists tend to be males who travel alone, pay cash, buy one-way tickets, and do not have luggage. Other warning signs include people who are traveling alone but seem to be communicating with others in the airplane, who are adjusting items underneath their clothes, or who seem overwrought or excessively nervous (Easterbrook 140). However, even using behavior patterns to identify potential terrorists is not without problems. After all, passengers involved in illegal activities would most likely know the kinds of behavior that airport security would be looking for and would go to great lengths to control their actions.

Conclusion

It is clear that the only acceptable way of ensuring the safety of airline passengers is to begin a program to issue Safe Traveler Cards or national ID cards to United States citizens.

*Paragraph needs
no documentation
because it contains
Caitlin's own ideas*

These cards would screen out those who are
unlikely to be terrorists and would also eliminate the delays that currently characterize air
travel. Most important, they would help prevent
terrorists from hijacking American planes. At
the same time, by making racial profiling unnecessary, these cards would help protect our
personal and civil liberties. Only by instituting a national ID card system can we make certain that the terrorists who attacked the United
States did not hijack the liberties that are so
precious to us.

Byrne 9

Works Cited

"Airlines, Passengers Confront Racial Profiling." CNN.com. 3 Oct. 2001. Cable News Network. 26 Jul. 2002 <http://www.cnn.com/2001
/TRAVEL/NEWS/10/03/rec.airlines.profiling
/index.html>.

Cambanis, Thanassis, and Mac Daniel. "Air Security under Fire: Travelers Irate over
Aggressive Airport Searches." Boston Globe.
17 Mar. 2002. 26 Jul. 2002 <http://
freerepublic.com/focus/news/648367/posts>.

Cole, David, and James X. Dempsey. Terrorism
and the Constitution: Sacrificing Civil
Liberties in the Name of National Security.
2nd ed. New York: New Press, 2002.

Dershowitz, Alan M. "Why Fear National ID
Cards?" Kirszner and Mandell 590-92.

Easterbrook, Gregg. "The All-Too-Friendly Skies:
Security as an Afterthought." How Did This
Happen? Terrorism and the New War. Ed.
James F. Hoge Jr. and Gideon Rose. New
York: Public Affairs, 2001. 163-82.

Kirszner, Laurie G., and Stephen R. Mandell,
eds. Patterns for College Writing. 9th ed.
New York: Bedford, 2004.

Mooney, Chris. "Smart — and Stupid — Profiling."
American Prospect. 23 Oct. 2001. 26 Jul.
2002 <http://www.prospect.org/
webfeatures/2001/10/mooney-c-10-23.html>.

Safire, William. "The Threat of National ID."
Kirszner and Mandell 586-88.

Taylor, Stuart Jr. "The Case for Using Racial
Profiling at Airports." Atlantic Online.
25 Sep. 2001. 26 Jul. 2002 <http://
www.theatlantic.com/politics/nj/
taylor2001-09-25.htm>.

Glossary

Abstract/Concrete language Abstract language names concepts or qualities that cannot be directly seen or touched: *love, emotion, evil, anguish.* Concrete language denotes objects or qualities that can be perceived by the senses: *fountain pen, leaky, shouting, rancid.* Abstract words are sometimes needed to express ideas, but they are very vague unless used with concrete supporting detail. The abstract phrase "The speaker was overcome with emotion" could mean almost anything, but the addition of concrete language clarifies the meaning: "He clenched his fist and shook it at the crowd" (anger).

Allusion A brief reference to literature, history, the Bible, mythology, popular culture, and so on that readers are expected to recognize. An allusion evokes a vivid impression in very few words. "The gardener opened the gate, and suddenly we found ourselves in Eden" suggests in one word (*Eden*) the stunning beauty of the garden.

Analogy A form of comparison that explains an unfamiliar element by comparing it to another that is more familiar. Analogies also enable writers to put abstract or technical information in simpler, more concrete terms: "The effect of pollution on the environment is like that of cancer on the body."

Annotating The technique of recording one's responses to a reading selection by writing notes in the margins of the text. Annotating a text might involve asking questions, suggesting possible parallels with other selections or with the reader's own experience, arguing with the writer's points, commenting on the writer's style, or defining unfamiliar terms or concepts.

Antithesis A viewpoint opposite to one expressed in a *thesis.* In an argumentative essay, the thesis must be debatable. If no antithesis exists, the writer's thesis is not debatable. (See also **Thesis**.)

Antonym A word opposite in meaning to another word. *Beautiful* is the antonym of *ugly. Synonym* is the antonym of *antonym.*

Argumentation The form of writing that takes a stand on an issue and attempts to convince readers by presenting a logical sequence of points supported by evidence. Unlike *persuasion,* which uses a number of different appeals, argumentation is primarily an appeal to reason. (See Chapter 12.)

Audience   The people "listening" to a writer's words. Writers who are sensitive to their audience will carefully choose a tone, examples, and allusions that their readers will understand and respond to. For instance, an effective article attempting to persuade high school students not to drink alcohol would use examples and allusions pertinent to a teenager's life. Different examples would be chosen if the writer were addressing middle-aged members of Alcoholics Anonymous.

Basis for comparison   A fundamental similarity between two or more things that enables a writer to compare them. In a comparison of how two towns react to immigrants, the basis of comparison might be that both towns have a rapidly expanding immigrant population. (If one of the towns did not have any immigrants, this comparison would be illogical.)

Body paragraphs   The paragraphs that develop and support an essay's thesis.

Brainstorming   An invention technique that can be done individually or in a group. When writers brainstorm on their own, they jot down every fact or idea that relates to a particular topic. When they brainstorm in a group, they discuss a topic with others and write down the useful ideas that come up.

Causal chain   A sequence of events in which one event causes another event, which in turn causes yet another event.

Cause and effect   The pattern of development that discusses either the reasons for an occurrence or the observed or predicted consequence of an occurrence. Often both causes and effects are discussed in the same essay. (See Chapter 8.)

Causes   The reasons for an event, situation, or phenomenon. An *immediate cause* is an obvious one; a *remote cause* is less easily perceived. The *main cause* is the most important cause, whether it is immediate or remote. Other, less important causes that nevertheless encourage the effect in some way (for instance, by speeding it up or providing favorable circumstances for it) are called *contributory causes.*

Chronological order   The time sequence in which events occur. Chronological order is often used to organize a narrative; it is also used to structure a process essay.

Claim   In Toulmin logic, the thesis or main point of an essay. Usually the claim is stated directly, but sometimes it is implied. (See also **Toulmin logic**.)

Classification and division   The pattern of development that uses these two related methods of organizing information. *Classification* involves searching for common characteristics among various items and grouping them accordingly, thereby imposing order on randomly organized information. *Division* breaks up an entity into smaller groups or elements. Classification generalizes; division specifies. (See Chapter 10.)

Cliché   An overused expression, such as *beauty is in the eye of the beholder, the good die young,* or *a picture is worth a thousand words.*

Clustering A method of invention whereby a writer groups ideas visually by listing the main topic in the center of a page, circling it, and surrounding it with words or phrases that identify the major points to be addressed. The writer then circles these words or phrases, creating new clusters or ideas for each of them.

Coherence The tight relationship between all the parts of an effective piece of writing. Such a relationship ensures that the writing will make sense to readers. For a piece of writing to be coherent, it must be logical and orderly, with effective *transitions* making the movement between sentences and paragraphs clear. Within and between paragraphs, coherence may also be enhanced by the repetition of key words and ideas, by the use of pronouns to refer to nouns mentioned previously, and by the use of parallel sentence structure.

Colloquialisms Expressions that are generally appropriate for conversation and informal writing but not usually acceptable for the writing you do in college, business, or professional settings. Examples of colloquial language include contractions; clipped forms (*dorm* for *dormitory, exam* for *examination*); vague expressions like *kind of* and *sort of*; conversation fillers like *you know*; and other informal words and expressions, such as *get across* for *communicate* and *kids* for *children*.

Common knowledge Factual information that is widely available in reference sources. Writers do not need to document common knowledge.

Comparison and contrast The pattern of development that focuses on similarities and/or differences between two or more subjects. In a general sense, *comparison* shows how two or more subjects are alike; *contrast* shows how they are different. (See Chapter 9.) (See also **Point-by-point comparison; Subject-by-subject comparison.**)

Conclusion The group of sentences or paragraphs that brings an essay to a close. To *conclude* means not only "to end" but also "to resolve." Although a conclusion does not resolve all the issues in an essay, the conclusion is the place to show that they *have* been resolved. An effective conclusion indicates that the writer is committed to what has been expressed, and it is the writer's last chance to leave an impression or idea with readers.

Concrete language See **Abstract/Concrete language**.

Connotation The associations, meanings, or feelings a word suggests beyond its literal meaning. Literally, the word *home* means one's place of residence, but *home* also connotes warmth and a sense of belonging. (See also **Denotation**.)

Contributory cause See **Causes**.

Deductive reasoning The method of reasoning that moves from a general premise to a specific conclusion. Deductive reasoning is the opposite of *inductive reasoning*. (See also **Syllogism**.)

Definition An explanation of a word's meaning; the pattern of development in which a writer explains what something or someone is. See Chapter 11. (See also **Extended definition; Formal definition**.)

Denotation The literal meaning of a word. The denotation of *home* is "one's place of residence." (See also **Connotation**.)

Description The pattern of development that presents a word picture of a thing, a person, a situation, or a series of events. (See Chapter 5.) (See also **Objective description; Subjective description**.)

Digression A remark or series of remarks that wanders from the main point of a discussion. In a personal narrative, a digression may be entertaining because of its irrelevance, but in other kinds of writing it is likely to distract and confuse readers.

Division See **Classification and division**.

Documentation The formal way of giving credit to the sources from which a writer borrows words or ideas. Documentation allows readers to evaluate a writer's sources and to consult them if they wish. Papers written for literature and writing classes use the documentation style recommended by the Modern Language Association (MLA). (See Appendix.)

Dominant impression The mood or quality that is central to a piece of writing.

Essay A short work of nonfiction writing on a single topic that usually expresses the author's impressions or opinions. An essay may be organized around one of the patterns of development presented in Chapters 4 through 12 of this book, or it may combine several of these patterns.

Euphemism A polite term for an unpleasant concept. (*Passed on* is a euphemism for *died.*)

Evidence Facts and opinions used to support a statement, position, or idea. *Facts,* which may include statistics, may be drawn from research or personal experience; *opinions* may represent the conclusions of experts or the writer's own ideas.

Example A concrete, specific illustration of a general point.

Exemplification The pattern of development that uses a single extended *example* or a series of shorter examples to support a thesis. (See Chapter 6.)

Extended definition A paragraph-, essay-, or book-length definition developed by means of one or more of the rhetorical strategies discussed in this book.

Fallacy A statement that resembles a logical argument but is actually flawed. Logical fallacies are often persuasive, but they unfairly manipulate readers to win agreement. Fallacies include begging the question; argument from analogy; personal (*ad hominem*) attacks; hasty or sweeping generalizations; false dilemmas (the either/or fallacy); equivocation; red herrings; you also (*tu quoque*); appeals to doubtful authority; distorting statistics; *post hoc* reasoning; and *non sequiturs.*

Figures of speech (also known as *figurative language*) Imaginative language used to suggest a special meaning or create a special effect. Three of the most common figures of speech are *similes, metaphors,* and *personification.*

Formal definition A brief explanation of a word's meaning as it appears in the dictionary.

Freewriting A method of invention that involves writing without stopping for a fixed period — perhaps five or ten minutes — without paying attention to spelling, grammar, or punctuation. The goal of freewriting is to let ideas flow and get them down on paper.

Grounds   In Toulmin logic, the material that a writer uses to support a claim. Grounds may be evidence (facts or expert opinions) or appeals to the emotions or values of an audience. (See also **Toulmin logic**.)

Highlighting   A technique used by a reader to record responses to a reading selection by marking the text with symbols. Highlighting a text might involve underlining important ideas, boxing key terms, numbering a series of related points, circling unfamiliar words (or placing question marks next to them), drawing vertical lines next to an interesting or important passage, drawing arrows to connect related points, or placing asterisks next to discussions of the selection's central issues or themes.

Hyperbole   Deliberate exaggeration for emphasis or humorous effect: "I froze to death out in the storm"; "She has hundreds of boyfriends"; "Senior year passed by in a second." The opposite of hyperbole is *understatement.*

Imagery   A set of verbal pictures of sensory experiences. These pictures, conveyed through concrete details, make a description vivid and immediate to the reader. Some images are literal ("The cows were so white they almost glowed in the dark"); others are more figurative ("The black and white cows looked like maps, with the continents in black and the seas in white"). A pattern of imagery (repeated images of, for example, shadows, forests, or fire) may run through a piece of writing.

Immediate cause   See **Causes**.

Inductive reasoning   The method of reasoning that moves from specific evidence to a general conclusion based on this evidence. Inductive reasoning is the opposite of *deductive reasoning.*

Instructions   A kind of process essay whose purpose is to enable readers to *perform* a process. Instructions use the present tense and speak directly to readers: "Walk at a moderate pace for twenty minutes."

Introduction   An essay's opening. Depending on the length of an essay, the introduction may be one paragraph or several paragraphs. In an introduction, a writer tries to encourage the audience to read the essay that follows. Therefore, the writer must choose tone and diction carefully, indicate what the paper is about, and suggest to readers what direction it will take.

Invention (also known as *prewriting*)   The stage of writing in which a writer explores the writing assignment, focuses ideas, and ultimately decides on a thesis for an essay. A writer might begin by thinking through the requirements of the assignment—the essay's purpose, length, and audience. Then, using one or more methods of invention—such as *freewriting, questions for probing, brainstorming, clustering,* and *journal writing*—the writer can formulate a tentative thesis and begin to write the essay.

Irony   Language that points to a discrepancy between two different levels of meaning. *Verbal irony* is characterized by a gap between what is stated and what is really meant, which often has the opposite meaning—for instance, "his humble abode" (referring to a millionaire's estate). *Situational irony* points to a discrepancy between what actually happens and what readers expect will happen. This kind of irony is present, for instance, when a character, trying to frighten a rival, ends up being frightened himself. *Dramatic irony* occurs when the reader understands more about what is happening in a story than the character who is telling the story does. For example, a narrator might tell an anecdote that he intends to illustrate how clever he is, while it is obvious to the reader from the story's events that the narrator has made a fool of himself because of his gullibility. (See also **Sarcasm**.)

Jargon The specialized vocabulary of a profession or academic field. Although the jargon of a particular profession is an efficient means of communication within that field, it may not be clear or meaningful to readers outside that profession.

Journal writing A method of invention that involves recording ideas that emerge from reading or other experiences and then exploring them in writing.

Looping A method of invention that involves isolating one idea from a piece of freewriting and using this idea as a focus for a new piece of freewriting.

Main cause See **Causes**.

Metaphor A comparison of two dissimilar things that does not use the words *like* or *as* ("Not yet would they veer southward to the caldron of the land that lay below" — N. Scott Momaday).

Narration The pattern of development that tells a story. (See Chapter 4.)

Objective description A detached, factual picture presented in plain and direct manner. Although pure objectivity is impossible to achieve, writers of science papers, technical reports, and news articles, among others, strive for precise language that is free of value judgments.

Paradox A statement that seems self-contradictory or absurd but is nonetheless true.

Paragraph The basic unit of an essay. A paragraph is composed of related sentences that together express a single idea. This main idea is often stated in a single *topic sentence*. Paragraphs are also graphic symbols on the page, mapping the progress of the ideas in the essay and providing visual breaks for readers.

Parallelism The use of similar grammatical elements within a sentence or sentences. "I like hiking, skiing, and to cook" is not parallel because *hiking* and *skiing* are gerund forms (*-ing*) while *to cook* is an infinitive form. Revised for parallelism, the sentence could read either "I like hiking, skiing, and cooking" or "I like to hike, to ski, and to cook." As a stylistic technique, parallelism can provide emphasis through repetition — for example, "Walk groundly, talk profoundly, drink roundly, sleep soundly" (William Hazlitt). Parallelism is also a powerful oratorical technique: "Until justice is blind to color, until education is unaware of race, until opportunity is unconcerned with the color of men's skins, emancipation will be a proclamation but not a fact" (Lyndon B. Johnson). Finally, parallelism can increase *coherence* within a paragraph or an essay.

Paraphrase The restatement of another person's words in one's own words, following the order and emphasis of the original. Paraphrase is frequently used in source-based papers, where the purpose is to use information gathered during research to support the ideas in the paper. For example, Jonathan Kozol's "Illiterates cannot travel freely. When they attempt to do so, they encounter risks that few of us can dream of" (page 233) might be paraphrased like this: "According to Jonathan Kozol, people who cannot read find travel extremely dangerous."

Personification Describing concepts or objects as if they were human ("the chair slouched"; "the wind sighed outside the window").

Persuasion The method by which a writer moves an audience to adopt a belief or follow a course of action. To persuade an audience, a writer relies on the various appeals — to the emotions, to reason, or to ethics. Persuasion is different from *argumentation,* which appeals primarily to reason.

Plagiarism Presenting the words or ideas of someone else as if they were one's own (whether intentionally or unintentionally). Plagiarism should always be avoided.

Point-by-point comparison A comparison in which the writer first makes a point about one subject and then follows it with a comparable point about the other subject. (See also **Subject-by-subject comparison**.)

***Post hoc* reasoning** A logical fallacy that involves looking back at two events that occurred in chronological sequence and wrongly assuming that the first event caused the second. For example, just because a car will not start after a thunderstorm, one cannot automatically assume that the storm caused the problem.

Prewriting See **Invention**.

Principle of classification In a classification-and-division essay, the quality the items have in common. For example, if a writer were classifying automobiles, one principle of classification might be "repair records."

Process The pattern of development that presents a series of steps in a procedure in chronological order and shows how this sequence of steps leads to a particular result. (See Chapter 7.)

Process explanation A kind of process essay whose purpose is to enable readers to understand a process rather than perform it.

Purpose A writer's reason for writing. A writer's purpose may, for example, be to entertain readers with an amusing story, to inform them about a dangerous disease, to move them to action by enraging them with an example of injustice, or to change their perspective by revealing a hidden dimension of a person or situation.

Quotation The exact words of a source, enclosed in quotation marks. A quotation should be used only to present a particularly memorable statement or to avoid a paraphrase that would change the meaning of the original.

Refutation The attempt to counter an opposing argument by revealing its weaknesses. Three of the most common weaknesses are logical flaws in the argument, inadequate evidence, and irrelevance. Refutation greatly strengthens an argument by showing that the writer is aware of the complexity of the issue and has considered opposing viewpoints.

Remote cause See **Causes**.

Rhetorical question A question asked for effect and not meant to be answered.

Rogerian argument A strategy put forth by psychologist Carl Rogers that rejects the adversarial approach that characterizes many arguments. Rather than attacking the opposition, Rogers suggests acknowledging the validity of opposing positions. By finding areas of agreement, a Rogerian argument reduces conflict and increases the chance that the final position will satisfy all parties.

Sarcasm Deliberately insincere and biting irony—for example, "That's okay—I love it when you borrow things and don't return them."

Satire Writing that uses wit, irony, and ridicule to attack foolishness, incompetence, or evil in a person or idea. Satire has a different purpose from comedy, which usually intends simply to entertain. For a classic example of satire, see Jonathan Swift's "A Modest Proposal," page 676.

Sexist language Language that stereotypes people according to gender. Writers often use plural constructions to avoid sexist language. For example, *the doctors . . . they* can be used instead of *the doctor . . . he*. Words such as *police officer* and *firefighter* can be used instead of *policeman* and *fireman*.

Simile A comparison of two dissimilar things using the words *like* or *as* ("Hills Like White Elephants"—Ernest Hemingway).

Slang Informal words whose meanings vary from locale to locale or change as time passes. Slang is frequently associated with a particular group of people—for example, bikers, musicians, or urban youth. Slang is inappropriate in college writing.

Subject-by-subject comparison A comparison that discusses one subject in full and then goes on to discuss the next subject. (See also **Point-by-point comparison**.)

Subjective description A description that contains value judgments (*a saintly person*, for example). Whereas objective language is distanced from an event or object, *subjective language* is involved. A subjective description focuses on the author's reaction to the event, conveying not just a factual record of details but also their significance. Subjective language may include poetic or colorful words that impart a judgment or an emotional response (*stride, limp, meander, hobble, stroll, plod*, or *shuffle* instead of *walk*). Subjective descriptions often include *figures of speech*.

Summary The ideas of a source as presented in one's own words. Unlike a paraphrase, a summary conveys only a general sense of a passage, without following the order and emphasis of the original.

Syllogism A basic form of deductive reasoning. Every syllogism includes three parts: a major premise that makes a general statement ("Confinement is physically and psychologically damaging"); a minor premise that makes a related but more specific statement ("Zoos confine animals"); and a conclusion drawn from these two premises ("Therefore, zoos are physically and psychologically damaging to animals").

Symbol A person, event, or object that stands for something more than its literal meaning.

Synonym   A word with the same basic meaning as another word. A synonym for *loud* is *noisy*. Most words in the English language have several synonyms, but each word has unique nuances or *connotations*.

Thesis   An essay's main idea; the idea that all the points in the body of the essay support. A thesis may be implied, but it is usually stated explicitly in the form of a *thesis statement*. In addition to conveying the essay's main idea, the thesis statement may indicate the writer's approach to the subject and the writer's purpose. It may also indicate the pattern of development that will structure the essay.

Topic sentence   A sentence stating the main idea of a paragraph. Often, but not always, the topic sentence opens the paragraph.

Toulmin logic   A method of structuring an argument according to the way arguments occur in everyday life. Developed by philosopher Stephen Toulmin, Toulmin logic divides an argument into three parts: the *claim*, the *grounds*, and the *warrant*.

Transitions   Words or expressions that link ideas in a piece of writing. Long essays frequently contain *transitional paragraphs* that connect one part of the essay to another. Writers use a variety of transitional expressions, such as *afterward, because, consequently, for instance, furthermore, however*, and *likewise*. See the list of transitions on page 43.

Understatement   Deliberate deemphasis for effect: "The people who live near the Mississippi River are not exactly looking forward to more flooding"; "Emily was a little upset about failing math." The opposite of understatement is *hyperbole*.

Unity   The desirable attribute of a paragraph in which every sentence relates directly to the paragraph's main idea. This main idea is often stated in a *topic sentence*.

Warrant   In Toulmin logic, the inference that connects the claim to the grounds. The warrant can be a belief that is taken for granted or an assumption that underlies the argument. (See also **Toulmin logic**.)

Writing process   The sequence of tasks a writer undertakes when writing an essay. During *invention*, or *prewriting*, the writer gathers information and ideas and develops a thesis. During the *arrangement* stage, the writer organizes material into a logical sequence. During *drafting and revision*, the essay is actually written and then rewritten. Finally, during *editing*, the writer puts the finishing touches on the essay by correcting misspellings, checking punctuation, searching for grammatical inaccuracies, and so on. These stages occur in no fixed order; many effective writers move back and forth among them. (See Chapter 1.)

George Orwell. "Shooting an Elephant." From *Shooting an Elephant and Other Essays* by George Orwell. Copyright © 1950 by Sonia Brownell Orwell and renewed 1978 by Sonia Pitt-Rivers. Reprinted by permission of Harcourt, Inc. and A.M. Heath.

Grace Paley. "Samuel." From *Enormous Changes at the Last Minute* by Grace Paley. Copyright © 1971, 1974 by Grace Paley. Reprinted by permission of Farrar, Straus & Giroux, LLC.

Lawrence J. Peter and Raymond Hull. Excerpt from *The Peter Principle* by Lawrence J. Peter and Raymond Hull. Copyright © 1969 by William Morrow & Company, Inc. Reprinted by permission of HarperCollins Publishers, Inc.

Joshua Piven, David Borgenicht and Jennifer Worick. "How to Escape from a Bad Date." From *Worst Case Scenario Handbook: Sex & Dating* by Joshua Piven, David Borgenicht and Jennifer Worick. Copyright © 2001 by Quirk Productions, Inc. Published by Chronicle Books, LLC, San Francisco. Used with permission. www.worstcasescenarios.com.

Katha Pollitt. "Why Boys Don't Play with Dolls." From *The New York Times*, October 8, 1995. Copyright © 1995 by the New York Times. Reprinted by permission.

Jedediah Purdy. "Shades of Green." From *American Prospect*, Vol. 11, No. 4 (January 3, 2000). Copyright © 2000. Reprinted by permission of the author.

Richard Rodriguez. "Strange Tools." From *The Hunger of Memory* by Richard Rodriguez. Copyright © 1982 by Richard Rodriguez. Reprinted by permission of David R. Godine Publisher, Inc.

William Safire. "The Threat of National ID." From *The New York Times*, December 24, 2001. Copyright © 2001 by The New York Times Company. Reprinted by permission.

Scott Russell Sanders. "The Men We Carry in Our Minds." From *The Paradise of Bombs* by Scott Russell Sanders. Copyright © 1984 by Scott Russell Sanders. Originally published in *Milkweed Chronicle*. Reprinted by permission of the author and the author's agent, Virginia Kidd, Literary Agent.

Eric Schlosser. "Your Trusted Friends." From *Fast Food Nation* by Eric Schlosser. Copyright © 2001 by Eric Schlosser. Reprinted by permission of Houghton Mifflin Company. All rights reserved.

David Sedaris. "Make That a Double." From *Me Talk Pretty One Day* by David Sedaris. Copyright © 2000 by David Sedaris. Reprinted by permission of Little, Brown and Company, Inc.

Gayle Rosenwald Smith. "T-shirt's Violent Nickname is an Ugly Fashion Statement." From *The Philadelphia Inquirer*, July 2, 2001. Copyright © 2001. Reprinted by permission.

Bonnie Smith-Yackel. "My Mother Never Worked." Reprinted by permission of the author.

Brent Staples. "Just Walk On By: A Black Man Ponders His Power to Alter Public Space." From *Harper's*, December 1986. Reprinted with the permission of the author.

Oliver Stone. "Memo to John Grisham — What's Next — 'A Movie Made Me Do It?'" From the *LA Weekly*, March 29–April 4, 1996, p. 39. Reprinted by permission of the author.

Amy Tan. "Mother Tongue." Copyright © 1990 by Amy Tan. First appeared in *The Threepenny Review*. Repinted by permission of the author and the Sandra Dijkstra Literary Agency.

Deborah Tannen. "Sex, Lies, and Conversation." From *You Just Don't Understand* by Deborah Tannen. Copyright © 1990 by Deborah Tannen. Reprinted by permission of HarperCollins Publishers, Inc.

Alice Walker. "In Search of Our Mothers' Gardens." From *In Search of Our Mothers' Gardens: Womanist Prose* by Alice Walker. Copyright © 1974 by Alice Walker. Reprinted by permission of Harcourt, Inc. "Women" from *Revolutionary Petunias & Other Poems* by Alice Walker. Copyright © 1970 and renewed 1998 by Alice Walker. Reprinted by permission of Harcourt, Inc.

E.B. White. "Once More to the Lake." From *One Man's Meat*, text copyright © 1941 by E.B. White. Copyright renewed. Reprinted by permission of Tilbury House, Publishers, Gardiner, Maine.

Juan Williams. "Slavery Isn't the Issue." From the *Wall Street Journal*, Europe, April 10, 2002. Copyright © 2002. Reprinted by permission of the author.

Marie Winn. "Family Life." From *The Plug-In Drug,* Revised and Updated 25th Anniversary Edition by Marie Winn. Copyright © 1977, 1985, 2002 by Marie Winn Miller. Used by permission of Viking Penguin, a division of Penguin Putnam, Inc.

Michael Zimecki. "Violent Films Cry 'Fire' in Crowded Theaters." From *The National Law Journal*, February 19, 1996. Michael Zimecki is an attorney in Pittsburgh, PA. Reprinted by permission of the author.

William Zinsser. "College Pressures." From *Blair & Ketchum's Country Journal*, Vol. VI, No. 4, April 1979. Copyright © 1979 by William K. Zinsser. Reprinted by permission of the author.

Picture Credits

Chapter 5: Girls and mural, Vincent LaForet/The New York Times.

Chapter 6: Tattoos (clockwise order), Alex Williams; Joel Gordon; Charles Gatewood/STOCK, BOSTON; Bob Daemmrich/STOCK, BOSTON.

Chapter 7: Jack-o'-Lantern, Michael P. Gadomski/PHOTO RESEARCHERS.

Chapter 8: Baseball fight, Louis Requena/AP/WIDE WORLD PHOTOS.

Chapter 9: (a) Auguste Rodin, THE KISS, Musee Rodin, Paris, France; The Bridgeman Art Library; (b) LOVE sculpture by Robert Indiana; photo by Jon Burbank/THE IMAGE WORKS.

Chapter 10: (a) Table on aliens, from The Annual Report of the Commissioner General on Immigration, 1931; courtesy, Immigration & Naturalization Service Library; (b) Health inspection, Courtesy, U.S. Public Health Service Historian.

Chapter 11: Courtesy, U.S. Dept. of Commerce/Bureau of the Census.

Chapter 12: Ad, Courtesy, American Civil Liberties Union; DeVito/Verdi Advertising, New York.

Index

Resources for
Instructors
to Accompany

PATTERNS
for College Writing
A Rhetorical Reader and Guide

NINTH EDITION

Laurie G. Kirszner • Stephen R. Mandell

Resources for Instructors
to Accompany

Patterns
for College
Writing

A RHETORICAL
READER
AND GUIDE

NINTH EDITION

LAURIE G. KIRSZNER
UNIVERSITY OF THE SCIENCES
IN PHILADELPHIA

STEPHEN R. MANDELL
DREXEL UNIVERSITY

with the assistance of
MARK GALLAHER

Bedford/St. Martin's
Boston ◆ New York

Manufactured in the United States of America.

8 7 6 5 4
f e d c b a

For information, write: Bedford/St. Martin's, 75 Arlington Street, Boston, MA 02116
(617-399-4000)

ISBN: 0-312-40941-9

PREFACE

Our main purpose in this manual to accompany the ninth edition of *Patterns for College Writing* is to save the instructor time in choosing assignments and in working with the questions that follow each selection. For each reading in *Patterns*, we include a paragraph or two on the teaching opportunities it affords, and we sometimes add a personal comment on how we like to approach a favorite selection in our own classes. We also supply the answers that we had in mind as we constructed the questions. Most of the questions are open to a range of worthwhile answers, some of them perhaps more pointed and interesting than our own; not only do we encourage and applaud interpretations that differ from ours, but we would be grateful to hear about them from anyone willing to take the time to write to us. (Wherever appropriate, paragraph numbers are included in the answers so that instructors can easily refer to the text.)

Except for the chapter on combining the patterns, the first selection in each chapter on a rhetorical pattern is not an essay, but a visual text—a photo, an ad, or a piece of fine art—that visually reinforces the chapter's basic rhetorical concept. It is followed by *Reading Images* questions, a *Journal Entry*, and *Thematic Connections*, which help students see how the rhetorical pattern operates in a visual format.

The reading selections in *Patterns* range in subject across much of the college curriculum. They are meant to acquaint students with the rhetorical options open to them as they write for their college courses, and to show how the reading techniques presented in the Introduction and the writing strategies discussed and illustrated in Chapter 1 and throughout the book become crucial to the effectiveness of a finished piece. The selections are also meant to stimulate class discussion and serve as springboards for student writing assignments.

After each essay by a professional writer we ask four types of questions: Comprehension, Purpose and Audience, Style and Structure, and Vocabulary Projects. *Comprehension* questions help students test their understanding of basic content. The questions focus attention on facts, details, and references that are necessary for comprehension; underscore the major points of each essay; and lead students through the logical progression of a writer's ideas.

Purpose and Audience questions focus on how the writer's intent and sense of his or her readers establish boundaries for the essay and govern other decisions the writer must make—for example, how much detail, or what different kinds of detail, must be supplied for one audience as opposed to another. These questions ask students to imagine themselves in the author's place and to consider, from the evidence of the essay, how the audience was perceived.

Style and Structure questions focus on the stylistic and structural options the authors have exercised. Particular attention is paid to organization, sentence structure, and word choice.

Vocabulary Projects are designed to help students build their vocabularies and increase their sensitivity to the various connotations and denotations of key words. These questions also focus on using synonyms and antonyms and on identifying figurative language.

Following the questions about each essay is a *Writing Workshop* prompt, which asks students to use a particular rhetorical strategy and to write something in response (though not necessarily in reply) to the essay they have read. Some of the assignments require students to assume various roles and to address different audiences; others ask them to write in their own voices, drawing as necessary on the materials in the essay for examples, facts, or quotations.

Except for the chapter on argumentation, each of the chapters on a single rhetorical pattern includes a poem or a short story that illustrates the pattern. After each of these poems or stories we ask *Reading Literature* questions that focus students on many of the same concerns that they consider for the essays—rhetorical organization, diction, imagery, and meaning. We want students to see that writers of various genres are involved in making many of the same choices.

After each selection by a professional writer, we include a *Journal Entry* prompt, a question that will stimulate students to examine and clarify their own value systems. We believe that regularly writing responses to these questions will assist students in developing good thinking, reading, and writing skills and, frequently, in generating paper topics. *Combining the Patterns* questions follow each professional essay. These encourage students to see other patterns at work within the dominant pattern of the essay.

Also included after each selection by a professional writer are *Thematic Connections*, which encourage students to perceive relationships between selections (including the student essays) they have read. The *Thematic Connections* can be used for classroom discussion or as topics for reading-based student essays.

At the end of each rhetorical chapter is a comprehensive list of *Writing Assignments*, some asking students to connect two or more selections. A suggested *Collaborative Activity* for writing follows this list. New to this edition is an *Internet Assignment* for each rhetorical pattern and each argument debate and casebook.

The final chapter, Combining the Patterns, presents one student essay and three professional essays, each of which demonstrates several different patterns within a single piece of writing. The student essay and the first professional essay have been annotated to identify these various patterns.

The Appendix includes a step-by-step discussion of writing a research paper as well as guidelines for citing and documenting both print and online sources. It gives advice about using quotation, paraphrase, and summary, as well as avoiding plagiarism, and it includes a new sample student research paper. An updated Glossary defines terms important to good writers. We have cross-referenced them, whenever useful, to discussions within the text.

Peer-editing worksheets, to be used with writing assignments for Chapters 4–13, appear in this manual and are also available as part of the transparency master package.

A Web site offering additional materials, access to online grammar practice through Exercise Central, the largest collection of exercises available, and access to the Toplinks database, with links on the most commonly chosen writing topics, can be found at <bedfordstmartins.com/patterns>.

Transparency masters, which include sample student essays from the textbook and peer-editing worksheets that students can use to evaluate each other's work, are available as a separate package.

In all cases we have tried to make the questions and writing assignments interesting, challenging, and accessible. We would be grateful for suggestions that might improve both this manual and *Patterns for College Writing*. Comments may be sent to us at our college addresses or c/o Bedford/St. Martin's, 33 Irving Place, New York, NY 10003.

Laurie G. Kirszner
Department of Humanities
University of the Sciences in Philadelphia
Philadelphia, Pennsylvania 19104

Stephen R. Mandell
Department of Humanities–Communications
Drexel University
Philadelphia, Pennsylvania 19104

CONTENTS

MODEL SYLLABI

We have included two sample syllabi that we hope will show you the flexibility you have with the ninth edition of *Patterns for College Writing*. The first uses the text's rhetorical approach for a 10-week term; the second uses both a thematic and a rhetorical approach for a 14-week term.*

SYLLABUS—RHETORICAL APPROACH:
10-week term, 3 meetings per week

Instructors can tailor readings to suit their own students' abilities and interests.

WEEK	ACTIVITIES
1	**Introduction** Introduction: Reading to Write Part 1: The Writing Process Diagnostic Essay
2	**Narration and Description, Chapters 4 and 5** Introduction Readings Narrative or Descriptive Essay
3	**Exemplification, Chapter 6** Introduction Readings Exemplification Essay
4	**Process Analysis, Chapter 7** Introduction Readings Process Analysis Essay
5	**Cause and Effect, Chapter 8** Introduction Readings Cause-and-Effect Essay
6	**Comparison and Contrast, Chapter 9** Introduction Readings Comparison-and-Contrast Essay
7	**Classification and Division, Chapter 10** Introduction Readings Classification-and-Division Essay

Suggestions for modifying these syllabi are discussed in this manual's introduction to Part I of text.

SYLLABUS—THEMATIC/RHETORICAL APPROACH:

14-week term, 3 meetings per week

This syllabus is organized primarily around a thematic approach; however, included with each theme is a rhetorical mode that the essays on the theme illustrate. Of course, instructors may modify the syllabus by deleting the rhetorical introductions and supplementing the units with additional selections (by professional or student writers) on the theme for each week.

WEEK	ACTIVITIES
1	**The Writing Process**

Introduction: Reading to Write
Part 1: The Writing Process
Writing Activity: Diagnostic Essay

2 Autobiography

Using Description: Introduction to Chapter 5
Family Relationships:
"Only Daughter," Sandra Cisneros
"Words Left Unspoken," Leah Hager Cohen
"The Way to Rainy Mountain," N. Scott Momaday
"Two Ways to Belong in America," Bharati Mukherjee
"Suicide Note," Janice Mirikitani
Writing Assignment: Essay on a Family Relationship

3 Autobiography

Using Narration: Introduction to Chapter 4
Life Lessons:
"Shooting an Elephant," George Orwell
"Once More to the Lake," E. B. White
"The Catbird Seat," David J. Birnbaum
"My First Conk," Malcolm X
"Strange Tools," Richard Rodriguez
Writing Assignment: Essay on an Epiphany
PEER EDITING WORKSHOP

4 Education

Using Exemplification: Introduction to Chapter 6
"Indian Education," Sherman Alexie
"The Human Cost of an Illiterate Society," Jonathan Kozol
"Brains versus Brawn," Mark Cotharn
"College Pressures," William Zinsser
"What I Learned (and Didn't Learn) in College," Kristy Bredin
Writing Assignment: Essay on Education

*Alternatively, the unit could focus on the reparations for slavery debate, with students reading the essays in the casebook "Should African Americans Receive Reparations for Slavery?"

USING THE END-OF-CHAPTER
COLLABORATIVE ACTIVITIES

Chapters 4–13 in this edition of *Patterns for College Writing* each conclude with a Collaborative Activity that allows students to work together to produce a paper or class presentation based on a particular rhetorical strategy. Although we don't expect that most instructors will assign a Collaborative Activity with every chapter for which they assign an individual paper, we do encourage you to give students at least one or two opportunities to complete an assignment collaboratively. A collaborative writing assignment allows students to witness a variety of writing styles and writing habits; it also provides a writing situation that students generally take seriously because they recognize that others' grades depend on their performance. Moreover, collaboration is a real-world activity; students should realize that much writing in business and professional settings is produced collaboratively, either with a different person taking on each different stage of the writing process (research, drafting, editing, and so forth) or with each person contributing a section to a larger report that is then refined and edited by the group. Finally, the assignments that call for class presentations give students practice in oral rhetoric, skills that have many academic and professional real-world applications.

Following are a few suggestions for setting up collaborative activities:

Make sure each group has a "leader." Although peer-editing groups can often be assigned randomly, collaborative groups generally work best if they are balanced in terms of individual members' abilities and the dynamics of the group. In assigning groups—particularly for the first few times—keep in mind that each should include at least one student you can depend on to motivate the others to keep the project moving forward. These "leaders" will not necessarily be the most adept writers but rather those students who are outgoing and responsible and who consistently make positive contributions to class discussion. For writing projects it can also be a good idea to see that each group has a good editor as well—a student whose command of grammar, mechanics, and spelling is strong.

Provide an explicit schedule. Most collaborative activities can be completed in one-and-a-half to two-and-a-half weeks (three to five class sessions); a few may require even less time. Generally, on the day you introduce the assignment, you should give students time in class to get started and provide a written schedule so they will know from the start what activities need to be divided up. Then, for each subsequent class session, students should come prepared to meet at least briefly with their group, bringing with them whatever materials are due for that session. It is up to you whether to require group meetings outside of class (although activities involving group drafting, like the one following Chapter 5, will almost have to involve some group work out of class, unless you're willing to devote several complete class sessions to the task).

Here's a typical schedule for the most common kind of Collaborative Activity, which asks each group member to contribute a paragraph or section individually. (Note that the suggested activities for any of the four days could be extended into an outside meeting.)

Day 1:   Give the assignment and allow class time for the group discussion suggested by the assignment or for planning.

Day 2:	Have students bring drafts of their contributions for review and revision suggestions by other group members; have groups discuss possible strategies for the introduction and conclusion and determine who will draft each.
Day 3:	Have students bring revised drafts of their contributions and the draft introduction and conclusion; have groups work to revise the individual parts into a whole essay and then determine which member will type the full draft.
Day 4:	Have groups meet to discuss and revise the full draft and then determine who will edit and type the final version.
Day 5:	Final version due; allow time for each group member to proofread quickly before collecting.

You might ask the groups to provide multiple copies of their final drafts to share in rotation with the other groups.

Allow for group self-evaluation. As groups are meeting in class, feel free to observe and even join each group for a few minutes to answer questions or make suggestions. If you observe a student behaving in a way seriously detrimental to the functioning of the group, you might want to talk to that student privately; but in general, try to give each group responsibility for "policing" lack of contribution or other inappropriate behavior. For example, if you grade a collaborative assignment, do so using points, and then require each group to determine collectively how many points each individual member will receive. Once the assignment is complete, you might also ask members to write a brief evaluation of the workings of their group to share—perhaps anonymously—with the rest of the group.

At several points during the semester, you may want to have students write briefly about their experience working with groups generally: what they've learned about group decision-making and group dynamics as well as their own usual function in groups.

USING THE END-OF-CHAPTER INTERNET ASSIGNMENTS

The Internet assignments at the ends of Chapters 4–13, revised and updated for this edition, give students an opportunity to access a wide variety of Internet sources. While these assignments will naturally interest students who are already experienced Internet users, they may be most useful for students who have little or no such experience. The sites listed are all reliable, and well designed; they are also easy to navigate. As a group, they suggest the wide range of information available online. (Novice users could benefit enormously by accessing the three comprehensive online guides to using the Internet listed at the end of Chapter 7, "Process.")

Before assigning these activities, make sure all the students in your class have easy access to the Internet. Most campuses now offer students at least some access to the Internet. If you are not already familiar with what is available at your school, check with your library or with the office that oversees such services. Generally, workshops introducing the Internet and other electronic services are offered at regularly scheduled times. Many of your students, of course, may have access at home or in their workplaces. Additionally, students may be able to use computers linked to the Internet in local public libraries or in commercial "cybercafes." (Alternatively, you could allow students to choose an Internet assignment for a paper in a particular mode but also allow them to complete the assignment by using the more traditional writing suggestions in the text. You might also allow the Internet assignments to be completed for extra credit.)

Each Internet assignment asks students to use information they find at suggested sites as support for an essay. (Complete URLs are provided for each site, along with a brief description of what the site has to offer.) By their nature, the assignments all involve at least some level of research, so before assigning them you might take the opportunity to have students practice documenting online sources; models are provided in the appendix, "Writing a Research Paper."

Although all the sites in these assignments are well regarded and reliable, you may want to warn students that not everything they find on the Internet can be trusted. Virtually anyone can create Internet sites and postings, and while most are harmless, they also provide a forum for biased arguments, crackpot theories, and even outright lies posing as fact. As with any research, students must view the sources of their information with a critical eye.

INTRODUCTION: READING TO WRITE

The introductory discussion of reading as it relates to the writing process is extremely important because many students have not learned to read actively. Instead, they do little more than move their eyes across the lines of print—reading their textbooks as if they were reading a light novel. The Introduction prepares students to read critically, so the activities you use with it can prepare students to read—and to discuss—the materials in this (and any) text. The Introduction is especially important if you are using the text as the source of material for reading-based essays.

READING CRITICALLY

One way to help students read and respond critically is to conduct a simple exercise with class members. As you discuss the concept that reading is "a two-way street," ask where students grew up—near your school, in distant areas of your state, in other states, or even in other countries. You can then discuss what differences such diversity can make in the reading and writing process. Similar questions can be asked about students' ages and backgrounds—ethnic, economic, etc. Also, review Henry Louis Gates's essay "'What's in a Name?'" and ask your class how various students' backgrounds are likely to affect their reading of the essay. Such discussion not only suggests that different responses are likely as various people read, but it also gives students a sense of their own audience for the essays they will be writing.

As you discuss the Introduction, you will want to stress differences between subjective and objective responses—and the extent to which each is appropriate in the reading/writing process. Students will need reminders of the "rules" for validating an interpretation because many have not learned to do close readings of a text. Push your students beyond the recall level, and insist that they turn to the text to support their interpretations. When students distort, overlook details, or add irrelevant details, systematically ask them to point to evidence in the text. At first, many students will expect you to signal the right answer. Not telling them that they are wrong reinforces the concept that a text may lend itself to more than one interpretation. When you ask students to turn to the text, you may also discover another valid interpretation—one you had not anticipated. Saying as much enlivens discussions throughout the term as you and your students become a community of scholars. Students will quickly learn to question and respond in appropriate ways.

READING ACTIVELY

Do more than merely assign the Introduction. As you assign it, go over the signals given by the text's formatting—the items discussed in the section *Before You Read*. Show students that the headnotes and headings can be turned into questions for them to keep in mind as they read. Ask them to consider questions you might ask during the discussion—questions such as those listed in *As You Read*—which move students from making inferences (questions 1–4), to forming judgments (questions 5–8), and finally to making connections with their own experience and with other selections in the text—the sort of connections from which paper topics can grow (questions 9–10). Define both *highlighting* and *annotating* and ask students to do both as they read the Introduction. When they come to class, you might ask them what questions would have been fair for you to have asked, had you quizzed them on their first reading assignment. Students will be happy to demonstrate that they read closely—and relieved that they are to receive reinforcement for good reading skills. Peer groups can also be used to reinforce the kinds of information students should have discovered in their first reading assignment.

READING THE SELECTION

As you discuss the Gates essay and the study questions that follow it, you will want to stress not only the ways the textbook can be used but also the kinds of questioning strategies that will make students better readers. You will also want to emphasize the questions that can lead to multiple answers—and consider reasons Gates might have had for leaving some details open to more than one interpretation. Explain that not every question has a single "right" answer, but explain as well that students need to be able to justify their responses from within an essay.

If your course calls for students to write reading-based (rather than personal) essays, you will want to focus very carefully on the discussions of *Thematic Connections.* Used throughout the text, these sections can be the source of subject matter for many essays. Using these in early discussions will illustrate for students the kinds of critical skills they will need in order to write effective essays based on selections from the text. (The student paper in the Appendix, Writing a Research Paper, is an example of an essay that draws on thematically linked readings in the text for its subject matter. Although this paper cites additional outside sources—to demonstrate documentation style for sources other than books—it can still show students how they may base their essays on readings linked by theme.)

You may also want to point out the questions under the Combining the Patterns section following the Gates essay. Questions about subsidiary patterns used within a dominant pattern follow every essay in the text. These questions can help students see that most writing mixes patterns at least to some degree, an idea that is reinforced in Chapter 13, Combining the Patterns, where we include three longer, more complex essays.

A final note about the questions following the readings. You may find, with the Gates essay as well as with the other essays throughout the book, that you do not want—or need—to deal with every question in class. For example, a class of fairly advanced readers might find the Comprehension questions a bit basic; or, you might want to stress style or audience rather than how patterns are combined. In fact, we have included more questions than we expect every instructor to use in order to provide the greatest degree of flexibility. You should certainly choose and assign questions for discussion according to your students' needs and the particular focus of your writing instruction.

PART ONE: THE WRITING PROCESS

Part One presents an overview of the entire writing process, from deciding on a topic through revising and editing the first draft. You may want to spend two or more weeks on these three chapters, having students work their way through the entire process as they complete their first paper for the class. You might even work through the three chapters in Part One in conjunction with the first pattern chapter you assign. For example, you might have your students read and discuss the essays in Chapter 4 and then have them draft and revise narrative essays of their own based on the guidelines in Part One. In any case, rather than assign students to read all of Part One at once, you will probably want to assign one chapter per class session.

Whatever your choice, you will want to link carefully the concepts discussed in Part One to those discussed in the Introduction: Reading to Write in order to make the reading/writing connection clear for students who see these activities as only loosely related. We have structured the introductions on reading and writing to assist you in making this connection: In Part One, Laura Bobnak's essay, with its multiple drafts, explicitly connects reading and writing since it responds to an assignment derived from the Gates essay—which is printed in the Introduction. As you work your way through other chapters in the text, remind students to read actively and to consider various ideas in their readings as potential paper topics. Encourage your students to read selections once for overall content and a second time to see the interplay between the writers' choices and their impact on readers. As you discuss various concepts in Part One, tell your students that throughout the term, you will ask them to identify the thesis statement in a selection; to point to major transitions; and to discuss stylistic and thematic subtleties that can only be understood by rereading difficult passages, looking up unfamiliar words, and considering them in context. Encourage students to continue using their highlighting and annotating skills. Ask them to use the questions after each selection to test their understanding before coming to class. Remind them that they will have to make many of the same choices the writers of the selections did; for this reason, developing greater awareness as readers will help them become better writers.

In class, closely focus your discussions on a writer's choices. Students will have a far clearer understanding of purpose, audience, occasion, and other concepts covered in Part One if you guide them both as they read and as they respond to your questions in class. Require students to keep journals with their responses to formal Journal Entries throughout the text as well as any other responses they may have to the text's selections. (You may wish to give a credit/no credit grade to encourage students to stretch and explore their own thinking.) Point out to students the value Laura Bobnak's journal entry (p. 27) had in the writing of her paper. Occasionally during the term, ask students to freewrite, brainstorm, or cluster using one or more of the Writing Workshop prompts at the end of reading selections so they see that what they read is vitally linked to what they write.

In Part One, by necessity, we discuss writing as a linear process, but as experienced writers know, it might more accurately be described as a series of spirals. We outline the steps of the writing process in succession but point out that they can also be performed simultaneously and recurrently. Whether or not you decide to stress this approach depends on the needs of your students. We prefer to give beginning writers a simple, concrete structure rather than overwhelm them with options they cannot fully understand or take advantage of.

Chapters 1 and 2 focus on the prewriting stage of the writing process. Most students entering college underrate prewriting. Thus the techniques we provide to narrow a topic, find something to say, develop a thesis, and arrange ideas will probably be new to them. You may find that, at first, students will resist using the techniques we present. Often a class or two devoted to illustrating prewriting can give students an understanding of how this preliminary work helps inform an entire essay. For example, you may want to tell students that using questions for probing closely parallels their normal thought processes. With these questions, students can construct a framework for the various topics they encounter. Your students should see these questions—and other techniques discussed in Chapters 1 and 2—as systematic ways both of exploring a topic's potential and of organizing the topic's presentation—whether the essay is personal or reading-based.

In Chapter 3 we focus on revision. Often students fail to understand that "finishing" a rough draft involves more than proofreading or correcting errors in grammar and spelling. They are unaware of the need to reconsider the quality of an essay's ideas and its organization into paragraphs and sentences. They do not realize that revision goes on throughout all the stages of their writing. To familiarize students with revision, we take them through three drafts of the sample essay; and, after each student essay in the chapter introductions, we include a Focus on Revision section, which suggests how an already effective essay could be made stronger. To guide your students as they revise, we include Revision and Editing Checklists for easy reference. Encourage students to use these aids.

We also include Guidelines for Peer Critiques and provide a sample peer critique following Laura Bobnak's first draft. (Model peer-editing worksheets for each chapter—like the one used to critique Bobnak's draft—appear on pages 179–88 of this manual and are also available as transparency masters.) Such critiques can be enormously useful in improving both a specific paper and students' overall sense of the connection between their writing and an audience's reading. As they critique their classmates' drafts, encourage students to be specific—to avoid simple "yes" or "no" answers, to refer to examples or passages within the draft, and to offer suggestions that might be incorporated into a subsequent draft. Also make it clear that, while they should take their peer readers' remarks seriously, writers need not follow every suggestion they receive. Ultimately, each writer must make his or her own decisions about how to go about revising a draft.

One possibility for peer critiquing in the classroom is to conduct class sessions as "writing workshops" on days when drafts are due. On these days you may require two or three students to photocopy their drafts and bring copies to class to distribute. After each of the students reads his or her paper aloud, a discussion (guided by the questions on the appropriate peer-editing worksheet) can follow. If possible, try to distribute drafts before the class in which they are to be discussed, so students can fill out peer-editing worksheets in advance. In any case, remind peer critics that their role is to make helpful suggestions, not to correct errors or impose their ideas on the draft they are critiquing. To reinforce this point, instruct them to write their comments on the worksheets, not directly on the photocopied draft.

If you want students to work in small groups, set up these groups well ahead of time so students know how many photocopies to make. (If you want to avoid the expense and possible confusion of making a number of photocopies, you can assign students to work in pairs; in this case they can simply exchange papers.)

Even if students are working in very small groups, with an "audience" of only one or two other students, it is still a good idea to require them to read their drafts aloud. Both student authors and their audiences will hear errors and inconsistencies that they may overlook when reading silently, and hearing students read aloud will sometimes alert you to reading difficulties they have.

Finally, be sure each student whose draft is the subject of a peer critique session knows to take careful notes about the other students' comments and suggestions and to ask for clarification when necessary.

As students revise their drafts—especially for your earlier assignments—you will want to make sure they recognize that an effective essay does not necessarily follow a five-paragraph formula. In fact, such a formula can impose restrictions on the development of a student's ideas. Students should see that, like Laura Bobnak's essay, their own work should proceed organically, with the structure and organization growing out of the development of their ideas. As the semester progresses, you should also eventually encourage students to depart from the confining structure of the informal outlines presented in the text. For example, they can certainly move beyond a "there are three reasons" thesis statement and a simple restatement of their thesis in the conclusion.

As students write and revise, encourage them to use computers. Although *Patterns* does not require students to use computers, we have made suggestions in Computer Strategy boxes throughout Part One for those who do. Whether you teach a computer-assisted course or a traditional one, your students will probably have access to computers in a writing lab, library, or computer center. If so, you can use a variety of techniques to facilitate computer revision. For example, you can encourage students to put topic sentences in a draft in bold print—a form of review outlining—to help them analyze their papers' structure. You can also demonstrate (or have demonstrated) the ease with which they can rearrange whole sections of a paper by cutting and pasting, and the use of spell checkers and interactive software that raises such questions as the number of *be* verbs in a draft. If students have compatible hardware and software, you can even have them critique each other's disks, and you may want to react to students' disks yourself, placing your comments wherever they will be most helpful. Make sure your students understand that they should print out a hard copy of a draft sometime before they present a finished essay. Too few of them notice their mechanical errors on the screen. Also insist that your students keep backup disks of all their work.

To reinforce the various concepts of Part One, we suggest that you have students complete the exercises included throughout Chapters 1–3. You can have students work on these exercises individually or in small groups. You may want to assign all the exercises or just some of them. Later, as you assign and discuss selections in the text, you may wish to adapt some of the exercises in Part One to help students generate and organize ideas for reading-based essays by using one or more *Thematic Connections* included with a particular selection. Of course you may wish to reproduce essays your students have written and ask your class to discuss them.

Following are discussions of the exercises in Part One, each labeled with its appropriate topic heading.

1: INVENTION

Exercise 1—Setting Limits (p. 19)

1. A history of animal testing in medical research labs is too broad a topic for a two- to three-page paper. Without further narrowing, this topic could not be treated adequately in such a short essay.

2. This kind of topic is typical of an essay examination. Before writing an answer, a student should narrow the topic by deciding what points to discuss about the effectiveness of bilingual education programs. The number of points and the depth of the discussion are determined by the two hours allotted for the exam and the number of other questions.

3. An interpretation of Andy Warhol's soup cans is an unlikely in-class essay assignment for courses other than art history. This topic requires more knowledge about art than most students ordinarily would have, and research would be impossible under the circumstances.

4. An examination of a school's policy on alcoholic beverages would be suitable for a letter to a college paper.

Exercise 2—Setting Limits (p. 20)

The purpose of this exercise is to make students aware of the different audiences they encounter daily. An even more important realization for students is that they accommodate themselves rhetorically to each of these audiences. Levels of diction, subjects, and strategies are adjusted to suit the various audiences.

Exercise 3—Questions for Probing (p. 22)

1. Limited topic
2. Limited topic
3. Limited topic
4. General subject
5. Limited topic
6. General subject
7. Limited topic
8. General subject
9. Limited topic
10. General subject

Exercise 4—Questions for Probing (p. 22)

Students should be encouraged to use the questions for probing. This exercise lets them practice generating limited topics from general subjects. Here, you can demonstrate to them that even the most mundane general subjects can yield several interesting and workable limited topics. This is the first step in breaking down many students' preconceptions that they have nothing to say.

Exercise 5—Freewriting (p. 24)

Your students may have difficulty at first and may begin several topics before they find one they can focus on. They may also wish to repeat Exercise 4, generating topics for different general subjects.

Exercise 6—Freewriting (p. 24)

Students who have narrowed their topics sufficiently in Exercise 5 should be able to continue to freewrite from the summaries they generate. However, you may have to provide assistance for some students.

Exercise 7—Freewriting, Brainstorming, Clustering, and Making an Informal Outline (p. 29)

This exercise not only reinforces the concepts introduced in the previous section, but enables a student to progress from a general subject, to a limited topic, to a list of ideas that could be discussed in a paper, and to a rough outline of the first draft. Depending on their own learning styles, students will likely develop a preference for either clustering or informal outlining. This is a good time to tell students that some assignments, such as midterm and final examination questions, result from the narrowing of general subjects to limited topics. Knowing this can help students to prepare for such assignments and to complete them effectively by practicing the techniques described.

Exercise 8—Formulating a Thesis (p. 33)

1. Many students' first thesis statements will resemble item (2). Although this statement now expresses an opinion, it still lacks the clear limits of a good thesis.
2. Like Item 1, this is still too broad to serve as an effective thesis.
3. This is an effective thesis statement; the paper that follows would discuss myths that express societal attitudes.
4. This is a statement of fact rather than opinion; therefore, it is not a thesis statement.
5. This is a thesis statement; the paper would discuss examples of skiing injuries.
6. This is a thesis statement; the paper would give examples of needed reforms.
7. This is a topic, not a thesis statement.
8. This is a thesis statement; the paper that follows would discuss techniques parents could use to help their preschool children learn.
9. You will want to compare this item to (10). Although this statement expresses an opinion, it still lacks the clear limits of a good thesis.
10. This is a thesis statement; the paper that follows would demonstrate how fiction can encourage social change.

Exercise 9—Formulating a Thesis (p. 34)

Students' thesis statements will vary. You may want to put several of them on a transparency for evaluation in class. Push your students beyond platitudes and stress clear wording.

Exercise 10—Formulating a Thesis (p. 34)

Even good statements of Sagan's thesis will vary somewhat. One possible statement might be the following: Because robots are becoming increasingly sophisticated and need no biological or safety provisions, we must overcome our "primitive chauvinisms" against using them in space.

Exercise 11—Formulating a Thesis (p. 35)

This exercise enables students to progress through the entire prewriting process. As students do this assignment, reinforce the importance of prewriting and tell them that this process should play a major part in all their writing assignments.

2: ARRANGEMENT

Exercise 1—The Introduction (p. 41)

Examples for each kind of introduction in the text include the following:

Background information: "Television: The Plug-In Drug" (Ch. 8)
Definition: "Make That a Double" (Ch. 6)
Anecdote or story: "Just Walk On By" (Ch. 6)
Question: "In Search of Our Mothers' Gardens" (Ch. 13)
Quotation: "Violent Films Cry 'Fire' in Crowded Theaters" (Ch. 12)
Surprising statement: "Shooting an Elephant" (Ch. 4)
Contradiction: "A Peaceful Woman Explains Why She Carries a Gun" (Ch. 8)
Fact or statistic: "Shades of Green" (Ch. 10)

Exercise 2—Body Paragraphs (p. 44)

Any essay in the text could be used for this exercise, but you should probably limit students to paragraphs of five or more sentences.

Exercise 3—Body Paragraphs (p. 46)

Good choices for this exercise include "Sex, Lies, and Conversation" (Ch. 9) or "Shades of Green" (Ch. 10).

Exercise 4—The Conclusion (p. 47)

Examples for each kind of conclusion in the text include the following:

Review of key points: "Slavery Isn't the Issue" (Ch. 12)
Recommendation: "Sex, Lies, and Conversation" (Ch. 9)
Prediction: "Shades of Green" (Ch. 10)
Quotation: "Violent Films Cry 'Fire' in Crowded Theaters" (Ch. 12)

Exercise 5—Formal Outlines (p. 49)

Some students find making formal topic outlines a difficult task. If you assign this exercise, you should carefully go over the sample outline in the text and also demonstrate how to construct an outline, using either the board or an overhead projector.

3: DRAFTING AND REVISING

Exercise 1—The First Draft (p. 53)

Remind students that first drafts do not have to be perfect. Encourage them to write as fluently as possible without stopping to make minor corrections or worrying too much about spelling and punctuation—particularly if doing so interrupts the flow of their writing.

Exercise 2 and Exercise 3—Revising the Draft (pp. 65–66)

You may wish to combine these two exercises, having students revise their drafts after they have been read and commented on by another student or students. You might also choose to comment yourself on their first drafts before having students revise.

Exercise 4—Editing (p. 66)

Remind students how crucial the editing process can be; call attention to mistakes in grammar, punctuation, and spelling that can seriously limit the effectiveness of a piece of writing, no matter how strong its content. This might be a good time to review with students their assigned handbook if you require one. If not, you might point out the importance of a good guide to grammar and punctuation, as well as a dictionary.

PART TWO: READINGS FOR WRITERS

The Introduction: Reading to Write, both in the text and in this manual, discusses how the readings in this part and their apparatus can be used.

Note that the headnotes in this edition have been revised or newly drafted to provide information not only about the author but also about the cultural or historical context crucial to understanding the reading. We have come to recognize that what we consider "common knowledge"—the extent of racial segregation prior to the 1960s, prevailing attitudes in the early days of the feminist movement, and how patterns of immigration have changed over the last hundred years, to cite a few examples—is not immediately available to many students in their teens and early twenties. In addition, some readings assume familiarity with certain historical facts or events that are *not* common knowledge today. In such cases, we have included in the headnote enough background information to help students read and understand the essay.

In other cases, we have used the headnotes to provide interesting background information—for example, statistics about homeless rates, women's entry into higher education and the professions since the 1970s, and so forth—to create a context for a reading.

We suggest that you review the headnotes with students—particularly the information provided in the second paragraphs—before discussing a reading selection. A good way to begin might be to summarize this information (perhaps by posing some version of a "Did you know before reading this . . . ?" question) and then apply the information to the reading itself.

4: NARRATION

Most first-year students seem to feel comfortable with narration because they have usually done a significant amount of first-person writing in high school. This does not necessarily mean, of course, that beginning students will already have mastered narrative writing. As the chapter moves through progressively more demanding narratives, you can gradually encourage your students to identify the techniques that can help them make their personal narratives more effective—

dialogue, sentence variety, sharp detail. Eventually, you may ask your classes to experiment with other kinds of narrative writing, such as narrative journalism.

One way of handling the unit on narration is to assign the chapter's readings in the sequence in which they appear in the text, beginning with the paragraph by Barry Lopez on page 71. The paragraph is useful because it allows you to illustrate the pattern quickly and helps you to teach the use of narrative examples as well. You might then have students work with the panels from the *Spider-Man* comic as a way of recognizing the visual aspects of narratives and how they can be translated into prose.

The first reading, Sandra Cisneros's "Only Daughter," uses a series of short, related narratives that occurred over a number of years as she traces her relationship with her father from childhood onward. With Maya Angelou's "Finishing School," you can emphasize thematic connections with the first reading: Both Cisneros and Angelou consider the chafing effects of discrimination, whether based on gender or on race. In terms of structure, "Finishing School" relates a pattern of events, then concludes by focusing on a single dramatic incident. From "Finishing School," you can move to "My Mother Never Worked," which remains relatively informal in style and simple in vocabulary but employs flashbacks and effective descriptive detail. After your students read Gansberg's "Thirty-Eight Who Saw Murder Didn't Call the Police," you can discuss the differences between personal and journalistic narrative. Barbara Ehrenreich's "Scrubbing in Maine" relates events that take place over the course of a week as Ehrenreich shares her experiences of first being trained by and then working for a housecleaning service she calls The Maids. Here again, you can point out the fact that the work performed by Ehrenreich and her coworkers in contemporary New England is not so far removed from the domestic service Angelou recalls being trained for as a child in the 1930s South. Next you can read Orwell's "Shooting an Elephant," which employs various narrative techniques to analyze political ideas as well as personal reactions. Finally, you can move your students from narrative essays into the realm of fiction with Sherman Alexie's "Indian Education." While clearly autobiographical, Alexie's short story is also a work of the imagination with a somewhat unconventional structure. Divided into thirteen sections—one for each of the narrator's first twelve school years and a final postscript ironically titled "Class Reunion"—it provides a perhaps startling insight into the cultural discrimination and personal difficulties faced by Native Americans living on reservations. Along with the nonfiction narratives, it also suggests the range of options available to writers of narration.

Thematic Connections at the end of each of these selections suggest other readings in the text that you may wish to assign during your narrative unit.

Marvel Comics, from *Spider-Man* (Comic Book)

Students are clearly going to be familiar with the sort of visual narrative represented here. The *Journal Entry* could allow some discussion of how narration involving visuals with some dialogue and brief verbal transitions differs with narration that relies solely on words.

READING IMAGES (p. 82)

1. First, the Vulture, having disposed of Spider-Man, soars off to carry out the next step of his evil plan. Meanwhile, Spider-Man, trapped inside a water tank, blames himself for his carelessness. Then, when he attempts to escape

by means of his web, he realizes that he has neglected to refill the ejector and so it is empty. Seeing that the sides of the tank are too slippery to allow him to climb out, he almost despairs but finally realizes that he does have the ability to escape.

2. A not-so-obvious visual element links the two opening panels: the water tower first glimpsed in the background behind the Vulture and then seen from the inside. In the following panels, the figure of Spider-Man floating in water—although seen from different angles—provides the linkage. The clearest verbal transition is "meanwhile" in the narration of panel two; Spider-Man's "well" (panel two), "Oh, No!" (panel three), "but" (panel four), and "Wait a minute!" (panel 5) can also be seen as transitions.

3. Clearly, prior to the first panel the Vulture used some devious ploy to trap Spider-Man in the water tank. Just as clearly, following the fifth panel Spider-Man will use his special strengths to effect his escape and set off in pursuit of the Vulture.

THEMATIC CONNECTIONS

Creating a Female Sleuth **(p. 265):** Here Marcia Muller describes how she created the fictional private investigator Sharon McCone and then went on to plot her first mystery novel. How might Muller's advice about characterization and plotting be applied to comic books?

On Fire **(p. 280):** Larry Brown's first-person, present-tense account of the life of a fire fighter offers a different kind of adventure story. Some students might want to experiment with turning one of its paragraphs into a series of cartoon panels.

Whodunit—The Media? **(p. 618):** Maggie Cutler's essay about the effects of viewing media violence does not deal specifically with comic books. Students might like to consider why comics—some of which are quite violent—have not come under the same attack as violent movies, television programs, and video games.

The Park **(p. 655):** In this student essay, Michael Huu Truong recalls acting out the adventures of superheroes with a childhood friend. Students might think about why characters with super powers have such appeal for children.

Sandra Cisneros, *Only Daughter*

Sandra Cisneros's essay presents a thought-provoking look at how a particular culture may define gender identity. You will want to make certain that students respect other cultures—even while they may question some cultural practices. One way of doing this is to point out that Cisneros's father was able to appreciate her accomplishment as an author when it became accessible to him in Spanish and when it related to his realm of experience. Students need to recognize that, to a certain extent, we appreciate what we have the experience to appreciate. They also need to recognize Cisneros's father's many positive qualities—his love of family, his love of Mexico, and his hard work to provide for his family, including his children's educations.

You may also help students suspend their judgments about Cisneros's father by pointing out that other cultures—for example, the more conservative cultures of the Arab world—have similar views of women. You may want to make students aware of historical male dominance in the Anglo culture, and of some religious or ethnic groups' continuing male dominance—the debates, for instance, in some sects over the possibility of female clergy. Remind them of the continuing pay differential between men and women in this country and the debate in the military about women's value as soldiers.

You may want to discuss changes in the mainstream culture that have affected our perceptions of women's roles—such as the need for women to work in factories during World War II, or today's high cost of living, which forces many women to work—and therefore to address such issues as equal pay and opportunity.

COMPREHENSION (p. 87)

1. Cisneros means that her male-oriented household shaped her identity, even those elements of her personality that developed contrary to her father's expectations. Her father's pride in having six sons was so pronounced that she felt negated, especially when he, in a confusion of languages, mistakenly claimed he had seven sons rather than six sons and one daughter. As a result, Cisneros developed her talents to please her father. She says, "In a sense, everything I have ever written has been for him, to win his approval" (7).

2. The expression *the only daughter* is neutral—merely a description of gender in the family; however, the expression *only a daughter* suggests the family's belief that sons are worth more than daughters—a belief Cisneros tried to overcome through her achievements.

3. As "the only daughter," Cisneros was isolated from other family members—which ironically gave her time to read and develop the abilities of a good writer. As "only a daughter," Cisneros was sent to college to meet a suitable husband—which gave her a good education. Since her father saw college as a way for her to marry a man who would earn a good living with his mind, he did not monitor her choice of a major or question her writing—which allowed her to major in English and further develop her writing abilities.

4. Her father thought she had wasted her years of education because, even after two years of graduate school, she did not have a husband. As a result, she longed to have her father affirm her for being *profesora*, not just teacher, and for being a writer.

5. When Cisneros's father asked for additional copies of her story in Spanish translation, he affirmed her as a person, independent of her gender.

PURPOSE AND AUDIENCE (p. 87)

1. Choosing to define and explain Spanish words is a clear indication that Cisneros's primary audience is not Hispanic. She wishes to take an Anglo audience below the surface of her family's strong male orientation—to help them understand its negative effects on her but at the same time to see her father as a sympathetic person, as someone whose approval was worth seeking. She makes the Spanish words accessible to Anglo readers—as the translation of her story into Spanish made it accessible to her father.

2. Cisneros's thesis is that being the only daughter of a working-class Mexican father and Mexican-American mother "had everything to do with who I am today" (2). Many details support her point. Her father's pride in having six sons and her brothers' leaving her alone gave her "time to think and think, to

imagine, to read and prepare myself" as a "would-be writer." Her father's belief that she would find herself a suitable husband while in college and his indifference to what she might be studying and writing further developed her abilities to teach and write. These abilities led her to two National Endowment for the Arts Fellowships, a guest professorship, and publications—including the one in Spanish translation that finally won her father's approval. Her teaching and publishing grew out of her need for her father's approval. He came to represent "a public who is uninterested in reading, and yet one whom I am writing about and for, and privately trying to woo" (8).

3. Cisneros felt diminished by her father's cultural attitudes toward gender, but she makes clear that his preference for sons was a result of his Mexican heritage, rather than a personal character flaw. Overall she presents him as sympathetic—as a hard-working man who loved his family and his homeland; as a father who wanted his children not to be poor; and, when able to read her story in Spanish, as a parent who was proud of her and wanted to share her accomplishment.

STYLE AND STRUCTURE (p. 87)

1. Each of Cisneros's episodes relates an experience or a cluster of experiences that helped to shape her, beginning with her writing of a contributor's note for an anthology, which caused her to recognize that being an only daughter of a Mexican father and Mexican-American mother has determined her identity. This awareness provides her with the thesis statement for "Only Daughter." Each of the short narratives that follows is accompanied by analysis, which explains how Cisneros felt herself "being erased" (12) but, at the same time, shaped as a writer. Consequently, when Cisneros tells about the Christmas her father affirmed her writing, readers fully understand the importance of that affirmation. The analysis following each episode helps readers understand Cisneros's thesis. Without it, readers would very likely not understand the development that grew out of her sense of diminishment and might also miss her father's positive qualities.

2. As the transitional expressions (question 3) show, episodes are generally presented in chronological order.

3. Transitional expressions indicating time introduce each new episode: *Once, several years ago* (1), *ever since* (2), *when I was in the fifth grade* (4), *After four years in college and two more in graduate school* (4), *Last year, after ten years of writing professionally* (15), and *At Christmas* (16).

4. When Cisneros quotes her father, she humanizes him by allowing him to reveal his pride in his sons, his hard physical work and desire for an easier life for his children, and his language limitations, which are partly responsible for Cisneros's feeling "erased." She also lets us see his doggedness in reading her story once it is presented to him in Spanish and lets us hear his desire to share it with relatives.

5. The details describing Cisneros's father in paragraphs 17–18 focus on evidence of his mortality. Although she says he recovered from a stroke he had two years earlier, the bland food, his horizontal position, the "vials of pills and balled Kleenex" and the "plastic urinal" undercut any sense of robustness that might come from her father's laughing at the movie he is watching. These details contrast strongly with details of her father's mobility in paragraphs 9–11.

13

VOCABULARY PROJECTS (p. 87)

1. *Embroidering,* in its context, ironically feminizes Cisneros's writing of poems and stories—activities that are not inherently gender-linked. Her father would no doubt see embroidering (needlework) as an appropriate—though insignificant—activity for women. Cisneros also conveys this irony when she calls the works she "embroiders" "little poems and stories." *Embroidering* may also suggest embellishing her "little poems and stories" beyond their inherent significance. Her father's early obliviousness to her writing makes his recognition at the end all the sweeter. *Stubbed* suggests that Mr. Cisneros's fingers are *worn down to stubs,* or *stumps,* by hard physical labor.
2. *Sons* suggests the continuation of a patriarchal lineage; *children* does not carry such associations. *Professor* may suggest greater status than *teacher.* Cisneros no doubt correctly interpreted the significance *sons* had for her father. One can argue that *professor* generally denotes an individual with advanced academic degrees, which *teacher* does not.

COMBINING THE PATTERNS (p. 88)

One difference that Cisneros mentions directly in paragraph 3 is that her brothers spent a lot of time together when they were growing up, while she was often alone. At this early point in the narrative, she might have offered other points of contrast between her brothers and herself in terms of family life during childhood and adolescence—for example, household responsibilities, restrictions on behavior (curfews and the like), methods of parental discipline. Later, after she mentions that her oldest brother graduated from medical school (13), she might have offered some more specific contrasts regarding her and her brothers' academic and career choices.

THEMATIC CONNECTIONS

My Field of Dreams (p. 77): Like Cisneros, Tiffany Forte must adjust to a culture that values male accomplishment more highly than it does female accomplishment. However, while Cisneros is ultimately able to achieve her dreams—and even to receive her father's approval for her work—Forte must abandon her childhood dream of becoming a major league baseball player because it is a role that is simply not open to women. You might ask students why they think women—who have broken barriers in so many fields—remain less visible than men in both college and professional sports, except perhaps for tennis, golf, and figure skating.

Words Left Unspoken (p. 153): Leah Hager Cohen also paints a portrait of an older immigrant relative, in this case her grandfather. These two essays provide an interesting opportunity for discussion of differences in relationships across generations. Cohen, for example, sees her grandfather more objectively than Cisneros sees her father, and Cohen doesn't need her grandfather's approval in the way that Cisneros needs her father's. At the same time, the next-to-last paragraph of Cohen's essay suggests how strongly she wanted to find an emotional connection with her grandfather. Cohen's essay can also allow you to talk about the differences between a piece of writing that is primarily narrative and one that is primarily descriptive.

Suicide Note (p. 357): See *Thematic Connections,* "Suicide Note," p. 87 of this manual.

The Men We Carry in Our Minds (p. 456): Scott Russell Sanders considers the roles that are available for men and women in our society, focusing particularly on how class and economic level further limit what anyone—male or female—can dream for oneself. Like Cisneros, Sanders was born into the working class and viewed education as a way to make something better of himself. For him, the lot of men in the working class in which he grew up was harder than the lot of women, and in college he couldn't accept the judgment of upper-class female acquaintances that he was privileged because he was male. Sanders tries to move away from a simple view of sexism to suggest a broader notion of what constitutes power in society.

Maya Angelou, *Finishing School*

"Finishing School" is a personal, colloquial narrative of seemingly unremarkable events. By using dialogue effectively and recording her emotions carefully, Angelou brings her story to life and makes it important and memorable. When you teach this essay, you may need to explain its setting to your students—for instance, providing some background about the Great Depression and perhaps also about black/white relations in the South at the time. Besides stressing Angelou's strengths as a narrator, you might point to the theme of class consciousness in the story, examining the significance of Miss Glory's loyalty to her employer, of Mrs. Cullinan's having married beneath her, and of the narrator's unfamiliarity with the white woman's domestic rituals. The idea of ethnic pride should also be considered.

COMPREHENSION (p. 93)

1. Angelou is required to learn a variety of household rituals: a rigid time schedule for various tasks, the names and uses of a vast array of dishes and silverware, and the proper location of each item—including the separate shelf on which her own and Miss Glory's water glasses were to be placed (4–7). Mrs. Cullinan's rituals were an attempt to hold onto the old South. In the discussion of tasks Angelou performed, we learn that Mrs. Cullinan "kept up the tradition of her wealthy parents," that Miss Glory was "a descendant of slaves that had worked for the Cullinans," and that Mr. Cullinan's family "hadn't had their money very long and what they had 'didn't mount to much.'"

2. At first Angelou feels sorry for Mrs. Cullinan because she is ugly and cannot have children. Her attitude changes when Mrs. Cullinan insults her by calling her "Mary." Angelou recognizes that the impulse to rename her and to discuss her name as if she were not present is based on disrespect for her because she is black.

3. Mrs. Cullinan's friend feels "Margaret" was too long a name and therefore too much trouble to say. This upsets Angelou because, as she notes in paragraph 26, every black person "had a hellish horror of being 'called out of his name.' "

4. Bailey advises his sister to get herself fired by breaking some of Mrs. Cullinan's favorite possessions, ones with symbolic value. Her "Mamma's china from Virginia," "the Virginia dishes," were part of Mrs. Cullinan's attempt to hold onto the traditions of the old South.

5.   Angelou's experience prepared her for adulthood; it taught her that she had to stand up to "white folks" in order to retain her pride.

PURPOSE AND AUDIENCE (p. 93)

1.   Angelou is clearly writing for a general audience. To help her audience understand circumstances with which they may be unfamiliar, she provides information in paragraph 2 about the activities of "Negro girls in small Southern towns" and explains in paragraph 26 why African Americans fear being called by names other than their own.
2.   Angelou uses this exchange to show that the white woman, while ignorant of what Angelou's childhood was like, was no more "ridiculous" in her assumptions about Angelou's life than were the southern blacks themselves in their expectations for their daughters.
3.   Angelou's thesis is that preparation for adulthood involves more than learning the social niceties; it involves learning what is important to you and how to get it.

STYLE AND STRUCTURE (p. 93)

1.   A *finishing school* is a private academy for young women that focuses on social graces and accomplishments. The phrase usually evokes images of young ladies in Victorian dress learning to play the piano and speak French. Ironically, in this selection it is not the superficial social skills Angelou learns but the difficult realities of society.
2.   Angelou signals the passage of time by using transitional phrases such as *During my tenth year* (2), *It took me a week* (5), *the next morning* (11), *For weeks after* (12), *Then one evening* (13), *That evening* (20), *The very next day* (21), and *For a week* (32).
3.   The difference between the standard speech of Mrs. Cullinan and her friends and Miss Glory's nonstandard speech underscores the gap between blacks and whites. This strengthens the narrative by making even clearer the idea that Angelou has to make a choice between her employer's values and her own.
4.   Angelou uses Mrs. Cullinan's wrinkles, the fat covering her fragile bones, and her drinking from unmarked bottles to highlight her unattractiveness and idleness. She uses Mrs. Cullinan's extensive collection of glasses, dishes, and silverware to contrast with what we assume to be the modest circumstances of Angelou's own house—and to suggest Mrs. Cullinan's rigid attempts to hold onto the rituals of the old South.

VOCABULARY PROJECTS (p. 94)

2.   Essentially, the words have similar meanings. The difference lies in the degree—*ludicrous* means that it is even more laughable; a *tureen* is a larger, perhaps fancier soup bowl. The first distinction suggests Angelou's purpose is emphasis; the second that she means to point up Mrs. Cullinan's pretensions.
3.   This exercise gives students an opportunity to see how important context is to word choice. Discuss some of their substitutions in class and have their classmates decide which word is more effective and why.

COMBINING THE PATTERNS (p. 95)

Descriptive passages include paragraphs 3 and 9 (Mrs. Cullinan), 11 (her husband's illegitimate daughters), and 34 (her reaction to Angelou's breaking of the casserole and cups). The descriptions are primarily visual. Students might suggest further descriptions of the setting (the Cullinan house) and of the objects that were broken.

THEMATIC CONNECTIONS

Midnight (p. 201): Grace Ku describes the abominable conditions under which her immigrant parents work in a large dry cleaning establishment, where they do dangerous, physically exhausting work that demands long hours at a substandard wage. Some students may be surprised that such conditions—only a few steps better than physical slavery—are allowed to exist in this country. In comparison with the days of Angelou's youth, few people today work as servants. But many, particularly immigrants with little English and even less knowledge of U.S. employment policies, labor in illegal sweatshops for considerably less than the minimum wage. Given the arguments for limiting immigration, do students think anyone else would take these jobs?

The "Black Table" Is Still There (p. 340): Lawrence Otis Graham's essay offers another African-American perspective on relations between blacks and whites. Graham focuses on the tendency of black students in the largely white junior high school he attended to segregate themselves from the white students—a practice he is sorry to see still exists some ten years after he was a student there. His essay and Angelou's provide an opportunity to compare what changes have occurred in race relations in the sixty years or so since Angelou attended Mrs. Cullinan's "finishing school"—and what hasn't changed.

Litigating the Legacy of Slavery (p. 627): In advocating for reparations for the descendents of slaves, African-American scholar Charles J. Ogletree Jr. writes in this essay that "the civil rights movement has long been organized, in part, around the notion that slavery and the century of legal discrimination that followed have had enduring and detrimental effects on American minorities." Angelou's essay provides some firsthand insight into this legacy of slavery.

Bonnie Smith-Yackel, *My Mother Never Worked*

A discussion of the rationale behind the injustices Smith-Yackel finds in our Social Security laws is bound to produce lively debate, as is the issue of whether Mrs. Smith really "worked." This narrative can be examined in light of its original appearance in *Women: A Journal of Liberation*, a small (now defunct) feminist publication, in the mid-1970s; its subsequent appearance in *Ms*; and its continued relevance today. Students may also want to talk about the differences between "men's work" and "women's work"; between the duties of farm wives and the duties of city wives who are not employed outside the home; and between the responsibilities of homemakers in Mrs. Smith's generation and in the present.

COMPREHENSION (p. 99)

1. Martha Smith worked very hard at raising her children, doing farm chores, and maintaining a household, but she did not work outside the home for pay—the only kind of work recognized by the government.

2. According to the government, Martha Smith is not eligible for a death benefit because she was never employed.
3. The government defines *work* as an activity performed for compensation.

PURPOSE AND AUDIENCE (p. 99)

1. The essay's thesis is that although Martha Smith did not work outside the home, the work she did should be considered valuable enough to entitle her to Social Security benefits. The thesis is never explicitly stated because the accumulation of concrete details argues the author's point more forcefully than would direct statement.
2. This essay might have found sympathetic audiences in other publications. For example, had it appeared in a magazine aimed at homemakers, many of these readers, regardless of their opinions about feminism, might have seen similarities between Martha Smith's story and their own (or their mothers') situations.
3. She mentions little about her father because the thesis of the essay does not concern him.
4. Students, depending on where they are from, may find the essay dated in that the rural way of life described is less common now. The issue the author raises, however, remains the same. A stay-at-home wife and mother is eligible for Social Security benefits only through her wage-earning husband.

STYLE AND STRUCTURE (p. 99)

1. Most students will find the title is effective because it introduces the irony that runs through the essay and is summed up in the conclusion.
2. The frame provides the bureaucratic definition of *work*, which is contrasted in the essay with the meaning of *work* for the individual. It also establishes the contrast between the impersonal efficiency of the present and the warm memories of the past. These contrasts produce the irony that makes the essay so effective.
3. She uses transitional words and phrases that mention the season or month and the year.
4. The many specific, concrete details make it clear that the writer, unlike the Social Security office, feels her mother *did* work.
5. This repetition adds to the enormity of Martha Smith's accomplishments by indicating that she continued to work even after illness and old age had set in.

VOCABULARY PROJECTS (p. 99)

2. Students will come up with a number of different examples, probably simpler and more modern in tone. Discuss how Smith-Yackel's choice of words fits the time in which the events occurred.
3. Smith-Yackel's use of concrete verbs clearly conveys the image of her mother that she wants to project: she shows Mrs. Smith constantly in motion.

COMBINING THE PATTERNS (p. 100)

Passages that suggest a process explanation include paragraphs 16–18 and 21; all relate the daily chores of a farm family. If Smith-Yackel had written her essay entirely as a process explanation, she would have had to eliminate most of the specifics regarding her mother's character and personality, particularly the passages about her parents' courtship (11–12), the births of their children (13, first sentence of 17, and 19), and the details about her mother's later years. The essay would no longer be about her mother.

THEMATIC CONNECTIONS

Midnight (p. 201): This student essay also focuses on hard-working parents, here Asian immigrants who labor in a dry cleaning sweatshop more than twelve hours a day for substantially less than the minimum wage. Although Grace Ku does not say so specifically, it is possible that her parents were working illegally; if so, no contributions were being made by their employer to Social Security. According to the bureaucracy that Smith-Yackel dealt with, Ku's parents may also have "never worked."

On Fire (p. 280): Larry Brown's essay focuses on a different, and certainly more dangerous, kind of labor: firefighting. One interesting question is whether Brown's job—dangerous (and sometimes tedious) though it may be—is more appealing than the backbreaking and precarious farm life Smith-Yackel describes. Note particularly paragraph 8 where Brown writes, "You learn to love a job that is not like sacking groceries or working in a factory or painting houses, because everybody watches you when you come down the street." Does Smith-Yackel's mother seem to have taken the same kind of satisfaction in her work?

I Want a Wife (p. 505): Judy Brady's highly ironic examination of "women's work" can provide an especially interesting pairing with "My Mother Never Worked." Both describe in detail what has traditionally been "expected" of a wife and mother, albeit in two different worlds—one rural and working class, the other urban and professional. Students might discuss the similarities and differences between these two images and what they suggest in terms of class and generational distinctions. They might also consider whether our ideas about the roles of wife and mother have changed in the twenty or so years since these pieces were written.

The Company Man (p. 517): Despite Martha Smith's fears of responsibility before her marriage, her total dedication to her family may be contrasted with Ellen Goodman's "company man," who feels responsibility only to his work—to the exclusion of his family. Students are sure to have strong feelings about the contrast and can discover paper ideas from discussion. Students can also be encouraged to see different ways in which we define *work* and to discuss the relative value of Phil's work and Mrs. Smith's.

Martin Gansberg, *Thirty-Eight Who Saw Murder Didn't Call the Police*

This is an essay that never fails to interest students. Some background about the 1964 incident and the public outcry it generated can open class discussion; the students will probably take it from there, volunteering information about similar incidents they have experienced or heard about. You might want to summarize for the class the psychological experiments described in the widely anthologized essay "Why People Don't Help in a Crisis" and try to examine the motives of those who watched but didn't act. You can also ask students to clip newspaper articles about similar situations—which are surprisingly easy to find. Finally, you can ask your students how they think they might react in such a situation.

COMPREHENSION (p. 104)

1. Kitty Genovese was first stabbed shortly after 3:20; the ambulance arrived at 4:25, but the people did not come out until after it drove away. Thus, over an hour elapsed.
2. The neighbors' excuses ranged from not wanting to get involved to assuming the attack was a lovers' quarrel to being tired or afraid. One woman replied, "I don't know."

PURPOSE AND AUDIENCE (p. 104)

1. The article was intended to make its audience aware of society's general apathy and of our responsibility to correct it. It probably has very much the same impact today as it did in 1964, leading readers to wonder whether they would have come to the victim's aid.
2. The article's main point is "If someone had called the police in time, Kitty Genovese might have been saved." Gansberg has Assistant Chief Inspector Lussen (who is accustomed to crime) express his being shocked by the "good people" who did not call the police. His responses are counterpointed by the weak excuses made by witnesses. An overt statement of the thesis would detract from the contrast.
3. Gansberg's description of Austin Street establishes the area as an ordinary American neighborhood. The idea that such a crime can happen anywhere, to anyone, increases the article's impact. In addition, many middle-class readers of the *New York Times,* Gansberg's original audience, could identify with the residents of such a neighborhood.
4. Gansberg prints the police department's telephone number both to inform his readers and to persuade them how simple it would have been to get help.

STYLE AND STRUCTURE (p. 104)

1. Gansberg's precision helps to establish him as an authority on his subject, someone who has investigated these events thoroughly. This precision makes the reader more likely to accept Gansberg's thesis.
2. The words and phrases that most clearly reveal the writer's anger include the ironic *respectable, law-abiding citizens* (1) and *good people* (4).
3. Many of the briefest paragraphs (3, for instance, or the concluding paragraph) are effective because their brevity makes them stand out. Others (16, for example) include a single line of dialogue and thus would stand as separate paragraphs in any essay. In general, then, the paragraphing probably is effective. Nevertheless, students may feel that the presentation of events is choppy and that combining paragraphs could eliminate this problem.
4. The dialogue makes the article more compelling by presenting the participants as real people with whom readers may identify.
5. The ironic comment by a police detective about the people finally coming out much too late expresses the writer's dismay.

VOCABULARY PROJECTS (p. 104)

2. The repetition of the word *assailant* matches the relentlessness of the attack. The word is also commonly used in reporting crimes. *Attacker* has the same meaning as *assailant,* although the latter is probably more commonly used in the media. *Murderer,* while it ultimately describes the crime, does not necessarily convey the sense of relentless attack since murders can seem relatively passive—in the case of a poisoning, for instance.

COMBINING THE PATTERNS (p. 105)

More descriptive detail about the neighborhood (6, 8–9, 18, and 25), about Kitty Genovese (7), and about her killer (22) would certainly add color and drama to the piece; the result would be something closer to a detailed magazine profile than to Gansberg's straightforward news story. The neighbors he interviewed do suggest some of their reasons for not getting involved, but if he were not reporting as a journalist, Gansberg might have concluded by offering his own analysis of causes. Students may be divided over the effectiveness of doing this because it would be difficult in such an analysis to go beyond simple moralizing about people's indifference. As it is, readers are left to struggle with their own conclusions and to consider what their own responses—and motivations—might be.

THEMATIC CONNECTIONS

Ground Zero (p. 158): Students might consider the 2001 attack on the World Trade Center in New York City and the many ensuing concerns over public safety in light of the uproar created some forty years earlier by the murder of Kitty Genovese. Are people of their generation more fearful of being the victim of a criminal attack than were people of earlier generations? Or are they more complacent about crime? Are they more or less willing to report to authorities what they suspect to be potential criminal behavior? Are they more or less willing to intervene if they witness a criminal attack?

Samuel (p. 239): Grace Paley's compact and thought-provoking short story offers an ironic contrast to the tragedy of Kitty Genovese. Here, it is a bystander's well-meaning attempt to intervene that results in the violent death of a boy recklessly fooling around on the platforms between two New York subway cars. In an interesting parallel to Gansberg's survey of Genovese's neighbors' reactions, Paley lets her readers inside the heads of the people in the subway car as they watch and judge the boys between the cars.

Who Killed Benny Paret? (p. 321): Norman Cousins's indictment of prizefighting focuses on another aspect of violence in the United States. Students may well want to broaden their discussion to include movies, cartoons, video games, contact sports, and other aspects of popular culture that suggest "prevailing mores" about violence in contemporary American society. Have we become so accustomed to violence that we are immune to shock when violence occurs in real life?

A Peaceful Woman Explains Why She Carries a Gun (p. 345): In this essay, Linda Hasselstrom makes the point that a "pistol is not the only way to avoid being raped or murdered in today's world, but, intelligently wielded, it can shift the balance of power and provide a measure of safety." Clearly, if Kitty Genovese had been carrying a gun, she probably would not have been murdered. Do students agree with Hasselstrom that carrying a gun is a good way of protecting oneself?

Barbara Ehrenreich, *Scrubbing in Maine*

One way to begin discussion of this selection is to ask why Ehrenreich, a successful journalist and social commentator, would have chosen to go under cover, so to speak, to work for a low-paying house cleaning service as she relates here. (In researching her book *Nickel and Dimed: On Not Getting By in America,* from which this is an excerpt, Ehrenreich also took jobs as a clerk in a discount store, a waitress in a diner, and a nurse's aide, among others.) Students should recognize that Ehrenreich's politics are fiercely liberal and that her ultimate goal was to show the serious plight of America's working poor by "walking a mile in their shoes." (Ironically, in a sense, the book turned into a best-seller and likely earned Ehrenreich a great deal of money.) Clearly, reporting firsthand as she does is more effective than simply presenting statistics about low-income wage earners, but ask students to think about the extent to which Ehrenreich's methods here are more or less effective than if she had simply relied on interviews with the sorts of working people she encounters. Ask them, as well, to consider the ethical issues involved. In some ways, Ehrenreich must have misrepresented herself to her employers ("The Maids," for example, would hardly have hired her had the company known she was out to expose the organization, even though she has changed the company's name and the names of its managers) as well as to her fellow employees. Do the ends justify the means here? Ehrenreich's critics have also charged that she didn't fully experience life at such menial jobs because she left them after only a few weeks to return to the comfort of her own home before setting out on her research again. Do students find this a legitimate criticism? (If *Nickel and Dimed* is available in your campus library, you might consider putting it on reserve; some students might be interested in reading more about Ehrenreich's experiences before evaluating her research methods.)

COMPREHENSION (p. 114)

1. Ehrenreich is an educated woman and a successful journalist who has chosen to work as a maid in order to research the lives of blue-collar workers. The maids themselves are women with little education and few other employment options.
2. At the end of paragraph 2, Ehrenreich suggests that the only advantages of working for the agency are that one doesn't need a "clientele or even a car. You can arrive straight from welfare . . . right off the boat."
3. The Maids system of cleaning uses very little water or soap; surfaces look clean even though bacteria may remain.
4. Specific cosmetic touches, including fluffing pillows and spraying floral scented air freshener, are described at the end of paragraph 6. The point is to give the illusion that the client's home is clean even though only a fairly superficial job has been done.
5. The Maids are expected to work much more quickly than they are depicted doing in the videos. The actual work is also quite a bit more strenuous.
6. The signs all point to the fact that these women have almost no money—even for minor purchases.

7. Ehrenreich suggests in paragraph 15 that scrubbing the floor on hands and knees gives the illusion that a better cleaning job is being done—and also makes the Maids look more like servants.
8. Economically, Ehrenreich has more in common with Mrs. W., but it is clear that she has greater sympathy for her coworkers. She implies that she herself does not employ a cleaning person. It is likely that Mrs. W. would react negatively if she realized that Ehrenreich was a journalist and would possibly be writing about her.

PURPOSE AND AUDIENCE (p. 114)

1. Her thesis might be restated as "I didn't realize how difficult and demeaning this work would be." Students' opinions may vary as to how much Ehrenreich is exaggerating her situation, but she does find the work exhausting and is literally down on her hands and knees scrubbing floors.
2. Again, students' opinions may vary. Certainly, a large part of Ehrenreich's purpose is to give readers who have never held such menial jobs a sympathetic glimpse into the lives of these workers. Some students may realize that, on a larger level, she is making an argument for a higher minimum wage.
3. For Ehrenreich, the Peruvian musicians represent "secret emissaries of a worldwide lower class conspiracy to snatch joy out of degradation and filth." Despite their circumstances, those at the bottom of the working class can still maintain a kind of dignity.

STYLE AND STRUCTURE (p. 115)

1. Examples of other transitional expressions include "At last, after . . ." (3), "After a day's training" (7), "The Friday of my first week . . ." (11), and "when I can find no more surfaces to wipe . . ." (15).
2. The paragraphs are necessary to Ehrenreich's purpose of suggesting how difficult it is to live on the wages paid by employers like The Maids. They help support her implied argument about raising the minimum wage.
3. Her negative attitude toward Mrs. W. is conveyed through such phrases as "grimacing with exasperation" (12), "now occupying herself by monitoring her investments and the baby's bowel movements" (13), and "every single doodad and *objet* through which she expresses her unique, individual self" (14). Students' opinions may vary as to whether this characterization is fair. It would appear that at least Maddy shares Ehrenreich's contempt when she refers to "Mrs. W. and her big-ass house" (11).
4. Students' opinions will probably vary as to the effectiveness of Ehrenreich's descriptions of her coworkers. In fact, we learn relatively little about them, and only Maddy and, to a lesser extent, Rosalie emerge very clearly as individuals. Dialogue might have strengthened their characterizations and could have been added during their commutes from house to house. However, such dialogue might detract from the sense of drudgery and exhaustion Ehrenreich is attempting to create.
5. Some other early examples of sarcasm include Ted "pausing the video to underscore a particularly dramatic moment" (4); Ehrenreich finding it "good to know . . . that in the hierarchy of the company's values I rank above Windex" (4); and Ehrenreich discovering that "life is nothing like the movies" (6).

Students should be able to find many more examples, and most will recognize that Ehrenreich's sarcasm adds to the humor and the ultimate purpose of her writing.

VOCABULARY PROJECTS (p. 115)

2. Some examples of brand names include Windex (4), Dobie (6), and Doritos (8). The use of brand names helps ground the narrative in an everyday reality. Some students may feel that more might have been effectively added.

COMBINING THE PATTERNS (p. 116)

Most students will probably feel that Ehrenreich adequately suggests the contrasts between her coworkers and herself. Had she done so more explicitly, Ehrenreich might have come off as something of a snob. For this to be a true essay of comparison and contrast, Ehrenreich would have to consider herself and one of her coworkers in terms of background, education, family life, income, goals and aspirations, and so forth. Or she might focus on two of her coworkers in similar terms.

THEMATIC CONNECTIONS

Finishing School (p. 89): In this autobiographical excerpt, Maya Angelou recalls being trained as a young girl for a life of domestic service in the segregated South of the 1930s. The role is not very different from that in which employees of maid services find themselves today.

The Peter Principle (p. 207): Students might compare Ted, The Maids franchise owner, and Tammy, the office manager, with the managers who have risen to the level of their incompetence, as described in this essay.

The Men We Carry in Our Minds (p. 454): Ehrenreich describes the sort of menial work generally accomplished by women. In this classification and division essay, Scott Russell Sanders describes the kinds of work generally assigned to unskilled, blue-collar male workers.

George Orwell, *Shooting an Elephant*

Before discussing "Shooting an Elephant," you will probably need to provide students with some background about imperialism. This should include the extent of the British Empire, the purposes and methods of imperialism, and its effects on native populations or on the system's enforcers. Parallels could be drawn with American military forces stationed abroad or with the Vietnam War, with which students may be more familiar. A more helpful way of illustrating Orwell's predicament might be to ask students to put themselves in the position of a white police officer responding to an emergency in a black ghetto during times of unrest. While the situations are certainly quite different, the inner conflicts they produce may be similar.

Many students probably will have read either *Animal Farm* or *1984*; Orwell's views about political oppression in these novels can enlighten the discussion of "Shooting an Elephant."

COMPREHENSION (p. 123)

1. Orwell is hated because he is a European police officer and therefore a symbol to the Burmese of British imperialism. Despite his position, Orwell had mixed feelings. "Theoretically . . . [he] was all for the Burmese" because he was convinced that imperialism was evil. But he also considered the Burmese "evil-spirited little beasts who tried to make [his] job impossible" (2).
2. The local officials want something done about the elephant because it has been running loose and damaging property. The crowd, on the other hand, wants to be entertained. Orwell notes that they want him to shoot just as an audience wants a magician to perform a trick; their faces were "happy and excited" (7) as they watched. Also, the crowd *expected* Orwell to shoot; they considered it his duty.
3. Orwell says he decided to kill the elephant "solely to avoid looking like a fool" (14). He realizes that he really has no choice; by accepting his position as an imperialist, he has destroyed his own freedom. Thus, like other imperial rulers, "in every crisis he has got to do what the 'natives' expect of him" (7). He hesitates because he feels it would be murder to shoot the elephant, which appears peaceful and harmless. He also feels that killing the elephant is "comparable to destroying a huge and costly piece of machinery" (6) and would cause a hardship for the beast's owner.
4. Orwell believed that the coolie's death justified his decision to shoot the elephant.

PURPOSE AND AUDIENCE (p. 123)

1. The narrative reveals the true nature of imperialism by showing how it oppresses the rulers as well as the ruled.
2. Orwell's essay is strongly persuasive; he hoped to convince his audience of the evils of imperialism, not just provide them with an informative account of his experiences in Burma. Orwell probably expected his audience to be surprised by his potentially controversial views on imperialism. As a consequence, he explains his mixed feelings, the incident, and his resulting recognitions in great detail so his audience can come to understand his perspective.
3. The essay's thesis is that imperialism is an evil practice that enslaves both the rulers and the ruled.

STYLE AND STRUCTURE (p. 123)

1. Orwell's first sentence attracts the reader's attention; the rest of the paragraph presents the story's setting and introduces the conflict between the Burmese and the Europeans. The actual narrative begins with paragraph 3, "One day something happened."
2. Orwell writes this narrative in order to show the effect the incident had on him; he is the story's dominant character. Therefore, his voice is logically the one heard above all others. Given Orwell's purpose, this narrative technique strengthens his essay.
3. Orwell devotes two paragraphs to the elephant's misery to show how much its death upset him. It is clear to the reader that the shooting is no casual event to Orwell.

4. The parenthetical comments in this essay may represent a sudden change in tone or subject, as in paragraph 4, or simply an explanatory aside to the reader, as in paragraphs 8 and 11. In both cases, the comments are isolated so they do not jar the reader with their abruptness.

5. The speaker feels he must choose between two worlds and that he is caught in a dichotomy. Paragraphs 4 and 14 reinforce this theme by showing sharply contrasted differences at all levels in the society.

VOCABULARY PROJECTS (p. 124)

2. Some equivalent expressions might be *cause trouble* for *raise a riot, called me* for *rang me up, garbage truck* for *rubbish van, damaged* for *inflicted violence, a little excitement* for *a bit of fun, I think* for *I daresay.* Your students will probably think of some equally acceptable examples. Other "Britishisms" include *chucked up my job* and *looking a fool* (14).

COMBINING THE PATTERNS (p. 125)

The contrasts Orwell implies between himself (along with others among the British ruling class in Burma) and the Burmese are primarily differences between those who rule and those who are ruled within an imperialist system. He is an intruder, and the Burmese are native to the country; he is comparatively well-off, and they are comparatively poor; he has power, and they are powerless (although he notes that, ironically, his "power" is basically a sham because, like other "tyrants," he "has got to do what the 'natives' expect of him . . . to appear resolute" even when he is uncertain). However, setting these contrasts in sharp opposition in a separate paragraph would tend to undercut Orwell's central point about the ambiguity inherent in the power relationships he describes.

THEMATIC CONNECTIONS

Thirty-Eight Who Saw Murder Didn't Call the Police (p. 101): The preceding piece by Martin Gansberg offers an interesting contrast to Orwell's story. Orwell was egged on to shoot the elephant by a crowd eager for a show, and Kitty Genovese's killer was abetted by thirty-eight neighbors who ignored her calls for help. Also, both stories raise issues of morality and personal responsibility. Orwell uses recalled experience to clarify his own failings; the episode is something of a turning point in his life. Is there any suggestion that Kitty Genovese's neighbors gained any similar insight?

Just Walk On By (p. 223): In this essay Brent Staples also considers issues of power and powerlessness and, in particular, the extent to which poor young black men may find themselves in a situation similar to the one Orwell describes: adopting a powerful persona—an intimidating mask of fearsomeness—that hides an essential powerlessness. The point Staples makes is that every day he must fight against such stereotypes that lead to suspicion and fear.

The Untouchable (p. 498): Orwell's essay can remind students that India had an additional "caste," one not described by Ajoy Mahtab in "The Untouchable"— British "sahibs." Students can quickly infer how Orwell, who was born in India, must have reacted to India's caste system and why. You can also remind your students of Mahatma Gandhi. Ask them to consider how Gandhi's passive resistance parallels the role of the Burmese natives in Orwell's shooting of the elephant and how his use of passive resistance further illustrates Orwell's thesis.

Sherman Alexie, *Indian Education*

This short story is unusual in that it is told as a series of vignettes, or short anecdotes, spanning the narrator's life from first through twelfth grades, with each section relating an incident that occurred in each grade. You might focus students' attention on the cumulative effect of this series of vignettes, a question that is discussed in the second item under *Reading Literature*. Another interesting topic of discussion is whether one of these vignettes might have been expanded into a more traditional narrative exploring the one incident in detail. Could the effect have been the same? Students might also consider how well they think Alexie succeeds in bringing his narrator to life. For example, does he seem to age appropriately from one vignette to the next? (Most will probably agree that he does, beginning as a little troublemaker and growing into an increasingly serious and sensitive thinker.) Finally, if you focus on literature in any detailed way in your course, you might ask students to think about the relationship between autobiography and fiction. As the headnote preceding the selection suggests, Alexie's own youth had much in common with that of his narrator, and life as he presents it fictionally on the reservation is actually very close to the truth. What does this autobiographical aspect contribute to Alexie's themes?

READING LITERATURE (p. 131)

1. Alexie indicates the passage of time by using headings that refer to each school year from the first to twelfth grade. Students should recognize that in a piece of fiction, this technique is quite efficient. Adding more traditional transitional phrases (such as, "When I was in the second grade") would make this read more like an essay—although varying such transitions from grade to grade could prove challenging.

2. In general, the incidents described for each grade have in common that they suggest the difficulties the narrator faced in his childhood, scorned by his reservation friends because he was different, stereotyped by the white world, surrounded by poverty and lack of opportunity. And yet, in face of this adversity, he learns to succeed on his own terms.

3. "There is more than one way to starve" suggests that those on the reservation become spiritually as well as economically deprived. "Sharing dark skin doesn't necessarily make two men brothers" follows from the story the narrator tells of being stereotyped as an alcoholic by a Chicano teacher. "[E]verything looks like a noose if you stare at it long enough" points to the sense of hopelessness many Native Americans face in contemplating what seems a history of failure following the arrival of Europeans.

THEMATIC CONNECTIONS

College Pressures (p. 447): Students might consider similarities and differences among the various kinds of pressure facing students from different ethnic and socioeconomic groups.

Burdens **(p. 507)**: John Kenneth Galbraith's essay focuses on the unequal distribution of wealth in the United States and the ways in which, in his view, government taxation and subsidy policies favor the wealthy and the upper middle classes over the poorest in the country. Those on reservations are clearly among the poorest.

The Declaration of Independence **(p. 557)**: This founding document of the United States, with its famous assertion that "all men are created equal," was never intended to apply to the native populations of North America. How has this fact and its subsequent interpretations affected the lives of Native Americans over the last two-and-a-quarter centuries?

An Idea Whose Time Has Come **(p. 637)**: An interesting topic for research might be the idea of economic reparations for Native Americans. Have such reparations been proposed, and how does the concept of such reparations differ from that of reparations for the descendents of slaves?

Strange Tools **(p. 697)**: Like Alexie, Richard Rodriguez reflects on a childhood marked by a thirst for education that others sometimes saw as odd. How might the narrator of "Indian Education" be defined as a "scholarship boy"?

5: DESCRIPTION

Many college students have previously written descriptions that involve painting verbal pictures of places or things, something the introductory paragraph by James Agee does with lush concreteness. Invoking the senses of sight, hearing, and touch, the paragraph is a good place to begin your descriptive unit. A subjective description, it offers colors, shapes, and movement, as well as a variety of tactile and auditory sensations, in both literal and figurative images. Although the language is a mixture of objective and subjective words and phrases, overall the paragraph focuses on the writer's impressions.

Having discussed the paragraph, students will need you to help them expand their ideas about the uses of description. The selections within this chapter were chosen to demonstrate stylistic diversity. Leah Hager Cohen describes her deaf grandfather's "strong, jutting chin" (1), the "shapeless, gusty sound" of his voice (2), and his "lithe, vital" hands (8) to paint a portrait that is both vivid and sympathetic. Suzanne Berne focuses on a place, the environs of rubble of the World Trade Center six months after it was destroyed by a horrifying terrorist attack, from two perspectives: her initial sense that what she is viewing is "absence" and her dawning realization that there is a great deal to take in visually surrounding the site. Annie Dillard takes a close look at weasels, describing them physically and in terms of their behavior, but also imagining for weasels an inner life that is in tune with the natural order. N. Scott Momaday uses recollections of his grandmother to describe a turning point in the history of his people. Perhaps the most difficult essay in this group is "Once More to the Lake" by E. B. White. White's vocabulary and intense imagery could be challenging for some students, and we recommend that you discuss several of the shorter essays before assigning his. If you include works of literature in your course, you will want to end your unit with Kate Chopin's short story "The Storm" to show the ways a fiction writer uses description of people as well as of the physical environment to heighten a story's impact and to contribute to a story's themes. Classroom discussions can focus on the uses that both essay and fiction writers make of description and the techniques they use to convey ideas and impressions to their readers. Students should be encouraged to experiment and to open themselves up to the possibilities inherent in description.

Also, classroom discussions can concentrate on thematic threads that run through the selections, which also reflect a variety of cultures. Several of the selections deal with death as a means of understanding life.

Vincent LaForet, *Girls in Front of 9/11 Mural* (Photo)

"A picture is worth a thousand words," it is said. Students should recognize, though, that a photograph can focus only on a single image. A writer encountering this scene could have incorporated it into a larger essay describing New York City a year after the World Trade Center attack.

READING IMAGES (p. 151)

1. The mural is dominated by an American flag (with eleven stripes and sixty-one stars, oddly enough). Beside it is a large drawing of stars within stars, under which is the epitaph "In Memory 9/11/01" with stars bracketing the date. To the other side of the flag are more stars within stars. The mural also includes the note "Please Respect No Tags"; "tags" are the way those who paint graffiti sign themselves. Students' opinions will differ as to what determines the arrangement of these details.
2. The intended dominant impression seems to be one of patriotic celebration. This is certainly not a mournful representation of the lives lost in the attack on the World Trade Center.
3. The positioning of the cheerful pair of girls skipping past the mural suggests an essentially subjective view of the image. The photographer seems to be trying to create an impression in readers' minds.

THEMATIC CONNECTIONS

Ground Zero (p. 158): Suzanne Berne offers a different kind of reflection on the destruction of the World Trade Center and the many lives that were lost there. Students might consider how their responses differ from this verbal reflection and from the photographer's visual one.

Who Killed Benny Paret? (p. 321): Norman Cousins writes here about the death in the ring of a boxer during a live televised match in the 1960s, much to the horror of viewers. The collapse of the twin towers was also broadcast live to a horrified viewing audience. Is there a difference between seeing such images in real time and seeing them after the fact on tape?

Five Ways to Kill a Man (p. 487): Here, poet Edwin Brock reflects on intolerance and war through the ages and the resulting loss of innocent life.

"Hope" Is the Thing with Feathers (p. 525): Emily Dickinson's famous poem is a bittersweet consideration of how human beings face difficult times with a sense of hope that cannot be easily extinguished.

Leah Hager Cohen, *Words Left Unspoken*

In this fond remembrance of her paternal grandfather, who died when she was thirteen, Cohen offers a number of details that relate specifically to his deafness: his ritual physical greeting, his wordless voice, the sound he made when eating "that, originating from other quarters, would have drawn chiding or expulsion from the table" (2), his delight in the visual antics of comics like Laurel and Hardy on television. But she also lets us see him as we might any grandfather: playing games, mimicking the way she ate, doing coin tricks, and ultimately aging. Students may want to begin by thinking about the final sentence of her first paragraph: "In all my life, I never heard him speak a word I could understand." How much does Cohen seem to regret this?

COMPREHENSION (p. 155)

1. Apparently deaf since birth, Cohen's grandfather communicated only in sign language. Cohen had not learned sign language before her grandfather died, so they could communicate only indirectly—through games, gestures, and shared physical jokes.
2. The relationship seems to have been as warm as it could be given the lack of verbal communication. Certainly, she seems to have found him a source of much fun.
3. Looking back, Cohen regrets not being able to know her grandfather better— as she might have if they had shared a language. During the walk with him she describes in paragraph 12, when she "found his rhythm, and breathed it in," she experienced a level of union that approached conversation.
4. Often when we lose a relative at an early age, we spend our lives trying to sort through the memories in order to reach a fuller understanding. In this sense "everything seems like a clue."
5. The "words left unspoken" represent conversations with her grandfather that Cohen didn't have. Her implied regret is that he died before she had a chance to learn to communicate with him. At another level, though, Cohen did communicate with her grandfather in ways that transcend speech.

PURPOSE AND AUDIENCE (p. 156)

1. The essay does not have an explicit thesis statement as is often the case with professional descriptive writing. The description stands for itself. You might have students create a thesis statement ("My grandfather was . . .") and discuss whether or not such a statement would contribute to the effectiveness of the essay.
2. Cohen seems to be trying to create a dominant impression of a funny, loving, good-natured grandfather who tried to close the emotional distance created by his deafness and her unfamiliarity with sign language.
3. Cohen neither explores deaf culture in much detail, nor expects her audience to be familiar with it. In some sense, she writes from the perspective of a child, which allows us to see her grandfather's world from an inexpert viewpoint.

STYLE AND STRUCTURE (p. 156)

1. As a child she found her grandfather's chin his most dominant feature. Moreover, he used his chin to nuzzle his grandchildren's cheeks as a means of silent, affectionate greeting.
2. The essay is organized for the most part chronologically, moving from the earliest to later memories. For Cohen's purposes, this probably creates the most effective organization.
3. Cohen gives relatively little physical description of her grandfather, except in paragraphs 1 and 8. She seems less interested in letting readers picture him than in giving a sense of his manner and personality.
4. Students will have different ideas about where Cohen could have provided more detail. Physical description is certainly one possibility.
5. Cohen uses similes in her early paragraphs: "like a chunk of honed granite" (1); "like a pair of bellows sending up sparks," "like a dreaming dog" (2); "like big white fish" (3); "motions as swift and implausible as a Saturday morning cartoon chase" (4). Paragraph 12 also includes strong images. Students may suggest that more figures of speech might have been included elsewhere as well.

VOCABULARY PROJECTS (p. 156)

2. Possible synonyms—honed: *sharpened;* expulsion: *banishment;* percussive: *staccato;* smirking: *smiling;* splayed: *spread;* abundant: *many;* prominent: *conspicuous;* lithe: *supple;* conduits: *channels;* gait: *stride.*

COMBINING THE PATTERNS (p. 157)

Paragraph 9 briefly recounts the bare facts of Sam Cohen's birth, his parents' emigration from Russia, and the discovery of his deafness. The narrative passage serves to create further sympathy for the man, whose childhood was obviously marked by poverty and hardship.

THEMATIC CONNECTIONS

Only Daughter (p. 84): Sandra Cisneros also writes about a complex relationship with a family member, her somewhat distant father who maintained old-fashioned expectations for the only daughter in the family. Both Cohen and Cisneros explore obstacles to communication, and both end their essays with a scene that shows the barriers to communication being breached.

The Way to Rainy Mountain (p. 169): N. Scott Momaday's remembrance of his grandmother as a keeper of tradition and an important connection to his Kiowa heritage provides an especially good companion piece to Cohen's remembrance of her deaf grandfather. Within very different contexts, both writers explore cross-generational relationships with great poignancy, suggesting a sense of intimacy but also the lost opportunities for communication. Momaday's inability to understand his grandmother's Kiowa prayers relates directly to Cohen's inability to use sign language with her grandfather.

Mother Tongue **(p. 462):** Amy Tan writes about communicating with her mother, a Chinese immigrant who speaks "broken" English. You might focus particularly on Tan's having to translate for her mother in dealing with authority figures. In what ways does lack of language put a person at a distinct disadvantage?

Suzanne Berne, *Ground Zero*

Here, Berne describes a visit to the site of the twin towers of the World Trade Center some six months after the devastating terrorist attacks of September 11, 2001. (It is interesting to note that nowhere in the essay does she refer to the attacks themselves, only in paragraph 12 to the "terrible images" of the towers collapsing; she assumes her readers' recognition of the events that led to the collapse.) Berne's first response is that there is nothing to see at the site but the "absence" of what was once there. Then, "what is not there becomes visible" as she begins to notice various signs that recall the collapse in paragraphs 8–9. Finally, she is able to find a vantage point from which she can actually see down into the pit (18), which turns into a highly sobering moment before "the day flowed back into itself" so that "the "space fills up again."

Berne is particularly adept at using adjectives in this piece. Dividing students into groups, you might assign each a different section of the essay and ask that they circle the adjectives Berne uses in that section; then have them share their responses to each section with the rest of the class. They should find that some sections contain many more adjectives than others. Where does Berne rely on vivid nouns and verbs rather than adjectives? An important point to make is that the overuse of adjectives in description is as problematic as their underuse.

If you have students who have visited the site described here, you might have them compare their responses to Berne's. A related topic for discussion or writing is the question Berne poses in paragraph 14 ("You want tickets to the disaster?"). Is visiting the site for those who did not directly lose loved ones there essentially an act of respect? Or is it more related to the rubbernecking people do at the site of a traffic accident?

COMPREHENSION (p. 161)

1. She means that one begins to realize the absence of what was at the site before: the destroyed towers of the World Trade Center and the lives they contained.
2. It takes "quite a while" to see all the details at ground zero because there are so many varied images to take in, from the nearby skyscraper "shrouded in black plastic" to the myriad flags that surround the site. Thinking of something to say requires confronting the unspeakable destruction that took place there.
3. At the point in time when Berne visits ground zero, most evidence of the horrific images broadcast in the days following the attack has been removed so it is difficult to "superimpose those images" when viewing the empty site.
4. Berne notes a kind of normalcy and "busyness" in the area surrounding ground zero that contrasts starkly with what occurred there, a contrast Berne finds both unsettling and oddly comforting.
5. She means, as she says in her final phrase, that because of the many visitors, "that space fills up again." She seems to be less ironic here than ambiguous about her feelings.

PURPOSE AND AUDIENCE (p. 161)

1. Berne comes closest to stating her thesis in her final sentence, although students will recognize that part of the central point regarding the "absence" she encounters is implied.
2. Berne's primary purpose seems to be to share with readers her own very personal responses to the site of ground zero where she visited.
3. On the surface, Berne seems to assume that her readers are curious about what it would be like to visit the site. However, writing for the *New York Times*, she must also know that more than a few of her readers would have visited the site themselves, so a further assumption may be that these readers would be interested in how another visitor to the site articulates her response.

STYLE AND STRUCTURE (p. 161)

1. Students' answers may vary. In part, at least, she is suggesting that she never felt any interest in visiting lower Manhattan prior to the destruction of the World Trade Center.
2. Berne's essay is organized chronologically, beginning with her arrival at the site and ending with final reflections about herself and the other visitors there. This structure allows her to mirror for readers her own deepening impressions as she surveys ground zero and its environs.
3. As suggested in the answer to the previous question, Berne's vision of the site changes according to her changing vantage point over the course of her visit.
4. It is at the end of paragraph 17 that Berne is finally in a position to see directly into the chasm where the remains of those killed as the towers collapsed can be found. The fact of the disaster hits home at this point.
5. Berne's conclusion reinforces the idea that the site is more than an empty space; life must continue despite such an awful tragedy.
6. Berne uses the word *suddenly* here to suggest that her attention is drawn to many disparate images in very quick succession after a long period when she has, in a sense, been able to see nothing. The effect is that readers are almost bombarded with images.

VOCABULARY PROJECTS (p. 162)

2. Some examples of paradox include "they were all craning to see across the street, where there was nothing to see" (2), "when absence begins to assume a material form, when what is not there becomes visible" (7), and "to stare at so much devastation, and know it for devastation, and yet recognize that it does not look like the devastation one has imagined" (12). Paradoxical statements like these reinforce Berne's point that the site itself is a paradox where death and life come together as one.
3. Such visual details can be readily found in paragraphs 2, 4, 7–9, 15, and 18–20. Students will differ as to whether there are other details she might have used.
4. Literally, *ground zero* is the point immediately over or below a nuclear bomb detonation. It connotes a place of great devastation, where life and property are destroyed in an act of military aggression.

COMBINING THE PATTERNS (p. 162)

The contrast is between the first impression that there is "nothing" to see at ground zero—that what one initially thinks about is the absence of what was once there—with the gradual and then sudden realization that there is a great deal to see, both in terms of what remains and the activity that now surrounds the site.

THEMATIC CONNECTIONS

Shooting an Elephant (p. 117): In this classic essay, George Orwell recounts a different kind of incident that becomes a magnet for crowds of curious onlookers. Students might use this and "Ground Zero" as a starting point for considering why people are drawn to such sites.

Once More to the Lake (p. 175): E. B. White's essay is a meditation on what Berne refers to in paragraph 13 as "mental revision," on how we remember what is no longer there, superimposing the past on the present.

On Fire (p. 280): Hundreds of firefighters were killed in the collapse of the World Trade Center following the terrorist attacks on September 11, 2001, while others heroically led survivors in the buildings to safety. In this essay, novelist and former firefighter Larry Brown describes the dangers and satisfactions of this crucial job.

Why Fear National ID Cards? (p. 590): In the wake of the 2001 terrorist attacks that destroyed the World Trade Center, a number of proposals to identify potential terrorists, including electronically encrypted national ID cards, have generated considerable controversy over civil liberties concerns.

Annie Dillard, *Living Like Weasels*

In this relatively sophisticated example of descriptive writing, Dillard goes beyond simply offering a sensory description of weasels. Indeed, the physical detail she provides about weasels is fairly limited, although details she does provide in paragraph 6 are quite effective. Her larger intention is to describe the profound emotional and spiritual impact she felt on first encountering a weasel in the wild. Indeed, everything that follows paragraph 6 is Dillard's attempt to communicate this deeply felt experience to her readers. There is no question that such an intense experience is difficult to put into words, but many who have read the essay since its publication in 1974 believe Dillard succeeds. Her point is that, in gazing into the startled weasel's eyes, she achieved an almost mystical oneness with this wild creature, a union of mind and spirit that offered her a glimpse into the unbending "necessity" of nature that the human intellect constantly struggles to control, in vain. Death is the ultimate end for all, and to give ourselves up to this fact, to realize that we are not in control of our fates and to live with that understanding without despair or anger, is to achieve a spiritual truth that is at the heart Zen Buddhism, a belief that Dillard herself practices.

Some students may be a little baffled at first ("She wants to live like a *weasel?* Is she crazy?"), and some may in fact find the central point of the essay difficult to grasp at all. More contemplative students, however, should be encouraged to see this essay as a way of thinking about how very difficult it is to put into words any sort of intensely spiritual experience without lapsing into triteness or incoherence. In a sense, Dillard is testing the very limits of language here in an attempt to explain what may, after all, be unexplainable.

COMPREHENSION (p. 167)

1. Dillard is thinking of weasels because she has just encountered one in the wild for the first time.
2. She admires the tenacity of weasels and the fact of their "yielding at every moment to the perfect freedom of single necessity" (14).
3. Dillard suggests that she would like to share with the weasel its instinctive grasp of its place in the natural order of things: "I might learn something of mindlessness, something of the purity of living in the physical senses and the dignity of living without bias or motive" (12).
4. As she has noted in the previous paragraphs, Dillard longs for a sort of spiritual oneness with the weasel, a chance to enter into its "mindlessness" and "choosing the given" (12). She feels disappointed that she failed to achieve this goal.

PURPOSE AND AUDIENCE (p. 167)

1. Dillard states her thesis most directly in the first sentence of paragraph 15. So complex an idea would be difficult to communicate if merely implied.
2. Students' opinions may vary as to Dillard's intended audience. The point should be made, however, that her work has reached a wide general audience and that her subject here goes beyond the interests of animal lovers or nature enthusiasts to something more deeply spiritual.
3. Students should easily recognize that while this essay may have begun as a series of journal entries, they have been carefully polished—and probably revised and expanded—for publication. Her purpose is clearly to communicate a deeply felt idea about human nature and the natural world.

STYLE AND STRUCTURE (p. 167)

1. The dominant impression Dillard wishes to create is stated in her first sentence: that weasels are "wild." In discussing how effectively she creates this impression, students will need to consider all the implications for Dillard of the adjective "wild."
2. In her first two paragraphs, Dillard describes the tenacity of the weasel's bite. Then, in paragraph 6, she describes what the weasel she encountered looked like. At the end of paragraph 12, she describes what might be referred to as the inner life of the weasel, and in paragraph 13 she imagines herself in the weasel's den. She returns in paragraph 14 to describing the weasel's inner life. This arrangement clearly serves her purpose of communicating the various aspects of the weasel's wildness.
3. Dillard wants readers to see the weasel and its actions objectively before she attempts to share her highly subjective impressions beginning in paragraph 8.
4. The image of the weasel skull clasping the eagle's throat is a symbol for Dillard of the weasel being "open to time and death painlessly" and "choosing the given with a fierce and pointed will" (12). It is this surrendering to the instinct and the spirit that she proposes humans should strive for.
5. Students' opinions may vary. Dillard does seem to suggest that she thinks one could actually live like a weasel, but ultimately her thoughts are metaphoric.

VOCABULARY PROJECTS (p. 168)

2. Some of these adjectives include *wild* and *obedient to instinct* in paragraph 1; those such as *thin, muscled,* and *brown* in the physical description in paragraph 5; and *open to time and death* in paragraph 12. She clearly admires the weasel and finds in it a kind of physical and spiritual beauty.

3. Similes include *two black eyes I did not see, any more than you see a window* (6), *a sudden beating of brains, with all the charge and intimate grate of rubbed balloons* (8), and *like blood pulsed into my gut through a jugular vein* (13). Metaphors include *a clearing blow to the gut* (8), *muttering through unique and secret tapes* (10), and *[h]is journal is tracks in clay, a spray of feathers, mouse blood and bone* (11). Personification can be found in the image of "two lovers, or deadly enemies" in paragraph 8 and the weasel feeling "the yank of separation" in paragraph 9. These figures of speech all serve to heighten Dillard's sense of becoming one with the weasel.

COMBINING THE PATTERNS (p. 168)

The paragraph sets up a contrast between the weasel's nature and human nature, a contrast that goes to the heart of Dillard's point here.

THEMATIC CONNECTIONS

Scrubbing in Maine (p. 106): Students might consider the extent to which the women working for The Maids are "living like weasels," giving in to necessity rather than grasping at choice. Ehrenreich's final reflections concerning the Peruvian musicians might also come into consideration here.

Shades of Green (p. 480): In this essay, Jedidiah Purdy describes three kinds of environmentalists. To which category does Dillard belong, and why?

Burdens (p. 509): Based on his comments in this essay, what might John Kenneth Galbraith make of Dillard's exhortation "to grasp your one necessity and not let it go, to dangle from it limp wherever it takes you" (15)?

N. Scott Momaday, *The Way to Rainy Mountain*

In this essay Momaday makes a pilgrimage to places his grandmother had described when telling him the history of the Kiowa people. Students should recognize Momaday's mythic sense of his people's past and his sense of loss at the passing of the old lifestyles and traditions. His calling the death of his people's religious rituals "deicide" (9), without railing against whites, clearly ascribes blame. He explains that the Kiowas were "forbidden without cause the essential act of their faith" (9), as herds of buffalo were slaughtered and left to rot and the Kiowas were scattered by soldiers from Fort Sill. Through his grandmother, Momaday learns about his heritage, but ironically he also participates in the loss of the past, since he does not speak Kiowa and could not understand his grandmother's prayers.

You might ask your students to interview their parents or grandparents to see if they can write a similar description of how their ancestors settled in the United States. You might also ask them to read other accounts of the settling of the American plains—selections from Willa Cather's *My Antonia*, for instance.

COMPREHENSION (p. 173)

1. The title describes both the journey of the Kiowas and his own journey.
2. He means that they were soon to leave their old lifestyles and traditions behind.
3. From the Crows they learned the Plains religion, obtained horses, and discovered courage and pride.
4. Because of the soldiers, they lost the opportunity to practice a sacred belief.
5. Momaday's grandmother gave him a connection to his Kiowa ancestry and the land of his forebears. She represents his heritage.

PURPOSE AND AUDIENCE (p. 173)

1. His purpose is to describe his ancestry and give it meaning.
2. He assumes we have some knowledge of the history of Native Americans. We know this because he omits many details about their lives.
3. This legend gives further meaning to the life and struggle of the Kiowas.

STYLE AND STRUCTURE (p. 173)

1. This description sets the mood and tone of the essay.
2. Momaday begins at her death, goes back to her childhood, and presents a chronological account that again ends in her death. This allows him to present details from different times in her life.
3. This description adds a timeless spiritual note to the essay.
4. One point Momaday stresses is the close connection Native-American people feel to the natural landscape. He uses descriptions of landscapes to point up his grandmother's spiritual bond to the lands occupied by her forebears.

VOCABULARY PROJECTS (p. 173)

2. Three examples include *memory in her blood, cauldron of the land,* and *land was like iron.* They convey the hardships, the difficulty of survival, and the endurance of the Kiowas.

COMBINING THE PATTERNS (p. 174)

Narrative passages include paragraphs 3 and 4, which trace the history of the Kiowas, the legend Momaday quotes in paragraph 8, and the story he relates from his grandmother's childhood in paragraph 9. Each of these suggests something of his grandmother's Kiowa heritage, a heritage that became increasingly distant with the conquest of the West by white settlers.

THEMATIC CONNECTIONS

Indian Education (p. 126): Sherman Alexie's short story provides an unsettling view of life on a contemporary Indian reservation. Momaday celebrates his ancestral culture; Alexie's narrator seems to suggest that his culture is almost lost because of government policies that relegate Native Americans to second-class citizenship. Students might contrast Momaday's sense of connection with his forebears to the overwhelming sense of hopelessness that prevails among residents of the reservation as described in Alexie's story. How are the goals of these authors, writing two generations apart, essentially different? What might account for this difference? The cultural context information in the headnotes might offer some insight here.

Only Daughter (p. 84): As Momaday does in "The Way to Rainy Mountain," Cisneros explores the role culture has played in her family. Although Momaday remembers the positive aspects of his grandmother and his Kiowa culture, Cisneros looks at a negative quality of her Hispanic culture—the higher value placed on a family's having sons rather than daughters. Interestingly, limits of language play a part in both essays. Momaday has not learned to speak Kiowa, which keeps him from understanding his grandmother's prayers—and no doubt some aspects of his heritage; Cisneros's father does not read English, a second language for him, which is at least partly responsible for his not affirming her as a writer—until he has a Spanish translation. Ask students to consider the importance that the language of someone's forebears has in transmitting his or her native culture and the importance that acquiring the mainstream culture's language has for someone living in a heterogeneous society. You might use these two essays as an opportunity to address the "English Only" movement. Also ask students to consider the delicate balance required to maintain one's cultural identity while rejecting a particular—perhaps even fundamental—cultural practice.

My Mother Never Worked (p. 96): Although of different cultures and genders, both Smith-Yackel and Momaday look to the lives of female family members to discover some meaning larger than themselves. After students discuss the social significance that each writer discovers in the life of a woman, you may want them to consider a family member who serves a similar function in each of their lives.

Words Left Unspoken (p. 153): Leah Hager Cohen's remembrance of her grandfather provides an interesting counterpoint to Momaday's remembrance of his grandmother. This could provide a good comparison-and-contrast assignment.

E. B. White, *Once More to the Lake*

In "Once More to the Lake" White evokes a vivid sense of a lake in Maine. The essay flows effortlessly and seems to be connected without a seam. White uses words masterfully, and students should be encouraged to see how he chooses just the right word to express his thoughts. Sense impressions abound as White attempts to convey to readers the way the lake looked and felt. At points the essay becomes a lyrical poem extolling the beauty and mystery of nature. It is important to tell students that White's essay is not intended as a model, but as a *tour de force* of descriptive writing.

COMPREHENSION (p. 180)

1. The similarities and differences between White and his son concern their childhood experiences. The son relives some of White's experiences during his one trip to the lake, but White made regular childhood trips there and enjoyed a lake that had changed perceptibly by the time he returned as an adult.

When he says, "I seemed to be living a dual existence," White means that, because he saw his son do the same things that he had done as a boy, he experienced the illusion that he was both father and son.

2. White keeps vacillating between the past and the present. In some ways the lake has remained the same as it was when he was a boy. But in other subtle ways the lake has changed and so has he.

3. White is disconcerted that he cannot sustain the impression that time has stood still at the lake. The change in the road shows that automobiles, not horses and wagons, now travel to the farmhouse. White seems to sense that, for him, life no longer holds the possibilities that it once did.

4. When White had visited the lake as a child, there were no outboard motors there. When he returned with his son, the sound of the roaring motors made the experience different than it had been years before.

5. White cannot maintain the illusion that he and his son are one. He realizes that like his father before him, he, too, will die.

PURPOSE AND AUDIENCE (p. 181)

1. The thesis is complex and does not become apparent until the last line of the essay. Even though at the lake time seems to stand still, it really does not. White realizes that he, like his father, and even his son, is moving inevitably toward death.

2. The ending of this essay may come as no surprise to a careful reader. Throughout the essay White foreshadows his realization of the advance of time. The peacefulness of the lake, for example, is shattered by the harsh sound of an outboard motor. White says that "this was the note that jarred, the one thing that would sometimes break the illusion and set the years moving" (10).

3. Although younger students will be able to grasp White's point, this essay appeals primarily to those in middle age. White's experience is not foreign to anyone who has watched his or her children growing up.

STYLE AND STRUCTURE (p. 181)

1. White mainly emphasizes similarities between his childhood visits and his visit with his son. The main difference he notes is in paragraph 10, where he describes the jarring noise of the outboard motors that hadn't been present when he was a child; he also mentions the two-track road (three-track before) and the waitresses having washed their hair (7).

2. White says over and over that he feels as if he were experiencing his own childhood. He also says that although at first the lake seems unchanged, he realizes there are differences. Finally, images of summer, such as swimming and bass fishing, occur repeatedly. These repetitions reinforce the main point of his essay.

3. White's use of precise sense imagery enables him to transport his readers to the lake and have them see what he saw and feel what he felt. Much of the effect of this essay would be lost if White's audience read with detachment.

4. In his conclusion White realizes his identity with his father. No longer identifying with his son, White understands that he has taken his father's place and, like him, will eventually die.

VOCABULARY PROJECTS (p. 181)

2. There are many words your students might list, as most of the essay relies on sensory description. Although many of these words refer to the same sense, each is used in a unique way, depending on the context. Students will discover that synonyms are easy to think of, but they do not convey White's meaning as completely.

COMBINING THE PATTERNS (p. 182)

By opening with a narration of his childhood visit to the lake, White sets the scene for his meditation on the inevitable advance of time that comes full circle in his concluding realization of his own mortality.

THEMATIC CONNECTIONS

Only Daughter (p. 84): White returns to the lake wondering how much his childhood spot will have changed. The site is mostly as it was when he was a child, which makes it difficult for him to distinguish the past from the present, but periodically he is jolted into acute awareness of the differences and therefore develops an awareness of his own mortality. Cisneros's father, on the other hand, assumes that past experiences for women will be exactly repeated for his daughter: her "destiny" is "to become someone's wife." He is so certain that old patterns will be repeated that he entirely misses the significance of Cisneros's plans for college. At least in his view of his daughter, he lacks White's sensitivity.

A father's mortality figures in both Cisneros's and White's accounts. White thinks of his dead father as his son pulls up his wet swimsuit. Cisneros does not mention her father's impending death, but her account of his sickroom with its "vials of pills and balled Kleenex" and her inability to ignore the "plastic urinal" are evidence that she is aware of his mortality. One can assume that both writers are aware of their own mortality, although only White discusses it explicitly.

How the Lawyers Stole Winter (p. 402): Like White, Christopher Daly looks back nostalgically to childhood pleasures—in Daly's case, the joy of skating in winter on local natural ponds. Also like White, Daly would like his sons to share his experience; but today many such ponds are declared off-limits by local governments fearful of lawsuits. Like the outboard motors that jar White back to the present, the lawyers represent for Daly the intrusive reality of modern life.

The Men We Carry in Our Minds (p. 456): Scott Russell Sanders's essay is also concerned with the relationships between fathers and sons, although the picture Sanders presents is a far cry from White's idyll by the lake. Writing from the perspective of a son, Sanders remembers the images of fatherhood he grew up with among the rural poor—men whose struggle to earn a living for their families left them little time for the sort of attention and love White can offer his son. Students might consider which of Sanders's categories a man like White comes closest to.

Kate Chopin, *The Storm*

Coming after the essays by Dillard, Momaday, and White, Chopin's story provides a relatively simple example of descriptive writing. Set in Louisiana Creole country in the late nineteenth century, the brief narrative describes a passionate encounter between former lovers, now married to others, precipitated when the two are thrown together at the home of the wife by the advent of a violent thunderstorm. (The storm is, quite obviously, a symbol of the sudden, overwhelming intensity of the lovers' feelings for one another.) Their lovemaking leaves the two exhilarated, which ultimately—and, perhaps ironically—brings them both into closer happiness with their own spouses and children. Most of the descriptive elements of the story focus on the physical presence of the central character, Calixta, and on the storm that rages outside.

Students will learn from the headnote preceding the story that it remained unpublished for many years because readers of its day would have been scandalized by the unpunished act of adultery it depicted—even celebrated—in what would then have been seen as shockingly graphic terms. Do any find it equally scandalous today, or are people now simply more open to sexual expression? Another point to make is that, within Creole culture, men were expected to have affairs, but they were condemned for married women. Does such a double standard exist in any cultures students are familiar with?

Another topic students might discuss or write about is how this very visual story might be turned into a short film. Would anything have to be added or left out of such an adaptation? Could a film version of the story have the same effect as the written version, or would it necessarily create a different effect?

READING LITERATURE (p. 187)

1. The storm requires that Calixta's husband and son arrive home from the store later than expected and also leads Alcée to seek shelter at Calixta's home. Later, a bolt of lightning startles Calixta into Alcée's embrace, which leads eventually to their lovemaking.
2. Students' opinions may vary, but the events of the day do indeed seem to have left everyone happy—although Calixta's husband, Bobinot, and Alcée's wife, Clarisse, would likely not be so happy if they knew the truth.
3. The details provided about Calixta suggest that she is attractive (12 and 22), nervous in the presence of Alcée (21), and passionate (23). She is also a devoted and loving wife and mother (33–36).

THEMATIC CONNECTIONS

The Men We Carry in Our Minds (p. 456): How might the kinds of class distinctions Scott Russell Sanders describes in this essay affect the actions of the characters in Chopin's story?

The Ways We Lie (p. 470): What kind of lie do Calixta and Alcée carry out? What might be Stephanie Ericsson's response to this lie? What seems to be the narrator's response? How do students themselves respond?

6: EXEMPLIFICATION

Before writing exemplification essays, students should understand that exemplification is a way of supporting assertions, not a rhetorical pattern. As the essays in this section show, examples can be organized in a number of ways. Jonathan Kozol uses a number of descriptive examples (as would students considering the four tattoos in the chapter's opening visual text), whereas Laurence J. Peter and

Raymond Hull rely on narrative examples, as does David Birnbaum. Regardless of their form, however, the main use of examples is to explain or persuade.

The biggest problem that students have when they write their first exemplification essays is knowing how many examples they need. Students should understand that the position they want to support determines how many examples they need. The Alleen Pace Nilsen paragraph in the chapter introduction begins this discussion. Although it is a topic sentence for a paragraph rather than a thesis for an essay, Nilsen's main idea presents general practice and therefore obligates her to provide a variety of examples. Of course, a general topic sentence can also be supported with one especially instructive example, and the same is true of essays. In most cases, though, essays will require more than a single example to fully support a thesis. For instance, Brent Staples is obliged to offer a variety of examples to support his statement that he can "alter public space in ugly ways" because of his black skin. His indication that his experience is not unique among black men requires him to offer—at the very least—one other black man's experience.

Students also should realize that a personal statement or observation might not be sufficient to support some assertions. If they say, for instance, "Women do not have to face the problems they once did being admitted to medical school," they cannot expect to overcome audience skepticism with examples telling how easy it was for friends or fellow students to be accepted. To support his statement they would need to report the findings of a study involving hundreds or thousands of female applicants.

Four Tattoos: Alex Williams, *"Lisa Karen"*; Bob Daemmrich, *Woman with "Jiminy Cricket"*; Joel Gordon, *Rose Tattoo on Woman's Shoulder*; Charles Gatewood, *Man with Body Art and Mirror* (Photos)

Question number 3 under *Reading Images* is an important question for students to consider here. The fact is that based on only these four tattoos—or even discussions with the four tattooed people themselves—students would probably not have enough information to form a valid general conclusion about people's reasons for getting tattoos. Most students would already have to have more familiarity with tattooed people to come to a thesis that could provide the basis for an essay.

READING IMAGES (p. 206)

1. One tattoo—on a man's bicep—is an example of a tribute to a girlfriend (ironically, the first girlfriend's name has been crossed out and replaced by another). One—on a woman's upper back—is an image of a well-known cartoon character, in this case Jiminy Cricket from Disney's animated version of *Pinocchio*. Another, on a woman's shoulder, is a detailed depiction of a rose. The most elaborate is a tattoo of a medieval Chinese warrior that covers a man's entire back and arms. The four actually have little in common other than the fact that they are all on the wearer's upper body, and they clearly reflect very different ways of expressing oneself with a tattoo.
2. Student answers will differ here (see the introductory paragraph above), but their statements could provide the topic sentence for a paragraph.

3. Again, student answers will differ. If you have no students with tattoos—or no students willing to share their reasons for having tattoos—you might ask students to talk about people they themselves know who have tattoos and why they chose to do so.

THEMATIC CONNECTIONS

Medium Ash Brown (p. 254): Here student Melany Hunt recalls her impulsive decision to dye her hair—with disastrous results. Students might think about this essay and the photos of tattoos in terms of what happens when people regret changes they make to their physical appearance.

My First Conk (p. 260): In this excerpt from his autobiography, Malcolm X recalls the intensely painful process of hair straightening that many African Americans endured during the middle years of the twentieth century in order to have "good" hair (that is, hair that resembled that of white people). The tattooing process is also painful. What are people's different reasons for enduring it?

The Embalming of Mr. Jones (p. 285): In another take on the impulse to "improve" appearances, Jessica Mitford examines the highly artificial ways used by morticians to make corpses look "life-like."

The Wife-Beater (p. 521): Many people associate tattoos—even those worn by women—with an attempt to enforce a sense of hypermasculinity, particularly when tattoos are large and prominently displayed. Does the popular name applied to the kind of T-shirts Gayle Rosenwald Smith writes about—shirts worn by both males and females and called "wife-beaters" by both—also suggest an emphasis on hypermasculine values? If so, what might this say about our culture?

Laurence J. Peter and Raymond Hull, *The Peter Principle*

Not all students will realize that this essay has a humorous edge to it. Peter and Hull present a number of examples to support their thesis, but a careful reading shows that there are not enough of them. To overcome this shortcoming the writers give the illusion of having carried out a systematic study and having more evidence by labeling their examples "Municipal Government File, Case No. 17" or "Military File, Case No. 8." Their purpose, however, is not to establish their case beyond a doubt or to engage in a statistical sampling. Indeed, their motivation seems to be to take a humorous poke at bureaucratic systems and, at the same time, to cause people to think.

COMPREHENSION (p. 211)

1. When he began teaching, Peter was disillusioned because many "teachers, school principals, supervisors, and superintendents appeared to be unaware of their professional responsibilities and incompetent in executing their duties" (1). He found out that "every organization contained a number of persons who could not do their jobs" (5).
2. The Peter Principle states that *"In a Hierarchy Every Employee Tends to Rise to His Level of Incompetence"* (30). When employees reach this level, they stay there. As Peter's Corollary observes, *"In time, every post tends to be occupied by an employee who is incompetent to carry out its duties"* (36).

3. By *hierarchiology* Peter and Hull mean "the study of hierarchies," organizations "whose members or employees are arranged in order of rank, grade, or class" (32). Observing how employees were promoted in such organizations and how they did their jobs led Peter to the Peter Principle.
4. In a hierarchy, work is done by the *"employees who have not yet reached their level of incompetence"* (37).

PURPOSE AND AUDIENCE (p. 212)

1. This essay is aimed at a general audience as its tone, its lack of technical vocabulary, and its humor indicate.
2. The statement of the Peter Principle (23) is the thesis. Because the thesis is controversial, Peter and Hull do not present it until they have explained to their audience how Peter arrived at his conclusion. They assume that their readers will more readily accept his assertion if they first understand his reasoning.
3. The writers intend for Peter's "theory" to be instructive, but also entertaining. Their use of exaggerated claims, such as "I had inadvertently founded a new science" (31) and "My Principle is the key to . . . an understanding of the whole structure of civilization" (34), brings humor into the essay. The names the writers give to people promoted to incompetence bring additional humor into the essay. Unfortunately, many students entirely miss, for example, that *E. Tinker at the G. Reece Auto Repair, Inc.* can be read as *He tinkers at grease Auto Repair, Inc.* The humor in the essay probably lowers the audience's resistance to its thesis.

STYLE AND STRUCTURE (p. 212)

1. Before they present the thesis, Peter and Hull demonstrate, through examples, that the conditions they describe exist. They use the opening example to show how, as a new teacher, Peter became aware of occupational incompetence. They then use a series of brief examples to widen the essay's focus and show that this incompetence is everywhere. After establishing this point, they analyze their typical case histories.
2. Peter and Hull mention that they collected hundreds of case histories in order to establish that they are authorities on hierarchies and that their conclusions about hierarchies are valid and based on fact. The three case histories analyzed in the essay are typical because they all illustrate the Peter Principle in operation. Moreover, each represents a different type of hierarchical organization, thus showing the general applicability of the Peter Principle.
3. The hypothetical examples come late enough in the discussion to compensate for any inherent weakness in using them. Examples early in the selection are persuasive, intended to convince readers that promotional incompetence occurs. The hypothetical examples are expository: having demonstrated the problem's existence, the writers can clarify how it occurs. Students should be made aware, however, that hypothetical examples alone are not enough to convince an academic audience.
4. Yes, the range is sufficient. The examples come from many different kinds of hierarchies.

VOCABULARY PROJECTS (p. 212)

2. Yes. They personify the characteristics of the environment they are describing. The personification adds a humorous note to the essay and reinforces Peter and Hull's thesis.

COMBINING THE PATTERNS (p. 215)

The narrative examples give the essay its humorous edge, and they also illustrate clearly the central concept of rising to the level of one's incompetence. A possible disadvantage of this strategy is that the examples might not be taken seriously or considered representative. Statistical examples might be hard to come by, however, and including them—while possibly strengthening the writers' point—would not only make the reading drier, but also more difficult for a general audience.

THEMATIC CONNECTIONS

Shooting an Elephant (p. 117): If your students have already read Orwell's essay, it will be interesting to return to it briefly to discuss whether his position as "subdivisional police officer" is an example of the Peter Principle at work. In what ways can he be seen as having been promoted to a position that he is incompetent to fill? Would a more "competent" police officer have performed differently? How often might incompetent workers act in a certain way "solely to avoid looking a fool"?

Walt and Ray: Your Trusted Friends (p. 414): In this essay comparing Walt Disney and Ray Kroc, the mastermind behind the McDonald's fast-food chain, Eric Schlosser provides a number of examples of business decisions made by the two corporate moguls and by some of the executives they managed. Students might consider the "competence" and "incompetence" of these decisions in terms of what they ultimately meant for each business. Students considering a major in business might want to expand their focus to include contemporary examples of corporate decision making as reported in the media.

The Company Man (p. 517): Phil, the company man, when considered in light of "The Peter Principle," can be seen as someone who may have worked himself to death for a promotion to his level of incompetence. The two selections also suggest a flaw in the company's criterion for assessing competence among its executives: the president, in order to replace Phil, asks, "Who's been working the hardest?" rather than "Who does the best work?"

David J. Birnbaum, *The Catbird Seat*

In this highly accessible essay, Birnbaum, a quadriplegic confined to a wheelchair following a car crash, enumerates the many ways in which his predicament has led to unexpected rewards because of the sympathy and special treatment the able-bodied extend to him. Ending with the story of a flight home from Jamaica when he was able to breeze through customs carrying a box of Cuban cigars without being searched and was bumped into first class by a sympathetic flight attendant, Birnbaum concludes with a surprising realization: When trying to push to the head of an elevator line, he is stopped cold by those he expected to humor him because he has jumped ahead of a blind man.

One interesting area of discussion here is Birnbaum's tone. He himself refers to his "cockiness" in paragraph 14. Do students find him at all cocky elsewhere in the essay, or does he basically come off to them as sympathetic? Another topic of discussion is the fact that Birnbaum plays down the limitations and inconveniences he endures because of his disability. Why might he have done so? Do students think he can be seen as representative of most people who live their lives in wheelchairs or with other serious disabilities? Students with disabilities themselves or who are close to others with disabilities may have some special insight into these questions. A final question is whether able-bodied students agree that that they are likely to defer to people with disabilities in the way that Birnbaum describes.

COMPREHENSION (p. 216)

1. His disability gains Birnbaum the sympathy of others and allows him, among other perks, to cut to the head of lines and avoid searches that might lead to the confiscation of beer at concerts and Cuban cigars at customs in airports.
2. See the answer to the preceding question. He also avoids traffic tickets, arrives late to work with impunity, and allows himself to be bumped into first class when flying.
3. These perks help compensate for his "physical limitations and for the difficulties caused by establishments not in compliance with the Americans with Disabilities Act."
4. He realizes this when he is stopped from cutting ahead of a blind man when boarding an elevator: "blind trumps wheelchair" (16).

PURPOSE AND AUDIENCE (p. 216)

1. He seems to assume that his readers share the same preconceptions as the able-bodied who defer to him: that being confined to wheelchair is a special liability that deserves special treatment.
2. Students' opinions may differ, but this concluding position for the thesis can be viewed as effective because the thesis comes as something of a surprise, supported by his final example.
3. Were Birnbaum writing for health-care professionals, he would likely adopt a different tone, one perhaps that was a bit more formal and took into account their more clinical interest in the attitudes that people with disabilities are faced with. If writing for other people with disabilities, he might adopt a more intimate tone, using phrases such as "have you ever noticed . . ." or "we've all had the experience . . ."
4. Birnbaum's purpose seems to be essentially informative; he wants general readers who may only see the limitations placed on the disabled to understand that a disability can also have some practical advantages.

STYLE AND STRUCTURE (p. 216)

1. For a personal essay such as this, beginning with an example engages readers' interest more immediately than a more formal introduction might do.
2. Students' opinions may vary. Certainly, the number of examples he provides from his own experiences seems convincing enough, but it is impossible to

tell from these examples whether all people confined to wheelchairs are treated similarly.

3. The arrangement is essentially chronological, beginning with his experiences immediately after being confined to a wheelchair and ending with his trip back from Jamaica "last January" (6–16). Such an arrangement seems natural, although students may note that he refers to past experiences again in paragraph 11, interrupting the chronology.

4. In his first example, a pregnant woman is criticized for complaining that he cut ahead of her getting onto an elevator. In his final example, he himself is criticized for cutting ahead of a blind man when getting onto an elevator: "blind trumps wheelchair; wheelchair trumps pregnant . . ."

VOCABULARY PROJECTS (p. 217)

2. Birnbaum refers to his condition with terms such as *quadriplegia* (1), *in a wheelchair* (2), *physical limitations* (11), and *disability* (11). Note that he avoids using *crippled* or *handicapped*, which many regard as somewhat negatively charged (although he does refer to his "handicap shower seat" when talking to the customs inspector). He also avoids such "politically correct" euphemisms as *differently abled* or *physically challenged*.

3. The term *catbird seat* in the title is more ironic than serious. His wheelchair is a catbird seat only insofar as it allows him to avoid a few minor inconveniences. Surely, these are far outweighed by the major inconveniences he faces on a daily basis.

COMBINING THE PATTERNS (p. 217)

His examples are presented primarily as narratives with enough description to make the anecdotes immediate for readers.

THEMATIC CONNECTIONS

Words Left Unspoken (p. 153): Leah Hager Cohen remembers her grandfather who coped with another kind of disability: deafness. Students might compare the lives of Birnbaum and Sam Cohen.

The Men We Carry in Our Minds (p. 456): Scott Russell Sanders considers another kind of disability: the lack of education and employment opportunities that confines many people to a life of grueling physical work and spiritual poverty.

On Dumpster Diving (p. 660): Lars Eighner also writes about what it means to be poor and lack economic opportunity. In this essay he describes a period in his life when he was homeless and forced to subsist on what he could scrounge from public garbage containers. Would passersby likely be as sympathetic to an able-bodied homeless person as to someone in a wheelchair?

David Sedaris, *Make That a Double*

Students will probably enjoy this basically humorous look at one of the biggest difficulties faced by native English speakers who are trying to learn French or another Romance language: the fact that nouns have gender, which is indicated in the singular by the articles and adjectives that accompany them.

Sedaris himself doesn't give examples in French, so you might want to share the following two, which students may already be familiar with even though they may never have noticed the gender markers before: in the common bakery name *Le Bon Pain* ("the good bread"), the noun *pain* is masculine and so takes the article form *le* and the adjective form *bon*, while in the common restaurant name *La Bonne Soupe* (literally, "the good soup") the noun *soupe* is feminine and so takes the article form *la* and the adjective form *bonne*. (The central question Sedaris raises is why, for example, *bread* should be masculine and *soup* should be feminine.) Sedaris concludes by making the not-so-serious claim that he now spares himself embarrassment when shopping by asking for multiples of everything so he can avoid the issue of gender. Sedaris's characterization of this avoidance is not entirely true, however; although the plural article is *les* for both masculine and feminine nouns, and numbers in French do not change form according to the gender of the noun, many plural adjectives still have masculine and feminine forms.

One way of beginning discussion is with Sedaris's title. A "double" in this phrase usually refers to a double shot of alcohol in a cocktail. For Sedaris it refers literally to asking for more than one of an item when shopping and perhaps, as well, to one possible response to the frustration of dealing with the gender of nouns.

If you have students whose first language marks nouns by gender, you might ask them to talk about the extent to which recognizing the gender of nouns becomes second nature at a very early age as Sedaris's French friend claims it does.

(Should you make it a practice of sharing such information, Sedaris is openly gay and the Hugh he refers to is his lover, as is made clear in other essays in the collection from which this is taken.)

COMPREHENSION (p. 220)

1. The "Hard Kind" is spoken by Americans who attempt to master the complexity of the French language, pretty much mangling it in the process. The "Easy Kind" is simply shouted English, based on the assumption that anyone should be able to understand the American tongue.
2. Because he can find no logic behind the gender assignment of French nouns, it is impossible for Sedaris to remember their gender; consequently, he constantly makes mistakes with the forms of the articles and adjectives that go with singular nouns.
3. He tries to make up qualities for objects that might distinguish them as masculine or feminine, he uses gender-specific pronouns when referring to objects when speaking English, and he assigns gender to the objects he uses every day, setting them up on blind dates. None of these strategies helps.
4. The same word in French can have two different meanings according to whether it is accompanied by a masculine or feminine article, so it is crucial that such articles be clearly pronounced.
5. Because plural articles and numbers are not marked by gender in French, one need not worry about making mistakes in gender when referring to plural nouns.

PURPOSE AND AUDIENCE (p. 221)

1. Certainly, Sedaris doesn't expect his readers to speak French: he uses no French vocabulary at all in the essay, translating every French word he cites into English. At the same time, readers who have studied some French will likely share his frustration and may have a greater appreciation for his humor.

2. The thesis ("Of all the stumbling blocks inherent in learning this language, the greatest for me is the principle that each noun has a corresponding sex that affects both its articles and adjectives.") is stated in paragraph 3.
3. Most students will agree that Sedaris's primary purpose is to entertain. It's unlikely, for example, that he is serious when he says he now buys everything in multiple quantities.

STYLE AND STRUCTURE (p. 221)

1. In his introduction Sedaris makes the point that most Americans who attempt to speak French while in Paris inevitably make mistakes because speaking French "involves the conjugation of tricky verbs and the science of placing them alongside various other words." Other Americans simply do not bother trying to speak French at all. Implicitly, he admires the former and is critical of the latter.
2. He doesn't establish this relationship directly, but his transition from discussing "Easy French" to stating his thesis ("That's *Mister* Steak to you, buddy.") does imply that gender is one of the difficulties of "Hard French." Students' opinions will differ as to whether the relationship should be clearer.
3. In paragraph 4, the contradictory examples support his point that there is no "secret code" governing the gender of nouns in French. In paragraphs 5–6, the examples of his attempts to assign gender to English nouns suggest just how difficult doing so is for native speakers of English. The examples of U.S. place names in paragraph 7 point up the arbitrariness of gender assignment in French, and the example in paragraph 8 points up Sedaris's frustration. In paragraph 9, the example of his French friend who claims that French children have no trouble with the gender of nouns adds to his frustration, leading to the amusing examples of avoiding singular nouns with which he concludes.
4. Students' opinions may vary, although most all probably see his use of examples as sufficient.
5. Again students' opinions may vary as to the effectiveness of the closing paragraph; it is meant to be a sort of comic zinger.

VOCABULARY PROJECTS (p. 221)

2. You might assign this activity to students in small groups. Some other examples include *fireman/firefighter, stewardess/flight attendant, policeman/police officer, businessman/business professional, salesman* (or *saleswoman*)*/sales representative* (or *sales associate*), and *girl Friday/personal assistant*. Students might also think of professions not identified by gender but to which they might sometimes attach gender identity: *male nurse, woman pilot*.

COMBINING THE PATTERNS (p. 222)

The first and second paragraphs are structured as comparison and contrast; however, the purpose here is more comic than informative. Paragraph 11 is a brief narrative. Students' opinions may differ as to the need for an additional paragraph comparing French and English; certainly, such a comparison is implied throughout.

THEMATIC CONNECTIONS

Mother Tongue (p. 462): The examples Amy Tan provides of her Chinese immigrant mother's use of English suggest the difficulties of mastering the spoken version of a new language later in life.

Sex, Lies, and Conversation (p. 407): In another essay focusing on language and gender, Deborah Tannen examines how differences between male and female conversational strategies can lead to misunderstanding and even conflict.

The Wife-Beater (p. 521): In this essay, Gayle Rosenwald Smith argues that language has the power to shape perceptions about gender relationships, using the example of a popular term for a kind of T-shirt—a term she suggests implicitly condones violence against women.

Strange Tools (p. 697): In this excerpt from his memoir, Richard Rodriguez, whose first language was Spanish, recalls his early attempts as a schoolboy to become comfortable speaking English in public.

Brent Staples, *Just Walk On By*

One way of approaching Staples's essay is to tell students about Lennel Geter, a black man in Texas who served jail time because of mistaken identity, which began when a woman saw him eating in a park each day and assumed his black skin was evidence that he was dangerous. She identified him as the man who had robbed a fast-food store. Students should also be aware of Yusuf Hawkins, a young black man who was killed in 1989 when he entered a white New York City neighborhood to inquire about a car that was for sale. You will want to ask students to consider the emotional effects of always being suspect. You will also want to stress Staples's fairness and ability to identify with his audience—a technique important for any writer of persuasion. Finally, you might ask students to identify Staples's clear topic sentences and to consider the number and kinds of examples he uses for each assertion.

COMPREHENSION (p. 226)

1. Calling the woman a "victim" has meaning on more than one level. Staples's description of the woman makes clear that she *feels* like a victim, which, in a sense, makes her one. Staples understands that her fear is genuine: "It was clear that she thought herself the quarry of a mugger, a rapist, or worse" (2). Primarily, however, the word *victim* is ironic. Since Staples was only "stalking sleep," *he* is the victim of her paranoia.

2. He has the power to "alter public space" because people, fearing him because he is black, react as if any public space were a danger zone. They flee from such zones or even become a hazard to Staples himself in an attempt to protect themselves from imaginary dangers.

3. Staples walks the streets at night because he is an insomniac (2). He also refers to his walks as "constitutionals" (14).

4. A "young thug" is created when he is "seduced" by the cultural idea that it is "only manly" to "frighten and intimidate." When he first robs someone who offers no resistance, he sees himself as a "tough guy," and "myth and reality merged" (8). Poor men are more likely to become thugs because they are

powerless in a culture that values power "in work and in play and even in love." Their powerlessness causes them to see chivalric, romantic nonsense as literal. Men with power are less apt to romanticize it.

5. Staples uses a variety of tactics to appear less threatening: He stays away from nervous people on subway platforms, especially when he is casually dressed; he waits before entering building lobbies when he sees nervous people; he is extremely pleasant when stopped by police; and he whistles well-known classical melodies when walking on relatively deserted streets.

PURPOSE AND AUDIENCE (p. 227)

1. Staples states his thesis in paragraph 6. He acknowledges that some people may experience genuine fear of blacks, but he says that "is no solace against the kind of alienation that comes of being ever the suspect, against being set apart, a fearsome entity"—solely because of the color of one's skin.

2. Staples presents his appeal logically ("This is what happens to me and other black men: these are the facts; these are the consequences"), but students are likely to feel that it is because they sympathize with Staples emotionally that they best come to understand the point he is trying to make.

3. Staples seems to presume a white audience, in which case the preconceptions he must challenge are (1) that it is reasonable to fear all black male strangers, or (2) that white people don't really discriminate between black and white male strangers. He uses the example of himself as a way of challenging these preconceptions.

4. Staples's first sentence is intentionally misleading because the woman he describes was a "victim" only in her own mind. Staples's intention is ironic surprise, which works well in context.

STYLE AND STRUCTURE (p. 227)

1. Podhoretz provides evidence that "New York mugging literature" exists. In addition, he illustrates a they/we approach to race relations when he says blacks "were tougher than we were, more ruthless"—as if all members of an ethnic community were identical. His remarks are, as Staples suggests, "infamous" (5); they create alienation.

2. The opening anecdote, developed with irony, is highly effective. In concrete detail, it presents a "victim" "running in earnest" from Staples's "beard and billowing hair" and "bulky military jacket." An insensitive reader might make the same mistake that the "victim" did in thinking that Staples is a thug. However, in the second paragraph, Staples makes clear that his appearance did not make him dangerous—which is the point he tries to make in the essay. A sensitive reader will recognize his ironic use of "victim" from the "discreet, uninflammatory distance" he maintained from the woman. Had Staples begun with an angry statement of his thesis, the unconscious bigot might have seen reason to be suspicious.

3. Staples offers many examples, but his assertion that "standard unpleasantries" occur with police and "others whose business it is to screen out troublesome individuals *before* there is any nastiness" (3) needs to be illustrated. He could also strengthen the essay with more examples of other innocent blacks who have

had experiences similar to his. Although he uses an example of one other reporter, his assertion that "such episodes are not uncommon" (11) is sweeping.
4. Staples presents his examples in essentially chronological order, beginning with the first time he realized as a young adult "the lethality nighttime pedestrians attributed to me," moving on to the late 1970s and early 1980s when he was working in Chicago, and ending in the present—although he breaks this order in paragraphs 4–6 when he jumps forward to the present. Some students might see a strictly chronological order as preferable.

VOCABULARY PROJECTS (p. 227)

2. Synonyms for *thug* include *hoodlum, gangster, mugger,* and *gunman.* The more general meaning of *thug* suits Staples's purpose. The connotations of the others are either too weak or too strong.

COMBINING THE PATTERNS (p. 228)

For the purposes of this essay, a narrative case study is probably more than is necessary—after all, Staples isn't writing about thugs, per se. You might direct students to another widely anthologized Staples's essay, "A Brother's Murder," in which he does trace his brother's evolution into a thug.

THEMATIC CONNECTIONS

The "Black Table" Is Still There (p. 340): Lawrence Otis Graham's essay offers a complementary perspective on black–white relationships and perceptions across racial lines.

Brains versus Brawn (p. 371): Student Mark Cotharn explores a different kind of stereotyping. As a student athlete at two different high schools, he found that teachers and administrators made unfounded assumptions about academic interest and capability.

The Ways We Lie (p. 470): Two of Stephanie Ericsson's categories of lying have particular pertinence to Staples's essay: facades (you might ask students the extent to which they think the actions Staples describes in his conclusion constitute a facade) and stereotypes/clichés.

The Wife-Beater (p. 521): Gayle Rosenwald Smith argues here that this popular nickname for a kind of sleeveless T-shirt creates "ugly stereotypes [that] are both obvious and toxic." She suggests that such stereotypes can create a cultural climate in which violence against women is acceptable.

Jonathan Kozol, *The Human Cost of an Illiterate Society*

This essay uses an appeal to emotion to argue for a commitment to literacy. Students may not, at first, believe that illiteracy exists to such an extent in our society. Some simple exercises in class may help them identify with the plight of the illiterate. You might, for example, use signs written in Russian, Chinese, or Hebrew to illustrate how English signs look to a nonreader.

COMPREHENSION (p. 236)

1. Illiteracy is a danger to democracy because governments will be elected by the small number of people who read well enough to vote.
2. If we believe in democracy, we will protect it by ensuring that citizens can make educated choices in elections.
3. Illiterates can participate in only a limited number of activities. They cannot buy, eat, or select from written choices such as menu items, product labels, or television listings.
4. They frequently do not pay bills, adhere to leases, meet insurance obligations, and the like because they cannot understand them.
5. According to Kozol's essay, virtually nothing is being done on a government level to solve the problem of illiteracy.

PURPOSE AND AUDIENCE (p. 236)

1. Kozol's thesis is that an illiterate society is in danger of becoming something other than a democracy. He discusses this point in paragraph 4 and states it specifically in paragraph 5.
2. Kozol writes of everyday experiences, familiar to a general audience. For an audience of reading experts or politicians, he might include a statistical analysis of the effects of illiteracy on a particular year's elections results.
3. His primary purpose is to persuade by giving numerous examples that create strong feelings in the reader, but he also means to inform and to express his own sense of anger and injustice. Additional purposes include identifying specific injustices inflicted upon the illiterate, such as their being denied the right to bear children.

STYLE AND STRUCTURE (p. 237)

1. Socrates and Madison were known as reasonable, responsible men. Their belief that knowledge is a moral imperative supports Kozol's thesis.
2. This anecdote puts the essay on a personal level. It introduces the reader to the emotional aspects of illiteracy and sets the tone for the examples that follow.
3. Kozol uses more than a dozen examples, the effect of which is to suggest the terrible extent of the problem. Fewer examples developed in more detail would not have this effect, although they might create greater sympathy for individual cases.
4. Kozol's use of statistics complements his personal illustrations because it presents the human cost in factual terms.

VOCABULARY PROJECTS (p. 237)

2. Students should select such words as *immobilized, paralysis, circumscribed.* The original version is more likely to appeal to a general audience and to reading teachers, the more objective version to sociologists.

Kozol wants the problems of illiteracy to be seen as personal rather than as statistical. Because of the persuasiveness of his narrative, readers must respond to the final paragraphs with a determination to do what they can to correct the situation.

THEMATIC CONNECTIONS

Words Left Unspoken **(p. 153):** Leah Hager Cohen's remembrance of her deaf grandfather who could communicate only in sign language presents a different kind of obstacle to being fully functional in society. Students might think about which of the two "disabilities"—being unable to hear and speak or being unable to read—poses the more serious problems. They might also do some research about the level of illiteracy support services offered in their communities as compared to the level of services offered for the deaf.

Mother Tongue **(p. 462):** Another aspect of reading and language is offered by Amy Tan in her description of her Chinese immigrant mother, who can read English with little difficulty but has considerable difficulty communicating orally with native English speakers, particularly those in positions of power or authority. How different are Tan's mother's problems from those of native English speakers who cannot read? Are people who cannot read likely to have problems with oral communication as well?

The Untouchable **(p. 498):** This student essay focuses on the lowest caste of Indian society. Students might consider the extent to which those who cannot read occupy the lowest "caste" of American society. Indeed, the description of the caste system in Indian society might provide a good starting point for discussion of class in American society and of the limitations on those who cannot read. Can students suggest any reforms to help the illiterate like those Gandhi instituted to help the untouchables?

Strange Tools **(p. 697):** In this excerpt from his memoir, Richard Rodriguez also considers issues of literacy. For his immigrant parents, "reading was something done out of necessity and as quickly as possible. Never did I see either of them read an entire book." As a grade school student, Rodriguez himself was assigned to remedial reading classes, and he eventually grew into a voracious reader—to his parents' gentle concern. Students might consider the role of reading in their parents' lives as well as their own.

Grace Paley, *Samuel*

Your students will likely find much to appreciate in this simply told but highly emphatic short story, most of which takes place on a moving subway train. The plot is quickly summarized. Four daredevil boys—three of them black—"jiggle and hop" on the platform between two cars. Adult passengers "don't like them to jiggle and jump but don't want to interfere" (2). The men think of "the brave things they had done when they were boys" (3). The women become angry ("their mothers never know where they are" [4]), and one opens the door to warn the boys that they should go into a car and sit down. The boys nod but don't move. When she returns to her seat, they begin laughing and pounding one another's backs. A man "whose boyhood had been more watchful than brave" (8) angrily pulls the emergency brake. The sudden stop causes one of the boys, Samuel, to fall, and he is killed instantly. His distraught mother eventually gives birth to another son but realizes that "never again will a boy exactly like Samuel be known" (12).

You might begin by asking which of the people in the story have the most clearly defined characters. We learn the most about the "tough" man who remembers riding the tail of a speeding truck as a boy, and we are given hints of the characters of several other passengers, particularly the two who contribute to the action. Samuel and the other boys, however, are hardly characterized at all—we know only that they are "tough," that they have been to the "missile exhibit," and that their mothers do in fact know where they are. They are much less differentiated than the passengers, yet each is given a name. Whom do students find most sympathetic?

READING LITERATURE (p. 241)

1. Like the men on the subway, Samuel sees himself as tough. But like all our lives, his life is ultimately fragile, extinguishable.
2. Students will probably differ as to who in the story is brave. Some will say no one; others may see the woman who risks humiliation to warn the boys as the bravest. An interesting further question is whether it is possible for young people like Samuel, who see themselves as indestructible, ever to be truly brave.
3. Certainly, the man who pulls the emergency cord "in a citizenly way" strikes us as pompous, and even the woman who warns the boys comes off as foolish in her fears. Ultimately, it is their interference that causes Samuel's death.

THEMATIC CONNECTIONS

Thirty-Eight Who Saw Murder Didn't Call the Police (p. 101): See *Thematic Connections*, "Thirty-Eight Who Saw Murder Didn't Call the Police," p. 21 of this manual.

Who Killed Benny Paret? (p. 323): In this argument against the sport of boxing, Norman Cousins refers to the example of a boxer who died after a vicious beating in the ring. Like the boys (and some of the men) in Paley's story, boxers willingly participate in risk-taking behavior that can all too commonly result in serious injury and even death. Students might consider the appeal that taking physical risks holds for certain types of people. Part of their discussion might center on contemporary "reality" game shows.

Why Boys Don't Play with Dolls (p. 337): The attitude of some of the male subway passengers in "Samuel" might be summarized in the cliché "boys will be boys." Based on the argument she makes in her essay, how would Katha Pollitt respond to such a sentiment?

The Men We Carry in Our Minds (p. 456): Scott Russell Sanders's essay considers the concept of manhood, particularly the idea of poor, disadvantaged boys growing into "tough" men. His essay connects closely to Paley's story of "tough" city boys—and their ultimate fragility. How close is Samuel to the boy Sanders describes himself as being? How much role-playing is involved in such youthful "toughness" as Samuel's, and to what extent does such role-playing result in an adult personality?

7: PROCESS

If your students have never written how-to essays, they are likely to assume that this pattern is useful only for recipes and scientific experiments. Even students who have written process essays will probably not have experimented much beyond "How to Play Monopoly." This, then, is your chance to introduce your classes to the possible uses and variations of process writing.

The paragraph in the chapter introduction from Hayakawa's *Language in Thought and Action* allows you to review the difference between instructions and process explanations and the differences in person and tense these forms require. Your students can easily see how Hayakawa would have altered the paragraph if he were giving instructions rather than explanations.

The first essay in the chapter, "My First Conk," draws on personal experience and uses process analysis as a vehicle for social criticism. Malcolm X uses his step-by-step account of how he got his hair conked for the first time to illustrate the degrading rituals African Americans were willing to go through to look like whites; his tone becomes increasingly angry. In "Creating a Female Sleuth," mystery writer Marcia Muller also draws on personal experience to explain the process she went through in developing her first novel and, in particular, her central character, one of the first fictional female private eyes; Muller's tone is far more objective than that of Malcolm X. "How to Escape from a Bad Date" is an ironic set of instructions that become increasingly far-fetched, all with an eye toward entertaining readers who recognize the "perils" of blind dates. In contrast, Larry Brown's "On Fire" is a personal, and often highly dramatic, account of the working life of a firefighter.

If you assign Jessica Mitford's "The Embalming of Mr. Jones," you will probably want to devote an entire class to the essay because the grisly subject matter and subtleties of tone and style will require a good deal of explanation. Shirley Jackson's "The Lottery" logically follows Mitford's essay since it also contains grisly subject matter used as a medium of social criticism.

By the end of the chapter, your students should have a dramatically altered sense of how flexible and significant process writing can be.

Michael P. Gadomski, *Jack-o'-Lantern* (Photo)

If students haven't themselves carved jack-o'-lanterns or haven't watched others do so, they can still probably figure out the steps in the process on their own.

READING IMAGES

1. The pumpkin has been cleaned out, and pieces of its shell have been cut out to create the face of the jack-o'-lantern.
2. The first step is choosing a nicely shaped pumpkin. Then, the top is cut off and the insides are scooped out. Next, a design is chosen and drawn or stenciled on the pumpkin using a pen or pencil, and a sharp knife is used to cut out pieces along the lines. As a final step, a candle is often placed inside the pumpkin and lit so that the features seem to glow before the "lid" of the pumpkin is replaced.

3. An important caution is to be careful when using the knife, making sure the fingers holding the pumpkin are not in its way in order to avoid cuts. One reminder might be to use one's creativity; all jack-o'-lanterns need not look alike.

THEMATIC CONNECTIONS

Why Boys Don't Play with Dolls (p. 335): Students might consider whether, in their own experience, carving jack-o'-lanterns is an activity associated more with males or with females or an activity that both genders share an equal interest in. How might they account for their response? A more whimsical issue is whether it is possible to create a female jack-o'-lantern, and, if so, what it should be called.

How the Lawyers Stole Winter (p. 402): Christopher B. Daly writes here about how the litigious nature of our society has limited the activities children can participate in because of the lawsuits that might be brought were an accident to occur. His focus is on a neighborhood public pond closed to skaters by municipal authorities, but it is equally unlikely that schools, for example, would allow students to create jack-o'-lanterns because of the potential dangers involved in using knives—let alone the dangers involved in having knives at school. Do students think Daly's concerns have merit? Another possible link involves the idea of rituals: for Daly, ice skating was a memorable winter ritual just as pumpkin carving is an autumn ritual. What other rituals are associated with particular times of year?

Tortillas (p. 513): For José Antonio Burciaga, tortillas are a cultural artifact of his Mexican heritage. In what sense are jack-o'-lanterns a cultural artifact? Students might do some research into the origins of jack-o'-lanterns. Are they more closely associated with any particular cultures?

Malcolm X, *My First Conk*

If you have a class composed largely of white eighteen-year-olds, you may have to provide some background on Malcolm X for them, although they may be familiar with Spike Lee's movie version of his life. Some explanation of the methodology of *The Autobiography of Malcolm X* is also in order. Although students may be familiar with Alex Haley's work, particularly the book and television versions of *Roots*, they will probably not know that Haley first met Malcolm X in the course of interviewing him for *Playboy* and that Malcolm X, pleased with this interview, proposed that he dictate an account of his life to Haley. For further information on the working relationship between Malcolm X and Haley, consult the epilogue of *The Autobiography of Malcolm X*.

COMPREHENSION (p. 263)

1. A conk is a smooth, thick mane of chemically straightened hair. Malcolm X wants to get his hair conked so that he will have hair "as straight as any white man's" (21). At the time the process was performed, the conk was a status symbol; at the time he writes about it, he considers it a symbol of degradation.
2. Shorty asks Malcolm X to buy lye, eggs, potatoes, Vaseline, soap, two combs, a rubber hose and apron, and a pair of gloves. The purpose of each is explained in the context of the process.

3. The major stages of the process include preparing the congolene, applying Vaseline, combing in the congolene, lathering and spray-rinsing, drying the hair, applying Vaseline, combing the hair, and trimming the conk with a razor. All the stages are presented in chronological sequence.

PURPOSE AND AUDIENCE (p. 263)

1. Malcolm X does not present the selection as a set of instructions because he does not intend his audience to perform the steps themselves; in fact, he advises against it. He merely explains an incident from his past.
2. The thesis is that trying to look like a white man is degrading and that blacks should concentrate on their brains, not their appearances, to get ahead.
3. Although conking is no longer a widespread practice, Malcolm X's general argument about black pride is still relevant. This thesis can be applied to many other instances of conformity (see Writing Workshop, p. 264, question 1) and to any race.
4. This emphasis on his discomfort supports his thesis by showing how much he was willing to endure for the dubious achievement of having straight hair.
5. Malcolm X's narrative is a personal illustration of his central point about the sacrifices people will make to conform.

STYLE AND STRUCTURE (p. 263)

1. Some of the transitional words Malcolm X uses to move from step to step are: *then, as, also, when, but, then, until,* and *finally.*
2. The process begins in paragraph 5; it ends in paragraph 19.
3. He uses the quotation marks to indicate sarcasm.

VOCABULARY PROJECTS (p. 263)

2. Suggested substitutions include *avoided* for *beat, room* for *pad, substance* for *glop, very* for *real, stylish* for *sharp, sophisticated* for *hip.* The substitutions weaken the essay because they are inconsistent with the overall tone.

COMBINING THE PATTERNS (p. 264)

A definition of a conk would certainly include description, showing in words what the result was intended to look like. (The result is briefly described in paragraph 21.) It might also include cause and effect, indicating more about how the chemical nature of the process worked, and perhaps set up a contrast with a natural style. Students may have different ideas about where such additions might be inserted.

THEMATIC CONNECTIONS

Finishing School (p. 89): Students can learn a lot about tone (as well as the mechanisms of discrimination) by comparing "My First Conk" to "Finishing School." Both Malcolm X and Maya Angelou describe situations in which parts of their African-American identities were challenged by white standards. Students should be able to explain at least some of the differences in tone by seeing that Malcolm X's anger was driven by self-contempt—by his having chosen to deny part of his identity—whereas Angelou refused the denial Mrs. Cullinan tried to force on her and even exacts revenge.

Medium Ash Brown (p. 254): This student essay in the introduction to this chapter seems in many ways patterned after "My First Conk." The process described by Melany Hunt is that of dyeing her hair using a commercial product. While not painful, as the process of conking was for Malcolm X, the dye job leaves Hunt's hair "the putrid greenish brown color of a winter lawn." As she concludes, "I still have no idea what prompted me to dye my hair." Students might want to consider why we want to change our appearances, and what happens when the attempt backfires.

Slavery Isn't the Issue (p. 632): In his argument against monetary reparations for the descendents of slaves, African-American journalist Juan Williams makes the point that today "black Americans are enjoying record levels of educational attainment and income" and says that rather than lobbying for reparations, black leaders should be working to ensure that minorities have a better chance at receiving strong educations. Students might do some research to quantify the gains black Americans have made since the 1940s, when Malcolm X's essay takes place, and the 1960s, when Malcolm X published his autobiography, and to consider the challenges that still face many minority citizens. Have all the goals of the civil rights movement been accomplished, or are there still important battles to be fought?

Marcia Muller, *Creating a Female Sleuth*

In 1974 Muller introduced mystery lovers to one of fiction's first female private investigators, Sharon McCone, whom she has since featured in a series of popular novels. In this essay, the writer describes her own process for developing the character and then goes on to describe the process she used in creating the plot of her first mystery. Students may note that she is not directly presenting a series of stages for writing in the sense of laying out a road map for other writers. Still, writers—and particularly budding mystery writers—can learn a great deal from Muller's description of her writing process. Students should find this an extremely accessible essay written in an immediately engaging style. It suggests how hard professional writers must work but also how much satisfaction they can take in their craft.

You might begin discussion by asking students what they think makes for a good fictional mystery—whether it be a novel, film, or television episode. If you have students who are particularly fans of mysteries, you might have them discuss their favorite writers—as well as those writers' fictional sleuths—as a way of getting at some of the conventions that Muller faced as she set out to write her first novel. For extra credit, you might allow students who wish to read *Edwin of the Iron Shoes* or another novel featuring McCone and then report on the book to the rest of the class.

Another creative assignment would be to have students—as Muller describes—write an in-depth (two- to three-page) biography of a fictional detective of their own; they could then describe the process they went through in developing this portrait.

COMPREHENSION (p. 270)

1. Muller created her sleuth because, as a fan of mysteries, she noticed there were no fictional female private investigators. She doesn't say so, but she probably felt there would be a market for a book featuring a woman detective.
2. Muller felt her detective could not be "too much of a superwoman" so that readers could identify with her; but she also felt her detective needed to be larger than life in order to take on difficult and dangerous assignments that ordinary people would likely avoid. To satisfy the first requirement, Muller gave her character a normal background and created life problems for her that readers would sympathize with. To satisfy the second, she made Sharon McCone taller than average and an expert at judo and gave her the qualities of independence, assertiveness, and bravery.
3. Her advantages as a female include "the qualities of empathy and intuition." The disadvantages include the possibility of responding emotionally to dangerous situations and the encumbrance of a purse.
4. The two unbreakable rules of plotting for Muller are knowing the solution to the mystery before beginning to draft and being flexible enough to alter that solution if necessary. The first of these is crucial because it allows her to develop her plot in a believable way. The second is crucial because, during the drafting process, unexpected situations may arise that require a different ending.
5. The main problems Muller encountered were that her original story was too short and that the culprit was too obvious. She solved these by having the original culprit killed off so another had to be discovered. Among the mechanical devices Muller used in plotting were a detailed biography of the detective, an initial sketch of the entire plot, a sketch of each main character, and a time chart to keep track of the characters' whereabouts.

PURPOSE AND AUDIENCE (p. 270)

1. Students' opinions will vary, but certainly Muller's advice about plotting is still relevant.
2. She seems to expect that readers will be familiar with the conventions of the detective novel because she covers them implicitly rather than spelling them out in detail.
3. A possible paraphrase of paragraph 3: Writing a mystery centering on a female private investigator posed several challenges, including how to make this groundbreaking character acceptable to readers.

STYLE AND STRUCTURE (p. 270)

1. The discussion of the process begins in paragraph 4, where Muller explains how she began to "reconcile these seeming opposites" that she has just discussed.
2. She first created the character's life story, including how she came to have the skills and training to work as a private investigator. She then developed her physical attributes. Finally, she thought about developing the character's "emotional balance."
3. Transitional expressions include "now" (10 and 14), "with this in mind" (16), "first" (24), "second" (25), "the most useful device" (26), and "during the final typing of the manuscript" (29).

4. There are not really any warnings or reminders here because Muller is sharing her own unique process rather than offering instructions.
5. Examples of informal language include "whodunit" (1), "hooked" (1), "nose for secrets" (2), "cops" (5), "smart-aleck" (7), "working out" (11), and "the game of 'what if'" (16).

VOCABULARY PROJECTS (p. 270)

2. Examples include *stalk her quarry* (5), *dead body* (15), *murder* (15), *clues* (17), *suspects* (17), and *killer* (19). Such language helps keep readers focused on the subject of developing a mystery novel.
3. The adjectives describing McCone are *normal* (6), *uncomplicated* (5), *taller* (10), *independent* (10), and *braver* (10). All could be used to describe a male detective.

COMBINING THE PATTERNS (p. 271)

Muller's description is basically objective. In fact, she made McCone's features strongly Indian in order to "dispense with a great deal of description" (9).

THEMATIC CONNECTIONS

Why Boys Don't Play with Dolls (p. 335): Katha Pollitt's essay focuses on gender stereotypes and how they can be perpetuated by even the most well-meaning parents. What issues of gender was Muller concerned with in creating Sharon McCone? What she attempting to avoid stereotypes? Would Pollitt likely see McCone as a positive role model for young women?

Sex, Lies, and Conversation (p. 407): Deborah Tannen writes here about differences in the way men and women communicate. In addition to those Muller mentions, what qualities might a woman bring to the job of detective?

Declaration of Sentiments and Resolutions (p. 563): Elizabeth Cady Stanton's manifesto regarding equal rights and opportunities for women was written more than a century before Muller created Sharon McCone. Why might it not have been until the 1970s that the reading public was ready for a female private detective?

Joshua Piven, David Borgenicht, and Jennifer Worick, *How to Escape from a Bad Date*

The authors here offer extremely detailed—and, in large part, intentionally ludicrous—advice for those who find themselves on blind dates with people they immediately realize they can't stand. Much of this is essentially a parody of more straightforward books providing tips for readers seeking "Mr. Right." (One interesting question is why there are so few books on the market for those seeking "Ms. Right"—or, for that matter, why "Mr. Right" is a familiar term while "Ms. Right" is never used. Side discussions here could include the spate of reality television programs in which a group of women vie for a man's attention.)

One way to begin discussion is to ask students how common blind dates are among their circles of friends. To what extent is this essay aimed at people who actually go on blind dates, and to what extent is it aimed at readers who will simply find the possibility amusing? A good class activity is to have students scan through the essay again and try to determine when they first began to realize that the writers here were not entirely serious—that is, when it became obvious that this advice was not meant to be taken literally. (This is the subject of item one under *Purpose and Audience.*) Students should realize that a great deal of the humor here lies in the very straight face with which these writers present their advice. Even at their most outrageous, they are careful to offer the warning, for example, that when breaking through a bathroom window, "use your heavily wrapped hand; be sure you wrap your arm as well, beyond the elbow."

COMPREHENSION (p. 277)

1. The four basic strategies are faking an emergency, slipping away unnoticed, slipping out a window, and getting the date to leave.
2. Students will probably agree that the most realistic of the four strategies is the first one because one can actually imagine oneself accomplishing it. In fact, some may have used this or a similar ploy to get out of an uncomfortable situation.
3. The date being imagined here is a blind date, which is made explicit in the section "Be Aware." It clearly takes place in a restaurant, as is seen in the first set of instructions, and presumably involves the participants having dinner together, as is suggested in the instructions for getting the date to leave. Students' opinions will likely vary as to whether these escape strategies could be used for other types of dates.

PURPOSE AND AUDIENCE (p. 277)

1. Once the authors begin to describe ways of altering one's appearance and, in particular, when they explain how to escape through a locked window, it is fairly clear that they don't mean to be taken entirely seriously.
2. The visuals for instructions usually help readers see how to accomplish a particular part of the task that can be shown more clearly in pictures than in words. Here, the visuals support the humor of the instructions.
3. A possible thesis: "When you find yourself on a blind date with someone you dislike, there are several strategies you can use to escape." While this thesis is implied by the title, students should be encouraged to see that such a thesis, as well as an introductory paragraph, would be needed to make this piece acceptable for college writing courses.
4. The instructions are primarily aimed at women as is implied by the fact that the hypothetical friends referred to are all female; in the section on getting your date to leave, the date is specifically referred to as "he." Students may note, however, that men can equally appreciate the humor here.
5. The writers assume that readers will all have their own definition of a bad date. Again, students might note that in a conventional college essay such information might be contained in the introduction.

STYLE AND STRUCTURE (p. 278)

1. One obvious inclusion here not found in the chapter's other essay are numbers to identify the steps in each process; another is the inclusion of several alternative processes as well as alternatives within each process. The most apparent absence is that of introductory and concluding paragraphs.

2. The verbs here are in the present tense and the imperative mood.
3. You might elicit responses to this question by asking students to point out where they would never be likely to follow these instructions.
4. Cautions and reminders here include the advice to leave swiftly (3), to disguise oneself quickly (6), not to look at the date when exiting in disguise (12), not to open alarmed emergency exits (13), and to avoid using a body part to break a window (17). Whether these cautions are necessary depends on whether the instructions are actually followed.
5. The authors use paragraphs and numbers to move readers from one step to the next. Students will probably agree that the numbers act as substitutes for transitional words and expressions.

VOCABULARY PROJECTS (p. 278)

2. Other examples include *locate* (1), *swiftly and without hesitation* (3), *cover role* (11), *implement* (17), and *fool's errand* (23). Most students will agree that such "serious" language adds to the humor of the essay.

COMBINING THE PATTERNS (p. 279)

Students' opinions will vary about what might cause one to want to escape from a date and what the effects of such an escape might be. Such causal analysis could have a place in an essay with a more conventional introduction and conclusion.

THEMATIC CONNECTIONS

Sex, Lies, and Conversation (p. 407): Deborah Tannen's analysis of the differences between men's and women's communication styles could spark some discussion about how differently men and women might respond to a disastrous blind date.

The Ways We Lie (p. 470): The authors of "How to Escape from a Bad Date" suggest that readers may lie with impunity and no sense of guilt in such situations. Do students agree? How might Stephanie Ericsson characterize this form of lying?

Larry Brown, *On Fire*

This essay is quite a bit more complex as a piece of process writing than the other essays in the chapter. Here, novelist Larry Brown, who served for many years as a firefighter in Oxford, Mississippi (four years as captain), evokes the full panoply of a firefighter's professional life in a style that is both intensely realistic and highly impressionistic. In fact, Brown presents a series of discrete processes, each making up a different facet of the job and all told in the second person. He begins dramatically by describing the action of entering a burning building (1–2), then jumps back to let us see the tension of the drive to the fire (3). Paragraphs 4 and 5 shift to the work of the pump operator, whose expertise the nozzlemen's lives depend on, and paragraph 6 describes the action of raising and climbing a ladder to the second floor of a burning building. Paragraph 7 focuses on some of the specific dangers firefighters face; then, paragraph 8 shifts to describe the way community members show their respect and gratitude. In paragraph 9 we see the crucial process of testing the fire hose. Paragraph 10 shows the firefighter helping human victims—as well as the more mundane tasks of retrieving lost pets. Finally, paragraphs 11–12 show the firefighter when no emergency looms, carefully checking equipment at the fire station and waiting "for whatever comes your way."

COMPREHENSION (p. 282)

1. This is a bit of a trick question. As noted above, Brown doesn't exactly describe steps in a single, discrete process but rather presents a number of different activities that add up to the firefighter's life. As he writes in paragraph 11, "no two days are ever the same"; his purpose is to suggest the many facets of the job.
2. There are two general stages in the firefighter's job: the actions involved in actually fighting fires and the preparations that take place at the firehouse.
3. Interestingly, Brown doesn't seem to suggest that any one part of the firefighter's job is of greater importance than the others. He gives as much weight to checking equipment and to waiting "for whatever comes your way" as he does to the more dangerous and dramatic activity of fighting a fire.
4. A firefighter lives with danger—even the threat of death—which is the job's main drawback. Also he or she also experiences much tedium in between being called to fight fires. The main benefits Brown describes are the feeling of helping others and the appreciation shown by the community.

PURPOSE AND AUDIENCE (p. 282)

1. The essay is intended for a general audience. The amount of detail provided suggests that Brown is not writing for experienced firefighters.
2. Brown is trying to convey both the danger and tension involved in the job as well as the quieter life at the firehouse. Students will probably think he is successful.
3. There is no explicitly stated thesis, but Brown does make his general point in several places: "You learn to do whatever is called for" (10); "you wait for whatever comes your way" (12), so no explicit thesis is necessary.

STYLE AND STRUCTURE (p. 283)

1. Throughout the essay, Brown repeats phrases at the beginnings of sentences: *you learn, you try, you see.* This repetition creates an overall coherence. Elsewhere, the repetition of words—for example, in paragraphs 6 (*difficulty*) and 7 (*sometimes*)—is used for emphasis.
2. Students may be surprised to discover that other than the simile in paragraph 1, Brown uses no other explicit figures of speech. His language is remarkably direct, which contributes to the simple frankness of his tone.
3. The different sentence structures add variety to the essay. The use of contractions contributes to an informal, straightforward tone. The juxtaposition of long and short paragraphs creates variety of rhythm.
4. One interpretation of the title is that it denotes an essay *about* fire. But Brown clearly intends his audience to read the title as a synonym for *burning* as well.

5. The use of the pronoun *you* (rather than *I* or *we*) throughout enables Brown to distance himself from his painful material. At the same time, paradoxically, it adds a sense of immediacy; although *you* does not refer to readers, it encourages readers to see through the firefighter's eyes, experiencing the job directly. (Note: You will need to remind students not to use *you* carelessly in their own essays, as it is nearly always too imprecise and informal for college writing.)
6. As noted in the introduction above, the essay is quite unlike a typical process explanation (except that it discusses materials and offers cautions). Brown's purpose is not to instruct readers so they can carry out a firefighter's duties, nor is it to explain just one function firefighters perform. Rather, his purpose is to create a sense of what it is like to be a firefighter by showing the variety of tasks a firefighter must fulfill.
7. Paragraph 8 is something of a digression because it is concerned not with the firefighter's duties but with the way the community responds. The details here are nevertheless effective because they suggest an everyday aspect of the firefighter's life.

VOCABULARY PROJECTS (p. 283)

2. Examples of slang include *puke* (7) and *dumps in* (8); examples of jargon include *charged inch-and-a-half line* (6), *friction loss* (7), and *three hundred psi* (9); students will quickly find an impolite expression in paragraph 5. This language contributes to the authenticity of Brown's voice. The jargon also establishes his credibility as an experienced professional firefighter.

COMBINING THE PATTERNS (p. 284)

The addition of an opening or concluding paragraph comparing firefighting to other occupations would not, in our view, strengthen the essay because it would dissipate the drama Brown establishes at these two crucial points in his essay. Also, it is quite obvious how firefighting differs from other jobs.

THEMATIC CONNECTIONS

Scrubbing in Maine (p. 96): These two very different essays focusing on the experience of working for a cleaning service as a maid and that of working in a small town as a firefighter provide students with an opportunity to think about different kinds of work. Are some kinds of work more valuable than others? How are people compensated for the work that they do? Are the most "valuable" jobs and professions always the ones that are the most highly compensated?

Midnight (p. 201): Student Grace Ku's essay about the difficult life of her immigrant parents, who work long and grueling hours at a dry cleaning establishment, can be paired interestingly with "On Fire." If Ku's parents are at the bottom of the employment hierarchy, where does a firefighter fall?

Ground Zero (p. 158): See the discussion of "On Fire" under *Thematic Connections* for "Ground Zero" (p. 34).

The Men We Carry in Our Minds (p. 456): Scott Russell Sanders also looks at hierarchies within the workforce, dividing the world of work into "toilers," "warriors," and "bosses." Where might firefighters fit within this scheme?

Jessica Mitford, *The Embalming of Mr. Jones*

You should have no trouble getting students to participate in a discussion of this essay; your problem will more likely be getting them to move beyond the essay's content to focus on style and organization. You might open the discussion by asking whether students feel embalming is a necessary process. You might also ask students whether they think Mitford is being fair in her attack, and where her bias is most obvious. An interesting footnote on the book from which this piece is excerpted is Mitford's essay "My Way of Life Since *The American Way of Death*," reprinted in her 1979 book *Poison Penmanship* (Knopf).

COMPREHENSION (p. 289)

1. Mitford asserts that the public actually knows less about embalming than they used to because embalming is no longer done at home.
2. Mitford compares the embalmer unfavorably to the surgeon, describing the embalmer's technique as "crudely imitative of the surgeon's" (5). Later, in paragraph 12, she likens the embalmer to a sculptor and a cosmetician, again unfavorably since the techniques described are neither artistic nor skillful.
3. The major stages of the process of embalming and restoration are laying out the body; draining out the blood and pumping in embalming fluid; removing the contents of the chest cavity and replacing them with cavity fluid; creaming the face; replacing any missing parts of the body; reducing swelling or filling out hollow areas; positioning the lips; shaving, washing, dressing, and applying makeup to the body; and, finally, casketing.

PURPOSE AND AUDIENCE (p. 290)

1. Her thesis is that, if the public knew more about embalming, they might wonder whether they really wanted or needed to have it done.
2. Mitford seems prepared to have her audience disagree with her controversial thesis. Using such a critical, ironic tone for a sensitive topic reveals this.
3. Yes, she is muckraking in this essay. As her thesis indicates, she views her purpose as a kind of public service and expects her remarks to surprise, even shock, her readers. She suggests that undertakers are guilty of concealing information from the public that might threaten their business.
4. Mitford's judgmental tone helps to persuade readers that the process is in some ways ridiculous. Although her tone may not encourage readers to trust her entirely, they trust her enough to consider her thesis seriously. If she had presented the material more factually, she would probably diminish the interest of her readers.

STYLE AND STRUCTURE (p. 290)

1. The essay is written in present tense, but its sentences are statements, not commands, and it employs third, not second, person.
2. Mitford's list of materials includes quasi-surgical tools, chemical preparations, and "aids to prop and stabilize" the body. The tools are described as "crudely imitative of the surgeon's," the oils and creams are labeled *bewildering,*

and one piece of equipment is given the negative connotation of *old-fashioned stocks*. In general, then, the effect on the reader is likely to be negative.

3. To reveal her negative feelings about the industry, Mitford stresses the way embalmers distort language. She points, for example, to corruptions like *demisurgeon* (5), understatements like *quite discouraging* (11), coinages like *casketing* (17), and euphemisms like *young female subjects* (8).

4. Mitford quotes experts out of context and then echoes their words in contexts of her own. Examples of this technique include *rudimentary, not to say haphazard* (7) and *intestinal fortitude* (11, 15). She thus presents her remarks in a negative light and supports her thesis that the consumer should beware.

5. Some of the transitions Mitford uses to move from one stage of the process to another are: *To return to Mr. Jones* (8), *The next step* (10), *This done* (10), *The embalmer . . . returns to the attack* (12), *The patching and filling completed* (16), and *Jones is now ready for casketing* (17).

6. Examples abound. See paragraphs 4, 7, 10, 11, 14, 15, 17, and 18. Mitford's many quotations from mortuary handbooks, even the brand names of the mortuary supplies, are also presented sarcastically throughout. The tone certainly serves Mitford's purpose, but it could put off some readers—particularly if they have recently lost a loved one.

VOCABULARY PROJECTS (p. 290)

2. Substitutions might include *landscape* for *territory; grisliness* for *gruesomeness; clever* for *ingenious; poked* for *jabbed; acceptable* for *presentable*. Many of the substitutions are less descriptive, which weakens the tone of the essay.

3. There are numerous examples of medical and cosmetic diction that your students might list. It should be apparent to them that the number of medical/surgical terms far exceeds the number of cosmetic terms, indicating that Mitford's intention is to ridicule that area of the embalming process more than the other.

COMBINING THE PATTERNS (p. 291)

Paragraph 8 describes the different colors of embalming fluid, and beginning with paragraph 11, every paragraph includes some description of the corpse before and after "restoration." Each of these descriptive details suggests the artificiality and gruesomeness of the process and supports Mitford's thesis that if people knew more about it, they might be less likely to subject deceased loved ones to the procedure.

THEMATIC CONNECTIONS

My First Conk (p. 260): The process described by Malcolm X earlier in this chapter is, like embalming, a gruesome procedure, and the restorative part of the embalming process serves a similar function: artificially creating an image that conforms to a culturally determined standard of attractiveness or acceptability. (As Mitford ironically notes, *il faut souffrir pour être belle*.) While embalming may not be a debasing act, as Malcolm X suggests conking is, students may certainly want to question its necessity.

The Ways We Lie (p. 470): Obviously, embalming—and much of the ritual of funerals in the United States—can be seen as a certain kind of self-protective lie.

Friends and family members want to see the deceased "one last time" so they can "say goodbye," but few would be willing to face a corpse *au naturel*. Stephanie Ericsson would probably classify our funeral practices in the category of *delusion*. Ask students to consider her final four paragraphs in particular. Is our avoidance of facing the reality of death a healthy aspect of our culture? If we began to treat death more honestly, would other aspects of our lives perhaps improve?

A Modest Proposal (p. 676): After reading Jonathan Swift's caustic satire, students might enjoy working out their own "modest proposal" for the American funeral industry. They should recognize that the more outrageous their proposals, the more effectively they may be able to cast a critical light on current funerary practices.

Shirley Jackson, *The Lottery*

Many of your students will have read Jackson's short story, but they will, in all likelihood, not have focused on it as detailing a process. Even more smoothly than Malcolm X's "My First Conk," it combines narration with process. Your discussion can help students differentiate between the two related forms of writing. Seeing the lottery that the villagers conduct each year as an inflexible process can also help students recognize that rituals are processes—although many evolve and change over time. Realizing that the villagers perform a traditional *scapegoating* will allow students to recognize other cruel traditions—traditions that continue to be observed for reasons similar to Mr. Warner's illogical justification that "there's *always* been a lottery" (32). You might point back, for example, to "Finishing School" and Mrs. Cullinan's trying to hold onto "the tradition of her wealthy parents"—that is, to the unjust traditions of the old South. Malcolm X also participated in a painful tradition when he conked his hair for many years without thinking about its significance. He later came to feel self-contempt precisely because he was unthinking in his observance of a harmful tradition. Discussing the conditions that make observing a particular tradition a valuable process and the conditions that make it harmful can help students become more thoughtful about themselves and about the world in which they live.

READING LITERATURE (p. 299)

1. The first step of the process is preparation the night before the lottery is to be held. A slip of paper for each of the villagers—including the one with the black spot—is placed in the black box. The second step occurs the next day when the villagers gather in the square—first the children, with the boys piling up the stones; then the women; and finally the men. When everyone is gathered, the black box is brought to the square and placed on a three-legged stool. Mr. Summers, the lottery official, is then sworn in, and a roll call checks the attendance of the villagers. The next step is the first drawing of lots. After the family holding the paper with the black marks is identified, a "ballot" for each individual in that family is placed back in the box. When the family member who draws the black spot is identified, the final step of the process—the stoning of that person—occurs.

   Although the villagers still perform all of the steps in the process, they no longer understand the original significance of the steps. The only clue to the original meaning comes when Mr. Warner says, "Used to be a saying about 'Lottery in June, corn be heavy soon'"—which suggests that the lottery must have been a fertility ritual. Now, however, a lack of logic marks the way each step is performed. The black box is used because "no one liked to upset even as much tradition as was represented by the black box" (5). Slips of paper are used instead of the original wood chips "because so much of the ritual had been forgotten or discarded"—which allows Mr. Summers to successfully argue that wood chips for a growing village take up too much space (6). The swearing-in used to involve "a recital of some sort . . . a perfunctory tuneless chant" with the lottery official standing "just so," but "this part of the ritual had been allowed to lapse" (7). During the drawing itself, Mr. Summers merely speaks to each participant. The original "ritual salute" has been forgotten—further evidence that the lottery is not held because of its original meaning to the villagers (7). When the second drawing occurs, Mr. Summers asks the family members because "it was the business of the official of the lottery to ask such questions formally" (13). "Although the villagers had forgotten the ritual and lost the original black box, they still remembered to use the stones" (74). These explanations are not particularly logical.

2. Although the village has forgotten the lottery's original significance, the fact that the villagers still perform all of the steps of the process, especially the stoning, suggests a dark, cruel side to the villagers, and perhaps to humankind in general—cruelty for its own sake and a sinister need to scapegoat.

3. As a scapegoat story, "The Lottery" has universal implications. Cruel, unthinking traditions are maintained in many places in modern civilization. For example, novices are still forced to undergo hazing in order to be accepted into some military schools, fraternities, and sororities. Periodically someone dies from the cruelty of these traditions. Certainly, the Star of David pinned to the chests of Jews in Nazi Germany was the equivalent of the black spot—on an almost incomprehensible scale. Wherever and whenever someone is scapegoated—because of position, skin color, ethnic background—the equivalent of the lottery occurs, and the individual is sacrificed to fill some dark need of the group.

THEMATIC CONNECTIONS

Thirty-Eight Who Saw Murder Didn't Call the Police (p. 101): Martin Gansberg's newspaper report about a woman in New York City being murdered while her neighbors listened to her screams for help, refusing to get involved, is another kind of horror story about an almost banal evil at the heart of a community. Although Kitty Genovese was not a scapegoat, the actions of her neighbors suggest a lack of human feeling that parallels that of the townspeople who turn on Tessie Hutchinson. Students may well say that "The Lottery" is fiction and that nothing like its story would actually happen, but they have to admit the reality of stories such as Kitty Genovese's. You might expand the discussion to include other examples of members of our society "not getting involved" in the problems of others, from abused spouses or children to homeless people to functional illiterates. We would all probably say that, unlike Kitty Genovese's neighbors, we wouldn't ignore a person being attacked outside our window. Why, then, do we so easily ignore others with different kinds of troubles?

Shooting an Elephant (p. 117): Students should be able to see that Orwell becomes a scapegoat when he feels forced by the Burmese crowd to kill the elephant. He feels he has to act as a traditional "sahib": "A sahib has got to act like a sahib"—

or be laughed at. He is, therefore, "an absurd puppet pushed to and fro by the will of those yellow faces behind." Tessie Hutchinson's protest at being scapegoated is more understandable than Orwell's lack of protest. She fears being stoned to death; he fears being laughed at. The Burmese natives show the same dark excitement that the villagers exhibit when they throw their stones at Tessie. The natives are a "sea of yellow faces . . . faces all happy and excited over this bit of fun." The natives' "devilish roar of glee," like the stonethrowing, comes from the dark side of humanity.

Samuel (p. 239): Grace Paley's is another kind of story about a community and the sometimes tragic roles people play in the functioning of that community and its mythology. There is an inevitability about Samuel's death that parallels in an interesting way the stoning of Tessie Hutchinson. The men on the subway car, recalling their own "tough" youths and "the brave things they had done as boys," tacitly egg Samuel and his friends on in their dangerous game between the cars. If one of these men had told the boys to get into one of the cars and sit down, they would perhaps have been intimidated into doing so. Unfortunately, action is left to others—who don't understand the boys—and the result is a horrible death. It is in death, however, that Samuel enters the realm of myth, a child the likes of whom will never be known again.

8: CAUSE AND EFFECT

Students are likely to find the concept of cause and effect intriguing but difficult; they may tend to oversimplify causal relationships or mistake chronology for causality. It is probably wise, then, to begin your discussion of cause and effect by illustrating terms such as main and contributory causes, and immediate and remote causes with concrete examples drawn from current news events or from your students' own experience.

When the class has a working knowledge of terms and can apply them accurately, you can proceed to the readings. Since so many students confuse cause and effect with narration, beginning with two shorter examples will be helpful—the paragraph by Tom Wicker, which emphasizes effects, and the student essay on the Irish famine, which emphasizes causes. Comparing the famine paper with "My Field of Dreams" or "Finishing School" will also be helpful; cause and effect principles operate in these essays too, of course, but the emphasis is not on finding causes or predicting effects but rather on presenting the events in sequence—on telling the story. You might have students freewrite briefly about the causes and effects in one of these Chapter 4 selections, and then discuss in class what they have written. Another way of clarifying the difference between narration and cause and effect is to ask students to infer the causes for the speaker's suicide in "Suicide Note," a narrative poem at the end of the chapter. Together you might brainstorm for a cause-and-effect paper to show students that their causal analysis must take a form different from the original.

Consider assigning "Who Killed Benny Paret?" with "Television: The Plug-In Drug." Both are clearly organized, but Cousins offers very little detail to support his assertions. The two selections therefore allow you to discuss the amount of support necessary for proving cause-and-effect relationships. Other selections in this chapter explore significant social and economic issues through cause-and-effect analysis.

Louis Requena, *Major League Baseball Brawl* (Photo)

In discussing this photo, you might have students think about jumping to conclusions in proposing causes and effects. Although, as is suggested in item 1 under *Reading Images* below, the most common instigating factor in a baseball brawl is the so-called "bean ball," based on the photograph alone one cannot be certain that this was the case. In fact, an Internet search about a brawl between the players that can be identified in this image suggests that it might have occurred during a 1996 game when then Mets pitcher Pete Harnisch punched then Cubs catcher Steve Servais.

READING IMAGES (p. 319)

1. Most brawls in baseball—which are, in fact, regrettably common—are precipitated when the pitcher hits the batter with the ball. Believing the action to be deliberate (which it often is—sometimes even on instructions from the coach), the batter charges the pitcher's mound, leading to an almost knee-jerk response as his teammates converge on the field behind him and the team on the field comes to the support of the pitcher. Remote causes can include an intense rivalry between the teams or between the pitcher and batter, a team member having been hurt in a previous game, and a perceived insult to the opposing team. Students may come up with different scenarios.
2. Student responses will vary. Players who are seen as instigating brawls or responding with excessive violence may face suspension for a certain number of games as well as fines. Critics often contend that the consequences for players who participate in on-field brawls are too light to be a real deterrent.
3. Again, student responses will vary depending on the scenarios they devise.

THEMATIC CONNECTIONS

My Field of Dreams (p. 77): Student writer Tiffany Forte recalls her love of baseball as a young girl and describes the excitement of attending her first major league game. Students might think about whether her ideas about baseball would have been different if a brawl had occurred during that game.

Who Killed Benny Paret? (p. 321) Norman Cousins's essay focuses on violence in the boxing ring, which contributes to serious injury and even death. What might be seen as the links between competitive sports and violence?

Whodunit—The Media? (p. 618): Here social critic Maggie Cutler argues that violence in the media is not a direct cause of violent behavior in real life. One might question, however, whether seeing sports heroes participate in brawls on the field would have no effect on the behavior of young amateur players.

Norman Cousins, *Who Killed Benny Paret?*

Violence in sports—particularly in hockey, soccer, and boxing—remains a topic of great interest to students, who frequently have experienced it as players and as spectators. For this reason, class discussion of "Who Killed Benny Paret?" is usually lively. In this discussion you might consider whether sports have become more or less violent since this essay was written in 1962 and ask the class to try to account for the change. Has increased television coverage of sports, for instance, had any effect on violence in sports? Do the fans really want to see violent confrontations? You might also examine the *results* of this type of violence. For instance, does violence among the players lead to violence in the audience? Could frequent exposure to brutality in sports make people more tolerant of violence in other situations?

COMPREHENSION (p. 323)

1. Jacobs believes people come to see a prizefight because they want to see a man hurt. Cousins strongly agrees, as the rest of the essay demonstrates.
2. The immediate cause of Paret's death was the blow to the head he suffered during the fight. Remote causes considered by the investigators included the referee's failure to stop the fight, the doctors' willingness to certify Paret's physical fitness, and the manager's role in encouraging Paret to fight. Cousins feels the main cause of Paret's death was the crowd that wanted to see him hurt.
3. Cousins feels it is senseless to investigate the referee's role because the referee did not have "primary responsibility" (9) for the outcome of the fight; he only acted as the crowd expected him to.
4. "The point" is that people want prizefighting to continue just as it is.

PURPOSE AND AUDIENCE (p. 323)

1. The thesis of this essay is that Paret did not have to die; he died because the crowd wanted to see a man get hurt.
2. The case received a lot of publicity at the time of Paret's death. Even a month later, the essay would have moved readers to feel vaguely guilty about Paret's death. Because boxers continue to be killed during fights, the essay still forces readers to question their own motives as spectators.
3. This essay, which first appeared in *Saturday Review*, is aimed at a well-educated general audience. It is probably too strongly negative to impress either of the other groups; for those readers, Cousins would have presented a subtler argument.
4. Cousins writes as if he expects his audience to be receptive to this thesis but not necessarily to agree with it. He tries to win sympathy for his position by building sympathy for Paret and other fighters.

STYLE AND STRUCTURE (p. 323)

1. Cousins is eloquent and forceful, but the amount of detail is adequate only for an audience predisposed to accept his thesis. Many people, however, would find his argument to be slight. The fight promoter's testimony is one important piece of supporting evidence—but only one. Instead of accumulating other support, Cousins uses loaded language, saying "it is futile to investigate the referee's role . . . [and] it is nonsense to talk about prize fighting as a test of boxing skills" (9). He asserts that "no crowd was ever brought to its feet screaming and cheering" because of skill in a boxing match, but he fails to describe crowds at contests of skill instead of mayhem. He also neglects to interview referees and other participants.

2. Because the crowd pays to see a fighter hurt, if the referee stops the fight, the crowd boos; if the fighters dodge and weave skillfully, the crowd is quiet; if the referee does not halt the fight, thus allowing a fighter to be hit hard, the crowd comes alive.

3. In his conclusion, Cousin again refutes the two most obvious—but erroneous—explanations of Paret's death. The conclusion is effective because it firmly reiterates the cause on which the essay focuses and it forcefully sums up the essay's position.

VOCABULARY PROJECTS (p. 323)

2. a. For football, acceptable substitutions might include *general manager* for *promoter; football games* for *prize fights; on the field* for *in the ring; temperamental quarterbacks* for *boxing artists; dodging, weaving, grabbing, punching, and running* for *feinting, parrying, weaving, jabbing and dancing; killers and hitters and maulers* for *killers and sluggers and maulers; victory* for *knockout, players/play* for *fighters/fight.* (*Referee* would stay the same.)

b. "The crowd wants the victory; it wants to see a man stretched out on the field. . . . It is nonsense to talk about football as a test of skills. No crowd was ever brought to its feet screaming and cheering at the sight of two teams beautifully running and breaking through each other's lines."

COMBINING THE PATTERNS (p. 324)

The narrative introduction establishes Jacobs as an authority on boxing, someone whose negative feelings about the crowd seem justified. Because of his authority, his opinions lend strong support to the thesis Cousins presents. Cousins might have returned to his meeting with Jacobs at the conclusion to offer a final quotation to clinch his argument.

THEMATIC CONNECTIONS

Thirty-Eight Who Saw Murder Didn't Call the Police (p. 101): Students can consider whether frequent exposure to prizefights (and to other forms of violence on television) can produce thirty-eight witnesses to murder who are not alarmed enough to call the police. (See also *Thematic Connections*, "Thirty-Eight Who Saw Murder Didn't Call the Police," p. 21 of this manual.)

Shooting an Elephant (p. 119): Both Cousins and Orwell discuss the power of public opinion. Looking at their essays together is one way of evaluating Cousins's use of evidence. Orwell recounts his own experience. Cousins, on the other hand, recounts no firsthand experience and fails to interview referees who, he says, continue fights because of pressure from spectators.

The Lottery (p. 292): Shirley Jackson's famous short story recounts, in fictional terms, a violent ritual that many have read as emblematic of human culture. As with the boxing fans who egg fighters on to greater brutality, the characters in "The Lottery" egg each other on to strike out violently themselves. Students may want to think about the roots of violence: Are humans at heart a violent species checked only by a veneer of civilization? Or is violent behavior an aberration that marks only a small number of people? Why are people drawn to violent spectacles? How, for example, do they account for the popularity of violent films and video games among so many people today?

Marie Winn, *Television: The Plug-In Drug*

Winn's essay presents a historical account of the changes that television has wrought on the American family. She relates the positive early attitudes of educators and parents and then contrasts them with her own negative view of what the effects have actually been. Most of your students will have been raised with television as a dominant force in their lives. You may be startled to discover that some of your students have been raised in homes where several television sets play all day long. Winn makes a number of statements that will stimulate students to be more critical of their families' viewing patterns, but they may also see Winn's criticisms as a bit overstated. Discuss whether they believe television has been largely a positive or a negative influence—and how television and its influence have changed in the more than twenty years since Winn's essay was written.

COMPREHENSION (p. 332)

1. Early observers saw television as a boon to society and to the education of children; Winn feels it has had the opposite effect.
2. The amount of time spent watching television has increased. In addition, families have drifted into separate rooms to watch different programs.
3. Television keeps family members apart in a physical sense, as mentioned above, and in an emotional sense because they do not have to talk directly to one another.
4. Winn defines family rituals as those regular, dependable, recurrent happenings that give a family a feeling of belonging. She believes television has destroyed them.
5. According to Winn, a rising divorce rate, increasing numbers of working mothers, and loss of identification with neighborhoods and communities also have a negative impact.

PURPOSE AND AUDIENCE (p. 332)

1. The thesis is that home and family life have deteriorated in important ways since the advent of television.
2. She expects the words of these experts to support her thesis.
3. These paragraphs present a concrete example of the changes that have occurred in social situations because of television. They also show how insidiously these changes occurred.
4. Much of Winn's evidence is anecdotal, based on reports by parents, a teacher, a therapist, and a nurse. She also quotes several authorities, including a sociologist and a psychiatrist who specializes in children (Bettelheim), and presents results from a survey of television viewing habits. Whether students feel she provides enough evidence to support her thesis will depend on how they respond to the essay in general and the extent to which they recognize the effects of television she describes in their own lives.
5. She wants to indicate that in some ways our advanced civilization is not advanced at all.

STYLE AND STRUCTURE (p. 333)

1. She establishes the opposite view through quotations and definitions taken from the early period of television.
2. These paragraphs are condensed, comprehensive statements that serve to hold together the material that follows.
3. She draws quotations from those who study the effects (educators, sociologists, psychologists) and from those who experience them (parents, children, teachers).
4. These headings divide the material into logical units and indicate a new direction in the development of the essay. Although they might be omitted without affecting Winn's point, they help guide the reader through her essay.
5. Students' opinions may vary here. Winn might have addressed the issue of whether the actual quality of the content of television adversely affects her thesis. In terms of the research study she cites, in a sense, it is only fair that if Winn is aware of legitimate research that contradicts her thesis she should share this information with readers and then go on to attempt some sort of refutation. Note, as well, that she suggests the study she cites is the only one to have found that television does not have a negative effect on family life. And her refutation is fairly persuasive in that it points out the relative passivity of relationships among family members who watch a lot of television together.
6. Students may feel that some of Winn's more overt moralizing could have been cut. Again, this will depend on their overall response to the essay.

VOCABULARY PROJECTS (p. 333)

2. Some new words and usages might include *prime time, made-for-TV movie, cable-ready, game show, talk show, preview, lineup,* and *pilot.*

COMBINING THE PATTERNS (p. 334)

Winn uses narration in paragraphs 12–14, 22–23, and 34. She uses definition in paragraphs 16 and 18. She uses exemplification in paragraphs 2–4, 7, 22, and 34. Each of these patterns helps her to explain and clarify her point. For example, her definition of family rituals in paragraph 18 and her narrative example in paragraph 22 support her argument that television has replaced beneficial rituals with a ritual that diminishes personal involvement.

THEMATIC CONNECTIONS

Once More to the Lake (p. 175): An informal survey of your students can elicit important information about their opportunities in a television-dominated world to have parent-child experiences like E. B. White's—either as a child or as a parent. Or, you may wish to ask them to consider how White's vacation with his son would have been different if the camp had included a television set.

The Human Cost of an Illiterate Society (p. 229): Worth exploring is the possibility that television contributes to illiteracy by consuming enormous amounts of time that could be devoted to reading—and also the possibility that television, in addition to offering programs that overtly teach reading, may help nonreaders recognize important words when an announcer pronounces them as they appear printed on the screen. You might also survey your students about the time they spend reading in contrast to the time they spend watching television.

Whodunit—The Media? **(p. 618):** More contentious than the debate over the effects of television viewing on family life is the debate over whether television viewing contributes to aggressive or violent behavior. In this essay, part of a case-book presenting different opinions regarding the issue, Maggie Cutler argues that no conclusive evidence exists linking television violence with real-life violence. She recommends that, rather than worrying about making movies, television shows, and video games less violent, policymakers should be concentrating on prison conditions, after-school programs, and help for at-risk children. At the same time, students may see that the study Cutler reports in paragraphs 9-12 tends to support Winn's call that children watch less television.

Katha Pollitt, *Why Boys Don't Play with Dolls*

Like any feminist critique of gender roles, Pollitt's essay is likely to elicit very different responses from students with various viewpoints. Traditionalists will argue that generally accepted gender roles are inevitable and have biological foundations. Feminists will agree with Pollitt that such roles are cultural con-structs reinforced by stereotypes long embedded in our society's archaic views of men and women and still promulgated by the media. Others will fall somewhere in between, noting that men and women do seem differently "wired" but that this does not mean that strict stereotypes should govern the lives of boys and girls, or men and women. One thing students should realize is that Pollitt wrote this in 1995 and that it is directed in large part to members of her own generation (she would have been in her mid-forties at this time). People of this age group would have grown up prior to the advances of the feminist movement and for this rea-son, according to Pollitt, they are likely to accept a full-scale discarding of gender distinctions only "tentatively" even if they support the breaking down of some barriers between male and female roles (4).

Students should also see that Pollitt's primary point is that as society evolves— as more girls feel free to play sports, and more women to become scientists; as more boys feel free to cook, and more men to become grade school teachers—then so will traditionally recognized gender roles. According to Pollitt, this is already happening. Whether students agree with her is another matter.

One issue students should consider is the extent to which Pollitt is correct in her assumption that the ways toys are marketed—along with other media images— affect whether they appeal primarily to girls or to boys. If children are, as she claims in her next to last paragraph, "bombarded . . . from morning to night" with "messages about what it means to be male and female," is it actually possible to change those messages? For example, what would happen if fast food companies, in offering promotional toys for children, did not blatantly create one intended for girls and one intended for boys, but rather a single toy intended to appeal to both? What if cartoon makers and television producers, rather than developing chil-dren's programming centering mainly on male characters or mainly on female characters, developed programming in which both sexes appeared together as equals? Could such different messages have an effect on how children saw no-tions of gender?

COMPREHENSION (p. 337)

1. In paragraph 3, Pollitt writes that the feminist movement "has done much for some women, and something for every woman, but it has hardly turned America into a playground free of sex roles." In the following paragraph, she calls the feminist revolution "unfinished."
2. The feminist revolution is unfinished, Pollitt claims, because the goals of the feminist movement are still only "tentatively . . . embraced" by many of the women and men who claim to support them.
3. Mothers continue to "transmit" Barbie to their daughters because Barbie is a reflection of the cultural ideals ("being sexy, thin, stylish") that surround them. Pollitt herself is ambivalent about Barbie. She says that giving Barbie dolls to little girls is "crazy," but she also says that Barbie "must be passed along" because "to reject her is to say that what Barbie represents . . . is unimportant, which is obviously not true."
4. She first makes the point that mothers are not likely to go against the wishes of fathers who want their sons to play sports. She goes on to suggest that mothers may fear that sons who don't play sports—who prefer writing or reading or working in the kitchen—are antisocial, lonely, even gay.
5. Pollitt is dismissive of such theories. In paragraph 2, she says that studies suggest only "small cognitive differences between the sexes" and that these claims may not even hold up under further study. Then in paragraphs 10–11 she makes the point that parents who embrace such theories are "let . . . off the hook" and can more easily "take the path of least resistance" to the dominant culture.
6. The problem, according to Pollitt, is that such play encourages the kinds of gender stereotypes already enforced by the media, stereotypes that she believes are already being disproved by, for example, the number of women in medical school.
7. The paradox she refers to is the fact that two contradictory things are occurring: while many men and women are accepting the idea that gender behavior is determined by biology, "the rigid and hierarchal sex roles evoked by determinist theories is already passing away" in the aspirations of today's young people.
8. She's saying several things here: first, that people can only live within the norms their culture allows them to; and, second, that these norms are ultimately not rigid but flexible, that what is "possible" can expand and what is "necessary" can become less restricting.

PURPOSE AND AUDIENCE (p. 338)

1. Pollitt states her thesis in paragraph 4. You might ask students whether they agree with some parts of this thesis but not others.
2. The anecdote helps Pollitt make her point that even women who consider themselves feminists may not fully follow through on their convictions when it comes to the lives of their children.
3. Students' opinions will likely vary. Certainly Pollitt hopes that readers sympathetic to the goals of feminism will regard encouraging gender-based play among children in a new light. In a sense, she is also encouraging parents not to limit their children to stereotypical gender roles.

STYLE AND STRUCTURE (p. 338)

1. Pollitt suggests that such preferences are culturally based and particularly reinforced by the media: Children who have been "watching commercials since birth" learn to want "unbelievably sexist junk" (11). Parents, in turn, find it easier to give in to these preferences rather than to discourage them. You might ask students whether they think the education young people receive in preschool and grade school could reinforce gender stereotypes as well.
2. One such chain might be summarized as follows: the child is bombarded with television commercials in which girls play with dolls and boys play with trucks; based on these images, she begs her parents for a doll; the parents try to interest her in something other than dolls, but she resists; so the parents allow her to play with dolls.
3. Pollitt is not guilty of *post hoc* reasoning here; she is suggesting that people who would come to such a conclusion are.
4. Students' opinions may vary. You might have students draft an alternative conclusion and evaluate the differences between that conclusion and Pollitt's.

VOCABULARY PROJECTS (p. 338)

2. The term *kids* is more informal than *children,* and it may also be seen as embracing a wider range of ages—from four-year-olds to teenagers. Students' opinions may vary about the effectiveness of this choice.

COMBINING THE PATTERNS (p. 339)

Pollitt focuses here on the culturally stereotyped differences between males and females. She herself does not accept such differences as biologically determined and clearly believes that they are gradually being broken down, so she would have little reason to develop a full-scale comparison and contrast.

THEMATIC CONNECTIONS

My Field of Dreams (p. 77): In this essay, student Tiffany Forte writes about her avid interest in team sports and her bitter disappointment as a child to realize that she could never become a major league baseball player—that she could only aspire to "something that was appropriate for a girl to do."

Sex, Lies, and Conversation (p. 407): Linguist Deborah Tannen is the kind of researcher Pollitt refers to who has published extensively about the differences between men and women, in Tannen's case focusing on how the differing conversation styles of women and men can lead to misunderstanding. In reading this essay, students might consider the extent to which Tannen might regard these differences as culturally influenced rather than biologically based.

I Want a Wife (p. 505): Writing in the 1970s, feminist Judy Brady takes an ironic look at stereotypical roles for women and men.

Lawrence Otis Graham, *The "Black Table" Is Still There*

Graham's essay about the "self-imposed" segregation of black students in his junior high school cafeteria—something he was saddened to see was still in effect when he returned to the school almost fifteen years after he had been a student there in the 1970s—is likely to spark interesting class discussion. For one thing, Graham describes himself as having had mostly white friends in junior high and so avoided the black table because he feared that if he sat there he would lose them. He also describes the "blatantly racist" behavior of some of his white friends—behavior he endured without protest, still blaming the black students, rather than "white bigotry," for their self-segregation. Finally he notes that his junior high school cafeteria in fact included a number of tables segregated by ethnicity, gender, and personal interests. Why, he asks, does a "black table" receive so much more criticism than these other forms of self-segregation? Opinion on these issues will vary, but it is likely that students can point to concrete examples of such self-segregation in their own lives—perhaps even on campus.

COMPREHENSION (p. 342)

1. The "black table" is the cafeteria table where the few black students in a largely white school choose to eat together, separate from other students.
2. He was surprised because he expected more integration after fourteen years.
3. See paragraph 14. Where students sat depended on race, religion, gender, ethnicity, and personal interests.
4. He was afraid he would lose all his white friends if he did.
5. As a student, he blamed the other black students for segregating themselves. Now he sees the causes as more complex: blacks wanting to associate with blacks as other groups tend to do and the lingering racism that continues to make blacks uncomfortable with whites.

PURPOSE AND AUDIENCE (p. 342)

1. Graham states his thesis in the first sentence of his final paragraph.
2. The opinions and anecdotal evidence Graham offers seem to be enough for his purpose of drawing a personal conclusion. But students may not think he succeeds in supporting a larger argumentative thesis.
3. Black and white students may respond differently to Graham's portrait of himself as a lone African-American man breaking color barriers in a largely white world. Some students may think that a bit more information about the racial/ethnic makeup of the school might be interesting.
4. Answers here will vary. To change his audience's view of "black tables" would seem to be his conscious purpose.
5. Throughout, Graham suggests that he was closer to white culture than to black culture as a youth.

STYLE AND STRUCTURE (p. 342)

1. Graham asks rhetorical questions in paragraphs 3, 7, and 10. These suggest his attempt to work through the issues both as a young student and as an adult.

2. These quotations suggest the dilemma he faced—scorned by blacks, yet a black "voice" for whites. Answers will vary as to the need for more quotations.
3. Graham focuses basically on finding causes.
4. Graham's personal, informal style is appropriate for the personal nature of his conclusions.

VOCABULARY PROJECTS (p. 343)

2. Again, black and white students may have different responses. You might ask if *African-American table* has different connotations. Students may offer some pejorative terms as they invent names for the other tables. If so, explore what this suggests about the nature of such labels.

COMBINING THE PATTERNS (p. 343)

Paragraph 14 classifies students according to where they sit in the lunchroom—and, by extension, according to how they identify themselves. Students will likely come up with other such categories. This strategy is appropriate because Graham's purpose is to get readers to think about the nature of such classifications.

THEMATIC CONNECTIONS

Just Walk On By (p. 223): Brent Staples offers another example of the dilemma facing an "integrating black person" who faces a certain level of stereotyping by whites.

College Pressures (p. 447): William Zinsser's essay focuses on education in a different sense: the burnout college students can experience, particularly at highly competitive institutions like those Graham helped to integrate.

Slavery Isn't the Issue (p. 632): In this essay, an African-American journalist takes exception to the claim that reparations for slavery will help poor blacks because they "contradict the moral authority of black America's claim to equal rights." Those lobbying for such reparations are, in Juan Williams's view, on a "sure road to racial separatism" at a time when "black Americans are enjoying record levels of educational attainment and income." How might Graham, clearly a beneficiary of the civil rights movement and the strides made by blacks in the intervening time, but still concerned about the "superficial inroads that integration has made in society," respond to Manning Marable and Juan Williams?

An Idea Whose Time Has Come (p. 637): This essay as well as the preceding one are part of a casebook offering differing viewpoints on the question of whether black Americans should receive monetary reparations for the long history of slavery many of their ancestors suffered. Here, African-American scholar Manning Marable urges that reparations are the only way to bridge the "equity inequality" between blacks and whites, arguing that "whites have a moral and political responsibility to acknowledge the continuing burden of structural racism."

Linda M. Hasselstrom, *A Peaceful Woman Explains Why She Carries a Gun*

This essay is a good example of a personal causal explanation—Hasselstrom is not attempting to explain the causes of some social phenomenon, but only to explain what led her, a self-described pacifist, to begin carrying a gun. At the same time, she raises larger questions about equality between women and men and about the power their greater strength gives men over women. One way to begin discussion would be to ask if any of the women in your class would consider—or have considered—carrying a gun to protect themselves specifically from sexual assault (as opposed to, say, robbery). Another is to question students about their experiences with the kinds of threatening situations in which Hasselstrom finds herself.

COMPREHENSION (p. 349)

1. Hasselstrom carries a gun for self-protection after having too often found herself in situations in which she felt threatened by men.
2. Students should easily be able to point to the specific events that led to her decision.
3. She considered acquiring a CB radio, and she studied kung fu. The first she rejected because she realized that in calling for help she might in fact attract an assailant, and she came to see that her kung fu skills required expertise if she were to protect herself successfully from a large man. In one instance, she mentions the possibility of carrying mace, but says that she was warned by local police that mace is illegal; in fact, mace remains an alternative to a gun.
4. She mentions her reluctance in paragraphs 12 and 25.
5. She again refers to the dangers of carrying a gun in her final paragraph.
6. She means that before she drew her gun, the men considered her an easy mark and felt no compunction about giving her a hard time. Once they realized she had a gun, though, they did what she requested.

PURPOSE AND AUDIENCE (p. 349)

1. In her introduction, Hasselstrom suggests that she writes only because others might find her personal reasoning interesting. Students may recognize, however, that her larger purpose is to examine the physical balance of power between women and men.
2. Paragraph 5 serves to suggest the extent to which women are vulnerable. While Hasselstrom doesn't say whether she herself has been raped, the story about an actual rape victim graphically demonstrates the danger.
3. Students will probably see the essay speaks more acutely to women; however, we believe it has something to say to men as well. After all, Hasselstrom's central point is that if men behaved differently, she wouldn't need to carry a gun.
4. If not necessarily to agree, Hasselstrom clearly wants readers to at least understand her decision. She most clearly responds to readers' challenges with her final story of using the gun to achieve respect from the men trespassing on her property.

STYLE AND STRUCTURE (p. 349)

1. Students might see it as a weakness that Hasselstrom doesn't try to explain the extent to which women generally are in danger of assault. But because she is not really arguing that other women should carry guns—only explaining her personal reasons for doing so—relying only on her own experiences seems appropriate.
2. The main cause is clearly Hasselstrom's encounters with threatening men. Contributory causes include the fact that she doesn't feel she has viable alternatives and, perhaps, the fact that her husband at the time carried a gun.
3. Try to get students to see that it's not so much the fact that she is a woman that Hasselstrom uses to justify her decision; it is the fact that some men use their greater strength to intimidate women. If this didn't happen, a gun wouldn't be necessary.
4. Students might have fun coming up with possible situations that might result from Hasselstrom's virtually always carrying a gun. The larger question is whether they can imagine her actually killing someone—and when, if ever, this might be justified, especially for a pacifist. (See paragraph 13, where she describes "rehearsing . . . the precise conditions that would be required before I would shoot someone." Why isn't she more specific here?)
5. We find Hasselstrom successful at presenting herself as a peaceful woman who only reluctantly carries a gun. Students may suggest, however, that she seems to take a certain ironic delight in brandishing her weapon.

VOCABULARY PROJECTS (p. 350)

2. Examples include *changed the balance of power* (24 and, with a variation, 26) and the revised Colt slogan in paragraph 25.

COMBINING THE PATTERNS (p. 350)

Narrative passages include paragraphs 4, 6, 7, 8, and 17–23. They are clearly essential to Hasselstrom's purpose in the essay. Students probably won't feel that any should be briefer or deleted.

THEMATIC CONNECTIONS

Shooting an Elephant (p. 117): As a member of the Imperial Police in Burma in the 1920s, George Orwell carried a gun for very different reasons. But the dilemma he faces in this essay—whether or not to shoot an elephant that no longer seems to be posing a danger—applies to Hasselstrom as well: that is, how much of a threat must one perceive before shooting to kill is justified? It is far from unusual, for example, for police officers to kill unarmed people whom they erroneously perceive to be reaching for a gun. Tragically, there have been similar instances of civilians killing people whom they mistakenly perceive as a threat.

How the Lawyers Stole Winter (p. 402): Christopher Daly's focus on risks and liabilities ties this essay to the preceding discussion of "Shooting an Elephant."

The Wife-Beater (p. 521): In discussing this popular name for a kind of T-shirt, Gayle Rosenwald Smith argues that such a term trivializes, if not actively encourages, violence against women. As part of her argument, she cites statistics regarding the levels of violence suffered by women at the hands of husbands and boyfriends. Do students agree that many young people take violence against women too lightly? Popular rap music lyrics, for example, have often been charged with misogyny. Should women feel as concerned about their physical well-being as Linda Hasselstrom is?

Malcolm Gladwell, *The Tipping Point*

Here, reporter Gladwell suggests two specific—and related—causes for the plummeting crime rates in New York City beginning in the late 1980s and continuing into the 1990s (statistics for these rates can be found in the headnote preceding the reading). In fact, according to the "Broken Windows" theory to which Gladwell and those experts he cites subscribe, this precipitous decline was the result of a causal chain, as is detailed in the answers to items 1 and 2 under *Style and Structure* below. In beginning to discuss this essay, be sure that students understand the concept of the "tipping point" (defined in detail in the headnote) as well as the Broken Windows theory of crime (defined in the answer to item 2 under *Comprehension* below).

In discussing this essay, students should be aware that the Broken Windows theory has its critics, many of whom claim that strict enforcement of laws against petty crime amounts, in many cases, to harassment and that no clear connection exists between such crackdowns on petty crime and decreases in the rates of more serious crimes. At best, they argue it is one among many contributing factors. In thinking about this possible relationship, students could consider crime rates in their own communities. Are they higher or lower than average? To what might be attributed these rates of crime relative to other areas? Does disorder always lead to higher crime rates, and order to lower rates?

If your campus library has a copy of Gladwell's *The Tipping Point*, you might put it on reserve for your students. In it, Gladwell describes ostensible tipping points in a number of different areas, including several related to young people. One in particular has to do with "trend-setters" who initiate the eventual tipping point in terms of fashion.

COMPREHENSION (p. 355)

1. Violent crime declined in the United States because of a decline in the crack cocaine trade, a growing economy that provided more legitimate jobs, and an aging of the population that led to a smaller percentage of the young men who are most likely to commit such crimes. In New York City, however, these factors did not so clearly apply: the city's economy was slower to improve than that of the country as a whole, welfare cuts hit the poorest neighborhoods, and an influx of immigrants meant that the population of the city was actually getting younger. In addition, the decrease in crime in New York City happened more quickly than in the country as a whole.
2. The Broken Windows theory claims that crime results from disorder—that, for example, one unrepaired broken window suggests no one is in charge and leads to more windows being broken and, ultimately, to the idea that "anything goes." By cracking down on disorderly conduct, the New York police were able to create an atmosphere in which no crime seemed to be tolerated.

3. By an "epidemic theory of crime," Gladwell means that crime rates grow because, as they see petty crime all around them, people increasingly feel that they will not be punished for committing a crime—even a more serious crime. The tipping point for such an epidemic is the obvious prevalence of wantonly unlawful behavior, such as subway trains covered with graffiti or large numbers of people jumping subway turnstiles.

4. New York City initiated steps to reduce crime based on the Broken Windows theory by beginning to crack down on apparently minor crimes that had previously not been policed aggressively. Subway director David Gunn started out by eliminating graffiti because, in his view, "graffiti was symbolic of the collapse of the system." Eliminate graffiti, and you send an "unambiguous message" that crime will not be tolerated.

5. Transit police chief William Bratton cracked down on fare-beating for the same reason that Gunn cracked down on graffiti. Doing so sent a signal that even petty crime would result in punishment.

6. Many fare-beaters, it turned out, had outstanding arrest warrants for more serious crimes or were found to be carrying an illegal weapon.

7. Mayor Rudolph Giuliani appointed Bratton New York City police chief, from which position he expanded the Broken Windows theory to crack down on petty misdemeanor crimes such as unsolicited "squeegee" automobile windshield cleaning, public drunkenness and urination, and minor property damage.

PURPOSE AND AUDIENCE (p. 355)

1. Students will probably find it acceptable that Gladwell launches into a definition of the "something else" (enactment of the Broken Windows theory of criminal behavior) at the start of the next paragraph. Because it is a complex definition, it could not easily be contained in the thesis. You might ask how the effect of the essay would be different if the Broken Windows theory had been defined before the specific case of New York City had been introduced.

2. Have students actually highlight and reread these quotations before they consider this question. They should see that such direct quotation helps to clarify what Gladwell is trying to explain and adds authority to the essay as a whole.

STYLE AND STRUCTURE (p. 355)

1. Students may have a little trouble reaching agreement here. In his first paragraph, Gladwell clearly focuses on causes, but once he begins his discussion of the Broken Windows theory and its application to law enforcement in New York City, he focuses on causes and effects simultaneously because the theory posits a causal chain (a cause leads to an effect that, in turn, causes another effect).

2. See the answer to the previous question: disorder leads to the belief that no one is in charge, which leads to the belief that crime will seldom be reported or punished, which leads to an increase in crime. When people realize that even minor crimes are likely to be punished, then they are less likely to commit a crime, which leads to an overall decrease in crime rates. The same sort of causal chain can be applied to fare-beating.

3. In part, Gladwell wishes to show that these seemingly minor crackdowns required considerable effort, which is why they had not been attempted systematically before.
4. Critics of the Broken Windows theory have, in fact, seen it as an example of *post hoc* reasoning and question whether its implementation contributed significantly to New York City's declining crime rate.

VOCABULARY PROJECTS (p. 356)

2. Student answers will vary.

COMBINING THE PATTERNS (p. 356)

Basically, Gladwell would only need to provide a clearer introduction and conclusion to each section in order to turn it into a self-contained process explanation.

THEMATIC CONNECTIONS

Thirty-Eight Who Saw Murder Didn't Call the Police (p. 101): This newspaper account of a violent crime in New York City during the early 1960s is an interesting counterpart to Gladwell's essay. Why did Kitty Genovese's neighbors choose not to come to her aid or report her assault?

Just Walk On By (p. 223): Brent Staples focuses on crime from a different perspective—that of a well-meaning black man who is suspected of criminal intentions simply because he is black. How might Staples respond to the use of the Broken Windows theory to crack down on petty crimes?

On Dumpster Diving (p. 660): In this essay Lars Eighner offers a firsthand account of what it is like to be homeless and reduced to scavenging food and personal items from garbage bins. Students might want to do some research about New York City's response to the homeless during the years of Giuliani's tenure as mayor and Bratton's as police commissioner. In fact, the homeless were banned from sleeping in most public places and were themselves treated essentially as perpetrators of quality-of-life crimes. How do students respond to lumping the homeless with vandals and aggressive panhandlers?

Janice Mirikitani, *Suicide Note*

Suicide, more than most subjects, calls for causal analysis, and teenage suicides are all too frequent in this country. In one way or another, suicide may have personally touched the lives of many of your students. Some may have heard of situations in which one teen's suicide, reported widely in the press, led to a series of others. They may also be aware of despairing college students who have killed themselves. Discussing such suicides and trying to understand them can be vital to many of your students. You may want to make your students aware of your campus's mental health resources.

You will want to focus on the raw materials Mirikitani gives in narrative form, which suggest the complex chain that causes her speaker to commit suicide.

In addition to discussing the cause-and-effect relationships in "Suicide Note," you will want to discuss Mirikitani's artistry. Her use of repetition and concrete image patterns will increase your students' sense of the ways in which language can be used.

READING LITERATURE (p. 359)

1. Being a daughter in a family that values sons more than daughters is a less immediate but fundamental cause of the student's suicide. The speaker says,

   > If only I were a son . . .
   > I would see the light in my mother's
   > eyes, or the golden pride reflected
   > in my father's dream
   > of my wide, male hands worthy of work
   > and comfort. (ll. 10, 12–16)

   A causal chain operates from the fundamental cause. As a daughter, she is not praised as she believes a son would be. This, in turn, causes a lack of self-esteem: she feels "not good enough   not pretty enough   not smart enough." Her lack of self-esteem is explicitly tied to her gender: if she were a son, she asserts, "I would swagger through life / muscled and bold and assured, / drawing praises to me" (ll. 17–19). Feeling that she has disappointed her parents by being a daughter, she cannot live with feeling that she has further let them down by not getting a perfect 4.0 grade point average.

2. She believes she would be loved and praised more and would be "virile / with confidence" (ll. 20–21). Whether she would have been happier as a son is difficult to determine. If her parents really do value sons more than daughters, a son would have very likely developed a stronger sense of self-worth—which is fundamental to happiness. However, she may also mistakenly blame her parents' cultural biases for her unhappiness.

3. Mirikitani uses repetition as a means of communicating the extent of the speaker's unhappiness and desperation. The refrain "not good enough   not pretty enough   not smart enough" makes her unhappiness and desperation all-encompassing. She is obsessed with her sense of unworthiness. Other repetitions—"I've worked very hard," "I apologize," and "sorries / sorries,"—suggest her driving need to live up to her parents' expectations and her sense of shame.

   Mirikitani also effectively uses image patterns to communicate the speaker's despair. Bird imagery communicates her fragile self-image. She feels weak and inadequate—only a "sparrow / sillied and dizzied by the wind" (l. 38). "Perched / on the ledge of [her] womanhood," she is "fragile as wings / sillied and dizzied by the wind / on the edge" (ll. 32–40), and her wings are "crippled" (l. 45). Her suicide note, "like birdprints in snow" (l. 2), will leave no lasting imprint.

   Repeated snow and ice imagery also communicates the speaker's despair. Snow and ice are frozen potential, not water in life-giving form. "Each failure [is] a glacier / . . . Each disappointment, / ice above my river" (ll. 25, 27–28). Her "Choices [are] thin as shaved / ice," and her "notes shredded / drift like snow" (ll. 49–51). She will fly from her ledge while "it is snowing," and "the snow burdens [her] crippled wings" (ll. 36, 45). Her "bird bones" will be buried beneath "this white and cold and silent / breast of earth." (ll. 58, 62–63). Ironically, her grave will be marked by an evergreen.

THEMATIC CONNECTIONS

Only Daughter **(p. 84):** Cisneros's sense that she was "only a daughter" in a Latino family can suggest to students that Asian cultures are not the only ones to historically devalue daughters. If they think carefully, students who have not been conscious of such partiality may remember subtle indications in their own lives that sons are "special." Cisneros also suggests to students a constructive way of handling being "only a daughter." She devoted herself to her own goals, and she turned the loneliness of being an only daughter into time to prepare herself to be a writer. Recognizing her father's goals for her college education, she took advantage of the opportunity to major in English. Ultimately, she was able to gain her father's affirmation for what she chose to be.

College Pressures **(p. 447):** The notes to Carlos at the beginning of "College Pressures" suggests the sense of desperation felt by many college students. Zinsser also analyzes the reasons many students become desperate—no doubt, in some cases, desperate enough to commit suicide. In a "brutal economy," they, their parents, and their peers feel they must major in "pre-rich" and compete without respite to find "an edge" over other students. Caught in "webs of love and duty and guilt," like Mirikitani's speaker, they fail to understand that they have "the right to fail" and to use their educations to discover who they are and enrich their lives. Zinsser is emphatic about the solution: "Ultimately it will be the students' own business to break the cycles in which they are trapped." (See also *Thematic Connections*, "College Pressures," p. 109.)

The Company Man **(p. 517):** Ellen Goodman describes another kind of death resulting from the pressure to succeed: an executive who works himself into a heart attack at the age of fifty-one. This essay can provide opportunities to discuss several different issues in relation to "Suicide Note." The most obvious is the debilitating influence in our society of the concept of "achievement" defined in terms of grades or income or status and divorced from any sense of personal satisfaction or individual worth. The second is the effect of the death of a loved one on those who survive. Look particularly at paragraphs 7–12 of Goodman's essay, and ask students to speculate about the reactions of the suicide note writer's survivors.

9: COMPARISON AND CONTRAST

Students have several problems with comparison and contrast. They often fail to appreciate the importance of prewriting when they write a comparison-and-contrast paper. The result can be a jumbled presentation that makes it difficult to understand the basis of comparison or, at times, exactly what elements are being compared. This situation occurs especially during examinations and in-class writings when time is short. In the chapter introduction we stress the necessity of planning when we discuss both point-by-point and subject-by-subject comparisons. Even so, we have found that you cannot repeat this advice enough to students.

Another problem students have is realizing that they have to compare the same or similar elements for each subject they discuss. Having your students outline one or two of the essays in this section can illustrate that writers do follow this strategy when they write. Make sure students understand that if they don't discuss the same or similar points for each subject, they are not actually comparing or contrasting anything.

Finally, students should understand that comparison-and-contrast essays need transitions to make them flow smoothly. Signals indicate movement from one point to another, highlight similarities and differences, and eliminate choppiness to help readers follow a discussion. Revision exercises concentrating on transitions can help students appreciate the importance of this concern.

We chose the two paragraphs in the introduction to illustrate the difference between comparison and analogy. You will need to explain both the value of a good analogy and its logical limits. Students should understand that analogies can be vivid, suggest important relationships, and draw readers into an essay by calling on whatever they already know, but they should also understand that analogies can be trivial or even faulty when similarities are assumed that do not exist.

We chose the selections in this chapter to illustrate the variety of ways that comparison and contrast can be used. The first, Bruce Catton's "Grant and Lee: A Study in Contrasts," offers a very clear-cut point-by-point comparison of the two Civil War generals and makes an excellent opening assignment. With Ian Frazier's "Dearly Disconnected," students will see how a writer can create a somewhat more complex point-by-point structure; the real focus of the essay is the subject of pay telephones, which Frazier feels will eventually disappear because of the proliferation of cell phones, the subject with which he contrasts pay phones. These are followed by three more point-by-point comparisons: Bharati Mukherjee's "Two Ways to Belong in America," Christopher Daly's "How the Lawyers Stole Winter," and Deborah Tannen's "Sex, Lies, and Conversation." Rounding out the chapter's essays is Eric Schlosser's "Walt and Ray: Your Trusted Friends," which is primarily a subject-by-subject comparison of Walt Disney and Ray Kroc but which also introduces the two men with a succinct point-by-point comparison. Finally, Gwendolyn Brooks's poem "Sadie and Maud" expands the use of comparison and contrast into the realm of literature.

Auguste Rodin, *"The Kiss"* and Robert Indiana, *"LOVE"* (Sculpture)

Students might be interested to learn that these two sculptures were created some eighty years apart, Rodin's in the mid-1880s and Indiana's in the mid-1960s. In part, their differences can be accounted for by the prevailing artistic movements of these two eras.

READING IMAGES (p. 385)

1. The two sculptures share the characteristic of being larger than life. In addition, both could be titled "Love." Their shared theme provides a sufficient basis for comparison.
2. Except in terms of theme, students are likely to find few, if any, similarities between the two sculptures, but they will be able to list a number of differences: "The Kiss" depicts figures, the "LOVE" sculpture depicts a word; "The Kiss" is essentially realistic, the "LOVE" sculpture is essentially conceptual; "The Kiss" suggests passion, the "LOVE" sculpture suggests whimsy; "The Kiss" focuses on the love between men and women, the "LOVE" sculpture focuses on love in a more generalized sense.

3. Students' responses will vary, but one possible statement that could be made based on the points of contrast between the two sculptures is "Rodin's 'The Kiss' and Robert Indiana's 'LOVE' sculpture both depict an image based on the idea of love, but 'The Kiss' is about carnal love while the 'LOVE' sculpture is about love as a force that can unite humanity."

THEMATIC CONNECTIONS

The Storm (p. 183): Kate Chopin's short story, like the Rodin sculpture, is a depiction of passionate lovemaking. Considering that the two were created at approximately the same time in the late 1880s, why might Chopin's story have been seen as so much more scandalous?

Sex, Lies, and Conversation (p. 407): Do the details of Rodin's "The Kiss" suggest any innate differences between men and women? If so, how might they be related to the kinds of differences Deborah Tannen writes about in this essay?

Bruce Catton, *Grant and Lee: A Study in Contrasts*

This essay is a classic point-by-point comparison. First Catton discusses Lee, the aristocratic representative of tidewater Virginia. Next he presents Grant, the son of a tanner, who was everything Lee was not. He moves from generalizations about each man to the ways they differed in character and orientation. You might point out to students how, beginning with paragraph 12, Catton sums up his discussion of Lee and Grant with a point-by-point comparison. This is a good opportunity to discuss strategy and to ask students why Catton uses both types of comparisons in his essay. In this essay, topic sentences and transitions are important. The questions in Style and Structure ask students to consider these elements, and you might want to go further, devoting an entire class to these issues.

COMPREHENSION (p. 389)

1. Grant and Lee met at Appomattox Court House to work out the terms for Lee's surrender, thus "bringing the Civil War to its virtual finish" (2).
2. Lee represented the aristocratic values of tidewater Virginia. He stood for a privileged class of landowners whose values and responsible leadership ideally were to repay the society that recognized their status. This regional ideal was embodied in Lee, "as if he himself was the Confederacy" (6). In contrast, Grant, who grew up on the western frontier, was independent, self-reliant, and democratic. He was committed to the nation as a whole and to its prosperity.
3. Grant and Lee contrast most strikingly in their attitudes about society. Lee saw himself in terms of his own locality: "He lived in a static society which could endure almost anything except change" (10). On the other hand, Grant believed in the nation as a whole, a "broader concept of society" defined by "growth, expansion, and a constantly widening horizon" (11).
4. Both men were "marvelous fighters" whose "fighting qualities were really very much alike" (13). Each had tenacity, fidelity, daring, and resourcefulness. And most importantly, each was able "to turn quickly from war to peace once the fighting was over" (16).

5. Catton suggests that "succeeding generations of Americans are in debt to Grant and Lee" because of the way they were able to "turn quickly from war to peace once the fighting was over."

PURPOSE AND AUDIENCE (p. 389)

1. The aristocratic current, represented by Lee, is based on a class structure ruled by the elite. The democratic current, represented by Grant, is based on individualism and a strong sense of national community. These differences have always defined two strong currents in America from Jefferson and Hamilton to Dole and Clinton, and they are still apparent in debates between conservative Republicans and liberal Democrats.
2. Catton uses Grant and Lee to represent "the strengths of two conflicting currents that, through them, had come into final collision" (3). Although their differences produced collision, their strengths made reconciliation possible. By comparing them, Catton makes a statement about the strengths of the American character and its ability to reconcile differences.
3. Catton's thesis is that Grant and Lee embodied two conflicting currents in America, the democratic and the aristocratic.

STYLE AND STRUCTURE (p. 389)

1. Catton uses point-by-point comparison since he includes too many points for an effective subject-by-subject comparison. An audience would have difficulty remembering all the details about the first subject once the essay moved to the second.
2. These topic sentences establish the comparison and contrast; moreover, they indicate whether Grant or Lee will be the focus of the paragraph. They also unify the essay by providing transitions from one paragraph to another.
3. Examples of transitions in this essay include *These men* (2), *They were two strong men* (3), *Grant . . . was everything Lee was not* (7), *Yet along with this feeling* (9), *And that, perhaps, is where the contrast . . . becomes most striking* (10), and so forth.
4. Catton uses the meeting at Appomattox as a frame for his essay. His major concern is Lee and Grant and the currents they represent, not the events during the meeting.

VOCABULARY PROJECTS (p. 390)

2. To do this exercise correctly, students will have to be sensitive to context. For example, although *manners* is a synonym for *deportment,* it does not convey the notion of *cultivated,* which is required by the context.

COMBINING THE PATTERNS (p. 390)

Paragraphs 9, 10, and 11 also use exemplification. Each suggests contrasting characteristics of the Westerner and the Virginia aristocrat.

THEMATIC CONNECTIONS

The Declaration of Independence **(p. 557):** The Declaration of Independence provides an underlying framework for discussing historical U.S. goals and values. Students might consider ways the Civil War tested the powers of this crucial document.

Letter from Birmingham Jail **(p. 570):** Catton asserts that Robert E. Lee fought for an ideal, but criticizes it by tying it to images from the Middle Ages—to the age of chivalry, knighthood, and English squires—dated images that depend on the existence of a subordinate class. Just as feudalism required the subjugation of peasants, so Lee's "feeling that it was somehow advantageous for human society to have a pronounced inequality in the social structure" required the subjugation of blacks. In his "Letter from Birmingham Jail," Martin Luther King Jr. shows that such inequalities continued to exist for blacks a century after the Civil War and calls on the ministers to whom he is writing—and by extension, all Americans—to stand up "for what is best in the American dream and for the most sacred values in our Judaeo-Christian heritage, thereby bringing our nation back to the great wells of democracy which were dug deeply by the founding fathers in the formulation of the Constitution and the Declaration of Independence."

An Idea Whose Time Has Come **(p. 637):** The fundamental issue that sparked the Civil War was that of slavery and its abolition. Today, almost a century and a half later, a movement is under way to gain monetary reparations for the descendents of slaves from the United Sates government, which for so long legalized slavery, and from corporations and other institutions that once benefited financially from the slave trade. This essay and the others that accompany it in the casebook on reparations for the descendents of slaves lay out the terms of this contentious debate.

Ian Frazier, *Dearly Disconnected*

Frazier writes here about pay telephones, a seemingly unlikely topic but one to which he brings great insight and heart. He recalls the days when people depended on pay phones for a variety of reasons and, in paragraph 4, even allows for the frustrations they often caused and, in paragraph 6, notes their sense of "seediness" and "sadness." He is at his best here when he nostalgically describes the pay phones he remembers from his past and the roles they played in his life. He goes on in paragraphs 9 through 11 to contrast pay phones with the cell phones that are rapidly replacing their use (see item number 2 under *Style and Structure* below). And he goes on to make a larger point at the end of paragraph 12: that pay phones represent a kind of "commonality," a sharing of community resources no matter what one's status, that contemporary society seems to be abandoning as well.

You might begin class discussion by asking students if they know where pay phones are located on campus and whether they have ever actually used them. You might also want to discuss the pros and cons of cell phones. They are certainly a convenience and can be invaluable in emergency situations, but they can also be surprisingly expensive, not to mention disruptive (if their users are not careful, they can ring in completely inappropriate situations—during class, for example). People who have them may also find that they are always within reach and that they no longer have an excuse for not checking in at the office or at home.

Another possible topic for discussion is the idea of nostalgia. What kinds of things to people remember nostalgically? For many of your younger students, television shows they watched as children may be among the few things they ever grow nostalgic about, but, if you have older students, you might get some more varied responses.

COMPREHENSION (p. 395)

1. The Florida pay phone is a landmark for Frazier because once, while living alone in Montana and estranged from his girlfriend who was living in Sarasota at the time without a phone, he called a nearby pay phone in a crazy attempt to reach her; she happened to be walking by and answered. He implies that this little miracle led to their eventual marriage.
2. Increasing use of cell phones means that pay phones are becoming less and less important for most people.
3. Frazier feels nostalgic about pay phones because he has so many memories associated with pay phones—some of which he enumerates in paragraph 8, where he notes that each phone he describes "is as specific as a birthmark, a point on earth unlike any other."
4. One primary difference is that people own their own cell phones whereas pay phones were a public commodity and "suggested a human average; they belonged to anybody who had a couple of coins" (12). Also, as Frazier suggests in paragraph 9, cell phones are "toylike, nearly magic," whereas pay phones are more prosaic. People can talk on cell phones while in motion, something not possible with pay phones. Yet pay phones allow privacy, which most people who use cell phones seem to regard with indifference (11).
5. Frazier says that "what drives me so nuts" about cell phones is that when people use them in public, they treat those who surround them as if they weren't there (11).

PURPOSE AND AUDIENCE (p. 395)

1. Frazier states his thesis in the first two sentences of paragraph 4. It follows the story of the pay phone that brought him and his wife together and introduces his many nostalgic memories of pay phones, both negative and positive.
2. Most immediately, Frazier seems to feel that his readers have not given much thought to pay phones or to the fact that they are an increasingly endangered species. Possible preconceptions might be that they could be a nuisance (4) and that they were often associated with "seediness," "sadness," and the "mundane" (6). At the same time, Frazier seems to feel that some readers, at least, might respond to his nostalgia with a sense of nostalgia of their own.
3. Essentially, Frazier's purpose seems to be to share his thoughts about pay phones and cell phones. The essay can be seen as instructive in that it attempts to remind readers of the important role pay phones once played in people's lives, to make the point that pay phones are being superseded by cell phones, and finally to make the larger point that "like public schools and public transportation, pay phones belong to a former commonality our culture is no longer quite so sure it needs" (12).
4. If students recognize the title's allusion to the phrase "dearly departed," used in eulogies to refer to the deceased, they will probably feel that it accurately—

and wittily—reflects the essay's thesis. (In fact, the essay can be read as a eulogy for the pay phone.) The other title possibilities are virtually endless, ranging from the straightforward ("The Disappearing Pay Phone") to the punny ("Pay Phones: Cell-ared Away").

STYLE AND STRUCTURE (p. 395)

1. The opening story serves to suggest how important a role pay phones played in Frazier's life, and by extension, many people's lives. The fact that, in later years, his family made a special detour to visit the pay phone that connected him to his future wife sets up the pay phone as a sort of shrine to an earlier, more romantic time.

2. The comparison of pay phones and cell phones, which occupies paragraphs 9 through 11, is essentially point-by-point. The two are compared in terms of how their users treat them and feel about them, their relationship to the idea of transience and to their user's air of importance, their relation to the public and private spheres, and the cultural values they reflect. Because Frazier wants to concentrate on pay phones rather than cell phones, a limited point-by-point comparison that takes up a relatively brief portion of his essay makes sense.

3. In fact, Frazier uses no traditional transitions to signal movement from one subject to the next in paragraphs 9 through 11. Several of his comparisons are actually implied rather stated directly. An interesting subject for discussion is whether students have difficulty recognizing the differences Frazier is suggesting. Ask students to try to insert transitions, and they will inevitably have difficulty doing so. They should recognize that Frazier's is a highly personal voice, moving from thought to thought seamlessly (although his use of paragraphing does serve to indicate some transitions).

4. Basically in paragraphs 9 through 11 Frazier contrasts pay phones and cell phones in similar terms: pay phones are the "difficult older sibling" while cell phones are the "cherished newborn"; people yelled at pay phones but don't yell at cell phones; cell phones are used "gently" while pay phones are "beat-up"; pay phones were a symbol of "transience" while cell phones are a symbol of "mobility and speed" (a clear step up from transience); pay phone callers talked within walls while, for cell phone users, the people around them are the "walls"; pay phones are open to the public while cell phones imply private privilege. One difference Frazier doesn't note is that people may have to wait to use pay phones while cell phones are always immediately available. This difference would not have contributed significantly to his main point.

5. Frazier turns decidedly lyrical in his conclusion, imagining the future as he would like to see it and resigning himself—albeit in highly abstract terms—to the future he actually foresees. It is arguable that paragraph 12 provides a more forceful ending because the point it makes is more concrete.

VOCABULARY PROJECTS (p. 395)

2. More accessible language in paragraph 6 might include *change* for *transience*, *secret meetings* for *assignations*, *thinking about* for *contemplating*, *surroundings* for *atmospherics*, *items* for *accessories*, *called up* for *evoked*, *ordinary* for *mundane*,

similar people for *undifferentiated humanity* and *silence* for *muteness*. What might be gained in simplicity by such substitutions is counterbalanced by the loss of nuance and connotation.

COMBINING THE PATTERNS (p. 396)

The many examples Frazier uses ground his essay in a specific reality. Such paragraphs help him evoke the look and feel of various pay phone booths.

THEMATIC CONNECTIONS

Once More to the Lake (p. 175): E. B. White's essay is also a kind of elegy for times past. In revisiting the rural lake where his family vacationed when he was a child, White calls up nostalgic memories, noting that, while much remains the same, technology has also brought change not entirely for the better. Students might also notice that White and Frazier write in a very similar style.

Television: The Plug-In Drug (p. 325): Marie Winn also questions society's thoughtless acceptance of new technologies. Her focus is on television and the way it has been allowed to interfere with close family relationships.

How the Lawyers Stole Winter (p. 402): Like Frazier, Daly writes about the passing of an era. He recalls his great pleasure as a boy in skating on a frozen pond in his neighborhood without regulation or supervision. Now, he finds this pleasure nearly impossible for his own sons because the potential for liability suits has caused his town to disallow skating on a public pond. Children today, he notes ruefully, have little opportunity to learn for themselves how to recognize danger because they are so protected from any potentially dangerous situations.

Bharati Mukherjee, *Two Ways to Belong in America*

In the wake of congressional proposals to restrict the rights and government benefits allowed to resident aliens—that is, foreign-born people who live legally in the United States (and in many cases work and pay taxes) but who choose not to become U.S. citizens—Indian-born Mukherjee contrasts her sister, a resident alien, with herself, a naturalized citizen. With mixed feelings, Mukherjee sympathizes with her sister's anger over America's changing "its rules in midstream" (8) but at the same time characterizes her sister's relationship with America as a "comfortable yet loveless marriage, without risk or recklessness" (9). Mukherjee, however, embraces "the trauma of self-transformation" (15) that becoming a citizen has required. This essay provides a good opportunity to introduce current controversies about immigration policy, which are debated in depth in the argument chapter.

COMPREHENSION (p. 400)

1. They expected to stay only two years to attend school, but both married, found fulfilling jobs, and so decided to stay.
2. The strain results in part from differing expectations for the wives of Indian-born men and those who marry westerners. Mukherjee says she renounced "3,000 years (at least) of caste-observant, 'pure culture' marriage" in her family (5).

3. Mira "clings passionately to her Indian citizenship and hopes to go home to India when she retires" (4). Mukherjee feels the need to be "a part of the community . . . to put roots down, to vote and make the difference that I can" (15). Rather than "maintain an identity" as her sister did, Mukherjee chose to "transform" hers. The two seem to have an affectionate relationship, but the differences between them make them "pity" each other.
4. Mira's employer asked her to stay in the United States because of her talents. She has contributed a great deal to her community, paid her taxes, "obeyed all the rules" (8). Now, after thirty years, she is angry because she stands to be denied benefits she has come to expect.
5. Because she hasn't become a citizen but has chosen to maintain her status as an "outsider," Mira stands to lose almost as much as "the millions of hard-working but effectively silenced documented immigrants as well as their less fortunate 'illegal' brothers and sisters" (12).

PURPOSE AND AUDIENCE (p. 400)

1. Her thesis is stated in her final sentence.
2. Mukherjee seems to have an audience of general readers in mind, which might include educated immigrant readers like her sister and herself.
3. Mukherjee's primary purpose is to explore the different mindsets of immigrants who choose to become citizens and those who don't (informative). But her purpose is also to create in her readers some sympathy for her sister's situation—and so, perhaps, to have an effect on the kinds of laws that are eventually passed (persuasive).

STYLE AND STRUCTURE (p. 400)

1. The basis of comparison is the sisters' differing attitudes toward becoming U.S. citizens. Mukherjee establishes it in her opening paragraph.
2. The comparison is essentially point-by-point, which helps Mukherjee to keep the focus on both her sister and herself throughout.
3. She discusses their different marital and career paths, their different decisions about becoming U.S. citizens, and the different situations they face now that government policies toward resident aliens have changed. She also refers to finding herself in a situation similar to her sister's—and feeling a similar sense of betrayal—when she was living in Canada at a time when anti-immigration sentiments ran high. Discussing other points isn't really necessary.
4. Transitional words and phrases include *instead* (3), *nearly twenty years ago* (13), and *however* (15). Students may note that Mukherjee uses relatively few transitional words and phrases, and those she uses are set up as direct oppositions.
5. The conclusion is an effective summary of Mukherjee's points.

VOCABULARY PROJECTS (p. 400)

2. An *immigrant* adopts his or her new country, whereas an *exile* maintains the customs of the native country, feels a strong connection there, and hopes to return. The connotations of the first are fairly neutral, but those of the second are more charged, either negatively or positively depending on the particular context.

COMBINING THE PATTERNS (p. 401)

Some causal analysis of the reasons for the two sisters' differences would be interesting—and she might have included such an analysis in a longer essay. This was written with the length limitations of the *New York Times*'s op-ed page in mind.

THEMATIC CONNECTIONS

Only Daughter (p. 84): Sandra Cisneros also writes about the experience of being an immigrant and the difficulties involved in adjusting to the mores of a new culture.

The Way to Rainy Mountain (p. 169): N. Scott Momaday's remembrances of his Kiowa grandmother suggest a different slant on maintaining traditional ways. Obviously not an immigrant, his grandmother nonetheless stood outside of mainstream U.S. culture and was in a sense denied full participation in the American system. But like Mira, she also chose not to assimilate.

The Big Move (p. 377): Student Margaret Depner's essay is about adjusting to life in England while living there for a year after her father was transferred. It provides a contrasting viewpoint—that of a U.S. citizen living abroad with the status of a resident alien. If your students found long-term careers in another country and married citizens there, how many of them would choose to give up their U.S. citizenship, as Mukherjee did, in order to participate more fully in their communities? How do their feelings about this color their views of Mukherjee and her sister?

The Untouchable (p. 498): Student Ajoy Mahtab's essay will provide students with some insight into the strict caste system of Indian life that Mukherjee refers to.

Strange Tools (p. 697): In another essay that focuses on the immigrant experience in the United States, Richard Rodriguez writes about growing up as the child of Mexican-American parents and about how learning to read was, for him, a means of cultural assimilation.

Christopher B. Daly, *How the Lawyers Stole Winter*

Daly contrasts the past with the present in this essay. Remembering with pleasure ice skating with friends on unsupervised natural ponds in rural Massachusetts, he laments the fact that today his sons are denied this activity because local governments (and their lawyers) have declared such ponds off-limits in order to avoid lawsuits. What his sons' generation loses, he says, is not only the freedom from adult intrusion that he and his childhood friends enjoyed playing hockey on the ice, but also the opportunity of learning to evaluate risks and handle them on one's own. By "not teaching our kids how to take risks," Daly says, "we are making the world more dangerous" (11). You might begin class discussion by raising this point: Are children today *too* protected? If so, to what extent does it make them more, rather than less, vulnerable? (See *Comprehension* question 5.)

COMPREHENSION (p. 404)

1. They put on play clothes and went outside to play until dinnertime—play that in winter often included ice skating and playing hockey.

2. Winter is "in danger of passing away" because towns, cities, and property holders are so afraid of lawsuits that they are declaring ponds off-limits for skating.

3. During his childhood, Daly and his friends tested the ice by "throwing heavy stones, hammering it with downed branches, and, finally, jumping on it" (2). (See also paragraph 9 for other ways they learned to gauge the ice.) Today, children are simply prohibited from skating on ponds, so they have no opportunity to learn these things.

4. As children, Daly and his friends learned to take risks judiciously; today children are encouraged not to take risks, and when they do anyway, Daly feels, they are likely to do so without the "collective wisdom" necessary to evaluate the risks accurately. Daly implicitly proposes that children be given more freedom to play on their own, unsupervised.

5. As suggested in the introduction above, Daly means that children who are denied the experience of taking risks don't learn how to evaluate dangerous situations for themselves and so are more likely to get into trouble when they face risks.

PURPOSE AND AUDIENCE (p. 405)

1. Daly's thesis is stated in the first sentence of paragraph 11. Delaying his thesis allows him to set up his contrast clearly before getting into his main argument.

2. His purpose is to get readers to think about the situation he describes and perhaps to effect change.

3. Daly seems to think readers will be neutral or even sympathetic to his ideas. His opening evokes a sense of nostalgia that he expects his readers to share.

4. Answers will vary here. Probably many contemporary parents and children would find Daly's remarks persuasive.

5. By mentioning StairMasters and health clubs, Daly is contrasting the "clean, free exercise" (5) of his youth with the more structured exercise of contemporary life. He would expect his readers to see the irony.

STYLE AND STRUCTURE (p. 405)

1. The introduction establishes the "ideal" past which leads Daly into his discussion of the very different present.

2. The arrangement is basically point-by-point: Paragraphs 1–2 stand in contrast with paragraphs 3–4; paragraphs 5–6 contain another contrast; paragraphs 7–9 contrast with paragraphs 10–11; and paragraph 12 contrasts with paragraphs 13–14. Because of the length of these sections, students might see the essay as a combination of point-by-point and subject-by-subject.

3. The words *thin ice* are used both literally and figuratively. Literally, thin ice is the reason skating is prohibited. Figuratively, "skating on thin ice" is a metaphor for taking a risk.

4. Daly's transitions mostly deal with time: *recently* (3), *nowadays* (5), *when* (7), *today* (10). The transitions, while not prominent, seem sufficient to keep Daly's organization clear.

5. Answers will vary. Given the informality of Daly's essay, a one-sentence conclusion is acceptable, but it might be combined with the previous paragraph.

VOCABULARY PROJECTS (p. 405)

2. These words occur in paragraphs 5, 10, 11, and 12 and basically have the same meaning in each case. The repetition provides coherence.

COMBINING THE PATTERNS (p. 406)

The narrative is detailed enough to make Daly's ironic point that the "ever vigilant" (15) town officials overreact to the dangers of skating.

THEMATIC CONNECTIONS

Ground Zero (p. 158): There are two possible connections between this essay and Suzanne Berne's reflections about her visit to the site of the World Trade Center six months after its destruction in the terrorist attack of September 2001. First, Daly's focus on risk can be considered in light of the risks people took to help save the lives of others in the collapsing towers. Second, students might think about the idea of security and risk when we feel threatened by potential terrorist attacks.

The Way to Rainy Mountain (p. 169): N. Scott Momaday's essay corresponds to Daly's in several ways, but particularly in terms of how different generations stand in relation to the natural world. Like Daly's sons, Momaday has not learned to "read" the landscape with the same kind of authority that his grandmother had. Momaday also senses that something is lost as later generations grow further from the land.

Once More to the Lake (p. 175): See the *Thematic Connections* entry for E. B. White's essay on p. 40 of this manual. These two essays (Momaday's and White's) could provide interesting topics for discussing or writing about parent–child relationships and generational differences. For a unit discussing how a person's perception of events changes as he or she matures, bring in Malcolm X's "My First Conk" (p. 260).

Television: The Plug-In Drug (p. 325): Like Daly, Marie Winn considers how contemporary societal changes have affected children for the worse. You might have students expand Winn's discussion of rituals to include the kinds of childhood rituals Daly describes. How, in your students' view, have these changed over the last twenty years or so? Are children today, to use Daly's words, better off or not?

Deborah Tannen, *Sex, Lies, and Conversation*

Tannen contrasts male and female communication styles, suggesting that many misunderstandings between heterosexual couples are due less to real personal differences than to misread conversational signals. She looks first at differences between the way girls communicate with girls and the way boys communicate with boys and the resulting "misalignments in the mechanics of conversation" among men and women (6–13). She then describes differences in the way males and females read their conversational partners' responses (14–20) and differences in men's and women's reasons for talking (21–22). Her concluding paragraphs offer hope that by recognizing these differences as "cross-cultural," unhappy couples will be able to better understand one another. A good place to begin discussion is by asking students whether they think Tannen's examples are basically superficial stereotypes or whether they can see themselves in the men or the women she describes.

Ask for specific exceptions to Tannen's generalizations. Do any such exceptions prove—or disprove—the rule?

COMPREHENSION (p. 411)

1. At the beginning of her article Tannen offers an example of a husband doing most of the talking in public and a wife doing most of the talking at home.
2. Women most often complain that their partners don't listen or talk to them.
3. Three basic behaviors give women the impression that men do not listen: men tend to face away from each other in conversation, they often switch topics instead of following up with questions, and they make less listener-noise than women.
4. Men often respond to listener-noise as overreaction or impatience. In addition, women are more likely to "finish each other's sentences, and anticipate what the other is about to say," which men interpret as "interruption, intrusion, and lack of attention" (18).
5. Understanding differences in communication style can lead couples to modify their conversational behavior in ways that the other will respond to more positively. Even without such modifications, women can recognize that a man's failure to participate in the kind of conversation she expects from her close female friends does not necessarily indicate a "failure of intimacy" (25) and simply accept the difference without taking offense.

PURPOSE AND AUDIENCE (p. 412)

1. Tannen's thesis is stated in two parts: in paragraph 2 and at the beginning of paragraph 8.
2. Tannen's purpose is basically to inform. She doesn't directly advocate any change in male and female communication styles, suggesting that understanding the differences can help couples avoid misunderstandings.
3. Tannen clearly intends an audience of general readers, both men and women. (The essay originally appeared in the *Washington Post*.) The terms she uses and the concepts she explains are accessible to virtually any educated person, and she doesn't limit her discussion to one gender.

STYLE AND STRUCTURE (p. 412)

1. Because she is writing to provide information most people are not aware of, it is best that she state her thesis early in order to orient readers so they can understand the specific points that follow.
2. This is a point-by-point comparison, which allows Tannen to enumerate clearly the differences in several specific conversational activities.
3. Tannen's use of scholarly studies and statistics helps her suggest that the differences she describes are not simply based on her own observations but that they are supported by the work of other experts and by objective research.
4. Tannen's tone is positive, generally hopeful that husbands and wives can reduce the frictions caused by problems of cross-cultural communication.
5. Tannen's concluding call for cross-cultural understanding in "these times of resurgent ethnic conflict" may strike some readers as a bit too far-reaching for her particular subject. Not everyone will agree that a resolution to racial and ethnic conflict might be more easily achieved if men and women in the United States learn to better understand their conversational differences.

VOCABULARY PROJECTS (p. 412)

2. Tannen doesn't use much professional jargon. Among the few examples are *organizational structures and interactive norms* (7), *physical alignment* and *topical alignment* (13), and *listener-noise* and *participatory listenership* (18). Opinion will differ as to the effectiveness of such jargon in the essay. She generally defines her terms directly or through example, and the professional jargon tends to make her authority more credible.

COMBINING THE PATTERNS (p. 413)

The anecdote provides an example of the point Tannen makes throughout her essay—that women and men communicate in different ways but remain largely unaware of these differences, which leads to misunderstandings. The story is itself amusing and serves to establish Tannen's informal, friendly style.

THEMATIC CONNECTIONS

Why Boys Don't Play with Dolls (p. 335): Katha Pollitt's essay examines some assumptions about gender differences in terms of biological predisposition and social construction. See "Sex, Lies, and Conversation" under *Thematic Connections* on p. 78 of this manual.

The Men We Carry in Our Minds (p. 456): Scott Russell Sanders also considers questions of gender difference and misunderstandings between himself and women friends in college. Sanders's point, however, is that he finds class differences more telling when it comes to issues of power and control.

I Want a Wife (p. 505): Judy Brady's essay also looks at conflicts between wives and husbands, in this case based on stereotypical assumptions about the roles each should fulfill within a marriage. How might Tannen respond to Brady's portrait of a wife? Do the differences Tannen suggests between men and women in any way justify the popularly held stereotypes of male-female roles?

The Wife-Beater (p. 521): This essay by Gayle Rosenwald Smith takes aim at the popular term for a fashionable kind of T-shirt worn by young people. To call a shirt a "wife-beater" is, for this writer, to suggest that violence against women is either something to joke about or to accept as the norm. Tannen does not consider the extent to which miscommunication between spouses may lead to angry altercations, but students might think about how differences between the way men and women communicate can lead to violence against women.

Eric Schlosser, *Walt and Ray: Your Trusted Friends*

This relatively lengthy essay is not so great a challenge as it might first appear because it focuses on elements of popular culture with which students will likely be familiar: the Walt Disney empire (spanning animated films to theme parks) and the McDonald's fast food empire created by Ray Kroc. Schlosser's central point here is that Disney and Kroc had a great deal in common, both in terms of their personal qualities and their influential marketing savvy. Students may not be familiar with these two icons of American commerce, but they will certainly recognize their product lines, their two companies' continuing influence on Americans' spending habits, and the "intangible" something (28) that both companies still sell to children.

You could begin discussion by asking students about their earliest memories of the "brands" Disney and McDonald's. What do they associate both of these names with? How did both companies use television as a way of capturing the interest of young viewers? Do they still feel the same way about Disney enterprises and McDonald's as they did when they were younger? If you have students who did not grow up in the United States, ask them to talk about the international reach of these companies. Was their earliest awareness of these brands and their products very different from that of students who grew up watching American television?

You could then turn students' attention to Walt Disney and Ray Kroc as Schlosser describes them here. What impressions of these two men do they come away with after reading this essay? Do they think they are models of what a successful entrepreneur should be (or must be)? Have their opinions of the respective worlds of Disney and McDonald's changed at all after reading Schlosser's portraits of Disney and Kroc and the business models they each created?

COMPREHENSION (p. 424)

1. Disney and Kroc were the same age and born in the Midwest, dropped out of high school, served together in World War I, relocated to California at an early age, created important American businesses that trained employees via "the trappings of formal education," had an obsessive need for control and cleanliness, shared a "faith in technology" and "the same conservative political viewpoints," and "were charismatic leaders" more adept at providing an overall vision that captured the public mood than at handling "creative and financial details" (5–6). In addition, both were ruthless businessmen (15–16) and shrewd marketers, especially to children (7; 24–28); Schlosser sees this latter point as their most significant achievement.

2. Kroc obtained from the brothers the right to turn the restaurant they had created into a nationwide franchise. They were not willing to put in the long hours of travel and selling that Kroc was already used to.

3. Disney's success came much sooner than Kroc's and so his production and marketing methods were influential to Kroc. Both were members of the Republican party (although Disney played a much more active role in politics than Kroc did), and both believed that society was governed by the rule of "survival of the fittest" (15–18).

4. For Schlosser the "great irony" of Disneyland is that its vision of a utopian future was so far removed from the urban sprawl that the theme park actually created in surrounding Anaheim—and, by extension, the urban sprawl that makes up so much of the American landscape.

5. The Magic Kingdom and McDonaldland had a similar physical appearance and similar theme songs and jingles; in addition, the fantasy characters who populated them were similar and "[a]lmost everything in [both] was for sale" (28).

PURPOSE AND AUDIENCE (p. 424)

1. The thesis, stated in the first two sentences of paragraph 5, is that both the Walt Disney Company and the McDonald's Corporation, as well as their

respective founders, were similar in many ways, and that their successes as salesmen in their respective businesses shaped future American business models, paving the way for countless other marketing programs targeting America's youth.

2. Schlosser's reference to Disney and Kroc as "your trusted friends" is essentially ironic. His point is that the two men gained the trust of consumers, particularly children, merely to market their products; their goals were exploitative rather than altruistic. Students may come up with a variety of alternative titles, probably ones such as "Two Corporate Masters" that emphasize their similarities or "Marketing Magicians" that emphasize their skills as salesmen.

3. Basically, Schlosser's point here in terms of his book's overall thesis is that Disney's methods of marketing to children paved the way for Kroc's and those of other fast food merchandisers. As has been widely reported since the book's publication, fast food has contributed greatly to increasing obesity in the United States, especially among children and teenagers.

STYLE AND STRUCTURE (p. 424)

1. Students' opinions will vary here. This opening certainly makes the point that there is a "common McDonald's culture," that the company is a marketing bonanza and a ubiquitous part of American life, and that Kroc himself was a larger-than-life figure enshrined by the museum. Students may recognize that as a section of a chapter in a book devoted to fast food, this opening makes sense because it connects the chapter to the book's theme. They may not see it as quite so effective as an opening for a free-standing essay because it focuses solely on Kroc rather than Kroc and Disney.

2. Schlosser emphasizes similarities, as the answer to item one under *Comprehension* suggests. The only differences he mentions are that Disney succeeded much earlier in life than Kroc did (14) and that Disney was active in politics while Kroc—with one exception—was not (17–18).

3. Students will probably notice that Schlosser uses both organizational patterns. His overview of the two men in paragraphs 5 through 7 is point-by-point, while the remainder of the essay treats the two men subject-by-subject. This allows Schlosser to introduce their similarities and then treat each man in more detail.

4. The basis of comparison is that the two used their similar personality traits and a similar marketing savvy to create two hugely successful corporations. The comparison is clearly justified.

5. He means that both Disney and Kroc sold an image that was tailored to encourage customer loyalty—or, less positively, to influence the buying habits of impressionable youngsters.

VOCABULARY PROJECTS (p. 425)

2. To describe Kroc, Schlosser uses adjectives such as *charming, funny,* and *indefatigable* in paragraph 8; *ambitious* in paragraph 11; and *clever* and *pragmatic* in paragraph 25. To describe Disney, he uses adjectives such as *famous* (14); *embittered* (15); *passionate* in his resistance to unions and government interference in free markets (19); *beloved* (22); and *cheerful, friendly,* and *patriotic* (24). The adjectives emphasize the qualities that helped Kroc persevere and succeed and the qualities that marked Disney as a highly contradictory personality.

COMBINING THE PATTERNS (p. 425)

Cause and effect provides the basis for paragraphs 15 (which explains why Disney became a strong anti-Communist), 17–18 (which explain Kroc's reasons for not backing political candidates), 19 (which explains why Disney came to contract for work with the federal government), 23 (which notes the effects of Disneyland on urban sprawl and Disney's subsequent plans for Disney World), and 28 (which shows how Kroc succeeded in capturing the attention of children).

THEMATIC CONNECTIONS

The Peter Principle (p. 207): This essay's focus on business practices can be tied into Schlosser's discussion of two business giants. See *Thematic Connections*, "The Peter Principle," p. 45 of this manual.

The Ways We Lie (p. 470): Beginning in paragraph 24, Schlosser describes the ways both the Walt Disney Company and the McDonald's Corporation tailored their messages to attract the youngest television audience members as consumers for their products. Students might consider the extent to which such appeals are deceptive, as well as the ethics of such advertising.

Tortillas (p. 513): In this lighthearted essay, Mexican-American writer José Antonio Burciaga offers a detailed definition of this staple of Mexican cuisine. Students might think about how food reflects culture in the United States and how the fast food industry has influenced American culture.

On Dumpster Diving (p. 660): Lars Eighner considers consumer culture from a different perspective. During a period when he was jobless and homeless and reduced to scavenging in dumpsters for the necessities of life, he learned some surprising things by discovering the perfectly good items that people throw away.

Gwendolyn Brooks, *Sadie and Maud*

Brooks's poem compares two sisters, one of whom conformed to convention and the other of whom rebelled against it. While a surface reading of the poem might suggest a "good sister"/"bad sister" dichotomy, students should recognize that Brooks is after something much more subtle here. Although Sadie may have been wild by nature and even irresponsible in her behavior, she lived life large and passionately; Maud's life, as suggested by the final stanza, was far more drab and confined. Sadie at least left a "heritage," albeit a difficult one; it appears that Maud will leave behind none. Students should note that the poem tells readers much more about Sadie (thirteen lines are devoted to her) than about Maud (seven lines, two of which also refer to "Ma and Pa") and that, although Maud is mentioned first in the poem itself, Sadie is mentioned first in the title. Ask students specifically how they interpret the image of Sadie scraping life "With a fine-tooth comb" and the repetition of this image at the poem's next-to-last stanza. Another interpretive question is why Brooks uses the phrases "said her last so-long" in line 13 and "thin brown mouse" in line 18.

READING LITERATURE (p. 427)

1. Brooks compares two extremes for women: One plays by the rules and pursues an education but ends up sadly "all alone"; the other breaks the rules,

pursuing life's pleasures and giving birth to two illegitimate children, then dies young (note, though, that "said her last so-long" is a surprisingly chipper way of noting someone's death). Brooks indicates her shifts in subject as simply as possible, by introducing each sister's name.

2. The poem may tempt some readers to see stereotypes—what might in Brooks's day have been called the "loose woman" on the one hand and on the other the "old maid." In fact, though, the sympathy the poet brings to describing both sisters' lives suggests that she doesn't see them as stereotypes at all, but as women who make choices and face the consequences of those choices. (It should also be noted that neither of these stereotypes need be confined to African-American women; they are familiar within all ethnic groups.)

3. Students' responses will likely vary. Getting an education is clearly associated with bettering oneself here, and it could be said that Brooks is commenting on the limited opportunities society made available to women—and particularly black women—at the time the poem was written. Note that while "Maud went to college," nowhere does the poem suggest that she had any sort of career.

THEMATIC CONNECTIONS

Finishing School (p. 89): Like Sadie, Maya Angelou shows herself in this excerpt from her memoirs to be a rebel as a child, chafing at the requirement that she do what is expected of her, and Angelou went on to break convention throughout her life—although not in quite the same way that Sadie does.

Declaration of Sentiments and Resolutions (p. 557): This call for women's rights, written almost a century before Brooks's poem, grew out of the larger abolitionist movement and its call for human rights more generally in the United States. Yet even by the 1940s, few of the goals of either movement had been fully achieved. How far along are we today in achieving the goals of equal rights and opportunities for all?

Strange Tools (p. 697): This excerpt from Richard Rodriguez's memoir focusing on his early education suggests that in some contexts education can be not only empowering but isolating as well.

10: CLASSIFICATION AND DIVISION

A natural way to begin studying classification and division is to look closely at Gregory Rawlings's paragraph from "Pregnant with Possibility." Note that the paragraph begins with a clear topic sentence defining three categories of people based on the effect that computer technology is having on their economic status. Rawlings then goes on to develop this central idea and to make an important point about the people in each category. Finally, he explains why he uses the word *races* in referring to his three categories in order to make a larger point about them.

Remind students that as they write any essay they are classifying and dividing—classifying bits of information into categories that may become paragraphs, dividing a topic into parts, and so on. You might also review the many ways we use classification and division to simplify our lives—in everything from libraries to classified ads, from biological hierarchies to technical reports. You can easily devise an exercise to illustrate how we classify and divide: items on a list of twenty-five television shows, for instance, can be classified according to format (sitcom, detective story, etc.), degree of popularity, time of broadcast, or any of several other principles. Once students have practiced arranging the titles in various groupings, you can show them how they might use these categories as support for several different thesis statements concerning television programming.

The selections in this chapter use classification and division for a wide range of purposes. The opening visual text is a somewhat shocking government document that charts how immigration authorities between 1892 and 1931 classified those not permitted entry to the United States based on the causes for which they were debarred. Then, students can readily relate to William Zinsser's essay "College Pressures," focusing on four kinds of pressures college students face. Next, Scott Russell Sanders uses classification to make a thoughtful point about class, gender, and power. In the following essay, novelist Amy Tan focuses on language, classifying the different "Englishes" she uses when communicating with different audiences; Stephanie Ericsson's essay uses division to suggest the many kinds of lies we tell ourselves and others, and Jedediah Purdy's essay uses division to suggest that there are three distinct types of environmentalists in the United States whose goals sometimes conflict with one another. Finally, Edwin Brock's poem enumerates "Five Ways to Kill a Man" as a bleak metaphor for the human condition.

Immigration and Naturalization Services Library, "Aliens Debarred from the United States by Causes: 1892–1931" (Chart) and Public Health Service Historian, Medical Exam of Male Immigrants (Photo)

During the period covered by the chart, many potential immigrants to the United States were fleeing poverty and persecution in their home countries. Disembarking from the cramped steerage decks of ocean liners, they first had to pass through grim processing centers, as depicted in the photograph, where they were met by a series of officials testing their "fitness" to enter the country. As the chart suggests, these officials found many reasons to debar entry, some of which may strike us now as almost entirely discriminary. Students should understand that labels such as "idiots" and "imbeciles," while considered scientific at the time, could in fact be highly subjective and have long since been discredited.

READING IMAGES (p. 445)

1. While other answers are possible, the most logical principle of classifying these categories is probably "reason for undesirability."
2. Based on the principle of classification in item 1, possible groupings include *mental defect, disease, inability to support oneself,* and *social undesirability* (or *likelihood of becoming a public nuisance*). Students may note that because the categories themselves overlap somewhat, there are different ways of placing them in these four groups.
3. The photograph shows medical inspectors checking potential immigrants for disease or conditions that might prevent them from earning a living. It is through such examinations that people were debarred from the United States and placed in the categories listed on the chart.

THEMATIC CONNECTIONS

Words Left Unspoken **(p. 153):** As Leah Hager Cohen explains in paragraph 9 of her essay, her grandfather's family immigrated to the United States in 1913 when he was a young child. Probably born deaf, he would not have been allowed to enter the country if immigration officials had detected his disability. Cohen also refers to another indignity many immigrants suffered at the hands of immigration officials: the altering of their names in order to "simplify" them for native English speakers.

The Catbird Seat **(p. 509):** David J. Birnbaum writes of being a quadriplegic confined to a wheelchair. Students might do some research to see how such a disability would have affected a potential immigrant's chance of entering the country early in the twentieth century and what effect it might have today.

Burdens **(p. 509):** John Kenneth Galbraith's essay suggests that current governmental policies increasingly favor the "haves" over the "have-nots," just as immigration policies did according to the 1892–1931 chart. Students might consider why the United States has continued to be seen as a "land of opportunity" for so many around the world. What types of legal immigrants are considered most valuable today?

Why Fear National ID Cards? **(p. 590):** Alan Dershowitz's essay is part of a debate about security concerns in light of the continued threat of terrorist attacks in the United States. The attacks of September 2001 were made possible, in part, by serious lapses by immigration authorities that only came to light after the fact, and the Immigration Service has continued to come under fire for admitting potential security risks. What sort of screening of potential immigrants do students think should take place in the changed world we find ourselves in today?

William Zinsser, *College Pressures*

You will probably want to discuss this essay first in your classification unit because its subject matter is so close to students and because it so clearly demonstrates meaningful use of the pattern. From Zinsser's essay, you can raise any number of classification issues: the basis for the system, the logic behind the order in which categories are presented, questions about any overlapping categories, and the significance of the system.

As you assign the essay, you might ask students to consider causes of student suicide in this country. Of course, the causes are varied and complex, but they often include academic pressures. As you discuss the selection, you will want to emphasize Zinsser's belief that students "have the power to shape their own future" (39) and to discuss ways in which they can do so. You might also ask your students how closely Yale students parallel students elsewhere. Are the concerns of most Yale students trivial compared to pressures faced by students at state universities or community colleges, for instance? (Don't forget to remind students that Yale students, too, may have severe financial problems.)

COMPREHENSION (p. 453)

1. Zinsser advises students that their futures are unpredictable, with turns they will not expect, and that there is time to make changes of careers, jobs, attitudes, and approaches.

2. He wishes them "some release from the clammy grip of the future" (13) so that they will have the chance to enjoy each stage of their education, to experiment, and to learn that failure is not fatal and can even be valuable. He believes his wish is naive because America worships achievement and lauds the successful in the media.

3. Zinsser identifies economic, parental, peer, and self-induced pressures.

4. Zinsser blames no one. He sees only victims, not villains because the pressures to compete are all too real.

5. Zinsser evaluates students by the range of their learning, their curiosity, and their willingness to take risks. He cares little about their grades. In contrast, he sees employers evaluating them on the basis of their having taken a narrow spectrum of safe subjects and earned uniformly high grades.

6. Women are under even more pressure than men because society is so slow to recognize their leadership potential for jobs traditionally reserved for men.

7. The "new pauperism" causes professors to spend their time publishing to avoid "perishing" in a shrinking profession. Consequently, they do not spend as much time with students as many would like.

8. Ultimately students themselves must accept responsibility for eliminating college pressures. They are the ones who can find faith in themselves and refuse to be shaped by external pressures.

9. Because students have too many choices for the limited time they have available, sports and other extracurricular activities cause them further anxiety. Students adapt by selecting activities with a foreseeable end rather than choosing ongoing activities.

PURPOSE AND AUDIENCE (p. 454)

1. Zinsser's thesis is that students who are victims of enormous economic, parental, peer, and self-induced pressures must, nonetheless, free themselves—as only they can. Without discounting the difficulties, Zinsser intends to effect change, to make students aware that they can free themselves from "the clammy grip of the future" (13).

2. Very likely students would most feel the impact from Zinsser's ideas since they generally feel pressured without realizing that they can free themselves. Other potential audiences have more experience with academic and professional life.

3. In paragraphs 42 through 46, Zinsser hopes to make readers aware that anxiety even drives students' extracurricular pursuits: he sees students as "largely ignoring the blithe spirit inside who keeps trying to come out and play" (46) because of faulty American values.

4. Zinsser believes that his readers, for the most part, share the values that cause student anxiety and obsession without being aware of the impact these values have. However, he also believes that they can be enlightened. His assumption about the materialism of his audience is not entirely valid; many parents are already enlightened and do not insist that their students major in "pre-rich," and many employers look for qualities not shown on transcripts. Of course, Zinsser's assumptions are not without some foundation, although they need to be qualified. Certainly his assumption that Yale students are typical of students nationally could lead him to overgeneralize.

STYLE AND STRUCTURE (p. 454)

1. Zinsser effectively uses the introductory notes to Carlos to personalize students' struggling for success.

2. Zinsser signals his classification in paragraph 15 with his explicit statement of the four types of pressure. He begins his first category in paragraph 16 when he discusses the typical question of today's students: How can they find an "edge" for getting into the professional schools that almost guarantee their earning large incomes after graduation? He indicates the completion of the final category when he asserts that the student, "as a driven creature who is largely ignoring the blithe spirit inside" (46), is the product of values that make him or her feel both driven and fearful.

3. Paragraphs 22 and 31 are transitional. Each introduces a new type of pressure by closely linking it to the one just discussed.

4. Zinsser has several options for referring to groups of mixed gender, including "he or she" and "he/she." The least obtrusive option is to make both antecedents and pronouns plural. Because it is unobtrusive, it is the preferred option. Certainly the most controversial option, at least in academic situations, is to use a plural pronoun to refer to a singular indefinite pronoun; however, this usage does sometimes appear in respected publications. Discuss your preferences and your logic with your students. The issue of gender usage creates an opportunity for you to discuss the notion of language as dynamic rather than fixed—a concept that will surprise some of your students.

5. Quotations from deans and students at Yale support Zinsser's thesis.

6. Economic pressures drive parents who, in turn, pressure students. Thus the two types of pressure overlap. Students feeling driven by economic and parental pressures are further pressured by seeing other students outclass them, and therefore they drive themselves even further. Zinsser's acknowledgment that the categories overlap strengthens the essay, making it clear that the pressures combine to trap students.

7. Zinsser discusses economic pressure first since it generates parental pressure. Both external pressures foster pressures inside the academic environment. Zinsser ends with self-induced pressure to emphasize the individual student who suffers.

VOCABULARY PROJECTS (p. 454)

2. Students who leave notes to Carlos are *supplicants* (9), and achievement is the *national god* that is venerated and glorified as the state religion (14). Colleges, students, and their parents, like religious ascetics, belong to a *brotherhood of paupers* (20). The language suggests that Zinsser believes American materialism has replaced (or even become) religion in American society.

COMBINING THE PATTERNS (p. 455)

In the opening paragraphs, Zinsser cites notes from students that exemplify the pressures they face, and he refers to specific students as examples in paragraphs 30 and 32. Other examples include the comments from deans in paragraph 16, the specifics about Yale and Harvard in paragraph 17, and the examples of the "brutal economy" in paragraphs 20–21. All the examples help make Zinsser's point more concrete. Additional examples of specific students might add to readers' understanding.

THEMATIC CONNECTIONS

The "Black Table" Is Still There **(p. 340):** See *Thematic Connections,* "The "Black Table" Is Still There," p. 80 of this manual. You might consider asking whether minority students like Graham face pressures in college that are different from those faced by the students Zinsser describes.

Suicide Note **(p. 357):** The suicide note written by Mirikitani's student and the accompanying note about an actual Asian-American student who leaped to her death from her dormitory suggest how intensely parental pressures, real or assumed, can weigh on students. In her note, the girl apologizes to her parents "for disappointing you," repeatedly explaining, "I've worked very hard." She clearly suffers from being caught in what Zinsser calls "one of the oldest webs of love and duty and guilt" (28). Zinsser does not mention suicide, but news articles appear with some frequency about student suicides that can be traced to academic pressures. Your students can benefit from discussing this link—and from your informing them about your school's resources for troubled students. Be sure they understand that Zinsser does not blame anyone for the pressures but does suggest a solution (See also *Thematic Connections,* "Suicide Note," p. 87 of this manual.)

The Company Man **(p. 517):** Students tend not to see beyond today's academic pressures. When asked to consider a connection between Zinsser's discussion and Goodman's, they should see that Phil, the company man, dies in the service of achievement, "the state religion." Zinsser's belief that students can "break the circles in which they are trapped" (39) has much longer-range implications than he discusses. Phil's situation should show them good reasons for breaking the circle.

Scott Russell Sanders, *The Men We Carry in Our Minds*

Sanders uses classification as a way of making a larger point in this essay. He begins by suggesting that the images of manhood he knew growing up among the rural poor fell into two groups: "the brute toiling animal and the boss" (1). In paragraph 4 he adds a third group: the "warriors," local GIs who did not "toil" but were similarly at the mercy of a "boss." "Toiler" and "warrior" were the only roles he could imagine for his peers. In paragraph 7 he turns to his central point: ultimately a scholarship student at "a university meant for the children of the rich," he could not understand why the women he met there envied the "joys and privileges" of men, why they held such "deep grievances" (8), since his experience was that women seemed to have easier lives than men. Sanders says that in many parts of the world "the fate of men is as grim and bleak as the fate of women" (9), but that the women he met at college saw men only as their fathers were—power wielders, "bosses." He concludes that he himself was not that kind of man, not an "enemy to their desires" but rather an "ally" (11), even though he could not make the privileged young women he knew understand this.

You might begin discussion by asking why Sanders titled his essay "The Men We Carry in Our Minds." How do the images we absorb in childhood color our view of reality throughout our lives?

COMPREHENSION (p. 459)

1. The convicts represent the "toilers," and the guards represent the "bosses."
2. He saw no options other than to become a "toiler," but he escaped that fate as a scholarship student at a prestigious university.
3. As a boy he "envied" women because they had time to cultivate an interest in the arts, to "enjoy a sense of ease," and because most women worked in their houses, which seemed to him "brighter, handsomer places than any factory" (8). He only became aware of the "grievances" of women, of the narrowness of their choices and their potential for victimization, when confronted by feminists in college.
4. The women he met at college carried in their minds the images of their powerful fathers, similar to Sanders's "bosses." All men, they charged, are "destined from birth" (11) to oppress women. Sanders argues that the men he knew in his youth, those he carries in his mind, are just as much victims, so he was really an ally, not an enemy.

PURPOSE AND AUDIENCE (p. 460)

1. Sanders seems to have intended this essay as a way of exploring his own complicated feelings. Moreover, he wants readers to recognize that a concept like "masculine power" is far too sweeping; not all men have power. Power, he seems to suggest, is far more the prerogative of economic class.
2. Sanders's thesis is summarized in the introduction to this entry. Student summaries should bring together the ideas expressed in paragraphs 10 and 11.
3. Sanders seems to have in mind an educated audience rather than workers such as those he grew up with. Directed equally at men and women, the essay might well have a greater impact on the latter.

STYLE AND STRUCTURE (p. 460)

1. Sanders begins by considering the categories of "toiler" and "warrior" and their "bosses." In another sense the essay focuses on the categories *men of privilege* and *women of privilege, men of the working class* and *women of the working class.*
2. Sanders's principles of classification are class and gender.
3. Sanders begins with those categories with which he is most familiar and then moves to the categories of privilege.
4. Sanders gives more attention to the categories of working people than to the categories of privileged people, assuming perhaps that many of his readers will know little about the lives of poor working people.

VOCABULARY PROJECTS (p. 460)

2. See number 1 under Style and Structure. Students' titles may be somewhat different.

Sanders uses description to characterize his subjects in paragraphs 1 (convicts), 3 (working men), and 4 (his father). He doesn't describe the GIs in detail (4), but he does provide a lot of detail about their actions.

THEMATIC CONNECTIONS

Scrubbing in Maine (p. 106): The women working for the cleaning service that Barbara Ehrenreich describes are further examples of toilers in our society and to some extent belie Sanders's assertion that women of limited resources work any less menially than do men. See "The Men We Carry in Our Minds" under *Thematic Connections* on p. 24 of this manual.

Midnight (p. 201): This student essay describes another kind of toiler: Asian immigrants working twelve hours and more a day in a dry cleaning sweatshop under uncomfortable, sometimes dangerous, conditions. Students should see an immediate connection between this essay and paragraph 9 of Sanders's essay, where he expands the category of toiler to include those "in mining country, in black ghettos, in Hispanic barrios, in the shadows of factories, in Third World nations—any place where the fate of men is as grim and bleak as the fate of women."

On Fire (p. 280): See *Thematic Connections*, "On Fire," p. 65 of this manual. Students might consider some of the similarities and differences between Larry Brown's job as a firefighter and the kinds of labor Sanders describes. In what sense does firefighting combine aspects of the "toiler" and the "warrior"? What are the greater advantages—and disadvantages—of the firefighter's job?

Amy Tan, *Mother Tongue*

The daughter of Chinese immigrant parents, Amy Tan describes the four "Englishes I grew up with" (2), focusing on their relation to her mother: the "simple" English she spoke to her mother, her mother's "broken" English, her "watered-down" translations of her mother's Chinese, and her imaginatively realized "perfect" translations of her mother's "internal language." Tan does not name these categories until her next-to-last paragraph, but she provides examples throughout: paragraphs 4–9 discuss her "simple" English and her mother's "broken" English, with Tan concluding ruefully that as a child she was embarrassed by her mother's English; paragraphs 10–14 give examples of her "watered-down" translations; and her final paragraphs describe her attempts to capture her mother's "internal language." In paragraphs 15–18, Tan suggests her purpose in considering these "Englishes": to explain the difficulties Asian-American students have with English, particularly English achievement tests, and the reason they end up pursuing degrees in math and science.

At some point you may want to ask students—even those whose families are native English speakers—how different their "home language" is from the language they encounter at school. What difficulties do they have adjusting to "academic English"?

COMPREHENSION (p. 467)

1. See the discussion of Tan's categories in the introduction above.
2. She identifies the categories in her next-to-last paragraph. Students might suggest that this identification could have come earlier to make the structure of the essay clearer from the start. You might point out that this might have made the essay seem more formal.
3. Only the final category is not clearly illustrated. Tan might have provided an example from one of her books to do so, but her conclusion might then have had less force.
4. Her mother's English was a handicap when her mother needed to communicate about important matters with native English speakers in positions of authority—her stockbroker, for example, and hospital personnel. Other examples might include dealings with the police, the courts, government agencies, and the like.
5. Tan was embarrassed by her mother's English as a child, and she also believes that the language she heard at home contributed to her lowered scores on language achievement tests. But in adulthood the same language became an inspiration to her as a novelist.
6. Tan attributes her difficulty in answering questions on achievement tests to the fact that she could not easily limit the possibilities; her mind, she suggests, didn't process language in a simple either/or pattern. It is certainly possible that Tan's imagination—which would lead to her success as a writer—contributed as much to the problem as did the level of her family's language skills.
7. Because they score higher on math achievement tests than on language tests, Tan suggests that many Asian-American students are being steered to majors in math and science, effectively cutting them off from creative writing. Other explanations might include the possibility that such students simply feel more comfortable with more technical subjects.

PURPOSE AND AUDIENCE (p. 467)

1. Tan uses her opening to show that she is writing from personal experience, not from extensive study. She doesn't intend her ultimate claims about Asian-American students to be definitive.
2. The level of detail she offers about immigrant culture suggests that Tan expects her audience to be composed largely of native English speakers.
3. Tan focuses fairly equally on her mother and on the subject of language, but her larger purpose is to make a point about language.

STYLE AND STRUCTURE (p. 467)

1. Both Tan's diction and her organizational structure are relatively informal. For an audience of nonexperts, such informality seems appropriate, but achieving credibility with a more expert audience would require a more formal style.
2. She includes the example to suggest what the "family talk" she grew up with sounds like. The impression it gives is that her mother's English is indeed "broken," which is the effect Tan intended.
3. These passages demonstrate the contrast between Tan's command of English and her mother's.

4. *Mother tongue* generally refers to one's native language. Here the phrase refers more exactly to Tan's mother's language, the language of home for the writer.
5. The "terrible" line shows Tan reaching to find an English suitable for formal expression—and in doing so, using diction that is artificial and stilted. The style she uses for the essay is more natural and fluid.

VOCABULARY PROJECTS (p. 468)

2. Students may have different opinions about this and, like Tan, will probably have difficulty coming up with a more neutral term. You might ask what this difficulty suggests about the way speakers like Tan's mother are viewed in American society.

COMBINING THE PATTERNS (p. 469)

The narration Tan uses adds color and vividness to the essay and is crucial to making her point concrete. No other strategy would be quite so appropriate, although the anecdotes do serve as examples.

THEMATIC CONNECTIONS

Only Daughter (p. 84): Sandra Cisneros also writes about growing up in an immigrant (Mexican-American) household. Although her focus isn't on language, her description of her relationship with her father—and the cultural assumptions against which she must struggle—have interesting parallels with Tan's experiences.

Words Left Unspoken (p. 153): In writing about her deaf grandfather, who could communicate only in sign, Leah Hager Cohen presents a different kind of language barrier, but one that can readily be compared to the barrier Tan's mother faces. If you have students who know sign language, they might want to explain for the class some differences between a spoken English sentence and its signed equivalent. How do these differences relate to Tan's translations of her mother's English into more formal prose?

The Human Cost of an Illiterate Society (p. 229): Students can compare the problems of people who can't read with those of people who speak limited English. See *Thematic Connections,* "The Human Cost of an Illiterate Society," p. 54 of this manual.

Stephanie Ericsson, *The Ways We Lie*

Ericsson analyzes the effect of lying by dividing lies into ten different categories, moving from the most personal to those that affect our world in the most profound ways. Admitting that we can't really eliminate lies entirely from our lives, Ericsson nonetheless suggests that to create a sea change that will grant us as a public "our *right* to trust" the media, politicians, and others, we must begin on the smallest level: "Maybe if I don't tell the bank the check's in the mail I'll be less tolerant of the lies told me every day" (37).

One way to begin discussion is to have students provide some examples of their own for Ericsson's categories, particularly white lies, deflecting, omission, dismissal, and delusion. Ask whether there are any times when they feel justified in telling a lie (most will say "yes"); then ask if there are any times when they feel it is justified for someone else to lie to them (a much more difficult question).

COMPREHENSION (p. 477)

1. (1) *White lies* are generally "harmless untruths." (2) *Facades* are roles we play, often to impress others. (3) *Ignoring the plain facts* is a kind of lying to oneself. (4) *Deflecting* is distracting others from something negative about oneself or refusing to respond when accused of inappropriate behavior. (5) *Omission* is the leaving out of pertinent facts that don't correspond with the image one wants to present. (6) *Stereotypes and clichés* "shut down original thinking" and result in "all the 'isms.'" (7) *Groupthink* is a combination of other forms of lying in which a group's loyalty to itself outweighs any other value, including the truth. (8) *Out-and-out lies* are attempts to "refute reality" and can be "easily confronted." (9) *Dismissal* is ignoring "feelings, perceptions, or even the raw facts of a situation," particularly as they relate to others. (10) *Delusion* is "the tendency to see excuses as facts," "the mind's ability . . . to support what it wants to be the truth."

2. Lies are often necessary to protect the feelings of others and to help us present the most positive images of ourselves. In addition, delusion is a "survival mechanism."

3. White lies can delude people into a false sense of security or hope. Facades can be used to "seduce others into an illusion" (11). Ignoring the plain facts can lead to all kinds of harm, particularly when criminal behavior is involved. Deflecting can let people hide what they don't want others to know by making it look as though they're being honest; it is also a way of resisting justified criticism. Omission on a historical level can keep people ignorant of their true past. Stereotypes "close minds and separate people" (22). Groupthink leads to poor decision making. Out-and-out lies can refute reality unless they are caught. Dismissal can result in mental illness. Delusion allows us to ignore our most serious problems.

4. Out-and-out lies are the most "honest" lies; that is, the liar knows he or she is lying and expects you to suspect the lie.

5. Dismissal often involves things that can't be "proved" unless we delve deeply. As long as we don't delve deeply, we can continue to believe that the problem doesn't exist.

PURPOSE AND AUDIENCE (p. 477)

1. Ultimately, Ericsson attacks lying. As she says in her conclusion, "Our acceptance of lies becomes a cultural cancer that eventually shrouds and reorders reality until moral garbage becomes as invisible to us as water is to a fish" (35). She ends by encouraging readers, at least implicitly, to think carefully before telling even little lies in order to become "less tolerant" (37) of the larger lies that surround us.

2. Ericsson's is a fairly liberal slant, most evident in the examples she offers in paragraphs 5, 12, 15, 18–20, 24–25, and 33. She seems to have imagined a fairly liberal audience, but it's clear that people of all political stripes are concerned about politicians' lying and lying in the media—although they might define those lies differently.

STYLE AND STRUCTURE (p. 477)

1. Ericsson's informal opening serves to draw readers in. She establishes common ground by telling about her own lies and noting that we all lie.
2. The quotations from a wide variety of time periods and sources serve to universalize the points she is making. Students, unfamiliar with many of these sources, may see them as interruptions.
3. Generally, each discussion includes an example or two, and Ericsson's evaluation of when that category of lie is beneficial and how it is harmful. Sometimes, however, she omits the discussion of benefits—one assumes because she sees no benefit in that category of lie. The discussions are not exactly balanced, however; some are more detailed than others. Students might feel that more balance would set up each category more clearly.
4. Ericsson basically moves from the least to the most problematic kinds of lies—although students will not necessarily agree with her ranking system. Some, for example, might see ignoring the plain facts as more harmful than deflecting or omission.
5. Rhetorical questions help emphasize the point that lying is a double-edged sword, sometimes beneficial, sometimes harmful. Ericsson wants us as a society to find alternatives to lying, yet she has no simple answer as to how this might be accomplished.
6. Ericsson cites historians and psychologists, the very sorts of experts one would expect in a research paper on lying. Student opinion will vary regarding the need for other citations.
7. Ericsson also uses the feminine indefinite pronoun in paragraph 4, but she uses the male indefinite pronoun in paragraph 8. It is unlikely that students would find these few shifts distracting.
8. In both her conclusion and her introduction, Ericsson uses personal experience, quotation, and rhetorical questions. Her conclusion echoes much of the important language in the introduction as well.

VOCABULARY PROJECTS (p. 478)

2. Colloquialisms include *Sure I Lie . . .* (3); *ducked out* (6); *looks great . . . looks like hell* (8); *crawls into a hole* (16); *mouth like a truck driver* (22); and *good-ole-boy* (25). They lend a certain informality and accessibility to her prose, which most readers should view positively.

COMBINING THE PATTERNS (p. 479)

The dictionary definition is probably not necessary, but it does allow Ericsson to establish common terminology before discussing behaviors that readers might not have thought of as lying before.

THEMATIC CONNECTIONS

"What's in a Name?" (p. 4): Henry Louis Gates's essay offers the story of a childhood incident that revealed to him the extent to which African Americans were considered inferior by whites. Ericsson's discussion of stereotypes is pertinent

here, as is her discussion of facades. Maya Angelou's "Finishing School," Brent Staples's "Just Walk On By," and student Mark Cotharn's "Brains versus Brawn" also deal with stereotypes.

Thirty-Eight Who Saw Murder Didn't Call the Police (p. 101): Have students decide, on the basis of the quotations in this newspaper article, what kind of lying the thirty-eight witnesses exhibited. The most likely categories are ignoring the plain facts and dismissal, with stereotypes playing a role in some instances.

The Lottery (p. 292): Students will easily see Shirley Jackson's short story as an example of groupthink. Tessie Hutchinson also uses deflection when she argues that the lottery drawing was unfair.

Jedediah Purdy, *Shades of Green*

In this essay, Purdy focuses on three distinct types of environmentalism, as defined under the answers to items 3, 4, and 5 under *Comprehension*. Advocates of each type are often at odds with one another in terms of goals and methods for achieving those goals, and Purdy offers as examples several rifts within the environmental movement as a whole. Yet he is optimistic that by working together, the three groups can achieve a new definition of environmentalism that focuses on the environments in which all of us live on a daily basis, one that can successfully preserve nature's wonders, encourage the sustainability of natural resources and species, and create healthy communities for people and ecosystems alike.

One way to begin is to discuss Purdy's title. This quite clever play on words points up the classification and division structure very neatly. You might also ask students if they agree with Purdy that student-age environmentalists today are more likely to sympathize with the goals of the environmental justice movement than with romantic environmentalism (5). Another possible topic of discussion is that of Purdy's optimism. Based on how Purdy describes the three environmentalisms here, along with any experience students have themselves had with environmental issues, do they agree with him that these groups can put aside their differences and work productively together to achieve common goals?

COMPREHENSION (p. 484)

1. Purdy says the environmental movement deserves a closer look because so many people with so many diverse viewpoints consider themselves environmentalists so that areas of consensus and division among them are worth examining.

2. In paragraph 2, Purdy writes that environmental politics has begun to expand "from its traditional concern with a limited number of wild places and species to a broader commitment to the environment as the place where we all live, all the time." He expands on this idea in his final five paragraphs.

3. "Romantic environmentalism" is based on "the love of beautiful landscapes," "a reverence for untamed places," and a "spiritual attachment" to nature (3). It originated in the late nineteenth century "when America's wealthy discovered outdoor recreation" and such organizations as the Sierra Club were born.

4. "Managerial environmentalism," according to paragraph 4, "puts the wild at our service" and "makes as its basic task the putting together of ecology and economy to advance human ends." Managerial environmentalists are basi-

cally government bureaucrats who work with businesses to hammer out compromises that will serve the environment without sacrificing profits too drastically. It is a fundamentally pragmatic approach, while romantic environmentalism is spiritual and idealistic.

5. The environmental justice movement is an activist movement focusing on minorities and the poor and the polluted environments these people often inhabit in inner cities and industrial areas, where waste dumps and other environmental hazards of industrialization are often clustered; its members rely on lawsuits to right what they see as social injustice. They have little patience for romantic environmentalists, who are predominately prosperous and white, because such romantics have sometimes sought to protect nature to the detriment of poor communities and because they do not see community health concerns as an "environmental" issue. They distrust managerial environmentalists because of their ties to big business; their passionate concern for social justice contrasts starkly with the managers' more "rational" concern for efficient resource use.

6. "Domesticated environmentalism" refers to the concept that we should concern ourselves with the environments that people actually live in, no matter what their economic or social status, with issues such as urban sprawl, the preservation of green space, and changing lifestyles in ways that benefit both people and the environment.

7. Purdy believes that the three approaches to the environment, if they can come together and find common ground, can help one another to achieve the ultimate goals of clean air and water, livable communities, sustained resource management, and wilderness preservation—goals that are important for everyone's future.

8. One possible result, as he notes in his conclusion, is "a broader, more effective environmental movement."

PURPOSE AND AUDIENCE (p. 484)

1. While this statement could be seen as the thesis were Purdy only describing the three environmentalisms, his essay does something more, as suggested by the final sentence of paragraph 2, his true thesis.

2. Students' opinions may differ, but he seems to find less negative to say about the environmental justice movement than about the other two, characterized as they are by a kind of elitism and blindness to the needs of the poor and disenfranchised.

3. Students will surely see Purdy's conclusion as optimistic (even, perhaps, overly so).

STYLE AND STRUCTURE (p. 484)

1. For each category, he covers historical roots and goals, but while he covers general methodologies for managerial environmentalism and the environmental justice movement, he really does not do so for romantic environmentalism. He might have noted that romantics tend to contribute money to environmental organizations, which in turn lobby government officials for wilderness and species protection and preservation.

2. Students will probably agree that phrases such as "oldest and most familiar version" (3), "Another type" (4), and "another thing entirely" (5) serve to clearly introduce each category. The transitions in paragraphs 11 and 12 also seem clear.
3. Students' opinions may differ. He certainly could have named his three categories in paragraph 2, but there seems to be little need for him to have done so.
4. Domesticated environmentalism, for Purdy, is a kind of amalgam of the best aspects of the three environmentalisms he originally discusses. It can be seen as at the same level as the other categories, but still in its very earliest stages.

VOCABULARY PROJECTS (p. 485)

2. *Encounters with the wild* means something like *communion with the wilderness, with spaces where one can escape civilization.* *Culture of perpetual embattlement* describes the activists' sense of always being outsiders fighting wealthy interests on the behalf of the downtrodden. *Smart growth* is a catch phrase referring to urban and suburban planning that is controlled in such a way that it benefits both human and natural interests. *Brushfire struggles* refers to the activists' habit of dealing with individual crises one at a time rather than taking a more long-term, systematic approach to the problems of environmental justice.

COMBINING THE PATTERNS (p. 486)

Students' opinions may vary. One possibility might have been for him to describe the kind of "romantic environmentalism" that is often depicted in car commercials: gas-guzzling SUVs being driven into pristine spaces, their drivers pictured as "rugged individualists." This, however, might have alienated some of the readers he was trying to reach.

THEMATIC CONNECTIONS

Living Like Weasels (p. 164): Annie Dillard might be classed as a romantic environmentalist, and her description of encountering a weasel in the wild and the almost spiritual revelation it brought to her is an extreme example of the "spiritual attachment" to nature that Purdy ascribes to the romantics. Students might do some research about Dillard to see where she currently stands on environmental issues.

Burdens (p. 509): John Kenneth Galbraith writes here about government policies that he sees as increasingly favoring those in our society who are well off while the poor are left to fend for themselves. It is likely that he would champion the goals of the environmental justice movement. Students might want to consider whether or not government should play a greater role in requiring that poor people and minorities in this country have safe environments to live in. Is this really a question of liberal versus conservative values and economic policies?

On Dumpster Diving (p. 660): Lars Eighner's description of a period of homelessness can be tied to the previous essay in terms of the sort of protections that government should provide to the disadvantaged. Additionally, students might think about the very practical hazards faced by those reduced to scrounging in dumpsters and garbage piles for the basic needs of daily life. Would helping such people, who are often homeless as well as hungry, come under the rubric of "domesticated environmentalism" as Purdy defines it?

Edwin Brock, *Five Ways to Kill a Man*

This intriguing poem was first published in 1963 before the escalation of hostilities in Vietnam that led to a wave of antiwar protests in the United States and Europe. Given that, it seems almost prescient in its antiwar sentiments. The poem's larger theme, however, is suggested in its final stanza: "living somewhere in the middle/of the twentieth century" is, for the speaker, also a version of death. The speaker does not go on to elaborate this point as he does the first four, so his meaning here can provide an interesting topic for discussion. Brock himself was British and had lived through World War II and witnessed much of the dismantling of the British empire, as described in the headnote to "Shooting an Elephant" on page 117 of the text. The poem was written at the height of the Cold War, when the threat of nuclear attacks between the United States and the former Soviet Union seemed uncomfortably real. At the same time, consumer culture, the values of which many critics questioned, was beginning to come into its full fruition. All of these factors may be read into the final stanza.

You may have to point out to students that the poem is not a literal example of classification and division. In fact, the speaker does not name any categories, but simply provides an example of each from which readers can extrapolate as discussed in the answer to item 2 below.

READING LITERATURE (p. 488)

1. The five ways are crucifixion, being pierced by an arrow during medieval battle, being gassed (as during World War I), being bombed from a fighter jet, and—metaphorically—living during the "middle/of the twentieth century," which suggests a spiritual rather than a physical death resulting, perhaps, from societies that are unfeeling and sterile.
2. The first category, suggesting capital punishment, would include beheading and hanging. The second, suggesting primitive battle, would include stabbing with a sword and beating with a club. The third, suggesting early twentieth century battle, would include using firearms and cannonry. The fourth, suggesting contemporary warfare, would include napalm, "smart" bombs, and perhaps terrorist attacks. Students will probably argue that the fifth category is of a different kind than the other four and so is not represented by other examples.
3. In some sense, the *you* can be seen as referring to something like "those who have the power to carry out executions and wage war," but other interpretations are certainly possible ranging from "God" to "all of humanity."

THEMATIC CONNECTIONS

Thirty-Eight Who Saw Murder Didn't Call the Police (p. 101): Students might want to think about why the kind of one-on-one murder described in Gansberg's essay is not included among Brock's categories. Is it any less inhumane than crucifixion or warfare? What might the exclusion of such murders suggest about the idea that Brock is trying to communicate in his poem?

Ground Zero **(p. 158):** Students might create a new stanza for this poem incorporating the terrorist attack on the World Trade Center to represent terrorist attacks more generally as another "way to kill a man." Be sure they recognize Brock's pattern of describing first "what you can do" and then "what you need to do it."

The Lottery **(p. 292):** Shirley Jackson's famous short story has been interpreted as a reflection on the human capacity for violence against others in the name of a "common good." Students might analyze the thematic similarities and differences between "The Lottery" and "Five Ways to Kill a Man."

11: DEFINITION

Because definition encompasses all the patterns of arrangement, this chapter presents a good opportunity for review. A logical beginning model for your discussion is Desmond Morris's paragraph defining *altruism* because it compactly illustrates the combination of two techniques. As you read the essays in this chapter, you can show your students that these definition techniques and others can structure not only paragraphs but also sections of longer pieces and even whole essays, poems, or stories. You should also emphasize that any essay can include examples of several rhetorical patterns studied throughout the text. This might also be a good time to look back at earlier essays in which a definition is central—*work* in "My Mother Never Worked" and *environmentalism* in "Shades of Green," for example.

U.S. Census Bureau, *U.S. Census 2000 Form*

Reproduced here is the box on the 2000 Census Form in which people were asked to identify themselves first as "Spanish/Hispanic/Latino" or not and then by "race." The form offered many more choices than the form used ten years earlier, and some critics have questioned whether the many choices included did not ultimately cause more confusion than clarity and perhaps even skew the reported results. For example, figures released by the Census Bureau in 2003 showed that Hispanics now account for a larger percentage of the total U.S. population than do blacks, and some attribute this to the fact that people could, for the first time, check off more than one box.

If questions regarding race might be a sensitive topic in your classroom, you might have students simply write about the questions posed below rather than conducting a class discussion.

READING IMAGES (p. 503)

1. Students' answers will vary. You might ask whether the request to define oneself in terms of "race, religion, or ethnicity" provides any students with too limited a set of options and, if so, why.
2. Again, students' answers will vary. You might note that the form uses the term *race* rather loosely; anthropologists generally define only three races: Caucasoid (roughly, white), Negroid (roughly, black), and Mongoloid (roughly, Asian). It is also becoming increasingly clear that genetically racial

differences are minuscule compared to the vast number of genes shared by all human beings.

3. Again, students' answers will vary. Students who consider themselves of mixed race may have the most to contribute to the conversation.

THEMATIC CONNECTIONS

The five essays listed here all focus on some aspect of the writer's ethnic and/or racial identity: Chicana ("Only Daughter"), American Indian ("Indian Education"), Asian Indian ("Two Ways to Belong in America"), African American ("The 'Black Table' Is Still There"), and Chinese ("Mother Tongue"). You might suggest that George Orwell's "Shooting an Elephant" (p. 117) is perhaps the only essay in the book in which the author writes in any direct way about being white—and that is because he is writing about a time when he was living in Asia. Is it more unusual in the United States for white people to consider themselves in terms of their "whiteness" than it is for other people to consider themselves in terms of a racial or ethnic identity? What about the so-called "hyphenated" white Americans—Irish-Americans, Italian-Americans, and so forth? Do they tend to identify with an ethnic identity? Why might such hyphenated European labels not be included as choices on the census form?

Judy Brady, *I Want a Wife*

This essay comments satirically on the demands placed on wives and mothers. You might begin by asking your students whether Brady overstates her case.

COMPREHENSION (p. 507)

1. She means a devoted "servant." This ideal wife exists in the pages of some women's magazines and in the minds of some men and women.
2. Some specific duties include washing clothes, cleaning, cooking, babysitting, and typing. The five categories are child care, household chores, cooking, managing social life, and providing for sexual needs.
3. She feels she must do the jobs of both husband and wife.
4. She might leave if she found a more suitable wife. In that case, her first wife would take care of the children.

PURPOSE AND AUDIENCE (p. 507)

1. It exaggerates the role of wife and mother to ridicule it. Most feminists would agree—perhaps in varying degrees—with her thesis. Students may not see this essay as likely to appear in any publication today.
2. The thesis, which is implied, is that too much is expected of wives.
3. No. She is merely using this to make her point.

STYLE AND STRUCTURE (p. 507)

1. This repetition reinforces her thesis and introduces a list of new reasons why she wants a wife.

2. No. In fact, the length of the paragraphs draws attention to the statements being made.
3. Students can find a number of verbs that are repeated, and they should be able to determine how they affect the tone of the essay.
4. She omits the pronouns because she means to suggest that her wife—or any wife—could just as easily be male as female.
5. These words help to convey the tone. There is to be no question that the wife described will be capable of easily and willingly performing all the tasks listed.

VOCABULARY PROJECTS (p. 508)

2. Students will readily see that many of these words are used sarcastically.

COMBINING THE PATTERNS (p. 508)

Brady uses exemplification and description as the major patterns in her definition—and contrasts between images of wives and husbands are implied. The implied contrasts might in fact be seen as the most important for Brady's purposes.

THEMATIC CONNECTIONS

My Mother Never Worked (p. 96): Even Brady's exhausting job description for a wife falls short of the work performed by Martha Smith. Students can discuss the extent to which a woman's life has improved since 1921, when Martha Smith became a wife, or make the necessary additions to turn Brady's essay into "I Want a Farm Wife."

Sex, Lies, and Conversation (p. 407): See *Thematic Connections*, "Sex, Lies, and Conversation," p. 100 of this manual. Deborah Tannen's essay provides a good opportunity to think about male-female stereotypes—and what actually governs gender roles.

The Men We Carry in Our Minds (p. 456): Scott Russell Sanders provides a different view of the roles of husbands and wives, focusing on the laboring classes. Here, he asserts, the lives of men are bound by the everyday "toil" of factories and mines; as a child, he saw the lives of women as far easier than the lives of men. As a young adult, he adjusted his view to recognize that the division is not so much between men and women as between the "bosses"—traditionally, professional-class males much like the husband Brady describes— and those who serve them, either as wives or as paid "toilers." The women he met at college have the same "grievances" against men that Brady implies.

John Kenneth Galbraith, *Burdens*

Galbraith's is a highly ironic use of definition; make sure students realize that the definition Galbraith offers is not one he agrees with. He defines the word *burden* specifically as it is used in the sense of "a burden imposed by government on the citizen" (1). (He doesn't say so directly, but his obvious reference is to taxes and to how tax dollars are distributed.) His point is that the term is used very selectively in this context. Expenditures for defense, for bailing out failed savings and loans, for Social Security, for farm supports, for Medicare, and for congressional health benefits are not seen as burdens, but expenditures for welfare programs, food stamps, Medicaid, and aid to inner-city schools are so defined. Galbraith's caustic conclusion is that government expenditures are not considered burdens when they benefit the rich, only when they benefit the poor. If there is a mix of political viewpoints in your classroom, this essay may spark some lively debate; some students will probably disagree strongly with Galbraith's implications about the role of government.

COMPREHENSION (p. 510)

1. Galbraith offers his formal definition in his final sentence. He does so as a way of clinching his implied argument.
2. By *good* he means language that is thoughtful and direct; *accepted,* however, implies that the language may be logically incorrect but widespread. The distinction is important because he wants to make the point that he disagrees with the accepted definition of *burden.*
3. Government spending to bail out the "costly financial misadventure" of the failed savings and loans—because it benefited well-off people—is not a burden.
4. See the introductory discussion above.
5. Education is a "special case" because it both *is* a burden (public education in inner-city schools) and is *not* a burden (private education, for which many are seeking tax relief).
6. Galbraith implies that funding for the arts and public broadcasting is a burden because these are seen as liberal interests.

PURPOSE AND AUDIENCE (p. 511)

1. The original title makes clear that Galbraith sees those who use *burden* in the way he describes as using language dishonestly, as serving their own interests at the expense of the poor. Students who disagree with him may see the title as overly provocative. (You might note the fact that one source for the title— "White man speaks with forked tongue"—suggests the kind of hypocritical exploitation Galbraith is criticizing. A "forked tongue" is also associated with snakes and poetically with Satan, as the serpent in the Garden of Eden.)
2. Galbraith's purpose is to criticize social priorities; he criticizes the use of the word *burden* in order to accomplish this larger goal. His primary targets are those politicians and commentators—and average citizens—who seek budget cuts affecting the poor but who benefit from other government subsidies.

STYLE AND STRUCTURE (p. 511)

1. Galbraith defines by enumeration throughout. He defines by negation in paragraphs 2–3 and briefly in paragraph 5. The strategy is effective because his point ultimately is to suggest the hypocrisy of the selective use of the word *burden;* thus, what it is *not* becomes especially important.
2. Discussing the origin of *burden* would not strengthen Galbraith's definition in this context because he is focusing on its use in the present. He might have included some synonyms early on and then provided an analogy to strengthen the contrast between what is a burden and what is not.
3. Galbraith is clearly disheartened, but his tone is more caustic and ironic than angry.
4. Students will find sarcasm in virtually every paragraph. Their responses to the sarcasm may vary based on their own political beliefs.

5. Answers will vary here. In a longer essay, such additions might be instructive, but they would detract from Galbraith's pithiness.
6. Similar language occurs in paragraphs 6 and 7. Galbraith holds such rule makers—conservative politicians and their supporters—in disdain.

VOCABULARY PROJECTS (p. 511)

2. The dictionary defines *burden* as "something that is carried," a "load, duty, responsibility." Galbraith's purpose is not to define the word literally but rather as it is used in current political discourse.

COMBINING THE PATTERNS (p. 512)

Galbraith relies primarily on exemplification, providing examples of burdens and non-burdens. He might have recounted the events leading up to the savings-and-loan bailout or to the current situation in which "no wholly plausible enemy" (2) can justify defense spending, but we don't see that such narrative additions would improve his argument. Telling the story of a family losing welfare benefits might be effective, but it would not really be in keeping with his tone.

THEMATIC CONNECTIONS

The Human Cost of an Illiterate Society (p. 229): Jonathan Kozol is similarly concerned with the plight of society's disadvantaged and with the lack of concern on the part of those in power. His tone, however, is quite different from Galbraith's. Students might consider which approach they find more persuasive.

The Ways We Lie (p. 470): Students might explore what kind of lie (or lies) Galbraith would consider for the selective use of the word *burden*. Do they see it as deflecting, groupthink, or simply an out-and-out lie?

On Dumpster Diving (p. 660): Lars Eighner's experiences suggest a different aspect of poverty—homelessness—but Eighner does not seem representative of the poor in the United States. To what extent do students think that someone like Eighner—intelligent, able-bodied, and capable of work but apparently not quite able to adapt to conventional workplaces—deserves government aid? They might even do some research about the kind of aid a person like Eighner would be eligible for.

A Modest Proposal (p. 676): The specific situation is quite different, but Jonathan Swift's classic essay is also an ironic attack on attitudes and policies toward the poor. Although far less outrageous than Swift, Galbraith is writing in much the same vein.

José Antonio Burciaga, *Tortillas*

This lighthearted look at a staple of Mexican cuisine is an especially good example of definition. Not only is it interesting and immediately accessible, but it also shows the combination of rhetorical techniques that can go into making an extended definition: narration (1, 3), cause and effect (2), process (4), exemplification (5, 7–8), description (6), and comparison (6). You might begin discussion by asking what students remember first when they think of tortillas as described by Burciaga; then have them decide why the technique used to make that point is particularly effective.

COMPREHENSION (p. 515)

1. A tortilla is a flat, round corn cake that is fried or steamed.
2. Tortillas may be filled with a variety of fillings and rolled into tacos. They may be filled with cheese and grilled (*quesadillas*). They may be deep-fried (*flautas* or *gorditas*). More whimsically, they can be used as a mask or hat, as an artist's canvas, or even as the basis for a miraculous vision.
3. Burciaga is not entirely serious here, yet he does mean to suggest the fundamental role tortillas play in Mexican culture.

PURPOSE AND AUDIENCE (p. 515)

1. The thesis might be paraphrased as "Although we take tortillas for granted, they are in fact a special part of Mexico's cultural heritage." Burciaga doesn't state his thesis sooner because he wants to lead us to this understanding in his conclusion.
2. Students may have different opinions about Burciaga's intended audience. He certainly assumes that his audience is already familiar with tortillas because he spends very little time describing them, but this doesn't necessarily mean that he expects readers to be of Mexican descent. Given the level of detail and the tone, it would seem that Burciaga is writing for a general audience that includes both Chicanos and non-Chicanos.
3. Burciaga is trying in a lighthearted, humorous way to "elevate" the tortilla in his readers' minds, to show how versatile, even meaningful, it is. If he tried to be more serious, he would probably be less convincing because he might seem to be overstating his case.
4. For Burciaga tortillas are a representation of his childhood and of his cultural heritage.

STYLE AND STRUCTURE (p. 515)

1. The brief formal definition comes in paragraph 6. It is clear that Burciaga assumes an audience that already knows what a tortilla is and so does not feel the need to provide an introductory definition. The definition in paragraph 6 serves to highlight the versatility of tortillas.
2. Burciaga doesn't define three Spanish words in paragraph 4: *mercado* (market), *masa* (the cornmeal dough from which tortillas are made), and *deliciosas* (delicious). He clearly assumes that readers will be familiar with these words or that their meanings will be clear in context. Note that he also doesn't define the Yiddish word *yarmulke* (skullcap) in paragraph 1.
3. Burciaga doesn't use synonyms, although he uses a helpful analogy at the beginning of paragraph 3; and he doesn't discuss the word's origin, although he traces its appearance in Mayan mythology. Neither does he use negation as part of his definition, probably because little would be gained by doing so.

VOCABULARY PROJECTS (p. 515)

2. See question 2 under *Style and Structure. Jalapeños* are hot green peppers used in much Mexican and southwestern cooking.

See the introduction to this entry for a survey of the rhetorical patterns Burciaga uses.

THEMATIC CONNECTIONS

Once More to the Lake (p. 175): Both Burciaga and E. B. White invoke childhood memories that represent their cultural heritage and that suggest deeply satisfying and meaningful rituals. In both cases the past seems to permeate the present, creating a warm feeling of nostalgia. Students might consider the differences in tone between the two essays.

Walt and Ray: Your Trusted Friends (p. 414) Burciaga and Schlosser discuss food in their essays. "Tortillas" deals with personal and ethnic associations with food, while "Walt and Ray: Your Trusted Friends" broadens the discussion to focus on the effect fast food has on American culture.

The Park (p. 655): Student Michael Huu Truong's essay is also a reminiscence of childhood that focuses on culture and assimilation. Note that except for Bruce Lee, the heroes the two boys (one Vietnamese, the other Korean) imagine themselves to be are all American icons: Abbott and Costello, Superman, Clint Eastwood, the Bionic Man. Does assimilation mean losing one's heritage, or can assimilation result in something "truly bicultural," like Burciaga's children putting peanut butter and jelly on tortillas?

Ellen Goodman, *The Company Man*

In her essay, Goodman uses a number of short examples to form a single extended definition. She suggests her thesis and then focuses on different aspects of Phil's life to support it. The result is a devastating portrait of a man who worked himself to death. Students should understand that Goodman is not trying to portray a specific individual. Phil is a corporate "everyman" who represents all people who give themselves to their jobs. Some students might miss the irony that Goodman uses throughout her presentation. For this reason, several of the questions in *Style and Structure* focus students' attention on this feature of the essay.

COMPREHENSION (p. 519)

1. The company man devotes all of his time, and literally his "life," to his job. A one-sentence definition fails to convey the tragedy Goodman reveals through her extended definition.
2. She means that working as he has been, he has actually been gone from the family for a long time.
3. He feels he never really knew his father and wants to get to know him now.
4. She's afraid her bitterness might show.
5. The president will seek someone just like Phil.

PURPOSE AND AUDIENCE (p. 519)

1. Goodman makes the point that Phil's compulsion cost him his happiness, his family, and ultimately his life. In a larger sense she suggests that people who live like Phil hurt not only themselves but also those who love and care for them.

2. Goodman assumes that her readers can identify in part with Phil. Her detached, unsentimental tone and her irony are designed to make her readers question their priorities.
3. To state her thesis directly could alienate her readers. By focusing on Phil and supplying her readers with details about his life, Goodman overcomes their skepticism and leads them to accept her point of view.

STYLE AND STRUCTURE (p. 519)

1. Goodman wants to assume the detached tone of a report or case study for her essay. The times at the beginning and end of her essay help her achieve this end.
2. The character Goodman creates is supposed to be representative of all workaholics. Therefore, before giving him a name she presents some general characteristics that all workaholics possess.
3. The dialogue adds an ironic dimension to the story and tells readers how Phil's family and employer feel about him. When a company friend says to Phil's widow that he knows she will miss her husband, she laconically replies, "I already have" (7). Phil's son makes the comment that both he and his father only board at home, and after the funeral, Phil's boss asks, "Who's been working the hardest?" (16). These comments indicate that Phil has sacrificed the love of his family for a job that another person can fill by 5:00, the afternoon of the funeral.
4. Goodman's tone is ironic and detached. She wants her readers to look at Phil without emotion. She is not trying to create a character for whom her audience will feel sympathy. Her tone enables her to keep her distance from Phil and to illustrate to her audience that Phil has foolishly wasted his life.
5. The quotation marks make the comments seem realistic and also draw attention to their irony.

VOCABULARY PROJECTS (p. 519)

2. Various substitutions are possible, but students should see that the more formal diction makes the tone less conversational and perhaps less ironic.

COMBINING THE PATTERNS (p. 520)

Narration is an effective choice because it allows Goodman to trace Phil's almost neurotic devotion to work—and his distance from family and friends. Goodman also uses exemplification and description.

THEMATIC CONNECTIONS

Midnight (p. 201): Student Grace Ku writes about the sacrifices her immigrant parents make to provide for their family's well-being. Working long hours in menial, physically demanding jobs—the only employment available because of their limited education and lack of English skills—the Kus provide an interesting contrast to Goodman's Phil: their "devotion" to work grows out of necessity, not choice. But students may also think about similarities between the two families. For example, in both cases family life suffers because of the demands of the workplace.

The Peter Principle (**p. 207**): See *Thematic Connections*, "The Peter Principle," p. 45 of this manual.

Suicide Note (**p. 357**): Janice Mirikitani's poem takes the form of a suicide note from a young Asian-American college student to her parents. It is an apology that reveals the intense pressure she feels to excel in order to meet her family's expectations. Students can relate the pressures they feel in college, and perhaps in their jobs as well, to those experienced by the author of the suicide note—and also by Phil. If Phil had been able to write a similar note to his family before his death, what might he have said?

Gayle Rosenwald Smith, *The Wife-Beater*

Depending on your age and fashion sense, you may or may not be familiar with the term "wife-beater" to describe a tank-style T-shirt. One way to begin discussion is to ask students whether they are familiar with this meaning of the term and whether they have used it themselves. If many have used it, ask whether Smith has opened their eyes in any way in arguing that the use of the term is disturbing and leads to a climate that tolerates violence against women. (You will surely have some students who will think Smith should "lighten up" and who will argue that the term is more a joke than anything else.)

You will probably want to have students consider contemporary culture more generally in terms of what Smith refers to in paragraph 11 as a return to male dominance. Many commentators have over the past decade noted a backlash against feminism that has younger men and women embracing more traditional gender roles in their relationships. Do students see such a trend? In addition, do male rappers, sports figures, and other celebrities popular with young men create a climate in which "manliness" is equated with violence, as Smith suggests in her conclusion?

In terms of teaching this essay as a rhetorical model, you'll need to point out that, while definition is central to the points Smith is trying to make, hers is not a conventional essay of definition, using a variety of patterns to define a particular object or concept. This is at heart an argumentative essay and, thus, provides an excellent transition to the next chapter.

COMPREHENSION (p. 523)

1. "Wife-beater" is the nickname for a white, skinny-ribbed, tank-style T-shirt originally worn by men as an undershirt and now fashionable with men and women as an outer garment or under a jacket.
2. Smith is disturbed by the name because its casual use suggests that spousal abuse is acceptable among those who use the term.
3. When she says "The name is the issue," she seems to mean that the fact that such shirts themselves are "all the rage" (3) is not a matter of concern to her—only what they are called. When she says "It's not just the name that worries me," she means that she fears the use of the term is an example of a possible "return . . . to male dominance where physical abuse is acceptable as a means of control." There's no real contradiction here.
4. In paragraphs 13 through 16 Smith suggests that she fears a causal connection between the acceptance of the term "wife-beater" and high rates of family

violence, particularly when she notes that most people who use the term are under 25 and that the average age of batterers is 31. Students should recognize, though, that she does not actually claim a causal connection.

5. This does not really undercut her argument because she has made the point earlier that it is not the popularity of the shirt that disturbs her, but rather the popularity of the slang term for it.

6. Smith feels that because many women find men who wear the shirt attractive and "manly," *manly* comes to equal *violent*, leading perhaps to young women tolerating violent behavior against themselves.

PURPOSE AND AUDIENCE (p. 523)

1. There are a number of possible reactions to Smith's opening sentence. Most immediately, readers are likely to be curious about what she means by "them" and so continue reading. In the context of her essay as a whole, this opening suggests that, if her concerns are correct, then the problem may be widespread.

2. Smith is clearly encouraging readers to think twice about using the term and even abandon its use altogether. But she also wants readers to recognize that violence against women is something our culture should be concerned about and should discourage in any way that we can.

3. She seems to have a fairly broad audience in mind including both young adults and older readers. She does not seem to be writing only to those who wear such T-shirts because she is careful to explain what they are to readers who may not have heard of them, but it is also clear that her imagined audience includes those who use the term.

4. A possible paraphrase of Smith's thesis: "Casual use of the term 'wife-beater' as the nickname for a popular style of T-shirt contributes to a cultural climate that condones and even encourages violence against women."

STYLE AND STRUCTURE (p. 523)

1. The fact that the T-shirt is so popular is part of the source of Smith's concern about what it is called. Students will probably see this as an effective opening.

2. One effect of including the dictionary definition is to show that the term has become so widely used that it has found its way into dictionaries. Another is to support her contention that the term refers openly to spousal abuse.

3. At the end of her first paragraph, Smith mentions that this particular style of T-shirt has not achieved such popularity since the leading male character in the film *A Streetcar Named Desire* made it popular in the 1950s. (For readers familiar with the film, this historical fact will immediately call up the image of Marlon Brando wearing such a shirt and so help them visualize it; for others, it probably serves little rhetorical purpose.) Then, in paragraphs 6 through 9, she traces several possible histories of the term to link it to spousal abuse.

4. Smith quotes three statistics in paragraph 13 to suggest a link between the popularity of the term "wife-beater" among young people and the high levels of violence against women.

VOCABULARY PROJECTS (p. 524)

2. Students' answers will vary. Based on Smith's suggestion that the shirt's name should connote flattery rather than violence, one possibility is "hunk-shirt."

COMBINING THE PATTERNS (p. 524)

Students' opinions will likely vary. She does not really establish a cause-and-effect relationship but rather suggests that even the possibility of one is reason enough to abandon the name. In fact, hard information is not available to establish such a relationship, although students might consider the extent to which the term reflects stereotypes of gender relations that are also seen in other aspects of contemporary culture.

THEMATIC CONNECTIONS

My First Conk (p. 260): In this excerpt from his 1964 autobiography, Malcolm X recalls undergoing the painful process of hair straightening popular among black men prior to the 1960s. He argues that the stereotype that "white" hair is more attractive than "black" hair, popularized by many entertainers, reflects a self-degrading attitude among blacks. Like Smith, he encourages a change in how a popular fashion statement is regarded as a way to combat pernicious stereotypes.

A Peaceful Woman Explains Why She Carries a Gun (p. 345): Linda Hasselstrom's essay describes a culture in which the possibility of violence against women is so prevalent that she has begun carrying a gun for protection. One theme students might consider is whether women have reason to fear violence in most parts of the United States and, if so, whether gender stereotypes may be responsible for such violence.

Violent Films Cry "Fire" in Crowded Theaters (p. 612): Michael Zimecki argues here that violent imagery in the media unquestionably contributes to violence in the real world. The essay is part of a casebook about the effects of media violence; it can be tied into Smith's argument about cultural images that may lead to violence against women.

Emily Dickinson, *"Hope" Is the Thing with Feathers*

Some students may already be familiar with Dickinson's famous poem from high school English classes. You might want to have the class try to paraphrase the definition here, to look into the metaphors Dickinson offers, and translate into plain language what they represent. For example, the first two stanzas might briefly be paraphrased as "Hope is a power that lives inside us and can always bring a kind of sweetness and sense of comfort to our lives no matter what adversity we are facing." What is lost and what is gained in such a straightforward statement?

READING LITERATURE (p. 526)

1. Hope, like a bird, "perches," "sings" a "tune without . . . words," can be heard during times of storm, can be found "in the chillest land—/ And on the strangest Sea—," and never asks "a crumb." Like a bird, hope can also be said to nest and to be fragile.

2. Students' interpretations will differ. Why might a tune without words be seen as especially comforting?
3. *Creature* could be substituted for *thing, sits* for *perches, coldest* for *chillest,* and *thing* for *crumb.* Students may come up with other substitutions, and they may have different ideas about how they might change the poem. In these examples, the final three substitutions are less specific and concrete, while the first is more specific, perhaps too specific.

THEMATIC CONNECTIONS

Ground Zero (p. 158): Describing a visit to the site of the demolished World Trade Center some six months after the terrorist attack that horrified the United States and much of the world, Suzanne Berne finds a certain comfort, even hope, in the fact that life continues on even in the face of such devastating death and destruction.

Suicide Note (p. 357): This poem, which takes the form of a college student's suicide note, sums up a sort of despair that is the opposite of Dickinson's hope. An analysis of the two poems could provide an interesting comparison and contrast.

The Declaration of Independence (p. 557): Ask students to think about how this founding document of the American republic reflects a sense of optimism and hope for a better future. Does the concept of hope underlie all successful enterprises? What kind of world would we inhabit if we had no concept of hope for the future?

12: ARGUMENTATION

Argumentation is a difficult rhetorical form for students to understand. In the chapter introduction we take pains to describe it and relate it to the other types of writing we have discussed. Although our primary emphasis is the appeal to reason, we recognize the emotional dimension that most good arguments possess. At the risk of oversimplifying the issue, however, we do not discuss in any depth the other appeals acceptable for persuasive writing. We choose to focus on argumentation because it is the principal form of persuasion used in college and because many beginning student writers confuse appeals to emotion with the feeling that "because I feel it is right, it must be."

Our suggestion is that you spend a good deal of time emphasizing the rhetoric of argumentation. You can illustrate to students that a good argument usually relies on a number of patterns of development. In order to convince an audience, they should use all of the rhetorical tools at their disposal.

Another point you will want to make is that argumentative essays are flexible and develop out of a writer's concept of audience and purpose. Many students are all too willing to apply simple formulas to their writing and fail to appreciate that effective arguments must be tailored to specific audiences. The paragraph taken from Jerome Groopman's "Holding Cell" provides a good opening example of a writer thinking clearly about his audience. He recognizes that people who oppose cloning for biomedical research based on deeply held moral or religious beliefs are unlikely to be swayed by any arguments in its favor and that many "scientists and . . . patients with incurable maladies" are already likely to be in favor of such research. His primary audience, therefore, consists of readers who have not made up their minds on the issue or who lean one way or the other but lack key facts to help them make an informed decision. In arguing in favor of cloning for biomedical research, therefore, he begins by summarizing the White House report's recommendation of a moratorium on cloning—which many readers might initially accept as authoritative—then goes on to point out what he sees as the flaws in the report and the negative effects the moratorium will have.

Carefully illustrate for students how writers support their assertions. You can, for example, ask students to point out the information Thomas Jefferson uses to support his points. You can also ask students to judge the quality and effectiveness of the deductive argument he presents. Elizabeth Cady Stanton's Declaration of Sentiments and Resolutions, which is modeled on Jefferson's Declaration, and other essays included in the unit can also be examined for their uses of evidence. Pointing out inadequate evidence is another effective way to teach students. Some of the questions at the ends of selections will help your students make such judgments.

One of the more exciting and challenging aspects of argumentation is refutation, which requires students to develop a dynamic and subtle sense of audience. Earlier in the semester students were concerned with presenting information to an audience, but now they not only have to evaluate an audience, they also must anticipate and react to its probable responses to a subject. We suggest you begin with "Letter from Birmingham Jail." You will want to explore King's excellent uses of induction and deduction and then to consider his care in refuting his opposition. If students use a highlighter to mark each time King addresses his opponents' view, they will see that these refutations organize King's tightly logical argument.

To further sharpen students' awareness of the need to identify audience and refute arguments, we have grouped essays into four widely debated subject areas. In the first grouping, William Safire and Alan M. Dershowitz debate the issue of national identity cards, proposed in the wake of increased terrorist threats, focusing on questions of privacy and civil liberties. The second grouping offers contrasting views from Tom Adkins and Becky Birtha on the controversial question of whether gay and lesbian couples should be allowed to adopt children. This is followed by a casebook in which writers debate issues of media violence: Does violence depicted in movies, on television, and in video games lead viewers to act violently? Should moviemakers bear responsibility for "copycat" crimes that seem related to their movies? How far should the law go in censoring violence in the entertainment media? A second casebook follows and focuses on the movement to grant contemporary African Americans monetary reparations for the legacy of slavery. Would such reparations, as their proponents argue, help to right a great injustice and promote racial reconciliation, or would they, as their critics charge, create a flawed special interest and act as a deeply polarizing force? In these two casebooks, students are presented with multiple sides of each issue. As a result, they can more clearly see refutations at work. Before asking students to write a full argumentative essay, have them write a short essay in which they refute a specific argument. This assignment will help them build up to more demanding argumentation assignments.

The section on deductive and inductive reasoning is intended as an introduction to logic. Our purpose is to give an overview of the basic principles of logic and to provide a list of the problems in reasoning that plague many student writers. You can use this section as the subject for a class discussion, or you can refer students to it as the need arises. For more information on reasoning and logic we suggest you consult *With Good Reason: An Introduction to Informal Fallacies* by S. Morris Engel (St. Martin's Press).

ACLU, *Thanks to Modern Science . . .* (Ad)

The American Civil Liberties Union (ACLU) is a public advocacy organization that is generally perceived as highly liberal in its outlook—even though it has taken on a number of civil liberties issues with which many liberals do not agree, particularly in areas related to free speech. Students should recognize that political advertisements such as this one are examples of advocacy rather than true argument.

In January of 2003, outgoing Governor George Ryan of Illinois took his moratorium on capital punishment a step further, commuting the sentences of all death row prisoners in the state to life in prison.

READING IMAGES (p. 556)

1. The headline might be summarized, "DNA testing has exonerated or raised questions about the guilt of seventeen people sentenced to death, while we know that twenty-three innocent people have been executed because of the current political climate." The ad does not fully support the headline because nowhere in its text does it refer specifically to the source of these two figures—although the *Chicago Tribune* series mentioned might provide the source. In fact, at the time the governor issued his moratorium, thirteen death row inmates in Illinois had recently been exonerated.
2. The picture is a brutal image of a man strapped to an electric chair, a form of capital punishment that is increasingly being viewed as unacceptable. The picture supports the sense in the ad that capital punishment too often results in injustice.
3. The appeal is primarily to the emotions, although in quoting the *Chicago Tribune* and Justice Brennan, it does make an appeal to authority.
4. Essentially, the ad makes the argument that a moratorium should be declared on capital punishment in its current form for two reasons: because innocent people are being executed and because the system is riddled with "incompetent lawyers, racial bias, and lack of access to DNA testing" and "preys on the poor." Students may think that the first point is supported, at least to some degree, by the two opening examples in the text and by the reference to the moratorium in Illinois. The text does not attempt to support the subsequent points. Students' responses to the ad will likely vary, but this is a good opportunity to discuss why formal argumentation should go beyond mere assertion of a position and provide solid evidence for that position.

THEMATIC CONNECTIONS

Thirty-Eight Who Saw Murder Didn't Call the Police (p. 101): Students may be interested to learn that Winston Moseley, convicted of Kitty Genovese's murder, was condemned to death, but an appeals court later reduced the sentence to life because, it noted, evidence of his mental condition should have been admitted at trial. Moseley later escaped prison and took five people hostage, raping a woman in front of her husband, before being recaptured by the police. He remains in prison, several requests for a retrial having been denied. How might the writers of the ACLU ad respond to the example of someone like Moseley?

A Peaceful Woman Explains Why She Carries a Gun (p. 345): Linda Hasselstrom suggests in her essay that we live in a culture in which the threat of violence is a constant matter of concern. How might this culture have contributed to popular support for the death penalty over the last twenty years?

Five Ways to Kill a Man (p. 487): Crucifixion, an ancient form of capital punishment, is the subject of the first stanza of Edwin Brock's poem. Students might do some research about forms of capital punishment, past and present. Are some more "humane" than others?

Whodunit—The Media? (p. 618): Maggie Cutler writes here about the link between media violence and the violent tendencies in children. Several capital cases over the last few years have focused on the age of young defendants who have been sentenced to deaths for their crimes. In a number of states, sixteen- and seventeen-year-olds can be sentenced to death even though many argue that confessions by young people may be more easily coerced than those of older suspects. Should there be a cut-off age for a death sentence?

Thomas Jefferson, *The Declaration of Independence*

The Declaration of Independence stands as a classic model of deductive argument. It begins with a major premise, progresses to a minor premise, and draws a logical conclusion. Often, students approach this document with a closed mind and see it as a musty, boring piece of history that has nothing to do with them. Many students have never read it and are surprised to see how clear and exciting it really is. You might point out to them how genuinely revolutionary it was and how it shocked the world when it first appeared. Once students realize this fact, they can have great fun analyzing the rhetorical strategy that Jefferson and the other writers employed. Especially interesting in this regard are the many grievances that the document lists. Not only do they make for an interesting class discussion, but they also show the lengths to which the writers felt they had to go to establish the reasonableness of their case.

COMPREHENSION (p. 560)

1. Paragraph 2 enumerates that self-evident truths that Jefferson asserts: "that all men are created equal, that they are endowed by their Creator with certain unalienable rights, that among these are life, liberty, and the pursuit of happiness. That to secure these rights, governments are instituted among men, deriving their just powers from the consent of the governed. That whenever any form of government becomes destructive of these ends, it is the right of the people to alter or abolish it, and to institute a new government, laying its foundation on such principles and organizing its powers in such form, as to them shall seem most likely to effect their safety and happiness."
2. Governments derive "their just powers from the consent of the governed" (2).
3. Paragraphs 3 through 31 list the reasons that justify the break with Great Britain.
4. Jefferson concludes that the British crown no longer deserves allegiance because it no longer protects the rights of the governed.

PURPOSE AND AUDIENCE (p. 560)

1. The major premise of Jefferson's argument is that all men are created equal. He could not have done more to establish that premise in this essay and still have accomplished his purpose.

2. Jefferson structures the Declaration like a formal argument in logic. In paragraph 2, he states the general premises upon which he bases his argument. In paragraphs 3 through 31, he states specific justifications for the actions of the colonies. Finally, in paragraph 32, he sums up his argument and states his conclusions.

3. Jefferson realized that he would have to address several very distinct audiences. The Declaration announced to Great Britain that the colonies no longer owed allegiance to the crown; to other European countries that the colonies were free states that would trade, wage war, and make alliances independent of Great Britain; and to the colonists themselves that some of their number were ready to fight for independence. Jefferson surely knew that some people would never accept his conclusions no matter how well reasoned they were—as evidenced by the strong and continued support of the king by many of the colonists.

4. In paragraphs 2, 30, and 31, Jefferson effectively anticipates the opposition and presents convincing evidence that all reasonable approaches have been attempted.

5. Jefferson speaks of his "British brethren" to emphasize the cultural bonds that connected the colonies with England. By doing this, he hopes to gain empathy from his audience. In part, this was also an effort to defuse the violent reaction that Jefferson expected from the British.

6. Jefferson states his thesis, so to speak, in the final paragraph. Because its claim is so decisively revolutionary, it is necessary that he present all pertinent evidence before stating it directly.

STYLE AND STRUCTURE (p. 561)

1. Jefferson primarily uses deductive reasoning. The Declaration of Independence resembles a syllogism. It begins with a major premise, progresses to a minor premise, and ends with a conclusion. Jefferson argues that his major premise is "self-evident." However, when he provides evidence that his minor premise is sound (3–29), he reasons inductively.

2. In addition to the syllogistic structure discussed above, Jefferson uses the language of formal logic to create transitions between sections. He introduces his premises by saying, "We hold these truths to be self-evident." He then prefaces the list of grievances by saying, "To prove this, let facts be submitted to a candid world" (2). Finally, he begins his conclusion by saying, "We, therefore, the Representatives of the United States of America" (32).

3. Jefferson includes all twenty-eight grievances to establish the reasonableness of the colonists' position. Summarizing them or stating only a few of them would materially weaken the Declaration, since anyone not already inclined to agree with the colonists would suspect they are being unfair to the king and his government.

4. Jefferson concludes with "We, therefore" to emphasize the deductive structure of the document and the reasonableness of his argument. He has effectively built to this conclusion with the long list of evidence that precedes it.

VOCABULARY PROJECTS (p. 561)

2. Your students will find numerous examples of words with negative connotations, including *abuses, usurpations, despotism, injuries, forbidden, invasions,*

135

obstructed, plundered, ravaged, and *burnt.* These words portray the actions of the king in a strongly negative light, justifying the Declaration of Independence. Had Jefferson used more neutral words, the case against the king would not have seemed so strong nor the action of the colonists so justified.

3. Jefferson's text includes a number of words that may be unfamiliar to students: *usurpations, evinces, prudence, sufferance, tyrant, dissolutions, quartering, perfidy,* and *magnanimity.* Whether students prefer their updated versions will depend to some extent on their sophistication as writers. Certainly, they are bound to sound less formal and incantatory.

COMBINING THE PATTERNS (p. 562)

History suggests that Jefferson's examples are relevant, representative, sufficient, and effective. Implicit in the examples is a pattern of cause and effect (the effects of British policies on the colonists); students might consider whether making this pattern more explicit would add to the argument.

THEMATIC CONNECTIONS

The "Black Table" Is Still There (p. 340): Pairing the Declaration of Independence with Lawrence Otis Graham's essay about self-segregation in a suburban junior high school provides an opportunity to consider the extent to which the values embodied in the Declaration have been achieved in contemporary U.S. life. Is it possible for groups to be separate but equal?

Grant and Lee: A Study in Contrasts (p. 386): Consulting both the Declaration and Bruce Catton's essay, students should determine how the Confederate cause differed from Jefferson's cause. Both involved throwing off a government that participants deemed to be unjust.

Letter from Birmingham Jail (p. 570): This country, founded on a belief that "all men are created equal," failed to extend that equality to blacks. Although slavery was discussed by the Founding Fathers, political differences led them to essentially ignore the problem. Students may not know that Jefferson himself was a slaveholder. Ask your students to read the Declaration of Independence a second time. As they reread the list of abuses the colonists believed justified their actions, ask them to keep in mind the injustices that Martin Luther King talks about. Many of Jefferson's complaints have parallels in slavery and, later, in segregation. Ask students to reread King's "Letter from Birmingham Jail" as well. Because of its length and complexity, they will need a second reading. As they reread, have them mark King's explicit and implicit references to Jefferson, the Declaration of Independence, and the Constitution. Doing so will help them appreciate and understand King's arguments and gain a stronger sense of their country's history.

Litigating the Legacy of Slavery (p. 627) The Declaration of Independence defines the basic principles on which the United States is founded; "Litigating the Legacy of Slavery," in discussing the residual effects of slavery on contemporary African Americans, suggests that the ideals of the Declaration of Independence may not have been fully realized.

Elizabeth Cady Stanton, *Declaration of Sentiments and Resolutions*

You will want to make sure that students read the headnote before tackling this selection because it provides important background information. You will probably also want to study this essay after the class has worked on the Declaration of Independence (or after you are sure that students are reasonably familiar with the Declaration of Independence) because Stanton's 1848 Declaration very deliberately echoes Jefferson's; she expected her audience to immediately recognize the parallels. Like Jefferson's Declaration, hers is also a justification for rebelling against the shackles of a despotic government, but her target is the governmental, legal, and society sanctions of the day that prevented women from sharing equally with men the "inalienable rights" of "life, liberty, and the pursuit of happiness."

It should be clear to students that women of Stanton's day were less than even second-class citizens; they barely shared in the rights of citizenship at all. As Stanton acknowledges, most men and many women themselves simply accepted as a given that women were intellectually and emotionally inferior to men and unfit for any pursuits beyond keeping house and raising a family. The only serious profession open to women was that of novelist and even this was considered somewhat suspect. At the same time, women were generally held to a far higher moral standard than were men, and any breach of decorum on their part was grounds for censure. Moreover, it was unusual for women to inherit property, and when they married, they and everything they owned became, by law, their husband's property. In its day, Stanton's Declaration was nothing less than revolutionary.

If you have a dramatic bent, you might enjoy reading some passages here aloud to students. It was intended as much as a document to be heard as to be read.

COMPREHENSION (p. 567)

1. The declaration of sentiments is necessary, out of "respect to the opinions of mankind," to "declare the causes" that have led "one portion of the family of man" (that is, women) to assume a new position in the world, one "to which the laws of nature and of nature's God entitle them."

2. These "self-evident" truths are that men and women are equals, that they share the basic rights of "life, liberty, and the pursuit of happiness," and that it is the government's responsibility to "to secure these rights" for all citizens.

3. The injuries are detailed in paragraphs 4 through 18. They include women not being allowed to vote and the consequences of this disenfranchisement (4–7); the legally restricted status of wives, including their inability to hold property on their own (8–11); the taxation of single women by a government that does not represent them (12); the highly restricted opportunities for women in terms of employment and education (13–15); the enforcement of a different moral code for men and women (16); the arbitrary assignment to women of a limited "sphere of action" (17); and the resulting lack of confidence and self-respect that make women "willing to lead a dependent and abject life" (18). Students' opinions may differ as to the relative importance of these injuries; they might consider how many paragraphs are devoted to each.

4. Stanton writes that she expects a reception marked by "misconception, mis-representation, and ridicule" (20) and that she and her fellow conventioneers "shall employ agents, circulate tracts, petition the State and National legislatures, and endeavor to enlist the pulpit and the press in our behalf."

5. Women, Stanton concludes, should share the same rights enjoyed by men—to choose one's "station in society" (23), to "speak and teach . . . in all religious assemblies" (26), to speak in public more generally (28), and to vote (30). In paragraph 32, she asserts as "self-evident" that "equally with man," women should be able to "promote every righteous cause with every righteous means." It is "self-evident falsehood" that women are incapable of doing this.

PURPOSE AND AUDIENCE (p. 567)

1. While Stanton's audience at the Seneca Falls Convention was made up primarily of women, she clearly expected her Declaration to be read by men. As the final paragraph makes clear, it is a call to action to both men and women. Given prevailing sentiments, women would, by and large, be more immediately receptive to the argument than men.

2. Perhaps Stanton's most effective strategy is couching her Declaration so that it echoes the Declaration of Independence, considered a model of reasonable argument. At the end of paragraph 3, she is also quick to offer proof to back up her assertions. Then in paragraph 21 she cites the great legal commentator Blackstone as a way of supporting her position. While some contemporary readers may think that Stanton is overstating the case, women of her day were, in fact, denied all the rights she claims.

3. Stanton states her thesis in paragraph 19, waiting until she has detailed the "disenfranchisement" and "degradation" of women before proposing her solution.

4. Stanton's primary purpose is to stir up the convention's delegates in order to encourage them to begin lobbying for change. At the same time, she hopes to provoke a debate that will ultimately serve to change people's ideas and behavior.

STYLE AND STRUCTURE (p. 567)

1. Modeled as it is on the Declaration of Independence, Stanton's argument is basically inductive, beginning with a major premise that is "self-evident," then moving on to a minor premise (that women are denied their basic rights); this minor premise she supports inductively in paragraphs 3 through 18.

2. The main advantage of this strategy was that the Declaration of Independence was given great moral weight and was seen as a model of rational argument. A disadvantage is that her use of the Declaration as a model might have be seen as a kind of sacrilege, a trivialization of this important document.

3. In fact, these truths were no more "self-evident" in Stanton's day than were the truths Thomas Jefferson posed as "self-evident" when the Declaration of Independence was written. Because these are beliefs, however, Stanton could have done little to establish their validity.

4. Stanton's major premise is that, equally with men, women are guaranteed certain rights and that when these rights are abridged, those affected may

seek change ("insist upon the institution of a new government"). Her minor premise is that men have abridged the rights of women. Logically, this leads to her conclusion that women must insist upon change.

5. "To prove this" provides a transition from the statement of the minor premise to supporting evidence in paragraph 3, while the transition "now" leads from the previous list of injuries to Stanton's conclusion in paragraph 19. Then, beginning in paragraph 22, each new item is introduced with *"Resolved."* Most students will see these transitions as effective.

6. Students' opinions may vary. Note that Stanton implicitly denies that opposition to her position has any validity whatsoever. She essentially bases her argument on the assertion that because the laws of God apply equally to men and women, so should the laws of man.

VOCABULARY PROJECTS (p. 568)

2. Paragraph 13 is a good possibility here. It might be paraphrased: "Men have set aside for themselves almost all ways of earning a living, and any jobs women can take pay only low wages. Women are barred from pursuing any career, valued by men, that leads to wealth or distinction. Women cannot be religious leaders, doctors, or lawyers."

COMBINING THE PATTERNS (p. 569)

Students should recognize that because they accurately summarize the way women of Stanton's time were subordinated, her examples are relevant and representative. She certainly offers sufficient examples, but the effectiveness of her examples will ultimately depend on one's beliefs regarding the equality of men and women.

THEMATIC CONNECTIONS

My Mother Never Worked **(p. 96):** Bonnie Smith-Yackel's essay suggests that what has traditionally been considered women's work is still undervalued in contemporary society. Students might consider why it continues to be uncommon for married men to take on the primary role of housekeeper and stay-at-home dad.

I Want a Wife **(p. 505):** This classic essay can be tied in neatly with the preceding entry under *Thematic Connections.*

The Declaration of Independence (p. 557): As suggested in the introductory remarks to this chapter, you will probably want to study the Declaration of Sentiments and Resolutions in conjunction with the Declaration of Independence, which provided Stanton with her rhetorical model. Students might compare the two, looking for places where Stanton adheres closely to her model and for places where she varies from it significantly. Why does she choose to follow Jefferson's words closely? Why are her variations necessary to her purpose?

In Search of Our Mothers' Gardens **(p. 686):** Alice Walker writes here about how the creativity of African-American women of the past was often thwarted by the role they were supposed to assume as "the *mule* of the world." Despite the "injuries" suffered by white women a century and more ago, the limits placed on black women were even greater.

Martin Luther King Jr., *Letter from Birmingham Jail*

King's letter is an excellent illustration of a complex argument. Many critics have pointed out the similarities between it and the Declaration of Independence. Both documents attack injustice and take pains to establish the reasonableness of their positions. Like Jefferson, King realizes that the specific audience he is addressing (the king and Parliament in Jefferson's case) is not the only audience to whom he must appeal. He is aware that people all over the world are watching the events in which he is involved. His carefully crafted argument aligns him with the three men to whom he feels he is spiritual heir: Jefferson, Thoreau, and Gandhi. Many students will not be familiar with these men or the fact that they all sought to influence public opinion by acts of civil disobedience. A short summary of their lives and causes will enable students to perceive some of the subtleties of King's argument. This essay offers a good opportunity to introduce the term *allusion* and to show students how King makes conscious reference to the Declaration of Independence, the Bible, and "Civil Disobedience."

COMPREHENSION (p. 582)

1. King says that he receives so much criticism. he would have to spend all his time answering it. He decided to answer this criticism because he feels that his fellow clergymen are men of good will and that their criticisms were sincerely set forth (1).
2. Since the demonstrations occurred after an election in Birmingham, the clergymen think that King and his associates have not allowed the new administration enough time to act.
3. King says that "Birmingham is probably the most thoroughly segregated city in the United States" (6) and mentions brutality, unfair courts, and bombings. Because the city fathers "consistently refused to engage in good-faith negotiation" (6) and because promises made by white merchants were broken (7), King says, "We had no alternative except to prepare for direct action" (8).
4. For African Americans, *wait* usually means never, as King observes in paragraph 13.
5. King defines two types of laws, *just* and *unjust:* "A just law is a man-made code that squares with the moral law or the law of God. An unjust law is a code that is out of harmony with the moral law" (16).
6. King says that condemning nonviolent protests because they precipitate violence is "like condemning a robbed man because his possession of money precipitated the evil act of robbery" (25). He goes on to say that "as the federal courts have consistently affirmed, it is wrong to urge an individual to cease his efforts to gain his basic constitutional rights because the quest may precipitate violence."
7. King is disappointed that the white churches did not support him. Some, he says, have been outright opponents.

PURPOSE AND AUDIENCE (p. 583)

1. King's purpose is to reach and inspire white clergymen in the South to support his cause. By establishing his setting as the Birmingham city jail, he hopes to make his audience sympathetic and to demonstrate his commitment to his

cause. By defining his audience as "fellow clergymen," King can address them as "men of genuine good will," an assumption that is basic to his argument.

2. Throughout his letter, King scolds his fellow clergymen for being insensitive to the moral rightness of his cause. He does this in paragraphs 5, 12, 13, 15, 23, 24, 25, 26, 27, 32, 33, 34, 35, and 36. Although King says he believes his audience comprises men of good will, it is clear from his didactic tone throughout these passages that he has his doubts about their altruism.

3. King is aware that his letter will be picked up by the press and read by a wide general audience. His detailed description of the situation in Birmingham (already familiar to the clergymen) is one indication of this fact.

4. King's implied thesis is that men of good will should support the demonstrations in Birmingham by the Southern Christian Leadership Conference.

STYLE AND STRUCTURE (p. 583)

1. In the first paragraph, King says that since his audience of clergymen are men of good will, he will try to answer their statements patiently and reasonably.

2. King addresses the possible objections of his audience in paragraphs 5, 12, 15, 25, and 27.

3. King makes the transition from one section of his argument to another with rhetorical questions and statements that directly address his audience. For instance, when moving from his introduction (4) to his definition of the problem (5), he says, "You deplore the demonstrations taking place in Birmingham." When turning from the end of his definition of the problem (9) to a discussion of direct action (10), he says, "You may well ask, 'Why direct action?'" After this section ends with paragraph 14, King introduces his discussion of just and unjust laws with the statement, "You express a great deal of anxiety over our willingness to break laws" (15).

4. King is seeking support from all of the United States' major religions; therefore, he carefully reinforces his arguments with references to Jewish, Catholic, and Protestant philosophers. Also, he wants to establish that his conclusions are basic to Western philosophical thought.

5. King uses appeals to authority to indicate that his argument is supported by the writings and teachings of famous philosophers and theologians.

6. King's explanation of why he came to Birmingham is an example of inductive reasoning. His examination of just and unjust laws is an example of deductive reasoning.

7. King tries to reestablish a harmonious relationship with his audience by first asking their forgiveness if he has overstated the truth (46). He then reasserts his common bond with the other clergymen and ends with a remark that asserts his optimism about the future (47). Students are likely to find King's strategy successful.

VOCABULARY PROJECTS (p. 583)

2. Allusions to the Bible appear in paragraphs 3, 21, 25, 26, and 31. These allusions refer to events or teachings in scripture that support King's position of justice, equality, and love.

3. King is alluding to the phrase "my cup runneth over" in Psalm 23. With this allusion, King reinforces the point that he, too, is walking "through the valley

of the shadow of death" and, because of his faith, "will fear no evil." Thus King effectively uses a biblical reference to express his impatience.

COMBINING THE PATTERNS (p. 584)

Passages of narration include paragraphs 7–9, 14, 32, and 35–36. Each of these narratives shows how King and his African-American followers have been disappointed by the policies of the white power elite.

THEMATIC CONNECTIONS

Finishing School (p. 89): The childhood incident described by Maya Angelou dramatically suggests the institutionalized bias and personal degradation faced daily by black people in the segregated South prior to the civil rights movement.

The "Black Table" Is Still There (p. 340): In writing about self-segregation in a suburban junior high school, Lawrence Otis Graham suggests the extent to which racial polarities continue to exist some thirty-five years after the height of the civil rights movement, when King's letter was written. You might ask students to consider how King would view the current state of race relations in the United States if he were alive today. Would he feel that most of his goals have been achieved? Or would he be disappointed at how little progress has been made?

Two Ways to Belong in America (p. 397) Bharati Mukherjee's essay focuses on the discrimination sometimes suffered by immigrants to the United States. Anti-immigrant sentiment has in the past been almost as virulent as racism, and in recent years there have been attempts by several states—and by the federal government—to limit the rights of immigrants who are not citizens. One issue students might consider is why the "silenced" immigrants Mukherjee describes in paragraph 12 are so much less likely to protest their condition than are African Americans.

DEBATE: Should U.S. Citizens Be Required to Carry National ID Cards?

You might begin by asking students whether they were already familiar with proposals following the terrorist attacks of September 2001 to institute a national ID card for all legal residents of the United States above a certain age. What were their own preconceptions of such ID cards? Has reading the arguments by Safire and Dershowitz raised any issues they had not considered before? You might even take a poll to determine how many students are in favor of and against such cards.

Then, in discussing these essays, you will need to make the point that while they may seem to be in disagreement, Safire and Dershowitz are actually arguing about different issues because they each define national ID cards differently. A national ID card that, as Dershowitz suggests, includes only "name, address, photo, and print" (8) is not what Safire is concerned about; rather, Safire's skepticism is of a national ID card with a computer chip that allows access to a wide variety of information about the holder, from medical records to credit card purchases to bank account information to product preferences to links to suspicious Web sites. Dershowitz makes clear that he sees the availability of "too much personal information" as a "separate issue"; likely, he would also oppose such a card. The question becomes whether Safire's fears are justified, but Dershowitz does not discuss this issue.

You might have students do some research about the current status of national ID cards. As of this writing, little congressional or presidential initiative seems to have been taken regarding national ID cards, and, for the moment, debate over the issue has dwindled significantly.

William Safire, *The Threat of National ID*

COMPREHENSION (p. 588)

1. Safire says that people are willing to give up some privacy "in return for greater safety" (3). He claims that law enforcement agencies are using fears over terrorist attacks as a way of "sweeping for suspects" (4) and abolishing habeas corpus (12).
2. Safire implies here that national identity cards will, in fact, do little to protect the United States from terrorists attacks while giving an illusion of doing so that diverts people from taking real precautions.
3. The card would be mandatory (4), and, Safire claims, even if it *were* possible to "opt out," those who did so would find their ability to travel, make purchases on credit, and more—including perhaps secure employment—severely curtailed.
4. Safire's point is that both governmental and business interests have reason to want to be able to legally track the behavior of individual citizens across the board. He compares this to the worst abuses of communism.
5. Students' opinions will differ as to the advantages of national ID cards. Safire does not mention any. According to him, the great danger of such cards is the loss of individual privacy they will allow.

PURPOSE AND AUDIENCE (p. 588)

1. Safire alludes to a potentially hostile audience in paragraph 12, but given that this was one of his columns published in the *New York Times*, he could expect both friendly and neutral readers.
2. His purpose seems to be to change people's minds; he is encouraging readers not to blindly support national ID cards as a protection against terrorist threats. He does not call readers to action—asking them to write to their congressional leaders, for example.
3. Safire assumes that most readers are essentially in favor of national ID cards and believe they can provide a way of tracking potential terrorists without inconveniencing average citizens; he notes in paragraph 12 that the proposal is "gaining popularity."

STYLE AND STRUCTURE (p. 588)

1. Students' opinions will vary as to the effectiveness of this opening. It seems to have little to do with the point he is making. (However, you might refer to the answer to item 6 below.)
2. The argument is basically deductive: "Anything that seriously limits U.S. citizens' right to privacy is a bad thing. A national ID card would seriously limit U.S. citizens' right to privacy. Therefore, a national ID card is a bad thing." He presents evidence inductively to support the second premise.

3. Safire offers evidence that law enforcement agencies are already using technology to essentially spy on citizens (5) as well as evidence that much data about individuals is already being collected through computer records (8–9) and evidence that the current Attorney General is willing to institute policies that limit privacy (12). His claim that a national ID card would enhance these tracking abilities is not really supported by any evidence here (although some readers will find that he only wants to make the case that the potential for abuse exists, which is reason enough to question the implementation of a national ID system).

4. Safire does not directly refute opposing arguments except to suggest that those who would call him "alarmist" are too quick not to take matters of privacy seriously (12).

5. Rhetorical questions are found in paragraphs 5, 10, and 11. (Note that the question in paragraph 8 is not rhetorical.) The questions in paragraphs 5 and 10 give the essay a more conversational tone than would statements or conventional transitions, while the questions in paragraph 11 are meant to provoke readers to think about what the loss of privacy might mean in practical terms.

6. The first two sentences summarize Safire's main points. The final sentence, which refers to his description in his introduction of a neck implant ID for pets, is meant to be a somewhat chilling image of a world in which we have no privacy and are tracked by our "owners." He probably means this to be seen as an exaggeration.

VOCABULARY PROJECTS (p. 589)

2. Students' opinions will likely vary here. The use of colloquialisms inevitably lends an essay a conversational style and a greater air of informality—of "plain speaking." Mixing colloquialisms with more difficult language is a hallmark of Safire's style.

COMBINING THE PATTERNS (p. 589)

Most of the evidence Safire presents, as detailed under the answer to item 3 under *Style and Structure,* is in the form of examples. Students' opinions may differ as to the effectiveness of his examples, particularly as his examples must ultimately provide the support for his argument.

THEMATIC CONNECTIONS

Ground Zero (p. 158): Suzanne Berne's visit to the site of the World Trade Center in lower Manhattan offers a stark reminder of the horrifying terrorist attacks in September 2001 that precipitated the call for national ID cards.

A Peaceful Woman Explains Why She Carries a Gun (p. 345): While Safire writes that law enforcement agencies have begun to go too far in ferreting out potential criminals, Linda Hasselstrom's experiences suggest that, at least in some instances, law enforcement agencies may be doing too little to protect citizens.

The Tipping Point (p. 351): Malcolm Gladwell's essay focuses on changes in policing practices that served to significantly lower the crime rate in New York City in the 1990s. What might Safire have to say about the wholesale arrest of people for petty crimes that led, in many cases, to additional, more serious charges?

Alan M. Dershowitz, *Why Fear National ID Cards?*

COMPREHENSION (p. 592)

1. EZ Pass transmitters are, in Dershowitz's words, "a trade-off between privacy and convenience," while national ID cards would offer "a similar kind of trade-off: a little less anonymity for a lot more security."
2. The trade-off is that while authorities can more easily track one's movements, one is able to get around "more expeditiously."
3. According to Dershowitz, fears concerning national ID cards are essentially based on the prospect of the government playing a more intrusive role in people's lives and being able to more easily deport illegal immigrants. He does not feel these fears are justified.
4. He says that the government could set criteria "for any official who demands to see the card" (6), limiting such occasions to serve legitimate purposes.
5. Dershowitz means here that while the right to privacy is protected, there is no similar right for citizens who wish to remain anonymous; some information about people is necessarily public.

PURPOSE AND AUDIENCE (p. 592)

1. He seems to be addressing those who might, like himself, be "skeptical" of the potential infringement of civil liberties such cards might allow (3). He is convinced otherwise, and he hopes to convice these skeptics as well.
2. Civil libertarians tend to oppose any infringement on Americans' basic freedoms. Dershowitz seems to feel that if he, an attorney well known for pursuing civil liberties cases, can accept the trade-off offered by national ID cards, others should be able to also. Students' opinions may vary as to how successful he is, but they should recognize that he goes on to claim that such ID cards can actually enhance the civil liberties of those who might otherwise face racial or ethnic profiling.
3. Dershowitz concedes the legitimacy of opposing arguments in paragraph 6 (concerning the deportation of illegal immigrants) and paragraph 7 (concerning the fact that a national ID card "would not prevent all threats of terrorism"). The parenthetical information at the end of paragraph 8 is also something of a concession in that he acknowledges as a separate issue the charge that national ID cards could be used to provide "too much personal information" and that the information could be "used improperly." The first two concessions are effective in that they admit the inevitable, but the third may be seen as raising more questions than it answers. In fact, this is exactly the issue that William Safire raises as the basis for his argument against national ID cards.

STYLE AND STRUCTURE (p. 592)

1. Because people are comfortable using EZ Pass transmitters, it is likely that the analogy will make readers more comfortable with the idea of national ID cards; Dershowitz's point is that Americans have nothing to fear from either.
2. He refutes the argument that national ID cards would lead to greater governmental intrusion in citizens' lives. While he does not refute the argument that

the cards would increase deportation of illegal immigrants, he suggests that many may soon be able to claim legal status anyway and that ID cards may be a benefit to legal immigrants. Because he is imagining an audience of readers skeptical of national ID cards, he naturally wants to refute their objections.

3. Again, writing to a skeptical audience, Dershowitz waits until he has refuted objections before he argues his own case that national ID cards can actually enhance civil liberties, an idea most readers would not accept immediately.

4. Essentially, Dershowitz offers the evidence that Americans are already required to show identification for many activities. He also writes that a fingerprint ID is harder to fake than a picture ID and so harder to forge or alter, so that it "would reduce the likelihood that someone could, intentionally or not, get lost in the cracks of multiple bureaucracies" (5). Potential terrorists would find it harder to "hide in open view, as many of the September 11 hijackers apparently managed to do" (7). Other evidence to strengthen his case might focus on how to make sure that too much personal information would not become readily available.

5. The final paragraph seems an effective summary of his argument. Although Dershowitz has not already specifically made the point that a "national ID card would be much more effective in preventing terrorism than profiling millions of men simply because of their appearance," he has prepared readers for this idea.

VOCABULARY PROJECTS (p. 593)

2. By *civil libertarian,* Dershowitz means "one who defines most broadly the freedoms guaranteed by the Constitution and argues for the enforcement of these freedoms." Students will differ as to the connotations of the term. While viewed in some circles as a radical brand of liberalism, civil libertarianism also lies at the heart of certain conservative positions such as the right to bear arms.

COMBINING THE PATTERNS (p. 593)

Students may feel that the distinction is not really made clearly in the paragraph. Have them compare dictionary definitions of *privacy* and *anonymity* to decide how including formal definitions might have made a difference here.

THEMATIC CONNECTIONS

Just Walk On By (p. 223): While Brent Staples doesn't use the term *racial profiling* in this selection, he does describe how innocent African-American males are often immediately assumed by white people to pose a threat. Would a national ID card alleviate this bias as Dershowitz claims it would the bias against those who seem to physically match the profile of a terrorist?

Two Ways to Belong in America (p. 397): This essay compares two sisters from India living in the United States, one a naturalized citizen, the other a long-term legal resident alien. According to Dershowitz, how would a national ID card affect the status of such legal immigrants who clearly look "foreign"? How might Bharati Mukherjee and her sister respond to carrying a national ID card?

Five Ways to Kill a Man (p. 487): In times of war, such as described in this poem, citizens' civil liberties may often be severely curtailed. Students may wish to do some research about past infringements on civil liberties during war times, then think about the extent to which governments have a legitimate right to do this.

The Declaration of Independence (p. 557): Thomas Jefferson's famous document claims that governments derive their powers "from the consent of the governed" in order to secure the rights of those governed. Abuse of citizens' rights deprives a government of its authority. In what sense does the whole idea of civil liberties in the United States have as its basis Jefferson's stirring words?

DEBATE: Should Gay and Lesbian Couples Be Allowed to Adopt?

The following two essays appeared on the op-ed page of the *Philadelphia Inquirer* in March of 2002, shortly after the American Academy of Pediatrics (AAP) released a policy statement recommending that the same-sex partner of a gay parent should have the right to adopt his or her partner's child so that the child would have two legal parents. (The recommendation was based, in part, on AAP studies indicating that growing up in a gay household may have few ill effects on children.) The recommendation was immediately misconstrued as a more general endorsement of gay adoption and thus prompted some heated debate about the legitimacy of gay parenting—an issue that will likely continue to be debated in the foreseeable future as more and more gay couples seek to adopt.

You might begin discussion by asking students whether they know any gay celebrities who have adopted children. Rosie O'Donnell may come immediately to mind; she has become an outspoken advocate for gay adoption. More interesting to this debate, however, might be rock star Melissa Etheridge. When Etheridge and her partner decided to have children, her partner bore them through artificial insemination, and they were adopted by Etheridge after their birth. The couple later separated amicably, and Etheridge continues to be a custodial mom. One thing students should recognize is that in gay households with children, particularly among lesbians, one parent as often as not is a biological parent. The real issue raised by the AAP report is whether the biological parent in such households should have the opportunity to allow the child to be adopted by his or her partner for purposes of insurance, medical decision making, and other joint legal responsibilities.

Students should also understand that with the availability of private adoptions and overseas adoptions, gay people with the proper resources can adopt singly relatively easily. The question becomes whether the state will recognize a joint adoption by a gay couple.

Tom Adkins, *Traditional Mother and Father: Still the Best Choice for Children*

COMPREHENSION (p. 598)

1. Adkins has, in the previous paragraph, used the word *prize* to refer to election to political office. Gays have rightfully won such prizes, he says, but the prize of children is a more critical one, not to be granted by the will of voters. The right to adopt children may be seen as a "prize" because it confers societal legitimacy.

2. The AAP policy statement said that children "could be brought up with equally good results by gay or by heterosexual parents" (3). This policy statement is controversial because gay men and lesbians have not been fully accepted by society and are seen in some circles as practicing a deviant lifestyle to which children should not be exposed.

3. One study has shown that "daughters of lesbian couples are more likely to be sexually promiscuous and engage in lesbian experimentation," and one sociologist has concluded that "same-sex parenting fosters homosexual behavior and confused gender roles," and that "such children often suffer serious psychological problems later in life." (Adkins does not show that such problems occur less often in children raised by heterosexual couples.)

4. Adkins claims that the AAP endorses gay parenting for political reasons, that the endorsement is in keeping with other liberal stances taken by the organization.

5. His point seems to be that children already living with gay parents benefit because they are having these special needs taken care of, not because they are being raised by gay parents. It is not clear what factors have been taken into consideration by the report.

6. They are responsible for making "the best certain choice": finding homes with a "loving, responsible mother and father" (10).

PURPOSE AND AUDIENCE (p. 599)

1. Adkins does not seem to assume that readers have a great deal of familiarity with issues of gay adoption. He provides a significant amount of background information.

2. Students' opinions will differ as to Adkins's attempts to convince readers that he is being fair. There are few examples to point to.

3. Adkins states his thesis twice: in the two sentences that end paragraph 10 and again in his final sentence. He takes time to refute the supposedly authoritative report before concluding with his thesis.

4. Students may point to paragraph 9 as direct evidence of bias on Adkins's part.

STYLE AND STRUCTURE (p. 599)

1. Students' opinions will probably differ. We find this distinction a bit difficult to follow and so not especially effective.

2. Adkins claims that the report ignores flaws in the studies on which it bases its conclusions, that it lacks a longitudinal perspective, and that its conclusion is politically motivated.

3. It is rather difficult to know how fair this assertion is without knowing more about the American Academy of Pediatrics; the fact that it has taken stands on two issues that may be viewed as "decidedly liberal" is not necessarily evidence of a political agenda. For Adkins, however, these stands mean that all its policy statements are suspect.

4. Adkins does not attempt to present a fair cross-section of opinion. To be broadly convincing, he probably should have included and refuted positive studies of gay parenting.

5. Again, student's opinions will probably vary. Implicitly, such an assertion assumes that gay parenting causes harm until proven otherwise, which is neither exactly fair nor logical, but it is also a view that may be widely held.

6. Adkins does, perhaps inadvertently, set this question up as a false dilemma because it implies that the choice is between allowing gay couples to adopt or heterosexual couples to adopt, but not both. Of course, this is not what he means. Better phrased, the question might read "Should gay couples have the same right to adopt that heterosexual couples currently have?" although this phrasing does not concede the point that both kinds of couples can make loving parents.

VOCABULARY PROJECTS (p. 599)

2. Students' opinions may vary. The phrase is informal but also suggests that the data was literally torn apart by the researchers, reducing it to hash, which clearly serves Adkins's purpose. A more formal term might be "thoroughly analyzed and discredited."

COMBINING THE PATTERNS (p. 600)

Students who accept Adkins's argument will probably find the examples sufficient, while those who do not will see the need for more. The examples do serve to support Adkins's contention that more studies—particularly long-term studies—are needed before a definitive conclusion can be reached about children who grow up with gay parents. The quandary is that, if gay couples cannot adopt, few such examples will be available for study.

THEMATIC CONNECTIONS

The Lottery (p. 292): In this classic short story, lots are drawn by a group of villagers to determine which among them will be stoned to death. If homosexuality is, indeed, genetic, then how might it be seen as the result of chance over which one has no control? What lessons might "The Lottery" have to offer here?

The Tipping Point (p. 351): Gay men and lesbians have come to achieve increasingly widespread acceptance. Has the movement already reached its tipping point? If not, is it likely to do so?

A Modest Proposal (p. 676): Swift's classic essay reminds us that the welfare of children has not always been a matter of concern for society. Why are matters of child welfare so important to us today?

Becky Birtha, *Laws Should Support Loving Households, Straight or Not*

COMPREHENSION (p. 603)

1. The academy recommended that "children born to or adopted by a parent in a same-sex couple [should] have the right to be adopted by their nonlegal parent."

2. Opponents argue that the data the policy recommendation is based on are "limited and flawed" (3), that the issue is political not medical (4), and that it is not clear whether "gay people are capable of making lasting commitments" (5).

3. Critics' greatest fear is that "children raised by gays or lesbians will be homosexual themselves" (7). Birtha counters this by noting that heterosexual couples already raise gay children, so it is likely that some gay couples will as well.

4. Should the recommendation become law, Birtha feels that more children languishing in foster care would have adoptive parents available to them.

5. Birtha seems to imply that as gay people are allowed to be parents, they come to participate more in traditional values, but the point is not entirely clear. Few students are likely to agree immediately because "traditional values" has become a buzz word for "families headed by a father and mother."

PURPOSE AND AUDIENCE (p. 603)

1. Both writers are responding to the policy statement by the AAP. Adkins chooses to offer a refutation of the policy statement before stating his thesis. Birtha chooses to open by endorsing the policy statement, then goes on to deal with the opposition.

2. She seems to envision a range of readers. She acknowledges opposing viewpoints and attempts to counter them, but she does not seem to be writing solely to those who might oppose adoptions by gay couples because she does not go on the offensive.

3. One strategy Birtha uses to calm readers' fears is to carefully explain that the policy statement applies to children who already live in households headed by gay parents; such children's welfare can depend on the legal recognition of both as parents. For readers who might fear that children with two gay parents are more likely to become homosexual themselves, she makes the point that heterosexual parents already produce homosexual children. She also makes the point that it is possible for healthy children to grow up without both a mother and a father in the household.

4. This information might have added authority to Birtha's views, at least in some readers' eyes, and, in fact, she was identified as a "writer, adoptive parent, and adoption professional" in the brief biography that accompanied this op-ed piece.

STYLE AND STRUCTURE (p. 603)

1. Birtha opens by suggesting that a prestigious medical organization has "taken a giant step forward" on behalf of children. She casts the policy statement as a victory for children rather than for their gay parents. Students' opinions will vary as to the effectiveness of this opening.

2. She likely addresses opposing arguments early on because she realizes the AAP recommendations will be controversial.

3. It certainly does not seem necessary that Birtha name potential opponents of the policy specifically; she is referring to general trends of opposition. Being more specific about the sources of the studies she cites, however, might have served to lend credibility to their findings.

4. Her evidence includes the fact the recommendation was based on thirty-one studies spanning a twenty-year period and her explanation that the policy is directed at the well-being of children already growing up in households headed by same-sex parents "who are not about to gain a parent of the opposite sex." Students' opinions will differ as to the effectiveness of this evidence.

5. It is important for students to realize that the AAP's recommendation focuses on households in which one gay parent has given birth to or adopted a child; it suggests that the nonlegal gay parent should have the right to adopt the child jointly, largely for legal purposes. The distinction Birtha is making does make sense in terms of the AAP statement. At the same time, it may be seen as a bit disingenuous in terms of her hope that the recommendations eventually "apply to other adoptions by gay couples and singles" (9).

6. It is not really clear why she waits until the conclusion to provide this information, except perhaps because New Jersey's lead on the issue seems to go beyond the AAP's position and might on its face seem less acceptable to some readers.

7. Birtha makes transitions in paragraphs 3 through 7 by referring in each opening sentence to a different point of opposition. The lack of transitional expressions may trouble some students, but the essay is not difficult to follow.

VOCABULARY PROJECTS (p. 604)

2. See the answer to item 2 under *Comprehension*. Because Birtha is attempting, in a sense, to co-opt this buzz word for her own purposes, a more precise term would not have served her purposes.

COMBINING THE PATTERNS (p. 604)

Birtha uses cause and effect to show an ostensible relation between certain childhood and adolescent behaviors and being raised by gay or straight parents. She might have chosen to more directly compare and contrast these behaviors.

THEMATIC CONNECTIONS

Why Boys Don't Play with Dolls (p. 335): Katha Pollitt suggests that parents encourage their children to pursue activities traditional to their gender for fear that they might otherwise be gay. What does current research suggest about why people are gay?

The Men We Carry in Our Minds (p. 345): Scott Russell Sanders also focuses on gender roles and how hard it can be to escape them. Students might think about how homosexuals are often stereotyped as crossing gender norms (gay men are effeminate, gay women are masculine), while, in fact, a large number of homosexuals are not identifiable in this way.

DEBATE CASEBOOK: Does Media Violence Cause Societal Violence?

This casebook presents four different perspectives on the issue of violence in the media and the possible effects of such violence on society. You might begin by asking students how they respond to media violence. Do they enjoy violent movies, television shows, and video games? What are some particular examples that have been especially popular? How do they account for this popularity? Do they see different levels or kinds of violence—that is, are some depictions of violence more graphic than others? More believable? More gruesome? What especially memorable images of movie or television, or video violence can they recall?

Then you might ask specifically about Oliver Stone's *Natural Born Killers*, the subject of the first two essays in the casebook. Encourage students who have seen the film to describe the plot and the level of violence depicted. (You might also consider screening some of the film for your class—it's available on video—but you will probably want to do so fairly selectively. Or you might suggest that students who are interested rent the film to view for themselves.)

Finally, ask students to talk about whether their experiences suggest a link between violence in the media and violence in life. Do they have friends or family members who have been influenced directly by media images? Have they ever noticed young children act out in ways that could reflect their television viewing? Have they read any news reports or other stories that suggest such linkages?

The three essays that follow are summarized in the text's introduction to the casebook, p. 605.

Oliver Stone, *Memo to John Grisham: What's Next?—"A Movie Made Me Do It?"*

COMPREHENSION (p. 609)

1. He means that artists have historically reflected the concerns of human beings during the times in which they live. He sees *Natural Born Killers* as a reflection of the world in which we live today.
2. The participants in a witch hunt go after innocent victims, claiming that they are the cause of some evil in the world. Students may consider whether Stone goes too far here.
3. Stone suggests Grisham's *post hoc* reasoning in paragraphs 4–6, stating that many factors other than his film are responsible for the violent behavior of Sarah and Ben.
4. He says the film can move some audience members toward "a heightened sensitivity toward violence" (5). He also says that watching "15,000 hours of mostly violent television programming" (6) is more likely to have an effect than watching a single movie.
5. Stone's other causes include alcohol and the availability of firearms. He talks earlier about how damaged families can produce violent children. Students' opinions will differ as to the persuasiveness of Stone's reasoning.

PURPOSE AND AUDIENCE (p. 610)

1. Stone doesn't believe that movie violence is responsible for real-life violence. His scathing tone indicates he assumes that his audience will agree.
2. Students may differ about Stone's attitude toward his audience. He seems fairly dismissive of those who would disagree with him.
3. Stone's essay is a direct response to Grisham's, and his purpose is to prove Grisham wrong.

4. Stone's argument does not seem likely to win many converts. He concedes virtually nothing to the opposition and is openly hostile toward Grisham— and those who might agree with him.

STYLE AND STRUCTURE (p. 610)

1. Such an exaggerated claim always risks alienating some readers.
2. Stone refutes Grisham's major points in paragraphs 3–6. Students may or may not see his refutations as successful.
3. Actually, Stone only pretends to concede points to his opposition here. He admits his movie had an impact on audiences, but not the one his critics claim.
4. Stone's loaded language is not likely to appeal to those who strongly support the Second Amendment. He may not exactly be overstating his case by referring to "gun-toting crazies," but he is tarring with a broad brush.
5. Stone doesn't so much restate his position in the conclusion as make a strongly worded plea for artistic freedom. The attack on lawyers here isn't *ad hominem*, but one in paragraph 7 is ("only a lawyer in search of a client"). And in paragraph 8 he refers to Grisham's novels as "brainless"—a sterling example of *ad hominem* argument.

VOCABULARY PROJECTS (p. 610)

2. Stone's feelings come through especially strongly in paragraphs 2, 5, 8, and 9. Students might find his tone somewhat arrogant. Is Stone unwilling to see beyond his own feelings?

COMBINING THE PATTERNS (p. 611)

Cause-and-effect analysis is found in paragraphs 3, 5, 6, and 9. Cause and effect supports Stone's thesis by suggesting causes other than *Natural Born Killers* for the crimes committed by Sarah and Ben and by claiming that "silencing artists" will lead to a "human hell" (9).

THEMATIC CONNECTIONS

Thirty-Eight Who Saw Murder Didn't Call the Police (p. 101): In a sense, Martin Gansberg writes of a less violent time, more than thirty years ago, when none of Kitty Genovese's neighbors did anything to help as she was being brutally murdered outside on the street. Are we more or less callous toward violence today? In a more violent society, are people more or less likely to intercede when they encounter a crime in progress?

Who Killed Benny Paret? (p. 321): Norman Cousins suggests that boxing is violent because those who watch want it that way. Is the same true of movies and television?

Burdens (p. 509): The link here is less one of subject matter than of tone and intent. Both Stone and John Kenneth Galbraith use biting sarcasm to lambaste what they see as self-righteous, self-serving, and wrong-headed propaganda. Students might analyze both essays to consider how effective such a style of argumentation can be.

Michael Zimecki, *Violent Films Cry "Fire" in Crowded Theaters*

COMPREHENSION (p. 615)

1. The courts have held that freedom of expression outweighs the cost to society of receiving such "odious" images.
2. He means that there is a link between what goes on in life and what goes on in movies. He then points out several examples of movie-inspired violence: a boy who was killed attempting to duplicate a scene in the movie *The Program,* and a group of boys who raped a nine-year-old girl with a bottle after seeing a similar rape in a television film.
3. As products, movies are meant to be seen, so their producers can't be held responsible just because audiences go to see them. The concept of incitement is legally limited to speech that results—or could result—in immediate action; action that takes place outside a theater after a movie is over is too far removed in time to be considered incited action.
4. Certain films glorify violence—and thus "advocate violence implicitly, if not explicitly" (18). This, for Zimecki, is tantamount to incitement.
5. He means that the courts have not recognized the effects of violence that "can fester for years" (20) and that they have not recognized the cause-and-effect relationship between media violence and real-life violence.

PURPOSE AND AUDIENCE (p. 616)

1. Zimecki states his thesis at the end of paragraph 22. One reason he waits so long is that he needs to introduce, clarify, and refine the concept of incitement.
2. The essay is aimed primarily at lawyers, as the many legal citations suggest. But Zimecki seems to be writing to his audience more as general readers, concerned about media violence, than as experts concerned with the fine points of the law.
3. His purpose is to contribute to the debate over how to curb violence in the media by redefining the concept of incitement so that it can apply to movies and television programs.

STYLE AND STRUCTURE (p. 616)

1. The quotation sets up the cause-and-effect relationship between images and actions that is the basis for his argument. He might have opened by dramatically recounting the torching of the New York City subway clerk, but this strategy would have been less appropriate for an audience of lawyers.
2. For a more general publication, Zimecki would need to get rid of—or simply summarize—most of the legal citations, revise his more specialized language, and explain more graphically why the courts should see that violent media images incite real-life violence.
3. This concession does seem to undercut his case, although he suggests that the relationship between the movie and the crime may still be established. But, particularly in writing for a legal publication, he has to admit contrary evidence.
4. His primary evidence is the examples in paragraphs 8–10, which suggest a direct link between depictions of violence in the media and violence in real life.

5. Students may differ over whether the concluding cliché is effective. Another possible conclusion would be to return to the idea of shouting "fire" in a crowded theater.

VOCABULARY PROJECTS (p. 616)

2. *Incitement* means "the act of spurring others to action." In legal parlance, it generally refers to "spurring others to violent action or action that will result in 'imminent harm'" but not to "abstract" action at some unspecified time in the future.

COMBINING THE PATTERNS (p. 617)

The analogy of shouting "fire" in a crowded theater has been legally established as an act of incitement. Zimecki wants to suggest that movies incite violent action in much the same way. He uses cause and effect elsewhere, so it is not necessary here.

THEMATIC CONNECTIONS

Thirty-Eight Who Saw Murder Didn't Call the Police (p. 101): See *Thematic Connections,* "Memo to John Grisham: What's Next?—'A Movie Made Me Do It?'" p. 153 of this manual.

How the Lawyers Stole Winter (p. 402): Christopher Daly decries the fact that the threat of lawsuits has put even the simple pleasure of ice skating on public property off-limits in many communities. Oliver Stone's essay also suggests that lawyers like John Grisham and Michael Zimecki, who wish to "stifle artistic expression," pose a threat to personal freedom. Do students agree that threats of such lawsuits are ultimately not to society's benefit?

The Wife-Beater (p. 521): Gayle Rosenwald Smith argues here that even a seemingly minor aspect of popular culture can contribute to the potential for violence within society. The fact that young people today casually refer to a popular style of T-shirt as a "wife-beater," she claims, can lead to an atmosphere in which violence against women is seen as acceptable.

Maggie Cutler, *Whodunit—The Media?*

COMPREHENSION (p. 622)

1. Cutler feels that any discussion of the problem of media violence is difficult because the issues are so complex that "any simple statement on the subject obscures the complexity of the facts, half-facts and 'results-suggest' findings of the last forty years" (2) and because "the phenomenon may be too complex to study conclusively" (3).
2. The issue is whether violence in the media encourages real-life violence among young people (a cause-and-effect relationship) or whether children prone to violence—temperamentally or through parental modeling—are simply more readily drawn to violent representations in the media (a correlation, but not necessarily cause and effect). Cutler believes that no studies can actually resolve this conflict because they "can't exactly show exactly how and why" some children are more violent than others.

3. Cutler's point is that it is difficult to define media violence in terms of how children perceive it. Children "process content differently" so that while some children perceive media images more critically, recognizing their unreality, other children may not have such critical abilities and see media violence as "real."

4. Rather than focusing on reducing exposure to media violence, the Stanford researchers focused on reducing exposure to media more generally; they found that the more self-control children exerted over their own use of media, the less they resorted to verbal and physical aggression. Cutler finds their approach quite effective, centered as it is on the idea that real-life experiences have greater influence on children than do mediated experiences.

5. Cutler's proposal is that, rather than attempting to regulate media violence, lawmakers should "push to reform prison policies, provide supervised after-school activities for teens, and get early, comprehensive help to high-risk children" (14).

PURPOSE AND AUDIENCE (p. 622)

1. Students' opinions may differ, but certainly there is more than a hint of sarcasm in Cutler's tone, particularly when she mocks the easy correlations and quick fixes for media violence suggested by political leaders (1–3, 10, 14). Elsewhere, she seems more concerned that the complexities of the issue be taken seriously.

2. Cutler uses transitional expressions such as "Like most complex issues" (2), "But" (3), "in other words" (4), "like Orrin Hatch's committee" (6), "Perhaps" (8), "At first blush" (10), "Although" (12), and "Without belittling the importance of media research" (14). In other cases, transitions are more subtle, as in the final sentence of paragraph 6, which provides the transition to paragraph 7.

3. Students' opinions may differ here. She might have done more to establish her own credentials as a media critic.

4. Cutler reveals her biases almost immediately in paragraph 2, where she refers to the Parents Television Council as "right-wing." She is clearly writing from a perspective that is opposed to censorship.

STYLE AND STRUCTURE (p. 622)

1. As mentioned under the answer to item 1 under *Purpose and Audience,* there is a kind of shift in Cutler's tone here. Students might consider how Cutler envisions her readers so that, for her, such an opening is appropriate.

2. Cutler wants to establish that many ambiguities have resulted from studies of media violence, so legislating reductions in media violence is no sure way to reduce violent behavior. This leads to her real argument—that there are better, more realistic ways to reduce youth violence.

3. This excerpt from paragraph 7 does not clearly establish that "for the kids most at risk, reducing representational violence is obviously no cure." However, earlier in the paragraph, Cutler's summary of the APA report suggests exactly this.

4. Essentially, Cutler's essay is one long refutation of the prevailing idea that regulating violence in the media will have much impact on actually reducing youth violence. Students will probably feel that she covers all the bases even if she is not entirely convincing. That is, one can ask: Why not regulate media violence *and* institute programs to help at-risk children?

5. As suggested in the answer to item 4, she feels the need to refute the prevailing idea before suggesting alternatives. This is, for the most part, an effective strategy, particularly since she hints at her argument at the end of paragraph 7.

VOCABULARY PROJECTS (p. 623)

2. Students should see that the informal, even colloquial, language here is appropriate for the fairly hip, liberal audience Cutler envisions. She is a good example of a writer who is not trying to persuade those who oppose her, but rather those who might have mixed feelings about the issue.

COMBINING THE PATTERNS (p. 624)

Cutler is actually *redefining* the term "media violence" here, suggesting that, even for child audiences, the concept is more complex than readers often credit it with being. If children do not all process media violence the same way, then simply regulating it is not the primary issue.

THEMATIC CONNECTIONS

Just Walk On By (p. 223): It has been suggested that, in addition to provoking violence, media violence tends to create an exaggerated sense in viewers of how likely they are to be a victim of violence or crime. After reading Brent Staples's essay, students might consider the extent to which media portrayals of various ethnic groups as criminals can contribute to larger perceptions about those groups.

Samuel (p. 239): Grace Paley's short story relates an event in which misguided adults attempt to protect children from their dangerous behavior, with tragic results for one of the children. Cutler suggests that, even at their best intentioned, adults who focus on regulating media violence are short-changing children because they are diverting attention from real solutions.

Who Killed Benny Paret? (p. 321): Cutler makes a distinction between media violence which isn't real and that which is, arguing that the latter is far worse for children. How might she respond to the kind of "real-life" media violence that led to boxer Benny Paret's death and to the injury and death of other boxers?

A Peaceful Woman Explains Why She Carries a Gun (p. 345): Students might use Linda Hasselstrom's essay as a jumping-off point for doing some research about crime in the United States. Who is most likely to be a perpetrator of violent crime, and who is most likely to be a victim? Do statistics change according to the demographics of different areas? Do media images of violence correspond to the actual numbers? What does all this suggest about reducing violent crime?

DEBATE CASEBOOK: Should African Americans Receive Reparations for Slavery?

Before they begin with the essays in this casebook, students should carefully read both the casebook introduction and the headnotes for each essay; these provide crucial background information most students will need in order to approach the readings in an informed manner. As you begin discussion of the essays, make sure that students understand the terms of reparations for slavery as proposed by Charles Ogletree Jr. and Manning Marable. Many people—including many African Americans—mistakenly believe that reparations would be paid to individuals or individual families somewhat in the manner of a class action suit. In fact, serious proponents of reparations propose placing reparations moneys in a fund supporting efforts to provide African Americans who continue to be disenfranchised with educational and other opportunities that would bring them into the mainstream. In addition, students should recognize that one goal of reparations litigation is to raise public awareness about how slavery benefited many businesses and other institutions that continue to be in operation today; another is to raise public awareness about the extent to which blacks still lag statistically behind whites according to many socioeconomic measures.

Your main challenge in guiding discussion of the essays in the casebook will likely be steering students away from knee-jerk responses, whether of the "my-family-never-had-slaves" or of the "all-whites-are-racist" variety. The question of social and economic justice for African Americans continues to be a complex issue that can all too easily be brushed aside by whites as somehow "all behind us" when it is clear that the gains of the Civil Rights movement have not benefited all blacks equally. The reparations movement, whether one feels it is misguided or not, should be seen as a means of opening a debate over questions of why so many African Americans have not been able to seize the opportunities white critics claim are open to them.

Charles J. Ogletree Jr., *Litigating the Legacy of Slavery*

COMPREHENSION (p. 627)

1. The goal of the suit is to bring to light the extent to which the government and private institutions benefited historically from slavery, "to bring American society to a new reckoning with how our past affects the current conditions of African-Americans," and to provide financial benefits to those who still suffer the legacy of slavery and its aftermath.
2. Naming the government is important because "public officials guaranteed the viability of slavery and the segregation that followed it" (4). It will also "generate a public debate on slavery and the role its legacy continues to play in our society" (8).
3. According to Ogletree, the legacy of slavery is responsible for "well-documented racial disparities in access to education, health care, housing, insurance, employment, and other social goods" (13).
4. Litigation will provide the opportunity to "use expert witnesses and conduct extensive discovery [part of the pretrial litigation process during which each party requests relevant information and documents from the other side in an attempt to "discover" pertinent facts], to get facts and documentation" (8).
5. Ogletree acknowledges that not all African Americans have suffered equally as a result of the legacy of slavery. Therefore, reparations must focus on the "bottom-stuck . . . who have not substantially benefited from integration or affirmative action" (13).

PURPOSE AND AUDIENCE (p. 629)

1. Basically, Ogletree desires to establish for readers the motivations behind and justifications for the recently filed reparations litigation. Ogletree hopes to establish good will.
2. Most readers would probably describe the tone here as calm and confident. Those who feel otherwise would need to justify their claim.
3. Noting that he himself is cochair of The Reparations Coordinating Committee certainly puts Ogletree in the thick of the debate and establishes his credentials to explain what underlies the litigation.
4. Although his thesis is implied throughout, it is perhaps most clearly summarized in the final sentence. This summary, implying healing rather than division, provides a strong conclusion.

STYLE AND STRUCTURE (p. 630)

1. The class action suit is the subject of his essay, so beginning by introducing it is an effective strategy; he can't be certain that his readers are familiar.
2. The examples—particularly the fact that a United Nations conference has declared slavery "a crime against humanity"—certainly help to make Ogletree's case that the issue has international dimensions that may affect the litigation in the United States.
3. His admission of this difference can be seen as strengthening his case, both because it deals immediately with a potential objection and because he goes on to suggest potential parallels that can strengthen the case for slavery reparations.
4. The statement is not exactly self-evident, but it is difficult to refute; objectors would be hard pressed to point to evidence of a "full and deep conversation on slavery and its legacy," at least in the public forum Ogletree is talking about. It would be just as difficult for Ogletree to present evidence that such a conversation had *not* taken place. He assumes most readers of good will will concede this point.
5. Students' opinions may vary as to whether Ogletree should have refuted opposing arguments. His attitude seems to be that the lawsuit has been filed despite any objections to the contrary. Matters of debate will take place during what he expects to be an extended hearing process.

VOCABULARY PROJECTS (p. 630)

2. *Litigation* is literally "the act or process of engaging in legal action," although among those who feel the U.S. courts are awash in frivolous lawsuits, it has begun to have somewhat negative connotations. Students' responses will vary, but they should see that Ogletree has little choice but to use the word because it best sums up what he means.

COMBINING THE PATTERNS (p. 631)

Because of the difference in spelling, it may not be immediately obvious that the root of "reparations" is "to repair," and so his definition may come as something of a surprise. Ogletree might have called more directly for support of the reparations lawsuit, but the definition serves to do so with some subtlety.

THEMATIC CONNECTIONS

Indian Education (p. 126): An interesting topic for research might be the idea of economic reparations for Native Americans, who have clearly suffered as a result of treaties that have proved disadvantageous. Have such reparations been proposed, and how does the concept of such reparations differ from that of reparations for the descendents of slaves?

My First Conk (p. 260): This excerpt from Malcolm X's autobiography offers some insight into the lives of African Americans in white-dominated America prior to the most important gains of the Civil Rights movement.

How the Lawyers Stole Winter (p. 402): In this essay, Christopher Daly makes a strong case against litigation run amok in contemporary society. Reading it in conjunction with this debate casebook might raise interesting questions of personal responsibility and the culture of "victimhood."

Juan Williams, *Slavery Isn't the Issue*

COMPREHENSION (p. 635)

1. Williams implies that lawyers for the reparations movement have determined that they are unlikely to win a case against the government and that private institutions and corporations might be more willing to settle out of court.

2. He feels that, if successful, the movement will result in "racial resentment" (3), a lower opinion of the abilities of African Americans (4), and loss of any existing support for affirmative action (5) and social policies to help poor blacks (6).

3. Williams claims that those who support the reparations movement are motivated by the "bonanza payday" for the lawyers involved and by misconceptions about what reparations would involve (8). Moreover, the movement can be seen "as an effort by the rising black middle class to take control of the massive budgets dedicated to social-welfare policy" (12).

4. Williams finds the continuing impact of slavery a "stretch" because of the record levels of income and educational opportunity now enjoyed by African Americans.

5. If a reparations treasury were established, it would be controlled by powerful black interests so that "[w]hat is now national policy for dealing with black poverty would become a matter of a black nationalist agenda."

6. He argues that time would be better spent improving educational opportunities for minority children.

PURPOSE AND AUDIENCE (p. 635)

1. Essentially, Williams states his thesis in the two sentences of his final paragraph: "Reparations . . . contradict the moral authority of black Americans' claim to equal rights. . . . Pushing them through would only hurt race relations . . ."

2. Writing as an African American, Williams wants to dissuade both blacks and whites from supporting the reparations movement. Students' opinions will vary as to whether he succeeds.

3. Students may feel that language such as "twisted into a strange scheme" (1), "misguided adventure in racial politics" (3), "bonanza payday for some of the lawyers" (8), "greed aside" (9), "obscene . . . profiting from the blood money" (13), "self-indulgent hysteria by people intoxicated by their rising power" (14), and "dangerous, even evil" (15) is hardly moderate. But, for us, the tone works in its suggestion of a stance of reasonably motivated righteous indignation.

4. Williams does not attempt to be fair to those spearheading the reparations movement, brushing them all with one stroke as having less than altruistic motives. He does, however, attempt to fairly assess the needs of poor blacks in paragraphs 5 and 14 and argue that reparations are not the solution to these problems.

STYLE AND STRUCTURE (p. 635)

1. Williams' fairy tale reference to a past unfulfilled promise suggests that the reparations movement is a fairy tale promise as well.

2. In addition to the points detailed in the answer to item 2 under *Comprehension*, he makes the points that the movement seems motivated by greed, that the connection between the legacy of slavery and today's African Americans is a "stretch," and that, if successful, the movement would result in racial separation. Students may see that he offers little hard evidence to support these points other than the fact that reparations have been rejected in the past (2), the statistic that 70 percent of whites oppose even an apology for slavery (6), and the fact that black Americans today are better off than ever (11). In particular, he offers no evidence to support his claim about the motives of leaders of the reparations movement. Otherwise, it would be hard to provide hard evidence because so much of his argument is based on speculation about the negative results of reparations.

3. The question provides a transition into his discussion of the motivations of reparations leaders.

4. Williams concedes here that the historical horrors of slavery should not be forgotten but should continue as the subject of an ongoing public discussion. He goes on to suggest that the need for such public forums is being twisted into claims that African Americans still suffer from the legacy of slavery. This is a point he goes on to try to refute.

5. There is overstatement throughout, as suggested in the answer to item 3 under *Purpose and Audience*. Students' reactions here will probably differ.

6. In his next-to-final paragraph, Williams returns to an implication made in his opening: The fairy tale of reparations is a "fantasy." He then again indicts the leaders of the reparations movement, offers an alternative to the push for reparations, and concludes by summarizing his thesis. The conclusion seems effective for his purposes.

VOCABULARY PROJECTS (p. 636)

2. Such adjectives include *strange* (1), *faltering* (2), *misguided* (3), *devastating* (7), *obscene* (13), *self-indulgent* (14), *intoxicated* (14), *dangerous* (15), and *evil* (15). There is little doubt as to his antipathy toward the movement and its leaders.

3. A *Trojan Horse* is an apparent gift that, in fact, will have dire consequences. (During the mythic Trojan War, the Greeks apparently surrendered, sailing

away from Troy, but left behind a large wooden horse in which was hidden a contingent of Greek soldiers. The Trojans were persuaded to take the horse within the walls of the city. Later that night the concealed soldiers attacked and their allies returned, leading to the Greeks' possession of Troy.) For Williams, reparations are also an apparent gift with potentially dire consequences.

COMBINING THE PATTERNS (p. 636)

In paragraphs 3 through 5, Williams speculates about the negative results that reparations would ultimately have on African Americans in the United States. It is these negative results that lead him to call on readers to reject reparations.

THEMATIC CONNECTIONS

The "Black Table" Is Still There (p. 340): Lawrence Otis Graham's essay suggests that "racial separatism," as Williams terms it, is an endemic part of American culture that has changed little with the passage of time. Is this simply a case of people being most comfortable with their "own kind," as Graham suggests, or are the causes more complex?

Two Ways to Belong in America (p. 397): One of Williams's arguments against reparations is that they will cause African Americans to be "demeaned as less able than any Mexican immigrant or Bosnian refugee." What does Bharati Mukherjee's essay suggest about the self-image of immigrants to the United States? Might this self-image differ in any way from that of poor African Americans?

Burdens (p. 509): Would John Kenneth Galbraith define reparations for the descendents of slaves as a "burden"? Why has aid to the underprivileged come to be viewed so negatively? Where might Williams stand on this issue?

Manning Marable, *An Idea Whose Time Has Come*

COMPREHENSION (p. 636)

1. Structural racism, according to Marable, is the deeply patterned social and economic racial inequality that results from the cumulative effects of past racial injustice, beginning with slavery. It is "the fundamental problem of democracy in the twenty-first century" because "these structural barriers . . . deny democratic rights and opportunities to millions" of African Americans.
2. These two struggles were the era of Reconstruction following the Civil War and the era of the Civil Rights movement. The first was not successful but rather a "dream deferred," and while the second achieved some notable successes, according to Marable many black Americans remain disadvantaged.
3. On a basic level, reparations could help close "the socioeconomic gaps between blacks and whites" (11); more broadly, demands for reparations would help "highlight the contemporary reality of 'racial deficits' of all kinds, the unequal conditions that impact blacks regardless of class" (7).
4. Marable feels whites bear this responsibility because the "disproportionate wealth that most whites enjoy today was first constructed from centuries of unpaid black labor" (6).

5. Marable believes that reparations should take the form of a trust fund with money "targeted specifically toward poor, disadvantaged communities with the greatest need, not to individuals." He does not say so specifically, but he implies that whites would benefit because blacks would have more money to spend and provide less of a drain on the health care system.

6. He meant that integration in itself was not enough to make up for African Americans' long history of racial inequality. Malcolm X's next sentence ("We are here to collect back wages.") could be a statement of Marable's thesis.

PURPOSE AND AUDIENCE (p. 639)

1. It is unlikely that Marable expects readers to agree with him immediately. For example, he offers extensive evidence to show readers that structural racism continues to put black Americans at a disadvantage (7–9).

2. He states his thesis in the first sentence of his final paragraph. He might have stated his thesis at the end of his second paragraph, but instead he asks a question here that leads to his ultimate thesis.

3. Marable works to create a sense of being fair when he compiles statistical evidence of black disadvantage in paragraphs 7 through 9 and when he acknowledges that "[w]hite Americans today aren't guilty of carrying out slavery and segregation" (10). Students' opinions will likely differ as to how successful he is.

STYLE AND STRUCTURE (p. 630)

1. Opening by writing about his great-grandfather allows Marable to establish a direct connection between his own life and the roots of slavery, a connection that may surprise white readers. Students will probably have differing ideas about possible alternative openings.

2. Marable's primary evidence is the statistics he cites to support the claim that a "pattern of white privilege and black inequality continues today" (6). Some students may argue that statistics do not tell the whole story, that many black families actually are better off than the average white family. Marable might have provided evidence to show that reparations could truly make a difference in people's lives.

3. Students' responses may vary, but Marable could hardly have avoided making this concession because it is so often used as an argument against reparations.

4. The argument is primarily inductive, based on evidence that structural racism exists and that it creates socioeconomic problems for blacks that reparations could begin to alleviate.

5. Referring to a Second and Third Reconstruction allows Marable to make the point that the First Reconstruction, when black Americans should have been given an equal footing with whites, was a failure that led to another century of Jim Crow segregation. His implication is that the business of "reconstruction" can only be finished when long overdue reparations are paid for slavery. Some students may see this as misleading because they will not accept the idea that the roots of slavery still affect black Americans' lives.

6. Students' opinions will vary as to the effectiveness of the essay's conclusion. From one perspective, reparations will not end racism. From another perspective, slavery has long been abolished, so the chapter is already closed.

2. The term is probably defined adequately for those who would agree that structural racism exists but not perhaps so effectively for those who need convincing. Marable certainly uses the term for its academic weight.

COMBINING THE PATTERNS (p. 641)

The paragraph makes the point that unpaid black labor enriched white people and their institutions. This point lies at the heart of Marable's argument that contemporary African Americans deserve some compensation for their ancestors' labor.

THEMATIC CONNECTIONS

Finishing School (p. 89): This excerpt from Maya Angelou's autobiography suggests the extent to which the legacy of slavery continued to dominate race relations and socioeconomic conditions in the South long after slavery had been abolished. Mrs. Cullinen's wealth was clearly inherited from parents who owned slaves. The story Angelou tells provides a vivid example of structural racism.

Shooting an Elephant (p. 117): Imperialism, as George Orwell describes it here, was also a means of economic exploitation by white interests. In paragraph 7, Orwell writes that "when the white man turns tyrant it is his own freedom that he destroys." Can this statement be applied to slaveholders and their descendents who continued to exploit African Americans through the threat of force?

Indian Education (p. 126): See "Indian Education" under *Thematic Connections*, "Litigating the Legacy of Slavery," page 160 of this manual.

Linda Chavez, *Demands for Reparations*

COMPREHENSION (p. 644)

1. According to Chavez, Robinson is not to be dismissed lightly because of his previous accomplishments, most notably his work to end apartheid in South Africa.
2. The United States has long allowed victims of some wrong and their heirs to sue for monetary compensation through the court system, and Japanese Americans were compensated by the government for their forced internment during the Second World War. The difference with slave reparations, says Chavez, is that the ills of slavery occurred so long ago.
3. She thinks Robinson's ideas will result in "racial hatred, not healing."
4. Chavez feels the time for reparations has long since passed because it is "impossible to know generations later what a particular loss or gain for an individual might mean for his ancestors" (5).
5. To remember a "litany of injustices, slights, and wrongs" is to perpetuate "wars, feuds, and racial animosity" as we see in parts of the world where "such memories are constantly reinforced and renewed."
6. Chavez believes that the proper course is to "recommit ourselves to the simple goal of treating all men as equals, and affording every American equal opportunity to achieve what he or she can" (9).

PURPOSE AND AUDIENCE (p. 644)

1. Chavez summarizes Robinson's argument, which suggests that she doesn't expect readers to be familiar with his book. Students might consider whether it would have made a difference had Chavez included some of the information about Robinson's book that appears in the headnote for this reading.
2. Chavez's thesis is that it is too late now for slavery reparations to be made consistently or fairly. She comes closest to stating it directly at the end of paragraph 8, probably waiting until this late point in order to present her arguments against reparations.
3. Her attack is never really personal, although she does suggest in paragraph 8 that Robinson is blind to the feelings of resentment his words can engender.

STYLE AND STRUCTURE (p. 644)

1. Chavez answers her opening question at the end of paragraph 8, even specifically using the word "no."
2. She focuses on questioning the feasibility of fairly compensating the descendents of slaves with reparations so many years later and on her belief that dwelling on past injustices leads to resentment among the races rather than healing. Students' thoughts will differ as to how effectively she refutes Robinson's ideas. Essentially, Chavez simply asserts her opinions as stronger than Robinson's.
3. Chavez provides almost no real evidence here, relying instead on stating ideas that she feels her readers will find self-evident once they have been presented. More evidence to suggest the difficulties of determining the amount of reparations, perhaps in the form of testimony from attorneys or economists, might have been included.
4. Chavez concedes that under slavery, blacks suffered more grievously than any other Americans ever had (4) and that Robinson's goal is less a monetary one than the achievement of "a kind of national catharsis over slavery" (5). These seem to be effective concessions because they are based on fact.
5. The question that opens paragraph 8 is a rhetorical question that Chavez feels no need to answer. Here Chavez makes her case that it is better to forget the injustices of the past and work for greater harmony in the present.
6. Students' opinions may vary as to the effectiveness of Chavez's conclusion. Some might feel she should have brought up the idea of "forty acres and a mule" earlier rather than introducing it at this late date. A possible alternative conclusion might have returned to Robinson and how she might hope he would respond.

VOCABULARY PROJECTS (p. 645)

2. The repetition seems effective rhetorically, particularly because of the initial reference to "short memories." It would be difficult to come up with any substitute synonyms.

COMBINING THE PATTERNS (p. 645)

Chavez contrasts Robinson's goal of "exorcism" with what she sees as an insistence upon assigning blame that can only enflame racial resentment. In the rest of her essay, she goes on to argue that blacks need to get over their anger about the evils of slavery and that we should all put aside our differences and work for common goals.

THEMATIC CONNECTIONS

The Human Cost of an Illiterate Society (p. 229): Access to the quality of education that promotes true literacy skills is fundamental to "affording every American equal opportunity to achieve what he or she can." This is, in fact, one of the goals for reparations that Robinson talks about in his book (as mentioned in the headnote) although Chavez does not acknowledge this goal. What are some other things our government and our society as whole can do to promote quality education for all Americans?

Five Ways to Kill a Man (p. 487): It can be argued that the legacy of slavery and racism in the United States has had a deadening effect on the spirits of its most disenfranchised African-American citizens, that they have been so alienated from the mainstream that only drastic measures can save them. In light of this, how might reparations work? If not reparations, then what?

Letter from Birmingham Jail (p. 570): Martin Luther King's famous letter defending the actions taken during the Civil Rights movement provides important background information about racism and its effects that could be read usefully with any essay in this casebook.

13: COMBINING THE PATTERNS

In this section are two essays—one student, one professional—that we have annotated to indicate each writer's use of multiple patterns, along with two further unannotated professional essays. You may not wish to wait until you have completed the chapter on argumentation to discuss these essays. In fact, a good time to have students look at the two annotated essays might be prior to Chapter 8 or Chapter 9. At that point it can be useful for students to recognize that although their papers may be structured primarily as cause-and-effect or comparison-and-contrast essays, for example, they may well include passages of narration, description, exemplification, and process.

Another approach would be to look at the student essay in conjunction with Chapter 4. Michael Huu Truong's "The Park" is primarily a narrative essay, and you might use it early in the course to point out the interplay in most writing of the various patterns to be practiced in subsequent chapters. Then, in conjunction with Chapter 11, you could repeat this point by having students look at Lars Eighner's "On Dumpster Diving"—an essay of definition that, like many extended definitions, uses virtually every technique in the writer's repertoire of development strategies. Similarly, Richard Rodriguez's "Strange Tools" could be read as an example of narration, Alice Walker's "In Search of Our Mothers' Gardens" could be read in conjunction with the other cause-and-effect essays in the text, and Jonathan Swift's "A Modest Proposal" could be read as a special form of argumentation. Alternatively, you might introduce these two essays independently at the end of the course, as examples of the complex purposes to which writing can be put.

Lars Eighner, *On Dumpster Diving*

Students are bound to find much to fascinate, appall, and stimulate discussion in Eighner's guide to living on the street out of garbage cans and Dumpsters. Writing with rueful good humor, an eye for telling detail, and an engagingly personal style, Eighner does more to suggest the day-to-day reality of homelessness than would any number of documentaries or clinical studies.

He begins with his situation and his terminology, which lead him to his thesis. Then he looks at the theory, technique, and dangers (mainly dysentery) of scavenging through garbage for food. (If your campus is a residential one, students might be especially interested in Eighner's description of why college students are among his best sources.) Then he turns to the "predictable series of stages a person goes through in learning to scavenge" (31). He next considers the collection of objects and why he hates people who scrounge for cans to turn in for cash. He explains why he has reservations about going through individual garbage cans, which leads him to think about the personal lives of those whose garbage he sifts through. He also explains the animal dangers—vermin, cats, fire ants—as well as why it is best to lower oneself into a Dumpster. He concludes by noting the two "rather deep lessons" (63) he has learned from scavenging.

It will probably be easy to get students talking about Eighner and his essay, but as part of your discussion, be sure to have students think about his intended purpose and audience. Does he really expect readers to follow his directions and advice? Or does he want to affect his audience in a different way?

COMPREHENSION (p. 673)

1. *Dumpster diving* might be defined as "a systematic method of scouring refuse containers for items useful for living on little or no money."
2. Fruits and vegetables may be discarded for minor imperfections; pizzas may end up in a pizzeria's Dumpster because they were ordered as a prank or incorrectly made: college students often throw away food when they are going on a break ("through carelessness, ignorance, or wastefulness" [22]).
3. He avoids "game, poultry, pork, and egg-based foods" (28) and "home leftovers" (29), as well as anything that looks or smells obviously bad.
4. Obvious drawbacks include the threat of dysentery, dealing with the fire ants, and the lack of medical care and storage space. Implied drawbacks include the nastiness of rooting through garbage and the hunger that could result from several days without a successful "dive."
5. The stages of learning to scavenge are (a) scavenging at first with a sense of disgust and loathing; (b) realizing that a lot of good, usable stuff is discarded and therefore taking pleasure in scavenging; (c) becoming obsessed with scavenging to the point of trying to acquire everything one finds.
6. He also scavenges for collectible items (pocket calculators and the like), personal needs (like warm bedding), and essential drugs (like antibiotics) because he has no access to health care.
7. Can scroungers, who are usually addicts and winos, "tend to tear up the Dumpsters, mixing the contents and littering the area" (44), and Eighner is contemptuous of them because they pass up many useful items.

8. He has learned "to take what you can use and let the rest go by" (63) and that material being is transient: "mental things are longer lived than other material things" (64).

PURPOSE AND AUDIENCE (p. 673)

1. He apparently also wants to encourage some compassion in his audience for those like himself, living on the fringe. And in his final paragraphs, he suggests an even larger purpose: to let his audience see that material things are transient.
2. Students may respond in a variety of ways to the essay—feeling everything from real sympathy to outright contempt. Try to get them to explore the reasons for their different responses.
3. There may be many reasons to explain why Eighner does not provide background information about himself. For one thing, not doing so makes him essentially anonymous—like the homeless people readers actually encounter on the streets. Also, the facts of his earlier life may not be particularly interesting—or flattering. Many students, however, are likely to think he could have explained in more detail why he ended up as he did.
4. His purpose in including such detail is probably twofold: he wants to provide an in-depth view of a subject most readers know nothing about, and he wants to suggest that homelessness is fraught with peril and difficulty.
5. His telling about the stages of scavenging is a way of helping readers imagine themselves in his place (everyone can imagine being "filled with disgust and self-loathing" [32]), and his scruples about going through individual cans is something readers can share. In addition, when he describes the process of going through a Dumpster, he does so in a way that puts his readers directly on the scene.
6. The last line is calculated to suggest that even in his distressed state he has reached a level of inner understanding through Dumpster diving that makes him better off than the "rat-race millions" (67).

STYLE AND STRUCTURE (p. 673)

1. He describes the source of the term *Dumpster* and offers alternatives to the phrase *Dumpster diving*. These opening definitions seem appropriate to establish the subject and Eighner's tone of clarity and preciseness.
2. The one-sentence paragraphs are 2, 7, 41, and the final paragraph. The first and last are for dramatic effect; the middle two each introduce a new section of discussion and might be combined with the following paragraph.
3. The present tense adds a greater sense of immediacy than the past tense would allow.
4. Other paragraphs of lists include 14–16, 24–25, 28, 38, 40, 53, and 55. As mentioned earlier, Eighner's goal seems to be to establish a very precise, even fastidious, tone; the careful listing helps accomplish this goal.

VOCABULARY PROJECTS (p. 674)

2. *Scrounging* seems less purposeful than *scavenging* (hence, his use of the term when he's trying "to be obscure"), and *foraging,* as he suggests, has come to be associated with finding food in the wilderness. *Diving,* he says, is too cute and not quite accurate in his case. So he prefers *scavenging.*

COMBINING THE PATTERNS (p. 675)

Students will have different responses here, but certainly the passages of exemplification, cause and effect, and process are particularly instructive.

THEMATIC CONNECTIONS

The Human Cost of an Illiterate Society **(p. 229):** As Jonathan Kozol's essay suggests, illiteracy and poverty often go hand in hand. Eighner, however, is clearly highly literate. What do students make of this seeming contradiction in his life? Is it easier to sympathize with those in our society who can't read and write than with someone in Eighner's situation who has obviously mastered these skills? (Kozol, by the way, has also written extensively about homelessness. Students interested in this subject might look at some of the other books mentioned in the headnote to his essay.)

Burdens **(p. 509):** John Kenneth Galbraith writes about how governmental aid to the poor in the United States has come to be regarded as a "burden," while government spending that aids the middle-class and the wealthy is not seen in this way. Eighner's description of his down-and-out existence suggests how little aid is actually available to the poor. Should welfare be available to people like Eighner? Students might research current policies concerning welfare recipients in their community, particularly "welfare-to-work" programs.

The Untouchable **(p. 498):** In this essay student Ajoy Mahtab defines the lowest level of the Indian caste system, "human beings treated worse than dogs and shunned far more than lepers." To what extent are the homeless in the United States the "untouchables" of our society? Based on Eighner's essay, how fair do students find the attitudes toward the homeless?

The Declaration of Independence **(p. 557):** The United States is founded on the notion that "all men are created equal, that they are endowed by their Creator with certain unalienable rights, that among these are life, liberty and the pursuit of happiness." What does *equality* mean in this context? Using "On Dumpster Diving" and "Burdens" as a starting point, students might consider issues of class, privilege, and power in the United States in terms of the ideals on which the country is based.

Jonathan Swift, *A Modest Proposal*

Swift's brilliant, scathingly ironic attack on the devastating policies of the British ruling class toward an impoverished Irish peasantry is one of the classics of English prose. It will also be a challenging essay for most first-year students. Not only is the complex eighteenth-century rhetoric unfamiliar, but the essay also includes many historical references that will be difficult for students, even with footnotes. In addition, students often have trouble recognizing that Swift is adopting a persona and some may take his horrifying proposal at face value. Unless you already know the essay well and have an affinity for explaining its complexities in terms of both language and tone, you probably should reserve this essay for a course for advanced students. Even then, you should provide some historical background and make students aware that they don't need to understand every reference in order to appreciate Swift's irony and ultimate compassion. You might also point out that the main thrust of Swift's argument comes in paragraphs 3–16 and 20–30; the long digression in paragraphs 17–19 often bogs students down.

COMPREHENSION (p. 683)

1. Swift notes the problem of poverty in Ireland and satirically proposes that such poverty could be eliminated if the children of the poor were sold to be butchered and eaten.
2. The advantages of the plan are that it would lessen the number of Catholics, that poor tenants would have an income with which to pay the landlord, that poor parents wouldn't have to maintain their children after two years of age, that taverns would benefit by increased business, and that it would encourage marriage.
3. Paragraph 29 enumerates the "alternatives," which involve the wealthy giving up a squanderous lifestyle, the uniting of the Irish people, and an increased compassion for the poor. These are what Swift is actually proposing.
4. The very outrageousness of the proposal suggests that Swift is not serious. Other clues include the over-attention to detail and, of course, the seriousness of his true proposals outlined in paragraphs 29–33.
5. See question 3 above. He rejects them to suggest the callousness with which his audience has treated the poor.

PURPOSE AND AUDIENCE (p. 683)

1. Many British readers would likely dismiss the proposal as the rantings of a madman. Irish readers, however—at least those who realized the harm British control was doing to the country of Ireland—would understand Swift's point.
2. Swift seems to have wanted to inspire change; only by shocking the sensibilities of his audience so thoroughly could he make readers stop and consider real solutions.
3. Such computations establish the "proposer" as a meticulous, even finicky, man.
4. Only those who took the proposal seriously—or who disagreed with Swift's politics—would likely be offended.
5. He expected his conclusion to be viewed as comically ironic.

STYLE AND STRUCTURE (p. 683)

1. The term suggests livestock; Swift's proposer is dehumanizing poor women as Swift would suggest the ruling classes have already done.
2. Paragraph 8 is a transition. Paragraph 20 is another brief transitional paragraph. Paragraphs 12 and 30 are brief for emphasis.
3. The "objections" in paragraph 29 aren't really refuted because they represent Swift's real proposals. In paragraph 30 he simply writes that there is little hope they will be put into practice.
4. Other examples include *food* (9), *excellent nutritive meat* (14), and *yearling child* (27). Again, these words dehumanize the peasantry.
5. He refers to "a very worthy person" in paragraph 17 and to "some persons of a desponding spirit" in paragraph 19. Such references lend an air of authenticity to the proposal by suggesting the proposer has conducted research.
6. Swift's essay is sharply ironic, and he is ridiculing the callousness of the ruling classes toward the peasants by wittily attacking their attitude.
7. By enumerating each advantage he adds a level of formality to the proposal.
8. The parenthetical asides—generally amplifications or qualifications—serve to suggest a tone of fastidious regard for exactitude.

9. He has been digressing from the subject of slaughtering infants for meat—to take up the subject of substituting adolescents for deer as the prey in hunting!

VOCABULARY PROJECTS (p. 684)

2. Swift's proposal is hardly a modest one, and the use of the word humbly is a common rhetorical device even today. ("I humbly propose" often introduces a major proposal.)

COMBINING THE PATTERNS (p. 685)

The patterns Swift uses are description (1), cause and effect (2–3), process (4), cause and effect (5), exemplification (6–7), description (9), process (10), description (11–12), cause and effect (13), description (14–16), comparison (17), exemplification (18), description (19), cause and effect (21–28), and argumentation (29–33).

THEMATIC CONNECTIONS

The Embalming of Mr. Jones (p. 285): Jessica Mitford uses irony in a more straightforward way to describe the fairly horrifying process of embalming.

The Irish Famine, 1845–1849 (p. 314): Student Evelyn Pellicane's essay-exam response, though focusing on a period more than a hundred years after Swift wrote, provides useful historical detail for understanding conditions of Irish life and the relationship between Ireland and Britain.

I Want a Wife (p. 505): Judy Brady's ironic look at gender expectations has a goal similar to "A Modest Proposal": to present an exaggerated, even outrageous, view of the status quo in order to get readers to see the situation in a new light.

The Declaration of Independence (p. 557): This important document, written only fifty years after "A Modest Proposal," employs many rhetorical strategies common to eighteenth-century composition—although in a completely straightforward way. Reading the Declaration might help students recognize some of the conventions Swift was playing with.

Alice Walker, *In Search of Our Mothers' Gardens*

Walker writes of the way the creative voices of African-American women have been stifled over the centuries—as a result of slavery, the denial of access to education, other forms of discrimination, grim economic realities, and their subjugation to the needs of menfolk and families. Yet, she writes, their creative spirit blossomed nonetheless: in the singing of spirituals, in the making of quilts, in the cultivation of spectacular flower gardens, and in the passing down of oral stories. As an artist, Walker has come to see herself (and other black women artists) as part of this tradition of untutored artistic expression, extending from mother to grandmother and back to female forebears in Africa painting "vivid and daring decorations," singing sweetly, weaving "the most stunning mats," telling "the most ingenious stories," perhaps even creating poetry (49).

COMPREHENSION (p. 694)

1. They had no outlet for their intense spirituality, their deep wells of creativity, so "the strain of enduring their unused and unwanted talent drove them insane" (10).

2. "Evil honey" refers to the lives of hard work that stifled their creativity. Black women have been referred to as "the mule of the world" because they occupied the lowest rung of the economic ladder, subject to the control even of black men—the metaphor implies a beast of burden.

3. This unwritten music represents the creative impulses stifled by their hard lives—"music" that would have to wait generations to emerge.

4. She sees these women as "Artists," as "Creators" forced to "throw away [their] spirituality. . .to lighten the soul to a weight their. . .abused bodies could bear" (10).

5. To "be an artist in our grandmothers' time" was to live in a kind of agony and to die "with their real gifts stifled within them" (13). Their creativity was kept alive in accepted venues, such as singing.

6. It is not the end of the story because the creativity of these thwarted souls lives on in the work of black female artists today.

7. Wheatley, a former slave, became a published poet despite the many odds against her. But her heritage made her a divided person, trying to please a white European audience that had once seen her as less than human. After she had children, the strain of not being able to find any outlet for her creativity led, according to Walker, to her early death. This woman, "who, had she been white, would have been easily considered the intellectual superior of all the women and most of the men in the society of her day" (18), was ultimately no more able to realize her true creativity than any other black woman.

8. Walker sees these mothers and grandmothers as positive examples in that they channeled their creativity in the ways that they could, but as negative examples in that they had so little freedom. The title suggests a search for these women's sources of creativity, which are the heritage of the contemporary black woman artist.

9. They have left the legacy of their own lives.

PURPOSE AND AUDIENCE (p. 695)

1. The sentiments of the essay are deeply feminist, locating a unique strain of female creativity.

2. She advises readers to tap into the roots of their mothers' and grandmothers' creativity, a creativity they may not immediately recognize. Women of other races will probably find the message relevant; men may also see roots of creativity from fathers, mothers, and other forebears.

3. Her thesis might be summed up most simply by a sentence in paragraph 46: "This ability to hold on, even in very simple ways, is work black women have done for a very long time." Walker's expectations for her audience seem fairly complex. Her tone suggests that she feels the need to convince her readers of the viability of the heritage she describes, but she also expects them to be sympathetic to her position.

STYLE AND STRUCTURE (p. 695)

1. The Toomer quotation is a way of introducing the concept of black women's deep inner spirituality being thwarted by societal and economic constraints. Students may have trouble seeing this.

2. Examples of figurative language can be found in paragraphs 5, 6, 9, 27, 44, and in the poem in paragraph 47. Students may find some of this imagery a little difficult.

3. Except for the stylistic similarities of the poem in paragraph 14 and Walker's poem, the excerpts don't have much in common. In fact, the Wheatley excerpt in paragraph 23 is meant to contrast with the more authentic voices of the other two. The excerpt from Woolf's *A Room of One's Own* allows Walker to apply that famous essay about the difficulties facing women writers to her own complementary thoughts about black women. Each quote has an important place in the essay.
4. Walker's tone is both sorrowful, in a sense, and celebratory; she laments the stifling of black female creativity but also celebrates the fact that this creativity has been passed down.
5. Walker summarizes her mother's life to provide an example of the kinds of women she is writing about—and also to make the connection between her own artistic creativity and her mother's. Wheatley's creativity was stifled in different, more tragic ways.
6. Other questions can be found in paragraphs 11–13, 18, 21, 29, and 33. As Walker's title suggests, hers has been a search for answers to these questions.

VOCABULARY PROJECTS (p. 695)

2. Gardens are associated with images of growth, of cultivation and nurturance, of beauty and natural abundance. Gardens are also refuges, havens into which one can escape from the everyday toils of the world. In addition to art, the word *garden* in Walker's essay suggests all of these images, as well as the central idea of creative expression.

COMBINING THE PATTERNS (p. 696)

The patterns Walker uses are narration and description (1–8), cause and effect (9–10), contrast (12), exemplification (13), exemplification and cause and effect (14–25), definition and cause and effect (26), exemplification (27–28), narration (29), process (30–31), cause and effect (32–33), example and description (34–35), cause and effect (36–37), contrast and cause and effect (38), process (39–40), narration and description (41–43), cause and effect (44–45), and narration and description (46–48). She concludes with an example of cause and effect (49–50).

THEMATIC CONNECTIONS

My Mother Never Worked (p. 96): Bonnie Smith-Yackel also writes to honor her hard-working mother, who—like Walker's mother—had little time for creative expression. Martha Smith exemplifies the way many women's lives have been constricted by the demands of work and family, resulting, in Virginia Woolf's phrase, in many a "lost novelist, a suppressed poet, . . . some mute and inglorious Jane Austen."

The Way to Rainy Mountain (p. 169): In this essay N. Scott Momaday honors the memory of his Kiowa grandmother. She is an artistic influence of a different kind, linking him to the traditions, legends, and religion of "the last culture to evolve in North America." Note that, interestingly, it is not to a male forebear that Momaday pays tribute. The relevance of Walker's essay to male readers might be considered here.

The Men We Carry in Our Minds (p. 456): Scott Russell Sanders meditates on the poor, working-class white men he grew up with, whose lives seem to have been just as stifled as those of the black women Walker writes about. For Sanders, it was women he envied because "they were the only people . . . who were interested in art or music or literature, the only ones who read books." You might ask students to consider why the working-class women Sanders remembers are so different, in this sense, from the poor black women of the same generation as described by Walker. Is race the operating factor?

Mother Tongue (p. 462): Amy Tan writes that her mother also provided artistic inspiration for her work. When she started writing stories, she says, she wrote artificially crafted sentences; not until she began writing with her mother in mind as her reader did she find an authentic voice using "all the Englishes" she grew up with. In her stories she wanted to capture her mother's "intent, her passion, her imagery, the rhythms of her speech and the nature of her thoughts." She argues that the artistic impulses of many Asian Americans are stifled because their language skills are wrongly seen as limited.

Richard Rodriguez, *Strange Tools*

COMPREHENSION (p. 701)

1. Rodriguez's parents read tax forms, letters from Mexico, "work manuals, prayer books, newspapers, recipes." They generally read out of necessity rather than for pleasure or learning. Books were essentially foreign to them.
2. Like Hoggart's "scholarship boy," Rodriguez grew up in a home without books, disconnected from the life of school.
3. The attitude toward books that Rodriguez encountered at school was one of respect: books can "open the doors of your mind," help you "learn," act as your "best friends."
4. Reading was difficult for Rodriguez: He had trouble with vocabulary, and he felt isolated as a reader. The nun helped Rodriguez realize that books could speak to him, that he had nothing to fear from books, that books could open worlds for him. Before, he had only seen reading as a chore.
5. Rodriguez's main interest in books was his realization that they could make him "educated" (4); this helped him "overcome [his] fear of the silence."
6. Rodriguez wanted to read "important books" because he felt he could learn from them. His mother did not understand his appetite for reading; she was not sure whether so much reading was healthy for him, whether it meant he was smart or was simply a way of getting out of chores.
7. He believed that a book's value to him lay in its theme and that understanding the themes of the books he read would help him become "learned" (7).
8. Among the benefits of his reading were that Rodriguez found pleasure in the activity and that by the time he got to high school, he had become proficient in speaking and writing English. Because he was able to "sense something of the shape, the major concerns, of Western thought" he was able to "achieve academic success" (11).

PURPOSE AND AUDIENCE (p. 701)

1. Rodriguez means that he accepted what he read uncritically, that he did not bring his own thinking to bear on what he read. It is clear that he has, as an

adult, acquired this critical "point of view" because he can look back and recognize the lack of "point of view" he brought to reading as an adolescent.

2. Rodriguez's purpose seems to be to communicate to readers his youthful approach to reading, in particular because he was an intelligent and sensitive child growing up in a household that provided no model for reading. He might even be seen as attempting to suggest to teachers what they should take into account when dealing with children like himself.

3. His comments clearly apply to any household in which parents are themselves not educated readers, meaning that their children, without models or encouragement, must negotiate the difficulties of reading essentially on their own. The "scholarship boys" Rodriguez identifies with were, in fact, lower-class British schoolboys.

STYLE AND STRUCTURE (p. 702)

1. The books Rodriguez mentions specifically suggest both the range of his reading and the fact that he did not discriminate much in choosing his books. Additionally, of course, readers see that he read many books that were more difficult than those read by most children his age. He could not have made these points without listing specific books.

2. The paragraph provides a transition; from here on Rodriguez tries, from his adult perspective, to answer his mother's question "What do you see in your books?"

3. The passage reveals Rodriguez as a solitary boy who took pleasure in quiet time by himself with his books.

4. Just as a fortune-teller completes a vision of the future and then moves on to the next customer, so do old-fashioned novels like those by Dickens end with "the futures of the major characters neatly resolved."

VOCABULARY PROJECTS (p. 702)

2. Rodriguez means that he read voraciously but indiscriminately, gleaning from books anything he could "to fill the hollow within [himself] and make [himself] feel educated," but not really thinking seriously about what he read. An alternative to the phrase "vacuumed books" might be "stuffed my head with books."

COMBINING THE PATTERNS (p. 703)

Rodriguez uses exemplification in paragraph 1, definition and comparison and contrast in paragraph 2, description in paragraph 3, narration in paragraphs 4 through 6, cause-and-effect analysis in paragraph 7, description in paragraph 8, exemplification in paragraph 9, cause-and-effect analysis in paragraph 10, and narration in paragraph 11.

THEMATIC CONNECTIONS

Only Daughter (p. 84): Like Rodriguez, Sandra Cisneros describes growing up in a working-class Mexican-American household. Interestingly, her father saw education as crucial for his sons, but not his daughter. Not until after she is an adult and he reads one of her stories does she feel she has won her father's approval.

The Human Cost of an Illiterate Society **(p. 229):** As Rodriguez makes clear, neither of his parents was illiterate; they had functioning reading skills that allowed them to read enough to get by. How might Rodriguez's life have been different if his parents had, in fact, been illiterate? What additional challenges might be faced by the child of illiterate parents?

Television: The Plug-In Drug **(p. 325):** Students might want to compare their television-watching habits with their reading habits. As television has become a ubiquitous part of most children's lives, do children necessarily read less than they might otherwise? Students might also consider comparing and contrasting watching television with reading. What might they see as the benefits and drawbacks of each?

Mother Tongue **(p. 462):** Amy Tan is also the child of immigrants to the United States who found that her background led her to a particular perception of herself as a student. For Tan, the issue is not so much one of reading as it is one of growing up in a household where her mother spoke a highly Chinese-inflected English. If students read Rodriguez's *Hunger of Memory*, from which "Strange Tools" is excerpted, they will see that he also writes in detail about growing up in a household where English was not his parents' native language.

APPENDIX: WRITING A RESEARCH PAPER

This appendix provides an overview of the entire research process: choosing a topic, looking for sources, narrowing a topic, doing research, taking notes, avoiding plagiarism, drafting a thesis statement, making an outline, writing the paper, and documenting sources. Each section offers specific advice and includes examples from the research process of a student writer. The appendix concludes with the final draft of the student's paper, which is based on the national ID card casebook in Chapter 12. (You might find this or another debate in Chapter 12 a good starting place for student research.)

For further resources on research, you might direct your students to the online English Research Room at <bedfordstmartins.com/english_research>. Here they will find interactive tutorials for conducting simple and advanced electronic searches; links to useful sites, including search engines, online writing centers, and reference works; and general advice on the research process and on evaluating and citing sources.

The appendix includes guidelines for citing sources using MLA documentation style and provides sample entries for a Works Cited page, including examples of citations for electronic sources. The sample research paper follows MLA guidelines and so has no separate cover page; if you require such a cover page, you should explain to students the format you prefer.

While you will want to use much of the material in the appendix in conjunction with a formal research paper if you have students write essays analyzing any of the readings in the book, you should probably cover the material on paraphrasing, summarizing, and using quotations early on. You might use the examples in the text and have students practice paraphrasing and summarizing in class—being careful to point out any inadvertent plagiarism.

PEER-EDITING WORKSHEETS

Following are models of peer-editing worksheets—one for each of the patterns discussed in Chapters 4 through 13 of the text. You may retype and duplicate these to distribute to students or adapt them to create versions of your own. The worksheets are also available as transparency masters. Advice about using the peer-editing worksheets appears on page 4 of the manual.

Peer-Editing Worksheet: Narration

1. What is the subject of this narrative essay?

2. What point is the writer making about the essay's subject? Is this point explicitly stated in a thesis statement? If so, where? If not, is the essay's thesis clearly implied? Would a stated thesis be more effective?

3. Does the writer include enough detail? Where could more detail be added? What kind of detail? Be specific.

4. Does the writer vary sentence structure and avoid monotonous strings of similar sentences? Should some sentences be combined? If so, which ones? Can you suggest different openings for any sentences?

5. Is the order in which events occur clear? Should any events be relocated? Should any transitions be added to clarify relationships between events?

6. Are verb tenses consistent? Identify any verb tenses that you believe are incorrect.

7. What could the writer *add* to this essay?

8. What could the writer *take out* of this essay?

9. What is the essay's greatest strength? Why?

10. What is the essay's greatest weakness? What steps should the writer take to correct this problem?

Peer-Editing Worksheet: Description

1. What is the essay's dominant impression or thesis?

2. What points does the writer emphasize in the introduction? Should any other points be included? If so, which ones?

3. Would you characterize the essay as primarily an objective or subjective description? What leads you to your conclusions?

4. Point out some examples of figures of speech. Could the writer use figures of speech in other places? If so, where?

5. What specific details does the writer use to help readers visualize what he or she is describing? Are there any places where the writer could use more details?

6. Are all the details necessary? Do any seem excessive or redundant? Are there enough details to support the thesis or reinforce the dominant impression?

7. How is the essay organized? Would another arrangement principle be clearer or more effective?

8. List some transitional words and phrases that the writer uses to help readers follow his or her discussion. Do any sentences need transitional words or phrases to link them to other sentences?

9. Copy down an example of a particularly clear sentence. Are any sentences wordy or choppy? If so, which ones?

10. How effective is the essay's conclusion? Does the conclusion reinforce the dominant impression?

Peer-Editing Worksheet: Exemplification

1. What strategy does the writer use in the essay's introduction? Would another strategy be more effective?

2. What is the essay's thesis? Is it specific enough? Does it prepare readers for the examples that follow?

3. What points do the body paragraphs make? Does each of these points develop one aspect of the thesis?

4. Does the writer use one example or many to illustrate his or her points? Should the writer use more examples? Fewer? Explain.

5. List the examples the writer uses. Is there a sufficient range of examples? Are the examples explained in enough depth?

6. Are the examples representative of the idea the writer is discussing?

7. How persuasive are the examples? List a few other examples that might be more persuasive.

8. What transitional words and phrases does the writer use to reinforce the connections between examples? At what other points should transitional words and phrases be used?

9. In what order are the examples presented? Would another order be more effective? Explain.

10. What strategy does the writer use in the conclusion? What other strategy could the writer use?

Peer-Editing Worksheet: Process

1. What process does this essay describe? How familiar were you with this process before you read the essay?

2. Does the writer include all the information the audience needs? Is any vital step or piece of information missing? Is any step or piece of information irrelevant? Is any necessary definition, explanation, or warning missing or incomplete?

3. Is the essay a set of instructions or a process explanation? How can you tell? Why do you think the writer chose this format rather than the alternative? Do you think this was the right choice?

4. Does the writer consistently follow the stylistic conventions for the format—instructions or process explanation—he or she has chosen? Identify any inconsistencies in mood, person, or tense.

5. Are the steps presented in clear, logical order? Are they grouped logically into paragraphs? Should any steps be combined or relocated? If so, which ones?

6. Does the writer use enough transitions to move readers through the process? Should any transitions be added? If so, where? Do the transitions clearly indicate the logical and sequential relationships between steps?

7. Is the essay interesting? What descriptive details would add interest to the essay?

8. How would you characterize the writer's opening strategy? Is it appropriate for his or her purpose and audience? What alternative strategy might be more effective?

9. How would you characterize the writer's closing strategy? Would a different conclusion be more effective? Explain.

10. Is anything unclear or confusing? What might the writer do to help you understand the process more fully?

Peer-Editing Worksheet: Cause and Effect

1. Paraphrase the essay's thesis. Is it explicitly stated? Should it be?

2. Does the essay focus on causes, effects, or both? Does the thesis statement clearly identify this focus? If not, how should the thesis statement be revised?

3. Does the writer consider *all* relevant causes and/or effects? Are any key causes or effects omitted? Are any irrelevant causes or effects included?

4. Make an informal outline of the essay in the space below.

   What determines the order in which the causes and/or effects are arranged? Is this the most effective order? If not, what revisions do you suggest?

5. What transitional words and phrases are used to indicate causal connections? List them below.

   Are any additional transitions needed? If so, where?

6. Does the writer avoid *post hoc* reasoning? Are all causal connections logical?

7. Does the writer explain each cause and/or effect clearly and convincingly? Are more examples or details needed to help readers understand causal connections? If so, where?

8. Do you agree with the writer's assessment of the cause-and-effect relationships examined in this essay? Do you agree with his or her conclusions? Why or why not?

9. Are any sentences worded in an imprecise, unclear, or awkward manner? If so, which ones?

10. Are any words used incorrectly? If so, suggest substitutes.

Peer-Editing Worksheet: Comparison and Contrast

1. Does the essay have a clearly stated thesis? What is it?

2. What two things are being compared? What basis for comparison exists between the two?

3. Does the essay treat the same or similar points for each of its two subjects? List the points discussed below.

First subject   **Second subject**

1.   1.

2.   2.

3.   3.

4.   4.

Are these points discussed in the same order for both subjects? Do any points need to be relocated? If so, which ones? Where should they go?

4. Does the essay use a point-by-point or subject-by-subject arrangement? Is this the best choice? Why?

5. Are transitional words and expressions used appropriately to make the points of comparison and contrast clear? List below some of the transitions that are used.

6. Are additional transitions needed? If so, where?

7. How could the introductory paragraph be improved?

8. How could the concluding paragraph be improved?

9. What could the writer add to this essay?

10. What could the writer take out of this essay?

Peer-Editing Worksheet: Classification and Division

Make an informal outline of the essay in the space below, and consult it as you answer the questions that follow.

1. What thesis does the body of the essay support? Is this thesis explicitly stated? Does it clearly indicate the purpose of the classification and division?

2. What whole is being divided into parts in this essay? Into what general categories is the whole divided?

3. Is each category clearly identified and defined? If not, what revisions can you suggest (for example, can you suggest a different title for a particular category?)

4. Are the categories arranged in a logical order, one that indicates their relationships to one another and their relative importance? If not, how might they be rearranged?

5. Do the individual items discussed in the essay seem to be classified logically in appropriate categories? Should any items be located elsewhere? Explain.

6. Does the writer treat all relevant categories and no irrelevant ones? Which categories, if any, should be added, deleted, or combined?

7. Does the writer include all necessary items, and no unnecessary ones, within each category? What additional items might be added?

8. Does the writer treat all categories similarly, discussing comparable points for each? What additional points should be discussed? Where?

9. Do topic sentences clearly signal the movement from one category to the next? Do they signal the writer's direction and emphasis? Should any topic sentences be strengthened to mark the boundaries between categories more clearly? If so, which ones?

10. Could the writer use another pattern of development to structure this essay, or is classification and division the best choice? Why?

Peer-Editing Worksheet: Definition

1. What term is the writer defining? Does the essay include a formal dictionary definition? If so, where? If not, should one be added?

2. Why is the writer defining the term? Does the essay include a thesis statement that makes this purpose clear?

3. What patterns does the writer use to develop the definition? What other patterns could be used?

4. Does the essay define the term appropriately for its audience? Does the definition help you understand the meaning of the term?

5. Does the writer use synonyms to develop the definition? If so, where? If not, where could synonyms be used to help communicate the term's meaning?

6. Does the writer use negation to develop the definition? If so, where? If not, could the writer strengthen the definition by stating what the term is not?

7. Does the writer use enumeration to develop the definition? If so, where? If not, where might the term's special characteristics be listed?

8. Does the writer use analogies to develop the definition? If so, where? Do you find these analogies helpful? What additional analogies might help readers understand the term more fully?

9. Does the writer explain the term's linguistic origin and development? If so, where? If not, do you believe this information should be added?

10. Reread the essay's introduction. If the writer uses a dictionary definition as an opening strategy, try to suggest an alternative opening.

Peer-Editing Worksheet: Argumentation

1. Does the essay take a stand? What is it? At what point does the writer state his or her thesis?

2. Does the writer consider the audience friendly, hostile, or neutral? How do you know?

3. What evidence does the writer include to support his or her position? What additional evidence could the writer supply?

4. Does the essay attempt to refute the opposition's arguments? List these arguments below.

5. How effective are the writer's refutations? What other arguments should the writer address?

6. Does the essay rely mainly on inductive or deductive reasoning, or both? Provide an example of each type of reasoning from the essay.

   Inductive reasoning:

   Deductive reasoning:

7. Does the essay contain any logical fallacies? List them below. How would you correct these fallacies?

8. How could the introduction be improved?

9. How could the conclusion be improved?

10. What would you add to make this essay more convincing?

Peer-Editing Worksheet: Combining the Patterns

1. Using the annotations for "The Park" (p. 655) or "On Dumpster Diving" (p. 660) as a guide, annotate the essay to identify the patterns of development it uses.

2. What is the essay's thesis? If it is not explicitly stated, write it in your own words. What pattern or patterns of development are suggested by the wording of the thesis statement?

3. What pattern of development determines the essay's overall structure? Could the writer use a different pattern for this purpose? Which one?

4. What patterns does the writer use to develop the body paragraphs of the essay? Explain why each pattern is used in a particular paragraph or group of paragraphs.

5. What patterns are not used? Where, if anywhere, might one of these absent patterns serve the writer's purpose?

6. Review the essay's topic sentences. Is the wording of each topic sentence consistent with the particular pattern it introduces? If not, suggest possible ways some of the topic sentences might be reworded.

BIBLIOGRAPHY

Rhetoric and Composition Theory

Bloom, Lynn Z., Donald A. Daiker, and Edward M. White. *Composition in the Twenty-First Century: Crisis and Change.* Carbondale: Southern Illinois UP, 1997.

Graves, Richard, ed. *Writing, Teaching, Learning: A Sourcebook.* Portsmouth: Heinemann, Boynton/Cook, 1999.

Graves, Richard, ed. *Rhetoric and Composition: A Sourcebook for Teachers and Writers.* 3rd ed. Portsmouth: Heinemann, Boynton/Cook, 1990.

Lindemann, Erika. *A Rhetoric for Writing Teachers.* 4th ed. New York: Oxford UP, 2001.

Lindemann, Erika, and Gary Tate. *An Introduction to Composition Studies.* New York: Oxford UP, 1994.

Reynolds, Mark, ed. *Two-Year College English: Essays for a New Century.* Urbana: NCTE, 1994.

The Composing Process

Perl, Sondra, ed. *Landmark Essays on Writing Process.* Davis: Hermagoras, 1994.

Tobin, Lad, and Thomas Newkirk, eds. *Taking Stock: The Writing Process Movement in the '90s.* Portsmouth: Heinemann, Boynton/Cook, 1994.

Young, Richard, and Yameng Liu, eds. *Landmark Essays on Rhetorical Invention in Writing.* Davis: Hermagoras, 1994.

Teaching Methods

Belanoff, Pat, and Marcia Dickson. *Portfolios: Process and Product.* Portsmouth: Heinemann, Boynton/Cook, 1991.

Brooke, Robert, Ruth Mirtz, and Rick Evans. *Small Groups in Writing Workshops.* Urbana: NCTE, 1994.

Handa, Carolyn, ed. *Computers and Community: Teaching Composition in the Twenty-First Century.* Portsmouth: Boynton/Cook, 1990.

Harnack, Andrew, and Eugene Kleppinger. *Online! A Reference Guide to Using Internet Sources.* 3rd ed., 2001 update. New York: Bedford, 2000, 2001.

Hunter, Susan, and Ray Wallace, eds. *The Place of Grammar in Writing Instruction: Past, Present, Future.* Portsmouth: Heinemann, Boynton/Cook, 1995.

Murray, Donald. *A Writer Teaches Writing.* 2nd ed. Boston: Houghton, 1990.

Tate, Gary, ed. *Teaching Composition: Twelve Biographical Essays.* Fort Worth: Texas Christian UP, 1987.

Tate, Gary, Edward P. J. Corbett, and Nancy Myers. *The Writing Teacher's Sourcebook.* 4th ed. New York: Oxford UP, 1999.

Spear, Karen. *Sharing Writing: Peer Response Groups in English Classes.* Portsmouth: Heinemann, Boynton/Cook, 1988.

Walvoord, Barbara E. Fassler. *Helping Students Write Well: A Guide for Teachers in All Disciplines.* 2nd ed. New York: MLA, 1990.

Cutler's point is that it is difficult to define media violence in a substantive way children perceive it. Children process content differentially and not while some children perceive media violence in a manner really experiencing confusion, younger children may not have such causal abilities and apparent disturbance as readily.

Rather than is coming or reducing the return to media violence the authors researchers focused on reducing exposure to media more externally found that the most self-control children suffered over the previous six months, the least they resorted to verbal and physical aggression. She contends, the project quite effectively contradicts it is on the idea that real-life experiences have greater influence on children than do simulated experiences.

Cutler's proposal is that, rather than attempting to regulate media violence, law makers should speak to reform juvenile policies, provide supervised after-school activities for teens, and generally comprehensively help to reduce the violence that

PURPOSE AND AUDIENCE (p. 152)

Students' opinions may differ, but certainly there is more than a dose of sarcasm in Cutler's tone, particularly when she mocks the easy connections and quick fixes for media violence suggested by political leaders ((10)/(9)/(5). Elsewhere, she seems more concerned that the complex issue of the issue be taken seriously.

Cutler uses transitional expressions such as "Like most countries sister" (2), "but" (3), "in other words" (4), "like Great Britain sommates" (6), "Indeed" (8), "At first-sight" (10), "Although" (12), and "without building the importance of media research" (11), in other cases, transitions are more subtle, as in the final sentence of paragraph 6, which provides the transition to paragraph 7.

Students' opinions may differ here. She may have done more to establish her own credentials as a media critic.

Cutler reveals her biases about television in paragraph 7, where she refers to the Parents Television Council as "following." She is clearly arguing from a perspective that is opposed to censorship.

STYLE AND STRUCTURE (p. 152)

As mentioned under the answer to item 1 under Purpose and Audience, there is a lot of irony in Cutler's tone here. Students must consider that Cutler employs a persona here that, for example, is not meant to be taken.

Cutler wants to establish that misinformation has resulted from simplistic media violence to everything, is harmful to children and has not established for children. The support for these claims comes from the research that suggest that sometimes

This aspect of their personality does not help to understand it, is the most direct. Nothing is comprehensive statement in the literary review at the outset of the paragraph, Cutler's summary of research there to suggest establishes

Essentially, Cutler's essay is one long refutation of the argument that real-life experience. Although the middle will address willing to concede the point that this is a refutation that individual criteria may the support paragraphs, it is ultimately convincing. This is why she chooses to support the media violence and includes references to help to be children.